128TH YEAR

WISDEN

CRICKETERS' ALMANACK

1991

EDITED BY GRAEME WRIGHT

PUBLISHED BY JOHN WISDEN & CO LTD

A COMPANY JOINTLY OWNED BY
GRAYS OF CAMBRIDGE (INTERNATIONAL) LIMITED
AND
BOWATER PLC

SOFT COVER EDITION £16.75   CASED EDITION £20.00

ISBN
Cased edition 0 947766 16 2
Soft cover edition 0 947766 17 0

John Wisden & Co Ltd
25 Down Road
Merrow
Guildford
Surrey
GU1 2PY

Computer typeset by SB Datagraphics, Colchester
Printed in Great Britain by William Clowes Limited, Beccles

PREFACE

If anyone doubted that the amount of cricket being played around the world has been increasing – and doing so in inverse proportion to those watching, it seems – he or she need only compare the pages of this *Wisden* with those of the 1990 edition. Nor is this increase limited to countries other than the United Kingdom. Although it is frequently said that there is too much cricket, the TCCB managed last year to squeeze a short tour by Sri Lanka into a fixture list already containing Test-match tours by New Zealand and India. Each year, it appears, the season begins earlier and finishes later. With the first game commencing on April 13, the season in 1991 has its earliest start since 1903 (also April 13), while the final game, a new fixture over four days between the new county champions and the Sheffield Shield winners, is scheduled to start on September 23. One ramification of the profusion, as far as *Wisden* is concerned, is an increase in the number of pages from 1296 in 1990 to 1360 in 1991.

Even so, the demands on space continue. More schools, with fixtures against schools currently in *Wisden*, ask to be included. Among them this year was Richard Huish, of Taunton, the first state school to win the Barclays Under-17 competition: one of their players appeared for Somerset in the final of the Bain Clarkson Trophy. Prompted perhaps by Rachael Heyhoe Flint's application for membership of MCC, Roedean School submitted their averages for the season, pointing out correctly that there was an absence of girls' schools in the section. Their letter arriving two months after the closing date, an editorial dilemma was postponed for a year.

For their co-operation my thanks are extended to the secretariats of MCC and the TCCB, to the county secretaries and their staffs, and in particular to the county scorers and statisticians, whose checking of scorecards is so valuable. I would also like to pay tribute to the work of Roy Smart, who developed the computer program which set up for *Wisden* a data base of the summer's cricket and, in addition to producing averages and other statistical highlights, provided the facility to send scorecards on disk to our typesetters, SB Datagraphics.

Once again I am indebted to the many journalists and statisticians who help in so many ways. To P. N. Sundaresan, who sent details of cricket in India to *Wisden* from the 1967 edition until last year's, I offer *Wisden's* thanks for his generous help to three editors. As always, Christine Forrest's contribution has been tireless, and Gordon Burling has again read the majority of the proofs with his customary diligence. Finally, a welcome to Harriet Monkhouse, who has joined John Wisden as an editor and whose assistance has already altered the work-pattern of more than a decade. For that I am especially grateful.

GRAEME WRIGHT

Eastcote
Middlesex

LIST OF CONTRIBUTORS

The editor acknowledges with gratitude the assistance in the preparation of the Almanack by the following:

Jack Arlidge (Sussex)
John Arlott (Books)
David Armstrong
Chris Aspin (Lancashire Leagues)
Philip Bailey
Jack Bannister (Warwickshire)
Simon Barnes
Colin Bateman
Brian Bearshaw (Lancashire)
Sir William Becher
Michael Berry
Edward Bevan (Glamorgan)
J. Watson Blair (Scotland)
Dick Brittenden
Robert Brooke (Births and Deaths)
Gordon Burling
C. R. Buttery (New Zealand)
John Callaghan (Yorkshire)
Terry Cooper (Middlesex)
Geoffrey Copinger
Tony Cozier (West Indies)
Brian Croudy
Jon Culley (Leicestershire)
Pat Culpan
Norman de Mesquita
Patrick Eagar
Paton Fenton (Oxford University)
David Field (Surrey)
Bill Frindall (Records)
Nigel Fuller (Essex)
Ghulam Mustafa Khan
David Hallett (Cambridge University)
David Hardy (The Netherlands)
Peter Hargreaves (Denmark)
Bob Harragan (Welsh Schools)
Chris Harte
Les Hatton
Frank Heydenrych (South Africa)
Eric Hill (Somerset)
Ted and Mary-Anne Hirst

Dr Grenville Holland (UAU)
Brian Hunt
Ken Ingman (ESCA)
Kate Jenkins
Abid Ali Kazi (Pakistan)
Michael Kennedy
John Kitchin (Obituaries)
Stephanie Lawrence
Alan Lee
David Leggat
Nick Lucy (Nottinghamshire)
John MacKinnon (Australia)
John Minshull-Fogg
R. Mohan (India)
Chris Moore (Worcestershire)
Dudley Moore (Kent)
Gerald Mortimer (Derbyshire)
Don Mosey
David Munden
Mike Neasom (Hampshire)
David Norrie
Graham Otway
Alwyn Pichanick (Zimbabwe)
Qamar Ahmed
Andrew Radd (Northamptonshire)
Rex Roberts
Carol Salmon (Women's Cricket)
Geoffrey Saulez
Derek Scott (Ireland)
Roy Smart
Bill Smith
Peter Smith
Richard Streeton
John Thicknesse
Sudhir Vaidya (India)
Gerry Vaidyasekera (Sri Lanka)
David Walsh (HMC Schools)
Geoffrey Wheeler (Gloucestershire)
John Woodcock
Peter Wynne-Thomas

Thanks are accorded also to the following for checking the scorecards of first-class matches: M. R. L. W. Ayers, L. Beaumont, G. R. Blackburn, Mrs C. Byatt, L. V. Chandler, B. H. Clarke, W. Davies, B. T. Denning, J. Foley, V. H. Isaacs, B. H. Jenkins, D. Kendix, D. A. Oldam, S. W. Tacey and R. D. Wilkinson.

CONTENTS

INDEX

Note: For reasons of space, certain entries which appear in alphabetical order in sections of the Almanack are not included in this index. These include names that appear in Test Cricketers, Births and Deaths of Cricketers, individual batting and bowling performances in the 1990 first-class season, and Oxford and Cambridge Blues.

c. = *catches; d.* = *dismissals; p'ship* = *partnership; r.* = *runs; w.* = *wickets.*
* Signifies not out or an unbroken partnership.

A

Aamer Malik (Pak.):– 2 hundreds on début, *136;* 2 Test hundreds, *255.*

Aamer Wasim (Sialkot):– LBW hat-trick, *159.*

Aaqib Javed (Pak.):– Test début at 16, *197.*

Abdul Azeem (H'bad):– 303* v Tamil Nadu, *134.*

Abdul Kadir (Pak.):– Test p'ship record, *239.*

Abdul Qadir (Pak.):– 230 w. in Tests, *189;* 131 w. in one-day ints, *266;* 103 w. in Pakistan season, *161;* 10 w. or more in Test (4), *225, 239;* 9 w. in Test innings, *185;* All-round in Tests, *191;* Test p'ship record, *259.*

Abel, R. (Eng.):– 33,124 r., *143;* 3,309 r. in season, *140;* Highest for Surrey, *135;* 74 hundreds, *139;* 357* v Somerset, *133, 135;* 2 Test hundreds, *201, 209;* Carrying bat in Test, *181;* 379 for 1st wkt, *150.*

Absolom, C. A. (Eng.):– Obstructing the field, *155.*

Adcock, N. A. T. (SA):– 104 w. in Tests, *188;* 26 w. in series, *212;* Test p'ship record, *241.*

Addresses of representative bodies, *1315-6.*

Adhikari, H. R. (Ind.):– Test captain, *244;* 1 Test hundred, *246;* Test p'ship records, *236, 256.*

Afaq Hussain (Pak.):– Test p'ship record, *239.*

Aftab Baloch (Pak.):– Test début at 16, *197;* 428 v Baluchistan, *133.*

Agha Zahid (HBL):– 2 hundreds in match (2), *137.*

Agnew, J. P. (Eng.):– Career figures, *1324.*

Ahad Khan (Pak. Rlwys):– 9 w. for 7 r., *157.*

Alabaster, J. C. (NZ):– 8 w. in Test, *242;* Test p'ship record, *244.*

Alderman, T. M. (Aust.):– 153 w. in Tests, *188;* 42 w. in series, *187, 207;* 41 w. in series, *187;* 10 w. or more in Test, *206;* Test p'ship record, *239.*

Alexander, F. C. M. (WI):– Test captain, *213, 244, 247;* 1 Test hundred, *231;* 23 d. in series, *193;* 5 c. in Test innings, *192.*

Ali Zia (UBL):– 2 hundreds in match (2), *137.*

Alim-ud-Din (Pak.):– 2 Test hundreds, *224, 255.*

Allan, P. J. (Aust.):– 10 w. in innings, *156.*

Allcott, C. F. W. (NZ):– 190* for 8th wkt, *153;* Test p'ship record, *242.*

Allen, D. A. (Eng.):– 122 w. in Tests, *187;* Test p'ship records, *225.*

Allen, Sir G. O. B. (Eng.):– Test captain, *200, 213, 220;* Test cricket at 45, *198;* 1 Test hundred, *218;* 10 w. in innings, *156;* 10 w. or more in Test (1), *223;* 246 for 8th wkt v New Zealand, *184, 219.*

Alletson, E. B. (Notts.):– Fast scoring, *145;* 34 r. in over, *147.*

Alley, W. E. (Som.):– 3,019 r. in season, *140.*

Alleyne, M. W. (Glos.):– 256 in 1990, *273.*

Allom, M. J. C. (Eng.):– Test hat-trick, *189, 220.*

Allott, P. J. W. (Eng.):– 116 for 10th wkt, *277;* Test p'ship records, *222, 226.*

Altaf Shah (HBFC):– 355 for 5th wkt, *152.*

Amarnath, L. (Ind.):– Test captain, *235, 244, 254;* Hundred on Test début, *174, 221;* 410 for 3rd wkt, *152.*

Amarnath, M. (Ind.):– 4,378 r. in Tests, *179;* 11 Test hundreds, *236, 246, 255, 257;* 2,234 r. in overseas season, *141;* 1,077 Test r. in year, *177;* Test p'ship records, *236, 256, 257.*

Amarnath, S. (Ind.):– Hundred on Test début, *175, 250;* Test p'ship record, *256.*

Ambrose, C. E. L. (WI):– 12 w. in match, *277;* 10 w. in Test, *216;* 8 w. in Test innings, *185.*

Ames, L. E. G. (Eng.):– Obituary, *1254-6;* 37,248 r., *143;* 2,434 r. in Tests, *178;* 1,000 r. (17), *141;* 3,058 r. in season, *140;* 102 hundreds, *138;* 8 Test hundreds, *201, 209, 214, 218;* 2 hundreds in match (3), *137;* 1,121 d., *168;* 100 d. in season (3), *167;* 8 d. in Test, *192;* 2,482 r. and 104 d. in season, *1,919 r.* and 122 d. in season, *1,795 r.* and 128 d. in season, *165;* 246 for 8th wkt v New Zealand, *184, 219;* Test p'ship records, *184, 211, 219.*

Amin Lakhani (Pak. Univs):– Double hat-trick, *159.*

Amir Elahi (Ind. and Pak.):– Test p'ship record, *256.*

Amiss, D. L. (Eng.):– 43,423 r., *142;* 7,040 r. in Sunday League, *843;* 3,612 r. in Tests, *177;* 1,950 r. in GC/NWB, *725;* 1,379 Test r. in year, *176;* 1,000 r. (24), *140;* 102 hundreds, *138;* 11 Test hundreds, *214, 218, 221, 224;* 2 hundreds in match (3), *137;* 262* v West Indies, *174, 214.*

Index

INDEX OF FILLERS

NOTES BY THE EDITOR

If only the introduction to these Notes could have echoed those written for the 1929 *Wisden*. A record number of hundreds in the English season under review, success for England in the home Test matches, the Ashes series in Australia already won as the Almanack went to press. It was not to be. Injuries to key England players in Australia, particularly to the captain, Graham Gooch, were a factor in England's failure to regain the Ashes during the winter. But more worrying were avoidable technical deficiencies and the attitude of the team in Gooch's absence. When, early on, the wheels fell off, it seemed that no-one knew how to put them back on, leaving the mule-team to drag the waggon backwards and forwards across Australia on its axles. To those who watch county cricket regularly, and critically, this will have come as less of a surprise than it may have to the gentleman who wrote, in the autumn, "A fine season. A settled English captain, settled England openers, a successful team. Good County Championship season. Excellent over-limit season. Not such gloomy introductory Notes next year, please."

The profession of cricketer

At the press conference, in March 1987, at which the Test and County Cricket Board announced the appointment of Micky Stewart as England team manager for three years from April 1 that year, it was suggested to Mr Stewart that England's success on their recent tour of Australia owed something to their itinerary: until the final Test, the first-class matches were uninterrupted by one-day internationals, which were all played at the end of the tour. Able to concentrate on one form of the game at a time, England won the Test series 2-1 and both one-day tournaments. Might it not, Mr Stewart was asked, be more difficult for the players to maintain such form in a domestic programme which required them to alternate between the first-class and the one-day game throughout the season. If I remember correctly, his reply was to the effect that the players were professional cricketers: they knew how to adjust. If little else has emerged from the past winter's tour of Australia, two things have. The Australians made sure that England did not have such a sensible itinerary two tours running, and England's cricketers did not find it an easy matter to adjust. Nothing new there.

They are professional cricketers. What does this mean? I think that today it means they are cricketers who play the game of cricket as a livelihood, as opposed to playing it as a recreation. They are in a job, in the same way that a Civil Servant or a bank clerk is in a job. There is not the same security, of course, but that is a hazard of the occupation – and there is more than there was. The danger is that in regarding cricket as a job rather than a sport, players not only derive a nine to five mentality towards cricket but also become accustomed to defeat. In limited-overs cricket – and there is so much of it – someone has to lose. Given that fact, what is wrong with losing? It becomes part of the job. There is as little discredit attached to defeat as there is to any job done poorly these days. The public, too, becomes accustomed to a winner and a loser, and the value of a draw loses its significance. It is, after all, better than losing, and yet in the County Championship the draw brings no reward other than the negative one of denying victory to the opposing team. I feel it should. Those who can't be winners don't always have to be losers: many of us try to live honourably drawn lives and have to work hard to do so.

What "professional cricketers" no longer means is that they are professionals as opposed to amateurs. I wonder, though, what kind of professional cricketer Mr Stewart was thinking of. I suspect he had in mind the kind of professional cricketer he was himself: the county cricketer to whom the job was secondary to the enjoyment of playing cricket and to the opportunity to practise his skills against his peers at the highest level. It was his livelihood, it was his work, but it was not just a job.

In modern times the game provides a greater reward. Not riches by any means; but since the advent of sponsorship and income from off-field activities by the counties, the established player can expect better remuneration and greater security. A car is provided; away from home the teams stay in hotels. It is not an uncomfortable life. The player who maintains his average from season to season can remain an average player for a good number of summers. Indeed there is something of the chocolate cream soldier about him. Young players, adventurous and ambitious, come through, but not so many as to upset the order of things. As in the Civil Service, it takes a genuine talent to unsettle the time-servers: a few years of apprenticeship in the Second Eleven knocks off the confidence and cockiness of youth and produces in good time the county cricketer – the professional cricketer.

The consequence of this is a county game that rather meanders along from one season to the next with a carefully regulated change of personnel. And while there are some very good cricketers, there are a lot of fairly ordinary ones. It is not surprising that the overall standard of first-class cricket played and occasionally watched is not particularly high. It would be interesting to know how many English county cricketers would hold a place in a first-class side in Australia, the West Indies or in the Currie Cup in South Africa.

Under the auspices of the TCCB and the National Cricket Association, a programme has been launched to develop and maintain higher standards. Cricketers are monitored in their age-groups, the aim being to build a sound base for a pyramid, the apex of which is the England team. Inherent in this, however, is that to reach the apex, the young cricketer has to commit himself to the life of a professional county cricketer. And on the pyramid, county cricket is not so much the final step to the top as a broad plateau which many cricketers traverse summer after summer. It can be argued that the greater the number who are on the plateau, the better are those who go on to reach the apex. The evidence suggests otherwise.

Time to think anew

Perhaps the plateau should be smaller, making the competition for places on it greater. For this to happen, the structure of county cricket would have to change. And while at present it is inconceivable that the first-class counties would agree to any such change, it is possible that the coming years will show change to be inevitable. A lot will depend on how English cricket views its role on the small stage of international cricket: a star performer or a player of supporting parts.

It will be said that this reflects undue concern with Test cricket; that the County Championship serves a purpose other than being a nursery for Test cricketers. Perhaps, and then again perhaps not. Without the income that international cricket produces, and the interest it arouses, the subsidy to first-class cricket would be cut drastically and the diet of one-day cricket would be increased. That the economic health of English cricket in its fully professional form depends on the image the game projects, on and off the field, should not be in dispute. I am surprised sometimes that the players themselves are not more aware how important this is. International success is part of that image.

The intended elevation of Durham from minor county to first-class status in 1992 brings with it an opportunity to reshape the County Championship more radically than merely by an increase in the number of counties for the first time since 1921. One possible change is the introduction of a Championship consisting of seventeen four-day games per county; this, basically, is the recommendation of the TCCB's England, Cricket and Marketing committees, which was rejected by a majority of the counties last spring. Whether this is sufficient to bring about a more competitive Championship is another matter.

What about dividing the counties into two leagues of nine, with the teams in each league playing the others home and away? Worthwhile prizemoney, plus the prospect of promotion and relegation, might provide the keen competition which to me seems to be missing from much County Championship cricket. The nature of the cricket would demand a higher standard from the leading players: the potential England players. It is élitist, no doubt, but the alternative is mediocrity.

Another possible change is in the way cricketers are employed. No doubt Durham, the newcomers, will be hoping to attract experienced players from other counties. It would not be unexpected if some of those who retired at the end of 1990 were to reappear in Durham's colours in 1992, their absence from the game in 1991 having anticipated the obstacle of contested registrations.

What would be enterprising is an initiative which opens the way for young cricketers who want to try themselves in the first-class game but do not wish to commit themselves to a career as a professional cricketer. Durham have sought, and must continue to seek, sponsorship to pay their players. But what if companies were to provide that sponsorship in players rather than in money? A cricketer, in the employ of a local firm, could be available for the season, while at the same time having a career outside cricket which offers him long-term prospects. Indeed, his employment need not be dependent simply on his cricket but also on his other skills. The sponsoring company, in turn, would benefit from the presence on its staff of a county cricketer. The county cricket club would have a cricketer who could look to playing his natural game and not to maintaining a good enough average to keep his contract. It would, I believe, give more cricketers the opportunity to pursue every boy's ambition to play for his country.

Attitude as well as ability

Whatever their value, such thoughts are meaningless if the cricketers themselves are found wanting. It is worrying that young cricketers, who look to have had a good grounding in the basics of batting and bowling, pick up and retain technical faults between youth cricket and first-class cricket. What are the county coaches doing? Impressionable youngsters are being allowed to ape their seniors without the period of consolidation which has led to the senior player developing his particular style. Gooch, for example, did not start out with his raised-bat style: that was a development, not a beginning.

For a young batsman to emulate him because he is successful is rather like a writer setting out to write in the style of James Joyce's *Ulysses* without even having the mastery of the Joyce who wrote *Dubliners*.

But it is in their running between the wickets and their fielding that cricketers reveal much about their approach to the game and their coaching. In his tribute to Sir Leonard Hutton on pages 53 to 55, John Woodcock writes: "Studying under Sutcliffe in his early days for Yorkshire would have shown him the need for conviction in calling and let him into the secrets of the short single." Few batsmen today look to have learned how to take the pace off the ball; to make the fielder come in for the ball while the batsmen run their single quickly. Perhaps heavier bats have cost them that touch; they give the ball away to the fielder. If so it is poor cricket, for it has taken from the batsman the tactical advantage of upsetting field placings. Similarly in the field: too often one sees fieldsmen waiting for the ball to come to them rather than "attacking" it and putting the batsman under pressure when judging a run. Such things come naturally to a few; for most they require practice and awareness. Both appear to be at a premium.

That bowling skills are in short supply was demonstrated starkly last season. In time they will return. In an age when spelling is not considered important by some teachers, it is hardly surprising that the standard of spelling has deteriorated. So it is with the skills that bowlers need. The TCCB has acted positively to make the bowler, and not the ball or the pitch, the wicket-taker. They should be commended, not criticised, for acting decisively and for having the resolve to resist the cries for leniency. Their determination to maintain acceptable standards of behaviour is also correct. If some cricketers find the disciplinary measures repressive, it is probably not too late for them to become football hooligans.

It used to be said that when English batting is at a low ebb, look first at the strength of English bowling. And English batting, over the seventeen counties, is technically poor. Good bowlers show it up, as they did even in the batsmen's conditions of 1990. Sadly for England's selectors, none of those bowlers was eligible for England. And that is the problem to which the TCCB has addressed itself.

Getting to the pitch

In 1928, when there were 312 first-class games, there was an aggregate of 1,000 or more runs in 72 of those games. Last summer, 1,000 runs were posted in 108 of the 241 first-class games and there were 428 individual hundreds, which passed the previous record of 414 in 1928. However, the 32 double-hundreds in 1990 did not quite match the record 34 in 1933, another summer when good weather produced an improvement in conditions for batsmen. To what extent the balance swung from the bowlers to the batsmen last summer can be seen from a comparison of County Championship aggregates: 154,232 runs and 5,260 wickets in 1989; 179,360 runs and 4,632 wickets in 1990. Perhaps to encourage the endeavours of the bowlers in the coming years, the TCCB might limit the weight of bats. In addition to widening the range of strokeplay, this would reduce the instances of the bat making up with power what the batsman lacks in skill.

Although in 1928 the heavy run-getting struck the dominant note for the editor of *Wisden*, "the outstanding achievements were accomplished by a bowler and wicket-keeper, A. P. Freeman taking 304 wickets and so beating

Tom Richardson's record of 290 (made in 1895) and Leslie Ames disposing of 121 batsmen" – a total upgraded to 122 in recent years, I notice. Freeman, a leg-spinner, bowled more than 1,900 overs that season and averaged a wicket every six and a half overs. But of greater significance than the number of overs he bowled was the benefit he received from the hard wickets of that summer. I doubt that he would have had quite the same strike-rate on the pitches of 1990. Despite all the sunshine, they were in the main slow enough for batsmen playing from the crease to watch the turn and adjust accordingly. England's batsmen, although inexperienced against this kind of bowling, illustrated that against the Indian leg-spinners.

In an attempt to find a more uniform, ideal pitch, experimental pitches have been laid down at ten county grounds, using several different combinations of loam and grass seed. The TCCB hopes they will be ready for use towards the end of the 1991 season. What is needed, I suspect, is a break from cricket to give groundsmen time to relay not just a pitch here and there but the entire square. Since the end of the Second World War there have been 45 summers of cricket: 45 autumns of top-dressing and remaking, with the result that layers of soils have been pressed together, binding in some places and not binding in others. This irregular binding, it seems, is a major cause of uneven bounce. Another problem is that to keep the pitch together, groundsmen have to water more, with the result that matches start on pitches containing too much moisture to provide pace early on or help for the spinners in the later stages.

Last year there was a move by Derbyshire, Kent, Northamptonshire and Yorkshire for a return to uncovered pitches in Championship cricket. It was not supported by the other counties. Given a summer such as that of 1990, and the difficulties which some groundsmen have in getting topsoil to bind, it strikes me that if pitches were not covered overnight, the players could arrive on the final day to find that the surface was blowing away. If it did rain, in all probability the ball would go through the top so quickly that batsmen would be calling for their heaviest bats, not to hit the ball with but to bash the pitch into some kind of shape. It sounds like a groundsman's nightmare.

As to the argument that batsmen would improve their skills on such pitches, I agree in theory. In practice I am less than certain. From what I saw last summer when pitch and ball had a chance to conspire, a good number of batsmen are more likely to get out than grit it out. Mike Gatting's innings at Derby was an example of how to bat in such conditions, but it was also a rare exception.

Pity the poor umpire

It is not as if the players aren't capable of making life difficult for themselves. Groundsmen have noticed an increasing tendency among batsmen to run on the pitch and damage it with their spikes. And such was the umpires' concern at the practice of roughening one side of the ball that the TCCB last summer felt it necessary to bring in stiffer penalties for the offence, in line with those for picking the seam. In either instance the umpire can now replace the ball with one of inferior condition to that previously used. It makes one wonder whence the provenance of the malpractices alleged by the New Zealand and West Indian touring teams in Pakistan late last year. In England last summer there were one or two bowlers who swung the ball much more effectively in their second spell than in their opening one. It is yet another example of how the spirit of the game, as well as the Law, is violated. It is yet another item to tax the umpires' vigilance.

When I first wrote the editor's Notes for *Wisden*, in the 1987 edition, I advocated an international panel of umpires. It would, I wrote then, "cost money, but Test matches are cricket's money-spinner. They are also the world's window on the sport." Just how little money is spun by Test cricket, and how much an international panel of umpires would cost, has become apparent in recent months. A sum of around half a million pounds a year has been estimated (less than £75,000 per country), but without sponsorship that is beyond the budget of world cricket. Sponsorship not being forthcoming, nor for the present is the panel of umpires, even though the International Cricket Council voted six to one in favour of its mandatory use in Test cricket. Australia opposed the motion, partly because of the cost and in part because they did not believe such a move would raise the standard of international umpiring.

I was disappointed that ICC's proposal precluded members of the panel from standing in matches played by their own country. It had seemed to me that it was not neutrality that was so necessary as the umpires' independence from the national boards of control which have appointed and paid them, and will now continue to do so. It was my conjecture that placing the umpires under the auspices of ICC would give them the security to control the game without any kind of outside pressure. It was not my thinking that an Australian should never stand in Australia, or that a Sri Lankan umpire could not take part in a Test match involving Sri Lanka.

An incident at Melbourne in January 1990, in the tour match between Victoria and the Pakistanis, highlights the problems facing an umpire who stands by the grace of a local governing body. After a final warning for following through on the pitch, the Pakistani leg-spinner, Mushtaq Ahmed, was barred from bowling by the umpire following a further transgression. This resulted in the Pakistani team, with their manager, Intikhab Alam, at the head, walking off the field, and the match did not resume until a compromise was reached which allowed Mushtaq to continue bowling. On the face of it, the authority of the umpire was undermined. Let us assume that something similar had happened in a Test match there, and that the touring team had threatened to go home, not only with the Test series unfinished but with the crowd-drawing World Series one-day games still to be played. Would the umpire feel more confident of making a similar decision (and being appointed to stand again) if he had been chosen by the Australian Board or if he was a member of an ICC panel?

Although for the moment there will not be an independent panel of umpires, ICC will have a paid referee at all international matches from October 1991. He will have powers, including the imposition of fines and the suspension of players, to discipline anyone who contravenes the Code of Conduct being drawn up by ICC. The referee, it has been stressed, will be there to support the umpires and will not be able to overrule a decision or interfere with the course of a game. It would be interesting to know what action he could have taken in the aforementioned hypothesis, or what he will do in the event of pitches being prepared to enhance the prospects of the home country. The Code of Conduct will cover "sledging", dissent, over-rates and, one hopes, short-pitched bowling. But it is a sad commentary on the game's players, and on those who have administered the game nationally, that the Code of Conduct has been deemed necessary. Such are the times in which we live.

DON'T BLAME THE BALL

By JACK BANNISTER

Facts and figures may be irrefutable. But just as beauty is often in the eye of the beholder, so too are analysis and interpretation. This is particularly so when the dramatic swing in balance between bat and ball in the English domestic season of 1990 is examined.

Only four counties lacked an individual County Championship double-hundred, while no fewer than 25 batsmen shared 30 Championship scores of 200 or more, including two triple-hundreds. There were seven Championship totals over 600, including two of more than 700 and Lancashire's 863 at The Oval – the second-highest score in the Championship (the highest for 94 years) and the ninth-largest in first-class cricket anywhere in the world.

The occurrence of such a pronounced change in favour of batsmen did not come about simply by coincidence. The previous winter, concerned at the declining standards of play in English first-class cricket, the Test and County Cricket Board had brought in new conditions with regard to the seam of the ball and the preparation of pitches. It was the former, the "new" nine-strand ball, which received universal criticism from players and spectators alike. Bowlers claimed that the big reduction from the previous fifteen-strand ball had rendered ineffective techniques which, in recent years, had produced a rich harvest of wickets. And certainly the division of batting and bowling bonus points won by the seventeen counties in the Britannic Assurance County Championship seemed to reinforce the general complaint that the dominance by batsmen had resulted in too many contrived finishes following a surfeit of meaningless cricket in the preceding days.

Season	Batting Points	Bowling Points
1987	916	1,154
1988	819	1,118
1989	828	1,141
1990	1,048	909

The above table shows that, in the three seasons from 1987 to 1989, an average of 283 more bowling bonus points than batting bonus points were won. And yet in 1990 the difference in favour of the bat was only 139. Over the years, parity has always eluded the authorities, but the smallest differential in four years suggests that they are on the right lines. This is especially so, given that the effect of the despised "new" ball could not really be evaluated accurately because of the additional influence of better pitches and an exceptionally hot and dry summer.

Before the declining quality of modern bowling standards comes under the microscope, another clutch of statistics – bowling ones, this time – shows that the shock to the systems of most county bowlers was almost terminal. In 1989, of all those who bowled more than 200 overs and took ten wickets in Championship cricket, thirteen secured their wickets at an average of less than 20 runs apiece. In 1990 only Ian Bishop and Malcolm Marshall managed this. In 1989, using the same qualification, 38 bowlers secured their wickets at an average cost of less than 26, but in 1990 only five did so, with Curtly Ambrose, Waqar Younis and Ole Mortensen completing a nap-hand of bowlers ineligible for England. In 1989, ten bowlers took 70 wickets or more in the Championship – all of them seamers – whereas in 1990 only five bowlers accomplished this: Neil Foster, Courtney Walsh, Marshall, Tim Munton and Richard Illingworth. Another telling statistic is that in 1989 24 bowlers took 60 or more wickets, but only one spinner, whereas in 1990, of the ten bowlers who passed this mark, three were slow left-arm spinners: Illingworth, Philip Tufnell and Richard Davis.

Most of the bowlers whose results declined so spectacularly last year shouted "foul", but their *cri de coeur* was really a self-critical lament rather than a justifiable complaint that they had been treated unfairly. Even allowing for the fact that the most sharp-witted cricketers need more than one season to adjust to what was, arguably, the biggest change in equipment for two decades, the best bowlers still took wickets. And while the critics of the less helpful ball could claim that fewer matches produced outright results – 93 last year compared with 103 in 1989 – they cannot argue with what is probably the most revealing statistic of all – the extra amount of spin bowling in 1990.

The following list of spinners is a fair representation of most counties' slow-bowling strength (or lack thereof), and the sixteen, except for Barnett and Williams in the first year, all bowled a minimum of 200 overs in the County Championship in 1989 and 1990: Kim Barnett, John Childs, David Graveney, Raj Maru, Davis, John Emburey, Tufnell, Nick Cook, Richard Williams, Eddie Hemmings, Andy Afford, Ian Swallow, Keith Medlycott, Ian Salisbury, Illingworth and Phil Carrick.

Season	Overs Bowled	Wickets Taken
1989	7,216.2	607
1990	9,931.2	693

Surely these figures prove the worth of the decision of the cricket committee of the TCCB to put a stop to too many cheap wickets on too many sub-standard pitches. Admittedly the strike-rate declined from a wicket in every twelve overs to one in fourteen, but even this shows that captains were prepared to put their faith in spin once it became clear that ordinary medium-pace bowling, previously so effective from one new ball to another, produced nothing more than easy runs.

The real benefits to English cricket from a more equal contest between bat and ball will manifest themselves only slowly, because a whole new generation of bowlers is having to go right back to the beginning and learn many of the arts of bowling which were in danger of disappearing completely. Of course, the old days of bowlers taking big totals of wickets have gone, now that the Championship programme comprises only 72 days. And if the lobby which wants an entire programme of four-day Championship cricket has its way, even that total will be reduced by eight days. Consequently, valid comparisons with giants of yesteryear are impossible.

Since the proliferation of regular one-day cricket in the English domestic season from 1969, today's bowlers lack the opportunity to bowl the same number of overs as the leading wicket-takers either side of the Second World War. The current 72-day programme allows for a maximum of just under 8,000 overs in the 22 games played by each county; i.e., 4,000 overs per side. In the days of 32 three-day games, in which at least 120 overs a day were the norm, a seasonal maximum of more than 11,000 overs gave each set of bowlers well over 5,000 overs to share out. Hence the 59 instances of 28 bowlers taking 200 wickets or more in an English season. Eight of those instances were performed by the Kent leg-spinner, "Tich" Freeman, the only man this century to bowl more than 2,000 overs in a season, which he did in 1933 when he took 298 wickets, six fewer than his record of 304 in 1928. This means that he bowled approximately 80 per cent of his county's overs from one end. After the resumption of first-class cricket in 1946, however, only Tony Lock (twice), Tom Goddard and Bob Appleyard passed the 200 mark.

The decline in bowling standards started around twenty years ago, with at least four factors responsible: poor pitches, overseas players, one-day cricket and a more helpful ball, though not necessarily in that order. Thankfully, the TCCB, if not quite at a stroke, gave their policy on pitches some teeth; and whatever the criticism of introducing the nine-strand ball at the same time, the combination of the two has undoubtedly shown up the average modern bowler for what he is: an unimaginative purveyor of the kind of seam bowling which relies more on containment than penetration.

The Reader balls used until 1989 made life easy for such bowlers. They just had to point it and wait for the hand-grenade to explode. Subtleties, such as swinging the ball, varying the point of delivery and change of pace – arts learned, it seems, much more readily by overseas bowlers – were ignored, simply because they were unnecessary. Now they are required, and any bowler who cannot master what used to be ordinary basics will have to look for another job. However, Warwickshire's Munton has set an example for his fellow seam bowlers to copy. His own captain, Andy Lloyd, confessed that he thought Munton was the last sort of bowler to prosper with the 1990 ball. He was delighted by his bowler's determination to learn to swing the ball and to develop the ability to adjust his point of delivery, and so his line, when necessary.

For 1990, the two principal ball manufacturers, Reader and Duke, produced two different balls, despite the firm specifications given them. (These included nine strands only, and a reduction in the height of the seam from the circumference from 0.9 to 0.7 millimetres – a difference of 22 per cent.) The Reader ball contained a golf-ball-type core, which meant it retained its shape better than the softer Duke, which still had a cork-bound centre. However, Duke's used looser stitching which, when waxed, gave a more prominent seam and much more swing. In addition to the moans from the seam bowlers, there was also a general complaint that the flatter seam did not give slow bowlers the grip necessary to obtain more purchase. But that is a teething problem which should be solved by the manufacturers, as well as by some extra determination from a breed of bowlers who, in recent years, had been almost actively discouraged.

The cricketers, through their Association, and the captains begged the TCCB to relent and increase the strands for 1991 either to twelve or fifteen. However, the cricket committee stuck to its guns. That means a lot of hard work for many young bowlers, the benefit of which will be reaped at international level as soon as they develop a more repetitive technique. At the moment, Angus Fraser glitters like a lone jewel among much dross in English cricket. And if it irritates the modern cricketer to remind him that there were half a dozen Frasers in county cricket in the first 25 years after the Second World War, so be it.

Now that it is no longer sufficient for seam bowlers to point and release, they will have to learn the mechanics of a good hand action. With most bowlers, the position of the feet dictates the body position which, in turn, governs the hand action at the moment of release. Nevertheless, history is littered with exceptions to the rule – the unorthodox open-chested bowler who still possessed a hand action to bowl the out-swinger, and vice versa. I watched Tom Cartwright, originally a batsman for Warwickshire, turn seam bowling into an art, simply by taking the construction of a flawless hand action to the ultimate. With an "old" ball (i.e., before the seam was *increased*) he took 1,058 wickets for Warwickshire in the later part of the 1950s and in he 1960s.

The "new" ball is similar to that used 30 years ago. The major difference in the game, though, is that pitches were uncovered then. The arguments against reverting to this environment are many, yet if the run-ups were also uncovered, fears that fast bowlers would be lethal after rain would be unfounded. Uncovered pitches brought about more rounded techniques for both batsmen and bowlers. With the ball, accuracy and a repetitive method were essential. But while that debate continues, unquestionably the TCCB has got it right with regard to the ball. The Board must not now bow to pressure to abandon a brave experiment which, if responded to with similar courage by county bowlers, will bring the rich reward of better standards for bowlers and batsmen alike.

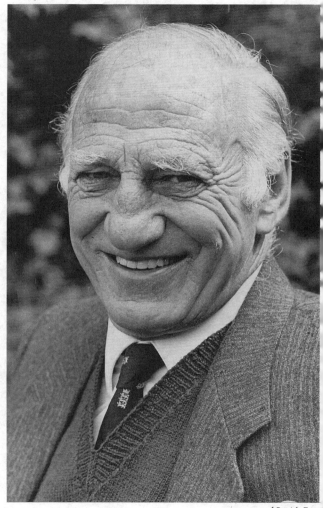

[*Patrick Eagar*

SIR LEONARD HUTTON

A CRICKETING LEGEND

By JOHN WOODCOCK

Between the end of the First World War in 1918 and the start of the Second in 1939, English cricket produced three great batsmen – Walter Hammond, Leonard Hutton and Denis Compton. Each one was endowed with a wonderful talent, Hammond's enabling him to play with rare splendour, Compton's with an irresistible *joie de vivre* and Hutton's with a style that was all-embracing. Although Herbert Sutcliffe had a comparable record, compiled between the wars, he was not in the same way a product of the 1920s or 1930s, having been on the point of breaking through in 1914.

Len Hutton died on September 6, 1990, at the age of 74. He had slipped into Lord's only five days earlier, to watch the final of the NatWest Bank Trophy from Paul Getty's box in the Mound Stand. He had been there, too, for the Test match against India in July, and seen Graham Gooch get to within 31 runs of his own most famous record, the 364 with which he tormented Australia at The Oval in 1938.

Hutton retained until the end the unassuming manner which marked his apprenticeship. Sir Jack Hobbs had been the same; as disarmingly unboastful after being knighted as before. There was also about Sir Len an apparent frailty at the crease, a characteristic which caused his son, Richard, who also played for Yorkshire and England, frequent anxiety until he was old and wise enough to recognise the artistry it disguised.

For the benefit of those who never saw Hutton bat, I have been trying to think of someone playing today who puts one in mind of him, and I am not sure that I can. This is surprising, for he was essentially orthodox and resolutely conventional. Except that he gives more of an impression of hitting the ball, and less of stroking it, than Hutton did, Stephen Waugh, the gifted Australian of similar build, probably comes as near to it as anyone. Mohammad Azharuddin is another who possesses that intuition which gives the great natural players such a start to life. There was something quite uncanny about the way, for example, in which Hutton coped with the mysteries of Sonny Ramadhin's spin while carrying his bat against West Indies at The Oval in 1950, just as there was in his handling of Jack Iverson's when doing the same against Australia at Adelaide only six months later. He was, hereabouts, at the meridian of his powers. So, besides Ramadhin and Iverson, were Keith Miller and Ray Lindwall. In fair weather and foul, at home and overseas, if Len failed the chances were that England would.

Whether his character was influenced by being born at Fulneck, the village near Pudsey where there was an isolated Moravian community ("protestants of rare missionary zeal") is a matter for conjecture. To some extent it probably was, their significance being quite considerable. But cricket, too, was a family religion. Those who didn't take to it would have been put back if that had been possible, and being chosen for Yorkshire when still a month short of his eighteenth birthday – his first match was against Cambridge University at Fenner's in May 1934 – made Hutton the youngest player to appear for the county since George Hirst in 1889. He came into a side that had won the Championship for the previous three years – Yorkshire had not

Sir Leonard Hutton

been out of the first four since 1911 – and, although they finished
disappointing fifth in 1934, to play regularly for them in those days gave
young man a distinct advantage. If the same applied today, Richard Blakey
and Ashley Metcalfe would, I am sure, be nearer to playing for England than
they probably are.

In Hutton's case, the transition from callow youth, cap steeply tilted, to one
of the world's most accomplished batsmen was achieved in an extraordinarily
short time. Yorkshire colts getting a game for the county side in the middle
1930s were left in no doubt that they were there to be seen and not heard. I
was an austere school, and Hutton was an astute observer. Within four years
of joining it he had become a household name. Nothing was more remarkable
about his *tour de force* at The Oval than that he was only just 22 at the time

Then came the war, claiming several summers when Hutton's play would
still have carried the bloom of youth, and leaving him, as the result of a
training accident, with his left arm two inches shorter than the right. With
the return of peace, the mantle that had been Hammond's passed to Hutton
whose batting, despite having been laid up for so long, had matured. Between
1934 and 1939 he had scored 11,658 runs at an average of 48.98. From 1945
when he played his next first-class innings, to his retirement in 1955 he made
another 28,292 at 58.81. Although, hardly surprisingly, he himself felt
handicapped by his disabled arm – its shortening was clearly visible – he
made miraculously light of it. If Compton and Bill Edrich were the spirit of
the immediate post-war years, Hutton was looked to to provide the stability
Between the three of them they did wonders for our rehabilitation.

That Compton rather than Hutton was made Freddie Brown's vice-captain
in Australia in 1950-51 was for reasons of compatibility. When, in 1952,
more egalitarian age was dawning and a captain was being sought to succeed
Brown, Len was the clear choice (although he had never led Yorkshire), and
it fell to him to regain the Ashes in England in 1953 and then retain them in
Australia two years later. In Australia he was quick to see the possibilities of
a Statham-Tyson combination, despite Tyson's rather lumbering early effort
and although it meant leaving out Alec Bedser, which he did without the con
sideration due to so great a figure in the game.

Hutton was not, in fact, an easy communicator. It could be said that he
distanced himself from his side when at times they needed a stronger lead
This was particularly so in the West Indies in 1953-54 on the first of his two
tours as captain. On the other hand, they were in awe of him as a player, and
that was a help. Just as Sir Henry Cotton dignified the status of the
professional golfer, so Hutton did of the professional cricketer.

Still good enough to make 145 against Australia at Lord's in 1953 – an
innings described by Neville Cardus as "one of the most regal and highly
pedigreed ever seen in an England and Australia Test match" – and to
average an astonishing 96.71 against West Indies that winter, by the summer
of 1954 Len was suddenly finding it much more of an effort to summon the
skill and nerve and concentration needed both to captain England and to
make runs. There were also suggestions that, although his side had staged a
epic recovery in the West Indies, they had not covered themselves with glory
in other respects. There were, accordingly, calls for a change of captain
These, happily, were resisted, and off to Australia he went in September 195
for his third and last tour there as a player. In the event it took so much ou
of him, once England had been horribly beaten in the First Test – not leas
because Hutton had put Australia in – that, within a few months of hi
getting home in the spring of 1955, he put his bats away. His back wa

laying him up, and after the heat and burden of the last two years a quiet retirement in Surrey, with a golf course nearby, had an obvious appeal. Famous Yorkshireman that he was, the south, with its less competitive responses, suited him better than the north.

For a decade Len Hutton was the model for English batsmen. As a first movement he slid his right foot back and across towards the middle stump, from where, basically, he did what came naturally. He had a lovely stance, as still as it was relaxed. He would play right back but seldom right forward, referring to let the ball come to him and playing it very late. Between bat and pad there was sometimes, dare I say it, a gap – the forward "prop" had yet to come into fashion – and through it he was liable to be bowled by an off-break. Early in the season, undergraduates at Oxford and Cambridge were known to get him out this way.

There were occasions, too, when, because of his arm, he played his cover drive not leaning into the ball so much as reaching for it. But his timing and balance were such that it was still pleasing to the eye. He had all the strokes if he wanted them, though only when no risk was involved did he loft the ball. In his nineteen Test hundreds he hit only two sixes, and one of those was to what was then the shortest straight boundary in Test cricket – Jamaica's Sabina Park. It was a drive off Gary Sobers, bowling orthodox left-arm spin.

Hutton never greatly cared for leaving his crease to the spinners, of whom there were vastly more then than there are now. Had he done so, the chances are that the generation which followed him, led by Peter May, Colin Cowdrey and Tom Graveney, would themselves have ventured forth rather more. Like all instinctively good judges of a run, he never looked to be in a hurry between the wickets. Studying under Sutcliffe in his early days for Yorkshire would have shown him the need for conviction in calling and let him into the secrets of the short single.

A broken nose gave Len a misleadingly rugged appearance. But to go with it he had a winning smile and blue eyes which regularly twinkled with his own brand of sometimes cryptic humour. He was full of paradoxes: self-contained yet vulnerable, reserved yet quizzical, shrewd yet enigmatic, gentle yet tenacious. He wanted to be judged as a person as much as in his role as a cricketer, and it may truthfully be said that, like Hobbs before him, he attracted widespread and genuine affection.

I see him on board ship in 1950 and again in 1954, bound for Australia and wrapped in contemplation. I see him working the ball around, seldom plundering the bowling, rather picking up runs as he went – a late cut here, a placed single there, and then, sometimes after a long wait, the cover drive that was his special glory. The modern game would have given us, inevitably, a different player: he would have had no chance to surpass himself, as he sometimes so memorably did, on drying pitches, and it is as dreadful to think of him in a helmet as it is to think of Compton, Hammond or W.G. in one.

I see him near the end of his tether, as a lot of us were, before the Ashes were safely in England's keeping in Australia in 1954-55. And I shall remember him at the Lord's Test match against India last year, going quietly and a little wearily off into the twilight, content, I fancy, that his record score for England was still intact, though certain to have been just as affable had it not been. He was not one to shower compliments around, but by then he knew when they were due and duly paid them. A cricketing legend, he won as many hearts with his beguiling albeit watchful charm as with the mastery of his batting.

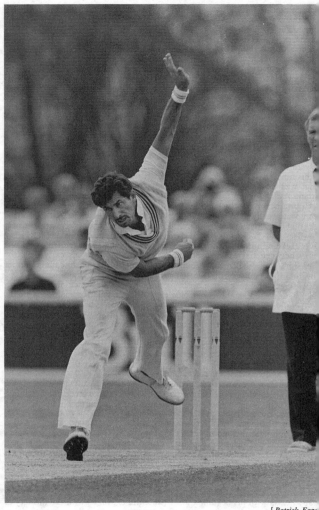

[*Patrick Eaga*

SIR RICHARD HADLEE

"VERY HAPPY, RELIEVED, PROUD"

By DON MOSEY

The international bowling career of Richard John Hadlee, KBE, by his own assessment may be divided into three distinct periods: the first five years when he was "erratic, inconsistent and without a great idea of how to get through three days, let alone four, or five"; the years 1977 to 1980 when, according to Glenn Turner, he "came of age"; and the final decade, when he positively raced to his record number of 431 Test wickets by summoning every resource of experience and guile.

It began on February 2, 1973, at the Basin Reserve, Wellington, where he took two wickets in the match against Pakistan for 112 runs, and it ended on July 10, 1990, at Edgbaston, Birmingham, when he was handed the ball with which he had taken five wickets in an innings for the 36th time. From that modest start he had averaged five wickets a match over the 86 Tests in which he had played in the subsequent seventeen and a half years, and he retired "very happy, relieved, proud".

That he was the most intelligent fast bowler the world has seen there can be little doubt or argument. He did not have the bumptious lovableness of Botham, the small boy's hero; he rarely, if ever, showed the fire and fury of Trueman in his pomp; he never besmirched his reputation with the gimmickry or histrionics of Lillee (the bowler he most admired). What Hadlee brought to fast bowling in the second half of his career was deep thought, intense academic study and immense concentration. Not only did he spend hours watching video-tapes of Lillee, considering the approach, the delivery, the grip, the release; he spent even more time searching for weaknesses in the defensive armoury of the greatest batsmen of his day, in the manner of a surgeon studying X-rays before probing for the source of the problem.

Hadlee's basic delivery (if, in fact, there was one) would be the ball which moved away from the bat after pitching on to an angled seam. He called it, in Southern hemisphere style, a leg-cutter – a delivery which in English terms requires a specific movement of the fingers at the moment of release – but such was his control and his ability to land the ball exactly as required that he might be said to have perfected a simplified version of the leg-cutter. He could nip one back the other way, usually from a little wider in the bowling crease to pose problems of line-judgement. Swing was not always the most potent weapon, but when atmospheric conditions were right his quicker ball moved late and away towards the slips; his slower ball, the one he called the "dangly", swung into the batsman. He used the quick bouncer sparingly, keeping it always in reserve to invest it with the additional element of surprise. There was subtlety in everything he did.

Hadlee's "placing" of these differing deliveries in the course of an over was as meticulously thoughtful as every other aspect of his campaign, for that is what a bowling spell was to him. In the manner of the great spin bowlers of earlier years, he plotted the downfall of his opponents on lines of long-term strategy, without necessarily feeling that each individual delivery deserved a wicket on its own merits. It was simply a factor in the Grand Design, a skirmish in the battle to put the batsman on the foot, back or front, where he was less assured or – the ultimate victory – to catch him in no-man's-land. There has been no greater fascination in modern cricket than watching an over from Richard Hadlee when there was some response from the pitch or some help in the atmosphere.

So great has been the impact of his bowling, for Nottinghamshire and for New Zealand, that it is possible to pay less regard to his batting than it merits. Yet on figures alone he stands among the greatest of post-war all-rounders. Only Botham, Kapil Dev and Imran Khan join him in the ranks of those who have scored more than 3,000 runs while taking more than 300 wickets in Test matches. His "double" in the County Championship of 1984 was the first to be performed in England since 1967 (by Fred Titmus), in an age when the feat seemed to be beyond modern cricketers. And consider his averages in accomplishing it: 1,179 runs at 51.26, 117 wickets costing 14.05 each. They are astonishing figures. In the 1987 NatWest Bank Trophy final, the game seemed irretrievably lost to Nottinghamshire when it spilled over into a second day because of rain; Hadlee's 70 not out from 61 balls on the Monday resulted in a victory which was something more than improbable.

At Test level, his eleven wickets for 102 and 51 runs in the first innings helped New Zealand to the victory which decided the 1979-80 series against West Indies; in the following match he completed a maiden Test century (as well as rounding off his Test "double") off 92 balls from Roberts, Holding, Garner and Croft. In February 1984, in Christchurch, he took eight wickets for 44 runs and scored 99 runs from 81 balls on a pitch where England mustered *totals* of only 82 and 93.

Even in a career as illustrious as his, however, there have been disappointments. "If the ultimate satisfaction for a bowler is to do the hat-trick, then the *ultimate* ultimate must be to take all ten wickets in an innings, and I never did that." The nearest Hadlee came to all ten was when he took nine for 52 in the innings victory over Australia in Brisbane in November 1985. But as he caught the tenth batsman, took six for 71 in the second innings, and in between hit 54 runs, that can scarcely amount to a deep disappointment. "No. That was, I suppose, as near-perfect a performance as one hopes to achieve, and one in which the whole team shared. Brilliant catches were held and the batting was consistent." It was a result which left Australia stunned.

For the real disappointment of his Test life, one has to turn to events in his own country, most particularly a widespread failure by press and public to understand and accept his adoption of the short run after 1980. There was a rather naïve insistence that New Zealand's principal strike bowler should *look* fast by continuing an approach from 25 yards. While sheer physical necessity demanded that he reduce this, Hadlee felt a sense of outrage that his professionalism was being questioned. The shaft which went deepest was a well-turned journalistic phrase of Don Cameron, the country's leading cricket-writer, who wrote of ". . . New Zealand's heaviest artillery operating off a pop-gun run-up". Ten years after the words were written, Richard Hadlee quotes them in a crescendo of indignant incredulity. It was that change which transformed him from a good Test bowler into a great one.

As his career developed, so did his public persona and the need for a highly developed sense of public relations. He acknowledges with gratitude the debt he owes to Grahame Felton, a management consultant in Christchurch, who changed the whole Hadlee character after a near-breakdown in 1983. His naturally strong personality became even more positive; he seemed able almost to anticipate all but the most asinine of questions, and in consequence an interview with Richard Hadlee has usually been a rewarding experience for the questioner. His replies are reasoned, succinct, humorous (where appropriate) and always to the point. If he has not suffered fools gladly, no-one but a fool would condemn him.

His is a character which his fellow New Zealanders have perhaps found easier to respect than to regard with warm affection, though his autobiography achieved a massive sale. His countrymen are less effusive about sporting heroes than in some other parts of the world. As a result of this, criticism at home, especially when ill-informed, has tended to irritate him more than might otherwise have been the case. (In this, he would find a ready ally in Glenn Turner.) One accusation of cupidity – the matter of a car awarded for an outstanding performance – was built up to a *cause célèbre* in New Zealand. Yet if one searches for the real heart of the man, one comes to his confession at the end of the 1980 season with Nottinghamshire: "I felt a cheat. I had had three awful seasons since first joining the club and commitments to New Zealand meant that I hadn't given Notts value for money. I was embarrassed to collect my pay-cheque." Hadlee has always been practical and pragmatic in financial matters, but he would shudder at the thought of anyone believing him capable of short-changing his employers or his colleagues.

He has been as industrious a worker outside cricket as he was on the field, involving himself in authorship, broadcasting (presenting his own programme), publicity and promotion, television commercials, journalism and public speaking. To these activities he now adds the commercial cultivation of exotic flowers, and it will be no surprise to anyone if that, in due course, becomes a highly successful enterprise. If Richard Hadlee appears to have the golden touch, it is largely because he works so hard for his success. Edison may well have been looking a century into the future when he defined genius as one per cent inspiration and 99 per cent perspiration.

The final distinction of a knighthood in the 1990 Birthday Honours' list came as near as anything has to overwhelming the man. He admits to "dreaming dreams" as a child without any real expectation of fulfilment. Personally, I have a few doubts about that. Richard John Hadlee seems always to have had a strong sense of his own destiny. At 39, feeling "very happy, relieved, proud", he could look forward to the second half of a life in which all things were possible. There will be no raised eyebrows – from New Zealand to Nottingham – at what he achieves.

While Hadlee's conversation is animated, bright and witty, it is perhaps a little difficult to think of him indulging his sense of humour in the middle of a Test match. When he bowled Devon Malcolm to end England's first innings at Edgbaston, however, he was laughing so much at the batsman's simulated aggression that he found it difficult to direct the ball at the target. The umpire, John Holder, confessed that *he* was laughing so heartily that it would have been difficult to answer an lbw appeal. Fortunately for the dignity of the game and of a distinguished career, the end of the second innings was a more serious matter, for that final five-wicket performance put New Zealand in with a chance of victory. It would have been unthinkable to look back on a bowling performance by Sir Richard Hadlee as any sort of laughing matter. The last spell of all put matters into perspective. Hadlee bade farewell to the game on a more characteristically thoughtful – and successful – note.

SIR RICHARD HADLEE

TEST CAREER – BATTING

		T	I	NO	R	HI	100s	50s	Avge	Ct
1972-73	v Pakistan†	1	1	0	46	46	0	0	46.00	2
1973	v England	1	2	1	4	4*	0	0	4.00	0
1973-74	v Australia	3	6	0	68	20	0	0	11.33	2
	v Australia†	2	3	0	37	23	0	0	12.33	1
1975-76	v India†	2	2	0	45	33	0	0	22.50	0
1976-77	v Pakistan	3	6	2	214	87	0	1	53.50	2
	v India	3	6	0	60	21	0	0	10.00	1
	v Australia†	2	4	0	143	81	0	1	35.75	2
1977-78	v England†	3	6	1	80	39	0	0	16.00	1
1978	v England	3	6	0	32	11	0	0	5.33	3
1978-79	v Pakistan†	3	5	1	115	53*	0	1	28.75	1
1979-80	v West Indies†	3	4	0	178	103	1	1	44.50	1
1980-81	v Australia	3	6	2	98	51*	0	1	24.50	1
	v India†	3	4	0	29	20	0	0	7.25	2
1981-82	v Australia†	3	5	1	92	40	0	0	23.00	2
1982-83	v Sri Lanka†	2	3	1	59	30	0	0	29.50	1
1983	v England	4	8	2	301	92*	0	3	50.16	1
1983-84	v England†	3	4	0	144	99	0	1	36.00	3
	v Sri Lanka	3	4	0	75	29	0	0	18.75	3
1984-85	v Pakistan†	3	4	0	131	89	0	1	32.75	0
	v West Indies	4	7	1	137	39*	0	0	22.83	2
1985-86	v Australia	3	4	0	111	54	0	1	27.75	2
	v Australia†	3	3	1	105	72*	0	1	52.50	2
1986	v England	3	3	0	93	68	0	1	31.00	0
1986-87	v West Indies†	3	4	2	74	35*	0	0	37.00	2
	v Sri Lanka	1	1	0	151	151*	1	0	—	1
1987-88	v Australia	3	6	1	111	36	0	0	22.20	0
	v England†	1	1	0	37	37	0	0	37.00	0
1988-89	v India	3	6	1	61	31	0	0	12.20	1
	v Pakistan†	2	3	1	53	32	0	0	26.50	0
1989-90	v India†	3	2	0	115	87	0	1	57.50	0
	v Australia†	1	1	0	18	18	0	0	18.00	0
1990	v England	3	4	0	107	86	0	1	26.75	2
		86	134	19	3,124	151*	2	15	27.16	39

* *Signifies not out.*   † *Series played in New Zealand.*

Highest innings: 151* v Sri Lanka at Colombo (CCC), 1986-87.

TEST CAREER – BOWLING

		T	O	M	R	W	BB	Avge	5W/i
1972-73	v Pakistan†	1	*25	0	112	2	2-84	56.00	0
1973	v England	1	45	8	143	1	1-79	143.00	0
1973-74	v Australia	3	*66.7	9	255	7	4-33	36.42	0
	v Australia†	2	*50.4	7	225	10	4-71	22.50	0
1975-76	v India†	2	*48.3	4	197	12	7-23	16.41	1‡

		T	O	M	R	W	BB	Avge	5W/i
1976-77	v Pakistan	3	*75.2	2	447	10	5-121	44.70	1
	v India	3	127	18	437	13	4-95	33.61	0
	v Australia†	2	*72	7	354	6	3-155	59.00	0
1977-78	v England†	3	*121.3	26	371	15	6-26	24.73	1‡
1978	v England	3	121.1	31	270	13	5-84	20.76	1
1978-79	v Pakistan†	3	*117.6	13	414	18	5-62	23.00	2
1979-80	v West Indies†	3	161.3	50	361	19	6-68	19.00	2‡
1980-81	v Australia	3	147.3	35	364	19	6-57	19.15	2
	v India†	3	119.3	37	288	10	5-47	28.80	1
1981-82	v Australia†	3	91.5	25	226	14	6-100	16.14	2
1982-83	v Sri Lanka†	2	77.3	27	141	10	4-33	14.10	0
1983	v England	4	232	65	559	21	6-53	26.61	2
1983-84	v England†	3	109.5	33	232	12	5-28	19.33	1
	v Sri Lanka	3	117.5	47	230	23	5-29	10.00	2‡
1984-85	v Pakistan†	3	118.5	29	306	16	6-51	19.12	1
	v West Indies	4	143	31	409	15	4-53	27.26	0
1985-86	v Australia	3	169.3	42	401	33	9-52	12.15	5§
	v Australia†	3	157.5	36	387	16	7-116	24.18	1
1986	v England	3	153.5	42	390	19	6-80	20.52	2‡
1986-87	v West Indies†	3	113.1	20	354	17	6-50	20.82	2
	v Sri Lanka	1	38.5	10	102	4	4-102	25.50	0
1987-88	v Australia	3	156	44	353	18	5-67	19.61	3‡
	v England†	1	18	3	50	0	0-50	—	0
1988-89	v India	3	100.5	25	252	18	6-49	14.00	2‡
	v Pakistan†	2	82	21	169	5	4-101	33.80	0
1989-90	v India†	3	105.5	24	319	12	4-69	26.58	0
	v Australia†	1	41.2	8	109	7	5-39	15.57	1
1990	v England	3	133.5	24	384	16	5-53	24.00	1
		86	2,883.3 & *577.1	803	9,611	431	9-52	22.29	36

* Eight-ball overs.   † Series played in New Zealand.

‡ *Signifies ten wickets in a match once; § twice. Sir Richard Hadlee took ten wickets in a Test match nine times.*

Best bowling: 9-52 v Australia at Brisbane, 1985-86.

SUMMARY v EACH COUNTRY

	T	O	M	R	W	BB	Avge	5W/i
v Australia	23	*189.3 & 764	213	2,674	130	9-52	20.56	14§
v England	21	*121.3 & 813.4	232	2,399	97	6-26	24.73	8‡
v India	14	*48.3 & 453.1	108	1,493	65	7-23	22.96	4‡
v Pakistan	12	*218 & 200.5	65	1,448	51	6-51	28.39	4
v West Indies	10	417.4	101	1,124	51	6-50	22.03	4†
v Sri Lanka	6	234.1	84	473	37	5-29	12.78	2†
	86	2,883.3 & *577.1	803	9,611	431	9-52	22.29	36

* Eight-ball overs.   † *Signifies ten wickets in a match once; ‡ twice; § three times.*

FIVE WICKETS IN AN INNINGS/TEN WICKETS IN A MATCH

4-35 ⎫
7-23 ⎭ v India, Wellington, 1975-76.

5-121 v Pakistan, Lahore, 1976-77.

4-74 ⎫
6-26 ⎭ v England, Wellington, 1977-78.

5-84 v England, Lord's, 1978.

5-62 v Pakistan, Christchurch, 1978-79.

5-104 v Pakistan, Auckland, 1978-79.

5-34 ⎫
6-68 ⎭ v West Indies, Dunedin, 1979-80.

5-87 v Australia, Perth, 1980-81.

6-57 v Australia, Melbourne, 1980-81.

5-47 v India, Christchurch, 1980-81.

5-63 v Australia, Auckland, 1981-82.

6-100 v Australia, Christchurch, 1981-82.

6-53 v England, The Oval, 1983.

5-93 v England, Lord's, 1983.

5-28 v England, Christchurch, 1983-84.

5-73 ⎫
5-29 ⎭ v Sri Lanka, Colombo (CCC), 1983-84.

6-51 ⎫
9-52 ⎬ v Pakistan, Dunedin, 1984-85.
6-71 ⎭

5-65 v Australia, Brisbane, 1985-86.

5-65 ⎫
6-90 ⎭ v Australia, Sydney, 1985-86.

7-116 v Australia, Perth, 1985-86.

6-80 v Australia, Christchurch, 1985-86.

6-80 ⎫
4-60 ⎭ v England, Lord's, 1986.

6-105 v England, Nottingham, 1986.

6-50 v West Indies, Auckland, 1986-87.

5-68 v West Indies, Christchurch, 1986-87.

5-109 ⎫
5-67 ⎭ v Australia, Adelaide, 1987-88.

5-65 v Australia, Melbourne, 1987-88.

6-49 ⎫
4-39 ⎭ v India, Bangalore, 1988-89.

5-39 v India, Bombay, 1988-89.

5-53 v Australia, Wellington, 1989-90.

v England, Birmingham, 1990.

FIRST-CLASS CAREER – BATTING

		M	I	NO	R	HI	100s	50s	Avge	Ct
1971-72		3	3	1	16	11	0	0	8.00	2
1972-73		6	8	1	126	50	0	1	18.00	7
	(Australia)	1	1	0	9	9	0	0	9.00	0
1973		12	7	2	74	30	0	0	14.80	0
1973-74		3	5	1	71	23	0	0	17.75	1
	(Australia)	7	11	0	197	49	0	0	17.90	3
1974-75		1	2	1	47	33	0	0	47.00	1
1975-76		9	12	3	200	53*	0	1	22.22	3
1976-77		7	11	1	328	81	0	2	32.80	4
	(Pakistan)	5	8	2	224	87	0	1	37.33	2
	(India)	3	6	0	60	21	0	0	10.00	1
1977-78		10	20	4	346	77	0	2	21.62	2
1978		17	21	4	342	101*	1	0	20.11	10
1978-79		10	16	4	329	79*	0	3	27.41	3
1979		12	16	4	193	41	0	0	16.08	5
1979-80		3	4	0	178	103	1	1	44.50	1
	(Australia)	6	10	3	160	33*	0	0	22.85	4
1980		8	9	1	231	68	0	1	28.87	0
1980-81		3	4	0	29	20	0	0	7.25	2
	(Australia)	5	8	2	249	103	1	1	41.50	2
1981		21	26	3	745	142*	1	3	32.39	14
1981-82		10	18	3	500	83*	0	3	33.33	5
1982		18	28	2	807	131	2	4	31.03	16
1982-83		4	7	1	171	46	0	0	28.50	5
1983		13	15	2	596	103	1	5	45.84	6
1983-84		6	9	1	305	99	0	2	38.12	7
	(Sri Lanka)	4	4	0	75	29	0	0	18.75	3
1984		24	31	8	1,179	210*	2	7	51.26	23
1984-85		8	12	2	221	89	0	1	22.10	0
	(West Indies)	4	7	1	137	39*	0	0	22.83	4
1985		19	29	11	592	73*	0	5	32.88	17

		M	I	NO	R	HI	100s	50s	Avge	Ct
1985-86		3	3	1	105	72*	0	1	52.50	2
	(Australia)	5	6	0	151	54	0	1	25.16	3
1986		17	21	5	813	129*	2	4	50.81	6
1986-87		11	17	5	281	50*	0	1	23.41	9
	(Sri Lanka)	1	1	1	151	151*	1	0	—	1
1987		21	28	7	1,111	133*	2	6	52.90	16
1987-88		1	1	0	37	37	0	0	37.00	0
	(Australia)	5	8	3	151	36	0	0	30.20	1
1988-89		3	4	1	90	37	0	0	30.00	0
	(India)	4	7	2	88	31	0	0	17.60	2
1989-90		4	3	0	133	87	0	1	44.33	0
1990		5	6	0	204	90	0	2	34.00	4
		342	473	93	12,052	210*	14	59	31.71	198

* *Signifies not out.*

Note: Sir Richard Hadlee appeared for Nottinghamshire from 1978 to 1987, and for Tasmania in 1979-80. In New Zealand he played for Canterbury.

Highest innings: 210*, Nottinghamshire v Middlesex at Lord's, 1984.

FIRST-CLASS CAREER – BOWLING

		O	M	R	W	BB	Avge	5W/i	10W/m
1971-72		*55	9	194	10	4-42	19.40	0	0
1972-73		*144	18	550	30	4-25	18.33	0	0
	(Australia)	*26	3	80	1	1-32	80.00	0	0
1973		355.1	72	1,058	38	5-56	27.84	1	0
1973-74		*79.5	11	340	16	4-64	21.25	0	0
	(Australia)	*175.7	18	728	16	4-33	45.50	0	0
1974-75		*27	6	82	3	2-32	27.33	0	0
1975-76		*222.7	31	751	40	7-23	18.77	2	1
1976-77		*181.5	20	721	18	3-21	40.05	0	0
	(Pakistan)	*109.5	3	610	18	5-47	33.88	2	0
	(India)	127	18	437	13	4-95	33.61	0	0
1977-78		*266.1	56	860	42	6-26	20.47	3	1
1978		497.1	120	1,269	78	7-77	16.26	6	2
1978-79		*299.1	56	909	50	6-28	18.18	4	0
1979		317	103	753	47	7-23	16.02	2	0
1979-80		161.3	50	361	19	6-68	19.00	2	1
	(Australia)	173.2	36	477	13	5-55	36.69	1	0
1980		222.1	82	410	29	5-32	14.13	1	0
1980-81		119.3	37	288	10	5-47	28.80	1	0
	(Australia)	229.3	52	567	27	6-57	21.00	3	0
1981		708.4	231	1,564	105	7-25	14.89	4	0
1981-82		424.2	131	867	59	6-26	14.69	7	2
1982		403.5	123	889	61	7-25	14.57	4	0
1982-83		152.5	52	277	23	6-43	12.04	1	1
1983		431.3	123	1,065	49	6-53	21.73	3	0
1983-84		181.5	62	329	24	5-28	13.70	1	0
	(Sri Lanka)	128.5	49	258	24	5-29	10.75	2	1
1984		772.2	248	1,645	117	7-35	14.05	6	1
1984-85		287.3	88	652	38	6-51	17.15	3	0
	(West Indies)	143	33	409	15	4-53	27.26	0	0
1985		473.5	136	1,026	59	8-41	17.38	2	0
1985-86		157.5	36	387	16	7-116	24.18	1	0
	(Australia)	241.3	65	537	37	9-52	14.51	5	2
1986		547.3	150	1,215	76	6-31	15.98	7	2
1986-87		407.2	106	935	62	7-49	15.08	8	1
	(Sri Lanka)	38.5	10	102	4	4-102	25.50	0	0
1987		591	189	1,227	97	6-20	12.64	9	2

		O	M	R	W	BB	Avge	5W/i	10W/m
1987-88		18	3	50	0	0-50	—	0	0
	(Australia)	237.4	63	564	29	5-30	19.44	5	2
1988-89		113	32	234	7	4-101	33.42	0	0
	(India)	124.5	30	307	27	9-55	11.37	3	1
1989-90		147.1	32	428	19	5-39	22.52	1	0
1990		201.5	39	586	24	5-27	24.41	2	0
		9,137.2 & *1,586.7	2,832	26,998	1,490	9-52	18.11	102	18

* *Eight-ball overs.*

Best bowling: 9-52, New Zealand v Australia at Brisbane, 1985-86.

LIMITED-OVERS CAREER – BATTING

	M	I	NO	R	HI	50s	Avge	Ct
One-day Internationals	115	98	17	1,749	79	4	21.59	27

Highest innings: 79 v England at Adelaide, 1982-83.

	M	I	NO	R	HI	50s	Avge	Ct
John Player/Refuge Assurance League	96	82	21	1,618	100*	3	26.52	32
Benson and Hedges Cup	44	37	9	920	70	5	32.85	15
Gillette Cup/NatWest Bank Trophy	19	17	3	412	70*	3	29.42	11
Australian domestic competition	9	7	1	86	30	0	14.33	3
New Zealand domestic competition . .	29	25	3	396	63	1	18.00	11

* *Signifies not out.*

Highest innings: 100*, Nottinghamshire v Gloucestershire at Cheltenham, 1982. This was Sir Richard Hadlee's only hundred in limited-overs matches.

LIMITED-OVERS CAREER – BOWLING

	Balls	R	W	BB	Avge	4W/i
One-day Internationals	6,182	3,407	158	5-25	21.56	6

Best bowling: 5-25 v Sri Lanka at Bristol, 1983.

	Balls	R	W	BB	Avge	4W/i
John Player/Refuge Assurance League	4,100	2,532	125	6-12	20.25	4
Benson and Hedges Cup	2,476	1,144	74	4-13	15.45	3
Gillette Cup/NatWest Bank Trophy .	1,184	480	32	5-17	15.00	1
Australian domestic competition	457	222	13	3-13	17.07	0
New Zealand domestic competition . .	1,545	647	46	4-15	14.06	3

Best bowling: 6-12, Nottinghamshire v Lancashire at Nottingham, 1980.

Statistics compiled by Philip Bailey.

WHERE WAS THE PROTECTION?

[*Patrick Eagar*

England's Robin Smith avoids yet another West Indies bouncer in the Antigua Test. As the barrage against him continued, the umpire did not intervene, even though such bowling not only was *likely to inflict physical injury* (Law 42.8) but actually did so.

THE 1990 NEW ZEALAND TEAM IN ENGLAND

[*Patrick Eagar*

Back row: A. C. Parore, D. K. Morrison, K. R. Rutherford, M. W. Priest. *Middle row*: R. S. Cunis (*coach*), T. J. Franklin, S. A. Thomson, A. H. Jones, M. J. Greatbatch, J. P. Millmow, P. N. Culpan (*scorer*), M. R. Plummer (*physiotherapist*). *Front row*: J. J. Crowe, M. C. Snedden, J. G. Bracewell,

THE 1990 INDIAN TEAM IN ENGLAND

[*Graham Morris*

Back row: Dr Ali Irani (*physiotherapist*), S. K. Sharma, S. L. V. Raju, W. V. Raman, A. S. Wassan, B. S. Bedi (*cricket manager*), A. Kumble, N. D. Hirwani, S. R. Tendulkar, N. R. Mongia, M. K. Mantri (*manager*). *Front row*: M. Prabhakar, K. S. More, D. B. Vengsarkar, M. Azharuddin (*captain*), R. J. Shastri (*vice-captain*), Kapil Dev, N. S. Sidhu, S. V. Manjrekar.

iv

THE DEVASTATING EFFECT OF THE FAST, IN-SWINGING YORKER

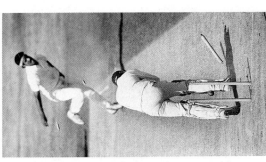

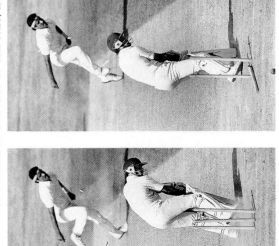

[*Adam Scott*]

The fast, full-pitched swing bowling of Waqar Younis for Surrey in 1990 led to the coining of a new word on the county circuit – Wackered! Leicestershire's Tim Boon (*left*), Peter Willey and James Whitaker learned its meaning during an eighteen-ball blitz on a hot August Saturday at The Oval.

CRICKET'S YOUNGEST TEEMED STAR

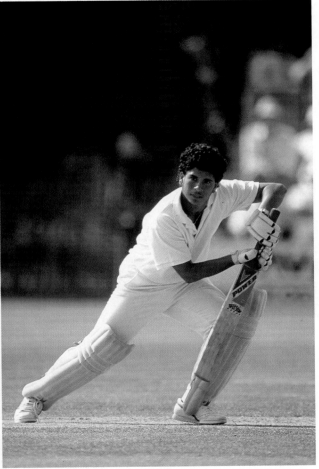

[*Patrick Eagar*

At sixteen India's youngest Test cricketer, at seventeen the maker of a Test hundred against England at Old Trafford : Sachin Tendulkar has the cricket world waiting to acclaim his prowess.

BEHIND THE SCREENS AT LORD'S

[*Patrick Eagar*

Masked by extended sightscreens, the construction of the Compton and Edrich stands at Lord's continued throughout the summer of 1990.

vii

AND THAT WAS ALL THE FAREWELL . . .

[*Patrick Eagar*]

[*Patrick Eagar*] [*Patrick Eagar*]

Alvin Kallicharran and Yorkshire wicket-keeper David Bairstow left the first-class game after two decades at Edgbaston and Headingley respectively.

FIVE CRICKETERS OF THE YEAR

[*David Munden*

A. R. Butcher (Glamorgan)

FIVE CRICKETERS OF THE YEAR

[*David Munden*

M. E. Waugh (Essex)

FIVE CRICKETERS OF THE YEAR

[*David Munden*

M. A. Atherton (Lancashire and England)

FIVE CRICKETERS OF THE YEAR

[*Patrick Eagar*

D. L. Haynes (Middlesex)

FIVE CRICKETERS OF THE YEAR

[*Patrick Eagar*

M. Azharuddin (India)

FIVE CRICKETERS OF THE YEAR

MOHAMMAD AZHARUDDIN

st summer, a new definition was given to oriental artistry as Mohammad
haruddin, India's captain, time and again placed the ball through square
g and mid-wicket with a wristy turn of the bat at the instant of impact. Line
emed to mean little, length everything, as he feasted on England's bowling
th hundreds at Lord's and Old Trafford to follow successively on one
ainst New Zealand in Auckland. They set the crackers bursting in the
smopolitan neighbourhood of Vithalwadi, in celebration not just of
haruddin's success, but also of the return of the touch which five years
rlier had launched his international career so spectacularly. Three hundreds
ainst England in his first three Tests. That was early in 1985, and the 21-
ar-old was hailed as a prophet among the Indian pantheon of batting demi-
ds. He was also beginning the struggle to cope with the expectations of a
tion and his awe of his own reputation.

MOHAMMAD AZHARUDDIN was born on February 8, 1963 in
yderabad, capital city of the Deccan plateau state of Andhra Pradesh. A
ting grandfather was the first to spot the youngster's passion for cricket,
d at the All Saints missionary school, Brother Joseph inculcated in him a
ve of the game. It was as a seam bowler, who could make the ball swing in
banana arc, that the young Azharuddin began playing for All Saints, but
progressed quickly to bat at No. 3, besides being the third seamer, for
yderabad Schools in the South Zone inter-state schools tournament. In
79-80 he turned out for South Zone Schools against the visiting English
hools side, and in 1981-82, at the age of eighteen, he made his first-class
but in the Ranji Trophy. Such exposure was rather easily attained in a
yderabad side which was going through a transition, but the experience
aped his batting even as it toughened him mentally.

National recognition came on the heels of a double-hundred for South
ne in January 1984, in the Duleep Trophy, with a place on the Under-25
ur of Zimbabwe. He did not make the short tour of Pakistan in October
at year, but only because it was thought that Pakistan was no place for
ooding youngsters. His breakthrough came later in the season after David
ower's England team, beaten in the First Test, had come back to square the
ries in Delhi. In contentious circumstances Kapil Dev was dropped from
e side and Azharuddin was brought in to replace Sandeep Patil for the
lcutta Test. The rest is history.

The soft-spoken, almost shy young man was also an instant hit in the
nited-overs game. Critics in Australia raved about his essentially back-foot
ay, which they thought had gone out of fashion along with good manners on
e field. His fielding, too, made him invaluable to the side, a factor which
me to his aid when his form could not match the impossibly high levels he
d set in his first international season. Azharuddin is emphatic that he did
t start out as a naturally gifted fielder and that he had to work hard to
tain the standards he has today.

While there were centuries to be made on the plumb pitches at home, there
ere none abroad until his first visit to Pakistan in 1989-90. By then,

following an unhappy tour of the West Indies, where fast and short-pitch
bowling had provided a searching test of his technique, his place in the si
was in doubt. Indeed, it was only because Raman Lamba was forced
withdraw from the First Test because of a broken toe that he played. F
saved his place for the next Test with a record-equalling five catches
Pakistan's first innings – four of them brilliant ones in the slips, where
had not always stood – but batting on a hard wicket had meant a return to t
horrors of his "blind" ducking against genuine fast bowling.

Advice from colleagues to stand up and hook if bowlers were trying
corner him with bouncers was not really what an uncertain and unwilli
player of the hook needed to hear. Sounder advice came from the form
Pakistan batsman, Zaheer Abbas, who advocated a readjustment of his gri
By wrapping his right hand further round the handle, Azharuddin found
could stroke the ball with greater control and assurance. In the seco
innings of the Faisalabad Test, having been dismissed for 0 in the fi
innings, he made his first century away from home. In the course of it,
found his confidence and his true touch returning. Changes in selection we
soon to thrust him further into the limelight, and although he had lit
experience of leading sides, he was made captain for the tour of New Zeala
in early 1990.

Such is Azharuddin's nature, however, that he takes everything in k
stride, not making a drama out of a crisis, or even a crisis out of the dran
that is so often Indian cricket. He set about tackling his new responsibilit
with the modesty that is a refreshing trait: the devout Muslim probal
believed in just praying extra hard and leaving his young team to play to t
best of their resources. Such a style was disastrous to begin with, but so
enough Azharuddin learned to assert himself as captain.

The Auckland Test, the last of the New Zealand series, brought
sensational twist to his career as a batsman, for it saw the fruition of F
counter-attacking style. Suddenly, everything he did came right and a tru
majestic innings of 192 unfolded. Marked by straight- and on-driving of
very high order, the innings was supreme also in that it was the highest by
Indian captain abroad. His match- and series-winning half-century at Tre
Bridge in the second of last summer's Texaco one-dayers was a furth
indication of how completely "Azhar" had rediscovered himself.

Having made his name as a stylist who used the power of his wrists
create the mesmeric effect of strokes played late, he had often been struggli
in his attempt to put percentages ahead of style. It was an index of his
emerging batting personality that he should score the centuries whi
fascinated Englishmen so. He explained away the seeming desperation whi
sparked India's strokeplay in the defeat at Lord's as the need for aggressi
which has always acted as a tonic for him. "It's not as if we were alwa
hitting the ball as if we wanted to take the cover off it. But there was so mu
loose bowling, especially from Malcolm, that it was easy to send the b
speeding down the slope." But at Old Trafford, and again at The Oval, whe
a century seemed his for the taking, Azharuddin reached the very heights
artistic batting. The Old Trafford hundred pleased him particularly.
always knew that the ball was going where I aimed to hit it." Watching sor
of the power developed, especially off the back foot, it was hard to believe
was playing with one of the lightest bats in modern cricket.

Since childhood, Azharuddin has believed in turning out neatly at a cricket match, be it a hit in the park or a Test. Notice how he always goes out to toss in a blazer. By his manner, he also promises to re-establish sporting standards in the game as well as sartorial ones. Certainly, if India's tour of England was a resounding success for the game, Azharuddin can take pride in being a leading contributor to it. This summer his contract with Derbyshire will see the oriental charmer return to England, with his one-year-old son, Asaduddin, in tow. The future beckons brightly. His only regret is that his grandfather, who used to stand under the trees on the boundary line watching him, did not live to see him play Test cricket. – R. Mohan.

ALAN BUTCHER

When Surrey decided not to renew Alan Butcher's contract in 1986, he thought seriously of retiring from first-class cricket. Instead, he accepted an offer to join Glamorgan, for whom his consistent batting and, latterly, his astute captaincy have been an inspiration. Moreover, and importantly, he began to enjoy his cricket again, something he had not experienced with Surrey for some seasons. Last season he thrived on his responsibilities as captain. While Glamorgan, who had propped up the County Championship for two years, rose to eighth, their best position for twenty years, the elegant left-hander, who many thought should have played for England more often than his solitary appearance in 1979, had his most successful season, finishing with an aggregate of 2,116 runs for an average of 58.77. He hit six Championship hundreds, but it was his unbeaten 104 against Middlesex in the NatWest Bank Trophy quarter-final at Lord's which best epitomised his many qualities. Glamorgan's early-order batsmen, including Viv Richards, were dismissed cheaply, but Butcher, on a slow, unresponsive pitch, countered the formidable Middlesex attack and batted throughout the innings. Despite the home side's emphatic nine-wicket win, this captain's innings earned him the Man of the Match award.

ALAN RAYMOND BUTCHER was born in Croydon on January 7, 1954, and after playing for Beckenham Under-11s he spent five and a half years in South Australia, where the family emigrated. He made a considerable impression with the Glenelg youth team, winning their Junior Cricketer award for outstanding performances, and was selected for the South Australia Under-15 side, and later for an all-Australia representative team. South Australia Under-15s included David Hookes, and had Alan's family decided to reside permanently in Australia he would almost certainly have played for his state team, and through qualification he would have been eligible for his adopted country.

After the family's return to England, he played for Surrey Young Cricketers before joining the county staff in 1972, having played two Sunday League games at the end of the previous season. In a Surrey side boasting a batting line-up which included John Edrich, Mike Edwards, Younis Ahmed, Graham Roope and Stewart Storey, he was selected primarily as a left-arm medium-fast bowler who batted at No. 8 or No. 9. In only his third first-class game he took six for 48 against Hampshire at Guildford, his wickets including Barry Richards, Gordon Greenidge and Roy Marshall, while two years later, in 1974, his three for 11 in Surrey's Benson and Hedges Cup semi-final against Lancashire was followed by an eleven-over spell in the final which yielded 23 runs as Leicestershire were beaten by 27 runs. However, the lively left-arm in-swingers are now only sparingly used, although some orthodox slow left-arm is occasionally revived in an attempt to break a partnership.

Butcher began opening the innings for Surrey midway through the 1973 season, partnering Edrich, a batsman whom he admired for his ability to concentrate fully, never to appear ruffled and never to play any differently. The following season he achieved his first Championship century, against Warwickshire at Edgbaston, and his consistent batting over the next three seasons earned him an England cap against India at The Oval in 1979. He made 14 and 20, succumbing to the spin of Venkataraghavan in the first innings and the swing of Ghavri in the second, but he was not given another chance at that level, although he was called up for a one-day international against Australia in 1980. Mike Brearley, who captained England in the 1979 series, rated Butcher as one of the best players of fast bowling in the county game, a view shared by many over the last fifteen years. His seasonal aggregates varied between 1,300 and 1,700, on good, bad and indifferent pitches, especially those at The Oval in the mid-1970s which lacked bounce and pace. Strangely, apart from a period when Geoff Howarth opened the Surrey innings with him, Butcher has always been involved in a left-handed opening combination. Grahame Clinton followed Edrich, and since he joined Glamorgan Butcher and Hugh Morris have developed a productive partnership which has yielded 4,845 runs at an average of 56.00, including eighteen century stands.

Readers of the coaching manual will not find many faults with Butcher's technique. He is well balanced, the weight evenly distributed on either foot enabling him to launch into a half-volley from the quicker bowlers or position himself for the hook and cut. Most batsmen of small stature, and most left handers, favour the latter, and Butcher's trademark is the slash past gully. While it sometimes gets him out, it also brings him lots of runs, and he revelled in the stroke last summer on flat pitches from which the ball rarely deviated. An abiding memory was Mike Gatting's field-placing when Butcher was batting at Lord's with a short Tavern boundary on his off side. There were two gullies slightly backward of square, with a third fielder in front and another posted ten yards deeper. Butcher relished the challenge and followed his century in the NatWest game several days earlier with fifties in the Championship and Sunday League matches.

Although Butcher's strokeplay is characterised by an attacking approach he is always prepared to graft when the occasion demands. In 1980 he scored 107 before lunch for Surrey at The Oval, ironically against Glamorgan; nine years later, on the same ground, he frustrated his former county with superb defensive innings of 88 not out that occupied 84 overs. On a pitch which provided exaggerated bounce and turn on the last day, he showed unwavering patience and concentration, denying himself any liberties and saving the game for his adopted county. It is this tough competitiveness allied to his professionalism and sportsmanship, which has always endeared him to his fellow-players. In addition to these qualities, he has shown that he possesses a shrewd cricket brain and the ability to be an inspiring leader. – Edward Bevan.

MIKE ATHERTON

It is quite possible that Mike Atherton would not yet have played Test cricket had Mike Gatting not taken a group of fellow-dissidents to South Africa in the winter of 1989-90. The announcement of a party which included eight players who had taken part in the 1989 series against Australia came during the Old Trafford Test. There were two Tests against Australia to go, and one of the new recruits, for the game at Trent Bridge, was Atherton, then 21 years old and having just completed his third and final year at Cambridge. His début was the sort of which nightmares are made – out second ball to the sixth ball of the match. Atherton's reaction was to respond with, "It bothered other people more than me. I hadn't suddenly become a bad player with one duck." He was top scorer in the second innings with 47, scored 12 and 14 in the final Test, and missed out on the tour of West Indies.

There was talk of protecting him, putting him in cotton wool, and he finished up instead with the gentler pleasures of Zimbabwean bowling. He was disappointed: he did not want to be protected, and hoped he had been omitted on the simple grounds of other players being better. But Zimbabwe helped his development, which continued in England in 1990 when he played in all six Tests and scored 735 runs in eleven innings, with hundreds at Trent Bridge, against New Zealand, and Old Trafford, against India, where he joined Geoff Pullar as the only Lancastrians to score centuries for England on their home ground. This was Atherton's first season as a full-time professional after three years split between Cambridge and Lancashire, and he responded with a total of 1,924 runs in first-class cricket for an average of 71.25.

MICHAEL ANDREW ATHERTON was born on March 23, 1968, a Mancunian like two of Lancashire's greatest players, Archie MacLaren and Brian Statham. He learned his cricket with Woodhouses, the Lancashire and Cheshire League club where his father also played. He was at Manchester Grammar School for seven years and his batting blossomed to take him into the Lancashire Schools', English Public Schools' and English Schools' teams. David Moss, his cricket mentor at Manchester Grammar School, recalled seeing Atherton play cricket at the age of nine and hoping he would pass his entrance examination so that the school would also benefit from his batting talent.

He captained the first team for three years, starting when he was fifteen, and for a time he, Mark Crawley and Gary Yates, all of whom played for Lancashire last year, were the first three in the batting order. Leadership qualities developed, and Mike went on to captain English Schools, Lancashire Federation and Young England – in Sri Lanka and Australia, where he had charge of such rising talent as Martin Bicknell, Mark Alleyne, Warren Hegg, Nasser Hussain, Chris Lewis, Mark Ramprakash, and Peter Martin.

Atherton went to Cambridge in 1987 and made his first-class début in a weak University side which sank to 20 for seven against a strong Essex team bristling with such bowling abilities as those of Neil Foster, John Lever, Hugh Page and John Childs. The team also included Graham Gooch and Keith Fletcher, who were later to play important parts in Atherton's progress. Batting at No. 3, he scored 73 not out in a total of 135 in the first innings and 33 out of 71 in the second. His first century was not far

behind. In his fifth match, opening the innings, Atherton carried his bat for
109 not out in a total of 185 against Derbyshire, an innings he looks back on
with pleasure. He also opened the batting in the University Match at Lord's
and scored 7 and 0 in the drawn game. Mark Crawley, on the other hand,
scored 140 for Oxford.

The second half of the season belonged to Lancashire, a pattern he was to
follow in his three years at Cambridge. There was a two-week gap in
Championship fixtures, so he went into the second team and scored 110 in
the match against Somerset at Taunton. His first-team début came at
Southport on July 22, 1987, and after Warwickshire had been bowled out for
116 on a soft, drying pitch, he scored 53 in 61 overs and shared in a stand of
108 with Fairbrother, helping Lancashire to a ten-wicket win in two days. He
had come to stay, and he played important parts in Lancashire's run of six
wins at the end of the season which almost swept them to the Championship.
With 602 runs in eleven games for Lancashire to add to his 411 for
Cambridge, he sneaked past 1,000 runs in his first season in first-class
cricket.

For those of us witnessing him for the first time, it was not just his class
which shone through; it was the temperament, his ability to adjust to any
situation and play accordingly. Atherton captained Cambridge in his next
two years and was also captain of Combined Universities, who beat Surrey
and the mighty Worcestershire in the qualifying stage of the 1989 Benson and
Hedges Cup before losing by 3 runs to Somerset in the quarter-finals. His best
summer at Cambridge was in 1988, when he scored two hundreds in a total
of 665 runs. Yet Lancashire, with a rare show of misjudgement, refused to
play him immediately he returned to Old Trafford, ignoring him for three
Championship matches. His reaction was to score two centuries in the eight
matches left to him and to finish top of the county's averages.

However, 1990 was to be the true testing time: a full, demanding season
with Lancashire, not just in Championship cricket but in limited-over
cricket, too. He started the Championship season with scores of 50, 191, 9,
and 51, the one-day matches with 63, 44, 5, 69 not out and 76 not out, and by
the end of May he had scored 856 runs in all competitions. Moreover, that
did not include a century denied him in a washed-out Benson and Hedges
Cup game with Hampshire. The recall to Test cricket was a near formality
although now it was as opener to leave the position of No. 3 available for
Graeme Hick in 1991. Atherton showed his taste for the game at its highest
level with innings of 151, 0, 54, 82 and 70 against New Zealand; 8, 72, 131,
74, 7 and 86 against India; a grand total of 735 runs and an average of 66.81.
Not bad for starters. – Brian Bearshaw.

DESMOND HAYNES

The death of Wilf Slack in January 1989 left a void in the Middlesex team
both on and off the field. The acquisition of the West Indian opening
batsman, Desmond Haynes, for the 1989 season undoubtedly filled the on-
field vacancy, and it quickly became apparent that he was the ideal man to
have in the dressing-room as well.

During 1989, Middlesex had a system of fines for such things as late
arrival, or not wearing a blazer or tie, with John Emburey in charge
of levying the fines. However, when he was away on Test-match duty

Middlesex at the time were playing two Championship matches at Uxbridge Haynes took it upon himself to bring to book his colleagues' misdemeanours. He did so with relish. He would be seen, lurking behind a pillar in the Uxbridge pavilion, waiting to leap out and surprise some unsuspecting young cricketer with the news that he owed a pound or two to the kitty.

This made it obvious that he was very much a part of the team, and he made no secret of the fact that his assimilation was made easier because of the West Indian members of the Middlesex side, most of whom he had met at some stage of his career. Emburey and Mike Gatting, of course, had been international opponents. He also found his introduction to county cricket made easier by virtue of the fact that the county was in the running for honours throughout the season. He thought that it would not have been quite so enjoyable playing for a county that was not in contention for at least one of the season's titles.

That first season was a good, rather than outstanding, one for Haynes. He scored 1,446 first-class runs at an average of just over 45, and his three centuries included the first double-century of his career – 206 not out against Kent at Uxbridge. In the limited-overs competitions, he made a fine start, winning the Gold Award in a Benson and Hedges group match against Surrey on his début for the county. In addition, he was Man of the Match in his first appearance in the NatWest Bank Trophy, scoring 83 against Durham at Darlington. He failed to score in the second round of the NatWest, against Nottinghamshire at Uxbridge, but this was only one of five ducks in seven innings which followed the award of his county cap. He returned to form with 88 in the quarter-finals, 80 in the semi-finals and 50 in the final. The Sunday game was not quite so much to his liking and he passed 50 only twice in ten games.

His avowed intention, at the end of 1989, was to score 2,000 first-class runs for Middlesex in 1990. He achieved that target with plenty to spare in what was an outstanding season. It culminated in Middlesex winning the County Championship and his being named both the Britannic Assurance and Nixdorf Middlesex Player of the Year.

DESMOND LEO HAYNES was born in the Holders Hill district of Barbados on February 15, 1956, the eldest of three brothers. There was no cricket-playing tradition in his family but, "Everyone in the area played cricket, and it's still very strong in high schools in the West Indies". He played in the Barbados Under-15 schools competition and made his first-class début for Barbados in January 1977. The following season, against Australia, came his first Test appearance for West Indies, and he has represented them early 100 times in Tests, as well as appearing in more than 170 limited-overs internationals. His opening partnership with Gordon Greenidge has left all others in its wake, and with Haynes showing no lessening of his skills or his enthusiasm in his mid-30s, there seems no reason why his international career should not continue for some years. Last winter, in the absence of Viv Richards, he captained West Indies in Pakistan and drew favourable comments for the way he led the side on a difficult tour.

He was one of many batsmen to take full advantage of last year's conditions, which were so much in favour of the bat, but he is realistic enough to accept that the ideal is somewhere between 1989 and 1990 in terms of which ball should be used in English cricket. He certainly started 1990

with a bang. Barely off the plane, he scored 107 not out on the first Sunday c
the season at Old Trafford, won Gold Awards in the first two Benson an
Hedges matches (80 against Minor Counties and 131 at Hove), and also h
116 in the second innings of Middlesex's opening Championship match
against Essex at Lord's. Before the end of April, he had scored 358 runs i
five innings in the three competitions. He was to score five more hal
centuries in the Refuge Assurance League and one more in the Cup, 75 n
out and 149 not out in the NatWest Trophy and, most important fc
Middlesex, 2,036 Championship runs at an average of 63.62. Besides tw
hundreds in the match against the New Zealanders at Lord's, he hit si
Championship hundreds, two of them, against Essex and Sussex, unbeate
double-centuries. He passed 50 on a further seven occasions and wa
consistency itself.

But it was not just the runs he scored, it was the way in which he score
them. Never slowly and always most attractively, without a slog in sight. H
cover driving, a combination of timing and barely evident power, remaine
in the mind's eye as a particular adornment of his batting. He was a mo
enthusiastic fielder and even took a couple of Championship wickets, as we
as providing several useful spells of bowling in the limited-overs game.

He wished he had played county cricket some years ago. "I would hav
liked to have come to it a bit earlier, but most counties are looking for a
overseas fast bowler rather than a batsman. Gordon [Greenidge] was
different case. He grew up over here and he was also playing at a time whe
counties could use more overseas players."

Desmond Haynes has a high regard for his Middlesex team-mates. "Ther
is a very good attitude, particularly on the part of the younger player
such as Mark Ramprakash and Mike Roseberry. Keith Brown doesn't get th
credit he deserves, and I would single him out for special mention. H
is reliable, difficult to get out and always seems to be able to play the righ
sort of innings for the situation." His Middlesex colleagues all spoke i
glowing terms of their West Indian opening batsman, not only with regard t
the runs he scored, but to his readiness to offer help and advice withou
having to be asked. Yet at the end of last season there was some doubt as t
whether the Middlesex committee would offer him a new contract for 199.
after the West Indies tour in 1991. Ask any Middlesex supporter, howeve
and you would get an unhesitating vote of confidence in Desmond Hayne
as well as the fervent hope that he would be playing for the county onc
again. – Norman de Mesquita.

MARK WAUGH

Australian cricket has two nurseries for its finest young players. One is in th
verdant grounds of Adelaide's glorious Oval, where the Australian Crick
Academy prepares a balanced squad of fourteen teenage prospects ever
year. The other is 12,000 miles away, in a country small enough to slip in
Australia's back pocket, but where the opportunities for cricketers are bi
England, of course, where the beer is warm, the climate cold and the Pon
live.

Despite these drawbacks, Allan Border, Australia's captain, knows th
value to a young cricketer's education of English cricket, with its diversity
players, pitches and pubs (for what would the game be without the bar-roo
analyst?). Border himself spent a few years enjoying all three with Essex, an

his Australian team has benefited from the skills of such as Steve Waugh and Terry Alderman, both of them graduates of the County Championship.

But while Border may have a deep affection for Essex, there was also some self-interest in the telephone call he made to Lancashire late in the summer of 1988. An investment for the future, as it were. Border was soon to leave England for training camp Down Under, prior to Australia's tour to Pakistan, and he was wondering if Mark Waugh would like to fill in at Essex for him for the rest of the season. Waugh, playing in Bolton League cricket, could hardly believe the conversation. You had to be either an established Test cricketer or a South African to get one of the plum jobs as an overseas professional at a county club. At 23, he was neither.

Waugh took the chance and did well. Well enough to be back in 1989 to watch with a mixture of anticipation and excitement as brother Steve, "A.B." and his Australian mates conquered England in the Ashes series. It was becoming a formidable batting line-up to break into. Back home, however, he topped the Sheffield Shield averages with New South Wales and forced Steve out of the Australian one-day side. "One of us had to go, and brotherly love stops short when it comes to playing for your country." Last summer he returned to Chelmsford to complete his education in readiness for the call-up to Test cricket.

He scored 2,072 first-class runs at an average of 76.74 which, even in a summer of indulgence for batsmen, showed him to be a performer of the highest calibre. He is the type who can have 30 on the board without the bowlers realising he has his pads strapped on. Undemonstrative, compact and still at the crease, he works the ball rather than crashing it about. And being a high-quality cricketer, he could supplement his batting with some useful medium-pace bowling and safe, adaptable fielding. Twice he improved on his highest score, first with 204 against Gloucestershire at Ilford and then with an unbeaten 207 against Yorkshire at Middlesbrough two months later. He also turned in career-best bowling figures of five for 37 against Northamptonshire late in the season and was voted Player of the Year by Essex supporters accustomed to fine batsmen from overseas.

What gave Waugh the greatest pleasure were his innings against the best bowlers in the world. His double-hundred against Gloucestershire came off an attack including Courtney Walsh; he scored 126 against Derbyshire and Ian Bishop, 125 against Hampshire and Malcolm Marshall, a one-day century against Lancashire and Wasim Akram, and 79 not out against Surrey's Pakistan Test discovery, Waqar Younis. "I'm confident I can handle it now", he said, explaining the satisfaction those scores had given him. "You never know as you progress in cricket how you will cope with the next step up. I realise that facing one West Indian quick at Ilford or Colchester may be different from facing four in Kingston, but the whole season has helped my confidence. I've faced those guys and survived. I feel ready for the next step when – if – it comes."

MARK EDWARD WAUGH was born in the Sydney suburb of Canterbury on June 2, 1965 a few moments after Steve went out to bat first for Rodger and Beverley Waugh. Next in the order was Dean, now 22 and following in Mark's footsteps in the Bolton League. At No. 4 is Danny, a sixteen-year-old in Sydney grade cricket: his older brothers think he is the best yet. The four Waugh boys had little option but be good at sport in a country which thrives on the outdoor life, has the ideal climate, and supplies its youth with excellent and cheap facilities. They also descend from a lineage rich in ball skills. One grandfather played rugby league for New South Wales Country; father Rodger once beat Tony Roche to win the New South Wales under-14 tennis title, and a few years later he picked up a national doubles title; mother Bev was a highly regarded tennis player, winning state and national titles as a teenager and later becoming a leading squash player in the state.

The Waugh twins were naturally good at soccer, tennis and cricket. Mark was playing Sheffield Shield cricket by twenty, a season later than Steve, but even then the brothers' careers were no longer running parallel. Already Steve was forging ahead into the Australian Test side, and after he had shown the benefits of county cricket at Somerset, Mark followed him to England to learn. At Essex it did not take long for the dressing-room wit to devise a nickname for the newcomer: "Afghan". Afghanistan, the forgotten war – simple when you know how. Relaxed and open, whereas Steve can be wary and cool, Mark soon found the company of Pringle, Hardie and Lilley as stimulating as the real ale he was being introduced to by a seriously social Essex side.

In this funny game, all cricketers have their little quirks, and Mark Waugh, for all his boy-next-door traits, has a ritual which is among the odder ones in the game. Like a Battle of Britain fighter pilot who painted swastikas outside his cockpit for every enemy aircraft downed, Waugh draws little matchstick men on his thigh pad for every century scored, with the name of the opponents below. Last summer another nine joined the ranks, and at that rate he may soon have enough for an army. – Colin Bateman.

LANCASHIRE'S REVIVAL – IS IT ENOUGH?

By MICHAEL KENNEDY

f Lancashire cricket is a religion for some of its supporters, we experience the doubts as well as the certainties of belief. Thanks to Cardus's imaginative prose, the giants of the distant past still have vivid life. We can almost delude ourselves that we saw MacLaren, Brearley, Spooner, J. T. Tyldesley, Johnny Briggs and Cecil Parkin. I did see Paynter and Washbrook before the war and have the brightest memories of the unfulfilled genius of Norman Oldfield, on the verge of greatness when war robbed him of six years, after which he took umbrage over pay and left Old Trafford (a mistake, as he later admitted).

Memories of watching Lancashire in the 45 seasons since the war are a mixture of frustration and elation: the former because of the maladroit administration which, for twenty years, sabotaged the efforts of several not always very wisely selected captains; the latter because of the pleasures afforded by such players as Washbrook, Statham, Clive Lloyd, Pullar, Tattersall, Hayes (the biggest "if only" of them all), Jack Simmons, the untiring Dick Pollard, Bond and Abrahams. So much talent and yet, until the advent of the one-day competitions, so little to show for it.

Thus, for someone born within a mile of the county cricket ground, the revival of Lancashire's fortunes under the captaincy of David Hughes has lifted the heart, especially as it has occurred during the presidency of Cyril Washbrook, illustrious link between the Lancashire of pre-1939 and the post-war side. Since Hughes was appointed captain at the end of 1986, Lancashire have been second, ninth, fourth and sixth in the County Championship, won the NatWest Bank Trophy and the Benson and Hedges Cup in the same season, 1990, and have been Refuge Assurance League champions in 1989 and runners-up in 1990; they were the first winners of the Refuge Assurance Cup in 1988. It is an impressive record, and all the more impressive when one recalls Lancashire's dismal eleven years in the County Championship from 1976 to 1986 when the highest they finished was twelfth.

If ever proof was needed that an inspired captain can re-motivate a team that has lost its bearings and confidence, then it was provided by Hughes in 1987, just as it was by Mike Brearley for England in 1981. The two cases are remarkably similar, since many people would have argued that neither was worth his place in the side on playing ability alone. Yet look what happened! Hughes was a legend because of the 1971 Gillette Cup semi-final against Gloucestershire at Old Trafford, when he struck Mortimore for 24 in an over in the gathering darkness of a late-July evening, but during the 1980s his form slipped and he played most of his cricket in the Second Eleven. In 1986 he played for the first team in only three one-day matches and was ready to resign, but delayed sending in his letter until he had captained Lancashire's second team to victory in the Second Eleven Championship. Lancashire finished 53 points ahead of the runners-up, Warwickshire, and were un-defeated. Hughes's part in the team's success was considerable: he had a batting average of 41.44, scoring 746 runs with a top score of 119 not out; he was second in the bowling averages, with 46 wickets at an average of 15.43. Lancashire's senior side had a wretched Championship season in 1986, but reached the NatWest Trophy final, only to be defeated by Sussex. A few days later, Jack Bond and Peter Lever, manager and coach respectively, were dismissed. Two months later Clive Lloyd was replaced as captain by the 39-year-old Hughes, to general Red Rose astonishment.

But the committee which made these changes was itself under fire, and in February 1987 its chairman since 1969, Cedric Rhoades, was compelled to resign. He was replaced by a former player, Bob Bennett; and Alan Ormrod who had joined Lancashire in 1984 after more than twenty years with Worcestershire and was Hughes's *aide-de-camp* in the Second Eleven triumph of 1986, became coach/manager. The Bennett-Hughes-Ormrod triumvirate has converted Lancashire into a team for which a run of success in the 1990s has been predicted by many commentators, not all of them northern in origin.

Hughes's leadership has been compared with that of the best amateur captains from between the wars. There is no doubt who is the boss when he is on the field, and his 100 per cent commitment to the game and to Lancashire has communicated itself to the other players, who now take the field with a spring in their step. The metamorphosis in 1987 will remain a glorious page in Lancashire's annals: the dejected side which had been fifteenth in the table the previous season now ended in second place, failing only at the last moment to draw level with Nottinghamshire by not gaining the full eight bonus points against Essex at Chelmsford. The 1988 season was disappointing by comparison, but the sense of buoyancy was maintained, and a new international star joined the side in Wasim Akram of Pakistan. After the retirement in 1986 of the great Clive Lloyd, Lancashire had lacked a glamorous figure of this stature and high hopes were built on Wasim.

The 1988 side was of special appeal, for it contained a piquant mixture of the old guard with the new. Hughes and the irrepressible Jack Simmons were survivors from the Lancashire team of the 1970s which, under the captaincy first of Bond and then of David Lloyd, twice finished third in the Championship, won the Gillette Cup three years running and again in 1975, and were regarded as the "one-day kings". The names of Barry Wood, Harry Pilling, Farokh Engineer, Frank Hayes, Peter Lee, Peter Lever and Ken Shuttleworth were a litany for Lancashire schoolboys as those of the pre-1939 players were for my generation.

Experience was also brought to the 1988 side by the batsmen, Graeme Fowler, Gehan Mendis and Trevor Jesty, and the diligent seam bowler, Paul Allott. They represented the "middle generation", as it were. The players of the future were the Cambridge University captain, Michael Atherton, who headed the batting averages although he played only fourteen innings (he had scored 602 runs for the county in 1987); Neil Fairbrother, a member of the side since 1982 and capped for England in 1987; the all-rounder, Mike Watkinson, another 1982 débutant; and the wicket-keeper, Warren Hegg, a more than useful batsman. In 1989 Phillip DeFreitas transferred to Lancashire from Leicestershire and David Lloyd's son, Graham, scored three centuries in essentially his first first-class season, drawing, it is said, from David Hughes the characteristically dry comment: "Good innings, lad. I don't know who coached you, but it can't have been your father!"

The 1990 season, still fresh in memory, belonged above all to Fairbrother His aggressive batting for Lancashire, heading the county first-class averages with 1,681 runs at 80.04, reminded older spectators of another little left-hander, Eddie Paynter, and made all the more inexplicable his failure in the

Test matches. The inevitable question was asked: does he lack the temperament for the big occasion? One is hesitant to be dogmatic, remembering the early Test careers of W. J. Edrich, Dennis Amiss and Mike Gatting. Yet one must doubt if he will receive many more chances, simply because there is a long queue of batsmen good enough to be picked for England, and the pressure to succeed means a low threshold of tolerance of failure. But about Atherton's temperament, there can be no doubt whatsoever; and if John Crawley remains with Lancashire (his elder brother, Mark, having already sadly refused the offer of a three-year contract), the batting strength should be formidable a season or two hence.

However high we Lancastrians throw our hats in the air over the team's successes last season, we are not really satisfied – nor, I am sure, is David Hughes – by one-day success. Lancashire have not won the County Championship outright since 1934, when Ernest Tyldesley scored 2,487 runs and Eddon more than 2,000, Len Hopwood did the double, and Frank Booth took 101 wickets. Their golden period was the five years from 1926 to 1930, when they won the Championship four times (three in succession) and were runners-up in 1929. Lancashire's batting side was strong in those years, with Harry Makepeace, Ernest Tyldesley, Charlie Hallows and Frank Watson, but they won because of their bowling, spearheaded by the wonderful Australian fast bowler, E. A. McDonald, who (in all matches) took 182 wickets in 1925, 175 in 1926, 150 in 1927 (a wet summer, so he turned to spin), 190 in 1928, 142 in 1929 and 108 in 1930. In those years, the Championship comprised up to 30 matches. McDonald was complemented by Dick Tyldesley, with Iddon, Hopwood and Sibbles in support – a combination of fast bowling, flight and spin. Yet the side was considered to play unattractive cricket, and in 1930 no less a partisan than Neville Cardus wrote that he hoped Gloucestershire would win the title!

In Lancashire's Championship hat-trick year, 1928, a total of 139 players scored 414 centuries. Such a batsmen's bonanza did not recur until last year, when 156 players scored 428 hundreds. But in 1928 Kent's "Tich" Freeman, a spin bowler, took 300 wickets and many bowlers passed the 100 wickets mark. In 1990 not one bowler in the land took 100 wickets; and whereas Atherton, Fairbrother and Mendis all averaged more than 50 with the bat, the most wickets taken for Lancashire were 47 by Watkinson at a cost of 33.57. DeFreitas's 34 wickets cost him 37.20 apiece and Wasim's 16 were even more expensive.

If Lancashire are to win the Championship, they must find bowlers who can be as consistent as McDonald and Tyldesley – and, of course, as Brian Statham was throughout his career from 1950 to 1968. Three attempts, in the persons of Croft, Holding and Patterson, to find a contemporary equivalent to McDonald have misfired on the benign Old Trafford post-war wicket. No successor to Statham for accuracy or silken grace has arisen. Wasim Akram and DeFreitas have only fitfully produced the form expected of them. Allott is in the second half of his career. Watkinson and Atherton offer the kind of variety that is needed, but a venomous strike bowler – preferably home-grown, like Statham – is an urgent requirement. Until he is found, no Lancashire supporter can be confident that the recent achievements of the Hughes-Ormrod partnership will be rewarded with the only accolade that matters – to be county champions.

[*Patrick Eagar*

A GENUINELY GREAT CRICKETER

AN ASSESSMENT OF GRAHAM GOOCH

By SIMON BARNES

Ian Botham has, in his time, managed to make a fair amount of trouble for himself. But not even Botham managed to get himself banned from Test cricket for three years, or made himself the hate-focus of an international political campaign, or caused an entire tour to be cancelled. Graham Gooch has done all those things. How extraordinary then, how absolutely extraordinary, to consider that this is the man we must begin to think of as the most important cricketer of his generation, and the most effective captain of England since Mike Brearley.

Yes, Gooch said famously, we've got the makings of a goodish side. The point is that this was not an understatement: it was an exact assessment of the facts. Gooch's achievement has been to maximise the resources of that goodish side. It has been a triumph of nothing less than leadership, and this from a man who resigned as captain of Essex because captaincy was affecting his form.

It is clear that captaincy affected his form as captain of England in the summer of 1990. To be accurate, captaincy inspired him. It took him to the enormous achievement of his innings of 333 against India at Lord's, and his breaking of Sir Donald Bradman's record for Test runs scored in an English summer.

Gooch had always been a man in search of greatness; he achieved that immodest aim last summer. He achieved greatness as a player – at the age of 37. Such preposterous scores are normally for younger men. The fitness, the reflexes, the ability to concentrate for session after session: these are things that the years take away from you. But they have not taken them from Gooch. Gooch is a fanatic for mere fitness, a passionate lover of work for its own sake, a true glutton for austerity. Furthermore, he has achieved something quite close to greatness as a leader. Before he was given the captaincy, England's cricket had become the material of cheap jokes: material the more discriminating joke-crackers avoided. A quip about England's defeats was simply too obvious, too hoary a joke.

The joke reached its apex in 1988, "the summer of the five captains". This was perhaps the most inept display of man-management in the history of sport; a summer in which Gatting, Emburey, Cowdrey, Gooch himself and Pringle all led England in the field, four of them as official appointees. When Gooch was asked to lead England in India, the tour was promptly cancelled because of Gooch's South African connections. Disaster followed disaster. After the West Indian hammering and the Indian débâcle, there came another traumatic summer. The opponents were Australia. England, captained now by Gower, were not only beaten but trampled on. For Gooch, as for Gower, the summer was a personal disaster. There was scarcely a scoreboard, it seemed, that did not carry details of Gooch lbw b Alderman, for not a lot. Gooch volunteered to stand down, to make room for fresh blood, and his offer was accepted. Perhaps that one incident summed up his summer: a personal nadir, a personal black hole. For some cricketers it would have been a disaster of career-ending proportions. Instead, Gooch used it as a springboard into greatness.

There is a case for saying that Headingley 1981 is one of the greatest disasters to have hit England's cricket. Certainly, it lunged into a pattern of self-destructiveness as the echoes of that extraordinary year died away. The England team became based around an Inner Ring, with Botham at its heart: Botham, self-justified by his prodigious feats during that unforgettable summer. To be accepted, you had to hate the press, hate practice, enjoy a few beers and what have you, and generally be one hell of a good ol' boy. Like all cliques, the England clique was defined by exclusion. Nothing could be more destructive to team spirit than a team within a team, but that was the situation in the England camp for years. It was the same at Somerset. It was the presence of an Inner Ring which created the furore in which Vivian Richards and Joel Garner were not offered new contracts, and Botham himself resigned. It needed the right man at the right time to destroy this unpleasant and destructive atmosphere in the England team. The old members of the Inner Ring were being lost to time, one by one. It needed someone to indicate that it was gone forever; that this was a new start, a new way forward. This was Gooch's moment, and he accepted it avidly.

It happened in India in the autumn of 1989. India had rejected an England team under Gooch's captaincy a year before. Now they accepted one. The Test-playing countries had at last come to an agreement about players with South African histories. Gooch was officially forgiven. The way was clear for the remaking of the England cricket team. The tour itself, a four-week trip for the Nehru Cup, a six-nation one-day tournament, was thought by all wise critics to be a complete waste of time. The widely used *mot juste* for the competition was "spurious". It was not spurious at all for Gooch.

It was on a practice ground in Delhi that one became aware of strong forces at work. The weather was hot, but the pace of the practice was still hotter. It was all sweat and Gatorade: everyone was competing as to who sweated the most. Micky Stewart, the manager, was like a man come into his own, taking fielding practice with all the camp affectations of a sergeant-major. It looked as if Stewart was having his way at last, but he was not. Gooch was. The two of them plainly saw eye to eye; not something that had always been the case with Stewart and his captains. They were dubbed "the Cockney Mafia" almost within hours.

The prevailing ethic of the old Inner Ring was that if you are as massively talented as us, you don't have to work as hard as ordinary players. Gooch has always believed that the difference between ordinariness and excellence lies in hard work. And if work will make that difference, then it is folly to be idle. He does not seek mindless conformity from his players. More than most team sports, cricket requires a motley bunch of assorted shapes, sizes, temperaments, talents and social backgrounds. What Gooch has managed is to inspire his own motley bunch with the same desire to work to a common goal: what is more, to work in the belief that the goal is attainable.

That has been his miracle. The results in the West Indies in the early months of 1990 did not surprise him. It was only everybody else who was surprised by the win and the near-win under his captaincy. Gooch would, I think, have escaped from the series on level terms at worst, had it not been for the injuries to himself and to Angus Fraser. Instead, England lost 2-1. The two 1-0 wins in the following summer's three-Test series against New

Zealand and India were consolidation. Suddenly, England had acquired the habit of winning Test matches. That was miracle enough to be going on with.

The central experience of Gooch's professional life was his trip to South Africa in 1982. He went to play on that "rebel" tour in the hopelessly naïve belief that he would not receive any form of punishment. He was made captain of the rebel team, though not as a recognition of any leading part in the plotting and deception involved in the setting-up of this tour: it was more an expression of the dressing-room's feelings about having Geoffrey Boycott as captain. But the responsibilities of the captaincy were not restricted to cricketing decisions. Gooch did not expect that. The captaincy made Gooch the spokesman of the tour. "Gooch's men" and "Gooch's rebel tour" were phrases that tripped nicely off page and microphone. Gooch himself had to face cameras and interviews: this was, as far as the Republic was concerned, a major public relations exercise. These were muddy waters, and Gooch hid behind his role of professional sportsman. "We're just here to play cricket, we're just professional cricketers." Would that life were as simple.

Gooch and his fellow-rebels were banned from Test cricket for three years. I am sure he still feels that this was desperately unjust; I suspect that even now, he finds this "wrong" an inspiration. For whereas many of his colleagues on that South African venture were well-known players slightly over the hill, Gooch was in his prime. His adventures robbed him of three years in which he might have established himself as the greatest batsman of his generation. Instead, he played for Essex and Western Province. Still, his career has been characterised as much by its troughs as by its peaks. He began his Test career with a pair in 1975; he chose not to tour Australia in 1986-87 because his wife, Brenda, was pregnant with twins; and Terry Alderman has turned up to blight his life more than once or twice. He even began his *annus mirabilis* of 1990 with a "king duck" against New Zealand.

Perhaps Gooch's greatest asset of all has been his ability to give equal treatment to Kipling's twin imposters, Triumph and Disaster. He remains consistent in everything in his life except shaving. His capricious changes from a clean shave, Zapata moustache, designer stubble or full beard have been the nearest he has come to a change of facial expression in fifteen years. But he is not an easy person. He does not forget those who, he believes, have done wrong by him. He has no appreciation of the necessary symbiosis of professional sport and mass media. His achievement in cutting down the number of compulsory captain's press conferences during a home Test from three to one was regarded as a major coup.

The chairman of the England selectors, Ted Dexter, when in his journalistic avatar, famously described Gooch as having the charisma of a wet fish. This has been thrown back at Dexter times without number, but it is, in fact, a fair remark – from a media person. All the same, Gooch cannot have achieved his success without great gifts of communication. It just so happens that these gifts are not apparent to those outside the charmed circle of his team. Nor does his team find Gooch's gifts readily communicable to the outside world. The nearest anyone ever gets to an explanation is to say that he leads "by example". But this means little. Plenty of leaders have worked themselves silly while inspiring only contempt. Gooch simply has, at a point that must be alarmingly close to the end of his cricketing life, come into his own. He has reconstructed and re-inspired the England cricket team: and it seems that he has done a similar job on himself. Yet he remains as hostile to outsiders as ever, and the team is probably even less approachable now tha it was in Botham's time. There is still an Inner Ring: the difference is tha Gooch appears to have made everyone in the team a member of it.

Right from the first moment that he took charge in Delhi, Gooch made clear that he wanted to be judged only by results. In those terms, he ha established himself as a genuinely great cricketer. His achievement i remaking the England team might yet be even more significant, and in thi much larger area he again bears the stamp of incipient greatness.

G. A. GOOCH – TEST CAREER

		T	I	NO	R	HI	100s	50s	Avge	
1975	v Australia	2	4	0	37	31	0	0	9.25	
1978	v Pakistan	2	2	0	74	54	0	1	37.00	
1978	v New Zealand	3	5	2	190	91*	0	2	63.33	
1978-79	v Australia	6	11	0	246	74	0	1	22.36	
1979	v India	4	5	0	207	83	0	2	41.40	
1979-80	v Australia	2	4	0	172	99	0	2	43.00	
	v India	1	2	1	57	49*	0	0	57.00	
1980	v West Indies	5	10	0	394	123	1	2	39.40	
	v Australia	1	2	0	24	16	0	0	12.00	
1980-81	v West Indies	4	8	0	460	153	2	1	57.50	
1981	v Australia	5	10	0	139	44	0	0	13.90	
1981-82	v India	6	10	1	487	127	1	4	54.11	
	v Sri Lanka	1	2	0	53	31	0	0	26.50	
1985	v Australia	6	9	0	487	196	1	2	54.11	
1985-86	v West Indies	5	10	0	276	53	0	4	27.60	
1986	v India	3	6	0	175	114	1	0	29.16	
	v New Zealand	3	5	0	268	183	1	0	53.60	
1987-88	v Pakistan	3	6	0	225	93	0	2	37.50	
1988	v West Indies	5	10	0	459	146	1	3	45.90	
	v Sri Lanka	1	2	0	111	75	0	1	55.50	
1989	v Australia	5	9	0	183	68	0	2	20.33	
1989-90	v West Indies	2	4	1	128	84	0	1	42.66	
1990	v New Zealand	3	5	0	306	154	1	1	61.20	
	v India	3	6	0	752	333	3	2	125.33	
		81	147	5	5,910	333	12	33	41.61	8

* *Signifies not out.*

Highest innings: 333 v India at Lord's, 1990.

Bowling: G. A. Gooch has taken 15 wickets for 717 runs (1,803 balls) at an average of 47.8 His best bowling figures are 2-12 v India at Delhi, 1981-82.

Note: In the 1990 calendar year, G. A. Gooch scored 1,264 runs (average 79.00) fro seventeen innings in nine Test matches.

SUMMARY v EACH COUNTRY

	T	I	NO	R	HI	100s	50s	Avge	
v Australia	27	49	0	1,288	196	1	7	26.28	2
v West Indies	21	42	1	1,717	153	4	11	41.87	2
v India	17	29	2	1,678	333	5	8	62.14	2
v New Zealand	9	15	2	764	183	2	3	58.76	1
v Pakistan	5	8	0	299	93	0	3	37.37	
v Sri Lanka	2	4	0	164	75	0	1	41.00	
	81	147	5	5,910	333	12	33	41.61	8

G. A. GOOCH – FIRST-CLASS CAREER

	M	I	NO	R	HI	100s	50s	Avge	Ct
1973	1	1	0	18	18	0	0	18.00	1
1974	15	25	3	637	114*	1	2	28.95	4
1975	24	42	0	1,147	100	1	7	27.30	16
1976	21	34	4	1,273	136	3	6	42.43	17
1977	23	37	6	837	105*	1	5	27.00	11
1978	21	33	3	1,254	129	2	9	41.80	22
1978-79 (Australia)	13	23	1	514	74	0	3	23.36	13
1979	17	25	2	838	109	1	6	36.43	28
1979-80 (Australia)	6	12	2	582	115	1	6	58.20	8
(India)	1	2	1	57	49*	0	0	57.00	1
1980	19	35	5	1,437	205	6	2	47.90	17
1980-81 (West Indies)	7	13	0	777	153	4	1	59.76	4
1981	16	31	0	1,345	164	5	5	43.38	11
1981-82 (India)	11	18	3	867	127	2	6	57.80	9
(Sri Lanka)	2	3	0	100	47	0	0	33.33	1
(South Africa)	4	7	0	396	109	1	3	56.57	6
1982	23	38	1	1,632	149	3	12	44.10	25
1982-83 (South Africa)	9	18	3	597	126	2	1	39.80	11
1983	26	38	1	1,481	174	4	7	40.02	35
1983-84 (South Africa)	7	13	1	615	171	2	1	51.25	5
1984	26	45	7	2,559	227	8	13	67.34	27
1985	21	33	2	2,208	202	7	9	71.22	25
1985-86 (West Indies)	9	18	0	443	53	0	5	24.61	10
1986	19	32	0	1,221	183	3	5	38.15	22
1987	24	41	6	1,361	171	3	7	38.88	20
1987-88 (Pakistan)	3	6	0	225	93	0	2	37.50	3
1988	21	37	1	2,324	275	6	15	64.55	28
1989	18	31	1	1,256	158	3	9	41.86	25
1989-90 (West Indies)	6	11	1	616	239	1	4	61.60	6
1990	18	30	3	2,746	333	12	8	101.70	16
	431	732	57	31,363	333	82	159	46.46	427

* *Signifies not out.*

Highest innings: 333, England v India at Lord's, 1990.

Bowling: G. A. Gooch has taken 213 wickets for 7,339 runs (16,329 balls) at an average of 34.45. His best bowling figures are 7-14, Essex v Worcestershire at Ilford, 1982.

G. A. GOOCH – LIMITED-OVERS CAREER

	M	I	NO	R	HI	100s	50s	Avge
One-day Internationals	85	83	5	3,305	142	8	19	42.37

Highest innings: 142 v Pakistan at Karachi, 1987-88.

	M	I	NO	R	HI	100s	50s	Avge
John Player/Refuge Assurance League	209	206	19	6,324	176	10	40	33.81
Benson and Hedges Cup	87	86	10	3,954	198*	9	28	52.02
Gillette Cup/NatWest Bank Trophy .	39	38	2	1,820	144	5	10	50.55
Nissan Shield (SA)	9	9	0	297	60	0	3	33.00
Benson and Hedges Trophy (SA)	11	11	0	546	106	1	3	49.63

* *Signifies not out.*

Highest innings: 198*, Essex v Sussex at Hove, 1982.

G. A. GOOCH in 1990

	M	I	NO	R	HI	100s	50s	Avge
First-class matches								
v New Zealand	3	5	0	306	154	1	1	61.20
v India	3	6	0	752	333	3	2	125.33
Britannic Assurance Championship	11	18	2	1,586	215	7	5	99.12
Other	1	1	1	102	102*	1	0	—
Limited-overs matches								
v New Zealand	2	2	1	167	112*	1	1	167.00
v India	2	2	0	52	45	0	0	26.00
Refuge Assurance League	10	10	0	386	136	1	3	38.60
Benson and Hedges Cup	4	4	1	285	102	1	2	95.00
NatWest Bank Trophy	2	2	1	247	144	2	0	247.00
Others	2	2	0	167	105	1	1	83.50
	40	52	6	4,050	333	18	15	88.04

* Signifies not out.   *Statistics compiled by Philip Bailey.*

[*Patrick Eagar*]

The scoreboard at Lord's following Gooch's dismissal for 333 against India in July 1990.

TEST CRICKETERS

FULL LIST FROM 1877 TO AUGUST 28, 1990

These lists have been compiled on a home and abroad basis, appearances abroad being printed in *italics*.

Abbreviations. E: England. A: Australia. SA: South Africa. WI: West Indies. NZ: New Zealand. In: India. P: Pakistan. SL: Sri Lanka.

All appearances are placed in this order of seniority. Hence, any England cricketer playing against Australia in England has that achievement recorded first and the remainder of his appearances at home (if any) set down before passing to matches abroad. Although the distinction between amateur and professional was abolished in 1963, initials of English professionals before that date are still given in brackets. The figures immediately following each name represent the total number of appearances in *all* Tests.

Where the season embraces two different years, the first year is given; i.e. 1876 indicates 1876-77.

ENGLAND

Number of Test cricketers: 546

Abel (R.) 13: v A 1888 (3) 1896 (3) 1902 (2); *v A 1891 (3); v SA 1888 (2)*

Absolom, C. A. 1: *v A 1878*

Agnew, J. P. 3: v A 1985 (1); v WI 1984 (1); v SL 1984 (1)

Allen (D. A.) 39: v A 1961 (4) 1964 (1); v SA 1960 (2); v WI 1963 (2) 1966 (1); v P 1962 (4); *v A 1962 (1) 1965 (4); v SA 1964 (4); v WI 1959 (5); v NZ 1965 (3); v In 1961 (5); v P 1961 (3)*

Allen, G. O. B. 25: v A 1930 (1) 1934 (2); v WI 1933 (1); v NZ 1931 (3); v In 1936 (3); *v A 1932 (5) 1936 (5); v WI 1947 (3); v NZ 1932 (2)*

Allom, M. J. C. 5: *v SA 1930 (1); v NZ 1929 (4)*

Allott, P. J. W. 13: v A 1981 (1) 1985 (4); v WI 1984 (3); v In 1982 (2); v SL 1984 (1); *v In 1981 (1); v SL 1981 (1)*

Ames (L. E. G.) 47: v A 1934 (5) 1938 (2); v SA 1929 (1) 1935 (4); v WI 1933 (3); v NZ 1931 (3) 1937 (3); v In 1932 (1); *v A 1932 (5) 1936 (5); v SA 1938 (5); v WI 1929 (4) 1934 (4); v NZ 1932 (2)*

Amiss, D. L. 50: v A 1968 (1) 1975 (2) 1977 (2); v WI 1966 (1) 1973 (3) 1976 (1); v NZ 1973 (3); v In 1967 (2) 1971 (1) 1974 (3); v P 1967 (1) 1971 (3) 1974 (3); *v A 1974 (5) 1976 (1); v WI 1973 (5) v NZ 1974 (2); v In 1972 (3) 1976 (5); v P 1972 (3)*

Andrew (K. V.) 2: v WI 1963 (1); *v A 1954 (1)*

Appleyard (R.) 9: v A 1956 (1); v SA 1955 (1); v P 1954 (1); *v A 1954 (4); v NZ 1954 (2)*

Archer, A. G. 1: *v SA 1898*

Armitage (T.) 2: *v A 1876 (2)*

Arnold (E. G.) 10: v A 1905 (4); v SA 1907 (2); *v A 1903 (4)*

Arnold, G. G. 34: v A 1972 (2) 1975 (1); v WI 1973 (3); v NZ 1969 (1) 1973 (3); v In 1974 (2); v P 1967 (2) 1974 (3); *v A 1974 (4); v WI 1973 (3); v NZ 1974 (2); v In 1972 (4); v P 1972 (3)*

Arnold (J.) 1: v NZ 1931

Astill (W. E.) 9: *v SA 1927 (5); v WI 1929 (4)*

Atherton, M. A. 8: v A 1989 (2); v NZ 1990 (3); v In 1990 (3)

Athey, C. W. J. 23: v A 1980 (1); v WI 1988 (1); v NZ 1986 (3); v In 1986 (2); v P 1987 (4); *v A 1986 (5) 1987 (1); v WI 1980 (2); v NZ 1987 (1); v P 1987 (3)*

Attewell (W.) 10: v A 1890 (1); *v A 1884 (5) 1887 (1) 1891 (3)*

Bailey, R. J. 4: v WI 1988 (1); *v WI 1989 (3)*

Bailey, T. E. 61: v A 1953 (5) 1956 (4); v SA 1951 (2) 1955 (5); v WI 1950 (2) 1957 (4); v NZ 1949 (4) 1958 (4); v P 1954 (3); *v A 1950 (4) 1954 (5) 1958 (5); v SA 1956 (5); v WI 1953 (5); v NZ 1950 (4) 1954 (2)*

Bairstow, D. L. 4: v A 1980 (1); v WI 1980 (1); v In 1979 (1); *v WI 1980 (1)*

Bakewell (A. H.) 6: v SA 1935 (2); v WI 1933 (1); v NZ 1931 (2); *v In 1933 (1)*

Balderstone J. C. 2: v WI 1976 (2)

Barber, R. W. 28: v A 1964 (1) 1968 (1); v SA 1960 (1) 1965 (3); v WI 1966 (2); v NZ 1965 (3); *v A 1965 (5); v SA 1964 (4); v In 1961 (5); v P 1961 (3)*

Barber (W.) 2: v SA 1935 (2)

Barlow, G. D. 3: v A 1977 (1); *v In 1976 (2)*

Barlow (R. G.) 17: v A 1882 (1) 1884 (3) 1886 (3); *v A 1881 (4) 1882 (4) 1886 (2)*

Barnes (S. F.) 27: v A 1902 (1) 1909 (3) 1912 (3); v SA 1912 (3); *v A 1901 (3) 1907 (5) 1911 (5), v SA 1913 (4)*

Barnes (W.) 21: v A 1880 (1) 1882 (1) 1884 (2) 1886 (2) 1888 (3) 1890 (2); *v A 1882 (4) 1884 (5) 1886 (1)*

Barnett (C. J.) 20: v A 1938 (3) 1948 (1); v SA 1947 (3); v WI 1933 (1); v NZ 1937 (3); v In 1936 (1); *v A 1936 (5); v In 1933 (3)*

Barnett, K. J. 4: v SL 1988 (1)

Barratt (F.) 5: v SA 1929 (1); *v NZ 1929 (4)*

Barrington (K. F.) 82: v A 1961 (5) 1964 (5) 1968 (5); v SA 1955 (2) 1960 (4) 1965 (3); v WI 1963 (5) 1966 (2); v In 1959 (5) 1967 (3); *v A 1962 (5) 1965 (5), v SA 1964 (5); v WI 1959 (5) 1967 (5); v NZ 1962 (3); v In 1961 (5) 1963 (5); v P 1961 (2)*

Barton (V. A.) 1: *v SA 1891*

Bates (W.) 15: *v A 1881 (4) 1882 (4) 1884 (5) 1886 (2)*

Bean (G.) 3: *v A 1891 (3)*

Bedser (A. V.) 51: v A 1948 (5) 1953 (5); v SA 1947 (2) 1951 (5) 1955 (1); v WI 1950 (3); v NZ 1949 (2); v In 1946 (3) 1952 (4); v P 1954 (2); *v A 1946 (5) 1950 (5) 1954 (1); v SA 1948 (5); v NZ 1946 (1) 1950 (2)*

Benson, M. R. 1: v In 1986

Berry (R.) 2: v WI 1950 (2)

Binks, J. G. 2: *v In 1963 (2)*

Bird M. C. 10: *v SA 1909 (5) 1913 (5)*

Birkenshaw J. 5: *v WI 1973 (2); v In 1972 (2); v P 1972 (1)*

Bligh, Hon. I. F. W. 4: *v A 1882 (4)*

Blythe (C.) 19: v A 1905 (1) 1909 (2); v SA 1907 (3); *v A 1901 (5) 1907 (1); v SA 1905 (5) 1909 (2)*

Board (J. H.) 6: *v SA 1898 (2) 1905 (4)*

Bolus, J. B. 7: v WI 1963 (2); *v In 1963 (5)*

Booth (M. W.) 2: *v SA 1913 (2)*

Bosanquet, B. J. T. 7: v A 1905 (3); *v A 1903 (4)*

Botham, I. T. 97: v A 1977 (2) 1980 (1) 1981 (6) 1985 (6) 1986 (3); v WI 1980 (5) 1984 (5); v NZ 1978 (3) 1983 (4) 1986 (1); v In 1979 (4) 1982 (3); v P 1978 (3) 1982 (3) 1987 (5); v SL 1984 (1); *v A 1978 (6) 1979 (3) 1982 (5) 1986 (4); v WI 1980 (4) 1985 (5); v NZ 1977 (3) 1983 (3); v In 1979 (1) 1981 (6); v P 1983 (1); v SL 1981 (1)*

Bowden, M. P. 2: *v SA 1888 (2)*

Bowes (W. E.) 15: v A 1934 (3) 1938 (2); v SA 1935 (4); v WI 1939 (2); v In 1932 (1) 1946 (1); *v A 1932 (1); v NZ 1932 (1)*

Bowley (E. H.) 5: v SA 1929 (2); *v NZ 1929 (3)*

Boycott, G. 108: v A 1964 (4) 1968 (3) 1972 (2) 1977 (3) 1980 (1) 1981 (6); v SA 1965 (2); v WI 1966 (4) 1969 (3) 1973 (3) 1980 (5); v NZ 1965 (2) 1969 (3) 1973 (3) 1978 (2); v In 1967 (2) 1971 (1) 1974 (1) 1979 (4); v P 1967 (1) 1971 (2); *v A 1965 (5) 1970 (5) 1978 (6) 1979 (3); v SA 1964 (5); v WI 1967 (5) 1973 (5) 1980 (4); v NZ 1965 (2) 1977 (3); v In 1979 (1) 1981 (4); v P 1977 (3)*

Bradley, W. M. 2: v A 1899 (2)

Braund (L. C.) 23: v A 1902 (5); v SA 1907 (3); *v A 1901 (5) 1903 (5) 1907 (5)*

Brearley, J. M. 39: v A 1977 (5) 1981 (4); v WI 1976 (2); v NZ 1978 (3); v In 1979 (4); v P 1978 (3); *v A 1976 (1) 1978 (6) 1979 (3); v In 1976 (5) 1979 (1); v P 1977 (2)*

Brearley, W. 4: v A 1905 (2) 1909 (1); v SA 1912 (1)

Brennan, D. V. 2: v SA 1951 (2)

Briggs (John) 33: v A 1886 (3) 1888 (3) 1893 (2) 1896 (1) 1899 (1); *v A 1884 (5) 1886 (2) 1887 (1) 1891 (3) 1894 (5) 1897 (5); v SA 1888 (2)*

Broad, B. C. 25: v A 1989 (2); v WI 1984 (4) 1988 (2); v P 1987 (4); v SL 1984 (1); *v A 1986 (5) 1987 (1); v NZ 1987 (3); v P 1987 (3)*

Brockwell (W.) 7: v A 1893 (1) 1899 (1); *v A 1894 (5)*

Bromley-Davenport, H. R. 4: *v SA 1895 (3) 1898 (1)*

Brookes (D.) 1: *v WI 1947*

Brown (A.) 2: *v In 1961 (1); v P 1961 (1)*

Brown, D. J. 26: v A 1968 (4); v SA 1965 (2); v WI 1966 (1) 1969 (3); v NZ 1969 (1); v In 1967 (2); *v A 1965 (4); v WI 1967 (4); v NZ 1965 (2); v P 1968 (3)*

Dewes, J. G. 5: v A 1948 (1); v WI 1950 (2); *v A 1950 (2)*

Dexter, E. R. 62: v A 1961 (5) 1964 (5) 1968 (2); v SA 1960 (5); v WI 1963 (5); v NZ 1958 (1) 196 (2); v In 1959 (2); v P 1962 (5); *v A 1958 (2) 1962 (5); v SA 1964 (5); v WI 1959 (5); v NZ 19. (2) 1962 (3); v In 1961 (5); v P 1961 (3)*

Dilley, G. R. 41: v A 1981 (3) 1989 (2); v WI 1980 (3) 1988 (4); v NZ 1983 (1) 1986 (2); v In 198 (2); v P 1987 (4); *v A 1979 (2) 1986 (4) 1987 (1); v WI 1980 (4); v NZ 1987 (3); v In 1981 (4); v 1983 (1) 1987 (1)*

Dipper (A. E.) 1: v A 1921

Doggart, G. H. G. 2: v WI 1950 (2)

D'Oliveira, B. L. 44: v A 1968 (2) 1972 (5); v WI 1966 (4) 1969 (3); v NZ 1969 (3); v In 1967 (1971 (3); v P 1967 (3) 1971 (3); *v A 1970 (6); v WI 1967 (5); v NZ 1970 (2); v P 1968 (.*

Dollery (H. E.) 4: v A 1948 (2); v SA 1947 (1); v WI 1950 (1)

Dolphin (A.) 1: *v A 1920*

Douglas, J. W. H. T. 23: v A 1912 (1) 1921 (5); v SA 1924 (1); *v A 1911 (5) 1920 (5) 1924 (1); v S 1913 (5)*

Downton, P. R. 30: v A 1981 (1) 1985 (6); v WI 1984 (5) 1988 (3); v In 1986 (1); v SL 1984 (1 *v WI 1980 (3) 1985 (5); v In 1984 (5)*

Druce, N. F. 5: *v A 1897 (5)*

Ducat (A.) 1: v A 1921

Duckworth (G.) 24: v A 1930 (5); v SA 1924 (1) 1929 (4) 1935 (1); v WI 1928 (1); v In 1936 (3 *v A 1928 (5); v SA 1930 (3); v NZ 1932 (1)*

Duleepsinhji, K. S. 12: v A 1930 (4); v SA 1929 (1); v NZ 1931 (3); *v NZ 1929 (4)*

Durston (F. J.) 1: v A 1921

Edmonds, P. H. 51: v A 1975 (2) 1985 (5); v NZ 1978 (3) 1983 (2) 1986 (3); v In 1979 (4) 1982 (1986 (2); v P 1978 (3) 1987 (5); *v A 1978 (1) 1986 (5); v WI 1985 (3); v NZ 1977 (3); v In 198 (5); v P 1977 (3)*

Edrich, J. H. 77: v A 1964 (3) 1968 (5) 1972 (5) 1975 (4); v SA 1965 (1); v WI 1963 (3) 1966 (1969 (3) 1976 (2); v NZ 1965 (1) 1969 (3); v In 1967 (2) 1971 (3) 1974 (3); v P 1971 (3) 1974 (*v A 1965 (5) 1970 (6) 1974 (4); v WI 1967 (5); v NZ 1965 (3) 1970 (2) 1974 (2); v In 1963 (2); v 1968 (3)*

Edrich, W. J. 39: v A 1938 (4) 1948 (5) 1953 (3); v SA 1947 (4); v WI 1950 (2); v NZ 1949 (4 v In 1946 (1); v P 1954 (1); *v A 1946 (5) 1954 (4); v SA 1938 (5); v NZ 1946 (1)*

Elliott (H.) 4: v WI 1928 (1); *v SA 1927 (1); v In 1933 (2)*

Ellison, R. M. 11: v A 1985 (2); v WI 1984 (1); v In 1986 (1); v SL 1984 (1); *v WI 1985 (3); v . 1984 (3)*

Emburey, J. E. 60: v A 1980 (1) 1981 (4) 1985 (6) 1989 (3); v WI 1980 (3) 1988 (3); v NZ 1978 (1986 (2); v In 1986 (3); v P 1987 (4); v SL 1988 (1); *v A 1978 (4) 1986 (5) 1987 (1); v WI 1980 (1985 (4); v NZ 1987 (3); v In 1979 (1) 1981 (3); v P 1987 (3); v SL 1981 (1)*

Emmett (G. M.) 1: v A 1948

Emmett (T.) 7: *v A 1876 (2) 1878 (1) 1881 (4)*

Evans, A. J. 1: v A 1921

Evans (T. G.) 91: v A 1948 (5) 1953 (5) 1956 (5); v SA 1947 (5) 1951 (5) 1955 (5); v WI 1950 (1957 (5); v NZ 1949 (4) 1958 (5); v In 1946 (1) 1952 (4) 1959 (2); v P 1954 (4); *v A 1946 (4) 19. (5) 1954 (4) 1958 (3); v SA 1948 (3) 1956 (5); v WI 1947 (4) 1953 (4); v NZ 1946 (1) 1950 (. 1954 (2)*

Fagg (A. E.) 5: v WI 1939 (1); v In 1936 (2); *v A 1936 (2)*

Fairbrother, N. H. 7: v NZ 1990 (3); v P 1987 (1); *v NZ 1987 (2); v P 1987 (1)*

Fane, F. L. 14: *v A 1907 (4); v SA 1905 (5) 1909 (5)*

Farnes, K. 15: v A 1934 (2) 1938 (4); *v A 1936 (2); v SA 1938 (5); v WI 1934 (2)*

Farrimond (W.) 4: v SA 1935 (1); *v SA 1930 (2); v WI 1934 (1)*

Fender, P. G. H. 13: v A 1921 (2); v SA 1924 (2) 1929 (1); *v A 1920 (3); v SA 1922 (5)*

Ferris, J. J. 1: *v SA 1891*

Fielder (A.) 6: *v A 1903 (2) 1907 (4)*

Fishlock (L. B.) 4: v In 1936 (2) 1946 (1); *v A 1946 (1)*

Flavell (J. A.) 4: v A 1961 (2) 1964 (2)

Fletcher, K. W. R. 59: v A 1968 (1) 1972 (1) 1975 (2); v WI 1973 (3); v NZ 1969 (2) 1973 (3); v } 1971 (2) 1974 (3); v P 1974 (3); *v A 1970 (5) 1974 (5) 1976 (1); v WI 1973 (4); v NZ 1970 (1) 197 (2); v In 1972 (5) 1976 (3) 1981 (6); v P 1968 (3) 1972 (3); v SL 1981 (1)*

Flowers (W.) 8: v A 1893 (1); *v A 1884 (5) 1886 (2)*

Ford, F. G. J. 5: *v A 1894 (5)*

Foster, F. R. 11: v A 1912 (3); v SA 1912 (3); *v A 1911* (5)
Foster, N. A. 28: v A 1985 (1) 1989 (3); v WI 1984 (1) 1988 (2); v NZ 1983 (1) 1986 (1); v In 1986 (1); v P 1987 (5); v SL 1988 (1); *v A 1987 (1)*; *v WI 1985* (3); *v NZ 1983* (2); *v In 1984* (2); *v P 1983* (2) *1987* (2)
Foster, R. E. 8: v SA 1907 (3); *v A 1903* (5)
Fothergill (A. J.) 2: *v SA 1888* (2)
Fowler, G. 21: v WI 1984 (5); v NZ 1983 (2); v P 1982 (1); v SL 1984 (1); *v A 1982 (3); v NZ 1983* (2); *v In* 1984 (5); *v P 1983* (2)
Fraser, A. R. C. 8: v A 1989 (3); v In 1990 (3); *v WI 1989* (2)
Freeman (A. P.) 12: v SA 1929 (3); v WI 1928 (3); *v A 1924* (2); *v SA 1927* (4)
French, B. N. 16: v NZ 1986 (3); v In 1986 (2); v P 1987 (4); *v A 1987 (1); v NZ 1987* (3); *v P 1987* (3)
Fry, C. B. 26: v A 1899 (5) 1902 (3) 1905 (4) 1909 (3) 1912 (3); v SA 1907 (3) 1912 (3); *v SA 1895* (2)

Gatting, M. W. 68: v A 1980 (1) 1981 (6) 1985 (6) 1989 (1); v WI 1980 (4) 1984 (1) 1988 (2); v NZ 1983 (2) 1986 (3); v In 1986 (3); v P 1982 (3) 1987 (5); *v A 1986 (5) 1987 (1); v WI 1980 (1) 1985 (1); v NZ 1977 (2) 1983* (2) *1987* (3); *v In 1981* (5) *1984* (5); *v P 1977 (1) 1983* (3) *1987* (3)
Gay, L. H. 1: *v A 1894*
Geary (G.) 14: v A 1926 (2) 1930 (1) 1934 (2); v SA 1924 (1) 1929 (2); *v A 1928* (4); *v SA 1927* (2)
Gibb, P. A. 8: v In 1946 (2); *v A 1946 (1); v SA 1938* (5)
Gifford, N. 15: v A 1964 (2) 1972 (3); v NZ 1973 (2); v In 1971 (2); v P 1971 (2); *v In 1972 (2); v P 1972* (2)
Gilligan, A. E. R. 11: v SA 1924 (4); *v A 1924* (5); *v SA 1922* (2)
Gilligan, A. H. H. 4: *v NZ 1929* (4)
Gimblett (H.) 3: v WI 1939 (1); v In 1936 (2)
Gladwin (C.) 8: v SA 1947 (2); v NZ 1949 (1); *v SA 1948* (5)
Goddard (T. W.) 8: v A 1930 (1); v WI 1939 (2); v NZ 1937 (2); *v SA 1938* (3)
Gooch, G. A. 81: v A 1975 (2) 1980 (1) 1981 (5) 1985 (6) 1989 (5); v WI 1980 (5) 1988 (5); v NZ 1978 (3) 1986 (3) 1990 (3); v In 1979 (4) 1986 (3) 1990 (3); v P 1978 (2); v SL 1988 (1); *v A 1978 (6) 1979 (2); v WI 1980 (4) 1985 (5) 1989 (2); v In 1979 (1) 1981 (6); v P 1987 (3); v SL 1981 (1)
Gover (A. R.) 4: v NZ 1937 (2); v In 1936 (1) 1946 (1)
Gower, D. I. 109: v A 1980 (1) 1981 (5) 1985 (6) 1989 (6); v WI 1980 (1) 1984 (5) 1988 (4); v NZ 1978 (3) 1983 (4) 1986 (3); v In 1979 (4) 1982 (3) 1986 (2) 1990 (3); v P 1978 (3) 1982 (3) 1987 (5); v SL 1984 (1); *v A 1978 (6) 1979 (3) 1982 (5) 1986 (5); v WI 1980 (4) 1985 (5); v NZ 1983 (3); v In 1979 (1) 1981 (6) 1984 (5); v P 1983 (3); v SL 1981 (1)
Grace, E. M. 1: v A 1880
Grace, G. F. 1: v A 1880
Grace, W. G. 22: v A 1880 (1) 1882 (1) 1884 (3) 1886 (3) 1888 (3) 1890 (2) 1893 (2) 1896 (3) 1899 (1); *v A 1891* (3)
Graveney (T. W.) 79: v A 1953 (5) 1956 (2) 1968 (5); v SA 1951 (1) 1955 (5); v WI 1957 (4) 1966 (4) 1969 (1); v NZ 1958 (4); v In 1952 (4) 1967 (3); v P 1954 (3) 1962 (4) 1967 (3); *v A 1954* (2) *1958* (5) *1962* (3); *v WI 1953* (5) *1967* (5); *v NZ 1954* (2) *1958* (2); *v In 1951* (4); *v P 1968* (3)
Greenhough (T.) 4: v SA 1960 (1); v In 1959 (3)
Greenwood (A.) 2: *v A 1876* (2)
Greig, A. W. 58: v A 1972 (5) 1975 (4) 1977 (5); v WI 1973 (3) 1976 (5); v NZ 1973 (3); v In 1974 (3); v P 1974 (3); *v A 1974 (6) 1976 (1); v WI 1973* (5); *v NZ 1974* (2); *v In 1972 (5) 1976* (5); *v P 1972* (3)
Greig, I. A. 2: v P 1982 (2)
Grieve, B. A. F. 2: *v SA 1888* (2)
Griffith, S. C. 3: *v SA 1948* (2); *v WI 1947* (1)
Gunn (G.) 15: v A 1909 (1); *v A 1907* (5) *1911* (5); *v WI 1929* (4)
Gunn (J.) 6: v A 1905 (1); *v A 1901* (5)
Gunn (W.) 11: v A 1888 (2) 1890 (2) 1893 (3) 1896 (1) 1899 (1); *v A 1886* (2)

Haig, N. E. 5: v A 1921 (1); *v WI 1929* (4)
Haigh (S.) 11: v A 1905 (2) 1909 (1) 1912 (1); *v SA 1898* (2) *1905* (5)
Hallows (C.) 2: v A 1921 (1); v WI 1928 (1)
Hammond, W. R. 85: v A 1930 (5) 1934 (5) 1938 (4); v SA 1929 (4) 1935 (5); v WI 1928 (3) 1933 (3) 1939 (3); v NZ 1931 (3) 1937 (3); v In 1932 (1) 1936 (2) 1946 (3); *v A 1928 (5) 1932 (5) 1936 (5) 1946 (4); v SA 1927 (5) 1930 (5) 1938 (5); v WI 1934 (4); v NZ 1932 (2) 1946 (1)
Hampshire, J. H. 8: v A 1972 (1) 1975 (1); v WI 1969 (2); *v A 1970 (2); v NZ 1970 (2)

Hardinge (H. T. W.) 1: v A 1921
Hardstaff (J.) 5: *v A 1907 (5)*
Hardstaff (J. jun.) 23: v A 1938 (2) 1948 (1); v SA 1935 (1); v WI 1939 (3); v NZ 1937 (3); v In
   1936 (2) 1946 (2); *v A 1936 (5) 1946 (1); v WI 1947 (3)*
Harris, Lord 4: v A 1880 (1) 1884 (2); *v A 1878 (1)*
Hartley, J. C. 2: *v SA 1905 (2)*
Hawke, Lord 5: *v SA 1895 (3) 1898 (2)*
Hayes (E. G.) 5: v A 1909 (1); v SA 1912 (1); *v SA 1905 (3)*
Hayes, F. C. 9: v WI 1973 (3) 1976 (2); *v WI 1973 (4)*
Hayward (T. W.) 35: v A 1896 (3) 1899 (5) 1902 (1) 1905 (5) 1909 (1); v SA 1907 (3); *v A 1897 (5)*
   1901 (5) 1903 (5); v SA 1895 (3)
Hearne (A.) 1: *v SA 1891*
Hearne (F.) 2: *v SA 1888 (2)*
Hearne (G. G.) 1: *v SA 1891*
Hearne (J. T.) 12: v A 1896 (3) 1899 (3); *v A 1897 (3); v SA 1891 (1)*
Hearne (J. W.) 24: v A 1912 (3) 1921 (1) 1926 (1); v SA 1912 (2) 1924 (3); *v A 1911 (5) 1920 (2)*
   1924 (4); v SA 1913 (3)
Hemmings, E. E. 15: v A 1989 (1); v NZ 1990 (3); v In 1990 (3); v P 1982 (2); *v A 1982 (3) 1987*
   (1); v NZ 1987 (1); v P 1987 (1)
Hendren (E. H.) 51: v A 1921 (2) 1926 (5) 1930 (2) 1934 (4); v SA 1924 (5) 1929 (4); v WI 1928
   (1); *v A 1920 (5) 1924 (5) 1928 (5); v SA 1930 (5); v WI 1929 (4) 1934 (4)*
Hendrick, M. 30: v A 1977 (3) 1980 (1) 1981 (2); v WI 1976 (2) 1980 (2); v NZ 1978 (2); v In 1974
   (3) 1979 (4); v P 1974 (2); *v A 1974 (2) 1978 (5); v NZ 1974 (1) 1977 (1)*
Heseltine, C. 2: v SA 1895 (2)
Higgs, K. 15: v A 1968 (1); v WI 1966 (5); v SA 1965 (1); v In 1967 (1); v P 1967 (3); *v A 1965 (1);*
   v NZ 1965 (3)
Hill (A.) 2: *v A 1876 (2)*
Hill, A. J. L. 3: *v SA 1895 (3)*
Hilton (M. J.) 4: v SA 1951 (1); v WI 1950 (1); *v In 1951 (2)*
Hirst (G. H.) 24: v A 1899 (1) 1902 (4) 1905 (3) 1909 (4); v SA 1907 (3); *v A 1897 (4) 1903 (5)*
Hitch (J. W.) 7: v A 1912 (1) 1921 (1); v SA 1912 (1); *v A 1911 (3) 1920 (1)*
Hobbs (J. B.) 61: v A 1909 (3) 1912 (3) 1921 (1) 1926 (5) 1930 (5); v SA 1912 (3) 1924 (4) 1929 (1);
   v WI 1928 (2); *v A 1907 (4) 1911 (5) 1920 (5) 1924 (5) 1928 (5); v SA 1909 (5) 1913 (5)*
Hobbs, R. N. S. 7: v In 1967 (5); v P 1967 (1) 1971 (1); *v WI 1967 (1); v P 1968 (1)*
Hollies (W. E.) 13: v A 1948 (1); v SA 1947 (3); v WI 1950 (2); v NZ 1949 (4); *v WI 1934 (3)*
Holmes, E. R. T. 5: v SA 1935 (1); *v WI 1934 (4)*
Holmes (P.) 7: v A 1921 (1); v In 1932 (1); *v SA 1927 (5)*
Hone, L. 1: *v A 1878*
Hopwood (J. L.) 2: v A 1934 (2)
Hornby, A. N. 3: v A 1882 (1) 1884 (1); *v A 1878 (1)*
Horton (M. J.) 2: v In 1959 (2)
Howard, N. D. 4: *v In 1951 (4)*
Howell (H.) 5: v A 1921 (1); v SA 1924 (1); *v A 1920 (3)*
Howorth (R.) 5: v SA 1947 (1); *v WI 1947 (4)*
Humphries (J.) 3: *v A 1907 (3)*
Hunter (J.) 5: *v A 1884 (5)*
Hussain, N. 3: *v WI 1989 (3)*
Hutchings, K. L. 7: v A 1909 (2); *v A 1907 (5)*
Hutton (L.) 79: v A 1938 (3) 1948 (4) 1953 (5); v SA 1947 (5) 1951 (5); v WI 1939 (3) 1950 (3);
   v NZ 1937 (3) 1949 (4); v In 1946 (3) 1952 (4); v P 1954 (2); *v A 1946 (5) 1950 (5) 1954 (5); v SA*
   1938 (4) 1948 (5); v WI 1947 (2) 1953 (5); v NZ 1950 (2) 1954 (2)
Hutton, R. A. 5: v In 1971 (3); v P 1971 (2)

Iddon (J.) 5: v SA 1935 (1); *v WI 1934 (4)*
Igglesden, A. P. 1: v A 1989
Ikin (J. T.) 18: v SA 1951 (3) 1955 (1); v In 1946 (2) 1952 (2); *v A 1946 (5); v NZ 1946 (1); v WI*
   1947 (4)
Illingworth (R.) 61: v A 1961 (2) 1968 (3) 1972 (5); v SA 1960 (4); v WI 1966 (2) 1969 (3) 1973 (3);
   v NZ 1958 (1) 1965 (1) 1969 (3) 1973 (3); v In 1959 (2) 1967 (3) 1971 (3); v P 1962 (1) 1967 (1)
   1971 (3); *v A 1962 (2) 1970 (6); v WI 1959 (5); v NZ 1962 (3) 1970 (2)*
Insole, D. J. 9: v A 1956 (1); v SA 1955 (1); v WI 1950 (1) 1957 (1); *v SA 1956 (5)*

ackman, R. D. 4: v P 1982 (2); *v WI 1980* (2)

ackson, F. S. 20: v A 1893 (2) 1896 (3) 1899 (5) 1902 (5) 1905 (5)

ackson (H. L.): v A 1961 (1); v NZ 1949 (1)

ameson, J. A. 4: v In 1971 (2); *v WI 1973* (2)

ardine, D. R. 22: v WI 1928 (2) 1933 (2); v NZ 1931 (3); v In 1932 (1); *v A 1928 (5) 1932 (5); v NZ 1932 (1); v In 1933* (3)

arvis, P. W. 6: v A 1989 (2); v WI 1988 (2); *v NZ 1987* (2)

enkins (R. O.) 9: v WI 1950 (2); v In 1952 (2); *v SA 1948* (5)

essop, G. L. 18: v A 1899 (1) 1902 (4) 1905 (1) 1909 (2); v SA 1907 (3) 1912 (2); *v A 1901* (5)

ones, A. O. 12: v A 1899 (1) 1905 (2) 1909 (2); *v A 1901 (5) 1907* (2)

ones, I. J. 15: v WI 1966 (2); *v A 1965 (4); v WI 1967 (5); v NZ 1965 (3); v In 1963* (1)

upp (H.) 2: *v A 1876* (2)

upp, V. W. C. 8: v A 1921 (2); v WI 1928 (2); *v SA 1922* (4)

Keeton (W. W.) 2: v A 1934 (1); v WI 1939 (1)

Kennedy (A. S.) 5: *v SA 1922* (5)

Kenyon (D.) 8: v A 1953 (2); v SA 1955 (3); *v In 1951* (3)

Killick, E. T. 2: v SA 1929 (2)

Kilner (R.) 9: v A 1926 (4); v SA 1924 (2); *v A 1924* (3)

King (J. H.) 1: v A 1909

Kinneir (S. P.) 1: *v A 1911*

Knight (A. E.) 3: *v A 1903* (3)

Knight (B. R.) 29: v A 1968 (2); v WI 1966 (1) 1969 (3); v NZ 1969 (2); v P 1962 (2); *v A 1962 (1) 1965 (2); v NZ 1962 (3) 1965 (2); v In 1961 (4) 1963 (5); v P 1961* (2)

Knight, D. J. 2: v A 1921 (2)

Knott, A. P. E. 95: v A 1968 (5) 1972 (5) 1975 (4) 1977 (5) 1981 (2); v WI 1969 (3) 1973 (3) 1976 (5) 1980 (4); v NZ 1969 (3) 1973 (3); v In 1971 (3) 1974 (3); v P 1967 (2) 1971 (3) 1974 (3); *v A 1970 (6) 1974 (6) 1976 (1); v WI 1967 (2) 1973 (5); v NZ 1970 (1) 1974 (2); v In 1972 (5) 1976 (5); v P 1968 (3) 1972* (3)

Knox, N. A. 2: v SA 1907 (2)

Laker (J. C.) 46: v A 1948 (3) 1953 (3) 1956 (5); v SA 1951 (2) 1955 (1); v WI 1950 (1) 1957 (4); v NZ 1949 (1) 1958 (4); v In 1952 (4); v P 1954 (1); *v A 1958 (4); v SA 1956 (5); v WI 1947 (4) 1953* (4)

Lamb, A. J. 67: v A 1985 (6) 1989 (1); v WI 1984 (5) 1988 (4); v NZ 1983 (4) 1986 (1) 1990 (3); v In 1982 (3) 1986 (2) 1990 (3); v P 1982 (3); v SL 1984 (1) 1988 (1); *v A 1982 (5) 1986 (5); v WI 1985 (5) 1989 (4); v NZ 1983 (3); v In 1984 (5); v P 1983* (3)

Langridge (James) 8: v SA 1935 (1); v WI 1933 (2); v In 1936 (1) 1946 (1); *v In 1933* (3)

Larkins, W. 10: v A 1981 (1); v WI 1980 (3); *v A 1979 (1); v WI 1989 (4); v In 1979* (1)

Larter (J. D. F.) 10: v SA 1965 (2); v NZ 1965 (1); v P 1962 (1); *v NZ 1962 (3); v In 1963* (3)

Larwood (H.) 21: v A 1926 (2) 1930 (3); v SA 1929 (3); v WI 1928 (2); v NZ 1931 (1); *v A 1928 (5) 1932* (5)

Lawrence, D. V. 1: v SL 1988

Leadbeater (E.) 1: *v In 1951* (2)

Lee (H. W.) 1: *v SA 1930*

Lees (W. S.) 5: *v SA 1905* (5)

Legge G. B. 5: *v SA 1927 (1); v NZ 1929* (4)

Leslie, C. F. H. 4: *v A 1882* (4)

Lever, J. K. 21: v A 1977 (3); v WI 1980 (1); v In 1979 (1) 1986 (1); *v A 1976 (1) 1978 (1) 1979 (1); v NZ 1977 (1); v In 1976 (5) 1979 (1) 1981 (2); v P 1977* (3)

Lever, P. 17: v A 1972 (1) 1975 (1); v In 1971 (1); v P 1971 (3); *v A 1970 (5) 1974 (2); v NZ 1970 (2) 1974* (2)

Leveson Gower, H. D. G. 3: *v SA 1909* (3)

Levett, W. H. V. 1: *v In 1933*

Lewis, A. R. 9: v NZ 1973 (1); *v In 1972 (5); v P 1972* (3)

Lewis, C. C. 3: v NZ 1990 (1); v In 1990 (2)

Leyland (M.) 41: v A 1930 (3) 1934 (5) 1938 (1); v SA 1929 (5) 1935 (4); v WI 1928 (1) 1933 (1); v In 1936 (2); *v A 1928 (1) 1932 (5) 1936 (5); v SA 1930 (5); v WI 1934* (3)

Lilley (A. A.) 35: v A 1896 (3) 1899 (4) 1902 (5) 1905 (5) 1909 (5); v SA 1907 (3); *v A 1901 (5) 1903* (5)

Lillywhite (James jun.) 2: *v A 1876* (2)

Lloyd, D. 9: v In 1974 (2); v P 1974 (3); *v A 1974* (4)

Lloyd, T. A. 1: v WI 1984
Loader (P. J.) 13: v SA 1955 (1); v WI 1957 (2); v NZ 1958 (3); v P 1954 (1); *v A 1958 (2); v SA 1956 (4)*
Lock (G. A. R.) 49: v A 1953 (2) 1956 (4) 1961 (3); v SA 1955 (3); v WI 1957 (3) 1963 (3); v NZ 1958 (5); v In 1952 (2); v P 1962 (3); *v A 1958 (4); v SA 1956 (1); v WI 1953 (5) 1967 (2); v NZ 1958 (2); v In 1961 (5); v P 1961 (2)*
Lockwood (W. H.) 12: v A 1893 (2) 1899 (1) 1902 (4); *v A 1894 (5)*
Lohmann (G. A.) 18: v A 1886 (3) 1888 (3) 1890 (2) 1896 (1); *v A 1886 (2) 1887 (1) 1891 (3); v SA 1895 (3)*
Lowson (F. A.) 7: v SA 1951 (2) 1955 (1); *v In 1951 (4)*
Lucas, A. P. 5: v A 1880 (1) 1882 (1) 1884 (2); *v A 1878 (1)*
Luckhurst, B. W. 21: v A 1972 (4); v WI 1973 (2); v In 1971 (3); v P 1971 (3); *v A 1970 (5) 1974 (2); v NZ 1970 (2)*
Lyttelton, Hon. A. 4: v A 1880 (1) 1882 (1) 1884 (2)

Macaulay (G. G.) 8: v A 1926 (1); v SA 1924 (1); v WI 1933 (2); *v SA 1922 (4)*
MacBryan, J. C. W. 1: v SA 1924
McConnon (J. E.) 2: v P 1954 (2)
McGahey, C. P. 2: *v A 1901 (2)*
MacGregor, G. 8: v A 1890 (2) 1893 (3); *v A 1891 (3)*
McIntyre (A. J. W.) 3: v SA 1955 (1); v WI 1950 (1); *v A 1950 (1)*
MacKinnon, F. A. 1: *v A 1878*
MacLaren, A. C. 35: v A 1896 (2) 1899 (4) 1902 (5) 1905 (4) 1909 (5); *v A 1894 (5) 1897 (5) 1901 (5)*
McMaster, J. E. P. 1: *v SA 1888*
Makepeace (J. W. H.) 4: *v A 1920 (4)*
Malcolm, D. E. 11: v A 1989 (1); v NZ 1990 (3); v In 1990 (3); *v WI 1989 (4)*
Mann, F. G. 7: v NZ 1949 (2); *v SA 1948 (5)*
Mann, F. T. 5: *v SA 1922 (5)*
Marks, V. J. 6: v NZ 1983 (1); v P 1982 (1); *v NZ 1983 (1); v P 1983 (3)*
Marriott, C. S. 1: v WI 1933
Martin (F.) 2: v A 1890 (1); *v SA 1891 (1)*
Martin, J. W. 1: v SA 1947
Mason, J. R. 5: *v A 1897 (5)*
Matthews (A. D. G.) 1: v NZ 1937
May, P. B. H. 66: v A 1953 (2) 1956 (5) 1961 (4); v SA 1951 (2) 1955 (5); v WI 1957 (5); v NZ 1958 (5); v In 1952 (4) 1959 (3); v P 1954 (4); *v A 1954 (5) 1958 (5); v SA 1956 (5); v WI 1953 (5) 1959 (3); v NZ 1954 (2) 1958 (2)*
Maynard, M. P. 1: v WI 1988
Mead (C. P.) 17: v A 1921 (2); *v A 1911 (4) 1928 (1); v SA 1913 (5) 1922 (5)*
Mead (W.) 1: v A 1899
Midwinter (W. E.) 4: *v A 1881 (4)*
Milburn, C. 9: v A 1968 (2); v WI 1966 (4); v In 1967 (1); v P 1967 (1); *v P 1968 (1)*
Miller, A. M. 1: *v SA 1895*
Miller, G. 34: v A 1977 (2); v WI 1976 (1) 1984 (2); v NZ 1978 (2); v In 1979 (3) 1982 (1); *v P 1978 (3) 1982 (1); v A 1978 (6) 1979 (1) 1982 (5); v WI 1980 (1); v NZ 1977 (3); v P 1977 (3)*
Milligan, F. W. 2: *v SA 1898 (2)*
Millman (G.) 6: v P 1962 (2); *v In 1961 (2); v P 1961 (2)*
Milton (C. A.) 6: v NZ 1958 (2); v In 1959 (2); *v A 1958 (2)*
Mitchell (A.) 6: v SA 1935 (2); v In 1936 (1); *v In 1933 (3)*
Mitchell, F. 2: *v SA 1898 (2)*
Mitchell (T. B.) 5: v A 1934 (2); v SA 1935 (1); *v A 1932 (1); v NZ 1932 (1)*
Mitchell-Innes, N. S. 1: v SA 1935
Mold (A. W.) 3: v A 1893 (3)
Moon, L. J. 4: *v SA 1905 (4)*
Morley (F.) 4: v A 1880 (1); *v A 1882 (3)*
Morris, J. E. 3: v In 1990 (3)
Mortimore (J. B.) 9: v A 1964 (1); v In 1959 (2); *v A 1958 (1); v NZ 1958 (2); v In 1963 (3)*
Moss (A. E.) 9: v A 1956 (1); v SA 1960 (2); v In 1959 (3); *v WI 1953 (1) 1959 (2)*
Moxon, M. D. 10: v A 1989 (1); v WI 1988 (2); v NZ 1986 (2); v P 1987 (1); *v A 1987 (1); v NZ 1987 (3)*
Murdoch, W. L. 1: *v SA 1891*

Murray, J. T. 21: v A 1961 (5); v WI 1966 (1); v In 1967 (3); v P 1962 (3) 1967 (1); *v A 1962 (1); v SA 1964 (1); v NZ 1962 (1) 1965 (1); v In 1961 (3); v P 1961 (1)*

Newham (W.) 1: *v A 1887*
Newport, P. J. 2: v A 1989 (1); v SL 1988 (1)
Nichols (M. S.) 14: v A 1930 (1); v SA 1935 (4); v WI 1933 (1) 1939 (1); *v NZ 1929 (4); v In 1933 (3)*

Oakman (A. S. M.) 2: v A 1956 (2)
O'Brien, Sir T. C. 5: v A 1884 (1) 1888 (1); *v SA 1895 (3)*
O'Connor (J.) 4: v SA 1929 (1); *v WI 1929 (3)*
Old, C. M. 46: v A 1975 (3) 1977 (2) 1980 (1) 1981 (2); v WI 1973 (1) 1976 (2) 1980 (1); v NZ 1973 (2) 1978 (1); v In 1974 (3); v P 1974 (3) 1978 (3); *v A 1974 (2) 1976 (1) 1978 (1); v WI 1973 (4) 1980 (1); v NZ 1974 (1) 1977 (2); v In 1972 (4) 1976 (4); v P 1972 (1) 1977 (1)*
Oldfield (N.) 1: v WI 1939

Padgett (D. E. V.) 2: v SA 1960 (2)
Paine (G. A. E.) 4: *v WI 1934 (4)*
Palairet, L. C. H. 2: v A 1902 (2)
Palmer, C. H. 1: *v WI 1953*
Palmer, K. E. 1: *v SA 1964*
Parfitt (P. H.) 37: v A 1964 (4) 1972 (3); v SA 1965 (2); v WI 1969 (1); v NZ 1965 (2); v P 1962 (5); *v A 1962 (2); v SA 1964 (5); v NZ 1962 (3) 1965 (3); v In 1961 (2) 1963 (3); v P 1961 (2)*
Parker (C. W. L.) 1: v A 1921
Parker, P. W. G. 1: v A 1981
Parkhouse (W. G. A.) 7: v WI 1950 (2); v In 1959 (2); *v A 1950 (2); v NZ 1950 (1)*
Parkin (C. H.) 10: v A 1921 (4); v SA 1924 (1); *v A 1920 (5)*
Parks (J. H.) 1: v NZ 1937
Parks (J. M.) 46: v A 1964 (5); v SA 1960 (5) 1965 (3); v WI 1963 (4) 1966 (4); v NZ 1965 (3); v P 1954 (1); *v A 1965 (5); v SA 1964 (5); v WI 1959 (1) 1967 (3); v NZ 1965 (2); v In 1963 (5)*
Pataudi sen., Nawab of, 3: v A 1934 (1); *v A 1932 (2)*
Paynter (E.) 20: v A 1938 (4); v WI 1939 (2); v NZ 1931 (1) 1937 (2); v In 1932 (1); *v A 1932 (3); v SA 1938 (5); v NZ 1932 (2)*
Peate (E.) 9: v A 1882 (1) 1884 (3) 1886 (1); *v A 1881 (4)*
Peebles, I. A. R. 13: v A 1930 (2); v NZ 1931 (3); *v SA 1927 (4) 1930 (4)*
Peel (R.) 20: v A 1888 (3) 1890 (1) 1893 (1) 1896 (1); *v A 1884 (5) 1887 (1) 1891 (3) 1894 (5)*
Penn, F. 1: v A 1880
Perks (R. T. D.) 2: v WI 1939 (1); *v SA 1938 (1)*
Philipson, (H.) 5: *v A 1891 (1) 1894 (4)*
Pigott, A. C. S. 1: *v NZ 1983*
Pilling (R.) 8: v A 1884 (1) 1886 (1) 1888 (1); *v A 1881 (4) 1887 (1)*
Place (W.) 3: *v WI 1947 (3)*
Pocock, P. I. 25: v A 1968 (1); v WI 1976 (2) 1984 (2); v SL 1984 (1); *v WI 1967 (2) 1973 (4); v In 1972 (4) 1984 (5); v P 1968 (1) 1972 (3)*
Pollard (R.) 4: v A 1948 (2); v In 1946 (1); *v NZ 1946 (1)*
Poole (C. J.) 3: *v In 1951 (3)*
Pope (G. H.) 1: v SA 1947
Pougher (A. D.) 1: *v SA 1891*
Price, J. S. E. 15: v A 1964 (2) 1972 (1); v In 1971 (3); v P 1971 (1); *v SA 1964 (4); v In 1963 (4)*
Price (W. F. F.) 1: v A 1938
Prideaux, R. M. 3: v A 1968 (1); *v P 1968 (2)*
Pringle, D. R. 21: v A 1989 (2); v WI 1984 (2) 1988 (4); v NZ 1986 (1); v In 1982 (3) 1986 (3); v P 1982 (1); v SL 1988 (1); *v A 1982 (3)*
Pullar (G.) 28: v A 1961 (5); v SA 1960 (3); v In 1959 (3); v P 1962 (2); *v A 1962 (4); v WI 1959 (5); v In 1961 (3); v P 1961 (3)*

Quaife (W. G.) 7: v A 1899 (2); *v A 1901 (5)*

Radford, N. V. 3: v NZ 1986 (1); v In 1986 (1); *v NZ 1987 (1)*
Radley, C. T. 8: v NZ 1978 (3); v P 1978 (3); *v NZ 1977 (2)*

Randall, D. W. 47: v A 1977 (5); v WI 1984 (1); v NZ 1983 (3); v In 1979 (3) 1982 (3); v P 198 (3); *v A 1976 (1) 1978 (6) 1979 (2) 1982 (4); v NZ 1977 (3) 1983 (3); v In 1976 (4); v P 1977 (3 1983 (3)*

Ranjitsinhji, K. S. 15: v A 1896 (2) 1899 (5) 1902 (3); *v A 1897 (5)*

Read, H. D. 1: v SA 1935

Read (J. M.) 17: v A 1882 (1) 1890 (2) 1893 (1); *v A 1884 (5) 1886 (2) 1887 (1) 1891 (3); v S/ 1888 (2)*

Read, W. W. 18: v A 1884 (2) 1886 (3) 1888 (3) 1890 (2) 1893 (2); *v A 1882 (4) 1887 (1); v S/ 1891 (1)*

Relf (A. E.) 13: v A 1909 (1); *v A 1903 (2); v SA 1905 (5) 1913 (5)*

Rhodes (H. J.) 2: v In 1959 (2)

Rhodes (W.) 58: v A 1899 (3) 1902 (5) 1905 (4) 1909 (4) 1912 (3) 1921 (1) 1926 (1); v SA 1912 (3); *v A 1903 (5) 1907 (5) 1911 (5) 1920 (5); v SA 1909 (5) 1913 (5); v WI 1929 (4)*

Richards, C. J. 8: v A 1988 (2); v P 1987 (1); *v A 1986 (5)*

Richardson (D. W.) 1: v WI 1957

Richardson (P. E.) 34: v A 1956 (5); v WI 1957 (5) 1963 (1); v NZ 1958 (4); *v A 1958 (4); v S/ 1956 (5); v NZ 1958 (2); v In 1961 (5); v P 1961 (3)*

Richardson (T.) 14: v A 1893 (1) 1896 (3); *v A 1894 (5) 1897 (5)*

Richmond (T. L.) 1: v A 1921

Ridgway (F.) 5: *v In 1951 (5)*

Robertson (J. D.) 11: v SA 1947 (1); v NZ 1949 (1); *v WI 1947 (4); v In 1951 (5)*

Robins, R. W. V. 19: v A 1930 (2); v SA 1929 (1) 1935 (3); v WI 1933 (2); v NZ 1931 (1) 1937 (3) v In 1932 (1) 1936 (2); *v A 1936 (4)*

Robinson, R. T. 29: v A 1985 (6) 1989 (1); v In 1986 (1); v P 1987 (5); v SL 1988 (1); *v A 1987 (1) v WI 1985 (4); v NZ 1987 (3); v In 1984 (5); v P 1987 (2)*

Roope, G. R. J. 21: v A 1975 (1) 1977 (2); v WI 1973 (1); v NZ 1973 (3) 1978 (1); v P 1978 (3) *v NZ 1977 (3); v In 1972 (2); v P 1972 (2) 1977 (3)*

Root (C. F.) 3: v A 1926 (3)

Rose, B. C. 9: v WI 1980 (3); *v WI 1980 (1); v NZ 1977 (2); v P 1977 (2)*

Royle, V. P. F. A. 1: *v A 1878*

Rumsey, F. E. 5: v A 1964 (1); v SA 1965 (1); v NZ 1965 (3)

Russell (A. C.) 10: v A 1921 (2); *v A 1920 (4); v SA 1922 (4)*

Russell, R. C. 17: v A 1989 (6); v NZ 1990 (3); v In 1990 (3); v SL 1988 (1); *v WI 1989 (4)*

Russell, W. E. 10: v A 1965 (1); v WI 1966 (2); v P 1967 (1); *v A 1965 (1); v NZ 1965 (3); v Ir 1961 (1); v P 1961 (1)*

Sandham (A.) 14: v A 1921 (1); v SA 1924 (2); *v A 1924 (2); v SA 1922 (5); v WI 1929 (4*

Schultz, S. S. 1: *v A 1878*

Scotton (W. H.) 15: v A 1884 (1) 1886 (3); *v A 1881 (4) 1884 (5) 1886 (2)*

Selby (J.) 6: *v A 1876 (2) 1881 (4)*

Selvey, M. W. W. 3: v WI 1976 (2); *v In 1976 (1)*

Shackleton (D.) 7: v SA 1951 (1); v WI 1950 (1) 1963 (4); *v In 1951 (1)*

Sharp (J.) 3: v A 1909 (3)

Sharpe (J. W.) 3: v A 1890 (1); *v A 1891 (2)*

Sharpe, P. J. 12: v A 1964 (2); v WI 1963 (3) 1969 (3); v NZ 1969 (3); *v In 1963 (1)*

Shaw (A.) 7: v A 1880 (1); *v A 1876 (2) 1881 (4)*

Sheppard, Rev. D. S. 22: v A 1956 (2); v WI 1950 (1) 1957 (2); v In 1952 (2); v P 1954 (2) 1962 (2); *v A 1950 (2) 1962 (5); v NZ 1950 (1) 1963 (3)*

Sherwin (M.) 3: v A 1888 (1); *v A 1886 (2)*

Shrewsbury (A.) 23: v A 1884 (3) 1886 (3) 1890 (2) 1893 (3); *v A 1881 (4) 1884 (5) 1886 (2) 1887 (1)*

Shuter, J. 1: v A 1888

Shuttleworth, K. 5: v P 1971 (1); *v A 1970 (2); v NZ 1970 (2)*

Sidebottom, A. 1: v A 1985

Simpson, R. T. 27: v A 1953 (3); v SA 1951 (3); v WI 1950 (3); v NZ 1949 (1); v In 1952 (2); v F 1954 (3); *v A 1950 (5) 1954 (1); v SA 1948 (1); v NZ 1950 (2) 1954 (2)*

Simpson-Hayward, G. H. 5: *v SA 1909 (5)*

Sims (J. M.) 4: v SA 1935 (1); v In 1936 (1); *v A 1936 (2)*

Sinfield (R. A.) 1: v A 1938

Slack, W. N. 3: v In 1986 (1); *v WI 1985 (2)*

Smailes (T. F.) 1: v In 1946

Small, G. C. 13: v A 1989 (1); v WI 1988 (1); v NZ 1986 (2) 1990 (3); *v A 1986 (2); v WI 1989 (4)*

Smith, A. C. 6: *v A 1962 (4); v NZ 1962 (2)*

Smith, C. A. 1: *v SA 1888*
Smith (C. I. J.) 5: v NZ 1937 (1); *v WI 1934 (4)*
Smith, C. L. 8: v NZ 1983 (2); v In 1986 (1); *v NZ 1983 (2); v P 1983 (3)*
Smith (D.) 2: v SA 1935 (2)
Smith D. M. 2: *v WI 1985 (2)*
Smith (D. R.) 5: *v In 1961 (5)*
Smith (D. V.) 3: v WI 1957 (3)
Smith (E. J.) 11: v A 1912 (3); v SA 1912 (3); *v A 1911 (4); v SA 1913 (1)*
Smith (H.) 1: v WI 1928
Smith, M. J. K. 50: v A 1961 (1) 1972 (1); v SA 1960 (4) 1965 (3); v WI 1966 (1); v NZ 1958 (3) 1965 (3); v In 1959 (2); *v A 1965 (5); v SA 1964 (5); v WI 1959 (5); v NZ 1965 (3); v In 1961 (4) 1963 (5); v P 1961 (3)*
Smith, R. A. 18: v A 1989 (5); v WI 1988 (2); v NZ 1990 (3); v In 1990 (3); v SL 1988 (1); *v WI 1989 (4)*
Smith (T. P. B.) 4: v In 1946 (1); *v A 1946 (2); v NZ 1946 (1)*
Smithson (G. A.) 2: *v WI 1947 (2)*
Snow, J. A. 49: v A 1968 (5) 1972 (5) 1975 (4); v SA 1965 (1); v WI 1966 (3) 1969 (3) 1973 (1) 1976 (3); v NZ 1965 (1) 1969 (2) 1973 (3); v In 1967 (3) 1971 (2); v P 1967 (1); *v A 1970 (6); v WI 1967 (4); v P 1968 (2)*
Southerton (J.) 2: *v A 1876 (2)*
Spooner, R. H. 10: v A 1905 (2) 1909 (2) 1912 (3); v SA 1912 (3)
Spooner (R. T.) 7: v SA 1955 (1); *v In 1951 (5); v WI 1953 (1)*
Stanyforth, R. T. 4: *v SA 1927 (4)*
Staples (S. J.) 3: *v SA 1927 (3)*
Statham (J. B.) 70: v A 1953 (1) 1956 (3) 1961 (4); v SA 1951 (2) 1955 (4) 1960 (5) 1965 (1); v WI 1957 (3) 1963 (2); v NZ 1958 (2); v In 1959 (3); v P 1954 (4) 1962 (3); *v A 1954 (5) 1958 (4) 1962 (5); v SA 1956 (4); v WI 1953 (4) 1959 (3); v NZ 1950 (1) 1954 (2); v In 1951 (5)*
Steel, A. G. 13: v A 1880 (1) 1882 (1) 1884 (3) 1886 (3) 1888 (1); *v A 1882 (4)*
Steele, D. S. 8: v A 1975 (3); v WI 1976 (5)
Stephenson, J. P. 1: v A 1989
Stevens, G. T. S. 10: v A 1926 (2); *v SA 1922 (1) 1927 (5); v WI 1929 (2)*
Stevenson, G. B. 2: *v WI 1980 (1); v In 1979 (1)*
Stewart, A. J. 7: v NZ 1990 (3); *v WI 1989 (4)*
Stewart (M. J.) 8: v WI 1963 (4); v P 1962 (2); *v In 1963 (2)*
Stoddart, A. E. 16: v A 1893 (3) 1896 (2); *v A 1887 (1) 1891 (3) 1894 (5) 1897 (2)*
Storer (W.) 6: v A 1899 (1); *v A 1897 (5)*
Street (W.) 1: *v SA 1922*
Strudwick (H.) 28: v A 1921 (2) 1926 (5); v SA 1924 (1); *v A 1911 (1) 1920 (4) 1924 (5); v SA 1909 (5) 1913 (5)*
Studd, C. T. 5: v A 1882 (1); *v A 1882 (4)*
Studd, G. B. 4: *v A 1882 (4)*
Subba Row, R. 13: v A 1961 (5); v SA 1960 (4); v NZ 1958 (1); v In 1959 (1); *v WI 1959 (2)*
Sugg (F. H.) 2: v A 1888 (2)
Sutcliffe (H.) 54: v A 1926 (5) 1930 (4) 1934 (4); v SA 1924 (5) 1929 (5) 1935 (2); v WI 1928 (3) 1933 (2); v NZ 1931 (2); v In 1932 (1); *v A 1924 (5) 1928 (4) 1932 (5); v SA 1927 (5); v NZ 1932 (2)*
Swetman (R.) 11: v In 1959 (3); *v A 1958 (2); v WI 1959 (4); v NZ 1958 (2)*

Tate (F. W.) 1: v A 1902
Tate (M. W.) 39: v A 1926 (5) 1930 (5); v SA 1924 (5) 1929 (3) 1935 (1); v WI 1928 (3); v NZ 1931 (1); *v A 1924 (5) 1928 (5); v SA 1930 (5); v NZ 1932 (1)*
Tattersall (R.) 16: v A 1953 (1); v SA 1951 (5); v P 1954 (1); *v A 1950 (2); v NZ 1950 (2); v In 1951 (5)*
Tavaré, C. J. 31: v A 1981 (2) 1989 (1); v WI 1980 (2) 1984 (1); v NZ 1983 (4); v In 1982 (3); v P 1982 (1); v SL 1984 (1); *v A 1982 (5); v NZ 1983 (2); v In 1981 (6); v SL 1981 (1)*
Taylor (K.) 3: v A 1964 (1); v In 1959 (2)
Taylor, L. B. 2: v A 1985 (2)
Taylor, R. W. 57: v A 1981 (3); v NZ 1978 (3) 1983 (4); v In 1979 (3) 1982 (3); v P 1978 (3) 1982 (3); *v A 1978 (6) 1979 (3) 1982 (5); v NZ 1970 (1) 1977 (3) 1983 (3); v In 1979 (1) 1981 (6); v P 1977 (3) 1983 (3); v SL 1981 (1)*
Tennyson, Hon. L. H. 9: v A 1921 (4); *v SA 1913 (5)*
Terry, V. P. 2: v WI 1984 (2)

Thomas, J. G. 5: v NZ 1986 (1); *v WI 1985 (4)*

Thompson (G. J.) 6: v A 1909 (1); *v SA 1909 (5)*

Thomson, N. I. 5: *v SA 1964 (5)*

Titmus (F. J.) 53: v A 1964 (5); v SA 1955 (2) 1965 (3); v WI 1963 (4) 1966 (3); v NZ 1965 (3); v P 1962 (2) 1967 (2); *v A 1962 (5) 1965 (5) 1974 (4); v SA 1964 (5); v WI 1967 (2); v NZ 1962 (3); v In 1963 (5)*

Tolchard, R. W. 4: *v In 1976 (4)*

Townsend, C. L. 2: v A 1899 (2)

Townsend, D. C. H. 3: *v WI 1934 (3)*

Townsend (L. F.) 4: *v WI 1929 (1); v In 1933 (3)*

Tremlett (M. F.) 3: *v WI 1947 (3)*

Trott (A. E.) 2: *v SA 1898 (2)*

Trueman (F. S.) 67: v A 1953 (1) 1956 (2) 1961 (4) 1964 (4); v SA 1955 (1) 1960 (5); v WI 1957 (5) 1963 (5); v NZ 1958 (5) 1965 (2); v In 1952 (4) 1959 (5); v P 1962 (4); *v A 1958 (3) 1962 (5); v WI 1953 (3) 1959 (5); v NZ 1958 (2) 1962 (2)*

Tufnell, N. C. 1: *v SA 1909*

Turnbull, M. J. 9: v WI 1933 (2); v In 1936 (1); *v SA 1930 (5); v NZ 1929 (1)*

Tyldesley (E.) 14: v A 1921 (3) 1926 (1); v WI 1928 (3); *v A 1928 (1); v SA 1927 (5)*

Tyldesley (J. T.) 31: v A 1899 (2) 1902 (5) 1905 (5) 1909 (4); v SA 1907 (3); *v A 1901 (5) 1903 (5); v SA 1898 (2)*

Tyldesley (R. K.) 7: v A 1930 (2); v SA 1924 (4); *v A 1924 (1)*

Tylecote, E. F. S. 6: v A 1886 (2); *v A 1882 (4)*

Tyler (E. J.) 1: *v SA 1895*

Tyson (F. H.) 17: v A 1956 (1); v SA 1955 (1); v P 1954 (1); *v A 1954 (5) 1958 (2); v SA 1956 (2); v NZ 1954 (2) 1958 (2)*

Ulyett (G.) 25: v A 1882 (1) 1884 (3) 1886 (3) 1888 (2) 1890 (1); *v A 1876 (2) 1878 (1) 1881 (4) 1884 (5) 1887 (1); v SA 1888 (2)*

Underwood, D. L. 86: v A 1968 (4) 1972 (2) 1975 (4) 1977 (5); v WI 1966 (2) 1969 (2) 1973 (3) 1976 (5) 1980 (1); v NZ 1969 (3) 1973 (1); v In 1971 (1) 1974 (3); v P 1967 (2) 1971 (1) 1974 (3); *v A 1970 (5) 1974 (5) 1976 (1) 1979 (3); v WI 1973 (4); v NZ 1970 (2) 1974 (2); v In 1972 (4) 1976 (5) 1979 (1) 1981 (6); v P 1968 (3) 1972 (2); v SL 1981 (1)*

Valentine, B. H. 7: *v SA 1938 (5); v In 1933 (2)*

Verity (H.) 40: v A 1934 (5) 1938 (4); v SA 1935 (4); v WI 1933 (2) 1939 (1); v NZ 1931 (2) 1937 (1); v In 1936 (3); *v A 1932 (4) 1936 (5); v SA 1938 (5); v NZ 1932 (1); v In 1933 (3)*

Vernon, G. F. 1: *v A 1882*

Vine (J.) 2: *v A 1911 (2)*

Voce (W.) 27: v NZ 1931 (1) 1937 (1); v In 1932 (1) 1936 (1) 1946 (1); *v A 1932 (4) 1936 (5) 1946 (2); v SA 1930 (5); v WI 1929 (4); v NZ 1932 (2)*

Waddington (A.) 2: *v A 1920 (2)*

Wainwright (E.) 5: v A 1893 (1); *v A 1897 (4)*

Walker (P. M.) 3: v SA 1960 (3)

Walters, C. F. 11: v A 1934 (5); v WI 1933 (3); *v In 1933 (3)*

Ward, A. 5: v WI 1976 (1); v NZ 1969 (3); v P 1971 (1)

Ward (A.) 7: v A 1893 (2); *v A 1894 (5)*

Wardle (J. H.) 28: v A 1953 (1) 1956 (1); v SA 1951 (2) 1955 (3); v WI 1950 (1) 1957 (1); v P 1954 (4); *v A 1954 (4); v SA 1956 (4); v WI 1947 (1) 1953 (2); v NZ 1954 (2)*

Warner, P. F. 15: v A 1909 (1) 1912 (1); v SA 1912 (1); *v A 1903 (5); v SA 1898 (2) 1905 (5)*

Warr, J. J. 2: *v A 1950 (2)*

Warren (A. R.) 1: v A 1905

Washbrook (C.) 37: v A 1948 (4) 1956 (3); v SA 1947 (5); v WI 1950 (2); v NZ 1937 (1) 1949 (2); v In 1946 (3); *v A 1946 (5) 1950 (5); v SA 1948 (5); v NZ 1946 (1) 1950 (1)*

Watkins (A. J.) 15: v A 1948 (1); v NZ 1949 (1); v In 1952 (3); *v SA 1948 (5); v In 1951 (5)*

Watson (W.) 23: v A 1953 (3) 1956 (2); v SA 1951 (1) 1955 (1); v NZ 1958 (2); v In 1952 (1); *v A 1958 (2); v WI 1953 (5); v NZ 1958 (2)*

Webbe, A. J. 1: *v A 1878*

Wellard (A. W.) 2: v A 1938 (1); v NZ 1937 (1)

Wharton (A.) 1: v NZ 1949

Whitaker, J. J. 1: *v A 1986*

White (D. W.) 2: *v P 1961 (2)*

White, J. C. 15: v A 1921 (1) 1930 (1); v WI 1928 (1); *v A 1928 (5); v SA 1930 (4)*
Whysall (W. W.) 4: v A 1930 (1); *v A 1924 (3)*
Wilkinson (L. L.) 3: *v SA 1938 (3)*
Willey, P. 26: v A 1980 (1) 1981 (4) 1985 (1); v WI 1976 (2) 1980 (5); v NZ 1986 (1); v In 1979 (1); *v A 1979 (3); v WI 1980 (4) 1985 (4)*
Williams, N. F. 1: v In 1990
Willis, R. G. D. 90: v A 1977 (5) 1981 (6); v WI 1973 (1) 1976 (2) 1980 (4) 1984 (3); v NZ 1978 (3) 1983 (4); v In 1974 (1) 1979 (3) 1982 (3); v P 1974 (1) 1978 (3) 1982 (2); *v A 1970 (4) 1974 (5) 1976 (1) 1978 (6) 1979 (3) 1982 (5); v WI 1973 (3); v NZ 1970 (1) 1977 (3) 1983 (3); v In 1976 (5) 1981 (5); v P 1977 (3) 1983 (1); v SL 1981 (1)*
Wilson, C. E. M. 2: *v SA 1898 (2)*
Wilson, D. 6: *v NZ 1970 (1); v In 1963 (5)*
Wilson, E. R. 1: *v A 1920*
Wood (A.) 4: v A 1938 (1); v WI 1939 (3)
Wood, B. 12: v A 1972 (1) 1975 (3); v WI 1976 (1); v P 1978 (1); *v NZ 1974 (2); v In 1972 (3); v P 1972 (1)*
Wood, G. E. C. 3: *v SA 1924 (3)*
Wood (H.) 4: v A 1888 (1); *v SA 1888 (2) 1891 (1)*
Wood (R.) 1: *v A 1886*
Woods S. M. J. 3: *v SA 1895 (3)*
Woolley (F. E.) 64: v A 1909 (1) 1912 (3) 1921 (5) 1926 (5) 1930 (2) 1934 (1); v SA 1912 (3) 1924 (5) 1929 (3); v NZ 1931 (1); v In 1932 (1); *v A 1911 (5) 1920 (5) 1924 (5); v SA 1909 (5) 1913 (5) 1922 (5); v NZ 1929 (4)*
Woolmer, R. A. 19: v A 1975 (2) 1977 (5) 1981 (2); v WI 1976 (5) 1980 (2); *v A 1976 (1); v In 1976 (2)*
Worthington (T. S.) 9: v In 1936 (2); *v A 1936 (3); v NZ 1929 (4)*
Wright, C. W. 3: *v SA 1895 (3)*
Wright (D. V. P.) 34: v A 1938 (3) 1948 (1); v SA 1947 (4); v WI 1939 (3) 1950 (1); v NZ 1949 (1); v In 1946 (2); *v A 1946 (5) 1950 (5); v SA 1938 (3) 1948 (3); v NZ 1946 (1) 1950 (2)*
Wyatt, R. E. S. 40: v A 1930 (1) 1934 (4); v SA 1929 (2) 1935 (5); v WI 1933 (2); v In 1936 (1); *v A 1932 (5) 1936 (2); v SA 1927 (5) 1930 (5); v WI 1929 (2) 1934 (4); v NZ 1932 (2)*
Wynyard, E. G. 3: v A 1896 (1); *v SA 1905 (2)*

Yardley, N. W. D. 20: v A 1948 (5); v SA 1947 (5); v WI 1950 (3); *v A 1946 (5); v SA 1938 (1); v NZ 1946 (1)*
Young (H. I.) 2: v A 1899 (2)
Young (J. A.) 8: v A 1948 (3); v SA 1947 (1); v NZ 1949 (2); *v SA 1948 (2)*
Young, R. A. 2: *v A 1907 (2)*

AUSTRALIA

Number of Test cricketers: 348

Beckett, E. L. 4: v E 1928 (2); v SA 1931 (1); *v E 1930 (1)*
Alderman, T. M. 36: v E 1982 (1); v WI 1981 (2) 1984 (3) 1988 (2); v NZ 1989 (1); v P 1981 (3) 1989 (2); v SL 1989 (2); *v E 1981 (6) 1989 (6); v NZ 1981 (3) 1989 (1); v P 1982 (1)*
Alexander, G. 2: v E 1884 (1); *v E 1880 (1)*
Alexander, H. H. 1: v E 1932
Allan, F. E. 1: v E 1878
Allan, P. J. 1: v E 1965
Allen, R. C. 1: v E 1886
Andrews, T. J. E. 16: v E 1924 (3); *v E 1921 (5) 1926 (5); v SA 1921 (3)*
Archer, K. A. 5: v E 1950 (3); v WI 1951 (2)
Archer, R. G. 19: v E 1954 (4); v SA 1952 (1); *v E 1953 (3) 1956 (5); v WI 1954 (5); v P 1956 (1)*
Armstrong, W. W. 50: v E 1901 (4) 1903 (3) 1907 (5) 1911 (5) 1920 (5); v SA 1910 (5); *v E 1902 (5) 1905 (5) 1909 (5) 1921 (5); v SA 1902 (3)*

Badcock, C. L. 7: v E 1936 (3); *v E 1938 (4)*
Bannerman, A. C. 28: v E 1878 (1) 1881 (3) 1882 (4) 1884 (4) 1886 (1) 1891 (2); *v E 1880 (1) 1882 (1) 1884 (3) 1888 (3) 1893 (3)*
Bannerman, C. 3: v E 1876 (2) 1878 (1)

Bardsley, W. 41 : v E 1911 (4) 1920 (5) 1924 (3); v SA 1910 (5); *v E 1909 (5) 1912 (3) 1921 (5) 19.* *(5); v SA 1912 (3) 1921 (3)*

Barnes, S. G. 13 : v E 1946 (4); v In 1947 (3); *v E 1938 (1) 1948 (4); v NZ 1945 (1)*

Barnett, B. A. 4: *v E 1938 (4)*

Barrett, J. E. 2: *v E 1890 (2)*

Beard, G. R. 3: *v P 1979 (3)*

Benaud, J. 3: *v P 1972 (2); v WI 1972 (1)*

Benaud, R. 63: v E 1954 (5) 1958 (5) 1962 (5); v SA 1952 (4) 1963 (4); v WI 1951 (1) 1960 (5); *v 1953 (3) 1956 (5) 1961 (4); v SA 1957 (5); v WI 1954 (5); v In 1956 (3) 1959 (5); v P 1956 (1959 (3)*

Bennett, M. J. 3: v WI 1984 (2); *v E 1985 (1)*

Blackham, J. McC. 35: v E 1876 (2) 1878 (1) 1881 (4) 1882 (1) 1884 (2) 1886 (1) 1887 (1) 1891 (. 1894 (1); *v E 1880 (1) 1882 (1) 1884 (3) 1886 (3) 1888 (3) 1890 (2) 1893 (3)*

Blackie, D. D. 3: v E 1928 (3)

Bonnor, G. J. 17: v E 1882 (4) 1884 (3); *v E 1880 (1) 1882 (1) 1884 (3) 1886 (2) 1888 (3)*

Boon, D. C. 48: v E 1986 (4) 1987 (1); v WI 1984 (3) 1988 (5); v NZ 1985 (3) 1987 (3) 1989 (1 v In 1985 (3); v P 1989 (2); v SL 1987 (1) 1989 (2); *v E 1985 (4) 1989 (6); v NZ 1985 (3) 1989 (1 v In 1986 (3); v P 1988 (3)*

Booth, B. C. 29: v E 1962 (5) 1965 (3); v SA 1963 (4); v P 1964 (1); *v E 1961 (2) 1964 (5); v W 1964 (5); v In 1964 (3); v P 1964 (1)*

Border, A. R. 115: v E 1978 (3) 1979 (3) 1982 (5) 1986 (5) 1987 (1); v WI 1979 (3) 1981 (3) 1984 (1988 (5); v NZ 1980 (3) 1985 (3) 1987 (3) 1989 (1); v In 1980 (3) 1985 (3); v P 1978 (2) 1981 (1983 (5) 1989 (3); v SL 1987 (1) 1989 (2); *v E 1980 (1) 1981 (6) 1985 (6) 1989 (6); v WI 1983 (5 v NZ 1981 (3) 1985 (3) 1989 (1); v In 1979 (6) 1986 (3); v P 1979 (3) 1982 (3) 1988 (3); v SL 198 (1)*

Boyle, H. F. 12: v E 1878 (1) 1881 (4) 1882 (1) 1884 (1); *v E 1880 (1) 1882 (1) 1884 (3)*

Bradman, D. G. 52: v E 1928 (4) 1932 (4) 1936 (5) 1946 (5); v SA 1931 (5); v WI 1930 (5); v ➤ 1947 (5); *v E 1930 (5) 1934 (5) 1938 (4) 1948 (5)*

Bright, R. J. 25: v E 1979 (1); v WI 1979 (1); v NZ 1985 (1); v In 1985 (1); *v E 1977 (3) 1980 (1981 (5); v NZ 1985 (2); v In 1986 (3); v P 1979 (3) 1982 (2)*

Bromley, E. H. 2: v E 1932 (1); *v E 1934 (1)*

Brown, W. A. 22: v E 1936 (2); v In 1947 (3); *v E 1934 (5) 1938 (4) 1948 (2); v SA 1935 (5); v N 1945 (1)*

Bruce, W. 14: v E 1884 (2) 1891 (3) 1894 (4); *v E 1886 (2) 1893 (3)*

Burge, P. J. 42: v E 1954 (1) 1958 (1) 1962 (3) 1965 (4); v SA 1963 (5); v WI 1960 (2); *v E 1956 (1961 (5) 1964 (5); v SA 1957 (1); v WI 1954 (1); v In 1956 (3) 1959 (2) 1964 (3); v P 1959 (1964 (1)*

Burke, J. W. 24: v E 1950 (2) 1954 (2) 1958 (5); v WI 1951 (1); *v E 1956 (5); v SA 1957 (5); v . 1956 (3); v P 1956 (1)*

Burn, K. E. 2: *v E 1890 (2)*

Burton, F. J. 2: v E 1886 (1) 1887 (1)

Callaway, S. T. 3: v E 1891 (2) 1894 (1)

Callen, I. W. 1: v In 1977

Campbell, G. D. 4: v P 1989 (1); v SL 1989 (1); *v E 1989 (1); v NZ 1989 (1)*

Carkeek, W. 6: *v E 1912 (3); v SA 1912 (3)*

Carlson, P. H. 2: v E 1978 (2)

Carter, H. 28: v E 1907 (5) 1911 (5) 1920 (2); v SA 1910 (5); *v E 1909 (5) 1921 (4); v SA 1921 (*

Chappell, G. S. 87: v E 1970 (5) 1974 (6) 1976 (1) 1979 (3) 1982 (5); v WI 1975 (6) 1979 (3) 198 (3); v NZ 1973 (3) 1980 (3); v In 1980 (3); v P 1972 (3) 1976 (3) 1981 (3) 1983 (5); *v E 1972 (1975 (4) 1977 (5) 1980 (1); v WI 1972 (5); v NZ 1973 (3) 1976 (2) 1981 (3); v P 1979 (3); v S 1982 (1)*

Chappell, I. M. 75: v E 1965 (2) 1970 (6) 1974 (6) 1979 (2); v WI 1968 (5) 1975 (6) 1979 (1); v N 1973 (3); v In 1967 (4); v P 1964 (1) 1972 (3); *v E 1968 (5) 1972 (5) 1975 (4); v SA 1966 (5) 196 (4); v WI 1972 (5); v NZ 1973 (3); v In 1969 (5)*

Chappell, T. M. 3: *v E 1981 (3)*

Charlton, P. C. 2: *v E 1890 (2)*

Chipperfield, A. G. 14: v E 1936 (3); *v E 1934 (5) 1938 (1); v SA 1935 (5)*

Clark, W. M. 10: v In 1977 (5); v P 1978 (1); *v WI 1977 (4)*

Colley, D. J. 3: *v E 1972 (3)*

Collins, H. L. 19: v E 1920 (5) 1924 (5); *v E 1921 (3) 1926 (3); v SA 1921 (3)*

Coningham, A. 1: v E 1894

onnolly, A. N. 29: v E 1965 (1) 1970 (1); v SA 1963 (3); v WI 1968 (5); v In 1967 (3); *v E 1968 (5); v SA 1969 (4); v In 1964 (2); 1969 (5)*

ooper, B. B. 1: v E 1876

ooper, W. H. 2: v E 1881 (1) 1884 (1)

orling, G. E. 5: *v E 1964 (5)*

osier, G. J. 18: v E 1976 (1) 1978 (2); v WI 1975 (3); v In 1977 (4); v P 1976 (3); *v WI 1977 (3); v NZ 1976 (2)*

ottam, W. J. 1: v E 1886

otter, A. 21: v E 1903 (2) 1907 (2) 1911 (4); v SA 1910 (5); *v E 1905 (3) 1909 (5)*

oulthard, G. 1: v E 1881

owper, R. M. 27: v E 1965 (4); v In 1967 (4); v P 1964 (1); *v E 1964 (1) 1968 (4); v SA 1966 (5); v WI 1964 (5); v In 1964 (2); v P 1964 (1)*

raig, I. D. 11: v SA 1952 (1); *v E 1956 (2); v SA 1957 (5); v In 1956 (2); v P 1956 (1)*

rawford, W. P. A. 4: *v E 1956 (1); v In 1956 (3)*

arling, J. 34: v E 1894 (5) 1897 (5) 1901 (3); *v E 1896 (3) 1899 (5) 1902 (5) 1905 (5); v SA 1902 (3)*

arling, L. S. 12: v E 1932 (2) 1936 (1); *v E 1934 (4); v SA 1935 (5)*

arling, W. M. 14: v E 1978 (4); v In 1977 (1); v P 1978 (1); *v WI 1977 (3); v In 1979 (5)*

avidson, A. K. 44: v E 1954 (3) 1958 (5) 1962 (5); v WI 1960 (4); *v E 1953 (5) 1956 (2) 1961 (5); v SA 1957 (5); v In 1956 (1) 1959 (5); v P 1956 (1) 1959 (3)*

avis, I. C. 15: v E 1976 (1); v NZ 1973 (3); v P 1976 (3); *v E 1977 (3); v NZ 1973 (3) 1976 (2)*

avis, S. P. 1: *v NZ 1985*

e Courcy, J. H. 3: *v E 1953 (3)*

ell, A. R. 2: v E 1970 (1); v NZ 1973 (1)

odemaide, A. I. C. 8: v E 1987 (1); v WI 1988 (2); v NZ 1987 (1); v SL 1987 (1); *v P 1988 (3)*

onnan, H. 5: v E 1891 (2); *v E 1896 (3)*

ooland, B. 3: v E 1946 (2); v In 1947 (1)

uff, R. A. 22: v E 1901 (4) 1903 (5); *v E 1902 (5) 1905 (5); v SA 1902 (3)*

uncan, J. R. F. 1: v E 1970

yer, G. C. 6: v E 1986 (1) 1987 (1); v NZ 1987 (3); v SL 1987 (1)

ymock, G. 21: v E 1974 (1) 1978 (3) 1979 (3); v WI 1979 (2); v NZ 1973 (1); v P 1978 (1); *v NZ 1973 (2); v In 1979 (5); v P 1979 (3)*

yson, J. 30: v E 1982 (5); v WI 1981 (2) 1984 (3); v NZ 1980 (3); v In 1977 (3) 1980 (3); *v E 1981 (5); v NZ 1981 (3); v P 1982 (3)*

ady, C. J. 2: v E 1901 (1); *v E 1896 (1)*

stwood, K. H. 1: v E 1970

eling, H. I. 1: *v E 1934*

dwards, J. D. 3: *v E 1888 (3)*

dwards, R. 20: v E 1974 (5); v P 1972 (2); *v E 1972 (4) 1975 (4); v WI 1972 (5)*

dwards, W. J. 3: v E 1974 (3)

mery, S. H. 4: *v E 1912 (2); v SA 1912 (2)*

vans, E. 6: v E 1881 (2) 1882 (1) 1884 (1); *v E 1886 (2)*

airfax, A. G. 10: v E 1928 (1); v WI 1930 (5); *v E 1930 (4)*

avell, L. E. 19: v E 1954 (4) 1958 (2); v WI 1960 (4); *v WI 1954 (2); v In 1959 (4); v P 1959 (3)*

rris, J. J. 8: v E 1886 (2) 1887 (1); *v E 1888 (3) 1890 (2)*

ngleton, J. H. 18: v E 1932 (3) 1936 (5); v SA 1931 (1); *v E 1938 (4); v SA 1935 (5)*

eetwood-Smith, L. O'B. 10: v E 1936 (3); *v E 1938 (4); v SA 1935 (5)*

ancis, B. C. 3: *v E 1972 (3)*

eeman, E. W. 11: v WI 1968 (4); v In 1967 (4); *v E 1968 (2); v SA 1969 (4); v In 1969 (1)*

eer, F. W. 1: v E 1946

annon, J. B. 3: v In 1977 (3)

arrett, T. W. 19: v E 1876 (2) 1878 (1) 1881 (3) 1882 (3) 1884 (3) 1886 (2) 1887 (1); *v E 1882 (1) 1886 (3)*

aunt, R. A. 3: v SA 1963 (1); *v E 1961 (1); v SA 1957 (1)*

ehrs, D. R. A. 6: v E 1903 (1); v SA 1910 (4); *v E 1905 (1)*

ffen, G. 31: v E 1881 (3) 1882 (4) 1884 (3) 1891 (3) 1894 (5); *v E 1882 (1) 1884 (3) 1886 (3) 1893 (3) 1896 (3)*

ffen, W. F. 3: v E 1886 (1) 1891 (2)

Gilbert, D. R. 9: v NZ 1985 (3); v In 1985 (2); *v E 1985 (1); v NZ 1985 (1); v In 1986 (2*

Gilmour, G. J. 15: v E 1976 (1); v WI 1975 (5); v NZ 1973 (2); v P 1976 (3); *v E 1975 (1); v N 1973 (1) 1976 (2)*

Gleeson, J. W. 29: v E 1970 (5); v WI 1968 (5); v In 1967 (4); *v E 1968 (5) 1972 (3); v SA 1969 (4 v In 1969 (3)*

Graham, H. 6: v E 1894 (2); *v E 1893 (3) 1896 (1)*

Gregory, D. W. 3: v E 1876 (2) 1878 (1)

Gregory, E. J. 1: v E 1876

Gregory, J. M. 24: v E 1920 (5) 1924 (5) 1928 (1); *v E 1921 (5) 1926 (5); v SA 1921 (3)*

Gregory, R. G. 2: v E 1936 (2)

Gregory, S. E. 58: v E 1891 (1) 1894 (5) 1897 (5) 1901 (5) 1903 (4) 1907 (2) 1911 (1); *v E 1890 (1893 (3) 1896 (3) 1899 (5) 1902 (5) 1905 (3) 1909 (5) 1912 (3); v SA 1902 (3) 1912 (3)*

Grimmett, C. V. 37: v E 1924 (1) 1928 (5) 1932 (3); v SA 1931 (5); v WI 1930 (5); *v E 1926 (1930 (5) 1934 (5); v SA 1935 (5)*

Groube, T. U. 1: *v E 1880*

Grout, A. T. W. 51: v E 1958 (5) 1962 (2) 1965 (5); v SA 1963 (5); v WI 1960 (5); *v E 1961 (5) 19* *(5); v SA 1957 (5); v WI 1964 (5); v In 1959 (4) 1964 (1); v P 1959 (3) 1964 (1)*

Guest, C. E. J. 1: v E 1962

Hamence, R. A. 3: v E 1946 (1); v In 1947 (2)

Hammond, J. R. 5: *v WI 1972 (5)*

Harry, J. 1: v E 1894

Hartigan, R. J. 2: v E 1907 (2)

Hartkopf, A. E. V. 1: v E 1924

Harvey, M. R. 1: v E 1946

Harvey, R. N. 79: v E 1950 (5) 1954 (5) 1958 (5) 1962 (5); v SA 1952 (5); v WI 1951 (5) 1960 (4 v In 1947 (2); *v E 1948 (2) 1953 (5) 1956 (5) 1961 (5); v SA 1949 (5) 1957 (4); v WI 1954 (5 v In 1956 (3) 1959 (5); v P 1956 (1) 1959 (3)*

Hassett, A. L. 43: v E 1946 (5) 1950 (5); v SA 1952 (5); v WI 1951 (4); v In 1947 (4); *v E 1938 (1948 (5) 1953 (5); v SA 1949 (5); v NZ 1945 (1)*

Hawke, N. J. N. 27: v E 1962 (1) 1965 (4); v SA 1963 (4); v In 1967 (1); v P 1964 (1); *v E 1964 (1968 (2); v SA 1966 (2); v WI 1964 (5); v In 1964 (1); v P 1964 (1)*

Hazlitt, G. R. 9: v E 1907 (2) 1911 (1); *v E 1912 (3); v SA 1912 (3)*

Healy, I. A. 21: v WI 1988 (5); v NZ 1989 (1); v P 1989 (3); v SL 1989 (2); *v E 1989 (6); v N 1989 (1); v P 1988 (3)*

Hendry, H. S. T. L. 11: v E 1924 (1) 1928 (4); *v E 1921 (4); v SA 1921 (2)*

Hibbert, P. A. 1: v In 1977

Higgs, J. D. 22: v E 1978 (5) 1979 (1); v WI 1979 (1); v NZ 1980 (3); v In 1980 (2); *v WI 1977 (4 v In 1979 (6)*

Hilditch, A. M. J. 18: v E 1978 (1); v WI 1984 (2); v NZ 1985 (1); v P 1978 (2); *v E 1985 (6); v 1979 (6)*

Hill, C. 49: v E 1897 (5) 1901 (5) 1903 (5) 1907 (5) 1911 (5); v SA 1910 (5); *v E 1896 (3) 1899 (1902 (5) 1905 (5); v SA 1902 (3)*

Hill, J. C. 3: *v E 1953 (2); v WI 1954 (1)*

Hoare, D. E. 1: v WI 1960

Hodges, J. H. 2: v E 1876 (2)

Hogan, T. G. 7: v P 1983 (1); *v WI 1983 (5); v SL 1982 (1)*

Hogg, R. M. 38: v E 1978 (6) 1982 (3); v WI 1979 (2) 1984 (4); v NZ 1980 (2); v In 1980 (2); *v 1978 (2) 1983 (4); v E 1981 (2); v WI 1983 (4); v In 1979 (6); v SL 1982 (1)*

Hohns, T. V. 7: v WI 1988 (2); *v E 1989 (5)*

Hole, G. B. 18: v E 1950 (1) 1954 (3); v SA 1952 (4); v WI 1951 (5); *v E 1953 (5)*

Holland, R. G. 11: v WI 1984 (3); v NZ 1985 (3); v In 1985 (1); *v E 1985 (4)*

Hookes, D. W. 23: v E 1976 (1) 1982 (5); v WI 1979 (1); v NZ 1985 (2); v In 1985 (2); *v E 19 (5); v WI 1983 (5); v P 1979 (1); v SL 1982 (1)*

Hopkins, A. J. Y. 20: v E 1901 (2) 1903 (5); *v E 1902 (5) 1905 (3) 1909 (2); v SA 1902 (.*

Horan, T. P. 15: v E 1876 (1) 1878 (1) 1881 (4) 1882 (4) 1884 (4); *v E 1882 (1)*

Hordern, H. V. 7: v E 1911 (5); v SA 1910 (2)

Hornibrook, P. M. 6: v E 1928 (1); *v E 1930 (5)*

Howell, W. P. 18: v E 1897 (3) 1901 (4) 1903 (3); *v E 1899 (5) 1902 (1); v SA 1902 (2)*

Hughes, K. J. 70: v E 1978 (6) 1979 (3) 1982 (5); v WI 1979 (3) 1981 (3) 1984 (4); v NZ 1980 (v In 1977 (2) 1980 (3); v P 1978 (2) 1981 (3) 1983 (5); *v E 1977 (1) 1980 (1) 1981 (6); v 1983 (5); v NZ 1981 (3); v In 1979 (6); v P 1979 (3) 1982 (3)*

ughes, M. G. 23: v E 1986 (4); v WI 1988 (4); v NZ 1987 (1) 1989 (1); v In 1985 (1); v P 1989 (3); v SL 1987 (1) 1989 (2); *v E 1989 (6)*
unt, W. A. 1: v SA 1931
urst, A. G. 12: v E 1978 (6); v NZ 1973 (1); v In 1977 (1); v P 1978 (2); *v In 1979 (2)*
urwood, A. 2: v WI 1930 (2)

verarity, R. J. 6: v WI 1968 (1); *v E 1968 (2) 1972 (3)*
edale, F. A. 14: v E 1894 (5) 1897 (4); *v E 1896 (2) 1899 (3)*
onmonger, H. 14: v E 1928 (2) 1932 (4); v SA 1931 (4); v WI 1930 (4)
erson, J. B. 5: v E 1950 (5)

ckson, A. 8: v E 1928 (2); v WI 1930 (4); *v E 1930 (2)*
rman, B. N. 19: v E 1962 (3); v WI 1968 (4); v In 1967 (4); v P 1964 (1); *v E 1968 (4); v In 1959 (1); 1964 (2)*
rvis, A. H. 11: v E 1884 (3) 1894 (4); *v E 1886 (2) 1888 (2)*
nner, T. J. 9: v E 1970 (2) 1974 (2); v WI 1975 (1); *v WI 1972 (4)*
nnings, C. B. 6: *v E 1912 (3); v SA 1912 (3)*
hnson I. W. 45: v E 1946 (4) 1950 (5) 1954 (4); v SA 1952 (1); v WI 1951 (4); v In 1947 (4); *v E 1948 (4) 1956 (5); v SA 1949 (5); v WI 1954 (5); v NZ 1945 (1); v In 1956 (2); v P 1956 (1)*
hnson, L. J. 1: v In 1947
hnston W. A. 40: v E 1950 (5) 1954 (4); v SA 1952 (5); v WI 1951 (5); v In 1947 (4); *v E 1948 (5) 1953 (3); v SA 1949 (5); v WI 1954 (4)*
nes, D. M. 34: v E 1986 (5) 1987 (1); v WI 1988 (5); v NZ 1987 (3) 1989 (1); v P 1989 (3); v SL 1987 (1) 1989 (2); *v E 1989 (6); v WI 1983 (2); v NZ 1989 (1); v In 1986 (3); v P 1988 (3)*
nes, E. 19: v E 1894 (1) 1897 (5) 1901 (2); *v E 1896 (3) 1899 (5) 1902 (2); v SA 1902 (1)*
nes, S. P. 12: v E 1881 (2) 1884 (4) 1886 (1) 1887 (1); *v E 1882 (1) 1886 (3)*
slin, L. R. 1: v In 1967

elleway, C. 26: v E 1911 (4) 1920 (5) 1924 (5) 1928 (1); v SA 1910 (5); *v E 1912 (3); v SA 1912 (3)*
elly, J. J. 36: v E 1897 (5) 1901 (5) 1903 (5); *v E 1896 (3) 1899 (5) 1902 (5) 1905 (5); v SA 1902 (3)*
elly, T. J. D. 2: v E 1876 (1) 1878 (1)
endall, T. 2: v E 1876 (2)
ent, M. F. 3: *v E 1981 (3)*
err, R. B. 2: v NZ 1985 (2)
ippax, A. F. 22: v E 1924 (1) 1928 (5) 1932 (1); v SA 1931 (4); v WI 1930 (5); *v E 1930 (5) 1934 (1)*
line L. F. 13: v E 1958 (2); v WI 1960 (2); *v SA 1957 (5); v In 1959 (3); v P 1959 (1)*

aird, B. M. 21: v E 1979 (2); v WI 1979 (3) 1981 (3); v P 1981 (3); *v E 1980 (1); v NZ 1981 (3); v P 1979 (3) 1982 (3)*
angley, G. R. A. 26: v E 1954 (2); v SA 1952 (5); v WI 1951 (5); *v E 1953 (4) 1956 (3); v WI 1954 (4); v In 1956 (2); v P 1956 (1)*
aughlin, T. J. 3: v E 1978 (1); *v WI 1977 (2)*
aver, F. 15: v E 1901 (1) 1903 (1); *v E 1899 (4) 1905 (5) 1909 (4)*
awry, W. M. 67: v E 1962 (5) 1965 (5) 1970 (5); v SA 1963 (5); v WI 1968 (5); v In 1967 (4); v P 1964 (1); *v E 1961 (5) 1964 (5) 1968 (4); v SA 1966 (5) 1969 (4); v WI 1964 (5); v In 1964 (3) 1969 (5); v P 1964 (1)*
awson, G. F. 46: v E 1982 (5) 1986 (1); v WI 1981 (1) 1984 (5) 1988 (1); v NZ 1980 (1) 1985 (2) 1989 (1); v P 1983 (5); v SL 1989 (1); *v E 1981 (3) 1985 (6) 1989 (6); v WI 1983 (5); v P 1982 (3)*
ee, P. K. 2: v E 1932 (1); v SA 1931 (1)
llee, D. K. 70: v E 1970 (2) 1974 (6) 1976 (1) 1979 (1) 1982 (1); v WI 1975 (5) 1979 (3) 1981 (3); v NZ 1980 (3); v In 1980 (3); v P 1972 (3) 1976 (3) 1981 (3) 1983 (5); *v E 1972 (5) 1975 (4) 1980 (1) 1981 (6); v WI 1972 (1); v NZ 1976 (2) 1981 (3); v P 1979 (3); v SL 1982 (1)*
indwall, R. R. 61: v E 1946 (4) 1950 (5) 1954 (4) 1958 (2); v SA 1952 (4); v WI 1951 (5); v In 1947 (5); *v E 1948 (5) 1953 (5) 1956 (4); v SA 1949 (4); v WI 1954 (5); v NZ 1945 (1); v In 1956 (3) 1959 (2); v P 1956 (1) 1959 (2)*
ive, H. S. B. 1: v E 1932
xton, S. J. E. 12: v E 1950 (3); v In 1947 (1); *v E 1948 (3); v SA 1949 (5)*
ons, J. J. 14: v E 1886 (1) 1891 (3) 1894 (3) 1897 (1); *v E 1888 (3) 1890 (2) 1893 (3)*

cAlister, P. A. 8: v E 1903 (2) 1907 (4); *v E 1909 (2)*
acartney, C. G. 35: v E 1907 (5) 1911 (1) 1920 (5); v SA 1910 (1); *v E 1909 (5) 1912 (3) 1921 (5) 1926 (5); v SA 1912 (3) 1921 (2)*

McCabe, S. J. 39: v E 1932 (5) 1936 (5); v SA 1931 (5); v WI 1930 (5); *v E 1930 (5) 1934 (5) 193*
(4); v SA 1935 (5)

McCool, C. L. 14: v E 1946 (5); v In 1947 (3); *v SA 1949 (5) v NZ 1945 (1)*

McCormick, E. L. 12: v E 1936 (4); *v E 1938 (3); v SA 1935 (5)*

McCosker, R. B. 25: v E 1974 (3) 1976 (1) 1979 (2); v WI 1975 (4) 1979 (1); v P 1976 (3); *v E 197*
(4) 1977 (5); v NZ 1976 (2)

McDermott, C. J. 24: v E 1986 (1) 1987 (1); v WI 1984 (2) 1988 (2); v NZ 1985 (2) 1987 (3); v ▮
1985 (2); v SL 1987 (1); *v E 1985 (6); v NZ 1985 (2); v In 1986 (2)*

McDonald, C. C. 47: v E 1954 (2) 1958 (5); v SA 1952 (5); v WI 1951 (1) 1960 (5); *v E 1956 (.*
1961 (3); v SA 1957 (5); v WI 1954 (5); v In 1956 (2) 1959 (5); v P 1956 (1) 1959 (3)

McDonald, E. A. 11: v E 1920 (3); *v E 1921 (5); v SA 1921 (3)*

McDonnell, P. S. 19: v E 1881 (4) 1882 (3) 1884 (2) 1886 (2) 1887 (1); *v E 1880 (1) 1884 (.*
1888 (3)

McIlwraith, J. 1: *v E 1886*

Mackay K. D. 37: v E 1958 (5) 1962 (3); v WI 1960 (5); *v E 1956 (3) 1961 (5); v SA 1957 (5); v ▮*
1956 (3) 1959 (5); v P 1959 (3)

McKenzie, G. D. 60: v E 1962 (5) 1965 (4) 1970 (3); v SA 1963 (5); v WI 1968 (5); v In 1967 (2);
P 1964 (1); *v E 1961 (3) 1964 (5) 1968 (5); v SA 1966 (5) 1969 (3); v WI 1964 (5); v In 1964 (.*
1969 (5) v P 1964 (1)

McKibbin, T. R. 5: v E 1894 (1) 1897 (2); *v E 1896 (2)*

McLaren, J. W. 1: v E 1911

Maclean, J. A. 4: v E 1978 (4)

McLeod, C. E. 17: v E 1894 (1) 1897 (5) 1901 (2) 1903 (3); *v E 1899 (1) 1905 (5)*

McLeod, R. W. 6: v E 1891 (3); *v E 1893 (3)*

McShane, P. G. 3: v E 1884 (1) 1886 (1) 1887 (1)

Maddocks, L. V. 7: v E 1954 (3); *v E 1956 (2); v WI 1954 (1); v In 1956 (1)*

Maguire, J. N. 3: v P 1983 (1); *v WI 1983 (2)*

Mailey, A. A. 21: v E 1920 (5) 1924 (5); *v E 1921 (3) 1926 (5); v SA 1921 (3)*

Mallett, A. A. 38: v E 1970 (2) 1974 (5) 1979 (1); v WI 1968 (1) 1975 (6) 1979 (1); v NZ 1973 (3'
v P 1972 (2); *v E 1968 (1) 1972 (2) 1975 (4) 1980 (1); v SA 1969 (1); v NZ 1973 (3); v In 1969 (:*

Malone, M. F. 1: *v E 1977*

Mann, A. L. 4: v In 1977 (4)

Marr, A. P. 1: v E 1884

Marsh, G. R. 36: v E 1986 (5) 1987 (1); v WI 1988 (5); v NZ 1987 (3); v In 1985 (3); v P 1989 (2
v SL 1987 (1); *v E 1989 (6); v NZ 1985 (3) 1989 (1); v In 1986 (3); v P 1988 (3)*

Marsh, R. W. 96: v E 1970 (6) 1974 (6) 1976 (1) 1979 (3) 1982 (5); v WI 1975 (6) 1979 (3) 1981 (3'
v NZ 1973 (3) 1980 (3); v In 1980 (3); v P 1972 (3) 1976 (3) 1981 (3) 1983 (5); *v E 1972 (5) 197*
(4) 1977 (5) 1980 (1) 1981 (6); v WI 1972 (5); v NZ 1973 (3) 1976 (2) 1981 (3); v P 1979 (.
1982 (3)

Martin, J. W. 8: v SA 1963 (1); v WI 1960 (3); *v SA 1966 (1); v In 1964 (2); v P 1964 (1'*

Massie, H. H. 9: v E 1881 (4) 1882 (3) 1884 (1); *v E 1882 (1)*

Massie, R. A. L. 6: v P 1972 (2); *v E 1972 (4)*

Matthews, C. D. 3: v E 1986 (2); v WI 1988 (1)

Matthews, G. R. J. 21: v E 1986 (4); v WI 1984 (1); v NZ 1985 (3); v In 1985 (3); v P 1983 (2); *v*
1985 (1); v WI 1983 (1); v NZ 1985 (3); v In 1986 (3)

Matthews, T. J. 8: v E 1911 (2); *v E 1912 (3); v SA 1912 (3)*

May, T. B. A. 7: v WI 1988 (3); v NZ 1987 (1); *v P 1988 (3)*

Mayne, E. R. 4: *v E 1912 (1); v SA 1912 (1) 1921 (2)*

Mayne, L. C. 6: *v SA 1969 (2); v WI 1964 (3); v In 1969 (1)*

Meckiff, I. 18: v E 1958 (4); v SA 1963 (1); v WI 1960 (2); *v SA 1957 (4); v In 1959 (5); v*
1959 (2)

Meuleman, K. D. 1: *v NZ 1945*

Midwinter, W. E. 8: v E 1876 (3) 1882 (1) 1886 (2); *v E 1884 (3)*

Miller, K. R. 55: v E 1946 (5) 1950 (5) 1954 (4); v SA 1952 (4); v WI 1951 (5); v In 1947 (5); *v*
1948 (5) 1953 (5) 1956 (5); v SA 1949 (5); v WI 1954 (5); v NZ 1945 (1); v P 1956 (1)

Minnett, R. B. 9: v E 1911 (5); *v E 1912 (1); v SA 1912 (3)*

Misson, F. M. 5: v WI 1960 (3); *v E 1961 (2)*

Moody, T. M. 4: v NZ 1989 (1); v P 1989 (1); v SL 1989 (2)

Moroney, J. R. 7: v E 1950 (1); v WI 1951 (1); *v SA 1949 (5)*

Morris, A. R. 46: v E 1946 (5) 1950 (5) 1954 (4); v SA 1952 (5); v WI 1951 (4); v In 1947 (4); *v*
1948 (5) 1953 (5); v SA 1949 (5); v WI 1954 (4)

Morris, S. 1: v E 1884

Moses, H. 6: v E 1886 (2) 1887 (1) 1891 (2) 1894 (1)
Moss, J. K. 1: v P 1978
Moule, W. H. 1: *v E 1880*
Murdoch, W. L. 18: v E 1876 (1) 1878 (1) 1881 (4) 1882 (4) 1884 (1); *v E 1880 (1) 1882 (1) 1884 (3) 1890 (2)*
Musgrove, H. 1: v E 1884

Nagel, L. E. 1: v E 1932
Nash, L. J. 2: v E 1936 (1); v SA 1931 (1)
Nitschke, H. C. 2: v SA 1931 (2)
Noble, M. A. 42: v E 1897 (4) 1901 (5) 1903 (5) 1907 (5); *v E 1899 (5) 1902 (5) 1905 (5) 1909 (5); v SA 1902 (3)*
Noblet, G. 3: v SA 1952 (1); v WI 1951 (1); *v SA 1949 (1)*
Nothling, O. E. 1: v E 1928

O'Brien, L. P. J. 5: v E 1932 (2) 1936 (1); *v SA 1935 (2)*
O'Connor, J. D. A. 4: v E 1907 (3); *v E 1909 (1)*
O'Donnell, S. P. 6: v NZ 1985 (1); *v E 1985 (5)*
Ogilvie, A. D. 5: v In 1977 (3); *v WI 1977 (2)*
O'Keeffe, K. J. 24: v E 1970 (2) 1976 (1); v NZ 1973 (3); v P 1972 (2) 1976 (3); *v E 1977 (3); v WI 1972 (5); v NZ 1973 (3) 1976 (2)*
Oldfield, W. A. 54: v E 1920 (3) 1924 (5) 1928 (5) 1932 (4) 1936 (5); v SA 1931 (5); v WI 1930 (5); *v E 1921 (1) 1926 (5) 1930 (5) 1934 (5); v SA 1921 (1) 1935 (5)*
O'Neill, N. C. 42: v E 1958 (5) 1962 (5); v SA 1963 (4); v WI 1960 (5); *v E 1961 (5) 1964 (4); v WI 1964 (4); v In 1959 (5) 1964 (2); v P 1959 (3)*
O'Reilly, W. J. 27: v E 1932 (5) 1936 (5); v SA 1931 (2); *v E 1934 (5) 1938 (4); v SA 1935 (5); v NZ 1945 (1)*
Oxenham, R. K. 7: v E 1928 (3); v SA 1931 (1); v WI 1930 (3)

Palmer, G. E. 17: v E 1881 (4) 1882 (4) 1884 (2); *v E 1880 (1) 1884 (3) 1886 (3)*
Park, R. L. 1: v E 1920
Pascoe, L. S. 14: v E 1979 (2); v WI 1979 (1) 1981 (1); v NZ 1980 (3); v In 1980 (3); *v E 1977 (3) 1980 (1)*
Pellew, C. E. 10: v E 1920 (4); *v E 1921 (5); v SA 1921 (1)*
Phillips, W. B. 27: v WI 1984 (2); v NZ 1985 (3); v In 1985 (3); v P 1983 (5); *v E 1985 (6); v WI 1983 (5); v NZ 1985 (3)*
Philpott, P. I. 8: v E 1965 (3); *v WI 1964 (5)*
Ponsford, W. H. 29: v E 1924 (5) 1928 (2) 1932 (3); v SA 1931 (4); v WI 1930 (5); *v E 1926 (2) 1930 (4) 1934 (4)*
Pope, R. J. 1: v E 1884

Rackemann, C. G. 11: v E 1982 (1); v WI 1984 (1); v NZ 1989 (1); v P 1983 (2) 1989 (3); v SL 1989 (1); *v WI 1983 (1); v NZ 1989 (1)*
Ransford, V. S. 20: v E 1907 (5) 1911 (5); v SA 1910 (5); *v E 1909 (5)*
Redpath, I. R. 66: v E 1965 (1) 1970 (6) 1974 (6); v SA 1963 (1); v WI 1968 (5) 1975 (6); v In 1967 (3); v P 1972 (3); *v E 1964 (5) 1968 (5); v SA 1966 (5) 1969 (4); v WI 1972 (5); v NZ 1973 (3); v In 1964 (2) 1969 (5); v P 1964 (1)*
Reedman, J. C. 1: v E 1894
Reid, B. A. 18: v E 1986 (5); v NZ 1987 (2); v In 1985 (3); *v NZ 1985 (3); v In 1986 (2); v P 1988 (3)*
Renneberg, D. A. 8: v In 1967 (3); *v SA 1966 (5)*
Richardson, A. J. 9: v E 1924 (4); *v E 1926 (5)*
Richardson, V. Y. 19: v E 1924 (3) 1928 (2) 1932 (5); *v E 1930 (4); v SA 1935 (5)*
Ring, D. T. 13: v SA 1952 (5); v WI 1951 (5); v In 1947 (1); *v E 1948 (1) 1953 (1)*
Ritchie, G. M. 30: v E 1986 (4); v WI 1984 (1); v NZ 1985 (3); v In 1985 (3); *v E 1985 (6); v WI 1983 (5); v NZ 1985 (3); v In 1986 (3); v P 1982 (3)*
Rixon, S. J. 13: v WI 1984 (3); v In 1977 (5); *v WI 1977 (5)*
Robertson, W. R. 1: v E 1884
Robinson, R. D. 3: *v E 1977 (3)*
Robinson, R. H. 1: v E 1936
Rorke, G. F. 4: v E 1958 (2); *v In 1959 (2)*

Rutherford, J. W. 1: *v In 1956*

Ryder, J. 20: v E 1920 (5) 1924 (3) 1928 (5); *v E 1926 (4); v SA 1921 (3)*

Saggers, R. A. 6: *v E 1948 (1); v SA 1949 (5)*

Saunders, J. V. 14: v E 1901 (1) 1903 (2) 1907 (5); *v E 1902 (4); v SA 1902 (2)*

Scott, H. J. H. 8: v E 1884 (2); *v E 1884 (3) 1886 (3)*

Sellers, R. H. D. 1: *v In 1964*

Serjeant, C. S. 12: v In 1977 (4); *v E 1977 (3); v WI 1977 (5)*

Sheahan, A. P. 31: v E 1970 (2); v WI 1968 (5); v NZ 1973 (2); v In 1967 (4); v P 1972 (2); *v E 1968 (5) 1972 (2); v SA 1969 (4); v In 1969 (5)*

Shepherd, B. K. 9: v E 1962 (2); v SA 1963 (4); v P 1964 (1); *v WI 1964 (2)*

Sievers, M. W. 3: v E 1936 (3)

Simpson, R. B. 62: v E 1958 (1) 1962 (5) 1965 (3); v SA 1963 (5); v WI 1960 (5); v In 1967 (3) 1977 (5); v P 1964 (1); *v E 1961 (5) 1964 (5); v SA 1957 (5) 1966 (5); v WI 1964 (5) 1977 (5); v In 1964 (3); v P 1964 (1)*

Sincock, D. J. 3: v E 1965 (1); v P 1964 (1); *v WI 1964 (1)*

Slater, K. N. 1: v E 1958

Sleep, P. R. 14: v E 1986 (3) 1987 (1); v NZ 1987 (3); v P 1978 (1) 1989 (1); v SL 1989 (1); *v In 1979 (2); v P 1982 (1) 1988 (1)*

Slight, J. 1: *v E 1880*

Smith, D. B. M. 2: *v E 1912 (2)*

Smith, S. B. 3: *v WI 1983 (3)*

Spofforth, F. R. 18: v E 1876 (1) 1878 (1) 1881 (1) 1882 (4) 1884 (3) 1886 (1); *v E 1882 (1) 1884 (3) 1886 (3)*

Stackpole, K. R. 43: v E 1965 (2) 1970 (6); v WI 1968 (5); v NZ 1973 (3); v P 1972 (1); *v E 1972 (5); v SA 1966 (5) 1969 (4); v WI 1972 (4); v NZ 1973 (3); v In 1969 (5)*

Stevens, G. B. 4: *v In 1959 (2); v P 1959 (2)*

Taber, H. B. 16: v WI 1968 (1); *v E 1968 (1); v SA 1966 (5); 1969 (4); v In 1969 (5)*

Tallon, D. 21: v E 1946 (5) 1950 (5); v In 1947 (5); *v E 1948 (4) 1953 (1); v NZ 1945 (1)*

Taylor, J. M. 20: v E 1920 (5) 1924 (5); *v E 1921 (5) 1926 (3); v SA 1921 (2)*

Taylor, M. A. 15: v WI 1988 (2); v NZ 1989 (1); v P 1989 (3); v SL 1989 (2); *v E 1989 (6); v NZ 1989 (1)*

Taylor, P. L. 10: v E 1986 (1) 1987 (1); v WI 1988 (2); v P 1989 (2); v SL 1987 (1); v NZ 1989 (1) *v P 1988 (2)*

Thomas, G. 8: v E 1965 (3); *v WI 1964 (5)*

Thompson, N. 2: v E 1876 (2)

Thoms, G. R. 1: v WI 1951

Thomson, A. L. 4: v E 1970 (4)

Thomson, J. R. 51: v E 1974 (5) 1979 (1) 1982 (4); v WI 1975 (6) 1979 (1) 1981 (2); v In 1977 (5); v P 1972 (1) 1976 (1) 1981 (3); *v E 1975 (4) 1977 (5) 1985 (2); v WI 1977 (5); v NZ 1981 (3); v P 1982 (3)*

Thurlow, H. M. 1: v SA 1931

Toohey, P. M. 15: v E 1978 (5) 1979 (1); v WI 1979 (1); v In 1977 (5); *v WI 1977 (3)*

Toshack, E. R. H. 12: v E 1946 (5); v In 1947 (2); *v E 1948 (4); v NZ 1945 (1)*

Travers, J. P. F. 1: v E 1901

Tribe, G. E. 3: v E 1946 (3)

Trott, A. E. 3: v E 1894 (3)

Trott, G. H. S. 24: v E 1891 (3) 1894 (5) 1897 (5); *v E 1888 (3) 1890 (2) 1893 (3) 1896 (3)*

Trumble, H. 32: v E 1894 (1) 1897 (5) 1901 (5) 1903 (4); *v E 1890 (2) 1893 (3) 1896 (3) 1899 (5) 1902 (3); v SA 1902 (1)*

Trumble, J. W. 7: v E 1884 (4); *v E 1886 (3)*

Trumper, V. T. 48: v E 1901 (5) 1903 (5) 1907 (5) 1911 (5); v SA 1910 (5); *v E 1899 (5) 1902 (5) 1905 (5) 1909 (5); v SA 1902 (3)*

Turner, A. 14: v WI 1975 (6); v P 1976 (3); *v E 1975 (3); v NZ 1976 (2)*

Turner, C. T. B. 17: v E 1886 (2) 1887 (1) 1891 (3) 1894 (3); *v E 1888 (3) 1890 (2) 1893 (3)*

Veivers, T. R. 21: v E 1965 (4); v SA 1963 (3); v P 1964 (1); *v E 1964 (5); v SA 1966 (4); v In 1964 (3); v P 1964 (1)*

Veletta, M. R. J. 8: v E 1987 (1); v WI 1988 (2); v NZ 1987 (3); v P 1989 (1); v SL 1987 (1)

Waite, M. G. 2: *v E 1938 (2)*

Walker, M. H. N. 34: v E 1974 (6); 1976 (1); v WI 1975 (3); v NZ 1973 (1); v P 1972 (2) 1976 (2); *v E 1975 (4); 1977 (5); v WI 1972 (5); v NZ 1973 (3) 1976 (2)*

all, T. W. 18: v E 1928 (1) 1932 (4); v SA 1931 (3); v WI 1930 (1); *v E 1930 (5) 1934 (4)*
alters, F. H. 1: v E 1884
alters, K. D. 74: v E 1965 (5) 1970 (6) 1974 (6) 1976 (1); v WI 1968 (4); v NZ 1973 (3) 1980 (3);
v In 1967 (2) 1980 (3); v P 1972 (1) 1976 (3); *v E 1968 (5) 1972 (4) 1975 (4) 1977 (5); v SA 1969
(4); v WI 1972 (5); v NZ 1973 (3) 1976 (2); v In 1969 (5)*
ard, F. A. 4: v E 1936 (4); *v E 1938 (1)*
atkins, J. R. 1: v P 1972
atson, G. D. 5: *v E 1972 (2); v SA 1966 (3)*
atson, W. 4: v E 1954 (1); *v WI 1954 (3)*
augh, S. R. 39: v E 1986 (5) 1987 (1); v WI 1988 (5); v NZ 1987 (3) 1989 (1); v In 1985 (2); v P
1989 (3); v SL 1987 (1) 1989 (2); *v E 1989 (6); v NZ 1985 (3) 1989 (1); v In 1986 (3); v P 1988 (3)*
ellham, D. M. 6: v E 1986 (1); v WI 1981 (1); v P 1981 (2); *v E 1981 (1) 1985 (1)*
essels, K. C. 24: v E 1982 (4); v WI 1984 (5); v NZ 1985 (1); v P 1983 (5); *v E 1985 (6); v WI
1983 (2); v SL 1982 (1)*
hatmore, D. F. 7: v P 1978 (2); *v In 1979 (5)*
hitney, M. R. 4: v WI 1988 (1); v NZ 1987 (1); *v E 1981 (2)*
hitty, W. J. 14: v E 1911 (2); v SA 1910 (5); *v E 1909 (1) 1912 (3); v SA 1912 (3)*
iener, J. M. 6: v E 1979 (2); v WI 1979 (2); *v P 1979 (2)*
ilson, J. W. 1: *v In 1956*
ood, G. M. 59: v E 1978 (6) 1982 (1); v WI 1981 (3) 1984 (5) 1988 (3); v NZ 1980 (3); v In 1977
(1) 1980 (3); v P 1978 (1) 1981 (3); *v E 1980 (1) 1981 (6) 1985 (5); v WI 1977 (5) 1983 (1); v NZ
1981 (3); v In 1979 (2); v P 1982 (3) 1988 (3); v SL 1982 (1)*
oodcock, A. J. 1: v NZ 1973
oodfull, W. M. 35: v E 1928 (5) 1932 (5); v SA 1931 (5); v WI 1930 (5); *v E 1926 (5) 1930 (5)
1934 (5)*
oods, S. M. J. 3: *v E 1888 (3)*
oolley, R. D. 2: *v WI 1983 (1); v SL 1982 (1)*
orrall, J. 11: v E 1884 (1) 1887 (1) 1894 (1) 1897 (1); *v E 1888 (3) 1899 (4)*
right, K. J. 10: v E 1978 (2); v P 1978 (2); *v In 1979 (6)*

llop, G. N. 39: v E 1978 (6); v WI 1975 (3) 1984 (1); v In 1977 (1); v P 1978 (1) 1981 (1) 1983
(5); *v E 1980 (1) 1981 (6); v WI 1977 (4); v In 1979 (6); v P 1979 (3); v SL 1982 (1)*
rdley, B. 33: v E 1978 (4) 1982 (5); v WI 1981 (3); v In 1977 (1) 1980 (2); v P 1978 (1) 1981 (3);
v WI 1977 (5); v NZ 1981 (3); v In 1979 (3); v P 1982 (2); v SL 1982 (1)

ehrer, T. J. 10: v E 1986 (4); *v NZ 1985 (3); v In 1986 (3)*

SOUTH AFRICA

Number of Test cricketers: 235

lcock, N. A. T. 26: v E 1956 (5); v A 1957 (5); v NZ 1953 (5) 1961 (2); *v E 1955 (4) 1960 (5)*
derson, J. H. 1: v A 1902
hley, W. H. 1: v E 1888

cher, A. 12: v A 1966 (5) 1969 (4); *v E 1965 (3)*
laskas, X. C. 9: v E 1930 (2) 1938 (1); v A 1935 (3); *v E 1935 (1); v NZ 1931 (2)*
rlow, E. J. 30: v E 1964 (5); v A 1966 (5) 1969 (4); v NZ 1961 (5); *v E 1965 (3); v A 1963 (5);
v NZ 1963 (3)*
umgartner, H. V. 1: v E 1913
aumont, R. 5: v E 1913 (2); *v E 1912 (1); v A 1912 (2)*
gbie, D. W. 5: v E 1948 (3); v A 1949 (2)
ll, A. J. 16: v E 1930 (3); *v E 1929 (3) 1935 (3); v A 1931 (5); v NZ 1931 (2)*
sset, M. 3: v E 1898 (2) 1909 (1)
ssett, G. F. 4: v E 1927 (4)
anckenberg, J. M. 18: v E 1913 (5) 1922 (5); v A 1921 (3); *v E 1924 (5)*
and, K. C. 21: v E 1964 (5); v A 1966 (1); v NZ 1961 (5); *v E 1965 (3); v A 1963 (4); v NZ
1963 (3)*
ck, E. G. 1: v A 1935
nd, G. E. 1: v E 1938

Botten, J. T. 3: *v E 1965 (3)*

Brann, W. H. 3: v E 1922 (3)

Briscoe, A. W. 2: v E 1938 (1); v A 1935 (1)

Bromfield, H. D. 9: v E 1964 (3); v NZ 1961 (5); *v E 1965 (1)*

Brown, L. S. 2: *v A 1931 (1); v NZ 1931 (1)*

Burger, C. G. de V. 2: v A 1957 (2)

Burke, S. F. 2: v E 1964 (1); v NZ 1961 (1)

Buys, I. D. 1: v E 1922

Cameron, H. B. 26: v E 1927 (5) 1930 (5); *v E 1929 (4) 1935 (5); v A 1931 (5); v NZ 1931 (*

Campbell, T. 5: v E 1909 (4); *v E 1912 (1)*

Carlstein, P. R. 8: v A 1957 (1); *v E 1960 (5); v A 1963 (2)*

Carter, C. P. 10: v E 1913 (2); v A 1921 (3); *v E 1912 (2) 1924 (3)*

Catterall, R. H. 24: v E 1922 (5) 1927 (5) 1930 (4); *v E 1924 (5) 1929 (5)*

Chapman, H. W. 2: v E 1913 (1); v A 1921 (1)

Cheetham, J. E. 24: v E 1948 (1); v A 1949 (3); v NZ 1953 (5); *v E 1951 (5) 1955 (3); v A 1952 (5)*
    v NZ 1952 (2)

Chevalier, G. A. 1: v A 1969

Christy, J. A. J. 10: v E 1930 (1); *v E 1929 (2); v A 1931 (5); v NZ 1931 (2)*

Chubb, G. W. A. 5: *v E 1951 (5)*

Cochran, J. A. K. 1: v E 1930

Coen, S. K. 2: v E 1927 (2)

Commaille, J. M. M. 12: v E 1909 (5) 1927 (2); *v E 1924 (5)*

Conyngham, D. P. 1: v E 1922

Cook, F. J. 1: v E 1895

Cooper, A. H. C. 1: v E 1913

Cox, J. L. 3: v E 1913 (3)

Cripps, G. 1: v E 1891

Crisp, R. J. 9: v A 1935 (4); *v E 1935 (5)*

Curnow, S. H. 7: v E 1930 (3); *v A 1931 (4)*

Dalton, E. L. 15: v E 1930 (1) 1938 (4); v A 1935 (1); *v E 1929 (1) 1935 (4); v A 1931 (2); v N*
    1931 (2)

Davies, E. Q. 5: v E 1938 (3); v A 1935 (2)

Dawson, O. C. 9: v E 1948 (4); *v E 1947 (5)*

Deane, H. G. 17: v E 1927 (5) 1930 (2); *v E 1924 (5) 1929 (5)*

Dixon, C. D. 1: v E 1913

Dower, R. R. 1: v E 1898

Draper, R. G. 2: v A 1949 (2)

Duckworth, C. A. R. 2: v E 1956 (2)

Dumbrill, R. 5: v A 1966 (2); *v E 1965 (3)*

Duminy, J. P. 3: v E 1927 (2); *v E 1929 (1)*

Dunell, O. R. 2: v E 1888 (2)

Du Preez, J. H. 2: v A 1966 (2)

Du Toit, J. F. 1: v E 1891

Dyer, D. V. 3: *v E 1947 (3)*

Elgie, M. K. 3: v NZ 1961 (3)

Endean, W. R. 28: v E 1956 (5); v A 1957 (5); v NZ 1953 (5); *v E 1951 (1) 1955 (5); v A 1952 (5)*
    v NZ 1952 (2)

Farrer, W. S. 6: v NZ 1961 (3); *v NZ 1963 (3)*

Faulkner, G. A. 25: v E 1905 (5) 1909 (5); *v E 1907 (3) 1912 (3) 1924 (1); v A 1910 (5) 1912 (*

Fellows-Smith, J. P. 4: *v E 1960 (4)*

Fichardt, C. G. 2: v E 1891 (1) 1895 (1)

Finlason, C. E. 1: v E 1888

Floquet, C. E. 1: v E 1909

Francis, H. H. 2: v E 1898 (2)

Francois, C. M. 5: v E 1922 (5)

Frank, C. N. 3: v A 1921 (3)

Frank, W. H. B. 1: v E 1895

Fuller, E. R. H. 7: v A 1957 (1); *v E 1955 (2); v A 1952 (2); v NZ 1952 (2)*

ullerton, G. M. 7: v A 1949 (2); *v E 1947 (2) 1951 (3)*
unston, K. J. 18: v E 1956 (3); v A 1957 (5); v NZ 1953 (3); *v A 1952 (5); v NZ 1952 (2)*

amsy, D. 2: v A 1969 (2)
leeson, R. A. 1: v E 1895
lover, G. K. 1: v E 1895
oddard, T. L. 41: v E 1956 (5) 1964 (5); v A 1957 (5) 1966 (5) 1969 (3); *v E 1955 (5) 1960 (5); v A 1963 (5); v NZ 1963 (3)*
ordon, N. 5: v E 1938 (5)
raham, R. 2: v E 1898 (2)
rieveson, R. E. 2: v E 1938 (2)
riffin, G. M. 2: *v E 1960 (2)*

all, A. E. 7: v E 1922 (4) 1927 (2) 1930 (1)
all, G. G. 1: v E 1964
alliwell, E. A. 8: v E 1891 (1) 1895 (3) 1898 (1); v A 1902 (3)
alse, C. G. 3: *v A 1963 (3)*
ands, P. A. M. 7: v E 1913 (5); v A 1921 (1); *v E 1924 (1)*
ands, R. H. M. 1: v E 1913
anley, M. A. 1: v E 1948
arris, T. A. 3: v E 1948 (1); *v E 1947 (2)*
artigan, G. P. D. 5: v E 1913 (3); *v E 1912 (1); v A 1912 (1)*
arvey, R. L. 2: v A 1935 (2)
athorn, C. M. H. 12: v E 1905 (5); v A 1902 (3); *v E 1907 (3); v A 1910 (1)*
earne, F. 4: v E 1891 (1) 1895 (3)
earne, G. A. L. 3: v E 1922 (2); *v E 1924 (1)*
eine, P. S. 14: v E 1956 (5); v A 1957 (4); v NZ 1961 (1); *v E 1955 (4)*
ime, C. F. W. 1: v E 1895
utchinson, P. 2: v E 1888 (2)

onside, D. E. J. 3: v NZ 1953 (3)
vine, B. L. 4: v A 1969 (4)

ohnson, C. L. 1: v E 1895

eith, H. J. 8: v E 1956 (3); *v E 1955 (4); v A 1952 (1)*
empis, G. A. 1: v E 1888
otze, J. J. 3: v A 1902 (2); *v E 1907 (1)*
uys, F. 1: v E 1898

ance, H. R. 13: v A 1966 (5) 1969 (3); v NZ 1961 (2); *v E 1965 (3)*
angton, A. B. C. 15: v E 1938 (5); v A 1935 (5); *v E 1935 (5)*
awrence, G. B. 5: v NZ 1961 (5)
e Roux, F. le S. 1: v E 1913
ewis, P. T. 1: v E 1913
ndsay, D. T. 19: v E 1964 (3); v A 1966 (5) 1969 (2); *v E 1965 (3); v A 1963 (3); v NZ 1963 (3)*
ndsay, J. D. 3: *v E 1947 (3)*
ndsay, N. V. 1: v A 1921
ng, W. V. S. 6: v E 1922 (3); v A 1921 (3)
ewellyn, C. B. 15: v E 1895 (1) 1898 (1); v A 1902 (3); *v E 1912 (3); v A 1910 (5) 1912 (2)*
ndie, E. B. 1: v E 1913

acaulay, M. J. 1: v E 1964
cCarthy, C. N. 15: v E 1948 (5); v A 1949 (5); *v E 1951 (5)*
cGlew, D. J. 34: v E 1956 (1); v A 1957 (5); v NZ 1953 (5) 1961 (5); *v E 1951 (2) 1955 (5) 1960 (5); v A 1952 (4); v NZ 1952 (2)*
cKinnon, A. H. 8: v E 1964 (2); v A 1966 (2); v NZ 1961 (1); *v E 1960 (1) 1965 (2)*
cLean, R. A. 40: v E 1956 (5) 1964 (2); v A 1957 (4); v NZ 1953 (4) 1961 (5); *v E 1951 (3) 1955 (5) 1960 (5); v A 1952 (5); v NZ 1952 (2)*
cMillan, Q. 13: v E 1930 (5); *v E 1929 (2); v A 1931 (4); v NZ 1931 (2)*
ann, N. B. F. 19: v E 1948 (5); v A 1949 (5); *v E 1947 (5) 1951 (4)*
ansell, P. N. F. 13: *v E 1951 (2) 1955 (4); v A 1952 (5); v NZ 1952 (2)*
arkham, L. A. 1: v E 1948

Marx, W. F. E. 3: v A 1921 (3)
Meintjes, D. J. 2: v E 1922 (2)
Melle, M. G. 7: v A 1949 (2); *v E 1951 (1); v A 1952* (4)
Melville, A. 11: v E 1938 (5) 1948 (1); *v E 1947* (5)
Middleton, J. 6: v E 1895 (2) 1898 (2); v A 1902 (2)
Mills, C. 1: v E 1891
Milton, W. H. 3: v E 1888 (2) 1891 (1)
Mitchell, B. 42: v E 1930 (5) 1938 (5) 1948 (5); v A 1935 (5); *v E 1929 (5) 1935 (5) 1947 (5); v. 1931* (5); *v NZ 1931* (2)
Mitchell, F. 3: *v E 1912 (1); v A 1912* (2)
Morkel, D. P. B. 16: v E 1927 (5); *v E 1929 (5); v A 1931 (5); v NZ 1931 (1)*
Murray, A. R. A. 10: v NZ 1953 (4); *v A 1952 (4); v NZ 1952* (2)

Nel, J. D. 6: v A 1949 (5) 1957 (1)
Newberry, C. 4: v E 1913 (4)
Newson, E. S. 3: v E 1930 (1) 1938 (2)
Nicholson, F. 4: v A 1935 (4)
Nicolson, J. F. W. 3: v E 1927 (3)
Norton, N. O. 1: v E 1909
Nourse, A. D. 34: v E 1938 (5) 1948 (5); v A 1935 (5) 1949 (5); *v E 1935 (4) 1947 (5) 1951 (5)*
Nourse, A. W. 45: v E 1905 (5) 1909 (5) 1913 (5) 1922 (5); v A 1902 (3) 1921 (3); *v E 1907 (3) 191 (3) 1924 (5); v A 1910 (5) 1912* (3)
Nupen, E. P. 17: v E 1922 (4) 1927 (5) 1930 (3); v A 1921 (2) 1935 (1); *v E 1924* (2)

Ochse, A. E. 2: v E 1888 (2)
Ochse, A. L. 3: v E 1927 (1); *v E 1929* (2)
O'Linn, S. 7: v NZ 1961 (2); *v E 1960* (5)
Owen-Smith, H. G. 5: *v E 1929* (5)

Palm, A. W. 1: v E 1927
Parker, G. M. 2: *v E 1924* (2)
Parkin, D. C. 1: v E 1891
Partridge, J. T. 11: v E 1964 (3); *v A 1963 (5); v NZ 1963* (3)
Pearse, O. C. 3: *v A 1910* (3)
Pegler, S. J. 16: v E 1909 (1); *v E 1912 (3) 1924 (5); v A 1910 (4) 1912* (3)
Pithey, A. J. 17: v E 1956 (3) 1964 (5); *v E 1960 (2); v A 1963 (4); v NZ 1963* (3)
Pithey, D. B. 8: v A 1966 (2); *v A 1963 (3); v NZ 1963* (3)
Plimsoll, J. B. 1: *v E 1947*
Pollock, P. M. 28: v E 1964 (5); v A 1966 (5) 1969 (4); v NZ 1961 (3); *v E 1965 (3); v A 1963 (5); v NZ 1963* (3)
Pollock, R. G. 23: v E 1964 (5); v A 1966 (5) 1969 (4); *v E 1965 (3); v A 1963 (5); v NZ 1963 (1)*
Poore, R. M. 3: v E 1895 (3)
Pothecary, J. E. 3: *v E 1960* (3)
Powell, A. W. 1: v E 1898
Prince, C. F. H. 1: v E 1898
Procter, M. J. 7: v A 1966 (3) 1969 (4)
Promnitz, H. L. E. 2: v E 1927 (2)

Quinn, N. A. 12: v E 1930 (1); *v E 1929 (4); v A 1931 (5); v NZ 1931* (2)

Reid, N. 1: v A 1921
Richards, A. R. 1: v E 1895
Richards, B. A. 4: v A 1969 (4)
Richards, W. H. 1: v E 1888
Robertson, J. B. 3: v A 1935 (3)
Rose-Innes, A. 2: v E 1888 (2)
Routledge, T. W. 4: v E 1891 (1) 1895 (3)
Rowan, A. M. B. 15: v E 1948 (5); *v E 1947 (5) 1951* (5)
Rowan, E. A. B. 26: v E 1938 (4) 1948 (4); v A 1935 (3); 1949 (5); *v E 1935 (5) 1951* (5)
Rowe, G. A. 5: v E 1895 (2) 1898 (2); v A 1902 (1)

Samuelson, S. V. 1: v E 1909
Schwarz, R. O. 20: v E 1905 (5) 1909 (4); *v E 1907 (3) 1912 (1); v A 1910 (5) 1912* (2)
Seccull, A. W. 1: v E 1895

eymour, M. A. 7: v E 1964 (2); v A 1969 (1); *v A 1963 (4)*
halders, W. A. 12: v E 1898 (1) 1905 (5); v A 1902 (3); *v E 1907 (3)*
hepstone, G. H. 2: v E 1895 (1) 1898 (1)
herwell, P. W. 13: v E 1905 (5); *v E 1907 (3); v A 1910 (5)*
edle, I. J. 18: v E 1927 (1) 1930 (5); v A 1935 (5); *v E 1929 (3) 1935 (4)*
nclair, J. H. 25: v E 1895 (3) 1898 (2) 1905 (5) 1909 (4); v A 1902 (3); *v E 1907 (3); v A 1910 (5)*
mith, C. J. E. 3: v A 1902 (3)
mith, F. W. 3: v E 1888 (2) 1895 (1)
mith, V. I. 9: v A 1949 (3) 1957 (1); *v E 1947 (4) 1955 (1)*
nooke, S. D. 1: *v E 1907*
nooke, S. J. 26: v E 1905 (5) 1909 (5) 1922 (3); *v E 1907 (3) 1912 (3); v A 1910 (5) 1912 (2)*
olomon, W. R. 1: v E 1898
ewart, R. B. 1: v E 1888
ricker, L. A. 13: v E 1909 (4); *v E 1912 (2); v A 1910 (5) 1912 (2)*
usskind, M. J. 5: *v E 1924 (5)*

aberer, H. M. 1: v A 1902
ancred, A. B. 2: v E 1888 (2)
ancred, L. J. 14: v E 1905 (5) 1913 (1); v A 1902 (3); *v E 1907 (1) 1912 (2); v A 1912 (2)*
ancred, V. M. 1: v E 1898
apscott, G. L. 1: v E 1913
apscott, L. E. 2: v E 1922 (2)
ayfield, H. J. 37: v E 1956 (5); v A 1949 (5) 1957 (2); v NZ 1953 (5); *v E 1955 (5) 1960 (5); v A 1952 (5); v NZ 1952 (2)*
aylor, A. I. 1: v E 1956
aylor, D. 2: v E 1913 (2)
aylor, H. W. 42: v E 1913 (5) 1922 (5) 1927 (5) 1930 (4); v A 1921 (3); *v E 1912 (3) 1924 (5) 1929 (3); v A 1912 (3) 1931 (5); v NZ 1931 (1)*
heunissen, N. H. G. de J. 1: v E 1888
hornton, P. G. 1: v A 1902
omlinson, D. S. 1: *v E 1935*
raicos, A. J. 3: v A 1969 (3)
rimborn, P. H. J. 4: v A 1966 (3) 1969 (1)
uckett, L. 9: v E 1948 (4); *v E 1947 (5)*
uckett, L. R. 1: v E 1913
wentyman-Jones, P. S. 1: v A 1902

an der Bijl, P. G. V. 5: v E 1938 (5)
an der Merwe, E. A. 2: v A 1935 (1); *v E 1929 (1)*
an der Merwe, P. L. 15: v E 1964 (2); v A 1966 (5); *v E 1965 (3); v A 1963 (3); v NZ 1963 (2)*
an Ryneveld, C. B. 19: v E 1956 (5); v A 1957 (4); v NZ 1953 (5); *v E 1951 (5)*
arnals, G. D. 3: v E 1964 (3)
iljoen, K. G. 27: v E 1930 (3) 1938 (4) 1948 (2); v A 1935 (4); *v E 1935 (4) 1947 (5); v A 1931 (4); v NZ 1931 (1)*
incent, C. L. 25: v E 1927 (5) 1930 (5); *v E 1929 (4) 1935 (4); v A 1931 (5); v NZ 1931 (2)*
intent, C. H. 3: v E 1888 (2) 1891 (1)
ogler, A. E. E. 15: v E 1905 (5) 1909 (5); *v E 1907 (3); v A 1910 (2)*

ade, H. F. 10: v A 1935 (5); *v E 1935 (5)*
ade, W. W. 11: v E 1938 (3) 1948 (5); v A 1949 (3)
aite, J. H. B. 50: v E 1956 (5); 1964 (2); v A 1957 (5); v NZ 1953 (5) 1961 (5); *v E 1951 (4) 1955 (5) 1960 (5); v A 1952 (5) 1963 (4); v NZ 1952 (2) 1963 (3)*
alter, K. A. 2: v NZ 1961 (2)
ard, T. A. 23: v E 1913 (5) 1922 (5); v A 1921 (3); *v E 1912 (2) 1924 (5); v A 1912 (3)*
atkins, J. C. 15: v E 1956 (2); v A 1949 (3); v NZ 1953 (3); *v A 1952 (5); v NZ 1952 (2)*
esley, C. 3: *v E 1960 (3)*
estcott, R. J. 5: v A 1957 (2); v NZ 1953 (3)
hite, G. C. 17: v E 1905 (5) 1909 (4); *v E 1907 (3) 1912 (2); v A 1912 (3)*
illoughby, J. T. I. 2: v E 1895 (2)
imble, C. S. 1: v E 1891
inslow, P. L. 5: v A 1949 (2); *v E 1955 (3)*
ynne, O. E. 6: v E 1948 (3); v A 1949 (3)

ulch, J. W. 16: v E 1909 (5) 1913 (3); v A 1921 (3); *v A 1910 (5)*

WEST INDIES

Number of Test cricketers: 195

Achong, E. 6: v E 1929 (1) 1934 (2); *v E 1933 (3)*

Alexander, F. C. M. 25: v E 1959 (5); v P 1957 (5); *v E 1957 (2); v A 1960 (5); v In 1958 (5); v 1958 (3)*

Ali, Imtiaz 1: v In 1975

Ali, Inshan 12: v E 1973 (2); v A 1972 (3); v In 1970 (1); v P 1976 (1); v NZ 1971 (3); *v E 197 (1); v A 1975 (1)*

Allan, D. W. 5: v A 1964 (1); v In 1961 (2); *v E 1966 (2)*

Ambrose, C. E. L. 20: v E 1989 (3); v In 1988 (4); v P 1987 (3); *v E 1988 (5); v A 1988 (5*

Arthurton, K. L. T. 5: v In 1988 (4); *v E 1988 (1)*

Asgarali, N. 2: *v E 1957 (2)*

Atkinson, D. St E. 22: v E 1953 (4); v A 1954 (4); v P 1957 (1); *v E 1957 (2); v A 1951 (2); v N. 1951 (1) 1955 (4); v In 1948 (4)*

Atkinson, E. St E. 8: v P 1957 (3); *v In 1958 (3); v P 1958 (2)*

Austin, R. A. 2: v A 1977 (2)

Bacchus, S. F. A. F. 19: v E 1977 (2); *v E 1980 (5); v A 1981 (2); v In 1978 (6); v P 1980 (4*

Baichan, L. 3: *v A 1975 (1); v P 1974 (2)*

Baptiste, E. A. E. 10: v E 1989 (1); v A 1983 (3); *v E 1984 (5); v In 1983 (1)*

Barrett, A. G. 6: v E 1973 (2); v In 1970 (2); *v In 1974 (2)*

Barrow, I. 11: v E 1929 (1) 1934 (1); *v E 1933 (3) 1939 (1); v A 1930 (5)*

Bartlett, E. L. 5: *v E 1928 (1); v A 1930 (4)*

Benjamin, W. K. M. 8: v In 1988 (1); v P 1987 (3); *v E 1988 (3); v In 1987 (1)*

Best, C. A. 6: v E 1985 (3) 1989 (3)

Betancourt, N. 1: v E 1929

Binns, A. P. 5: v A 1954 (1); v In 1952 (1); *v NZ 1955 (3)*

Birkett, L. S. 4: *v A 1930 (4)*

Bishop, I. R. 8: v E 1989 (4); v In 1988 (4)

Boyce, K. D. 21: v E 1973 (4); v A 1972 (4); v In 1970 (1); *v E 1973 (3); v A 1975 (4); v In 197 (3); v P 1974 (2)*

Browne, C. R. 4: v E 1929 (2); *v E 1928 (2)*

Butcher, B. F. 44: v E 1959 (2) 1967 (5); v A 1964 (5); *v E 1963 (5) 1966 (5) 1969 (3); v A 1968 (5 v NZ 1968 (3); v In 1958 (5) 1966 (3); v P 1958 (5)*

Butler, L. 1: v A 1954

Butts, C. G. 7: v NZ 1984 (1); *v NZ 1986 (1); v In 1987 (3); v P 1986 (2)*

Bynoe, M. R. 4: *v In 1966 (3); v P 1958 (1)*

Camacho, G. S. 11: v E 1967 (5); v In 1970 (2); *v E 1969 (2); v A 1968 (2)*

Cameron, F. J. 5: *v In 1948 (5)*

Cameron, J. H. 2: *v E 1939 (2)*

Carew, G. M. 4: v E 1934 (1) 1947 (2); *v In 1948 (1)*

Carew, M. C. 19: v E 1967 (1); v NZ 1971 (3); v In 1970 (3); *v E 1963 (2) 1966 (1) 1969 (1); v 1968 (5); v NZ 1968 (3)*

Challenor, G. 3: *v E 1928 (3)*

Chang, H. S. 1: *v In 1978*

Christiani, C. M. 4: v E 1934 (4)

Christiani, R. J. 22: v E 1947 (4) 1953 (1); v In 1952 (2); *v E 1950 (4); v A 1951 (5); v NZ 1951 (1 v In 1948 (5)*

Clarke, C. B. 3: *v E 1939 (3)*

Clarke, S. T. 11: v A 1977 (1); *v A 1981 (1); v In 1978 (5); v P 1980 (4)*

Constantine, L. N. 18: v E 1929 (3) 1934 (3); *v E 1928 (3) 1933 (1) 1939 (3); v A 1930 (5)*

Croft, C. E. H. 27: v E 1980 (4); v A 1977 (2); v P 1976 (5); *v E 1980 (5); v A 1979 (3) 1981 (3 v NZ 1979 (3); v P 1980 (4)*

Da Costa, O. C. 5: v E 1929 (1) 1934 (1); *v E 1933 (3)*

Daniel, W. W. 10: v A 1983 (2); v In 1975 (1); *v E 1976 (4); v In 1983 (3)*

Davis, B. A. 4: v A 1964 (4)

Davis, C. A. 15: v A 1972 (2); v NZ 1971 (5); v In 1970 (4); *v E 1969 (3); v A 1968 (1)*

avis, W. W. 15: v A 1983 (1); v NZ 1984 (2); v In 1982 (1); *v E 1984 (1); v In 1983 (6) 1987 (4)*
 Caires, F. I. 3: v E 1929 (3)
epeiza, C. C. 5: v A 1954 (3); *v NZ 1955 (2)*
ewdney, T. 9: v A 1954 (2); v P 1957 (3); *v E 1957 (1); v NZ 1955 (3)*
owe, U. G. 4: v A 1972 (1); v NZ 1971 (1); v In 1970 (2)
ujon, P. J. L. 68: v E 1985 (4) 1989 (4); v A 1983 (5); v NZ 1984 (4); v In 1982 (5) 1988 (4); v P
 1987 (3); *v E 1984 (5) 1988 (5); v A 1981 (3) 1984 (5) 1988 (5); v NZ 1986 (3); v In 1983 (6) 1987
 (4); v P 1986 (3)*

dwards, R. M. 5: *v A 1968 (2); v NZ 1968 (3)*

rguson, W. 8: v E 1947 (4) 1953 (1); *v In 1948 (3)*
rnandes, M. P. 2: v E 1929 (1); *v E 1928 (1)*
ndlay, T. M. 10: v A 1972 (1); v NZ 1971 (5); v In 1970 (2); *v E 1969 (2)*
ster, M. L. C. 14: v E 1973 (1); v A 1972 (4) 1977 (1); v NZ 1971 (3); v In 1970 (2); v P 1976
 (1); *v E 1969 (1) 1973 (1)*
ancis, G. N. 10: v E 1929 (1); *v E 1928 (3) 1933 (1); v A 1930 (5)*
ederick, M. C. 1: v E 1953
edericks, R. C. 59: v E 1973 (5); v A 1972 (5); v NZ 1971 (5); v In 1970 (4) 1975 (4); v P 1976
 (5); *v E 1969 (3) 1973 (3) 1976 (5); v A 1968 (4) 1975 (6); v NZ 1968 (3); v In 1974 (5); v P
 1974 (2)*
ller, R. L. 1: v E 1934
rlonge, H. A. 3: v A 1954 (1); *v NZ 1955 (2)*

anteaume, A. G. 1: v E 1947
arner, J. 58: v E 1980 (4) 1985 (5); v A 1977 (2) 1983 (5); v NZ 1984 (4); v In 1982 (4); v P 1976
 (5); *v E 1980 (5) 1984 (5); v A 1979 (3) 1981 (3) 1984 (5); v NZ 1979 (3) 1986 (2); v P 1980 (3)*
askin, B. B. M. 2: v E 1947 (2)
bbs, G. L. R. 1: v A 1954
bbs, L. R. 79: v E 1967 (5) 1973 (5); v A 1964 (5) 1972 (5); v NZ 1971 (2); v In 1961 (5) 1970
 (1); v P 1957 (4); *v E 1963 (5) 1966 (5) 1969 (3) 1973 (3); v A 1960 (3) 1968 (5) 1975 (6); v NZ
 1968 (3); v In 1958 (1) 1966 (3) 1974 (5); v P 1958 (3) 1974 (2)*
lchrist, R. 13: v P 1957 (5); *v E 1957 (4); v In 1958 (4)*
adstone, G. 1: v E 1929
addard, J. D. C. 27: v E 1947 (4); *v E 1950 (4) 1957 (5); v A 1951 (4); v NZ 1951 (2) 1955 (3);
 v In 1948 (5)*
omes, H. A. 60: v E 1980 (4) 1985 (5); v A 1977 (3) 1983 (2); v NZ 1984 (4); v In 1982 (5); *v E
 1976 (2) 1984 (5); v A 1981 (3) 1984 (5); v NZ 1986 (3); v In 1978 (6) 1983 (6); v P 1980 (4)
 1986 (3)*
omez, G. E. 29: v E 1947 (4) 1953 (4); v In 1952 (4); *v E 1939 (2) 1950 (4); v A 1951 (5); v NZ
 1951 (1); v In 1948 (5)*
ant, G. C. 12: v E 1934 (4); *v E 1933 (3); v A 1930 (5)*
ant, R. S. 7: v E 1934 (4); *v E 1939 (3)*
ay, A. H. 5: *v NZ 1986 (2); v P 1986 (3)*
eenidge, A. E. 6: v A 1977 (2); *v In 1978 (4)*
eenidge, C. G. 100: v E 1980 (4) 1985 (5) 1989 (4); v A 1977 (2) 1983 (5); v NZ 1984 (4); v In
 1982 (5) 1988 (4); v P 1976 (5) 1987 (3); *v E 1976 (5) 1980 (5) 1984 (5) 1988 (4); v A 1975 (2)
 1979 (3) 1981 (2) 1984 (5) 1988 (5); v NZ 1979 (3) 1986 (3); v In 1974 (5) 1983 (6) 1987 (3); v P
 1986 (3)*
eenidge, G. A. 5: v A 1972 (3); v NZ 1971 (2)
ell, M. G. 1: v E 1929
iffith, C. C. 28: v E 1959 (1) 1967 (4); v A 1964 (5); *v E 1963 (5) 1966 (5); v A 1968 (3); v NZ
 1968 (2); v In 1966 (3)*
iffith, H. C. 13: v E 1929 (3); *v E 1928 (3) 1933 (2); v A 1930 (5)*
illen, S. C. 5: *v A 1951 (3); v NZ 1951 (2)*

ll, W. W. 48: v E 1959 (5) 1967 (4); v A 1964 (5); v In 1961 (5); *v E 1963 (5) 1966 (5); v A 1960
 5) 1968 (2); v NZ 1968 (1); v In 1958 (5) 1966 (5); v P 1958 (3)*
rper, R. A. 24: v E 1985 (2); v A 1983 (4); v NZ 1984 (1); *v E 1984 (5) 1988 (3); v A 1984 (2)
 1988 (1); v In 1983 (2) 1987 (1); v P 1986 (3)*
ynes, D. L. 89: v E 1980 (4) 1985 (5) 1989 (4); v A 1977 (3) 1983 (5); v NZ 1984 (4); v In 1982
 5) 1988 (4); v P 1987 (3); *v E 1980 (5) 1984 (5) 1988 (4); v A 1979 (3) 1981 (3) 1984 (5) 1988 (5);
 v NZ 1979 (3) 1986 (3); v In 1983 (6) 1987 (4); v P 1980 (4) 1986 (3)*

Headley, G. A. 22: v E 1929 (4) 1934 (4) 1947 (1) 1953 (1); *v E 1933* (3) *1939* (3); *v A 1930* (5); *v 1948* (1)

Headley, R. G. A. 2: *v E 1973* (2)

Hendriks, J. L. 20: v A 1964 (4); v In 1961 (1); *v E 1966* (3) *1969* (1); *v A 1968* (5); *v NZ 1968* (5) *v In 1966* (3)

Hoad, E. L. G. 4: v E 1929 (1); *v E 1928* (1) *1933* (2)

Holder, V. A. 40: v E 1973 (1); v A 1972 (3) 1977 (3); v NZ 1971 (4); v In 1970 (3) 1975 (1); v 1976 (1); *v E 1969* (3) *1973* (2) *1976* (4); *v A 1975* (3); *v In 1974* (4) *1978* (6); *v P 1974* (

Holding, M. A. 60: v E 1980 (4) 1985 (4); v A 1983 (3); v NZ 1984 (3); v In 1975 (4) 1982 (5); v 1976 (4) 1980 (5) 1984 (4); *v A 1975* (5) *1979* (3) *1981* (3) *1984* (3); *v NZ 1979* (3) *1986* (1); *v 1983* (6)

Holford, D. A. J. 24: v E 1967 (4); v NZ 1971 (5); v In 1970 (1) 1975 (2); v P 1976 (1); *v E 19 (5); v A 1968* (2); *v NZ 1968* (2); *v In 1966* (1)

Holt, J. K. 17: v E 1953 (5); v A 1954 (5); *v In 1958* (5); *v P 1958* (2)

Hooper, C. L. 19: v E 1989 (3); v P 1987 (3); *v E 1988* (5); *v A 1988* (5); *v In 1987* (3)

Howard, A. B. 1: v NZ 1971

Hunte, C. C. 44: v E 1959 (5); v A 1964 (5); v In 1961 (5); v P 1957 (5); *v E 1963* (5) *1966* (5); *v 1960* (5); *v In 1958* (5) *1966* (3); *v P 1958* (1)

Hunte, E. A. C. 3: v E 1929 (3)

Hylton, L. G. 6: v E 1934 (4); *v E 1939* (2)

Johnson, H. H. H. 3: v E 1947 (1); *v E 1950* (2)

Johnson, T. F. 1: *v E 1939*

Jones, C. M. 4: v E 1929 (1) 1934 (3)

Jones, P. E. 9: v E 1947 (1); *v E 1950* (2); *v A 1951* (1); *v In 1948* (5)

Julien, B. D. 24: v E 1973 (5); v In 1975 (4); v P 1976 (1); *v E 1973* (3) *1976* (2); *v A 1975* (3); *v 1974* (4); *v P 1974* (2)

Jumadeen, R. R. 12: v A 1972 (1) 1977 (2); v NZ 1971 (1); v In 1975 (4); v P 1976 (1); *v E 19 (1); v In 1978* (2)

Kallicharran, A. I. 66: v E 1973 (5); v A 1972 (5) 1977 (5); v NZ 1971 (2); v In 1975 (4); v P 19 (5); *v E 1973* (3) *1976* (3) *1980* (5); *v A 1975* (6) *1979* (3); *v NZ 1979* (3); *v In 1974* (5) *1978* (6 *v P 1974* (2) *1980* (4)

Kanhai, R. B. 79: v E 1959 (5) 1967 (5) 1973 (5); v A 1964 (5) 1972 (5); v In 1961 (5) 1970 (5); v 1957 (5); *v E 1957* (5) *1963* (5) *1966* (5) *1973* (3); *v A 1960* (5) *1968* (5); *v In 1958* (5) *1966* (3); *v 1958* (3)

Kentish, E. S. M. 2: v E 1947 (1) 1953 (1)

King, C. L. 9: v P 1976 (1); *v E 1976* (3) *1980* (1); *v A 1979* (1); *v NZ 1979* (3)

King, F. M. 14: v E 1953 (3); v A 1954 (4); v In 1952 (5); *v NZ 1955* (2)

King, L. A. 2: v E 1967 (1); v In 1961 (1)

Lashley, P. D. 4: *v E 1966* (2); *v A 1960* (2)

Legall, R. 4: v In 1952 (4)

Lewis, D. M. 3: v In 1970 (3)

Lloyd, C. H. 110: v E 1967 (5) 1973 (5) 1980 (4); v A 1972 (3) 1977 (2) 1983 (4); v NZ 1971 (; v In 1970 (5) 1975 (4) 1982 (5); v P 1976 (5); *v E 1969* (3) *1973* (3) *1976* (5) *1980* (4) *1984* (; *v A 1968* (4) *1975* (6) *1979* (2) *1981* (3) *1984* (5); *v NZ 1968* (3) *1979* (3); *v In 1966* (3) *1974 1983* (6); *v P 1974* (2) *1980* (4)

Logie, A. L. 40: v E 1989 (3); v A 1983 (1); v NZ 1984 (4); v In 1982 (5) 1988 (4); v P 1987 (3); 1988* (5); *v A 1988* (5); *v NZ 1986* (3); *v In 1983* (3) *1987* (4)

McMorris, E. D. A. 13: v E 1959 (4); v In 1961 (5); v P 1957 (1); *v E 1963* (2) *1966* (2)

McWatt, C. A. 6: v E 1953 (5); v A 1954 (1)

Madray, I. S. 2: v P 1957 (2)

Marshall, M. D. 68: v E 1980 (1) 1985 (5) 1989 (2); v A 1983 (4); v NZ 1984 (4); v In 1982 1988 (3); v P 1987 (2); *v E 1980* (4) *1984* (4) *1988* (5); *v A 1984* (5) *1988* (5); *v NZ 1986* (3); *v 1978* (3) *1983* (6); *v P 1980* (4) *1986* (3)

Marshall, N. E. 1: v A 1954

Marshall, R. E. 4: *v A 1951* (2); *v NZ 1951* (2)

Martin, F. R. 9: v E 1929 (1); *v E 1928* (3); *v A 1930* (5)

Martindale, E. A. 10: v E 1934 (4); *v E 1933* (3) *1939* (3)

Mattis, E. H. 4: v E 1980 (4)

Mendonca, I. L. 2: v In 1961 (2)
Merry, C. A. 2: *v E 1933 (2)*
Miller, R. 1: v In 1952
Moodie, G. H. 1: v E 1934
Moseley, E. A. 2: v E 1989 (2)
Murray, D. A. 19: v E 1980 (4); v A 1977 (3); *v A 1981 (2); v In 1978 (6); v P 1980 (4)*
Murray, D. L. 62: v E 1967 (5) 1973 (5); v A 1972 (4) 1977 (2); v In 1975 (4); v P 1976 (5); *v E 1963 (5) 1973 (3) 1976 (5) 1980 (5); v A 1975 (6) 1979 (3); v NZ 1979 (3); v In 1974 (5); v P 1974 (2)*

Nanan, R. 1: *v P 1980*
Neblett, J. M. 1: v E 1934
Noreiga, J. M. 4: v In 1970 (4)
Nunes, R. K. 4: v E 1929 (1); *v E 1928 (3)*
Nurse, S. M. 29: v E 1959 (1) 1967 (5); v A 1964 (4); v In 1961 (1); *v E 1966 (5); v A 1960 (3) 1968 (5); v NZ 1968 (3); v In 1966 (2)*

Padmore, A. L. 2: v In 1975 (1); *v E 1976 (1)*
Pairaudeau, B. H. 13: v E 1953 (2); v In 1952 (5): *v E 1957 (2); v NZ 1955 (4)*
Parry, D. R. 12: v A 1977 (5); *v NZ 1979 (1); v In 1978 (6)*
Passailaigue, C. C. 1: v E 1929
Patterson, B. P. 18: v E 1985 (5) 1989 (1); v P 1987 (1); *v E 1988 (2); v A 1988 (4); v In 1987 (4); v P 1986 (1)*
Payne, T. R. O. 1: v E 1985
Phillip, N. 9: v A 1977 (3); *v In 1978 (6)*
Pierre, L. R. 1: v E 1947

Rae, A. F. 15: v In 1952 (2); *v E 1950 (4); v A 1951 (3); v NZ 1951 (1); v In 1948 (5)*
Ramadhin, S. 43: v E 1953 (5) 1959 (4); v A 1954 (4); v In 1952 (4); *v E 1950 (4) 1957 (5); v A 1951 (5) 1960 (2); v NZ 1951 (1) 1955 (4); v In 1958 (2); v P 1958 (2)*
Richards, I. V. A. 111: v E 1980 (4) 1985 (5) 1989 (3); v A 1977 (2) 1983 (5); v NZ 1984 (4); v In 1975 (4) 1982 (5) 1988 (4); v P 1976 (5) 1987 (2); *v E 1976 (4) 1980 (5) 1984 (5) 1988 (5); v A 1975 (6) 1979 (3) 1981 (3) 1984 (5) 1988 (5); v NZ 1986 (3); v In 1974 (5) 1983 (6) 1987 (4); v P 1974 (2) 1980 (4) 1986 (3)*
Richardson, R. B. 49: v E 1985 (5) 1989 (4); v A 1983 (5); v NZ 1984 (4); v In 1988 (4); v P 1987 (3); *v E 1988 (3); v A 1984 (5) 1988 (5); v NZ 1986 (3); v In 1983 (1) 1987 (4); v P 1986 (3)*
Rickards, K. R. 2: v E 1947 (1); *v A 1951 (1)*
Roach, C. A. 16: v E 1929 (4) 1934 (1); *v E 1928 (3) 1933 (3); v A 1930 (5)*
Roberts, A. M. E. 47: v E 1973 (1) 1980 (3); v A 1977 (2); v In 1975 (2) 1982 (5); v P 1976 (5); *v E 1976 (5) 1980 (5); v A 1975 (5) 1979 (3) 1981 (2); v NZ 1979 (2); v In 1974 (5) 1983 (2); v P 1974 (2)*
Roberts, A. T. 1: *v NZ 1955*
Rodriguez, W. V. 5: v E 1967 (1); v A 1964 (1); v In 1961 (2); *v E 1963 (1)*
Rowe, L. G. 30: v E 1973 (5); v A 1972 (3); v NZ 1971 (4); v In 1975 (4); *v E 1976 (2); v A 1975 (6) 1979 (3); v NZ 1979 (3)*

St Hill, E. L. 2: v E 1929 (2)
St Hill, W. H. 3: v E 1929 (1); *v E 1928 (2)*
Scarlett, R. O. 3: v E 1959 (3)
Scott, A. P. H. 1: v In 1952
Scott, O. C. 8: v E 1929 (1); *v E 1928 (2); v A 1930 (5)*
Sealey, B. J. 1: *v E 1933*
Sealy, J. E. D. 11: v E 1929 (2) 1934 (4); *v E 1939 (3); v A 1930 (2)*
Shepherd, J. N. 5: v In 1970 (2); *v E 1969 (3)*
Shillingford, G. C. 7: v NZ 1971 (2); v In 1970 (3); *v E 1969 (2)*
Shillingford, I. T. 4: v A 1977 (1); v P 1976 (3)
Shivnarine, S. 8: v A 1977 (3); *v In 1978 (5)*
Simmons, P. V. 2: v P 1987 (1); *v In 1987 (1)*
Singh, C. K. 2: v E 1959 (2)
Small, J. A. 3: v E 1929 (1); *v E 1928 (2)*
Small, M. A. 2: v A 1983 (1); *v E 1984 (1)*
Smith, C. W. 5: v In 1961 (1); *v A 1960 (4)*
Smith, O. G. 26: v A 1954 (4); v P 1957 (5); *v E 1957 (5); v NZ 1955 (4); v In 1958 (5); v P 1958 (3)*

Sobers, G. S. 93 : v E 1953 (1) 1959 (5) 1967 (5) 1973 (4); v A 1954 (4) 1964 (5); v NZ 1971 (5); v In 1961 (5); 1970 (5); v P 1957 (5); *v E 1957 (5) 1963 (5) 1966 (5) 1969 (3) 1973 (3); v A 1960 (5) 1968 (5); v NZ 1955 (4) 1968 (3); v In 1958 (5) 1966 (3); v P 1958 (3)*

Solomon, J. S. 27 : v E 1959 (2); v A 1964 (4); v In 1961 (4); *v E 1963 (5); v A 1960 (5); v In 1958 (4); v P 1958 (3)*

Stayers, S. C. 4 : v In 1961 (4)

Stollmeyer, J. B. 32 : v E 1947 (2) 1953 (5); v A 1954 (2); v In 1952 (5); *v E 1939 (1) 1950 (4); v A 1951 (5); v NZ 1951 (2); v In 1948 (4)*

Stollmeyer, V. H. 1 : *v E 1939*

Taylor, J. 3 : v P 1957 (1); *v In 1958 (1); v P 1958 (1)*

Trim, J. 4 : v E 1947 (1); *v A 1951 (1); v In 1948 (2)*

Valentine, A. L. 36 : v E 1953 (3); v A 1954 (3); v In 1952 (5) 1961 (2); v P 1957 (1); *v E 1950 (4) 1957 (2); v A 1951 (5) 1960 (5); v NZ 1951 (2) 1955 (4)*

Valentine, V. A. 2 : *v E 1933 (2)*

Walcott, C. L. 44 : v E 1947 (4) 1953 (5) 1959 (2); v A 1954 (5); v In 1952 (5); v P 1957 (4); *v E 1950 (4) 1957 (5); v A 1951 (3); v NZ 1951 (2); v In 1948 (5)*

Walcott, L. A. 1 : v E 1929

Walsh, C. A. 37 : v E 1985 (1) 1989 (5); v NZ 1984 (1); v In 1988 (4); v P 1987 (3); *v E 1988 (5); v A 1984 (5) 1988 (5); v NZ 1986 (3); v In 1987 (4); v P 1986 (3)*

Watson, C. 7 : v E 1959 (5); v In 1961 (1); *v A 1960 (1)*

Weekes, E. D. 48 : v E 1947 (4) 1953 (4); v A 1954 (5) v In 1952 (5); v P 1957 (5); *v E 1950 (4) 1957 (5); v A 1951 (5); v NZ 1951 (2) 1955 (4); v In 1948 (5)*

Weekes, K. H. 2 : *v E 1939 (2)*

White, W. A. 2 : v A 1964 (2)

Wight, C. V. 2 : v E 1929 (1); *v E 1928 (1)*

Wight, G. L. 1 : v In 1952

Wiles, C. A. 1 : *v E 1933*

Willett, E. T. 5 : v A 1972 (3); *v In 1974 (2)*

Williams, A. B. 7 : v A 1977 (3); *v In 1978 (4)*

Williams, E. A. V. 4 : v E 1947 (3); *v E 1939 (1)*

Wishart, K. L. 1 : v E 1934

Worrell, F. M. M. 51 : v E 1947 (3) 1953 (4) 1959 (4); v A 1954 (4); v In 1952 (5) 1961 (5); *v E 1950 (4) 1957 (5) 1963 (5); v A 1951 (5) 1960 (5); v NZ 1951 (2)*

NEW ZEALAND

Number of Test cricketers: 171

Alabaster, J. C. 21 : v E 1962 (2); v WI 1955 (1); v In 1967 (4); *v E 1958 (2); v SA 1961 (5); v WI 1971 (2); v In 1955 (4); v P 1955 (1)*

Allcott, C. F. W. 6 : v E 1929 (2); v SA 1931 (1); *v E 1931 (3)*

Anderson, R. W. 9 : v E 1977 (3); *v E 1978 (3); v P 1976 (3)*

Anderson, W. M. 1 : v A 1945

Andrews, B. 2 : *v A 1973 (2)*

Badcock, F. T. 7 : v E 1929 (3) 1932 (2); v SA 1931 (2)

Barber, R. T. 1 : v WI 1955

Bartlett, G. A. 10 : v E 1965 (2); v In 1967 (2); v P 1964 (1); *v SA 1961 (5)*

Barton, P. T. 7 : v E 1962 (3); *v SA 1961 (4)*

Beard, D. D. 4 : v WI 1951 (2) 1955 (2)

Beck, J. E. F. 8 : v WI 1955 (4); *v SA 1953 (4)*

Bell, W. 2 : *v SA 1953 (2)*

Bilby, G. P. 2 : v E 1965 (2)

Blain, T. E. 3 : *v E 1986 (1); v In 1988 (2)*

Blair, R. W. 19 : v E 1954 (1) 1958 (2) 1962 (2); v SA 1952 (2) 1963 (3); v WI 1955 (2); *v E 1958 (3); v SA 1953 (4)*

Blunt, R. C. 9 : v E 1929 (4); v SA 1931 (2); *v E 1931 (3)*

Bolton, B. A. 2 : v E 1958 (2)

Boock, S. L. 30 : v E 1977 (3) 1983 (2) 1987 (1); v WI 1979 (3) 1986 (2); v P 1978 (3) 1984 (2) 1988 (1); *v E 1978 (3); v A 1985 (1); v WI 1984 (3); v P 1984 (3); v SL 1983 (3)*

Bracewell, B. P. 6: v P 1978 (1) 1984 (1); *v E 1978 (3); v A 1980 (I)*

Bracewell, J. G. 41: v E 1987 (3); v A 1985 (2) 1989 (1); v WI 1986 (3); v In 1980 (1) 1989 (2); v P 1988 (2); *v E 1983 (4) 1986 (3) 1990 (3); v A 1980 (3) 1985 (2) 1987 (3); v WI 1984 (I); v In 1988 (3); v P 1984 (2); v SL 1983 (2) 1986 (I)*

Bradburn, W. P. 2: v SA 1963 (2)

Brown, V. R. 2: *v A 1985 (2)*

Burgess, M. G. 50: v E 1970 (1) 1977 (3); v A 1973 (1) 1976 (2); v WI 1968 (3); v In 1967 (4) 1975 (3); v P 1972 (3) 1978 (3); *v E 1969 (2) 1973 (3) 1978 (3); v A 1980 (3); v WI 1971 (5); v In 1969 (3) 1976 (3); v P 1969 (3) 1976 (3)*

Burke, C. 1: v A 1945

Burtt, T. B. 10: v E 1946 (1) 1950 (2); v SA 1952 (1); v WI 1951 (2); *v E 1949 (4)*

Butterfield, L. A. 1: v A 1945

Cairns, B. L. 43: v E 1974 (1) 1977 (1) 1983 (3); v A 1976 (1) 1981 (3); v WI 1979 (3); v In 1975 (1) 1980 (3); v P 1978 (3) 1984 (3); v SL 1982 (2); *v E 1978 (2) 1983 (4); v A 1973 (I) 1980 (3) 1985 (I); v WI 1984 (2); v In 1976 (2); v P 1976 (2); v SL 1983 (2)*

Cairns, C. L. 1: *v A 1989*

Cameron, F. J. 19: v E 1962 (3); v SA 1963 (3); v P 1964 (3); *v E 1965 (2); v SA 1961 (5); v In 1964 (I); v P 1964 (2)*

Cave, H. B. 19: v E 1954 (2); v WI 1955 (3); *v E 1949 (4) 1958 (2); v In 1955 (5); v P 1955 (3)*

Chapple, M. E. 14: v E 1954 (1) 1965 (1); v SA 1952 (1) 1963 (3); v WI 1955 (1); *v SA 1953 (5) 1961 (2)*

Chatfield, E. J. 43: v E 1974 (1) 1977 (1) 1983 (3) 1987 (3); v A 1976 (2) 1981 (1) 1985 (3); v WI 1986 (3); v P 1984 (3) 1988 (2); v SL 1982 (2); *v E 1983 (3) 1986 (I); v A 1985 (2) 1987 (2); v WI 1984 (4); v In 1988 (3); v P 1984 (I); v SL 1983 (2) 1986 (I)*

Cleverley, D. C. 2: v SA 1931 (1); v A 1945 (1)

Collinge, R. O. 35: v E 1970 (2) 1974 (2) 1977 (3); v A 1973 (3); v In 1967 (2) 1975 (3); v P 1964 (3) 1972 (2); *v E 1965 (3) 1969 (I) 1973 (3) 1978 (I); v In 1964 (2) 1976 (I); v P 1964 (3) 1976 (2)*

Colquhoun, I. A. 2: v E 1954 (2)

Coney, J. V. 52: v E 1983 (3); v A 1973 (2) 1981 (3) 1985 (3); v WI 1979 (3) 1986 (3); v In 1980 (3); v P 1978 (3) 1984 (3); v SL 1982 (2); *v E 1983 (4) 1986 (3); v A 1973 (2) 1980 (2) 1985 (3); v WI 1984 (4); v P 1984 (3); v SL 1983 (3)*

Congdon, B. E. 61: v E 1965 (3) 1970 (2) 1974 (2) 1977 (3); v A 1973 (3) 1976 (2); v WI 1968 (3); v In 1967 (4) 1975 (3); v P 1964 (3) 1972 (3); *v E 1965 (3) 1969 (3) 1973 (3) 1978 (3); v A 1973 (3); v WI 1971 (5); v In 1964 (3) 1969 (3); v P 1964 (I) 1969 (3)*

Cowie, J. 9: v E 1946 (1); v A 1945 (1); *v E 1937 (3) 1949 (4)*

Cresswell, G. F. 3: v E 1950 (2); *v E 1949 (I)*

Cromb, I. B. 5: v SA 1931 (2); *v E 1931 (3)*

Crowe, J. J. 39: v E 1983 (3) 1987 (2); v A 1989 (1); v WI 1986 (3); v P 1984 (3) 1988 (2); v SL 1982 (2); *v E 1983 (2) 1986 (3); v A 1985 (3) 1987 (3) 1989 (I); v WI 1984 (4); v P 1984 (3); v SL 1983 (3) 1986 (I)*

Crowe, M. D. 51: v E 1983 (3) 1987 (3); v A 1981 (3) 1985 (3); v WI 1986 (3); v In 1989 (3); v P 1984 (3) 1988 (2); *v E 1983 (4) 1986 (3) 1990 (3); v A 1985 (3) 1987 (3) 1989 (I); v WI 1984 (4); v P 1984 (3); v SL 1983 (3) 1986 (I)*

Cunis, R. S. 20: v E 1965 (3) 1970 (2); v SA 1963 (1); v WI 1968 (3); *v E 1969 (I); v WI 1971 (5); v In 1969 (3); v P 1969 (2)*

D'Arcy, J. W. 5: *v E 1958 (5)*

Dempster, C. S. 10: v E 1929 (4) 1932 (2); v SA 1931 (2); *v E 1931 (2)*

Dempster, E. W. 5: v SA 1952 (1); *v SA 1953 (4)*

Dick, A. E. 17: v E 1962 (3); v SA 1963 (3); v P 1964 (3); *v E 1965 (2); v SA 1961 (5); v P 1964 (3)*

Dickinson, G. R. 3: v E 1929 (2); v SA 1931 (1)

Donnelly, M. P. 7: *v E 1937 (3) 1949 (4)*

Dowling, G. T. 39: v E 1962 (3) 1970 (2); v In 1967 (4); v SA 1963 (1); v WI 1968 (3); v P 1964 (2); *v E 1965 (3) 1969 (3); v SA 1961 (4); v WI 1971 (2); v In 1964 (4) 1969 (3); v P 1964 (2) 1969 (3)*

Dunning, J. A. 4: v E 1932 (1); *v E 1937 (3)*

Edgar, B. A. 39: v E 1983 (3); v A 1981 (3) 1985 (3); v WI 1979 (3); v In 1980 (3); v P 1978 (3); v SL 1982 (2); *v E 1978 (3) 1983 (4) 1986 (3); v A 1980 (3) 1985 (3); v P 1984 (3)*

Edwards, G. N. 8: v E 1977 (1); v A 1976 (2); v In 1980 (3); *v E 1978 (2)*

Emery, R. W. G. 2: v WI 1951 (2)

Fisher, F. E. 1: v SA 1952
Foley, H. 1: v E 1929
Franklin, T. J. 15: v E 1987 (3); v A 1985 (1) 1989 (1); v In 1989 (3); *v E 1983 (1) 1990 (3); v In 1988 (3)*
Freeman, D. L. 2: v E 1932 (2)

Gallichan, N. 1: *v E 1937*
Gedye, S. G. 4: v SA 1963 (3); v P 1964 (1)
Gillespie, S. R. 1: v A 1985
Gray, E. J. 10: *v E 1983 (2) 1986 (3); v A 1987 (1); v In 1988 (1); v P 1984 (2); v SL 1986 (1)*
Greatbatch, M. J. 14: v E 1987 (2); v A 1989 (1); v In 1989 (3); v P 1988 (1); *v E 1990 (3); v A 1989 (1); v In 1988 (3)*
Guillen, S. C. 3: v WI 1955 (3)
Guy, J. W. 12: v E 1958 (2); v WI 1955 (2); *v SA 1961 (2); v In 1955 (5); v P 1955 (1)*

Hadlee, D. R. 26: v E 1974 (2) 1977 (1); v A 1973 (3) 1976 (1); v In 1975 (3); v P 1972 (2); *v E 1969 (2) 1973 (3); v A 1973 (3); v In 1969 (3); v P 1969 (3)*
Hadlee, Sir R. J. 86: v E 1977 (3) 1983 (3) 1987 (1); v A 1973 (2) 1976 (2) 1981 (3) 1985 (3) 1989 (1); v WI 1979 (3) 1986 (3); v In 1975 (2) 1980 (3) 1989 (3); v P 1972 (1) 1978 (3) 1984 (3) 1988 (2); v SL 1982 (2); *v E 1973 (1) 1978 (3) 1983 (4) 1986 (3) 1990 (3); v A 1973 (3) 1980 (3) 1985 (3) 1987 (3); v WI 1984 (4); v In 1976 (3) 1988 (3); v P 1976 (3); v SL 1983 (3) 1986 (1)*
Hadlee, W. A. 11: v E 1946 (1) 1950 (2); v A 1945 (1); *v E 1937 (3) 1949 (4)*
Harford, N. S. 8: *v E 1958 (4); v In 1955 (2); v P 1955 (2)*
Harford, R. I. 3: v In 1967 (3)
Harris, P. G. Z. 9: v P 1964 (1); *v SA 1961 (5); v In 1955 (1); v P 1955 (2)*
Harris, R. M. 2: v E 1958 (2)
Hastings, B. F. 31: v E 1974 (2); v A 1973 (3); v WI 1968 (3); v In 1975 (1); v P 1972 (3); *v E 1969 (2); v A 1973 (3); v WI 1971 (5); v In 1969 (2); v P 1969 (3)*
Hayes, J. A. 15: v E 1950 (2) 1954 (1); v WI 1951 (2); *v E 1958 (4); v In 1955 (5); v P 1955 (1)*
Henderson, M. 1: v E 1929
Horne, P. A. 3: v WI 1986 (1); *v A 1987 (1); v SL 1986 (1)*
Hough, K. W. 2: v E 1958 (2)
Howarth, G. P. 47: v E 1974 (2) 1977 (3) 1983 (3); v A 1976 (2) 1981 (3); v WI 1979 (3); v In 1980 (3); v P 1978 (3) 1984 (3); v SL 1982 (2); *v E 1978 (3) 1983 (4); v A 1980 (2); v WI 1984 (4); v In 1976 (2); v P 1976 (2); v SL 1983 (3)*
Howarth, H. J. 30: v E 1970 (2) 1974 (2); v A 1973 (3) 1976 (2); v In 1975 (3); v P 1972 (3); *v E 1969 (3) 1973 (2); v WI 1971 (5); v In 1969 (3); v P 1969 (3)*

James, K. C. 11: v E 1929 (4) 1932 (2); v SA 1931 (2); *v E 1931 (3)*
Jarvis, T. W. 13: v E 1965 (1); v P 1972 (3); *v WI 1971 (4); v In 1964 (2); v P 1964 (3)*
Jones, A. H. 17: v E 1987 (1); v A 1989 (1); v In 1989 (3); v P 1988 (2); *v E 1990 (3); v A 1987 (3); v In 1988 (3); v SL 1986 (1)*

Kerr, J. L. 7: v E 1932 (2); v SA 1931 (1); *v E 1931 (2) 1937 (2)*
Kuggeleijn, C. M. 2: *v In 1988 (2)*

Lees, W. K. 21: v E 1977 (2); v A 1976 (1); v WI 1979 (3); v P 1978 (3); v SL 1982 (2); *v E 1983 (2); v A 1980 (2); v In 1976 (3); v P 1976 (3)*
Leggat, I. B. 1: *v SA 1953*
Leggat, J. G. 9: v E 1954 (1); v SA 1952 (1); v WI 1951 (1) 1955 (1); *v In 1955 (3); v P 1955 (2)*
Lissette, A. F. 2: v WI 1955 (2)
Lowry, T. C. 7: v E 1929 (4); *v E 1931 (3)*

MacGibbon, A. R. 26: v E 1950 (2) 1954 (2); v SA 1952 (1); v WI 1955 (3); *v E 1958 (5); v SA 1953 (5); v In 1955 (5); v P 1955 (3)*
McEwan, P. E. 4: v WI 1979 (1); *v A 1980 (2); v P 1984 (1)*
McGirr, H. M. 2: v E 1929 (2)
McGregor, S. N. 25: v E 1954 (2) 1958 (2); v SA 1963 (3); v WI 1955 (4); v P 1964 (2); *v SA 1961 (5); v In 1955 (4); v P 1955 (3)*
McLeod E. G. 1: v E 1929
McMahon T. G. 5: v WI 1955 (1); *v In 1955 (3); v P 1955 (1)*
McRae, D. A. N. 1: v A 1945

Matheson, A. M. 2: v E 1929 (1); *v E 1931 (1)*
Meale, T. 2: *v E 1958 (2)*
Merritt, W. E. 6: v E 1929 (4); *v E 1931 (2)*
Meuli, E. M. 1: v SA 1952
Milburn, B. D. 3: v WI 1968 (3)
Miller, L. S. M. 13: v SA 1952 (2); v WI 1955 (3); *v E 1958 (4); v SA 1953 (4)*
Mills, J. E. 7: v E 1929 (3) 1932 (1); *v E 1931 (3)*
Moir, A. M. 17: v E 1950 (2) 1954 (2) 1958 (2); v SA 1952 (1); v WI 1951 (2) 1955 (1); *v E 1958 (2); v In 1955 (2); v P 1955 (3)*
Moloney D. A. R. 3: *v E 1937 (3)*
Mooney, F. L. H. 14: v E 1950 (2); v SA 1952 (2); v WI 1951 (2); *v E 1949 (3); v SA 1953 (5)*
Morgan, R. W. 20: v E 1965 (2) 1970 (2); v WI 1968 (1); v P 1964 (2); *v E 1965 (3); v WI 1971 (3); v In 1964 (4); v P 1964 (3)*
Morrison, B. D. 1: v E 1962
Morrison, D. K. 16: v E 1987 (3); v A 1989 (1); v In 1989 (3); v P 1988 (1); *v E 1990 (3); v A 1987 (3) 1989 (1); v In 1988 (3)*
Morrison, J. F. M. 17: v E 1974 (2); v A 1973 (3) 1981 (3); v In 1975 (3); *v A 1973 (3); v In 1976 (3); v P 1976 (2)*
Motz, R. C. 32: v E 1962 (2) 1965 (3); v SA 1963 (2); v WI 1968 (3); v In 1967 (4); v P 1964 (3); *v E 1965 (3) 1969 (3); v SA 1961 (5); v In 1964 (3); v P 1964 (1)*
Murray, B. A. G. 13: v E 1970 (1); v In 1967 (4); *v E 1969 (2); v In 1969 (3); v P 1969 (3)*

Newman J. 3: v E 1932 (2); v SA 1931 (1)

O'Sullivan, D. R. 11: v In 1975 (1); v P 1972 (1); *v A 1973 (3); v In 1976 (3); v P 1976 (3)*
Overton, G. W. F. 3: *v SA 1953 (3)*

Page, M. L. 14: v E 1929 (4) 1932 (2); v SA 1931 (2); *v E 1931 (3) 1937 (3)*
Parker, J. M. 36: v E 1974 (2) 1977 (3); v A 1973 (3) 1976 (2); v WI 1979 (3); v In 1975 (3); v P 1972 (1) 1978 (2); *v E 1973 (3) 1978 (2); v A 1973 (3) 1980 (3); v In 1976 (3); v P 1976 (3)*
Parker, N. M. 3: *v In 1976 (2); v P 1976 (1)*
Parore, A. C. 1: *v E 1990*
Patel, D. N. 8: v WI 1986 (3); v P 1988 (1); *v A 1987 (3) 1989 (1)*
Petherick, P. J. 6: v A 1976 (1); *v In 1976 (3); v P 1976 (2)*
Petrie, E. C. 14: v E 1958 (2) 1965 (3); *v E 1958 (5); v In 1955 (2); v P 1955 (2)*
Playle, W. R. 8: v E 1962 (3); *v E 1958 (5)*
Pollard, V. 32: v E 1965 (3) 1970 (1); v WI 1968 (3); v In 1967 (4); v P 1972 (1); *v E 1965 (3) 1969 (3) 1973 (3); v In 1964 (4) 1969 (1); v P 1964 (3) 1969 (3)*
Poore, M. B. 14: v E 1954 (1); v SA 1952 (1); *v SA 1953 (5); v In 1955 (4); v P 1955 (3)*
Priest, M. W. 1: *v E 1990*
Puna, N. 3: v E 1965 (3)

Rabone, G. O. 12: v E 1954 (2); v SA 1952 (1); v WI 1951 (2); *v E 1949 (4); v SA 1953 (3)*
Redmond, R. E. 1: v P 1972
Reid, J. F. 19: v A 1985 (3); v In 1980 (3); v P 1978 (1) 1984 (3); *v A 1985 (3); v P 1984 (3); v SL 1983 (3)*
Reid, J. R. 58: v E 1950 (2) 1954 (2) 1958 (2) 1962 (3); v SA 1952 (2) 1963 (3); v WI 1951 (2) 1955 (4); v P 1964 (3); *v E 1949 (2) 1958 (5) 1965 (3); v SA 1953 (5) 1961 (5); v In 1955 (5) 1964 (4); v P 1955 (3) 1964 (3)*
Roberts, A. D. G. 7: v In 1975 (2); *v In 1976 (3); v P 1976 (2)*
Roberts, A. W. 5: v E 1929 (1); v SA 1931 (2); *v E 1937 (2)*
Robertson, G. K. 1: v A 1985
Rowe, C. G. 1: v A 1945
Rutherford, K. R. 22: v E 1987 (2); v A 1985 (3) 1989 (1); v WI 1986 (2); v In 1989 (3); *v E 1986 (1) 1990 (2); v A 1987 (1); v WI 1984 (4); v In 1988 (2); v SL 1986 (1)*

Scott, R. H. 1: v E 1946
Scott, V. J. 10: v E 1946 (1) 1950 (2); v A 1945 (1); v WI 1951 (2); *v E 1949 (4)*
Shrimpton, M. J. F. 10: v E 1962 (2) 1965 (3) 1970 (2); v SA 1963 (1); *v A 1973 (2)*
Sinclair, B. W. 21: v E 1962 (3) 1965 (3); v SA 1963 (3); v In 1967 (2); v P 1964 (2); *v E 1965 (3); v In 1964 (3); v P 1964 (3)*
Sinclair, I. M. 2: v WI 1955 (2)

Smith, F. B. 4: v E 1946 (1); v WI 1951 (1); *v E 1949 (2)*
Smith, H. D. 1: v E 1932
Smith, I. D. S. 55: v E 1983 (3) 1987 (3); v A 1981 (3) 1985 (3) 1989 (1); v WI 1986 (3); v In 1980 (3) 1989 (3); v P 1984 (3) 1988 (2); *v E 1983 (2) 1986 (2) 1990 (2); v A 1980 (1) 1985 (3) 1987 (3) 1989 (1); v WI 1984 (4); v In 1988 (3); v P 1984 (3); v SL 1983 (3) 1986 (1)*
Snedden, C. A. 1: v E 1946
Snedden, M. C. 25: v E 1983 (1) 1987 (2); v A 1981 (3) 1989 (1); v WI 1986 (1); v In 1980 (3) 1989 (3); v SL 1982 (2); *v E 1983 (1) 1990 (3); v A 1985 (1) 1987 (1) 1989 (1); v In 1988 (1); v SL 1986 (1)*
Sparling, J. T. 11: v E 1958 (2) 1962 (1); v SA 1963 (2); *v E 1958 (3); v SA 1961 (3)*
Stirling, D. A. 6: *v E 1986 (2); v WI 1984 (1); v P 1984 (3)*
Sutcliffe, B. 42: v E 1946 (1) 1950 (2) 1954 (2) 1958 (2); v SA 1952 (2); v WI 1951 (2) 1955 (2); *v E 1949 (4) 1958 (4) 1965 (1); v SA 1953 (5); v In 1955 (5) 1964 (4); v P 1955 (3) 1964 (3)*

Taylor, B. R. 30: v E 1965 (1); v WI 1968 (3); v In 1967 (3); v P 1972 (3); *v E 1965 (2) 1969 (2) 1973 (3); v WI 1971 (4); v In 1964 (3) 1969 (2); v P 1964 (3) 1969 (1)*
Taylor, D. D. 3: v E 1946 (1); v WI 1955 (2)
Thomson, K. 2: v In 1967 (2)
Thomson, S. A. 1: v In 1989
Tindill, E. W. T. 5: v E 1946 (1); v A 1945 (1); *v E 1937 (3)*
Troup, G. B. 15: v A 1981 (2) 1985 (2); v WI 1979 (3); v In 1980 (2); v P 1978 (2); *v A 1980 (2); v WI 1984 (1); v In 1976 (1)*
Truscott, P. B. 1: v P 1964
Turner, G. M. 41: v E 1970 (2) 1974 (2); v A 1973 (3) 1976 (2); v WI 1968 (3); v In 1975 (3); v P 1972 (3); v SL 1982 (2); *v E 1969 (2) 1973 (3); v A 1973 (2); v WI 1971 (5); v In 1969 (3) 1976 (3); v P 1969 (1) 1976 (2)*

Vance, R. H. 4: v E 1987 (1); v P 1988 (2); *v A 1989 (1)*
Vivian, G. E. 5: *v WI 1971 (4); v In 1964 (1)*
Vivian, H. G. 7: v E 1932 (1); v SA 1931 (1); *v E 1931 (2) 1937 (3)*

Wadsworth, K. J. 33: v E 1970 (2) 1974 (2); v A 1973 (3); v In 1975 (3); v P 1972 (3); *v E 1969 (3) 1973 (3); v A 1973 (3); v WI 1971 (5); v In 1969 (3); v P 1969 (3)*
Wallace, W. M. 13: v E 1946 (1) 1950 (2); v A 1945 (1); v SA 1952 (2); *v E 1937 (3) 1949 (4)*
Ward, J. T. 8: v SA 1963 (1); v In 1967 (1); v P 1964 (1); *v E 1965 (1); v In 1964 (4)*
Watson, W. 3: *v E 1986 (2); v A 1989 (1)*
Watt, L. 1: v E 1954
Webb, M. G. 3: v E 1970 (1); v A 1973 (1); *v WI 1971 (1)*
Webb, P. N. 2: v WI 1979 (2)
Weir, G. L. 11: v E 1929 (3) 1932 (2); v SA 1931 (2); *v E 1931 (3) 1937 (1)*
Whitelaw, P. E. 2: v E 1932 (2)
Wright, J. G. 71: v E 1977 (3) 1983 (3) 1987 (3); v A 1981 (3) 1985 (2) 1989 (1); v WI 1979 (3) 1986 (3); v In 1980 (3) 1989 (3); v P 1978 (3) 1984 (3) 1988 (2); v SL 1982 (2); *v E 1978 (2) 1983 (3) 1986 (3) 1990 (3); v A 1980 (3) 1985 (3) 1987 (3) 1989 (1); v WI 1984 (4); v In 1988 (3); v P 1984 (3); v SL 1983 (3)*

Yuile, B. W. 17: v E 1962 (2); v WI 1968 (3); v In 1967 (1); v P 1964 (3); *v E 1965 (1); v In 1964 (3) 1969 (1); v P 1964 (1) 1969 (2)*

INDIA

Number of Test cricketers: 192

Abid Ali, S. 29: v E 1972 (4); v A 1969 (1); v WI 1974 (2); v NZ 1969 (3); *v E 1971 (3) 1974 (3); v A 1967 (4); v WI 1970 (5); v NZ 1967 (4)*
Adhikari, H. R. 21: v E 1951 (3); v A 1956 (2); v WI 1948 (5) 1958 (1); v P 1952 (2); *v E 1952 (3); v A 1947 (5)*
Amarnath, L. 24: v E 1933 (3) 1951 (3); v WI 1948 (5); v P 1952 (5); *v E 1946 (3); v A 1947 (5)*
Amarnath, M. 69: v E 1976 (2) 1984 (5); v A 1969 (1) 1979 (1) 1986 (3); v WI 1978 (2) 1983 (3) 1987 (3); v NZ 1976 (3); v P 1983 (2) 1986 (5); v SL 1986 (2); *v E 1979 (2) 1986 (2); v A 1977 (3) 1985 (3); v WI 1975 (4) 1982 (5); v NZ 1975 (3); v P 1978 (3) 1982 (6) 1984 (2); v SL 1985 (2)*

Amarnath, S. 10: v E 1976 (2); *v WI 1975 (2); v NZ 1975 (3); v P 1978 (3)*

Amar Singh 7: v E 1933 (3); *v E 1932 (1) 1936 (3)*

Amir Elahi 1: *v A 1947*

Ankola, S. A. 1: *v P 1989*

Apte, A. L. 1: *v E 1959*

Apte, M. L. 7: v P 1952 (2); *v WI 1952 (5)*

Arshad Ayub 13: v WI 1987 (4); v NZ 1988 (3); *v WI 1988 (4); v P 1989 (2)*

Arun, B. 2: v SL 1986 (2)

Arun Lal 16: v WI 1987 (4); v NZ 1988 (3); v P 1986 (1); v SL 1982 (1); *v WI 1988 (4); v P 1982 (3)*

Azad, K. 7: v E 1981 (3); v WI 1983 (2); v P 1983 (1); *v NZ 1980 (1)*

Azharuddin, M. 40: v E 1984 (3); v A 1986 (3); v WI 1987 (3); v NZ 1988 (3); v P 1986 (5); v SL 1986 (1); *v E 1986 (3) 1990 (3); v A 1985 (3); v WI 1988 (3); v NZ 1989 (3); v P 1989 (4); v SL 1985 (3)*

Baig, A. A. 10: v A 1959 (3); v WI 1966 (2); v P 1960 (3); *v E 1959 (2)*

Banerjee, S. A. 1: v WI 1948

Banerjee, S. N. 1: v WI 1948

Baqa Jilani, M. 1: *v E 1936*

Bedi, B. S. 67: v E 1972 (5) 1976 (5); v A 1969 (5); v WI 1966 (2) 1974 (4) 1978 (3); v NZ 1969 (3) 1976 (3); *v E 1967 (3) 1971 (3) 1974 (3) 1979 (3); v A 1967 (2) 1977 (5); v WI 1970 (5) 1975 (4); v NZ 1967 (4) 1975 (2); v P 1978 (3)*

Bhandari, P. 3: v A 1956 (1); v NZ 1955 (1); *v P 1954 (1)*

Bhat, A. R. 2: v WI 1983 (1); v P 1983 (1)

Binny, R. M. H. 27: v E 1979 (1); v WI 1983 (6); v P 1979 (6) 1983 (2) 1986 (3); *v E 1986 (3); v A 1980 (1) 1985 (2); v NZ 1980 (1); v P 1984 (1); v SL 1985 (1)*

Borde, C. G. 55: v E 1961 (5) 1963 (5); v A 1959 (5) 1964 (3) 1969 (1); v WI 1958 (4) 1966 (3); v NZ 1964 (4); v P 1960 (5); *v E 1959 (4) 1967 (3); v A 1967 (4); v WI 1961 (5); v NZ 1967 (4)*

Chandrasekhar, B. S. 58: v E 1963 (4) 1972 (5) 1976 (5); v A 1964 (2); v WI 1966 (3) 1974 (4) 1978 (4); v NZ 1964 (2) 1976 (3); *v E 1967 (3) 1971 (3) 1974 (2) 1979 (1); v A 1967 (2) 1977 (5); v WI 1975 (4); v NZ 1975 (3); v P 1978 (3)*

Chauhan, C. P. S. 40: v E 1972 (2); v A 1969 (1) 1979 (6); v WI 1978 (6); v NZ 1969 (2); v P 1979 (6); *v E 1979 (4); v A 1977 (4) 1980 (3); v NZ 1980 (3); v P 1978 (3)*

Chowdhury, N. R. 2: v E 1951 (1); v WI 1948 (1)

Colah, S. H. M. 2: v E 1933 (1); *v E 1932 (1)*

Contractor, N. J. 31: v E 1961 (5); v A 1956 (1) 1959 (5); v WI 1958 (5); v NZ 1955 (4); v P 1960 (5); *v E 1959 (4); v WI 1961 (2)*

Dani, H. T. 1: v P 1952

Desai, R. B. 28: v E 1961 (4) 1963 (2); v A 1959 (3); v WI 1958 (1); v NZ 1964 (3); v P 1960 (5); *v E 1959 (5); v A 1967 (1); v WI 1961 (3); v NZ 1967 (1)*

Dilawar Hussain 3: v E 1933 (2); *v E 1936 (1)*

Divecha, R. V. 5: v E 1951 (2); v P 1952 (1); *v E 1952 (2)*

Doshi, D. R. 33: v E 1979 (1) 1981 (6); v A 1979 (6); v P 1979 (6) 1983 (1); v SL 1982 (1); *v E 1982 (3); v A 1980 (3); v NZ 1980 (2); v P 1982 (3)*

Durani, S. A. 29: v E 1961 (5) 1963 (5) 1972 (3); v A 1959 (1) 1964 (3); v WI 1966 (1); v NZ 1964 (3); *v WI 1961 (5) 1970 (3)*

Engineer, F. M. 46: v E 1961 (4) 1972 (5); v A 1969 (5); v WI 1966 (1) 1974 (5); v NZ 1964 (4) 1969 (2); *v E 1967 (3) 1971 (3) 1974 (3); v A 1967 (4); v WI 1961 (3); v NZ 1967 (4)*

Gadkari, C. V. 6: *v WI 1952 (3); v P 1954 (3)*

Gaekwad, A. D. 40: v E 1976 (4) 1984 (3); v WI 1974 (3) 1978 (5) 1983 (6); v NZ 1976 (3); v P 1983 (3); *v E 1979 (2); v A 1977 (1); v WI 1975 (3) 1982 (5); v P 1984 (2)*

Gaekwad, D. K. 11: v WI 1958 (1); v P 1952 (2) 1960 (1); *v E 1952 (1) 1959 (4); v WI 1952 (2)*

Gaekwad, H. G. 1: v P 1952

Gandotra, A. 2: v A 1969 (1); v NZ 1969 (1)

Gavaskar, S. M. 125: v E 1972 (5) 1976 (5) 1979 (1) 1981 (6) 1984 (5); v A 1979 (6) 1986 (3); v WI 1974 (2) 1978 (6) 1983 (6); v NZ 1976 (3); v P 1979 (6) 1983 (3) 1986 (4); v SL 1982 (1) 1986 (3); *v E 1971 (3) 1974 (3) 1979 (4) 1982 (3) 1986 (3); v A 1977 (4) 1980 (3) 1985 (3); v WI 1970 (4) 1975 (4) 1982 (5); v NZ 1975 (3) 1980 (3); v P 1978 (3) 1982 (6) 1984 (2); v SL 1985 (3)*

Ghavri, K. D. 39: v E 1976 (3) 1979 (1); v A 1979 (6); v WI 1974 (3) 1978 (6); v NZ 1976 (2); v P 1979 (6); *v E 1979 (4); v A 1977 (3) 1980 (3); v NZ 1980 (1); v P 1978 (1)*

Ghorpade, J. M. 8: v A 1956 (1); v WI 1958 (1); v NZ 1955 (1); *v E 1959 (3); v WI 1952 (2)*

Ghulam Ahmed 22: v E 1951 (2); v A 1956 (2); v WI 1948 (3) 1958 (2); v NZ 1955 (1); v P 1952 (4); *v E 1952 (4); v P 1954 (4)*

Gopalan, M. J. 1: v E 1933

Gopinath, C. D. 8: v E 1951 (3); v A 1959 (1); v P 1952 (1); *v E 1952 (1); v P 1954 (2)*

Guard, G. M. 2: v A 1959 (1); v WI 1958 (1)

Guha, S. 4: v A 1969 (3); *v E 1967 (1)*

Gul Mahomed 8: v P 1952 (2); *v E 1946 (1); v A 1947 (5)*

Gupte, B. P. 3: v E 1963 (1); v NZ 1964 (1); v P 1960 (1)

Gupte, S. P. 36: v E 1951 (1) 1961 (2); v A 1956 (3); v WI 1958 (5); v NZ 1955 (5); v P 1952 (2) 1960 (3); *v E 1959 (5); v WI 1952 (5); v P 1954 (5)*

Gursharan Singh 1: *v NZ 1989*

Hafeez, A. 3: *v E 1946 (3)*

Hanumant Singh 14: v E 1963 (2); v A 1964 (3); v WI 1966 (2); v NZ 1964 (4) 1969 (1); *v E 1967 (2)*

Hardikar, M. S. 2: v WI 1958 (2)

Hazare, V. S. 30: v E 1951 (5); v WI 1948 (5); v P 1952 (3); *v E 1946 (3) 1952 (4); v A 1947 (5); v WI 1952 (5)*

Hindlekar, D. D. 4: *v E 1936 (1) 1946 (3)*

Hirwani, N. D. 13: v WI 1987 (1); v NZ 1988 (3); *v E 1990 (3); v WI 1988 (3); v NZ 1989 (3)*

Ibrahim, K. C. 4: v WI 1948 (4)

Indrajitsinhji, K. S. 4: v A 1964 (3); v NZ 1969 (1)

Irani, J. K. 2: *v A 1947 (2)*

Jahangir Khan, M. 4: *v E 1932 (1) 1936 (3)*

Jai, L. P. 1: v E 1933

Jaisimha, M. L. 39: v E 1961 (5) 1963 (5); v A 1959 (1) 1964 (3); v WI 1966 (2); v NZ 1964 (4) 1969 (1); v P 1960 (4); *v E 1959 (1); v A 1967 (2); v WI 1961 (4) 1970 (3); v NZ 1967 (4)*

Jamshedji, R. J. 1: v E 1933

Jayantilal, K. 1: *v WI 1970*

Joshi, P. G. 12: v E 1951 (2); v A 1959 (1); v WI 1958 (1); v P 1952 (1) 1960 (1); *v E 1959 (3); v WI 1952 (3)*

Kanitkar, H. S. 2: v WI 1974 (2)

Kapil Dev 109: v E 1979 (1) 1981 (6) 1984 (4); v A 1979 (6) 1986 (3); v WI 1978 (6) 1983 (6) 1987 (4); v NZ 1988 (3); v P 1979 (6) 1983 (3) 1986 (5); v SL 1982 (1) 1986 (3); *v E 1979 (4) 1982 (3) 1986 (3) 1990 (3); v A 1980 (3) 1985 (3); v WI 1982 (5) 1988 (4); v NZ 1980 (3) 1989 (3); v P 1978 (3) 1982 (6) 1984 (2) 1989 (4); v SL 1985 (3)*

Kardar, A. H. (*see* Hafeez)

Kenny, R. B. 5: v A 1959 (4); v WI 1958 (1)

Kirmani, S. M. H. 88: v E 1976 (5) 1979 (1) 1981 (6) 1984 (5); v A 1979 (6); v WI 1978 (6) 1983 (6); v NZ 1976 (3); v P 1979 (6) 1983 (3); v SL 1982 (1); *v E 1982 (3); v A 1977 (5) 1980 (3) 1985 (3); v WI 1975 (4) 1982 (5); v NZ 1975 (3) 1980 (3); v P 1978 (3) 1982 (6) 1984 (2)*

Kischenchand, G. 5: v P 1952 (1); *v A 1947 (4)*

Kripal Singh, A. G. 14: v E 1961 (3) 1963 (2); v A 1956 (2) 1964 (1); v WI 1958 (1); v NZ 1955 (4); *v E 1959 (1)*

Krishnamurthy, P. 5: *v WI 1970 (5)*

Kulkarni, R. R. 3: v A 1986 (1); v P 1986 (2)

Kulkarni, U. N. 4: *v A 1967 (3); v NZ 1967 (1)*

Kumar, V. V. 2: v E 1961 (1); v P 1960 (1)

Kumble, A. 1: *v E 1990*

Kunderan, B. K. 18: v E 1961 (1) 1963 (5); v A 1959 (3); v WI 1966 (2); v NZ 1964 (1); v P 1960 (2); *v E 1967 (2); v WI 1961 (2)*

Lall Singh 1: *v E 1932*

Lamba, R. 4: v WI 1987 (1); v SL 1986 (3)

Madan Lal 39: v E 1976 (2) 1981 (6); v WI 1974 (2) 1983 (2); v NZ 1976 (1); v P 1983 (3); v SL 1982 (1); *v E 1974 (2) 1982 (3) 1986 (1); v A 1977 (2); v WI 1975 (4) 1982 (2); v NZ 1975 (3); v P 1982 (3) 1984 (1)*

Maka, E. S. 2: v P 1952 (1); *v WI 1952 (1)*

Malhotra, A. 7: v E 1981 (2) 1984 (1); v WI 1983 (3); *v E 1982 (1)*

Maninder Singh 34: v A 1986 (3); v WI 1983 (4) 1987 (3); v P 1986 (4); v SL 1986 (3); *v E 1986 (3); v WI 1982 (3); v P 1982 (5) 1984 (1) 1989 (3); v SL 1985 (3)*

Manjrekar, S. V. 15: v WI 1987 (1); *v E 1990 (3); v WI 1988 (4); v NZ 1989 (3); v P 1989 (4)*

Manjrekar, V. L. 55: v E 1951 (2) 1961 (5) 1963 (4); v A 1956 (3) 1964 (3); v WI 1958 (4); v NZ 1955 (5) 1964 (1); v P 1952 (3) 1960 (5); *v E 1952 (4) 1959 (2); v WI 1952 (4) 1961 (5); v P 1954 (5)*

Mankad, A. V. 22: v E 1976 (1); v A 1969 (5); v WI 1974 (1); v NZ 1969 (2) 1976 (3); *v E 1971 (3) 1974 (1); v A 1977 (3); v WI 1970 (3)*

Mankad, V. 44: v E 1951 (5); v A 1956 (3); v WI 1948 (5) 1958 (2); v NZ 1955 (5); v P 1952 (4); *v E 1946 (3) 1952 (3); v A 1947 (5); v WI 1952 (5); v P 1954 (5)*

Mansur Ali Khan (*see* Pataudi)

Mantri, M. K. 4: v E 1951 (1); *v E 1952 (2); v P 1954 (1)*

Meherhomji, K. R. 1: *v E 1936*

Mehra, V. L. 8: v E 1961 (1) 1963 (2); v NZ 1955 (2); *v WI 1961 (3)*

Merchant, V. M. 10: v E 1933 (3) 1951 (1); *v E 1936 (3) 1946 (3)*

Milkha Singh, A. G. 4: v E 1961 (1); v A 1959 (1); v P 1960 (2)

Modi, R. S. 10: v E 1951 (1); v WI 1948 (5); v P 1952 (1); *v E 1946 (3)*

More, K. S. 34: v A 1986 (2); v WI 1987 (4); v NZ 1988 (3); v P 1986 (5); v SL 1986 (3); *v E 1986 (3) 1990 (3); v WI 1988 (4); v NZ 1989 (3); v P 1989 (4)*

Muddiah, V. M. 2: v A 1959 (1); v P 1960 (1)

Mushtaq Ali, S. 11: v E 1933 (2) 1951 (1); v WI 1948 (3); *v E 1936 (3) 1946 (2)*

Nadkarni, R. G. 41: v E 1961 (1) 1963 (5); v A 1959 (5) 1964 (3); v WI 1958 (1) 1966 (1); v NZ 1955 (1) 1964 (4); v P 1960 (4); *v E 1959 (4); v A 1967 (3); v WI 1961 (5); v NZ 1967 (4)*

Naik, S. S. 3: v WI 1974 (2); *v E 1974 (1)*

Naoomal Jeoomal 3: v E 1933 (2); *v E 1932 (1)*

Narasimha Rao, M. V. 4: v A 1979 (2); v WI 1978 (2)

Navle, J. G. 2: v E 1933 (1); *v E 1932 (1)*

Nayak, S. V. 2: *v E 1982 (2)*

Nayudu, C. K. 7: v E 1933 (3); *v E 1932 (1) 1936 (3)*

Nayudu, C. S. 11: v E 1933 (2) 1951 (1); *v E 1936 (2) 1946 (2); v A 1947 (4)*

Nazir Ali, S. 2: v E 1933 (1); *v E 1932 (1)*

Nissar, Mahomed 6: v E 1933 (2); *v E 1932 (1) 1936 (3)*

Nyalchand, S. 1: v P 1952

Pai, A. M. 1: v NZ 1969

Palia, P. E. 2: *v E 1932 (1) 1936 (1)*

Pandit, C. S. 3: v A 1986 (2); *v E 1986 (1)*

Parkar, G. A. 1: *v E 1982*

Parkar, R. D. 2: v E 1972 (2)

Parsana, D. D. 2: v WI 1978 (2)

Patankar, C. T. 1: v NZ 1955

Pataudi sen., Nawab of, 3: *v E 1946 (3)*

Pataudi jun., Nawab of (now Mansur Ali Khan) 46: v E 1961 (1) 1963 (5) 1972 (3); v A 1964 (3) 1969 (5); v WI 1966 (3) 1974 (4); v NZ 1964 (4) 1969 (3); *v E 1967 (3); v A 1967 (3); v WI 1961 (3); v NZ 1967 (4)*

Patel, B. P. 21: v E 1976 (5); v WI 1974 (3); v NZ 1976 (3); *v E 1974 (2); v A 1977 (2); v WI 1975 (3); v NZ 1975 (3)*

Patel, J. M. 7: v A 1956 (2) 1959 (3); v NZ 1955 (1); *v P 1954 (1)*

Patel, R. 1: v NZ 1988

Patiala, Yuvraj of, 1: v E 1933

Patil, S. M. 29: v E 1979 (1) 1981 (4) 1984 (2); v WI 1983 (2); v P 1979 (2) 1983 (3); v SL 1982 (1); *v E 1982 (2); v A 1980 (3); v NZ 1980 (3); v P 1982 (4) 1984 (2)*

Patil, S. R. 1: v NZ 1955

Phadkar, D. G. 31: v E 1951 (4); v A 1956 (1); v WI 1948 (4) 1958 (1); v NZ 1955 (4); v P 1952 (2); *v E 1952 (4); v A 1947 (4); v WI 1952 (4); v P 1954 (3)*

Prabhakar, M. 12: v E 1984 (2); *v E 1990 (2); v NZ 1989 (3); v P 1989 (4)*

Prasanna, E. A. S. 49: v E 1961 (1) 1972 (3) 1976 (4); v A 1969 (5); v WI 1966 (1) 1974 (5); v NZ 1969 (3); *v E 1967 (3) 1974 (2); v A 1967 (4) 1977 (4); v WI 1961 (1) 1970 (3) 1975 (1); v NZ 1967 (4) 1975 (3); v P 1978 (2)*

Punjabi, P. H. 5: *v P 1954 (5)*

Rai Singh, K. 1: *v A 1947*

Rajinder Pal 1: v E 1963

Rajindernath, V. 1: v P 1952

Rajput, L. S. 2: *v SL 1985 (2)*

Raju, S. L. V. 2: *v NZ 1989 (2)*

Raman, W. V. 6: v WI 1987 (1); v NZ 1988 (1); *v WI 1988 (1); v NZ 1989 (3)*

Ramaswami, C. 2: *v E 1936 (2)*

Ramchand, G. S. 33: v A 1956 (3) 1959 (5); v WI 1958 (3); v NZ 1955 (5); v P 1952 (3); *v E 195. (4); v WI 1952 (3); v P 1954 (5)*

Ramji, L. 1: v E 1933

Rangachary, C. R. 4: v WI 1948 (2); *v A 1947 (2)*

Rangnekar, K. M. 3: *v A 1947 (3)*

Ranjane, V. B. 7: v E 1961 (3) 1963 (1); v A 1964 (1); v WI 1958 (1); *v WI 1961 (1)*

Razdan, V. 2: *v P 1989 (2)*

Reddy, B. 4: *v E 1979 (4)*

Rege, M. R. 1: v WI 1948

Roy, A. 4: v A 1969 (2); v NZ 1969 (2)

Roy, Pankaj 43: v E 1951 (5); v A 1956 (3) 1959 (5); v WI 1958 (5); v NZ 1955 (3); v P 1952 (3 1960 (1); *v E 1952 (4) 1959 (5); v WI 1952 (4); v P 1954 (5)*

Roy, Pranab 2: v E 1981 (2)

Sandhu, B. S. 8: v WI 1983 (1); *v WI 1982 (4); v P 1982 (3)*

Sardesai, D. N. 30: v E 1961 (1) 1963 (5) 1972 (1); v A 1964 (3) 1969 (1); v WI 1966 (2); v NZ 1964 (3); *v E 1967 (1) 1971 (3); v A 1967 (2); v WI 1961 (3) 1970 (5)*

Sarwate, C. T. 9: v E 1951 (1); v WI 1948 (2); *v E 1946 (1); v A 1947 (5)*

Saxena, R. C. 1: *v E 1967*

Sekar, T. A. P. 2: *v P 1982 (2)*

Sen, P. 14: v E 1951 (2); v WI 1948 (5); v P 1952 (2); *v E 1952 (2); v A 1947 (3)*

Sengupta, A. K. 1: v WI 1958

Sharma, Ajay 1: v WI 1987

Sharma, Chetan 23: v E 1984 (3); v A 1986 (2); v WI 1987 (3); v SL 1986 (2); *v E 1986 (2); v A 1985 (2); v WI 1988 (4); v P 1984 (2); v SL 1985 (3)*

Sharma, Gopal 4: v E 1984 (1); v P 1986 (2); *v SL 1985 (1)*

Sharma, P. 5: v E 1976 (2); v WI 1974 (2); *v WI 1975 (1)*

Sharma, Sanjeev 2: v NZ 1988 (1); *v E 1990 (1)*

Shastri, R. J. 72: v E 1981 (6) 1984 (5); v A 1986 (2); v WI 1983 (6) 1987 (4); v NZ 1988 (3); v F 1983 (2) 1986 (5); v SL 1986 (3); *v E 1982 (3) 1986 (3) 1990 (3); v A 1985 (3); v WI 1982 (5) 1988 (4); v NZ 1980 (3); v P 1982 (2) 1984 (2) 1989 (4); v SL 1985 (3)*

Shinde, S. G. 7: v E 1951 (3); v WI 1948 (1); *v E 1946 (1) 1952 (2)*

Shodhan, R. H. 3: v P 1952 (1); *v WI 1952 (2)*

Shukla, R. C. 1: v SL 1982

Sidhu, N. S. 17: v WI 1983 (2); v NZ 1988 (3); *v E 1990 (3); v WI 1988 (4); v NZ 1989 (1); v F 1989 (4)*

Sivaramakrishnan, L. 9: v E 1984 (5); *v A 1985 (2); v WI 1982 (1); v SL 1985 (1)*

Sohoni, S. W. 4: v E 1951 (1); *v E 1946 (2); v A 1947 (1)*

Solkar, E. D. 27: v E 1972 (5) 1976 (1); v A 1969 (4); v WI 1974 (4); v NZ 1969 (1); *v E 1971 (3 1974 (3); v WI 1970 (5) 1975 (1)*

Sood, M. M. 1: v A 1959

Srikkanth, K. 39: v E 1981 (4) 1984 (2); v A 1986 (2); v WI 1987 (4); v NZ 1988 (3); v P 1986 (5) v SL 1986 (3); *v E 1986 (3); v A 1985 (3); v P 1982 (2) 1989 (4); v SL 1985 (3)*

Srinivasan, T. E. 1: *v NZ 1980*

Subramanya, V. 9: v WI 1966 (2); v NZ 1964 (1); *v E 1967 (2); v A 1967 (2); v NZ 1967 (2)*

Sunderram, G. 2: v NZ 1955 (2)

Surendranath, R. 11: v A 1959 (2); v WI 1958 (2); v P 1960 (2); *v E 1959 (5)*

Surti, R. F. 26: v E 1963 (1); v A 1964 (2) 1969 (1); v WI 1966 (2); v NZ 1964 (1) 1969 (2); v P 1960 (2); *v E 1967 (2); v A 1967 (4); v WI 1961 (5); v NZ 1967 (4)*

Swamy, V. N. 1: v NZ 1955

Tamhane, N. S. 21: v A 1956 (3) 1959 (1); v WI 1958 (4); v NZ 1955 (4); v P 1960 (2); *v E 1959 (2); v P 1954 (5)*

Tarapore, K. K. 1: v WI 1948

Tendulkar, S. R. 10: *v E 1990 (3); v NZ 1989 (3); v P 1989 (4)*

Umrigar, P. R. 59: v E 1951 (5) 1961 (4); v A 1956 (3) 1959 (3); v WI 1948 (1) 1958 (5); v NZ 1955 (5); v P 1952 (5) 1960 (5); *v E 1952 (4) 1959 (4); v WI 1952 (5) 1961 (5); v P 1954 (5)*

Vengsarkar, D. B. 110: v E 1976 (1) 1979 (1) 1981 (6) 1984 (5); v A 1979 (6) 1986 (2); v WI 1978 (6) 1983 (5) 1987 (3); v NZ 1988 (3); v P 1979 (5) 1983 (1) 1986 (5); v SL 1982 (1) 1986 (3); *v E 1979 (4) 1982 (3) 1986 (3) 1990 (3); v A 1977 (5) 1980 (3) 1985 (3); v WI 1975 (2) 1982 (5) 1988 (4); v NZ 1975 (3) 1980 (3) 1989 (2); v P 1978 (3) 1982 (6) 1984 (2); v SL 1985 (3)*

Venkataraghavan, S. 57: v E 1972 (2) 1976 (1); v A 1969 (5) 1979 (3); v WI 1966 (2) 1974 (2) 1978 (6); v NZ 1964 (4) 1969 (2) 1976 (3); v P 1983 (2); *v E 1967 (1) 1971 (3) 1974 (2) 1979 (4); v A 1977 (1); v WI 1970 (5) 1975 (3) 1982 (5); v NZ 1975 (1)*

Venkataramana, M. 1: *v WI 1988*

Viswanath, G. R. 91: v E 1972 (5) 1976 (5) 1979 (1) 1981 (6); v A 1969 (4) 1979 (6); v WI 1974 (5) 1978 (6); v NZ 1976 (3); v P 1979 (6); v SL 1982 (1); *v E 1971 (3) 1974 (3) 1979 (4) 1982 (3); v A 1977 (5) 1980 (3); v WI 1970 (3) 1975 (4); v NZ 1975 (3) 1980 (3); v P 1978 (3) 1982 (6)*

Viswanath, S. 3: *v SL 1985 (3)*

Vizianagram, Maharaj Sir Vijaya 3: *v E 1936 (3)*

Wadekar, A. L. 37: v E 1972 (5); v A 1969 (5); v WI 1966 (2); v NZ 1969 (3); *v E 1967 (3) 1971 (3) 1974 (3); v A 1967 (4); v WI 1970 (5); v NZ 1967 (4)*

Wassan, A. S. 4: *v E 1990 (1); v NZ 1989 (3)*

Wazir Ali, S. 7: v E 1933 (3); *v E 1932 (1) 1936 (3)*

Yadav, N. S. 35: v E 1979 (1) 1981 (1) 1984 (4); v A 1979 (5) 1986 (3); v WI 1983 (3); v P 1979 (5) 1986 (4); v SL 1986 (2); *v A 1980 (2) 1985 (3); v NZ 1980 (1); v P 1984 (1)*

Yajurvindra Singh 4: v E 1976 (2); v A 1979 (1); *v E 1979 (1)*

Yashpal Sharma 37: v E 1979 (1) 1981 (2); v A 1979 (6); v WI 1983 (1); v P 1979 (6) 1983 (3); v SL 1982 (1); *v E 1979 (3) 1982 (3); v A 1980 (3); v WI 1982 (5); v NZ 1980 (1); v P 1982 (2)*

Yograj Singh 1: *v NZ 1980*

Note: Hafeez, on going later to Oxford University, took his correct name, Kardar.

PAKISTAN

Number of Test cricketers: 117

Aamer Malik 12: v E 1987 (2); v A 1988 (1); v In 1989 (4); *v A 1989 (2); v WI 1987 (1); v NZ 1988 (2)*

Aaqib Javed 2: *v A 1989 (1); v NZ 1988 (1)*

Abdul Kadir 4: v E 1964 (1); *v A 1964 (1); v NZ 1964 (2)*

Abdul Qadir 63: v E 1977 (3) 1983 (3) 1987 (3); v A 1982 (3) 1988 (3); v WI 1980 (2) 1986 (3); v NZ 1984 (3); v In 1982 (5) 1984 (1) 1989 (4); v SL 1985 (3); *v E 1982 (3) 1987 (4); v A 1983 (5); v WI 1987 (3); v NZ 1984 (2) 1988 (2); v In 1979 (3) 1986 (3); v SL 1985 (2)*

Afaq Hussain 2: v E 1961 (1); *v A 1964 (1)*

Aftab Baloch 2: v WI 1974 (1); v NZ 1969 (1)

Aftab Gul 6: v E 1968 (2); v NZ 1969 (1); *v E 1971 (3)*

Agha Saadat Ali 1: v NZ 1955

Agha Zahid 1: v WI 1974

Akram Raza 1: v In 1989

Alim-ud-Din 25: v E 1961 (2); v A 1956 (1) 1959 (1); v WI 1958 (1); v NZ 1955 (3); v In 1954 (5); *v E 1954 (3) 1962 (3); v WI 1957 (5); v In 1960 (1)*

Amir Elahi 5: *v In 1952 (5)*

Anil Dalpat 9: v E 1983 (3); v NZ 1984 (3); *v NZ 1984 (3)*

Anwar Hussain 4: *v In 1952 (4)*

Anwar Khan 1: *v NZ 1978*

Arif Butt 3: *v A 1964 (1); v NZ 1964 (2)*

Ashraf Ali 8: v E 1987 (3); v In 1984 (2); v SL 1981 (2) 1985 (1)

Asif Iqbal 58: v E 1968 (3) 1972 (3); v A 1964 (1); v WI 1974 (2); v NZ 1964 (3) 1969 (3) 1976 (3); v In 1978 (3); *v E 1967 (3) 1971 (3) 1974 (3); v A 1964 (1) 1972 (3) 1976 (3) 1978 (2); v WI 1976 (3); v NZ 1964 (3) 1972 (3) 1978 (2); v In 1979 (6)*

Asif Masood 16: v E 1968 (2) 1972 (1); v WI 1974 (2); v NZ 1969 (1); *v E 1971 (3) 1974 (3); v A 1972 (3) 1976 (1)*

Asif Mujtaba 3: v E 1987 (1); v WI 1986 (2)

Azeem Hafeez 18: v E 1983 (2); v NZ 1984 (3); v In 1984 (2); *v A 1983 (5); v NZ 1984 (3); v In 1983 (3)*

Azhar Khan 1: v A 1979

Azmat Rana 1: v A 1979

Burki, J. 25: v E 1961 (3); v A 1964 (1); v NZ 1964 (3) 1969 (1); *v E 1962 (5) 1967 (3); v A 1964 (1); v NZ 1964 (3); v In 1960 (5)*

D'Souza, A. 6: v E 1961 (2); v WI 1958 (1); *v E 1962 (3)*

Ehtesham-ud-Din 5: v A 1979 (1); *v E 1982 (1); v In 1979 (3)*

Farooq Hamid 1: *v A 1964*

Farrukh Zaman 1: v NZ 1976

Fazal Mahmood 34: v E 1961 (1); v A 1956 (1) 1959 (2); v WI 1958 (3); v NZ 1955 (2); v In 1954 (4); *v E 1954 (4) 1962 (2); v WI 1957 (5); v In 1952 (5) 1960 (5)*

Ghazali, M. E. Z. 2: *v E 1954 (2)*

Ghulam Abbas 1: *v E 1967*

Gul Mahomed 1: v A 1956

Hanif Mohammad 55: v E 1961 (3) 1968 (3); v A 1956 (1) 1959 (3) 1964 (1); v WI 1958 (1); v NZ 1955 (3) 1964 (3) 1969 (1); v In 1954 (5); *v E 1954 (4) 1962 (5) 1967 (3); v A 1964 (1); v WI 1957 (5); v NZ 1964 (3); v In 1952 (5) 1960 (5)*

Haroon Rashid 23: v E 1977 (3); v A 1979 (2) 1982 (3); v In 1982 (1); v SL 1981 (2); *v E 1978 (3) 1982 (1); v A 1976 (1) 1978 (1); v WI 1976 (5); v NZ 1978 (1)*

Haseeb Ahsan 12: v E 1961 (2); v A 1959 (1); v WI 1958 (1); *v WI 1957 (3); v In 1960 (5)*

Ibadulla, K. 4: v A 1964 (1); *v E 1967 (2); v NZ 1964 (1)*

Ijaz Ahmed 16: v E 1987 (3); v A 1988 (3); *v E 1987 (4); v A 1989 (3); v WI 1987 (2); v In 1986 (1)*

Ijaz Butt 8: v A 1959 (2); v WI 1958 (3); *v E 1962 (3)*

Ijaz Faqih 5: v WI 1980 (1); *v A 1981 (1); v WI 1987 (2); v In 1986 (1)*

Imran Khan 82: v A 1979 (2) 1982 (3); v WI 1980 (4) 1986 (3); v NZ 1976 (3); v In 1978 (3) 1982 (6) 1989 (4); v SL 1981 (1) 1985 (3); *v E 1971 (1) 1974 (3) 1982 (3) 1987 (5); v A 1976 (3) 1978 (2) 1981 (3) 1983 (2) 1989 (3); v WI 1976 (5) 1987 (3); v NZ 1978 (2) 1988 (2); v In 1979 (5) 1986 (5); v SL 1985 (3)*

Imtiaz Ahmed 41: v E 1961 (3); v A 1956 (1) 1959 (3); v WI 1958 (3); v NZ 1955 (3); v In 1954 (5); *v E 1954 (4) 1962 (4); v WI 1957 (5); v In 1952 (5) 1960 (5)*

Intikhab Alam 47: v E 1961 (2) 1968 (3) 1972 (3); v A 1959 (1) 1964 (1); v WI 1974 (2); v NZ 1964 (3) 1969 (3) 1976 (3); *v E 1962 (3) 1967 (3) 1971 (3) 1974 (3); v A 1964 (1) 1972 (3); v WI 1976 (1); v NZ 1964 (3) 1972 (3); v In 1960 (3)*

Iqbal Qasim 50: v E 1977 (3) 1987 (3); v A 1979 (3) 1982 (2) 1988 (3); v WI 1980 (4); v NZ 1984 (3); v In 1978 (3) 1982 (2); v SL 1981 (3); *v E 1978 (3); v A 1976 (3) 1981 (2); v WI 1976 (2); v NZ 1984 (1); v In 1979 (6) 1983 (1) 1986 (3)*

Israr Ali 4: v A 1959 (2); *v In 1952 (2)*

Jalal-ud-Din 6: v A 1982 (1); v In 1982 (2) 1984 (2); v SL 1985 (1)

Javed Akhtar 1: *v E 1962*

Javed Miandad 104: v E 1977 (3) 1987 (3); v A 1979 (3) 1982 (3) 1988 (3); v WI 1980 (4) 1986 (3); v NZ 1976 (3) 1984 (3); v In 1978 (3) 1982 (6) 1984 (2) 1989 (4); v SL 1981 (3) 1985 (3); *v E 1978 (3) 1982 (3) 1987 (5); v A 1976 (3) 1978 (2) 1981 (3) 1983 (5) 1989 (3); v WI 1976 (1) 1987 (3); v NZ 1978 (3) 1984 (3) 1988 (2); v In 1979 (6) 1983 (3) 1986 (4); v SL 1985 (3)*

Kardar, A. H. 23: v A 1956 (1); v NZ 1955 (3); v In 1954 (5); *v E 1954 (4); v WI 1957 (5); v In 1952 (5)*

Khalid Hassan 1: *v E 1954*

Khalid Wazir 2: *v E 1954 (2)*

Khan Mohammad 13: v A 1956 (1); v NZ 1955 (3); v In 1954 (4); *v E 1954 (2); v WI 1957 (2); v In 1952 (1)*

Liaqat Ali 5: v E 1977 (2); v WI 1974 (1); *v E 1978 (2)*

Mahmood Hussain 27: v E 1961 (1); v WI 1958 (3); v NZ 1955 (1); v In 1954 (5); *v E 1954 (2) 1962 (3); v WI 1957 (3); v In 1952 (4) 1960 (5)*

Majid Khan 63: v E 1968 (3) 1972 (3); v A 1964 (1) 1979 (3); v WI 1974 (2) 1980 (4); v NZ 1964 (3) 1976 (3); v In 1978 (3) 1982 (1); v SL 1981 (1); *v E 1967 (3) 1971 (2) 1974 (3) 1982 (1); v A 1972 (3) 1976 (3) 1978 (2) 1981 (3); v WI 1976 (5); v NZ 1972 (3) 1978 (2); v In 1979 (6)*

Mansoor Akhtar 19: v A 1982 (3); v WI 1980 (2); v In 1982 (3); v SL 1981 (1); *v E 1982 (3) 1987 (5); v A 1981 (1) 1989 (1)*

Manzoor Elahi 4: v NZ 1984 (1); v In 1984 (1); *v In 1986 (2)*

Maqsood Ahmed 16: v NZ 1955 (2); v In 1954 (5); *v E 1954 (4); v In 1952 (5)*

Mathias, Wallis 21: v E 1961 (1); v A 1956 (1) 1959 (2); v WI 1958 (3); v NZ 1955 (1); *v E 1962 (3); v WI 1957 (5); v In 1960 (5)*

Miran Bux 2: v In 1954 (2)

Mohammad Aslam 1: *v E 1954*

Mohammad Farooq 7: v NZ 1964 (3); *v E 1962 (2); v In 1960 (2)*

Mohammad Ilyas 10: v E 1968 (2); v NZ 1964 (3); *v E 1967 (1); v A 1964 (1); v NZ 1964 (3)*

Mohammad Munaf 4: v E 1961 (2); v A 1959 (2)

Mohammad Nazir 14: v E 1972 (1); v WI 1980 (4); v NZ 1969 (3); *v A 1983 (3); v In 1983 (3)*

Mohsin Kamal 7: v E 1983 (1); v SL 1985 (1); *v E 1987 (4); v SL 1985 (1)*

Mohsin Khan 48: v E 1977 (1) 1983 (3); v A 1982 (3); v WI 1986 (3); v NZ 1984 (2); v In 1982 (6) 1984 (2); v SL 1981 (2) 1985 (2); *v E 1978 (3) 1982 (3); v A 1978 (1) 1981 (2) 1983 (5); v NZ 1978 (1) 1984 (3); v In 1983 (3); v SL 1985 (3)*

Mudassar Nazar 76: v E 1977 (3) 1983 (1) 1987 (3); v A 1979 (3) 1982 (3) 1988 (3); v WI 1986 (2); v NZ 1984 (3); v In 1978 (2) 1982 (6) 1984 (2); v SL 1981 (1) 1985 (3); *v E 1978 (3) 1982 (3) 1987 (5); v A 1976 (1) 1978 (1) 1981 (3) 1983 (5); v WI 1987 (3); v NZ 1978 (1) 1984 (3) 1988 (2); v In 1979 (5) 1983 (3); v SL 1985 (3)*

Mufasir-ul-Haq 1: *v NZ 1964*

Munir Malik 3: v A 1959 (1); *v E 1962 (2)*

Mushtaq Ahmed 1: *v A 1989*

Mushtaq Mohammad 57: v E 1961 (3) 1968 (3) 1972 (3); v WI 1958 (1) 1974 (2); v NZ 1969 (2) 1976 (3); v In 1978 (3); *v E 1962 (5) 1967 (3) 1971 (3) 1974 (3); v A 1972 (3) 1976 (3) 1978 (2); v WI 1976 (5); v NZ 1972 (2) 1978 (3); v In 1960 (5)*

Nadeem Abbasi 3: v In 1989 (3)

Nadeem Ghauri 1: *v A 1989*

Nasim-ul-Ghani 29: v E 1961 (2); v A 1959 (2) 1964 (1); v WI 1958 (3); *v E 1962 (5) 1967 (2); v A 1964 (1) 1972 (1); v WI 1957 (5); v NZ 1964 (3); v In 1960 (4)*

Naushad Ali 6: v NZ 1964 (3); *v NZ 1964 (3)*

Naved Anjum 1: v In 1989

Nazar Mohammad 5: *v In 1952 (5)*

Nazir Junior (*see* Mohammad Nazir)

Niaz Ahmed 2: v E 1968 (1); *v E 1967 (1)*

Pervez Sajjad 19: v E 1968 (1) 1972 (2); v A 1964 (1); v NZ 1964 (3) 1969 (3); *v E 1971 (3); v NZ 1964 (3) 1972 (3)*

Qasim Omar 26: v E 1983 (3); v WI 1986 (3); v NZ 1984 (3); v In 1984 (2); v SL 1985 (3); *v A 1983 (5); v NZ 1984 (3); v In 1983 (1); v SL 1985 (3)*

Ramiz Raja 31: v E 1983 (2) 1987 (3); v A 1988 (3); v WI 1986 (3); v In 1989 (4); v SL 1985 (1); *v E 1987 (2); v A 1989 (2); v WI 1987 (3); v SL 1985 (3)*

Rashid Khan 4: v SL 1981 (2); *v A 1983 (1); v NZ 1984 (1)*

Rehman, S. F. 1: *v WI 1957*

Rizwan-uz-Zaman 11: v WI 1986 (1); v SL 1981 (2); *v A 1981 (1); v NZ 1988 (2); v In 1986 (5)*

Sadiq Mohammad 41: v E 1972 (3) 1977 (2); v WI 1974 (1) 1980 (2); v NZ 1969 (3) 1976 (3); v In 1978 (1); *v E 1971 (3) 1974 (3) 1978 (3); v A 1972 (3) 1976 (2); v WI 1976 (5); v NZ 1972 (3); v In 1979 (3)*

Saeed Ahmed 41: v E 1961 (3) 1968 (3); v A 1959 (2) 1964 (1); v WI 1958 (3); v NZ 1964 (3); *v E 1962 (5) 1967 (3) 1971 (1); v A 1964 (1) 1972 (2); v WI 1957 (5); v NZ 1964 (3); v In 1960 (5)*

Salah-ud-Din 5: v E 1968 (1); v NZ 1964 (3) 1969 (1)

Saleem Jaffer 10: v E 1987 (1); v A 1988 (2); v WI 1986 (1); v In 1989 (1); *v WI 1987 (1); v NZ 1988 (2); v In 1986 (2)*

Salim Altaf 21: v E 1972 (3); v NZ 1969 (2); v In 1978 (1); *v E 1967 (2) 1971 (2); v A 1972 (3) 1976 (2); v WI 1976 (3); v NZ 1972 (3)*

Salim Malik 57: v E 1983 (3) 1987 (3); v A 1988 (3); v WI 1986 (1); v NZ 1984 (3); v In 1982 (6) 1984 (2) 1989 (4); v SL 1981 (2) 1985 (3); *v E 1987 (5); v A 1983 (3) 1989 (1); v WI 1987 (3); v NZ 1984 (3) 1988 (2); v In 1983 (2) 1986 (5); v SL 1985 (3)*

Salim Yousuf 28: v A 1988 (3); v WI 1986 (3); v In 1989 (1); v SL 1981 (1) 1985 (2); *v E 1987 (5); v A 1989 (3); v WI 1987 (3); v NZ 1988 (2); v In 1986 (5)*

Sarfraz Nawaz 55: v E 1968 (1) 1972 (2) 1977 (2) 1983 (3); v A 1979 (3); v WI 1974 (2) 1980 (2); v NZ 1976 (3); v In 1978 (3) 1982 (6); *v E 1974 (3) 1978 (2) 1982 (1); v A 1972 (2) 1976 (2) 1978 (2) 1981 (3) 1983 (3); v WI 1976 (4); v NZ 1972 (3) 1978 (3)*

Shafiq Ahmad 6: v E 1977 (3); v WI 1980 (2); *v E 1974 (1)*

Shafqat Rana 5: v E 1968 (2); v A 1964 (1); v NZ 1969 (2)

Shahid Israr 1: v NZ 1976

Shahid Mahboob 1: v In 1989

Shahid Mahmood 1: *v E 1962*

Shahid Saeed 1: v In 1989

Sharpe, D. 3: v A 1959 (3)

Shoaib Mohammad 29: v E 1983 (1) 1987 (1); v A 1988 (3); v NZ 1984 (1); v In 1989 (4); v SL 1985 (1); *v E 1987 (4); v A 1989 (3); v WI 1987 (3); v NZ 1984 (1) 1988 (2); v In 1983 (2) 1986 (3)*

Shuja-ud-Din 19: v E 1961 (2); v A 1959 (3); v WI 1958 (3); v NZ 1955 (3); v In 1954 (5); *v E 1954 (3)*

Sikander Bakht 26: v E 1977 (2); v WI 1980 (1); v NZ 1976 (1); v In 1978 (2) 1982 (1); *v E 1978 (3) 1982 (2); v A 1978 (2) 1981 (3); v WI 1976 (1); v NZ 1978 (3); v In 1979 (5)*

Tahir Naqqash 15: v A 1982 (3); v In 1982 (2); v SL 1981 (3); *v E 1982 (2); v A 1983 (1); v NZ 1984 (1); v In 1983 (3)*

Talat Ali 10: v E 1972 (3); *v E 1978 (2); v A 1972 (1); v NZ 1972 (1) 1978 (3)*

Taslim Arif 6: v A 1979 (3); v WI 1980 (2); *v In 1979 (1)*

Tauseef Ahmed 31: v E 1983 (2) 1987 (2); v A 1979 (3) 1988 (3); v WI 1986 (3); v NZ 1984 (1); v In 1984 (1); v SL 1981 (3) 1985 (1); *v E 1987 (2); v A 1989 (3); v NZ 1988 (1); v In 1986 (4); v SL 1985 (2)*

Waqar Hassan 21: v A 1956 (1) 1959 (1); v WI 1958 (1); v NZ 1955 (3); v In 1954 (5); *v E 1954 (4); v WI 1957 (1); v In 1952 (5)*

Waqar Younis 5: v In 1989 (2); *v A 1989 (3)*

Wasim Akram 32: v E 1987 (2); v WI 1986 (2); v In 1989 (4); v SL 1985 (3); *v E 1987 (5); v A 1989 (3); v WI 1987 (3); v NZ 1984 (2); v In 1986 (5); v SL 1985 (3)*

Wasim Bari 81: v E 1968 (3) 1972 (3) 1977 (3); v A 1982 (3); v WI 1974 (2) 1980 (2); v NZ 1969 (3) 1976 (2); v In 1978 (3) 1982 (6); *v E 1967 (3) 1971 (3) 1974 (3) 1978 (3) 1982 (3); v A 1972 (3) 1976 (3) 1978 (2) 1981 (3) 1983 (5); v WI 1976 (5); v NZ 1972 (3) 1978 (3); v In 1979 (6) 1983 (3)*

Wasim Raja 57: v E 1972 (1) 1977 (3) 1983 (3); v A 1979 (3); v WI 1974 (2) 1980 (4); v NZ 1976 (1) 1984 (1); v In 1982 (1) 1984 (1); v SL 1981 (3); *v E 1974 (2) 1978 (3) 1982 (1); v A 1978 (1) 1981 (3) 1983 (2); v WI 1976 (5); v NZ 1972 (3) 1978 (3) 1984 (2); v In 1979 (6) 1983 (3)*

Wazir Mohammad 20: v A 1956 (1) 1959 (1); v WI 1958 (3); v NZ 1955 (2); v In 1954 (5); *v E 1954 (2); v WI 1957 (5); v In 1952 (1)*

Younis Ahmed 4: v NZ 1969 (2); *v In 1986 (2)*

Zaheer Abbas 78: v E 1972 (2) 1983 (3); v A 1979 (2) 1982 (3); v WI 1974 (2) 1980 (3); v NZ 1969 (1) 1976 (3) 1984 (3); v In 1978 (3) 1982 (6) 1984 (2); v SL 1981 (1) 1985 (2); *v E 1971 (3) 1974 (3) 1982 (3); v A 1972 (3) 1976 (3) 1978 (2) 1981 (2) 1983 (5); v WI 1976 (3); v NZ 1972 (3) 1978 (2) 1984 (2); v In 1979 (5) 1983 (3)*

Zakir Khan 2: v In 1989 (1); *v SL 1985 (1)*

Zulfiqar Ahmed 9: v A 1956 (1); v NZ 1955 (1); *v E 1954 (2); v In 1952 (3)*

Zulqarnain 3: *v SL 1985 (3)*

SRI LANKA

Number of Test cricketers: 45

Ahangama, F. S. 3: v In 1985 (3)

Amalean, K. N. 2: v P 1985 (1); *v A 1987 (1)*

Amerasinghe, A. M. J. G. 2: v NZ 1983 (2)

Anurasiri, S. D. 4: v NZ 1986 (1); v P 1985 (2); *v In 1986 (1)*

TWO COUNTRIES

Twelve cricketers have appeared for two countries in Test matches, namely:

Amir Elahi, *India and Pakistan*.
J. J. Ferris, *Australia and England*.
S. C. Guillen, *West Indies and NZ*.
Gul Mahomed, *India and Pakistan*.
F. Hearne, *England and South Africa*.
A. H. Kardar, *India and Pakistan*.

W. E. Midwinter, *England and Australia*.
F. Mitchell, *England and South Africa*.
W. L. Murdoch, *Australia and England*.
Nawab of Pataudi, sen., *England and India*.
A. E. Trott, *Australia and England*.
S. M. J. Woods, *Australia and England*.

MOST TEST APPEARANCES FOR EACH COUNTRY

England: M. C. Cowdrey 114.
Australia: A. R. Border 115.
South Africa: J. H. B. Waite 50.
West Indies: I. V. A. Richards 111.

New Zealand: Sir R. J. Hadlee 86.
India: S. M. Gavaskar 125.
Pakistan: Javed Miandad 104.
Sri Lanka: A. Ranatunga 26.

MOST TEST APPEARANCES AS CAPTAIN FOR EACH COUNTRY

England: P. B. H. May 41.
Australia: A. R. Border 52.
South Africa: H. W. Taylor 18.
West Indies: C. H. Lloyd 74.

New Zealand: J. R. Reid 34.
India: S. M. Gavaskar 47.
Pakistan: Imran Khan 42.
Sri Lanka: L. R. D. Mendis 19.

ENGLAND v REST OF THE WORLD

The following were awarded England caps for playing against the Rest of the World in England in 1970, although the five matches played are now generally considered not to have rated as full Tests: D. L. Amiss (1), G. Boycott (2), D. J. Brown (2), M. C. Cowdrey (4), M. H. Denness (1), B. L. D'Oliveira (4), J. H. Edrich (2), K. W. R. Fletcher (4), A. W. Greig (3), R. Illingworth (5), A. Jones (1), A. P. E. Knott (5), P. Lever (1), B. W. Luckhurst (5), C. M. Old (2), P. J. Sharpe (1), K. Shuttleworth (1), J. A. Snow (5), D. L. Underwood (3), A. Ward (1), D. Wilson (2).

CRICKET RECORDS

Amended by BILL FRINDALL to end of the 1990 season in England

Unless stated to be of a minor character, all records apply only to first-class cricket including some performances in the distant past which have always been recognised as of exceptional merit.

* Denotes not out or an unbroken partnership.

(A), (SA), (WI), (NZ), (I), (P) or (SL) indicates either the nationality of the player, or the country in which the record was made.

FIRST-CLASS RECORDS

BATTING RECORDS

BOWLING RECORDS

ALL-ROUND RECORDS

WICKET-KEEPING RECORDS

FIELDING RECORDS

TEAM RECORDS

TEST MATCH RECORDS

BATTING RECORDS

BOWLING RECORDS

ALL-ROUND RECORDS

WICKET-KEEPING RECORDS

FIELDING RECORDS

TEAM RECORDS

TEST SERIES

LIMITED-OVERS INTERNATIONAL RECORDS

MISCELLANEOUS

FIRST-CLASS RECORDS

BATTING RECORDS

HIGHEST INDIVIDUAL SCORES

499	Hanif Mohammad	Karachi v Bahawalpur at Karachi	1958-59
452*	D. G. Bradman	NSW v Queensland at Sydney	1929-30
443*	B. B. Nimbalkar	Maharashtra v Kathiawar at Poona	1948-49
437	W. H. Ponsford	Victoria v Queensland at Melbourne	1927-28
429	W. H. Ponsford	Victoria v Tasmania at Melbourne	1922-23
428	Aftab Baloch	Sind v Baluchistan at Karachi	1973-74
424	A. C. MacLaren	Lancashire v Somerset at Taunton	1895
405*	G. A. Hick	Worcestershire v Somerset at Taunton	1988
385	B. Sutcliffe	Otago v Canterbury at Christchurch	1952-53
383	C. W. Gregory	NSW v Queensland at Brisbane	1906-07
369	D. G. Bradman	South Australia v Tasmania at Adelaide	1935-36
366	N. H. Fairbrother	Lancashire v Surrey at The Oval	1990
365*	C. Hill	South Australia v NSW at Adelaide	1900-01
365*	G. S. Sobers	West Indies v Pakistan at Kingston	1957-58
364	L. Hutton	England v Australia at The Oval	1938
359*	V. M. Merchant	Bombay v Maharashtra at Bombay	1943-44
359	R. B. Simpson	NSW v Queensland at Brisbane	1963-64
357*	R. Abel	Surrey v Somerset at The Oval	1899
357	D. G. Bradman	South Australia v Victoria at Melbourne	1935-36
356	B. A. Richards	South Australia v Western Australia at Perth ...	1970-71
355*	G. R. Marsh	Western Australia v South Australia at Perth ...	1989-90
355	B. Sutcliffe	Otago v Auckland at Dunedin	1949-50
352	W. H. Ponsford	Victoria v NSW at Melbourne	1926-27
350	Rashid Israr	Habib Bank v National Bank at Lahore	1976-77
345	C. G. Macartney	Australians v Nottinghamshire at Nottingham ...	1921
344*	A. G. A. Headley	Jamaica v Lord Tennyson's XI at Kingston	1931-32
344	W. G. Grace	MCC v Kent at Canterbury	1876
343*	P. A. Perrin	Essex v Derbyshire at Chesterfield	1904
341	G. H. Hirst	Yorkshire v Leicestershire at Leicester	1905
340*	D. G. Bradman	NSW v Victoria at Sydney	1928-29
340	S. M. Gavaskar	Bombay v Bengal at Bombay	1981-82
338*	R. C. Blunt	Otago v Canterbury at Christchurch	1931-32
338	W. W. Read	Surrey v Oxford University at The Oval	1888
337*	Pervez Akhtar	Railways v Dera Ismail Khan at Lahore	1964-65
337†	Hanif Mohammad	Pakistan v West Indies at Bridgetown	1957-58
336*	W. R. Hammond	England v New Zealand at Auckland	1932-33
336	W. H. Ponsford	Victoria v South Australia at Melbourne	1927-28
334	D. G. Bradman	Australia v England at Leeds	1930
333	K. S. Duleepsinhji	Sussex v Northamptonshire at Hove	1930
333	G. A. Gooch	England v India at Lord's	1990
332	W. H. Ashdown	Kent v Essex at Brentwood	1934
331*	J. D. Robertson	Middlesex v Worcestershire at Worcester	1949
325*	H. L. Hendry	Victoria v New Zealanders at Melbourne	1925-26
325	A. Sandham	England v West Indies at Kingston	1929-30
325	C. L. Badcock	South Australia v Victoria at Adelaide	1935-36
324	J. B. Stollmeyer	Trinidad v British Guiana at Port-of-Spain	1946-47
324	Waheed Mirza	Karachi Whites v Quetta at Karachi	1976-77
323	A. L. Wadekar	Bombay v Mysore at Bombay	1966-67
322	E. Paynter	Lancashire v Sussex at Hove	1937
322	I. V. A. Richards	Somerset v Warwickshire at Taunton	1985
321	W. L. Murdoch	NSW v Victoria at Sydney	1881-82
320	R. Lamba	North Zone v West Zone at Bhilai	1987-88
319	Gul Mahomed	Baroda v Holkar at Baroda	1946-47
318*	W. G. Grace	Gloucestershire v Yorkshire at Cheltenham	1876
317	W. R. Hammond	Gloucestershire v Nottinghamshire at Gloucester ...	1936

317	K. R. Rutherford	New Zealanders v D. B. Close's XI at Scarborough .	1986
316*	J. B. Hobbs	Surrey v Middlesex at Lord's	1926
316*	V. S. Hazare	Maharashtra v Baroda at Poona	1939-40
316	R. H. Moore	Hampshire v Warwickshire at Bournemouth	1937
315*	T. W. Hayward	Surrey v Lancashire at The Oval	1898
315*	P. Holmes	Yorkshire v Middlesex at Lord's	1925
315*	A. F. Kippax	NSW v Queensland at Sydney	1927-28
314*	C. L. Walcott	Barbados v Trinidad at Port-of-Spain	1945-46
313*	S. J. Cook	Somerset v Glamorgan at Cardiff	1990
313	H. Sutcliffe	Yorkshire v Essex at Leyton	1932
313	W. V. Raman	Tamil Nadu v Goa at Panaji	1988-89
312*	W. W. Keeton	Nottinghamshire v Middlesex at The Oval‡	1939
312*	J. M. Brearley	MCC Under 25 v North Zone at Peshawar	1966-67
311*	G. M. Turner	Worcestershire v Warwickshire at Worcester	1982
311	J. T. Brown	Yorkshire v Sussex at Sheffield	1897
311	R. B. Simpson	Australia v England at Manchester	1964
311	Javed Miandad	Karachi Whites v National Bank at Karachi	1974-75
310*	J. H. Edrich	England v New Zealand at Leeds	1965
310	H. Gimblett	Somerset v Sussex at Eastbourne	1948
309	V. S. Hazare	The Rest v Hindus at Bombay	1943-44
308*	F. M. M. Worrell	Barbados v Trinidad at Bridgetown	1943-44
307	M. C. Cowdrey	MCC v South Australia at Adelaide	1962-63
307	R. M. Cowper	Australia v England at Melbourne	1965-66
306*	A. Ducat	Surrey v Oxford University at The Oval	1919
306*	E. A. B. Rowan	Transvaal v Natal at Johannesburg	1939-40
306*	D. W. Hookes	South Australia v Tasmania at Adelaide	1986-87
305*	F. E. Woolley	MCC v Tasmania at Hobart	1911-12
305*	F. R. Foster	Warwickshire v Worcestershire at Dudley	1914
305*	W. H. Ashdown	Kent v Derbyshire at Dover	1935
304*	A. W. Nourse	Natal v Transvaal at Johannesburg	1919-20
304*	P. H. Tarilton	Barbados v Trinidad at Bridgetown	1919-20
304*	E. D. Weekes	West Indians v Cambridge University at Cambridge	1950
304	R. M. Poore	Hampshire v Somerset at Taunton	1899
304	D. G. Bradman	Australia v England at Leeds	1934
303*	W. W. Armstrong	Australians v Somerset at Bath	1905
303*	Mushtaq Mohammad	Karachi Blues v Karachi University at Karachi . . .	1967-68
303*	Abdul Azeem	Hyderabad v Tamil Nadu at Hyderabad	1986-87
302*	P. Holmes	Yorkshire v Hampshire at Portsmouth	1920
302*	W. R. Hammond	Gloucestershire v Glamorgan at Bristol	1934
302*	Arjan Kripal Singh	Tamil Nadu v Goa at Panaji	1988-89
302	W. R. Hammond	Gloucestershire v Glamorgan at Newport	1939
302	L. G. Rowe	West Indies v England at Bridgetown	1973-74
301*	E. H. Hendren	Middlesex v Worcestershire at Dudley	1933
301	W. G. Grace	Gloucestershire v Sussex at Bristol	1896
300*	V. T. Trumper	Australians v Sussex at Hove	1899
300*	F. B. Watson	Lancashire v Surrey at Manchester	1928
300*	Imtiaz Ahmed	PM's XI v Commonwealth XI at Bombay	1950-51
300	J. T. Brown	Yorkshire v Derbyshire at Chesterfield	1898
300	D. C. S. Compton	MCC v N. E. Transvaal at Benoni	1948-49
300	R. Subba Row	Northamptonshire v Surrey at The Oval	1958

    † *Hanif Mohammad batted for 16 hours 10 minutes – the longest innings in first-class cricket.*
    ‡ *Played at The Oval because Lord's was required for Eton v Harrow.*
Note: W. V. Raman (313) and Arjan Kripal Singh (302*) provide the only instance of two triple-hundreds in the same innings.

HIGHEST FOR TEAMS

For English Teams in Australia

| 307 | M. C. Cowdrey | MCC v South Australia at Adelaide . . . . | 1962-63 |
| 287 | R. E. Foster | England v Australia at Sydney . . . . | 1903-04 |

Against Australians in England

364	L. Hutton	England v Australia at The Oval	1938
219	A. Sandham	Surrey at The Oval (record for any county)	1934

For Australian Teams in England

345	C. G. Macartney	v Nottinghamshire at Nottingham	1921
334	D. G. Bradman	Australia v England at Leeds	1930

Against English Teams in Australia

307	R. M. Cowper	Australia v England at Melbourne	1965-66
280	A. J. Richardson	South Australia v MCC at Adelaide	1922-23

For Each First-Class County

Derbyshire	274	G. Davidson v Lancashire at Manchester		1896
Essex	343*	P. A. Perrin v Derbyshire at Chesterfield		1904
Glamorgan	287*	D. E. Davies v Gloucestershire at Newport		1939
Gloucestershire	318*	W. G. Grace v Yorkshire at Cheltenham		1876
Hampshire	316	R. H. Moore v Warwickshire at Bournemouth		1937
Kent	332	W. H. Ashdown v Essex at Brentwood		1934
Lancashire	424	A. C. MacLaren v Somerset at Taunton		1895
Leicestershire	252*	S. Coe v Northamptonshire at Leicester		1914
Middlesex	331*	J. D. Robertson v Worcestershire at Worcester		1949
Northamptonshire	300	R. Subba Row v Surrey at The Oval		1958
Nottinghamshire	312*	W. W. Keeton v Middlesex at The Oval†		1939
Somerset	322	I. V. A. Richards v Warwickshire at Taunton		1985
Surrey	357*	R. Abel v Somerset at The Oval		1899
Sussex	333	K. S. Duleepsinhji v Northamptonshire at Hove		1930
Warwickshire	305*	F. R. Foster v Worcestershire at Dudley		1914
Worcestershire	405*	G. A. Hick v Somerset at Taunton		1988
Yorkshire	341	G. H. Hirst v Leicestershire at Leicester		1905

† *Played at The Oval because Lord's was required for Eton v Harrow.*

HUNDRED ON DEBUT IN BRITISH ISLES

(The following list does not include instances of players who have previously appeared in first-class cricket outside the British Isles or who performed the feat before 1946. Particulars of the latter are in *Wisdens* prior to 1984.)

114	F. W. Stocks	Nottinghamshire v Kent at Nottingham	1946
108	A. Fairbairn	Middlesex v Somerset at Taunton	†‡1947
124	P. Hearn	Kent v Warwickshire at Gillingham	1947
215*	G. H. G. Doggart	Cambridge University v Lancashire at Cambridge	1948
106	J. R. Gill	Ireland v MCC at Dublin	1948
107*	G. Barker	Essex v Canadians at Clacton	†1954
135	J. K. E. Slack	Cambridge University v Middlesex at Cambridge	1954
100*	E. A. Clark	Middlesex v Cambridge University at Cambridge	1959
113	G. J. Chidgey	Free Foresters v Cambridge U. at Cambridge	1962
100*	D. R. Shepherd	Gloucestershire v Oxford University at Oxford	1965
110*	A. J. Harvey-Walker	Derbyshire v Oxford University at Burton upon Trent	†1971
173	J. Whitehouse	Warwickshire v Oxford University at Oxford	1971
106	J. B. Turner	Minor Counties v Pakistanis at Jesmond	1974
112	J. A. Claughton	Oxford University v Gloucestershire at Oxford	†1976
100*	A. W. Lilley	Essex v Nottinghamshire at Nottingham	†1978
146*	J. S. Johnson	Minor Counties v Indians at Wellington	1979
110	N. R. Taylor	Kent v Sri Lankans at Canterbury	1979
146*	D. G. Aslett	Kent v Hampshire at Bournemouth	1981
116	M. D. Moxon	Yorkshire v Essex at Leeds	†1981
100	D. A. Banks	Worcestershire v Oxford University at Oxford	1983
122	A. A. Metcalfe	Yorkshire v Nottinghamshire at Bradford	1983
117*	K. T. Medlycott	Surrey v Cambridge University at Banstead	§1984
101*	N. J. Falkner		
106	A. C. Storie	Northamptonshire v Hampshire at Northampton	†1985
102	M. P. Maynard	Glamorgan v Yorkshire at Swansea	1985

117*	R. J. Bartlett	Somerset v Oxford University at Oxford	1986
100*	P. D. Bowler	Leicestershire v Hampshire at Leicester	1986
145	I. L. Philip	Scotland v Ireland at Glasgow	1986
114*	P. D. Atkins	Surrey v Cambridge University at The Oval	1988
100	B. M. W. Patterson	Scotland v Ireland at Dumfries	1988
116*	J. J. B. Lewis	Essex v Surrey at The Oval	1990

† *In his second innings.*

‡ *A. Fairbairn (Middlesex) in 1947 scored hundreds in the second innings of his first two matches in first-class cricket: 108 as above, 110* Middlesex v Nottinghamshire at Nottingham.*

§ *The only instance in England of two players performing the feat in the same match.*

Notes: A number of players abroad have also made a hundred on a first appearance.

The highest innings on début was hit by W. F. E. Marx when he made 240 for Transvaal against Griqualand West at Johannesburg in 1920-21.

There are three instances of a cricketer making two separate hundreds on début: A. R. Morris, New South Wales, 148 and 111 against Queensland in 1940-41, N. J. Contractor, Gujarat, 152 and 102* against Baroda in 1952-53, and Aamer Malik, Lahore "A", 132* and 110* against Railways in 1979-80.

J. S. Solomon, British Guiana, scored a hundred in each of his first three innings in first-class cricket: 114* v Jamaica; 108 v Barbados in 1956-57; 121 v Pakistanis in 1957-58.

R. Watson-Smith, Border, scored 310 runs before he was dismissed in first-class cricket, including not-out centuries in his first two innings: 183* v Orange Free State and 125* v Griqualand West in 1969-70.

G. R. Viswanath and D. M. Wellham alone have scored a hundred on both their début in first-class cricket and in Test cricket. Viswanath scored 230 for Mysore v Andhra in 1967-68 and 137 for India v Australia in 1969-70. Wellham scored 100 for New South Wales v Victoria in 1980-81 and 103 for Australia v England in 1981.

TWO DOUBLE-HUNDREDS IN A MATCH

| A. E. Fagg . . . . | 244 | 202* | Kent v Essex at Colchester . . . . | 1938 |

HUNDRED AND DOUBLE-HUNDRED IN A MATCH

C. B. Fry	125	229	Sussex v Surrey at Hove	1900
W. W. Armstrong .	157*	245	Victoria v South Australia at Melbourne.	1920-21
H. T. W. Hardinge .	207	102*	Kent v Surrey at Blackheath	1921
C. P. Mead	113	224	Hampshire v Sussex at Horsham	1921
K. S. Duleepsinhji .	115	246	Sussex v Kent at Hastings	1929
D. G. Bradman . . .	124	225	Woodfull's XI v Ryder's XI at Sydney . . .	1929-30
B. Sutcliffe	243	100*	New Zealanders v Essex at Southend . . .	1949
M. R. Hallam	210*	157	Leicestershire v Glamorgan at Leicester .	1959
M. R. Hallam	203*	143*	Leicestershire v Sussex at Worthing	1961
Hanumant Singh . .	109	213*	Rajasthan v Bombay at Bombay	1966-67
Salah-ud-Din	256	102*	Karachi v East Pakistan at Karachi	1968-69
K. D. Walters	242	103	Australia v West Indies at Sydney	1968-69
S. M. Gavaskar . . .	124	220	India v West Indies at Port-of-Spain . . .	1970-71
L. G. Rowe	214	100*	West Indies v New Zealand at Kingston .	1971-72
G. S. Chappell	247*	133	Australia v New Zealand at Wellington .	1973-74
L. Baichan	216*	102	Berbice v Demerara at Georgetown	1973-74
Zaheer Abbas	216*	156*	Gloucestershire v Surrey at The Oval . . .	1976
Zaheer Abbas	230*	104*	Gloucestershire v Kent at Canterbury . . .	1976
Zaheer Abbas	205*	108*	Gloucestershire v Sussex at Cheltenham .	1977
Saadat Ali	141	222	Income Tax v Multan at Multan	1977-78
Talat Ali	214*	104	PIA v Punjab at Lahore	1978-79
Shafiq Ahmed	129	217*	National Bank v MCB at Karachi	1978-79
D. W. Randall	209	146	Nottinghamshire v Middlesex at Nottingham	1979
Zaheer Abbas	215*	150*	Gloucestershire v Somerset at Bath	1981

asim Omar	210*	110	MCB v Lahore at Lahore 1982-83
. I. Kallicharran .	200*	117*	Warwickshire v Northamptonshire at Birmingham 1984
izwan-uz-Zaman .	139	217*	PIA v PACO at Lahore 1989-90
. A. Gooch	333	123	England v India at Lord's 1990
. A. Hick	252*	100*	Worcestershire v Glamorgan at Abergavenny 1990
. R. Taylor	204	142	Kent v Surrey at Canterbury 1990

TWO SEPARATE HUNDREDS IN A MATCH

Eight times: Zaheer Abbas.

Seven times: W. R. Hammond.

Six times: J. B. Hobbs, G. M. Turner.

Five times: C. B. Fry.

Four times: D. G. Bradman, G. S. Chappell, J. H. Edrich, L. B. Fishlock, T. W. Graveney, . G. Greenidge, H. T. W. Hardinge, E. H. Hendren, Javed Miandad, G. L. Jessop, P. A. errin, B. Sutcliffe, H. Sutcliffe.

Three times: L. E. G. Ames, G. Boycott, I. M. Chappell, D. C. S. Compton, M. C. Cowdrey, . Denton, K. S. Duleepsinhji, R. E. Foster, R. C. Fredericks, S. M. Gavaskar, W. G. Grace, . Gunn, M. R. Hallam, Hanif Mohammad, M. J. Harris, T. W. Hayward, V. S. Hazare, D. W. ookes, L. Hutton, A. Jones, P. N. Kirsten, R. B. McCosker, P. B. H. May, C. P. Mead, izwan-uz-Zaman A. C. Russell, Sadiq Mohammad, J. T. Tyldesley.

Twice: Agha Zahid, Ali Zia, D. L. Amiss, C. W. J. Athey, L. Baichan, Basit Ali, A. R. Border, . J. T. Bosanquet, R. J. Boyd-Moss, S. J. Cook, C. C. Dacre, G. M. Emmett, A. E. Fagg, L. E. avell, H. Gimblett, G. A. Gooch, C. Hallows, R. A. Hamence, A. L. Hassett, G. A. Headley, . A. Hick, A. I. Kallicharran, J. H. King, A. F. Kippax, J. G. Langridge, H. W. Lee, E. Lester, . B. Llewellyn, C. G. Macartney, C. A. Milton, A. R. Morris, H. Morris, P. H. Parfitt, Nawab f Pataudi jun., E. Paynter, C. Pinch, R. G. Pollock, R. M. Prideaux, Qasim Omar, M W. Rhodes, . A. Richards, I. V. A. Richards, R. T. Robinson, Pankaj Roy, James Seymour, Shafiq hmed, R. B. Simpson, G. S. Sobers, M. A. Taylor, E. Tyldesley, C. L. Walcott, K. C. Wessels, . W. Whysall, G. N. Yallop.

Notes: W. Lambert scored 107 and 157 for Sussex v Epsom at Lord's in 1817 and it was not until V. G. Grace made 130 and 102* for South of the Thames v North of the Thames at Canterbury 1868 that the feat was repeated.

T. W. Hayward (Surrey) set up a unique record in 1906 when in one week – six days – he hit our successive hundreds, 144 and 100 v Nottinghamshire at Nottingham and 143 and 125 v eicestershire at Leicester.

L. G. Rowe is alone in scoring hundreds in each innings on his first appearance in Test ricket: 214 and 100* for West Indies v New Zealand at Kingston in 1971-72.

Zaheer Abbas (Gloucestershire) set a unique record in 1976 by twice scoring a double undred and a hundred in the same match without being dismissed: 216* and 156* v Surrey at he Oval and 230* and 104* v Kent at Canterbury. In 1977 he achieved this feat for a third me, scoring 205* and 108* v Sussex at Cheltenham, and in 1981 for a fourth time, scoring 15* and 150* v Somerset at Bath.

M. R. Hallam (Leicestershire), opening the batting each time, achieved the following treble: 0* and 157 v Glamorgan at Leicester, 1959; 203* and 143* v Sussex at Worthing, 1961; 107* nd 149* v Worcestershire at Leicester, 1965. In the last two matches he was on the field the whole time.

C. J. B. Wood, 107* and 117* for Leicestershire v Yorkshire at Bradford in 1911, and S. J. Cook, 120* and 131* for Somerset v Nottinghamshire at Nottingham in 1989, are alone in arrying their bats and scoring hundreds in each innings.

W. L. Foster, 140 and 172*, and R. E. Foster, 134 and 101*, for Worcestershire v Hampshire t Worcester in July 1899, were the first brothers each to score two separate hundreds in the ame first-class match.

The brothers I. M. Chappell, 145 and 121, and G. S. Chappell, 247* and 133, for Australia v New Zealand at Wellington in 1973-74, became the first players on the same side each to score a undred in each innings of a Test match.

G. Gunn, 183, and G. V. Gunn, 100*, for Nottinghamshire v Warwickshire at Birmingham n 1931, provide the only instance of father and son each hitting a century in the same innings of first-class match.

Most recent instances

In 1989-90

Basit Ali (2)	106	127	Karachi Blues v Multan at Karachi.
	128*	157	PACO v ADBP at Lahore.
J. Cox	175	102	Tasmania v New South Wales at Hobart.
D. M. Jones	116	121*	Australia v Pakistan at Adelaide.
R. B. Parikh	198	115*	Baroda v Gujarat at Baroda.
Rizwan-uz-Zaman	139	217*	PIA v PACO at Lahore.
M. W. Rushmere	150*	151*	SA Invitation XI v English XI at Pietermaritzburg.
Tariq Baig	103	103	Lahore City v Bahawalpur at Lahore.
M. A. Taylor	127	100	New South Wales v Queensland at Sydney.
Zahoor Elahi	122	133	ADBP v PNSC at Rawalpindi.

In 1990: See Features of 1990.

FOUR HUNDREDS OR MORE IN SUCCESSION

Six in succession: C. B. Fry 1901; D. G. Bradman 1938-39; M. J. Procter 1970-71.

Five in succession: E. D. Weekes 1955-56.

Four in succession: C. W. J. Athey 1987; M. Azharuddin 1984-85; A. R. Border 1985; D. G Bradman 1931-32, 1948-49; D. C. S. Compton 1946-47; N. J. Contractor 1957-58; S. J. Cox 1989; K. S. Duleepsinhji 1931; C. B. Fry 1911; C. G. Greenidge 1986; W. R. Hammon 1936-37, 1945-46; H. T. W. Hardinge 1913; T. W. Hayward 1906; J. B. Hobbs 1920, 192: D. W. Hookes 1976-77; P. N. Kirsten 1976-77; J. G. Langridge 1949; C. G. Macartney 192: K. S. McEwan 1977; P. B. H. May 1956-57; V. M. Merchant 1941-42; A. Mitchell 1933; Nawa of Pataudi sen. 1931; L. G. Rowe 1971-72; Pankaj Roy 1962-63; Rizwan-uz-Zaman 1989-9(Sadiq Mohammad 1976; Saeed Ahmed 1961-62; H. Sutcliffe 1931, 1939; E. Tyldesley 192(W. W. Whysall 1930; F. E. Woolley 1929; Zaheer Abbas 1970-71, 1982-83.

Note: The most fifties in consecutive innings is ten – by E. Tyldesley in 1926 and by D. G Bradman in the 1947-48 and 1948 seasons.

MOST HUNDREDS IN A SEASON

Eighteen: D. C. S. Compton in 1947. These included six hundreds against the South African in which matches his average was 84.78. His aggregate for the season was 3,816, also a recore

Sixteen: J. B. Hobbs in 1925, when aged 42, played 16 three-figure innings in first-cla: matches. It was during this season that he exceeded the number of hundreds obtained in firs class cricket by W. G. Grace.

Fifteen: W. R. Hammond in 1938.

Fourteen: H. Sutcliffe in 1932.

Thirteen: G. Boycott in 1971, D. G. Bradman in 1938, C. B. Fry in 1901, W. R. Hammond i 1933 and 1937, T. W. Hayward in 1906, E. H. Hendren in 1923, 1927 and 1928, C. P. Mead i 1928, and H. Sutcliffe in 1928 and 1931.

MOST HUNDREDS IN A CAREER

(35 or more)

	Hundreds Total	Abroad	100th 100		Hundreds Total	Abroad	100th 100
J. B. Hobbs	197	22	1923	D. G. Bradman	117	41†	1947-4
E. H. Hendren	170	19	1928-29	I. V. A. Richards	109	90†	1988-8!
W. R. Hammond	167	33	1935	Zaheer Abbas	108	70†	1982-8
C. P. Mead	153	8	1927	M. C. Cowdrey	107	27	197
G. Boycott	151	27	1977	A. Sandham	107	20	193
H. Sutcliffe	149	14	1932	T. W. Hayward	104	4	191
F. E. Woolley	145	10	1929	J. H. Edrich	103	13	197
L. Hutton	129	24	1951	G. M. Turner	103	85†	198
W. G. Grace	126	1	1895	L. E. G. Ames	102	13	195
D. C. S. Compton	123	31	1952	D. L. Amiss	102	15	198
T. W. Graveney	122	31	1964	E. Tyldesley	102	8	193

† *"Abroad" for D. G. Bradman is outside Australia; for Zaheer Abbas, outside Pakistan; for M. Turner, outside New Zealand; for I. V. A. Richards, outside the West Indies.*
E. H. Hendren, D. G. Bradman and I. V. A. Richards scored their 100th hundreds in Australia, Zaheer Abbas scored his in Pakistan. Zaheer Abbas and G. Boycott did so in Test matches.

W. Hearne ... 96	A. Jones ... 56	C. Hill ... 45
B. Fry ... 94	C. A. Milton ... 56	N. C. O'Neill ... 45
G. Greenidge ... 90	C. Hallows ... 55	E. Paynter ... 45
I. Kallicharran ... 87	Hanif Mohammad ... 55	Rev. D. S. Sheppard ... 45
. J. Edrich ... 86	W. Watson ... 55	K. D. Walters ... 45
S. Sobers ... 86	J. G. Wright ... 55	H. H. I. Gibbons ... 44
T. Tyldesley ... 86	M. D. Crowe ... 54	V. M. Merchant ... 44
B. H. May ... 85	G. A. Hick ... 54	A. Mitchell ... 44
E. S. Wyatt ... 85	D. J. Insole ... 54	P. E. Richardson ... 44
Hardstaff, jun. ... 83	W. W. Keeton ... 54	B. Sutcliffe ... 44
B. Kanhai ... 83	W. Bardsley ... 53	G. R. Viswanath ... 44
A. Gooch ... 82	B. F. Davison ... 53	P. Willey ... 44
M. Gavaskar ... 81	A. E. Dipper ... 53	E. J. Barlow ... 43
. Leyland ... 80	G. L. Jessop ... 53	S. J. Cook ... 43
A. Richards ... 80	James Seymour ... 53	B. L. D'Oliveira ... 43
H. Lloyd ... 79	E. H. Bowley ... 52	J. H. Hampshire ... 43
ved Miandad ... 78	D. B. Close ... 52	A. F. Kippax ... 43
. F. Barrington ... 76	A. Ducat ... 52	J. W. H. Makepeace ... 43
G. Langridge ... 76	Shafiq Ahmed ... 52	A. R. Butcher ... 42
Washbrook ... 76	E. R. Dexter ... 51	James Langridge ... 42
T. W. Hardinge ... 75	J. M. Parks ... 51	Mudassar Nazar ... 42
Abel ... 74	W. W. Whysall ... 51	H. W. Parks ... 42
S. Chappell ... 74	G. Cox jun. ... 50	T. F. Shepherd ... 42
Kenyon ... 74	H. E. Dollery ... 50	V. T. Trumper ... 42
S. McEwan ... 73	K. S. Duleepsinhji ... 50	M. J. Harris ... 41
ajid Khan ... 73	H. Gimblett ... 50	K. R. Miller ... 41
ushtaq Mohammad ... 72	W. M. Lawry ... 50	A. D. Nourse ... 41
O'Connor ... 72	Sadiq Mohammad ... 50	J. H. Parks ... 41
. G. Quaife ... 72	D. B. Vengsarkar ... 50	R. M. Prideaux ... 41
S. Ranjitsinhji ... 72	F. B. Watson ... 50	G. Pullar ... 41
Brookes ... 71	W. Larkins ... 49	W. E. Russell ... 41
C. Russell ... 71	C. G. Macartney ... 49	C. L. Smith ... 41
Denton ... 69	M. J. Stewart ... 49	R. C. Fredericks ... 40
J. K. Smith ... 69	K. G. Suttle ... 49	J. Gunn ... 40
E. Marshall ... 68	P. R. Umrigar ... 49	P. W. G. Parker ... 40
N. Harvey ... 67	W. M. Woodfull ... 49	M. J. Smith ... 40
Holmes ... 67	C. J. Barnett ... 48	C. L. Walcott ... 40
D. Robertson ... 67	W. Gunn ... 48	D. M. Young ... 40
J. Lamb ... 66	E. G. Hayes ... 48	W. H. Ashdown ... 39
A. Perrin ... 66	B. W. Luckhurst ... 48	J. B. Bolus ... 39
G. Pollock ... 64	M. J. Procter ... 48	W. A. Brown ... 39
T. Simpson ... 64	C. E. B. Rice ... 48	R. J. Gregory ... 39
W. R. Fletcher ... 63	A. C. MacLaren ... 47	W. R. D. Payton ... 39
Gunn ... 62	W. H. Ponsford ... 47	J. R. Reid ... 39
R. Border ... 61	D. I. Gower ... 46	R. T. Robinson ... 39
S. Hazare ... 60	J. Iddon ... 46	C. J. Tavaré ... 39
. H. Hirst ... 60	P. N. Kirsten ... 46	F. M. M. Worrell ... 39
B. Simpson ... 60	A. R. Morris ... 46	F. L. Bowley ... 38
F. Warner ... 60	C. T. Radley ... 46	P. J. Burge ... 38
M. Chappell ... 59	D. W. Randall ... 46	J. F. Crapp ... 38
L. Hassett ... 59	K. C. Wessels ... 46	D. L. Haynes ... 38
Shrewsbury ... 59	Younis Ahmed ... 46	D. Lloyd ... 38
E. Fagg ... 58	W. W. Armstrong ... 45	V. L. Manjrekar ... 38
. W. Gatting ... 58	Asif Iqbal ... 45	A. W. Nourse ... 38
H. Parfitt ... 58	L. G. Berry ... 45	N. Oldfield ... 38
. Rhodes ... 58	J. M. Brearley ... 45	Rev. J. H. Parsons ... 38
B. Fishlock ... 56	A. W. Carr ... 45	W. W. Read ... 38

J. Sharp 38	H. W. Lee 37	E. Oldroyd ....
L. J. Todd 38	M. A. Noble 37	W. Place ....
J. Arnold 37	B. P. Patel 37	A. L. Wadekar .....
Arshad Pervez 37	H. S. Squires 37	E. D. Weekes ......
B. C. Broad 37	R. T. Virgin 37	C. W. J. Athey ....
G. Brown 37	C. J. B. Wood 37	C. S. Dempster ....
G. Cook 37	N. F. Armstrong 36	D. R. Jardine .....
G. M. Emmett 37	G. D. Mendis 36	B. H. Valentine ...

3,000 RUNS IN A SEASON

	Season	I	NO	R	HI	100s	Avg
D. C. S. Compton	1947	50	8	3,816	246	18	90.8
W. J. Edrich	1947	52	8	3,539	267*	12	80.4
T. W. Hayward	1906	61	8	3,518	219	13	66.3
L. Hutton	1949	56	6	3,429	269*	12	68.5
F. E. Woolley	1928	59	4	3,352	198	12	60.9
H. Sutcliffe	1932	52	7	3,336	313	14	74.1
W. R. Hammond	1933	54	5	3,323	264	13	67.8
E. H. Hendren	1928	54	7	3,311	209*	13	70.4
R. Abel	1901	68	8	3,309	247	7	55.1
W. R. Hammond	1937	55	5	3,252	217	13	65.0
M. J. K. Smith	1959	67	11	3,245	200*	8	57.9
E. H. Hendren	1933	65	9	3,186	301*	11	56.8
C. P. Mead	1921	52	6	3,179	280*	10	69.1
T. W. Hayward	1904	63	5	3,170	203	11	54.6
K. S. Ranjitsinhji ..	1899	58	8	3,159	197	8	63.1
C. B. Fry	1901	43	3	3,147	244	13	78.6
K. S. Ranjitsinhji ..	1900	40	5	3,065	275	11	87.5
L. E. G. Ames	1933	57	5	3,058	295	9	58.8
J. T. Tyldesley	1901	60	5	3,041	221	9	55.2
C. P. Mead	1928	50	10	3,027	180	13	75.6
J. B. Hobbs	1925	48	5	3,024	266*	16	70.3
E. Tyldesley	1928	48	10	3,024	242	10	79.5
W. E. Alley	1961	64	11	3,019	221*	11	56.9
W. R. Hammond	1938	42	2	3,011	271	15	75.2
E. H. Hendren	1923	51	12	3,010	200*	13	77.1
H. Sutcliffe	1931	42	11	3,006	230	13	96.9
J. H. Parks	1937	63	4	3,003	168	11	50.8
H. Sutcliffe	1928	44	5	3,002	228	13	76.9

Notes: W. G. Grace scored 2,739 runs in 1871 – the first batsman to reach 2,000 runs in a season. He made ten hundreds and twice exceeded 200, with an average of 78.25 in all first-class matches. At the time, the over consisted of four balls.

The highest aggregate in a season since the reduction of County Championship matches in 1969 is 2,746 by G. A. Gooch (30 innings) in 1990.

1,000 RUNS IN A SEASON MOST TIMES

(Includes Overseas Tours and Seasons)

28 times: W. G. Grace 2,000 (6); F. E. Woolley 3,000 (1), 2,000 (12).
27 times: M. C. Cowdrey 2,000 (2); C. P. Mead 3,000 (2), 2,000 (9).
26 times: G. Boycott 2,000 (3); J. B. Hobbs 3,000 (1), 2,000 (16).
25 times: E. H. Hendren 3,000 (3), 2,000 (12).
24 times: D. L. Amiss 2,000 (3); W. G. Quaife 2,000 (1); H. Sutcliffe 3,000 (3), 2,000 (12)

23 times: A. Jones.

22 times: T. W. Graveney 2,000 (7); W. R. Hammond 3,000 (3), 2,000 (9).

21 times: D. Denton 2,000 (5); J. H. Edrich 2,000 (6); W. Rhodes 2,000 (2).

20 times: D. B. Close; K. W. R. Fletcher; G. Gunn; T. W. Hayward 3,000 (2), 2,000); James Langridge 2,000 (1); J. M. Parks 2,000 (3); A. Sandham 2,000 (8); M. J. K. Smith 000 (1), 2,000 (5); C. Washbrook 2,000 (2).

19 times: J. W. Hearne 2,000 (4); G. H. Hirst 2,000 (3); D. Kenyon 2,000 (7); E. Tyldesley 000 (1), 2,000 (5); J. T. Tyldesley 3,000 (1), 2,000 (4).

18 times: L. G. Berry 2,000 (1); H. T. W. Hardinge 2,000 (5); R. E. Marshall 2,000 (6); A. Perrin; G. M. Turner 2,000 (3); R. E. S. Wyatt 2,000 (5).

17 times: L. E. G. Ames 3,000 (1), 2,000 (5); T. E. Bailey 2,000 (1); D. Brookes 2,000 (6); C. S. Compton 3,000 (1), 2,000 (5); C. G. Greenidge 2,000 (1); L. Hutton 3,000 (1), 2,000 (8); G. Langridge 2,000 (11); M. Leyland 2,000 (3); K. G. Suttle 2,000 (1), Zaheer Abbas 2,000 (2).

16 times: D. G. Bradman 2,000 (4); D. E. Davies 2,000 (1); E. G. Hayes 2,000 (2); C. A. ilton 2,000 (1); J. O'Connor 2,000 (4); C. T. Radley; I. V. A. Richards 2,000 (1); James ymour 2,000 (1).

15 times: G. Barker; K. F. Barrington 2,000 (3); E. H. Bowley 2,000 (4); M. H. Denness; E. Dipper 2,000 (5); H. E. Dollery 2,000 (2); W. J. Edrich 3,000 (1), 2,000 (8); G. A. Gooch 000 (4); J. H. Hampshire; P. Holmes 2,000 (7); Mushtaq Mohammad; R. B. Nicholls 2,000); P. H. Parfitt 2,000 (3); W. G. A. Parkhouse 2,000 (1); B. A. Richards 2,000 (1); J. D. obertson 2,000 (9); G. S. Sobers; M. J. Stewart 2,000 (1).

otes: F. E. Woolley reached 1,000 runs in 28 consecutive seasons (1907-1938). C. P. Mead did 27 seasons in succession (1906-1936).

Outside England, 1,000 runs in a season has been reached most times by D. G. Bradman (in seasons in Australia).

Three batsmen have scored 1,000 runs in a season in each of four different countries: G. S. bers in West Indies, England, India and Australia; M. C. Cowdrey and G. Boycott in ngland, South Africa, West Indies and Australia.

HIGHEST AGGREGATES OUTSIDE ENGLAND

	Season	I	NO	R	HI	100s	Avge
Australia							
G. Bradman	1928-29	24	6	1,690	340*	7	93.88
South Africa							
R. Reid	1961-62	30	2	1,915	203	7	68.39
West Indies							
H. Hendren	1929-30	18	5	1,765	254*	6	135.76
New Zealand							
. D. Crowe	1986-87	21	3	1,676	175*	8	93.11
India							
G. Borde	1964-65	28	3	1,604	168	6	64.16
Pakistan							
adat Ali	1983-84	27	1	1,649	208	4	63.42
Sri Lanka							
Ranatunga	1985-86	16	2	739	135*	3	52.78

ote: In more than one country, the following aggregates of over 2,000 runs have been corded.

	Season	I	NO	R	HI	100s	Avge
. Amarnath (P/I/WI)	1982-83	34	6	2,234	207	9	79.78
R. Reid (SA/A/NZ) .	1961-62	40	2	2,188	203	7	57.57
M. Gavaskar (I/P) .	1978-79	30	6	2,121	205	10	88.37
B. Simpson (I/P/A/WI)	1964-65	34	4	2,063	201	8	68.76

HIGHEST AVERAGES IN AN ENGLISH SEASON

(Qualification: 12 innings)

	Season	I	NO	R	HI	100s	Avge
D. G. Bradman	1938	26	5	2,429	278	13	115.6
G. Boycott	1979	20	5	1,538	175*	6	102.5
W. A. Johnston	1953	17	16	102	28*	0	102.0
G. A. Gooch	1990	30	3	2,746	333	12	101.7
G. Boycott	1971	30	5	2,503	233	13	100.1
D. G. Bradman	1930	36	6	2,960	334	10	98.6
H. Sutcliffe	1931	42	11	3,006	230	13	96.9
R. M. Poore	1899	21	4	1,551	304	7	91.2
D. R. Jardine	1927	14	3	1,002	147	5	91.0
D. C. S. Compton	1947	50	8	3,816	246	18	90.8
G. A. Hick	1990	35	9	2,347	252*	8	90.2
G. M. Turner	1982	16	3	1,171	311*	5	90.0
D. G. Bradman	1948	31	4	2,428	187	11	89.9
T. M. Moody	1990	15	2	1,163	168	7	89.4
D. M. Jones	1989	20	3	1,510	248	5	88.8
Zaheer Abbas	1981	36	10	2,306	215*	10	88.6
K. S. Ranjitsinhji	1900	40	5	3,065	275	11	87.5
D. R. Jardine	1928	17	4	1,133	193	3	87.1
W. R. Hammond	1946	26	5	1,783	214	7	84.9
D. G. Bradman	1934	27	3	2,020	304	7	84.1
R. B. Kanhai	1975	22	9	1,073	178*	3	82.5
Mudassar Nazar	1982	16	6	825	211*	4	82.5
C. G. Greenidge	1984	16	3	1,069	223	4	82.2
J. B. Hobbs	1928	38	7	2,542	200*	12	82.0
C. B. Fry	1903	40	7	2,683	234	9	81.3
W. J. Edrich	1947	52	8	3,539	267*	12	80.4

25,000 RUNS IN A CAREER

Dates in italics denote the first half of an overseas season; i.e. *1945* denotes the 1945-46 season

	Career	R	I	NO	HI	100s	Avge
J. B. Hobbs	1905-34	61,237	1,315	106	316*	197	50.6
F. E. Woolley	1906-38	58,969	1,532	85	305*	145	40.7
E. H. Hendren	1907-38	57,611	1,300	166	301*	170	50.8
C. P. Mead	1905-36	55,061	1,340	185	280*	153	47.6
W. G. Grace	1865-1908	54,896	1,493	105	344	126	39.5
W. R. Hammond	1920-51	50,551	1,005	104	336*	167	56.1
H. Sutcliffe	1919-45	50,138	1,088	123	313	149	51.9
G. Boycott	1962-86	48,426	1,014	162	261*	151	56.8
T. W. Graveney	1948-*71*	47,793	1,223	159	258	122	44.9
T. W. Hayward	1893-1914	43,551	1,138	96	315*	104	41.7
D. L. Amiss	1960-87	43,423	1,139	126	262*	102	42.8
M. C. Cowdrey	1950-76	42,719	1,130	134	307	107	42.8
A. Sandham	1911-37	41,284	1,000	79	325	107	44.8
L. Hutton	1934-60	40,140	814	91	364	129	55.5
M. J. K. Smith	1951-75	39,832	1,091	139	204	69	41.8
W. Rhodes	1898-1930	39,802	1,528	237	267*	58	30.8
J. H. Edrich	1956-78	39,790	979	104	310*	103	45.4
R. E. S. Wyatt	1923-57	39,405	1,141	157	232	85	40.0
D. C. S. Compton ...	1936-64	38,942	839	88	300	123	51.8
E. Tyldesley	1909-36	38,874	961	106	256*	102	45.4
J. T. Tyldesley	1895-1923	37,897	994	62	295*	86	40.6
K. W. R. Fletcher ...	1962-88	37,665	1,167	170	228*	63	37.7

	Career	R	I	NO	HI	100s	Avge
W. Hearne	1909-36	37,252	1,025	116	285*	96	40.98
E. G. Ames	1926-51	37,248	951	95	295	102	43.51
. Kenyon	1946-67	37,002	1,159	59	259	74	33.63
'. J. Edrich	1934-58	36,965	964	92	267*	86	42.39
M. Parks	1949-76	36,673	1,227	172	205*	51	34.76
. Denton	1894-1920	36,479	1,163	70	221	69	33.37
. G. Greenidge	1970-90	36,434	860	72	273*	90	46.23
. H. Hirst	1891-1929	36,323	1,215	151	341	60	34.13
. Jones	1957-83	36,049	1,168	72	204*	56	32.89
V. G. Quaife	1894-1928	36,012	1,203	185	255*	72	35.37
. E. Marshall	*1945-72*	35,725	1,053	59	228*	68	35.94
. Gunn	1902-32	35,208	1,061	82	220	62	35.96
. B. Close	1949-86	34,994	1,225	173	198	52	33.26
aheer Abbas	*1965-86*	34,843	768	92	274	108	51.54
G. Langridge	1928-55	34,380	984	66	250*	76	37.45
. M. Turner	*1964-82*	34,346	792	101	311*	103	49.70
. Washbrook	1933-64	34,101	906	107	251*	76	42.67
4. Leyland	1920-48	33,660	932	101	263	80	40.50
. T. W. Hardinge	1902-33	33,519	1,021	103	263*	75	36.51
. Abel	1881-1904	33,124	1,007	73	357*	74	35.46
V. A. Richards	*1971-90*	33,033	708	50	322	109	50.20
. I. Kallicharran	*1966-90*	32,650	834	86	243*	87	43.64
. A. Milton	1948-74	32,150	1,078	125	170	56	33.73
D. Robertson	1937-59	31,914	897	46	331*	67	37.50
Hardstaff, jun.	1930-55	31,847	812	94	266	83	44.35
ames Langridge	1924-53	31,716	1,058	157	167	42	35.20
.. F. Barrington	1953-68	31,714	831	136	256	76	45.63
. A. Gooch	1973-90	31,363	732	57	333	82	46.46
. H. Lloyd	*1963-86*	31,232	730	96	242*	79	49.26
Aushtaq Mohammad	1956-85	31,091	843	104	303*	72	42.07
. B. Fry	1892-*1921*	30,886	658	43	258*	94	50.22
*. Brookes	1934-59	30,874	925	70	257	71	36.10
. Holmes	1913-35	30,573	810	84	315*	67	42.11
. T. Simpson	*1944-*63	30,546	852	55	259	64	38.32
. G. Berry	1924-51	30,225	1,056	57	232	45	30.25
.. G. Suttle	1949-71	30,225	1,064	92	204*	49	31.09
. A. Perrin	1896-1928	29,709	918	91	343*	66	35.92
. F. Warner	1894-1929	29,028	875	75	244	60	36.28
ᵣ. B. Kanhai	*1954-81*	28,774	669	82	256	83	49.01
. O'Connor	1921-39	28,764	903	79	248	72	34.90
. E. Bailey	1945-67	28,641	1,072	215	205	28	33.42
. H. Bowley	1912-34	28,378	859	47	283	52	34.94
. A. Richards	*1964-82*	28,358	576	58	356	80	54.74
ᵢ. S. Sobers	*1952-*74	28,315	609	93	365*	86	54.87
. E. Dipper	1908-32	28,075	865	69	252*	53	35.27
*. G. Bradman	*1927-48*	28,067	338	43	452*	117	95.14
. H. Hampshire	1961-84	28,059	924	112	183*	43	34.55
. B. H. May	1948-63	27,592	618	77	285*	85	51.00
ᵢ. F. Davison	*1967-87*	27,453	766	79	189	53	39.96
1ajid Khan	*1961-84*	27,444	700	62	241	73	43.01
ᵢ. C. Russell	1908-30	27,358	717	59	273	71	41.57
. G. Hayes	1896-1926	27,318	896	48	276	48	32.21
. E. Fagg	1932-57	27,291	803	46	269*	58	36.05
ames Seymour	1900-26	27,237	911	62	218*	53	32.08
aved Miandad	*1973-89*	27,010	584	90	311	78	54.67
. H. Parfitt	1956-*73*	26,924	845	104	200*	58	36.33
ᵢ. L. Jessop	1894-1914	26,698	855	37	286	53	32.63
. Mead	1924-54	26,564	1,032	80	287*	32	27.90
. Shrewsbury	1875-1902	26,505	813	90	267	59	36.65
4. J. Stewart	1954-72	26,492	898	93	227*	49	32.90

	Career	R	I	NO	HI	100s	Avge
C. T. Radley	1964-87	26,441	880	134	200	46	35.44
K. S. McEwan	1972-89	26,309	698	66	218	73	41.62
Younis Ahmed	1961-86	26,063	762	118	221*	46	40.47
P. E. Richardson	1949-65	26,055	794	41	185	44	34.60
M. H. Denness	1959-80	25,886	838	65	195	33	33.48
S. M. Gavaskar	1966-87	25,834	563	61	340	81	51.46
J. W. H. Makepeace .	1906-30	25,799	778	66	203	43	36.23
D. W. Randall	1972-90	25,727	754	69	237	46	37.55
W. Gunn	1880-1904	25,691	850	72	273	48	33.02
W. Watson	1939-64	25,670	753	109	257	55	39.86
G. Brown	1908-33	25,649	1,012	52	232*	37	26.71
G. M. Emmett	1936-59	25,602	865	50	188	37	31.41
J. B. Bolus	1956-75	25,598	833	81	202*	39	34.03
W. E. Russell	1956-72	25,525	796	64	193	41	34.87
C. E. B. Rice	1969-89	25,417	732	118	246	48	41.39
C. J. Barnett	1927-53	25,389	821	45	259	48	32.71
L. B. Fishlock	1931-52	25,376	699	54	253	56	39.34
D. J. Insole	1947-63	25,241	743	72	219*	54	37.61
J. M. Brearley	1961-83	25,185	768	102	312*	45	37.81
J. Vine	1896-1922	25,171	920	79	202	34	29.92
R. M. Prideaux	1958-74	25,136	808	75	202*	41	34.29
J. H. King	1895-1926	25,122	988	69	227*	34	27.33

Note: Some works of reference provide career figures which differ from those in this list, owing to the exclusion or inclusion of matches recognised or not recognised as first-class by *Wisden.* Those figures are:

	Career	R	I	NO	HI	100s	Avge
J. B. Hobbs	1905-34	61,760	1,325	107	316*	199	50.66
F. E. Woolley	1906-38	58,959	1,530	84	305*	145	40.77
W. G. Grace	1865-1908	54,211	1,478	104	344	124	39.45
H. Sutcliffe	1919-45	50,670	1,098	124	313	151	52.02
W. Rhodes	1898-1930	39,969	1,534	237	267*	58	30.58
D. Denton	1894-1920	36,440	1,161	70	221	69	33.40
G. H. Hirst	1891-1929	36,356	1,217	152	341	60	34.13

CAREER AVERAGE OVER 50

(Qualification: 10,000 runs)

Avge		Career	I	NO	R	HI	100s
95.14	D. G. Bradman	1927-48	338	43	28,067	452*	117
71.22	V. M. Merchant	1929-51	229	43	13,248	359*	44
65.18	W. H. Ponsford	1920-34	235	23	13,819	437	47
64.99	W. M. Woodfull	1921-34	245	39	13,388	284	49
64.17	G. A. Hick	1983-90	269	34	15,080	405*	54
58.24	A. L. Hassett	1932-53	322	32	16,890	232	59
58.19	V. S. Hazare	1934-66	365	45	18,621	316*	60
57.23	M. D. Crowe	1979-90	321	50	15,512	242*	54
57.22	A. F. Kippax	1918-35	256	33	12,762	315*	43
56.83	G. Boycott	1962-86	1,014	162	48,426	261*	151
56.55	C. L. Walcott	1941-63	238	29	11,820	314*	40
56.37	K. S. Ranjitsinhji	1893-1920	500	62	24,692	285*	72
56.22	R. B. Simpson	1952-77	436	62	21,029	359	60
56.10	W. R. Hammond	1920-51	1,005	104	50,551	336*	167
55.51	L. Hutton	1934-60	814	91	40,140	364	129
55.34	E. D. Weekes	1944-64	241	24	12,010	304*	36
54.87	G. S. Sobers	1952-74	609	93	28,315	365*	86

Avge		Career	I	NO	R	HI	100s
54.74	B. A. Richards	1964-82	576	58	28,358	356	80
54.67	Javed Miandad	1973-89	584	90	27,010	311	78
54.67	R. G. Pollock	1960-86	437	54	20,940	274	64
54.24	F. M. M. Worrell	1941-64	326	49	15,025	308*	39
53.78	R. M. Cowper	1959-69	228	31	10,595	307	26
53.67	A. R. Morris	1940-63	250	15	12,614	290	46
53.15	A. R. Border	1976-89	476	76	21,261	205	61
52.32	Hanif Mohammad	1951-75	371	45	17,059	499	55
52.27	P. R. Umrigar	1944-67	350	41	16,154	252*	49
52.20	G. S. Chappell	1966-83	542	72	24,535	247*	74
51.95	H. Sutcliffe	1919-45	1,088	123	50,138	313	149
51.85	D. C. S. Compton	1936-64	839	88	38,942	300	123
51.58	D. B. Vengsarkar	1975-90	360	48	16,095	210	50
51.54	Zaheer Abbas	1965-86	768	92	34,843	274	108
51.53	A. D. Nourse	1931-52	269	27	12,472	260*	41
51.46	S. M. Gavaskar	1966-87	563	61	25,834	340	81
51.44	W. A. Brown	1932-49	284	15	13,838	265*	39
51.00	P. B. H. May	1948-63	618	77	27,592	285*	85
50.95	N. C. O'Neill	1955-67	306	34	13,859	284	45
50.93	R. N. Harvey	1946-62	461	35	21,699	231*	67
50.90	W. M. Lawry	1955-71	417	49	18,734	266	50
50.90	A. V. Mankad	1963-82	326	71	12,980	265	31
50.80	E. H. Hendren	1907-38	1,300	166	57,611	301*	170
50.65	J. B. Hobbs	1905-34	1,315	106	61,237	316*	197
50.22	C. B. Fry	1892-1921	658	43	30,886	258*	94
50.20	I. V. A. Richards	1971-90	708	50	33,033	322	109

FAST FIFTIES

Minutes			
11	C. I. J. Smith (66)	Middlesex v Gloucestershire at Bristol	1938
14	S. J. Pegler (50)	South Africans v Tasmania at Launceston	1910-11
14	F. T. Mann (53)	Middlesex v Nottinghamshire at Lord's	1921
14	H. B. Cameron (56)	Transvaal v Orange Free State at Johannesburg ...	1934-35
14	C. I. J. Smith (52)	Middlesex v Kent at Maidstone	1935

Note: The following fast fifties were scored in contrived circumstances when runs were given from full tosses and long hops to expedite a declaration: C. C. Inman (8 minutes), Leicestershire v Nottinghamshire at Nottingham, 1965; T. M. Moody (11 minutes), Warwickshire v Glamorgan at Swansea, 1990; M. P. Maynard (14 minutes), Glamorgan v Yorkshire at Cardiff, 1987.

FASTEST HUNDREDS

Minutes			
35	P. G. H. Fender (113*)	Surrey v Northamptonshire at Northampton ..	1920
40	G. L. Jessop (101)	Gloucestershire v Yorkshire at Harrogate	1897
42	G. L. Jessop (191)	Gentlemen of South v Players of South at Hastings	1907
43	A. H. Hornby (106)	Lancashire v Somerset at Manchester	1905
43	D. W. Hookes (107)	South Australia v Victoria at Adelaide	1982-83
44	R. N. S. Hobbs (100)	Essex v Australians at Chelmsford	1975

Notes: The fastest recorded hundred in terms of balls received was scored off 34 balls by D. W. Hookes (above).

Research of the scorebook has shown that P. G. H. Fender scored his hundred from between 40 and 46 balls. He contributed 113 to an unfinished sixth-wicket partnership of 171 in 42 minutes with H. A. Peach.

E. B. Alletson (Nottinghamshire) scored 189 out of 227 runs in 90 minutes against Sussex at Hove in 1911. It has been estimated that his last 139 runs took 37 minutes.

The following fast hundreds were scored in contrived circumstances when runs were given from full tosses and long hops to expedite a declaration: T. M. Moody (26 minutes), Warwickshire v Glamorgan at Swansea, 1990; S. J. O'Shaughnessy (35 minutes), Lancashire v Leicestershire at Manchester, 1983; C. M. Old (37 minutes), Yorkshire v Warwickshire at Birmingham, 1977; N. F. M. Popplewell (41 minutes), Somerset v Gloucestershire at Bath, 1983.

FASTEST DOUBLE-HUNDREDS

Minutes
113	R. J. Shastri (200*)	Bombay v Baroda at Bombay	1984-85
120	G. L. Jessop (286)	Gloucestershire v Sussex at Hove	1903
120	C. H. Lloyd (201*)	West Indians v Glamorgan at Swansea	1976
130	G. L. Jessop (234)	Gloucestershire v Somerset at Bristol	1905
131	V. T. Trumper (293)	Australians v Canterbury at Christchurch	1913-14

FASTEST TRIPLE-HUNDREDS

Minutes
181	D. C. S. Compton (300)	MCC v N. E. Transvaal at Benoni	1948-49
205	F. E. Woolley (305*)	MCC v Tasmania at Hobart	1911-12
205	C. G. Macartney (345)	Australians v Nottinghamshire at Nottingham	1921
213	D. G. Bradman (369)	South Australia v Tasmania at Adelaide	1935-36

300 RUNS IN ONE DAY

345	C. G. Macartney	Australians v Nottinghamshire at Nottingham	1921
334	W. H. Ponsford	Victoria v New South Wales at Melbourne	1926-27
333	K. S. Duleepsinhji	Sussex v Northamptonshire at Hove	1930
331*	J. D. Robertson	Middlesex v Worcestershire at Worcester	1949
325*	B. A. Richards	S. Australia v W. Australia at Perth	1970-71
322†	E. Paynter	Lancashire v Sussex at Hove	1937
322	I. V. A. Richards	Somerset v Warwickshire at Taunton	1985
318	C. W. Gregory	New South Wales v Queensland at Brisbane	1906-07
317	K. R. Rutherford	New Zealanders v D. B. Close's XI at Scarborough	1986
316†	R. H. Moore	Hampshire v Warwickshire at Bournemouth	1937
315*	R. C. Blunt	Otago v Canterbury at Christchurch	1931-32
312*	J. M. Brearley	MCC Under 25 v North Zone at Peshawar	1966-67
311*	G. M. Turner	Worcestershire v Warwickshire at Worcester	1982
311*	N. H. Fairbrother	Lancashire v Surrey at The Oval	1990
309*	D. G. Bradman	Australia v England at Leeds	1930
307*	W. H. Ashdown	Kent v Essex at Brentwood	1934
306*	A. Ducat	Surrey v Oxford University at The Oval	1919
305*	F. R. Foster	Warwickshire v Worcestershire at Dudley	1914

† *E. Paynter's 322 and R. H. Moore's 316 were scored on the same day: July 28, 1937.*

1,000 RUNS IN MAY

		Runs	*Avge*
W. G. Grace, May 9 to May 30, 1895 (22 days):			
13, 103, 18, 25, 288, 52, 257, 73*, 18, 169		1,016	112.88
Grace was within two months of completing his 47th year.			
W. R. Hammond, May 7 to May 31, 1927 (25 days):			
27, 135, 108, 128, 17, 11, 99, 187, 4, 30, 83, 7, 192, 14		1,042	74.42
Hammond scored his 1,000th run on May 28, thus equalling			
Grace's record of 22 days.			
C. Hallows, May 5 to May 31, 1928 (27 days):			
100, 101, 51*, 123, 101*, 22, 74, 104, 58, 34*, 232		1,000	125.00

1,000 RUNS IN APRIL AND MAY

T. W. Hayward, April 16 to May 31, 1900:
  120*, 55, 108, 131*, 55, 193, 120, 5, 6, 3, 40, 146, 92   1,074   97.63

D. G. Bradman, April 30 to May 31, 1930:
  236, 185*, 78, 9, 48*, 66, 4, 44, 252*, 32, 47*   1,001   143.00
  On April 30 Bradman scored 75 not out.

D. G. Bradman, April 30 to May 31, 1938:
  258, 58, 137, 278, 2, 143, 145*, 5, 30*   1,056   150.85
  Bradman scored 258 on April 30, and his 1,000th run on May 27.

W. J. Edrich, April 30 to May 31, 1938:
  104, 37, 115, 63, 20*, 182, 71, 31, 53*, 45, 15, 245, 0, 9, 20*   1,010   84.16
  Edrich scored 21 not out on April 30. All his runs were scored at
  Lord's.

G. M. Turner, April 24 to May 31, 1973:
  41, 151*, 143, 85, 7, 8, 17*, 81, 13, 53, 44, 153*, 3, 2, 66*, 30, 10*,
  111   1,018   78.30

G. A. Hick, April 17 to May 29, 1988:
  61, 37, 212, 86, 14, 405*, 8, 11, 6, 7, 172   1,019   101.90
  Hick scored a record 410 runs in April, and his 1,000th run on
  May 28.

1,000 RUNS IN TWO SEPARATE MONTHS

Only four batsmen, C. B. Fry, K. S. Ranjitsinhji, H. Sutcliffe and L. Hutton, have scored over 1,000 runs in each of two months in the same season. L. Hutton, by scoring 1,294 in June 1949, made more runs in a single month than anyone else. He also made 1,050 in August 1949.

MOST RUNS SCORED OFF ONE OVER

(All instances refer to six-ball overs)

36	G. S. Sobers	off M. A. Nash, Nottinghamshire v Glamorgan at Swansea (six sixes)	1968
36	R. J. Shastri	off Tilak Raj, Bombay v Baroda at Bombay (six sixes) . . .	1984-85
34	E. B. Alletson	off E. H. Killick, Nottinghamshire v Sussex at Hove (46604446; including two no-balls)	1911
34	F. C. Hayes	off M. A. Nash, Lancashire v Glamorgan at Swansea (646666)	1977
32	I. T. Botham	off I. R. Snook, England XI v Central Districts at Palmerston North (466466)	1983-84
32	C. C. Inman	off N. W. Hill, Leicestershire v Nottinghamshire at Nottingham (466664; full tosses were provided for him to hit)	1965
32	T. E. Jesty	off R. J. Boyd-Moss, Hampshire v Northamptonshire at Southampton (666662)	1984
32	P. W. G. Parker	off A. I. Kallicharran, Sussex v Warwickshire at Birmingham (666664)	1982
32	I. R. Redpath	off N. Rosendorff, Australians v Orange Free State at Bloemfontein (666664)	1969-70
32	C. C. Smart	off G. Hill, Glamorgan v Hampshire at Cardiff (664664) .	1935
31	M. H. Bowditch (1) and M. J. Procter (30)	off A. A. Mallett, Western Province v Australians at Cape Town (Procter hit five sixes)	1969-70
31	A. W. Wellard	off F. E. Woolley, Somerset v Kent at Wells (666661) . . .	1938
30	I. T. Botham	off P. A. Smith, Somerset v Warwickshire at Taunton (4466460 including one no-ball)	1982

30	D. G. Bradman	off A. P. Freeman, Australians v England XI at Folkestone (466464)	1934
30	H. B. Cameron	off H. Verity, South Africans v Yorkshire at Sheffield (444666)	1935
30	G. A. Gooch	off S. R. Gorman, Essex v Cambridge U. at Cambridge (662664)	1985
30	A. J. Lamb	off A. I. Kallicharran, Northamptonshire v Warwickshire at Birmingham (644664)	1982
30	D. T. Lindsay	off W. T. Greensmith, South African Fezela XI v Essex at Chelmsford (066666 to win the match)	1961
30	Majid Khan	off R. C. Davis, Pakistanis v Glamorgan at Swansea (606666)	1967
30	M. P. Maynard	off K. Sharp, Glamorgan v Yorkshire at Cardiff (464466) (runs were offered to expedite a declaration)	1987
30	A. W. Wellard	off T. R. Armstrong, Somerset v Derbyshire at Wells (066666)	1936
30	D. Wilson	off R. N. S. Hobbs, Yorkshire v MCC at Scarborough (466266)	1966
30	P. L. Winslow	off J. T. Ikin, South Africans v Lancashire at Manchester (446646)	1955
30	Zaheer Abbas	off D. Breakwell, Gloucestershire v Somerset at Taunton (466626)	1979

Notes: The greatest number of runs scored off an eight-ball over is 34 (40446664) by R. M. Edwards off M. C. Carew, Governor-General's XI v West Indians at Auckland, 1968-69.

In a Shell Trophy match against Canterbury at Christchurch in 1989-90, R. H. Vance (Wellington), acting on the instructions of his captain, deliberately conceded 77 runs in an over of full tosses which contained seventeen no-balls, owing to the umpire's miscalculation, only five legitimate deliveries.

MOST SIXES IN AN INNINGS

15	J. R. Reid (296)	Wellington v N. Districts at Wellington	1962-63
13	Majid Khan (147*)	Pakistanis v Glamorgan at Swansea	1967
13	C. G. Greenidge (273*)	D. H. Robins' XI v Pakistanis at Eastbourne	1974
13	C. G. Greenidge (259)	Hampshire v Sussex at Southampton	1975
13	G. W. Humpage (254)	Warwickshire v Lancashire at Southport	1982
13	R. J. Shastri (200*)	Bombay v Baroda at Bombay	1984-85
12	Gulfraz Khan (207)	Railways v Universities at Lahore	1976-77
12	I. T. Botham (138*)	Somerset v Warwickshire at Birmingham	1985
12	R. A. Harper (234)	Northamptonshire v Gloucestershire at Northampton	1986
12	D. M. Jones (248)	Australians v Warwickshire at Birmingham	1989
11	C. K. Nayudu (153)	Hindus v MCC at Bombay	1926-27
11	C. J. Barnett (194)	Gloucestershire v Somerset at Bath	1934
11	R. Benaud (135)	Australians v T. N. Pearce's XI at Scarborough	1953
11	G. A. Hick (405*)	Worcestershire v Somerset at Taunton	1988

Note: W. J. Stewart (Warwickshire) hit seventeen sixes in the match v Lancashire, at Blackpool, 1959; ten in his first innings of 155 and seven in his second innings of 125.

MOST SIXES IN A SEASON

80   I. T. Botham   1985   66   A. W. Wellard   1935

Note: A. W. Wellard hit 50 or more sixes in a season four times. His number of sixes in 1935 has in the past been given as 72, but later research has caused this to be adjusted.

MOST BOUNDARIES IN AN INNINGS

68	P. A. Perrin (343*)	Essex v Derbyshire at Chesterfield	1904
65	A. C. MacLaren (424)	Lancashire v Somerset at Taunton	1895
64	Hanif Mohammad (499)	Karachi v Bahawalpur at Karachi	1958-59
57	J. H. Edrich (310*)	England v New Zealand at Leeds	1965
55	C. W. Gregory (383)	NSW v Queensland at Brisbane	1906-07
55	G. R. Marsh (355*)	Western Australia v South Australia at Perth	1989-90
54	G. H. Hirst (341)	Yorkshire v Leicestershire at Leicester	1905
53	A. W. Nourse (304*)	Natal v Transvaal at Johannesburg	1919-20
53	K. R. Rutherford (317)	New Zealanders v D. B. Close's XI at Scarborough.	1986
52	N. H. Fairbrother (366)	Lancashire v Surrey at The Oval	1990
51	C. G. Macartney (345)	Australians v Nottinghamshire at Nottingham	1921
50	D. G. Bradman (369)	South Australia v Tasmania at Adelaide	1935-36
50	A. Ducat (306*)	Surrey v Oxford University at The Oval	1919
50	B. B. Nimbalkar (443*)	Maharashtra v Kathiawar at Poona	1948-49
50	J. R. Reid (296)	Wellington v N. Districts at Wellington	1962-63
50	I. V. A. Richards (322)	Somerset v Warwickshire at Taunton	1985

Note: Boundaries include sixes.

HIGHEST PARTNERSHIPS

577	V. S. Hazare (288) and Gul Mahomed (319), fourth wicket, Baroda v Holkar at Baroda	1946-47
574*	F. M. M. Worrell (255*) and C. L. Walcott (314*), fourth wicket, Barbados v Trinidad at Port-of-Spain	1945-46
561	Waheed Mirza (324) and Mansoor Akhtar (224*), first wicket, Karachi Whites v Quetta at Karachi	1976-77
555	P. Holmes (224*) and H. Sutcliffe (313), first wicket, Yorkshire v Essex at Leyton	1932
554	J. T. Brown (300) and J. Tunnicliffe (243), first wicket, Yorkshire v Derbyshire at Chesterfield	1898
502*	F. M. M. Worrell (308*) and J. D. C. Goddard (218*), fourth wicket, Barbados v Trinidad at Bridgetown	1943-44
490	E. H. Bowley (283) and J. G. Langridge (195), first wicket, Sussex v Middlesex at Hove	1933
487*	G. A. Headley (344*) and C. C. Passailaigue (261*), sixth wicket, Jamaica v Lord Tennyson's XI at Kingston	1931-32
470	A. I. Kallicharran (230*) and G. W. Humpage (254), fourth wicket, Warwickshire v Lancashire at Southport	1982
465*	J. A. Jameson (240*) and R. B. Kanhai (213*), second wicket, Warwickshire v Gloucestershire at Birmingham	1974
462*	D. W. Hookes (306*) and W. B. Phillips (213*), fourth wicket, South Australia v Tasmania at Adelaide	1986-87
456	W. H. Ponsford (248) and E. R. Mayne (209), first wicket, Victoria v Queensland at Melbourne	1923-24
456	Khalid Irtiza (290) and Aslam Ali (236), third wicket, United Bank v Multan at Karachi	1975-76
455	K. V. Bhandarkar (205) and B. B. Nimbalkar (443*), second wicket, Maharashtra v Kathiawar at Poona	1948-49
451	D. G. Bradman (244) and W. H. Ponsford (266), second wicket, Australia v England, Fifth Test, at The Oval	1934
451*	S. Desai (218*) and R. M. H. Binny (211*), first wicket, Karnataka v Kerala at Chikmagalur	1977-78
451	Mudassar Nazar (231) and Javed Miandad (280*), third wicket, Pakistan v India, Fourth Test, at Hyderabad	1982-83

PARTNERSHIPS FOR FIRST WICKET

561	Waheed Mirza and Mansoor Akhtar, Karachi Whites v Quetta at Karachi	1976-77
555	P. Holmes and H. Sutcliffe, Yorkshire v Essex at Leyton	1932
554	J. T. Brown and J. Tunnicliffe, Yorkshire v Derbyshire at Chesterfield	1898
490	E. H. Bowley and J. G. Langridge, Sussex v Middlesex at Hove	1933
456	E. R. Mayne and W. H. Ponsford, Victoria v Queensland at Melbourne ...	1923-24
451*	S. Desai and R. M. H. Binny, Karnataka v Kerala at Chikmagalur	1977-78
431	M. R. J. Veletta and G. R. Marsh, Western Australia v South Australia at Perth	1989-90
428	J. B Hobbs and A. Sandham, Surrey v Oxford University at The Oval ...	1926
424	J. F. W. Nicholson and I. J. Siedle, Natal v Orange Free State at Bloemfontein	1926-27
421	S. M. Gavaskar and G. A. Parkar, Bombay v Bengal at Bombay	1981-82
418	Kamal Najamuddin and Khalid Alvi, Karachi v Railways at Karachi	1980-81
413	V. Mankad and Pankaj Roy, India v New Zealand at Madras (world Test record)	1955-56
405	C. P. S. Chauhan and M. S. Gupte, Maharashtra v Vidarbha at Poona ...	1972-73
395	D. M. Young and R. B. Nicholls, Gloucestershire v Oxford University at Oxford	1962
391	A. O. Jones and A. Shrewsbury, Nottinghamshire v Gloucestershire at Bristol	1899
390	G. L. Wight and G. L. R. Gibbs, B. Guiana v Barbados at Georgetown ...	1951-52
390	B. Dudleston and J. F. Steele, Leicestershire v Derbyshire at Leicester	1979
389	Majid Khan and Shafiq Ahmed, Punjab A v Sind A at Karachi	1974-75
389	Mudassar Nazar and Mansoor Akhtar, United Bank v Rawalpindi at Lahore	1981-82
388	K. C. Wessels and R. B. Kerr, Queensland v Victoria at St Kilda, Melbourne	1982-83
387	G. M. Turner and T. W. Jarvis, New Zealand v West Indies at Georgetown	1971-72
382	R. B. Simpson and W. M. Lawry, Australia v West Indies at Bridgetown .	1964-65
380	H. Whitehead and C. J. B. Wood, Leicestershire v Worcestershire at Worcester	1906
379	R. Abel and W. Brockwell, Surrey v Hampshire at The Oval	1897
378	J. T. Brown and J. Tunnicliffe, Yorkshire v Sussex at Sheffield	1897
377*	N. F. Horner and Khalid Ibadulla, Warwickshire v Surrey at The Oval ...	1960
375	W. H. Ponsford and W. M. Woodfull, Victoria v New South Wales at Melbourne	1926-27

FIRST-WICKET HUNDREDS IN BOTH INNINGS

There have been three instances of two double-century opening stands in the same match: B. Sutcliffe and D. D. Taylor, 220 and 286 for Auckland v Canterbury at Auckland in 1948-49; P. R. Pollard and R. T. Robinson, 222 and 282 for Nottinghamshire v Kent at Nottingham in 1989; and G. A. Gooch and J. P. Stephenson, 227 and 220 for Essex v Northamptonshire at Northampton in 1990.

T. W. Hayward and J. B. Hobbs in 1907 accomplished a performance without parallel by scoring over 100 together for Surrey's first wicket four times in one week: 106 and 125 v Cambridge University at The Oval, and 147 and 105 v Middlesex at Lord's.

L. Hutton and C. Washbrook, in three consecutive Test match innings which they opened together for England v Australia in 1946-47, made 138 in the second innings at Melbourne, and 137 and 100 at Adelaide. They also opened with 168 and 129 at Leeds in 1948.

J. B. Hobbs and H. Sutcliffe, in three consecutive Test match innings which they opened together for England v Australia in 1924-25, made 157 and 110 at Sydney and 283 at Melbourne. On 26 occasions – 15 times in Test matches – Hobbs and Sutcliffe took part in a three-figure first-wicket partnership. Seven of these stands exceeded 200.

G. Boycott and J. H. Edrich, in three consecutive Test match innings which they opened together for England v Australia in 1970-71, made 161* in the second innings at Melbourne, and 107 and 103 at Adelaide.

In 1971 R. G. A. Headley and P. J. Stimpson of Worcestershire shared in first-wicket hundred partnerships on each of the first four occasions they opened the innings together: 125 and 147 v Northamptonshire at Worcester, and 102 and 128* v Warwickshire at Birmingham.

J. B. Hobbs during his career, which extended from 1905 to 1934, helped to make 100 or more for the first wicket in first-class cricket 166 times – 15 of them in 1926, when in consecutive innings he helped to make 428, 182, 106 and 123 before a wicket fell. As many as 117 of the 166 stands were made for Surrey. In all first-class matches Hobbs and A. Sandham shared 66 first-wicket partnerships of 100 or more runs.

P. Holmes and H. Sutcliffe made 100 or more runs for the first wicket of Yorkshire on 69 occasions; J. B. Hobbs and A. Sandham for Surrey on 63 occasions; W. W. Keeton and C. B. Harris of Nottinghamshire on 46; T. W. Hayward and J. B. Hobbs of Surrey on 40; G. Gunn and W. W. Whysall of Nottinghamshire on 40; J. D. Robertson and S. M. Brown of Middlesex on 34; C. B. Fry and J. Vine of Sussex on 33; R. E. Marshall and J. R. Gray of Hampshire on 33; and D. E. Davies and A. H. Dyson of Glamorgan on 32.

J. Douglas and A. E. Stoddart in 1896 scored over 150 runs for the Middlesex first wicket three times within a fortnight. In 1901, J. Iremonger and A. O. Jones obtained over 100 for the Nottinghamshire first wicket four times within eight days, scoring 134 and 144* v Surrey at The Oval, 238 v Essex at Leyton, and 119 v Derbyshire at Welbeck.

J. W. Lee and F. S. Lee, brothers, for Somerset in 1934, scored over 100 runs thrice in succession in the County Championship.

W. G. Grace and A. E. Stoddart, in three consecutive innings against the Australians in 1893, made over 100 runs for each opening partnership.

C. Hallows and F. B. Watson, in consecutive innings for Lancashire in 1928, opened with 200, 202, 107, 118; reached three figures twelve times, 200 four times.

H. Sutcliffe, in the period 1919-1939 inclusive, shared in 145 first-wicket partnerships of 100 runs or more.

There were four first-wicket hundred partnerships in the match between Somerset and Cambridge University at Taunton in 1960. G. Atkinson and R. T. Virgin scored 172 and 112 for Somerset and R. M. Prideaux and A. R. Lewis 198 and 137 for Cambridge University.

PARTNERSHIP RECORDS FOR ALL COUNTRIES

Best First-Wicket Stands

Pakistan	561	Waheed Mirza (324) and Mansoor Akhtar (224*), Karachi Whites v Quetta at Karachi	1976-77
English	555	P. Holmes (224*) and H. Sutcliffe (313), Yorkshire v Essex at Leyton	1932
Australian	456	W. H. Ponsford (248) and E. R. Mayne (209), Victoria v Queensland at Melbourne	1923-24
Indian	451*	S. Desai (218*) and R. M. H. Binny (211*), Karnataka v Kerala at Chikmagalur	1977-78
South African	424	J. F. W. Nicolson (252*) and I. J. Siedle (174), Natal v Orange Free State at Bloemfontein	1926-27
West Indian	390	G. L. Wight (262*) and G. L. R. Gibbs (216), British Guiana v Barbados at Georgetown	1951-52
New Zealand	387	G. M. Turner (259) and T. W. Jarvis (182), New Zealand v West Indies at Georgetown	1971-72

Best Second-Wicket Stands

English	465*	J. A. Jameson (240*) and R. B. Kanhai (213*), Warwickshire v Gloucestershire at Birmingham	1974
Indian	455	K. V. Bhandarkar (205) and B. B. Nimbalkar (443*), Maharashtra v Kathiawar at Poona	1948-49
Australian	451	W. H. Ponsford (266) and D. G. Bradman (244), Australia v England at The Oval	1934
West Indian	446	C. C. Hunte (260) and G. S. Sobers (365*), West Indies v Pakistan at Kingston	1957-58
Pakistan	426	Arshad Pervez (220) and Mohsin Khan (220), Habib Bank v Income Tax Dept at Lahore	1977-78
New Zealand	317	R. T. Hart (167*) and P. S. Briasco (157), Central Districts v Canterbury at New Plymouth	1983-84
South African	305	S. K. Coen (165) and J. M. M Commaille (186), Orange Free State v Natal at Bloemfontein	1926-27

Best Third-Wicket Stands

Pakistan	456	Khalid Irtiza (290) and Aslam Ali (236), United Bank v Multan at Karachi	1975-76
New Zealand	445	P. E. Whitelaw (195) and W. N. Carson (290), Auckland v Otago at Dunedin (in 268 minutes)	1936-37
West Indian	434	J. B. Stollmeyer (324) and G. E. Gomez (190), Trinidad v British Guiana at Port-of-Spain	1946-47
English	424*	W. J. Edrich (168*) and D. C. S. Compton (252*), Middlesex v Somerset at Lord's	1948
Indian	410	L. Amarnath (262) and R. S. Modi (156), India in England v The Rest at Calcutta	1946-47
Australian	390*	J. M. Wiener (221*) and J. K. Moss (200*), Victoria v Western Australia at St Kilda, Melbourne	1981-82
South African	341	E. J. Barlow (201) and R. G. Pollock (175), South Africa v Australia at Adelaide	1963-64

Best Fourth-Wicket Stands

Indian	577	V. S. Hazare (288) and Gul Mahomed (319), Baroda v Holkar at Baroda	1946-47
West Indian	574*	C. L. Walcott (314*) and F. M. M. Worrell (255*), Barbados v Trinidad at Port-of-Spain	1945-46
English	470	A. I. Kallicharran (230*) and G. W. Humpage (254), Warwickshire v Lancashire at Southport	1982
Australian	462*	D. W. Hookes (306*) and W. B. Phillips (213*), South Australia v Tasmania at Adelaide	1986-87
Pakistan	350	Mushtaq Mohammad (201) and Asif Iqbal (175), Pakistan v New Zealand at Dunedin	1972-73
South African	342	E. A. B. Rowan (196) and P. J. M. Gibb (203), Transvaal v N. E. Transvaal at Johannesburg	1952-53
New Zealand	324	J. R. Reid (188*) and W. M. Wallace (197), New Zealanders v Cambridge University at Cambridge	1949

Best Fifth-Wicket Stands

Australian	405	S. G. Barnes (234) and D. G. Bradman (234), Australia v England at Sydney	1946-47
English	393	E. G. Arnold (200*) and W. B. Burns (196), Worcestershire v Warwickshire at Birmingham	1909
Indian	360	U. M. Merchant (217) and M. N. Raiji (170), Bombay v Hyderabad at Bombay	1947-48
Pakistan	355	Altaf Shah (276) and Tariq Bashir (196), House Building Finance Corporation v Multan at Multan	1976-77
South African	355	A. J. Lamb (294) and J. J. Strydom (107), OFS v Eastern Province at Bloemfontein	1987-88
New Zealand	341	G. R. Larsen (161) and E. B. McSweeney (205*), Wellington v Central Districts at Levin	1987-88
West Indian	335	B. F. Butcher (151) and C. H. Lloyd (201*), West Indians v Glamorgan at Swansea	1969

Best Sixth-Wicket Stands

West Indian	487*	G. A. Headley (344*) and C. C. Passailaigue (261*), Jamaica v Lord Tennyson's XI at Kingston	1931-32
Australian	428	M. A. Noble (284) and W. W. Armstrong (172*), Australians v Sussex at Hove	1902
English	411	R. M. Poore (304) and E. G. Wynyard (225), Hampshire v Somerset at Taunton	1899
Indian	371	V. M. Merchant (359*) and R. S. Modi (168), Bombay v Maharashtra at Bombay	1943-44

akistan ...... 353 Salah-ud-Din (256) and Zaheer Abbas (197), Karachi v East
Pakistan at Karachi 1968-69
outh African .. 259 S. A. Jones (209*) and O. Henry (125), Boland v Border at
East London 1987-88
ew Zealand .. 246* J. J. Crowe (120*) and R. J. Hadlee (151*), New Zealand v
Sri Lanka at Colombo (CCC) 1986-87

est Seventh-Wicket Stands

est Indian ... 347 D. St E. Atkinson (219) and C. C. Depeiza (122), West Indies
v Australia at Bridgetown 1954-55
nglish .... 344 K. S. Ranjitsinhji (230) and W. Newham (153), Sussex v
Essex at Leyton 1902
ustralian ..... 335 C. W. Andrews (253) and E. C. Bensted (155), Queensland v
New South Wales at Sydney 1934-35
akistan ...... 308 Waqar Hassan (189) and Imtiaz Ahmed (209), Pakistan v
New Zealand at Lahore 1955-56
outh African .. 299 B. Mitchell (159) and A. Melville (153), Transvaal v
Griqualand West at Kimberley 1946-47
ndian .... 274 K. C. Ibrahim (250) and K. M. Rangnekar (138), Bijapur XI
v Bengal XI at Bombay 1942-43
ew Zealand .. 265 J. L. Powell (164) and N. Dorreen (105*), Canterbury v
Otago at Christchurch 1929-30

est Eighth-Wicket Stands

ustralian ..... 433 A. Sims (184*) and V. T. Trumper (293), An Australian XI v
Canterbury at Christchurch 1913-14
nglish .... 292 R. Peel (210*) and Lord Hawke (166), Yorkshire v
Warwickshire at Birmingham 1896
est Indian ... 255 E. A. V. Williams (131*) and E. A. Martindale (134),
Barbados v Trinidad at Bridgetown 1935-36
akistan ...... 240 Gulfraz Khan (207) and Raja Sarfraz (102), Railways v
Universities at Lahore 1976-77
ndian .... 236 C. T. Sarwate (235) and R. P. Singh (88), Holkar v Delhi and
District at Delhi 1949-50
outh African .. 222 D. P. B. Morkel (114) and S. S. L. Steyn (261*), Western
Province v Border at Cape Town 1929-30
ew Zealand .. 190* J. E. Mills (104*) and C. F. W. Allcott (102*), New
Zealanders v Civil Service at Chiswick 1927

est Ninth-Wicket Stands

nglish .... 283 J. Chapman (165) and A. Warren (123), Derbyshire v
Warwickshire at Blackwell 1910
ndian .... 245 V. S. Hazare (316*) and N. D. Nagarwalla (98), Maharashtra
v Baroda at Poona 1939-40
ew Zealand .. 239 H. B. Cave (118) and I. B. Leggat (142*), Central Districts v
Otago at Dunedin 1952-53
ustralian ..... 232 C. Hill (365*) and E. Walkley (53), South Australia v New
South Wales at Adelaide 1900-01
outh African .. 221 N. V. Lindsay (160*) and G. R. McCubbin (97), Transvaal v
Rhodesia at Bulawayo 1922-23
akistan ...... 190 Asif Iqbal (146) and Intikhab Alam (51), Pakistan v England
at The Oval 1967
est Indian ... 161 C. H. Lloyd (161*) and A. M. E. Roberts (68), West Indies v
India at Calcutta 1983-84

Best Tenth-Wicket Stands

Australian 307	A. F. Kippax (260*), and J. E. H. Hooker (62), New South Wales v Victoria at Melbourne	1928-2
Indian 249	C. T. Sarwate (124*) and S. N. Banerjee (121), Indians v Surrey at The Oval	194
English 235	F. E. Woolley (185) and A. Fielder (112*), Kent v Worcestershire at Stourbridge	190
Pakistan 196*	Nadim Yousuf (202*) and Maqsood Kundi (109*) Muslim Commercial Bank v National Bank at Lahore	1981-8
New Zealand .. 184	R. C. Blunt (338*) and W. Hawkesworth (21), Otago v Canterbury at Christchurch	1931-3
South African .. 174	H. R. Lance (168) and D. Mackay-Coghill (57*), Transvaal v Natal at Johannesburg	1965-6
West Indian ... 138	E. L. G. Hoad (149*) and H. C. Griffith (84), West Indians v Sussex at Hove	193

Note: All the English record wicket partnerships were made in the County Championship

OUT HANDLED THE BALL

J. Grundy	MCC v Kent at Lord's	185
G. Bennett	Kent v Sussex at Hove	187
W. H. Scotton	Smokers v Non-Smokers at East Melbourne	1886-8
C. W. Wright	Nottinghamshire v Gloucestershire at Bristol	189
E. Jones	South Australia v Victoria at Melbourne	1894-9
A. W. Nourse	South Africans v Sussex at Hove	190
E. T. Benson	MCC v Auckland at Auckland	1929-3
A. W. Gilbertson	Otago v Auckland at Auckland	1952-5
W. R. Endean	South Africa v England at Cape Town	1956-5
P. J. Burge	Queensland v New South Wales at Sydney	1958-5
Dildar Awan	Services v Lahore at Lahore	1959-6
Mahmood-ul-Hasan	Karachi University v Railways-Quetta at Karachi	1960-6
Ali Raza	Karachi Greens v Hyderabad at Karachi	1961-6
Mohammad Yusuf	Rawalpindi v Peshawar at Peshawar	1962-6
A. Rees	Glamorgan v Middlesex at Lord's	196
Pervez Akhtar	Multan v Karachi Greens at Sahiwal	1971-7
Javed Mirza	Railways v Punjab at Lahore	1972-7
R. G. Pollock	Eastern Province v Western Province at Cape Town	1973-7
C. I. Dey	Northern Transvaal v Orange Free State at Bloemfontein	1973-7
Nasir Valika	Karachi Whites v National Bank at Karachi	1974-7
Haji Yousuf	National Bank v Railways at Lahore	1974-7
Masood-ul-Hasan	PIA v National Bank B at Lyallpur	1975-7
D. K. Pearse	Natal v Western Province at Cape Town	1978-7
A. M. J. Hilditch	Australia v Pakistan at Perth	1978-7
Musleh-ud-Din	Railways v Lahore at Lahore	1979-8
Jalal-ud-Din	IDBP v Habib Bank at Bahawalpur	1981-8
Mohsin Khan	Pakistan v Australia at Karachi	1982-8
D. L. Haynes	West Indies v India at Bombay	1983-8
K. Azad	Delhi v Punjab at Amritsar	1983-8
Athar A. Khan	Allied Bank v HBFC at Sialkot	1983-8
A. Pandya	Saurashtra v Baroda at Baroda	1984-8
G. N. Linton	Barbados v Windward Islands at Bridgetown	1985-8
R. B. Gartrell	Tasmania v Victoria at Melbourne	1986-8
R. Nayyar	Himachal Pradesh v Punjab at Una	1988-8

OUT OBSTRUCTING THE FIELD

A. Absolom	Cambridge University v Surrey at The Oval	1868
Straw	Worcestershire v Warwickshire at Worcester	1899
Straw	Worcestershire v Warwickshire at Birmingham	1901
P. Whiteside	Leicestershire v Lancashire at Leicester	1901
Hutton	England v South Africa at The Oval	1951
A. Hayes	Canterbury v Central Districts at Christchurch	1954-55
D. Deshpande	Madhya Pradesh v Uttar Pradesh at Benares	1956-57
M. Mehra	Railways v Delhi at Delhi	1959-60
Ibadulla	Warwickshire v Hampshire at Coventry	1963
aiser Khan	Dera Ismail Khan v Railways at Lahore	1964-65
az Ahmed	Lahore Greens v Lahore Blues at Lahore	1973-74
asim Feroze	Bahawalpur v Universities at Lahore	1974-75
Quirk	Northern Transvaal v Border at East London	1978-79
ahmood Rashid	United Bank v Muslim Commercial Bank at Bahawalpur	1981-82
rshad Ali	Sukkur v Quetta at Quetta	1983-84
Wasu	Vidarbha v Rajasthan at Akola	1984-85
halid Javed	Railways v Lahore at Lahore	1985-86

OUT HIT THE BALL TWICE

E. Bull	MCC v Oxford University at Lord's	1864
R. J. Charlwood	Sussex v Surrey at Hove	1872
G. Barlow	North v South at Lord's	1878
S. Wimble	Transvaal v Griqualand West at Kimberley	1892-93
B. Nicholls	Somerset v Gloucestershire at Bristol	1896
A. Lilley	Warwickshire v Yorkshire at Birmingham	1897
H. King	Leicestershire v Surrey at The Oval	1906
P. Binns	Jamaica v British Guiana at Georgetown	1956-57
Bavanna	Andhra v Mysore at Guntur	1963-64
aheer Abbas	PIA A v Karachi Blues at Karachi	1969-70
nwar Miandad	IDBP v United Bank at Lahore	1979-80
nwar Iqbal	Hyderabad v Sukkur at Hyderabad	1983-84
qtidar Ali	Allied Bank v Muslim Commercial Bank at Lahore	1983-84
aziz Malik	Lahore Division v Faisalabad at Sialkot	1984-85
aved Mohammad	Multan v Karachi Whites at Sahiwal	1986-87

BOWLING RECORDS

TEN WICKETS IN ONE INNINGS

	O	M	R		
Hinkly (Kent)				v England at Lord's	1848
Wisden (North)				v South at Lord's	1850
E. Walker (England)	43	17	74	v Surrey at The Oval	1859
E. Walker (Middlesex)	44.2	5	104	v Lancashire at Manchester	1865
Wootton (All England)	31.3	9	54	v Yorkshire at Sheffield	1865
W. Hickton (Lancashire)	36.2	19	46	v Hampshire at Manchester	1870
E. Butler (Oxford)	24.1	11	38	v Cambridge at Lord's	1871
ames Lillywhite (South)	60.2	22	129	v North at Canterbury	1872
A. Shaw (MCC)	36.2	8	73	v North at Lord's	1874
Barratt (Players)	29	11	43	v Australians at The Oval	1878
Giffen (Australian XI)	26	10	66	v The Rest at Sydney	1883-84
W. G. Grace (MCC)	36.2	17	49	v Oxford University at Oxford	1886
Burton (Middlesex)	52.3	25	59	v Surrey at The Oval	1888
A. E. Moss (Canterbury)	21.3	10	28	v Wellington at Christchurch	1889-90
M. J. Woods (Cambridge U.)	31	6	69	v Thornton's XI at Cambridge	1890
Richardson (Surrey)	15.3	3	45	v Essex at The Oval	1894

	O	M	R		
H. Pickett (Essex)	27	11	32	v Leicestershire at Leyton	189
E. J. Tyler (Somerset)	34.3	15	49	v Surrey at Taunton	189
W. P. Howell (Australians)	23.2	14	28	v Surrey at The Oval	189*
C. H. G. Bland (Sussex)	25.2	10	48	v Kent at Tonbridge	189
J. Briggs (Lancashire)	28.5	7	55	v Worcestershire at Manchester	190*
A. E. Trott (Middlesex)	14.2	5	42	v Somerset at Taunton	190(
F. Hinds (A. B. St Hill's XI)	19.1	6	36	v Trinidad at Port-of-Spain	1900-0
A. Fielder (Players)	24.5	1	90	v Gentlemen at Lord's	190*
E. G. Dennett (Gloucestershire)	19.4	7	40	v Essex at Bristol	190(
A. E. E. Vogler (E. Province)	12	2	26	v Griqualand West at Johannesburg	1906-0;
C. Blythe (Kent)	16	7	30	v Northamptonshire at Northampton	190;
A. Drake (Yorkshire)	8.5	0	35	v Somerset at Weston-super-Mare	1914
W. Bestwick (Derbyshire)	19	2	40	v Glamorgan at Cardiff	192)
A. A. Mailey (Australians)	28.4	5	66	v Gloucestershire at Cheltenham	192*
C. W. L. Parker (Glos.)	40.3	13	79	v Somerset at Bristol	192
T. Rushby (Surrey)	17.5	4	43	v Somerset at Taunton	192)
J. C. White (Somerset)	42.2	11	76	v Worcestershire at Worcester	192)
G. C. Collins (Kent)	19.3	4	65	v Nottinghamshire at Dover	192:
H. Howell (Warwickshire)	25.1	5	51	v Yorkshire at Birmingham	192:
A. S. Kennedy (Players)	22.4	10	37	v Gentlemen at The Oval	192;
G. O. B. Allen (Middlesex)	25.3	10	40	v Lancashire at Lord's	192)
A. P. Freeman (Kent)	42	9	131	v Lancashire at Maidstone	192)
G. Geary (Leicestershire)	16.2	8	18	v Glamorgan at Pontypridd	192)
C. V. Grimmett (Australians)	22.3	8	37	v Yorkshire at Sheffield	193(
A. P. Freeman (Kent)	30.4	8	53	v Essex at Southend	193(
H. Verity (Yorkshire)	18.4	6	36	v Warwickshire at Leeds	193)
A. P. Freeman (Kent)	36.1	9	79	v Lancashire at Manchester	193)
V. W. C. Jupp (Northants)	39	6	127	v Kent at Tunbridge Wells	1932
H. Verity (Yorkshire)	19.4	16	10	v Nottinghamshire at Leeds	1932
T. W. Wall (South Australia)	12.4	2	36	v New South Wales at Sydney	1932-33
T. B. Mitchell (Derbyshire)	19.1	4	64	v Leicestershire at Leicester	193!
J. Mercer (Glamorgan)	26	10	51	v Worcestershire at Worcester	193(
T. W. Goddard (Glos.)	28.4	4	113	v Worcestershire at Cheltenham	193;
T. F. Smailes (Yorkshire)	17.1	5	47	v Derbyshire at Sheffield	193)
E. A. Watts (Surrey)	24.1	8	67	v Warwickshire at Birmingham	193)
*W. E. Hollies (Warwickshire)	20.4	4	49	v Nottinghamshire at Birmingham	194(
J. M. Sims (East)	18.4	2	90	v West at Kingston	1948
T. E. Bailey (Essex)	39.4	9	90	v Lancashire at Clacton	194)
J. K. Graveney (Glos.)	18.4	2	66	v Derbyshire at Chesterfield	194)
R. Berry (Lancashire)	36.2	9	102	v Worcestershire at Blackpool	195:
S. P. Gupte (President's XI)	24.2	7	78	v Combined XI at Bombay	1954-5!
J. C. Laker (Surrey)	46	18	88	v Australians at The Oval	195(
J. C. Laker (England)	51.2	23	53	v Australia at Manchester	195(
G. A. R. Lock (Surrey)	29.1	18	54	v Kent at Blackheath	195(
K. Smales (Nottinghamshire)	41.3	20	66	v Gloucestershire at Stroud	195(
P. Chatterjee (Bengal)	19	11	20	v Assam at Jorhat	1956-57
J. D. Bannister (Warwickshire)	23.3	11	41	v Comb. Services at Birmingham	195)
A. J. G. Pearson (Cambridge University)	30.3	8	78	v Leicestershire at Loughborough	196)
N. I. Thomson (Sussex)	34.2	19	49	v Warwickshire at Worthing	196(
P. J. Allan (Queensland)	15.6	3	61	v Victoria at Melbourne	1965-66
I. J. Brayshaw (W. Australia)	17.6	4	44	v Victoria at Perth	1967-68
Shahid Mahmood (Karachi Whites)	25	5	58	v Khairpur at Karachi	1969-70
E. E. Hemmings (International XI)	49.3	14	175	v West Indies XI at Kingston	1982-83
P. Sunderam (Rajasthan)	22	5	78	v Vidarbha at Jodhpur	1985-86

	O	M	R		
T. Jefferies (W. Province) ..	22.5	7	59	v Orange Free State at Cape Town	1987-88
aran Adil (Bahawalpur)	22.5	3	92	v Faisalabad at Faisalabad	1989-90

* J. Wisden and W. E. Hollies achieved the feat without the direct assistance of a fielder. Wisden's ten ere all bowled; Hollies bowled seven and had three leg-before-wicket.
† On debut in first-class cricket.

ote: The following instances were achieved in 12-a-side matches:

	O	M	R		
M. Grace (MCC)	32.2	7	69	v Gents of Kent at Canterbury ..	1862
. G. Grace (MCC)	46.1	15	92	v Kent at Canterbury	1873

OUTSTANDING ANALYSES

	O	M	R	W		
. Verity (Yorkshire)	19.4	16	10	10	v Nottinghamshire at Leeds	1932
. Elliott (Victoria)	19	17	2	9	v Tasmania at Launceston	1857-58
had Khan (Railways)	6.3	4	7	9	v Dera Ismail Khan at Lahore ...	1964-65
C. Laker (England)	14	12	2	8	v The Rest at Bradford	1950
. Shackleton (Hampshire)..	11.1	7	4	8	v Somerset at Weston-super-Mare	1955
. Peate (Yorkshire)	16	11	5	8	v Surrey at Holbeck	1883
. R. Spofforth (Australians).	8.3	6	3	7	v England XI at Birmingham ...	1884
. A. Henderson (N.E. Transvaal)	9.3	7	4	7	v Orange Free State at Bloemfontein	1937-38
ajinder Goel (Haryana) ...	7	4	4	7	v Jammu and Kashmir at Chandigarh	1977-78
. I. Smith (South Africans) .	4.5	3	1	6	v Derbyshire at Derby	1947
. Costick (Victoria)	21.1	20	1	6	v Tasmania at Melbourne	1868-69
srar Ali (Bahawalpur)	11	10	1	6	v Dacca U. at Bahawalpur	1957-58
. D. Pougher (MCC)	3	3	0	5	v Australians at Lord's	1896
. R. Cox (Sussex)	6	6	0	5	v Somerset at Weston-super-Mare	1921
. K. Tyldesley (Lancashire).	5	5	0	5	v Leicestershire at Manchester ..	1924
. T. Mills (Gloucestershire).	6.4	6	0	5	v Somerset at Bristol	1928

MOST WICKETS IN A MATCH

9-90	J. C. Laker	England v Australia at Manchester	1956
7-48	C. Blythe	Kent v Northamptonshire at Northampton	1907
7-50	C. T. B. Turner	Australians v England XI at Hastings	1888
7-54	W. P. Howell	Australians v Western Province at Cape Town ...	1902-03
7-56	C. W. L. Parker	Gloucestershire v Essex at Gloucester	1925
7-67	A. P. Freeman	Kent v Sussex at Hove	1922
7-89	W. G. Grace	Gloucestershire v Nottinghamshire at Cheltenham.	1877
7-89	F. C. L. Matthews	Nottinghamshire v Northants at Nottingham	1923
7-91	H. Dean	Lancashire v Yorkshire at Liverpool	1913
7-91	H. Verity	Yorkshire v Essex at Leyton	1933
7-92	A. P. Freeman	Kent v Warwickshire at Folkestone	1932
7-103	W. Mycroft	Derbyshire v Hampshire at Southampton	1876
7-106	G. R. Cox	Sussex v Warwickshire at Horsham	1926
7-106	T. W. Goddard	Gloucestershire v Kent at Bristol	1939
7-119	W. Mead	Essex v Hampshire at Southampton	1895
7-137	W. Brearley	Lancashire v Somerset at Manchester	1905
7-159	S. F. Barnes	England v South Africa at Johannesburg	1913-14
7-201	G. Giffen	South Australia v Victoria at Adelaide	1885-86
7-212	J. C. Clay	Glamorgan v Worcestershire at Swansea	1937

Notes: H. A. Arkwright took eighteen wickets for 96 runs in a 12-a-side match for Gentlemen of

MCC v Gentlemen of Kent at Canterbury in 1861.

W. Mead took seventeen wickets for 205 runs for Essex v Australians at Leyton in 1893, the year before Essex were raised to first-class status.

F. P. Fenner took seventeen wickets for Cambridge Town Club v University of Cambridge at Cambridge in 1844.

SIXTEEN OR MORE WICKETS IN A DAY

17-48	C. Blythe	Kent v Northamptonshire at Northampton	190
17-91	H. Verity	Yorkshire v Essex at Leyton	193
17-106	T. W. Goddard	Gloucestershire v Kent at Bristol	193
16-38	T. Emmett	Yorkshire v Cambridgeshire at Hunslet	186
16-52	J. Southerton	South v North at Lord's	187
16-69	T. G. Wass	Nottinghamshire v Lancashire at Liverpool	190
16-38	A. E. E. Vogler	E. Province v Griqualand West at Johannesburg .	1906-0
16-103	T. G. Wass	Nottinghamshire v Essex at Nottingham	190
16-83	J. C. White	Somerset v Worcestershire at Bath	191

FOUR WICKETS WITH CONSECUTIVE BALLS

J. Wells	Kent v Sussex at Brighton	186
G. Ulyett	Lord Harris's XI v New South Wales at Sydney	1878-7
G. Nash	Lancashire v Somerset at Manchester	188
J. B. Hide	Sussex v MCC and Ground at Lord's	189
F. J. Shacklock	Nottinghamshire v Somerset at Nottingham	189
A. D. Downes	Otago v Auckland at Dunedin	1893-9
F. Martin	MCC and Ground v Derbyshire at Lord's	189
A. W. Mold	Lancashire v Nottinghamshire at Nottingham	189
W. Brearley†	Lancashire v Somerset at Manchester	190
S. Haigh	MCC v Army XI at Pretoria	1905-0
A. E. Trott‡	Middlesex v Somerset at Lord's	190
F. A. Tarrant	Middlesex v Gloucestershire at Bristol	190
A. Drake	Yorkshire v Derbyshire at Chesterfield	191
S. G. Smith	Northamptonshire v Warwickshire at Birmingham	191
H. A. Peach	Surrey v Sussex at The Oval	192
A. F. Borland	Natal v Griqualand West at Kimberley	1926-2
J. E. H. Hooker†	New South Wales v Victoria at Sydney	1928-2
R. K. Tyldesley†	Lancashire v Derbyshire at Derby	192
R. J. Crisp	Western Province v Griqualand West at Johannesburg ..	1931-3
R. J. Crisp	Western Province v Natal at Durban	1933-3
A. R. Gover	Surrey v Worcestershire at Worcester	193
W. H. Copson	Derbyshire v Warwickshire at Derby	193
W. A. Henderson	N.E. Transvaal v Orange Free State at Bloemfontein ...	1937-3
F. Ridgway	Kent v Derbyshire at Folkestone	195
A. K. Walker§	Nottinghamshire v Leicestershire at Leicester	195
S. N. Mohol	Board of Control President's XI v Minister for Small Savings' XI at Poona	1965-6
P. I. Pocock	Surrey v Sussex at Eastbourne	197
S. S. Saini†	Delhi v Himachal Pradesh at Delhi	1988-8

† Not all in the same innings.

‡ Trott achieved another hat-trick in the same innings of this, his benefit match.

§ Walker dismissed Firth with the last ball of the first innings and Lester, Tompkin and Smithson with the first three balls of the second innings, a feat without parallel.

Notes: In their match with England at The Oval in 1863, Surrey lost four wickets in the course of a four-ball over from G. Bennett.

Sussex lost five wickets in the course of the final (six-ball) over of their match with Surrey at Eastbourne in 1972. P. I. Pocock, who had taken three wickets in his previous over, captured four more, taking in all seven wickets with eleven balls, a feat unique in first-class matches. (The eighth wicket fell to a run-out.)

HAT-TRICKS

Double Hat-Trick

Besides Trott's performance, which is given in the preceding section, the following instances are recorded of players having performed the hat-trick twice in the same match, Rao doing so in the same innings.

A. Shaw	Nottinghamshire v Gloucestershire at Nottingham	1884
T. J. Matthews	Australia v South Africa at Manchester	1912
C. W. L. Parker	Gloucestershire v Middlesex at Bristol	1924
R. O. Jenkins	Worcestershire v Surrey at Worcester	1949
S. Rao	Services v Northern Punjab at Amritsar	1963-64
Amin Lakhani	Combined XI v Indians at Multan	1978-79

Five Wickets with Six Consecutive Balls

W. H. Copson	Derbyshire v Warwickshire at Derby	1937
W. A. Henderson	NE Transvaal v Orange Free State at Bloemfontein	1937-38
P. I. Pocock	Surrey v Sussex at Eastbourne	1972

Most Hat-Tricks

Seven times: D. V. P. Wright.

Six times: T. W. Goddard, C. W. L. Parker.

Five times: S. Haigh, V. W. C. Jupp, A. E. G. Rhodes, F. A. Tarrant.

Four times: R. G. Barlow, J. T. Hearne, J. C. Laker, G. A. R. Lock, G. G. Macaulay, T. J. Matthews, M. J. Procter, T. Richardson, F. R. Spofforth, F. S. Trueman.

Three times: W. M. Bradley, H. J. Butler, S. T. Clarke, W. H. Copson, R. J. Crisp, J. W. H. T. Douglas, J. A. Flavell, A. P. Freeman, G. Giffen, K. Higgs, A. Hill, W. A. Humphries, R. D. Jackman, R. O. Jenkins, A. S. Kennedy, W. H. Lockwood, E. A. McDonald, T. L. Pritchard, S. Rao, A. Shaw, J. B. Statham, M. W. Tate, H. Trumble, D. Wilson, G. A. Wilson.

Unusual Hat-Tricks

All "Stumped":	by W. H. Brain off C. L. Townsend, Gloucestershire v Somerset at Cheltenham	1893
All "Caught":	by G. J. Thompson off S. G. Smith, Northamptonshire v Warwickshire at Birmingham	1914
	by C. de L. White off R. Beesly, Border v Griqualand West at Queenstown	1946-47
	by G. O. Dawkes (wicket-keeper) off H. L. Jackson, Derbyshire v Worcestershire at Kidderminster	1958
All "LBW":	H. Fisher, Yorkshire v Somerset at Sheffield	1932
	J. A. Flavell, Worcestershire v Lancashire at Manchester	1963
	M. J. Procter, Gloucestershire v Essex at Westcliff	1972
	B. J. Ikin, Griqualand West v OFS at Kimberley	1973-74
	M. J. Procter, Gloucestershire v Yorkshire at Cheltenham	1979
	Aamer Wasim, Zone C v Lahore at Lahore	1985-86

Most recent instances

In 1989-90

Ayaz Jilani	PACO v United Bank at Sialkot.
D. A. Beard	Northern Districts v Central Districts at Nelson.
Haaris Khan	Karachi Blues v Lahore City at Lahore.
M. B. Halangoda	Sinhalese SC v Sinha SC at Sinhalese SC, Colombo.
H. C. Lindenberg	Border v Natal B at East London.
Masood Anwar	United Bank v National Bank at Karachi.
S. Mukherjee	Bengal v Hyderabad at Secunderabad (*on début*).
R. J. Ratnayake	Western Province v Southern Province at Galle.
A. Singla	Haryana v Services at Gurgaon.
J. Srinath	Karnataka v Hyderabad at Secunderabad (*on début*).

In 1990: See Features of 1990.

200 WICKETS IN A SEASON

	Season	O	M	R	W	Avge
A. P. Freeman	1928	1,976.1	423	5,489	304	18.05
A. P. Freeman	1933	2,039	651	4,549	298	15.26
T. Richardson	1895‡	1,690.1	463	4,170	290	14.37
C. T. B. Turner**	1888†	2,427.2	1,127	3,307	283	11.68
A. P. Freeman	1931	1,618	360	4,307	276	15.60
A. P. Freeman	1930	1,914.3	472	4,632	275	16.84
T. Richardson	1897‡	1,603.4	495	3,945	273	14.45
A. P. Freeman	1929	1,670.5	381	4,879	267	18.27
W. Rhodes	1900	1,553	455	3,606	261	13.81
J. T. Hearne	1896	2,003.1	818	3,670	257	14.28
A. P. Freeman	1932	1,565.5	404	4,149	253	16.39
W. Rhodes	1901	1,565	505	3,797	251	15.12
T. W. Goddard	1937	1,478.1	359	4,158	248	16.76
W. C. Smith	1910	1,423.3	420	3,225	247	13.05
T. Richardson	1896‡	1,656.2	526	4,015	246	16.32
A. E. Trott	1899‡	1,772.4	587	4,086	239	17.09
T. W. Goddard	1947	1,451.2	344	4,119	238	17.30
M. W. Tate	1925	1,694.3	472	3,415	228	14.97
J. T. Hearne	1898‡	1,802.2	781	3,120	222	14.05
C. W. L. Parker	1925	1,512.3	478	3,311	222	14.91
G. A. Lohmann	1890‡	1,759.1	737	2,998	220	13.62
M. W. Tate	1923	1,608.5	331	3,061	219	13.97
C. F. Root	1925	1,493.2	416	3,770	219	17.21
C. W. L. Parker	1931	1,320.4	386	3,125	219	14.26
H. Verity	1936	1,289.3	463	2,847	216	13.18
G. A. R. Lock	1955	1,408.4	497	3,109	216	14.39
C. Blythe	1909	1,273.5	343	3,128	215	14.54
E. Peate	1882†	1,853.1	868	2,466	214	11.52
A. W. Mold	1895‡	1,629	598	3,400	213	15.96
W. Rhodes	1902	1,306.3	405	2,801	213	13.15
C. W. L. Parker	1926	1,739.5	556	3,920	213	18.40
J. T. Hearne	1893‡	1,741.4	667	3,492	212	16.47
A. P. Freeman	1935	1,503.2	320	4,562	212	21.51
G. A. R. Lock	1957	1,194.1	449	2,550	212	12.02
A. E. Trott	1900	1,547.1	363	4,923	211	23.33
G. G. Macaulay	1925	1,338.2	307	3,268	211	15.48
H. Verity	1935	1,279.2	453	3,032	211	14.36
J. Southerton	1870†	1,876.5	709	3,074	210	14.63
G. A. Lohmann	1888†	1,649.1	783	2,280	209	10.90
C. H. Parkin	1923	1,356.2	356	3,543	209	16.95
G. H. Hirst	1906	1,306.1	271	3,434	208	16.50
F. R. Spofforth	1884†	1,577	653	2,654	207	12.82
A. W. Mold	1894‡	1,288.3	456	2,548	207	12.30
C. W. L. Parker	1922	1,294.5	445	2,712	206	13.16
A. S. Kennedy	1922	1,346.4	366	3,444	205	16.80
M. W. Tate	1924	1,469.5	465	2,818	205	13.74
E. A. McDonald	1925	1,249.4	282	3,828	205	18.67
A. P. Freeman	1934	1,744.4	440	4,753	205	23.18
C. W. L. Parker	1924	1,303.5	411	2,913	204	14.27
G. A. Lohmann	1889‡	1,614.1	646	2,714	202	13.43
H. Verity	1937	1,386.2	487	3,168	202	15.68
A. Shaw	1878†	2,630	1,586	2,203	202	10.89
E. G. Dennett	1907	1,216.2	305	3,227	201	16.05
A. R. Gover	1937	1,219.4	191	3,816	201	18.98
C. H. Parkin	1924	1,162.5	357	2,735	200	13.67
T. W. Goddard	1935	1,553	384	4,073	200	20.36
A. R. Gover	1936	1,159.2	185	3,547	200	17.73
T. W. Goddard	1939§	819	139	2,973	200	14.86
R. Appleyard	1951	1,313.2	391	2,829	200	14.14

† *Indicates 4-ball overs;* ‡ *5-ball overs. All others were 6-ball overs except* § *8-ball overs.*
** *Exclusive of matches not reckoned as first-class.*

?otes: In four consecutive seasons (1928-31), A. P. Freeman took 1,122 wickets, and in eight ?onsecutive seasons (1928-35), 2,090 wickets. In each of these eight seasons he took over 200 ?ickets.

T. Richardson took 1,005 wickets in four consecutive seasons (1894-97).

In 1896, J. T. Hearne took his 100th wicket as early as June 12. In 1931, C. W. L. Parker did ?e same and A. P. Freeman obtained his 100th wicket a day later.

The most wickets in a season since the reduction of Championship matches in 1969 is 134 by ?. D. Marshall (822 overs) in 1982.

100 WICKETS IN A SEASON MOST TIMES

(Includes Overseas Tours and Seasons)

23 times: W. Rhodes 200 wkts (3).

20 times: D. Shackleton (In successive seasons – 1949 to 1968 inclusive).

17 times: A. P. Freeman 300 wkts (1), 200 wkts (7).

16 times: T. W. Goddard 200 wkts (4), C. W. L. Parker 200 wkts (5), R. T. D. Perks, . J. Titmus.

15 times: J. T. Hearne 200 wkts (3), G. H. Hirst 200 wkts (1), A. S. Kennedy 200 wkts (1).

14 times: C. Blythe 200 wkts (1), W. E. Hollies, G. A. R. Lock 200 wkts (2), M. W. Tate 200 ?kts (3), J. C White.

13 times: J. B. Statham.

12 times: J. Briggs, E. G. Dennett 200 wkts (1), C. Gladwin, D. J. Shepherd, N. I. Thomson, '. S. Trueman.

11 times: A. V. Bedser, G. Geary, S. Haigh, J. C. Laker, M. S. Nichols, A. E. Relf.

10 times: W. Attewell, W. G. Grace, R. Illingworth, H. L. Jackson, V. W. C. Jupp, G. G. ?acaulay 200 wkts (1), W. Mead, T. B. Mitchell, T. Richardson 200 wkts (3), J. Southerton 200 ?kts (1), R. K. Tyldesley, D. L. Underwood, J. H. Wardle, T. G. Wass, D. V. P. Wright.

9 times: W. E. Astill, T. E. Bailey, W. E. Bowes, C. Cook, R. Howorth, J. Mercer, A. W. Mold ?00 wkts (2), J. A. Newman, C. F. Root 200 wkts (1), A. Shaw 200 wkts (1), H. Verity 200 wkts ?).

8 times: T. W. Cartwright, H. Dean, J. A. Flavell, A. R. Gover 200 wkts (2), H. Larwood, ?. A. Lohmann 200 wkts (3), R. Peel, J. M. Sims, F. A. Tarrant, R. Tattersall, G. J. Thompson, ?. E. Tribe, A. W. Wellard, F. E. Woolley, J. A. Young.

100 WICKETS IN A SEASON OUTSIDE ENGLAND

W		Season	Country	R	Avge
?16	M. W. Tate	1926-27	India/Ceylon	1,599	13.78
?07	Ijaz Faqih	1985-86	Pakistan	1,719	16.06
?06	C. T. B. Turner ...	1887-88	Australia	1,441	13.59
?06	R. Benaud	1957-58	South Africa	2,056	19.39
?04	S. F. Barnes	1913-14	South Africa	1,117	10.74
?04	Sajjad Akbar	1989-90	Pakistan	2,328	22.38
?03	Abdul Qadir	1982-83	Pakistan	2,367	22.98

1,500 WICKETS IN A CAREER

?ates in italics denote the first half of an overseas season; i.e. *1970* denotes the 1970-71 season.

	Career	W	R	Avge
V. Rhodes	1898-1930	4,187	69,993	16.71
?. P. Freeman	1914-36	3,776	69,577	18.42
?. W. L. Parker	1903-35	3,278	63,817	19.46
?. T. Hearne	1888-1923	3,061	54,352	17.75
. W. Goddard	1922-52	2,979	59,116	19.84
V. G. Grace	1865-1908	2,876	51,545	17.92

	Career	W	R	Avg
A. S. Kennedy	1907-36	2,874	61,034	21.2
D. Shackleton	1948-69	2,857	53,303	18.6
G. A. R. Lock	1946-*70*	2,844	54,709	19.2
F. J. Titmus	1949-82	2,830	63,313	22.3
M. W. Tate	1912-37	2,784	50,571	18.1
G. H. Hirst	1891-1929	2,739	51,282	18.7
C. Blythe	1899-1914	2,506	42,136	16.8
D. L. Underwood	1963-87	2,465	49,993	20.2
W. E. Astill	1906-39	2,431	57,783	23.7
J. C. White	1909-37	2,356	43,759	18.5
W. E. Hollies	1932-57	2,323	48,656	20.9
F. S. Trueman	1949-69	2,304	42,154	18.2
J. B. Statham	1950-68	2,260	36,995	16.3
R. T. D. Perks	1930-55	2,233	53,770	24.0
J. Briggs	1879-1900	2,221	35,430	15.9
D. J. Shepherd	1950-72	2,218	47,302	21.3
E. G. Dennett	1903-26	2,147	42,571	19.8
T. Richardson	1892-1905	2,104	38,794	18.4
T. E. Bailey	1945-67	2,082	48,170	23.1
R. Illingworth	1951-83	2,072	42,023	20.2
N. Gifford	1960-88	2,068	48,731	23.5
F. E. Woolley	1906-38	2,068	41,066	19.8
G. Geary	1912-38	2,063	41,339	20.0
D. V. P. Wright	1932-57	2,056	49,307	23.9
J. A. Newman	1906-30	2,032	51,111	25.1
†A. Shaw	1864-97	2,027	24,580	12.1
S. Haigh	1895-1913	2,012	32,091	15.9
H. Verity	1930-39	1,956	29,146	14.9
W. Attewell	1881-1900	1,950	29,896	15.3
J. C. Laker	1946-*64*	1,944	35,791	18.4
A. V. Bedser	1939-60	1,924	39,279	20.4
W. Mead	1892-1913	1,916	36,388	18.9
A. E. Relf	1900-21	1,897	39,724	20.9
P. G. H. Fender	1910-36	1,894	47,458	25.0
J. W. H. T. Douglas	1901-30	1,893	44,159	23.3
J. H. Wardle	1946-*67*	1,846	35,027	18.9
G. R. Cox	1895-1928	1,843	42,136	22.8
G. A. Lohmann	1884-97	1,841	25,295	13.7
J. W. Hearne	1909-36	1,839	44,926	24.4
G. G. Macaulay	1920-35	1,837	32,440	17.6
M. S. Nichols	1924-39	1,833	39,666	21.6
J. B. Mortimore	1950-75	1,807	41,904	23.1
C. Cook	1946-64	1,782	36,578	20.5
R. Peel	1882-99	1,753	28,442	16.2
H. L. Jackson	1947-63	1,733	30,101	17.3
J. K. Lever	1967-89	1,722	41,772	24.2
T. P. B. Smith	1929-52	1,697	45,059	26.5
J. Southerton	1854-79	1,681	24,290	14.4
A. E. Trott	*1892*-1911	1,674	35,317	21.0
A. W. Mold	1889-1901	1,673	26,010	15.5
T. G. Wass	1896-1920	1,666	34,092	20.4
V. W. C. Jupp	1909-38	1,658	38,166	23.0
C. Gladwin	1939-58	1,653	30,265	18.3
W. E. Bowes	1928-47	1,639	27,470	16.7
A. W. Wellard	1927-50	1,614	39,302	24.3
P. I. Pocock	1964-86	1,607	42,648	26.5
N. I. Thomson	1952-72	1,597	32,867	20.5
J. Mercer	1919-47	1,591	37,210	23.3
G. J. Thompson	1897-1922	1,591	30,058	18.8
J. M. Sims	1929-53	1,581	39,401	24.9
T. Emmett	1866-88	1,571	21,314	13.5

	Career	W	R	Avge
ntikhab Alam	1957-82	1,571	43,474	27.67
s. S. Bedi	1961-81	1,560	33,843	21.69
V. Voce	1927-52	1,558	35,961	23.08
A. R. Gover	1928-48	1,555	36,753	23.63
T. W. Cartwright	1952-77	1,536	29,357	19.11
K. Higgs	1958-86	1,536	36,267	23.61
ames Langridge	1924-53	1,530	34,524	22.56
. A. Flavell	1949-67	1,529	32,847	21.48
C. F. Root	1910-33	1,512	31,933	21.11
R. K. Tyldesley	1919-35	1,509	25,980	17.21

† *The figures for A. Shaw exclude one wicket for which no analysis is available.*

Note: Some works of reference provide career figures which differ from those in this list, owing to the exclusion or inclusion of matches recognised or not recognised as first-class by *Wisden.* Those figures are:

	Career	W	R	Avge
W. Rhodes	1898-1930	4,204	70,322	16.72
W. G. Grace	1865-1908	2,808	50,982	18.15
G. H. Hirst	1891-1929	2,742	51,372	18.73
C. Blythe	1899-1914	2,503	42,099	16.81
E. G. Dennett	1903-26	2,151	42,640	19.82
F. E. Woolley	1906-38	2,066	41,058	19.87
J. A. Newman	1906-30	2,054	51,397	25.03
R. Peel	1882-99	1,776	28,758	16.19

ALL-ROUND RECORDS

HUNDRED AND TEN WICKETS IN ONE INNINGS

V. E. Walker, England v Surrey at The Oval; 20*, 108, ten for 74, and four for 17.		1859
W. G. Grace, MCC v Oxford University at Oxford; 104, two for 60, and ten for 49.		1886

Note: E. M. Grace, for MCC v Gentlemen of Kent in a 12-a-side match at Canterbury in 1862, scored 192* and took five for 77 and ten for 69.

TWO HUNDRED RUNS AND SIXTEEN WICKETS

G. Giffen, South Australia v Victoria at Adelaide; 271, nine for 96, and seven for 70.   1891-92

HUNDRED IN EACH INNINGS AND FIVE WICKETS TWICE

G. H. Hirst, Yorkshire v Somerset at Bath; 111, 117*, six for 70, and five for 45.   1906

HUNDRED IN EACH INNINGS AND TEN WICKETS

B. J. T. Bosanquet, Middlesex v Sussex at Lord's; 103, 100*, three for 75, and
eight for 53   1905
F. D. Stephenson, Nottinghamshire v Yorkshire at Nottingham; 111, 117, four for
105, and seven for 117   1988

HUNDRED AND HAT-TRICK

G. Giffen, Australians v Lancashire at Manchester; 13, 113, and six for 55 including
    hat-trick 1884

W. E. Roller, Surrey v Sussex at The Oval; 204, four for 28 including hat-trick, and
    two for 16. (Unique instance of 200 and hat-trick.) 1885

W. B. Burns, Worcestershire v Gloucestershire at Worcester; 102*, three for 56
    including hat-trick, and two for 21 1913

V. W. C. Jupp, Sussex v Essex at Colchester; 102, six for 61 including hat-trick, and
    six for 78 1921

R. E. S. Wyatt, MCC v Ceylon at Colombo; 124 and five for 39 including hat-trick. 1926-27

L. N. Constantine, West Indians v Northamptonshire at Northampton; seven for 45
    including hat-trick, 107 (five 6s), and six for 67 1928

D. E. Davies, Glamorgan v Leicestershire at Leicester; 139, four for 27, and three for
    31 including hat-trick 1937

V. M. Merchant, Dr C. R. Pereira's XI v Sir Homi Mehta's XI at Bombay; 1, 142,
    three for 31 including hat-trick, and no wicket for 17 1946-47

M. J. Procter, Gloucestershire v Essex at Westcliff-on-Sea; 51, 102, three for 43, and
    five for 30 including hat-trick (all lbw) 1972

M. J. Procter, Gloucestershire v Leicestershire at Bristol; 122, no wkt for 32, and
    seven for 26 including hat-trick 1979

Note: W. G. Grace, for MCC v Kent in a 12-a-side match at Canterbury in 1874, scored 123 and
took five for 82 and six for 47 including a hat-trick.

SEASON DOUBLES

2,000 RUNS AND 200 WICKETS

1906	G. H. Hirst	2,385 runs and 208 wickets

3,000 RUNS AND 100 WICKETS

1937	J. H. Parks	3,003 runs and 101 wickets

2,000 RUNS AND 100 WICKETS

	Season	R	W		Season	R	W
W. G. Grace	1873	2,139	106	F. E. Woolley	1914	2,272	125
W. G. Grace	1876	2,622	129	J. W. Hearne	1920	2,148	142
C. L. Townsend	1899	2,440	101	V. W. C. Jupp	1921	2,169	121
G. L. Jessop	1900	2,210	104	F. E. Woolley	1921	2,101	167
G. H. Hirst	1904	2,501	132	F. E. Woolley	1922	2,022	163
G. H. Hirst	1905	2,266	110	F. E. Woolley	1923	2,091	101
W. Rhodes	1909	2,094	141	L. F. Townsend	1933	2,268	100
W. Rhodes	1911	2,261	117	D. E. Davies	1937	2,012	103
F. A. Tarrant	1911	2,030	111	James Langridge	1937	2,082	101
J. W. Hearne	1913	2,036	124	T. E Bailey	1959	2,011	100
J. W. Hearne	1914	2,116	123				

1,000 RUNS AND 200 WICKETS

	Season	R	W		Season	R	W
A. E. Trott	1899	1,175	239	M. W. Tate	1923	1,168	219
A. E. Trott	1900	1,337	211	M. W. Tate	1924	1,419	205
A. S. Kennedy	1922	1,129	205	M. W. Tate	1925	1,290	228

1,000 RUNS AND 100 WICKETS

Sixteen times: W. Rhodes.   **Fourteen times:** G. H. Hirst.
Ten times: V. W. C. Jupp.   **Nine times:** W. E. Astill.
Eight times: T. E. Bailey, W. G. Grace, M. S. Nichols, A. E. Relf, F. A. Tarrant, M. W. Tate†, F. J. Titmus, F. E. Woolley.
Seven times: G. E. Tribe.
Six times: P. G. H. Fender, R. Illingworth, James Langridge.
Five times: J. W. H. T. Douglas, J. W. Hearne, A. S. Kennedy, J. A. Newman.
Four times: E. G. Arnold, J. Gunn, R. Kilner, B. R. Knight.
Three times: W. W. Armstrong (Australians), L. C. Braund, G. Giffen (Australians), N. E. Haig, R. Howorth, C. B. Llewellyn, J. B. Mortimore, Ray Smith, S. G. Smith, L. F. Townsend, A. W. Wellard.

† *M. W. Tate also scored 1,193 runs and took 116 wickets for MCC in first-class matches on the 1926-27 MCC tour of India and Ceylon.*

Note: R. J. Hadlee (1984) and F. D. Stephenson (1988) are the only players to perform the feat since the reduction of County Championship matches. A complete list of those performing the feat before then will be found on p. 202 of the 1982 *Wisden*.

WICKET-KEEPERS' DOUBLE

	Season	R	D
L. E. G. Ames	1928	1,919	122
L. E. G. Ames	1929	1,795	128
L. E. G. Ames	1932	2,482	104
J. T. Murray	1957	1,025	104

20,000 RUNS AND 2,000 WICKETS IN A CAREER

	Career	R	Avge	W	Avge	'Doubles'
W. E. Astill	1906-39	22,731	22.55	2,431	23.76	9
T. E. Bailey	1945-67	28,642	33.42	2,082	23.13	8
W. G. Grace	1865-1908	54,896	39.55	2,876	17.92	8
G. H. Hirst	1891-1929	36,323	34.13	2,739	18.72	14
R. Illingworth	1951-83	24,134	28.06	2,072	20.28	6
W. Rhodes	1898-1930	39,802	30.83	4,187	16.71	16
M. W. Tate	1912-37	21,717	25.01	2,784	18.16	8
F. J. Titmus	1949-82	21,588	23.11	2,830	22.37	8
F. E. Woolley	1906-38	58,969	40.75	2,068	19.85	8

WICKET-KEEPING RECORDS

MOST DISMISSALS IN AN INNINGS

8 (all ct)	A. T. W. Grout	Queensland v Western Australia at Brisbane	1959-60
8 (all ct)†	D. E. East	Essex v Somerset at Taunton	1985
7 (4ct, 3st)	E. J. Smith	Warwickshire v Derbyshire at Birmingham	1926
7 (6ct, 1st)	W. Farrimond	Lancashire v Kent at Manchester	1930
7 (all ct)	W. F. F. Price	Middlesex v Yorkshire at Lord's	1937
7 (3ct, 4st)	D. Tallon	Queensland v Victoria at Brisbane	1938-39
7 (all ct)	R. A. Saggers	New South Wales v Combined XI at Brisbane	1940-41
7 (1ct, 6st)	H. Yarnold	Worcestershire v Scotland at Dundee	1951
7 (4ct, 3st)	J. Brown	Scotland v Ireland at Dublin	1957
7 (6ct, 1st)	N. Kirsten	Border v Rhodesia at East London	1959-60
7 (all ct)	M. S. Smith	Natal v Border at East London	1959-60
7 (all ct)	K. V. Andrew	Northamptonshire v Lancashire at Manchester	1962

7 (all ct)	A. Long	Surrey v Sussex at Hove	1964
7 (all ct)	R. M. Schofield	Central Districts v Wellington at Wellington	1964-65
7 (all ct)	R. W. Taylor	Derbyshire v Glamorgan at Derby	1966
7 (6ct, 1st)	H. B. Taber	New South Wales v South Australia at Adelaide ..	1968-69
7 (6ct, 1st)	E. W. Jones	Glamorgan v Cambridge University at Cambridge.	1970
7 (6ct, 1st)	S. Benjamin	Central Zone v North Zone at Bombay	1973-74
7 (all ct)	R. W. Taylor	Derbyshire v Yorkshire at Chesterfield	1975
7 (6ct, 1st)	Shahid Israr	Karachi Whites v Quetta at Karachi	1976-77
7 (4ct, 3st)	Wasim Bari	PIA v Sind at Lahore	1977-78
7 (all ct)	J. A. Maclean	Queensland v Victoria at Melbourne	1977-78
7 (5ct, 2st)	Taslim Arif	National Bank v Punjab at Lahore	1978-79
7 (all ct)	Wasim Bari	Pakistan v New Zealand at Auckland	1978-79
7 (all ct)	R. W. Taylor	England v India at Bombay	1979-80
7 (all ct)	D. L. Bairstow	Yorkshire v Derbyshire at Scarborough	1982
7 (6ct, 1st)	R. B. Phillips	Queensland v New Zealanders at Bundaberg	1982-83
7 (3ct, 4st)	Masood Iqbal	Habib Bank v Lahore at Lahore	1982-83
7 (3ct, 4st)	Arif-ud-Din	United Bank v PACO at Sahiwal	1983-84
7 (6ct, 1st)	R. J. East	OFS v Western Province B at Cape Town	1984-85
7 (all ct)	B. A. Young	Northern Districts v Canterbury at Christchurch ..	1986-87
7 (all ct)	D. J. Richardson	Eastern Province v OFS at Bloemfontein	1988-89
7 (6ct, 1st)	Dildar Malik	Multan v Faisalabad at Sahiwal	1988-89
7 (all ct)	W. K. Hegg	Lancashire v Derbyshire at Chesterfield	1989
7 (all ct)	Imran Zia	Bahawalpur v Faisalabad at Faisalabad	1989-90

† *The first eight wickets to fall.*

WICKET-KEEPERS' HAT-TRICKS

W. H. Brain, Gloucestershire v Somerset at Cheltenham, 1893 – three stumpings off successive balls from C. L. Townsend.

G. O. Dawkes, Derbyshire v Worcestershire at Kidderminster, 1958 – three catches off successive balls from H. L. Jackson.

R. C. Russell, Gloucestershire v Surrey at The Oval, 1986 – three catches off successive balls from C. A. Walsh and D. V. Lawrence (2).

MOST DISMISSALS IN A MATCH

12 (8ct, 4st)	E. Pooley	Surrey v Sussex at The Oval	1868
12 (9ct, 3st)	D. Tallon	Queensland v New South Wales at Sydney	1938-39
12 (9ct, 3st)	H. B. Taber	New South Wales v South Australia at Adelaide.	1968-69
11 (all ct)	A. Long	Surrey v Sussex at Hove	1964
11 (all ct)	R. W. Marsh	Western Australia v Victoria at Perth	1975-76
11 (all ct)	D. L. Bairstow	Yorkshire v Derbyshire at Scarborough	1982
11 (all ct)	W. K. Hegg	Lancashire v Derbyshire at Chesterfield	1989
11 (all ct)	A. J. Stewart	Surrey v Leicestershire at Leicester	1989
10 (5ct, 5st)	H. Phillips	Sussex v Surrey at The Oval	1872
10 (2ct, 8st)	E. Pooley	Surrey v Kent at The Oval	1878
10 (9ct, 1st)	T. W. Oates	Nottinghamshire v Middlesex at Nottingham ..	1906
10 (1ct, 9st)	F. H. Huish	Kent v Surrey at The Oval	1911
10 (9ct, 1st)	J. C. Hubble	Kent v Gloucestershire at Cheltenham	1923
10 (8ct, 2st)	H. Elliott	Derbyshire v Lancashire at Manchester	1935
10 (7ct, 3st)	P. Corrall	Leicestershire v Sussex at Hove	1936
10 (9ct, 1st)	R. A. Saggers	New South Wales v Combined XI at Brisbane .	1940-41
10 (all ct)	A. E. Wilson	Gloucestershire v Hampshire at Portsmouth ..	1953
10 (7ct, 3st)	B. N. Jarman	South Australia v New South Wales at Adelaide.	1961-62
10 (all ct)	L. A. Johnson	Northamptonshire v Sussex at Worthing	1963
10 (all ct)	R. W. Taylor	Derbyshire v Hampshire at Chesterfield	1963
10 (8ct, 2st)	L. A. Johnson	Northamptonshire v Warwickshire at Birmingham	1965

0 (9ct, 1st)	R. C. Jordon	Victoria v South Australia at Melbourne	1970-71
0 (all ct)	R. W. Marsh†	Western Australia v South Australia at Perth	1976-77
0 (6ct, 4st)	Taslim Arif	National Bank v Punjab at Lahore	1978-79
0 (9ct, 1st)	Arif-ud-Din	United Bank v Karachi B at Karachi	1978-79
0 (all ct)	R. W. Taylor	England v India at Bombay	1979-80
0 (all ct)	R. J. Parks	Hampshire v Derbyshire at Portsmouth	1981
0 (9ct, 1st)	A. Ghosh	Bihar v Assam at Bhagalpur	1981-82
0 (8ct, 2st)	Z. Parkar	Bombay v Maharashtra at Bombay	1981-82
0 (all ct)	R. V. Jennings	Transvaal v Arosa Sri Lankans at Johannesburg	1982-83
0 (9ct, 1st)	Kamal Najamuddin	Karachi v Lahore at Multan	1982-83
0 (all ct)	D. A. Murray	West Indies XI v South Africa at Port Elizabeth.	1983-84
0 (7ct, 3st)	Azhar Abbas	Bahawalpur v Lahore City Greens at Bahawalpur	1983-84
0 (7ct, 3st)	B. N. French	Nottinghamshire v Oxford University at Oxford.	1984
0 (8ct, 2st)	R. J. Ryall	Western Province v Transvaal at Cape Town	1984-85
0 (all ct)	S. J. Rixon	Australian XI v South Africa at Johannesburg	1985-86
0 (8ct, 2st)	Anil Dalpat	Karachi v United Bank at Lahore	1985-86
0 (all ct)	R. V. Jennings	Transvaal v Northern Transvaal at Verwoerdburg	1986-87
0 (all ct)	S. J. Rixon	Australian XI v South Africa at Johannesburg	1986-87
0 (all ct)	R. V. Jennings	Transvaal v Orange Free State at Johannesburg	1986-87
0 (9ct, 1st)	C. J. Richards	Surrey v Sussex at Guildford	1987
0 (all ct)	C. W. Scott	Nottinghamshire v Derbyshire at Derby	1988
0 (all ct)	D. J. Richardson	Eastern Province v OFS at Bloemfontein	1988-89
0 (all ct)	A. N. Aymes	Hampshire v Oxford University at Oxford	1989
0 (all ct)	L. R. Fernando	Moratuwa v Panadura at Moratuwa	1989-90
0 (all ct)	Imran Zia	Bahawalpur v Faisalabad at Faisalabad	1989-90
0 (9ct, 1st)	D. J. Richardson	Eastern Province v N. Transvaal at Verwoerdburg	1989-90

† *Marsh also scored a hundred (104), a unique "double".*

MOST DISMISSALS IN A SEASON

128 (79ct, 49st)	L. E. G. Ames	Kent	1929
122 (70ct, 52st)	L. E. G. Ames	Kent	1928
110 (63ct, 47st)	H. Yarnold	Worcestershire	1949
107 (77ct, 30st)	G. Duckworth	Lancashire	1928
107 (96ct, 11st)	J. G. Binks	Yorkshire	1960
104 (40ct, 64st)	L. E. G. Ames	Kent	1932
104 (82ct, 22st)	J. T. Murray	Middlesex	1957
102 (69ct, 33st)	F. H. Huish	Kent	1913
102 (95ct, 7st)	J. T. Murray	Middlesex	1960
101 (62ct, 39st)	F. H. Huish	Kent	1911
101 (85ct, 16st)	R. Booth	Worcestershire	1960
100 (91ct, 9st)	R. Booth	Worcestershire	1964

MOST DISMISSALS IN A CAREER

Dates in italics denote the first half of an overseas season; i.e. *1914* denotes the 1914-15 season.

	Career	M	Ct	St	Total
R. W. Taylor	1960-88	639	1,473	176	1,649
J. T. Murray	1952-75	635	1,270	257	1,527
H. Strudwick	1902-27	675	1,242	255	1,497
A. P. E. Knott	1964-85	511	1,211	133	1,344
F. H. Huish	1895-1914	497	933	377	1,310
B. Taylor	1949-73	572	1,083	211	1,294
D. Hunter	1889-1909	548	906	347	1,253

	Career	M	Ct	St	Total
H. R. Butt	1890-1912	550	953	275	1,228
J. H. Board	1891-*1914*	525	852	355	1,207
H. Elliott	1920-47	532	904	302	1,206
J. M. Parks	1949-76	739	1,088	93	1,181
R. Booth	1951-70	468	948	178	1,126
L. E. G. Ames	1926-51	593	703	418	1,121
D. L. Bairstow	1970-90	459	961	138	1,099
G. Duckworth	1923-47	504	753	343	1,096
H. W. Stephenson	1948-64	462	748	334	1,082
J. G. Binks	1955-75	502	895	176	1,071
T. G. Evans	1939-69	465	816	250	1,066
A. Long	1960-80	452	922	124	1,046
G. O. Dawkes	1937-61	482	895	148	1,043
R. W. Tolchard	1965-83	483	912	125	1,037
W. L. Cornford	1921-47	496	675	342	1,017

FIELDING RECORDS

(Excluding wicket-keepers)

Most Catches in an Innings

7	M. J. Stewart	Surrey v Northamptonshire at Northampton	1957
7	A. S. Brown	Gloucestershire v Nottinghamshire at Nottingham	1966

Most Catches in a Match

10	W. R. Hammond†	Gloucestershire v Surrey at Cheltenham	1928
8	W. B. Burns	Worcestershire v Yorkshire at Bradford	1907
8	A. H. Bakewell	Northamptonshire v Essex at Leyton	1928
8	W. R. Hammond	Gloucestershire v Worcestershire at Cheltenham	1932
8	K. J. Grieves	Lancashire v Sussex at Manchester	1951
8	C. A. Milton	Gloucestershire v Sussex at Hove	1952
8	G. A. R. Lock	Surrey v Warwickshire at The Oval	1957
8	J. M. Prodger	Kent v Gloucestershire at Cheltenham	1961
8	P. M. Walker	Glamorgan v Derbyshire at Swansea	1970
8	Javed Miandad	Habib Bank v Universities at Lahore	1977-78
8	Masood Anwar	Rawalpindi v Lahore Division at Rawalpindi	1983-84

† *Hammond also scored a hundred in each innings.*

Most Catches in a Season

78	W. R. Hammond	1928		65	D. W. Richardson	1961
77	M. J. Stewart	1957		64	K. F. Barrington	1957
73	P. M. Walker	1961		64	G. A. R. Lock	1957
71	P. J. Sharpe	1962		63	J. Tunnicliffe	1896
70	J. Tunnicliffe	1901		63	J. Tunnicliffe	1904
69	J. G. Langridge	1955		63	K. J. Grieves	1950
69	P. M. Walker	1960		63	C. A. Milton	1956
66	J. Tunnicliffe	1895		61	J. V. Wilson	1955
65	W. R. Hammond	1925		61	M. J. Stewart	1958
65	P. M. Walker	1959				

Note: The most catches by a fielder since the reduction of County Championship matches in 1969 is 49 by C. J. Tavaré in 1979.

Most Catches in a Career

Dates in italics denote the first half of an overseas season; i.e. *1970* denotes the 1970-71 season.

1,018	F. E. Woolley (1906-38)		784	J. G. Langridge (1928-55)
887	W. G. Grace (1865-1908)		764	W. Rhodes (1898-1930)
830	G. A. R. Lock (1946-*70*)		758	C. A. Milton (1948-74)
819	W. R. Hammond (1920-51)		754	E. H. Hendren (1907-38)
813	D. B. Close (1949-86)			

TEAM RECORDS

HIGHEST TOTALS

1,107	Victoria v New South Wales at Melbourne	1926-27
1,059	Victoria v Tasmania at Melbourne	1922-23
951-7 dec.	Sind v Baluchistan at Karachi	1973-74
918	New South Wales v South Australia at Sydney	1900-01
912-8 dec.	Holkar v Mysore at Indore	1945-46
910-6 dec.	Railways v Dera Ismail Khan at Lahore	1964-65
903-7 dec.	England v Australia at The Oval	1938
887	Yorkshire v Warwickshire at Birmingham	1896
863	Lancashire v Surrey at The Oval	1990
860-6 dec.†	Tamil Nadu v Goa at Panaji	1988-89
849	England v West Indies at Kingston	1929-30
843	Australians v Oxford and Cambridge Universities Past and Present at Portsmouth	1893

† *Tamil Nadu's final total of 912-6 dec. included 52 penalty runs from their opponents' failure to meet the required bowling rate by 13 overs.*

Note: North Zone totalled 868 v West Zone at Bhilai in 1987-88. However, this included 68 penalty runs for West Zone's failure to meet the required bowling rate by 17 overs.

HIGHEST FOR EACH FIRST-CLASS COUNTY

Derbyshire	645	v Hampshire at Derby	1898
Essex	761-6	v Leicestershire at Chelmsford	1990
Glamorgan	587-8	v Derbyshire at Cardiff	1951
Gloucestershire	653-6	v Glamorgan at Bristol	1928
Hampshire	672-7	v Somerset at Taunton	1899
Kent	803-4	v Essex at Brentwood	1934
Lancashire	863	v Surrey at The Oval	1990
Leicestershire	701-4	v Worcestershire at Worcester	1906
Middlesex .	642-3	v Hampshire at Southampton	1923
Northamptonshire .	636-6	v Essex at Chelmsford	1990
Nottinghamshire ...	739-7	v Leicestershire at Nottingham	1903
Somerset	675-9	v Hampshire at Bath	1924
Surrey	811	v Somerset at The Oval	1899
Sussex	705-8	v Surrey at Hastings	1902
Warwickshire	657-6	v Hampshire at Birmingham	1899
Worcestershire	633	v Warwickshire at Worcester	1906
Yorkshire	887	v Warwickshire at Birmingham	1896

LOWEST TOTALS

12	Oxford University v MCC and Ground at Oxford	....	†1877
12	Northamptonshire v Gloucestershire at Gloucester	....	1907
13	Auckland v Canterbury at Auckland	....	1877-78
13	Nottinghamshire v Yorkshire at Nottingham	....	1901
14	Surrey v Essex at Chelmsford	....	1983
15	MCC v Surrey at Lord's	....	1839
15	Victoria v MCC at Melbourne	....	†1903-04
15	Northamptonshire v Yorkshire at Northampton	....	†1908
15	Hampshire v Warwickshire at Birmingham	....	1922
	(Following on, Hampshire scored 521 and won by 155 runs.)		
16	MCC and Ground v Surrey at Lord's	....	1872
16	Derbyshire v Nottinghamshire at Nottingham	....	1879
16	Surrey v Nottinghamshire at The Oval	....	1880
16	Warwickshire v Kent at Tonbridge	....	1913
16	Trinidad v Barbados at Bridgetown	....	1942-43
16	Border v Natal at East London (first innings)	....	1959-60
17	Gentlemen of Kent v Gentlemen of England at Lord's	....	1850
17	Gloucestershire v Australians at Cheltenham	....	1896
18	The Bs v England at Lord's	....	1831
18	Kent v Sussex at Gravesend	....	†1867
18	Tasmania v Victoria at Melbourne	....	1868-69
18	Australians v MCC and Ground at Lord's	....	†1896
18	Border v Natal at East London (second innings)	....	1959-60
19	Sussex v Surrey at Godalming	....	1830
19	Sussex v Nottinghamshire at Hove	....	†1873
19	MCC and Ground v Australians at Lord's	....	1878
19	Wellington v Nelson at Nelson	....	1885-86

† *Signifies that one man was absent.*

Note: At Lord's in 1810, The Bs, with one man absent, were dismissed by England for 6.

LOWEST TOTAL IN A MATCH

34	(16 and 18) Border v Natal at East London	....	1959-60
42	(27 and 15) Northamptonshire v Yorkshire at Northampton	....	1908

Note: Northamptonshire batted one man short in each innings.

LOWEST FOR EACH FIRST-CLASS COUNTY

Derbyshire	16	v Nottinghamshire at Nottingham	1879
Essex	30	v Yorkshire at Leyton	1901
Glamorgan	22	v Lancashire at Liverpool	1924
Gloucestershire	17	v Australians at Cheltenham	1896
Hampshire	15	v Warwickshire at Birmingham	1922
Kent	18	v Sussex at Gravesend	1867
Lancashire	25	v Derbyshire at Manchester	1871
Leicestershire	25	v Kent at Leicester	1912
Middlesex	20	v MCC at Lord's	1864
Northamptonshire	12	v Gloucestershire at Gloucester	1907
Nottinghamshire	13	v Yorkshire at Nottingham	1901
Somerset	25	v Gloucestershire at Bristol	1947
Surrey	14	v Essex at Chelmsford	1983
Sussex	19	v Nottinghamshire at Hove	1873
Warwickshire	16	v Kent at Tonbridge	1913
Worcestershire	24	v Yorkshire at Huddersfield	1903
Yorkshire	23	v Hampshire at Middlesbrough	1965

HIGHEST MATCH AGGREGATES

2,376 for 38 wickets	Maharashtra v Bombay at Poona	1948-49
2,078 for 40 wickets	Bombay v Holkar at Bombay	1944-45
1,981 for 35 wickets	England v South Africa at Durban	1938-39
1,929 for 39 wickets	New South Wales v South Australia at Sydney	1925-26
1,911 for 34 wickets	New South Wales v Victoria at Sydney	1908-09
1,905 for 40 wickets	Otago v Wellington at Dunedin	1923-24

In England

1,723 for 31 wickets	England v Australia at Leeds	1948
1,650 for 19 wickets	Surrey v Lancashire at The Oval	1990
1,641 for 16 wickets	Glamorgan v Worcestershire at Abergavenny	1990
1,614 for 30 wickets	England v India at Manchester	1990
1,603 for 28 wickets	England v India at Lord's	1990
1,601 for 29 wickets	England v Australia at Lord's	1930
1,570 for 29 wickets	Essex v Kent at Chelmsford	1988
1,530 for 19 wickets	Essex v Leicestershire at Chelmsford	1990
1,509 for 36 wickets	Somerset v Worcestershire at Taunton	1990
1,507 for 28 wickets	England v West Indies at The Oval	1976
1,502 for 28 wickets	MCC v New Zealanders at Lord's	1927

LOWEST AGGREGATE IN A COMPLETED MATCH

105 for 31 wickets	MCC v Australians at Lord's	1878

Note: The lowest aggregate since 1900 is 158 for 22 wickets, Surrey v Worcestershire at The Oval, 1954.

HIGHEST FOURTH-INNINGS TOTALS

(Unless otherwise stated, the side making the runs won the match.)

654-5	England v South Africa at Durban	1938-39
	(After being set 696 to win. The match was left drawn on the tenth day.)	
604	Maharashtra v Bombay at Poona	1948-49
	(After being set 959 to win.)	
576-8	Trinidad v Barbados at Port-of-Spain	1945-46
	(After being set 672 to win. Match drawn on fifth day.)	
572	New South Wales v South Australia at Sydney	1907-08
	(After being set 593 to win.)	
529-9	Combined XI v South Africans at Perth	1963-64
	(After being set 579 to win. Match drawn on fourth day.)	
518	Victoria v Queensland at Brisbane	1926-27
	(After being set 753 to win.)	
507-7	Cambridge University v MCC and Ground at Lord's	1896
502-6	Middlesex v Nottinghamshire at Nottingham	1925
	(Game won by an unfinished stand of 271; a county record.)	
502-8	Players v Gentlemen at Lord's	1900
500-7	South African Universities v Western Province at Stellenbosch	1978-79

LARGEST VICTORIES

Largest Innings Victories

Inns and 851 runs:	Railways (910-6 dec.) v Dera Ismail Khan (Lahore)	1964-6:
Inns and 666 runs:	Victoria (1,059) v Tasmania (Melbourne)	1922-2:
Inns and 656 runs:	Victoria (1,107) v New South Wales (Melbourne)	1926-2'
Inns and 605 runs:	New South Wales (918) v South Australia (Sydney)	1900-0]
Inns and 579 runs:	England (903-7 dec.) v Australia (The Oval)	1938
Inns and 575 runs:	Sind (951-7 dec.) v Baluchistan (Karachi)	1973-7¢
Inns and 527 runs:	New South Wales (713) v South Australia (Adelaide)	1908-0¶
Inns and 517 runs:	Australians (675) v Nottinghamshire (Nottingham)	192]

Largest Victories by Runs Margin

685 runs:	New South Wales (235 and 761-8 dec.) v Queensland (Sydney)	1929-3C
675 runs:	England (521 and 342-8 dec.) v Australia (Brisbane)	1928-29
638 runs:	New South Wales (304 and 770) v South Australia (Adelaide)	1920-21
625 runs:	Sargodha (376 and 416) v Lahore Municipal Corporation (Faisalabad)	1978-79
609 runs:	Muslim Commercial Bank (575 and 282-0 dec.) v WAPDA (Lahore).	1977-78
571 runs:	Victoria (304 and 649) v South Australia (Adelaide)	1926-27
562 runs:	Australia (701 and 327) v England (The Oval)	1934

Victory Without Losing a Wicket

Lancashire (166-0 dec. and 66-0) beat Leicestershire by ten wickets (Manchester)	1956
Karachi A (277-0 dec.) beat Sind A by an innings and 77 runs (Karachi)	1957-58
Railways (236-0 dec. and 16-0) beat Jammu and Kashmir by ten wickets (Srinagar)	1960-6]
Karnataka (451-0 dec.) beat Kerala by an innings and 186 runs (Chikmagalur) .	1977-78

TIED MATCHES IN FIRST-CLASS CRICKET

There have been 37 tied matches since the First World War.

Somerset v Sussex at Taunton	1919
(The last Sussex batsman was not allowed to bat under Law 45 [subsequently Law 17 and now Law 31].)	
Orange Free State v Eastern Province at Bloemfontein	1925-26
(Eastern Province had two wickets to fall.)	
Essex v Somerset at Chelmsford	1926
(Although Essex had one man to go in, MCC ruled that the game should rank as a tie. The ninth wicket fell half a minute before time.)	
Gloucestershire v Australians at Bristol	1930
Victoria v MCC at Melbourne	1932-33
(Victoria's third wicket fell to the last ball of the match when one run was needed to win.)	
Worcestershire v Somerset at Kidderminster	1939
Southern Punjab v Baroda at Patiala	1945-46
Essex v Northamptonshire at Ilford	1947
Hampshire v Lancashire at Bournemouth	1947
D. G. Bradman's XI v A. L. Hassett's XI at Melbourne	1948-49
Hampshire v Kent at Southampton	1950
Sussex v Warwickshire at Hove	1952
Essex v Lancashire at Brentwood	1952
Northamptonshire v Middlesex at Peterborough	1953
Yorkshire v Leicestershire at Huddersfield	1954
Sussex v Hampshire at Eastbourne	1955
Victoria v New South Wales at Melbourne	1956-57
T. N. Pearce's XI v New Zealanders at Scarborough	1958
Essex v Gloucestershire at Leyton	1959

Australia v West Indies (First Test) at Brisbane	1960-61
Bahawalpur v Lahore B at Bahawalpur	1961-62
Hampshire v Middlesex at Portsmouth	1967
England XI v England Under-25 XI at Scarborough	1968
Yorkshire v Middlesex at Bradford	1973
Sussex v Essex at Hove	1974
South Australia v Queensland at Adelaide	1976-77
Central Districts v England XI at New Plymouth	1977-78
Victoria v New Zealanders at Melbourne	1982-83
Muslim Commercial Bank v Railways at Sialkot	1983-84
Sussex v Kent at Hastings	1984
Northamptonshire v Kent at Northampton	1984
Eastern Province B v Boland at Albany SC, Port Elizabeth	1985-86
Natal B v Eastern Province B at Pietermaritzburg	1985-86
India v Australia (First Test) at Madras	1986-87
Gloucestershire v Derbyshire at Bristol	1987
Bahawalpur v Peshawar at Bahawalpur	1988-89
Wellington v Canterbury at Wellington	1988-89

Note: Since 1948 a tie has been recognised only when the scores are level with all the wickets down in the fourth innings. This ruling applies to all grades of cricket, and in the case of a one-day match to the second innings, provided that the match has not been brought to a further conclusion.

MATCHES BEGUN AND FINISHED ON FIRST DAY

Since 1900. A fuller list may be found in the Wisden *of 1981 and preceding editions.*

Yorkshire v Worcestershire at Bradford, May 7	1900
MCC and Ground v London County at Lord's, May 20	1903
Transvaal v Orange Free State at Johannesburg, December 30	1906
Middlesex v Gentlemen of Philadelphia at Lord's, July 20	1908
Gloucestershire v Middlesex at Bristol, August 26	1909
Eastern Province v Orange Free State at Port Elizabeth, December 26	1912
Kent v Sussex at Tonbridge, June 21	1919
Lancashire v Somerset at Manchester, May 21	1925
Madras v Mysore at Madras, November 4	1934
Ireland v New Zealanders at Dublin, September 11	1937
Derbyshire v Somerset at Chesterfield, June 11	1947
Lancashire v Sussex at Manchester, July 12	1950
Surrey v Warwickshire at The Oval, May 16	1953
Somerset v Lancashire at Bath, June 6 (H. T. F. Buse's benefit)	1953
Kent v Worcestershire at Tunbridge Wells, June 15	1960

TEST MATCH RECORDS

BATTING RECORDS

HIGHEST INDIVIDUAL INNINGS

365*	G. S. Sobers, West Indies v Pakistan at Kingston	1957-58
364	L. Hutton, England v Australia at The Oval	1938
337	Hanif Mohammad, Pakistan v West Indies at Bridgetown	1957-58
336*	W. R. Hammond, England v New Zealand at Auckland	1932-33
334	D. G. Bradman, Australia v England at Leeds	1930
333	G. A. Gooch, England v India at Lord's	1990
325	A. Sandham, England v West Indies at Kingston	1929-30

311	R. B. Simpson, Australia v England at Manchester	1964
310*	J. H. Edrich, England v New Zealand at Leeds	1965
307	R. M. Cowper, Australia v England at Melbourne	1965-66
304	D. G. Bradman, Australia v England at Leeds	1934
302	L. G. Rowe, West Indies v England at Bridgetown	1973-74
299*	D. G. Bradman, Australia v South Africa at Adelaide	1931-32
291	I. V. A. Richards, West Indies v England at The Oval	1976
287	R. E. Foster, England v Australia at Sydney	1903-04
285*	P. B. H. May, England v West Indies at Birmingham	1957
280*	Javed Miandad, Pakistan v India at Hyderabad	1982-83
278	D. C. S. Compton, England v Pakistan at Nottingham	1954
274	R. G. Pollock, South Africa v Australia at Durban	1969-70
274	Zaheer Abbas, Pakistan v England at Birmingham	1971
271	Javed Miandad, Pakistan v New Zealand at Auckland	1988-89
270*	G. A. Headley, West Indies v England at Kingston	1934-35
270	D. G. Bradman, Australia v England at Melbourne	1936-37
268	G. N. Yallop, Australia v Pakistan at Melbourne	1983-84
266	W. H. Ponsford, Australia v England at The Oval	1934
262*	D. L. Amiss, England v West Indies at Kingston	1973-74
261	F. M. M. Worrell, West Indies v England at Nottingham	1950
260	C. C. Hunte, West Indies v Pakistan at Kingston	1957-58
260	Javed Miandad, Pakistan v England at The Oval	1987
259	G. M. Turner, New Zealand v West Indies at Georgetown	1971-72
258	T. W. Graveney, England v West Indies at Nottingham	1957
258	S. M. Nurse, West Indies v New Zealand at Christchurch	1968-69
256	R. B. Kanhai, West Indies v India at Calcutta	1958-59
256	K. F. Barrington, England v Australia at Manchester	1964
255*	D. J. McGlew, South Africa v New Zealand at Wellington	1952-53
254	D. G. Bradman, Australia v England at Lord's	1930
251	W. R. Hammond, England v Australia at Sydney	1928-29
250	K. D. Walters, Australia v New Zealand at Christchurch	1976-77
250	S. F. A. F. Bacchus, West Indies v India at Kanpur	1978-79

The highest individual innings for other countries are:

236*	S. M. Gavaskar, India v West Indies at Madras	1983-84
201*	D. S. B. P. Kuruppu, Sri Lanka v New Zealand at Colombo (CCC)	1986-87

HUNDRED ON TEST DEBUT

C. Bannerman (165*)	Australia v England at Melbourne	1876-77
W. G. Grace (152)	England v Australia at The Oval	1880
H. Graham (107)	Australia v England at Lord's	1893
†K. S. Ranjitsinhji (154*) ..	England v Australia at Manchester	1896
†P. F. Warner (132*)	England v South Africa at Johannesburg	1898-99
†R. A. Duff (104)	Australia v England at Melbourne	1901-02
R. E. Foster (287)	England v Australia at Sydney	1903-04
G. Gunn (119)	England v Australia at Sydney	1907-08
†R. J. Hartigan (116)	Australia v England at Adelaide	1907-08
†H. L. Collins (104)	Australia v England at Sydney	1920-21
W. H. Ponsford (110)	Australia v England at Sydney	1924-25
A. A. Jackson (164)	Australia v England at Adelaide	1928-29
†G. A. Headley (176)	West Indies v England at Bridgetown	1929-30
J. E. Mills (117)	New Zealand v England at Wellington	1929-30
Nawab of Pataudi sen. (102)	England v Australia at Sydney	1932-33
B. H. Valentine (136)	England v India at Bombay	1933-34
†L. Amarnath (118)	India v England at Bombay	1933-34
†P. A. Gibb (106)	England v South Africa at Johannesburg	1938-39
S. C. Griffith (140)	England v West Indies at Port-of-Spain	1947-48
A. G. Ganteaume (112) ...	West Indies v England at Port-of-Spain	1947-48

†J. W. Burke (101*)	Australia v England at Adelaide	1950-51
P. B. H. May (138)	England v South Africa at Leeds	1951
R. H. Shodhan (110)	India v Pakistan at Calcutta	1952-53
B. H. Pairaudeau (115)	West Indies v India at Port-of-Spain	1952-53
†O. G. Smith (104)	West Indies v Australia at Kingston	1954-55
A. G. Kripal Singh (100*) .	India v New Zealand at Hyderabad	1955-56
C. C. Hunte (142)	West Indies v Pakistan at Bridgetown	1957-58
C. A. Milton (104*)	England v New Zealand at Leeds	1958
†A. A. Baig (112)	India v England at Manchester	1959
Hanumant Singh (105)	India v England at Delhi	1963-64
Khalid Ibadulla (166)	Pakistan v Australia at Karachi	1964-65
B. R. Taylor (105)	New Zealand v India at Calcutta	1964-65
K. D. Walters (155)	Australia v England at Brisbane	1965-66
J. H. Hampshire (107)	England v West Indies at Lord's	1969
†G. R. Viswanath (137)	India v Australia at Kanpur	1969-70
G. S. Chappell (108)	Australia v England at Perth	1970-71
‡L. G. Rowe (214, 100*) . . .	West Indies v New Zealand at Kingston	1971-72
A. I. Kallicharran (100*) . .	West Indies v New Zealand at Georgetown . . .	1971-72
R. E. Redmond (107)	New Zealand v Pakistan at Auckland	1972-73
†F. C. Hayes (106*)	England v West Indies at The Oval	1973
†C. G. Greenidge (107)	West Indies v India at Bangalore	1974-75
†L. Baichan (105*)	West Indies v Pakistan at Lahore	1974-75
G. J. Cosier (109)	Australia v West Indies at Melbourne	1975-76
S. Amarnath (124)	India v New Zealand at Auckland	1975-76
Javed Miandad (163)	Pakistan v New Zealand at Lahore	1976-77
†A. B. Williams (100)	West Indies v Australia at Georgetown	1977-78
†D. M. Wellham (103)	Australia v England at The Oval	1981
†Salim Malik (100*)	Pakistan v Sri Lanka at Karachi	1981-82
K. C. Wessels (162)	Australia v England at Brisbane	1982-83
W. B. Phillips (159)	Australia v Pakistan at Perth	1983-84
§M. Azharuddin (110)	India v England at Calcutta	1984-85
D. S. B. P. Kuruppu (201*)	Sri Lanka v New Zealand at Colombo (CCC) .	1986-87
†M. J. Greatbatch (107*) . .	New Zealand v England at Auckland	1987-88

† *In his second innings of the match.*
‡ *L. G. Rowe is the only batsman to score a hundred in each innings on début.*
§ *M. Azharuddin is the only batsman to score hundreds in each of his first three Tests.*

Note: L. Amarnath and S. Amarnath provide the only instance of a father and son scoring a hundred on début.

300 RUNS IN FIRST TEST

314	L. G. Rowe (214, 100*)	West Indies v New Zealand at Kingston	1971-72
306	R. E. Foster (287, 19)	England v Australia at Sydney	1903-04

TWO SEPARATE HUNDREDS IN A TEST

Three times: S. M. Gavaskar v West Indies (1970-71), v Pakistan (1978-79), v West Indies (1978-79).

Twice in one series: C. L. Walcott v Australia (1954-55).

Twice: H. Sutcliffe v Australia (1924-25), v South Africa (1929); G. A. Headley v England (1929-30 and 1939); G. S. Chappell v New Zealand (1973-74), v West Indies (1975-76); ‡A. R. Border v Pakistan (1979-80), v New Zealand (1985-86).

Once: W. Bardsley v England (1909); A. C. Russell v South Africa (1922-23); W. R. Hammond v Australia (1928-29); E. Paynter v South Africa (1938-39); D. C. S. Compton v Australia (1946-47); A. R. Morris v England (1946-47); A. Melville v England (1947); B. Mitchell v England (1947); D. G. Bradman v India (1947-48); V. S. Hazare v Australia (1947-48); E. D. Weekes v India (1948-49); J. Moroney v South Africa (1949-50); G. S. Sobers v Pakistan (1957-58); R. B. Kanhai v Australia (1960-61); Hanif Mohammad v England (1961-62); R. B. Simpson v Pakistan (1964-65); K. D. Walters v West Indies (1968-69); †L. G. Rowe v New Zealand (1971-72); I. M. Chappell v New Zealand (1973-74); G. M. Turner v Australia (1973-74); C. G. Greenidge v England (1976); G. P. Howarth v England (1977-78); L. R. D. Mendis v India (1982-83); Javed Miandad v New Zealand (1984-85); D. M. Jones v Pakistan (1989-90); G. A. Gooch v India (1990).

† *L. G. Rowe's two hundreds were on his Test début.*

‡ *A. R. Border scored 150* and 153 against Pakistan to become the first batsman to score 150 in each innings of a Test match.*

HUNDRED AND DOUBLE-HUNDRED IN SAME TEST

K. D. Walters (Australia)	242 and 103 v West Indies at Sydney	1968-69
S. M. Gavaskar (India)	124 and 220 v West Indies at Port-of-Spain	1970-71
†L. G. Rowe (West Indies)	214 and 100* v New Zealand at Kingston	1971-72
G. S. Chappell (Australia)	247* and 133 v New Zealand at Wellington	1973-74
‡G. A. Gooch (England)	333 and 123 v India at Lord's	1990

† *On Test début.*

‡ *G. A. Gooch became the first to score a hundred and a triple-hundred in the same first-class match.*

MOST RUNS IN A SERIES

	T	I	NO	R	HI	100s	Avge		
D. G. Bradman ...	5	7	0	974	334	4	139.14	A v E	1930
W. R. Hammond .	5	9	1	905	251	4	113.12	E v A	1928-29
M. A. Taylor	6	11	1	839	219	2	83.90	A v E	1989
R. N. Harvey	5	9	0	834	205	4	92.66	A v SA	1952-53
I. V. A. Richards .	4	7	0	829	291	3	118.42	WI v E	1976
C. L. Walcott	5	10	0	827	155	5	82.70	WI v A	1954-55
G. S. Sobers	5	8	2	824	365*	3	137.33	WI v P	1957-58
D. G. Bradman ...	5	9	0	810	270	3	90.00	A v E	1936-37
D. G. Bradman ...	5	5	1	806	299*	4	201.50	A v SA	1931-32
E. D. Weekes ...	5	7	0	779	194	4	111.28	WI v I	1948-49
†S. M. Gavaskar ..	4	8	3	774	220	4	154.80	I v WI	1970-71
Mudassar Nazar ..	6	8	2	761	231	4	126.83	P v I	1982-83
D. G. Bradman ...	5	8	0	758	304	2	94.75	A v E	1934
D. C. S. Compton	5	8	0	753	208	4	94.12	E v SA	1947
‡G. A. Gooch	3	6	0	752	333	3	125.33	E v I	1990

† *Gavaskar's aggregate was achieved in his first Test series.*

‡ *G. A. Gooch is alone in scoring 1,000 runs in Test cricket during an English season with 1,058 runs in eleven innings against New Zealand and India in 1990.*

1,000 TEST RUNS IN A CALENDAR YEAR

	T	I	NO	R	HI	100s	Avge	Year
I. V. A. Richards (WI)	11	19	0	1,710	291	7	90.00	1976
S. M. Gavaskar (I)	18	27	1	1,555	221	5	59.80	1979
G. R. Viswanath (I)	17	26	3	1,388	179	5	60.34	1979
R. B. Simpson (A)	14	26	3	1,381	311	3	60.04	1964
D. L. Amiss (E)	13	22	2	1,379	262*	5	68.95	1974

	T	I	NO	R	HI	100s	Avge	Year
S. M. Gavaskar (I)	18	32	4	1,310	236*	5	46.78	1983
G. A. Gooch (E)	9	17	1	1,264	333	4	79.00	1990‡
M. A. Taylor (A)	11	20	1	1,219	219	4	64.15	1989†
G. S. Sobers (WI)	7	12	3	1,193	365*	5	132.55	1958
D. B. Vengsarkar (I)	18	27	4	1,174	146*	5	51.04	1979
K. J. Hughes (A)	15	28	4	1,163	130*	2	48.45	1979
D. C. S. Compton (E)	9	15	1	1,159	208	6	82.78	1947
C. G. Greenidge (WI)	14	22	4	1,149	223	4	63.83	1984
A. R. Border (A)	11	20	3	1,099	196	4	64.64	1985
D. M. Jones (A)	11	18	3	1,099	216	4	73.26	1989
I. T. Botham (E)	14	22	0	1,095	208	3	49.77	1982
K. W. R. Fletcher (E)	13	22	4	1,090	178	2	60.55	1973
M. Amarnath (I)	14	24	1	1,077	120	4	46.82	1983
A. R. Border (A)	14	27	3	1,073	162	3	44.70	1979
C. Hill (A)	12	21	2	1,061	142	2	55.84	1902
D. I. Gower (E)	14	25	2	1,061	114	1	46.13	1982
D. I. Gower (E)	14	25	1	1,059	136	2	44.12	1986
W. M. Lawry (A)	14	27	2	1,056	157	2	42.24	1964
S. M. Gavaskar (I)	9	15	2	1,044	205	4	80.30	1978
K. F. Barrington (E)	12	22	2	1,039	132*	3	51.95	1963
E. R. Dexter (E)	11	15	1	1,038	205	2	74.14	1962
K. F. Barrington (E)	10	17	4	1,032	172	4	79.38	1961
Mohsin Khan (P)	10	17	3	1,029	200	4	73.50	1982
D. G. Bradman (A)	8	13	4	1,025	201	5	113.88	1948
S. M. Gavaskar (I)	11	20	1	1,024	156	4	53.89	1976
A. R. Border (A)	11	19	3	1,000	140	5	62.50	1986

† *The year of his début.*   ‡ *Amended to December 1990.*
Notes: The earliest date for completing 1,000 runs is May 3 by M. Amarnath in 1983.
    D. G. Bradman (A) scored 1,005 runs in five consecutive Tests, all against England, in 1936-37 and 1938: 13, 270, 26, 212, 169, 51, 144*, 18, 102*.

MOST RUNS IN A CAREER

(Qualification: 2,000 runs)

ENGLAND

	T	I	NO	R	HI	100s	Avge
G. Boycott	108	193	23	8,114	246*	22	47.72
D. I. Gower	109	189	15	7,674	215	16	44.10
M. C. Cowdrey	114	188	15	7,624	182	22	44.06
W. R. Hammond	85	140	16	7,249	336*	22	58.45
L. Hutton	79	138	15	6,971	364	19	56.67
K. F. Barrington	82	131	15	6,806	256	20	58.67
G. A. Gooch	81	147	5	5,910	333	12	41.61
D. C. S. Compton	78	131	15	5,807	278	17	50.06
J. B. Hobbs	61	102	7	5,410	211	15	56.94
J. H. Edrich	77	127	9	5,138	310*	12	43.54
I. T. Botham	97	154	5	5,119	208	14	34.35
T. W. Graveney	79	123	13	4,882	258	11	44.38
H. Sutcliffe	54	84	9	4,555	194	16	60.73
P. B. H. May	66	106	9	4,537	285*	13	46.77
E. R. Dexter	62	102	8	4,502	205	9	47.89
A. P. E. Knott	95	149	15	4,389	135	5	32.75
A. J. Lamb	67	118	10	3,981	139	13	36.86
M. W. Gatting	68	117	14	3,870	207	9	37.57
D. L. Amiss	50	88	10	3,612	262*	11	46.30
A. W. Greig	58	93	4	3,599	148	8	40.43
E. H. Hendren	51	83	9	3,525	205*	7	47.63

	T	I	NO	R	HI	100s	Avge
F. E. Woolley	64	98	7	3,283	154	5	36.07
K. W. R. Fletcher	59	96	14	3,272	216	7	39.90
M. Leyland	41	65	5	2,764	187	9	46.06
C. Washbrook	37	66	6	2,569	195	6	42.81
B. L. D'Oliveira	44	70	8	2,484	158	5	40.06
D. W. Randall	47	79	5	2,470	174	7	33.37
W. J. Edrich	39	63	2	2,440	219	6	40.00
T. G. Evans	91	133	14	2,439	104	2	20.49
L. E. G. Ames	47	72	12	2,434	149	8	40.56
W. Rhodes	58	98	21	2,325	179	2	30.19
T. E. Bailey	61	91	14	2,290	134*	1	29.74
M. J. K. Smith	50	78	6	2,278	121	3	31.63
P. E. Richardson	34	56	1	2,061	126	5	37.47

AUSTRALIA

	T	I	NO	R	HI	100s	Avge
A. R. Border	115	199	36	8,701	205	23	53.38
G. S. Chappell	87	151	19	7,110	247*	24	53.86
D. G. Bradman	52	80	10	6,996	334	29	99.94
R. N. Harvey	79	137	10	6,149	205	21	48.41
K. D. Walters	74	125	14	5,357	250	15	48.26
I. M. Chappell	75	136	10	5,345	196	14	42.42
W. M. Lawry	67	123	12	5,234	210	13	47.15
R. B. Simpson	62	111	7	4,869	311	10	46.81
I. R. Redpath	66	120	11	4,737	171	8	43.45
K. J. Hughes	70	124	6	4,415	213	9	37.41
R. W. Marsh	96	150	13	3,633	132	3	26.51
A. R. Morris	46	79	3	3,533	206	12	46.48
C. Hill	49	89	2	3,412	191	7	39.21
G. M. Wood	59	112	6	3,374	172	9	31.83
D. C. Boon	48	88	7	3,186	200	8	39.33
V. T. Trumper	48	89	8	3,163	214*	8	39.04
C. C. McDonald	47	83	4	3,107	170	5	39.32
A. L. Hassett	43	69	3	3,073	198*	10	46.56
K. R. Miller	55	87	7	2,958	147	7	36.97
W. W. Armstrong	50	84	10	2,863	159*	6	38.68
K. R. Stackpole	43	80	5	2,807	207	7	37.42
N. C. O'Neill	42	69	8	2,779	181	6	45.55
G. N. Yallop	39	70	3	2,756	268	8	41.13
S. J. McCabe	39	62	5	2,748	232	6	48.21
D. M. Jones	34	59	8	2,637	216	5	51.70
W. Bardsley	41	66	5	2,469	193*	6	40.47
W. M. Woodfull	35	54	4	2,300	161	7	46.00
P. J. Burge	42	68	8	2,290	181	4	38.16
S. E. Gregory	58	100	7	2,282	201	4	24.53
R. Benaud	63	97	7	2,201	122	3	24.45
C. G. Macartney	35	55	4	2,131	170	7	41.78
G. R. Marsh	36	66	3	2,129	138	4	33.79
W. H. Ponsford	29	48	4	2,122	266	7	48.22
R. M. Cowper	27	46	2	2,061	307	5	46.84

SOUTH AFRICA

	T	I	NO	R	HI	100s	Avge
B. Mitchell	42	80	9	3,471	189*	8	48.88
A. D. Nourse	34	62	7	2,960	231	9	53.81
H. W. Taylor	42	76	4	2,936	176	7	40.77
E. J. Barlow	30	57	2	2,516	201	6	45.74
T. L. Goddard	41	78	5	2,516	112	1	34.46

	T	I	NO	R	HI	100s	Avge
D. J. McGlew	34	64	6	2,440	255*	7	42.06
J. H. B. Waite	50	86	7	2,405	134	4	30.44
R. G. Pollock	23	41	4	2,256	274	7	60.97
A. W. Nourse	45	83	8	2,234	111	1	29.78
R. A. McLean	40	73	3	2,120	142	5	30.28

WEST INDIES

	T	I	NO	R	HI	100s	Avge
G. S. Sobers	93	160	21	8,032	365*	26	57.78
I. V. A. Richards	111	166	10	7,990	291	24	51.21
C. H. Lloyd	110	175	14	7,515	242*	19	46.67
C. G. Greenidge	100	170	15	7,134	223	18	46.02
R. B. Kanhai	79	137	6	6,227	256	15	47.53
D. L. Haynes	89	153	17	5,711	184	14	41.99
E. D. Weekes	48	81	5	4,455	207	15	58.61
A. I. Kallicharran	66	109	10	4,399	187	12	44.43
R. C. Fredericks	59	109	7	4,334	169	8	42.49
F. M. M. Worrell	51	87	9	3,860	261	9	49.48
C. L. Walcott	44	74	7	3,798	220	15	56.68
R. B. Richardson	49	83	7	3,515	194	10	46.25
C. C. Hunte	44	78	6	3,245	260	8	45.06
H. A. Gomes	60	91	11	3,171	143	9	39.63
B. F. Butcher	44	78	6	3,104	209*	7	43.11
P. J. L. Dujon	68	96	11	2,994	139	5	35.22
S. M. Nurse	29	54	1	2,523	258	6	47.60
G. A. Headley	22	40	4	2,190	270*	10	60.83
J. B. Stollmeyer	32	56	5	2,159	160	4	42.33
L. G. Rowe	30	49	2	2,047	302	7	43.55

NEW ZEALAND

	T	I	NO	R	HI	100s	Avge
J. G. Wright	71	126	6	4,377	185	10	36.47
B. E. Congdon	61	114	7	3,448	176	7	32.22
J. R. Reid	58	108	5	3,428	142	6	33.28
M. D. Crowe	51	83	9	3,384	188	11	44.52
Sir R. J. Hadlee	86	134	19	3,124	151*	2	27.16
G. M. Turner	41	73	6	2,991	259	7	44.64
B. Sutcliffe	42	76	8	2,727	230*	5	40.10
M. G. Burgess	50	92	6	2,684	119*	5	31.20
J. V. Coney	52	85	14	2,668	174*	3	37.57
G. P. Howarth	47	83	5	2,531	147	6	32.44
G. T. Dowling	39	77	3	2,306	239	3	31.16

INDIA

	T	I	NO	R	HI	100s	Avge
S. M. Gavaskar	125	214	16	10,122	236*	34	51.12
D. B. Vengsarkar	110	175	22	6,703	166	17	43.81
G. R. Viswanath	91	155	10	6,080	222	14	41.93
Kapil Dev	109	158	13	4,521	163	7	31.17
M. Amarnath	69	113	10	4,378	138	11	42.50
P. R. Umrigar	59	94	8	3,631	223	12	42.22
R. J. Shastri	72	109	14	3,372	187	10	35.49
V. L. Manjrekar	55	92	10	3,208	189*	7	39.12
C. G. Borde	55	97	11	3,061	177*	5	35.59

	T	I	NO	R	HI	100s	Avge
M. Azharuddin	40	60	3	2,953	199	10	51.80
Nawab of Pataudi jun.	46	83	3	2,793	203*	6	34.91
S. M. H. Kirmani	88	124	22	2,759	102	2	27.04
F. M. Engineer	46	87	3	2,611	121	2	31.08
Pankaj Roy	43	79	4	2,442	173	5	32.56
V. S. Hazare	30	52	6	2,192	164*	7	47.65
A. L. Wadekar	37	71	3	2,113	143	1	31.07
V. Mankad	44	72	5	2,109	231	5	31.47
C. P. S. Chauhan ...	40	68	2	2,084	97	0	31.57
M. L. Jaisimha	39	71	4	2,056	129	3	30.68
D. N. Sardesai	30	55	4	2,001	212	5	39.23

PAKISTAN

	T	I	NO	R	HI	100s	Avge
Javed Miandad	104	158	18	7,891	280*	22	56.36
Zaheer Abbas	78	124	11	5,062	274	12	44.79
Mudassar Nazar	76	116	8	4,114	231	10	38.09
Majid Khan	63	106	5	3,931	167	8	38.92
Hanif Mohammad ...	55	97	8	3,915	337	12	43.98
Mushtaq Mohammad .	57	100	7	3,643	201	10	39.17
Asif Iqbal	58	99	7	3,575	175	11	38.85
Imran Khan	82	118	22	3,541	136	6	36.88
Saeed Ahmed	41	78	4	2,991	172	5	40.41
Wasim Raja	57	92	14	2,821	125	4	36.16
Salim Malik	57	79	14	2,718	119*	7	41.81
Mohsin Khan	48	79	6	2,709	200	7	37.10
Sadiq Mohammad	41	74	2	2,579	166	5	35.81
Imtiaz Ahmed	41	72	1	2,079	209	3	29.28

SRI LANKA: The highest aggregate is 1,621, average 36.84, by A. Ranatunga in 26 Tests.

HIGHEST AVERAGES

(Qualification: 20 innings)

Avge		T	I	NO	R	HI	100s
99.94	D. G. Bradman (A)	52	80	10	6,996	334	29
64.72	M. A. Taylor (A)	15	27	2	1,618	219	6
60.97	R. G. Pollock (SA)	23	41	4	2,256	274	7
60.83	G. A. Headley (WI)	22	40	4	2,190	270*	10
60.73	H. Sutcliffe (E)	54	84	9	4,555	194	16
59.23	E. Paynter (E)	20	31	5	1,540	243	4
58.67	K. F. Barrington (E)	82	131	15	6,806	256	20
58.61	E. D. Weekes (WI)	48	81	5	4,455	207	15
58.45	W. R. Hammond (E)	85	140	16	7,249	336*	22
57.78	G. S. Sobers (WI)	93	160	21	8,032	365*	26
56.94	J. B. Hobbs (E)	61	102	7	5,410	211	15
56.68	C. L. Walcott (WI)	44	74	7	3,798	220	15
56.67	L. Hutton (E)	79	138	15	6,971	364	19
56.36	Javed Miandad (P)	104	158	18	7,891	280*	22
55.00	E. Tyldesley (E)	14	20	2	990	122	3
54.20	C. A. Davis (WI)	15	29	5	1,301	183	4
53.94	M. J. Greatbatch (NZ)	14	21	4	917	146*	2
53.86	G. S. Chappell (A)	87	151	19	7,110	247*	24

Avge		T	I	NO	R	HI	100s
53.81	A. D. Nourse (SA)	34	62	7	2,960	231	9
53.73	R. A. Smith (E)	18	34	8	1,397	143	4
53.38	A. R. Border (A)	115	199	36	8,701	205	23
51.80	M. Azharuddin (I)	40	60	3	2,953	199	10
51.70	D. M. Jones (A)	34	59	8	2,637	216	9
51.62	J. Ryder (A)	20	32	5	1,394	201*	3
51.21	I. V. A. Richards (WI)	111	166	10	7,990	291	24
51.12	S. M. Gavaskar (I)	125	214	16	10,122	236*	34
50.06	D. C. S. Compton (E)	78	131	15	5,807	278	17

MOST HUNDREDS

Total		E	A	SA	WI	NZ	I	P	SL
34	S. M. Gavaskar (I)	4	8	—	13	2	—	5	2
29	D. G. Bradman (A)	19	—	4	2	—	4	—	—
26	G. S. Sobers (WI)	10	4	—	—	1	8	3	—
24	G. S. Chappell (A)	9	—	5	3	1	6	0	
24	I. V. A. Richards (WI)	8	5	—	—	1	8	2	—
23	A. R. Border (A)	7	—	—	2	4	4	6	0
22	W. R. Hammond (E)	—	9	6	1	4	2	—	
22	M. C. Cowdrey (E)	—	5	3	6	2	3	3	—
22	G. Boycott (E)	—	7	1	5	2	4	3	—
22	Javed Miandad (P)	1	6	—	2	7	5	—	1
21	R. N. Harvey (A)	6	—	8	3	—	4	0	—
20	K. F. Barrington (E)	—	5	2	3	3	3	4	—

CARRYING BAT THROUGH TEST INNINGS

(Figures in brackets show side's total)

A. B. Tancred	26* (47)	South Africa v England at Cape Town ..	1888-89
J. E. Barrett	67* (176)	Australia v England at Lord's	1890
R. Abel	132* (307)	England v Australia at Sydney	1891-92
P. F. Warner	132* (237)	England v South Africa at Johannesburg .	1898-99
W. W. Armstrong ..	159* (309)	Australia v South Africa at Johannesburg	1902-03
J. W. Zulch	43* (103)	South Africa v England at Cape Town ..	1909-10
W. Bardsley	193* (383)	Australia v England at Lord's	1926
W. M. Woodfull ..	30* (66)‡	Australia v England at Brisbane	1928-29
W. M. Woodfull ..	73* (193)†	Australia v England at Adelaide	1932-33
W. A. Brown	206* (422)	Australia v England at Lord's	1938
L. Hutton	202* (344)	England v West Indies at The Oval	1950
L. Hutton	156* (272)	England v Australia at Adelaide	1950-51
Nazar Mohammad ..	124* (331)	Pakistan v India at Lucknow	1952-53
F. M. M. Worrell ..	191* (372)	West Indies v England at Nottingham ...	1957
T. L. Goddard	56* (99)	South Africa v Australia at Cape Town ..	1957-58
D. J. McGlew	127* (292)	South Africa v New Zealand at Durban ..	1961-62
C. C. Hunte	60* (131)	West Indies v Australia at Port-of-Spain .	1964-65
G. M. Turner	43* (131)	New Zealand v England at Lord's	1969
W. M. Lawry	49* (107)	Australia v India at Delhi	1969-70
W. M. Lawry	60* (116)†	Australia v England at Sydney	1970-71
G. M. Turner	223* (386)	New Zealand v West Indies at Kingston .	1971-72
I. R. Redpath	159* (346)	Australia v New Zealand at Auckland ...	1973-74
G. Boycott	99* (215)	England v Australia at Perth	1979-80
S. M. Gavaskar ...	127* (286)	India v Pakistan at Faisalabad	1982-83
Mudassar Nazar ...	152* (323)	Pakistan v India at Lahore	1982-83
S. Wettimuny	63* (144)	Sri Lanka v New Zealand at Christchurch	1982-83
D. C. Boon	58* (103)	Australia v New Zealand at Auckland ...	1985-86
D. L. Haynes	88* (211)	West Indies v Pakistan at Karachi	1986-87

† *One man absent.*   ‡ *Two men absent.*

Notes: G. M. Turner (223*) holds the record for the highest score by a player carrying his bat through a Test innings. He is also the youngest player to do so, being 22 years 63 days old when he first achieved the feat (1969).

Nazar Mohammad and Mudassar Nazar provide the only instance of a father and son carrying their bat through a Test innings.

D. L. Haynes (55 and 105) opened the batting and was last man out in each innings for West Indies v New Zealand at Dunedin, 1979-80.

FASTEST FIFTIES

Minutes

28	J. T. Brown	England v Australia at Melbourne	1894-95
29	S. A. Durani	India v England at Kanpur	1963-64
30	E. A. V. Williams .	West Indies v England at Bridgetown	1947-48
30	B. R. Taylor	New Zealand v West Indies at Auckland	1968-69
33	C. A. Roach	West Indies v England at The Oval	1933
34	C. R. Browne	West Indies v England at Georgetown	1929-30

The fastest fifties in terms of balls received (where recorded) are:

Balls

30	Kapil Dev	India v Pakistan at Karachi (2nd Test)	1982-83
32	I. T. Botham	England v New Zealand at The Oval	1986
32	I. V. A. Richards . .	West Indies v India at Kingston	1982-83
33	R. C. Fredericks . .	West Indies v Australia at Perth	1975-76
33	Kapil Dev	India v Pakistan at Karachi	1978-79
33	Kapil Dev	India v England at Manchester	1982
33	I. V. A. Richards . .	West Indies v England at St John's	1985-86

FASTEST HUNDREDS

Minutes

70	J. M. Gregory	Australia v South Africa at Johannesburg	1921-22
75	G. L. Jessop	England v Australia at The Oval	1902
78	R. Benaud	Australia v West Indies at Kingston	1954-55
80	J. H. Sinclair	South Africa v Australia at Cape Town	1902-03
81	I. V. A. Richards . .	West Indies v England at St John's	1985-86
86	B. R. Taylor	New Zealand v West Indies at Auckland	1968-69

The fastest hundreds in terms of balls received (where recorded) are:

Balls

56	I. V. A. Richards . .	West Indies v England at St John's	1985-86
67	J. M. Gregory	Australia v South Africa at Johannesburg	1921-22
71	R. C. Fredericks . .	West Indies v Australia at Perth	1975-76
74	Kapil Dev	India v Sri Lanka at Kanpur	1986-87
76	G. L. Jessop	England v Australia at The Oval	1902
77	Majid Khan	Pakistan v New Zealand at Karachi	1976-77

FASTEST DOUBLE-HUNDREDS

Minutes

214	D. G. Bradman . . .	Australia v England at Leeds	1930
223	S. J. McCabe	Australia v England at Nottingham	1938
226	V. T. Trumper	Australia v South Africa at Adelaide	1910-11
234	D. G. Bradman . . .	Australia v England at Lord's	1930
240	W. R. Hammond . .	England v New Zealand at Auckland	1932-33
241	S. E. Gregory	Australia v England at Sydney	1894-95
245	D. C. S. Compton .	England v Pakistan at Nottingham	1954

The fastest double-hundreds in terms of balls received (where recorded) are:

Balls

220	I. T. Botham	England v India at The Oval	1982
232	C. G. Greenidge . . .	West Indies v England at Lord's	1984
240	C. H. Lloyd	West Indies v India at Bombay	1974-75
241	Zaheer Abbas	Pakistan v India at Lahore	1982-83
242	D. G. Bradman	Australia v England at The Oval	1934
242	I. V. A. Richards . .	West Indies v Australia at Melbourne	1984-85

FASTEST TRIPLE-HUNDREDS

Minutes

288	W. R. Hammond . .	England v New Zealand at Auckland	1932-33
336	D. G. Bradman . . .	Australia v England at Leeds	1930

MOST RUNS IN A DAY BY A BATSMAN

309	D. G. Bradman	Australia v England at Leeds	1930
295	W. R. Hammond	England v New Zealand at Auckland	1932-33
273	D. C. S. Compton	England v Pakistan at Nottingham	1954
271	D. G. Bradman	Australia v England at Leeds	1934

SLOWEST INDIVIDUAL BATTING

2* in 80 minutes	C. E. H. Croft, West Indies v Australia at Brisbane	1979-80
3* in 100 minutes	J. T. Murray, England v Australia at Sydney	1962-63
5 in 102 minutes	Nawab of Pataudi jun, India v England at Bombay	1972-73
7 in 123 minutes	G. Miller, England v Australia at Melbourne	1978-79
9 in 125 minutes	T. W. Jarvis, New Zealand v India at Madras	1964-65
10* in 133 minutes	T. G. Evans, England v Australia at Adelaide	1946-47
16* in 147 minutes	D. B. Vengsarkar, India v Pakistan at Kanpur	1979-80
17* in 166 minutes	G. M. Ritchie, Australia v India at Sydney	1985-86
18 in 194 minutes	W. R. Playle, New Zealand v England at Leeds	1958
19 in 217 minutes	M. D. Crowe, New Zealand v Sri Lanka at Colombo (SSC) . . .	1983-84
28* in 250 minutes	J. W. Burke, Australia v England at Brisbane	1958-59
31 in 264 minutes	K. D. Mackay, Australia v England at Lord's	1956
34* in 271 minutes	Younis Ahmed, Pakistan v India at Ahmedabad	1986-87
35 in 332 minutes	C. J. Tavaré, England v India at Madras	1981-82
55 in 336 minutes	B. A. Edgar, New Zealand v Australia at Wellington	1981-82
57 in 346 minutes	G. S. Camacho, West Indies v England at Bridgetown	1967-68
58 in 367 minutes	Ijaz Butt, Pakistan v India at Karachi	1959-60
60 in 390 minutes	D. N. Sardesai, India v West Indies at Bridgetown	1961-62
62 in 408 minutes	Ramiz Raja, Pakistan v West Indies at Karachi	1986-87
68 in 458 minutes	T. E. Bailey, England v Australia at Brisbane	1958-59
99 in 505 minutes	M. L. Jaisimha, India v Pakistan at Kanpur	1960-61
105 in 575 minutes	D. J. McGlew, South Africa v Australia at Durban	1957-58
114 in 591 minutes	Mudassar Nazar, Pakistan v England at Lahore	1977-78
120* in 609 minutes	J. J. Crowe, New Zealand v Sri Lanka, Colombo (CCC) .	1986-87
158 in 648 minutes	C. T. Radley, England v New Zealand at Auckland	1977-78
163 in 720 minutes	Shoaib Mohammad, Pakistan v New Zealand at Wellington	1988-89
337 in 970 minutes	Hanif Mohammad, Pakistan v West Indies at Bridgetown	1957-58

SLOWEST HUNDREDS

557 minutes	Mudassar Nazar, Pakistan v England at Lahore	1977-78
545 minutes	D. J. McGlew, South Africa v Australia at Durban	1957-58
515 minutes	J. J. Crowe, New Zealand v Sri Lanka, Colombo (CCC)	1986-87
488 minutes	P. E. Richardson, England v South Africa at Johannesburg	1956-57

Notes: The slowest hundred for any Test in England is 458 minutes (329 balls) by K. W. R.

Fletcher, England v Pakistan, The Oval, 1974.

The slowest double-hundred in a Test was scored in 777 minutes (548 balls) by D. S. B. P. Kuruppu for Sri Lanka v New Zealand at Colombo (CCC), 1986-87, on his début. It is also the slowest-ever first-class double-hundred.

HIGHEST PARTNERSHIPS FOR EACH WICKET

413 for 1st	V. Mankad (231)/Pankaj Roy (173)........	I v NZ	Madras	1955-56
451 for 2nd	W. H. Ponsford (266)/D. G. Bradman (244).	A v E	The Oval	1934
451 for 3rd	Mudassar Nazar (231)/Javed Miandad (280*)	P v I	Hyderabad	1982-83
411 for 4th	P. B. H. May (285*)/M. C. Cowdrey (154)..	E v WI	Birmingham	1957
405 for 5th	S. G. Barnes (234)/D. G. Bradman (234) ...	A v E	Sydney	1946-47
346 for 6th	J. H. W. Fingleton (136)/D. G. Bradman (270)	A v E	Melbourne	1936-37
347 for 7th	D. St E. Atkinson (219)/C. C. Depeiza (122)	WI v A	Bridgetown	1954-55
246 for 8th	L. E. G. Ames (137)/G. O. B. Allen (122) ..	E v NZ	Lord's	1931
190 for 9th	Asif Iqbal (146)/Intikhab Alam (51)	P v E	The Oval	1967
151 for 10th	B. F. Hastings (110)/R. O. Collinge (68*)...	NZ v P	Auckland	1972-73

PARTNERSHIPS OF 300 AND OVER

451 for 2nd	W. H. Ponsford (266)/D. G. Bradman (244) ...	A v E	The Oval	1934
451 for 3rd	Mudassar Nazar (231)/Javed Miandad (280*)..	P v I	Hyderabad	1982-83
446 for 2nd	C. C. Hunte (260)/G. S. Sobers (365*)	WI v P	Kingston	1957-58
413 for 1st	V. Mankad (231)/Pankaj Roy (173)	I v NZ	Madras	1955-56
411 for 4th	P. B. H. May (285*)/M. C. Cowdrey (154) ...	E v WI	Birmingham	1957
405 for 5th	S. G. Barnes (234)/D. G. Bradman (234)	A v E	Sydney	1946-47
399 for 4th	G. S. Sobers (226)/F. M. M. Worrell (197*) ...	WI v E	Bridgetown	1959-60
397 for 3rd	Qasim Omar (206)/Javed Miandad (203*)	P v SL	Faisalabad	1985-86
388 for 4th	W. H. Ponsford (181)/D. G. Bradman (304) ...	A v E	Leeds	1934
387 for 1st	G. M. Turner (259)/T. W. Jarvis (182)	NZ v WI	Georgetown	1971-72
382 for 2nd	L. Hutton (364)/M. Leyland (187)	E v A	The Oval	1938
382 for 1st	W. M. Lawry (210)/R. B. Simpson (201)	A v WI	Bridgetown	1964-65
370 for 3rd	W. J. Edrich (189)/D. C. S. Compton (208) ...	E v SA	Lord's	1947
369 for 2nd	J. H. Edrich (310*)/K. F. Barrington (163)	E v NZ	Leeds	1965
359 for 1st	L. Hutton (158)/C. Washbrook (195)	E v SA	Johannesburg	1948-49
351 for 2nd	G. A. Gooch (196)/D. I. Gower (157)	E v A	The Oval	1985
350 for 4th	Mushtaq Mohammad (201)/Asif Iqbal (175) ...	P v NZ	Dunedin	1972-73
347 for 7th	D. St E. Atkinson (219)/C. C. Depeiza (122) ...	WI v A	Bridgetown	1954-55
346 for 6th	J. H. Fingleton (136)/D. G. Bradman (270) ...	A v E	Melbourne	1936-37
344* for 2nd	S. M. Gavaskar (182*)/D. B. Vengsarkar (157*)	I v WI	Calcutta	1978-79
341 for 3rd	E. J. Barlow (201)/R. G. Pollock (175)	SA v A	Adelaide	1963-64
338 for 3rd	E. D. Weekes (206)/F. M. M. Worrell (167) ...	WI v E	Port-of-Spain	1953-54
336 for 4th	W. M. Lawry (151)/K. D. Walters (242)	A v WI	Sydney	1968-69
331 for 2nd	R. T. Robinson (148)/D. I. Gower (215)	E v A	Birmingham	1985
329 for 1st	G. R. Marsh (138)/M. A. Taylor (219)	A v E	Nottingham	1989
323 for 1st	J. B. Hobbs (178)/W. Rhodes (179)	E v A	Melbourne	1911-12
319 for 3rd	A. Melville (189)/A. D. Nourse (149)	SA v E	Nottingham	1947
316† for 3rd	G. R. Viswanath (222)/Yashpal Sharma (140) .	I v E	Madras	1981-82
308 for 7th	Waqar Hassan (189)/Imtiaz Ahmed (209)	P v NZ	Lahore	1955-56
308 for 3rd	R. B. Richardson (154)/I. V. A. Richards (178)	WI v A	St John's	1983-84
308 for 3rd	G. A. Gooch (333)/A. J. Lamb (139)	E v I	Lord's	1990
303 for 3rd	I. V. A. Richards (232)/A. I. Kallicharran (97).	WI v E	Nottingham	1976
301 for 2nd	A. R. Morris (182)/D. G. Bradman (173*)	A v E	Leeds	1948

† 415 runs were scored for this wicket in two separate partnerships: D. B. Vengsarkar retired hurt when he and Viswanath had added 99 runs.

BOWLING RECORDS

MOST WICKETS IN AN INNINGS

10-53	J. C. Laker	England v Australia at Manchester	1956
9-28	G. A. Lohmann	England v South Africa at Johannesburg	1895-96
9-37	J. C. Laker	England v Australia at Manchester	1956
9-52	R. J. Hadlee	New Zealand v Australia at Brisbane	1985-86
9-56	Abdul Qadir	Pakistan v England at Lahore	1987-88
9-69	J. M. Patel	India v Australia at Kanpur	1959-60
9-83	Kapil Dev	India v West Indies at Ahmedabad	1983-84
9-86	Sarfraz Nawaz	Pakistan v Australia at Melbourne	1978-79
9-95	J. M. Noreiga	West Indies v India at Port-of-Spain	1970-71
9-102	S. P. Gupte	India v West Indies at Kanpur	1958-59
9-103	S. F. Barnes	England v South Africa at Johannesburg	1913-14
9-113	H. J. Tayfield	South Africa v England at Johannesburg	1956-57
9-121	A. A. Mailey	Australia v England at Melbourne	1920-21
8-7	G. A. Lohmann	England v South Africa at Port Elizabeth	1895-96
8-11	J. Briggs	England v South Africa at Cape Town	1888-89
8-29	S. F. Barnes	England v South Africa at The Oval	1912
8-29	C. E. H. Croft	West Indies v Pakistan at Port-of-Spain	1976-77
8-31	F. Laver	Australia v England at Manchester	1909
8-31	F. S. Trueman	England v India at Manchester	1952
8-34	I. T. Botham	England v Pakistan at Lord's	1978
8-35	G. A. Lohmann	England v Australia at Sydney	1886-87
8-38	L. R. Gibbs	West Indies v India at Bridgetown	1961-62
8-43†	A. E. Trott	Australia v England at Adelaide	1894-95
8-43	H. Verity	England v Australia at Lord's	1934
8-43	R. G. D. Willis	England v Australia at Leeds	1981
8-45	C. E. L. Ambrose	West Indies v England at Bridgetown	1989-90
8-51	D. L. Underwood	England v Pakistan at Lord's	1974
8-52	V. Mankad	India v Pakistan at Delhi	1952-53
8-53	G. B. Lawrence	South Africa v New Zealand at Johannesburg	1961-62
8-53†	R. A. L. Massie	Australia v England at Lord's	1972
8-55	V. Mankad	India v England at Madras	1951-52
8-56	S. F. Barnes	England v South Africa at Johannesburg	1913-14
8-58	G. A. Lohmann	England v Australia at Sydney	1891-92
8-58	Imran Khan	Pakistan v Sri Lanka at Lahore	1981-82
8-59	C. Blythe	England v South Africa at Leeds	1907
8-59	A. A. Mallett	Australia v Pakistan at Adelaide	1972-73
8-60	Imran Khan	Pakistan v India at Karachi	1982-83
8-61†	N. D. Hirwani	India v West Indies at Madras	1987-88
8-65	H. Trumble	Australia v England at The Oval	1902
8-68	W. Rhodes	England v Australia at Melbourne	1903-04
8-69	H. J. Tayfield	South Africa v England at Durban	1956-57
8-69	Sikander Bakht	Pakistan v India at Delhi	1979-80
8-70	S. J. Snooke	South Africa v England at Johannesburg	1905-06
8-71	G. D. McKenzie	Australia v West Indies at Melbourne	1968-69
8-72	S. Venkataraghavan	India v New Zealand at Delhi	1964-65
8-75†	N. D. Hirwani	India v West Indies at Madras	1987-88
8-76	E. A. S. Prasanna	India v New Zealand at Auckland	1975-76
8-79	B. S. Chandrasekhar	India v England at Delhi	1972-73
8-81	L. C. Braund	England v Australia at Melbourne	1903-04
8-83	J. R. Ratnayeke	Sri Lanka v Pakistan at Sialkot	1985-86
8-84†	R. A. L. Massie	Australia v England at Lord's	1972
8-85	Kapil Dev	India v Pakistan at Lahore	1982-83
8-86	A. W. Greig	England v West Indies at Port-of-Spain	1973-74
8-87	M. G. Hughes	Australia v West Indies at Perth	1988-89
8-92	M. A. Holding	West Indies v England at The Oval	1976
8-94	T. Richardson	England v Australia at Sydney	1897-98
8-103	I. T. Botham	England v West Indies at Lord's	1984

8-104†	A. L. Valentine	...	West Indies v England at Manchester	....	1950
8-106	Kapil Dev	....	India v Australia at Adelaide	....	1985-86
8-107	B. J. T. Bosanquet	.	England v Australia at Nottingham	....	1905
8-107	N. A. Foster	......	England v Pakistan at Leeds	....	1987
8-112	G. F. Lawson	.....	Australia v West Indies at Adelaide	....	1984-85
8-126	J. C. White	....	England v Australia at Adelaide	....	1928-29
8-141	C. J. McDermott	..	Australia v England at Manchester	....	1985
8-143	M. H. N. Walker	..	Australia v England at Melbourne	....	1974-75

† *On Test début.*

OUTSTANDING ANALYSES

	O	*M*	*R*	*W*		
J. C. Laker (E)	51.2	23	53	10	v Australia at Manchester	1956
G. A. Lohmann (E)	14.2	6	28	9	v South Africa at Johannesburg	1895-96
J. C. Laker (E)	16.4	4	37	9	v Australia at Manchester	1956
G. A. Lohmann (E)	9.4	5	7	8	v South Africa at Port Elizabeth	1895-96
J. Briggs (E)	14.2	5	11	8	v South Africa at Cape Town ..	1888-89
J. Briggs (E)	19.1	11	17	7	v South Africa at Cape Town ..	1888-89
M. A. Noble (A)	7.4	2	17	7	v England at Melbourne	1901-02
W. Rhodes (E)	11	3	17	7	v Australia at Birmingham	1902
A. E. R. Gilligan (E)	6.3	4	7	6	v South Africa at Birmingham ..	1924
S. Haigh (E)	11.4	6	11	6	v South Africa at Cape Town ..	1898-99
D. L. Underwood (E)	11.6	7	12	6	v New Zealand at Christchurch	1970-71
H. J. Tayfield (SA)	14	7	13	6	v New Zealand at Johannesburg.	1953-54
C. T. B. Turner (A)	18	11	15	6	v England at Sydney	1886-87
M. H. N. Walker (A)	16	8	15	6	v Pakistan at Sydney	1972-73
E. R. H. Toshack (A)	2.3	1	2	5	v India at Brisbane	1947-48
H. Ironmonger (A)	7.2	5	6	5	v South Africa at Melbourne ...	1931-32
Pervez Sajjad (P)	12	8	5	4	v New Zealand at Rawalpindi ..	1964-65
K. Higgs (E)	9	7	5	4	v New Zealand at Christchurch.	1965-66
P. H. Edmonds (E)	8	6	6	4	v Pakistan at Lord's	1978
J. C. White (E)	6.3	2	7	4	v Australia at Brisbane	1928-29
J. H. Wardle (E)	5	2	7	4	v Australia at Manchester	1953
R. Appleyard (E)	6	3	7	4	v New Zealand at Auckland ...	1954-55
R. Benaud (A)	3.4	3	0	3	v India at Delhi	1959-60

MOST WICKETS IN A MATCH

19-90	J. C. Laker	....	England v Australia at Manchester	....	1956
17-159	S. F. Barnes	......	England v South Africa at Johannesburg	......	1913-14
16-136†	N. D. Hirwani	....	India v West Indies at Madras	....	1987-88
16-137†	R. A. L. Massie	..	Australia v England at Lord's	....	1972
15-28	J. Briggs	....	England v South Africa at Cape Town	....	1888-89
15-45	G. A. Lohmann	...	England v South Africa at Port Elizabeth	.....	1895-96
15-99	C. Blythe	....	England v South Africa at Leeds	....	1907
15-104	H. Verity	....	England v Australia at Lord's	....	1934
15-123	R. J. Hadlee	......	New Zealand v Australia at Brisbane	....	1985-86
15-124	W. Rhodes	....	England v Australia at Melbourne	....	1903-04
14-90	F. R. Spofforth	....	Australia v England at The Oval	....	1882
14-99	A. V. Bedser	......	England v Australia at Nottingham	....	1953
14-102	W. Bates	....	England v Australia at Melbourne	....	1882-83
14-116	Imran Khan	......	Pakistan v Sri Lanka at Lahore	....	1981-82
14-124	J. M. Patel	....	India v Australia at Kanpur	....	1959-60
14-144	S. F. Barnes	......	England v South Africa at Durban	....	1913-14
14-149	M. A. Holding	...	West Indies v England at The Oval	....	1976
14-199	C. V. Grimmett	...	Australia v South Africa at Adelaide	....	1931-32

† *On Test début.*

Notes: The best for South Africa is 13-165 by H. J. Tayfield against Australia at Melbourne, 1952-53.

The best for Sri Lanka is 9-125 by R. J. Ratnayake against India at Colombo (PSS), 1985-86.

MOST WICKETS IN A SERIES

	T	R	W	Avge		
S. F. Barnes	4	536	49	10.93	England v South Africa	1913-14
C. Laker	5	442	46	9.60	England v Australia	1956
C. V. Grimmett	5	642	44	14.59	Australia v South Africa	1935-36
T. M. Alderman	6	893	42	21.26	Australia v England	1981
R. M. Hogg	6	527	41	12.85	Australia v England	1978-79
T. M. Alderman	6	712	41	17.36	Australia v England	1989
Imran Khan	6	558	40	13.95	Pakistan v India	1982-83
A. V. Bedser	5	682	39	17.48	England v Australia	1953
D. K. Lillee	6	870	39	22.30	Australia v England	1981
M. W. Tate	5	881	38	23.18	England v Australia	1924-25
W. J. Whitty	5	632	37	17.08	Australia v South Africa	1910-11
H. J. Tayfield	5	636	37	17.18	South Africa v England	1956-57
A. E. E. Vogler	5	783	36	21.75	South Africa v England	1909-10
A. A. Mailey	5	946	36	26.27	Australia v England	1920-21
G. A. Lohmann	3	203	35	5.80	England v South Africa	1895-96
B. S. Chandrasekhar	5	662	35	18.91	India v England	1972-73
M. D. Marshall	5	443	35	12.65	West Indies v England	1988

MOST WICKETS IN A CAREER

(Qualification: 100 wickets)

ENGLAND

	T	Balls	R	W	Avge	5 W/i	10 W/m
I. T. Botham	97	21,281	10,633	376	28.27	27	4
R. G. D. Willis	90	17,357	8,190	325	25.20	16	—
F. S. Trueman	67	15,178	6,625	307	21.57	17	3
D. L. Underwood	86	21,862	7,674	297	25.83	17	6
J. B. Statham	70	16,056	6,261	252	24.84	9	1
A. V. Bedser	51	15,918	5,876	236	24.89	15	5
J. A. Snow	49	12,021	5,387	202	26.66	8	1
J. C. Laker	46	12,027	4,101	193	21.24	9	3
S. F. Barnes	27	7,873	3,106	189	16.43	24	7
G. A. R. Lock	49	13,147	4,451	174	25.58	9	3
M. W. Tate	39	12,523	4,055	155	26.16	7	1
F. J. Titmus	53	15,118	4,931	153	32.22	7	—
H. Verity	40	11,173	3,510	144	24.37	5	2
C. M. Old	46	8,858	4,020	143	28.11	4	—
A. W. Greig	58	9,802	4,541	141	32.20	6	2
G. R. Dilley	41	8,192	4,107	138	29.76	6	—
J. E. Emburey	60	14,227	5,105	138	36.99	6	—
T. E. Bailey	61	9,712	3,856	132	29.21	5	1
W. Rhodes	58	8,231	3,425	127	26.96	6	1
P. H. Edmonds	51	12,028	4,273	125	34.18	2	—
D. A. Allen	39	11,297	3,779	122	30.97	4	—
R. Illingworth	61	11,934	3,807	122	31.20	3	—
J. Briggs	33	5,332	2,094	118	17.74	9	4
G. G. Arnold	34	7,650	3,254	115	28.29	6	—
G. A. Lohmann	18	3,821	1,205	112	10.75	9	5
D. V. P. Wright	34	8,135	4,224	108	39.11	6	1
R. Peel	20	5,216	1,715	102	16.81	6	2
J. H. Wardle	28	6,597	2,080	102	20.39	5	1
C. Blythe	19	4,546	1,863	100	18.63	9	4

AUSTRALIA

	T	Balls	R	W	Avge	5 W/i	10 W/r
D. K. Lillee	70	18,467	8,493	355	23.92	23	7
R. Benaud	63	19,108	6,704	248	27.03	16	1
G. D. McKenzie	60	17,681	7,328	246	29.78	16	3
R. R. Lindwall	61	13,650	5,251	228	23.03	12	—
C. V. Grimmett	37	14,513	5,231	216	24.21	21	7
J. R. Thomson	51	10,535	5,601	200	28.00	8	—
A. K. Davidson	44	11,587	3,819	186	20.53	14	2
G. F. Lawson	46	11,118	5,501	180	30.56	11	2
K. R. Miller	55	10,461	3,906	170	22.97	7	1
W. A. Johnston	40	11,048	3,826	160	23.91	7	—
T. M. Alderman	35	9,152	4,083	153	26.68	13	1
W. J. O'Reilly	27	10,024	3,254	144	22.59	11	3
H. Trumble	32	8,099	3,072	141	21.78	9	3
M. H. N. Walker	34	10,094	3,792	138	27.47	6	—
A. A. Mallett	38	9,990	3,940	132	29.84	6	1
B. Yardley	33	8,909	3,986	126	31.63	6	1
R. M. Hogg	38	7,633	3,503	123	28.47	6	2
M. A. Noble	42	7,159	3,025	121	25.00	9	2
I. W. Johnson	45	8,780	3,182	109	29.19	3	—
G. Giffen	31	6,391	2,791	103	27.09	7	1
A. N. Connolly	29	7,818	2,981	102	29.22	4	—
C. T. B. Turner	17	5,179	1,670	101	16.53	11	2

SOUTH AFRICA

	T	Balls	R	W	Avge	5 W/i	10 W/r
H. J. Tayfield	37	13,568	4,405	170	25.91	14	2
T. L. Goddard	41	11,736	3,226	123	26.22	5	—
P. M. Pollock	28	6,522	2,806	116	24.18	9	1
N. A. T. Adcock	26	6,391	2,195	104	21.10	5	—

WEST INDIES

	T	Balls	R	W	Avge	5 W/i	10 W/r
M. D. Marshall	68	15,221	6,831	329	20.76	22	4
L. R. Gibbs	79	27,115	8,989	309	29.09	18	2
J. Garner	58	13,169	5,433	259	20.97	7	—
M. A. Holding	60	12,680	5,898	249	23.68	13	2
G. S. Sobers	93	21,599	7,999	235	34.03	6	—
A. M. E. Roberts	47	11,136	5,174	202	25.61	11	2
W. W. Hall	48	10,421	5,066	192	26.38	9	1
S. Ramadhin	43	13,939	4,579	158	28.98	10	1
A. L. Valentine	36	12,953	4,215	139	30.32	8	2
C. A. Walsh	37	7,177	3,201	134	23.88	5	1
C. E. H. Croft	27	6,165	2,913	125	23.30	3	—
V. A. Holder	40	9,095	3,627	109	33.27	3	—

NEW ZEALAND

	T	Balls	R	W	Avge	5 W/i	10 W/r
Sir R. J. Hadlee	86	21,918	9,611	431	22.29	36	9
B. L. Cairns	43	10,628	4,280	130	32.92	6	1
E. J. Chatfield	43	10,360	3,958	123	32.17	3	1
R. O. Collinge	35	7,689	3,392	116	29.24	3	—
B. R. Taylor	30	6,334	2,953	111	26.60	4	—
J. G. Bracewell	41	8,403	3,653	102	35.81	4	1
R. C. Motz	32	7,034	3,148	100	31.48	5	—

INDIA

	T	Balls	R	W	Avge	5 W/i	10 W/m
Kapil Dev	109	23,037	11,199	371	30.18	21	2
B. S. Bedi	67	21,364	7,637	266	28.71	14	1
B. S. Chandrasekhar . .	58	15,963	7,199	242	29.74	16	2
E. A. S. Prasanna	49	14,353	5,742	189	30.38	10	2
V. Mankad	44	14,686	5,236	162	32.32	8	2
S. Venkataraghavan . .	57	14,877	5,634	156	36.11	3	1
S. P. Gupte	36	11,284	4,403	149	29.55	12	1
R. J. Shastri	72	15,103	5,914	143	41.35	2	—
D. R. Doshi	33	9,322	3,502	114	30.71	6	—
K. D. Ghavri	39	7,042	3,656	109	33.54	4	—
N. S. Yadav	35	8,349	3,580	102	35.09	3	—

PAKISTAN

	T	Balls	R	W	Avge	5 W/i	10 W/m
Imran Khan	82	19,290	8,188	358	22.87	23	6
Abdul Qadir	63	16,592	7,458	230	32.42	15	5
Sarfraz Nawaz	55	13,927	5,798	177	32.75	4	1
Iqbal Qasim	50	13,019	4,807	171	28.11	8	2
Fazal Mahmood	34	9,834	3,434	139	24.70	13	4
Intikhab Alam	47	10,474	4,494	125	35.95	5	2
Wasim Akram	32	7,017	2,967	111	26.72	8	2

SRI LANKA: The highest aggregate is 59 wickets, average 36.94, by A. L. F. de Mel in 17 Tests.

WICKET WITH FIRST BALL IN TEST CRICKET

	Batsman dismissed			
A. Coningham	A. C. MacLaren	A v E	Melbourne	1894-95
W. M. Bradley	F. Laver	E v A	Manchester	1899
E. G. Arnold	V. T. Trumper	E v A	Sydney	1903-04
G. Macaulay	G. A. L. Hearne	E v SA	Cape Town	1922-23
M. W. Tate	M. J. Susskind	E v SA	Birmingham	1924
M. Henderson	E. W. Dawson	NZ v E	Christchurch	1929-30
H. D. Smith	E. Paynter	NZ v E	Christchurch	1932-33
T. F. Johnson	W. W. Keeton	WI v E	The Oval	1939
R. Howorth	D. V. Dyer	E v SA	The Oval	1947
Intikhab Alam	C. C. McDonald	P v A	Karachi	1959-60

HAT-TRICKS

F. R. Spofforth	Australia v England at Melbourne	1878-79
W. Bates	England v Australia at Melbourne	1882-83
J. Briggs	England v Australia at Sydney	1891-92
G. A. Lohmann	England v South Africa at Port Elizabeth	1895-96
J. T. Hearne	England v Australia at Leeds	1899
H. Trumble	Australia v England at Melbourne	1901-02
H. Trumble	Australia v England at Melbourne	1903-04
T. J. Matthews† . . . T. J. Matthews	} Australia v South Africa at Manchester	1912
M. J. C. Allom‡ . . .	England v New Zealand at Christchurch	1929-30

T. W. Goddard	England v South Africa at Johannesburg	1938-39
P. J. Loader	England v West Indies at Leeds	1957
L. F. Kline	Australia v South Africa at Cape Town	1957-58
W. W. Hall	West Indies v Pakistan at Lahore	1958-59
G. M. Griffin	South Africa v England at Lord's	1960
L. R. Gibbs	West Indies v Australia at Adelaide	1960-61
P. J. Petherick‡ . . .	New Zealand v Pakistan at Lahore	1976-77
C. A. Walsh§	West Indies v Australia at Brisbane	1988-89
M. G. Hughes§	Australia v West Indies at Perth	1988-89

    † *T. J. Matthews did the hat-trick in each innings of the same match.*
    ‡ *On Test début.*
    § *Not all in the same innings.*

MOST BALLS BOWLED IN A TEST

S. Ramadhin (West Indies) sent down 774 balls in 129 overs against England at Birmingham, 1957. It was the most delivered by any bowler in a Test, beating H. Verity's 766 for England against South Africa at Durban, 1938-39. In this match Ramadhin also bowled the most balls (588) in any single first-class innings, including Tests.

    It should be noted that six balls were bowled to the over in the Australia v England Test series of 1928-29 and 1932-33, when the eight-ball over was otherwise in force in Australia.

ALL-ROUND RECORDS

100 RUNS AND FIVE WICKETS IN AN INNINGS

England

A. W. Greig	148	6-164	v West Indies	Bridgetown	1973-74
I. T. Botham	103	5-73	v New Zealand	Christchurch	1977-78
I. T. Botham	108	8-34	v Pakistan	Lord's	1978
I. T. Botham	114	6-58 7-48 }	v India	Bombay	1979-80
I. T. Botham	149*	6-95	v Australia	Leeds	1981
I. T. Botham	138	5-59	v New Zealand	Wellington	1983-84

Australia

C. Kelleway	114	5-33	v South Africa	Manchester	1912
J. M. Gregory	100	7-69	v England	Melbourne	1920-21
K. R. Miller	109	6-107	v West Indies	Kingston	1954-55
R. Benaud	100	5-84	v South Africa	Johannesburg	1957-58

South Africa

J. H. Sinclair	106	6-26	v England	Cape Town	1898-99
G. A. Faulkner	123	5-120	v England	Johannesburg	1909-10

West Indies

D. St E. Atkinson	219	5-56	v Australia	Bridgetown	1954-55
O. G. Smith	100	5-90	v India	Delhi	1958-59
G. S. Sobers	104	5-63	v India	Kingston	1961-62
G. S. Sobers	174	5-41	v England	Leeds	1966

New Zealand

B. R. Taylor†	105	5-86	v India	Calcutta	1964-65

India

V. Mankad	184	5-196	v England	Lord's	1952
P. R. Umrigar	172*	5-107	v West Indies	Port-of-Spain	1961-62

Pakistan

Mushtaq Mohammad	201	5-49	v New Zealand	Dunedin	1972-73
Mushtaq Mohammad	121	5-28	v West Indies	Port-of-Spain	1976-77
Imran Khan	117	6-98 5-82 }	v India	Faisalabad	1982-83
Wasim Akram	123	5-100	v Australia	Adelaide	1989-90

    † *On début.*

100 RUNS AND FIVE DISMISSALS IN AN INNINGS

D. T. Lindsay	182	6ct	SA v A	Johannesburg	1966-67
D. S. Smith	113*	4ct, 1st	NZ v E	Auckland	1983-84
A. R. Silva	111	5ct	SL v I	Colombo (PSS)	1985-86

100 RUNS AND TEN WICKETS IN A TEST

A. K. Davidson	44 80	5-135 } 6-87 }	A v WI	Brisbane	1960-61
I. T. Botham	114	6-58 } 7-48 }	E v I	Bombay	1979-80
Imran Khan	117	6-98 } 5-82 }	P v I	Faisalabad	1982-83

1,000 RUNS AND 100 WICKETS IN A CAREER

	Tests	Runs	Wkts	Tests for Double
England				
T. E. Bailey	61	2,290	132	47
I. T. Botham	97	5,119	376	21
J. E. Emburey	60	1,540	138	46
A. W. Greig	58	3,599	141	37
R. Illingworth	61	1,836	122	47
W. Rhodes	58	2,325	127	44
M. W. Tate	39	1,198	155	33
F. J. Titmus	53	1,449	153	40
Australia				
R. Benaud	63	2,201	248	32
A. K. Davidson	44	1,328	186	34
G. Giffen	31	1,238	103	30
I. W. Johnson	45	1,000	109	45
R. R. Lindwall	61	1,502	228	38
K. R. Miller	55	2,958	170	33
M. A. Noble	42	1,997	121	27
South Africa				
T. L. Goddard	41	2,516	123	36
West Indies				
M. D. Marshall	68	1,457	329	49
G. S. Sobers	93	8,032	235	48
New Zealand				
J. G. Bracewell	41	1,001	102	41
Sir R. J. Hadlee	86	3,124	431	28
India				
Kapil Dev	109	4,521	371	25
V. Mankad	44	2,109	162	23
R. J. Shastri	72	3,372	143	44
Pakistan				
Abdul Qadir	63	1,022	230	62
Imran Khan	82	3,541	358	30
Intikhab Alam	47	1,493	125	41
Sarfraz Nawaz	55	1,045	177	55

1,000 RUNS, 100 WICKETS AND 100 CATCHES

	Tests	Runs	Wkts	Ct
I. T. Botham	97	5,119	376	112
G. S. Sobers	93	8,032	235	109

WICKET-KEEPING RECORDS

Most Dismissals in an Innings

7 (all ct)	Wasim Bari	Pakistan v New Zealand at Auckland ...	1978-79
7 (all ct)	R. W. Taylor	England v India at Bombay	1979-80
6 (all ct)	A. T. W. Grout ...	Australia v South Africa at Johannesburg	1957-58
6 (all ct)	D. T. Lindsay	South Africa v Australia at Johannesburg	1966-67
6 (all ct)	J. T. Murray	England v India at Lord's	1967
6 (5ct, 1st)	S. M. H. Kirmani .	India v New Zealand at Christchurch ...	1975-76
6 (all ct)	R. W. Marsh	Australia v England at Brisbane	1982-83
6 (all ct)	S. A. R. Silva	Sri Lanka v India at Colombo (SSC)	1985-86

Note: The most stumpings in an innings is 5 by K. S. More for India v West Indies at Madras in 1987-88.

Most Dismissals in One Test

10 (all ct)	R. W. Taylor	England v India at Bombay	1979-80
9 (8ct, 1st)	G. R. A. Langley ..	Australia v England at Lord's	1956
9 (all ct)	D. A. Murray	West Indies v Australia at Melbourne ...	1981-82
9 (all ct)	R. W. Marsh	Australia v England at Brisbane	1982-83
9 (all ct)	S. A. R. Silva	Sri Lanka v India at Colombo (SSC)	1985-86
9 (8ct, 1st)	S. A. R. Silva	Sri Lanka v India at Colombo (PSS)	1985-86
8 (all ct)	J. J. Kelly	Australia v England at Sydney	1901-02
8 (6ct, 2st)	L. E. G. Ames	England v West Indies at The Oval	1933
8 (all ct)	G. R. A. Langley ..	Australia v West Indies at Kingston	1954-55
8 (6ct, 2st)	A. T. W. Grout ...	Australia v Pakistan at Lahore	1959-60
8 (all ct)	A. T. W. Grout ...	Australia v England at Lord's	1961
8 (all ct)	J. M. Parks	England v New Zealand at Christchurch .	1965-66
8 (all ct)	D. T. Lindsay	South Africa v Australia at Johannesburg	1966-67
8 (7ct, 1st)	H. B. Taber	Australia v South Africa at Johannesburg	1966-67
8 (all ct)	Wasim Bari	Pakistan v England at Leeds...........	1971
8 (all ct)	R. W. Marsh	Australia v West Indies at Melbourne ...	1975-76
8 (all ct)	R. W. Marsh	Australia v New Zealand at Christchurch	1976-77
8 (7ct, 1st)	R. W. Marsh	Australia v India at Sydney	1980-81
8 (all ct)	W. K. Lees	New Zealand v Sri Lanka at Wellington .	1982-83
8 (all ct)	R. W. Marsh	Australia v England at Adelaide	1982-83

Notes: S. A. R. Silva made 18 dismissals in two successive Tests.

The most stumpings in a match is 6 by K. S. More for India v West Indies at Madras in 1987-88.

Most Dismissals in a Series

(Played in 5 Tests unless otherwise stated)

28 (all ct)	R. W. Marsh	Australia v England	1982-83
26 (23ct, 3st)	J. H. B. Waite	South Africa v New Zealand	1961-62
26 (all ct)	R. W. Marsh	Australia v West Indies (6 Tests)	1975-76
24 (22ct, 2st)	D. L. Murray	West Indies v England	1963
24 (all ct)	D. T. Lindsay	South Africa v Australia	1966-67

(21ct, 3st)	A. P. E. Knott	England v Australia (6 Tests)	1970-71
(16ct, 7st)	J. H. B. Waite	South Africa v New Zealand	1953-54
(22ct, 1st)	F. C. M. Alexander.	West Indies v England	1959-60
(20ct, 2st)	A. T. W. Grout	Australia v West Indies	1960-61
(21ct, 2st)	A. E. Dick	New Zealand v South Africa	1961-62
(21ct, 2st)	R. W. Marsh	Australia v England	1972
(22ct, 1st)	A. P. E. Knott	England v Australia (6 Tests)	1974-75
(all ct)	R. W. Marsh	Australia v England (6 Tests)	1981
(all ct)	S. J. Rixon	Australia v India	1977-78
(21ct, 1st)	S. A. R. Silva	Sri Lanka v India (3 Tests)	1985-86
(15ct, 6st)	H. Strudwick	England v South Africa	1913-14
(13ct, 8st)	R. A. Saggers	Australia v South Africa	1949-50
(16ct, 5st)	G. R. A. Langley ..	Australia v West Indies	1951-52
(20ct, 1st)	A. T. W. Grout ...	Australia v England	1961
(all ct)	R. W. Marsh	Australia v Pakistan	1983-84
(16ct, 4st)	D. Tallon	Australia v England	1946-47
(16ct, 4st)	G. R. A. Langley ..	Australia v West Indies (4 Tests)	1954-55
(18ct, 2st)	T. G. Evans	England v South Africa	1956-57
(17ct, 3st)	A. T. W. Grout ...	Australia v England	1958-59
(19ct, 1st)	H. B. Taber	Australia v South Africa	1966-67
(18ct, 2st)	R. W. Taylor	England v Australia (6 Tests)	1978-79
(19ct, 1st)	P. J. L. Dujon	West Indies v Australia	1983-84
(19ct, 1st)	P. R. Downton	England v Australia (6 Tests)	1985
(all ct)	P. J. L. Dujon	West Indies v England	1988

Most Dismissals in a Career

	T	Ct	St	Total
R. W. Marsh (Australia)	96	343	12	355
A. P. E. Knott (England)	95	250	19	269
Wasim Bari (Pakistan)	81	201	27	228
P. J. L. Dujon (West Indies)	68	218	5	223
T. G. Evans (England)	91	173	46	219
S. M. H. Kirmani (India)	88	160	38	198
D. L. Murray (West Indies)	62	181	8	189
A. T. W. Grout (Australia)..................	51	163	24	187
R. W. Taylor (England)	57	167	7	174
I. D. S. Smith (New Zealand)	55	143	8	151
J. H. B. Waite (South Africa)	50	124	17	141
W. A. Oldfield (Australia)..................	54	78	52	130
J. M. Parks (England)	46	103	11	114

Notes: The records for P. J. L. Dujon and J. M. Parks each include two catches taken when not keeping wicket in two and three Tests respectively.

S. A. R. Silva (33ct, 1st) has made most dismissals for Sri Lanka.

FIELDING RECORDS

(Excluding wicket-keepers)

Most Catches in an Innings

V. Y. Richardson	Australia v South Africa at Durban	1935-36
Yajurvindra Singh	India v England at Bangalore	1976-77
M. Azharuddin	India v Pakistan at Karachi	1989-90

Most Catches in One Test

7	G. S. Chappell	Australia v England at Perth	1974-7
7	Yajurvindra Singh	India v England at Bangalore	1976-7
6	A. Shrewsbury	England v Australia at Sydney	1887-8
6	A. E. E. Vogler	South Africa v England at Durban	1909-1
6	F. E. Woolley	England v Australia at Sydney	1911-1
6	J. M. Gregory	Australia v England at Sydney	1920-2
6	B. Mitchell	South Africa v Australia at Melbourne	1931-3
6	V. Y. Richardson	Australia v South Africa at Durban	1935-3
6	R. N. Harvey	Australia v England at Sydney	1962-6
6	M. C. Cowdrey	England v West Indies at Lord's	196
6	E. D. Solkar	India v West Indies at Port-of-Spain	1970-7
6	G. S. Sobers	West Indies v England at Lord's	197
6	I. M. Chappell	Australia v New Zealand at Adelaide	1973-7
6	A. W. Greig	England v Pakistan at Leeds	197
6	D. F. Whatmore	Australia v India at Kanpur	1979-8
6	A. J. Lamb	England v New Zealand at Lord's	198

Most Catches in a Series

15	J. M. Gregory	Australia v England	1920-2
14	G. S. Chappell	Australia v England (6 Tests)	1974-7
13	R. B. Simpson	Australia v South Africa	1957-5
13	R. B. Simpson	Australia v West Indies	1960-6

Most Catches in a Career

A. R. Border (Australia)	125 in 115 matches
G. S. Chappell (Australia)	122 in 87 matches
M. C. Cowdrey (England)	120 in 114 matches
I. V. A. Richards (West Indies) .	116 in 111 matches
I. T. Botham (England)	112 in 97 matches
R. B. Simpson (Australia)	110 in 62 matches
W. R. Hammond (England)	110 in 85 matches
G. S. Sobers (West Indies)	109 in 93 matches
S. M. Gavaskar (India)	108 in 125 matches
I. M. Chappell (Australia)	105 in 75 matches

TEAM RECORDS

HIGHEST INNINGS TOTALS

903-7 dec.	England v Australia at The Oval	19.
849	England v West Indies at Kingston	1929-
790-3 dec.	West Indies v Pakistan at Kingston	1957-
758-8 dec.	Australia v West Indies at Kingston	1954-
729-6 dec.	Australia v England at Lord's	19
708	Pakistan v England at The Oval	19
701	Australia v England at The Oval	19
699-5	Pakistan v India at Lahore	1989-
695	Australia v England at The Oval	19
687-8 dec.	West Indies v England at The Oval	19
681-8 dec.	West Indies v England at Port-of-Spain	1953-
676-7	India v Sri Lanka at Kanpur	1986-
674-6	Pakistan v India at Faisalabad	1984-
674	Australia v India at Adelaide	1947-
668	Australia v West Indies at Bridgetown	1954-
659-8 dec.	Australia v England at Sydney	1946-
658-8 dec.	England v Australia at Nottingham	19
657-8 dec.	Pakistan v West Indies at Bridgetown	1957-
656-8 dec.	Australia v England at Manchester	19

54-5	England v South Africa at Durban	1938-39
53-4 dec.	England v India at Lord's	1990
52-7 dec.	England v India at Madras	1984-85
52-8 dec.	West Indies v England at Lord's	1973
52	Pakistan v India at Faisalabad	1982-83
50-6 dec.	Australia v West Indies at Bridgetown	1964-65

The highest innings for the countries not mentioned above are:

22-9 dec.	South Africa v Australia at Durban	1969-70
53-7 dec.	New Zealand v Australia at Brisbane	1985-86
91-7 dec.	Sri Lanka v England at Lord's	1984

HIGHEST FOURTH-INNINGS TOTALS

o win

06-4	India (needing 403) v West Indies at Port-of-Spain	1975-76
04-3	Australia (needing 404) v England at Leeds	1948
52-7	Australia (needing 359) v West Indies at Georgetown	1977-78
48-5	West Indies (needing 345) v New Zealand at Auckland	1968-69
44-1	West Indies (needing 342) v England at Lord's	1984

o tie

47	India v Australia at Madras	1986-87

o draw

54-5	England (needing 696 to win) v South Africa at Durban	1938-39
29-8	India (needing 438 to win) v England at The Oval	1979
23-7	South Africa (needing 451 to win) v England at The Oval	1947
08-5	West Indies (needing 836 to win) v England at Kingston	1929-30

o lose

45	India (lost by 47 runs) v Australia at Adelaide	1977-78
40	New Zealand (lost by 38 runs) v England at Nottingham	1973
17	England (lost by 45 runs) v Australia at Melbourne	1976-77
11	England (lost by 193 runs) v Australia at Sydney	1924-25

MOST RUNS IN A DAY (BOTH SIDES)

88	England (398-6), India (190-0) at Manchester (2nd day)	1936
22	England (503-2), South Africa (19-0) at Lord's (2nd day)	1924
08	England (221-2), South Africa (287-6) at The Oval (3rd day)	1935

MOST RUNS IN A DAY (ONE SIDE)

03	England (503-2) v South Africa at Lord's (2nd day)	1924
94	Australia (494-6) v South Africa at Sydney (1st day)	1910-11
75	Australia (475-2) v England at The Oval (1st day)	1934
71	England (471-8) v India at The Oval (1st day)	1936
58	Australia (458-3) v England at Leeds (1st day)	1930
55	Australia (455-1) v England at Leeds (2nd day)	1934

MOST WICKETS IN A DAY

27	England (18-3 to 53 out and 62) v Australia (60) at Lord's (2nd day)	188
25	Australia (112 and 48-5) v England (61) at Melbourne (1st day)	1901-0

HIGHEST MATCH AGGREGATES

Runs	Wkts			Days played
1,981	35	South Africa v England at Durban	1938-39	10†
1,815	34	West Indies v England at Kingston	1929-30	9‡
1,764	39	Australia v West Indies at Adelaide	1968-69	5
1,753	40	Australia v England at Adelaide	1920-21	6
1,723	31	England v Australia at Leeds	1948	5
1,661	36	West Indies v Australia at Bridgetown	1954-55	6

 † *No play on one day.*   ‡ *No play on two days.*

LOWEST INNINGS TOTALS

26	New Zealand v England at Auckland	1954-5
30	South Africa v England at Port Elizabeth	1895-9
30	South Africa v England at Birmingham	192
35	South Africa v England at Cape Town	1898-9
36	Australia v England at Birmingham	190
36	South Africa v Australia at Melbourne	1931-3
42	Australia v England at Sydney	1887-8
42	New Zealand v Australia at Wellington	1945-4
42†	India v England at Lord's	197
43	South Africa v England at Cape Town	1888-8
44	Australia v England at The Oval	189
45	England v Australia at Sydney	1886-8
45	South Africa v Australia at Melbourne	1931-3
47	South Africa v England at Cape Town	1888-8
47	New Zealand v England at Lord's	195

The lowest innings for the countries not mentioned above are:

53	West Indies v Pakistan at Faisalabad	1986-8
62	Pakistan v Australia at Perth	1981-8
93	Sri Lanka v New Zealand at Wellington	1982-8

 † *Batted one man short.*

FEWEST RUNS IN A FULL DAY'S PLAY

95	At Karachi, October 11, 1956. Australia 80 all out; Pakistan 15 for two (first day, 5 hours).
104	At Karachi, December 8, 1959. Pakistan 0 for no wicket to 104 for five v Australia (fourth day, 5½ hours).
106	At Brisbane, December 9, 1958. England 92 for two to 198 all out v Australia (fourth day 5 hours). *England were dismissed five minutes before the close of play, leaving no time fc Australia to start their second innings.*
112	At Karachi, October 15, 1956. Australia 138 for six to 187 all out; Pakistan 63 for on (fourth day, 5½ hours).
115	At Karachi, September 19, 1988. Australia 116 for seven to 165 all out and 66 for fiv following on v Pakistan (fourth day, 5½ hours).
117	At Madras, October 19, 1956. India 117 for five v Australia (first day, 5½ hours).
117	At Colombo (SSC), March 21, 1984. New Zealand 6 for no wicket to 123 for four (fift day, 5 hours, 47 minutes).

n England

51 At Lord's, August 26, 1978. England 175 for two to 289 all out; New Zealand 37 for seven (third day, 6 hours).
59 At Leeds, July 10, 1971. Pakistan 208 for four to 350 all out; England 17 for one (third day, 6 hours).

LOWEST MATCH AGGREGATES

(For a completed match)

Runs	Wkts			Days played
234	29	Australia v South Africa at Melbourne	1931-32	3†
291	40	England v Australia at Lord's	1888	2
295	28	New Zealand v Australia at Wellington	1945-46	2
309	29	West Indies v England at Bridgetown	1934-35	3
323	30	England v Australia at Manchester	1888	2

† *No play on one day.*

YOUNGEST TEST PLAYERS

Years	Days			
15	124	Mushtaq Mohammad	Pakistan v West Indies at Lahore	1958-59
16	189	Aaqib Javed	Pakistan v New Zealand at Wellington	1988-89
16	205	S. R. Tendulkar	India v Pakistan at Karachi	1989-90
16	221	Aftab Baloch	Pakistan v New Zealand at Dacca	1969-70
16	248	Nasim-ul-Ghani	Pakistan v West Indies at Bridgetown	1957-58
16	352	Khalid Hassan	Pakistan v England at Nottingham	1954
17	118	L. Sivaramakrishnan	India v West Indies at St John's	1982-83
17	122	J. E. D. Sealy	West Indies v England at Bridgetown	1929-30
17	189	C. D. U. S. Weerasinghe	Sri Lanka v India at Colombo (PSS)	1985-86
17	193	Maninder Singh	India v Pakistan at Karachi	1982-83
17	239	I. D. Craig	Australia v South Africa at Melbourne	1952-53
17	245	G. S. Sobers	West Indies v England at Kingston	1953-54
17	265	V. L. Mehra	India v New Zealand at Bombay	1955-56
17	300	Hanif Mohammad	Pakistan v India at Delhi	1952-53
17	341	Intikhab Alam	Pakistan v Australia at Karachi	1959-60
17	364	Waqar Younis	Pakistan v India at Karachi	1989-90

Note: The youngest Test players for countries not mentioned above are: England – D. B. Close, 18 years 149 days, v New Zealand at Manchester, 1949; New Zealand – D. L. Freeman, 18 years 197 days, v England at Christchurch, 1932-33; South Africa – A. E. Ochse, 19 years 1 day, v England at Port Elizabeth, 1888-89.

OLDEST PLAYERS ON TEST DEBUT

Years	Days			
49	119	J. Southerton	England v Australia at Melbourne	1876-77
47	284	Miran Bux	Pakistan v India at Lahore	1954-55
46	253	D. D. Blackie	Australia v England at Sydney	1928-29
46	237	H. Ironmonger	Australia v England at Brisbane	1928-29
42	242	N. Betancourt	West Indies v England at Port-of-Spain	1929-30
41	337	E. R. Wilson	England v Australia at Sydney	1920-21
41	27	R. J. D. Jamshedji	India v England at Bombay	1933-34

Years	Days			
40	345	C. A. Wiles	West Indies v England at Manchester ..	193
40	216	S. P. Kinneir ...	England v Australia at Sydney	1911-1
40	110	H. W. Lee	England v South Africa at Johannesburg	1930-3
40	56	G. W. A. Chubb	South Africa v England at Nottingham .	195
40	37	C. Ramaswami ..	India v England at Manchester	193

Note: The oldest Test player on début for New Zealand was H. M. McGirr, 38 years 101 days v England at Auckland, 1929-30; for Sri Lanka, D. S. de Silva, 39 years 251 days, v England a Colombo (PSO), 1981-82.

OLDEST TEST PLAYERS

(Age on final day of their last Test match)

Years	Days			
52	165	W. Rhodes	England v West Indies at Kingston ...	1929-3
50	327	H. Ironmonger	Australia v England at Sydney	1932-33
50	320	W. G. Grace	England v Australia at Nottingham ...	1899
50	303	G. Gunn	England v West Indies at Kingston ...	1929-3
49	139	J. Southerton	England v Australia at Melbourne	1876-7
47	302	Miran Bux	Pakistan v India at Peshawar	1954-5
47	249	J. B. Hobbs	England v Australia at The Oval	1930
47	87	F. E. Woolley	England v Australia at The Oval	1934
46	309	D. D. Blackie	Australia v England at Adelaide	1928-29
46	206	A. W. Nourse	South Africa v England at The Oval ..	1924
46	202	H. Strudwick	England v Australia at The Oval	1926
46	41	E. H. Hendren	England v West Indies at Kingston ...	1934-35
45	245	G. O. B. Allen	England v West Indies at Kingston ...	1947-48
45	215	P. Holmes	England v India at Lord's	1932
45	140	D. B. Close	England v West Indies at Manchester .	1976

MOST TEST MATCH APPEARANCES

For	Total		E	A	SA	WI	NZ	I	P	SL
England	114	M. C. Cowdrey	—	43	14	21	18	8	10	—
Australia	115	A. R. Border	36	—	—	21	17	15	22	4
South Africa	50	J. H. B. Waite	21	14	—	—	15	—	—	—
West Indies	111	I. V. A. Richards	31	29	—	—	7	28	16	—
New Zealand	86	Sir R. J. Hadlee	21	23	—	10	—	14	12	6
India	125	S. M. Gavaskar	38	20	—	27	9	—	24	7
Pakistan	104	Javed Miandad	17	25	—	11	14	28	—	9
Sri Lanka	26	A. Ranatunga	3	4	—	—	4	7	8	—

MOST CONSECUTIVE TEST APPEARANCES

112	A. R. Border (Australia)	March 1979 to March 1990
106	S. M. Gavaskar (India)	January 1975 to February 1987
87	G. R. Viswanath (India)	March 1971 to February 1983
85	G. S. Sobers (West Indies)	April 1955 to April 1972
72	D. L. Haynes (West Indies)	December 1979 to June 1988
71	I. M. Chappell (Australia)	January 1966 to February 1976
66	Kapil Dev (India)	October 1978 to December 1984
65	I. T. Botham (England)	February 1978 to March 1984
65	A. P. E. Knott (England)	March 1971 to August 1977

The most consecutive Test appearances for the countries not mentioned above are:

58†	J. R. Reid (New Zealand)	July 1949 to July 1965
53	Javed Miandad (Pakistan)	December 1977 to January 1984
45†	A. W. Nourse (South Africa) ...	October 1902 to August 1924
22	A. Ranatunga (Sri Lanka)	April 1983 to December 1989

† *Indicates complete Test career.*

SUMMARY OF ALL TEST MATCHES

To end of 1990 season in England

		Tests				Won by					Tied	Drawn
			E	A	SA	WI	NZ	I	P	SL		
England	v Australia	269	88	101	–	–	–	–	–	–	–	80
	v South Africa	102	46	–	18	–	–	–	–	–	–	38
	v West Indies	99	22	–	–	41	–	–	–	–	–	36
	v New Zealand	69	31	–	–	–	4	–	–	–	–	34
	v India	78	31	–	–	–	–	11	–	–	–	36
	v Pakistan	47	13	–	–	–	–	–	5	–	–	29
	v Sri Lanka	3	2	–	–	–	–	–	–	0	–	1
Australia	v South Africa	53	–	29	11	–	–	–	–	–	–	13
	v West Indies	67	–	28	–	22	–	–	–	–	1	16
	v New Zealand	26	–	10	–	–	6	–	–	–	–	10
	v India	45	–	20	–	–	–	8	–	–	1	16
	v Pakistan	34	–	12	–	–	–	–	9	–	–	13
	v Sri Lanka	4	–	3	–	–	–	–	–	0	–	1
South Africa	v New Zealand	17	–	–	9	–	2	–	–	–	–	6
West Indies	v New Zealand	24	–	–	–	8	4	–	–	–	–	12
	v India	62	–	–	–	26	–	6	–	–	–	30
	v Pakistan	25	–	–	–	9	–	–	6	–	–	10
New Zealand	v India	31	–	–	–	–	6	12	–	–	–	13
	v Pakistan	29	–	–	–	–	3	–	10	–	–	16
	v Sri Lanka	6	–	–	–	–	4	–	–	0	–	2
India	v Pakistan	44	–	–	–	–	–	4	7	–	–	33
	v Sri Lanka	7	–	–	–	–	–	2	–	1	–	4
Pakistan	v Sri Lanka	9	–	–	–	–	–	–	5	1	–	3
		1,150	233	203	38	106	29	43	42	2	2	452

	Tests	Won	Lost	Drawn	Tied	Toss Won
England	667	233	180	254	–	330
Australia	498	203	144	149	2	250
South Africa	172	38	77	57	–	80
West Indies	277	106	66	104	1	145
New Zealand	202	29	80	93	–	100
India	267	43	91	132	1	132
Pakistan	188	42	42	104	–	98
Sri Lanka	29	2	16	11	–	15

ENGLAND v AUSTRALIA

Captains

Season	England	Australia	T	E	A	D
1876-77	James Lillywhite	D. W. Gregory	2	1	1	0
1878-79	Lord Harris	D. W. Gregory	1	0	1	0
1880	Lord Harris	W. L. Murdoch	1	1	0	0
1881-82	A. Shaw	W. L. Murdoch	4	0	2	2
1882	A. N. Hornby	W. L. Murdoch	1	0	1	0

THE ASHES

Season	England	Australia	T	E	A	D	Held by
1882-83	Hon. Ivo Bligh	W. L. Murdoch	4*	2	2	0	E
1884	Lord Harris[1]	W. L. Murdoch	3	1	0	2	E
1884-85	A. Shrewsbury	T. Horan[2]	5	3	2	0	E
1886	A. G. Steel	H. J. H. Scott	3	3	0	0	E
1886-87	A. Shrewsbury	P. S. McDonnell	2	2	0	0	E
1887-88	W. W. Read	P. S. McDonnell	1	1	0	0	E
1888	W. G. Grace[3]	P. S. McDonnell	3	2	1	0	E
1890†	W. G. Grace	W. L. Murdoch	2	2	0	0	E
1891-92	W. G. Grace	J. McC. Blackham	3	1	2	0	A
1893	W. G. Grace[4]	J. McC. Blackham	3	1	0	2	E
1894-95	A. E. Stoddart	G. Giffen[5]	5	3	2	0	E
1896	W. G. Grace	G. H. S. Trott	3	2	1	0	E
1897-98	A. E. Stoddart[6]	G. H. S. Trott	5	1	4	0	A
1899	A. C. MacLaren[7]	J. Darling	5	0	1	4	A
1901-02	A. C. MacLaren	J. Darling[8]	5	1	4	0	A
1902	A. C. MacLaren	J. Darling	5	1	2	2	A
1903-04	P. F. Warner	M. A. Noble	5	3	2	0	E
1905	Hon. F. S. Jackson	J. Darling	5	2	0	3	E
1907-08	A. O. Jones[9]	M. A. Noble	5	1	4	0	A
1909	A. C. MacLaren	M. A. Noble	5	1	2	2	A
1911-12	J. W. H. T. Douglas	C. Hill	5	4	1	0	E
1912	C. B. Fry	S. E. Gregory	3	1	0	2	E
1920-21	J. W. H. T. Douglas	W. W. Armstrong	5	0	5	0	A
1921	Hon. L. H. Tennyson[10]	W. W. Armstrong	5	0	3	2	A
1924-25	A. E. R. Gilligan	H. L. Collins	5	1	4	0	A
1926	A. W. Carr[11]	H. L. Collins[12]	5	1	0	4	E
1928-29	A. P. F. Chapman[13]	J. Ryder	5	4	1	0	E
1930	A. P. F. Chapman[14]	W. M. Woodfull	5	1	2	2	A
1932-33	D. R. Jardine	W. M. Woodfull	5	4	1	0	E
1934	R. E. S. Wyatt[15]	W. M. Woodfull	5	1	2	2	A
1936-37	G. O. B. Allen	D. G. Bradman	5	2	3	0	A
1938†	W. R. Hammond	D. G. Bradman	4	1	1	2	A
1946-47	W. R. Hammond[16]	D. G. Bradman	5	0	3	2	A
1948	N. W. D. Yardley	D. G. Bradman	5	0	4	1	A
1950-51	F. R. Brown	A. L. Hassett	5	1	4	0	A
1953	L. Hutton	A. L. Hassett	5	1	0	4	E
1954-55	L. Hutton	I. W. Johnson[17]	5	3	1	1	E
1956	P. B. H. May	I. W. Johnson	5	2	1	2	E
1958-59	P. B. H. May	R. Benaud	5	0	4	1	A
1961	P. B. H. May[18]	R. Benaud[19]	5	1	2	2	A
1962-63	E. R. Dexter	R. Benaud	5	1	1	3	A
1964	E. R. Dexter	R. B. Simpson	5	0	1	4	A
1965-66	M. J. K. Smith	R. B. Simpson[20]	5	1	1	3	A
1968	M. C. Cowdrey[21]	W. M. Lawry[22]	5	1	1	3	A
1970-71†	R. Illingworth	W. M. Lawry[23]	6	2	0	4	E
1972	R. Illingworth	I. M. Chappell	5	2	2	1	E
1974-75	M. H. Denness[24]	I. M. Chappell	6	1	4	1	A
1975	A. W. Greig[25]	I. M. Chappell	4	0	1	3	A
1976-77‡	A. W. Greig	G. S. Chappell	1	0	1	0	—
1977	J. M. Brearley	G. S. Chappell	5	3	0	2	E
1978-79	J. M. Brearley	G. N. Yallop	6	5	1	0	E
1979-80‡	J. M. Brearley	G. S. Chappell	3	0	3	0	—
1980‡	I. T. Botham	G. S. Chappell	1	0	0	1	—
1981	J. M. Brearley[26]	K. J. Hughes	6	3	1	2	E
1982-83	R. G. D. Willis	G. S. Chappell	5	1	2	2	A
1985	D. I. Gower	A. R. Border	6	3	1	2	E
1986-87	M. W. Gatting	A. R. Border	5	2	1	2	E
1987-88‡	M. W. Gatting	A. R. Border	1	0	0	1	—
1989	D. I. Gower	A. R. Border	6	0	4	2	A
	In Australia		140	51	67	22	
	In England		129	37	34	58	
	Totals		269	88	101	80	

* The Ashes were awarded in 1882-83 after a series of three matches which England won 2-1. A
ourth unofficial match was played, each innings being played on a different pitch, and this was won by
Australia.

† The matches at Manchester in 1890 and 1938 and at Melbourne (Third Test) in 1970-71 were
abandoned without a ball being bowled and are excluded.

‡ The Ashes were not at stake in these series.

Notes: The following deputised for the official touring captain or were appointed by the home
authority for only a minor proportion of the series:
[1]A. N. Hornby (First). [2]W. L. Murdoch (First), H. H. Massie (Third), J. McC. Blackham
(Fourth). [3]A. G. Steel (First). [4]A. E. Stoddart (First). [5]J. McC. Blackham (First). [6]A. C.
MacLaren (First, Second and Fifth). [7]W. G. Grace (First). [8]H. Trumble (Fourth and Fifth).
F. L. Fane (First, Second and Third). [10]J. W. H. T. Douglas (First and Second). [11]A. P. F.
Chapman (Fifth). [12]W. Bardsley (Third and Fourth). [13]J. C. White (Fifth). [14]R. E. S. Wyatt
(Fifth). [15]C. F. Walters (First). [16]N. W. D. Yardley (Fifth). [17]A. R. Morris (Second). [18]M. C.
Cowdrey (First and Second). [19]R. N. Harvey (Second). [20]B. C. Booth (First and Third). [21]T. W.
Graveney (Fourth). [22]B. N. Jarman (Fourth). [23]I. M. Chappell (Seventh). [24]J. H. Edrich
(Fourth). [25]M. H. Denness (First). [26]I. T. Botham (First and Second).

HIGHEST INNINGS TOTALS

For England in England: 903-7 dec. at The Oval	....	1938
in Australia: 636 at Sydney	....	1928-29
For Australia in England: 729-6 dec. at Lord's	....	1930
in Australia: 659-8 dec. at Sydney	....	1946-47

LOWEST INNINGS TOTALS

For England in England: 52 at The Oval	....	1948
in Australia: 45 at Sydney	....	1886-87
For Australia in England: 36 at Birmingham	....	1902
in Australia: 42 at Sydney	....	1887-88

INDIVIDUAL HUNDREDS

For England (192)

R. Abel (1)				**I. T. Botham** (4)	
132*‡	Sydney	1891-92		119*	Melbourne .. 1979-80
L. E. G. Ames (1)				149*	Leeds 1981
120	Lord's	1934		118	Manchester .. 1981
R. W. Barber (1)				138	Brisbane 1986-87
185	Sydney 1965-66			**G. Boycott** (7)	
W. Barnes (1)				113	The Oval ... 1964
134	Adelaide.... 1884-85			142*	Sydney 1970-71
C. J. Barnett (2)				119*	Adelaide ... 1970-71
129	Adelaide 1936-37			107	Nottingham . 1977
126	Nottingham . 1938			191	Leeds 1977
K. F. Barrington (5)				128*	Lord's 1980
132*	Adelaide 1962-63			137	The Oval ... 1981
101	Sydney 1962-63			**L. C. Braund** (2)	
256	Manchester . 1964			103*	Adelaide 1901-02
102	Adelaide 1965-66			102	Sydney 1903-04
115	Melbourne .. 1965-66				

J. Briggs (1)		
121	Melbourne ..	1884-85
B. C. Broad (4)		
162	Perth	1986-87
116	Adelaide ...	1986-87
112	Melbourne ..	1986-87
139	Sydney	1987-88
J. T. Brown (1)		
140	Melbourne ..	1894-95
A. P. F. Chapman (1)		
121	Lord's	1930
D. C. S. Compton (5)		
102†	Nottingham .	1938
147 }	Adelaide	1946-47
103* }		
184	Nottingham .	1948
145*	Manchester .	1948

M. C. Cowdrey (5)
102 Melbourne .. 1954-55
100* Sydney 1958-59
113 Melbourne .. 1962-63
104 Melbourne .. 1965-66
104 Birmingham . 1968

M. H. Denness (1)
188 Melbourne .. 1974-75

E. R. Dexter (2)
180 Birmingham . 1961
174 Manchester . 1964

B. L. D'Oliveira (2)
158 The Oval ... 1968
117 Melbourne .. 1970-71

K. S. Duleepsinhji (1)
173† Lord's 1930

J. H. Edrich (7)
120† Lord's 1964
109 Melbourne .. 1965-66
103 Sydney 1965-66
164 The Oval ... 1968
115* Perth 1970-71
130 Adelaide 1970-71
175 Lord's 1975

W. J. Edrich (2)
119 Sydney 1946-47
111 Leeds 1948

K. W. R. Fletcher (1)
146 Melbourne .. 1974-75

R. E. Foster (1)
287† Sydney 1903-04

C. B. Fry (1)
144 The Oval ... 1905

M. W. Gatting (3)
160 Manchester . 1985
100* Birmingham . 1985
100 Adelaide 1986-87

G. A. Gooch (1)
196 The Oval ... 1985

D. I. Gower (7)
102 Perth 1978-79
114 Adelaide 1982-83
166 Nottingham . 1985
215 Birmingham . 1985
157 The Oval ... 1985
136 Perth 1986-87
106 Lord's 1989

W. G. Grace (2)
152† The Oval ... 1880
170 The Oval ... 1886

T. W. Graveney (1)
111 Sydney 1954-55

A. W. Greig (1)
110 Brisbane ... 1974-75

G. Gunn (2)
119† Sydney 1907-08
122* Sydney 1907-08

W. Gunn (1)
102* Manchester . 1893

W. R. Hammond (9)
251 Sydney 1928-29
200 Melbourne .. 1928-29
119* }
177 } Adelaide 1928-29
113 Leeds 1930
112 Sydney 1932-33
101 Sydney 1932-33
231* Sydney 1936-37
240 Lord's 1938

J. Hardstaff jun. (1)
169* The Oval ... 1938

T. W. Hayward (2)
130 Manchester . 1899
137 The Oval ... 1899

J. W. Hearne (1)
114 Melbourne .. 1911-12

E. H. Hendren (3)
127* Lord's 1926
169 Brisbane ... 1928-29
132 Manchester . 1934

J. B. Hobbs (12)
126* Melbourne .. 1911-12
187 Adelaide 1911-12
178 Melbourne .. 1911-12
107 Lord's 1912
122 Melbourne .. 1920-21
123 Adelaide 1920-21
115 Sydney 1924-25
154 Melbourne .. 1924-25
119 Adelaide 1924-25
119 Lord's 1926
100 The Oval ... 1926
142 Melbourne .. 1928-29

K. L. Hutchings (1)
126 Melbourne .. 1907-08

L. Hutton (5)
100† Nottingham . 1938
364 The Oval ... 1938
122* Sydney 1946-47
156*‡ Adelaide 1950-51
145 Lord's 1953

Hon. F. S. Jackson (5)
103 The Oval ... 1893
118 The Oval ... 1899
128 Manchester . 1902
144* Leeds 1905
113 Manchester . 1905

G. L. Jessop (1)
104 The Oval ... 1902

A. P. E. Knott (2)
106* Adelaide 1974-75
135 Nottingham . 1977

A. J. Lamb (1)
125 Leeds 1989

M. Leyland (7)
137† Melbourne .. 1928-29
109 Lord's 1934
153 Manchester . 1934
110 The Oval ... 1934
126 Brisbane 1936-37
111* Melbourne .. 1936-37
187 The Oval ... 1938

B. W. Luckhurst (2)
131 Perth ...... 1970-7[1]
109 Melbourne .. 1970-7[1]

A. C. MacLaren (5)
120 Melbourne .. 1894-9[5]
109 Sydney ..... 1897-9[8]
124 Adelaide .... 1897-9[8]
116 Sydney ..... 1901-0[2]
140 Nottingham . 190[5]

J. W. H. Makepeace (1)
117 Melbourne .. 1920-2[1]

P. B. H. May (3)
104 Sydney ..... 1954-5[5]
101 Leeds ...... 195[6]
113 Melbourne .. 1958-5[9]

C. P. Mead (1)
182* The Oval ... 192[1]

Nawab of Pataudi sen. (1)
102† Sydney ..... 1932-3[3]

E. Paynter (1)
216* Nottingham . 193[8]

D. W. Randall (3)
174† Melbourne .. 1976-7[7]
150 Sydney ..... 1978-7[9]
115 Perth ...... 1982-8[3]

K. S. Ranjitsinhji (2)
154*† Manchester . 189[6]
175 Sydney ..... 1897-9[8]

W. W. Read (1)
117 The Oval ... 188[4]

W. Rhodes (1)
179 Melbourne .. 1911-1[2]

C. J. Richards (1)
133 Perth ...... 1986-8[7]

P. E. Richardson (1)
104 Manchester . 195[6]

R. T. Robinson (2)
175† Leeds ...... 198[5]
148 Birmingham . 198[5]

A. C. Russell (3)
135* Adelaide .... 1920-2[1]
101 Manchester . 192[1]
102* The Oval ... 192[1]

R. C. Russell (1)
128* Manchester . 198[9]

J. Sharp (1)
105 The Oval ... 190[9]

Rev. D. S. Sheppard (2)
113 Manchester . 195[6]
113 Melbourne .. 1962-6[3]

A. Shrewsbury (3)
105* Melbourne .. 1884-8[5]
164 Lord's ...... 188[6]
106 Lord's ...... 189[3]

R. T. Simpson (1)
156* Melbourne .. 1950-5[1]

R. A. Smith (2)
143 Manchester . 198[9]
101 Nottingham . 198[9]

A. G. Steel (2)
135* Sydney ..... 1882-8[3]
148 Lord's ...... 188[4]

A. E. Stoddart (2)		
34	Adelaide	1891-92
73	Melbourne ..	1894-95

R. Subba Row (2)		
112†	Birmingham .	1961
37	The Oval	1961

H. Sutcliffe (8)		
15†	Sydney	1924-25
76	} Melbourne ..	1924-25
27		1924-25
43	Melbourne ..	1924-25
61	The Oval	1926

135	Melbourne ..	1928-29
161	The Oval	1930
194	Sydney	1932-33

J. T. Tyldesley (3)		
138	Birmingham .	1902
100	Leeds	1905
112*	The Oval	1905

G. Ulyett (1)		
149	Melbourne ..	1881-82

A. Ward (1)		
117	Sydney	1894-95

C. Washbrook (2)		
112	Melbourne ..	1946-47
143	Leeds	1948

W. Watson (1)		
109†	Lord's	1953

F. E. Woolley (2)		
133*	Sydney	1911-12
123	Sydney	1924-25

R. A. Woolmer (3)		
149	The Oval	1975
120	Lord's	1977
137	Manchester .	1977

† *Signifies hundred on first appearance in England–Australia Tests.*
‡ *Carried his bat.*

Note: In consecutive innings in 1928-29, W. R. Hammond scored 251 at Sydney, 200 and 32 at Melbourne, and 119* and 177 at Adelaide.

For Australia (211)

W. W. Armstrong (4)		
33*	Melbourne ..	1907-08
58	Sydney	1920-21
21	Adelaide	1920-21
23*	Melbourne ..	1920-21

C. L. Badcock (1)		
18	Melbourne ..	1936-37

C. Bannerman (1)		
165*†	Melbourne ..	1876-77

W. Bardsley (3)		
136	} The Oval ...	1909
30		1909
193*‡	Lord's	1926

S. G. Barnes (2)		
234	Sydney	1946-47
141	Lord's	1948

S. J. Bonnor (1)		
128	Sydney	1884-85

D. C. Boon (2)		
103	Adelaide	1986-87
184*	Sydney	1987-88

B. C. Booth (2)		
112	Brisbane	1962-63
103	Melbourne ..	1962-63

A. R. Border (7)		
115	Perth	1979-80
123*	Manchester .	1981
106*	The Oval	1981
196	Lord's	1985
146*	Manchester .	1985
125	Perth	1986-87
100*	Adelaide	1986-87

D. G. Bradman (19)		
112	Melbourne ..	1928-29
123	Melbourne ..	1928-29
131	Nottingham .	1930
254	Lord's	1930
334	Leeds	1930
232	The Oval	1930
103*	Melbourne ..	1932-33
304	Leeds	1934
244	The Oval	1934

270	Melbourne ..	1936-37
212	Adelaide	1936-37
169	Melbourne ..	1936-37
144*	Nottingham .	1938
102*	Lord's	1938
103	Leeds	1938
187	Brisbane	1946-47
234	Sydney	1946-47
138	Nottingham .	1948
173*	Leeds	1948

W. A. Brown (3)		
105	Lord's	1934
133	Nottingham .	1938
206*‡	Lord's	1938

P. J. Burge (4)		
181	The Oval	1961
103	Sydney	1962-63
160	Leeds	1964
120	Melbourne ..	1965-66

J. W. Burke (1)		
101*†	Adelaide	1950-51

G. S. Chappell (9)		
108†	Perth	1970-71
131	Lord's	1972
113	The Oval	1972
144	Sydney	1974-75
102	Melbourne ..	1974-75
112	Manchester .	1977
114	Melbourne ..	1979-80
117	Perth	1982-83
115	Adelaide	1982-83

I. M. Chappell (4)		
111	Melbourne ..	1970-71
104	Adelaide	1970-71
118	The Oval	1972
192	The Oval	1975

H. L. Collins (3)		
104†	Sydney	1920-21
162	Adelaide	1920-21
114	Sydney	1924-25

R. M. Cowper (1)		
307	Melbourne ..	1965-66

J. Darling (3)		
101	Sydney	1897-98
178	Adelaide	1897-98
160	Sydney	1897-98

R. A. Duff (2)		
104†	Melbourne ..	1901-02
146	The Oval	1905

J. Dyson (1)		
102	Leeds	1981

R. Edwards (2)		
170*	Nottingham .	1972
115	Perth	1974-75

J. H. Fingleton (2)		
100	Brisbane	1936-37
136	Melbourne ..	1936-37

G. Giffen (1)		
161	Sydney	1894-95

H. Graham (2)		
107†	Lord's	1893
105	Sydney	1894-95

J. M. Gregory (1)		
100	Melbourne ..	1920-21

S. E. Gregory (4)		
201	Sydney	1894-95
103	Lord's	1896
117	The Oval	1899
112	Adelaide	1903-04

R. J. Hartigan (1)		
116†	Adelaide	1907-08

R. N. Harvey (6)		
112†	Leeds	1948
122	Manchester .	1953
162	Brisbane	1954-55
167	Melbourne ..	1958-59
114	Birmingham .	1961
154	Adelaide	1962-63

A. L. Hassett (4)		
128	Brisbane	1946-47
137	Nottingham .	1948
115	Nottingham .	1953
104	Lord's	1953

H. S. T. L. Hendry (1)
112 Sydney 1928-29
A. M. J. Hilditch (1)
119 Leeds 1985
C. Hill (4)
188 Melbourne .. 1897-98
135 Lord's 1899
119 Sheffield 1902
160 Adelaide 1907-08
T. P. Horan (1)
124 Melbourne .. 1881-82
K. J. Hughes (3)
129 Brisbane 1978-79
117 Lord's 1980
137 Sydney 1982-83
F. A. Iredale (2)
140 Adelaide 1894-95
108 Manchester . 1896
A. A. Jackson (1)
164† Adelaide 1928-29
D. M. Jones (3)
184* Sydney 1986-87
157 Birmingham . 1989
122 The Oval ... 1989
C. Kelleway (1)
147 Adelaide 1920-21
A. F. Kippax (1)
100 Melbourne .. 1928-29
W. M. Lawry (7)
130 Lord's 1961
102 Manchester . 1961
106 Manchester . 1964
166 Brisbane 1965-66
119 Adelaide 1965-66
108 Melbourne .. 1965-66
135 The Oval ... 1968
R. R. Lindwall (1)
100 Melbourne .. 1946-47
J. J. Lyons (1)
134 Sydney 1891-92
C. G. Macartney (5)
170 Sydney 1920-21
115 Leeds 1921
133* Lord's 1926
151 Leeds 1926
109 Manchester . 1926
S. J. McCabe (4)
187* Sydney 1932-33
137 Manchester . 1934
112 Melbourne .. 1936-37
232 Nottingham . 1938
C. L. McCool (1)
104* Melbourne .. 1946-47
R. B. McCosker (2)
127 The Oval ... 1975
107 Nottingham . 1977

C. C. McDonald (2)
170 Adelaide 1958-59
133 Melbourne .. 1958-59
P. S. McDonnell (3)
147 Sydney 1881-82
103 The Oval ... 1884
124 Adelaide 1884-85
C. E. McLeod (1)
112 Melbourne .. 1897-98
G. R. Marsh (2)
110† Brisbane 1986-87
138 Nottingham . 1989
R. W. Marsh (1)
110* Melbourne .. 1976-77
K. R. Miller (3)
141* Adelaide 1946-47
145* Sydney 1950-51
109 Lord's 1953
A. R. Morris (8)
155 Melbourne .. 1946-47
122 ⎫
124* ⎬ Adelaide 1946-47
105 Lord's 1948
182 Leeds 1948
196 The Oval ... 1948
206 Adelaide 1950-51
153 Brisbane 1954-55
W. L. Murdoch (2)
153* The Oval ... 1880
211 The Oval ... 1884
M. A. Noble (1)
133 Sydney 1903-04
N. C. O'Neill (2)
117 The Oval ... 1961
100 Adelaide 1962-63
C. E. Pellew (2)
116 Melbourne .. 1920-21
104 Adelaide 1920-21
W. H. Ponsford (5)
110† Sydney 1924-25
128 Melbourne .. 1924-25
110 The Oval ... 1930
181 Leeds 1934
266 The Oval ... 1934
V. S. Ransford (1)
143* Lord's 1909
I. R. Redpath (2)
171 Perth 1970-71
105 Sydney 1974-75
A. J. Richardson (1)
100 Leeds 1926
V. Y. Richardson (1)
138 Melbourne .. 1924-25
G. M. Ritchie (1)
146 Nottingham . 1985

J. Ryder (2)
201* Adelaide 1924-25
112 Melbourne .. 1928-29
H. J. H. Scott (1)
102 The Oval ... 1884
R. B. Simpson (2)
311 Manchester . 1964
225 Adelaide 1965-66
K. R. Stackpole (3)
207 Brisbane 1970-71
136 Adelaide 1970-71
114 Nottingham . 1972
J. M. Taylor (1)
108 Sydney 1924-25
M. A. Taylor (2)
136† Leeds 1989
219 Nottingham . 1989
G. H. S. Trott (1)
143 Lord's 1896
V. T. Trumper (6)
135* Lord's 1899
104 Manchester . 1902
185* Sydney 1903-04
113 Adelaide 1903-04
166 Sydney 1907-08
113 Sydney 1911-12
K. D. Walters (4)
155† Brisbane 1965-66
115 Melbourne .. 1965-66
112 Brisbane 1970-71
103 Perth 1974-75
S. R. Waugh (2)
177* Leeds 1989
152* Lord's 1989
D. M. Wellham (1)
103† The Oval ... 1981
K. C. Wessels (1)
162† Brisbane 1982-83
G. M. Wood (3)
100 Melbourne .. 1978-79
112 Lord's 1980
172 Nottingham . 1981
W. M. Woodfull (6)
141 Leeds 1926
117 Manchester . 1926
111 Sydney 1928-29
107 Melbourne .. 1928-29
102 Melbourne .. 1928-29
155 Lord's 1930
G. N. Yallop (3)
102† Brisbane 1978-79
121 Sydney 1978-79
114 Manchester . 1981

† *Signifies hundred on first appearance in England–Australia Tests.*

‡ *Carried his bat.*

Notes: D. G. Bradman's scores in 1930 were 8 and 131 at Nottingham, 254 and 1 at Lord's, 334 at Leeds, 14 at Manchester, and 232 at The Oval.

D. G. Bradman scored a hundred in eight successive Tests against England in which he batted – three in 1936-37, three in 1938 and two in 1946-47. He was injured and unable to bat at the Oval in 1938.

W. H. Ponsford and K. D. Walters each hit hundreds in their first two Tests.

C. Bannerman and H. Graham each scored their maiden hundred in first-class cricket in their first Test.

No right-handed batsman has obtained two hundreds for Australia in a Test match against England, and no left-handed batsman for England against Australia.

H. Sutcliffe, in his first two games for England, scored 59 and 115 at Sydney and 176 and 127 at Melbourne in 1924-25. In the latter match, which lasted into the seventh day, he was on the field throughout except for 86 minutes, namely 27 hours and 52 minutes.

C. Hill made 98 and 97 at Adelaide in 1901-02, and F. E. Woolley 95 and 93 at Lord's in 1921.

H. Sutcliffe in 1924-25, C. G. Macartney in 1926 and A. R. Morris in 1946-47 made three hundreds in consecutive innings.

J. B. Hobbs and H. Sutcliffe shared eleven first-wicket three-figure partnerships.

L. Hutton and C. Washbrook twice made three-figure stands in each innings, at Adelaide in 1946-47 and at Leeds in 1948.

H. Sutcliffe, during his highest score of 194, v Australia in 1932-33, took part in three stands each exceeding 100, viz. 112 with R. E. S. Wyatt for the first wicket, 188 with W. R. Hammond for the second wicket, and 123 with the Nawab of Pataudi sen. for the third wicket. In 1903-04 R. E. Foster, in his historic innings of 287, added 192 for the fifth wicket with L. C. Braund, 115 for the ninth wicket with A. E. Relf, and 130 for the tenth with W. Rhodes.

When L. Hutton scored 364 at The Oval in 1938 he added 382 for the second wicket with M. Leyland, 135 for the third wicket with W. R. Hammond and 215 for the sixth wicket with Hardstaff jun.

D. C. S. Compton and A. R. Morris at Adelaide in 1946-47 provide the only instance of a player on each side hitting two separate hundreds in a Test match.

G. S. and I. M. Chappell at The Oval in 1972 provide the first instance in Test matches of brothers each scoring hundreds in the same innings.

RECORD PARTNERSHIPS FOR EACH WICKET

For England

323 for 1st	J. B. Hobbs and W. Rhodes at Melbourne	1911-12
382 for 2nd†	L. Hutton and M. Leyland at The Oval	1938
262 for 3rd	W. R. Hammond and D. R. Jardine at Adelaide	1928-29
222 for 4th	W. R. Hammond and E. Paynter at Lord's	1938
206 for 5th	E. Paynter and D. C. S. Compton at Nottingham	1938
215 for 6th	{ L. Hutton and J. Hardstaff jun. at The Oval	1938
	{ G. Boycott and A. P. E. Knott at Nottingham	1977
143 for 7th	F. E. Woolley and J. Vine at Sydney	1911-12
124 for 8th	E. H. Hendren and H. Larwood at Brisbane	1928-29
151 for 9th	W. H. Scotton and W. W. Read at The Oval	1884
130 for 10th†	R. E. Foster and W. Rhodes at Sydney	1903-04

For Australia

329 for 1st	G. R. Marsh and M. A. Taylor at Nottingham	1989
451 for 2nd†	W. H. Ponsford and D. G. Bradman at The Oval	1934
276 for 3rd	D. G. Bradman and A. L. Hassett at Brisbane	1946-47
388 for 4th†	W. H. Ponsford and D. G. Bradman at Leeds	1934
405 for 5th†‡	S. G. Barnes and D. G. Bradman at Sydney	1946-47
346 for 6th†	J. H. Fingleton and D. G. Bradman at Melbourne	1936-37
165 for 7th	C. Hill and H. Trumble at Melbourne	1897-98
243 for 8th†	R. J. Hartigan and C. Hill at Adelaide	1907-08
154 for 9th†	S. E. Gregory and J. McC. Blackham at Sydney	1894-95
127 for 10th†	J. M. Taylor and A. A. Mailey at Sydney	1924-25

† *Denotes record partnership against all countries.*
‡ *Record fifth-wicket partnership in first-class cricket.*

MOST RUNS IN A SERIES

England in England	732 (average 81.33)	D. I. Gower	198
England in Australia	905 (average 113.12)	W. R. Hammond ..	1928-2
Australia in England	974 (average 139.14)	D. G. Bradman ...	193
Australia in Australia	810 (average 90.00)	D. G. Bradman ...	1936-3

TEN WICKETS OR MORE IN A MATCH

For England (37)

13-163 (6-42, 7-121)	S. F. Barnes, Melbourne	1901-0
14-102 (7-28, 7-74)	W. Bates, Melbourne	1882-8
10-105 (5-46, 5-59)	A. V. Bedser, Melbourne	1950-5
14-99 (7-55, 7-44)	A. V. Bedser, Nottingham	195
11-102 (6-44, 5-58)	C. Blythe, Birmingham	190
11-176 (6-78, 5-98)	I. T. Botham, Perth	1979-8
10-253 (6-125, 4-128)	I. T. Botham, The Oval	198
11-74 (5-29, 6-45)	J. Briggs, Lord's	188
12-136 (6-49, 6-87)	J. Briggs, Adelaide	1891-9
10-148 (5-34, 5-114)	J. Briggs, The Oval	189
10-104 (6-77, 4-27)†	R. M. Ellison, Birmingham	198
10-179 (5-102, 5-77)†	K. Farnes, Nottingham	193
10-60 (6-41, 4-19)	J. T. Hearne, The Oval	189
11-113 (5-58, 6-55)	J. C. Laker, Leeds	195
19-90 (9-37, 10-53)	J. C. Laker, Manchester	195
10-124 (5-96, 5-28)	H. Larwood, Sydney	1932-3
11-76 (6-48, 5-28)	W. H. Lockwood, Manchester	190
12-104 (7-36, 5-68)	G. A. Lohmann, The Oval	188
10-87 (8-35, 2-52)	G. A. Lohmann, Sydney	1886-8
10-142 (8-58, 2-84)	G. A. Lohmann, Sydney	1891-9
12-102 (6-50, 6-52)†	F. Martin, The Oval	189
10-58 (5-18, 5-40)	R. Peel, Sydney	1887-8
11-68 (7-31, 4-37)	R. Peel, Manchester	188
15-124 (7-56, 8-68)	W. Rhodes, Melbourne	1903-0
10-156 (5-49, 5-107)†	T. Richardson, Manchester	189
11-173 (6-39, 5-134)	T. Richardson, Lord's	189
13-244 (7-168, 6-76)	T. Richardson, Manchester	189
10-204 (8-94, 2-110)	T. Richardson, Sydney	1897-9
11-228 (6-130, 5-98)†	M. W. Tate, Sydney	1924-2
11-88 (5-58, 6-30)	F. S. Trueman, Leeds	196
10-130 (4-45, 6-85)	F. H. Tyson, Sydney	1954-5
10-82 (4-37, 6-45)	D. L. Underwood, Leeds	197
11-215 (7-113, 4-102)	D. L. Underwood, Adelaide	1974-7
15-104 (7-61, 8-43)	H. Verity, Lord's	193
10-57 (6-41, 4-16)	W. Voce, Brisbane	1936-3
13-256 (5-130, 8-126)	J. C. White, Adelaide	1928-2
10-49 (5-29, 5-20)	F. E. Woolley, The Oval	191

For Australia (36)

10-151 (5-107, 5-44)	T. M. Alderman, Leeds	198
10-239 (4-129, 6-110)	L. O'B. Fleetwood-Smith, Adelaide	1936-3
10-160 (4-88, 6-72)	G. Giffen, Sydney	1891-9
11-82 (5-45, 6-37)†	C. V. Grimmett, Sydney	1924-2
10-201 (5-107, 5-94)	C. V. Grimmett, Nottingham	193
10-122 (5-65, 5-57)	R. M. Hogg, Perth	1978-7
10-66 (5-30, 5-36)	R. M. Hogg, Melbourne	1978-7
12-175 (5-85, 7-90)†	H. V. Hordern, Sydney	1911-1

0-161 (5-95, 5-66)	H. V. Hordern, Sydney	1911-12
0-164 (7-88, 3-76)	E. Jones, Lord's	1899
1-134 (6-47, 5-87)	G. F. Lawson, Brisbane	1982-83
0-181 (5-58, 5-123)	D. K. Lillee, The Oval	1972
1-165 (6-26, 5-139)	D. K. Lillee, Melbourne	1976-77
1-138 (6-60, 5-78)	D. K. Lillee, Melbourne	1979-80
1-159 (7-89, 4-70)	D. K. Lillee, The Oval	1981
1-85 (7-58, 4-27)	C. G. Macartney, Leeds	1909
0-302 (5-160, 5-142)	A. A. Mailey, Adelaide	1920-21
3-236 (4-115, 9-121)	A. A. Mailey, Melbourne	1920-21
6-137 (8-84, 8-53)†	R. A. L. Massie, Lord's	1972
0-152 (5-72, 5-80)	K. R. Miller, Lord's	1956
3-77 (7-17, 6-60)	M. A. Noble, Melbourne	1901-02
1-103 (5-51, 6-52)	M. A. Noble, Sheffield	1902
0-129 (5-63, 5-66)	W. J. O'Reilly, Melbourne	1932-33
1-129 (4-75, 7-54)	W. J. O'Reilly, Nottingham	1934
0-122 (5-66, 5-56)	W. J. O'Reilly, Leeds	1938
1-165 (7-68, 4-97)	G. E. Palmer, Sydney	1881-82
0-126 (7-65, 3-61)	G. E. Palmer, Melbourne	1882-83
3-110 (6-48, 7-62)	F. R. Spofforth, Melbourne	1878-79
4-90 (7-46, 7-44)	F. R. Spofforth, The Oval	1882
1-117 (4-73, 7-44)	F. R. Spofforth, Sydney	1882-83
0-144 (4-54, 6-90)	F. R. Spofforth, Sydney	1884-85
2-89 (6-59, 6-30)	H. Trumble, The Oval	1896
0-128 (4-75, 6-53)	H. Trumble, Manchester	1902
2-173 (8-65, 4-108)	H. Trumble, The Oval	1902
2-87 (5-44, 7-43)	C. T. B. Turner, Sydney	1887-88
0-63 (5-27, 5-36)	C. T. B. Turner, Lord's	1888

† *Signifies ten wickets or more on first appearance in England–Australia Tests.*

Note: J. Briggs, J. C. Laker, T. Richardson in 1896, R. M. Hogg, A. A. Mailey, H. Trumble and C. T. B. Turner took ten wickets or more in successive Tests. J. Briggs was omitted, however, from the England team for the first Test match in 1893.

MOST WICKETS IN A SERIES

England in England	46 (average 9.60)	J. C. Laker	1956
England in Australia	38 (average 23.18)	M. W. Tate	1924-25
Australia in England	42 (average 21.26)	T. M. Alderman (6 Tests)	1981
Australia in Australia	41 (average 12.85)	R. M. Hogg (6 Tests)	1978-79

WICKET-KEEPING – MOST DISMISSALS

	M	Ct	St	Total
†R. W. Marsh (Australia)	42	141	7	148
A. P. E. Knott (England)	34	97	8	105
†W. A. Oldfield (Australia)	38	59	31	90
A. A. Lilley (England)	32	65	19	84
A. T. W. Grout (Australia)	22	69	7	76
T. G. Evans (England)	31	63	12	75

† *The number of catches by R. W. Marsh (141) and stumpings by W. A. Oldfield (31) are respective records in England–Australia Tests.*

SCORERS OF OVER 2,000 RUNS

	T		I		NO		R		HI		Avge
D. G. Bradman	37	..	63	..	7	..	5,028	..	334	..	89.78
J. B. Hobbs	41	..	71	..	4	..	3,636	..	187	..	54.26
G. Boycott	38	..	71	..	9	..	2,945	..	191	..	47.50
D. I. Gower	37	..	67	..	3	..	2,862	..	215	..	44.71
W. R. Hammond	33	..	58	..	3	..	2,852	..	251	..	51.85
A. R. Border	36	..	66	..	17	..	2,834	..	196	..	57.83
H. Sutcliffe	27	..	46	..	5	..	2,741	..	194	..	66.85
C. Hill	41	..	76	..	1	..	2,660	..	188	..	35.46
J. H. Edrich	32	..	57	..	3	..	2,644	..	175	..	48.96
G. S. Chappell	35	..	65	..	8	..	2,619	..	144	..	45.94
M. C. Cowdrey	43	..	75	..	4	..	2,433	..	113	..	34.26
L. Hutton	27	..	49	..	6	..	2,428	..	364	..	56.46
R. N. Harvey	37	..	68	..	5	..	2,416	..	167	..	38.34
V. T. Trumper	40	..	74	..	5	..	2,263	..	185*	..	32.79
W. M. Lawry	29	..	51	..	5	..	2,233	..	166	..	48.54
S. E. Gregory	52	..	92	..	7	..	2,193	..	201	..	25.80
W. W. Armstrong	42	..	71	..	9	..	2,172	..	158	..	35.03
I. M. Chappell	30	..	56	..	4	..	2,138	..	192	..	41.11
K. F. Barrington	23	..	39	..	6	..	2,111	..	256	..	63.96
A. R. Morris	24	..	43	..	2	..	2,080	..	206	..	50.73

BOWLERS WITH 100 WICKETS

	T		Balls		R		W		5 W/i		Avge
D. K. Lillee	29	..	8,516	..	3,507	..	167	..	11	..	21.00
I. T. Botham	36	..	8,479	..	4,093	..	148	..	9	..	27.65
H. Trumble	31	..	7,895	..	2,945	..	141	..	9	..	20.88
R. G. D. Willis	35	..	7,294	..	3,346	..	128	..	7	..	26.14
M. A. Noble	39	..	6,845	..	2,860	..	115	..	9	..	24.86
R. R. Lindwall	29	..	6,728	..	2,559	..	114	..	6	..	22.44
W. Rhodes	41	..	5,791	..	2,616	..	109	..	6	..	24.00
S. F. Barnes	20	..	5,749	..	2,288	..	106	..	12	..	21.58
C. V. Grimmett	22	..	9,224	..	3,439	..	106	..	11	..	32.44
D. L. Underwood	29	..	8,000	..	2,770	..	105	..	4	..	26.38
A. V. Bedser	21	..	7,065	..	2,859	..	104	..	7	..	27.49
G. Giffen	31	..	6,325	..	2,791	..	103	..	7	..	27.09
W. J. O'Reilly	19	..	7,864	..	2,587	..	102	..	8	..	25.36
R. Peel	20	..	5,216	..	1,715	..	102	..	6	..	16.81
C. T. B. Turner	17	..	5,195	..	1,670	..	101	..	11	..	16.53
J. R. Thomson	21	..	4,951	..	2,418	..	100	..	5	..	24.18

ENGLAND v SOUTH AFRICA

Season	England	Captains	South Africa	T	E	SA	L
1888-89	C. A. Smith[1]		O. R. Dunell[2]	2	2	0	
1891-92	W. W. Read		W. H. Milton	1	1	0	
1895-96	Lord Hawke[3]		E. A. Halliwell[4]	3	3	0	
1898-99	Lord Hawke		M. Bisset	2	2	0	
1905-06	P. F. Warner		P. W. Sherwell	5	1	4	
1907	R. E. Foster		P. W. Sherwell	3	1	0	
1909-10	H. D. G. Leveson Gower[5]		S. J. Snooke	5	2	3	
1912	C. B. Fry		F. Mitchell[6]	3	3	0	
1913-14	J. W. H. T. Douglas		H. W. Taylor	5	4	0	

Captains

Season	England	South Africa	T	E	SA	D
1922-23	F. T. Mann	H. W. Taylor	5	2	1	2
1924	A. E. R. Gilligan[7]	H. W. Taylor	5	3	0	2
1927-28	R. T. Stanyforth[8]	H. G. Deane	5	2	2	1
1929	J. C. White[9]	H. G. Deane	5	2	0	3
1930-31	A. P. F. Chapman	H. G. Deane[10]	5	0	1	4
1935	R. E. S. Wyatt	H. F. Wade	5	0	1	4
1938-39	W. R. Hammond	A. Melville	5	1	0	4
1947	N. W. D. Yardley	A. Melville	5	3	0	2
1948-49	F. G. Mann	A. D. Nourse	5	2	0	3
1951	F. R. Brown	A. D. Nourse	5	3	1	1
1955	P. B. H. May	J. E. Cheetham[11]	5	3	2	0
1956-57	P. B. H. May	C. B. van Ryneveld[12]	5	2	2	1
1960	M. C. Cowdrey	D. J. McGlew	5	3	0	2
1964-65	M. J. K. Smith	T. L. Goddard	5	1	0	4
1965	M. J. K. Smith	P. L. van der Merwe	3	0	1	2
	In South Africa		58	25	13	20
	In England		44	21	5	18
	Totals		102	46	18	38

Notes: The following deputised for the official touring captain or were appointed by the home authority for only a minor proportion of the series:

[1]M. P. Bowden (Second). [2]W. H. Milton (Second). [3]Sir T. C. O'Brien (First). [4]A. R. Richards (Third). [5]F. L. Fane (Fourth and Fifth). [6]L. J. Tancred (Second and Third). [7]J. W. H. T. Douglas (Fourth). [8]G. T. S. Stevens (Fifth). [9]A. W. Carr (Fourth and Fifth). [10]E. P. Nupen (First), H. B. Cameron (Fourth and Fifth). [11]D. J. McGlew (Third and Fourth). [12]D. J. McGlew (Second).

HIGHEST INNINGS TOTALS

For England in England: 554-8 dec. at Lord's		1947
in South Africa: 654-5 at Durban		1938-39
For South Africa in England: 538 at Leeds		1951
in South Africa: 530 at Durban		1938-39

LOWEST INNINGS TOTALS

For England in England: 76 at Leeds		1907
in South Africa: 92 at Cape Town		1898-99
For South Africa in England: 30 at Birmingham		1924
in South Africa: 30 at Port Elizabeth		1895-96

INDIVIDUAL HUNDREDS

For England (87)

R. Abel (1)
120   Cape Town . 1888-89

L. E. G. Ames (2)
148*   The Oval ... 1935
115   Cape Town . 1938-39

K. F. Barrington (2)
148*   Durban 1964-65
121   Johannesburg 1964-65

G. Boycott (1)
117   Pt Elizabeth . 1964-65

L. C. Braund (1)
104†   Lord's 1907

D. C. S. Compton (7)
163†   Nottingham . 1947
208   Lord's 1947
115   Manchester . 1947

113   The Oval ... 1947
114   Johannesburg 1948-49
112   Nottingham . 1951
158   Manchester . 1955

M. C. Cowdrey (3)
101   Cape Town . 1956-57
155   The Oval ... 1960
105   Nottingham . 1965

D. Denton (1)
104   Johannesburg 1909-10

E. R. Dexter (1)
172   Johannesburg 1964-65

J. W. H. T. Douglas (1)
119†   Durban 1913-14

W. J. Edrich (3)
219   Durban 1938-39
189   Lord's 1947
191   Manchester . 1947

F. L. Fane (1)
143   Johannesburg 1905-06

C. B. Fry (1)
129   The Oval ... 1907

P. A. Gibb (2)
106†   Johannesburg 1938-39
120   Durban 1938-39

W. R. Hammond (6)
138*   Birmingham . 1929
101*   The Oval ... 1929
136*   Durban 1930-31
181   Cape Town . 1938-39
120   Durban 1938-39
140   Durban 1938-39

T. W. Hayward (1)
122   Johannesburg 1895-96

E. H. Hendren (2)
132   Leeds 1924
142   The Oval ... 1924

A. J. L. Hill (1)
124   Cape Town . 1895-96

J. B. Hobbs (2)
187   Cape Town . 1909-10
211   Lord's 1924

L. Hutton (4)
100   Leeds 1947
158   Johannesburg 1948-49
123   Johannesburg 1948-49
100   Leeds 1951

D. J. Insole (1)
110*   Durban 1956-57

M. Leyland (2)
102   Lord's 1929
161   The Oval ... 1935

F. G. Mann (1)
136*   Pt Elizabeth 1948-49

P. B. H. May (3)
138†   Leeds 1951
112   Lord's 1955
117   Manchester . 1955

C. P. Mead (3)
102   Johannesburg 1913-14
117   Pt Elizabeth 1913-14
181   Durban 1922-23

P. H. Parfitt (1)
122*   Johannesburg 1964-65

J. M. Parks (1)
108*   Durban 1964-65

E. Paynter (3)
117 }
100 }†Johannesburg 1938-39
243   Durban 1938-39

G. Pullar (1)
175   The Oval ... 1960

W. Rhodes (1)
152   Johannesburg 1913-14

P. E. Richardson (1)
117†   Johannesburg 1956-57

R. W. V. Robins (1)
108   Manchester . 1935

A. C. Russell (2)
140 }
111 }Durban 1922-23

R. T. Simpson (1)
137   Nottingham . 1951

M. J. K. Smith (1)
121   Cape Town . 1964-65

R. H. Spooner (1)
119†   Lord's 1912

H. Sutcliffe (6)
122   Lord's 1924
102   Johannesburg 1927-28
114   Birmingham . 1929
100   Lord's 1929
104 }
109* }The Oval ... 1929

M. W. Tate (1)
100*   Lord's 1929

E. Tyldesley (2)
122   Johannesburg 1927-28
100   Durban 1927-28

J. T. Tyldesley (1)
112   Cape Town . 1898-99

B. H. Valentine (1)
112   Cape Town . 1938-39

P. F. Warner (1)
132*†‡Johannesburg 1898-99

C. Washbrook (1)
195   Johannesburg 1948-49

A. J. Watkins (1)
111   Johannesburg 1948-49

H. Wood (1)
134*   Cape Town . 1891-92

F. E. Woolley (3)
115*   Johannesburg 1922-23
134*   Lord's 1924
154   Manchester . 1929

R. E. S. Wyatt (2)
113   Manchester . 1929
149   Nottingham . 1935

For South Africa (58)

E. J. Barlow (1)
138   Cape Town . 1964-65

K. C. Bland (2)
144*   Johannesburg 1964-65
127   The Oval ... 1965

R. H. Catterall (3)
120   Birmingham . 1924
120   Lord's 1924
119   Durban 1927-28

E. L. Dalton (2)
117   The Oval ... 1935
102   Johannesburg 1938-39

W. R. Endean (1)
116*   Leeds 1955

G. A. Faulkner (1)
123   Johannesburg 1909-10

T. L. Goddard (1)
112   Johannesburg 1964-65

C. M. H. Hathorn (1)
102   Johannesburg 1905-06

D. J. McGlew (2)
104*   Manchester . 1955
133   Leeds 1955

R. A. McLean (3)
142   Lord's 1955
100   Durban 1956-57
109   Manchester . 1960

A. Melville (4)
189
104* }Nottingham . 1947
117   Lord's 1947

B. Mitchell (7)
123   Cape Town . 1930-31
164*   Leeds 1935
128   The Oval ... 1935
109   Durban 1938-39
120 }
189* }The Oval ... 1947
120   Cape Town . 1948-49

A. D. Nourse (7)
120   Cape Town . 1938-39
103   Durban 1938-39
149   Nottingham . 1947
115   Manchester . 1947
112   Cape Town . 1948-49
129*   Johannesburg 1948-49
208   Nottingham . 1951

H. G. Owen-Smith (1)
129   Leeds 1929

A. J. Pithey (1)
154   Cape Town . 1964-65

R. G. Pollock (2)
137   Pt Elizabeth . 1964-65
125   Nottingham . 1965

E. A. B. Rowan (2)
156*   Johannesburg 1948-49
236   Leeds 1951

P. W. Sherwell (1)
115   Lord's 1907

I. J. Siedle (1)	102 Durban 1922-23	**W. W. Wade** (1)
141 Cape Town . 1930-31	101 Johannesburg 1927-28	125 Pt Elizabeth . 1948-49
J. H. Sinclair (1)	121 The Oval ... 1929	**J. H. B. Waite** (1)
106 Cape Town . 1898-99	117 Cape Town . 1930-31	113 Manchester . 1955
H. W. Taylor (7)	**P. G. V. van der Bijl** (1)	**G. C. White** (2)
109 Durban 1913-14	125 Durban 1938-39	147 Johannesburg 1905-06
176 Johannesburg 1922-23	**K. G. Viljoen** (1)	118 Durban 1909-10
101 Johannesburg 1922-23	124 Manchester . 1935	**P. L. Winslow** (1)
		108 Manchester . 1955

† *Signifies hundred on first appearance in England–South Africa Tests.*

‡ *P. F. Warner carried his bat through the second innings.*

Notes: The highest score by a South African batsman on début is 93* by A. W. Nourse at Johannesburg in 1905-06.

    P. N. F. Mansell made 90 at Leeds in 1951, the best on début in England.

    A. Melville's four hundreds were made in successive Test innings.

    H. Wood scored the only hundred of his career in a Test match.

RECORD PARTNERSHIP FOR EACH WICKET

For England

359 for 1st†	L. Hutton and C. Washbrook at Johannesburg	1948-49
280 for 2nd	P. A. Gibb and W. J. Edrich at Durban	1938-39
370 for 3rd†	W. J. Edrich and D. C. S. Compton at Lord's	1947
197 for 4th	W. R. Hammond and L. E. G. Ames at Cape Town	1938-39
237 for 5th	D. C. S. Compton and N. W. D. Yardley at Nottingham	1947
206* for 6th	K. F. Barrington and J. M. Parks at Durban	1964-65
115 for 7th	M. C. Bird and J. W. H. T. Douglas at Durban	1913-14
154 for 8th	C. W. Wright and H. R. Bromley-Davenport at Johannesburg ..	1895-96
71 for 9th	H. Wood and J. T. Hearne at Cape Town	1891-92
92 for 10th	A. C. Russell and A. E. R. Gilligan at Durban	1922-23

For South Africa

260 for 1st†	I. J. Siedle and B. Mitchell at Cape Town	1930-31
198 for 2nd†	E. A. B. Rowan and C. B. van Ryneveld at Leeds	1951
319 for 3rd	A. Melville and A. D. Nourse at Nottingham	1947
214 for 4th†	H. W. Taylor and H. G. Deane at The Oval	1929
157 for 5th†	A. J. Pithey and J. H. B. Waite at Johannesburg	1964-65
171 for 6th	J. H. B. Waite and P. L. Winslow at Manchester	1955
123 for 7th	H. G. Deane and E. P. Nupen at Durban	1927-28
109* for 8th	B. Mitchell and L. Tuckett at The Oval	1947
137 for 9th†	E. L. Dalton and A. B. C. Langton at The Oval	1935
103 for 10th†	H. G. Owen-Smith and A. J. Bell at Leeds	1929

† *Denotes record partnership against all countries.*

MOST RUNS IN A SERIES

England in England	753 (average 94.12)	D. C. S. Compton .	1947
England in South Africa	653 (average 81.62)	E. Paynter	1938-39
South Africa in England	621 (average 69.00)	A. D. Nourse	1947
South Africa in South Africa .	582 (average 64.66)	H. W. Taylor	1922-23

TEN WICKETS OR MORE IN A MATCH

For England (23)

11-110 (5-25, 6-85)†	S. F. Barnes, Lord's	1912
10-115 (6-52, 4-63)	S. F. Barnes, Leeds	1912
13-57 (5-28, 8-29)	S. F. Barnes, The Oval	1912
10-105 (5-57, 5-48)	S. F. Barnes, Durban	1913-14
17-159 (8-56, 9-103)	S. F. Barnes, Johannesburg	1913-14
14-144 (7-56, 7-88)	S. F. Barnes, Durban	1913-14
12-112 (7-58, 5-54)	A. V. Bedser, Manchester	1951
11-118 (6-68, 5-50)	C. Blythe, Cape Town	1905-06
15-99 (8-59, 7-40)	C. Blythe, Leeds	1907
10-104 (7-46, 3-58)	C. Blythe, Johannesburg	1909-10
15-28 (7-17, 8-11)	J. Briggs, Cape Town	1888-89
13-91 (6-54, 7-37)†	J. J. Ferris, Cape Town	1891-92
10-207 (7-115, 3-92)	A. P. Freeman, Leeds	1929
12-171 (7-71, 5-100)	A. P. Freeman, Manchester	1929
12-130 (7-70, 5-60)	G. Geary, Johannesburg	1927-28
11-90 (6-7, 5-83)	A. E. R. Gilligan, Birmingham	1924
10-119 (4-64, 6-55)	J. C. Laker, The Oval	1951
15-45 (7-38, 8-7)†	G. A. Lohmann, Port Elizabeth	1895-96
12-71 (9-28, 3-43)	G. A. Lohmann, Johannesburg	1895-96
11-97 (6-63, 5-34)	J. B. Statham, Lord's	1960
12-101 (7-52, 5-49)	R. Tattersall, Lord's	1951
12-89 (5-53, 7-36)	J. H. Wardle, Cape Town	1956-57
10-175 (5-95, 5-80)	D. V. P. Wright, Lord's	1947

For South Africa (6)

11-112 (4-49, 7-63)†	A. E. Hall, Cape Town	1922-23
11-150 (5-63, 6-87)	E. P. Nupen, Johannesburg	1930-31
10-87 (5-53, 5-34)	P. M. Pollock, Nottingham	1965
12-127 (4-57, 8-70)	S. J. Snooke, Johannesburg	1905-06
13-192 (4-79, 9-113)	H. J. Tayfield, Johannesburg	1956-57
12-181 (5-87, 7-94)	A. E. E. Vogler, Johannesburg	1909-10

† *Signifies ten wickets or more on first appearance in England–South Africa Tests.*

Note: S. F. Barnes took ten wickets or more in his first five Tests v South Africa and in six of his seven Tests v South Africa. A. P. Freeman and G. A. Lohmann took ten wickets or more in successive matches.

MOST WICKETS IN A SERIES

England in England	34 (average 8.29)	S. F. Barnes	1912
England in South Africa	49 (average 10.93)	S. F. Barnes	1913-14
South Africa in England	26 (average 21.84)	H. J. Tayfield	1955
South Africa in England	26 (average 22.57)	N. A. T. Adcock . .	1960
South Africa in South Africa .	37 (average 17.18)	H. J. Tayfield	1956-57

ENGLAND v WEST INDIES

	Captains					
Season	England	West Indies	T	E	WI	D
1928	A. P. F. Chapman	R. K. Nunes	3	3	0	0
1929-30	Hon. F. S. G. Calthorpe	E. L. G. Hoad[1]	4	1	1	2
1933	D. R. Jardine[2]	G. C. Grant	3	2	0	1
1934-35	R. E. S. Wyatt	G. C. Grant	4	1	2	1
1939	W. R. Hammond	R. S. Grant	3	1	0	2
1947-48	G. O. B. Allen[3]	J. D. C. Goddard[4]	4	0	2	2
1950	N. W. D. Yardley[5]	J. D. C. Goddard	4	1	3	0
1953-54	L. Hutton	J. B. Stollmeyer	5	2	2	1
1957	P. B. H. May	J. D. C. Goddard	5	3	0	2
1959-60	P. B. H. May[6]	F. C. M. Alexander	5	1	0	4

THE WISDEN TROPHY

	Captains						
Season	England	West Indies	T	E	WI	D	Held by
1963	E. R. Dexter	F. M. M. Worrell	5	1	3	1	WI
1966	M. C. Cowdrey[7]	G. S. Sobers	5	1	3	1	WI
1967-68	M. C. Cowdrey	G. S. Sobers	5	1	0	4	E
1969	R. Illingworth	G. S. Sobers	3	2	0	1	E
1973	R. Illingworth	R. B. Kanhai	3	0	2	1	WI
1973-74	M. H. Denness	R. B. Kanhai	5	1	1	3	WI
1976	A. W. Greig	C. H. Lloyd	5	0	3	2	WI
1980	I. T. Botham	C. H. Lloyd[8]	5	0	1	4	WI
1980-81†	I. T. Botham	C. H. Lloyd	4	0	2	2	WI
1984	D. I. Gower	C. H. Lloyd	5	0	5	0	WI
1985-86	D. I. Gower	I. V. A. Richards	5	0	5	0	WI
1988	J. E. Emburey[9]	I. V. A. Richards	5	0	4	1	WI
1989-90‡	G. A. Gooch[10]	I. V. A. Richards[11]	4	1	2	1	WI
	In England		54	14	24	16	
	In West Indies		45	8	17	20	
	Totals		99	22	41	36	

† *The Second Test, at Georgetown, was cancelled owing to political pressure.*
‡ *The Second Test, at Georgetown, was abandoned without a ball being bowled and is excluded.*

Notes: The following deputised for the official touring captain or were appointed by the home authority for only a minor proportion of the series:
[1]N. Betancourt (Second), M. P. Fernandes (Third), R. K. Nunes (Fourth). [2]R. E. S. Wyatt (Third). [3]K. Cranston (First). [4]G. A. Headley (First), G. E. Gomez (Second). [5]F. R. Brown (Fourth). [6]M. C. Cowdrey (Fourth and Fifth). [7]M. J. K. Smith (First), D. B. Close (Fifth). [8]I. V. A. Richards (Fifth). [9]M. W. Gatting (First), C. S. Cowdrey (Fourth), G. A. Gooch (Fifth). [10]A. J. Lamb (Fourth and Fifth). [11]D. L. Haynes (Third).

HIGHEST INNINGS TOTALS

For England in England: 619-6 dec. at Nottingham		1957
in West Indies: 849 at Kingston		1929-30
For West Indies in England: 687-8 dec. at The Oval		1976
in West Indies: 681-8 dec. at Port-of-Spain		1953-54

LOWEST INNINGS TOTALS

For England in England: 71 at Manchester 1976
         in West Indies: 103 at Kingston 1934-35

For West Indies in England: 86 at The Oval 1957
          in West Indies: 102 at Bridgetown 1934-35

INDIVIDUAL HUNDREDS

For England (85)

L. E. G. Ames (3)
105   Port-of-Spain 1929-30
149   Kingston ... 1929-30
126   Kingston ... 1934-35
D. L. Amiss (4)
174   Port-of-Spain 1973-74
262* Kingston ... 1973-74
118   Georgetown . 1973-74
203   The Oval ... 1976
A. H. Bakewell (1)
107† The Oval ... 1933
K. F. Barrington (3)
128† Bridgetown . 1959-60
121   Port-of-Spain 1959-60
143   Port-of-Spain 1967-68
G. Boycott (5)
116   Georgetown . 1967-68
128   Manchester . 1969
106   Lord's 1969
112   Port-of-Spain 1973-74
104* St John's 1980-81
D. C. S. Compton (2)
120† Lord's 1939
133   Port-of-Spain 1953-54
M. C. Cowdrey (6)
154† Birmingham . 1957
152   Lord's 1957
114   Kingston ... 1959-60
119   Port-of-Spain 1959-60
101   Kingston ... 1967-68
148   Port-of-Spain 1967-68
E. R. Dexter (2)
136*† Bridgetown . 1959-60
110   Georgetown . 1959-60
J. H. Edrich (1)
146   Bridgetown . 1967-68
T. G. Evans (1)
104   Manchester . 1950
K. W. R. Fletcher (1)
129* Bridgetown . 1973-74
G. Fowler (1)
106   Lord's 1984

G. A. Gooch (4)
123   Lord's 1980
116   Bridgetown . 1980-81
153   Kingston ... 1980-81
146   Nottingham . 1988
D. I. Gower (1)
154* Kingston ... 1980-81
T. W. Graveney (5)
258   Nottingham . 1957
164   The Oval ... 1957
109   Nottingham . 1966
165   The Oval ... 1966
118   Port-of-Spain 1967-68
A. W. Greig (3)
148   Bridgetown . 1973-74
121   Georgetown . 1973-74
116   Leeds 1976
S. C. Griffith (1)
140† Port-of-Spain 1947-48
W. R. Hammond (1)
138   The Oval ... 1939
J. H. Hampshire (1)
107† Lord's 1969
F. C. Hayes (1)
106*† The Oval ... 1973
E. H. Hendren (2)
205* Port-of-Spain 1929-30
123   Georgetown . 1929-30
J. B. Hobbs (1)
159   The Oval ... 1928
L. Hutton (5)
196† Lord's 1939
165* The Oval ... 1939
202*‡ The Oval ... 1950
169   Georgetown . 1953-54
205   Kingston ... 1953-54
R. Illingworth (1)
113   Lord's 1969
D. R. Jardine (1)
127   Manchester . 1933
A. P. E. Knott (1)
116   Leeds 1976

A. J. Lamb (6)
110   Lord's 1984
100   Leeds 1984
100* Manchester . 1984
113   Lord's 1988
132   Kingston ... 1989-90
119   Bridgetown . 1989-90
P. B. H. May (3)
135   Port-of-Spain 1953-54
285* Birmingham . 1957
104   Nottingham . 1957
C. Milburn (1)
126* Lord's 1966
J. T. Murray (1)
112† The Oval ... 1966
J. M. Parks (1)
101*† Port-of-Spain 1959-60
W. Place (1)
107   Kingston ... 1947-48
P. E. Richardson (2)
126   Nottingham . 1957
107   The Oval ... 1957
J. D. Robertson (1)
133   Port-of-Spain 1947-48
A. Sandham (2)
152† Bridgetown . 1929-30
325   Kingston ... 1929-30
M. J. K. Smith (1)
108   Port-of-Spain 1959-60
D. S. Steele (1)
106† Nottingham . 1976
R. Subba Row (1)
100† Georgetown . 1959-60
E. Tyldesley (1)
122† Lord's 1928
C. Washbrook (2)
114† Lord's 1950
102   Nottingham . 1950
W. Watson (1)
116† Kingston ... 1953-54
P. Willey (1)
100* The Oval ... 1980
102* St John's 1980-81

For West Indies (96)

I. Barrow (1)
105 Manchester . 1933
C. A. Best (1)
164 Bridgetown . 1989-90
B. F. Butcher (2)
133 Lord's 1963
209* Nottingham . 1966
G. M. Carew (1)
107 Port-of-Spain 1947-48
C. A. Davis (1)
103 Lord's 1969
P. J. L. Dujon (1)
101 Manchester . 1984
R. C. Fredericks (3)
150 Birmingham . 1973
138 Lord's 1976
109 Leeds 1976
A. G. Ganteaume (1)
112† Port-of-Spain 1947-48
H. A. Gomes (2)
143 Birmingham . 1984
104* Leeds 1984
C. G. Greenidge (7)
134 ⎱
101 ⎰ Manchester . 1976
115 Leeds 1976
214* Lord's 1984
223 Manchester . 1984
103 Lord's 1988
149 St John's . . 1989-90
D. L. Haynes (5)
184 Lord's 1980
125 The Oval . . . 1984
131 St John's 1985-86
109 Bridgetown . 1989-90
167 St John's 1989-90
G. A. Headley (8)
176† Bridgetown . 1929-30
114 ⎱
112 ⎰ Georgetown . 1929-30
223 Kingston . . . 1929-30
169* Manchester . 1933
270† Kingston . . . 1934-35

106 ⎱
107 ⎰ Lord's 1939
D. A. J. Holford (1)
105* Lord's 1966
J. K. Holt (1)
166 Bridgetown . 1953-54
C. C. Hunte (3)
182 Manchester . 1963
108* The Oval . . . 1963
135 Manchester . 1966
B. D. Julien (1)
121 Lord's 1973
A. I. Kallicharran (2)
158 Port-of-Spain 1973-74
119 Bridgetown . 1973-74
R. B. Kanhai (5)
110 Port-of-Spain 1959-60
104 The Oval . . . 1966
153 Port-of-Spain 1967-68
150 Georgetown . 1967-68
157 Lord's 1973
C. H. Lloyd (5)
118† Port-of-Spain 1967-68
113* Bridgetown . 1967-68
132 The Oval . . . 1973
101 Manchester . 1980
100 Bridgetown . 1980-81
S. M. Nurse (2)
137 Leeds 1966
136 Port-of-Spain 1967-68
A. F. Rae (2)
106 Lord's 1950
109 The Oval 1950
I. V. A. Richards (8)
232† Nottingham . 1976
135 Manchester . 1976
291 The Oval . . . 1976
145 Lord's 1980
182* Bridgetown . 1980-81
114 St John's 1980-81
117 Birmingham . 1984
110* St John's . . . 1985-86

R. B. Richardson (2)
102 Port-of-Spain 1985-86
160 Bridgetown . 1985-86
C. A. Roach (2)
122 Bridgetown . 1929-30
209 Georgetown . 1929-30
L. G. Rowe (3)
120 Kingston . . . 1973-74
302 Bridgetown . 1973-74
123 Port-of-Spain 1973-74
O. G. Smith (2)
161† Birmingham . 1957
168 Nottingham . 1957
G. S. Sobers (10)
226 Bridgetown . 1959-60
147 Kingston . . . 1959-60
145 Georgetown . 1959-60
102 Leeds 1963
161 Manchester . 1966
163* Lord's 1966
174 Leeds 1966
113* Kingston . . . 1967-68
152 Georgetown . 1967-68
150* Lord's 1973
C. L. Walcott (4)
168* Lord's 1950
220 Bridgetown . 1953-54
124 Port-of-Spain 1953-54
116 Kingston . . . 1953-54
E. D. Weekes (3)
141 Kingston . . 1947-48
129 Nottingham . 1950
206 Port-of-Spain 1953-54
K. H. Weekes (1)
137 The Oval . . . 1939
F. M. M. Worrell (6)
131† Georgetown . 1947-48
261 Nottingham . 1950
138 The Oval . . . 1950
167 Port-of-Spain 1953-54
191*‡ Nottingham . 1957
191* Bridgetown . 1959-60

† *Signifies hundred on first appearance in England–West Indies Tests. S. C. Griffith provides the only instance for England of a player hitting his maiden century in first-class cricket in his first Test.*
‡ *Carried his bat.*

RECORD PARTNERSHIPS FOR EACH WICKET

For England

212 for 1st	C. Washbrook and R. T. Simpson at Nottingham	1950
266 for 2nd	P. E. Richardson and T. W. Graveney at Nottingham	1957
264 for 3rd	L. Hutton and W. R. Hammond at The Oval	1939
411 for 4th†	P. B. H. May and M. C. Cowdrey at Birmingham	1957
130* for 5th	C. Milburn and T. W. Graveney at Lord's	1966

163 for 6th	A. W. Greig and A. P. E. Knott at Bridgetown	1973-74
197 for 7th†	M. J. K. Smith and J. M. Parks at Port-of-Spain	1959-60
217 for 8th	T. W. Graveney and J. T. Murray at The Oval	1966
109 for 9th	G. A. R. Lock and P. I. Pocock at Georgetown	1967-68
128 for 10th	K. Higgs and J. A. Snow at The Oval	1966

For West Indies

298 for 1st†	C. G. Greenidge and D. L. Haynes at St John's	1989-90
287* for 2nd	C. G. Greenidge and H. A. Gomes at Lord's	1984
338 for 3rd†	E. D. Weekes and F. M. M. Worrell at Port-of-Spain	1953-54
399 for 4th†	G. S. Sobers and F. M. M. Worrell at Bridgetown	1959-60
265 for 5th†	S. M. Nurse and G. S. Sobers at Leeds	1966
274* for 6th†	G. S. Sobers and D. A. J. Holford at Lord's	1966
155* for 7th‡	G. S. Sobers and B. D. Julien at Lord's	1973
99 for 8th	C. A. McWatt and J. K. Holt at Georgetown	1953-54
150 for 9th	E. A. E. Baptiste and M. A. Holding at Birmingham	1984
67* for 10th	M. A. Holding and C. E. H. Croft at St John's	1980-81

† *Denotes record partnership against all countries.*

‡ *231 runs were added for this wicket in two separate partnerships: G. S. Sobers retired ill and was replaced by K. D. Boyce when 155 had been added.*

TEN WICKETS OR MORE IN A MATCH

For England (11)

11-98 (7-44, 4-54)	T. E. Bailey, Lord's	1957
10-93 (5-54, 5-39)	A. P. Freeman, Manchester	1928
13-156 (8-86, 5-70)	A. W. Greig, Port-of-Spain	1973-74
11-48 (5-28, 6-20)	G. A. R. Lock, The Oval	1957
10-137 (4-60, 6-77)	D. E. Malcolm, Port-of-Spain	1989-90
11-96 (5-37, 6-59)†	C. S. Marriott, The Oval	1933
10-142 (4-82, 6-60)	J. A. Snow, Georgetown	1967-68
10-195 (5-105, 5-90)†	G. T. S. Stevens, Bridgetown	1929-30
11-152 (6-100, 5-52)	F. S. Trueman, Lord's	1963
12-119 (5-75, 7-44)	F. S. Trueman, Birmingham	1963
11-149 (4-79, 7-70)	W. Voce, Port-of-Spain	1929-30

For West Indies (12)

10-127 (2-82, 8-45)	C. E. L. Ambrose, Bridgetown	1989-90
11-147 (5-70, 6-77)†	K. D. Boyce, The Oval	1973
11-229 (5-137, 6-92)	W. Ferguson, Port-of-Spain	1947-48
11-157 (5-59, 6-98)†	L. R. Gibbs, Manchester	1963
10-106 (5-37, 5-69)	L. R. Gibbs, Manchester	1966
14-149 (8-92, 6-57)	M. A. Holding, The Oval	1976
10-96 (5-41, 5-55)†	H. H. H. Johnson, Kingston	1947-48
10-92 (6-32, 4-60)	M. D. Marshall, Lord's	1988
11-152 (5-66, 6-86)	S. Ramadhin, Lord's	1950
10-123 (5-60, 5-63)	A. M. E. Roberts, Lord's	1976
11-204 (8-104, 3-100)†	A. L. Valentine, Manchester	1950
10-160 (4-121, 6-39)	A. L. Valentine, The Oval	1950

† *Signifies ten wickets or more on first appearance in England–West Indies Tests.*

Note: F. S. Trueman took ten wickets or more in successive matches.

ENGLAND v NEW ZEALAND

Captains

Season	England	New Zealand	T	E	NZ	D
1929-30	A. H. H. Gilligan	T. C. Lowry	4	1	0	3
1931	D. R. Jardine	T. C. Lowry	3	1	0	2
1932-33	D. R. Jardine[1]	M. L. Page	2	0	0	2
1937	R. W. V. Robins	M. L. Page	3	1	0	2
1946-47	W. R. Hammond	W. A. Hadlee	1	0	0	1
1949	F. G. Mann[2]	W. A. Hadlee	4	0	0	4
1950-51	F. R. Brown	W. A. Hadlee	2	1	0	1
1954-55	L. Hutton	G. O. Rabone	2	2	0	0
1958	P. B. H. May	J. R. Reid	5	4	0	1
1958-59	P. B. H. May	J. R. Reid	2	1	0	1
1962-63	E. R. Dexter	J. R. Reid	3	3	0	0
1965	M. J. K. Smith	J. R. Reid	3	3	0	0
1965-66	M. J. K. Smith	B. W. Sinclair[3]	3	0	0	3
1969	R. Illingworth	G. T. Dowling	3	2	0	1
1970-71	R. Illingworth	G. T. Dowling	2	1	0	1
1973	R. Illingworth	B. E. Congdon	3	2	0	1
1974-75	M. H. Denness	B. E. Congdon	2	1	0	1
1977-78	G. Boycott	M. G. Burgess	3	1	1	1
1978	J. M. Brearley	M. G. Burgess	3	3	0	0
1983	R. G. D. Willis	G. P. Howarth	4	3	1	0
1983-84	R. G. D. Willis	G. P. Howarth	3	0	1	2
1986	M. W. Gatting	J. V. Coney	3	0	1	2
1987-88	M. W. Gatting	J. J. Crowe[4]	3	0	0	3
1990	G. A. Gooch	J. G. Wright	3	1	0	2
	In New Zealand		32	11	2	19
	In England		37	20	2	15
	Totals		69	31	4	34

Notes: The following deputised for the official touring captain or were appointed by the home authority for only a minor proportion of the series:
[1]R. E. S. Wyatt (Second). [2]F. R. Brown (Third and Fourth). [3]M. E. Chapple (First). [4]J. G. Wright (Third).

HIGHEST INNINGS TOTALS

For England in England: 546-4 dec. at Leeds	1965
in New Zealand: 593-6 dec. at Auckland	1974-75
For New Zealand in England: 551-9 dec. at Lord's	1973
in New Zealand: 537 at Wellington	1983-84

LOWEST INNINGS TOTALS

For England in England: 158 at Birmingham	1990
in New Zealand: 64 at Wellington	1977-78
For New Zealand in England: 47 at Lord's	1958
in New Zealand: 26 at Auckland	1954-55

INDIVIDUAL HUNDREDS

For England (71)

G. O. B. Allen (1)
122† Lord's 1931
L. E. G. Ames (2)
137† Lord's 1931
103 Christchurch. 1932-33
D. L. Amiss (2)
138*† Nottingham . 1973
164* Christchurch. 1974-75
M. A. Atherton (1)
151† Nottingham . 1990
T. E. Bailey (1)
134* Christchurch. 1950-51
K. F. Barrington (3)
126† Auckland ... 1962-63
137 Birmingham . 1965
163 Leeds 1965
I. T. Botham (3)
103 Christchurch. 1977-78
103 Nottingham . 1983
138 Wellington . 1983-84
E. H. Bowley (1)
109 Auckland ... 1929-30
G. Boycott (2)
115 Leeds 1973
131 Nottingham . 1978
B. C. Broad (1)
114† Christchurch. 1987-88
D. C. S. Compton (2)
114 Leeds 1949
116 Lord's 1949
M. C. Cowdrey (2)
128* Wellington . 1962-63
119 Lord's 1965
M. H. Denness (1)
181 Auckland ... 1974-75
E. R. Dexter (1)
141 Christchurch. 1958-59
B. L. D'Oliveira (1)
100 Christchurch. 1970-71

K. S. Duleepsinhji (2)
117 Auckland ... 1929-30
109 The Oval ... 1931
J. H. Edrich (3)
310*† Leeds 1965
115 Lord's 1969
155 Nottingham . 1969
W. J. Edrich (1)
100 The Oval ... 1949
K. W. R. Fletcher (2)
178 Lord's 1973
216 Auckland ... 1974-75
G. Fowler (1)
105† The Oval ... 1983
M. W. Gatting (1)
121 The Oval ... 1986
G. A. Gooch (2)
183 Lord's 1986
154 Birmingham . 1990
D. I. Gower (4)
111† The Oval ... 1978
112* Leeds 1983
108 Lord's 1983
131 The Oval 1986
A. W. Greig (1)
139† Nottingham . 1973
W. R. Hammond (4)
100* The Oval ... 1931
227 Christchurch. 1932-33
336* Auckland ... 1932-33
140 Lord's 1937
J. Hardstaff jun. (2)
114† Lord's 1937
103 The Oval ... 1937
L. Hutton (3)
100 Manchester . 1937
101 Leeds 1949
206 The Oval ... 1949

B. R. Knight (1)
125† Auckland ... 1962-6
A. P. E. Knott (1)
101 Auckland ... 1970-7
A. J. Lamb (2)
102*† The Oval ... 198
137* Nottingham . 198
G. B. Legge (1)
196 Auckland ... 1929-3
P. B. H. May (3)
113* Leeds 195
101 Manchester . 195
124* Auckland ... 1958-5
C. A. Milton (1)
104*† Leeds 195
P. H. Parfitt (1)
131*† Auckland ... 1962-6
C. T. Radley (1)
158 Auckland ... 1977-78
D. W. Randall (2)
164 Wellington . 1983-84
104 Auckland ... 1983-8
P. E. Richardson (1)
100† Birmingham . 195
J. D. Robertson (1)
121† Lord's 194
P. J. Sharpe (1)
111 Nottingham . 196
R. T. Simpson (1)
103† Manchester . 194
H. Sutcliffe (2)
117† The Oval ... 193
109* Manchester . 193
C. J. Tavaré (1)
109† The Oval ... 198
C. Washbrook (1)
103* Leeds 194

For New Zealand (34)

J. G. Bracewell (1)
110 Nottingham . 1986
M. G. Burgess (2)
104 Auckland ... 1970-71
105 Lord's 1973
J. V. Coney (1)
174* Wellington .. 1983-84
B. E. Congdon (3)
104 Christchurch. 1965-66
176 Nottingham . 1973
175 Lord's 1973

J. J. Crowe (1)
128 Auckland ... 1983-84
M. D. Crowe (3)
100 Wellington .. 1983-84
106 Lord's 1986
143 Wellington .. 1987-88
C. S. Dempster (2)
136 Wellington .. 1929-30
120 Lord's 1931
M. P. Donnelly (1)
206 Lord's 1949

T. J. Franklin (1)
101 Lord's 1990
M. J. Greatbatch (1)
107*† Auckland ... 1987-88
W. A. Hadlee (1)
116 Christchurch. 1946-47
G. P. Howarth (3)
122 ⎫
122 ⎬ Auckland ... 1977-78
123 Lord's 1978

. E. Mills (1)			J. R. Reid (1)			B. Sutcliffe (2)		
17†	Wellington ..	1929-30	100	Christchurch.	1962-63	101	Manchester .	1949
A. L. Page (1)			**K. R. Rutherford** (1)			116	Christchurch.	1950-51
04	Lord's	1931	107*	Wellington ..	1987-88	**J. G. Wright** (3)		
. M. Parker (1)			**B. W. Sinclair** (1)			130	Auckland ...	1983-84
21	Auckland ...	1974-75	114	Auckland ...	1965-66	119	The Oval ...	1986
. Pollard (2)			**I. D. S. Smith** (1)			103	Auckland ...	1987-88
16	Nottingham .	1973	113*	Auckland ...	1983-84			
05*	Lord's	1973						

† *Signifies hundred on first appearance in England–New Zealand Tests.*

RECORD PARTNERSHIPS FOR EACH WICKET

For England

23 for 1st	G. Fowler and C. J. Tavaré at The Oval	1983
69 for 2nd	J. H. Edrich and K. F. Barrington at Leeds	1965
45 for 3rd	W. R. Hammond and J. Hardstaff jun. at Lord's	1937
66 for 4th	M. H. Denness and K. W. R. Fletcher at Auckland	1974-75
42 for 5th	W. R. Hammond and L. E. G. Ames at Christchurch	1932-33
40 for 6th†	P. H. Parfitt and B. R. Knight at Auckland	1962-63
49 for 7th	A. P. E. Knott and P. Lever at Auckland	1970-71
46 for 8th†	L. E. G. Ames and G. O. B. Allen at Lord's	1931
63* for 9th†	M. C. Cowdrey and A. C. Smith at Wellington	1962-63
59 for 10th	A. P. E. Knott and N. Gifford at Nottingham	1973

For New Zealand

276 for 1st	C. S. Dempster and J. E. Mills at Wellington	1929-30
31 for 2nd	B. Sutcliffe and J. R. Reid at Christchurch	1950-51
10 for 3rd	B. A. Edgar and M. D. Crowe at Lord's	1986
55 for 4th	M. D. Crowe and M. J. Greatbatch at Wellington	1987-88
77 for 5th	B. E. Congdon and V. Pollard at Nottingham	1973
34 for 6th	K. R. Rutherford and J. G. Bracewell at Wellington	1987-88
04 for 7th	B. Sutcliffe and V. Pollard at Birmingham	1965
04 for 8th	D. A. R. Moloney and A. W. Roberts at Lord's	1937
18 for 9th	J. V. Coney and B. L. Cairns at Wellington	1983-84
57 for 10th	F. L. H. Mooney and J. Cowie at Leeds	1949

† *Denotes record partnership against all countries.*

TEN WICKETS OR MORE IN A MATCH

For England (7)

1-140 (6-101, 5-39)	I. T. Botham, Lord's	1978
0-149 (5-98, 5-51)	A. W. Greig, Auckland	1974-75
1-65 (4-14, 7-51)	G. A. R. Lock, Leeds	1958
1-84 (5-31, 6-53)	G. A. R. Lock, Christchurch	1958-59
1-70 (4-38, 7-32)†	D. L. Underwood, Lord's	1969
2-101 (6-41, 6-60)	D. L. Underwood, The Oval	1969
2-97 (6-12, 6-85)	D. L. Underwood, Christchurch	1970-71

For New Zealand (4)

0-144 (7-74, 3-70)	B. L. Cairns, Leeds	1983
0-140 (4-73, 6-67)	J. Cowie, Manchester	1937
0-100 (4-74, 6-26)	R. J. Hadlee, Wellington	1977-78
0-140 (6-80, 4-60)	R. J. Hadlee, Nottingham	1986

† *Signifies ten wickets or more on first appearance in England–New Zealand Tests.*
Note: D. L. Underwood took twelve wickets in successive matches against New Zealand in 1969 and 1970-71.

HAT-TRICK AND FOUR WICKETS IN FIVE BALLS

M. J. C. Allom, in his first Test match, v New Zealand at Christchurch in 1929-30, dismissed C. S. Dempster, T. C. Lowry, K. C. James, and F. T. Badcock to take four wickets in five balls (w-www).

ENGLAND v INDIA

Season	England	Captains	India	T	E	I	D
1932	D. R. Jardine		C. K. Nayudu	1	1	0	0
1933-34	D. R. Jardine		C. K. Nayudu	3	2	0	1
1936	G. O. B. Allen	Maharaj of Vizianagram		3	2	0	1
1946	W. R. Hammond		Nawab of Pataudi sen.	3	1	0	2
1951-52	N. D. Howard[1]		V. S. Hazare	5	1	1	3
1952	L. Hutton		V. S. Hazare	4	3	0	1
1959	P. B. H. May[2]		D. K. Gaekwad[3]	5	5	0	0
1961-62	E. R. Dexter		N. J. Contractor	5	0	2	3
1963-64	M. J. K. Smith	Nawab of Pataudi jun.		5	0	0	5
1967	D. B. Close	Nawab of Pataudi jun.		3	3	0	0
1971	R. Illingworth		A. L. Wadekar	3	0	1	2
1972-73	A. R. Lewis		A. L. Wadekar	5	1	2	2
1974	M. H. Denness		A. L. Wadekar	3	3	0	0
1976-77	A. W. Greig		B. S. Bedi	5	3	1	1
1979	J. M. Brearley		S. Venkataraghavan	4	1	0	3
1979-80	J. M. Brearley		G. R. Viswanath	1	1	0	0
1981-82	K. W. R. Fletcher		S. M. Gavaskar	6	0	1	5
1982	R. G. D. Willis		S. M. Gavaskar	3	1	0	2
1984-85	D. I. Gower		S. M. Gavaskar	5	2	1	2
1986	M. W. Gatting[4]		Kapil Dev	3	0	2	1
1990	G. A. Gooch		M. Azharuddin	3	1	0	2
	In England			38	21	3	14
	In India			40	10	8	22
	Totals			78	31	11	36

Notes: The 1932 Indian touring team was captained by the Maharaj of Porbandar but he did not play in the Test match.

The following deputised for the official touring captain or were appointed by the home authority for only a minor proportion of the series:
[1]D. B. Carr (Fifth). [2]M. C. Cowdrey (Fourth and Fifth). [3]Pankaj Roy (Second). [4]D. I. Gower (First).

HIGHEST INNINGS TOTALS

For England in England: 653-4 dec. at Lord's	1990
in India: 652-7 dec. at Madras	1984-85
For India in England: 606-9 dec. at The Oval	1990
in India: 553-8 dec. at Kanpur	1984-85

LOWEST INNINGS TOTALS

For England in England: 101 at The Oval	1971
in India: 102 at Bombay	1981-82
For India in England: 42 at Lord's	1974
in India: 83 at Madras	1976-77

INDIVIDUAL HUNDREDS

For England (70)

D. L. Amiss (2)		
188	Lord's	1974
179	Delhi	1976-77
M. A. Atherton (1)		
131	Manchester	1990
K. F. Barrington (3)		
151*	Bombay	1961-62
172	Kanpur	1961-62
113*	Delhi	1961-62
I. T. Botham (5)		
137	Leeds	1979
114	Bombay	1979-80
142	Kanpur	1981-82
128	Manchester	1982
208	The Oval	1982
G. Boycott (4)		
246*†	Leeds	1967
155	Birmingham	1979
125	The Oval	1979
105	Delhi	1981-82
M. C. Cowdrey (3)		
160	Leeds	1959
107	Calcutta	1963-64
151	Delhi	1963-64
M. H. Denness (2)		
118	Lord's	1974
100	Birmingham	1974
E. R. Dexter (2)		
126*	Kanpur	1961-62
B. L. D'Oliveira (1)		
109†	Leeds	1967
J. H. Edrich (1)		
100*	Manchester	1974
T. G. Evans (1)		
104	Lord's	1952
K. W. R. Fletcher (2)		
113	Bombay	1972-73
123*	Manchester	1974

G. Fowler (1)		
201	Madras	1984-85
M. W. Gatting (3)		
136	Bombay	1984-85
207	Madras	1984-85
183*	Birmingham	1986
G. A. Gooch (5)		
127	Madras	1981-82
114	Lord's	1986
333	} Lord's	1990
123		
116	Manchester	1990
D. I. Gower (2)		
200*†	Birmingham	1979
157*	The Oval	1990
T. W. Graveney (2)		
175†	Bombay	1951-52
151	Lord's	1967
A. W. Greig (3)		
148	Bombay	1972-73
106	Lord's	1974
103	Calcutta	1976-77
W. R. Hammond (2)		
167	Manchester	1936
217	The Oval	1936
J. Hardstaff jun. (1)		
205*	Lord's	1946
L. Hutton (2)		
150	Lord's	1952
104	Manchester	1952
R. Illingworth (1)		
107	Manchester	1971
B. R. Knight (1)		
127	Kanpur	1963-64

A. J. Lamb (3)		
107	The Oval	1982
139	Lord's	1990
109	Manchester	1990
A. R. Lewis (1)		
125	Kanpur	1972-73
D. Lloyd (1)		
214*	Birmingham	1974
B. W. Luckhurst (1)		
101	Manchester	1971
P. B. H. May (1)		
106	Nottingham	1959
P. H. Parfitt (1)		
121	Kanpur	1963-64
G. Pullar (2)		
131	Manchester	1959
119	Kanpur	1961-62
D. W. Randall (1)		
126	Lord's	1982
R. T. Robinson (1)		
160	Delhi	1984-85
D. S. Sheppard (1)		
119	The Oval	1952
M. J. K. Smith (1)		
100†	Manchester	1959
R. A. Smith (2)		
100*†	Lord's	1990
121*	Manchester	1990
C. J. Tavaré (1)		
149	Delhi	1981-82
B. H. Valentine (1)		
136†	Bombay	1933-34
C. F. Walters (1)		
102	Madras	1933-34
A. J. Watkins (1)		
137*†	Delhi	1951-52
T. S. Worthington (1)		
128	The Oval	1936

For India (56)

L. Amarnath (1)		
118†	Bombay	1933-34
M. Azharuddin (5)		
110†	Calcutta	1984-85
105	Madras	1984-85
122	Kanpur	1984-85
121	Lord's	1990
179	Manchester	1990
A. A. Baig (1)		
112†	Manchester	1959
F. M. Engineer (1)		
121	Bombay	1972-73
S. M. Gavaskar (4)		
101	Manchester	1974
108	Bombay	1976-77

221	The Oval	1979
172	Bangalore	1981-82
Hanumant Singh (1)		
105†	Delhi	1963-64
V. S. Hazare (2)		
164*	Delhi	1951-52
155	Bombay	1951-52
M. L. Jaisimha (2)		
127	Delhi	1961-62
129	Calcutta	1963-64
Kapil Dev (2)		
116	Kanpur	1981-82
110	The Oval	1990
S. M. H. Kirmani (1)		
102	Bombay	1984-85

B. K. Kunderan (2)		
192	Madras	1963-64
100	Delhi	1963-64
V. L. Manjrekar (3)		
133	Leeds	1952
189*	Delhi	1961-62
108	Madras	1963-64
V. Mankad (1)		
184	Lord's	1952
V. M. Merchant (3)		
114	Manchester	1936
128	The Oval	1946
154	Delhi	1951-52
Mushtaq Ali (1)		
112	Manchester	1936

R. G. Nadkarni (1)
122*   Kanpur   1963-64
Nawab of Pataudi jun. (3)
103   Madras   1961-62
203*   Delhi   1963-64
148   Leeds   1967
S. M. Patil (1)
129*   Manchester   .   1982
D. G. Phadkar (1)
115   Calcutta   1951-52
Pankaj Roy (2)
140   Bombay   1951-52
111   Madras   1951-52

R. J. Shastri (4)
142   Bombay   1984-85
111   Calcutta   1984-85
100   Lord's   1990
187   The Oval   ...   1990
S. R. Tendulkar (1)
119*   Manchester   .   1990
P. R. Umrigar (3)
130*   Madras   1951-52
118   Manchester   .   1959
147*   Kanpur   1961-62
D. B. Vengsarkar (5)
103   Lord's   1979

157   Lord's   1982
137   Kanpur   1984-85
126*   Lord's   1986
102*   Leeds   1986
G. R. Viswanath (4)
113   Bombay   1972-73
113   Lord's   1979
107   Delhi   1981-82
222   Madras   1981-82
Yashpal Sharma (1)
140   Madras   1981-82

† *Signifies hundred on first appearance in England–India Tests.*

Notes: G. A. Gooch's match aggregate of 456 (333 and 123) for England at Lord's in 1990 is the record in Test matches and provides the only instance of a batsman scoring a triple-hundred and a hundred in the same first-class match. His 333 is the highest innings in any match at Lord's.
    M. Azharuddin scored hundreds in each of his first three Tests.

RECORD PARTNERSHIPS FOR EACH WICKET

For England

225 for 1st	G. A. Gooch and M. A. Atherton at Manchester	1990
241 for 2nd	G. Fowler and M. W. Gatting at Madras	1984-85
308 for 3rd	G. A. Gooch and A. J. Lamb at Lord's	1990
266 for 4th	W. R. Hammond and T. S. Worthington at The Oval	1936
254 for 5th†	K. W. R. Fletcher and A. W. Greig at Bombay	1972-73
171 for 6th	I. T. Botham and R. W. Taylor at Bombay	1979-80
125 for 7th	D. W. Randall and P. H. Edmonds at Lord's	1982
168 for 8th	R. Illingworth and P. Lever at Manchester	1971
83 for 9th	K. W. R. Fletcher and N. Gifford at Madras	1972-73
70 for 10th	P. J. W. Allott and R. G. D. Willis at Lord's	1982

For India

213 for 1st	S. M. Gavaskar and C. P. S. Chauhan at The Oval	1979
192 for 2nd	F. M. Engineer and A. L. Wadekar at Bombay	1972-73
316 for 3rd†‡	G. R. Viswanath and Yashpal Sharma at Madras	1981-82
222 for 4th†	V. S. Hazare and V. L. Manjrekar at Leeds	1952
214 for 5th†	M. Azharuddin and R. J. Shastri at Calcutta	1984-85
130 for 6th	S. M. H. Kirmani and Kapil Dev at The Oval	1982
235 for 7th†	R. J. Shastri and S. M. H. Kirmani at Bombay	1984-85
128 for 8th	R. J. Shastri and S. M. H. Kirmani at Delhi	1981-82
104 for 9th	R. J. Shastri and Madan Lal at Delhi	1981-82
51 for 10th	{ R. G. Nadkarni and B. S. Chandrasekhar at Calcutta	1963-64
	{ S. M. H. Kirmani and Chetan Sharma at Madras	1984-85

† *Denotes record partnership against all countries.*

‡ *415 runs were added between the fall of the 2nd and 3rd wickets: D. B. Vengsarkar retired hurt when he and Viswanath had added 99 runs.*

TEN WICKETS OR MORE IN A MATCH

For England (7)

10-78 (5-35, 5-43)†	G. O. B. Allen, Lord's	1936
11-145 (7-49, 4-96)†	A. V. Bedser, Lord's	1946
11-93 (4-41, 7-52)	A. V. Bedser, Manchester	1946
13-106 (6-58, 7-48)	I. T. Botham, Bombay	1979-80
11-163 (6-104, 5-59)†	N. A. Foster, Madras	1984-85
10-70 (7-46, 3-24)†	J. K. Lever, Delhi	1976-77
11-153 (7-49, 4-104)	H. Verity, Madras	1933-34

For India (4)

10-177 (6-105, 4-72)	S. A. Durani, Madras	1961-62
12-108 (8-55, 4-53)	V. Mankad, Madras	1951-52
10-188 (4-130, 6-58)	Chetan Sharma, Birmingham	1986
12-181 (6-64, 6-117)†	L. Sivaramakrishnan, Bombay	1984-85

† *Signifies ten wickets or more on first appearance in England–India Tests.*

Note: A. V. Bedser took eleven wickets in a match in the first two Tests of his career.

ENGLAND v PAKISTAN

Season	England	Captains	Pakistan	T	E	P	D
1954	L. Hutton[1]		A. H. Kardar	4	1	1	2
1961-62	E. R. Dexter		Imtiaz Ahmed	3	1	0	2
1962	E. R. Dexter[2]		Javed Burki	5	4	0	1
1967	D. B. Close		Hanif Mohammad	3	2	0	1
1968-69	M. C. Cowdrey		Saeed Ahmed	3	0	0	3
1971	R. Illingworth		Intikhab Alam	3	1	0	2
1972-73	A. R. Lewis		Majid Khan	3	0	0	3
1974	M. H. Denness		Intikhab Alam	3	0	0	3
1977-78	J. M. Brearley[3]		Wasim Bari	3	0	0	3
1978	J. M. Brearley		Wasim Bari	3	2	0	1
1982	R. G. D. Willis[4]		Imran Khan	3	2	1	0
1983-84	R. G. D. Willis[5]		Zaheer Abbas	3	0	1	2
1987	M. W. Gatting		Imran Khan	5	0	1	4
1987-88	M. W. Gatting		Javed Miandad	3	0	1	2
	In England			29	12	3	14
	In Pakistan			18	1	2	15
	Totals			47	13	5	29

Notes: The following deputised for the official touring captain or were appointed by the home authority for only a minor proportion of the series:
[1]D. S. Sheppard (Second and Third). [2]M. C. Cowdrey (Third). [3]G. Boycott (Third). [4]D. I. Gower (Second). [5]D. I. Gower (Second and Third).

HIGHEST INNINGS TOTALS

For England in England: 558-6 dec. at Nottingham		1954
in Pakistan: 546-8 dec. at Faisalabad		1983-84
For Pakistan in England: 708 at The Oval		1987
in Pakistan: 569-9 dec. at Hyderabad		1972-73

LOWEST INNINGS TOTALS

For England in England: 130 at The Oval 1954
             in Pakistan: 130 at Lahore 1987-88

For Pakistan in England: 87 at Lord's 1954
             in Pakistan: 191 at Faisalabad 1987-88

INDIVIDUAL HUNDREDS

For England (41)

D. L. Amiss (3)
112   Lahore 1972-73
158   Hyderabad .. 1972-73
183   The Oval ... 1974
C. W. J. Athey (1)
123   Lord's 1987
K. F. Barrington (4)
139† Lahore 1961-62
148   Lord's 1967
109* Nottingham . 1967
142   The Oval ... 1967
I. T. Botham (2)
100† Birmingham . 1978
108   Lord's 1978
G. Boycott (3)
121* Lord's 1971
112   Leeds 1971
100* Hyderabad .. 1977-78
B. C. Broad (1)
116   Faisalabad .. 1987-88
D. C. S. Compton (1)
278   Nottingham . 1954

M. C. Cowdrey (3)
159† Birmingham . 1962
182   The Oval ... 1962
100   Lahore 1968-69
E. R. Dexter (2)
205   Karachi 1961-62
172   The Oval ... 1962
B. L. D'Oliveira (1)
114* Dacca 1968-69
K. W. R. Fletcher (1)
122   The Oval ... 1974
M. W. Gatting (2)
124   Birmingham . 1987
150* The Oval ... 1987
D. I. Gower (2)
152   Faisalabad .. 1983-84
173* Lahore 1983-84
T. W. Graveney (3)
153   Lord's 1962
114   Nottingham . 1962
105   Karachi 1968-69

A. P. E. Knott (1)
116   Birmingham . 1971
B. W. Luckhurst (1)
108*† Birmingham . 1971
C. Milburn (1)
139   Karachi 1968-69
P. H. Parfitt (4)
111   Karachi 1961-62
101* Birmingham . 1962
119   Leeds 1962
101* Nottingham . 1962
G. Pullar (1)
165   Dacca 1961-62
C. T. Radley (1)
106† Birmingham . 1978
D. W. Randall (1)
105   Birmingham . 1982
R. T. Robinson (1)
166† Manchester . 1987
R. T. Simpson (1)
101   Nottingham . 1954

For Pakistan (30)

Alim-ud-Din (1)
109   Karachi 1961-62
Asif Iqbal (3)
146   The Oval ... 1967
104* Birmingham . 1971
102   Lahore 1972-73
Hanif Mohammad (3)
111 ⎫
104 ⎬Dacca 1961-62
187* Lord's 1967
Haroon Rashid (2)
122† Lahore 1977-78
108   Hyderabad .. 1977-78
Imran Khan (1)
118   The Oval ... 1987

Intikhab Alam (1)
138   Hyderabad .. 1972-73
Javed Burki (3)
138† Lahore 1961-62
140   Dacca 1961-62
101   Lord's 1962
Javed Miandad (1)
260   The Oval ... 1987
Mohsin Khan (2)
200   Lord's 1982
104   Lahore 1983-84
Mudassar Nazar (3)
114† Lahore 1977-88
124   Birmingham . 1987
120   Lahore 1987-88

Mushtaq Mohammad (3)
100* Nottingham . 1962
100   Birmingham . 1971
157   Hyderabad .. 1972-73
Nasim-ul Ghani (1)
101   Lord's 1962
Sadiq Mohammad (1)
119   Lahore 1972-73
Salim Malik (2)
116   Faisalabad .. 1983-84
102   The Oval ... 1987
Wasim Raja (1)
112   Faisalabad .. 1983-84
Zaheer Abbas (2)
274† Birmingham . 1971
240   The Oval ... 1974

† *Signifies hundred on first appearance in England–Pakistan Tests.*

Note: Three batsmen – Majid Khan, Mushtaq Mohammad and D. L. Amiss – were dismissed for 99 at Karachi, 1972-73: the only instance in Test matches.

RECORD PARTNERSHIPS FOR EACH WICKET

For England

198 for 1st	G. Pullar and R. W. Barber at Dacca	1961-62
248 for 2nd	M. C. Cowdrey and E. R. Dexter at The Oval	1962
201 for 3rd	K. F. Barrington and T. W. Graveney at Lord's	1967
188 for 4th	E. R. Dexter and P. H. Parfitt at Karachi	1961-62
192 for 5th	D. C. S. Compton and T. E. Bailey at Nottingham	1954
153* for 6th	P. H. Parfitt and D. A. Allen at Birmingham	1962
167 for 7th	D. I. Gower and V. J. Marks at Faisalabad	1983-84
99 for 8th	P. H. Parfitt and D. A. Allen at Leeds	1962
76 for 9th	T. W. Graveney and F. S. Trueman at Lord's	1962
79 for 10th	R. W. Taylor and R. G. D. Willis at Birmingham	1982

For Pakistan

173 for 1st	Mohsin Khan and Shoaib Mohammad at Lahore	1983-84
291 for 2nd†	Zaheer Abbas and Mushtaq Mohammad at Birmingham	1971
180 for 3rd	Mudassar Nazar and Haroon Rashid at Lahore	1977-78
234 for 4th	Javed Miandad and Salim Malik at The Oval	1987
197 for 5th	Javed Burki and Nasim-ul-Ghani at Lord's	1962
145 for 6th	Mushtaq Mohammad and Intikhab Alam at Hyderabad	1972-73
89 for 7th	Ijaz Ahmed and Salim Yousuf at The Oval	1987
130 for 8th†	Hanif Mohammad and Asif Iqbal at Lord's	1967
190 for 9th†	Asif Iqbal and Intikhab Alam at The Oval	1967
62 for 10th	Sarfraz Nawaz and Asif Masood at Leeds	1974

† *Denotes record partnership against all countries.*

TEN WICKETS OR MORE IN A MATCH

For England (2)

11-83 (6-65, 5-18)†	N. G. B. Cook, Karachi	1983-84
13-71 (5-20, 8-51)	D. L. Underwood, Lord's	1974

For Pakistan (6)

10-194 (5-84, 5-110)	Abdul Qadir, Lahore	1983-84
13-101 (9-56, 4-45)	Abdul Qadir, Lahore	1987-88
10-186 (5-88, 5-98)	Abdul Qadir, Karachi	1987-88
10-211 (7-96, 3-115)	Abdul Qadir, The Oval	1987
12-99 (6-53, 6-46)	Fazal Mahmood, The Oval	1954
10-77 (3-37, 7-40)	Imran Khan, Leeds	1987

† *Signifies ten wickets or more on first appearance in England–Pakistan Tests.*

FOUR WICKETS IN FIVE BALLS

C. M. Old, v Pakistan at Birmingham in 1978, dismissed Wasim Raja, Wasim Bari, Iqbal Qasim and Sikander Bakht to take four wickets in five balls (ww-ww).

ENGLAND v SRI LANKA

Captains

Season	England	Sri Lanka	T	E	SL	D
1981-82	K. W. R. Fletcher	B. Warnapura	1	1	0	0
1984	D. I. Gower	L. R. D. Mendis	1	0	0	1
1988	G. A. Gooch	R. S. Madugalle	1	1	0	0
	In England		2	1	0	1
	In Sri Lanka		1	1	0	0
	Totals		3	2	0	1

INNINGS TOTALS

Highest innings total for England: 429 at Lord's 1988
　　　　　　　　　　　for Sri Lanka: 491-7 dec. at Lord's 1984

Lowest innings total for England: 223 at Colombo (PSS) 1981-82
　　　　　　　　　　　for Sri Lanka: 175 at Colombo (PSS) 1981-82

INDIVIDUAL HUNDREDS

For England (1)

A. J. Lamb (1)
107† Lord's 1984

For Sri Lanka (3)

L. R. D. Mendis (1)	**S. A. R. Silva** (1)	**S. Wettimuny** (1)
111 Lord's 1984	102*† Lord's 1984	190 Lord's 1984

† *Signifies hundred on first appearance in England–Sri Lanka Tests.*

BEST BOWLING

Best bowling in an innings for England: 6-33 by J. E. Emburey at Colombo (PSS) 1981-82
　　　　　　　　　　　　　for Sri Lanka: 4-70 by A. L. F. de Mel at Colombo (PSS) 1981-82

RECORD PARTNERSHIPS FOR EACH WICKET

For England

73 for 1st	G. A. Gooch and R. T. Robinson at Lord's	1988
131 for 2nd	G. A. Gooch and R. C. Russell at Lord's	1988
85 for 3rd	B. C. Broad and D. I. Gower at Lord's	1984
87 for 4th	K. J. Barnett and A. J. Lamb at Lord's	1988
38 for 5th	A. J. Lamb and R. A. Smith at Lord's	1988
87 for 6th	A. J. Lamb and R. M. Ellison at Lord's	1984
49 for 7th	A. J. Lamb and P. R. Downton at Lord's	1984
9 for 8th	R. W. Taylor and P. J. W. Allott at Colombo (PSS)	1981-82
37 for 9th	P. J. Newport and N. A. Foster at Lord's	1988
9 for 10th	N. A. Foster and D. V. Lawrence at Lord's	1988

For Sri Lanka

43 for 1st	D. S. B. P. Kuruppu and S. A. R. Silva at Lord's	1988
83 for 2nd	B. Warnapura and R. L. Dias at Colombo (PSS)	1981-82
101 for 3rd	S. Wettimuny and R. L. Dias at Lord's	1984
148 for 4th	S. Wettimuny and A. Ranatunga at Lord's	1984
150 for 5th†	S. Wettimuny and L. R. D. Mendis at Lord's	1984
138 for 6th	S. A. R. Silva and L. R. D. Mendis at Lord's	1984
59 for 7th	L. R. D. Mendis and J. R. Ratnayeke at Lord's	1988
27* for 8th	A. L. F. de Mel and J. R. Ratnayeke at Lord's	1984
12 for 9th	J. R. Ratnayeke and G. F. Labrooy at Lord's	1988
64 for 10th†	J. R. Ratnayeke and G. F. Labrooy at Lord's	1988

† *Denotes record partnership against all countries.*

ENGLAND v REST OF THE WORLD

In 1970, owing to the cancellation of the South African tour to England, a series of matches was arranged, with the trappings of a full Test series, between England and the Rest of the World. It was played for the Guinness Trophy.

The following players represented the Rest of the World: E. J. Barlow (5), F. M. Engineer (2), L. R. Gibbs (4), Intikhab Alam (5), R. B. Kanhai (5), C. H. Lloyd (5), G. D. McKenzie (3), D. L. Murray (3), Mushtaq Mohammad (2), P. M. Pollock (1), R. G. Pollock (5), M. J. Procter (5), B. A. Richards (5), G. S. Sobers (5).

A list of players who appeared for England in these matches may be found on page 128.

AUSTRALIA v SOUTH AFRICA

Captains

Season	Australia	South Africa	T	A	SA	D
1902-03S	J. Darling	H. M. Taberer[1]	3	2	0	1
1910-11A	C. Hill	P. W. Sherwell	5	4	1	0
1912E	S. E. Gregory	F. Mitchell[2]	3	2	0	1
1921-22S	H. L. Collins	H. W. Taylor	3	1	0	2
1931-32A	W. M. Woodfull	H. B. Cameron	5	5	0	0
1935-36S	V. Y. Richardson	H. F. Wade	5	4	0	1
1949-50S	A. L. Hassett	A. D. Nourse	5	4	0	1
1952-53A	A. L. Hassett	J. E. Cheetham	5	2	2	1
1957-58S	I. D. Craig	C. B. van Ryneveld[3]	5	3	0	2
1963-64A	R. B. Simpson[4]	T. L. Goddard	5	1	1	3
1966-67S	R. B. Simpson	P. L. van der Merwe	5	1	3	1
1969-70S	W. M. Lawry	A. Bacher	4	0	4	0
	In South Africa		30	15	7	8
	In Australia		20	12	4	4
	In England		3	2	0	1
	Totals		53	29	11	13

S Played in South Africa. A Played in Australia. E Played in England.

Notes: The following deputised for the official touring captain or were appointed by the home authority for only a minor proportion of the series:
[1]J. H. Anderson (Second), E. A. Halliwell (Third). [2]L. J. Tancred (Third). [3]D. J. McGlew (First). [4]R. Benaud (First).

HIGHEST INNINGS TOTALS

For Australia in Australia: 578 at Melbourne		1910-11
in South Africa: 549-7 dec. at Port Elizabeth		1949-50
For South Africa in Australia: 595 at Adelaide		1963-64
in South Africa: 622-9 dec. at Durban		1969-70

LOWEST INNINGS TOTALS

For Australia in Australia: 153 at Melbourne 1931-32
          in South Africa: 75 at Durban 1949-50

For South Africa in Australia: 36† at Melbourne 1931-32
            in South Africa: 85 at Johannesburg 1902-03

† *Scored 45 in the second innings giving the smallest aggregate of 81 (12 extras) in Test cricket.*

INDIVIDUAL HUNDREDS

For Australia (55)

W. W. Armstrong (2)
159*‡ Johannesburg 1902-03
132 Melbourne .. 1910-11
W. Bardsley (3)
132† Sydney 1910-11
121 Manchester . 1912
164 Lord's 1912
R. Benaud (2)
122 Johannesburg 1957-58
100 Johannesburg 1957-58
B. C. Booth (2)
169† Brisbane 1963-64
102* Sydney 1963-64
D. G. Bradman (4)
226† Brisbane 1931-32
112 Sydney 1931-32
167 Melbourne .. 1931-32
299* Adelaide 1931-32
W. A. Brown (1)
121 Cape Town . 1935-36
J. W. Burke (1)
189 Cape Town . 1957-58
A. G. Chipperfield (1)
109† Durban 1935-36
H. L. Collins (1)
203 Johannesburg 1921-22
J. H. Fingleton (3)
112 Cape Town . 1935-36

108 Johannesburg 1935-36
118 Durban 1935-36
J. M. Gregory (1)
119 Johannesburg 1921-22
R. N. Harvey (8)
178 Cape Town . 1949-50
151* Durban 1949-50
100 Johannesburg 1949-50
116 Pt Elizabeth . 1949-50
109 Brisbane 1952-53
190 Sydney 1952-53
116 Adelaide 1952-53
205 Melbourne .. 1952-53
A. L. Hassett (3)
112† Johannesburg 1949-50
167 Pt Elizabeth . 1949-50
163 Adelaide 1952-53
C. Hill (3)
142† Johannesburg 1902-03
191 Sydney 1910-11
100 Melbourne .. 1910-11
C. Kelleway (2)
114 Manchester . 1912
102 Lord's 1912
W. M. Lawry (1)
157 Melbourne .. 1963-64
S. J. E. Loxton (1)
101† Johannesburg 1949-50

C. G. Macartney (2)
137 Sydney 1910-11
116 Durban 1921-22
S. J. McCabe (1)
189* Johannesburg 1935-36
C. C. McDonald (1)
154 Adelaide 1952-53
J. Moroney (2)
118 ⎫
101* ⎬ Johannesburg 1949-50
A. R. Morris (2)
111 Johannesburg 1949-50
157 Pt Elizabeth . 1949-50
K. E. Rigg (1)
127† Sydney 1931-32
J. Ryder (1)
142 Cape Town . 1921-22
R. B. Simpson (1)
153 Cape Town . 1966-67
K. R. Stackpole (1)
134 Cape Town . 1966-67
V. T. Trumper (2)
159 Melbourne .. 1910-11
214* Adelaide 1910-11
W. M. Woodfull (1)
161 Melbourne .. 1931-32

For South Africa (36)

E. J. Barlow (5)
114† Brisbane 1963-64
109 Melbourne .. 1963-64
201 Adelaide 1963-64
127 Cape Town . 1969-70
110 Johannesburg 1969-70
K. C. Bland (1)
126 Sydney 1963-64
W. R. Endean (1)
162* Melbourne .. 1952-53
G. A. Faulkner (3)
204 Melbourne .. 1910-11
115 Adelaide 1910-11
122* Manchester . 1912
C. N. Frank (1)
152 Johannesburg 1921-22
B. L. Irvine (1)
102 Pt Elizabeth . 1969-70

D. T. Lindsay (3)
182 Johannesburg 1966-67
137 Durban 1966-67
131 Johannesburg 1966-67
D. J. McGlew (2)
108 Johannesburg 1957-58
105 Durban 1957-58
A. D. Nourse (2)
231 Johannesburg 1935-36
114 Cape Town . 1949-50
A. W. Nourse (1)
111 Johannesburg 1921-22
R. G. Pollock (5)
122 Sydney 1963-64
175 Adelaide 1963-64
209 Cape Town . 1966-67
105 Pt Elizabeth . 1966-67
274 Durban 1969-70

B. A. Richards (2)
140 Durban 1969-70
126 Pt Elizabeth . 1969-70
E. A. B. Rowan (1)
143 Durban 1949-50
J. H. Sinclair (2)
101 Johannesburg 1902-03
104 Cape Town . 1902-03
S. J. Snooke (1)
103 Adelaide 1910-11
K. G. Viljoen (1)
111 Melbourne .. 1931-32
J. H. B. Waite (2)
115 Johannesburg 1957-58
134 Durban 1957-58
J. W. Zulch (2)
105 Adelaide 1910-11
150 Sydney 1910-11

† *Signifies hundred on first appearance in Australia–South Africa Tests.*
‡ *Carried his bat.*

RECORD PARTNERSHIPS FOR EACH WICKET

For Australia

233 for 1st	J. H. Fingleton and W. A. Brown at Cape Town	1935-36
275 for 2nd	C. C. McDonald and A. L. Hassett at Adelaide	1952-53
242 for 3rd	C. Kelleway and W. Bardsley at Lord's	1912
168 for 4th	R. N. Harvey and K. R. Miller at Sydney	1952-53
143 for 5th	W. W. Armstrong and V. T. Trumper at Melbourne	1910-11
107 for 6th	C. Kelleway and V. S. Ransford at Melbourne	1910-11
160 for 7th	R. Benaud and G. D. McKenzie at Sydney	1963-64
83 for 8th	A. G. Chipperfield and C. V. Grimmett at Durban	1935-36
78 for 9th	{ D. G. Bradman and W. J. O'Reilly at Adelaide	1931-32
	{ K. D. Mackay and I. Meckiff at Johannesburg	1957-58
82 for 10th	V. S. Ransford and W. J. Whitty at Melbourne	1910-11

For South Africa

176 for 1st	D. J. McGlew and T. L. Goddard at Johannesburg	1957-58
173 for 2nd	L. J. Tancred and C. B. Llewellyn at Johannesburg	1902-03
341 for 3rd†	E. J. Barlow and R. G. Pollock at Adelaide	1963-64
206 for 4th	C. N. Frank and A. W. Nourse at Johannesburg	1921-22
129 for 5th	J. H. B. Waite and W. R. Endean at Johannesburg	1957-58
200 for 6th†	R. G. Pollock and H. R. Lance at Durban	1969-70
221 for 7th	D. T. Lindsay and P. L. van der Merwe at Johannesburg	1966-67
124 for 8th†	A. W. Nourse and E. A. Halliwell at Johannesburg	1902-03
85 for 9th	R. G. Pollock and P. M. Pollock at Cape Town	1966-67
53 for 10th	L. A. Stricker and S. J. Pegler at Adelaide	1910-11

† *Denotes record partnership against all countries.*

TEN WICKETS OR MORE IN A MATCH

For Australia (5)

14-199 (7-116, 7-83)	C. V. Grimmett, Adelaide	1931-32
10-88 (5-32, 5-56)	C. V. Grimmett, Cape Town	1935-36
10-110 (3-70, 7-40)	C. V. Grimmett, Johannesburg	1935-36
13-173 (7-100, 6-73)	C. V. Grimmett, Durban	1935-36
11-24 (5-6, 6-18)	H. Ironmonger, Melbourne	1931-32

For South Africa (2)

10-116 (5-43, 5-73)	C. B. Llewellyn, Johannesburg	1902-03
13-165 (6-84, 7-81)	H. J. Tayfield, Melbourne	1952-53

Note: C. V. Grimmett took ten wickets or more in three consecutive matches in 1935-36.

AUSTRALIA v WEST INDIES

Captains

Season	Australia	West Indies	T	A	WI	T	D
1930-31*A*	W. M. Woodfull	G. C. Grant	5	4	1	0	0
1951-52*A*	A. L. Hassett[1]	J. D. C. Goddard[2]	5	4	1	0	0
1954-55*W*	I. W. Johnson	D. St E. Atkinson[3]	5	3	0	0	2
1960-61*A*	R. Benaud	F. M. M. Worrell	5	2	1	1	1

THE FRANK WORRELL TROPHY

Captains

Season	Australia	West Indies	T	A	WI	T	D	Held by
1964-65 *W*	R. B. Simpson	G. S. Sobers	5	1	2	0	2	WI
1968-69 *A*	W. M. Lawry	G. S. Sobers	5	3	1	0	1	A
1972-73 *W*	I. M. Chappell	R. B. Kanhai	5	2	0	0	3	A
1975-76 *A*	G. S. Chappell	C. H. Lloyd	6	5	1	0	0	A
1977-78 *W*	R. B. Simpson	A. I. Kallicharran[4]	5	1	3	0	1	WI
1979-80 *A*	G. S. Chappell	C. H. Lloyd[5]	3	0	2	0	1	WI
1981-82 *A*	G. S. Chappell	C. H. Lloyd	3	1	1	0	1	WI
1983-84 *W*	K. J. Hughes	C. H. Lloyd[6]	5	0	3	0	2	WI
1984-85 *A*	A. R. Border[7]	C. H. Lloyd	5	1	3	0	1	WI
1988-89 *A*	A. R. Border	I. V. A. Richards	5	1	3	0	1	WI
	In Australia		42	21	14	1	6	
	In West Indies		25	7	8	0	10	
	Totals		67	28	22	1	16	

A Played in Australia. W Played in West Indies.

Notes: The following deputised for the official touring captain or were appointed by the home authority for only a minor proportion of the series:
[1] A. R. Morris (Third). [2] J. B. Stollmeyer (Fifth). [3] J. B. Stollmeyer (Second and Third). [4] C. H. Lloyd (First and Second). [5] D. L. Murray (First). [6] I. V. A. Richards (Second). [7] K. J. Hughes (First and Second).

HIGHEST INNINGS TOTALS

For Australia in Australia: 619 at Sydney		1968-69
in West Indies: 758-8 dec. at Kingston		1954-55
For West Indies in Australia: 616 at Adelaide		1968-69
in West Indies: 573 at Bridgetown		1964-65

LOWEST INNINGS TOTALS

For Australia in Australia: 76 at Perth		1984-85
in West Indies: 90 at Port-of-Spain		1977-78
For West Indies in Australia: 78 at Sydney		1951-52
in West Indies: 109 at Georgetown		1972-73

INDIVIDUAL HUNDREDS

For Australia (67)

R. G. Archer (1)
128　Kingston ... 1954-55
R. Benaud (1)
121　Kingston ... 1954-55
D. C. Boon (1)
149　Sydney 1988-89
B. C. Booth (1)
117　Port-of-Spain 1964-65
A. R. Border (2)
126　Adelaide 1981-82
100*　Port-of-Spain 1983-84
D. G. Bradman (2)
223　Brisbane 1930-31
152　Melbourne .. 1930-31

G. S. Chappell (5)
106　Bridgetown . 1972-73
123 ⎫
109* ⎬ ‡Brisbane ... 1975-76
182*　Sydney 1975-76
124　Brisbane 1979-80
I. M. Chappell (5)
117†　Brisbane 1968-69
165　Melbourne .. 1968-69
106*　Bridgetown . 1972-73
109　Georgetown . 1972-73
156　Perth 1975-76
G. J. Cosier (1)
109†　Melbourne .. 1975-76

R. M. Cowper (2)
143　Port-of-Spain 1964-65
102　Bridgetown . 1964-65
J. Dyson (1)
127*†　Sydney 1981-82
R. N. Harvey (3)
133　Kingston ... 1954-55
133　Port-of-Spain 1954-55
204　Kingston ... 1954-55
A. L. Hassett (2)
132　Sydney 1951-52
102　Melbourne .. 1951-52
A. M. J. Hilditch (1)
113†　Melbourne .. 1984-85

K. J. Hughes (2)
130*† Brisbane 1979-80
100*   Melbourne .. 1981-82
D. M. Jones (1)
216   Adelaide 1988-89
A. F. Kippax (1)
146†   Adelaide 1930-31
W. M. Lawry (4)
210   Bridgetown . 1964-65
105   Brisbane 1968-69
205   Melbourne .. 1968-69
151   Sydney 1968-69
R. R. Lindwall (1)
118   Bridgetown . 1954-55
R. B. McCosker (1)
109*   Melbourne .. 1975-76
C. C. McDonald (2)
110   Port-of-Spain 1954-55
127   Kingston ... 1954-55
K. R. Miller (4)
129   Sydney 1951-52

147   Kingston ... 1954-55
137   Bridgetown . 1954-55
109   Kingston ... 1954-55
A. R. Morris (1)
111   Port-of-Spain 1954-55
N. C. O'Neill (1)
181†   Brisbane 1960-61
W. B. Phillips (1)
120   Bridgetown . 1983-84
W. H. Ponsford (2)
183   Sydney 1930-31
109   Brisbane 1930-31
I. R. Redpath (4)
132   Sydney 1968-69
102   Melbourne .. 1975-76
103   Adelaide 1975-76
101   Melbourne .. 1975-76
C. S. Serjeant (1)
124   Georgetown . 1977-78
R. B. Simpson (1)
201   Bridgetown . 1964-65

K. R. Stackpole (1)
142   Kingston ... 1972-73
P. M. Toohey (1)
122   Kingston ... 1977-78
A. Turner (1)
136   Adelaide 1975-76
K. D. Walters (6)
118   Sydney 1968-69
110   Adelaide 1968-69
242 } Sydney 1968-69
103 }
102*   Bridgetown . 1972-73
112   Port-of-Spain 1972-73
K. C. Wessels (1)
173   Sydney 1984-85
G. M. Wood (2)
126   Georgetown . 1977-78
111   Perth 1988-89

‡ *G. S. Chappell is the only player to score hundreds in both innings of his first Test as captain.*

For West Indies (69)

F. C. M. Alexander (1)
108   Sydney 1960-61
D. St E. Atkinson (1)
219   Bridgetown . 1954-55
B. F. Butcher (3)
117   Port-of-Spain 1964-65
101   Sydney 1968-69
118   Adelaide 1968-69
C. C. Depeiza (1)
122   Bridgetown . 1954-55
P. J. L. Dujon (2)
130   Port-of-Spain 1983-84
139   Perth 1984-85
M. L. C. Foster (1)
125†   Kingston ... 1972-73
R. C. Fredericks (1)
169   Perth 1975-76
H. A. Gomes (6)
101†   Georgetown . 1977-78
115   Kingston ... 1977-78
126   Sydney 1981-82
124*   Adelaide 1981-82
127   Perth 1984-85
120*   Adelaide 1984-85
C. G. Greenidge (3)
120*   Georgetown . 1983-84
127   Kingston ... 1983-84
104   Adelaide 1988-89
D. L. Haynes (4)
103*   Georgetown . 1983-84
145   Bridgetown . 1983-84
100   Perth 1988-89

143   Sydney 1988-89
G. A. Headley (2)
102*   Brisbane 1930-31
105   Sydney 1930-31
C. C. Hunte (1)
110   Melbourne .. 1960-61
A. I. Kallicharran (4)
101   Brisbane 1975-76
127   Port-of-Spain 1977-78
126   Kingston ... 1977-78
106   Adelaide 1979-80
R. B. Kanhai (5)
117 } Adelaide ... 1960-61
115 }
129   Bridgetown . 1964-65
121   Port-of-Spain 1964-65
105   Bridgetown . 1972-73
C. H. Lloyd (6)
129†   Brisbane 1968-69
178   Georgetown . 1972-73
149   Perth 1975-76
102   Melbourne .. 1975-76
121   Adelaide 1979-80
114   Brisbane 1984-85
F. R. Martin (1)
123*   Sydney 1930-31
S. M. Nurse (2)
201   Bridgetown . 1964-65
137   Sydney 1968-69
I. V. A. Richards (5)
101   Adelaide 1975-76
140   Brisbane 1979-80

178   St John's 1983-84
208   Melbourne .. 1984-85
146   Perth 1988-89
R. B. Richardson (5)
131*   Bridgetown . 1983-84
154   St John's 1983-84
138   Brisbane 1984-85
122   Melbourne .. 1988-89
106   Adelaide 1988-89
L. G. Rowe (1)
107   Brisbane 1975-76
O. G. Smith (1)
104†   Kingston ... 1954-55
G. S. Sobers (4)
132   Brisbane 1960-61
168   Sydney 1960-61
110   Adelaide 1968-69
113   Sydney 1968-69
J. B. Stollmeyer (1)
104   Sydney 1951-52
C. L. Walcott (5)
108   Kingston ... 1954-55
126 } Port-of-Spain 1954-55
110 }
155 } Kingston ... 1954-55
110 }
E. D. Weekes (1)
139   Port-of-Spain 1954-55
A. B. Williams (1)
100†   Georgetown . 1977-78
F. M. M. Worrell (1)
108   Melbourne .. 1951-52

† *Signifies hundred on first appearance in Australia–West Indies Tests.*

Note: F. C. M. Alexander and C. C. Depeiza scored the only hundreds of their careers in a Test match.

RECORD PARTNERSHIPS FOR EACH WICKET

For Australia

382 for 1st†	W. M. Lawry and R. B. Simpson at Bridgetown	1964-65
298 for 2nd	W. M. Lawry and I. M. Chappell at Melbourne	1968-69
295 for 3rd†	C. C. McDonald and R. N. Harvey at Kingston	1954-55
336 for 4th	W. M. Lawry and K. D. Walters at Sydney	1968-69
220 for 5th	K. R. Miller and R. G. Archer at Kingston	1954-55
206 for 6th	K. R. Miller and R. G. Archer at Bridgetown	1954-55
134 for 7th	A. K. Davidson and R. Benaud at Brisbane	1960-61
137 for 8th	R. Benaud and I. W. Johnson at Kingston	1954-55
114 for 9th	D. M. Jones and M. G. Hughes at Adelaide	1988-89
97 for 10th	T. G. Hogan and R. M. Hogg at Georgetown	1983-84

For West Indies

250* for 1st	C. G. Greenidge and D. L. Haynes at Georgetown	1983-84
167 for 2nd	D. L. Haynes and R. B. Richardson at Adelaide	1988-89
308 for 3rd	R. B. Richardson and I. V. A. Richards at St John's	1983-84
198 for 4th	L. G. Rowe and A. I. Kallicharran at Brisbane	1975-76
210 for 5th	R. B. Kanhai and M. L. C. Foster at Kingston	1972-73
165 for 6th	R. B. Kanhai and D. L. Murray at Bridgetown	1972-73
347 for 7th†‡	D. St E. Atkinson and C. C. Depeiza at Bridgetown	1954-55
82 for 8th	H. A. Gomes and A. M. E. Roberts at Adelaide	1981-82
122 for 9th	D. A. J. Holford and J. L. Hendriks at Adelaide	1968-69
56 for 10th	J. Garner and C. E. H. Croft at Brisbane	1979-80

† *Denotes record partnership against all countries.*
‡ *Record seventh-wicket partnership in first-class cricket.*

TEN WICKETS OR MORE IN A MATCH

For Australia (11)

11-96 (7-46, 4-50)	A. R. Border, Sydney	1988-89
11-222 (5-135, 6-87)†	A. K. Davidson, Brisbane	1960-61
11-183 (7-87, 4-96)†	C. V. Grimmett, Adelaide	1930-31
10-115 (6-72, 4-43)	N. J. N. Hawke, Georgetown	1964-65
10-144 (6-54, 4-90)	R. G. Holland, Sydney	1984-85
13-217 (5-130, 8-87)	M. G. Hughes, Perth	1988-89
11-79 (7-23, 4-56)	H. Ironmonger, Melbourne	1930-31
11-181 (8-112, 3-69)	G. F. Lawson, Adelaide	1984-85
10-127 (7-83, 3-44)	D. K. Lillee, Melbourne	1981-82
10-159 (8-71, 2-88)	G. D. McKenzie, Melbourne	1968-69
10-185 (3-87, 7-98)	B. Yardley, Sydney	1981-82

For West Indies (3)

10-113 (7-55, 3-58)	G. E. Gomez, Sydney	1951-52
11-107 (5-45, 6-62)	M. A. Holding, Melbourne	1981-82
10-107 (5-69, 5-38)	M. D. Marshall, Adelaide	1984-85

† *Signifies ten wickets or more on first appearance in Australia–West Indies Tests.*

AUSTRALIA v NEW ZEALAND

Captains

eason	Australia	New Zealand	T	A	NZ	D
)45-46N	W. A. Brown	W. A. Hadlee	1	1	0	0
)73-74A	I. M. Chappell	B. E. Congdon	3	2	0	1
)73-74N	I. M. Chappell	B. E. Congdon	3	1	1	1
)76-77N	G. S. Chappell	G. M. Turner	2	1	0	1
)80-81A	G. S. Chappell	G. P. Howarth[1]	3	2	0	1
)81-82N	G. S. Chappell	G. P. Howarth	3	1	1	1

TRANS-TASMAN TROPHY

Captains

eason	Australia	New Zealand	T	A	NZ	D	Held by
)85-86A	A. R. Border	J. V. Coney	3	1	2	0	NZ
)85-86N	A. R. Border	J. V. Coney	3	0	1	2	NZ
)87-88A	A. R. Border	J. J. Crowe	3	1	0	2	A
)89-90A†	A. R. Border	J. G. Wright	1	0	0	1	—
)89-90N†	A. R. Border	J. G. Wright	1	0	1	0	—
	In Australia		13	6	2	5	
	In New Zealand		13	4	4	5	
	Totals		26	10	6	10	

Played in Australia. N Played in New Zealand.

† The Trans-Tasman Trophy was not at stake in these series.

'ote: The following deputised for the official touring captain: [1]M. G. Burgess (Second).

HIGHEST INNINGS TOTALS

or Australia in Australia: 521-9 dec. at Perth		1989-90
in New Zealand: 552 at Christchurch		1976-77
or New Zealand in Australia: 553-7 dec. at Brisbane		1985-86
in New Zealand: 484 at Wellington		1973-74

LOWEST INNINGS TOTALS

or Australia in Australia: 162 at Sydney		1973-74
in New Zealand: 103 at Auckland		1985-86
or New Zealand in Australia: 121 at Perth		1980-81
in New Zealand: 42 at Wellington		1945-46

INDIVIDUAL HUNDREDS

For Australia (23)

'. C. Boon (2)
43 Brisbane 1987-88
00 Perth 1989-90

. R. Border (4)
52* Brisbane 1985-86
40 ⎫
14* ⎬ Christchurch . 1985-86
05 Adelaide 1987-88

. S. Chappell (3)
47* ⎫
33 ⎬ Wellington .. 1973-74
76 Christchurch. 1981-82

I. M. Chappell (2)
145 ⎫
121 ⎬ Wellington .. 1973-74

G. J. Gilmour (1)
101 Christchurch. 1976-77

G. R. Marsh (1)
118 Auckland ... 1985-86

R. W. Marsh (1)
132 Adelaide 1973-74

G. R. J. Matthews (2)
115† Brisbane 1985-86
130 Wellington .. 1985-86

I. R. Redpath (1)
159*‡ Auckland ... 1973-74

K. R. Stackpole (1)
122† Melbourne .. 1973-74

K. D. Walters (3)
104* Auckland ... 1973-74
250 Christchurch. 1976-77
107 Melbourne .. 1980-81

G. M. Wood (2)
111† Brisbane 1980-81
100 Auckland ... 1981-82

For New Zealand (17)

J. V. Coney (1)
101* Wellington .. 1985-86

B. E. Congdon (2)
132 Wellington ... 1973-74
107* Christchurch. 1976-77

M. D. Crowe (3)
188 Brisbane 1985-86
137 Christchurch. 1985-86
137 Adelaide 1987-88

B. A. Edgar (1)
161 Auckland ... 1981-82

M. J. Greatbatch (1)
146*† Perth 1989-90

B. F. Hastings (1)
101 Wellington .. 1973-74

A. H. Jones (1)
150 Adelaide 1987-88

J. F. M. Morrison (1)
117 Sydney 1973-74

J. M. Parker (1)
108 Sydney 1973-7

J. F. Reid (1)
108† Brisbane 1985-8

G. M. Turner (2)
101 ⎫
110* ⎬ Christchurch. 1973-7

J. G. Wright (2)
141 Christchurch. 1981-8
117* Wellington .. 1989-9

† *Signifies hundred on first appearance in Australia–New Zealand Tests.*
‡ *Carried his bat.*

Notes: G. S. and I. M. Chappell at Wellington in 1973-74 provide the only instance in Tes
matches of brothers both scoring a hundred in each innings and in the same Test.

RECORD PARTNERSHIPS FOR EACH WICKET

For Australia

106 for 1st	B. M. Laird and G. M. Wood at Auckland	1981-8.
168 for 2nd	G. R. Marsh and W. B. Phillips at Auckland	1985-8
264 for 3rd	I. M. Chappell and G. S. Chappell at Wellington	1973-7
116 for 4th	A. R. Border and S. R. Waugh at Adelaide	1987-8
213 for 5th	G. M. Ritchie and G. R. J. Matthews at Wellington	1985-8
197 for 6th	A. R. Border and G. R. J. Matthews at Brisbane	1985-8
217 for 7th†	K. D. Walters and G. J. Gilmour at Christchurch	1976-7
93 for 8th	G. J. Gilmour and K. J. O'Keeffe at Auckland	1976-7
61 for 9th	A. I. C. Dodemaide and C. J. McDermott at Melbourne	1987-8
60 for 10th	K. D. Walters and J. D. Higgs at Melbourne	1980-8

For New Zealand

107 for 1st	G. M. Turner and J. M. Parker at Auckland	1973-7
128* for 2nd	J. G. Wright and A. H. Jones at Wellington	1989-9
224 for 3rd	J. F. Reid and M. D. Crowe at Brisbane	1985-8
229 for 4th†	B. E. Congdon and B. F. Hastings at Wellington	1973-7
88 for 5th	J. V. Coney and M. G. Burgess at Perth	1980-8
109 for 6th	K. R. Rutherford and J. V. Coney at Wellington	1985-8
132* for 7th	J. V. Coney and R. J. Hadlee at Wellington	1985-8
88* for 8th	M. J. Greatbatch and M. C. Snedden at Perth	1989-9
73 for 9th	H. J. Howarth and D. R. Hadlee at Christchurch	1976-7
124 for 10th	J. G. Bracewell and S. L. Boock at Sydney	1985-8

† *Denotes record partnership against all countries.*

TEN WICKETS OR MORE IN A MATCH

For Australia (2)

10-174 (6-106, 4-68)	R. G. Holland, Sydney	1985-8
11-123 (5-51, 6-72)	D. K. Lillee, Auckland	1976-7

For New Zealand (4)

10-106 (4-74, 6-32)	J. G. Bracewell, Auckland	1985-8
15-123 (9-52, 6-71)	R. J. Hadlee, Brisbane.......................	1985-8
11-155 (5-65, 6-90)	R. J. Hadlee, Perth	1985-8
10-176 (5-109, 5-67)	R. J. Hadlee, Melbourne	1987-8

AUSTRALIA v INDIA

Captains

eason	*Australia*	*India*	T	A	I	T	D
947-48A	D. G. Bradman	L. Amarnath	5	4	0	0	1
956-57I	I. W. Johnson[1]	P. R. Umrigar	3	2	0	0	1
959-60I	R. Benaud	G. S. Ramchand	5	2	1	0	2
964-65I	R. B. Simpson	Nawab of Pataudi jun.	3	1	1	0	1
967-68A	R. B. Simpson[2]	Nawab of Pataudi jun.[3]	4	4	0	0	0
969-70I	W. M. Lawry	Nawab of Pataudi jun.	5	3	1	0	1
977-78A	R. B. Simpson	B. S. Bedi	5	3	2	0	0
979-80I	K. J. Hughes	S. M. Gavaskar	6	0	2	0	4
980-81A	G. S. Chappell	S. M. Gavaskar	3	1	1	0	1
985-86A	A. R. Border	Kapil Dev	3	0	0	0	3
986-87I	A. R. Border	Kapil Dev	3	0	0	1	2
	In Australia		20	12	3	0	5
	In India		25	8	5	1	11
	Totals		45	20	8	1	16

Played in Australia.   I Played in India.

otes: The following deputised for the official touring captain or were appointed by the home
*a*thority for only a minor proportion of the series:
[1]R. R. Lindwall (Second). [2]W. M. Lawry (Third and Fourth). [3]C. G. Borde (First).

HIGHEST INNINGS TOTALS

*o*r Australia in Australia: 674 at Adelaide 1947-48
           in India: 574-7 dec. at Madras 1986-87

*o*r India in Australia: 600-4 dec. at Sydney 1985-86
      in India: 517-5 dec. at Bombay 1986-87

LOWEST INNINGS TOTALS

*o*r Australia in Australia: 83 at Melbourne 1980-81
           in India: 105 at Kanpur 1959-60

*o*r India in Australia: 58 at Brisbane 1947-48
      in India: 135 at Delhi 1959-60

INDIVIDUAL HUNDREDS

For Australia (45)

G. Barnes (1)	**J. W. Burke** (1)	102 Bombay 1959-60
2 Adelaide 1947-48	161 Bombay 1956-57	**A. L. Hassett** (1)
. C. Boon (3)	**G. S. Chappell** (1)	198* Adelaide 1947-48
23† Adelaide 1985-86	204† Sydney 1980-81	**K. J. Hughes** (2)
1 Sydney 1985-86	**I. M. Chappell** (2)	100 Madras 1979-80
2 Madras 1986-87	151 Melbourne .. 1967-68	213 Adelaide 1980-81
. R. Border (4)	138 Delhi 1969-70	**D. M. Jones** (1)
2† Madras 1979-80	**R. M. Cowper** (2)	210† Madras 1986-87
4 Melbourne .. 1980-81	108 Adelaide 1967-68	**W. M. Lawry** (1)
3 Melbourne .. 1985-86	165 Sydney 1967-68	100 Melbourne .. 1967-68
6 Madras 1986-87	**L. E. Favell** (1)	**A. L. Mann** (1)
. G. Bradman (4)	101 Madras 1959-60	105 Perth 1977-78
5† Brisbane 1947-48	**R. N. Harvey** (4)	**G. R. Marsh** (1)
2 ⎫ Melbourne .. 1947-48	153 Melbourne .. 1947-48	101 Bombay 1986-87
*7** ⎬	140 Bombay 1956-57	**G. R. J. Matthews** (1)
1 Adelaide 1947-48	114 Delhi 1959-60	100* Melbourne .. 1985-86

A. R. Morris (1)			R. B. Simpson (4)			G. M. Wood (1)		
100*	Melbourne ..	1947-48	103	Adelaide	1967-68	125	Adelaide	1980-8
N. C. O'Neill (2)			109	Melbourne ..	1967-68	G. N. Yallop (2)		
163	Bombay	1959-60	176	Perth	1977-78	121†	Adelaide	1977-7
113	Calcutta	1959-60	100	Adelaide	1977-78	167	Calcutta	1979-8
G. M. Ritchie (1)			K. R. Stackpole (1)					
128†	Adelaide	1985-86	103†	Bombay	1969-70			
A. P. Sheahan (1)			K. D. Walters (1)					
114	Kanpur	1969-70	102	Madras	1969-70			

For India (31)

M. Amarnath (2)			M. L. Jaisimha (1)			R. J. Shastri (1)		
100	Perth	1977-78	101	Brisbane	1967-68	121*	Bombay	1986-8
138	Sydney	1985-86	Kapil Dev (1)			K. Srikkanth (1)		
N. J. Contractor (1)			119	Madras	1986-87	116	Sydney	1985-8
108	Bombay	1959-60	S. M. H. Kirmani (1)			D. B. Vengsarkar (2)		
S. M. Gavaskar (8)			101*	Bombay	1979-80	112	Bangalore ...	1979-8
113†	Brisbane	1977-78	V. Mankad (2)			164*	Bombay	1986-8
127	Perth	1977-78	116	Melbourne ..	1947-48	G. R. Viswanath (4)		
118	Melbourne ..	1977-78	111	Melbourne ..	1947-48	137†	Kanpur	1969-7
115	Delhi	1979-80	Nawab of Pataudi jun. (1)			161*	Bangalore ...	1979-8
123	Bombay	1979-80	128*†	Madras	1964-65	131	Delhi	1979-8
166*	Adelaide	1985-86	S. M. Patil (1)			114	Melbourne ..	1980-8
172	Sydney	1985-86	174	Adelaide	1980-81	Yashpal Sharma (1)		
103	Bombay	1986-87	D. G. Phadkar (1)			100*	Delhi	1979-8
V. S. Hazare (2)			123	Adelaide	1947-48			
116			G. S. Ramchand (1)					
145	} Adelaide	1947-48	109	Bombay	1956-57			

† *Signifies hundred on first appearance in Australia–India Tests.*

RECORD PARTNERSHIPS FOR EACH WICKET

For Australia

217 for 1st	D. C. Boon and G. R. Marsh at Sydney	1985-8
236 for 2nd	S. G. Barnes and D. G. Bradman at Adelaide	1947-4
222 for 3rd	A. R. Border and K. J. Hughes at Madras	1979-8
178 for 4th	D. M. Jones and A. R. Border at Madras	1986-8
223* for 5th	A. R. Morris and D. G. Bradman at Melbourne	1947-4
151 for 6th	T. R. Veivers and B. N. Jarman at Bombay	1964-6
66 for 7th	G. R. J. Matthews and R. J. Bright at Melbourne	1985-8
73 for 8th	T. R. Veivers and G. D. McKenzie at Madras	1964-6
87 for 9th	I. W. Johnson and W. P. A. Crawford at Madras	1956-5
77 for 10th	A. R. Border and D. R. Gilbert at Melbourne	1985-8

For India

192 for 1st	S. M. Gavaskar and C. P. S. Chauhan at Bombay	1979-8
224 for 2nd	S. M. Gavaskar and M. Amarnath at Sydney	1985-8
159 for 3rd	S. M. Gavaskar and G. R. Viswanath at Delhi	1979-8
159 for 4th	D. B. Vengsarkar and G. R. Viswanath at Bangalore	1979-8
109 for 5th	A. A. Baig and R. B. Kenny at Bombay	1959-6
298* for 6th†	D. B. Vengsarkar and R. J. Shastri at Bombay	1986-8
132 for 7th	V. S. Hazare and H. R. Adhikari at Adelaide	1947-4
127 for 8th	S. M. H. Kirmani and K. D. Ghavri at Bombay	1979-8
57 for 9th	{ S. M. H. Kirmani and K. D. Ghavri at Sydney .... { Kapil Dev and N. S. Yadav at Madras	1980-8 1986-8
94 for 10th	S. M. Gavaskar and N. S. Yadav at Adelaide	1985-8

† *Denotes record partnership against all countries.*

TEN WICKETS OR MORE IN A MATCH

For Australia (8)

⬩-105 (6-52, 5-53)	R. Benaud, Calcutta	1956-57
2-124 (5-31, 7-93)	A. K. Davidson, Kanpur	1959-60
2-166 (5-99, 7-67)	G. Dymock, Kanpur	1979-80
⬩-91 (6-58, 4-33)†	G. D. McKenzie, Madras	1964-65
⬩-151 (7-66, 3-85)	G. D. McKenzie, Melbourne	1967-68
⬩-144 (5-91, 5-53)	A. A. Mallett, Madras	1969-70
⬩-249 (5-103, 5-146)	G. R. J. Matthews, Madras	1986-87
⬩-31 (5-2, 6-29)†	E. R. H. Toshack, Brisbane	1947-48

For India (6)

⬩-194 (5-89, 5-105)	B. S. Bedi, Perth	1977-78
2-104 (6-52, 6-52)	B. S. Chandrasekhar, Melbourne	1977-78
⬩-130 (7-49, 3-81)	Ghulam Ahmed, Calcutta	1956-57
⬩-122 (5-31, 6-91)	R. G. Nadkarni, Madras	1964-65
4-124 (9-69, 5-55)	J. M. Patel, Kanpur	1959-60
⬩-174 (4-100, 6-74)	E. A. S. Prasanna, Madras	1969-70

† *Signifies ten wickets or more on first appearance in Australia–India Tests.*

AUSTRALIA v PAKISTAN

	Captains				
Season Australia	Pakistan	T	A	P	D
1956-57 *P* I. W. Johnson	A. H. Kardar	1	0	1	0
1959-60 *P* R. Benaud	Fazal Mahmood[1]	3	2	0	1
1964-65 *P* R. B. Simpson	Hanif Mohammad	1	0	0	1
1964-65 *A* R. B. Simpson	Hanif Mohammad	1	0	0	1
1972-73 *A* I. M. Chappell	Intikhab Alam	3	3	0	0
1976-77 *A* G. S. Chappell	Mushtaq Mohammad	3	1	1	1
1978-79 *A* G. N. Yallop[2]	Mushtaq Mohammad	2	1	1	0
1979-80 *P* G. S. Chappell	Javed Miandad	3	0	1	2
1981-82 *A* G. S. Chappell	Javed Miandad	3	2	1	0
1982-83 *P* K. J. Hughes	Imran Khan	3	0	3	0
1983-84 *A* K. J. Hughes	Imran Khan[3]	5	2	0	3
1988-89 *A* A. R. Border	Javed Miandad	3	0	1	2
1989-90 *A* A. R. Border	Imran Khan	3	1	0	2
In Pakistan		14	2	6	6
In Australia		20	10	3	7
Totals		34	12	9	13

A Played in Australia. *P* Played in Pakistan.

Notes: The following deputised for the official touring captain or were appointed by the home authority for only a minor proportion of the series:
[1] Imtiaz Ahmed (Second). [2] K. J. Hughes (Second). [3] Zaheer Abbas (First, Second and Third).

HIGHEST INNINGS TOTALS

For Australia in Australia: 585 at Adelaide		1972-73
in Pakistan: 617 at Faisalabad		1979-80
For Pakistan in Australia: 624 at Adelaide		1983-84
in Pakistan: 501-6 dec. at Faisalabad		1982-83

LOWEST INNINGS TOTALS

For Australia in Australia: 125 at Melbourne 1981-8
            in Pakistan: 80 at Karachi 1956-5

For Pakistan in Australia: 62 at Perth 1981-8
           in Pakistan: 134 at Dacca 1959-6

INDIVIDUAL HUNDREDS

For Australia (37)

J. Benaud (1)
142   Melbourne .. 1972-73
A. R. Border (6)
105†   Melbourne .. 1978-79
150* ⎫
153   ⎬Lahore 1979-80
118   Brisbane 1983-84
117* Adelaide 1983-84
113* Faisalabad .. 1988-89
G. S. Chappell (6)
116* Melbourne .. 1972-73
121   Melbourne .. 1976-77
235   Faisalabad .. 1979-80
201   Brisbane 1981-82
150* Brisbane 1983-84
182   Sydney 1983-84
I. M. Chappell (1)
196   Adelaide 1972-73
G. J. Cosier (1)
168   Melbourne .. 1976-77

I. C. Davis (1)
105† Adelaide 1976-77
K. J. Hughes (2)
106   Perth 1981-82
106   Adelaide 1983-84
D. M. Jones (2)
116 ⎫
121* ⎬Adelaide 1989-90
R. B. McCosker (1)
105   Melbourne .. 1976-77
R. W. Marsh (1)
118† Adelaide 1972-73
N. C. O'Neill (1)
134   Lahore 1959-60
W. B. Phillips (1)
159† Perth 1983-84
I. R. Redpath (1)
135   Melbourne .. 1972-73

G. M. Ritchie (1)
106* Faisalabad .. 1982-8
A. P. Sheahan (1)
127   Melbourne .. 1972-7
R. B. Simpson (2)
153 ⎫
115 ⎬†Karachi 1964-6
M. A. Taylor (2)
101† Melbourne .. 1989-9
101* Sydney 1989-9
K. D. Walters (1)
107   Adelaide 1976-7
K. C. Wessels (1)
179   Adelaide 1983-8
G. M. Wood (1)
100   Melbourne .. 1981-8
G. N. Yallop (3)
172   Faisalabad .. 1979-8
141   Perth 1983-8
268   Melbourne .. 1983-8

For Pakistan (31)

Asif Iqbal (3)
152* Adelaide 1976-77
120   Sydney 1976-77
134* Perth 1978-79
Hanif Mohammad (2)
101* Karachi 1959-60
104   Melbourne .. 1964-65
Ijaz Ahmed (2)
122   Faisalabad .. 1988-89
121   Melbourne .. 1989-90
Imran Khan (1)
136   Adelaide 1989-90
Javed Miandad (6)
129* Perth 1978-79
106* Faisalabad .. 1979-80
138   Lahore 1982-83

131   Adelaide 1983-84
211   Karachi 1988-89
107   Faisalabad .. 1988-89
Khalid Ibadulla (1)
166† Karachi 1964-65
Majid Khan (3)
158   Melbourne .. 1972-73
108   Melbourne .. 1978-79
110* Lahore 1979-80
Mansoor Akhtar (1)
111   Faisalabad .. 1982-83
Mohsin Khan (3)
135   Lahore 1982-83
149   Adelaide 1983-84
152   Melbourne .. 1983-84

Mushtaq Mohammad (1)
121   Sydney 1972-7
Qasim Omar (1)
113   Adelaide 1983-8
Sadiq Mohammad (2)
137   Melbourne .. 1972-7
105   Melbourne .. 1976-7
Saeed Ahmed (1)
166   Lahore 1959-6
Taslim Arif (1)
210* Faisalabad .. 1979-8
Wasim Akram (1)
123   Adelaide 1989-9
Zaheer Abbas (2)
101   Adelaide 1976-7
126   Faisalabad .. 1982-8

† *Signifies hundred on first appearance in Australia–Pakistan Tests.*

RECORD PARTNERSHIPS FOR EACH WICKET

For Australia

34 for 1st	I. C. Davis and A. Turner at Melbourne	1976-77
59 for 2nd	W. B. Phillips and G. N. Yallop at Perth	1983-84
03 for 3rd	G. N. Yallop and K. J. Hughes at Melbourne	1983-84
17 for 4th	G. S. Chappell and G. N. Yallop at Faisalabad	1979-80
71 for 5th	{ G. S. Chappell and G. J. Cosier at Melbourne	1976-77
	A. R. Border and G. S. Chappell at Brisbane	1983-84
39 for 6th	R. M. Cowper and T. R. Veivers at Melbourne	1964-65
85 for 7th	G. N. Yallop and G. R. J. Matthews at Melbourne	1983-84
17 for 8th	G. J. Cosier and K. J. O'Keeffe at Melbourne	1976-77
83 for 9th	J. R. Watkins and R. A. L. Massie at Sydney	1972-73
52 for 10th	{ D. K. Lillee and M. H. N. Walker at Sydney	1976-77
	G. F. Lawson and T. M. Alderman at Lahore	1982-83

For Pakistan

?49 for 1st†	Khalid Ibadulla and Abdul Kadir at Karachi	1964-65
?33 for 2nd	Mohsin Khan and Qasim Omar at Adelaide	1983-84
?23* for 3rd	Taslim Arif and Javed Miandad at Faisalabad	1979-80
?55 for 4th	Mansoor Akhtar and Zaheer Abbas at Faisalabad	1982-83
?86 for 5th	Javed Miandad and Salim Malik at Adelaide	1983-84
?91 for 6th	Imran Khan and Wasim Akram at Adelaide	1989-90
?04 for 7th	Intikhab Alam and Wasim Bari at Adelaide	1972-73
?11 for 8th	Majid Khan and Imran Khan at Lahore	1979-80
?56 for 9th	Intikhab Alam and Afaq Hussain at Melbourne	1964-65
?87 for 10th	Asif Iqbal and Iqbal Qasim at Adelaide	1976-77

† *Denotes record partnership against all countries.*

TEN WICKETS OR MORE IN A MATCH

For Australia (3)

?0-111 (7-87, 3-24)†	R. J. Bright, Karachi	1979-80
?0-135 (6-82, 4-53)	D. K. Lillee, Melbourne	1976-77
?1-118 (5-32, 6-86)†	C. G. Rackemann, Perth	1983-84

For Pakistan (6)

11-218 (4-76, 7-142)	Abdul Qadir, Faisalabad	1982-83
13-114 (6-34, 7-80)†	Fazal Mahmood, Karachi	1956-57
12-165 (6-102, 6-63)	Imran Khan, Sydney	1976-77
11-118 (4-69, 7-49)	Iqbal Qasim, Karachi	1979-80
11-125 (2-39, 9-86)	Sarfraz Nawaz, Melbourne	1978-79
11-160 (6-62, 5-98)	Wasim Akram, Melbourne	1989-90

† *Signifies ten wickets or more on first appearance in Australia–Pakistan Tests.*

AUSTRALIA v SRI LANKA

		Captains				
Season	Australia	Sri Lanka	T	A	SL	D
1982-83*SL*	G. S. Chappell	L. R. D. Mendis	1	1	0	0
1987-88*A*	A. R. Border	R. S. Madugalle	1	1	0	0
1989-90*A*	A. R. Border	A. Ranatunga	2	1	0	1
	In Australia		3	2	0	1
	In Sri Lanka		1	1	0	0
	Totals		4	3	0	1

A Played in Australia. SL Played in Sri Lanka.

INNINGS TOTALS

Highest innings total for Australia: 514-4 dec. at Kandy 1982-83
                     for Sri Lanka: 418 at Brisbane 1989-90

Lowest innings total for Australia: 224 at Hobart 1989-90
                  for Sri Lanka: 153 at Perth 1987-88

INDIVIDUAL HUNDREDS

For Australia (8)

D. W. Hookes (1)	**T. M. Moody** (1)	**S. R. Waugh** (1)
143*† Kandy 1982-83	106† Brisbane 1989-90	134* Hobart 1989-90
D. M. Jones (2)	**M. A. Taylor** (2)	**K. C. Wessels** (1)
102† Perth 1987-88	164† Brisbane 1989-90	141† Kandy 1982-83
118* Hobart 1989-90	108 Hobart 1989-90	

For Sri Lanka (1)

P. A. de Silva (1)
167 Brisbane 1989-90

† *Signifies hundred on first appearance in Australia–Sri Lanka Tests.*

BEST BOWLING

Best bowling in an innings for Australia: 5-66 by T. G. Hogan at Kandy 1982-83
                   for Sri Lanka: 6-66 by R. J. Ratnayake at Hobart . . . 1989-90

PARTNERSHIPS

Best wicket partnership for Australia: 260* for 6th by D. M. Jones and
                       S. R. Waugh at Hobart 1989-90
                 for Sri Lanka: 144 for 7th† by P. A. de Silva
                       and J. R. Ratnayeke at Brisbane 1989-90

† *Denotes record partnership against all countries.*

SOUTH AFRICA v NEW ZEALAND

Season	South Africa	*Captains* New Zealand	T	SA	NZ	D
1931-32*N*	H. B. Cameron	M. L. Page	2	2	0	0
1952-53*N*	J. E. Cheetham	W. M. Wallace	2	1	0	1
1953-54*S*	J. E. Cheetham	G. O. Rabone[1]	5	4	0	1
1961-62*S*	D. J. McGlew	J. R. Reid	5	2	2	1
1963-64*N*	T. L. Goddard	J. R. Reid	3	0	0	3
	In New Zealand		7	3	0	4
	In South Africa		10	6	2	2
	Totals		17	9	2	6

N Played in New Zealand.   S Played in South Africa.

Note: The following deputised for the official touring captain:
[1]B. Sutcliffe (Fourth and Fifth).

HIGHEST INNINGS TOTALS

| For South Africa in South Africa: 464 at Johannesburg | 1961-62 |
| in New Zealand: 524-8 at Wellington | 1952-53 |

| For New Zealand in South Africa: 505 at Cape Town | 1953-54 |
| in New Zealand: 364 at Wellington | 1931-32 |

LOWEST INNINGS TOTALS

| For South Africa in South Africa: 148 at Johannesburg | 1953-54 |
| in New Zealand: 223 at Dunedin | 1963-64 |

| For New Zealand in South Africa: 79 at Johannesburg | 1953-54 |
| in New Zealand: 138 at Dunedin | 1963-64 |

INDIVIDUAL HUNDREDS

For South Africa (11)

X. C. Balaskas (1)
122* Wellington . . 1931-32
J. A. J. Christy (1)
103† Christchurch. 1931-32
W. R. Endean (1)
116   Auckland . . . 1952-53
D. J. McGlew (3)
255*† Wellington . . 1952-53

127*‡ Durban 1961-62
120   Johannesburg 1961-62
R. A. McLean (2)
101   Durban 1953-54
113   Cape Town . 1961-62
B. Mitchell (1)
113† Christchurch. 1931-32

A. R. A. Murray (1)
109† Wellington . . 1952-53
J. H. B. Waite (1)
101   Johannesburg 1961-62

For New Zealand (7)

P. T. Barton (1)
109   Pt Elizabeth . 1961-62
P. G. Z. Harris (1)
101   Cape Town . 1961-62
G. O. Rabone (1)
107   Durban 1953-54

J. R. Reid (2)
135   Cape Town . 1953-54
142   Johannesburg 1961-62
B. W. Sinclair (1)
138   Auckland . . . 1963-64

H. G. Vivian (1)
100† Wellington . . 1931-32

† *Signifies hundred on first appearance in South Africa–New Zealand Tests.*
‡ *Carried his bat.*

RECORD PARTNERSHIPS FOR EACH WICKET

For South Africa

196 for 1st	J. A. J. Christy and B. Mitchell at Christchurch	1931-32
76 for 2nd	J. A. J. Christy and H. B. Cameron at Wellington	1931-32
112 for 3rd	D. J. McGlew and R. A. McLean at Johannesburg	1961-62
135 for 4th	K. J. Funston and R. A. McLean at Durban	1953-54
130 for 5th	W. R. Endean and J. E. Cheetham at Auckland	1952-53
83 for 6th	K. C. Bland and D. T. Lindsay at Auckland	1963-64
246 for 7th†	D. J. McGlew and A. R. A. Murray at Wellington	1952-53
95 for 8th	J. E. Cheetham and H. J. Tayfield at Cape Town	1953-54
60 for 9th	P. M. Pollock and N. A. T. Adcock at Port Elizabeth	1961-62
47 for 10th	D. J. McGlew and H. D. Bromfield at Port Elizabeth	1961-62

For New Zealand

126 for 1st	G. O. Rabone and M. E. Chapple at Cape Town	1953-54
51 for 2nd	W. P. Bradburn and B. W. Sinclair at Dunedin	1963-64
94 for 3rd	M. B. Poore and B. Sutcliffe at Cape Town	1953-54
171 for 4th	B. W. Sinclair and S. N. McGregor at Auckland	1963-64
174 for 5th	J. R. Reid and J. E. F. Beck at Cape Town	1953-54
100 for 6th	H. G. Vivian and F. T. Badcock at Wellington	1931-32
84 for 7th	J. R. Reid and G. A. Bartlett at Johannesburg	1961-62
73 for 8th	P. G. Z. Harris and G. A. Bartlett at Durban	1961-62
69 for 9th	C. F. W. Allcott and I. B. Cromb at Wellington	1931-32
49* for 10th	A. E. Dick and F. J. Cameron at Cape Town	1961-62

† *Denotes record partnership against all countries.*

TEN WICKETS OR MORE IN A MATCH

For South Africa (1)

11-196 (6-128, 5-68)†   S. F. Burke, Cape Town 1961-62

† *Signifies ten wickets or more on first appearance in South Africa–New Zealand Tests.*

Note: The best match figures by a New Zealand bowler are 8-180 (4-61, 4-119), J. C. Alabaster at Cape Town, 1961-62.

WEST INDIES v NEW ZEALAND

Captains

Season	West Indies	New Zealand	T	WI	NZ	D
1951-52N	J. D. C. Goddard	B. Sutcliffe	2	1	0	1
1955-56N	D. St E. Atkinson	J. R. Reid[1]	4	3	1	0
1968-69N	G. S. Sobers	G. T. Dowling	3	1	1	1
1971-72W	G. S. Sobers	G. T. Dowling[2]	5	0	0	5
1979-80N	C. H. Lloyd	G. P. Howarth	3	0	1	2
1984-85W	I. V. A. Richards	G. P. Howarth	4	2	0	2
1986-87N	I. V. A. Richards	J. V. Coney	3	1	1	1
	In New Zealand		15	6	4	5
	In West Indies		9	2	0	7
	Totals		24	8	4	12

N Played in New Zealand.   W Played in West Indies.

Notes: The following deputised for the official touring captain or were appointed by the home authority for only a minor proportion of the series:
[1]H. B. Cave (First). [2]B. E. Congdon (Third, Fourth and Fifth).

HIGHEST INNINGS TOTALS

For West Indies in West Indies: 564-8 at Bridgetown	1971-72
in New Zealand: 546-6 dec. at Auckland	1951-52
For New Zealand in West Indies: 543-3 dec. at Georgetown	1971-72
in New Zealand: 460 at Christchurch	1979-80

LOWEST INNINGS TOTALS

For West Indies in West Indies: 133 at Bridgetown	1971-72
in New Zealand: 77 at Auckland	1955-56
For New Zealand in West Indies: 94 at Bridgetown	1984-85
in New Zealand: 74 at Dunedin	1955-56

INDIVIDUAL HUNDREDS

By West Indies (25)

M. C. Carew (1)
109† Auckland ... 1968-69
C. A. Davis (1)
183 Bridgetown . 1971-72
R. C. Fredericks (1)
163 Kingston ... 1971-72
C. G. Greenidge (2)
100 Port-of-Spain 1984-85
213 Auckland ... 1986-87
D. L. Haynes (3)
105† Dunedin 1979-80
122 Christchurch. 1979-80
121 Wellington . 1986-87
A. I. Kallicharran (2)
100*† Georgetown . 1971-72

101 Port-of-Spain 1971-72
C. L. King (1)
100* Christchurch. 1979-80
S. M. Nurse (2)
168† Auckland ... 1968-69
258 Christchurch. 1968-69
I. V. A. Richards (1)
105 Bridgetown . 1984-85
R. B. Richardson (1)
185 Georgetown . 1984-85
L. G. Rowe (3)
214 ⎫ †Kingston .. 1971-72
100* ⎬
100 Christchurch. 1979-80

G. S. Sobers (1)
142 Bridgetown . 1971-72
J. B. Stollmeyer (1)
152 Auckland ... 1951-52
C. L. Walcott (1)
115 Auckland ... 1951-52
E. D. Weekes (3)
123 Dunedin 1955-56
103 Christchurch. 1955-56
156 Wellington . 1955-56
F. M. M. Worrell (1)
100 Auckland ... 1951-52

By New Zealand (17)

M. G. Burgess (1)
101 Kingston ... 1971-72
B. E. Congdon (2)
166* Port-of-Spain 1971-72
126 Bridgetown . 1971-72
J. J. Crowe (1)
112 Kingston ... 1984-85
M. D. Crowe (3)
188 Georgetown . 1984-85
119 Wellington .. 1986-87

104 Auckland ... 1986-87
B. A. Edgar (1)
127 Auckland ... 1979-80
R. J. Hadlee (1)
103 Christchurch. 1979-80
B. F. Hastings (2)
117* Christchurch. 1968-69
105 Bridgetown . 1971-72
G. P. Howarth (1)
147 Christchurch. 1979-80

T. W. Jarvis (1)
182 Georgetown . 1971-72
B. R. Taylor (1)
124† Auckland ... 1968-69
G. M. Turner (2)
223*‡ Kingston ... 1971-72
259 Georgetown . 1971-72
J. G. Wright (1)
138 Wellington .. 1986-87

† *Signifies hundred on first appearance in West Indies–New Zealand Tests.*
‡ *Carried his bat.*

Notes: E. D. Weekes in 1955-56 made three hundreds in consecutive innings.
L. G. Rowe and A. I. Kallicharran each scored hundreds in their first two innings in Test cricket, Rowe being the only batsman to do so in his first match.

RECORD PARTNERSHIPS FOR EACH WICKET

For West Indies

225 for 1st	C. G. Greenidge and D. L. Haynes at Christchurch	1979-80
269 for 2nd	R. C. Fredericks and L. G. Rowe at Kingston	1971-72
185 for 3rd	C. G. Greenidge and R. B. Richardson at Port-of-Spain	1984-85
162 for 4th	{ E. D. Weekes and O. G. Smith at Dunedin	1955-56
	{ C. G. Greenidge and A. I. Kallicharran at Christchurch	1979-80
189 for 5th	F. M. M. Worrell and C. L. Walcott at Auckland	1951-52
254 for 6th	C. A. Davis and G. S. Sobers at Bridgetown	1971-72
143 for 7th	D. St E. Atkinson and J. D. C. Goddard at Christchurch	1955-56
83 for 8th	I. V. A. Richards and M. D. Marshall at Bridgetown	1984-85
70 for 9th	M. D. Marshall and J. Garner at Bridgetown	1984-85
31 for 10th	T. M. Findlay and G. C. Shillingford at Bridgetown	1971-72

For New Zealand

387 for 1st†	G. M. Turner and T. W. Jarvis at Georgetown	1971-72
210 for 2nd†	G. P. Howarth and J. J. Crowe at Kingston	1984-85
241 for 3rd†	J. G. Wright and M. D. Crowe at Wellington	1986-87
175 for 4th	B. E. Congdon and B. F. Hastings at Bridgetown	1971-72
142 for 5th	M. D. Crowe and J. V. Coney at Georgetown	1984-85
220 for 6th	G. M. Turner and K. J. Wadsworth at Kingston	1971-72
143 for 7th	M. D. Crowe and I. D. S. Smith at Georgetown	1984-85
136 for 8th†	B. E. Congdon and R. S. Cunis at Port-of-Spain	1971-72
62* for 9th	V. Pollard and R. S. Cunis at Auckland	1968-69
41 for 10th	B. E. Congdon and J. C. Alabaster at Port-of-Spain	1971-72

† *Denotes record partnership against all countries.*

TEN WICKETS OR MORE IN A MATCH

For West Indies (1)

11-120 (4-40, 7-80)	M. D. Marshall, Bridgetown	1984-85

For New Zealand (3)

10-124 (4-51, 6-73)†	E. J. Chatfield, Port-of-Spain	1984-85
11-102 (5-34, 6-68)†	R. J. Hadlee, Dunedin	1979-80
10-166 (4-71, 6-95)	G. B. Troup, Auckland	1979-80

† *Signifies ten wickets or more on first appearance in West Indies–New Zealand Tests.*

WEST INDIES v INDIA

Captains

Season	West Indies	India	T	WI	I	D
1948-49*I*	J. D. C. Goddard	L. Amarnath	5	1	0	4
1952-53*W*	J. B. Stollmeyer	V. S. Hazare	5	1	0	4
1958-59*I*	F. C. M. Alexander	Ghulam Ahmed[1]	5	3	0	2
1961-62*W*	F. M. M. Worrell	N. J. Contractor[2]	5	5	0	0
1966-67*I*	G. S. Sobers	Nawab of Pataudi jun.	3	2	0	1
1970-71*W*	G. S. Sobers	A. L. Wadekar	5	0	1	4
1974-75*I*	C. H. Lloyd	Nawab of Pataudi jun.[3]	5	3	2	0
1975-76*W*	C. H. Lloyd	B. S. Bedi	4	2	1	1
1978-79*I*	A. I. Kallicharran	S. M. Gavaskar	6	0	1	5
1982-83*W*	C. H. Lloyd	Kapil Dev	5	2	0	3
1983-84*I*	C. H. Lloyd	Kapil Dev	6	3	0	3
1987-88*I*	I. V. A. Richards	D. B. Vengsarkar[4]	4	1	1	2
1988-89*W*	I. V. A. Richards	D. B. Vengsarkar	4	3	0	1
In India	....		34	13	4	17
In West Indies	....		28	13	2	13
Totals	....		62	26	6	30

I Played in India.   W Played in West Indies.

Notes: The following deputised for the official touring captain or were appointed by the home authority for only a minor proportion of the series:
[1]P. R. Umrigar (First), V. Mankad (Fourth), H. R. Adhikari (Fifth). [2]Nawab of Pataudi jun. (Third, Fourth and Fifth). [3]S. Venkataraghavan (Second). [4]R. J. Shastri (Fourth).

HIGHEST INNINGS TOTALS

For West Indies in West Indies: 631-8 dec. at Kingston 1961-62
           in India: 644-8 dec. at Delhi 1958-59

For India in West Indies: 469-7 at Port-of-Spain 1982-83
           in India: 644-7 dec. at Kanpur 1978-79

LOWEST INNINGS TOTALS

For West Indies in West Indies: 214 at Port-of-Spain 1970-71
           in India: 127 at Delhi 1987-88

For India in West Indies: 97† at Kingston 1975-76
           in India: 75 at Delhi 1987-88

† *Five men absent hurt. The lowest with eleven men batting is 98 at Port-of-Spain, 1961-62.*

INDIVIDUAL HUNDREDS

For West Indies (76)

S. F. A. F. Bacchus (1)
250   Kanpur 1978-79
B. F. Butcher (2)
103   Calcutta 1958-59
142   Madras 1958-59
R. J. Christiani (1)
107† Delhi 1948-49
C. A. Davis (2)
125* Georgetown . 1970-71
105   Port-of-Spain 1970-71
P. J. L. Dujon (1)
110   St John's 1982-83
R. C. Fredericks (2)
100   Calcutta 1974-75
104   Bombay 1974-75
H. A. Gomes (1)
123   Port-of-Spain 1982-83
G. E. Gomez (1)
101† Delhi 1948-49
C. G. Greenidge (5)
107† Bangalore ... 1974-75
154* St John's 1982-83
194   Kanpur 1983-84
141   Calcutta 1987-88
117   Bridgetown . 1988-89
D. L. Haynes (2)
136   St John's 1982-83
112* Bridgetown . 1988-89
J. K. Holt (1)
123   Delhi 1958-59
C. L. Hooper (1)
100* Calcutta 1987-88
C. C. Hunte (1)
101   Bombay 1966-67

A. I. Kallicharran (3)
124† Bangalore ... 1974-75
103* Port-of-Spain 1975-76
187   Bombay 1978-79
R. B. Kanhai (4)
256   Calcutta 1958-59
138   Kingston ... 1961-62
139   Port-of-Spain 1961-62
158* Kingston ... 1970-71
C. H. Lloyd (7)
163   Bangalore ... 1974-75
242* Bombay 1974-75
143   Port-of-Spain 1975-76
102   Bridgetown . 1975-76
106   St John's 1982-83
103   Delhi 1983-84
161* Calcutta 1983-84
A. L. Logie (2)
130   Bridgetown . 1982-83
101   Calcutta 1987-88
E. D. A. McMorris (1)
125† Kingston ... 1961-62
B. H. Pairaudeau (1)
115† Port-of-Spain 1952-53
A. F. Rae (2)
104   Bombay 1948-49
109   Madras 1948-49
I. V. A. Richards (8)
192* Delhi 1974-75
142   Bridgetown . 1975-76
130   Port-of-Spain 1975-76
177   Port-of-Spain 1975-76
109   Georgetown . 1982-83
120   Bombay 1983-84
109* Delhi 1987-88
110   Kingston ... 1988-89

R. B. Richardson (2)
194   Georgetown . 1988-89
156   Kingston ... 1988-89
O. G. Smith (1)
100   Delhi 1958-59
G. S. Sobers (8)
142*† Bombay 1958-59
198   Kanpur 1958-59
106* Calcutta 1958-59
153   Kingston ... 1961-62
104   Kingston ... 1961-62
108* Georgetown . 1970-71
178* Bridgetown . 1970-71
132   Port-of-Spain 1970-71
J. S. Solomon (1)
100* Delhi 1958-59
J. B. Stollmeyer (2)
160   Madras 1948-49
104* Port-of-Spain 1952-53
C. L. Walcott (4)
152† Delhi 1948-49
108   Calcutta 1948-49
125   Georgetown . 1952-53
118   Kingston ... 1952-53
E. D. Weekes (7)
128† Delhi 1948-49
194   Bombay 1948-49
162   ⎫
101   ⎬ Calcutta 1948-49
207   Port-of-Spain 1952-53
161   Port-of-Spain 1952-53
109   Kingston ... 1952-53
A. B. Williams (1)
111   Calcutta 1978-79
F. M. M. Worrell (1)
237   Kingston ... 1952-53

For India (55)

H. R. Adhikari (1)			**120**	Delhi	.....	1978-79	**R. J. Shastri** (2)		
114*†	Delhi	 1948-49	**147***	Georgetown	.	1982-83	102	St John's	1982-83
M. Amarnath (3)			**121**	Delhi	....	1983-84	107	Bridgetown .	1988-89
101*	Kanpur	 1978-79	**236***	Madras	.....	1983-84	**N. S. Sidhu** (1)		
117	Port-of-Spain	1982-83	**V. S. Hazare** (2)				116	Kingston	1988-89
116	St John's	1982-83	**134***	Bombay	....	1948-49	**E. D. Solkar** (1)		
M. L. Apte (1)			**122**	Bombay	....	1948-49	102	Bombay	1974-75
163*	Port-of-Spain	1952-53	**Kapil Dev** (3)				**P. R. Umrigar** (3)		
C. G. Borde (3)			**126***	Delhi	.....	1978-79	130	Port-of-Spain	1952-53
109	Delhi	 1958-59	**100***	Port-of-Spain		1982-83	117	Kingston	1952-53
121	Bombay	 1966-67	**109**	Madras	....	1987-88	172*	Port-of-Spain	1961-62
125	Madras	 1966-67	**S. V. Manjrekar** (1)				**D. B. Vengsarkar** (6)		
S. A. Durani (1)			**108**	Bridgetown	.	1988-89	157*	Calcutta	1978-79
104	Port-of-Spain	1961-62	**V. L. Manjrekar** (1)				109	Delhi	1978-79
F. M. Engineer (1)			**118**	Kingston	...	1952-53	159	Delhi	1983-84
109	Madras	 1966-67	**R. S. Modi** (1)				100	Bombay	1983-84
A. D. Gaekwad (1)			**112**	Bombay	....	1948-49	102	Delhi	1987-88
102	Kanpur	 1978-79	**Mushtaq Ali** (1)				102*	Calcutta	1987-88
S. M. Gavaskar (13)			**106†**	Calcutta	....	1948-49	**G. R. Viswanath** (4)		
116	Georgetown	. 1970-71	**B. P. Patel** (1)				139	Calcutta	1974-75
117*	Bridgetown	. 1970-71	**115***	Port-of-Spain		1975-76	112	Port-of-Spain	1975-76
124 220 }	Port-of-Spain	. 1970-71	**Pankaj Roy** (1)				124	Madras	1978-79
156	Port-of-Spain	1975-76	**150**	Kingston	...	1952-53	179	Kanpur	1978-79
102	Port-of-Spain	1975-76	**D. N. Sardesai** (3)						
205	Bombay	 1978-79	**212**	Kingston	...	1970-71			
107 182* }	Calcutta	1978-79	**112**	Port-of-Spain		1970-71			
			150	Bridgetown	.	1970-71			

† *Signifies hundred on first appearance in West Indies–India Tests.*

RECORD PARTNERSHIPS FOR EACH WICKET

For West Indies

296 for 1st	C. G. Greenidge and D. L. Haynes at St John's	1982-83
255 for 2nd	E. D. A. McMorris and R. B. Kanhai at Kingston	1961-62
220 for 3rd	I. V. A. Richards and A. I. Kallicharran at Bridgetown	1975-76
267 for 4th	C. L. Walcott and G. E. Gomez at Delhi	1948-49
219 for 5th	E. D. Weekes and B. H. Pairaudeau at Port-of-Spain	1952-53
250 for 6th	C. H. Lloyd and D. L. Murray at Bombay	1974-75
130 for 7th	C. G. Greenidge and M. D. Marshall at Kanpur	1983-84
124 for 8th†	I. V. A. Richards and K. D. Boyce at Delhi	1974-75
161 for 9th†	C. H. Lloyd and A. M. E. Roberts at Calcutta	1983-84
98* for 10th†	F. M. M. Worrell and W. W. Hall at Port-of-Spain	1961-62

For India

153 for 1st	S. M. Gavaskar and C. P. S. Chauhan at Bombay	1978-79
344* for 2nd†	S. M. Gavaskar and D. B. Vengsarkar at Calcutta	1978-79
159 for 3rd	M. Amarnath and G. R. Viswanath at Port-of-Spain	1975-76
172 for 4th	G. R. Viswanath and A. D. Gaekwad at Kanpur	1978-79
204 for 5th	S. M. Gavaskar and B. P. Patel at Port-of-Spain	1975-76
170 for 6th	S. M. Gavaskar and R. J. Shastri at Madras	1983-84
186 for 7th	D. N. Sardesai and E. D. Solkar at Bridgetown	1970-71
107 for 8th	Yashpal Sharma and B. S. Sandhu at Kingston	1982-83
143* for 9th	S. M. Gavaskar and S. M. H. Kirmani at Madras	1983-84
62 for 10th	D. N. Sardesai and B. S. Bedi at Bridgetown	1970-71

† *Denotes record partnership against all countries.*

TEN WICKETS OR MORE IN A MATCH

For West Indies (4)

11-126 (6-50, 5-76)	W. W. Hall, Kanpur	1958-59
11-89 (5-34, 6-55)	M. D. Marshall, Port-of-Spain	1988-89
12-121 (7-64, 5-57)	A. M. E. Roberts, Madras	1974-75
10-101 (6-62, 4-39)	C. A. Walsh, Kingston	1988-89

For India (4)

11-235 (7-157, 4-78)†	B. S. Chandrasekhar, Bombay	1966-67
10-223 (9-102, 1-121)	S. P. Gupte, Kanpur	1958-59
16-136 (8-61, 8-75)†	N. D. Hirwani, Madras	1987-88
10-135 (1-52, 9-83)	Kapil Dev, Ahmedabad	1983-84

† *Signifies ten wickets or more on first appearance in West Indies–India Tests.*

WEST INDIES v PAKISTAN

	Captains					
Season	West Indies	Pakistan	T	WI	P	D
1957-58W	F. C. M. Alexander	A. H. Kardar	5	3	1	1
1958-59P	F. C. M. Alexander	Fazal Mahmood	3	1	2	0
1974-75P	C. H. Lloyd	Intikhab Alam	2	0	0	2
1976-77W	C. H. Lloyd	Mushtaq Mohammad	5	2	1	2
1980-81P	C. H. Lloyd	Javed Miandad	4	1	0	3
1986-87P	I. V. A. Richards	Imran Khan	3	1	1	1
1987-88W	I. V. A. Richards[1]	Imran Khan	3	1	1	1
In West Indies			13	6	3	4
In Pakistan			12	3	3	6
Totals			25	9	6	10

P Played in Pakistan. W Played in West Indies.

Note: The following was appointed by the home authority for only a minor proportion of the series:
[1]C. G. Greenidge (First).

HIGHEST INNINGS TOTALS

For West Indies in West Indies: 790-3 dec. at Kingston		1957-58
in Pakistan: 493 at Karachi		1974-75
For Pakistan in West Indies: 657-8 dec. at Bridgetown		1957-58
in Pakistan: 406-8 dec. at Karachi		1974-75

LOWEST INNINGS TOTALS

For West Indies in West Indies: 154 at Port-of-Spain		1976-77
in Pakistan: 53 at Faisalabad		1986-87
For Pakistan in West Indies: 106 at Bridgetown		1957-58
in Pakistan: 77 at Lahore		1986-87

INDIVIDUAL HUNDREDS

For West Indies (19)

L. Baichan (1)	114 Georgetown . 1957-58	123 Port-of-Spain 1987-88
105*† Lahore 1974-75	**B. D. Julien** (1)	**I. T. Shillingford** (1)
P. J. L. Dujon (1)	101 Karachi 1974-75	120 Georgetown . 1976-77
106* Port-of-Spain 1987-88	**A. I. Kallicharran** (1)	**G. S. Sobers** (3)
R. C. Fredericks (1)	115 Karachi 1974-75	365* Kingston . . . 1957-58
120 Port-of-Spain 1976-77	**R. B. Kanhai** (1)	125 ⎫
C. G. Greenidge (1)	217 Lahore 1958-59	109* ⎬ Georgetown . . 1957-58
100 Kingston . . . 1976-77	**C. H. Lloyd** (1)	**C. L. Walcott** (1)
C. C. Hunte (3)	157 Bridgetown . 1976-77	145 Georgetown . 1957-58
142† Bridgetown . 1957-58	**I. V. A. Richards** (2)	**E. D. Weekes** (1)
260 Kingston . . . 1957-58	120* Multan 1980-81	197† Bridgetown . 1957-58

For Pakistan (16)

Asif Iqbal (1)	**Javed Miandad** (2)	**Saeed Ahmed** (1)
135 Kingston . . . 1976-77	114 Georgetown . 1987-88	150 Georgetown . 1957-58
Hanif Mohammad (2)	102 Port-of-Spain 1987-88	**Wasim Raja** (2)
337† Bridgetown . 1957-58	**Majid Khan** (2)	107* Karachi 1974-75
103 Karachi 1958-59	100 Karachi 1974-75	117* Bridgetown . 1976-77
Imtiaz Ahmed (1)	167 Georgetown . 1976-77	**Wazir Mohammad** (2)
122 Kingston . . . 1957-58	**Mushtaq Mohammad** (2)	106 Kingston . . . 1957-58
Imran Khan (1)	123 Lahore 1974-75	189 Port-of-Spain 1957-58
123 Lahore 1980-81	121 Port-of-Spain 1976-77	

† *Signifies hundred on first appearance in West Indies–Pakistan Tests.*

RECORD PARTNERSHIPS FOR EACH WICKET

For West Indies

182 for 1st	R. C. Fredericks and C. G. Greenidge at Kingston	1976-77
446 for 2nd†	C. C. Hunte and G. S. Sobers at Kingston	1957-58
162 for 3rd	R. B. Kanhai and G. S. Sobers at Lahore	1958-59
188* for 4th	G. S. Sobers and C. L. Walcott at Kingston	1957-58
185 for 5th	E. D. Weekes and O. G. Smith at Bridgetown	1957-58
151 for 6th	C. H. Lloyd and D. L. Murray at Bridgetown	1976-77
70 for 7th	C. H. Lloyd and J. Garner at Bridgetown	1976-77
50 for 8th	B. D. Julien and V. A. Holder at Karachi	1974-75
61* for 9th	P. J. L. Dujon and W. K. M. Benjamin at Bridgetown	1987-88
44 for 10th	R. Nanan and S. T. Clarke at Faisalabad	1980-81

For Pakistan

159 for 1st‡	Majid Khan and Zaheer Abbas at Georgetown	1976-77
178 for 2nd	Hanif Mohammad and Saeed Ahmed at Karachi	1958-59
169 for 3rd	Saeed Ahmed and Wazir Mohammad at Port-of-Spain	1957-58
154 for 4th	Wazir Mohammad and Hanif Mohammad at Port-of-Spain	1957-58
87 for 5th	Mushtaq Mohammad and Asif Iqbal at Kingston	1976-77
166 for 6th	Wazir Mohammad and A. H. Kardar at Kingston	1957-58
128 for 7th	Wasim Raja and Wasim Bari at Karachi	1974-75
94 for 8th	Salim Malik and Salim Yousuf at Port-of-Spain	1987-88
73 for 9th	Wasim Raja and Sarfraz Nawaz at Bridgetown	1976-77
133 for 10th†	Wasim Raja and Wasim Bari at Bridgetown	1976-77

† *Denotes record partnership against all countries.*

‡ *219 runs were added for this wicket in two separate partnerships: Sadiq Mohammad retired hurt and was replaced by Zaheer Abbas when 60 had been added. The highest partnership by two opening batsmen is 152 by Hanif Mohammad and Imtiaz Ahmed at Bridgetown, 1957-58.*

TEN WICKETS OR MORE IN A MATCH

For Pakistan (2)

-100 (6-34, 6-66)	Fazal Mahmood, Dacca	1958-59
-121 (7-80, 4-41)	Imran Khan, Georgetown	1987-88

ote: The best match figures by a West Indian bowler are 9-95 (8-29, 1-66) by C. E. H. Croft at *rt-of-Spain, 1976-77.

NEW ZEALAND v INDIA

		Captains				
ason	*New Zealand*	*India*	*T*	*NZ*	*I*	*D*
55-56*I*	H. B. Cave	P. R. Umrigar[1]	5	0	2	3
64-65*I*	J. R. Reid	Nawab of Pataudi jun.	4	0	1	3
67-68*N*	G. T. Dowling[2]	Nawab of Pataudi jun.	4	1	3	0
69-70*I*	G. T. Dowling	Nawab of Pataudi jun.	3	1	1	1
75-76*N*	G. M. Turner	B. S. Bedi[3]	3	1	1	1
76-77*I*	G. M. Turner	B. S. Bedi	3	0	2	1
80-81*N*	G. P. Howarth	S. M. Gavaskar	3	1	0	2
88-89*I*	J. G. Wright	D. B. Vengsarkar	3	1	2	0
89-90*N*	J. G. Wright	M. Azharuddin	3	1	0	2
	In India		18	2	8	8
	In New Zealand		13	4	4	5
	Totals		31	6	12	13

I Played in India. N Played in New Zealand.

otes: The following deputised for the official touring captain or were appointed by the home *thority for a minor proportion of the series:*
[1]Ghulam Ahmed (First). [2]B. W. Sinclair (First). [3]S. M. Gavaskar (First).

HIGHEST INNINGS TOTALS

*r New Zealand in New Zealand: 502 at Christchurch		1967-68
in India: 462-9 dec. at Calcutta		1964-65
*r India in New Zealand: 482 at Auckland		1989-90
in India: 537-3 dec. at Madras		1955-56

LOWEST INNINGS TOTALS

*r New Zealand in New Zealand: 100 at Wellington		1980-81
in India: 124 at Hyderabad		1988-89
*r India in New Zealand: 81 at Wellington		1975-76
in India: 88 at Bombay.......................................		1964-65

INDIVIDUAL HUNDREDS

For New Zealand (21)

M. D. Crowe (1)		**J. M. Parker** (1)		230* Delhi 1955-
113 Auckland ... 1989-90		104 Bombay 1976-77		151* Calcutta .... 1964-(
G. T. Dowling (3)		**J. F. Reid** (1)		**B. R. Taylor** (1)
120 Bombay 1964-65		123* Christchurch. 1980-81		105† Calcutta .... 1964-(
143 Dunedin 1967-68		**J. R. Reid** (2)		**G. M. Turner** (2)
239 Christchurch. 1967-68		119* Delhi 1955-56		117 Christchurch. 1975-
J. W. Guy (1)		120 Calcutta 1955-56		113 Kanpur .... 1976-"
102† Hyderabad .. 1955-56		**I. D. S. Smith** (1)		**J. G. Wright** (3)
G. P. Howarth (1)		173 Auckland ... 1989-90		110 Auckland ... 1980-!
137* Wellington .. 1980-81		**B. Sutcliffe** (3)		185 Christchurch. 1989-"
A. H. Jones (1)		137*† Hyderabad .. 1955-56		113* Napier 1989-
170* Auckland ... 1989-90				

For India (22)

S. Amarnath (1)		177 Delhi 1955-56		**D. N. Sardesai** (2)
124† Auckland ... 1975-76		102* Madras 1964-65		200* Bombay .... 1964-(
M. Azharuddin (1)		**V. Mankad** (2)		106 Delhi ...... 1964-(
192 Auckland ... 1989-90		223 Bombay 1955-56		**N. S. Sidhu** (1)
C. G. Borde (1)		231 Madras 1955-56		116† Bangalore .. 1988-!
109 Bombay 1964-65		**Nawab of Pataudi jun.** (2)		**P. R. Umrigar** (1)
S. M. Gavaskar (2)		153 Calcutta 1964-65		223† Hyderabad .. 1955-
116† Auckland ... 1975-76		113 Delhi 1964-65		**G. R. Viswanath** (1)
119 Bombay 1976-77		**G. S. Ramchand** (1)		103* Kanpur .... 1976-"
A. G. Kripal Singh (1)		106* Calcutta 1955-56		**A. L. Wadekar** (1)
100*† Hyderabad .. 1955-56		**Pankaj Roy** (2)		143 Wellington .. 1967-
V. L. Manjrekar (3)		100 Calcutta 1955-56		
118† Hyderabad .. 1955-56		173 Madras 1955-56		

† *Signifies hundred on first appearance in New Zealand–India Tests. B. R. Taylor provides* \
only instance for New Zealand of a player scoring his maiden hundred in first-class cricket in \
first Test.

RECORD PARTNERSHIPS FOR EACH WICKET

For New Zealand

149 for 1st	T. J. Franklin and J. G. Wright at Napier	1989-"
155 for 2nd	G. T. Dowling and B. E. Congdon at Dunedin	1967-(
222* for 3rd	B. Sutcliffe and J. R. Reid at Delhi	1955-!
125 for 4th	J. G. Wright and M. J. Greatbatch at Christchurch	1989-"
119 for 5th	G. T. Dowling and K. Thomson at Christchurch	1967-(
87 for 6th	J. W. Guy and A. R. MacGibbon at Hyderabad	1955-
163 for 7th	B. Sutcliffe and B. R. Taylor at Calcutta	1964-(
103 for 8th	R. J. Hadlee and I. D. S. Smith at Auckland	1989-(
136 for 9th†	I. D. S. Smith and M. C. Snedden at Auckland	1989-"
61 for 10th	J. T. Ward and R. O. Collinge at Madras	1964-(

For India

413 for 1st†	V. Mankad and Pankaj Roy at Madras	1955-
204 for 2nd	S. M. Gavaskar and S. Amarnath at Auckland	1975-
238 for 3rd	P. R. Umrigar and V. L. Manjrekar at Hyderabad	1955-
171 for 4th	P. R. Umrigar and A. G. Kripal Singh at Hyderabad	1955-!
127 for 5th	V. L. Manjrekar and G. S. Ramchand at Delhi	1955-!
193* for 6th	D. N. Sardesai and Hanumant Singh at Bombay	1964-(
128 for 7th	S. R. Tendulkar and K. S. More at Napier	1989-"
143 for 8th†	R. G. Nadkarni and F. M. Engineer at Madras	1964-(
105 for 9th {	S. M. H. Kirmani and B. S. Bedi at Bombay	1976-"
	S. M. H. Kirmani and N. S. Yadav at Auckland	1980-"
57 for 10th	R. B. Desai and B. S. Bedi at Dunedin	1967-(

† *Denotes record partnership against all countries.*

TEN WICKETS OR MORE IN A MATCH

For New Zealand (2)

-58 (4-35, 7-23)	R. J. Hadlee, Wellington	1975-76
-88 (6-49, 4-39)	R. J. Hadlee, Bombay	1988-89

For India (2)

-140 (3-64, 8-76)	E. A. S. Prasanna, Auckland	1975-76
-152 (8-72, 4-80)	S. Venkataraghavan, Delhi	1964-65

NEW ZEALAND v PAKISTAN

eason	*New Zealand*	*Captains* *Pakistan*	*T*	*NZ*	*P*	*D*
*55-56P	H. B. Cave	A. H. Kardar	3	0	2	1
*64-65N	J. R. Reid	Hanif Mohammad	3	0	0	3
*64-65P	J. R. Reid	Hanif Mohammad	3	0	2	1
*69-70P	G. T. Dowling	Intikhab Alam	3	1	0	2
*72-73N	B. E. Congdon	Intikhab Alam	3	0	1	2
*76-77P	G. M. Turner[1]	Mushtaq Mohammad	3	0	2	1
*78-79N	M. G. Burgess	Mushtaq Mohammad	3	0	1	2
*84-85P	J. V. Coney	Zaheer Abbas	3	0	2	1
*84-85N	G. P. Howarth	Javed Miandad	3	2	0	1
*88-89N†	J. G. Wright	Imran Khan	2	0	0	2
	In Pakistan		15	1	8	6
	In New Zealand		14	2	2	10
	Totals		29	3	10	16

Played in New Zealand. P Played in Pakistan.
The First Test at Dunedin was abandoned without a ball being bowled and is excluded.

ote: The following deputised for the official touring captain:
[1]J. M. Parker (Third).

HIGHEST INNINGS TOTALS

or New Zealand in New Zealand 492 at Wellington		1984-85
in Pakistan: 482-6 dec. at Lahore		1964-65
or Pakistan in New Zealand: 616-5 dec. at Auckland		1988-89
in Pakistan: 565-9 dec. at Karachi		1976-77

LOWEST INNINGS TOTALS

or New Zealand in New Zealand: 156 at Dunedin		1972-73
in Pakistan: 70 at Dacca		1955-56
or Pakistan in New Zealand: 169 at Auckland		1984-85
in Pakistan: 114 at Lahore		1969-70

INDIVIDUAL HUNDREDS

For New Zealand (17)

M. G. Burgess (2)
119* Dacca 1969-70
111 Lahore 1976-77
J. V. Coney (1)
111* Dunedin 1984-85
M. D. Crowe (1)
174 Wellington .. 1988-89
B. A. Edgar (1)
129† Christchurch. 1978-79
B. F. Hastings (1)
110 Auckland ... 1972-73

G. P. Howarth (1)
114 Napier 1978-79
W. K. Lees (1)
152 Karachi 1976-77
S. N. McGregor (1)
111 Lahore 1955-56
R. E. Redmond (1)
107† Auckland ... 1972-73
J. F. Reid (3)
106 Hyderabad .. 1984-85
148 Wellington .. 1984-85

158* Auckland ... 1984-85
J. R. Reid (1)
128 Karachi 1964-
B. W. Sinclair (1)
130 Lahore 1964-
G. M. Turner (1)
110† Dacca 1969-
J. G. Wright (1)
107 Karachi 1984-

For Pakistan (30)

Asif Iqbal (3)
175 Dunedin 1972-73
166 Lahore 1976-77
104 Napier 1978-79
Hanif Mohammad (3)
103 Dacca 1955-56
100* Christchurch. 1964-65
203* Lahore 1964-65
Imtiaz Ahmed (1)
209 Lahore 1955-56
Javed Miandad (7)
163† Lahore 1976-77
206 Karachi 1976-77
160* Christchurch. 1978-79

104 } Hyderabad .. 1984-85
103* }
118 Wellington .. 1988-89
271 Auckland ... 1988-89
Majid Khan (3)
110 Auckland ... 1972-73
112 Karachi 1976-77
119* Napier 1978-79
Mohammad Ilyas (1)
126 Karachi 1964-65
Mudassar Nazar (1)
106 Hyderabad .. 1984-85
Mushtaq Mohammad (3)
201 Dunedin 1972-73
101 Hyderabad .. 1976-77

107 Karachi 1976-
Sadiq Mohammad (2)
166 Wellington .. 1972-
103* Hyderabad .. 1976-
Saeed Ahmed (1)
172 Karachi 1964-
Salim Malik (1)
119* Karachi 1984-
Shoaib Mohammad (2)
163 Wellington .. 1988-
112 Auckland ... 1988-
Waqar Hassan (1)
189 Lahore 1955-
Zaheer Abbas (1)
135 Auckland ... 1978-

† *Signifies hundred on first appearance in New Zealand–Pakistan Tests.*

Note: Mushtaq and Sadiq Mohammad, at Hyderabad in 1976-77, provide the fourth instance Test matches, after the Chappells (thrice), of brothers each scoring hundreds in the sar innings.

RECORD PARTNERSHIPS FOR EACH WICKET

For New Zealand

159 for 1st	R. E. Redmond and G. M. Turner at Auckland	1972-
195 for 2nd	J. G. Wright and G. P. Howarth at Napier	1978-
178 for 3rd	B. W. Sinclair and J. R. Reid at Lahore	1964-
128 for 4th	B. F. Hastings and M. G. Burgess at Wellington	1972-
183 for 5th†	M. G. Burgess and R. W. Anderson at Lahore	1976-
145 for 6th	J. F. Reid and R. J. Hadlee at Wellington	1984-
186 for 7th†	W. K. Lees and R. J. Hadlee at Karachi	1976-
100 for 8th	B. W. Yuile and D. R. Hadlee at Karachi	1969-
96 for 9th	M. G. Burgess and R. S. Cunis at Dacca	1969-
151 for 10th†	B. F. Hastings and R. O. Collinge at Auckland	1972-

For Pakistan

147 for 1st‡	Sadiq Mohammad and Majid Khan at Karachi	1976-
114 for 2nd	Mohammad Ilyas and Saeed Ahmed at Rawalpindi	1964-
248 for 3rd	Shoaib Mohammad and Javed Miandad at Auckland	1988-
350 for 4th†	Mushtaq Mohammad and Asif Iqbal at Dunedin	1972-

for 5th†	Javed Miandad and Asif Iqbal at Lahore	1976-77
7 for 6th†	Hanif Mohammad and Majid Khan at Lahore	1964-65
8 for 7th†	Waqar Hassan and Imtiaz Ahmed at Lahore	1955-56
9 for 8th	Anil Dalpat and Iqbal Qasim at Karachi	1984-85
2 for 9th	Intikhab Alam and Arif Butt at Auckland	1964-65
5 for 10th	Salah-ud-Din and Mohammad Farooq at Rawalpindi	1964-65

† *Denotes record partnership against all countries.*
‡ *In the preceding Test of this series, at Hyderabad, 164 runs were added for this wicket by Sadiq ohammad, Majid Khan and Zaheer Abbas. Sadiq Mohammad retired hurt after 136 had been ored.*

TEN WICKETS OR MORE IN A MATCH

For Pakistan (4)

-182 (5-91, 5-91)	Intikhab Alam, Dacca	1969-70
-130 (7-52, 4-78)	Intikhab Alam, Dunedin	1972-73
-128 (5-56, 5-72)	Wasim Akram, Dunedin	1984-85
-79 (5-37, 6-42)†	Zulfiqar Ahmed, Karachi	1955-56

† *Signifies ten wickets or more on first appearance in New Zealand–Pakistan Tests.*
ote: The best match figures by a New Zealand bowler are 9-70 (4-36, 5-34), F. J. Cameron at uckland, 1964-65.

NEW ZEALAND v SRI LANKA

	Captains					
ason	*New Zealand*	*Sri Lanka*	T	NZ	SL	D
'82-83N	G. P. Howarth	D. S. de Silva	2	2	0	0
'83-84S	G. P. Howarth	L. R. D. Mendis	3	2	0	1
'86-87S†	J. J. Crowe	L. R. D. Mendis	1	0	0	1
	In New Zealand		2	2	0	0
	In Sri Lanka		4	2	0	2
	Totals		6	4	0	2

Played in New Zealand. S Played in Sri Lanka.
† *The Second and Third Tests were cancelled owing to civil disturbances.*

HIGHEST INNINGS TOTALS

or New Zealand in New Zealand: 344 at Christchurch		1982-83
in Sri Lanka: 459 at Colombo (CCC)		1983-84
or Sri Lanka in New Zealand: 240 at Wellington		1982-83
in Sri Lanka: 397-9 dec. at Colombo (CCC)		1986-87

LOWEST INNINGS TOTALS

or New Zealand in New Zealand: 201 at Wellington		1982-83
in Sri Lanka: 198 at Colombo (SSC)		1983-84
or Sri Lanka in New Zealand: 93 at Wellington		1982-83
in Sri Lanka: 97 at Kandy		1983-84

INDIVIDUAL HUNDREDS

For New Zealand (3)

J. J. Crowe (1)	**R. J. Hadlee** (1)	**J. F. Reid** (1)
120* Colombo	151* Colombo	180 Colombo
(CCC) 1986-87	(CCC) 1986-87	(CCC) 1983-

For Sri Lanka (2)

R. L. Dias (1)	**D. S. B. P. Kuruppu** (1)
108† Colombo	201*† Colombo
(SSC) 1983-84	(CCC) 1986-87

† *Signifies hundred on first appearance in New Zealand–Sri Lanka Tests.*

PARTNERSHIPS

Best wicket partnership for New Zealand: 246* for the 6th† by J. J. Crowe and
R. J. Hadlee at Colombo (CCC) 1986-
for Sri Lanka: 159* for the 3rd†‡ by S. Wettimuny and
R. L. Dias at Colombo (SSC) 1983-

† *Denotes record partnership against all countries.*
‡ *163 runs were added for this wicket in two separate partnerships: S. Wettimuny retired hurt a*
was replaced by L. R. D. Mendis when 159 had been added.

TEN WICKETS OR MORE IN A MATCH

For New Zealand (1)

10-102 (5-73, 5-29)   R. J. Hadlee, Colombo (CCC) 1983-

Note: The best match figures by a Sri Lankan bowler are 8-159 (5-86, 3-73), V. B. John
Kandy, 1983-84.

INDIA v PAKISTAN

	Captains				
Season	India	Pakistan	T	I	P
1952-53*I*	L. Amarnath	A. H. Kardar	5	2	1
1954-55*P*	V. Mankad	A. H. Kardar	5	0	0
1960-61*I*	N. J. Contractor	Fazal Mahmood	5	0	0
1978-79*P*	B. S. Bedi	Mushtaq Mohammad	3	0	2
1979-80*I*	S. M. Gavaskar[1]	Asif Iqbal	6	2	0
1982-83*P*	S. M. Gavaskar	Imran Khan	6	0	3
1983-84*I*	Kapil Dev	Zaheer Abbas	3	0	0
1984-85*P*	S. M. Gavaskar	Zaheer Abbas	2	0	0
1986-87*I*	Kapil Dev	Imran Khan	5	0	1
1989-90*P*	K. Srikkanth	Imran Khan	4	0	0
	In India		24	4	2
	In Pakistan		20	0	5
	Totals		44	4	7

I Played in India. P Played in Pakistan.

Note: The following was appointed by the home authority for only a minor proportion of
series:
[1]G. R. Viswanath (Sixth).

HIGHEST INNINGS TOTALS

For India in India: 539-9 dec. at Madras	....	1960-61
in Pakistan: 509 at Lahore	....	1989-90
For Pakistan in India: 487-9 dec. at Madras	....	1986-87
in Pakistan: 699-5 at Lahore	....	1989-90

LOWEST INNINGS TOTALS

For India in India: 106 at Lucknow	....	1952-53
in Pakistan: 145 at Karachi	....	1954-55
For Pakistan in India: 116 at Bangalore	....	1986-87
in Pakistan: 158 at Dacca	....	1954-55

INDIVIDUAL HUNDREDS

For India (31)

M. Amarnath (4)
109* Lahore 1982-83
120 Lahore 1982-83
103* Karachi 1982-83
101* Lahore 1984-85
M. Azharuddin (3)
141 Calcutta 1986-87
110 Jaipur 1986-87
109 Faisalabad .. 1989-90
C. G. Borde (1)
177* Madras 1960-61
A. D. Gaekwad (1)
201 Jullundur ... 1983-84
S. M. Gavaskar (5)
111 ⎫
137 ⎭ Karachi 1978-79

166 Madras 1979-80
127*‡ Faisalabad .. 1982-83
103* Bangalore ... 1983-84
V. S. Hazare (1)
146* Bombay 1952-53
S. V. Manjrekar (2)
113*† Karachi 1989-90
218 Lahore 1989-90
S. M. Patil (1)
127 Faisalabad .. 1984-85
R. J. Shastri (3)
128 Karachi 1982-83
139 Faisalabad .. 1984-85
125 Jaipur 1986-87
R. H. Shodhan (1)
110† Calcutta 1952-53

K. Srikkanth (1)
123 Madras 1986-87
P. R. Umrigar (5)
102 Bombay 1952-53
108 Peshawar ... 1954-55
115 Kanpur 1960-61
117 Madras 1960-61
112 Delhi 1960-61
D. B. Vengsarkar (2)
146* Delhi 1979-80
109 Ahmedabad .. 1986-87
G. R. Viswanath (1)
145† Faisalabad .. 1978-79

For Pakistan (41)

Aamer Malik (2)
117 Faisalabad .. 1989-90
113 Lahore 1989-90
Alim-ud-Din (1)
103* Karachi 1954-55
Asif Iqbal (1)
104† Faisalabad .. 1978-79
Hanif Mohammad (2)
142 Bahawalpur . 1954-55
160 Bombay 1960-61
Ijaz Faqih (1)
105† Ahmedabad . 1986-87
Imtiaz Ahmed (1)
135 Madras 1960-61
Imran Khan (3)
117 Faisalabad .. 1982-83
135* Madras 1986-87
109* Karachi 1989-90
Javed Miandad (5)
154*† Faisalabad .. 1978-79
100 Karachi 1978-79

126 Faisalabad .. 1982-83
280* Hyderabad .. 1982-83
145 Lahore 1989-90
Mohsin Khan (1)
101*† Lahore 1982-83
Mudassar Nazar (6)
119 Karachi 1982-83
231 Hyderabad .. 1982-83
152*‡ Lahore 1982-83
152 Karachi 1982-83
199 Faisalabad .. 1984-85
Mushtaq Mohammad (1)
101 Delhi 1960-61
Nazar Mohammad (1)
124*‡ Lucknow ... 1952-53
Qasim Omar (1)
210 Faisalabad .. 1984-85
Ramiz Raja (1)
114 Jaipur 1986-87

Saeed Ahmed (2)
121† Bombay 1960-61
103 Madras 1960-61
Salim Malik (3)
107 Faisalabad .. 1982-83
102* Faisalabad .. 1984-85
102* Karachi 1989-90
Shoaib Mohammad (2)
101 Madras 1986-87
203* Lahore 1989-90
Wasim Raja (1)
125 Jullundur ... 1983-84
Zaheer Abbas (6)
176† Faisalabad .. 1978-79
235* Lahore 1978-79
215 Lahore 1982-83
186 Karachi 1982-83
168 Faisalabad .. 1982-83
168* Lahore 1984-85

† *Signifies hundred on first appearance in India–Pakistan Tests.*
‡ *Carried his bat.*

RECORD PARTNERSHIPS FOR EACH WICKET

For India

200 for 1st	S. M. Gavaskar and K. Srikkanth at Madras	1986-8
135 for 2nd	N. S. Sidhu and S. V. Manjrekar at Karachi	1989-9
190 for 3rd	M. Amarnath and Yashpal Sharma at Lahore	1982-8
186 for 4th	S. V. Manjrekar and R. J. Shastri at Lahore	1989-9
200 for 5th	S. M. Patil and R. J. Shastri at Faisalabad	1984-8
143 for 6th	M. Azharuddin and Kapil Dev at Calcutta	1986-8
155 for 7th	R. M. H. Binny and Madan Lal at Bangalore	1983-8
122 for 8th	S. M. H. Kirmani and Madan Lal at Faisalabad	1982-8
149 for 9th†	P. G. Joshi and R. B. Desai at Bombay	1960-6
109 for 10th†	H. R. Adhikari and Ghulam Ahmed at Delhi	1952-5

For Pakistan

162 for 1st	Hanif Mohammad and Imtiaz Ahmed at Madras	1960-6
250 for 2nd	Mudassar Nazar and Qasim Omar at Faisalabad	1984-8
451 for 3rd†	Mudassar Nazar and Javed Miandad at Hyderabad	1982-8
287 for 4th	Javed Miandad and Zaheer Abbas at Faisalabad	1982-8
213 for 5th	Zaheer Abbas and Mudassar Nazar at Karachi	1982-8
207 for 6th	Salim Malik and Imran Khan at Faisalabad	1982-8
154 for 7th	Imran Khan and Ijaz Faqih at Ahmedabad	1986-8
112 for 8th	Imran Khan and Wasim Akram at Madras	1986-8
60 for 9th	Wasim Bari and Iqbal Qasim at Bangalore	1979-8
104 for 10th	Zulfiqar Ahmed and Amir Elahi at Madras	1952-5

† *Denotes record partnership against all countries.*

TEN WICKETS OR MORE IN A MATCH

For India (3)

11-146 (4-90, 7-56)	Kapil Dev, Madras	1979-8
10-126 (7-27, 3-99)	Maninder Singh, Bangalore	1986-8
13-131 (8-52, 5-79)†	V. Mankad, Delhi	1952-5

For Pakistan (5)

12-94 (5-52, 7-42)	Fazal Mahmood, Lucknow	1952-5
11-79 (3-19, 8-60)	Imran Khan, Karachi	1982-8
11-180 (6-98, 5-82)	Imran Khan, Faisalabad	1982-8
10-175 (4-135, 6-40)	Iqbal Qasim, Bombay	1979-8
11-190 (8-69, 3-121)	Sikander Bakht, Delhi	1979-8

† *Signifies ten wickets or more on first appearance in India–Pakistan Tests.*

INDIA v SRI LANKA

Season	India	Sri Lanka	T	I	SL	
		Captains				
1982-83*I*	S. M. Gavaskar	B. Warnapura	1	0	0	
1985-86*S*	Kapil Dev	L. R. D. Mendis	3	0	1	
1986-87*I*	Kapil Dev	L. R. D. Mendis	3	2	0	
	In India		4	2	0	
	In Sri Lanka		3	0	1	
	Totals		7	2	1	4

I Played in India. S Played in Sri Lanka.

HIGHEST INNINGS TOTALS

For India in India: 676-7 at Kanpur 1986-87
     in Sri Lanka: 325-5 dec. at Kandy 1985-86

For Sri Lanka in India: 420 at Kanpur 1986-87
     in Sri Lanka: 385 at Colombo (PSS) 1985-86

LOWEST INNINGS TOTALS

For India in India: 400 at Cuttack 1986-87
     in Sri Lanka: 198 at Colombo (PSS) 1985-86

For Sri Lanka in India: 141 at Nagpur 1986-87
     in Sri Lanka: 198 at Kandy 1985-86

INDIVIDUAL HUNDREDS

For India (9)

M. Amarnath (2)
116* Kandy 1985-86
131 Nagpur 1986-87
M. Azharuddin (1)
199 Kanpur 1986-87

S. M. Gavaskar (2)
155† Madras 1982-83
176 Kanpur 1986-87
Kapil Dev (1)
163 Kanpur 1986-87

S. M. Patil (1)
114*† Madras 1982-83
D. B. Vengsarkar (2)
153 Nagpur 1986-87
166 Cuttack 1986-87

For Sri Lanka (7)

R. L. Dias (1)
106 Kandy 1985-86
R. S. Madugalle (1)
103 Colombo
  (SSC) 1985-86
L. R. D. Mendis (3)
105
105 }†Madras 1982-83
124 Kandy 1985-86

A. Ranatunga (1)
111 Colombo
  (SSC) 1985-86
S. A. R. Silva (1)
111 Colombo
  (PSS) 1985-86

† *Signifies hundred on first appearance in India–Sri Lanka Tests.*

RECORD PARTNERSHIPS FOR EACH WICKET

For India

56 for 1st	S. M. Gavaskar and Arun Lal at Madras	1982-83
73 for 2nd	S. M. Gavaskar and D. B. Vengsarkar at Madras	1982-83
73 for 3rd	M. Amarnath and D. B. Vengsarkar at Nagpur	1986-87
63 for 4th	S. M. Gavaskar and M. Azharuddin at Kanpur	1986-87
78 for 5th	M. Amarnath and M. Azharuddin at Kandy	1985-86
72 for 6th	M. Azharuddin and Kapil Dev at Kanpur	1986-87
78* for 7th	S. M. Patil and Madan Lal at Madras	1982-83
70 for 8th	Kapil Dev and L. Sivaramakrishnan at Colombo (PSS)........	1985-86
16 for 9th	S. M. Gavaskar and Gopal Sharma at Colombo (SSC)	1985-86
29 for 10th	Kapil Dev and Chetan Sharma at Colombo (PSS)	1985-86

For Sri Lanka

159 for 1st†	S. Wettimuny and J. R. Ratnayeke at Kanpur	1986-87
95 for 2nd	S. A. R. Silva and R. S. Madugalle at Colombo (PSS)	1985-86
153 for 3rd	R. L. Dias and L. R. D. Mendis at Madras	1982-83
216 for 4th	R. L. Dias and L. R. D. Mendis at Kandy	1985-86
144 for 5th	R. S. Madugalle and A. Ranatunga at Colombo (SSC)	1985-86
89 for 6th	L. R. D. Mendis and A. N. Ranasinghe at Madras	1982-83
77 for 7th	R. S. Madugalle and D. S. de Silva at Madras	1982-83
40* for 8th	P. A. de Silva and A. L. F. de Mel at Kandy	1985-86
42 for 9th	J. R. Ratnayeke and A. L. F. de Mel at Madras	1982-83
44 for 10th	R. J. Ratnayake and E. A. R. de Silva at Nagpur	1986-87

† *Denotes record partnership against all countries.*

TEN WICKETS OR MORE IN A MATCH

For India (1)

10-107 (3-56, 7-51)   Maninder Singh, Nagpur 1986-87

Note: The best match figures by a Sri Lankan bowler are 9-125 (4-76, 5-49) by R. J. Ratnayake against India at Colombo (PSS), 1985-86.

PAKISTAN v SRI LANKA

	Captains					
Season	Pakistan	Sri Lanka	T	P	SL	D
1981-82P	Javed Miandad	B. Warnapura[1]	3	2	0	1
1985-86P	Javed Miandad	L. R. D. Mendis	3	2	0	1
1985-86S	Imran Khan	L. R. D. Mendis	3	1	1	1
	In Pakistan		6	4	0	2
	In Sri Lanka		3	1	1	1
	Totals		9	5	1	3

P Played in Pakistan. S Played in Sri Lanka.

Note: The following deputised for the official touring captain:
   [1] L. R. D. Mendis (Second).

HIGHEST INNINGS TOTALS

For Pakistan in Pakistan: 555-3 at Faisalabad	1985-86
in Sri Lanka: 318 at Colombo (PSS)	1985-86
For Sri Lanka in Pakistan: 479 at Faisalabad	1985-86
in Sri Lanka: 323-3 at Colombo (PSS)	1985-86

LOWEST INNINGS TOTALS

For Pakistan in Pakistan: 259 at Sialkot	1985-86
in Sri Lanka: 132 at Colombo (CCC)	1985-86
For Sri Lanka in Pakistan: 149 at Karachi	1981-82
in Sri Lanka: 101 at Kandy	1985-86

INDIVIDUAL HUNDREDS

For Pakistan (7)

Haroon Rashid (1)
153† Karachi 1981-82
Javed Miandad (1)
203* Faisalabad .. 1985-86
Mohsin Khan (1)
129 Lahore 1981-82
Qasim Omar (1)
206† Faisalabad .. 1985-86

Ramiz Raja (1)
122 Colombo
   (PSS) 1985-86
Salim Malik (1)
100*† Karachi 1981-82
Zaheer Abbas (1)
134† Lahore 1981-82

For Sri Lanka (6)

P. A. de Silva (2)
122† Faisalabad .. 1985-86
105 Karachi 1985-86
R. L. Dias (1)
109 Lahore 1981-82
A. P. Gurusinha (1)
116* Colombo
   (PSS) 1985-86

A. Ranatunga (1)
135* Colombo
   (PSS) 1985-86
S. Wettimuny (1)
157 Faisalabad .. 1981-82

† *Signifies hundred on first appearance in Pakistan–Sri Lanka Tests.*

RECORD PARTNERSHIPS FOR EACH WICKET

For Pakistan

98* for 1st	Mudassar Nazar and Mohsin Khan at Karachi	1985-86
151 for 2nd	Mohsin Khan and Majid Khan at Lahore	1981-82
397 for 3rd	Qasim Omar and Javed Miandad at Faisalabad	1985-86
162 for 4th	Salim Malik and Javed Miandad at Karachi	1981-82
102 for 5th	Mudassar Nazar and Salim Malik at Kandy	1985-86
100 for 6th	Zaheer Abbas and Imran Khan at Lahore	1981-82
104 for 7th	Haroon Rashid and Tahir Naqqash at Karachi	1981-82
29 for 8th	Ashraf Ali and Iqbal Qasim at Faisalabad	1981-82
	Salim Yousuf and Abdul Qadir at Sialkot	1985-86
	Salim Yousuf and Abdul Qadir at Karachi	1985-86
127 for 9th	Haroon Rashid and Rashid Khan at Karachi	1981-82
48 for 10th	Rashid Khan and Tauseef Ahmed at Faisalabad	1981-82

For Sri Lanka

77 for 1st	S. Wettimuny and H. M. Goonatillake at Faisalabad	1981-82
217 for 2nd†	S. Wettimuny and R. L. Dias at Faisalabad	1981-82
85 for 3rd	S. Wettimuny and R. L. Dias at Faisalabad	1985-86
240* for 4th†	A. P. Gurusinha and A. Ranatunga at Colombo (PSS)	1985-86
58 for 5th	R. L. Dias and L. R. D. Mendis at Lahore	1981-82
121 for 6th	A. Ranatunga and P. A. de Silva at Faisalabad	1985-86
66 for 7th	P. A. de Silva and J. R. Ratnayeke at Faisalabad	1985-86
61 for 8th†	R. S. Madugalle and D. S. de Silva at Faisalabad	1981-82
52 for 9th†	P. A. de Silva and R. J. Ratnayeke at Faisalabad	1985-86
36 for 10th	R. J. Ratnayake and R. G. C. E. Wijesuriya at Faisalabad	1985-86

† *Denotes record partnership against all countries.*

TEN WICKETS OR MORE IN A MATCH

For Pakistan (1)

14-116 (8-58, 6-58)   Imran Khan, Lahore 1981-82

Note: The best match figures by a Sri Lankan bowler are 9-162 (4-103, 5-59), D. S. de Silva at Faisalabad, 1981-82.

TEST MATCH GROUNDS

In Chronological Sequence

City and Ground	Date of First Test	Match
1. Melbourne, Melbourne Cricket Ground	March 15, 1877	Australia v England
2. London, Kennington Oval	September 6, 1880	England v Australia
3. Sydney, Sydney Cricket Ground (No. 1)	February 17, 1882	Australia v England
4. Manchester, Old Trafford	July 11, 1884	England v Australia

This match was due to have started on July 10, but rain prevented any play.

5. London, Lord's	July 21, 1884	England v Australia
6. Adelaide, Adelaide Oval	December 12, 1884	Australia v England
7. Port Elizabeth, St George's Park	March 12, 1889	South Africa v England
8. Cape Town, Newlands	March 25, 1889	South Africa v England
9. Johannesburg, Old Wanderers*	March 2, 1896	South Africa v England
10. Nottingham, Trent Bridge	June 1, 1899	England v Australia
11. Leeds, Headingley	June 29, 1899	England v Australia
12. Birmingham, Edgbaston	May 29, 1902	England v Australia
13. Sheffield, Bramall Lane*	July 3, 1902	England v Australia
14. Durban, Lord's*	January 21, 1910	South Africa v England
15. Durban, Kingsmead	January 18, 1923	South Africa v England
16. Brisbane, Exhibition Ground*	November 30, 1928	Australia v England
17. Christchurch, Lancaster Park	January 10, 1930	New Zealand v England
18. Bridgetown, Kensington Oval	January 11, 1930	West Indies v England
19. Wellington, Basin Reserve	January 24, 1930	New Zealand v England
20. Port-of-Spain, Queen's Park Oval	February 1, 1930	West Indies v England
21. Auckland, Eden Park	February 17, 1930	New Zealand v England

This match was due to have started on February 14, but rain prevented any play on the first two days. February 16 was a Sunday.

22. Georgetown, Bourda	February 21, 1930	West Indies v England
23. Kingston, Sabina Park	April 3, 1930	West Indies v England
24. Brisbane, Woolloongabba	November 27, 1931	Australia v South Africa
25. Bombay, Gymkhana Ground*	December 15, 1933	India v England
26. Calcutta, Eden Gardens	January 5, 1934	India v England
27. Madras, Chepauk (Chidambaram Stadium)	February 10, 1934	India v England
28. Delhi, Feroz Shah Kotla	November 10, 1948	India v West Indies
29. Bombay, Brabourne Stadium*	December 9, 1948	India v West Indies
30. Johannesburg, Ellis Park*	December 27, 1948	South Africa v England
31. Kanpur, Green Park (Modi Stadium)	January 12, 1952	India v England
32. Lucknow, University Ground*	October 25, 1952	India v Pakistan
33. Dacca, Dacca Stadium*	January 1, 1955	Pakistan v India
34. Bahawalpur, Dring Stadium	January 15, 1955	Pakistan v India
35. Lahore, Lawrence Gardens (Bagh-i-Jinnah)*	January 29, 1955	Pakistan v India
36. Peshawar, Services Club Ground	February 13, 1955	Pakistan v India
37. Karachi, National Stadium	February 26, 1955	Pakistan v India
38. Dunedin, Carisbrook	March 11, 1955	New Zealand v England
39. Hyderabad, Fateh Maidan (Lal Bahadur Stadium)	November 19, 1955	India v New Zealand

City and Ground	Date of First Test	Match
40. Madras, Corporation Stadium*	January 6, 1956	India v New Zealand
41. Johannesburg, New Wanderers	December 24, 1956	South Africa v England
42. Lahore, Gaddafi Stadium	November 21, 1959	Pakistan v Australia
43. Rawalpindi, Pindi Club Ground	March 27, 1965	Pakistan v New Zealand
44. Nagpur, Vidarbha Cricket Association Ground	October 3, 1969	India v New Zealand
45. Perth, Western Australian Cricket Association Ground	December 11, 1970	Australia v England
46. Hyderabad, Niaz Stadium	March 16, 1973	Pakistan v England
47. Bangalore, Karnataka State Cricket Association Ground (Chinnaswamy Stadium)	November 22, 1974	India v West Indies
48. Bombay, Wankhede Stadium	January 23, 1975	India v West Indies
49. Faisalabad, Iqbal Stadium	October 16, 1978	Pakistan v India
50. Napier, McLean Park	February 16, 1979	New Zealand v Pakistan
51. Multan, Ibn-e-Qasim Bagh Stadium	December 30, 1980	Pakistan v West Indies
52. St John's (Antigua), Recreation Ground	March 27, 1981	West Indies v England
53. Colombo, P. Saravanamuttu Stadium	February 17, 1982	Sri Lanka v England
54. Kandy, Asgiriya Stadium	April 22, 1983	Sri Lanka v Australia
55. Jullundur, Burlton Park	September 24, 1983	India v Pakistan
56. Ahmedabad, Gujarat Stadium	November 12, 1983	India v West Indies
57. Colombo, Sinhalese Sports Club Ground	March 16, 1984	Sri Lanka v New Zealand
58. Colombo, Colombo Cricket Club Ground	March 24, 1984	Sri Lanka v New Zealand
59. Sialkot, Jinnah Stadium	October 27, 1985	Pakistan v Sri Lanka
60. Cuttack, Barabati Stadium	January 4, 1987	India v Sri Lanka
61. Jaipur, Sawai Mansingh Stadium	February 21, 1987	India v Pakistan
62. Hobart, Bellerive Oval	December 16, 1989	Australia v Sri Lanka

* *Denotes no longer used for Test matches. In some instances the ground is no longer in existence.*

FAMILIES IN TEST CRICKET

FATHERS AND SONS

England
M. C. Cowdrey (114 Tests, 1954-55–1974-75) and C. S. Cowdrey (6 Tests, 1984-85–1988).
J. Hardstaff (5 Tests, 1907-08) and J. Hardstaff jun. (23 Tests, 1935–1948).
L. Hutton (79 Tests, 1937–1954-55) and R. A. Hutton (5 Tests, 1971).
F. T. Mann (5 Tests, 1922-23) and F. G. Mann (7 Tests, 1948-49–1949).
J. H. Parks (1 Test, 1937) and J. M. Parks (46 Tests, 1954–1967-68).
M. J. Stewart (8 Tests, 1962–1963-64) and A. J. Stewart (7 Tests, 1989-90–1990).
F. W. Tate (1 Test, 1902) and M. W. Tate (39 Tests, 1924–1935).
C. L. Townsend (2 Tests, 1899) and D. C. H. Townsend (3 Tests, 1934-35).

Australia
E. J. Gregory (1 Test, 1876-77) and S. E. Gregory (58 Tests, 1890–1912).

South Africa
F. Hearne (4 Tests, 1891-92–1895-96) and G. A. L. Hearne (3 Tests, 1922-23–1924).
    F. Hearne also played 2 Tests for England in 1888-89.
J. D. Lindsay (3 Tests, 1947) and D. T. Lindsay (19 Tests, 1963-64–1969-70).
A. W. Nourse (45 Tests, 1902-03–1924) and A. D. Nourse (34 Tests, 1935–1951).
L. R. Tuckett (1 Test, 1913-14) and L. Tuckett (9 Tests, 1947–1948-49).

West Indies
G. A. Headley (22 Tests, 1929-30–1953-54) and R. G. A. Headley (2 Tests, 1973).
O. C. Scott (8 Tests, 1928–1930-31) and A. P. H. Scott (1 Test, 1952-53).

New Zealand

W. M. Anderson (1 Test, 1945-46) and R. W. Anderson (9 Tests, 1976-77–1978).

B. L. Cairns (43 Tests, 1973-74–1985-86) and C. L. Cairns (1 Test, 1989-90).

W. A. Hadlee (11 Tests, 1937–1950-51) and D. R. Hadlee (26 Tests, 1969–1977-78); Sir R. J. Hadlee (86 Tests, 1972-73–1990).

H. G. Vivian (7 Tests, 1931–1937) and G. E. Vivian (5 Tests, 1964-65–1971-72).

India

L. Amarnath (24 Tests, 1933-34–1952-53) and M. Amarnath (69 Tests, 1969-70–1987-88); S. Amarnath (10 Tests, 1975-76–1978-79).

D. K. Gaekwad (11 Tests, 1952–1960-61) and A. D. Gaekwad (40 Tests, 1974-75–1984-85).

Nawab of Pataudi (Iftikhar Ali Khan) (3 Tests, 1946) and Nawab of Pataudi (Mansur Ali Khan) (46 Tests, 1961-62–1974-75).

Nawab of Pataudi sen. also played 3 Tests for England, 1932-33–1934.

V. L. Manjrekar (55 Tests, 1951-52–1964-65) and S. V. Manjrekar (15 Tests, 1987-88–1990).

V. Mankad (44 Tests, 1946–1958-59) and A. V. Mankad (22 Tests, 1969-70–1977-78).

Pankaj Roy (43 Tests, 1951-52–1960-61) and Pranab Roy (2 Tests, 1981-82).

India and Pakistan

M. Jahangir Khan (4 Tests, 1932–1936) and Majid Khan (63 Tests, 1964-65–1982-83).

S. Wazir Ali (7 Tests, 1932–1936) and Khalid Wazir (2 Tests, 1954).

Pakistan

Hanif Mohammad (55 Tests, 1954–1969-70) and Shoaib Mohammad (29 Tests, 1983-84–1989-90).

Nazar Mohammad (5 Tests, 1952-53) and Mudassar Nazar (76 Tests, 1976-77–1988-89).

GRANDFATHERS AND GRANDSONS

Australia

V. Y. Richardson (19 Tests, 1924-25–1935-36) and G. S. Chappell (87 Tests, 1970-71–1983-84); I. M. Chappell (75 Tests, 1964-65–1979-80); T. M. Chappell (3 Tests, 1981).

GREAT-GRANDFATHER AND GREAT-GRANDSON

Australia

W. H. Cooper (2 Tests, 1881-82 and 1884-85) and A. P. Sheahan (31 Tests, 1967-68–1973-74).

BROTHERS IN SAME TEST TEAM

England

E. M., G. F. and W. G. Grace: 1 Test, 1880.

C. T. and G. B. Studd: 4 Tests, 1882-83.

A. and G. G. Hearne: 1 Test, 1891-92.

F. Hearne, their brother, played in this match for South Africa.

D. W. and P. E. Richardson: 1 Test, 1957.

Australia

E. J. and D. W. Gregory: 1 Test, 1876-77.

C. and A. C. Bannerman: 1 Test, 1878-79.

G. and W. F. Giffen: 2 Tests, 1891-92.

G. H. S. and A. E. Trott: 3 Tests, 1894-95.

I. M. and G. S. Chappell: 43 Tests, 1970-71–1979-80.

South Africa

S. J. and S. D. Snooke: 1 Test, 1907.
D. and H. W. Taylor: 2 Tests, 1913-14.
R. H. M. and P. A. M. Hands: 1 Test, 1913-14.
E. A. B. and A. M. B. Rowan: 9 Tests, 1948-49–1951.
P. M. and R. G. Pollock: 23 Tests, 1963-64–1969-70.
A. J. and D. B. Pithey: 5 Tests, 1963-64.

West Indies

G. C. and R. S. Grant: 4 Tests, 1934-35.
J. B. and V. H. Stollmeyer: 1 Test, 1939.
D. St E. and E. St E. Atkinson: 1 Test, 1957-58.

New Zealand

J. J. and M. D. Crowe: 34 Tests, 1983–1989-90.
D. R. and R. J. Hadlee: 10 Tests, 1973–1977-78.
H. J. and G. P. Howarth: 4 Tests, 1974-75–1976-77.
J. M. and N. M. Parker: 3 Tests, 1976-77.
B. P. and J. G. Bracewell: 1 Test, 1980-81.

India

S. Wazir Ali and S. Nazir Ali: 2 Tests, 1932–1933-34.
L. Ramji and Amar Singh: 1 Test, 1933-34.
C. K. and C. S. Nayudu: 4 Tests, 1933-34–1936.
A. G. Kripal Singh and A. G. Milkha Singh: 1 Test, 1961-62.
S. and M. Amarnath: 8 Tests, 1975-76–1978-79.

Pakistan

Wazir and Hanif Mohammad: 18 Tests, 1952-53–1959-60.
Wazir and Mushtaq Mohammad: 1 Test, 1958-59.
Hanif and Mushtaq Mohammad: 19 Tests, 1960-61–1969-70.
Hanif, Mushtaq and Sadiq Mohammad: 1 Test, 1969-70.
Mushtaq and Sadiq Mohammad: 26 Tests, 1969-70–1978-79.
Wasim and Ramiz Raja: 2 Tests, 1983-84.

Sri Lanka

A. and D. Ranatunga: 2 Tests, 1989-90.
M. D. and S. Wettimuny: 2 Tests, 1982-83.

THE ASHES

"In affectionate remembrance of English cricket which died at The Oval, 29th August, 1882. Deeply lamented by a large circle of sorrowing friends and acquaintances, R.I.P. N.B. The body will be cremated and the Ashes taken to Australia."

Australia's first victory on English soil over the full strength of England, on August 29, 1882, inspired a young London journalist, Reginald Shirley Brooks, to write this mock "obituary". It appeared in the *Sporting Times*.

Before England's defeat at The Oval, by 7 runs, arrangements had already been made for the Hon. Ivo Bligh, afterwards Lord Darnley, to lead a team to Australia. Three weeks later they set out, now with the popular objective of recovering the Ashes. In the event, Australia won the First Test by nine wickets, but with England winning the next two it became generally accepted that they brought back the Ashes.

It was long accepted that the real Ashes – a small urn believed to contain the ashes of a bail used in the third match – were presented to Bligh by a group of Melbourne women. At the time of the 1982 centenary of The Oval Test match, however, evidence was produced which suggested that these ashes were the remains of a ball and that they were given to the England captain by Sir William Clarke, the presentation taking place before the Test matches in Australia in 1883. The certain origin of the Ashes, therefore, is the subject of some dispute.

After Lord Darnley's death in 1927, the urn was given to MCC by Lord Darnley's Australian-born widow, Florence. It can be seen in the cricket museum at Lord's, together with a red and gold velvet bag, made specially for it, and the scorecard of the 1882 match.

LIMITED-OVERS INTERNATIONAL RECORDS

Note: Limited-overs international matches do not have first-class status.

SUMMARY OF ALL LIMITED-OVERS INTERNATIONALS

To November 1, 1990

		Matches	\multicolumn{11}{c}{Won by}	Tied	NR
			E	A	I	NZ	P	SL	WI	B	C	EA	Z		
England	v Aust.	47	24	21	–	–	–	–	–	–	–	–	–	1	1
	v India	22	12	–	10	–	–	–	–	–	–	–	–	–	–
	v NZ	29	14	–	–	12	–	–	–	–	–	–	–	–	3
	v Pak.	29	19	–	–	–	10	–	–	–	–	–	–	–	–
	v SL	8	7	–	–	–	–	1	–	–	–	–	–	–	–
	v WI	39	14	–	–	–	–	–	23	–	–	–	–	–	2
	v Canada	1	1	–	–	–	–	–	–	–	0	–	–	–	–
	v E. Africa	1	1	–	–	–	–	–	–	–	–	0	–	–	–
Australia	v India	33	–	18	12	–	–	–	–	–	–	–	–	–	3
	v NZ	43	–	29	–	12	–	–	–	–	–	–	–	–	2
	v Pak.	33	–	15	–	–	16	–	–	–	–	–	–	–	2
	v SL	20	–	15	–	–	–	3	–	–	–	–	–	–	2
	v WI	53	–	17	–	–	–	–	35	–	–	–	–	1	–
	v Bangl.	1	–	1	–	–	–	–	–	0	–	–	–	–	–
	v Canada	1	–	1	–	–	–	–	–	–	0	–	–	–	–
	v Zimb.	4	–	3	–	–	–	–	–	–	–	–	1	–	–
India	v NZ	28	–	–	16	12	–	–	–	–	–	–	–	–	–
	v Pak.	34	–	–	10	–	22	–	–	–	–	–	–	–	2
	v SL	20	–	–	14	–	–	5	–	–	–	–	–	–	1
	v WI	33	–	–	6	–	–	–	27	–	–	–	–	–	–
	v Bangl.	1	–	–	1	–	–	–	–	0	–	–	–	–	–
	v E. Africa	1	–	–	1	–	–	–	–	–	–	0	–	–	–
	v Zimb.	4	–	–	4	–	–	–	–	–	–	–	0	–	–
New Zealand	v Pak.	20	–	–	–	11	8	–	–	–	–	–	–	–	1
	v SL	19	–	–	–	15	–	4	–	–	–	–	–	–	–
	v WI	13	–	–	–	1	–	–	11	–	–	–	–	–	1
	v Bangl.	1	–	–	–	1	–	–	–	0	–	–	–	–	–
	v E. Africa	1	–	–	–	1	–	–	–	–	–	0	–	–	–
	v Zimb.	2	–	–	–	2	–	–	–	–	–	–	0	–	–
Pakistan	v SL	28	–	–	–	–	22	5	–	–	–	–	–	–	1
	v WI	48	–	–	–	–	13	–	35	–	–	–	–	–	–
	v Bangl.	2	–	–	–	–	2	–	–	0	–	–	–	–	–
	v Canada	1	–	–	–	–	1	–	–	–	0	–	–	–	–
Sri Lanka	v WI	11	–	–	–	–	–	1	10	–	–	–	–	–	–
	v Bangl.	2	–	–	–	–	–	2	–	0	–	–	–	–	–
West Indies	v Zimb.	2	–	–	–	–	–	–	2	–	–	–	0	–	–
		635	92	120	74	67	94	21	143	0	0	0	1	2	21

	Matches	Won	Lost	Tied	No Result
England	176	92	77	1	6
Australia	235	120	103	2	10
India	176	74	96	–	6
New Zealand	156	67	82	–	7
Pakistan	195	94	95	–	6
Sri Lanka	108	21	83	–	4
West Indies	199	143	52	1	3
Bangladesh	7	–	7	–	–
Canada	3	–	3	–	–
East Africa	3	–	3	–	–
Zimbabwe	12	1	11	–	–

3,500 OR MORE RUNS

	M	I	NO	R	HI	100s	Avge
I. V. A. Richards (West Indies) ...	179	160	24	6,501	189*	11	47.80
D. L. Haynes (West Indies)	174	173	23	6,471	152*	16	43.14
Javed Miandad (Pakistan)	169	162	32	5,610	119*	6	43.15
A. R. Border (Australia)	210	195	29	5,263	127*	3	31.70
C. G. Greenidge (West Indies)	120	119	12	4,981	133*	11	46.55
D. M. Jones (Australia)	100	98	19	3,857	121	6	48.82
R. B. Richardson (West Indies) ...	126	123	17	3,795	110	3	35.80
K. Srikkanth (India)	126	125	3	3,541	123	4	29.02
D. B. Vengsarkar (India)	128	120	19	3,508	105	1	34.73

The leading aggregates for the countries not mentioned above are:

	M	I	NO	R	HI	100s	Avge
J. G. Wright (New Zealand)	127	126	1	3,416	101	1	27.32
A. J. Lamb (England)	99	95	16	3,306	118	4	41.84
A. Ranatunga (Sri Lanka)	88	85	15	2,173	86*	0	31.04

HIGHEST INDIVIDUAL SCORE FOR EACH COUNTRY

189*	I. V. A. Richards	**West Indies** v England at Manchester	1984
175*	Kapil Dev	**India** v Zimbabwe at Tunbridge Wells	1983
171*	G. M. Turner	**New Zealand** v East Africa at Birmingham	1975
158	D. I. Gower	**England** v New Zealand at Brisbane	1982-83
138*	G. S. Chappell	**Australia** v New Zealand at Sydney	1980-81
126*	Shoaib Mohammad	**Pakistan** v New Zealand at Wellington	1988-89
121	R. L. Dias	**Sri Lanka** v India at Bangalore	1982-83

SEVEN OR MORE HUNDREDS

Total		E	A	WI	NZ	I	P	SL	Others
16	D. L. Haynes (West Indies)	1	6	–	2	2	4	1	0
11	C. G. Greenidge (West Indies) ..	0	1	–	3	3	2	1	0
11	I. V. A. Richards (West Indies) ..	3	3	–	1	3	0	1	0
8	G. A. Gooch (England)	–	4	1	1	1	1	0	0
7	D. I. Gower (England)	–	2	0	3	0	1	1	0
7	G. R. Marsh (Australia)	1	–	0	2	3	1	0	0
7	Zaheer Abbas (Pakistan)	0	2	0	1	3	–	1	0

HIGHEST PARTNERSHIP FOR EACH WICKET

212 for 1st	G. R. Marsh (104) and D. C. Boon (111), Australia v India at Jaipur	1986-87
221 for 2nd	C. G. Greenidge (115) and I. V. A. Richards (149), West Indies v India at Jamshedpur	1983-84
224* for 3rd	D. M. Jones (99*) and A. R. Border (118*), Australia v Sri Lanka at Adelaide	1984-85
173 for 4th	D. M. Jones (121) and S. R. Waugh (82), Australia v Pakistan at Perth	1986-87
152 for 5th	I. V. A. Richards (98) and C. H. Lloyd (89*), West Indies v Sri Lanka at Brisbane	1984-85
144 for 6th	Imran Khan (102*) and Shahid Mahboob (77), Pakistan v Sri Lanka at Leeds	1983
115 for 7th	P. J. L. Dujon (57*) and M. D. Marshall (66), West Indies v Pakistan at Gujranwala	1986-87
117 for 8th	D. L. Houghton (141) and I. P. Butchart (54), Zimbabwe v New Zealand at Hyderabad (India)	1987-88
126* for 9th	Kapil Dev (175*) and S. M. H. Kirmani (24*), India v Zimbabwe at Tunbridge Wells	1983
106* for 10th	I. V. A. Richards (189*) and M. A. Holding (12*), West Indies v England at Manchester	1984

100 OR MORE WICKETS

	M	Balls	R	W	BB	4W/i	Avge
Kapil Dev (India)	157	7,941	4,977	185	5-43	2	26.90
Imran Khan (Pakistan)	149	6,337	4,063	165	6-14	4	24.62
R. J. Hadlee (New Zealand) ..	115	6,182	3,407	158	5-25	6	21.56
J. Garner (West Indies)	98	5,330	2,752	146	5-31	5	18.84
M. A. Holding (West Indies) ..	102	5,473	3,034	142	5-26	6	21.36
E. J. Chatfield (New Zealand)..	114	6,065	3,621	140	5-34	3	25.86
M. D. Marshall (West Indies) .	113	5,993	3,412	137	4-23	5	24.90
Abdul Qadir (Pakistan)	101	4,948	3,340	131	5-44	6	25.49
Wasim Akram (Pakistan)	97	4,833	3,072	130	5-21	5	23.63
I. T. Botham (England)	98	5,269	3,511	118	4-56	1	29.75
I. V. A. Richards (West Indies)	179	5,542	4,144	118	6-41	3	35.11
M. C. Snedden (New Zealand).	93	4,519	3,235	114	4-34	1	28.37
R. J. Shastri (India)	123	5,756	4,025	114	4-38	2	35.30
Mudassar Nazar (Pakistan) ...	122	4,855	3,431	111	5-28	2	30.90
D. K. Lillee (Australia)	63	3,593	2,145	103	5-34	6	20.82
C. A. Walsh (West Indies)	88	4,659	2,977	101	5-1	5	29.47

The leading aggregate for Sri Lanka is:

	M	Balls	R	W	BB	4W/i	Avge
J. R. Ratnayeke	78	3,573	2,865	85	4-23	1	33.70

BEST BOWLING FOR EACH COUNTRY

7-51	W. W. Davis	**West Indies** v Australia at Leeds	1983
6-14	G. J. Gilmour	**Australia** v England at Leeds	1975
6-14	Imran Khan	**Pakistan** v India at Sharjah	1984-85
5-20	V. J. Marks	**England** v New Zealand at Wellington	1983-84
5-21	Arshad Ayub	**India** v Pakistan at Dhaka	1988-89
5-23	R. O. Collinge	**New Zealand** v India at Christchurch	1975-76
5-26	S. H. U. Karnain	**Sri Lanka** v New Zealand at Moratuwa	1983-84

HAT-TRICKS

Jalal-ud-Din	Pakistan v Australia at Hyderabad	1982-83
B. A. Reid	Australia v New Zealand at Sydney	1985-86
Chetan Sharma	India v New Zealand at Nagpur	1987-88
Wasim Akram	Pakistan v West Indies at Sharjah	1989-90
Wasim Akram	Pakistan v Australia at Sharjah	1989-90

MOST DISMISSALS IN A MATCH

5 (all ct)	R. W. Marsh	Australia v England at Leeds	1981
5 (all ct)	R. G. de Alwis	Sri Lanka v Australia at Colombo (PSS)	1982-83
5 (all ct)	S. M. H. Kirmani ..	India v Zimbabwe at Leicester	1983
5 (3 ct, 2 st)	S. Viswanath	India v England at Sydney	1984-85
5 (3 ct, 2 st)	K. S. More	India v New Zealand at Sharjah	1987-88

50 OR MORE DISMISSALS

	M	Ct	St	Total
P. J. L. Dujon (West Indies)	155	170	18	188
R. W. Marsh (Australia)	92	120	4	124
Salim Yousuf (Pakistan)	79	73	18	91
I. D. S. Smith (New Zealand)	73	60	5	65
Wasim Bari (Pakistan)	51	52	10	62
K. S. More (India)	58	32	24	56
I. A. Healy (Australia)	38	45	6	51

MOST CATCHES IN A MATCH

(Excluding wicket-keepers)

Salim Malik	Pakistan v New Zealand at Sialkot	1984-85
S. M. Gavaskar	India v Pakistan at Sharjah	1984-85

Note: While fielding as substitute, J. G. Bracewell held 4 catches for New Zealand v Australia
at Adelaide, 1980-81.

50 OR MORE CATCHES

	M	Ct		M	Ct
I. V. A. Richards (WI)	179	99	Javed Miandad (P)	169	58
A. R. Border (A)	210	96	Kapil Dev (I)	157	57

ALL-ROUND

1,000 Runs and 100 Wickets

	M	R	W
I. T. Botham (England)	98	1,730	118
R. J. Hadlee (New Zealand)	115	1,749	158
Imran Khan (Pakistan)	149	3,051	165
Kapil Dev (India)	157	3,087	185
Mudassar Nazar (Pakistan)	122	2,654	111
I. V. A. Richards (West Indies)	179	6,501	118
R. J. Shastri (India)	123	2,391	114

1,000 Runs and 100 Dismissals

	M	R	D
P. J. L. Dujon (West Indies)	155	1,785	188
R. W. Marsh (Australia)	92	1,225	124

HIGHEST INNINGS TOTALS

360-4	(50 overs)	**West Indies** v Sri Lanka at Karachi	1987-88
338-4	(50 overs)	**New Zealand** v Bangladesh at Sharjah	1989-90
338-5	(60 overs)	**Pakistan** v Sri Lanka at Swansea	1983
334-4	(60 overs)	**England** v India at Lord's	1975
333-8	(45 overs)	West Indies v India at Jamshedpur	1983-84
333-9	(60 overs)	England v Sri Lanka at Taunton	1983
332-3	(50 overs)	**Australia** v Sri Lanka at Sharjah	1989-90
330-6	(60 overs)	Pakistan v Sri Lanka at Nottingham	1975

Note: The highest score by **India** is 299-4 (40 overs) v Sri Lanka at Bombay, 1986-87, and the
highest by **Sri Lanka** is 289-7 (40 overs) v India at Bombay, 1986-87.

HIGHEST TOTALS BATTING SECOND

Winning

298-6	(54.5 overs)	New Zealand v England at Leeds	1990
297-6	(48.5 overs)	New Zealand v England at Adelaide	1982-83

Losing

289-7	(40 overs)	Sri Lanka v India at Bombay	1986-87
288-9	(60 overs)	Sri Lanka v Pakistan at Swansea	1983

HIGHEST MATCH AGGREGATES

626-14	(120 overs)	Pakistan v Sri Lanka at Swansea	1983
619-19	(118 overs)	England v Sri Lanka at Taunton	1983
604-9	(120 overs)	Australia v Sri Lanka at The Oval	1975
603-11	(100 overs)	Pakistan v Sri Lanka at Adelaide	1989-90

LOWEST INNINGS TOTALS

45	(40.3 overs)	Canada v England at Manchester	1979
55	(28.3 overs)	**Sri Lanka** v West Indies at Sharjah	1986-87
63	(25.5 overs)	**India** v Australia at Sydney	1980-81
64	(35.5 overs)	**New Zealand** v Pakistan at Sharjah	1985-86
70	(25.2 overs)	**Australia** v England at Birmingham	1977
70	(26.3 overs)	Australia v New Zealand at Adelaide	1985-86
74	(29 overs)	New Zealand v Australia at Wellington	1981-82
74	(31.1 overs)	New Zealand v Pakistan at Sharjah	1989-90
78	(24.1 overs)	India v Sri Lanka at Kanpur	1986-87
79	(34.2 overs)	India v Pakistan at Sialkot	1978-79
85	(47 overs)	**Pakistan** v England at Manchester	1978

Notes: This section does not take into account those matches in which the number of overs was reduced.

The lowest innings total by **England** is 93 (36.2 overs) v Australia at Leeds, 1975, and the lowest by **West Indies** is 111 (41.4 overs) v Pakistan at Melbourne, 1983-84.

LARGEST VICTORIES

232 runs	Australia (323-2 in 50 overs) v Sri Lanka (91 in 35.5 overs) at Adelaide	1984-85
206 runs	New Zealand (276-7 in 50 overs) v Australia (70 in 26.3 overs) at Adelaide	1985-86
202 runs	England (334-4 in 60 overs) v India (132-3 in 60 overs) at Lord's	1975

By ten wickets: There have been seven instances of victory by ten wickets.

TIED MATCHES

West Indies 222-5 (50 overs), Australia 222-9 (50 overs) at Melbourne	1983-84
England 226-5 (55 overs), Australia 226-8 (55 overs) at Nottingham	1989

WORLD CUP FINALS

1975 (60 overs)	West Indies (291-8) beat Australia (274) by 17 runs at Lord's.
1979 (60 overs)	West Indies (286-9) beat England (194) by 92 runs at Lord's.
1983 (60 overs)	India (183) beat West Indies (140) by 43 runs at Lord's.
1987 (50 overs)	Australia (253-5) beat England (246-8) by 7 runs at Calcutta.

MISCELLANEOUS

LARGE ATTENDANCES

Test Series

943,000	Australia v England (5 Tests)	1936-37
In England		
549,650	England v Australia (5 Tests)	1953

Test Match

†350,534	Australia v England, Melbourne (Third Test)	1936-37
325,000+	India v England, Calcutta (Second Test)	1972-73
In England		
158,000+	England v Australia, Leeds (Fourth Test)	1948
137,915	England v Australia, Lord's (Second Test)	1953

Test Match Day

90,800	Australia v West Indies, Melbourne (Fifth Test, 2nd day)	1960-61

Other First-Class Matches in England

80,000+	Surrey v Yorkshire, The Oval (3 days)	1906
78,792	Yorkshire v Lancashire, Leeds (3 days)	1904
76,617	Lancashire v Yorkshire, Manchester (3 days)	1926

One-day International

86,133‡	Australia v West Indies, Melbourne	1983-84

† *Although no official figures are available, the attendance at the Fourth Test between India and England at Calcutta, 1981-82, was thought to have exceeded this figure.*

‡ *It is estimated that a crowd of more than 90,000 attended the one-day international between India and Pakistan at Calcutta, 1986-87. However, this figure has not been confirmed.*

LORD'S CRICKET GROUND

Lord's and the MCC were founded in 1787. The Club has enjoyed an uninterrupted career since that date, but there have been three grounds known as Lord's. The first (1787-1810) was situated where Dorset Square now is; the second (1809-13), at North Bank, had to be abandoned owing to the cutting of the Regent's Canal; and the third, opened in 1814, is the present one at St John's Wood. It was not until 1866 that the freehold of Lord's was secured by the MCC. The present pavilion was erected in 1890 at a cost of £21,000.

HIGHEST INDIVIDUAL SCORES MADE AT LORD'S

333	G. A. Gooch	England v India	1990
316*	J. B. Hobbs	Surrey v Middlesex	1926
315*	P. Holmes	Yorkshire v Middlesex	1925
281*	W. H. Ponsford	Australians v MCC	1934
278	W. Ward	MCC v Norfolk (with E. H. Budd, T. Vigne and F. Ladbroke)	1820
278	D. G. Bradman	Australians v MCC	1938
277*	E. H. Hendren	Middlesex v Kent	1922

Note: The longest innings in a first-class match at Lord's was played by S. Wettimuny (636 minutes, 190 runs) for Sri Lanka v England, 1984.

HIGHEST TOTALS OBTAINED AT LORD'S

First-Class Matches

729-6 dec.	Australia v England	1930
665	West Indians v Middlesex	1939
653-4 dec.	England v India	1990
652-8 dec.	West Indies v England	1973
629	England v India	1974
612-8 dec.	Middlesex v Nottinghamshire	1921
610-5 dec.	Australians v Gentlemen	1948
609-8 dec.	Cambridge University v MCC and Ground	1913
608-7 dec.	Middlesex v Hampshire	1919
607	MCC and Ground v Cambridge University	1902

Minor Match

735-9 dec.	MCC and Ground v Wiltshire	1888

BIGGEST HIT AT LORD'S

The only known instance of a batsman hitting a ball over the present pavilion at Lord's occurred when A. E. Trott, appearing for MCC against Australians on July 31, August 1, 2, 1899, drove M. A. Noble so far and high that the ball struck a chimney pot and fell behind the building

HIGHEST SCORE IN A MINOR COUNTY MATCH

323*	F. E. Lacey	Hampshire v Norfolk at Southampton	1887

HIGHEST SCORE IN MINOR COUNTIES CHAMPIONSHIP

282	E. Garnett	Berkshire v Wiltshire at Reading	1908
254	H. E. Morgan	Glamorgan v Monmouthshire at Cardiff	1901
253*	G. J. Whittaker	Surrey II v Gloucestershire II at The Oval	1950
253	A. Booth	Lancashire II v Lincolnshire at Grimsby	1950
252	J. A. Deed	Kent II v Surrey II at The Oval (on début)	1924

HIGHEST SCORE FOR ENGLISH PUBLIC SCHOOL

278	J. L. Guise	Winchester v Eton at Eton	1921

HIGHEST SCORES IN OTHER MATCHES

628*	A. E. J. Collins, Clark's House v North Town at Clifton College. (A Junior House match. His innings of 6 hours 50 minutes was spread over four afternoons.)	1899
566	C. J. Eady, Break-o'-Day v Wellington at Hobart	1901-02
515	D. R. Havewalla, B.B. and C.I. Rly v St Xavier's at Bombay	1933-34
506*	J. C. Sharp, Melbourne GS v Geelong College at Melbourne	1914-15
502*	Chaman Lal, Mahendra Coll., Patiala v Government Coll., Rupar at Patiala	1956-57
485	A. E. Stoddart, Hampstead v Stoics at Hampstead	1886
475*	Mohammad Iqbal, Muslim Model HS v Islamia HS, Sialkot at Lahore	1958-59
466*	G. T. S. Stevens, Beta v Lambda (University College School House match) at Neasden	1919
459	J. A. Prout, Wesley College v Geelong College at Geelong	1908-09

HIGHEST PARTNERSHIP IN MINOR CRICKET

664* for 3rd   V. G. Kambli and S. R. Tendulkar, Sharadashram Vidyamandir
School v St Xavier's High School at Bombay 1987-88

RECORD HIT

The Rev. W. Fellows, while at practice on the Christ Church ground at Oxford in 1856, drove a
ball bowled by Charles Rogers 175 yards from hit to pitch.

THROWING THE CRICKET BALL

140 yards 2 feet, Robert Percival, on the Durham Sands, Co. Durham Racecourse   c 1882
140 yards 9 inches, Ross Mackenzie, at Toronto 1872

Notes: W. F. Forbes, on March 16, 1876, threw 132 yards at the Eton College sports. He was
then eighteen years of age.

Onochie Onuorah, on June 5, 1987, threw a 4¾oz ball 100 yards 1 foot 8½ inches (91.94 metres)
at The Abbey School, Westgate, sports. He was then thirteen years of age.

William Yardley, while a boy at Rugby, threw 100 yards with his right hand and 78 yards with
his left.

Charles Arnold, of Cambridge, once threw 112 yards with the wind and 108 against.

W. H. Game, at The Oval in 1875, threw the ball 111 yards and then back the same distance.
W. G. Grace threw 109 yards one way and back 105, and George Millyard 108 with the wind
and 103 against. At The Oval in 1868, W. G. Grace made three successive throws of 116, 117
and 118 yards, and then threw back over 100 yards. D. G. Foster (Warwickshire) threw 133
yards, and in 1930 he made a Danish record with 120.1 metres – about 130 yards.

DATES OF FORMATION OF COUNTY CLUBS NOW
FIRST-CLASS

County	First known county organisation	Original date	Present Club Reorganisation, if substantial
Derbyshire	November 4, 1870	November 4, 1870	—
Essex	By May, 1790	January 14, 1876	—
Glamorgan	1863	July 6, 1888	—
Gloucestershire	November 3, 1863	1871	—
Hampshire	April 3, 1849	August 12, 1863	July, 1879
Kent	August 6, 1842	March 1, 1859	December 6, 1870
Lancashire	January 12, 1864	January 12, 1864	—
Leicestershire	By August, 1820	March 25, 1879	—
Middlesex	December 15, 1863	February 2, 1864	—
Northamptonshire ..	1820	1820	July 31, 1878
Nottinghamshire	March/April, 1841	March/April, 1841	December 11, 1866
Somerset	October 15, 1864	August 18, 1875	—
Surrey	August 22, 1845	August 22, 1845	—
Sussex	June 16, 1836	March 1, 1839	August, 1857
Warwickshire	May, 1826	1882	—
Worcestershire	1844	March 5, 1865	—
Yorkshire	March 7, 1861	January 8, 1863	December 10, 1891

DATES OF FORMATION OF CLUBS IN THE CURRENT MINOR COUNTIES CHAMPIONSHIP

County	First known county organisation	Present Club
Bedfordshire	May, 1847	November 3, 1899
Berkshire	By May, 1841	March 17, 1895
Buckinghamshire	November, 1864	January 15, 1891
Cambridgeshire	March 13, 1844	June 6, 1891
Cheshire	1819	September 29, 1908
Cornwall	1813	November 12, 1894
Cumberland	January 2, 1884	April 10, 1948
Devon	1824	November 26, 1899
Dorset	1862 *or* 1871	February 5, 1896
Durham	January 24, 1874	May 10, 1882
Hertfordshire	1838	March 8, 1876
Lincolnshire	1853	September 28, 1906
Norfolk	January 11, 1827	October 14, 1876
Northumberland	1834	December, 1895
Oxfordshire	1787	December 14, 1921
Shropshire	1819 or 1829	June 28, 1956
Staffordshire	November 24, 1871	November 24, 1871
Suffolk	July 27, 1864	August, 1932
Wiltshire	February 24, 1881	January, 1893

CONSTITUTION OF COUNTY CHAMPIONSHIP

There are references in the sporting press to a champion county as early as 1825, but the list is not continuous and in some cases only two counties contested the title. The earliest reference in any cricket publication is from 1864, and at this time there were eight leading counties who have come to be regarded as first-class from that date – Cambridgeshire, Hampshire, Kent, Middlesex, Nottinghamshire, Surrey, Sussex and Yorkshire. The newly formed Lancashire club began playing inter-county matches in 1865, Gloucestershire in 1870 and Derbyshire in 1871, and they are therefore regarded as first-class from these respective dates. Cambridgeshire dropped out after 1871, Hampshire, who had not played inter-county matches in certain seasons, after 1885, and Derbyshire after 1887. Somerset, who had played matches against the first-class counties since 1879, were regarded as first-class from 1882 to 1885, and were admitted formally to the Championship in 1891. In 1894, Derbyshire, Essex, Leicestershire and Warwickshire were granted first-class status, but did not compete in the Championship until 1895 when Hampshire returned. Worcestershire, Northamptonshire and Glamorgan were admitted to the Championship in 1899, 1905 and 1921 respectively and are regarded as first-class from these dates. An invitation in 1921 to Buckinghamshire to enter the Championship was declined, owing to the lack of necessary playing facilities, and an application by Devon in 1948 was unsuccessful.

MOST COUNTY CHAMPIONSHIP APPEARANCES

763	W. Rhodes	Yorkshire	1898-1930
707	F. E. Woolley	Kent	1906-38
665	C. P. Mead	Hampshire	1906-36

MOST CONSECUTIVE COUNTY CHAMPIONSHIP APPEARANCES

423	K. G. Suttle	Sussex	1954-69
412	J. G. Binks	Yorkshire	1955-69
399	J. Vine	Sussex	1899-1914
344	E. H. Killick	Sussex	1898-1912
326	C. N. Woolley	Northamptonshire	1913-31
305	A. H. Dyson	Glamorgan	1930-47
301	B. Taylor	Essex	1961-72

Notes: J. Vine made 417 consecutive appearances for Sussex in all first-class matches between July 1900 and September 1914.

J. G. Binks did not miss a Championship match for Yorkshire between making his début in June 1955 and retiring at the end of the 1969 season.

FEATURES OF 1990

Double-Hundreds (32)

M. W. Alleyne	256	Gloucestershire v Northamptonshire at Northampton.
R. J. Bailey	204*	Northamptonshire v Sussex at Northampton.
P. D. Bowler	210	Derbyshire v Kent at Chesterfield.
B. C. Broad	227*	Nottinghamshire v Kent at Tunbridge Wells.
K. R. Brown	200*	Middlesex v Nottinghamshire at Lord's.
S. J. Cook	313*	Somerset v Glamorgan at Cardiff.
P. A. de Silva	221*	Sri Lankans v Hampshire at Southampton.
N. H. Fairbrother (2)	366†	Lancashire v Surrey at The Oval.
		The second-highest first-class score by an Englishman.
	203*	Lancashire v Warwickshire at Coventry.
A. Fordham	206*	Northamptonshire v Yorkshire at Leeds.
G. A. Gooch (2)	215	Essex v Leicestershire at Chelmsford.
	333†	England v India (First Test) at Lord's.
I. A. Greig	291	Surrey v Lancashire at The Oval.
D. L. Haynes (2)	220*	Middlesex v Essex at Ilford.
	255*	Middlesex v Sussex at Lord's.
G. A. Hick	252*	Worcestershire v Glamorgan at Abergavenny.
S. G. Hinks	234	Kent v Middlesex at Canterbury.
A. J. Lamb	235	Northamptonshire v Yorkshire at Leeds.
W. Larkins	207	Northamptonshire v Essex at Northampton.
A. J. Moles	224*	Warwickshire v Glamorgan at Swansea.
M. D. Moxon	218*	Yorkshire v Sussex at Eastbourne.
P. J. Prichard	245	Essex v Leicestershire at Chelmsford.
D. A. Reeve	202*	Warwickshire v Northamptonshire at Northampton.
R. T. Robinson	220*	Nottinghamshire v Yorkshire at Nottingham.
P. M. Roebuck	201*	Somerset v Worcestershire at Worcester.
J. P. Stephenson	202*	Essex v Somerset at Bath.
C. J. Tavaré	219	Somerset v Sussex at Hove.
N. R. Taylor	204	Kent v Surrey at Canterbury.
D. M. Ward (2)	263	Surrey v Kent at Canterbury.
	208	Surrey v Essex at The Oval.
M. E. Waugh (2)	204	Essex v Gloucestershire at Ilford.
	207*	Essex v Yorkshire at Middlesbrough.

† *Ground record for all matches.*

Note: The three triple-hundreds in 1990 equal the record number in an English season (1899 and 1934).

Hundred on First-Class Début

J. J. B. Lewis	116*	Essex v Surrey at The Oval.

Three Hundreds in Successive Innings

K. J. Barnett (Derbyshire)	107, 123 and 109.
G. A. Gooch (Essex and England)	177, 333 and 123.
M. R. Ramprakash (Middlesex)	146*, 100* and 125.
I. V. A. Richards (Glamorgan)	111, 118* and 127.

Hundred in Each Innings of a Match (12)

C. W. J. Athey	108*	122	Gloucestershire v Warwickshire at Bristol.
G. A. Gooch (2)	333	123	England v India (First Test) at Lord's.
			The record individual aggregate in a Test match.
	174	126	Essex v Northamptonshire at Northampton.
M. J. Greatbatch	168*	128*	Michael Parkinson's World XI v Indians at Scarborough.
D. L. Haynes	181	129	Middlesex v New Zealanders at Lord's.
G. A. Hick	252*	100*	Worcestershire v Glamorgan at Abergavenny.
A. A. Metcalfe	194*	107	Yorkshire v Nottinghamshire at Nottingham.
H. Morris	110	102*	Glamorgan v Nottinghamshire at Worksop.
J. E. Morris	122	109	Derbyshire v Somerset at Taunton.
M. R. Ramprakash .	100*	125	Middlesex v Kent at Canterbury.
I. V. A. Richards ...	111	118*	Glamorgan v Essex at Southend.
N. R. Taylor	204	142	Kent v Surrey at Canterbury.

Fastest Hundred

(*For the Walter Lawrence Trophy*)

T. M. Moody ...... 36 balls   Warwickshire v Glamorgan at Swansea.

In 26 minutes and including seven sixes and eleven fours. The fastest hundred in first-class cricket but achieved against "soft" bowling used to expedite a declaration.

300 Runs in a Day

N. H. Fairbrother .. 311*   Lancashire v Surrey at The Oval (3rd day).

Hundred Before Lunch

B. C. Broad	101*	Nottinghamshire v Kent at Tunbridge Wells (1st day).
N. H. Fairbrother ..	100*†	Lancashire v Surrey at The Oval (3rd day).
I. A. Greig	145*	Surrey v Lancashire at The Oval (2nd day).
D. L. Haynes (2) ...	102*	Middlesex v Sussex at Lord's (1st day).
	110*	Middlesex v Yorkshire at Leeds (1st day).
A. A. Metcalfe	107*	Yorkshire v Gloucestershire at Cheltenham (1st day).
D. A. Reeve	102*	Warwickshire v Cambridge University at Cambridge (2nd day).
R. A. Smith	127*	Hampshire v Sussex at Southampton (2nd day).

† *N. H. Fairbrother scored 100 or more in each session – 100, 108, 103.*

Hundred Entirely with the Aid of a Runner

M. P. Speight 131   Sussex v Glamorgan at Hove.

500 Runs Without Being Dismissed

G. A. Hick (Worcestershire)..... 645: 171*, 69*, 252*, 100* and 53.

Hick scored seven successive fifties (also twelve in thirteen consecutive innings).

Fifty Boundaries in an Innings

N. H. Fairbrother. . . . . 52 (5 sixes, 47 fours)   Lancashire v Surrey at The Oval.

Most Sixes off Successive Balls

4. . . . . Kapil Dev (off E. E. Hemmings)   India v England (First Test) at Lord's.
      The first instance in Test matches.
3. . . . . M. R. Ramprakash (off C. J. Tavaré)   Middlesex v Somerset at Uxbridge.

First to 1,000 Runs

S. J. Cook (Somerset) on June 7.

First to 2,000 Runs

S. J. Cook (Somerset) on August 4.

Carrying Bat Through Completed Innings

N. E. Briers . . . . 157*†   Leicestershire (359) v Nottinghamshire at Leicester.
P. M. Roebuck . . . . . 114*   Somerset (270) v Warwickshire at Taunton.
   † *One man retired hurt.*

Most Successive First-Class Innings Without Scoring

12. . . . . M. A. Robinson (Northamptonshire): 0, 0*, 0*, 0*, 0*, 0*, 0, 0, 0, 0*, 0*, 0.

First-Wicket Partnership of 200 in Each Innings

227   220   G. A. Gooch/J. P. Stephenson, Essex v Northamptonshire at Northampton.
         Only the third instance in all first-class cricket.

First-Wicket Partnership of 100 in Each Innings

145   170   T. J. Boon/N. E. Briers, Leicestershire v Essex at Chelmsford.
140   256   A. R. Butcher/H. Morris, Glamorgan v Worcestershire at Abergavenny.

Other Notable Partnerships

First Wicket
321   D. J. Bicknell/G. S. Clinton, Surrey v Northamptonshire at The Oval.
306   D. L. Haynes/M. A. Roseberry, Middlesex v Essex at Ilford.
292   V. P. Terry/T. C. Middleton, Hampshire v Northamptonshire at Bournemouth.
264   V. P. Terry/C. L. Smith, Hampshire v Oxford University at Oxford.
256   D. J. Bicknell/D. M. Ward, Surrey v Oxford University at Oxford.
256   A. R. Butcher/H. Morris, Glamorgan v Worcestershire at Abergavenny.
255* A. R. Butcher/H. Morris, Glamorgan v Kent at Swansea.
251   R. J. Shastri/N. S. Sidhu, Indians v Gloucestershire at Bristol.

Second Wicket

403†	G. A. Gooch/P. J. Prichard, Essex v Leicestershire at Chelmsford.
366†	S. G. Hinks/N. R. Taylor, Kent v Middlesex at Canterbury.
264	T. S. Curtis/G. A. Hick, Worcestershire v Somerset at Taunton.
258	P. M. Roebuck/A. N. Hayhurst, Somerset v Worcestershire at Worcester.

Third Wicket

413†	D. J. Bicknell/D. M. Ward, Surrey v Kent at Canterbury.
393†	A. Fordham/A. J. Lamb, Northamptonshire v Yorkshire at Leeds.
364†	M. A. Atherton/N. H. Fairbrother, Lancashire v Surrey at The Oval.
308	G. A. Gooch/A. J. Lamb, England v India (First Test) at Lord's.
293*	A. A. Metcalfe/P. E. Robinson, Yorkshire v Derbyshire at Scarborough.
285*	S. J. Cook/C. J. Tavaré, Somerset v Glamorgan at Cardiff.
268	M. R. Benson/G. R. Cowdrey, Kent v Essex at Maidstone.
264	G. A. Hick/D. B. D'Oliveira, Worcestershire v Glamorgan at Abergavenny.
256	D. I. Gower/R. A. Smith, Hampshire v Sussex at Southampton.

Fourth Wicket

285	B. C. Broad/D. W. Randall, Nottinghamshire v Kent at Tunbridge Wells.
263	P. A. de Silva/H. P. Tillekeratne, Sri Lankans v Hampshire at Southampton.
258	S. G. Hinks/G. R. Cowdrey, Kent v Leicestershire at Leicester.
256	C. J. Tavaré/R. J. Harden, Somerset v New Zealanders at Taunton.

Sixth Wicket

226	D. B. D'Oliveira/S. J. Rhodes, Worcestershire v Lancashire at Manchester.

Seventh Wicket

229	K. M. Curran/R. C. Russell, Gloucestershire v Somerset at Bristol.

Eighth Wicket

205†	I. A. Greig/M. P. Bicknell, Surrey v Lancashire at The Oval.

Ninth Wicket

183†	C. J. Tavaré/N. A. Mallender, Somerset v Sussex at Hove.

Tenth Wicket

116	G. Yates/P. J. W. Allott, Lancashire v Nottinghamshire at Nottingham.
107	G. Miller/S. J. Base, Derbyshire v Yorkshire at Chesterfield.

* Unbroken partnership.   † County record.

Twelve Wickets in a Match

C. E. L. Ambrose ...	12-155	Northamptonshire v Leicestershire at Leicester.
J. G. Bracewell	12-227	New Zealanders v Oxford & Cambridge Universities at Cambridge.

Eight Wickets in an Innings

G. D. Harrison	9-113	Ireland v Scotland at Edinburgh.
C. A. Walsh	8-58	Gloucestershire v Northamptonshire at Cheltenham.

Hat-Tricks

D. V. Lawrence	Gloucestershire v Nottinghamshire at Nottingham.
S. M. McEwan	Worcestershire v Leicestershire at Leicester.
P. A. Smith	Warwickshire v Sussex at Eastbourne.

Wicket with First Ball in First-Class Cricket

J. E. R. Gallian .... Lancashire v Oxford University at Oxford.

100 Wickets

For the second season in succession no bowler took 100 wickets. The highest aggregate was 94 by N. A. Foster (Essex).

1,000 Runs and 50 Wickets

K. M. Curran (Gloucestershire) ...	1,267 runs and 64 wickets.
A. I. C. Dodemaide (Sussex)	1,001 runs and 61 wickets.
G. D. Rose (Somerset)	1,000 runs and 53 wickets.

Nine Wicket-Keeping Dismissals in a Match

R. J. Blakey (9 ct) .... Yorkshire v Sussex at Eastbourne.

Six Wicket-Keeping Dismissals in an Innings

R. J. Blakey (6 ct)	Yorkshire v Sussex at Eastbourne.
C. P. Metson (2) (6 ct)......	Glamorgan v Hampshire at Southampton.
(6 ct)......	Glamorgan v Warwickshire at Birmingham.
P. A. Nixon (5 ct, 1 st)	Leicestershire v Glamorgan at Hinckley.
K. J. Piper (5 ct, 1 st)	Warwickshire v Somerset at Taunton.

Highest Innings Totals

(28 of 500 or more)

863†	Lancashire v Surrey at The Oval.
761-6 dec. ...	Essex v Leicestershire at Chelmsford.
707-9 dec. ...	Surrey v Lancashire at The Oval.
653-4 dec. ...	England v India (First Test) at Lord's.
648	Surrey v Kent at Canterbury.
636-6 dec. ...	Northamptonshire v Essex at Chelmsford.
613-6 dec. ...	Surrey v Essex at The Oval.
606-9 dec. ...	India v England (Third Test) at The Oval.
600-8 dec. ...	Hampshire v Sussex at Southampton.
592-6 dec. ...	Northamptonshire v Essex at Northampton.
574	Gloucestershire v Yorkshire at Cheltenham.
558-6 dec. ...	Lancashire v Oxford University at Oxford.
551-8 dec. ...	Gloucestershire v Worcestershire at Bristol.
539	Essex v Surrey at The Oval.
535-2 dec. ...	Somerset v Glamorgan at Cardiff.
525-9 dec. ...	Somerset v Sussex at Hove.
521	Gloucestershire v Northamptonshire at Northampton.
520-9 dec. ...	Worcestershire v Somerset at Taunton.
520	Leicestershire v Essex at Chelmsford.
519	England v India (Second Test) at Manchester.
517	Surrey v Hampshire at Southampton.
514-4 dec. ...	Worcestershire v Glamorgan at Abergavenny.
514-5 dec. ...	Derbyshire v Kent at Chesterfield.
512-6 dec. ...	Indians v Minor Counties at Trowbridge.
510-5 dec. ...	Middlesex v Nottinghamshire at Lord's.
508-9 dec. ...	Essex v Kent at Chelmsford.
506-7 dec. ...	Sri Lankans v Hampshire at Southampton.
500-5 dec. ...	Somerset v Sussex at Taunton.

† *The second-highest total in County Championship matches.*

Highest Fourth-Innings Totals

493-6 .... Glamorgan v Worcestershire at Abergavenny (set 495).
446-8 .... Hampshire v Gloucestershire at Southampton (set 445).

Lowest Innings Totals

50† ...... Northamptonshire v Derbyshire at Northampton.
72 .... Derbyshire v Gloucestershire at Derby.
96 .... Warwickshire v Worcestershire at Worcester.
99 .... Middlesex v Derbyshire at Derby.

   † *Three men absent.*

Match Aggregates of 1,400 Runs

Runs-Wkts
1,650-19 .. Surrey v Lancashire at The Oval.
1,641-16 .. Glamorgan v Worcestershire at Abergavenny.
1,614-30 .. England v India (Second Test) at Manchester.
1,603-28 .. England v India (First Test) at Lord's.
1,530-19 .. Essex v Leicestershire at Chelmsford.
1,509-36 .. Somerset v Worcestershire at Taunton.
1,451-29 .. Kent v Surrey at Canterbury.
1,430-17 .. Glamorgan v Somerset at Cardiff.
1,423-23 .. England v India (Third Test) at The Oval.

Fifty Extras in an Innings

	b	l-b	w	n-b	
71	33	26	2	10	Nottinghamshire v Leicestershire at Leicester.
56	15	26	11	4	Nottinghamshire v Worcestershire at Worcester.
55	16	22	5	12	England v India (Third Test) at The Oval.
54	10	29	2	13	Northamptonshire v Essex at Chelmsford.
50	11	12	9	18	Kent v Leicestershire at Leicester.

Career Aggregate Milestones†

30,000 runs .... G. A. Gooch
20,000 runs .... A. R. Butcher, C. J. Tavaré.
10,000 runs .... R. J. Bailey, N. H. Fairbrother, R. A. Smith, V. P. Terry.

   † *Achieved since September 1989.*

FIRST-CLASS AVERAGES, 1990

BATTING

(Qualification: 8 innings, average 10.00)

* Signifies not out.   † Denotes a left-handed batsman.

	M	I	NO	R	HI	100s	50s	Avge
G. A. Gooch (*Essex*)	18	30	3	2,746	333	12	8	101.70
G. A. Hick (*Worcs.*)	21	35	9	2,347	252*	8	14	90.26
T. M. Moody (*Warwicks.*)	9	15	2	1,163	168	7	1	89.46
A. N. Aymes (*Hants*)	5	8	4	317	75*	0	3	79.25
M. E. Waugh (*Essex*)	22	33	6	2,072	207*	8	8	76.74
D. M. Ward (*Surrey*)	24	34	7	2,072	263	7	3	76.74
S. J. Cook (*Somerset*)	24	41	7	2,608	313*	9	11	76.70
B. R. Hardie (*Essex*)	12	17	7	728	125	2	4	72.80
M. A. Atherton (*Lancs.*)	20	31	4	1,924	191	7	12	71.25
†N. H. Fairbrother (*Lancs.*)	22	32	7	1,740	366	4	9	69.60
†D. J. Bicknell (*Surrey*)	15	23	4	1,317	186	5	6	69.31
M. A. Crawley (*OUCC & Lancs.*).	11	14	3	762	105*	2	5	69.27
D. L. Haynes (*Middx*)	23	39	5	2,346	255*	8	7	69.00
R. A. Smith (*Hants*)	18	30	8	1,454	181	6	7	66.09
R. J. Bailey (*Northants*)	23	39	8	1,987	204*	7	9	64.09
A. J. Lamb (*Northants*)	17	29	4	1,596	235	6	5	63.84
I. V. A. Richards (*Glam.*)	18	28	5	1,425	164*	7	3	61.95
N. R. Taylor (*Kent*)	22	37	5	1,979	204	7	10	61.84
C. L. Smith (*Hants*)	22	38	7	1,886	148	4	12	60.83
R. J. Harden (*Somerset*)	24	31	7	1,460	104*	3	12	60.83
†A. R. Butcher (*Glam.*)	23	41	5	2,116	151*	6	15	58.77
C. J. Tavaré (*Somerset*)	24	32	4	1,638	219	3	12	58.50
A. N. Hayhurst (*Somerset*)	22	35	8	1,559	170	4	8	57.74
†M. J. Greatbatch (*New Zealanders & M. Parkinson's World XI*) ...	11	16	3	744	168*	2	4	57.23
J. P. Stephenson (*Essex*)	25	44	8	1,887	202*	4	13	57.18
M. W. Gatting (*Middx*)	23	37	7	1,704	170*	4	9	56.80
T. S. Curtis (*Worcs.*)	22	39	8	1,731	197*	4	7	55.83
G. D. Rose (*Somerset*)	24	29	11	1,000	97*	0	8	55.55
†H. Morris (*Glam.*)	25	46	5	2,276	160*	10	10	55.51
I. A. Greig (*Surrey*)	24	29	6	1,259	291	2	5	54.73
D. A. Reeve (*Warwicks.*)	25	38	12	1,412	202*	3	5	54.30
†B. C. Broad (*Notts.*)	22	43	2	2,226	227*	9	3	54.29
J. E. Morris (*Derbys.*)	21	33	6	1,459	157*	6	6	54.03
K. R. Brown (*Middx*)	24	36	8	1,505	200*	5	8	53.75
G. D. Mendis (*Lancs.*)	21	35	6	1,551	180	4	8	53.48
C. W. J. Athey (*Glos.*)	23	35	7	1,474	131	3	9	52.64
R. I. Alikhan (*Surrey*)	11	16	2	726	138	2	4	51.85
†W. M. van der Merwe (*OUCC*) .	8	9	3	310	84	0	3	51.66
A. A. Metcalfe (*Yorks.*)	23	44	4	2,047	194*	6	7	51.17
K. M. Curran (*Glos.*)	23	33	8	1,267	144*	3	5	50.68
K. J. Barnett (*Derbys.*)	24	39	6	1,648	141	5	9	49.93
N. E. Briers (*Leics.*)	24	44	4	1,996	176	5	11	49.90
P. M. Roebuck (*Somerset*)	18	28	5	1,134	201*	2	6	49.30
†M. R. Benson (*Kent*)	16	25	1	1,171	159	5	5	48.79
A. J. Moles (*Warwicks.*)	24	46	8	1,854	224*	4	10	48.78
P. J. Prichard (*Essex*)	22	32	3	1,407	245	5	4	48.51
M. R. Ramprakash (*Middx*)	24	42	10	1,541	146*	5	6	48.15
M. D. Moxon (*Yorks.*)	22	40	6	1,633	218*	3	7	48.02
G. R. Cowdrey (*Kent*)	22	39	6	1,576	135	3	8	47.75
T. C. Middleton (*Hants*)	18	29	3	1,238	127	5	5	47.61

	M	I	NO	R	HI	100s	50s	Avge
). J. Capel (*Northants*)	18	29	6	1,092	123	3	7	47.47
*. W. G. Parker (*Sussex*)	15	25	4	985	107	2	6	46.90
). I. Gower (*Hants*)	20	32	5	1,263	157*	3	3	46.77
ĵ. R. Dilley (*Worcs.*)	10	8	4	185	45*	0	0	46.25
ĵ. S. Clinton (*Surrey*)	20	32	4	1,292	146	1	8	46.14
. P. Evans (*Notts.*)	15	25	9	738	100*	1	4	46.12
. R. Ayling (*Hants*)	9	11	3	368	62*	0	3	46.00
Л. D. Marshall (*Hants*)	18	24	3	962	117	2	6	45.80
ĵ. J. Lord (*Worcs.*)	13	24	2	1,003	190	3	5	45.59
N. Shahid (*Essex*)	19	29	7	1,003	125	1	6	45.59
Л. A. Lynch (*Surrey*)	24	32	5	1,227	104	1	9	45.44
N. J. Speak (*Lancs.*)	6	9	0	409	138	1	3	45.44
. J. Whitaker (*Leics.*)	24	45	6	1,767	124*	4	8	45.30
Я. E. Morris (*OUCC*)	9	12	1	498	96	0	6	45.27
ҫ. J. Rhodes (*Worcs.*)	22	25	10	672	96	0	5	44.80
Я. D. B. Croft (*Glam.*)	16	26	11	672	91*	0	4	44.80
Ҙ. A. Neale (*Worcs.*)	21	32	10	976	122	2	3	44.36
Ō. Bainbridge (*Glos.*)	20	28	3	1,107	152	2	5	44.28
ĵ. D. Lloyd (*Lancs.*)	14	20	2	796	96	0	8	44.22
A. Fordham (*Northants*)	24	42	2	1,767	206*	4	9	44.17
M. P. Maynard (*Glam.*)	23	41	7	1,501	125*	2	11	44.14
M. J. Kilborn (*OUCC*)	6	8	1	309	95	0	2	44.14
Ō. E. Robinson (*Yorks.*)	23	39	7	1,402	150*	1	12	43.81
Я. T. Robinson (*Notts.*)	23	45	5	1,747	220*	4	8	43.67
Т. E. Jesty (*Lancs.*)	17	24	6	785	98	0	7	43.61
A. P. Wells (*Sussex*)	24	44	7	1,611	144*	4	7	43.54
A. J. Stewart (*Surrey*)	17	29	6	984	100*	1	9	42.78
ĵ. C. Holmes (*Glam.*)	10	15	4	465	125*	1	2	42.27
W. K. Hegg (*Lancs.*)	21	22	6	674	100*	1	3	42.12
Ō. D. Bowler (*Derbys.*)	22	39	5	1,428	210	3	7	42.00
J. P. Terry (*Hants*)	22	35	3	1,332	165	5	4	41.62
N. J. Lenham (*Sussex*)	22	41	1	1,663	123	4	9	41.57
N. A. Felton (*Northants*)	22	39	2	1,538	122	4	9	41.56
A. M. Brown (*Derbys.*)	8	12	2	413	139*	1	1	41.30
N. G. Cowley (*Glam.*)	14	17	4	536	76	0	6	41.23
. Smith (*Glam.*)	7	10	2	328	112*	1	2	41.00
С. S. Cowdrey (*Kent*)	13	24	6	733	107*	3	2	40.72
Т. J. G. O'Gorman (*Derbys.*)	7	12	1	448	100	1	4	40.72
M. W. Alleyne (*Glos.*)	13	21	0	854	256	2	3	40.66
M. P. Speight (*Sussex*)	23	41	7	1,375	131	2	11	40.44
M. A. Roseberry (*Middx*)	24	44	4	1,593	135	3	11	39.82
К. Sharp (*Yorks.*)	9	13	5	318	53*	0	1	39.75
N. D. Burns (*Somerset*)	24	34	10	951	166	1	5	39.62
R. M. Ellison (*Kent*)	15	19	7	473	81	0	3	39.41
Ō. Miller (*Derbys.*)	14	14	8	233	47*	0	0	38.83
P. A. J. DeFreitas (*Lancs.*)	18	20	3	660	102	2	2	38.82
M. P. Bicknell (*Surrey*)	21	16	8	310	50*	0	1	38.75
D. B. D'Oliveira (*Worcs.*)	23	35	2	1,263	155	2	7	38.27
J. W. Lloyds (*Glos.*)	24	34	12	839	93	0	4	38.13
P. Johnson (*Notts.*)	23	43	3	1,518	165*	3	9	37.95
R. C. Russell (*Glos.*)	17	23	2	794	120	2	3	37.80
M. V. Fleming (*Kent*)	19	32	6	980	102	1	5	37.69
N. Hussain (*Essex*)	16	23	3	752	197	1	2	37.60
T. J. Boon (*Leics.*)	24	45	4	1,539	138	2	11	37.53
ҫ. G. Hinks (*Kent*)	24	45	0	1,588	234	4	6	36.93
Ĝ. D. Hodgson (*Glos.*)	24	40	4	1,320	126	2	10	36.66
D. W. Randall (*Notts.*)	15	28	1	987	178	2	5	36.55
A. P. Grayson (*Yorks.*)	5	8	4	145	44*	0	0	36.25
Л. Watkinson (*Lancs.*)	19	23	2	754	138	1	4	35.90
M. C. J. Nicholas (*Hants*)	23	35	10	895	104	1	5	35.80
B. Roberts (*Derbys.*)	24	38	7	1,108	124*	2	4	35.74

	M	I	NO	R	HI	100s	50s	Avge
P. J. Newport (*Worcs.*)	21	18	6	424	98	0	3	35.33
I. T. Botham (*Worcs.*)	13	18	1	595	113	1	4	35.00
G. W. Humpage (*Warwicks.*)	13	22	4	628	74	0	5	34.88
J. D. R. Benson (*Leics.*)	18	27	6	725	106	1	3	34.52
S. P. James (*CUCC & Glam.*)	16	31	2	1,000	131*	4	5	34.48
I. P. Butcher (*Glos.*)	12	19	4	513	102	1	2	34.20
C. S. Pickles (*Yorks.*)	16	22	8	478	57*	0	3	34.14
D. R. Pringle (*Essex*)	17	15	2	443	84	0	3	34.07
M. Newell (*Notts.*)	15	27	2	851	112	1	6	34.04
P. Willey (*Leics.*)	22	40	6	1,150	177	2	5	33.82
S. A. Marsh (*Kent*)	24	35	8	911	114*	1	5	33.74
W. K. M. Benjamin (*Leics.*)	12	15	2	437	101*	1	4	33.61
P. A. Cottey (*Glam.*)	20	35	5	1,001	156	3	4	33.36
A. I. C. Dodemaide (*Sussex*)	24	38	8	1,001	112	2	4	33.36
C. M. Wells (*Sussex*)	20	33	5	933	113*	2	4	33.32
R. K. Illingworth (*Worcs.*)	23	22	6	532	117	1	3	33.25
C. C. Lewis (*Leics.*)	17	26	5	697	189*	1	2	33.19
†R. C. J. Williams (*Glos.*)	8	8	4	132	50*	0	1	33.00
†J. J. E. Hardy (*Somerset*)	9	16	5	361	91	0	1	32.81
P. W. Romaines (*Glos.*)	7	11	2	295	95	0	2	32.77
L. Potter (*Leics.*)	23	38	5	1,080	109*	1	7	32.72
J. W. Hall (*Sussex*)	20	37	2	1,140	125	2	5	32.57
P. A. Smith (*Warwicks.*)	12	20	4	520	117	1	3	32.50
†G. Fowler (*Lancs.*)	21	35	6	938	126	2	2	32.34
T. R. Ward (*Kent*)	15	28	1	863	175	2	5	31.96
†A. L. Penberthy (*Northants*)	12	17	3	435	101*	1	3	31.07
C. J. Adams (*Derbys.*)	23	34	4	932	111*	2	5	31.06
S. A. Kellett (*Yorks.*)	16	28	3	774	75*	0	6	30.96
N. M. K. Smith (*Warwicks.*)	10	14	2	370	83*	0	1	30.83
P. N. Hepworth (*Leics.*)	4	8	2	185	55*	0	1	30.83
P. D. Lunn (*OUCC*)	8	10	4	184	44*	0	0	30.66
†I. D. Austin (*Lancs.*)	13	15	6	276	58	0	1	30.66
†M. Saxelby (*Notts.*)	8	15	4	335	73	0	2	30.45
R. J. Blakey (*Yorks.*)	25	43	9	1,033	111	1	6	30.38
B. T. P. Donelan (*Sussex*)	11	13	6	211	53	0	1	30.14
D. J. R. Martindale (*Notts.*)	17	28	3	751	138	2	2	30.04
D. P. Ostler (*Warwicks.*)	11	19	2	510	71	0	5	30.00
D. Ripley (*Northants*)	21	28	6	656	109*	1	2	29.81
M. A. Garnham (*Essex*)	24	28	7	615	84*	0	2	29.28
M. A. Feltham (*Surrey*)	15	16	3	379	101	1	2	29.15
R. J. Maru (*Hants*)	25	20	2	520	59	0	3	28.88
P. Bent (*Worcs.*)	7	12	0	346	79	0	2	28.83
F. D. Stephenson (*Notts.*)	20	35	7	807	121	1	4	28.82
†D. Byas (*Yorks.*)	19	29	4	704	83	0	5	28.16
J. E. Emburey (*Middx*)	23	32	7	702	111*	1	2	28.08
W. Larkins (*Northants*)	15	25	0	701	207	2	2	28.04
Waqar Younis (*Surrey*)	14	9	7	56	14	0	0	28.00
J. D. Ratcliffe (*Warwicks.*)	16	31	3	780	81*	0	5	27.85
Asif Din (*Warwicks.*)	22	39	4	974	100*	1	5	27.82
I. R. Bishop (*Derbys.*)	13	16	4	333	103*	1	0	27.75
†G. P. Thorpe (*Surrey*)	18	28	6	608	86	0	3	27.6
†P. A. Nixon (*Leics.*)	19	23	8	411	46	0	0	27.48
C. A. Walsh (*Glos.*)	20	20	3	464	63*	0	3	27.29
R. G. Williams (*Northants*)	17	26	5	566	96	0	4	26.95
J. E. Benjamin (*Warwicks.*)	15	14	7	188	41	0	0	26.85
†R. G. Twose (*Warwicks.*)	6	10	1	241	64*	0	3	26.7
P. R. Downton (*Middx*)	16	24	2	587	63	0	4	26.68
N. A. Foster (*Essex*)	22	22	2	530	101	1	2	26.50
G. Cook (*Northants*)	9	12	1	287	87	0	1	26.09
A. J. Wright (*Glos.*)	23	38	3	911	112	1	5	26.02
P. Carrick (*Yorks.*)	18	22	2	515	64	0	3	25.77

	M	I	NO	R	HI	100s	50s	Avge
C. T. Medlycott (*Surrey*)	23	25	9	410	44	0	0	25.62
N. A. Mallender (*Somerset*)	20	10	3	177	87*	0	1	25.28
D. M. Smith (*Sussex*)	9	16	2	353	71	0	2	25.21
A. N. Jones (*Somerset*)	22	9	5	100	41	0	0	25.00
T. A. Lloyd (*Warwicks.*)	15	27	1	646	101	1	4	24.84
G. J. Turner (*OUCC*)	9	12	0	298	59	0	2	24.83
C. A. Connor (*Hants*)	22	10	4	148	46	0	0	24.66
A. I. Kallicharran (*Warwicks.*)	7	10	1	221	72	0	2	24.55
I. D. K. Salisbury (*Sussex*)	20	23	10	313	68	0	1	24.07
A. P. Kuiper (*Derbys.*)	12	17	0	407	68	0	2	23.94
D. P. Hughes (*Lancs.*)	18	17	7	237	57	0	1	23.70
I. J. Gould (*Sussex*)	8	12	2	235	73	0	2	23.50
V. J. Wells (*Kent*)	8	15	0	352	58	0	2	23.46
S. M. McEwan (*Worcs.*)	15	12	5	164	54	0	1	23.42
K. J. Piper (*Warwicks.*)	16	21	1	461	111	1	1	23.05
M. J. Lowrey (*CUCC*)	10	18	2	363	72	0	2	22.68
E. E. Hemmings (*Notts.*)	17	20	5	333	83	0	2	22.20
R. Heap (*CUCC*)	10	19	2	376	63	0	2	22.11
P. S. de Villiers (*Kent*)	12	15	3	264	37	0	0	22.00
P. C. R. Tufnell (*Middx*)	23	22	9	283	37	0	0	21.76
P. Moores (*Sussex*)	25	36	4	694	106*	1	2	21.68
N. F. Williams (*Middx*)	21	24	3	448	55*	0	1	21.33
P. R. Pollard (*Notts.*)	7	13	0	277	72	0	1	21.30
P. Farbrace (*Middx*)	8	8	2	124	79	0	1	20.66
M. J. Cann (*Glam.*)	6	10	0	206	64	0	2	20.60
R. A. Pick (*Notts.*)	17	16	6	204	35	0	0	20.40
B. N. French (*Notts.*)	22	34	9	506	105*	1	0	20.24
D. H. Shufflebotham (*CUCC*)	8	9	3	121	29	0	0	20.16
J. C. M. Atkinson (*CUCC*)	11	21	2	374	72	0	2	19.68
R. J. Parks (*Hants*)	20	21	10	216	36*	0	0	19.63
S. J. Base (*Derbys.*)	13	13	2	215	58	0	2	19.54
A. R. C. Fraser (*Middx*)	15	13	2	214	92	0	1	19.45
P. J. Bakker (*Hants*)	16	9	4	95	20	0	0	19.00
J. Turner (*CUCC*)	9	16	0	302	38	0	0	18.87
A. C. S. Pigott (*Sussex*)	21	29	5	451	64*	0	4	18.79
S. R. Lampitt (*Worcs.*)	23	24	5	356	45*	0	0	18.73
M. G. Swallow (*Somerset*)	23	17	7	187	32	0	0	18.70
K. M. Krikken (*Derbys.*)	22	29	2	488	77*	0	2	18.07
R. J. Scott (*Hants*)	6	10	2	144	71	0	1	18.00
G. B. A. Dyer (*CUCC*)	4	8	2	107	23	0	0	17.83
P. W. Jarvis (*Yorks.*)	15	16	4	212	43*	0	0	17.66
J. D. Robinson (*Surrey*)	8	10	0	175	72	0	1	17.50
R. P. Davis (*Kent*)	24	32	3	504	59	0	2	17.37
P. A. Booth (*Warwicks.*)	10	16	2	240	60	0	2	17.14
N. V. Radford (*Worcs.*)	12	8	1	118	43*	0	0	16.85
S. C. Goldsmith (*Derbys.*)	12	17	1	267	51	0	1	16.68
J. D. Fitton (*Lancs.*)	15	13	5	133	25*	0	0	16.62
R. P. Lefebvre (*Somerset*)	17	16	3	214	53	0	1	16.46
G. C. Small (*Warwicks.*)	15	22	4	296	55	0	1	16.44
A. Dale (*Glam.*)	9	14	0	229	92	0	1	16.35
C. P. Metson (*Glam.*)	23	27	5	352	50*	0	1	16.00
H. A. G. Anthony (*Glam.*)	6	8	0	127	39	0	0	15.87
C. E. L. Ambrose (*Northants*)	15	18	5	203	55*	0	1	15.61
P. J. Hartley (*Yorks.*)	17	15	1	218	75	0	1	15.57
N. M. Kendrick (*Surrey*)	13	12	4	124	52*	0	1	15.50
M. C. Ilott (*Essex*)	9	10	2	123	42*	0	0	15.37
J. G. Thomas (*Northants*)	12	13	3	152	48	0	0	15.20
M. M. Patel (*Kent*)	9	12	5	104	41*	0	0	14.85
M. J. Morris (*Glam.*)	10	17	3	206	45	0	0	14.71
D. A. Hagan (*OUCC*)	9	12	0	175	47	0	0	14.58
A. R. K. Pierson (*Warwicks.*)	11	9	5	57	16*	0	0	14.25

	M	I	NO	R	HI	100s	50s	Avg
C. White (*Yorks.*)	10	11	2	127	38	0	0	14.1
M. Jean-Jacques (*Derbys.*)	12	13	5	107	25	0	0	13.3
S. J. W. Andrew (*Essex*)	18	16	7	119	35	0	0	13.2
A. P. Igglesden (*Kent*)	14	17	9	105	24	0	0	13.
N. G. B. Cook (*Northants*)	19	19	8	143	30	0	0	13.0
N. G. Cowans (*Middx*)	18	17	7	127	46*	0	0	12.7
D. J. M. Kelleher (*Kent*)	5	8	0	101	44	0	0	12.6
†Wasim Akram (*Lancs.*)	8	11	0	135	32	0	0	12.2
J. P. Agnew (*Leics.*)	22	26	5	257	46*	0	0	12.2
D. A. Graveney (*Glos.*)	13	13	4	107	46*	0	0	11.8
†K. E. Cooper (*Notts.*)	21	26	6	227	35*	0	0	11.3
P. S. Gerrans (*OUCC*)	9	9	0	102	39	0	0	11.3
†G. J. Parsons (*Leics.*)	10	13	3	112	20	0	0	11.2
†J. H. Childs (*Essex*)	23	16	5	123	26	0	0	11.?
D. Gough (*Yorks.*)	14	17	6	123	24	0	0	11.?
S. L. Watkin (*Glam.*)	24	25	8	187	25*	0	0	11.0
T. A. Merrick (*Kent*)	7	8	2	66	35	0	0	11.0
R. A. Bunting (*Sussex*)	15	13	5	85	24*	0	0	10.6
M. J. Weston (*Worcs.*)	6	10	1	90	38*	0	0	10.0
O. H. Mortensen (*Derbys.*)	12	11	9	20	5*	0	0	10.0

BOWLING

(Qualification: 10 wickets in 10 innings)

† *Denotes a left-arm bowler.*

	O	M	R	W	BB	5W/i	Avg
I. R. Bishop (*Derbys.*)	407.3	94	1,124	59	6-71	3	19.0
M. D. Marshall (*Hants*)	554.2	142	1,381	72	7-47	4	19.1
D. J. Millns (*Leics.*)	206.4	36	662	31	6-63	2	21.3
O. H. Mortensen (*Derbys.*)	316.2	91	785	35	4-22	0	22.4
C. E. L. Ambrose (*Northants*)	503.4	127	1,413	61	7-89	5	23.1
Waqar Younis (*Surrey*)	422	70	1,357	57	7-73	3	23.8
M. W. Alleyne (*Glos.*)	112	29	391	16	3-23	0	24.4
P. A. Smith (*Warwicks.*)	148.5	34	497	20	5-48	1	24.8
N. A. Foster (*Essex*)	819.2	175	2,502	94	6-32	6	26.6
A. R. C. Fraser (*Middx*)	596	144	1,533	57	6-30	4	26.8
M. P. Bicknell (*Surrey*)	671.1	157	1,827	67	5-34	1	27.2
G. J. Parsons (*Leics.*)	304.5	77	963	35	6-75	2	27.5
J. E. Benjamin (*Warwicks.*)	388.3	68	1,205	43	5-29	4	28.0
C. A. Walsh (*Glos.*)	612.1	107	2,022	72	8-58	3	28.0
†R. K. Illingworth (*Worcs.*)	875.5	280	2,122	75	5-59	1	28.2
D. J. Capel (*Northants*)	234	51	711	25	5-74	0	28.4
D. A. Reeve (*Warwicks.*)	377.4	111	940	33	4-42	0	28.4
T. A. Merrick (*Kent*)	184.3	45	488	17	4-66	0	28.7
M. A. Feltham (*Surrey*)	349.4	61	1,150	40	6-53	2	28.7
T. A. Munton (*Warwicks.*)	827.1	199	2,254	78	5-33	2	28.8
K. J. Barnett (*Derbys.*)	293.3	54	757	26	4-28	0	29.1
D. R. Pringle (*Essex*)	358.3	91	994	34	5-66	1	29.2
I. T. Botham (*Worcs.*)	194.4	38	614	21	4-65	0	29.2
N. F. Williams (*Middx*)	530.1	98	1,618	54	7-61	2	29.9
C. C. Lewis (*Leics.*)	536.2	102	1,697	56	6-55	2	30.3
S. Bastien (*Glam.*)	317.1	57	1,187	39	6-75	2	30.4
K. M. Curran (*Glos.*)	598.3	111	1,961	64	5-63	1	30.6
W. K. M. Benjamin (*Leics.*)	284.3	63	858	28	5-73	2	30.6
M. A. Atherton (*Lancs.*)	433.3	104	1,398	45	6-78	3	31.0
N. A. Mallender (*Somerset*)	553.2	116	1,585	51	5-46	2	31.0

	O	M	R	W	BB	5W/i	Avge
M. McEwan (*Worcs.*)	375.2	75	1,189	38	3-31	0	31.28
. J. Newport (*Worcs.*)	626.2	116	2,001	63	6-54	4	31.76
N. G. Cowans (*Middx*)	460	124	1,247	39	5-67	1	31.97
E. Emburey (*Middx*)	942.3	275	1,957	61	5-32	2	32.08
G. A. Hick (*Worcs.*)	208.5	41	645	20	5-37	1	32.25
. D. Topley (*Essex*)	223	34	713	22	4-67	0	32.40
D. E. Malcolm (*Derbys.*)	518.2	99	1,688	52	5-46	2	32.46
R. A. Pick (*Notts.*)	494.5	83	1,657	51	7-128	1	32.49
. R. Lampitt (*Worcs.*)	565.3	98	1,889	58	5-34	2	32.56
A. P. Kuiper (*Derbys.*)	125.3	29	393	12	4-69	0	32.75
M. C. Ilott (*Essex*)	322.1	65	1,036	31	5-34	2	33.41
M. Watkinson (*Lancs.*)	508.2	122	1,578	47	5-65	3	33.57
G. R. Dilley (*Worcs.*)	224.2	30	818	24	5-62	2	34.08
N. G. B. Cook (*Northants*)	527.1	167	1,364	40	5-44	2	34.10
D. V. Lawrence (*Glos.*)	497.3	53	1,979	58	5-51	2	34.12
P. Carrick (*Yorks.*)	601	173	1,570	46	5-49	3	34.13
P. J. Hartley (*Yorks.*)	491	80	1,781	52	6-57	2	34.25
M. Frost (*Glam.*)	557.1	74	2,047	59	5-40	2	34.69
B. P. Patterson (*Lancs.*)	281.4	45	1,015	29	4-52	0	35.00
A. H. Gray (*Surrey*)	239.5	43	666	19	4-83	0	35.05
* C. R. Tufnell (*Middx*)	1,036.5	281	2,635	74	6-79	2	35.60
. D. Fletcher (*Yorks.*)	292.5	60	1,035	29	5-94	1	35.68
P. M. Such (*Essex*)	272.4	67	715	20	3-34	0	35.75
A. P. Igglesden (*Kent*)	326	47	1,150	32	4-79	0	35.93
A. L. Penberthy (*Northants*)	207.4	29	791	22	4-91	0	35.95
* A. J. DeFreitas (*Lancs.*)	489.3	109	1,440	40	6-39	2	36.00
E. E. Hemmings (*Notts.*)	688.2	197	1,844	51	6-58	2	36.15
K. P. Evans (*Notts.*)	356	78	1,232	34	4-50	0	36.23
R. J. Maru (*Hants*)	851.1	219	2,420	66	6-97	2	36.66
A. N. Jones (*Somerset*)	572.4	92	2,055	56	6-75	2	36.69
G. D. Rose (*Somerset*)	571.4	99	1,951	53	5-52	1	36.81
A. C. S. Pigott (*Sussex*)	541	94	1,997	54	5-52	3	36.98
D. Gough (*Yorks.*)	279.4	49	1,037	28	4-68	0	37.03
G. C. Small (*Warwicks.*)	425.4	105	1,190	32	6-94	2	37.18
P. Agnew (*Leics.*)	612	108	2,196	59	5-54	5	37.22
G. Miller (*Derbys.*)	461	114	1,308	35	6-45	1	37.37
M. A. Crawley (*OUCC & Lancs.*)	224.5	38	750	20	6-92	1	37.50
A. A. Donald (*Warwicks.*)	391	89	1,089	29	3-28	0	37.55
S. N. Barnes (*Glos.*)	207	45	602	16	4-51	0	37.62
P. W. Jarvis (*Yorks.*)	405.2	68	1,393	37	4-53	0	37.64
A. D. Mullally (*Leics.*)	487.2	117	1,446	38	4-59	0	38.05
C. A. Connor (*Hants*)	510.1	88	1,789	47	5-96	1	38.06
D. P. Hughes (*Lancs.*)	280.4	61	918	24	4-25	0	38.25
D. A. Graveney (*Glos.*)	485.4	136	1,189	31	5-45	3	38.35
A. R. K. Pierson (*Warwicks.*)	302.4	55	965	25	5-101	1	38.60
R. G. Williams (*Northants*)	432.3	119	1,204	31	4-94	0	38.83
F. D. Stephenson (*Notts.*)	610.4	94	2,098	54	6-84	2	38.85
P. J. Bakker (*Hants*)	436.2	90	1,439	37	5-101	1	38.89
R. P. Davis (*Kent*)	908.1	221	2,844	73	6-40	5	38.95
K. T. Medlycott (*Surrey*)	748.5	170	2,382	61	7-92	3	39.04
S. L. Watkin (*Glam.*)	796.1	137	2,712	69	5-100	1	39.30
T. M. Tremlett (*Hants*)	120.5	30	393	10	3-33	0	39.30
K. J. Shine (*Hants*)	156.4	30	552	14	4-52	0	39.42
P. J. Martin (*Lancs.*)	275.3	52	868	22	4-68	0	39.45
P. S. de Villiers (*Kent*)	304.5	58	992	25	6-70	1	39.68
Wasim Akram (*Lancs.*)	204	44	640	16	3-76	0	40.00
S. J. Base (*Derbys.*)	414.3	68	1,402	35	6-105	2	40.05
G. J. F. Ferris (*Leics.*)	138.2	29	482	12	4-44	0	40.16
A. I. C. Dodemaide (*Sussex*)	763.1	130	2,457	61	6-106	1	40.27
A. E. Warner (*Derbys.*)	393.3	67	1,330	33	3-56	0	40.30

	O	M	R	W	BB	5W/i	Avg
J. G. Thomas (*Northants*)	305.2	51	1,171	29	7-75	1	40.3
P. J. W. Allott (*Lancs.*)	266	77	730	18	4-23	0	40.5
K. E. Cooper (*Notts.*)	703.4	153	2,203	54	5-56	3	40.7
S. D. Udal (*Hants*)	238.3	46	900	22	4-139	0	40.9
S. J. W. Andrew (*Essex*)	503	93	1,897	46	5-55	1	41.2
R. P. Lefebvre (*Somerset*)	506.1	137	1,281	31	5-30	1	41.3
C. S. Pickles (*Yorks.*)	325.1	72	1,163	28	3-56	0	41.5
†M. M. Patel (*Kent*)	297.5	72	836	20	6-57	2	41.8
A. J. Murphy (*Surrey*)	404.2	76	1,367	30	5-67	2	45.5
†J. A. Afford (*Notts.*)	688	209	1,944	42	4-137	0	46.2
C. White (*Yorks.*)	159	23	608	13	5-74	1	46.7
P. Bainbridge (*Glos.*)	162.4	30	515	11	3-23	0	46.8
†A. J. Buzza (*CUCC*)	287	47	1,086	23	4-87	0	47.2
M. A. Robinson (*Northants*)	559.1	104	1,889	40	3-47	0	47.2
P. Willey (*Leics.*)	421.4	119	1,091	23	2-7	0	47.4
R. D. B. Croft (*Glam.*)	397.1	83	1,335	28	3-10	0	47.6
†N. M. Kendrick (*Surrey*)	348	66	1,194	25	4-110	0	47.7
M. J. Lowrey (*CUCC*)	151.2	33	483	10	2-13	0	48.3
†S. J. Dennis (*Glam.*)	322	61	1,071	22	5-76	1	48.6
M. V. Fleming (*Kent*)	394.5	94	1,072	22	3-65	0	48.7
†P. A. Booth (*Warwicks.*)	250.5	75	636	13	4-55	0	48.9
I. D. K. Salisbury (*Sussex*)	601.1	113	2,075	42	5-32	2	49.4
B. T. P. Donelan (*Sussex*)	304.4	56	1,000	20	3-79	0	50.0
R. A. Bunting (*Sussex*)	360	62	1,314	26	2-36	0	50.5
R. M. Ellison (*Kent*)	291.5	51	963	19	4-76	0	50.6
J. R. Ayling (*Hants*)	181.2	46	572	11	2-48	0	52.0
R. J. Bailey (*Northants*)	168.2	29	604	11	3-82	0	54.9
I. D. Austin (*Lancs.*)	245	76	662	12	3-42	0	55.1
J. W. Lloyds (*Glos.*)	382.5	60	1,429	25	4-11	0	57.1
C. Penn (*Kent*)	186	35	636	11	3-45	0	57.8
P. S. Gerrans (*OUCC*)	208	40	695	12	3-86	0	57.9
†J. H. Childs (*Essex*)	655.5	211	1,590	27	4-56	0	58.8
J. D. Batty (*Yorks.*)	195	29	722	12	4-76	0	60.1
W. W. Davis (*Northants*)	237.5	28	812	13	3-28	0	62.4
R. A. Pyman (*CUCC*)	308.4	81	938	15	2-29	0	62.5
Asif Din (*Warwicks.*)	159.1	30	635	10	3-17	0	63.5
R. H. J. Jenkins (*CUCC*)	281.4	41	959	15	5-100	1	63.9
I. G. Swallow (*Somerset*)	689.1	161	2,174	34	3-88	0	63.9
A. N. Hayhurst (*Somerset*)	321.2	50	1,087	17	3-58	0	63.9
M. E. Waugh (*Essex*)	191	33	771	12	5-37	1	64.2
I. A. Greig (*Surrey*)	216.1	21	858	13	3-60	0	66.0
N. V. Radford (*Worcs.*)	302	49	1,195	18	4-55	0	66.3
C. M. Wells (*Sussex*)	374	68	1,237	17	3-48	0	72.7
N. G. Cowley (*Glam.*)	316.3	64	900	12	3-84	0	75.0
G. J. Turner (*OUCC*)	212.2	39	819	10	3-100	0	81.9
J. D. Fitton (*Lancs.*)	454.4	91	1,447	14	3-69	0	103.3

The following bowlers took ten wickets but bowled in fewer than ten innings:

	O	M	R	W	BB	5W/i	Avg
V. J. Wells (*Kent*)	85	19	257	12	5-43	1	21.4
H. A. G. Anthony (*Glam.*)	142.4	32	466	12	3-95	0	38.8
C. Pringle (*New Zealanders & M. Parkinson's World XI*)	149	32	483	10	2-49	0	48.3

INDIVIDUAL SCORES OF 100 AND OVER

here were 428 three-figure innings in first-class cricket in 1990, 180 more than in 1989 and ourteen more than in any other season. The total passed the previous record of 414 hundreds cored in 1928, of which 329 were scored in the County Championship and 75 in other latches. In 1990 there were three triple-hundreds, a record equalled only in 1899 and 1934, nd 29 other double-hundreds. The record number of double-hundreds is 34 in 1933. In 1928, hen 312 first-class matches were played, compared with 241 in 1990, there was one triple-undred and 28 double-hundreds. In that year, 139 batsmen recorded three-figure innings, ompared with 156 in 1990, and thirteen each were played by E. H. Hendren, C. P. Mead and I. Sutcliffe, while the most in 1990 was twelve by G. A. Gooch. The following list includes 27 hit in the County Championship, two by the Zimbabwean touring team and 71 in other rst-class games, but not the fifteen scored by the Indian touring team, the seven scored by ie Sri Lankan touring team, nor the six scored by the New Zealand touring team, which may e found in their respective sections.

Note: Players' hundreds are listed in chronological order. Previously they have been listed n descending order.

* *Signifies not out.*

. A. Gooch (12)

37	Essex v Middx, Lord's
15	Essex v Leics., Chelmsford
21	Essex v Worcs., Worcester
20	Essex v Middx, Ilford
02*	Essex v New Zealanders, Chelmsford
54	England v New Zealand, Birmingham
77	Essex v Lancs., Colchester
33 23 }	England v India, Lord's
16	England v India, Manchester
74 26 }	Essex v Northants, Northampton

. Morris (10)

03	Glam. v Oxford U., Oxford
00*	Glam. v Kent, Swansea
02	Glam. v Yorks., Cardiff
19	Glam. v Worcs., Abergavenny
06	Glam. v Warwicks., Swansea
00	Glam. v Middx, Lord's
10 02* }	Glam. v Notts., Worksop
26	Glam. v Sri Lankans, Ebbw Vale
60*	Glam. v Derbys., Cardiff

. C. Broad (9)

80	Notts. v Derbys., Nottingham
19	Notts. v Warwicks., Birmingham
27*	Notts. v Kent, Tunbridge Wells
12*	Notts. v Leics., Nottingham
26	Notts. v Yorks., Scarborough
22	Notts. v Lancs., Southport
40	Notts. v Middx, Nottingham
56	Notts. v Worcs., Nottingham
22	Notts. v Lancs., Nottingham

S. J. Cook (9)

313*	Somerset v Glam., Cardiff
117*	Somerset v New Zealanders, Taunton
197	Somerset v Sussex, Taunton
112*	Somerset v Northants, Taunton
137	Somerset v Warwicks., Taunton
152	Somerset v Middx, Uxbridge
116*	Somerset v Surrey, Weston-super-Mare
114	Somerset v Hants, Taunton
143	Somerset v Worcs., Taunton

D. L. Haynes (8)

116	Middx v Essex, Lord's
181 129 }	Middx v New Zealanders, Lord's
220*	Middx v Essex, Ilford
108	Middx v Somerset, Uxbridge
173	Middx v Glam., Lord's
255*	Middx v Sussex, Lord's
131	Middx v Yorks., Leeds

G. A. Hick (8)

106*	Worcs. v Lancs., Manchester
171*	Worcs. v Somerset, Worcester
252* 100* }	Worcs. v Glam., Abergavenny
102	Worcs. v Leics., Leicester
110	Worcs. v Glos., Bristol
154	Worcs. v Somerset, Taunton
138*	Worcs. v Glam., Worcester

M. E. Waugh (8)

166*	Essex v Worcs., Worcester
125	Essex v Hants, Southampton
204	Essex v Glos., Ilford
103	Essex v Warwicks., Birmingham
126	Essex v Derbys., Colchester
103*	Essex v Sussex, Chelmsford
207*	Essex v Yorks., Middlesbrough
169	Essex v Kent, Chelmsford

M. A. Atherton (7)

191	Lancs. v Surrey, The Oval
151	England v New Zealand, Nottingham
117	Lancs. v Oxford U., Oxford
101	Lancs. v Kent, Maidstone
108*	Lancs. v Essex, Colchester
131	England v India, Manchester
108	Lancs. v Yorks., Manchester

R. J. Bailey (7)

101	Northants v Somerset, Taunton
138*	Northants v Kent, Northampton
204*	Northants v Sussex, Northampton
134*	Northants v Derbys., Chesterfield
105	Northants v Glos., Northampton
108	Northants v Essex, Northampton
107	Northants v Essex, Chelmsford

T. M. Moody (7)

147	Warwicks. v Cambridge U., Cambridge
106	Warwicks. v New Zealanders, Birmingham
168	Warwicks. v Derbys., Derby
103*	Warwicks. v Glam., Swansea
101*	Warwicks. v Hants, Birmingham
110	Warwicks. v Sussex, Eastbourne
117	Warwicks. v Leics., Birmingham

I. V. A. Richards (7)

119	Glam. v Leics., Cardiff
118*	Glam. v Sussex, Hove
109	Glam. v Northants, Northampton
164*	Glam. v Hants, Southampton
111	Glam. v Essex, Southend
118*	
127	Glam. v Notts., Worksop

N. R. Taylor (7)

106	Kent v Glam., Swansea
124*	Kent v Yorks., Tunbridge Wells
120	Kent v Cambridge U., Cambridge
107*	Kent v Indians, Canterbury
152*	Kent v Middx, Canterbury
204	Kent v Surrey, Canterbury
142	

D. M. Ward (7)

181	Surrey v Oxford U., Oxford
129*	Surrey v Hants, The Oval
154*	Surrey v Notts., Nottingham
126	Surrey v Warwicks., The Oval
191	Surrey v Hants, Southampton
263	Surrey v Kent, Canterbury
208	Surrey v Essex, The Oval

A. R. Butcher (6)

139	Glam. v Sussex, Hove
151*	Glam. v Kent, Swansea
115	Glam. v Leics., Hinckley
130	Glam. v Worcs., Abergavenny
116	Glam. v Warwicks., Swansea
121*	Glam. v Notts., Worksop

A. J. Lamb (6)

235	Northants v Yorks., Leeds
135*	Northants v Sussex, Northampton
139	England v India, Lord's
109	England v India, Manchester
134	Northants v Essex, Northampton
165	Northants v Essex, Chelmsford

A. A. Metcalfe (6)

162	Yorks. v Glos., Cheltenham
102	Yorks. v Somerset, Scarborough
146	Yorks. v Lancs., Leeds
150*	Yorks. v Derbys., Scarborough
194*	Yorks. v Notts., Nottingham
107	

J. E. Morris (6)

122	Derbys. v Somerset, Taunton
109	
103	Derbys. v Notts., Derby
103*	Derbys. v Warwicks., Derby
157*	Derbys. v Hants, Portsmouth
109	Derbys. v Yorks., Scarborough

R. A. Smith (6)

181	Hants v Sussex, Southampton
114*	Hants v Surrey, The Oval
153	Hants v Glam., Southampton
100*	England v India, Lord's
121*	England v India, Manchester
124	Hants v Glos., Southampton

K. J. Barnett (5)

141	Derbys. v Yorks., Chesterfield
131	Derbys. v Warwicks., Derby
107	Derbys. v Glos., Derby
123	Derbys. v Sussex, Hove
109	Derbys. v Lancs., Liverpool

M. R. Benson (5)

109	Kent v Sussex, Folkestone
116	Kent v Somerset, Canterbury
159	Kent v Essex, Maidstone
107	Kent v Leics., Dartford
115*	Kent v Sussex, Hove

D. J. Bicknell (5)

169	Surrey v Northants, The Oval
143	Surrey v Sussex, Guildford
111	Surrey v Leics., The Oval
186	Surrey v Kent, Canterbury
114	Surrey v Middx, The Oval

N. E. Briers (5)

104	Leics. v Essex, Chelmsford
157*	Leics. v Notts., Leicester
150*	Leics. v Indians, Leicester
111	Leics. v Worcs., Leicester
176	Leics. v Northants, Leicester

K. R. Brown (5)

141	Middx v Essex, Lord's
109*	Middx v Yorks., Uxbridge
120	Middx v Glam., Lord's
200*	Middx v Notts., Lord's
116	Middx v Sussex, Hove

. C. Middleton (5)
27	Hants v Kent, Canterbury
04*	Hants v Essex, Southampton
23	Hants v Northants, Bournemouth
17*	Hants v Worcs., Worcester
04	Hants v Kent, Bournemouth

. J. Prichard (5)
45	Essex v Leics., Chelmsford
16	Essex v Cambridge U., Cambridge
15	Essex v Somerset, Bath
03	Essex v Derbys., Derby
02	Essex v Kent, Chelmsford

1. R. Ramprakash (5)
18*	Middx v Cambridge U., Cambridge
46*	Middx v Somerset, Uxbridge
00* }	Middx v Kent, Canterbury
25 }	
32	Middx v Notts., Lord's

. P. Terry (5)
07	Hants v Kent, Canterbury
12	Hants v Oxford U., Oxford
19*	Hants v Warwicks., Birmingham
65	Hants v Northants, Bournemouth
20	Hants v Sri Lankans, Southampton

. S. Curtis (4)
11*	Worcs. v Glam., Abergavenny
51*	Worcs. v Leics., Leicester
97*	Worcs. v Warwicks., Worcester
56	Worcs. v Somerset, Taunton

. H. Fairbrother (4)
66	Lancs. v Surrey, The Oval
05	Lancs. v Oxford U., Oxford
03*	Lancs. v Warwicks., Coventry
09*	Lancs. v Essex, Colchester

N. A. Felton (4)
19*	Northants v Notts., Nottingham
22	Northants v Glam., Northampton
01	Northants v Somerset, Taunton
06	Northants v Yorks., Northampton

A. Fordham (4)
06*	Northants v Yorks., Leeds
28	Northants v Somerset, Taunton
72	Northants v Lancs., Northampton
59	Northants v Essex, Chelmsford

M. W. Gatting (4)
70*	Middx v Somerset, Uxbridge
01	Middx v Kent, Canterbury
69*	Middx v Notts., Nottingham
19*	Middx v Derbys., Derby

A. N. Hayhurst (4)
10*	Somerset v Glam., Cardiff
70	Somerset v Sussex, Taunton
19	Somerset v Worcs., Worcester
70	Somerset v Yorks., Scarborough

S. G. Hinks (4)
107	Kent v Glam., Swansea
120	Kent v Surrey, Guildford
234	Kent v Middx, Canterbury
163	Kent v Leics., Leicester

S. P. James (4)
116	Cambridge U. v Glos., Cambridge
104*	Cambridge U. v Notts., Cambridge
131*	Oxford & Camb. Univs v New Zealanders, Cambridge
102	Cambridge U. v Sussex, Hove

N. J. Lenham (4)
121	Sussex v Hants, Southampton
108	Sussex v Somerset, Taunton
109*	Sussex v Surrey, Guildford
123	Sussex v Somerset, Hove

G. D. Mendis (4)
102	Lancs. v Surrey, The Oval
113	Lancs. v Leics., Manchester
114	Lancs. v Middx, Manchester
180	Lancs. v Notts., Southport

A. J. Moles (4)
128*	Warwicks. v Middx, Lord's
100*	Warwicks. v Lancs., Coventry
224*	Warwicks. v Glam., Swansea
117	Warwicks. v Sri Lankans, Birmingham

R. T. Robinson (4)
125*	Notts. v Somerset, Weston-super-Mare
123	Notts. v Glos., Nottingham
105	Notts. v Middx, Lord's
220*	Notts. v Yorks., Nottingham

C. L. Smith (4)
148	Hants v Oxford U., Oxford
128	Hants v Essex, Southampton
132*	Hants v Sussex, Arundel
111	Hants v Surrey, Southampton

J. P. Stephenson (4)
202*	Essex v Somerset, Bath
147	Essex v New Zealanders, Chelmsford
131*	Essex v Leics., Leicester
116	TCCB Under-25 XI v Indians, Birmingham

A. P. Wells (4)
137	Sussex v Cambridge U., Hove
102*	Sussex v Northants, Northampton
144*	Sussex v Warwicks., Eastbourne
109*	Sussex v Leics., Leicester

J. J. Whitaker (4)
107*	Leics. v Lancs., Manchester
124*	Leics. v Oxford U., Oxford
116	Leics. v Derbys., Leicester
100	Leics. v Kent, Leicester

C. W. J. Athey (3)
131   Glos. v Sussex, Hove
108* ⎫
122 ⎬ Glos. v Warwicks., Bristol

P. D. Bowler (3)
120   Derbys. v Warwicks., Derby
115*   Derbys. v Lancs., Liverpool
210   Derbys. v Kent, Chesterfield

D. J. Capel (3)
113   Northants v Glam., Northampton
123   Northants v New Zealanders,
        Northampton
103*   Northants v Derbys., Chesterfield

P. A. Cottey (3)
156   Glam. v Oxford U., Oxford
125   Glam. v Leics., Hinckley
100*   Glam. v Worcs., Abergavenny

C. S. Cowdrey (3)
107   Kent v Hants, Canterbury
102*   Kent v Cambridge U., Cambridge
107*   Kent v Northants, Northampton

G. R. Cowdrey (3)
116   Kent v Essex, Maidstone
119*   Kent v Surrey, Guildford
135   Kent v Leics., Leicester

K. M. Curran (3)
103*   Glos. v Somerset, Bristol
144*   Glos. v Sussex, Bristol
101*   Glos. v Hants, Southampton

D. I. Gower (3)
145   Hants v Sussex, Southampton
126*   Hants v Indians, Southampton
157*   England v India, The Oval

R. J. Harden (3)
104   Somerset v New Zealanders,
        Taunton
101   Somerset v Yorks., Scarborough
104*   Somerset v Surrey, Weston-super-
        Mare

P. Johnson (3)
165*   Notts. v Northants, Nottingham
112*   Notts. v Oxford U., Oxford
149   Notts. v Yorks., Scarborough

G. J. Lord (3)
101   Worcs. v Lancs., Kidderminster
190   Worcs. v Hants, Worcester
127   Worcs. v Glam., Worcester

M. D. Moxon (3)
130   Yorks. v Zimbabweans, Leeds
123   Yorks. v Notts., Scarborough
218*   Yorks. v Sussex, Eastbourne

D. A. Reeve (3)
102*   Warwicks. v Cambridge U.,
        Cambridge
202*   Warwicks. v Northants,
        Northampton
121*   Warwicks. v Lancs., Manchester

M. A. Roseberry (3)
122   Middx v Surrey, Lord's
135   Middx v Essex, Ilford
115   Middx v Northants, Luton

C. J. Tavaré (3)
120*   Somerset v Glam., Cardiff
156   Somerset v New Zealanders,
        Taunton
219   Somerset v Sussex, Hove

C. J. Adams (2)
111*   Derbys. v Cambridge U., Cambridge
101   Derbys. v Yorks., Scarborough

R. I. Alikhan (2)
119   Surrey v Middx, The Oval
138   Surrey v Essex, The Oval

M. W. Alleyne (2)
118   Glos. v Surrey, Cheltenham
256   Glos. v Northants, Northampton

P. Bainbridge (2)
152   Glos. v Yorks., Cheltenham
129   Glos. v Worcs., Bristol

T. J. Boon (2)
128   Leics. v Somerset, Leicester
138   Leics. v Glos., Gloucester

M. A. Crawley (2)
103*   Oxford U. v Glam., Oxford
105*   Oxford U. v Leics., Oxford

P. A. J. DeFreitas (2)
102   Lancs. v Oxford U., Oxford
100*   Lancs. v Northants, Northampton

A. I. C. Dodemaide (2)
110*   Sussex v New Zealanders, Hove
112   Sussex v Somerset, Hove

D. B. D'Oliveira (2)
155   Worcs. v Lancs., Manchester
121   Worcs. v Glam., Abergavenny

G. Fowler (2)
115*   Lancs. v Leics., Manchester
126   Lancs. v Glos., Manchester

M. J. Greatbatch (2)
168* ⎫ M. Parkinson's World XI v Indians,
128* ⎬ Scarborough

A. Greig (2)
91   Surrey v Lancs., The Oval
23*   Surrey v Somerset, Weston-super-Mare

J. W. Hall (2)
20*   Sussex v New Zealanders, Hove
25   Sussex v Notts., Nottingham

B. R. Hardie (2)
125   Essex v Hants, Southampton
110* Essex v Glos., Ilford

G. D. Hodgson (2)
126   Glos. v Zimbabweans, Bristol
109   Glos. v Worcs., Bristol

W. Larkins (2)
107   Northants v Surrey, The Oval
207   Northants v Essex, Northampton

M. D. Marshall (2)
117   Hants v Yorks., Leeds
112   Hants v Leics., Leicester

D. J. R. Martindale (2)
108* Notts. v Northants, Nottingham
138   Notts. v Cambridge U., Cambridge

M. P. Maynard (2)
125* Glam. v Northants, Northampton
115   Glam. v Notts., Worksop

P. A. Neale (2)
122   Worcs. v Notts., Worcester
119* Worcs. v Kent, Canterbury

P. W. G. Parker (2)
100   Sussex v Surrey, Hove
107   Sussex v Kent, Folkestone

D. W. Randall (2)
120   Notts. v Leics., Leicester
178   Notts. v Kent, Tunbridge Wells

B. Roberts (2)
124* Derbys. v Yorks., Chesterfield
100* Derbys. v Kent, Chesterfield

P. M. Roebuck (2)
114* Somerset v Warwicks., Taunton
201* Somerset v Worcs., Worcester

R. C. Russell (2)
120   Glos. v Somerset, Bristol
103* Glos. v Notts., Nottingham

M. P. Speight (2)
131   Sussex v Glam., Hove
108   Sussex v Surrey, Guildford

T. R. Ward (2)
124   Kent v Derbys., Chesterfield
175   Kent v Hants, Bournemouth

C. M. Wells (2)
113* Sussex v New Zealanders, Hove
107   Sussex v Hants, Arundel

P. Willey (2)
177   Leics. v Oxford U., Oxford
112   Leics. v Sussex, Leicester

The following each played one three-figure innings:

Asif Din, 100*, Warwicks. v Cambridge U., Cambridge.
W. K. M. Benjamin, 101*, Leics. v Derbys., Leicester; J. D. R. Benson, 106, Leics. v Indians, Leicester; I. R. Bishop, 103*, Derbys. v Yorks., Scarborough; R. J. Blakey, 111, Yorks. v Somerset, Scarborough; I. T. Botham, 113, Worcs. v Surrey, The Oval; A. M. Brown, 139*, Derbys. v Northants, Chesterfield; G. K. Brown, 103, Minor Counties v Indians, Trowbridge; N. D. Burns, 166, Somerset v Glos., Taunton; I. P. Butcher, 102, Glos. v Middx, Lord's.
G. S. Clinton, 146, Surrey v Northants, The Oval; R. M. F. Cox, 104*, Hants v Worcs., Worcester.
J. E. Emburey, 111*, Middx v Hants, Bournemouth; K. P. Evans, 100*, Notts. v Somerset, Weston-super-Mare.
M. A. Feltham, 101, Surrey v Middx, The Oval; M. V. Fleming, 102, Kent v Notts., Tunbridge Wells; N. A. Foster, 101, Essex v Leics., Chelmsford; B. N. French, 105*, Notts. v Derbys., Derby.
K. Greenfield, 102*, Sussex v Cambridge U., Hove.
W. K. Hegg, 100*, Lancs. v Essex, Colchester; G. C. Holmes, 125*, Glam. v Somerset, Cardiff; N. Hussain, 197, Essex v Surrey, The Oval.
R. K. Illingworth, 117, Worcs. v Notts., Worcester.
K. D. James, 104*, Hants v Kent, Canterbury.
C. C. Lewis, 189*, Leics. v Essex, Chelmsford; J. J. B. Lewis, 116*, Essex v Surrey, The Oval; T. A. Lloyd, 101, Warwicks. v Glam., Swansea; M. A. Lynch, 104, Surrey v Somerset, Weston-super-Mare.

S. A. Marsh, 114*, Kent v Notts., Tunbridge Wells; P. Moores, 106*, Sussex v Glam., Hove;
  Mudassar Nazar, 107*, M. Parkinson's World XI v Indians, Scarborough.
M. Newell, 112, Notts. v Sri Lankans, Cleethorpes; M. C. J. Nicholas, 104, Hants v Indians,
  Southampton.
T. J. G. O'Gorman, 100, Derbys. v Leics., Derby.
A. L. Penberthy, 101*, Northants v Cambridge U., Cambridge; I. L. Philip, 100, Scotland
  v Ireland, Edinburgh (Myreside); K. J. Piper, 111, Warwicks. v Somerset, Birmingham;
  L. Potter, 109*, Leics. v Yorks., Sheffield.
D. Ripley, 109*, Northants v Leics., Leicester; C. M. Robertson, 125, Zimbabweans v Lancs.,
  Manchester; P. E. Robinson, 150*, Yorks. v Derbys., Scarborough.
A. H. Shah, 185, Zimbabweans v Glos., Bristol; N. Shahid, 125, Essex v Lancs., Colchester;
  I. Smith, 112*, Glam. v Lancs., Colwyn Bay; P. A. Smith, 117, Warwicks. v Glam.,
  Birmingham; N. J. Speak, 138, Lancs. v Zimbabweans, Manchester; F. D. Stephenson,
  121, Notts. v Leics., Nottingham; A. J. Stewart, 100*, Surrey v Hants, The Oval.
S. J. S. Warke, 100*, Ireland v Scotland, Edinburgh (Myreside); M. Watkinson, 138, Lancs.
  v Yorks., Manchester; A. J. Wright, 112, Glos. v Northants, Cheltenham.
G. Yates, 106, Lancs. v Notts., Nottingham.

TEN WICKETS IN A MATCH

There were thirteen instances of bowlers taking ten or more wickets in a match in first-class
cricket in 1990, seventeen fewer than in 1989. The list includes twelve in the County
Championship and one by the New Zealand touring team. Two of the instances occurred in
the same match and for the same side, when R. P. Davis and M. M. Patel shared all twenty
wickets for Kent against Leicestershire at Dartford.

M. D. Marshall (2): 10-107, Hants v Derbys., Portsmouth; 11-92, Hants v Glam., Pontypridd.

The following each took ten wickets in a match on one occasion:

C. E. L. Ambrose, 12-155, Northants v Leics., Leicester.
J. G. Bracewell, 12-227, New Zealanders v Oxford & Cambridge Univs, Cambridge.
R. P. Davis, 10-142, Kent v Leics., Dartford.
N. A. Foster, 11-76, Essex v Surrey, Chelmsford; M. Frost, 10-82, Glam. v Glos., Bristol.
D. A. Graveney, 10-104, Glos. v Sussex, Bristol.
C. C. Lewis, 10-119, Leics. v Glam., Cardiff.
M. M. Patel, 10-148, Kent v Leics., Dartford; R. A. Pick, 10-184, Notts. v Leics., Leicester.
C. A. Walsh, 11-99, Glos. v Northants, Cheltenham.
Waqar Younis, 11-128, Surrey v Warwicks., The Oval.

COUNTY BENEFITS AWARDED IN 1991

Essex	D. E. East.	Middlesex	S. P. Hughes.
Glamorgan	G. C. Holmes.	Nottinghamshire	B. N. French.
Gloucestershire	P. W. Romaines.	Surrey	M. A. Lynch.
Hampshire	M. C. J. Nicholas.	Sussex	A. C. S. Pigott.
Kent	M. R. Benson.	Yorkshire	K. Sharp.
Lancashire	G. Fowler.		

  *No benefit was awarded by Derbyshire, Leicestershire, Northamptonshire, Somerset, Warwick-
shire or Worcestershire.*

THE CRICKET COUNCIL

The Cricket Council, which was set up in 1968 and reconstituted in 1974 and 1983, acts as the governing body for cricket in the British Isles. It comprises the following, the officers listed being those for 1989-90.

Chairman: R. Subba Row.
Vice-Chairman: J. D. Robson.
8 Representatives of the Test and County Cricket Board: R. Subba Row, C. R. M. Atkinson, D. J. Insole, F. G. Mann, M. P. Murray, D. N. Perry, H. J. Pocock, F. M. Turner.
5 Representatives of the National Cricket Association: J. D. Robson, F. R. Brown, F. H. Elliott, E. K. Ingman, J. G. Overy.
3 Representatives of the Marylebone Cricket Club: G. H. G. Doggart, N. E. J. Pocock, Sir Denys Roberts.
1 Representative (non-voting) of the Minor Counties Cricket Association: G. L. B. August.
1 Representative (non-voting) of the Irish Cricket Union: D. Scott.
1 Representative (non-voting) of the Scottish Cricket Union: R. W. Barclay.

Secretary: A. C. Smith.

THE TEST AND COUNTY CRICKET BOARD

The TCCB was set up in 1968 to be responsible for Test matches, official tours, and first-class and minor county competitions. It is composed of representatives of the seventeen first-class counties; Marylebone Cricket Club; Minor Counties Cricket Association; Oxford University Cricket Club, Cambridge University Cricket Club, the Irish Cricket Union and the Scottish Cricket Union.

Officers 1989-90

Chairman: R. Subba Row.

Chairmen of Committees: R. Subba Row (Executive); D. B. Carr (County Pitches); O. S. Wheatley (Cricket); D. J. Insole (Overseas Tours); P. R. Bromage (Discipline); M. P. Murray (Finance); C. R. M. Atkinson (PR and Marketing); D. R. W. Silk (Registration); E. R. Dexter (England Committee); A. C. Smith (Umpires); Revd M. D. Vockins (Under-25 and Second XI Competitions).

Chief Executive: A. C. Smith. *Cricket Secretary:* T. M. Lamb. *Assistant Secretary (Administration):* A. S. Brown. *Accountant:* C. A. Barker. *England Tour Manager:* P. M. Lush. *England Team Manager:* M. J. Stewart. *Media Relations Manager:* P. W. Smith.

THE NATIONAL CRICKET ASSOCIATION

With the setting up of the Cricket Council in 1968 it was necessary to form a separate organisation to represent the interests of all cricket below the first-class game, and it is the National Cricket Association that carries out this function. It comprises representatives from 51 county cricket associations and seventeen national cricketing organisations.

Officers 1989-90

President: F. R. Brown.
Chairman: J. D. Robson.
Vice-Chairman: F. H. Elliott.

Chief Executive: K. V. Andrew.
General Secretary: B. J. Aspital.
Hon. Treasurer: D. W. Carter.

THE NEW ZEALANDERS IN ENGLAND, 1990

New Zealand arrived for their twelfth tour of England with realistic hopes of winning their second successive Test series there. When they left, having lost the three-match series 1-0, there was a distinct feeling among their supporters that the side had played below their potential. Certainly, through no particular fault, the tour fell somewhat flat. In a summer as memorable for high temperatures as high scores, it was blighted at crucial stages by poor weather, and the succeeding tour by India, with its dazzling batting, did the New Zealanders no favours in comparison. Moreover, they came up against an England side with a significantly stiffer backbone than that of a year earlier.

The touring team, spearheaded by their amiable captain, John Wright, and their greatest player, Richard Hadlee, was one of considerable talent and vast experience, with, in addition to their traditional doughty fighters, a clutch of players selected with an eye to the future. Although losing the one-day fixture against MCC, they made a promising start. Inspired perhaps by an enterprising sponsorship of the eight three-day matches against the counties, their cricket was entertaining, even if at times it was, through necessity, contrived at the business end.

However, there was a school of thought which, with the benefit of hindsight, held that the emphasis of the tour should have changed once the tourists were no longer eligible for the Tetley Challenge bonus for winning all the county matches. At least one senior player believed that, rather than continuing to play positive, spectator-pleasing cricket, the New Zealanders should have approached the remaining county games with the Test matches in mind. If that meant batting for the first day and a half of a three-day match, it was suggested, then so be it.

By the final Test, at Edgbaston early in July, the touring team had had wins over Worcestershire – on the liveliest pitch of the tour – Somerset, Sussex and Derbyshire, and had drawn with England twice, Middlesex, Warwickshire, Northamptonshire and Essex. Their one first-class defeat had been to the combined Oxford & Cambridge Universities – whose first win it was over a touring side – and they had shared the two-match one-day series, though failing on run-rate to win the Texaco Trophy. It was suggested by Wright that the success of the tour would be judged by the result of the final Test, for the Test matches are history's criteria. In the event England won, deservedly, by 114 runs after the New Zealand captain had erred badly by putting them in.

The Birmingham Test brought down the curtain on Hadlee's remarkable career. With his impeccable sense of occasion, he took his 431st and final wicket with his last ball in a Test. Although past his finest days, he showed he could still severely embarrass the world's top batsmen. Before the Lord's Test Hadlee had been awarded a knighthood for his services to the game, the first New Zealander so honoured, and if there was criticism of the timing of the announcement, there was precious little doubt about the worthiness of the recipient. Hadlee's knighthood also made the Lord's Test scorecard a unique modern-day sporting document.

Before the tour began, it was felt that run-scoring would not be a problem, but bowling out the opposition would. That suspicion was well founded, especially when the Test and County Cricket Board's edicts on the summer's pitches and the ball's seam were added to the equation. The New Zealanders simply did not have sufficient penetration. Even Sussex, destined to finish last in the 1990 County Championship, managed 570 runs against them for the loss of only six wickets. The most successful bowler was the experienced off-spinner, John Bracewell, who was making his third tour of England. He missed eight matches with a finger injury at the start but, always competitive, he finished with 34 first-class wickets, having, despite his absences, bowled the most overs. His four dismissals in the second innings at Birmingham gave him 102 Test wickets and, after he had passed 1,000 Test runs in the first innings, made him only the second New Zealander, after Hadlee, to complete such a double. By then he had also proved himself to be the world's best attacking off-spinner.

Martin Snedden, another to retire from international cricket at the end of the visit, bowled his nagging medium pace as well as ever for much of the tour. But the sustained aggression expected from Danny Morrison was seen all too infrequently. Nor did injuries help. Chris Pringle and the former Test player, Willie Watson, both just above medium pace, were called into the side from the Bradford and Northern Leagues respectively to cover during a time when the tour party had just one fit fast bowler, the gangling Jonathan Millmow. Misfortune eventually caught up with him at Northampton, with shin splints ending his first senior tour.

Although all the batsmen had their moments, only the tall opener, Trevor Franklin, was able to look back with any real satisfaction. Unspectacular but effective, he arrived in England as a batsman still trying to establish a regular Test place. He finished the tour having topped the Test and first-class aggregates, and only the England opening pair, Graham Gooch and Michael Atherton, bettered his average of 56.75 in the Tests. With Wright he set a New Zealand first-wicket record for Tests in England, putting on 185 at Lord's, and he went on to his maiden Test hundred. Wright, however, fell 2 runs short of his eleventh Test century, a personal disappointment on his final overseas tour. He scored fewer runs than he would have liked, but he proved himself to be perhaps New Zealand's most popular captain ever, even if his Test leadership tended towards a safety-first approach.

New Zealand's premier batsman, Martin Crowe, had a disappointing tour. Runmaking appeared to come all too easily in the county matches, but he passed 50 only once in the Tests. Mark Greatbatch's centuries in the one-day internationals, innings of clean, powerful strokeplay, were probably the finest of the tour. However, impetuosity was his downfall more than once, and he did not really do himself justice. Nor did Andrew Jones, another of whom much was expected. Jones did as well as anyone against the counties, but England found a technical weakness against the short ball and capitalised on it in the Tests. Ken Rutherford did not recover fully from a nasty blow above the left eyebrow in the second one-day international, while Jeff Crowe was always battling for a Test place.

Of the younger players, none did better than the wicket-keeper, Adam Parore, and the left-arm spinner, Mark Priest. Parore, aged nineteen, made his Test début at Edgbaston when injury ruled out the experienced Ian Smith, and although showing that some fine tuning of his glovework was needed, he revealed that he was a technically sound batsman of whom much more should be heard. Priest worked hard at his game, played in one Test and should have had a second chance. He struggled for wickets but fielded well and performed tidily with the bat. – David Leggat.

NEW ZEALAND TOUR RESULTS

Test matches – Played 3: Lost 1, Drawn 2.
First-class matches – Played 12: Won 4, Lost 2, Drawn 6.
Wins – Derbyshire, Somerset, Sussex, Worcestershire.
Losses – England, Oxford & Cambridge Universities.
Draws – England (2), Essex, Middlesex, Northamptonshire, Warwickshire.
One-day internationals – Played 2: Won 1, Lost 1.
Other non first-class matches – Played 5: Won 3, Lost 2. *Wins* – Ireland (2), Lavinia Duchess of Norfolk's XI. *Losses* – Leicestershire, MCC.

TEST MATCH AVERAGES

ENGLAND – BATTING

	T	I	NO	R	HI	100s	Avge
M. A. Atherton	3	5	0	357	151	1	71.40
G. A. Gooch	3	5	0	306	154	1	61.20
G. C. Small	3	4	2	84	44*	0	42.00
A. J. Lamb	3	5	1	129	84*	0	32.25
R. A. Smith	3	5	0	152	64	0	30.40
A. J. Stewart	3	5	0	147	54	0	29.40
P. A. J. DeFreitas	2	2	0	52	38	0	26.00
R. C. Russell	3	4	0	84	43	0	21.00
N. H. Fairbrother	3	5	1	59	33*	0	14.75
E. E. Hemmings	3	4	0	33	20	0	11.00
D. E. Malcolm	3	4	2	4	4*	0	2.00

Played in one Test: C. C. Lewis 32, 1.

* *Signifies not out.*

BOWLING

	O	M	R	W	BB	5W/i	Avge
D. E. Malcolm	118.4	38	269	15	5-46	2	17.93
E. E. Hemmings	107.3	44	215	10	6-58	1	21.50
P. A. J. DeFreitas	59.4	9	175	6	5-53	1	29.16
G. C. Small	104	27	290	5	2-49	0	58.00

Also bowled: M. A. Atherton 10-6-17-0; G. A. Gooch 13-7-25-0; C. C. Lewis 41-8-127-4.

NEW ZEALAND – BATTING

	T	I	NO	R	HI	100s	Avge
T. J. Franklin	3	5	1	227	101	1	56.75
J. G. Wright	3	5	0	177	98	0	35.40
I. D. S. Smith	2	2	1	29	27	0	29.00
M. J. Greatbatch	3	4	0	115	47	0	28.75
A. H. Jones	3	5	0	143	49	0	28.60
Sir R. J. Hadlee	3	4	0	107	86	0	26.75
M. D. Crowe	3	4	0	96	59	0	24.00
M. C. Snedden	3	4	2	36	21*	0	18.00
K. R. Rutherford	2	3	0	47	29	0	15.66
J. G. Bracewell	3	4	0	57	28	0	14.25
D. K. Morrison	3	5	2	9	6	0	3.00

Played in one Test: A. C. Parore 12*, 20; M. W. Priest 26.

* *Signifies not out.*

BOWLING

	O	M	R	W	BB	5W/i	Avge
r R. J. Hadlee	133.5	24	384	16	5-53	1	24.00
G. Bracewell	148	41	400	12	4-38	0	33.33
. C. Snedden	101	30	264	6	3-106	0	44.00
. K. Morrison	85.4	15	351	7	4-64	0	50.14

Also bowled: A. H. Jones 13–3–42–1; M. W. Priest 12–4–26–1; K. R. Rutherford 3–0–18–0.

NEW ZEALAND AVERAGES – FIRST-CLASS MATCHES

BATTING

	M	I	NO	R	HI	100s	Avge
. D. Crowe	9	13	3	537	123*	1	53.70
. H. Jones	10	16	3	692	121*	1	53.23
G. Wright	9	15	2	653	121	1	50.23
. R. Rutherford	8	13	5	376	68*	0	47.00
. J. Franklin	11	17	1	731	103	2	45.68
J. Crowe	8	15	4	493	132	1	44.81
. W. Priest	9	11	3	345	72	0	43.12
. J. Greatbatch	10	14	1	448	85	0	34.46
r R. J. Hadlee	5	6	0	204	90	0	34.00
G. Bracewell	8	8	3	169	40*	0	33.80
A. Thomson	5	5	4	32	20	0	32.00
. C. Parore	7	6	1	131	43	0	26.20
D. S. Smith	6	4	1	65	34	0	21.66
. C. Snedden	7	6	3	38	21*	0	12.66
. Pringle	4	1	0	6	6	0	6.00
. K. Morrison	9	6	2	14	6	0	3.50

Played in five matches: J. P. Millmow 2*. Played in two matches: W. Watson 17*.

* Signifies not out.

BOWLING

	O	M	R	W	BB	5W/i	Avge
ir R. J. Hadlee	201.5	39	586	24	5-27	2	24.41
. C. Snedden	231.5	56	633	23	5-63	1	27.52
. G. Bracewell	383.3	102	1,120	34	7-120	2	32.94
. P. Millmow	105	14	391	11	3-66	0	35.54
). K. Morrison	234.4	36	889	21	4-64	0	42.33
. Pringle	130	31	398	8	2-67	0	49.75
. W. Priest	312.4	90	907	14	3-35	0	64.78
. A. Thomson	106.2	18	435	5	2-84	0	87.00

Also bowled: M. D. Crowe 8–3–20–0; A. H. Jones 26–4–87–3; K. R. Rutherford 2–3–196–0; W. Watson 54–10–177–3.

FIELDING

5 – A. C. Parore (14 ct, 1 st); 7 – K. R. Rutherford; 6 – J. J. Crowe, M. W. Priest; 5 – J. G. Bracewell, M. D. Crowe, M. J. Greatbatch, I. D. S. Smith, S. A. Thomson; 4 – Sir R. J. Hadlee; 3 – T. J. Franklin, A. H. Jones, D. K. Morrison, M. C. Snedden, Substitutes; 2 – J. P. Millmow, C. Pringle, J. G. Wright.

HUNDREDS FOR NEW ZEALANDERS

The following eight three-figure innings were played for the New Zealanders, six in first-class matches and two in non first-class matches.

T. J. Franklin (2)
   103 v Somerset, Taunton
   101 v England, Lord's (Second Test)

M. J. Greatbatch (2)
   †102* v England, Leeds (First Texaco Trophy)
   †111 v England, The Oval (Second Texaco Trophy)

J. J. Crowe (1)
   132 v Oxford & Cambridge Univs, Cambridge

M. D. Crowe (1)
   123* v Essex, Chelmsford

A. H. Jones (1)
   121* v Derbys., Derby

J. G. Wright (1)
   121 v Essex, Chelmsford

   * Signifies not out.   † *Not first-class.*

Note: Those matches which follow which were not first-class are signified by the use of dagger.

†LAVINIA, DUCHESS OF NORFOLK'S XI v NEW ZEALANDERS

At Arundel, May 6. New Zealanders won by seven wickets. Toss: Lavinia, Duchess of Norfolk's XI. A crowd of 8,000 saw acting-captain Martin Crowe and Rutherford run up 96 in ten overs to win the tourists' opening fixture with nearly three overs to spare. Crowe's 89 not out came from 58 deliveries, and included two sixes and ten fours, six of them in the last sixteen balls, which brought him 39 runs. Earlier his brother, Jeff, and Franklin had given the team a solid start with 81 from 19 overs for the first wicket, Franklin hitting powerfully for his 82. The highlight of the invitation team's innings was Dodemaide's century. Sussex's Australian all-rounder took 143 balls to make 131, and put on 180 with Parker, his county captain, against an attack which was missing Hadlee.

Lavinia, Duchess of Norfolk's XI

I. J. F. Hutchinson b Priest 19	†I. J. Gould not out . . . .
A. I. C. Dodemaide c sub b Snedden . . 131	
*P. W. G. Parker c Priest b Millmow . 90	L-b 16, w 1, n-b 1 1
A. P. Wells c M. D. Crowe b Millmow. 16	
M. P. Speight lbw b Snedden 0	1/59 2/239 3/262 (6 wkts, 50 overs) 27
C. M. Wells run out 2	4/263 5/274 6/277

V. J. Marks, J. K. Lever, A. R. Hansford and J. Boiling did not bat.

Bowling: Millmow 10-2-55-2; Thomson 10-2-58-0; Priest 10-1-42-1; Snedden 10-1-42-2; Bracewell 9-0-57-0; Rutherford 1-0-7-0.

New Zealanders

J. J. Crowe b Hansford 43	K. R. Rutherford not out 3
T. J. Franklin b Lever 82	B 1, l-b 11 1
M. J. Greatbatch c Hansford b Boiling . 20	
*M. D. Crowe not out 89	1/81 2/114 3/182 (3 wkts, 47.2 overs) 27

S. A. Thomson, M. W. Priest, J. G. Bracewell, †A. C. Parore, M. C. Snedden and J. P. Millmow did not bat.

Bowling: Lever 9-1-48-1; C. M. Wells 10-1-39-0; Marks 10-0-63-0; Boiling 9-0-57-1; Hansford 9-0-58-1; Parker 0.2-0-1-0.

Umpires: C. Cook and J. G. Langridge.

†MCC v NEW ZEALANDERS

At Lord's, May 7. MCC won by six wickets. Toss: MCC. Gower's fluent 97 in 104 balls provided handsome entertainment for a good Bank Holiday crowd, whose appetite had earlier been whetted by the powerful strokeplay of Greatbatch and enjoyable cameos from Jones and Martin Crowe. The former Essex and England left-armer, Lever, playing in his second match against the tourists, had accounted for the elder Crowe with a breathtaking caught and bowled, low and to his right, in the opening overs. Gower, captaining an MCC side made up otherwise of players from Gloucestershire, Hampshire and Middlesex, drove his first ball to the cover boundary and, helped by 17 runs in one over from Morrison, went to 52 off 47 balls with the fifth of his eleven fours. He also hit two sixes. Brown, who added 109 with Gower, reached his fifty from 70 balls and stayed to see MCC to victory with four overs in hand. For the New Zealanders, Snedden bowled well and Parore's wicket-keeping again made a good impression.

Man of the Match: K. R. Brown.

New Zealanders

T. J. Franklin c Tufnell b Tremlett	29	†A. C. Parore run out	6
M. J. Crowe c and b Lever	1	M. C. Snedden not out	8
A. H. Jones st Parks b Bainbridge	49	B 1, l-b 2, w 15	18
M. J. Greatbatch c Wright b Jarvis	52		
S. A. Thomson b Bainbridge	5	1/8 2/44 3/129 (8 wkts, 55 overs) 222	
†M. D. Crowe c Parks b Tremlett	26	4/153 5/164 6/178	
M. W. Priest c Bainbridge b Jarvis	28	7/206 8/222	

D. K. Morrison and J. P. Millmow did not bat.

Bowling: Jarvis 11–1–49–2; Lever 11–1–45–1; Tufnell 11–1–42–0; Tremlett 11–0–50–2; Bainbridge 11–1–33–2.

MCC

V. P. Terry b Millmow	4	P. Bainbridge not out	19
A. J. Wright c Parore b Snedden	8		
D. I. Gower c Parore b Snedden	97	B 4, l-b 3, w 4	11
M. R. Ramprakash c M. D. Crowe b Snedden	6		
K. R. Brown not out	79	1/8 2/46 3/62 (4 wkts, 50.5 overs) 224	
		4/171	

P. M. Tremlett, †R. J. Parks, J. K. Lever, P. C. R. Tufnell and K. B. S. Jarvis did not bat.

Bowling: Morrison 5–1–33–0; Millmow 10–0–43–1; Snedden 10–3–28–3; Thomson 9.5–1–40–0; Priest 11–0–40–0; Jones 5–0–33–0.

Umpires: J. D. Bond and R. Julian.

†IRELAND v NEW ZEALANDERS

At Downpatrick, May 9. New Zealanders won by seven wickets. Toss: New Zealanders. The first New Zealand touring team to visit Ireland since 1965, when a first-class match was played in Belfast, had no difficulty winning the first of two one-day matches sponsored by Gilbey's Ulster Games. Only Lamba, the Indian Test cricketer, playing his first game as Ireland's professional, really came to terms with the New Zealanders' bowling, adding 69 for the third wicket with Warke. Wright, in his first game of the tour, set the New Zealanders on their way with a brisk 49 in an opening stand of 71, and Crowe hit three sixes and a four in a rapid 48 before the visitors won with eighteen overs to spare.

Ireland

M. F. Cohen c Hadlee b Millmow	8	*†P. B. Jackson b Hadlee	6
R. Lamba c Smith b Hadlee	52	P. McCrum not out	1
M. A. F. Nulty c Franklin b Millmow	1	P. O'Reilly not out	1
S. J. S. Warke c Smith b Hadlee	23	B 2, l-b 8, w 4, n-b 9	23
G. D. Harrison lbw b Millmow	6		
D. A. Lewis b Snedden	19	1/25 2/30 3/99 (9 wkts, 55 overs) 151	
S. J. T. Patterson run out	9	4/100 5/120 6/138	
N. E. Thompson b Snedden	2	7/138 8/149 9/149	

Bowling: Hadlee 11–1–25–3; Millmow 11–1–28–3; Snedden 11–1–27–2; Thomso
11–3–30–0; Priest 11–1–31–0.

New Zealanders

T. J. Franklin c O'Reilly b Thompson . 26	S. A. Thomson not out . . . .
*J. G. Wright run out 49	L-b 3, w 8, n-b 4 I
M. D. Crowe c Jackson b McCrum . . . 48	
K. R. Rutherford not out 13	1/71 2/89 3/150 (3 wkts, 36.3 overs) 15

A. H. Jones, R. J. Hadlee, †I. D. S. Smith, M. W. Priest, M. C. Snedden and J. P. Millmov
did not bat.

Bowling: McCrum 7.3–2–26–1; O'Reilly 4–0–22–0; Thompson 7–0–23–1; Harriso
11–3–42–0; Lamba 6–1–27–0; Lewis 1–0–9–0.

Umpires: L. Hogan and M. Moore.

†IRELAND v NEW ZEALANDERS

At Ormeau, Belfast, May 10. New Zealanders won by 40 runs. Toss: Ireland. Althoug
Ireland's bowlers, off-spinner Harrison in particular, did well to hold the New Zealanders
203, their batsmen quickly fell behind the asking-rate on a slow pitch of low bounce onc
Hadlee had removed Cohen and Nulty in his first three overs. Water had seeped under th
covers at one end, and Hadlee was a distinctly unpleasant prospect for the Irish so soon i
their season.

New Zealanders

*J. G. Wright c Thompson b Harrison . 44	M. W. Priest not out I
J. J. Crowe st Jackson b Harrison 19	†A. C. Parore not out . . . .
A. H. Jones b Thompson 32	B 1, l-b 4, w 2, n-b 6 I
M. J. Greatbatch b O'Reilly 32	
K. R. Rutherford c Lamba b O'Reilly . . 2	1/61 2/72 3/135 (7 wkts, 50 overs) 2C
R. J. Hadlee b McCrum 20	4/139 5/142
I. D. S. Smith c Patterson b Lamba . . . 19	6/173 7/191

M. C. Snedden and D. K. Morrison did not bat.

Bowling: McCrum 10–0–42–1; Lamba 10–1–40–1; Harrison 10–2–25–2; O'Reill
10–0–56–2; Thompson 10–0–35–1.

Ireland

M. F. Cohen b Hadlee 2	*†P. B. Jackson st Parore b Smith I
R. Lamba c Hadlee b Snedden 5	P. McCrum not out . . . .
M. A. F. Nulty lbw b Hadlee 6	P. O'Reilly not out . . . .
S. J. S. Warke run out 44	B 9, l-b 2, w 1 I
G. D. Harrison c Hadlee b Priest 17	
D. A. Lewis c Crowe b Rutherford . . . 18	1/2 2/12 3/20 (9 wkts, 50 overs) 1€
T. J. T. Patterson b Rutherford 23	4/57 5/104 6/104
N. E. Thompson b Rutherford 8	7/112 8/143 9/160

Bowling: Hadlee 6–2–13–2; Morrison 8–1–20–0; Snedden 5–2–4–1; Priest 10–1–39–
Rutherford 10–1–38–3; Jones 8–1–27–0; Smith 2–0–8–1; Greatbatch 1–0–3–0.

Umpires: B. Arlow and H. Henderson.

WORCESTERSHIRE v NEW ZEALANDERS

At Worcester, May 12, 13, 14. New Zealanders won by six wickets. Toss: New Zealanders.
game of fluctuating fortunes finally swung the tourists' way through a captain's innings fro
Wright, who was only 1 run short of a century when he stepped back on his wicket. Set 245

in from a minimum of 81 overs, the New Zealanders achieved the target with 7.1 overs to [sp]are. The injury-hit county champions, without Botham, Curtis, Dilley and Rhodes, were [fu]rther handicapped by the early loss of Hick, when the index finger of his left hand was [br]oken by a rising delivery from Morrison. Yet a magnificent all-round performance from [N]ewport gave them a scent of victory. His five for 18 in 14.2 immaculate overs left the tourists [in] dire straits at 113 for eight at the end of the first day, after Hadlee, with five for 27, had [ca]rried Worcestershire out for 171. Next morning, however, Hadlee added 67 out of 74 runs [of] the bat to engineer a lead of 30. The New Zealanders strengthened their position by [re]ducing Worcestershire to 59 for four – effectively five without Hick – only to meet resistance [fr]om Newport and Illingworth, who added 179 in 50 overs. Newport was just 2 runs short of a [m]aiden century when his career-best innings, laced with eighteen fours, came to an end after [24]0 minutes. Wright and Franklin then provided the platform for victory with an opening [st]and of 163, broken when Franklin, for the second time in the match, was caught at slip off [M]cEwan by S. Herzberg, one of several substitute fielders.

Close of play: First day, New Zealanders 113-8 (R. J. Hadlee 23*); Second day, [W]orcestershire 248-7 (S. R. Lampitt 5*, S. R. Bevins 1*).

[W]orcestershire

Bent b Morrison	22	– lbw b Hadlee	9
[T]. J. Weston c Rutherford b Hadlee	3	– c Priest b Morrison	7
[G]. A. Hick retired hurt	2	– absent injured	
[G]. B. D'Oliveira c Greatbatch b Hadlee	48	– (3) c Morrison b Hadlee	24
[P]. A. Neale b Millmow	5	– (4) lbw b Millmow	15
[S.] R. Lampitt b Hadlee	40	– (7) b Millmow	30
[R.] K. Illingworth c Rutherford b Hadlee	0	– (5) c Crowe b Morrison	74
[P.] J. Newport c Greatbatch b Morrison	7	– (6) c Rutherford b Priest	98
[N.] V. Radford c Priest b Millmow	13	– (8) c and b Morrison	1
[S.] R. Bevins lbw b Hadlee	10	– (9) lbw b Millmow	1
[C.] M. McEwan not out	1	– (10) not out	0
L-b 12, w 1, n-b 7	20	B 1, l-b 8, n-b 6	15
	171		**274**

1/1 2/46 3/90 4/102 5/102 6/109 7/133 8/170 9/171

1/9 2/21 3/55 4/59 5/238 6/238 7/241 8/269 9/274

the first innings G. A. Hick retired hurt at 23.

Bowling: First Innings—Hadlee 15-7-27-5; Morrison 20-5-46-2; Millmow 16-2-59-2; [R]utherford 8-2-25-0; Priest 2-1-2-0. *Second Innings*—Morrison 16-2-60-3; Hadlee [1]4-3-72-2; Millmow 20.2-3-66-3; Priest 22-7-40-1; Rutherford 7-0-27-0.

[N]ew Zealanders

[T.] J. Franklin c sub b McEwan	28	– c sub b McEwan	50
[J.] G. Wright lbw b Newport	8	– hit wkt b Illingworth	99
[A.] H. Jones c Bevins b Newport	1	– c Radford b Illingworth	9
[M.] J. Greatbatch c sub b Newport	1	– c Radford b Illingworth	19
[K.] R. Rutherford lbw b Weston	4	– not out	26
[M.] J. Crowe c Bevins b McEwan	13		
[M.] W. Priest c sub b McEwan	13	– (6) not out	16
[R.] J. Hadlee c Bevins b McEwan	90		
[I.] D. S. Smith c sub b Newport	2		
[J.] K. Morrison lbw b Newport	5		
[G.] P. Millmow not out	2		
B 8, l-b 12, w 10, n-b 4	34	B 4, l-b 15, w 4, n-b 3	26
	201		**(4 wkts) 245**

1/16 2/20 3/25 4/29 5/68 6/69 7/111 8/113 9/152

1/163 2/172 3/196 4/203

Bowling: First Innings—Newport 26-8-54-6; McEwan 16.3-2-49-3; Weston 7-1-32-1; [Illin]gworth 12-6-13-0; Radford 10-1-33-0. *Second Innings*—Radford 13-3-47-0; McEwan [1]5-3-69-1; Newport 19-4-56-0; Illingworth 17-5-35-3; Weston 7-1-19-0.

Umpires: J. H. Hampshire and B. J. Meyer.

SOMERSET v NEW ZEALANDERS

At Taunton, May 16, 17, 18. New Zealanders won by five wickets. Toss: Somerset. The ba[t]
dominated after Somerset's faltering start. From being 70 for three, they recovered thanks t[o]
centuries from Tavaré, whose 156 took 217 balls and included 28 fours, and Harden. Togethe[r]
they put on 256 in 62 overs, and Somerset were able to declare in time to snatch a wicke[t]
before the close. Franklin, who needed 219 balls for his 103 (thirteen fours), and night
watchman Parore responded with a second-wicket stand of 113 in 43 overs, and when Jone[s]
and Martin Crowe had added half-centuries the New Zealanders declared 65 runs behind
Again Somerset lost their first three wickets quickly, but Cook stayed for a hundred that too[k]
him to 567 first-class runs for the season to date; Burns and Rose provided the support, th[e]
latter hitting three sixes and six fours in 59 from 63 balls. Another declaration left the Ne[w]
Zealanders needing 322 from 65 overs. Runs came crisply throughout their effort, with the
highlights and impetus supplied by Martin Crowe's fifty and Greatbatch, whose 85 from 8[1]
balls featured six fours and two sixes, one into the River Tone. After them, the stead[y]
Rutherford saw the tourists home with three balls to spare.

Close of play: First day, New Zealanders 22-1 (T. J. Franklin 11*, A. C. Parore 1*); Secon[d]
day, Somerset 113-3 (S. J. Cook 51*, N. D. Burns 43*).

Somerset

S. J. Cook c Parore b Thomson	31	– not out 117
P. M. Roebuck lbw b Snedden	17	– lbw b Snedden 6
J. J. E. Hardy c Parore b Snedden	13	– c Parore b Millmow 5
*C. J. Tavaré b Snedden	156	
R. J. Harden c Millmow b Priest	104	
†N. D. Burns c Parore b Snedden	1	– (5) c J. J. Crowe b Priest 59
A. N. Hayhurst not out	3	– (4) run out 2
G. D. Rose not out	12	– (6) not out 59
L-b 5, n-b 1	6	L-b 6, n-b 2 8

1/44 2/48 3/70 4/326   (6 wkts dec.) 343   1/23 2/34 3/48   (4 wkts dec.) 256
5/328 6/329   4/148

I. G. Swallow, J. C. Hallett and A. N. Jones did not bat.

Bowling: *First Innings*—Millmow 16–4–55–0; Snedden 30–7–79–4; Thomson 17–2–104–1
Priest 27–8–79–1; Rutherford 3–0–13–0; Jones 2–0–8–0. *Second Innings*—Millmow 8–1–35–1
Snedden 18–3–49–1; Rutherford 10–1–62–0; Priest 28.3–11–80–1; Jones 4–0–8–0; M. D[.]
Crowe 5–1–16–0.

New Zealanders

T. J. Franklin lbw b Swallow	103	– (2) lbw b Hallett 30
J. J. Crowe c and b Jones	0	– (1) c Hardy b Hallett 30
†A. C. Parore c Jones b Swallow	43	
A. H. Jones not out	57	– (3) c Tavaré b Roebuck 53
*M. D. Crowe not out	55	– (4) b Jones 64
M. J. Greatbatch (did not bat)		– (5) b Rose 85
K. R. Rutherford (did not bat)		– (6) not out 46
S. A. Thomson (did not bat)		– (7) not out 4
B 9, l-b 9, w 1, n-b 1	20	B 4, l-b 4, w 1, n-b 1 10

1/9 2/122 3/201   (3 wkts dec.) 278   1/57 2/64 3/174   (5 wkts) 322
                                                4/201 5/312

M. W. Priest, M. C. Snedden and J. P. Millmow did not bat.

Bowling: *First Innings*—Jones 9–2–20–1; Rose 16–4–33–0; Hayhurst 17–3–55–0; Hallet[t]
14–2–52–0; Swallow 19–5–52–2; Roebuck 11–3–26–0; Harden 3–0–22–0. *Second Innings*—
Jones 8–1–28–1; Rose 11–0–74–1; Hayhurst 13–1–58–0; Swallow 15–0–68–0; Hallet[t]
11.3–0–51–2; Roebuck 6–0–35–1.

Umpires: D. J. Constant and D. R. Shepherd.

MIDDLESEX v NEW ZEALANDERS

At Lord's, May 19, 20, 21. Drawn. Toss: Middlesex. Haynes, continuing his prolific form, was the dominant figure on the first day, with 146 of his 181 runs resulting from boundaries; he took fourteen fours off Morrison and twelve off Priest. Hadlee was less hostile than usual, but the accurate Snedden sniped away at the other batsmen. Although Middlesex fielded an under-strength attack – Thursfield and Weekes were making their first-class débuts – the bowlers were not mastered until Rutherford and Priest shared a fluent stand of 114. In the second innings a more restrained Haynes hit two sixes and sixteen fours in his 129, his two hundreds for Middlesex against a touring team emulating P. H. Parfitt's feat in 1962 against the Pakistanis. Set a target of 300 in 51 overs, the New Zealanders were eager to keep alive their prospects of the bonus for winning all county games. Jones and Greatbatch added 103 from eighteen overs, but when Tufnell's four wickets put Middlesex in sight of victory, Martin Crowe, who had avoided batting because of hamstring trouble, was required to come in and secure the draw.

Close of play: First day, New Zealanders 13-0 (J. J. Crowe 8*, J. G. Wright 5*); Second day, Middlesex 64-1 (D. L. Haynes 25*, M. R. Ramprakash 36*).

Middlesex

D. L. Haynes lbw b Hadlee	181	– c and b Jones	129
M. A. Roseberry c Rutherford b Snedden	9	– c Hadlee b Morrison	0
M. R. Ramprakash c Hadlee b Snedden	21	– c Priest b Snedden	62
K. R. Brown lbw b Snedden	23	– not out	24
†O. Butcher lbw b Snedden	0	– not out	22
†P. R. Downton not out	57		
P. N. Weekes lbw b Snedden	22		
L-b 14, n-b 5	19	B 1, l-b 9, n-b 4	14

1/48 2/96 3/159 4/161   (6 wkts dec.) 332   1/4 2/143 3/226   (3 wkts dec.) 251
5/286 6/332

N. J. Thursfield, S. P. Hughes, N. G. Cowans and P. C. R. Tufnell did not bat.

Bowling: First Innings—Hadlee 22-3-78-1; Morrison 22-1-100-0; Snedden 27.5-7-63-5; Priest 22-7-77-0. *Second Innings*—Hadlee 11-2-25-0; Morrison 17-1-67-1; Priest 9-3-73-0; Jones 5-0-28-1; Snedden 8-2-22-1; Rutherford 6-0-26-0.

New Zealanders

J. J. Crowe c Downton b Cowans	14	– lbw b Cowans	20
J. G. Wright c Weekes b Hughes	54	– c Butcher b Thursfield	18
A. H. Jones lbw b Hughes	41	– run out	70
M. D. Crowe c Downton b Tufnell	13	– (9) not out	13
M. J. Greatbatch b Hughes	34	– (4) b Weekes	52
K. R. Rutherford not out	68	– (5) st Downton b Tufnell	2
M. W. Priest not out	51	– b Tufnell	19
†I. D. S. Smith (did not bat)		– (6) c Weekes b Tufnell	34
R. J. Hadlee (did not bat)		– (8) c Roseberry b Tufnell	7
M. C. Snedden (did not bat)		– not out	0
B 7, l-b 1, n-b 1	9	B 4, l-b 3, w 1	8

1/44 2/77 3/103 4/148 5/170   (5 wkts dec.) 284   1/34 2/40 3/143 4/150   (8 wkts) 243
5/173 6/213 7/223 8/242

D. K. Morrison did not bat.

Bowling: First Innings—Cowans 21-4-56-1; Hughes 23.2-6-87-3; Tufnell 20-5-64-1; Thursfield 16-7-41-0; Weekes 13-6-28-0. *Second Innings*—Cowans 6-0-25-1; Hughes 10-0-38-0; Thursfield 9-0-44-1; Tufnell 17-3-76-4; Weekes 13-3-53-1.

Umpires: J. C. Balderstone and N. T. Plews.

†ENGLAND v NEW ZEALAND

First Texaco Trophy Match

At Leeds, May 23. New Zealand won by four wickets. Toss: New Zealand. With Snedde
troubled by a stomach strain, the New Zealanders recruited Pringle from the Bradfor
League, and he it was who made the vital breakthrough, on the point of lunch, after Gooc
(88 balls) and Smith had put on 113 in 27 overs. Smith, dropped when 16 off a return catch t
Morrison, went on impressively to his first one-day hundred for England and had hit sixtee
fours in his 128 (168 balls) when he was fifth out. Stewart's 33 from 25 balls helped th
scoring-rate, and England's Pringle reached 30 from seventeen balls by hitting Hadlee's las
four deliveries to the boundary. Wright and Jones gave New Zealand a sound start, averagin
more than 4 an over while putting on 97, and when Gooch dismissed them both, Crowe an
the left-handed Greatbatch added 118 in twenty overs. With twelve overs remaining and eigh
wickets in hand the target was 72. But three wickets by Lewis and a brilliant catch by Gowe
at short mid-wicket left them needing 37 at approximately 9 runs an over. Smith, howeve
responded to the crisis ebulliently, and with Greatbatch saw his side to a dramatic wir
Greatbatch reached his first one-day international hundred in the final over, having hit tw
sixes and nine fours in 104 deliveries.

Man of the Match: M. J. Greatbatch.   *Attendance:* 12,000 (est.); *receipts* £179,007.

England

*G. A. Gooch c Millmow b Pringle ... 55	P. A. J. DeFreitas not out	
D. I. Gower c Priest b Hadlee 1		
R. A. Smith c Crowe b Hadlee 128	L-b 10, w 1, n-b 5 1	
A. J. Lamb run out 18	—	
A. J. Stewart lbw b Morrison 33	1/5 (2) 2/118 (1) (6 wkts, 55 overs) 29.	
D. R. Pringle not out 30	3/168 (4) 4/225 (5)	
†R. C. Russell c Crowe b Pringle 13	5/261 (3) 6/274 (7)	

C. C. Lewis, G. C. Small and E. E. Hemmings did not bat.

Bowling: Hadlee 11–4–46–2; Pringle 11–2–45–2; Morrison 11–0–70–1; Millmov
11–0–65–0; Priest 11–0–59–0.

New Zealand

*J. G. Wright c Stewart b Gooch 52	†I. D. S. Smith not out 1	
A. H. Jones st Russell b Gooch 51		
M. D. Crowe c Russell b Lewis 46	B 5, l-b 7, w 3, n-b 1 1	
M. J. Greatbatch not out 102	—	
K. R. Rutherford lbw b Lewis 0	1/97 (2) 2/106 (1) (6 wkts, 54.5 overs) 29.	
R. J. Hadlee c Lamb b Lewis 12	3/224 (3) 4/224 (5)	
M. W. Priest c Gower b Small 2	5/254 (6) 6/259 (7)	

C. Pringle, J. P. Millmow and D. K. Morrison did not bat.

Bowling: Small 11–1–43–1; DeFreitas 10.5–0–70–0; Pringle 7–0–45–0; Lewis 11–0–54–3
Hemmings 11–0–51–0; Gooch 4–0–23–2.

Umpires: B. J. Meyer and N. T. Plews.

†ENGLAND v NEW ZEALAND

Second Texaco Trophy Match

At The Oval, May 25. England won by six wickets. Toss: England. Some fine fast bowling b
Malcolm and Lewis, on a pitch providing pace and bounce, had New Zealand in all kinds c
trouble. Wright, Jones and Crowe were out with only 53 on the board, and they then los
Rutherford and Hadlee to injuries before the fourth wicket fell. Rutherford was hit above th
left eye, trying to hook Lewis early in his innings; Hadlee, struck on the right hand by Lewis

did not resume after lunch and X-rays revealed a broken bone below the knuckle. Greatbatch held the innings together, advancing defiantly to his second hundred of the series. Priest helped him add 81 and Smith 28 before Greatbatch sliced Malcolm to third man in the 54th over. His 111, from 130 balls, contained a six and ten fours. New Zealand's target hardly looked enough, but when Hadlee, despite his injured hand, removed Gower and Smith in a lovely opening spell, and Pringle trapped Lamb in the sixth over, England were themselves struggling. Gooch saw off the openers and then weathered a dangerous spell by Morrison. He lost Stewart straight after tea, having added 75 for the fourth wicket in 80 minutes, but Russell then joined him in a match-winning stand producing 109 runs in 97 minutes. Gooch hit fifteen fours in his 112 not out (152 balls), and ensured that England not only squared the series but, by winning with 5.3 overs to spare, took the Texaco Trophy on run-rate.

Man of the Match: D. E. Malcolm.   *Attendance:* 13,909; *receipts* £238,490.

Men of the Series: England – G. A. Gooch; New Zealand – M. J. Greatbatch.

New Zealand

*J. G. Wright c Small b Malcolm	15	†I. D. S. Smith not out	25
A. H. Jones run out	15	C. Pringle b Small	1
M. D. Crowe c Russell b Lewis	7	L-b 2, w 3	5
M. J. Greatbatch c Smith b Malcolm	111		
K. R. Rutherford retired hurt	0	(6 wkts, 55 overs)	212
R. J. Hadlee retired hurt	9		
M. W. Priest c Smith b DeFreitas	24		

1/25 (1) 2/34 (2) 3/53 (3) 4/174 (7) 5/202 (4) 6/212 (9)

J. P. Millmow and D. K. Morrison did not bat.

K. R. Rutherford retired hurt at 53; R. J. Hadlee retired hurt at 93.

Bowling: DeFreitas 11–1–47–1; Malcolm 11–5–19–2; Lewis 11–1–51–1; Small 11–0–59–1; Hemmings 11–2–34–0.

England

*G. A. Gooch not out	112	†R. C. Russell not out	47
D. I. Gower b Hadlee	4	L-b 7, w 5, n-b 1	13
R. A. Smith c Smith b Hadlee	5		
A. J. Lamb lbw b Pringle	4	(4 wkts, 49.3 overs)	213
A. J. Stewart c Morrison b Priest	28		

1/5 (2) 2/15 (3) 3/29 (4) 4/104 (5)

C. C. Lewis, P. A. J. DeFreitas, G. C. Small, E. E. Hemmings and D. E. Malcolm did not bat.

Bowling: Hadlee 11–2–34–2; Pringle 9.3–0–53–1; Millmow 9–1–47–0; Morrison 9–0–38–0; Priest 11–2–34–1.

Umpires: D. J. Constant and J. H. Hampshire.

SUSSEX v NEW ZEALANDERS

At Hove, May 26, 27, 28. New Zealanders won by seven wickets. Toss: Sussex. The New Zealanders won an entertaining game with fourteen balls to spare after their captain, Wright, had given them an ideal start with a fluent 82. He put on 147 with Franklin, who, having been stuck on 0 until the tenth over, eventually hit thirteen fours in his 78, and as the innings gained momentum, Jeff Crowe and Greatbatch provided belligerent half-centuries. Nevertheless Sussex, who had lost just six wickets in the match, emerged with great credit. Hall, whose previous four innings in County Championship cricket had all been in single figures, scored his maiden first-class hundred in just under six hours (322 balls), and in their second innings Dodemaide also made a maiden first-class century, his unbeaten 110 including fourteen fours and a six. Dodemaide added 188 in 49 overs with acting-captain Colin Wells, who reached 113 not out in 141 deliveries (four sixes, fourteen fours) before asking the tourists to score 341 from 71 overs.

Close of play: First day, New Zealanders 22-1 (J. J. Crowe 7*, M. W. Priest 15*); Second day, Sussex 144-2 (A. I. C. Dodemaide 52*, C. M. Wells 45*).

Sussex

N. J. Lenham b Morrison	64	– c Parore b Pringle	6
J. W. Hall not out	120	– run out	40
A. I. C. Dodemaide b Morrison	4	– not out	110
A. P. Wells c Parore b Thomson	86		
*C. M. Wells c Greatbatch b Pringle	8	– (4) not out	113
I. J. Gould not out	6		
B 1, l-b 5, w 1, n-b 5	12	L-b 1	1

1/99 2/103 3/269 4/294   (4 wkts dec.) 300   1/12 2/82   (2 wkts dec.) 270

†P. Moores, I. D. K. Salisbury, B. T. P. Donelan, R. A. Bunting and A. M. Babington did not bat.

Bowling: First Innings—Morrison 10-2-35-2; Pringle 19-3-66-1; Thomson 18.4-6-52-1; Bracewell 34.2-9-99-0; Priest 16-4-42-0. *Second Innings*—Pringle 25-5-61-1; M. D. Crowe 3-2-4-0; Bracewell 34-5-138-0; Priest 20-3-66-0.

New Zealanders

T. J. Franklin b Dodemaide	0	– b Bunting	78
J. J. Crowe b Salisbury	48	– (3) not out	81
M. W. Priest c Moores b Donelan	72		
M. J. Greatbatch c C. M. Wells b Bunting	26	– (5) not out	51
M. D. Crowe c Donelan b Babington	65	– (4) c Gould b Salisbury	24
*J. G. Wright not out	10	– (2) c C. M. Wells b Dodemaide	82
S. A. Thomson not out	3		
B 3, l-b 1, n-b 2	6	B 15, l-b 7, n-b 3	25

1/0 2/114 3/139 4/193 5/223   (5 wkts dec.) 230   1/147 2/204 3/268   (3 wkts) 341

J. G. Bracewell, †A. C. Parore, C. Pringle and D. K. Morrison did not bat.

Bowling: First Innings—Dodemaide 14-2-56-1; Bunting 14-3-42-1; C. M. Wells 5-1-22-0; Babington 9-0-36-1; Salisbury 16-2-55-1; Donelan 9-3-15-1. *Second Innings*—Dodemaide 19-6-57-1; Babington 11-0-54-0; C. M. Wells 3-0-20-0; Bunting 7-0-45-1; Salisbury 14-0-80-1; Donelan 14-0-62-0; Gould 0.4-0-1-0.

Umpires: B. Hassan and D. R. Shepherd.

WARWICKSHIRE v NEW ZEALANDERS

At Birmingham, May 30, 31, June 1. Drawn. Toss: New Zealanders. Rain on the third day put paid to the possibility of an interesting finish, after a fine hundred from Moody had enabled Warwickshire to leave the tourists a target of 326 in 73 overs. The Australian's batting in both innings showed his immense power off the front foot, and he hit three sixes and fifteen fours in his 106. There were also promising performances from Warwickshire's youngsters. Ratcliffe and Twose, the latter making his highest first-class score, gave both innings a good start; Booth hit his maiden first-class fifty from 59 balls, with ten fours; and Smith hurried to 41 in 36 balls as the county looked to their second declaration. The New Zealanders' bowling, with Pringle and Watson drafted in in the absence of Hadlee and Morrison, lacked penetration, but half-centuries on the second day from Wright, Jones and Martin Crowe (47 balls) underlined the strength of their batting.

Close of play: First day, New Zealanders 12-1 (J. G. Wright 6*, M. C. Snedden 2*); Second day, Warwickshire 141-2 (T. M. Moody 42*, G. W. Humpage 30*).

Warwickshire

J. D. Ratcliffe c J. J. Crowe b Watson	29	– c and b Bracewell 43
R. G. Twose c Pringle b Watson	64	– c Wright b Millmow 21
T. M. Moody c Jones b Snedden	44	– b Bracewell 106
A. I. Kallicharran c Smith b Millmow	3	
*†G. W. Humpage c Smith b Pringle	9	– (4) b Pringle 46
D. P. Ostler c and b Snedden	19	– (5) b Pringle 0
N. M. K. Smith c Franklin b Bracewell	24	– (6) c Pringle b Bracewell 41
P. A. Booth not out	51	
A. A. Donald not out	25	– (7) b Millmow 1
J. E. Benjamin (did not bat)		– (8) not out 3
T. A. Munton (did not bat)		– (9) b Bracewell 4
B 4, l-b 9, w 2, n-b 14	29	L-b 5, n-b 4 9

1/69 2/133 3/154 4/167 5/171   (7 wkts dec.) 297   1/52 2/93 3/186   (8 wkts dec.) 274
6/218 7/218   4/200 5/259 6/267
                                                            7/269 8/274

Bowling: *First Innings*—Millmow 18–2–64–1; Pringle 13–1–57–1; Snedden 24–3–69–2; Watson 22–6–67–2; Bracewell 17–5–27–1. *Second Innings*—Millmow 11–1–47–2; Pringle 15–3–67–2; Snedden 5–0–32–0; Bracewell 10.2–1–66–4; Watson 12–0–57–0.

New Zealanders

T. J. Franklin b Benjamin	2	
*J. G. Wright c sub b Twose	51	– not out 2
M. C. Snedden b Benjamin	2	
A. H. Jones b Benjamin	82	
M. D. Crowe c sub b Smith	52	
J. J. Crowe not out	9	– (1) not out 10
J. G. Bracewell not out	31	
B 3, l-b 6, w 6, n-b 2	17	W 3 3

1/7 2/25 3/109 4/203 5/207   (5 wkts dec.) 246   (no wkt) 15

†I. D. S. Smith, C. Pringle, W. Watson and J. P. Millmow did not bat.

Bowling: *First Innings*—Donald 13–3–24–0; Benjamin 18–4–45–3; Munton 15–3–33–0; Twose 14–6–44–1; Smith 24–8–63–1; Moody 3–0–28–0. *Second Innings*—Donald 2–0–9–0; Benjamin 1–0–2–0; Munton 2.4–0–3–0; Humpage 2–1–1–0.

Umpires: M. J. Kitchen and R. C. Tolchard.

DERBYSHIRE v NEW ZEALANDERS

At Derby, June 2, 3, 4. New Zealanders won by 82 runs. Toss: Derbyshire. Rain nearly ruined the match, although the captains were able to make something of it through declarations. There was little more than half an hour's play on the first day and none before lunch on the second, after which Jones dominated the New Zealanders' innings with an exciting 121 not out from 144 balls. Making great use of his bottom hand to place his cover drives, he hit fourteen fours, and was given lively support by Bracewell. Cork, making his first-class début, dismissed Franklin with his third ball, and the opener also became a first victim for Adams in the second innings. Derbyshire declared at their overnight total of 30 without loss and fed the tourists cheap runs before setting out to chase a target of 333 in 80 overs. Barnett was out to the first ball of the innings, and only Kuiper and Krikken diverted attention from Hadlee, practising in the nets, or threatened the New Zealanders, who won with all but two balls of the last twenty overs to spare.

Close of play: First day, New Zealanders 9-0 (T. J. Franklin 5*, J. J. Crowe 1*); Second day, Derbyshire 30-0 (K. J. Barnett 14*, P. D. Bowler 11*).

New Zealanders

T. J. Franklin c Bowler b Cork	19	– (2) c and b Adams	9
J. J. Crowe lbw b Jean-Jacques	1	– (1) c Morris b Roberts	47
A. H. Jones not out	121		
*M. D. Crowe c Krikken b Kuiper	32		
M. J. Greatbatch c and b Kuiper	3		
M. W. Priest c Bowler b Jean-Jacques	20	– (4) c Krikken b Cork	10
J. G. Bracewell not out	40	– (5) not out	3
†A. C. Parore (did not bat)		– (3) lbw b Jean-Jacques	37
L-b 11, w 1, n-b 4	16	L-b 2, w 1, n-b 1	4

1/11 2/55 3/123 4/132 5/191   (5 wkts dec.) 252   1/20 2/83 3/104   (4 wkts dec.) 110
4/110

M. C. Snedden, D. K. Morrison and J. P. Millmow did not bat.

Bowling: *First Innings*—Bishop 12–3–37–0; Malcolm 12–1–36–0; Jean-Jacques 14–2–67–2; Cork 14–2–49–1; Kuiper 10–2–52–2. *Second Innings*—Morris 7–0–47–0; Adams 6–1–20–1; Bowler 3–0–25–0; Roberts 3–0–10–1; Cork 1–0–4–1; Jean-Jacques 0.4–0–2–1.

Derbyshire

*K. J. Barnett not out	14	– lbw b Morrison	0
P. D. Bowler not out	11	– lbw b Snedden	9
J. E. Morris (did not bat)		– b Millmow	20
B. Roberts (did not bat)		– c M. D. Crowe b Morrison	25
A. P. Kuiper (did not bat)		– lbw b Bracewell	68
C. J. Adams (did not bat)		– c J. J. Crowe b Priest	21
†K. M. Krikken (did not bat)		– c M. D. Crowe b Snedden	62
M. Jean-Jacques (did not bat)		– b Snedden	14
I. R. Bishop (did not bat)		– c Greatbatch b Bracewell	7
D. E. Malcolm (did not bat)		– lbw b Snedden	0
D. G. Cork (did not bat)		– not out	2
L-b 1, n-b 4	5	L-b 15, n-b 7	22

(no wkt dec.) 30   1/0 2/24 3/36 4/79 5/159   250
6/169 7/233 8/248 9/248

Bowling: *First Innings*—Morrison 4–0–16–0; Millmow 4–1–13–0. *Second Innings*—Morrison 9–2–40–2; Millmow 8–0–36–1; Snedden 18–4–55–4; Priest 10–1–46–1; Bracewell 15.2–3–58–2.

Umpires: M. J. Kitchen and R. A. White.

ENGLAND v NEW ZEALAND

First Cornhill Test

At Nottingham, June 7, 8, 9, 11, 12. Drawn. Toss: New Zealand. Pre-series prognostication indicated general expectation of three high-scoring draws, given that batting strength on both sides appeared rather more solid than bowling, and pitches were to be hard and true. In the event, the weather proved the decisive factor in the First Test, curtailing play to a degree which made a positive result impossible and shifting the emphasis to seam bowling. More than two hours were lost on the first day, when New Zealand scored 171 runs and lost five wickets. Only 23 minutes of play were possible on the second day, the tourists adding 18 runs for another wicket, and the innings was duly completed, a disappointing 208, before noon on Saturday.

The outstanding batting came from Martin Crowe, who hit five fours and a six in his 94-ball innings, which was of a higher class than anything else offered by New Zealand. Uncharacteristically, he was hitting across the line when he was bowled by DeFreitas. Although the conditions did not help England's fastest bowler, Malcolm, DeFreitas found them very much to his liking, and he bowled a consistently better line and length than on any previous occasion in his Test career. His reward was five wickets for 53 and the figures were well deserved. The one statistical curio was provided by Snedden, whose runless innings was spread over three days.

Hadlee received a warm and sentimental reception from the crowd when he emerged to play his last innings at Trent Bridge, his former county ground, but was unable to acknowledge it as he would have liked; he played on when trying to withdraw his bat before he had scored. He compensated, however, in suitably dramatic style by dismissing the England captain, Gooch, with the first delivery of the innings – his 416th Test wicket, to which he added three more before England declared at 345 for nine on Tuesday afternoon.

In terms of England's Test future the most significant event of the match was Atherton's innings of 151, in his first appearance as an opening bat at that level of cricket. His admirable temperament was illustrated by the way he assumed heavy responsibilities after seeing his captain depart so abruptly, to be followed – after a dashing little knock from Stewart – by the vice-captain, Lamb, who also failed to score.

There had been a certain inevitability about Atherton's progress, from his early days at Manchester Grammar School, through three years at Cambridge and late-summer appearances in the Lancashire side. His patience, concentration and selectivity of strokeplay were almost Boycott-like in his stay of 494 minutes, during which he faced 382 balls and struck sixteen boundaries. His choice as a partner to Gooch was to some extent forced upon the selectors by injury to Larkins, but it proved inspired. Together with the bonus of his leg-spin bowling (which Lancashire had not been afraid to use extensively in their earlier games) it provided the England Committee with a welcome number of new options.

In conditions which at one time or another helped swing and seam bowling, Hadlee showed that, even though his 39th birthday was less than a month away, he remained a dangerous practitioner with new ball or old. Snedden bowled with magnificent accuracy, Bracewell with more of a loop than most English spinners, and the slow left-arm débutant, Priest, with commendable economy to add to his sprightly fielding. Morrison alone would have been disappointed with his figures, probably the result of striving too hard on a pitch which suited him no better than it had Malcolm. – Don Mosey.

Man of the Match: M. A. Atherton. *Attendance:* 17,886; *receipts* £272,693.

Close of play: First day, New Zealand 171-5 (M. W. Priest 23*, M. C. Snedden 0*); Second day, New Zealand 189-6 (M. C. Snedden 0*, J. G. Bracewell 15*); Third day, England 4-1 (M. A. Atherton 3*, A. J. Stewart 1*); Fourth day, England 187-5 (M. A. Atherton 78*, R. C. Russell 4*).

New Zealand

T. J. Franklin b Malcolm	33	– not out	22
*J. G. Wright c Stewart b Small	8	– c Russell b Small	1
A. H. Jones c Stewart b Malcolm	39	– c Russell b DeFreitas	13
M. D. Crowe b DeFreitas	59		
M. J. Greatbatch b Hemmings	1		
M. W. Priest c Russell b DeFreitas	26		
M. C. Snedden c Gooch b DeFreitas	0		
J. G. Bracewell c Gooch b Small	28		
R. J. Hadlee b DeFreitas	0		
†I. D. S. Smith not out	2		
D. K. Morrison lbw b DeFreitas	0	– (4) not out	0
B 1, l-b 10, w 1	12		

1/16 (2) 2/75 (1) 3/110 (3) 4/121 (5) 208 1/8 (2) 2/36 (3) (2 wkts) 36
5/170 (4) 6/174 (6) 7/191 (7)
8/191 (9) 9/203 (8) 10/208 (11)

Bowling: *First Innings*—Small 29-9-49-2; Malcolm 19-7-48-2; Hemmings 19-6-47-1; DeFreitas 22-6-53-5. *Second Innings*—Malcolm 7-2-22-0; Small 6-2-14-1; DeFreitas 2-2-0-1; Hemmings 2-2-0-0.

England

*G. A. Gooch lbw b Hadlee	0	G. C. Small c Crowe b Hadlee 26
M. A. Atherton c Snedden b Priest 151		E. E. Hemmings not out 13
A. J. Stewart c Smith b Hadlee 27		D. E. Malcolm not out 4
A. J. Lamb lbw b Hadlee 0		B 2, l-b 3, n-b 3 8
R. A. Smith c Smith b Bracewell 55		
N. H. Fairbrother c Franklin b Snedden 19		1/0 (1) 2/43 (3) 3/45 (4) (9 wkts dec.) 345
†R. C. Russell c Snedden b Morrison .. 28		4/141 (5) 5/168 (6) 6/260 (7)
P. A. J. DeFreitas lbw b Bracewell 14		7/302 (2) 8/306 (8) 9/340 (9)

Bowling: Hadlee 33–6–89–4; Morrison 22–3–96–1; Snedden 36–17–54–1; Bracewell 35–8–75–2; Priest 12–4–26–1.

Umpires: H. D. Bird and J. H. Hampshire.

†LEICESTERSHIRE v NEW ZEALANDERS

At Leicester, June 14. Leicestershire won by four wickets. Toss: Leicestershire. Put in by Leicestershire on a slow pitch, the tourists delivered one of their poorer batting performances, finishing their 55 overs with a paltry 165 for nine. Only their captain, Wright, played with much conviction. After taking Jeff Crowe's wicket with his loosener, Mullally went from strength to strength to return impressive figures of six for 38 from his eleven overs. Lewis was unusually expensive, conceding 57 runs, but the young England prospect achieved much more success with the bat. Leicestershire had begun unconvincingly, losing three wickets for 29, but Lewis's calmly authoritative 51, made over 90 minutes, and his fourth-wicket partnership of 86 with the opener, Boon, ensured that the home side completed a comfortable victory with fourteen balls to spare.

New Zealanders

*J. G. Wright c Potter b Mullally	62	M. C. Snedden c Potter b Mullally	1
J. J. Crowe b Mullally	7	D. K. Morrison lbw b Willey	2
M. J. Greatbatch b Mullally	0	J. P. Millmow not out	2
K. R. Rutherford b Mullally	19	L-b 1, w 3, n-b 3	7
M. D. Crowe b Agnew	20		
S. A. Thomson c Nixon b Benjamin	25	1/23 2/23 3/50 (9 wkts, 55 overs)	165
M. W. Priest c Lewis b Mullally	1	4/76 5/128 6/139	
†A. C. Parore not out	19	7/141 8/142 9/149	

Bowling: Benjamin 11–1–27–1; Agnew 11–1–21–1; Lewis 11–1–57–0; Mullally 11–3–38–6; Willey 11–3–21–1.

Leicestershire

T. J. Boon c M. D. Crowe b Priest	40	J. D. R. Benson run out	19
*N. E. Briers b Morrison	7	W. K. M. Benjamin not out	0
J. J. Whitaker c Rutherford b Millmow	9	L-b 10, w 3, n-b 1	14
P. Willey c Parore b Snedden	4		
C. C. Lewis c J. J. Crowe b Thomson	51	1/8 2/23 3/29 (6 wkts, 52.4 overs)	171
L. Potter not out	27	4/115 5/119 6/165	

†P. A. Nixon, J. P. Agnew and A. D. Mullally did not bat.

Bowling: Morrison 11–1–27–1; Millmow 11–4–28–1; Snedden 9–2–32–1; Thomson 10–0–42–1; Priest 11–3–26–1; M. D. Crowe 0.4–0–6–0.

Umpires: A. A. Jones and V. A. Holder.

NORTHAMPTONSHIRE v NEW ZEALANDERS

At Northampton, June 16, 17, 18. Drawn. Toss: Northamptonshire. In the absence of Hadlee, whose knighthood was announced on the eve of the match, the headlines were stolen by Capel. He registered Northamptonshire's first hundred against the New Zealanders since D. W. Barrick's 147 in 1949, and hit a six and sixteen fours during his 232-minute innings, adding 167 in 59 overs with Williams. This followed an eventful opening session in which Millmow held a return catch to dismiss Bailey after the ball rebounded off the fielder at silly mid-off. The same bowler limped from the field shortly afterwards, with the shin injury which was to finish his tour, but Bracewell, completing Millmow's over, trapped Fordham with his first ball. Lamb also enlivened the proceedings by striking five boundaries in his 21. New Zealand's reply featured a fine display from Franklin, whose 92 took 201 minutes and included three sixes and ten fours, before he became one of three victims for Ambrose in the space of thirteen deliveries. Wright kept the match alive by declaring 14 runs behind, but an uninterrupted final day would have been necessary to secure a result. In the event only 36 overs could be bowled, and Capel again took centre stage with his unbeaten 65.

Close of play: First day, New Zealanders 28-0 (T. J. Franklin 16*, J. G. Wright 9*); Second day, Northamptonshire 71-2 (R. J. Bailey 12*, A. J. Lamb 6*).

Northamptonshire

A. Fordham lbw b Bracewell	20	– run out	23
N. A. Felton c Rutherford b Morrison	3	– c sub b Bracewell	22
R. J. Bailey c and b Millmow	0	– lbw b Morrison	22
*A. J. Lamb lbw b Morrison	21	– c Parore b Thomson	42
D. J. Capel c and b Priest	123	– not out	65
R. G. Williams c Wright b Priest	73	– not out	11
†W. M. Noon lbw b Morrison	2		
N. G. B. Cook b Priest	10		
W. W. Davis not out	5		
C. E. L. Ambrose lbw b Bracewell	0		
B 13, l-b 4, w 1, n-b 4	22	B 2, l-b 6, w 1, n-b 2	11

1/22 2/23 3/33 4/73 5/240   (9 wkts dec.) 279   1/45 2/50 3/92 4/139   (4 wkts) 196
6/253 7/267 8/274 9/279

M. A. Robinson did not bat.

Bowling: *First Innings*—Morrison 21-4-68-3; Millmow 3.4-0-16-1; Bracewell 30-9-78-2; Thomson 13-0-65-0; Priest 27-10-35-3. *Second Innings*—Morrison 11-2-49-1; Thomson 21-3-97-1; Bracewell 23-13-27-1; Priest 7.5-1-14-0; Rutherford 1-0-1-0.

New Zealanders

T. J. Franklin c Noon b Ambrose	92	S. A. Thomson not out	4
*J. G. Wright b Davis	31		
A. H. Jones lbw b Ambrose	46	B 1, l-b 5, w 2, n-b 10	18
M. J. Greatbatch c Capel b Ambrose	0		
K. R. Rutherford not out	42	1/67 2/176 3/182	(5 wkts dec.) 265
M. W. Priest run out	32	4/186 5/249	

†A. C. Parore, J. G. Bracewell, J. P. Millmow and D. K. Morrison did not bat.

Bowling: Davis 21-2-65-1; Ambrose 20-3-60-3; Robinson 17-1-53-0; Williams 15-3-39-0; Cook 16-5-42-0.

Umpires: B. Dudleston and D. S. Thompsett.

ENGLAND v NEW ZEALAND

Second Cornhill Test

At Lord's, June 21, 22, 23, 25, 26. Drawn. Toss: New Zealand. A number of factors combined to make this a less than remarkable Test. The pitch was too easy-paced, the bowling was not good enough to dismiss batsmen intent on survival, and the weather intervened.

There were some memorable features, however, the first of which came before the match started. Hadlee had received a knighthood in the Queen's Birthday Honours and there was much discussion as to how he should be designated on the scoreboard. In the event, "Sir R. Hadlee" was settled on, but not everyone was pleased. One senior statistician wrote to MCC complaining, mistakenly as it happened, that Hadlee could not use the title until his official investiture. But most cricket devotees were delighted by the honour and anxious that it should be used. So, fifteen minutes late because of damp conditions, Sir Richard Hadlee led New Zealand on to the field and was warmly received.

It was Morrison, however, who struck first for the visitors when Atherton was bowled in the second over, following his Trent Bridge century with a Lord's duck. This seemed to support Wright's decision to put England in, but it was the only incident of note on the first day, as rain drove the players off after only 50 minutes. The main statistical feature of the 11.3 overs bowled had been eight no-balls, four of them from Morrison. Extras continued to make a valuable contribution the next morning, adding 16 of the 74 runs scored after another late start.

The England captain, Gooch, completed his half-century soon after lunch. It had taken 142 minutes and contained six fours, which increased to twelve fours as he advanced to 85. Stewart's fifty took twenty minutes longer and he was out in the next over, lbw to Hadlee for 54. Lamb, on the other hand, started as though the fastest century of the season was in his sights. His first scoring stroke was an edged four to third man, but he handsomely off-drove Hadlee next delivery and 36 of his 39 runs, made in 46 balls, came in boundaries. Only 7 runs were scored by Smith in a fourth-wicket partnership of 38, which ended when Lamb was lbw to Snedden. Fairbrother, still looking for a big Test score, was missed at second slip off his third ball, and a halt for rain brought him no benefit; he made only 2 before giving Morrison a straightforward catch at mid-on off Bracewell. When Russell was bowled by Hadlee for 13, England were unhealthily placed at 255 for six, but DeFreitas joined Smith and they repaired some of the damage. Smith passed 1,000 runs in Test cricket and completed a half-century in 113 minutes, only to go 14 runs later to a fine catch from Bracewell at deep mid-on. With their last three wickets falling for 12 runs in 22 balls, England's total was a disappointing 334.

As New Zealand replied, none of the bowlers troubled Wright and Franklin. They gleaned runs at their own pace, interrupted only by a delay of nearly three hours caused by rain, which extended play until seven o'clock on Saturday. The openers had put on 185 in four and a half hours when Wright, 2 short of his hundred, was well caught at forward short leg, left-handed, by Stewart off Small. Jones helped Franklin add 93 in two hours before he gave Stewart a second catch, at cover point, 1 short of his half-century.

The wait for Franklin's maiden Test hundred was proving a long one. Missed at second slip by Gooch when 88, he spent threequarters of an hour on 98 before reaching three figures with a two from Malcolm. It had taken him seven hours eleven minutes, and in 309 balls he had hit just eight fours. Next ball he edged Malcolm to Russell and was gone. With Crowe and Rutherford then adding 1 run between them, the New Zealanders had lost four wickets for 7 runs and their innings was losing momentum when Hadlee strode to the middle for his last Test innings at Lord's. His second scoring stroke was a six over long-on off Hemmings, and two overs later he despatched Small over long-off, inspiring Greatbatch to flick Malcolm into the Grand Stand at square leg. Hadlee's fifty came in an hour from only 42 deliveries, and included six fours as well as the two sixes. He had put on 123 for the sixth wicket with Greatbatch, and struck another six fours, when he swung at Hemmings once too often and was bowled. There were many who wished they were saluting his hundred as the great New Zealand all-rounder paused before climbing the pavilion steps and lifted his bat high to acknowledge the applause all round the ground.

Wright declared at 462 for nine, after Malcolm had taken five wickets in a Test innings for the second time. But with less than a day remaining, the match drifted towards a draw. For England, Gooch confirmed his excellent form with 37 unforced runs before losing his off stump to Hadlee, while Atherton made up for his first-innings failure with 54, becoming Jones's first Test victim. An opportunity to move Fairbrother up the order was not taken, but when Smith trod on his wicket without having scored, he came in with just over an hour remaining to advantage himself of batting practice at Test level without excessive pressure. He added 97 with Lamb, whose unbeaten 84 from 99 balls contained fourteen fours and a six, but by this stage of the match Hadlee had returned to the dressing-room – where Snedden was already nursing his shoulder injury – to rest a strained hamstring. – *Norman de Mesquita.*

Man of the Match: Sir R. J. Hadlee. *Attendance:* 58,047; *receipts* £891,983.

Close of play: First day, England 27-1 (G. A. Gooch 16*, A. J. Stewart 3*); Second day, England 329-8 (P. A. J. DeFreitas 33*, E. E. Hemmings 0*); Third day, New Zealand 156-0 (T. J. Franklin 60*, J. G. Wright 84*); Fourth day, New Zealand 440-8 (I. D. S. Smith 20*, M. C. Snedden 0*).

England

*G. A. Gooch c and b Bracewell	85	– b Hadlee	37
M. A. Atherton b Morrison	0	– c Bracewell b Jones	54
A. J. Stewart lbw b Hadlee	54	– c sub (M. W. Priest) b Bracewell	54
A. J. Lamb lbw b Snedden	39	– not out	84
R. A. Smith c Bracewell b Morrison	64	– hit wkt b Bracewell	0
N. H. Fairbrother c Morrison b Bracewell	2	– not out	33
†R. C. Russell b Hadlee	13		
P. A. J. DeFreitas c Franklin b Morrison	38		
G. C. Small b Morrison	3		
E. E. Hemmings b Hadlee	0		
D. E. Malcolm not out	0		
L-b 13, w 1, n-b 22	36	B 8, l-b 8, n-b 6	22

1/3 (2) 2/151 (3) 3/178 (1) 4/216 (4)   334   1/68 (1) 2/135 (2)   (4 wkts dec.) 272
5/226 (6) 6/255 (7) 7/319 (5)   3/171 (3) 4/175 (5)
8/322 (9) 9/332 (10) 10/334 (8)

Bowling: *First Innings*—Hadlee 29–5–113–3; Morrison 18.4–4–64–4; Snedden 21–4–72–1; Bracewell 21–3–72–2. *Second Innings*—Hadlee 13–2–32–1; Morrison 16–0–81–0; Bracewell 4–13–85–2; Jones 12–3–40–1; Rutherford 3–0–18–0.

New Zealand

T. J. Franklin c Russell b Malcolm	101	M. C. Snedden not out	13
J. G. Wright c Stewart b Small	98	D. K. Morrison not out	2
A. H. Jones c Stewart b Malcolm	49		
M. D. Crowe c Russell b Hemmings	1	B 12, l-b 15, w 2, n-b 5	34
M. J. Greatbatch b Malcolm	47		
K. R. Rutherford c Fairbrother b Malcolm	0		(9 wkts dec.) 462
Sir R. J. Hadlee b Hemmings	86		
J. G. Bracewell run out	4		
I. D. S. Smith c Small b Malcolm	27		

1/185 (2) 2/278 (3) 3/281 (1) 4/284 (4) 5/285 (6) 6/408 (7) 7/415 (8) 8/425 (5) 9/448 (9)

Bowling: Malcolm 43–14–94–5; Small 35–4–127–1; DeFreitas 35.4–1–122–0; Hemmings 30–13–67–2; Gooch 13–7–25–0; Atherton 1–1–0–0.

Umpires: M. J. Kitchen and D. R. Shepherd.

OXFORD & CAMBRIDGE UNIVERSITIES v NEW ZEALANDERS

At Cambridge, June 27, 28, 29. Oxford & Cambridge Universities won by two wickets. Toss: Oxford & Cambridge Universities. Chasing 263 in a minimum of 71 overs, the Universities batted with flair and determination to win with ten balls to spare and inflict on the touring side their first defeat in first-class fixtures. The first New Zealand team to tour England, that of 1927, had also lost at Fenner's, to Cambridge University. Perhaps, then, it was fitting that the innings which accomplished defeat on the same ground in 1990 came from the Cambridge opener, James. On a pitch providing helpful turn for off-spinner Bracewell, he batted with great skill for his unbeaten 131, facing 224 balls and winning the match with his sixteenth four. He and Morris, heroes of the Universities' first innings, had taken up the tourists' challenge by putting on 93 at 4 runs an over until Morris, the Oxford captain, became the first of seven wickets for Bracewell. The previous day, Morris had batted for three hours before he was last out for 75, giving Thomson his third catch at short leg and Bracewell his fifth wicket of the Universities' first innings. On the opening day, Crowe underpinned the New Zealanders' batting, hitting 23 fours in his 132. However, both he and Greatbatch were dropped off Pyman (when 11 and 10 respectively), and Crowe spent an hour in the 90s before reaching his hundred in 281 minutes from 246 balls. He played with greater freedom on the second afternoon as the tourists built on a lead of just 24.

Close of play: First day, Oxford & Cambridge Universities 37-1 (S. P. James 30*, M. J. Kilborn 7*); Second day, New Zealanders 125-2 (K. R. Rutherford 33*, A. C. Parore 0*).

New Zealanders

M. J. Crowe c Crawley b Gerrans	132	– c G. J. Turner b Crawley	64
T. J. Franklin c Kilborn b Gerrans	19		
M. J. Greatbatch c van der Merwe b Crawley	62		
K. R. Rutherford c van der Merwe b Buzza	21	– (3) c and b Buzza	38
A. W. Priest not out	55	– (6) c Gerrans b Buzza	31
S. A. Thomson not out	1	– (2) b Gerrans	20
A. C. Parore (did not bat)		– (4) c R. J. Turner b Buzza	15
J. G. Bracewell (did not bat)		– (5) c R. J. Turner b Buzza	38
W. Watson (did not bat)		– (7) not out	17
C. Pringle (did not bat)		– (8) c Atkinson b Crawley	6
L-b 8, w 1, n-b 2	11	B 4, l-b 2, n-b 3	9

1/33 2/130 3/199 4/297 (4 wkts dec.) 301 1/47 2/124 3/145 (7 wkts dec.) 238 4/146 5/205 6/224 7/238

*I. D. S. Smith did not bat.

Bowling: *First Innings*—van der Merwe 11-3-28-0; Gerrans 18-6-59-2; Pyman 17-3-56-0
G. J. Turner 21-3-76-0; Buzza 13-5-44-1; Crawley 14-5-30-1. *Second Innings*—van de
Merwe 8-1-30-0; Gerrans 9-3-18-1; G. J. Turner 14-0-63-0; Buzza 17-0-87-4; Pyma
6-2-12-0; Crawley 6.3-0-22-2.

Oxford & Cambridge Universities

S. P. James c Thomson b Bracewell	67	– not out 13
P. S. Gerrans c Parore b Pringle	0	– (8) b Bracewell ....
M. J. Kilborn c Parore b Watson	27	– run out ....
M. A. Crawley c Smith b Bracewell	47	– (5) lbw b Bracewell ....
R. E. Morris c Thomson b Bracewell	75	– (2) c Greatbatch b Bracewell ... 5
*J. C. M. Atkinson c Bracewell b Priest	10	– b Bracewell ....
G. J. Turner c Crowe b Priest	14	– (4) c Crowe b Bracewell ... 2
W. M. van der Merwe b Priest	24	– (7) c Parore b Bracewell ... 1
†R. J. Turner b Bracewell	5	– b Bracewell ... 1
R. A. Pyman c Thomson b Bracewell	4	– not out ....
A. J. Buzza not out	0	
L-b 4	4	B 2, l-b 8, n-b 3 1

1/5 2/74 3/121 4/154 5/177   277   1/93 2/106 3/164 4/178   (8 wkts) 26
6/199 7/237 8/264 9/276   5/184 6/220 7/230 8/262

Bowling: *First Innings*—Pringle 10-2-28-1; Watson 13-3-26-1; Priest 36-16-93-3
Bracewell 38.3-10-107-5; Thomson 6-0-19-0. *Second Innings*—Thomson 5-1-14-0; Watso
7-1-27-0; Bracewell 33-6-120-7; Priest 25.2-7-79-0; Pringle 6-2-16-0.

Umpires: G. I. Burgess and R. Palmer.

ESSEX v NEW ZEALANDERS

At Chelmsford, June 30, July 1, 2. Drawn. Toss: New Zealanders. The game ended in a dr
draw after Gooch decided to bat on during the final day, apparently because the tourists we
not interested in manufacturing a finish. Ideal batting conditions enabled Wright, who hit 2
fours in his 121, and Martin Crowe, whose unbeaten 123 contained seventeen fours and tw
sixes, to prosper with ease. And when the home team replied, Gooch and Stephenson als
reached three figures. The Essex captain had hit sixteen boundaries by the time he limped o
of the action with a jarred knee, immediately after completing his hundred. His fellow-opene
went on to 147, which spanned 426 minutes and 332 balls. Gooch's was not the only injury i
the run-up to the Birmingham Test; Franklin dislocated his right-hand little finger whil
attempting to catch Gooch at second slip, and Martin Crowe needed stitches when he was h
in the face by a ball deflected by Parore off Stephenson's bat. Neither took part in the Ne
Zealanders' second innings, which gave Jones and Rutherford some useful practice befor
Edgbaston.

Close of play: First day, New Zealanders 388-4 (M. D. Crowe 123*, J. J. Crowe 9*); Secon
day, Essex 306-2 (J. P. Stephenson 107*, M. E. Waugh 55*).

New Zealanders

T. J. Franklin c Gooch b Topley	74	
*J. G. Wright lbw b Childs	121	
A. H. Jones c Garnham b Topley	3	– not out 6
M. D. Crowe not out	123	
K. R. Rutherford st Garnham b Stephenson	42	– (4) not out 4
J. J. Crowe not out	9	– (1) c Hussain b Topley ... 1
†A. C. Parore (did not bat)		– (2) lbw b Pringle ...
B 2, l-b 3, w 1, n-b 10	16	L-b 4, w 2, n-b 12 1

1/169 2/180 3/205 4/322   (4 wkts dec.) 388   1/9 2/53   (2 wkts) 14

M. W. Priest, S. A. Thomson, C. Pringle and D. K. Morrison did not bat.

Bowling: *First Innings*—Andrew 14–3–45–0; Pringle 9–4–25–0; Thomas 16–3–76–0; Topley 2–2–57–2; Childs 23–6–76–1; Hussain 7–1–28–0; Waugh 5–0–24–0; Stephenson 8–0–52–1. *Second Innings*—Andrew 8–1–16–0; Pringle 6–0–15–1; Topley 10–0–45–1; Thomas 2.2–0–5–0; Childs 5.4–0–22–0; Stephenson 5–1–15–0; Waugh 3–0–16–0; Hussain 1–0–5–0.

Essex

G. A. Gooch retired hurt	102	T. D. Topley not out	23
P. Stephenson c Thomson b Priest	147	K. O. Thomas c Priest b Thomson	2
J. P. Prichard c M. D. Crowe b Priest	15	S. J. W. Andrew b Thomson	0
N. Hussain c M. D. Crowe b Jones	1	L-b 25, w 1, n-b 3	29
M. E. Waugh c Priest b Pringle	63		
D. R. Pringle c Thomson b Priest	67	1/209 2/218 3/315 4/404 (8 wkts dec.) 449	
M. A. Garnham lbw b Pringle	0	5/408 6/438 7/449 8/449	

J. H. Childs did not bat.

G. A. Gooch retired hurt at 168.

Bowling: Morrison 19–2–57–0; Pringle 42–15–103–2; Thomson 25.4–6–84–2; Priest 48–7–155–3; Jones 2–1–1–1; Rutherford 4–0–24–0.

Umpires: P. J. Eele and K. E. Palmer.

ENGLAND v NEW ZEALAND

Third Cornhill Test

At Birmingham, July 5, 6, 7, 9, 10. England won by 114 runs. Toss: New Zealand. Even the relief of seeing Sir Richard Hadlee bound up the pavilion steps in a Test for the last time failed to match England's delight at saying goodbye to their worst-ever run in Tests at home. In nearly five years, England had beaten only Sri Lanka, in a one-off Test at Lord's in 1988; their previous success in a series had been in 1985, when Gower's side regained the Ashes. Since then, the Ashes had been retained in Australia and lost at home, and England had failed to win any of their subsequent 24 home Tests in six series. This victory at Edgbaston was also England's first win over New Zealand for seven years, and it provided an exciting finale to a dull Cornhill series which had been disrupted by the weather.

Hadlee's departure and the Test were not the only losses suffered by the tourists. Snedden announced his retirement prior to the match, and the New Zealand captain, Wright, confirmed that this was his final tour. Wright also confessed to his part in New Zealand's first defeat in ten Tests. "I was wrong to put England in. No two ways about it. It was a bad decision." Gooch, England's captain, could have faced two decisions as the home team searched for that elusive win. But he was excused both. Wright won the toss; then, with Gooch pondering on when to declare on the fourth day, England collapsed to their lowest total against the Kiwis in England. That gave New Zealand more time to score fewer runs than Gooch had planned, yet ultimately England's batting failure may have eased their path to victory. Hadlee bowed out with an inspired spell after lunch on the fourth day to open up the contest, and those wickets took his final Test tally to 431 as he claimed five wickets in an innings for a record 36th time. Malcolm provided the final breakthrough for England's success, but Hemmings, Gooch and Atherton all played a crucial part in the victory.

Gooch had been reappointed as captain for the India series after the Lord's Test, and England named an unchanged twelve for Edgbaston. Fraser, as Middlesex had no game, was added to the squad to give him match practice following the rib injury which had caused him to withdraw from the Fourth Test in Barbados three months earlier. And when DeFreitas left Wednesday's practice feeling feverish, then eventually dropped out with hamstring trouble, there was speculation that he might make an earlier return. In the event Lewis, although in some doubt earlier because of knee trouble – as was Stewart, with an ankle problem – came in to make his Test début. England's traditional pre-match dinner was abandoned in favour of a buffet so that the players could watch the soccer World Cup semi-final between England and

West Germany. For New Zealand, Franklin had recovered from a dislocated finger, bu
Smith was ruled out with a sore hamstring, giving a chance to the promising nineteen-year-ol
wicket-keeper, Parore, who had been brought on the tour to prepare him as Smith's successo
New Zealand's last Edgbaston Test had been in 1965, when they lost by nine wickets, but th
Birmingham ground had become England's favourite Test venue. They went into this matc
with fourteen wins and just two defeats in 26 matches at Warwickshire's headquarters.

Rain delayed the start on the first day until 2.45 p.m.; and although play might not hav
been possible so soon without the Brumbrella covering, this was damaged while bein
removed and was put out of action for the rest of the match. England responded positively t
Wright's insertion and finished the day at 191 for one. The three-and-a-half-hour openin
partnership of 170 between Gooch and Atherton was England's best since Broad and Athey
stand of 223 at Perth in 1986-87, and as well as Gooch becoming the eleventh Englishman t
reach 5,000 Test runs, both openers passed 1,000 first-class runs for the season. Gooch too
the first 40 minutes of the second morning to add the 5 runs he needed for his ninth Tes
hundred, his first in 26 innings, and his 394-minute 154 (281 balls) held the innings together a
England's middle order failed to capitalise on the good start. It was left to Lewis, Russel
Hemmings and Small to help England to their first total of 400 in eleven Tests. New Zealand
attack was made to work hard, but there was consolation in Parore's display behind th
stumps, despite his dropping Lewis.

Saturday belonged to Hemmings. The 41-year-old off-spinner entered the match with a
eight-year, eleven-Test record that had yielded only nineteen wickets. In the space of 9
deliveries and two hours, Hemmings induced a New Zealand collapse from 163 for four to 24
all out with his spell of six for 33, finishing with the best figures by an England spinner sinc
J. E. Emburey's seven for 78 at Sydney in 1986-87. Hemmings, who had started his count
career at Edgbaston 24 years earlier, was helped by slick close catching, a receptive pitch, an
his captain's attacking policy; it was the first time he had played three consecutive Tests an
the first time he had taken more than four wickets in a Test innings. Malcolm made the earl
breakthrough as the tourists' front-line batsmen paid for their positive approach, and Lew
took his first Test wicket when Crowe was adjudged lbw. Crowe initially refused to look a
umpire Meyer's response to England's appeal, and the umpire had to raise his finger a secon
time before Crowe, who later apologised, departed. Franklin was again the most difficult t
dislodge, his 66 taking four and a half hours and 207 balls, and New Zealand's inning
disintegrated just before tea when he and Greatbatch were dismissed. However, despit
Hemmings, New Zealand managed to escape the follow-on by 13 runs before the close.

England, with a lead of 186, started positively on Monday, posting 50 in 49 minutes, but th
quest for quick runs was exploited by Hadlee and Bracewell. The last seven wickets fell for 2
runs, with only Atherton keeping his nerve in a stay of almost three and a quarter hours
England's four middle-order batsmen had a disastrous Test, managing just 68 runs betwee
them, and while it put Stewart's Test future in doubt, Fairbrother seemed certain to pay th
penalty for failing to reproduce his county form for his country. The talented Lancashire left
hander had scored 64 runs in seven Tests and, apart from his undefeated 33 at Lord's, ha
never looked comfortable in this three-match series. Bracewell became the second Nev
Zealander to complete the Test double of 1,000 runs and 100 wickets. The first was, of course
Hadlee, who signed off in style with an eight-over spell of three for 17. Malcolm was just a
proud of being Hadlee's 431st and last Test victim as he was of dismissing cricket's lates
knight in his final Test innings.

With New Zealand wanting 345 runs for victory in eight and a half hours, Monday
evening session was crucial to both sides. The tourists were 101 runs nearer their target by th
close, but England settled for that as they had the wickets of Wright and Franklin. O
Tuesday, however, Jones, Greatbatch and Crowe were all denied the big innings needed t
give their side a platform for victory, and even the New Zealand romantics had to conced
defeat when Hadlee had his stumps splattered by Malcolm. England's fast bowler receive
good support from Lewis and the England fielders, especially Gooch and Atherton in th
slips. Atherton was named England's Man of the Series, while Hadlee picked up the Nev
Zealand award. That was no sentimental gesture; the world's leading Test wicket-taker ha
called it a day at the peak of his powers. – David Norrie.

Man of the Match: D. E. Malcolm.   *Attendance:* 33,963; *receipts* £402,962.

Close of play: First day, England 191-1 (G. A. Gooch 95*, A. J. Stewart 8*); Second day
New Zealand 9-0 (T. J. Franklin 8*, J. G. Wright 1*); Third day, New Zealand 249; Fourt
day, New Zealand 101-2 (A. H. Jones 37*, M. D. Crowe 10*).

England

G. A. Gooch c Hadlee b Morrison	154	– b Snedden	30
M. A. Atherton lbw b Snedden	82	– c Rutherford b Bracewell	70
N. J. Stewart c Parore b Morrison	9	– lbw b Bracewell	15
A. J. Lamb c Parore b Hadlee	2	– st Parore b Bracewell	4
R. A. Smith c Jones b Bracewell	19	– c and b Hadlee	14
J. H. Fairbrother lbw b Snedden	2	– lbw b Bracewell	3
R. C. Russell b Snedden	43	– c sub (J. J. Crowe) b Hadlee	0
C. C. Lewis c Rutherford b Bracewell	32	– c Parore b Hadlee	1
G. C. Small not out	44	– not out	11
E. E. Hemmings c Parore b Hadlee	20	– b Hadlee	0
D. E. Malcolm b Hadlee	0	– lbw b Hadlee	0
B 4, l-b 15, n-b 9	28	L-b 6, n-b 4	10

1/170 (2) 2/193 (3) 3/198 (4) 4/245 (5)   435   1/50 (1) 2/87 (3) 3/99 (4)   158
5/254 (6) 6/316 (1) 7/351 (7)   4/129 (5) 5/136 (6) 6/141 (7)
8/381 (8) 9/435 (10) 10/435 (11)   7/146 (8) 8/157 (2)
                                     9/158 (10) 10/158 (11)

Bowling: *First Innings*—Hadlee 37.5–8–97–3; Morrison 26–7–81–2; Snedden 35–9–106–3; Bracewell 42–12–130–2; Jones 1–0–2–0. *Second Innings*—Hadlee 21–3–53–5; Morrison 8–1–29–0; Snedden 9–0–32–1; Bracewell 16–5–38–4.

New Zealand

T. J. Franklin c Smith b Hemmings	66	– lbw b Malcolm	5
*J. G. Wright c Russell b Malcolm	24	– c Smith b Lewis	46
A. H. Jones c Russell b Malcolm	2	– c Gooch b Small	40
M. D. Crowe lbw b Lewis	11	– lbw b Malcolm	25
M. J. Greatbatch b Malcolm	45	– c Atherton b Hemmings	22
K. R. Rutherford c Stewart b Hemmings	29	– c Lamb b Lewis	18
Sir R. J. Hadlee c Atherton b Hemmings	8	– b Malcolm	13
J. G. Bracewell b Hemmings	25	– (9) c Atherton b Malcolm	0
†A. C. Parore not out	12	– (8) c Lamb b Lewis	20
M. C. Snedden lbw b Hemmings	2	– not out	21
D. K. Morrison b Hemmings	1	– b Malcolm	6
B 9, l-b 11, w 2, n-b 2	24	L-b 9, w 1, n-b 4	14

1/45 (2) 2/67 (3) 3/90 (4) 4/161 (5)   249   1/25 (1) 2/85 (2) 3/111 (3)   230
5/163 (1) 6/185 (7) 7/223 (8)   4/125 (4) 5/155 (5) 6/163 (6)
8/230 (6) 9/243 (10) 10/249 (11)   7/180 (7) 8/180 (9)
                                     9/203 (8) 10/230 (11)

Bowling: *First Innings*—Small 18–7–44–0; Malcolm 25–7–59–3; Lewis 19–5–51–1; Hemmings 27.3–10–58–6; Atherton 9–5–17–0. *Second Innings*—Malcolm 24.4–8–46–5; Small 16–5–56–1; Lewis 22–3–76–3; Hemmings 29–13–43–1.

Umpires: J. W. Holder and B. J. Meyer.

THE INDIANS IN ENGLAND, 1990

The theatrical impresarios of London's West End would have been proud to have put on a spectacle like this. The sporting plot was played out on arena larger than any stage along Shaftesbury Avenue, and it fascinated by it natural twists and turns, supported by bravura performances. Most importantly, the patrons went away delighted by what they had seen. The show was a winner.

The supremacy of cricket as England's summer sport was in question. The preceding Tests against New Zealand had struggled to compete against the circus of soccer's quadrennial showpiece, the World Cup, and neither the knighting of Richard Hadlee nor England's first win in a home series for five years made the impact of the Indian summer which followed.

A certain amateur spirit was needed if cricket was to recapture its glory and the Indian tourists, led by Mohammad Azharuddin, had that spirit. The fear of losing has often been responsible for dull Test cricket, but India, accustomed to winning abroad once in a blue moon, had none of that fear. Moreover, with conditions so dry that hosepipe bans were being imposed in Britain, the Indian batsmen found themselves in their element. They scored heavily from their earliest games, making fifteen first-class hundreds, six of them in Tests, and their double victory in the Texaco Trophy one-day internationals suggested how attractively they could perform. The Tests would revolve around their success in using these batting skills to support the notoriously weak bowling.

The fate of the series lay in the toss at Lord's. With so many batsmen among the runs, most captains would have grabbed first strike the moment the coin came down in their favour. This is where captaincy may have let India down. Graham Gooch, soon to make this summer his *annus mirabilis*, may not have believed his ears or his luck when England were asked to bat. For while the mild cloud cover at the time of the toss was contrary to the forecast, any moisture in the pitch could only have been imagined. Not without reason did the sagacious Mike Brearley write that the decision was pusillanimous. Moreover, the divisions in Indian cricket were soon emphasised as the team's cricket manager, Bishan Bedi, was reported to have disassociated himself from the decision to put England in, though he made a belated attempt to assuage the players' feelings by denying the words attributed to him.

The die had been cast for a glorious display of batting, and record books were constantly open as the unflappable Gooch piled on the runs to achieve the first Test triple-hundred since L. G. Rowe's 302 for West Indies against England at Bridgetown in 1973-74. The England captain was to score a second century in his next innings, giving him the record Test match aggregate of 456 runs, and another at Old Trafford. All in all, in eleven Test innings during the summer he made 1,058 runs for an average of 96.18, batting with the voracity of a Bradman, whose record of 974 Test runs in an English season he passed at The Oval. Gooch's understanding of Indian bowling, easily tamed by patience and a straight bat, was perfect, and his opening partnership with Mike Atherton went from strength to strength. They confirmed its efficacy at Lord's as they compiled a record opening stand against India of 204, and again as they beat it by 21 runs the next time they walked out together, in Manchester, where Atherton became only the second Lancastrian, after G. Pullar, to make a Test hundred for England at Old Trafford. Their stand of 176 at The Oval was their fourth century partnership in as many Tests; yet opening was an unaccustomed role for Atherton, used to batting at No. 3 for his county.

Although they sometimes seemed to be reduced to supporting players, the contributions of Robin Smith and Allan Lamb, both of whom scored centuries at Lord's and Old Trafford, should not be forgotten. The competent Smith must have put himself among the world's top ten batsmen. Over the series he was only twice out in making 361 runs, and his refreshingly orthodox technique, coupled with amazing power through the off side, gave him ample command of the Indian bowlers, whether pace or spin. No believer in the bat-behind-pad and forward-prod school of batting, he gave an object lesson with his handling of spin when the ball was turning on the second day at Old Trafford. In that innings Lamb's performance against spin was much criticised, but he overcame his supposed weakness later in the match to steer his team away from trouble and towards the chance of victory.

Until the last Test, India's batsmen were always left to battle against the odds, chasing one massive England total after another, but their talented line-up, and especially the brilliant Azharuddin, did much to re-establish the virtues of positive batting. The Indian captain's breathtakingly audacious hundred at Lord's signified the difference between the English straight bat, wielded with control rather than subtlety, and oriental wristiness, which lends itself to innovation. There were also solid and professional innings from Ravi Shastri and Sanjay Manjrekar, but the most spectacular effort came from Kapil Dev at Lord's. With the last man in and 24 needed to save the follow-on, he lifted four sixes in as many deliveries into the uncompleted stands of the Nursery End – just in time, for Narendra Hirwani was to fall next ball.

Despite such heroics, India were let down by their lack of cold-blooded professionalism, most obvious when they failed in the task of batting just under four sessions for the draw at Lord's. Under the pressure of having to remain at the wicket, rather than being able to bat with uninhibited aggression, they succumbed more easily than one would have imagined, while at the same time continuing their spectacular strokeplay. It was after the senior batsmen had displayed the same lack of commitment on the final day at Old Trafford that Sachin Tendulkar completed his conquest of English hearts, saving his side from defeat and scoring the sixth century of the match en route. There should be many more Test hundreds for Tendulkar; what made his first so special were the circumstances in which he made it, as a seventeen-year-old coming to the rescue of his country. Yet those who had seen him stand up to a barrage of bouncers from the Pakistani fast bowlers at Sialkot the previous winter would have had no doubts about his genius, or his capacity to set an example to colleagues old enough to be father figures. He had already shown his character in the first innings at Manchester when, after waiting nearly an hour for his first run, he went on to regain his one-day touch, and he had dazzled the crowd at Lord's with an unbelievably athletic catch of the sort that only players of his age can attempt.

How different the series might have been was suggested by the way India performed when they batted first in the final Test, on a parched Oval pitch as close to their native conditions as they were likely to find. They made the most of it with their highest score against England, who came to appreciate the difference now that it was their turn to bat after the opposition had ground out a huge total. The ball was spinning on the third day, and when England followed on before lunch on Monday, conditions pointed to India's first victory in an overseas Test since Leeds in 1986. But their bowling was exposed yet again. Inflexible tactics and lack of penetration led the Indians to accept the draw long before England could relax to enjoy their first summer without a defeat since 1979.

Throughout the tour the Indian bowlers had been expensive and rarely looked better than club class, although leg-spinner Hirwani may have been handicapped by a bleeding index finger, which troubled him all summer. Additionally, their wicket-keeper, Kiran More, was generally agreed to have had a poor tour behind the stumps. Nor was there any relief in the county fixtures. The tourists drew all but two of these, beating Kent and losing to Hampshire, with whom they shared the financial rewards provided by the sponsorship of Tetley Bitter. But it was not a summer for bowlers, and England's Angus Fraser was the only one in the series who rose above mediocrity. Getting lift from closer to a length than the quicker Malcolm, he bowled the off-stump line designed to bring out the worst in Indian batsmen. At 28.75 his average was half that of the most economical of his opponents, Anil Kumble, the second of the leg-spinners, who played in only one Test.

But it was the batting which made the series such a success, and one of the finest examples came on its last day at The Oval, with the elegant century of David Gower. The former England captain, if his critics were to be believed, had spent the series inventing ways of getting out, but the threat of having to go to Australia as a tour host rather than as a member of the England team seemed to bring out the best in him. The timing of his strokes was impeccable in a charming 157 not out, and with England not yet out of the woods, so was the timing of the innings. A lot was at stake, for Gower and for his team; he did not disappoint himself or the crowd.

The happy ending for England brought down the curtain on a popular show. The Indians had been model tourists, ever willing to please the spectators and never once questioning the umpiring, the crowded itinerary (twice they went straight from a Test into six days of first-class cricket), the long coach rides in a criss-cross programme, or even some hotels with less than adequate service. Relations between the teams were excellent. Neither two poor umpiring decisions in successive overs at Old Trafford, when India were poised to match England's total, nor the couple of warnings for attempting to interfere with the ball were allowed to dampen the good cheer.

The Indians left England happier for their visit, convinced that the future would be brighter and that a nucleus of players had been found to serve them for some time to come. In the Texaco series they had also rediscovered their talent in the one-day game. Their hosts were similarly pleased. The triumphs in two Test series confirmed that English cricket had emerged from the shadows, and that the brave performances in the Caribbean in the spring had been no flash in the pan. The fact that only twelve players were used in the series against India, as opposed to the 29 who appeared against Australia in 1989, reflected a settled look and greater wisdom among the selectors. Most of all, the series did more for the game than many recent ones, and that in itself was cause for celebration. – R. Mohan.

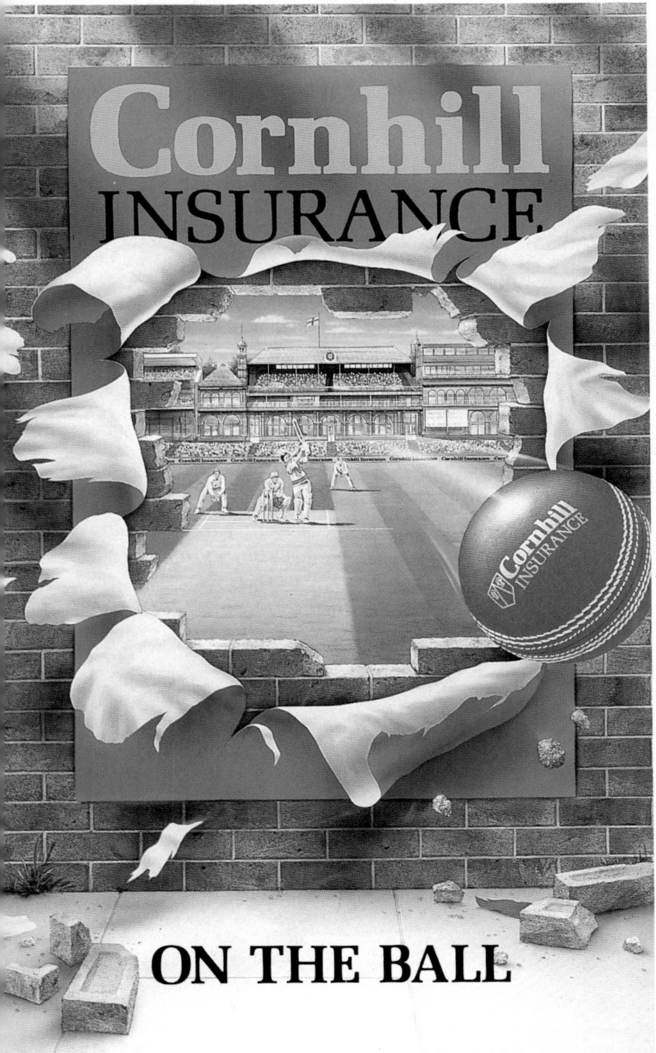
Cornhill
INSURANCE
Cornhill
INSURANCE
ON THE BALL

WELL HELD.

INDIAN TOUR RESULTS

Test matches – Played 3: Lost 1, Drawn 2.
First-class matches – Played 13: Won 1, Lost 2, Drawn 10.
Win – Kent.
Losses – England, Hampshire.
Draws – England (2), Glamorgan, Gloucestershire, Leicestershire, Michael Parkinson's World XI, Minor Counties, Surrey, TCCB Under-25 XI, Yorkshire.
One-day internationals – Played 2: Won 2.
Other non first-class matches – Played 3: Won 3. *Wins* – Derbyshire, League Cricket Conference, Scotland.

TEST MATCH AVERAGES

ENGLAND – BATTING

	T	I	NO	R	HI	100s	Avge
R. A. Smith	3	6	4	361	121*	2	180.50
G. A. Gooch	3	6	0	752	333	3	125.33
D. I. Gower	3	6	2	291	157*	1	72.75
M. A. Atherton	3	6	0	378	131	1	63.00
A. J. Lamb	3	6	0	364	139	2	60.66
E. E. Hemmings	3	2	0	70	51	0	35.00
R. C. Russell	3	3	1	59	35	0	29.50
D. E. Malcolm	3	2	1	28	15*	0	28.00
J. E. Morris	3	5	2	71	32	0	23.66

Played in three Tests: A. R. C. Fraser 1, 0. Played in two Tests: C. C. Lewis 3. Played in one Test: N. F. Williams 38.

* *Signifies not out.*

BOWLING

	O	M	R	W	BB	5W/i	Avge
A. R. C. Fraser	159.1	41	460	16	5-104	2	28.75
E. E. Hemmings	137.2	26	454	11	3-75	0	41.27
C. C. Lewis	65	8	281	5	2-26	0	56.20
D. E. Malcolm	110	16	436	7	2-65	0	62.28

Also bowled: M. A. Atherton 28-3-161-1; G. A. Gooch 18-4-70-1; N. F. Williams 41-5-148-2.

INDIA – BATTING

	T	I	NO	R	HI	100s	Avge
M. Azharuddin	3	5	0	426	179	2	85.20
R. J. Shastri	3	5	0	336	187	2	67.20
S. R. Tendulkar	3	5	1	245	119*	1	61.25
Kapil Dev	3	5	1	220	110	1	55.00
S. V. Manjrekar	3	5	0	216	93	0	43.20
M. Prabhakar	3	5	1	132	67*	0	33.00
D. B. Vengsarkar	3	5	0	158	52	0	31.60
K. S. More	3	4	1	91	61*	0	30.33
N. D. Hirwani	3	4	3	17	15*	0	17.00
N. S. Sidhu	3	5	0	56	30	0	11.20

Played in one Test: A. Kumble 2; S. K. Sharma 0, 38; A. S. Wassan 15.

* *Signifies not out.*

BOWLING

	O	M	R	W	BB	5W/i	Avge
A. Kumble	60	10	170	3	3-105	0	56.66
A. S. Wassan	37	5	173	3	2-79	0	57.66
Kapil Dev	128	23	445	7	2-66	0	63.57
N. D. Hirwani	212	41	586	9	4-174	0	65.11
S. K. Sharma	48	5	197	3	2-75	0	65.66
M. Prabhakar	155	28	554	8	4-74	0	69.25
R. J. Shastri	95.5	6	341	2	1-29	0	170.50

INDIAN AVERAGES – FIRST-CLASS MATCHES

BATTING

	M	I	NO	R	HI	100s	Avge
M. Azharuddin	9	11	1	770	179	3	77.00
R. J. Shastri	9	11	1	644	187	4	64.40
S. R. Tendulkar	11	19	4	945	119*	2	63.00
S. V. Manjrekar	11	17	3	814	158*	2	58.14
D. B. Vengsarkar ...	10	14	4	576	83*	0	57.60
W. V. Raman	8	15	2	623	127	1	47.92
N. S. Sidhu	9	17	3	639	142	2	45.64
N. R. Mongia	8	11	4	269	63*	0	38.42
Kapil Dev	9	12	2	377	110	1	37.70
S. K. Sharma	9	7	3	132	38	0	33.00
K. S. More	9	11	2	295	95	0	32.77
M. Prabhakar	10	14	3	296	76	0	26.90
S. L. V. Raju	6	6	2	105	40*	0	26.25
A. S. Wassan	9	3	1	47	24	0	23.50
A. Kumble	7	5	2	63	35*	0	21.00
N. D. Hirwani	9	5	3	17	15*	0	8.50

* Signifies not out.

BOWLING

	O	M	R	W	BB	5W/i	Avge
N. D. Hirwani	399.2	59	1,280	31	5-117	1	41.29
A. Kumble	212	40	660	14	6-49	1	47.14
A. S. Wassan	207.3	24	886	18	6-89	1	49.22
Kapil Dev	246.4	59	744	13	2-28	0	57.23
S. L. V. Raju	182.3	41	528	9	4-73	0	58.66
M. Prabhakar	281	47	994	16	4-74	0	62.12
S. K. Sharma	229	36	873	13	2-53	0	67.15
R. J. Shastri	199.2	30	607	7	2-80	0	86.71

Also bowled: K. S. More 8–0–54–0; W. V. Raman 15–2–72–1; S. R. Tendulkar 79–12–268–3.

FIELDING

18 – K. S. More (17 ct, 1 st); 12 – N. R. Mongia (9 ct, 3 st); 6 – S. V. Manjrekar, W. V. Raman, R. J. Shastri; 5 – S. R. Tendulkar; 4 – M. Prabhakar, D. B. Vengsarkar; 3 – M. Azharuddin, N. D. Hirwani, Kapil Dev; 2 – S. K. Sharma; 1 – A. Kumble, N. S. Sidhu, Substitute.

HUNDREDS FOR INDIANS

The following sixteen three-figure innings were played for the Indians, fifteen in first-class matches and one in a non first-class match.

R. J. Shastri (4)
105 v Minor Counties, Trowbridge
100 v England, Lord's (First Test)
133 v Glos., Bristol
187 v England, The Oval (Third Test)

M. Azharuddin (3)
105 v Minor Counties, Trowbridge
121 v England, Lord's (First Test)
179 v England, Manchester (Second Test)

S. R. Tendulkar (3)
†105* v Derbys., Chesterfield
119* v England, Manchester (Second Test)
108 v Michael Parkinson's World XI, Scarborough

S. V. Manjrekar (2)
158* v Yorks., Leeds
116 v TCCB Under-25 XI, Birmingham

N. S. Sidhu (2)
142 v Glos., Bristol
108* v TCCB Under-25 XI, Birmingham

Kapil Dev (1)
110 v England, The Oval (Third Test)

W. V. Raman (1)
127 v Surrey, The Oval

* *Signifies not out.*   † *Not first-class.*

Note: Those matches which follow which were not first-class are signified by the use of a dagger.

†LEAGUE CRICKET CONFERENCE v INDIANS

At Sunderland, June 28. Indians won by 40 runs. Toss: Indians. Although the Indians began their tour with a win, it was hard earned, and they would have been harder pressed had there been more support for McLeod. The West Indian all-rounder and Radcliffe professional hit two sixes and four fours in his late assault before running out of overs just 4 runs short of his half-century. Holmes, a 21-year-old medium-pace bowler from Kearsley in the Bolton League, was the pick of the Conference attack, which was promising to embarrass the touring team until More and Raju added 67 for the seventh wicket.

Indians

W. V. Raman b Walcott	0	S. K. Sharma c Lambert b Walcott	5
N. S. Sidhu b Day	17	A. S. Wassan c Ingham b McLeod	10
S. R. Tendulkar c Wundke b Holmes	19	A. Kumble not out	1
D. B. Vengsarkar c Borthwick b Day	28	B 7, l-b 9, w 19, n-b 4	39
M. Azharuddin b Wundke	20		
Kapil Dev c Tuckwell b Wundke	0	1/1 2/51 3/51	(9 wkts, 55 overs) 231
K. S. More b Wundke	58	4/87 5/89 6/128	
L. V. Raju not out	34	7/195 8/216 9/227	

Bowling: McLeod 11–1–44–1; Walcott 11–2–37–2; Holmes 11–3–20–1; Day 11–1–73–2; Wundke 11–0–41–3.

League Cricket Conference

C. B. Lambert c Kapil Dev b Sharma	. 22	V. D. Walcott b Kapil Dev ....
D. Lampitt c Vengsarkar b Sharma	... 15	A. C. Day c More b Sharma ....
D. A. Tuckwell c Vengsarkar b Wassan	17	B. L. Holmes not out ....
*N. J. Heaton st More b Kumble	41	B 10, w 3, n-b 6 .... 1*
M. J. Ingham lbw b Sharma	26	
S. C. Wundke c More b Kumble	3	1/41 2/48 3/82 (9 wkts, 55 overs) 19
K. W. McLeod not out	46	4/119 5/127 6/189
†D. Borthwick lbw b Kapil Dev	1	7/190 8/190 9/191

Bowling: Kapil Dev 10–3–29–2; Sharma 10–2–25–4; Wassan 7–0–39–1; Tendulka 6–1–16–0; Kumble 11–4–32–2; Raju 11–0–40–0.

Umpires: J. Atkinson and B. Johnson.

YORKSHIRE v INDIANS

At Leeds, June 30, July 1, 2. Drawn. Toss: Indians. The tourists took full advantage of a favourable pitch and a weakened Yorkshire attack, in which left-arm spinner Doidge wa making his début, to score at more than 4 runs an over. Manjrekar led the way, striking hi unbeaten 158 from 181 balls, and sharing partnerships of 110 in 24 overs with Sidhu and 15ᵉ from 35 overs with Vengsarkar. Bad light and rain reduced the first day to 69.5 overs and the second to 24, but both sides declared at their overnight totals to create a competitive situation Moxon and Metcalfe having scored briskly in the time available on the second day. The hig standards of batting were maintained by Shastri and Azharuddin, who finally set a target o 343 in 75 overs, five of which were lost to a brief shower. Taking up the challenge, Moxon an Metcalfe put on 152 in 33 overs, and the Yorkshire captain's fluent strokeplay brought him 93 runs from 111 balls, including one six and fifteen fours. The momentum could not be maintained, however, and Yorkshire, whose highest fourth-innings total to win a match wa 331 for eight against Middlesex at Lord's in 1910, settled for a draw. For the Indians, Kapi Dev and Hirwani bowled with restraint under pressure.

Close of play: First day, Indians 294-2 (S. V. Manjrekar 158*, D. B. Vengsarkar 47*) Second day, Yorkshire 88-0 (M. D. Moxon 45*, A. A. Metcalfe 40*).

Indians

W. V. Raman c Byas b Fletcher	12	– b Houseman	(
N. S. Sidhu c Blakey b Fletcher	61	– c Blakey b Houseman	3
S. V. Manjrekar not out	158		
D. B. Vengsarkar not out	47		
R. J. Shastri (did not bat)		– (3) not out	53
*M. Azharuddin (did not bat)		– (4) not out	79
L-b 3, n-b 13	16	L-b 2, n-b 3	5

1/25 2/135   (2 wkts dec.) 294   1/0 2/12   (2 wkts dec.) 136

Kapil Dev, †K. S. More, M. Prabhakar, A. S. Wassan and N. D. Hirwani did not bat.

Bowling: *First Innings*—Houseman 13–2–43–0; Sidebottom 12.5–1–46–0; Fletche 18–2–82–2; Byas 5–0–29–0; White 7–2–37–0; Doidge 14–2–54–0. *Second Innings*—Housemar 7–1–26–2; Sidebottom 4–1–23–0; Doidge 10–3–52–0; Fletcher 6–0–17–0; Byas 3–0–16–0.

Yorkshire

*M. D. Moxon not out	45	– c Kapil Dev b Hirwani	93
A. A. Metcalfe not out	40	– b Shastri	74
K. Sharp (did not bat)		– c Shastri b Hirwani	2
S. A. Kellett (did not bat)		– not out	36
†R. J. Blakey (did not bat)		– b Kapil Dev	2
D. Byas (did not bat)		– not out	8
L-b 1, n-b 2	3	B 1, l-b 8, w 1	10

(no wkt dec.) 88   1/152 2/161 3/192   (4 wkts) 225
4/208

M. J. Doidge, C. White, A. Sidebottom, I. J. Houseman and S. D. Fletcher did not bat.

Bowling: *First Innings*—Kapil Dev 8–2–13–0; Prabhakar 8–1–38–0; Wassan 5–0–31–0; Shastri 3–2–5–0. *Second Innings*—Kapil Dev 10–3–37–1; Prabhakar 8–0–48–0; Shastri 6–2–54–1; Wassan 6–2–24–0; Hirwani 13–1–45–2; Raman 3–1–8–0.

Umpires: H. D. Bird and J. H. Hampshire.

HAMPSHIRE v INDIANS

At Southampton, July 4, 5, 6. Hampshire won by seven wickets. Toss: Indians. Azharuddin's willingness to contribute to a genuine contest, rather than to seek batting practice after the first day had been lost to the weather, provided Hampshire with a chance to defeat a touring side for the first time for eight years. The Indian captain's second declaration challenged them to score 305 in a minimum of 62 overs, and after the early loss of Terry and Smith, Nicholas played with characteristic power and authority. With Gower, also at his best, he added 155 in 40 overs, mostly of spin, before being bowled for 104. His only first-class century of the summer, it came from 133 balls and included fourteen boundaries. Gower was undefeated at the close with 126, his second first-class hundred for his new county, having hit two sixes and fourteen fours to secure Hampshire's win with three overs to spare. As well as a victory to savour, the match also gave the Hampshire public the opportunity to assess the exciting potential of Tendulkar, and the seventeen-year-old did not disappoint them in two innings of considerable maturity.

Close of play: First day, No play; Second day, Hampshire 117-2 (M. C. J. Nicholas 37*, D. I. Gower 44*).

Indians

W. V. Raman c Terry b Joseph	26	– c Maru b Connor	22
N. S. Sidhu c Terry b Joseph	6	– not out	58
S. R. Tendulkar c Terry b Bakker	32	– not out	58
D. B. Vengsarkar c Parks b Connor	21		
*M. Azharuddin b Ayling	74		
M. Prabhakar c and b Maru	76		
†N. R. Mongia not out	14		
S. L. V. Raju c Parks b Maru	18		
B 6, l-b 3, w 2	11	B 1, l-b 3, n-b 1	5

1/22 2/39 3/78 4/92 5/240   (7 wkts dec.) 278   1/38   (1 wkt dec.) 143
6/246 7/278

S. K. Sharma, A. Kumble and N. D. Hirwani did not bat.

Bowling: *First Innings*—Bakker 22–1–84–1; Joseph 10–2–28–2; Connor 14–4–43–1; Ayling 5–2–45–1; Maru 16.4–1–69–2. *Second Innings*—Connor 8–3–28–1; Bakker 13–2–37–0; Ayling 8–1–26–0; Maru 6–0–31–0; Nicholas 4–0–17–0.

Hampshire

V. P. Terry c Raman b Prabhakar	5	– lbw b Sharma	11
C. L. Smith c Raman b Hirwani	24	– lbw b Prabhakar	36
*M. C. J. Nicholas not out	37	– b Prabhakar	104
D. I. Gower not out	44	– not out	126
J. R. Ayling (did not bat)		– not out	21
L-b 1, n-b 6	7	B 2, l-b 7, n-b 1	10

1/13 2/55   (2 wkts dec.) 117   1/26 2/85 3/240   (3 wkts) 308

T. C. Middleton, L. A. Joseph, †R. J. Parks, R. J. Maru, C. A. Connor and P. J. Bakker did not bat.

Bowling: *First Innings*—Prabhakar 8–1–20–1; Sharma 8–0–34–0; Hirwani 7–1–25–1; Raju 9–2–28–0; Kumble 2–0–9–0. *Second Innings*—Prabhakar 19–0–102–2; Sharma 16–3–79–1; Raju 13–1–56–0; Hirwani 8–0–39–0; Kumble 5–0–23–0.

Umpires: N. T. Plews and D. R. Shepherd.

KENT v INDIANS

At Canterbury, July 7, 8, 9. Indians won by seven wickets. Toss: Kent. Hinks and Benson gave Kent a solid start, with Taylor built on with an unbeaten 107, hitting seventeen fours in a stay of 241 minutes before Chris Cowdrey declared. Opening the innings because of sickness in the Indian team, Tendulkar stroked fourteen fours as he made 92 of the first 154 runs, facing 156 balls. The tourists declared well behind and were rewarded with a target of 265 to win in a minimum of 62 overs. After another fine performance from Tendulkar, who this time scored his 70 runs in 99 balls with eight fours, Vengsarkar (105 balls, thirteen fours) and Kapi Dev (72 balls) applied the finishing touches, adding 137 in 25 overs to win the game convincingly with three overs to spare. This was to be the Indians' only victory in the county games.

Close of play: First day, Kent 257-2 (N. R. Taylor 58*, G. R. Cowdrey 24*); Second day, Kent 25-0 (S. A. Marsh 16*, M. V. Fleming 8*).

Kent

S. G. Hinks b Raju	62				
M. R. Benson b Hirwani	90				
N. R. Taylor not out	107				
G. R. Cowdrey c More b Wassan	44	– (6) not out	27
*C. S. Cowdrey not out	20	– (4) c Tendulkar b Hirwani	12
†S. A. Marsh (did not bat)		– (1) c Sharma b Raju	44
M. V. Fleming (did not bat)		– (2) c Hirwani b Wassan	21
R. M. Ellison (did not bat)		– (3) not out	29
T. A. Merrick (did not bat)		– (5) b Hirwani	6
B 7, l-b 8, w 2, n-b 10	27	B 4, l-b 5	9

1/126 2/196 3/295   (3 wkts. dec.) 350   1/44 2/82 3/96   (4 wkts. dec.) 148
                                                      4/104

C. Penn and R. P. Davis did not bat.

Bowling: *First Innings*—Kapil Dev 21-6-58-0; Prabhakar 10-1-34-0; Sharma 11-3-37-0; Wassan 24-3-101-1; Shastri 10-2-37-0; Hirwani 14-2-41-1; Raju 14-7-27-1. *Second Innings*—Kapil Dev 8-3-20-0; Sharma 3-0-11-0; Raju 17.3-5-41-1; Hirwani 16-4-48-2; Wassan 3-0-19-1.

Indians

†K. S. More c Taylor b Fleming	32	– c Penn b Fleming	27
S. R. Tendulkar c Davis b Merrick	92	– st Marsh b Davis	70
S. V. Manjrekar c Davis b Penn	20	– c Marsh b Fleming	9
D. B. Vengsarkar not out	50	– not out	83
Kapil Dev c Ellison b Davis	17	– not out	59
S. L. V. Raju lbw b Penn	4		
S. K. Sharma not out	13		
L-b 3, n-b 3	6	B 8, l-b 9, n-b 2	19

1/75 2/125 3/154 4/189 5/204   (5 wkts. dec.) 234   1/66 2/96 3/130   (3 wkts) 267

*R. J. Shastri, M. Prabhakar, A. S. Wassan and N. D. Hirwani did not bat.

Bowling: *First Innings*—Merrick 17-2-75-1; Penn 16-2-40-2; Davis 23-4-66-1; G. R. Cowdrey 1-1-0-0; Ellison 11-2-27-0; Fleming 8.3-2-23-1. *Second Innings*—Merrick 4.1-1-17-0; Penn 12-0-61-0; Davis 17.5-0-90-1; Ellison 8-1-23-0; Fleming 11-5-28-2; C. S. Cowdrey 4-0-19-0; G. R. Cowdrey 2-0-12-0.

Umpires: M. J. Kitchen and N. T. Plews.

MINOR COUNTIES v INDIANS

At Trowbridge, July 11, 12, 13. Drawn. Toss: Minor Counties. On a pitch perfect for batting both sides laid out a feast of runs as the Minor Counties entertained a touring side a Trowbridge for the third year in succession. Brown of Durham, brother of the Middles: middle-order batsman, and Buckinghamshire's Roberts were the principal beneficiaries on th opening day before Kumble changed the emphasis with six for 27 in nine overs after tea

Roberts posted his fifty in 78 balls in their partnership of 178 in 64 overs, and Brown was still savouring his maiden first-class hundred, which included a six off Raju and eleven fours, when he was smartly stumped off Kumble in the first over after tea. Three balls later the leg-spinner had the left-handed Folland lbw as he attempted to sweep, and the Minor Counties went into a decline. Next day, with the sun blazing down, Raman hit eleven boundaries while racing to his fifty, and Shastri revealed his aptitude as an opening bat. Stuck in the 90s for thirteen overs, he danced to three figures by straight-driving the steady, 46-year-old medium-pacer, Greensword, for six. Azharuddin stroked fifteen fours in his hundred, two and a half hours of great charm, and Tendulkar and Kapil Dev (four sixes in 47 from 39 balls) made sure the entertainment matched the temperature. A lead of 219 offered the Indians a prospect of victory. Instead, Brown and Folland added 157 in 44 overs, and with play scheduled to finish at four o'clock to accommodate their travel arrangements, the tourists settled for a draw. However, the decision to draw stumps after only eight of the last twenty overs robbed Brown of the chance to record two hundreds in the match, leaving him unbeaten with 89 after 4 hours 21 minutes (215 balls, fourteen fours). The first-class status of the match, uncertain at the time, was later confirmed by the TCCB.

Close of play: First day, Indians 24-0 (R. J. Shastri 15*, W. V. Raman 5*); Second day, Indians 512-6 dec.

Minor Counties

G. K. Brown st Mongia b Kumble	103 – not out	89
M. J. Roberts b Shastri	85 – c Azharuddin b Sharma	1
P. Burn c Mongia b Sharma	0 – (4) not out	47
N. A. Folland lbw b Kumble	26 – (3) b Raju	82
T. A. Lester c Raman b Kumble	4	
D. R. Thomas c Shastri b Kumble	27	
*S. Greensword c Mongia b Kapil Dev	1	
†A. R. Fothergill b Kumble	3	
R. A. Evans not out	4	
N. R. Taylor b Kumble	0	
B 8, l-b 17, w 6, n-b 9	40	B 20, l-b 2, n-b 2 24

1/178 2/183 3/245 4/246 5/250   (9 wkts dec.) 293   1/6 2/163   (2 wkts) 243
6/253 7/264 8/293 9/293

K. A. Arnold did not bat.

Bowling: *First Innings*—Kapil Dev 14-6-27-1; Sharma 15-4-43-1; Wassan 9-1-36-0; Raju 21-4-67-0; Kumble 18-3-49-6; Shastri 20-4-43-1; Tendulkar 1-0-3-0. *Second Innings*—Kapil Dev 16-9-20-0; Sharma 15-4-47-1; Wassan 9-0-42-0; Kumble 16-4-54-0; Raju 18-4-58-1.

Indians

R. J. Shastri b Evans	105	†N. R. Mongia not out 43
W. V. Raman c Greensword b Arnold	55	S. L. V. Raju not out 33
S. V. Manjrekar run out	40	B 5, l-b 4, w 3, n-b 7 19
*M. Azharuddin c Arnold b Taylor	105	
Kapil Dev c Arnold b Evans	47	1/102 2/201 3/238 (6 wkts dec.) 512
S. R. Tendulkar lbw b Brown	65	4/312 5/426 6/449

S. K. Sharma, A. S. Wassan and A. Kumble did not bat.

Bowling: Taylor 23-2-87-1; Arnold 28-6-113-1; Evans 28-1-147-2; Thomas 15-1-65-0; Greensword 19-6-52-0; Brown 9-1-39-1.

Umpires: D. J. Halfyard and G. A. Stickley.

†SCOTLAND v INDIANS

At Titwood, Glasgow, July 14. Indians won by seven wickets. Toss: Indians. Put in on a pitch containing some moisture and with cloud overhead, Scotland struggled to 89 for five at lunch, with the slow left-armer, Raju, taking three wickets courtesy of catches by the bat-pad fieldsmen. Patterson and Salmond, the latter in his first match for Scotland, were out to successive balls. The afternoon brought sunshine and something of a recovery as Henry, who hit a six and eight fours in his 74, and Russell took their sixth-wicket stand to 122 in 81 minutes together. In reply, the Indians batted attractively but well within themselves, and neither the Scottish bowling nor a bomb alert could disturb their serenity.

Scotland

I. L. Philip run out	14	D. Cowan not out	1
C. G. Greenidge lbw b Sharma	34	A. Bee not out	2
B. M. W. Patterson c Manjrekar b Raju	0	L-b 13, w 3, n-b 1	17
G. Salmond c Manjrekar b Raju	0		—
*O. Henry c Raman b Kapil Dev	74	1/44 2/45 3/45 (7 wkts, 55 overs) 196	
†D. J. Haggo c Tendulkar b Raju	6	4/56 5/71	
A. B. Russell c and b Kapil Dev	48	6/193 7/194	

C. T. McKnight and J. D. Moir did not bat.

Bowling: Kapil Dev 10-2-25-2; Prabhakar 10-2-43-0; Sharma 11-1-27-1; Tendulkar 3-1-9-0; Raju 11-3-22-3; Kumble 10-0-57-0.

Indians

N. S. Sidhu c McKnight b Henry	50	Kapil Dev not out	11
W. V. Raman c Haggo b Bee	89	B 2, l-b 2, w 1, n-b 4	9
S. V. Manjrekar c Greenidge b Bee	31		—
S. R. Tendulkar not out	10	1/98 2/160 3/183 (3 wkts, 51.3 overs) 200	

*M. Azharuddin, M. Prabhakar, S. L. V. Raju, †K. S. More, S. K. Sharma and A. Kumble did not bat.

Bowling: Moir 9-1-34-0; Cowan 9.3-0-48-0; Bee 11-1-35-2; McKnight 11-2-29-0; Henry 11-0-50-1.

Umpires: J. van Geloven and A. Wood.

†DERBYSHIRE v INDIANS

At Chesterfield, July 16. Indians won by two wickets. Toss: Derbyshire. Barnett's fine hundred, scored freely against undemanding bowling, was capped by an exquisite innings from Tendulkar. The Derbyshire captain began in rich form, though he was dropped by More on 10, and his 115 took his total of runs in July to 784. His century included a six and ten fours, and the opening stand of 137 with Bowler was their seventh hundred partnership in all cricket during the season. While the experienced batsmen failed in the Indians' reply, Tendulkar shaped the innings as he wished, impressing the Derbyshire crowd and players not so much by his obvious quality as by his astonishing maturity. He completed his hundred from 147 balls, by hooking Bishop over the trees at square leg, and he clinched the game with his seventh four. But Derbyshire's undisciplined bowling also helped the Indians; they gave away 17 runs in wides and 16 in no-balls.

Derbyshire

*K. J. Barnett c Sidhu b Kapil Dev	115	†K. M. Krikken not out	0
P. D. Bowler b Raju	59		
J. E. Morris c sub b Kapil Dev	37	L-b 7, w 4, n-b 2	13
B. Roberts c Azharuddin b Kapil Dev	8		—
C. J. Adams run out	0	1/137 2/208 3/223 (6 wkts, 55 overs) 235	
S. C. Goldsmith run out	3	4/224 5/235 6/235	

G. Miller, I. R. Bishop, S. J. Base and O. H. Mortensen did not bat.

Bowling: Kapil Dev 11-1-76-3; Prabhakar 11-2-29-0; Sharma 11-0-51-0; Kumble 11-1-26-0; Raju 11-0-46-1.

dians

. V. Raman b Base	17	S. L. V. Raju c Roberts b Miller	1
. S. Sidhu lbw b Bishop	0	S. K. Sharma not out	8
R. Tendulkar not out	105		
M. Azharuddin lbw b Miller	7	L-b 2, w 17, n-b 16	35
apil Dev c Barnett b Mortensen	1		
. Prabhakar run out	31	1/5 2/59 3/80 (8 wkts, 54.4 overs) 239
K. S. More c Barnett b Miller	6	4/81 5/134 6/144
. B. Vengsarkar st Krikken b Miller	28	7/210 8/212

Kumble did not bat.

Bowling: Mortensen 11-1-31-1; Bishop 11-2-44-1; Base 11-0-45-1; Goldsmith
.4-0-71-0; Miller 11-0-46-4.

Umpires: H. D. Bird and M. J. Kitchen.

†ENGLAND v INDIA

First Texaco Trophy Match

k Leeds, July 18. India won by six wickets. Toss: India. The touring side won comfortably
ter their bowlers, under-rated in the pre-match forecasts, had dismissed England for 229
side 55 overs. Such a total seemed unlikely as Gooch and Gower were putting on 64
troubled runs for the second wicket. But when Gooch was beaten by cleverly disguised
ght in Shastri's fifth over and Kumble bowled Gower with a ball that turned a long way,
en undid Smith with bounce in his next over, England found themselves 142 for four with
irteen overs remaining. Their next six wickets managed 87, with the last four falling in
teen deliveries. Although the pitch was on the slow side for one-day batting, all credit was
e to the Indian bowlers. Kumble, a leg-spinner, did not concede a boundary in taking two
r 29, and he and Shastri bowled their overs straight through. India lost Raman to the first
gitimate ball of their innings, DeFreitas having begun with a no-ball. Thereafter they
asted along. Sidhu was out just before tea; afterwards Tendulkar roused the crowd by
iving Hemmings straight for six, Manjrekar (133 balls) and Azharuddin (50 balls) added 68
ten overs, and finally Shastri hit four fours in his 23 to hurry India to victory with two overs
spare.
Man of the Match: A. Kumble.   *Attendance*: 16,000 est.; *receipts* £229,819.

ngland

G. A. Gooch c and b Shastri	45	A. R. C. Fraser not out	4
. A. Atherton lbw b Prabhakar	7	D. E. Malcolm c Kapil Dev b Prabhakar	4
I. Gower b Kumble	50		
. J. Lamb c Prabhakar b Kapil Dev	56	B 6, l-b 8, w 9	23
A. Smith c More b Kumble	6		
R. C. Russell c Manjrekar b Kapil Dev	14	1/22 (2) 2/86 (1) 3/134 (3) (54.3 overs) 229
A. J. DeFreitas b Sharma	11	4/142 (5) 5/186 (6) 6/196 (4)
C. Lewis lbw b Prabhakar	6	7/211 (8) 8/221 (9)
E. Hemmings b Sharma	3	9/224 (7) 10/229 (11)

Bowling: Kapil Dev 11-1-49-2; Prabhakar 10.3-1-40-3; Sharma 11-1-57-2; Shastri
-0-40-1; Kumble 11-2-29-2.

ndia

. V. Raman c Atherton b DeFreitas	0	R. J. Shastri not out	23
. S. Sidhu lbw b Lewis	39	L-b 5, w 9, n-b 1	15
V. Manjrekar c Gower b Lewis	82		
R. Tendulkar b Malcolm	19	1/1 (1) 2/76 (2) (4 wkts, 53 overs) 233
M. Azharuddin not out	55	3/115 (4) 4/183 (3)

K. S. More, Kapil Dev, M. Prabhakar, S. K. Sharma and A. Kumble did not bat.

Bowling: DeFreitas 10-1-40-1; Malcolm 11-0-57-1; Fraser 11-3-37-0; Lewis 10-0-58-2;
emmings 11-0-36-0.

Umpires: J. H. Hampshire and J. W. Holder.

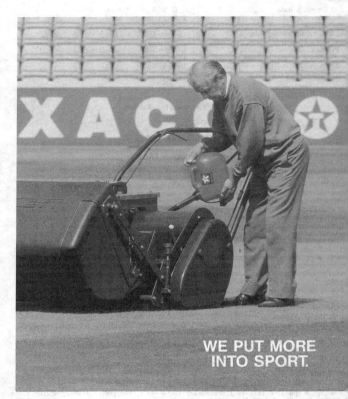

†ENGLAND v INDIA

Second Texaco Trophy Match

At Nottingham, July 20. India won by five wickets. Toss: India. The Indian batsmen revelled gloriously in ideal batting conditions; England's failed to do them, or themselves, justice. Gooch lost his off stump in the fourth over, offering no stroke to an in-swinger, and Gower and Lamb had been run out by the twentieth over. Having hit 24 of his 25 runs in boundaries, Gower was a victim of his own inattentiveness and the quick thinking of wicket-keeper More, whose throw hit the stumps at the non-striker's end. Smith gave the innings its purpose, reaching fifty from 42 balls and thumping most of the eleven fours in his 103 (105 balls). He added 111 in eighteen overs with the admirable Atherton (95 balls), and then 73 in twelve overs with Russell (50 balls); but when he was bowled in the 49th over, England's next five wickets realised just 35 runs. Small gave the Indians a flying start, conceding 12 runs in his first over, and when later he bowled Sidhu, Manjrekar held the innings together with 59 in 94 balls. By the time he was stumped he had caught the infectious mood of Vengsarkar's batting. India required 145 from the last twenty overs, and Tendulkar (26 balls) played some outrageous shots while adding 63 in seven overs with the felicitous Azharuddin, who went on to score 63 from 44 balls as India again won with two overs in hand. The defeat was England's tenth in their last eleven completed one-day internationals.

Man of the Match: R. A. Smith.   *Attendance:* 11,996; *receipts* £217,631.
Men of the Series: England – R. C. Russell; India – M. Azharuddin.

England

*G. A. Gooch b Prabhakar	7	G. C. Small c Azharuddin b Kapil Dev	4
M. A. Atherton c More b Prabhakar	59	E. E. Hemmings run out	0
D. I. Gower run out	25	A. R. C. Fraser not out	0
A. J. Lamb run out	3		
R. A. Smith b Shastri	103		
†R. C. Russell c Azharuddin		B 1, l-b 12, w 8, n-b 1	22
b Kapil Dev	50		
P. A. J. DeFreitas c Vengsarkar		1/12 (1) 2/47 (3) 3/62 (4) (55 overs) 281	
b Sharma	1	4/173 (2) 5/246 (5) 6/254 (7)	
C. C. Lewis lbw b Prabhakar	7	7/275 (8) 8/280 (9)	
		9/281 (10) 10/281 (6)	

Bowling: Kapil Dev 11–2–40–2; Prabhakar 11–0–58–3; Sharma 10–0–50–1; Shastri 11–0–52–1; Kumble 11–1–58–0; Tendulkar 1–0–10–0.

India

R. J. Shastri c Atherton b Hemmings	33	Kapil Dev not out	5
N. S. Sidhu b Small	23	L-b 5, w 9	14
S. V. Manjrekar st Russell b Hemmings	59		
D. B. Vengsarkar b Lewis	54	1/42 (2) 2/69 (1) (5 wkts, 53 overs) 282	
*M. Azharuddin not out	63	3/166 (3) 4/186 (4)	
S. R. Tendulkar b Fraser	31	5/249 (6)	

†K. S. More, M. Prabhakar, S. K. Sharma and A. Kumble did not bat.

Bowling: Small 10–0–73–1; DeFreitas 11–0–59–0; Fraser 11–1–38–1; Hemmings 11–1–53–2; Lewis 10–0–54–1.

Umpires: M. J. Kitchen and D. R. Shepherd.

LEICESTERSHIRE v INDIANS

At Leicester, July 21, 22, 23. Drawn. Toss: Leicestershire. Noisily supported by members of Leicester's large Indian community, the visitors found an opportunity to practise their strokes for the Lord's Test in their first innings, averaging 4 runs an over. Leicestershire's batsmen were also among the runs, however, and their captain, Briers, dominated the first day with his

unbeaten 150. Having survived a chance when 42, he went on to bat for six hours, hitting
seventeen fours and passing 1,000 first-class runs for the season. Whitaker helped him put on
131 for the second wicket and later he added 86 for the seventh with Benjamin, who struck
three sixes in his 55. The West Indian fast bowler removed Prabhakar on the first evening,
but the Leicestershire attack, already missing the injured Agnew, was weakened the next day
when Lewis withdrew because of a headache. Manjrekar, Vengsarkar and Mongia made the
most of it, and the Indians' reserve wicket-keeper hit seven fours and a six in his 63 not out.
The match was destined to drift towards a draw once Azharuddin chose to bat on for almost
an hour after tea on the second day, but Benson enlivened the final day's play by striking
twelve fours and three sixes in his maiden first-class hundred. Leicestershire's declaration left
the tourists to score an unrealistic 248 from a minimum of 31 overs, only nineteen of which
were bowled.

Close of play: First day, Indians 23-1 (N. S. Sidhu 8*, S. V. Manjrekar 8*); Second day,
Leicestershire 35-1 (L. Potter 10*, J. D. R. Benson 8*).

Leicestershire

T. J. Boon b Sharma	1	– c Hirwani b Wassan	16
*N. E. Briers not out	150		
J. J. Whitaker b Hirwani	61	– (9) not out	7
P. Willey c Tendulkar b Hirwani	5	– b Raju	76
L. Potter b Wassan	22	– (2) b Hirwani	30
C. C. Lewis c Manjrekar b Raju	1	– (5) c Prabhakar b Raju	28
J. D. R. Benson c Sharma b Wassan	0	– (3) c Prabhakar b Hirwani	106
W. K. M. Benjamin c Mongia b Wassan	55	– (7) b Raju	0
†P. A. Nixon not out	3	– (6) hit wkt b Raju	13
G. J. Parsons (did not bat)		– (8) not out	11
B 8, w 1, n-b 3	12	L-b 8, w 1, n-b 2	11

1/1 2/132 3/150 4/199 5/216   (7 wkts dec.) 310   1/25 2/108 3/181   (7 wkts dec.) 298
6/217 7/303   4/234 5/274
                                                           6/274 7/281

A. D. Mullally did not bat.

Bowling: *First Innings*—Prabhakar 10-1-35-0; Sharma 16-5-41-1; Tendulkar 1-0-9-0;
Wassan 17-1-76-3; Raju 30-7-62-1; Hirwani 22-1-79-2. *Second Innings*—Prabhakar
5-3-6-0; Sharma 13-2-52-0; Wassan 15-0-56-1; Raju 28-6-73-4; Hirwani 21-0-103-2.

Indians

M. Prabhakar c Potter b Benjamin	2	– c Nixon b Lewis	13
N. S. Sidhu c Nixon b Lewis	25	– lbw b Lewis	6
S. V. Manjrekar c Nixon b Mullally	66	– not out	3
S. R. Tendulkar c Benson b Parsons	30	– not out	25
D. B. Vengsarkar c Whitaker b Potter	80		
*M. Azharuddin c Mullally b Willey	46		
†N. R. Mongia not out	63		
S. L. V. Raju run out	3		
S. K. Sharma not out	23		
B 10, l-b 9, n-b 4	23	L-b 6, n-b 1	7

1/8 2/76 3/131 4/135 5/227   (7 wkts dec.) 361   1/20 2/25   (2 wkts) 54
6/285 7/302

A. S. Wassan and N. D. Hirwani did not bat.

Bowling: *First Innings*—Benjamin 20-2-81-1; Lewis 11-3-28-1; Parsons 16-2-73-1;
Mullally 18-1-78-1; Willey 17-5-42-1; Potter 12-1-40-1. *Second Innings*—Lewis 8-3-23-2;
Benjamin 4-1-8-0; Mullally 5-0-17-0; Parsons 2-2-0-0.

Umpires: J. H. Harris and J. W. Holder.

ENGLAND v INDIA

First Cornhill Test

At Lord's, July 26, 27, 28, 30, 31. England won by 247 runs. Toss: India. The Indians, and especially their captain, Azharuddin, had small reason to think so by the end, but the First Test was as brilliant a match as the players could hope to take part in, or spectators to watch. England's winning margin made it look one-sided; and no-one would dispute that, from lunch on the first day, when they were 82 for one after being put in, England were in control until the end. Certainly England's win, inspired by Gooch's historic innings of 333 and 123, which broke all kinds of records, was the result of a powerful performance by his team, and following the victory over New Zealand in the last Test of the previous series, it provided the first instance of England winning successive Tests since 1985. Yet it would not have been the match it was without the vibrant batting of the tourists. Shastri and Azharuddin made splendid hundreds of contrasting styles, and Kapil Dev struck a high-velocity 77 not out, jauntily rounded off with four successive sixes to limit England's lead to 199 and thus save the follow-on. Each was straight-driven off Hemmings's off-spin into the building works that throughout the season masqueraded as the Nursery End. When India were challenged by Gooch's second declaration to make 472 to win, or bat seven hours on a crusting pitch to draw, it was possible retrospectively to see that they were fighting a losing battle once Fraser and Malcolm had dismissed their openers in eight overs on the fourth evening.

Such was the depth of their batting, however, and the dash and artistry with which Vengsarkar and Azharuddin batted on the last morning as they put on 51 at 4 an over, that it was not until the former was caught at the wicket, trying not to play an off-break, that it became obvious there could be only one result. When Azharuddin followed twenty minutes later, superbly caught at third slip as he tried to turn a straight ball into the leg side, India's spirit cracked, and the score, at one stage 114 for three, was eroded to 181 for eight. A flourish by the last two wickets added 43 and so raised the match aggregate to 1,603, 2 runs more than the previous record for the ground, established in England's 1930 classic with Australia.

In similar conditions of pitch and outfield, true and fast respectively, Bradman had scored 254 in that Test, Woodfull 155, Duleepsinhji 173 and Chapman 121. What, if anything, could be inferred from the fact that in 1990 the average scoring-rate was 4.08 per over, whereas in the four-day Test of 1930 it had been 3.16? A different lbw Law, favouring the modern bowler, and the swing to heavier bats, supposedly favouring the batsmen – Gooch hit seven sixes with a three-pound Stuart Surridge Grand Prix Turbo – left too many imponderables for the question to be answered.

Of England's winning team against New Zealand at Edgbaston, Fairbrother and Small were dropped, while Stewart was put out of the reckoning by an injured back. They were replaced by Gower, returning after seven Tests, Morris of Derbyshire, a new cap, and Fraser, recovered at last from a rib injury suffered while in the Caribbean. Gower, debatably given out caught at point in the first innings, was outshone, while through no fault of his own, Morris faced only 21 balls. The 6ft 5in Fraser, however, played a leading part. Figures of five for 104 and three for 39 were due reward for his accuracy, bounce and movement at a lively pace. By using Shastri to open the batting, India made room to play the seventeen-year-old Bombay student, Tendulkar, who in England's second innings brought off as wonderful an outfield catch as Lord's has seen, holding Lamb's straight drive one-handed at knee height after hurtling more than 30 yards while long-off to a point behind the bowler.

At close of play on the first day, when England were 359 for two, Azharuddin tried to justify his decision to field by pointing out that had More, the wicket-keeper, held a routine chance when Gooch was 36, the score would have been 61 for two after 90 minutes' play. But 653 for four declared, with hundreds also from Lamb (in 276 minutes and 187 balls) and Smith (194 minutes, 155 balls), painted the picture truly. Azharuddin had made a bad misjudgement, and England made the most of it. Gooch, sharing with his vice-captain, Lamb, an all-wicket England v India record of 308, went on to make in 627 minutes (485 balls, three sixes, 43 fours) the highest score at Lord's, the third highest by an Englishman in Tests, and the sixth highest Test score overall before being bowled by medium-pacer Prabhakar, missing an off-drive. He was just 32 runs short of the world record of 365 not out, scored by Sir Garfield Sobers for West Indies against Pakistan in 1957-58.

Shastri, who made his hundred in 246 minutes and 184 balls, absorbed England's fast bowling like a born Test opener, only to mistime an on-drive off Hemmings. By contrast, Azharuddin dazzled. Not a few strokes early in his innings would have been hard to excuse had they cost him his wicket; but his luck held, and a capacity Saturday crowd was treated to a rare exhibition of audacious, wristy strokeplay which, with twenty fours, took him into three figures off only 88 balls. At close of play that day, when he was 117 not out, a draw looked the likeliest result. In Monday's third over, however, Azharuddin was bowled by Hemmings with an off-break that turned up the slope to hit leg stump as he was framing an expansive back-foot stroke through extra cover. Just 40 minutes later, when Fraser dismissed More and Sharma in three balls, India were 430 for nine, needing 24 to save the follow-on. Kapil Dev watched Hirwani survive the last ball of Fraser's over, played the first two of Hemmings's defensively, then ripped into the next four and drove each one for six. Three of them were enormous, clattering the scaffolding, one was simply big; all were magnificent. With the very next delivery, Fraser had Hirwani lbw. India had scored 78 in 15.1 overs, and the devil-may-care Kapil had become the first man to hit four sixes running in a Test. It was an unexpected way to save a follow-on.

Gooch, flicking Kapil Dev off his toes to the 65-yard Tavern boundary, at once set the tempo of England's 218-minute second innings, in which runs came at 5 an over. When he was out with the score 204, caught at extra cover after hitting four sixes and thirteen fours in 148 minutes and 113 balls, he had beaten G. S. Chappell's previous aggregate record for a Test by 76 runs. With Atherton, he had established a new record for England's first wicket against India. Answering in kind, India reached 57 for two in 56 minutes by the close and, despite the early loss of Manjrekar on the last morning, they were still batting as though they believed they had a winning chance at noon. Then, from the Nursery End, Hemmings caught Vengsarkar in two minds with a ball that pitched narrowly outside off stump. At the last moment the batsman decided not to play it, but it hurried through and brushed his gloves, heralding the final chapter of a memorable Test. Fittingly, it was Gooch who brought proceedings to a close midway through the sun-baked afternoon, flattening the middle stump at the bowler's end to run out Sharma from mid-on. – John Thicknesse.

Man of the Match: G. A. Gooch.   *Attendance:* 60,924; *receipts* £919,500.

Close of play: First day, England 359-2 (G. A. Gooch 194*, A. J. Lamb 104*); Second day, India 48-0 (R. J. Shastri 27*, N. S. Sidhu 20*); Third day, India 376-6 (M. Azharuddin 117*, Kapil Dev 14*); Fourth day, India 57-2 (S. V. Manjrekar 29*, D. B. Vengsarkar 14*).

England

*G. A. Gooch b Prabhakar	333	– c Azharuddin b Sharma 123
M. A. Atherton c Lamb b Kapil Dev	8	– c Vengsarkar b Sharma 72
D. I. Gower c Manjrekar b Hirwani	40	– not out 32
A. J. Lamb c Manjrekar b Sharma	139	– c Tendulkar b Hirwani 19
R. A. Smith not out	100	– b Prabhakar 15
J. E. Morris not out	4	
B 2, l-b 21, w 2, n-b 4	29	L-b 11 11

1/14 (2) 2/141 (3) 3/449 (4)   (4 wkts dec.) 653   1/204 (1) 2/207 (2)   (4 wkts dec.) 272
4/641 (1)   3/250 (4) 4/272 (5)

†R. C. Russell, C. C. Lewis, E. E. Hemmings, A. R. C. Fraser and D. E. Malcolm did not bat.

Bowling: *First Innings*—Kapil Dev 34–5–120–1; Prabhakar 43–6–187–1; Sharma 33–5–122–1; Shastri 22–0–99–0; Hirwani 30–1–102–1. *Second Innings*—Kapil Dev 10–0–53–0; Prabhakar 11.2–2–45–1; Shastri 7–0–38–0; Sharma 15–0–75–2; Hirwani 11–0–50–1.

India

R. J. Shastri c Gooch b Hemmings	100	– c Russell b Malcolm 12
N. S. Sidhu c Morris b Fraser	30	– c Morris b Fraser 1
S. V. Manjrekar c Russell b Gooch	18	– c Russell b Malcolm 33
D. B. Vengsarkar c Russell b Fraser	52	– c Russell b Hemmings 35
*M. Azharuddin b Hemmings	121	– c Atherton b Lewis 37
S. R. Tendulkar b Lewis	10	– c Gooch b Fraser 27
M. Prabhakar c Lewis b Malcolm	25	– lbw b Lewis 8
Kapil Dev not out	77	– c Lewis b Hemmings 7
†K. S. More c Morris b Fraser	8	– lbw b Fraser 16
S. K. Sharma c Russell b Fraser	0	– run out 38
N. D. Hirwani lbw b Fraser	0	– not out 0
L-b 1, w 4, n-b 8	13	B 3, l-b 1, n-b 6 10

1/63 (2) 2/102 (3) 3/191 (1) 4/241 (4)   454   1/9 (2) 2/23 (1) 3/63 (3)   224
5/288 (6) 6/348 (7) 7/393 (5)   4/114 (4) 5/127 (5) 6/140 (7)
8/430 (9) 9/430 (10) 10/454 (11)   7/158 (8) 8/181 (6)
                                                         9/206 (9) 10/224 (10)

Bowling: *First Innings*—Malcolm 25-1-106-1; Fraser 39.1-9-104-5; Lewis 24-3-108-1; ...och 6-3-26-1; Hemmings 20-3-109-2. *Second Innings*—Fraser 22-7-39-3; Malcolm ...0-65-2; Hemmings 21-2-79-2; Atherton 1-0-11-0; Lewis 8-1-26-2.

Umpires: H. D. Bird and N. T. Plews.

SURREY v INDIANS

At The Oval, August 1, 2, 3. Drawn. Toss: Surrey. The Indians had a poor day in the field in [th]e aftermath of their Test defeat at Lord's, not being helped by a spate of dropped catches [an]d some erratic bowling by the lively seamer, Wassan. The bespectacled leg-spinner, [Hi]rwani, suffered most from his team-mates' errors. A studious 97 from Clinton, 82 from [Ste]wart, with three sixes and six fours, and Lynch's robust 94 were the major contributions as [Su]rrey ran up 384 for seven in 90 overs. Next day, however, the touring team were lifted by a [sm]oothly assembled century from the tall left-hander, Raman, augmented by Vengsarkar's [m]eticulous half-century, and Shastri kept the game open by declaring 95 runs in arrears. [Be]fore the close Clinton had passed 50 for the second time in the match, in 61 balls, and next [da]y Greig, having hit five sixes and five fours to revive Surrey's stuttering innings, invited the [In]dians to chase 351 in 65 overs for victory. This was probably a stiffer target than Shastri had [be]en hoping for, given that the Indians were resting some of their top batsmen, and they [set]tled instead for batting practice.

Close of play: First day, Indians 35-1 (W. V. Raman 21*, S. V. Manjrekar 3*); Second day, [Su]rrey 96-1 (G. S. Clinton 53*, A. J. Stewart 22*).

Surrey

. J. Bicknell b Wassan	22		
. S. Clinton c Shastri b Kumble	97	– c sub b Shastri	74
. J. Stewart b Hirwani	82	– lbw b Shastri	22
. M. Ward c Mongia b Kumble	20	– b Hirwani	28
. A. Lynch c Raman b Hirwani	94	– c Manjrekar b Hirwani	3
. A. Greig st More b Hirwani	36	– not out	76
. A. Feltham c Mongia b Raju	1	– c Vengsarkar b Hirwani	5
. T. Medlycott not out	2	– not out	15
N. F. Sargeant (did not bat)		– (1) c Raman b Hirwani	18
B 5, l-b 8, w 9, n-b 8	30	B 2, l-b 9, n-b 3	14

1/34 2/189 3/233 4/282 5/351   (7 wkts dec.) 384   1/57 2/96 3/149   (6 wkts dec.) 255
6/352 7/384   4/149 5/170 6/190

. M. Kendrick and A. H. Gray did not bat.

Bowling: *First Innings*—Sharma 10-0-29-0; Wassan 13-1-81-1; Raju 22-4-64-1; Hirwani ...2-0-122-3; Kumble 21-1-75-2. *Second Innings*—Sharma 3-0-7-0; Wassan 4-0-19-0; ...astri 27.3-5-80-2; Hirwani 15-0-71-4; Kumble 3-0-15-0; Raju 1-0-52-0.

Indians

. V. Raman c Gray b Kendrick	127	– c sub b Kendrick	58
. R. Mongia c Kendrick b Feltham	10	– c Feltham b Kendrick	41
V. Manjrekar c Kendrick b Gray	9	– not out	52
. B. Vengsarkar c Stewart b Gray	55		
R. J. Shastri st Sargeant b Medlycott	8		
K. S. More c Sargeant b Medlycott	12	– (4) not out	12
L. V. Raju c and b Medlycott	7		
K. Sharma c Gray b Kendrick	15		
. Kumble c Kendrick b Gray	19		
. S. Wassan not out	8		
B 5, l-b 7, n-b 7	19	L-b 1, n-b 3	4

1/18 2/46 3/183 4/209 5/237   (9 wkts dec.) 289   1/94 2/111   (2 wkts) 167
6/242 7/261 8/261 9/289

. D. Hirwani did not bat.

Bowling: *First Innings*—Gray 18.1–0–69–3; Feltham 11–2–48–1; Medlycott 35–8–102–
Kendrick 20–4–58–2. *Second Innings*—Gray 9–0–41–0; Feltham 4–0–20–0; Medlyco
24–7–55–0; Kendrick 20–5–50–2.

Umpires: A. G. T. Whitehead and P. B. Wight.

GLOUCESTERSHIRE v INDIANS

At Bristol, August 4, 5, 6. Drawn. Toss: Indians. Although fifteen wickets fell on the first da
it was hard to perceive much malice in the pitch or bowling; many batsmen were out throu;
careless strokes. More and Raju pulled the touring side round after Walsh, captaini
Gloucestershire for the first time, had juggled his limited bowling resources to such effect th
eight wickets went for 112. The ninth-wicket pair added 127, but Raju's brave innings was l
last of the tour. His left hand was broken by a ball from Walsh. Milburn and Williams, wi
his maiden first-class fifty, helped Athey earn Gloucestershire a lead of 67, which prove
insignificant as openers Shastri and Sidhu thrilled their Indian supporters in a partnership
251. The second highest for any wicket by an Indian side in England, it ended shortly befo
lunch on the final day when Sidhu was caught going for his seventh six. He also hit sixtee
fours, while Shastri hit nineteen. The Indians' declaration, when the lead was 324 and only
overs remained, seemed no more than a token until Kapil Dev and Prabhakar, swinging t
ball about, caused Gloucestershire further embarrassment by taking four cheap wickets befo
the game was given up.

Close of play: First day, Gloucestershire 90-5 (C. W. J. Athey 11*, E. T. Milburn 0*
Second day, Indians 140-0 (R. J. Shastri 70*, N. S. Sidhu 69*).

Indians

R. J. Shastri b Walsh	5	– b Alleyne	1
N. S. Sidhu c Williams b Lawrence	31	– c Barnes b Lloyds	14
W. V. Raman c Williams b Walsh	0	– not out	
S. R. Tendulkar c Williams b Milburn	13	– c Lawrence b Romaines	
*M. Azharuddin b Alleyne	23		
M. Prabhakar c Hodgson b Alleyne	12	– (5) not out	
Kapil Dev c Butcher b Alleyne	12		
K. S. More c Williams b Milburn	95		
†N. R. Mongia c Alleyne b Lawrence	1		
S. L. V. Raju not out	40		
N. D. Hirwani c Williams b Milburn	0		
L-b 1, n-b 6	7	L-b 1, n-b 1	

1/13 2/19 3/42 4/54 5/79   239   1/251 2/301 3/374   (3 wkts dec.) 3
6/86 7/103 8/112 9/239

Bowling: *First Innings*—Walsh 17–4–45–2; Lawrence 12–1–65–2; Barnes 5–1–18–
Milburn 14.3–3–43–3; Alleyne 10–3–41–3; Lloyds 9–1–24–0; Athey 1–0–2–0. *Second Innings*
Lawrence 13–1–42–0; Walsh 11–5–16–0; Alleyne 15–1–54–1; Milburn 11–0–73–0; Lloy
21–0–136–1; Athey 13–1–39–0; Romaines 6–0–30–1.

Gloucestershire

G. D. Hodgson c Hirwani b Tendulkar	16	– not out	
I. P. Butcher b Hirwani	41	– b Prabhakar	
P. W. Romaines c Mongia b Tendulkar	2	– c More b Prabhakar	
C. W. J. Athey c Azharuddin b Hirwani	80		
M. W. Alleyne c Shastri b Tendulkar	0	– (4) c More b Kapil Dev	
J. W. Lloyds c Kapil Dev b Hirwani	8	– (5) c More b Kapil Dev	
E. T. Milburn c Mongia b Hirwani	35	– (6) not out	
†R. C. J. Williams not out	50		
*C. A. Walsh c Prabhakar b Hirwani	0		
D. V. Lawrence c Mongia b Prabhakar	35		
S. N. Barnes not out	12		
B 7, l-b 7, w 1, n-b 12	27	L-b 1, n-b 3	

1/54 2/66 3/71 4/73 5/89   (9 wkts dec.) 306   1/2 2/14 3/15 4/42   (4 wkts)
6/188 7/211 8/219 9/266

Bowling: *First Innings*—Prabhakar 18–4–53–1; Tendulkar 32–6–79–3; Hirwani 43–9–117–5; Shastri 22–6–36–0; Raman 1–0–7–0. *Second Innings*—Kapil Dev 11–1–28–2; Prabhakar 11–2–26–2; Tendulkar 5–1–6–0; Hirwani 4–0–4–0; Raman 1–0–1–0.

Umpires: B. Dudleston and D. S. Thompsett.

ENGLAND v INDIA

Second Cornhill Test

At Manchester, August 9, 10, 11, 13, 14. Drawn. Toss: England. Of the six individual centuries scored in this fascinating contest, none was more outstanding than Tendulkar's, which rescued India on the final afternoon. At 17 years and 112 days, he was only 30 days older than Mushtaq Mohammad was when, against India at Delhi in 1960-61, he became the youngest player to score a Test hundred. More significantly, after several of his colleagues had fallen to reckless strokes, Tendulkar held the England attack at bay with a disciplined display of immense maturity.

India were placed on the defensive once Gooch chose to bat first. The Old Trafford groundsman, Peter Marron, wrong-footed by a cold change in the weather after watering, had predicted even bounce but little pace, and England quickly grasped the opportunity. Leading an unchanged side, Gooch put on 73 untroubled runs with Atherton in the first hour, and India soon resorted to their leg-spinners, Hirwani and Kumble, the latter replacing seamer Sharma from the team at Lord's. They slowed down England's progress, but could do little to prevent a 225-run opening partnership, which overtook by 21 runs the record Gooch and Atherton had set at Lord's a fortnight earlier. In scoring 116, Gooch became the first English batsman for nineteen years to record centuries in three successive Test innings, but on the day he was eclipsed by his junior partner. In five and a half hours, Atherton carefully constructed 131, exactly matching the feat of G. Pullar, the only other Lancastrian to score a Test century for England at Old Trafford, against India 31 years earlier. Smith batted for just over four hours, passing his century during a last-wicket partnership of 60 with Malcolm, an unexpectedly supportive ally, as England reached 519.

The loss of three quick wickets for 57 to the seam movement of Fraser, in the final hour of the second day, placed India in immediate peril. On Saturday, however, they were rescued in style by their captain, Azharuddin, and Manjrekar, whose fourth-wicket stand of 189 set the pace for an entertaining day's play in which 355 runs were scored. Manjrekar made 93 in three and threequarter hours before falling to a bat-pad catch at silly point off the tireless Hemmings, but Azharuddin could not be stopped so easily. In a breathtaking 281-minute stay for 179, he hit 21 fours and a six, and between lunch and tea he became the first player to score 100 runs for India in a Test session. After he had miscued a drive off Fraser to Atherton, the second new ball accounted for most of the remaining Indian batting, although Tendulkar, after taking 54 minutes to get off the mark, gave warning of his talents in scoring 68 from 136 balls to reduce the England lead to just 87.

As England's second innings began on the fourth morning, Gooch suffered a rare failure in a rich summer, departing for 7. But Atherton added a further 74 to his first-innings hundred, and a winning position was achieved through the efforts of Lamb. Earlier in the game he had looked out of his depth against the Indian spinners, but, relishing the challenge, hit Hirwani for two successive sixes early on, and his 109 from 141 balls, followed by Smith's unbeaten 61, allowed Gooch to declare 25 minutes into the final day.

To win and square the series, India were offered a minimum of 88 overs in which to score 408, 2 runs more than their own record for the highest winning total by a side batting second in a Test. From the seventh ball of their innings, when Sidhu was brilliantly caught off Fraser by the substitute, Adams, at short leg, it looked a tall order. On a slowly wearing pitch Hemmings produced just enough deviation to have both Manjrekar and Azharuddin caught in the leg trap – but it was the gay abandon of three senior Indian batsmen which might have set Tendulkar a bad example. Shastri dragged a wide ball on to his stumps, Vengsarkar offered no stroke to Lewis, and Kapil Dev sallied down the pitch to Hemmings.

When the all-rounder, Prabhakar, joined Tendulkar, India were 183 for six and there were two and a half hours of the match remaining. Gooch crowded the bat and shuffled his bowlers like a croupier, but England were to be denied by their own mistakes. Hemmings put down a simple return catch when Tendulkar was 10, and Gooch failed to get a hand at second slip to a chance offered by Prabhakar. England could ill afford such lapses, and the pair had seen India to safety when the game was halted with two of the final twenty overs still to be bowled.

Tendulkar remained undefeated on 119, having batted for 224 minutes and hit seventeen fours. He looked the embodiment of India's famous opener, Gavaskar, and indeed was wearing a pair of his pads. While he displayed a full repertoire of strokes in compiling his maiden Test hundred, most remarkable were his off-side shots from the back foot. Though only 5ft 5in tall, he was still able to control without difficulty short deliveries from the English pacemen. – Graham Otway.

Man of the Match: S. R. Tendulkar.   *Attendance:* 42,424; *receipts* £521,100.

Close of play: First day, England 322-3 (A. J. Lamb 20*, R. C. Russell 7*); Second day, India 77-3 (S. V. Manjrekar 21*, M. Azharuddin 4*); Third day, India 432; Fourth day, England 290-4 (R. A. Smith 49*, J. E. Morris 15*).

England

*G. A. Gooch c More b Prabhakar	116	– c More b Prabhakar 7
M. A. Atherton c More b Hirwani	131	– lbw b Kapil Dev 74
D. I. Gower c Tendulkar b Kapil Dev	38	– b Hirwani 16
A. J. Lamb c Manjrekar b Kumble	38	– b Kapil Dev 109
†R. C. Russell c More b Hirwani	8	– (7) not out 16
R. A. Smith not out	121	– (5) not out 61
J. E. Morris b Kumble	13	– (6) retired hurt 15
C. C. Lewis b Hirwani	3	
E. E. Hemmings lbw b Hirwani	19	
A. R. C. Fraser c Tendulkar b Kumble	1	
D. E. Malcolm b Shastri	13	
B 2, l-b 9, w 1, n-b 6	18	L-b 15, n-b 7 22

1/225 (1) 2/292 (3) 3/312 (2) 4/324 (5)	519	1/15 (1) 2/46 (3)	(4 wkts dec.) 320
5/366 (6) 6/392 (7) 7/404 (8)			3/180 (2) 4/248 (4)
8/434 (9) 9/459 (10) 10/519 (11)

In the second innings J. E. Morris retired hurt at 290.

Bowling: *First Innings*—Kapil Dev 13–2–67–1; Prabhakar 25–2–112–1; Kumble 43–7–105–3; Hirwani 62–10–174–4; Shastri 17.5–2–50–1. *Second Innings*—Kapil Dev 22–4–69–2; Prabhakar 18–1–80–1; Hirwani 15–0–52–1; Kumble 17–3–65–0; Shastri 9–0–39–0.

India

R. J. Shastri c Gooch b Fraser	25	– b Malcolm 12
N. S. Sidhu c Gooch b Fraser	13	– c sub (C. J. Adams) b Fraser ... 0
S. V. Manjrekar c Smith b Hemmings	93	– c sub (C. J. Adams) b Hemmings 50
D. B. Vengsarkar c Russell b Fraser	6	– b Lewis 32
*M. Azharuddin c Atherton b Fraser	179	– c Lewis b Hemmings 11
S. R. Tendulkar c Lewis b Hemmings	68	– not out 119
M. Prabhakar c Russell b Malcolm	4	– (8) not out 67
Kapil Dev lbw b Lewis	0	– (7) b Hemmings 26
†K. S. More b Fraser	6	
A. Kumble run out	2	
N. D. Hirwani not out	15	
B 5, l-b 4, n-b 12	21	B 17, l-b 3, n-b 6 26

1/26 (2) 2/48 (1) 3/57 (4) 4/246 (3)	432	1/4 (2) 2/35 (1)	(6 wkts) 343
5/358 (5) 6/364 (7) 7/365 (8)			3/109 (3) 4/109 (4)
8/396 (9) 9/401 (10) 10/432 (6)			5/127 (5) 6/183 (7)

Bowling: *First Innings*—Malcolm 26–3–96–1; Fraser 35–5–124–5; Hemmings 29.2–8–74–2; Lewis 13–1–61–1; Atherton 16–3–68–0. *Second Innings*—Malcolm 14–5–59–1; Fraser 21–3–81–1; Hemmings 31–10–75–3; Atherton 4–0–22–0; Lewis 20–3–86–1.

Umpires: J. H. Hampshire and J. W. Holder.

TCCB UNDER-25 XI v INDIANS

At Birmingham, August 15, 16, 17. Drawn. Toss: TCCB Under-25 XI. A slow pitch, and the inhibitions young batsmen invariably feel under the eye of an England selector, made a draw the likeliest outcome, even though Stephenson declared 61 runs in arrears in the hope of being set a target. However, Shastri, captaining the touring team, made it a difficult one – 300 in 56 overs. Shastri himself was unable to bowl because of an injured hand, and having been put in on a pitch which promised to help the seam bowlers, but subsequently reneged, he probably felt he owed few favours. On the opening day, Bicknell enjoyed some success with the second new ball, taking three for 20 in nine overs. But by then Raman and Manjrekar had captivated with a partnership of 85 in 80 minutes, and Manjrekar and Vengsarkar had consolidated the innings with a century stand in 114. Manjrekar, with dancing footwork and supple wrists, was always quick to show up any weakness in line and length, hitting fourteen fours in his three-and-a-quarter-hour stay (197 balls). Sidhu, who missed out in the first innings, took his chance in the second and hit an unbeaten 108 from 189 balls (three sixes, thirteen fours), while Raman hit ten boundaries in his 56 as they opened with 134 in 151 minutes. Stephenson batted soundly for almost four hours in the Under-25s' first innings, his 116 from 242 balls including seventeen fours, and when his side lost three second-innings wickets in the first nine overs, he and Blakey ensured there was no further collapse.

Close of play: First day, Indians 293-6 (M. Prabhakar 2*, N. R. Mongia 1*); Second day, Indians 87-0 (N. S. Sidhu 48*, W. V. Raman 36*).

Indians

W. V. Raman lbw b Stephenson	61 –	(2) lbw b Munton 56
N. S. Sidhu c Blakey b Lampitt	13 –	(1) not out 108
S. V. Manjrekar c Stephenson b Medlycott	116	
D. B. Vengsarkar c Hussain b Bicknell	54	
S. R. Tendulkar c Lampitt b Bicknell	39 –	not out 30
*R. J. Shastri lbw b Bicknell	4	
M. Prabhakar not out	2 –	(4) st Blakey b Medlycott 23
†N. R. Mongia not out	1 –	(3) b Illingworth 11
L-b 2, n-b 1	3	B 3, l-b 6, n-b 1 10

1/33 2/118 3/220 4/278 5/287 6/290 (6 wkts dec.) 293   1/134 2/167 3/194 (3 wkts dec.) 238

S. K. Sharma, A. Kumble and A. S. Wassan did not bat.

Bowling: *First Innings*—Munton 23–9–49–0; Bicknell 22–6–50–3; Medlycott 9–1–46–1; Stephenson 6–2–18–1; Illingworth 24–5–66–0. *Second Innings*—Bicknell 9–2–26–0; Lampitt 8–0–33–0; Shahid 5–0–41–0; Munton 14–6–26–1; Stephenson 6–2–16–0; Illingworth 17–3–58–1; Medlycott 5–0–29–1.

TCCB Under-25 XI

*J. P. Stephenson c Mongia b Kumble	116 –	not out 41
N. Shahid st Mongia b Shastri	39 –	lbw b Prabhakar 0
G. P. Thorpe b Sharma	18 –	lbw b Sharma 5
N. Hussain not out	37	
P. Johnson b Wassan	3 –	(4) lbw b Prabhakar 1
†R. J. Blakey (did not bat)	–	(5) not out 40
B 8, l-b 1, n-b 10	19	B 7, l-b 15, n-b 1 23

1/118 2/175 3/214 4/232 (4 wkts dec.) 232   1/1 2/12 3/19 (3 wkts) 110

K. T. Medlycott, R. K. Illingworth, S. R. Lampitt, M. P. Bicknell and T. A. Munton did not bat.

Bowling: *First Innings*—Prabhakar 5–0–13–0; Sharma 18–1–57–1; Wassan 19.3–1–74–1; Tendulkar 14–3–40–0; Shastri 5–3–11–1; Kumble 19–8–28–1. *Second Innings*—Prabhakar 7–3–13–2; Sharma 10–3–24–1; Wassan 14–6–18–0; Kumble 5–1–9–0; Tendulkar 6–1–24–0.

Umpires: M. J. Harris and D. O. Oslear.

GLAMORGAN v INDIANS

At Swansea, August 18, 19, 20. Drawn. Toss: Indians. Although the loss of the second day spoiled the match as a contest, the spectators were treated to some spectacular strokeplay by Raman, Sidhu and Tendulkar on the first day, and later in the game only the staunch resistance of Croft and Metson denied the touring team a second victory over county opposition. The Indian openers put on 115 in even time, and after four wickets had fallen for just 13 runs, Tendulkar hit three sixes as he launched the recovery with some quality strokes. Even so, the Indians needed a ninth-wicket partnership of 90 between Mongia and Kumble to see them past 300. Glamorgan lost two quick wickets in the evening, and after Sunday's rain Butcher declared at the overnight 39 for two to help set up an interesting finish. The Indians then batted for an hour before leaving the home county the formidable task of scoring 390 from 79 overs. Despite another fluent innings from Morris, in pursuit of his county's record of nine hundreds in a season, Glamorgan seemed to be facing defeat when they were 170 for seven in the first over after tea, having just lost four wickets for 3 runs. However, Croft and Metson defied the tourists for 33 overs and put on 103, a county record for that wicket against the Indians. Both completed half-centuries, while figures of six for 89 from the medium-pacer, Wassan, ensured him of a place in India's team for the final Test at The Oval.

Close of play: First day, Glamorgan 39-2 (H. Morris 23*, M. P. Maynard 4*); Second day, No play.

Indians

N. S. Sidhu c James b Dale	54	– not out	76
W. V. Raman b Dale	59	– not out	20
S. V. Manjrekar lbw b Anthony	4		
Kapil Dev b Anthony	0		
*M. Azharuddin c Maynard b Anthony	21		
S. R. Tendulkar c Cottey b Croft	68		
K. S. More c Metson b Croft	8		
†N. R. Mongia b Dale	60		
S. K. Sharma c Morris b Croft	9		
A. Kumble not out	35		
L-b 8, w 3, n-b 1	12	W 2	2

1/115 2/126 3/126 4/128 5/168   (9 wkts dec.) 330   (no wkt dec.) 98
6/210 7/227 8/240 9/330

A. S. Wassan did not bat.

Bowling: *First Innings*—Anthony 25-3-95-3; Bastien 22-7-61-0; Dennis 15-2-63-0; Croft 17-3-82-3; Dale 8.3-1-21-3. *Second Innings*—Maynard 9-1-34-0; Dale 9-0-62-0; Anthony 1-0-2-0.

Glamorgan

S. P. James c More b Sharma	7	– c More b Wassan	15
H. Morris not out	23	– c Sidhu b Wassan	73
P. A. Cottey lbw b Kapil Dev	0	– c More b Wassan	29
M. P. Maynard not out	4	– b Wassan	26
*A. R. Butcher (did not bat)		– lbw b Wassan	12
A. Dale (did not bat)		– c More b Kumble	0
R. D. B. Croft (did not bat)		– not out	50
H. A. G. Anthony (did not bat)		– c More b Wassan	0
†C. P. Metson (did not bat)		– not out	50
L-b 1, n-b 4	5	B 8, l-b 2, n-b 8	18

1/14 2/31   (2 wkts dec.) 39   1/63 2/116 3/132 4/167 (7 wkts) 273
                              5/168 6/170 7/170

S. J. Dennis and S. Bastien did not bat.

Bowling: *First Innings*—Kapil Dev 6-3-8-1; Sharma 5-1-23-1; Wassan 1-0-5-0; Kumble 1-0-2-0. *Second Innings*—Kapil Dev 19-3-58-0; Sharma 9-2-48-0; Wassan 23-3-89-6; Tendulkar 1-0-5-0; Kumble 21-8-51-1; Raman 2-0-12-0.

Umpires: A. A. Jones and K. J. Lyons.

ENGLAND v INDIA

Third Cornhill Test

At The Oval, August 23, 24, 25, 27, 28. Drawn. Toss: India. Gower's sublime strokeplay, unwavering determination and considerable stamina throughout the final day erased India's chances of squaring the series, though their hopes were high when they enforced the follow-on after scoring their third-best score of all time. England thus won 1-0 to complete their first unbeaten Test season at home since 1979, having beaten New Zealand by the same margin earlier in the summer. The six-hour *tour de force* was Gower's sixteenth hundred in Tests and his fourth on the Kennington ground; with Shastri and Kapil Dev he brought the tally of centuries scored by the two teams to fifteen, a record for a three-match series. But while Gower's innings was conclusive in saving the game, Gooch had also continued his record-breaking summer, unchecked by a lightweight Indian attack never capable of marrying its industry to quality and penetration.

This time when Azharuddin won the toss, he needed no persuasion to take first use of an outstanding batting pitch. India had decided against the attacking option of an extra bowler, and at the same time preferred the lively Wassan to Kumble's sharp leg-spin. Just before the toss Lewis suffered a migraine attack during outfield practice, and Williams, the Middlesex seamer, was thrust into his first Test after being named twelfth man.

While Lewis sought rest and aspirin in the plush dressing-rooms of the new stand flanking the pavilion, Shastri settled in to give England their own headache. Gooch, who had lost the toss for the fifth time in six Tests, went through his tactical repertoire but found the tall, upright opener moulding a solid percentage game: playing permanently straight, waiting to punish the wayward delivery, and progressing to his tenth Test hundred and highest Test score. England's main strike bowler, Malcolm, looked jaded, but Williams moved the ball more than anyone else and was rewarded with Azharuddin's wicket just as the Indian captain was threatening to post his fourth hundred in as many Tests. The dependable Fraser was once more England's prime bowler on a day which began with Russell claiming two acrobatic catches in little more than an hour, and ended with India in undisputed command at 324 for four; Shastri 135 not out. It was a neat reversal of fortunes from Lord's and Old Trafford, where the touring team had been completely overrun in the field on the first day.

England had to keep India to a score of 450 or less to retain any hope of victory. But by tea on the second day, their concern was to salvage the match. India had already passed their previous highest total of 510 in England, made at Leeds in 1967, and they marched on to their biggest score against England in either country. The campaign was carried on by Kapil Dev, who added 110 with Shastri until Malcolm had the vice-captain caught at first slip for 187, after 561 minutes and 435 balls, including 23 fours. Kapil, meanwhile, used the wide open space of the playing area to his advantage and resisted the risky shots in the air which England might have expected. After the slowest of his seven Test hundreds – taking 130 balls – he was stumped off Hemmings twelve balls later, having struck sixteen fours, and a late flourish from the pugnacious More enabled India to declare at 606 for nine.

The target of 407 to avoid the follow-on was ultimately beyond England. A rare failure from Atherton that evening brought in Williams as night-watchman, but after he had contributed a useful 38 in 72 minutes, the rock-solid Gooch, understandably unadventurous, then had to watch his middle order being summarily despatched. However, Smith's resourceful half-century and spirited batting from Russell promised a lifeline until Gooch was caught, mis-sweeping Hirwani, for 85 after five and a half hours. His first 5 runs had taken him past Zaheer Abbas's record aggregate of 583 in a three-match series, but he was still 4 short of D. G. Bradman's total of 974 in an English summer. Once Russell had been wastefully run out by a direct hit from Wassan on the fourth morning, England were prepared for the worst, although Hemmings, helped in a last-wicket stand of 41 by Malcolm, seized the opportunity to score his second Test fifty before England were dismissed for 340.

When Gooch and Atherton returned to centre stage, India were soon to regret their lack of firepower. Azharuddin limped off with a sore heel and Shastri, taking over the reins, was to spurn the second new ball, instead keeping Hirwani's leg-breaks probing away into the footmarks in a marathon – and largely unrewarded – 59 consecutive overs from the Vauxhall End. Gooch quickly took the 5 runs he needed to pass Bradman (though he had taken four more innings) and the opening pair collected their third stand of a hundred in as many Tests. They were poised to make it a third double-century partnership when Gooch, after 225 minutes, was superbly caught, one-handed at backward short leg by Vengsarkar, off the bowling of Hirwani. Joined now by Gower, who was soon displaying some dazzling shots, Atherton advanced to 86, surviving a chance to backward square leg only to fall lbw to Kapil Dev after 5 hours 40 minutes of defensive endeavour. Morris failed to capitalise on a chance to impress the selectors, but for two hours Lamb was under little pressure in making 52 and England saved the match comfortably. Thanks to Gower's elegant, day-long guidance, they finished 211 ahead with six wickets in reserve. His unbeaten 157, from 271 balls and graced with 21 boundaries, provided a satisfying climax to his 109th Test, and convinced spectators that the former captain would, after all, be in the England team to tour Australia. – David Field.

Man of the Match: R. J. Shastri.		*Attendance:* 55,405; *receipts* £681,400.

Men of the Series: England – G. A. Gooch; India – M. Azharuddin.

Close of play: First day, India 324-4 (R. J. Shastri 135*, M. Prabhakar 20*); Second day, England 36-1 (G. A. Gooch 5*, N. F. Williams 15*); Third day, England 293-7 (R. C. Russell 34*, E. E. Hemmings 26*); Fourth day, England 215-1 (M. A. Atherton 71*, D. I. Gower 32*).

India

R. J. Shastri c Lamb b Malcolm	187	A. S. Wassan b Hemmings	15
N. S. Sidhu c Russell b Fraser	12	N. D. Hirwani not out	2
S. V. Manjrekar c Russell b Malcolm	22	B 7, l-b 8, w 6, n-b 16	37
D. B. Vengsarkar c and b Atherton	33		
*M. Azharuddin c Russell b Williams	78	1/16 (2) 2/61 (3)	(9 wkts dec.) 606
M. Prabhakar lbw b Fraser	28	3/150 (4) 4/289 (5)	
S. R. Tendulkar c Lamb b Williams	21	5/335 (6) 6/368 (7)	
Kapil Dev st Russell b Hemmings	110	7/478 (1) 8/552 (8)	
†K. S. More not out	61	9/576 (10)	

Bowling: Malcolm 35–7–110–2; Fraser 42–7–112–2; Williams 41–5–148–2; Gooch 12–1–44–0; Hemmings 36–3–117–2; Atherton 7–0–60–1.

England

*G. A. Gooch c Shastri b Hirwani	85	– c Vengsarkar b Hirwani	88
M. A. Atherton c More b Prabhakar	7	– lbw b Kapil Dev	86
N. F. Williams lbw b Prabhakar	38		
D. I. Gower lbw b Wassan	8	– (3) not out	157
J. E. Morris c More b Wassan	7	– (4) c More b Wassan	32
A. J. Lamb b Kapil Dev	7	– (5) c Shastri b Kapil Dev	52
R. A. Smith c Manjrekar b Shastri	57	– (6) not out	7
†R. C. Russell run out	35		
E. E. Hemmings c Vengsarkar b Prabhakar	51		
A. R. C. Fraser c More b Prabhakar	0		
D. E. Malcolm not out	15		
B 8, l-b 9, w 4, n-b 9	30	B 16, l-b 22, w 5, n-b 12	55

1/18 (2) 2/92 (3) 3/111 (4) 4/120 (5)	340	1/176 (1) 2/251 (2)	(4 wkts dec.) 477
5/139 (6) 6/231 (7) 7/233 (1) 8/295 (8)		3/334 (4) 4/463 (5)	
9/299 (10) 10/340 (9)			

Bowling: *First Innings*—Kapil Dev 25–7–70–1; Prabhakar 32.4–9–74–4; Wassan 19–3–79–2; Hirwani 35–12–71–1; Shastri 12–2–29–1. *Second Innings*—Prabhakar 25–8–56–0; Kapil Dev 24–5–66–2; Wassan 18–2–94–1; Hirwani 59–18–137–1; Shastri 28–2–86–0.

Umpires: N. T. Plews and D. R. Shepherd.

MICHAEL PARKINSON'S WORLD XI v INDIANS

At Scarborough, August 29, 30, 31. Drawn. Toss: Michael Parkinson's World XI. Their official matches behind them, the Indians ended their tour in the festival atmosphere of Scarborough with a privately arranged, first-class fixture against Michael Parkinson's invitation side. Conditions typically favoured the batsmen, and the Indians were not helped by the loss of Wassan early in the match with an ankle injury. However, their batsmen provided rich entertainment with their elegant strokeplay, and on the final day, when they were invited to chase 388 in four and a half hours, they were seen towards the safety of a draw by the precocious skills of Tendulkar. The seventeen-year-old hit seventeen fours in reaching his third hundred of the tour from 131 balls. Greatbatch, who had missed out on a first-class century for the New Zealanders earlier in the summer, made amends with two powerful three-figure innings, his 168 not out on the first day coming off 162 balls and containing two sixes and 25 fours. During the match, Bairstow took his tally of dismissals to 1,099 and moved into fourteenth place above G. Duckworth on the all-time list of wicket-keepers.

Close of play: First day, Indians 7-0 (W. V. Raman 3*, N. R. Mongia 0*); Second day, Michael Parkinson's World XI 172-2 (Mudassar Nazar 61*, M. J. Greatbatch 50*).

Michael Parkinson's World XI

Mudassar Nazar c Kapil Dev b Wassan	29	– not out	107
*C. G. Greenidge lbw b Sharma	23	– b Sharma	0
R. B. Richardson c Prabhakar b Kumble	65	– c Raman b Sharma	42
M. J. Greatbatch not out	168	– not out	128
R. A. Harper st Mongia b Raman	17		
P. R. Sleep c Kumble b Kapil Dev	42		
B 2, l-b 18, n-b 15	35	B 1, l-b 15, n-b 7	23

1/44 2/72 3/189 4/252 5/379   (5 wkts dec.) 379   1/6 2/77   (2 wkts dec.) 300

†D. L. Bairstow, E. A. Moseley, Chetan Sharma, M. R. Whitney and C. Pringle did not bat.

Bowling: *First Innings*—Sharma 20-3-91-1; Prabhakar 4-0-7-0; Wassan 8-1-42-1; Tendulkar 12-1-70-0; Kumble 24-4-103-1; Raman 8-1-44-1; Kapil Dev 0.4-0-2-1. *Second Innings*—Prabhakar 13-3-45-0; Sharma 9-0-53-2; Tendulkar 7-0-32-0; Kumble 17-1-72-0; More 8-0-54-0; Kapil Dev 5-0-28-0.

Indians

W. V. Raman c Greenidge b Pringle	58	– b Whitney	13
†N. R. Mongia c Bairstow b Whitney	10	– c Bairstow b Moseley	15
*S. V. Manjrekar c Whitney b Sleep	59	– (5) c Bairstow b Whitney	62
S. R. Tendulkar c Pringle b Harper	23	– c Pringle b Sleep	108
D. B. Vengsarkar b Greatbatch b Whitney	3	– (6) not out	25
M. Prabhakar b Harper	15	– (7) c Greatbatch b Harper	10
Kapil Dev c Harper b Pringle	19	– (3) c Richardson b Whitney	3
A. Kumble lbw b Harper	2	– not out	5
K. S. More c Bairstow b Sleep	18		
S. K. Sharma not out	34		
A. S. Wassan b Harper	24		
B 8, l-b 8, w 4, n-b 7	27	L-b 6, n-b 6	12

1/59 2/114 3/154 4/168 5/169   292   1/34 2/34 3/43   (6 wkts) 253
6/199 7/206 8/229 9/245   4/198 5/225 6/243

Bowling: *First Innings*—Moseley 9-2-22-0; Whitney 14-4-51-2; Pringle 12-0-49-2; C. Sharma 8-0-39-0; Sleep 17.4-4-68-4; Harper 12-1-36-1; Whitney 13-1-46-3; Pringle 7-1-36-0; C. Sharma 5-0-30-0; Harper 16-4-36-1; Sleep 12-1-63-1.

Umpires: J. H. Hampshire and B. Leadbeater.

THE SRI LANKANS IN ENGLAND, 1990

Towards the end of a busy English summer, a young Sri Lankan team made a five-week tour, with matches against eight first-class counties. From the Sri Lankan viewpoint, the purpose of the visit was threefold: to allow some of their cricketers to gain first-class experience abroad before the Asia Cup tournament and the tour of New Zealand in 1990-91; secondly, to accustom them to English conditions in preparation for the tour in 1991 by the full-strength Sri Lankan side, which was to play a Test match at Lord's; and thirdly, to impress on the English public the ability of Sri Lankan cricketers to hold their own against county sides.

All of these objectives were obtained, and if a record of one win and five draws in the first-class games does not in itself reflect the positive attitude shown by Aravinda de Silva's team, the draws against Sussex and Lancashire came when the counties were well short of not unrealistic targets with more than half their batting gone. Moreover, the win against Warwickshire provided Sri Lanka with a win over an English county to accompany the victories of the 1979 team over Oxford University and the 1981 team over a TCCB XI.

The decision of the Sri Lankan Board not to select five of their front-line players, including the current captain and vice-captain, plus injuries during the tour to two experienced players – Saliya Ahangama and Asanka Gurusinha – put considerable responsibility on the remaining players, four of whom were teenagers. That their only defeats came in the two one-day games was a reflection of the depth of playing strength in Sri Lanka. The captain, de Silva, set a good example by the positive way he went about his batting and his declarations, and his chanceless double-hundred to save the match against Hampshire was a gem of an innings. He played in every game and averaged 70.37 in his first-class innings.

In a further indication of their playing strength, the team included two fine wicket-keeper-batsmen, and so could enjoy the advantage of playing seven specialist batsmen. Hashan Tillekeratne hit two hundreds and, like his fellow-keeper, Brendon Kuruppu, was capable of batting anywhere in the order. Both performed their duties behind the stumps well. Roshan Mahanama and Chandika Hathurusinghe put on 210 the first time they opened together, against Nottinghamshire, and generally gave the side a sound start. In the middle order, Sanath Jayasuriya, a left-hander who had hit successive unbeaten double-hundreds against Pakistan B in 1988-89, and Marvan Atapattu, who averaged 60 on the tour, provided solidity or attractive strokeplay according to the team's needs.

The brunt of the bowling was borne by four players. Ranjith Madurasinghe had improved immensely since he toured England in 1988, and with 21 wickets at 26.66 in four games, he showed himself to be an off-spinner of some class. At the same time, the slow left-armer, Piyal Wijetunge, the youngster of the side, suggested that he could become a very good bowler with more experience. Of the faster bowlers, Graeme Labrooy, though at times beset by injury, reminded English spectators that he could trouble the best of batsmen, and Champaka Ramanayake also proved his effectiveness in the batsmen's conditions of 1990.

The team was managed excellently by Mumtaz Yusuf, who had toured ngland with the 1984 team, and his assistant manager, Jansa Severatne. ike their predecessors, the Sri Lankans were a credit to the game, both in heir behaviour and their approach to their cricket. – Pat Culpan.

SRI LANKAN TOUR RESULTS

irst-class matches – Played 6: Won 1, Drawn 5.
/in – Warwickshire.
raws – Glamorgan, Hampshire, Lancashire, Nottinghamshire, Sussex.
on first-class matches – Played 2: Lost 2. *Losses* – Somerset, Surrey.

SRI LANKAN AVERAGES – FIRST CLASS MATCHES

BATTING

	M	I	NO	R	HI	100s	Avge
A. de Silva	6	12	4	563	221*	1	70.37
. S. Atapattu	6	8	4	241	74*	0	60.25
. P. Tillekeratne	5	9	2	349	109*	2	49.85
. S. Mahanama	6	10	0	494	114	2	49.40
T. Jayasuriya	6	9	2	345	105*	1	49.28
. P. Gurusinha	3	6	3	138	58	0	46.00
. C. Hathurusinghe	5	10	0	385	136	1	38.50
. S. B. P. Kuruppu	5	10	1	259	56*	0	28.77
. W. R. Madurasinghe	4	3	1	43	28*	0	21.50
. F. Labrooy	4	6	0	121	69	0	20.16
. P. Wickremansinghe	3	2	0	17	17	0	8.50

Played in four matches: C. P. H. Ramanayake 8*, 3*, 5*, 9*; K. I. W. Wijegunawardene 0; . K. Wijetunge 5*. Played in one match: F. S. Ahangama did not bat.

* *Signifies not out.*

BOWLING

	O	M	R	W	BB	5W/i	Avge
. P. Gurusinha	40	8	113	5	3-38	0	22.60
. W. R. Madurasinghe	176.2	28	560	21	5-108	1	26.66
. F. Labrooy	111	13	440	16	5-97	1	27.50
. I. W. Wijegunawardene	87.3	13	318	9	2-30	0	35.33
. K. Wijetunge	129.4	24	438	12	4-133	0	36.50
. P. Wickremansinghe	79	17	251	6	3-95	0	41.83
. P. H. Ramanayake	133	12	510	12	3-96	0	42.50

Also bowled: F. S. Ahangama 1.3–0–4–0; M. S. Atapattu 4–0–21–0; P. A. de Silva 5–3–81–2; U. C. Hathurusinghe 21.1–8–58–3; S. T. Jayasuriya 7–1–18–1.

FIELDING

0 – P. A. de Silva, R. S. Mahanama; 9 – H. P. Tillekeratne (7 ct, 2 st); 8 – D. S. B. P. .uruppu (7ct, 1 st); 7 – M. S. Atapattu; 5 – S. T. Jayasuriya, K. I. W. Wijegunawardene; – P. K. Wijetunge; 1 – U. C. Hathurusinghe, G. F. Labrooy, A. W. R. Madurasinghe, ubstitute.

HUNDREDS FOR SRI LANKANS

The following seven three-figure innings were played for the Sri Lankans.

R. S. Mahanama (2)
 114 v Notts., Cleethorpes
 103 v Lancs., Manchester

H. P. Tillekeratne (2)
 109* v Warwicks., Birmingham
 100 v Hants, Southampton

 * *Signifies not out.*

P. A. de Silva (1)
 221* v Hants, Southampton

U. C. Hathurusinghe (1)
 136 v Sussex, Hove

S. T. Jayasuriya (1)
 105* v Lancs., Manchester

GLAMORGAN v SRI LANKANS

At Ebbw Vale, August 22, 23, 24. Drawn. Toss: Glamorgan. The Sri Lankans began the short, eight-match tour by contributing to an enjoyable three days, the highlight of which f Glamorgan supporters was Morris's ninth hundred of the season. Morris, captainir Glamorgan in Butcher's absence, passed the county record for a season, established by Jave Miandad in 1981, as he scored 126 in the second innings. Labrooy, bowling effectively medium pace on a pitch which helped the quicker bowlers, claimed five Glamorgan wicke in the first innings, though he was the most prodigal of the Sri Lankan bowlers when it can to no-balls. James, in his second match of the season for the county, batted for four hours afte remaining in single figures for nineteen overs. Gurusinha struck a forceful half-century as th visitors provided an attractive reply, and after declaring 23 runs ahead they soon ha Glamorgan in trouble at 33 for three. However, a partnership of 191 between Morris ar Holmes saved the innings and enabled Morris to set a target of 333 in 66 overs. At 109 for si defeat for the Sri Lankans appeared imminent, but they were rescued by an attacking stand 112 in sixteen overs between Atapattu and Labrooy. Labrooy struck Croft for 20 in one ov which included three sixes, but when he departed, caught off a ball that lifted, the touris settled for a draw.

Close of play: First day, Sri Lankans 78-1 (D. S. B. P. Kuruppu 38*, A. P. Gurusinha 29* Second day, Glamorgan 227-4 (H. Morris 101*, A. Dale 0*).

Glamorgan

S. P. James c Mahanama b Wijegunawardene	47	– c Mahanama b Labrooy	
*H. Morris c Tillekeratne b Labrooy	37	– c Mahanama b Wijegunawardene	12
P. A. Cottey lbw b Wijegunawardene	0	– c Atapattu b Ramanayake	
M. P. Maynard c Atapattu b Labrooy	20	– b Labrooy	
G. C. Holmes c Jayasuriya b Labrooy	0	– c Wijegunawardene b Labrooy	9
A. Dale b Wijetunge	36	– c Kuruppu b Gurusinha	
R. D. B. Croft b Labrooy	20	– c de Silva b Wijegunawardene	3
†M. L. Roberts lbw b Labrooy	25	– c Mahanama b Wijetunge	2
H. A. G. Anthony c Atapattu b Wijetunge	12	– st Tillekeratne b Wijetunge	
S. L. Watkin lbw b Ramanayake	1	– not out	
M. Frost not out	2		
B 1, l-b 6, w 1, n-b 27	35	B 2, l-b 10, w 3, n-b 24	3

1/53 2/54 3/86 4/90 5/154	235	1/0 2/8 3/33 (9 wkts dec.) 3!
6/165 7/190 8/208 9/214		4/224 5/260 6/287
		7/327 8/336 9/355

Bowling: *First Innings*—Labrooy 21-2-97-5; Ramanayake 14-1-61-1; Wijegunawarde. 13-2-30-2; Wijetunge 24-6-40-2. *Second Innings*—Labrooy 23-5-84-3; Ramanaya 15-0-64-1; Wijegunawardene 15-1-79-2; Gurusinha 15-6-31-1; Wijetunge 18.4-1-85-2.

Sri Lankans

R. S. Mahanama lbw b Anthony	9	– lbw b Frost	35
D. S. B. P. Kuruppu lbw b Watkin	45	– c Watkin b Dale	15
A. P. Gurusinha c Roberts b Watkin	58	– c Morris b Frost	23
*P. A. de Silva b Croft	45	– lbw b Holmes	2
†H. P. Tillekeratne c Cottey b Dale	30	– c Roberts b Frost	5
S. T. Jayasuriya lbw b Watkin	24	– c James b Croft	19
M. S. Atapattu c Roberts b Dale	23	– not out	71
G. F. Labrooy c Roberts b Dale	7	– c Maynard b Watkin	69
C. P. H. Ramanayake not out	8	– not out	3
L-b 5, w 1, n-b 3	9	B 4, l-b 2, w 1, n-b 1	8

1/21 2/99 3/152 4/186 5/207   (8 wkts dec.) 258   1/34 2/74 3/81   (7 wkts) 250
6/225 7/238 8/258   4/81 5/87 6/109 7/221

K. I. W. Wijegunawardene and P. K. Wijetunge did not bat.

Bowling: *First Innings*—Watkin 21–5–92–3; Anthony 12–2–47–1; Frost 14–3–51–0; Croft 10–3–38–1; Dale 9.3–3–25–3. *Second Innings*—Anthony 4–2–14–0; Watkin 15–7–48–1; Frost 14–3–44–3; Croft 13–1–89–1; Dale 12–1–43–1; Holmes 6–1–6–1.

Umpires: M. J. Harris and R. Palmer.

NOTTINGHAMSHIRE v SRI LANKANS

At Cleethorpes, August 25, 26, 27. Drawn. Toss: Nottinghamshire. Leaving the county and going off to the seaside for the Bank Holiday, Nottinghamshire found the weather most pleasant. However, they lost three wickets rather cheaply, and only a dour innings by Newell, 112 off 261 balls, and Evans's fifty made much of an impact on some modest bowling. The Nottinghamshire bowlers then failed to disturb the Sri Lankan opening pair before the close, and on Sunday Mahanama and Hathurusinghe took the score on to 210 before they were parted. The former hit seventeen fours and faced 231 balls for his 114. Although de Silva kept the game alive by declaring behind, Nottinghamshire failed to score at a reasonable rate on the last day until Stephenson hit out. The result was that the tourists felt a target of 274 off 59 overs was too high, and the game meandered to a draw.

Close of play: First day, Sri Lankans 43-0 (R. S. Mahanama 16*, U. C. Hathurusinghe 19*); Second day, Nottinghamshire 73-2 (R. T. Robinson 21*, P. Johnson 37*).

Nottinghamshire

P. R. Pollard b Ramanayake	5	– c Jayasuriya b Labrooy	5
M. Newell c Tillekeratne b Gurusinha	112	– c Atapattu b Labrooy	6
R. T. Robinson c Mahanama b Gurusinha	18	– run out	36
*P. Johnson c Mahanama b Gurusinha	1	– c Mahanama b Wickremasinghe	54
D. J. R. Martindale c Tillekeratne b Labrooy	26	– c Mahanama b Ramanayake	13
K. P. Evans c Jayasuriya b Wickremasinghe	55	– (7) run out	2
F. D. Stephenson not out	27	– (6) c Labrooy b Wickremasinghe	65
†C. W. Scott not out	13	– b Wickremsinghe	31
K. E. Cooper (did not bat)		– not out	10
R. A. Pick (did not bat)		– b Labrooy	5
J. A. Afford (did not bat)		– c sub b Labrooy	2
B 9, l-b 17, n-b 20	46	B 1, l-b 7, w 1, n-b 13	22

1/13 2/55 3/60 4/139   (6 wkts dec.) 303   1/13 2/22 3/101 4/117 5/129   251
5/259 6/261   6/145 7/232 8/234 9/239

Bowling: *First Innings*—Labrooy 19.4–2–68–1; Ramanayake 14–0–60–1; Wickremasinghe 24–9–63–1; Gurusinha 15–2–38–3; Hathurusinghe 3–3–0–0; Wijetunge 9–1–29–0; de Silva 6–1–19–0. *Second Innings*—Labrooy 14.2–3–60–4; Wickremasinghe 26–3–95–3; Ramanayake 15–0–70–1; de Silva 2–1–5–0; Wijetunge 1–0–13–0.

Sri Lankans

R. S. Mahanama lbw b Stephenson	114		
U. C. Hathurusinghe lbw b Cooper	84	– (1) lbw b Pick	44
A. P. Gurusinha not out	37	– (4) not out	17
*P. A. de Silva c Pollard b Cooper	1	– (3) not out	14
†H. P. Tillekeratne c Evans b Pick	0	– (2) lbw b Cooper	22
S. T. Jayasuriya c Johnson b Afford	15		
M. S. Atapattu not out	9		
B 4, l-b 10, n-b 7	21	B 2, l-b 8, n-b 3	13

1/210 2/221 3/223 4/224 5/250   (5 wkts dec.) 281   1/69 2/81   (2 wkts) 110

G. F. Labrooy, C. P. H. Ramanayake, P. K. Wijetunge and G. P. Wickremansinghe did not bat.

Bowling: *First Innings*—Pick 19-3-54-1; Cooper 25-10-67-2; Afford 22-5-74-1; Evans 14-0-38-0; Stephenson 12-3-34-1; Newell 1-1-0-0. *Second Innings*—Pick 11-3-33-1; Evans 6-0-19-0; Stephenson 6-1-17-0; Cooper 11-2-31-1.

Umpires: B. Leadbeater and H. J. Rhodes.

WARWICKSHIRE v SRI LANKANS

At Birmingham, August 29, 30, 31. Sri Lankans won by eight wickets. Toss: Warwickshire. While Warwickshire became the first county to lose a first-class match to the Sri Lankans in their five tours of England since 1979, the visitors did well to achieve victory on a typical slow-paced Edgbaston pitch after the home side had scored 349 for nine on the opening day. Moles was five hours over his 117, and he received good support from Ostler, Green and Twose, all young players. The Sri Lankans were unlucky in losing Ahangama so early in the day with a groin injury, but they were well served by their off-spinner, Madurasinghe, who finished the match with eight wickets. The tourists kept the game open by declaring 22 runs in arrears, the left-handed Tillekeratne and Jayasuriya having put on 163 in an unbroken fifth-wicket partnership. Earlier de Silva, the captain, had hit four sixes, as well as six fours, in his 67. Warwickshire, already in some trouble overnight at 37 for three, collapsed unaccountably on the final day and were bowled out for 133 in 57 overs and one ball by an attack which was accurate but not penetrative. With de Silva hitting his second attractive half-century of the match, the Sri Lankans won easily with more than twenty overs in hand.

Close of play: First day, Warwickshire 349-9 (R. G. Twose 64*, A. A. Donald 4*); Second day, Warwickshire 37-3 (A. J. Moles 15*, D. A. Reeve 0*).

Warwickshire

A. J. Moles b Wijegunawardene	117	– c Atapattu b Madurasinghe	38
J. D. Ratcliffe c Atapattu b Ramanayake	5	– c Tillekeratne b Wijegunawardene	14
D. P. Ostler c Wijegunawardene b Madurasinghe	56	– lbw b Ramanayake	3
S. J. Green c Jayasuriya b Madurasinghe	44	– c Kuruppu b Wijegunawardene	0
R. G. Twose not out	64	– (6) c Atapattu b Madurasinghe	4
*D. A. Reeve lbw b Madurasinghe	5	– (5) lbw b Ramanayake	1
N. M. K. Smith b Ramanayake	1	– c de Silva b Hathurusinghe	43
†K. J. Piper lbw b Ramanayake	19	– b Madurasinghe	0
J. E. Benjamin b Madurasinghe	2	– (10) b Hathurusinghe	14
P. A. Booth b Wijegunawardene	8	– (9) lbw b Madurasinghe	1
A. A. Donald not out	4	– not out	0
L-b 8, n-b 16	24	B 4, l-b 7, n-b 4	15

1/10 2/142 3/209 4/270 5/281   (9 wkts dec.) 349   1/23 2/30 3/33 4/46 5/57   133
6/293 7/321 8/324 9/345   6/83 7/83 8/101 9/132

Bowling: *First Innings*—Ramanayake 27-4-96-3; Ahangama 13-1-40-0; Wijegunawardene 19.3-4-82-2; Hathurusinghe 6-2-14-0; Madurasinghe 40-6-120-4; de Silva 9-1-25-0. *Second Innings*—Ramanayake 22-5-53-2; Wijegunawardene 15-3-31-2; Madurasinghe 17-6-35-4; Hathurusinghe 3.1-1-3-2.

Sri Lankans

R. S. Mahanama lbw b Benjamin	30		
U. C. Hathurusinghe b Twose	19	– lbw b Donald	19
D. S. B. P. Kuruppu c sub b Reeve	1	– (1) c Piper b Booth	40
*P. A. de Silva lbw b Reeve	67	– (3) not out	54
†H. P. Tillekeratne not out	109	– (4) not out	29
S. T. Jayasuriya not out	78		
B 4, l-b 8, w 1, n-b 10	23	B 5, l-b 6, n-b 4	15

1/42 2/44 3/58 4/164   (4 wkts dec.) 327   1/59 2/107   (2 wkts) 157

C. P. H. Ramanayake, M. S. Atapattu, K. I. W. Wijegunawardene, A. W. R. Madurasinghe and F. S. Ahangama did not bat.

Bowling: *First Innings*—Donald 11.5–4–33–0; Benjamin 12–0–59–1; Reeve 14–3–46–2; Twose 13–4–40–1; Booth 17–1–77–0; Smith 22–3–60–0. *Second Innings*—Donald 9–1–35–1; Benjamin 5–0–22–0; Reeve 6–1–29–0; Booth 11.3–3–41–1; Smith 2–0–19–0.

Umpires: M. J. Harris and R. Julian.

†SURREY v SRI LANKANS

At The Oval, September 2. Surrey won by 14 runs. Toss: Sri Lankans. Although Labrooy kept pulses racing in the closing stages with 28 from nineteen balls, before being caught at extra cover in the 54th over, Surrey had looked to have the match won through some excellent work in the field. Victory was much less certain during the morning as Labrooy, Gurusinha and Madurasinghe held them to 125 for one from 38 overs. However, Thorpe went on to 63 from 82 balls and Bicknell to 86 as Surrey set about the bowling in order to achieve a defendable total.

Surrey

D. J. Bicknell c and b de Silva	86	K. T. Medlycott c Tillekeratne b Labrooy	20
R. I. Alikhan b Gurusinha	22	C. K. Bullen not out	1
*G. P. Thorpe c Atapattu b de Silva	63		
J. D. Robinson c Wickremasinghe b de Silva	33	B 2, l-b 10, w 14	26
A. D. Brown c Wickremasinghe b de Silva	2	1/70 2/164 3/200 (6 wkts, 55 overs) 253
		4/205 5/239 6/253	

†N. F. Sargeant, N. M. Kendrick, A. H. Gray and A. J. Murphy did not bat.

Bowling: Labrooy 11–2–49–1; Wickremasinghe 8–1–45–0; Gurusinha 8–2–20–1; Madurasinghe 11–1–33–0; Wijegunawardene 9–1–39–0; de Silva 8–0–55–4.

Sri Lankans

D. S. B. P. Kuruppu c Murphy b Bullen	33	A. W. R. Madurasinghe not out	1
†H. P. Tillekeratne c Bullen b Murphy	45	K. I. W. Wijegunawardene c Medlycott b Murphy	1
A. P. Gurusinha lbw b Bullen	4		
*P. A. de Silva c Robinson b Kendrick	35		
S. T. Jayasuriya c Bicknell b Kendrick	32	L-b 3, w 2	5
R. S. Mahanama hit wkt b Kendrick	24		
M. S. Atapattu b Gray	19	1/64 2/77 3/97 (53.5 overs) 239
G. F. Labrooy c Bullen b Murphy	28	4/145 5/169 6/191	
G. P. Wickremasinghe b Gray	12	7/207 8/237 9/237	

Bowling: Gray 10–1–35–2; Murphy 10.5–0–61–3; Thorpe 3–1–15–0; Robinson 5–0–25–0; Bullen 11–1–37–2; Medlycott 8–0–42–0; Kendrick 6–0–21–3.

Umpires: B. Hassan and R. Julian.

†SOMERSET v SRI LANKANS

At Taunton, September 3. Somerset won by 71 runs. Toss: Sri Lankans. Roebuck (106 balls) and Townsend (112 balls) added 170 in 32 overs after Somerset were put in on a cloudy morning, with the pitch rather fresh. Three wickets fell quickly, but Burns and Harden then added 51 in five overs. The Sri Lankans never recovered from an opening spell of four for 15 in 25 deliveries from Rose. With the result not in doubt, Atapattu and Wickremansinghe put on 72 in the final fourteen overs, largely against the change bowlers.

Somerset

S. J. Cook c Mahanama b Ramanayake	13	†N. D. Burns not out	29
G. T. J. Townsend run out	77	*C. J. Tavaré not out	5
P. M. Roebuck c and b Madurasinghe	95	L-b 14, n-b 2	16
G. D. Rose c Wickremansinghe			
b Gurusinha	2	1/23 2/193 3/198 (5 wkts, 48 overs) 262	
R. J. Harden c Kuruppu b Ramanayake	25	4/200 5/251	

M. Lathwell, P. J. Rendell, A. R. Kaddick and A. N. Jones did not bat.

Bowling: Ramanayake 8–0–47–2; Wickremansinghe 10–1–45–0; Gurusinha 11–0–59–1; Wijegunawardene 9–0–50–0; Madurasinghe 10–0–47–1.

Sri Lankans

†D. S. B. P. Kuruppu lbw b Rose	1	C. P. H. Ramanayake lbw b Roebuck	12
H. P. Tillekeratne c Cook b Rose	23	G. P. Wickremansinghe not out	24
A. P. Gurusinha c Burns b Rose	1	L-b 7, w 7, n-b 3	17
*P. A. de Silva c Burns b Rendell	33		
S. T. Jayasuriya c Rendell b Rose	6	1/4 2/21 3/31 (7 wkts, 48 overs) 191	
R. S. Mahanama c and b Rendell	11	4/47 5/72	
M. S. Atapattu not out	63	6/88 7/119	

K. I. W. Wijegunawardene and A. W. R. Madurasinghe did not bat.

Bowling: Jones 6–0–31–0; Rose 11–1–16–4; Rendell 11–1–46–2; Kaddick 6–1–19–0; Roebuck 11–0–30–1; Lathwell 7–1–35–0; Harden 1–0–7–0.

Umpires: A. A. Jones and P. B. Wight.

SUSSEX v SRI LANKANS

At Hove, September 5, 6, 7. Drawn. Toss: Sussex. An uninspiring game, affected by rain, ended with Sussex holding out for a draw after some reckless batting had given the touring team a chance of victory. Hathurusinghe was the cornerstone of the Sri Lankans' first innings, revealing great promise in a maiden first-class hundred which included 22 fours, and when he was out de Silva and Atapattu put on 72 in fifteen overs. Sussex, to help make up the time lost to rain on the first day, declared 108 behind. Parker hastened the declaration with three sixes off Madurasinghe as he made a vigorous return to the side after a five-week absence because of injury. Threlfall sparked a potential crisis when he took two cheap wickets before the close, but Atapattu again batted with determination and the home team were left needing 297 from 47 overs to win. They went for the runs early on, but when six wickets had gone for 102, they shut up shop. Dodemaide and Moores, scoring only 45 runs off the final twenty overs, ensured that those members not at Eastbourne, watching the championship-winning Second Eleven, had departed long before the end.

Close of play: First day, Sri Lankans 229-2 (U. C. Hathurusinghe 114*, S. T. Jayasuriya 32*); Second day, Sri Lankans 28-3 (U. C. Hathurusinghe 8*, M. S. Atapattu 2*).

Sri Lankans

D. S. B. P. Kuruppu b Threlfall	51	– (4) lbw b Threlfall	4
U. C. Hathurusinghe c Moores b Dodemaide	136	– run out	31
A. P. Gurusinha not out	3	– c Moores b Threlfall	0
R. S. Mahanama run out	8	– (1) b Dodemaide	14
S. T. Jayasuriya c Moores b Threlfall	32	– (7) c Parker b Lenham	0
P. A. de Silva c Wells b Pigott	43	– c Hall b Threlfall	5
M. S. Atapattu not out	49	– (5) not out	74
G. F. Labrooy c Hall b Pigott	0	– (9) b Dodemaide	22
A. W. R. Madurasinghe (did not bat)		– (8) run out	11
G. P. Wickremansinghe (did not bat)		– c Wells b Pigott	17
K. K. Wijetunge (did not bat)		– not out	5
B 2, l-b 20, n-b 3	25	L-b 1, w 3, n-b 1	5

1/99 2/164 3/234 4/268 5/340   (6 wkts dec.) 347   1/20 2/21 3/25   (9 wkts dec.) 188
6/341   4/62 5/85 6/94
                                          7/118 8/148 9/182

A. P. Gurusinha, when 3, retired hurt at 123 and resumed at 341.

Bowling: First Innings—Dodemaide 23–6–73–1; Threlfall 14–3–44–2; Pigott 20.5–5–74–2; Lenham 14.1–4–31–0; Salisbury 25–5–103–0. *Second Innings*—Dodemaide 26–4–65–2; Threlfall 16–5–45–3; Pigott 4–1–7–1; Lenham 11–3–29–1; Salisbury 11–3–41–0.

Sussex

N. J. Lenham c Kuruppu b Labrooy	1	– c Kuruppu b Labrooy	1
J. W. Hall c Jayasuriya b Wijetunge	40	– (7) c de Silva b Madurasinghe	0
D. M. Smith lbw b Labrooy	0	– (2) c Wijetunge b Gurusinha	29
A. P. Wells c Kuruppu b Madurasinghe	96	– c de Silva b Wickremansinghe	20
P. W. G. Parker not out	83	– (3) b Wickremansinghe	21
M. P. Speight not out	5	– (5) c de Silva b Wijetunge	21
A. I. C. Dodemaide (did not bat)		– (6) not out	33
P. Moores (did not bat)		– not out	14
B 1, l-b 7, n-b 6	14	L-b 1, n-b 7	8

1/11 2/11 3/104 4/197   (4 wkts dec.) 239   1/7 2/49 3/67 4/84   (6 wkts) 147
                                          5/101 6/102

A. C. S. Pigott, I. D. K. Salisbury and P. W. Threlfall did not bat.

Bowling: First Innings—Labrooy 12–0–38–2; Wickremansinghe 13–3–41–0; Wijetunge 10–0–40–1; Hathurusinghe 2–0–12–0; Madurasinghe 16.5–1–92–1; Gurusinha 3–0–8–0. *Second Innings*—Labrooy 9–0–40–1; Wickremansinghe 12–2–30–2; Gurusinha 7–0–36–1; Madurasinghe 9–1–17–1; Wijetunge 9–4–15–1; Jayasuriya 1–0–4–0; Atapattu 1–0–4–0.

Umpires: G. I. Burgess and J. H. Harris.

LANCASHIRE v SRI LANKANS

At Manchester, September 8, 9, 10. Drawn. Toss: Sri Lankans. Lancashire fielded a virtual second team, playing only three capped players in Fairbrother, Folley and Austin, and giving a début to Crawley, the former Oxford University captain. Mahanama and de Silva led the Sri Lankans' recovery after two early wickets had fallen to Martin, and on the second morning de Silva allowed Jayasuriya to complete his century before declaring. An eighth-wicket stand between Yates and Folley made certain that Lancashire avoided the follow-on, after the middle order had failed to build on a century opening partnership from Lloyd, who faced only 87 balls for his 96, and Speak. On the final day, Mahanama missed his second century of the match by only 7 runs, being bowled by a full toss to become Speak's maiden first-class victim, and Lancashire were set a victory target of 293 in 58 overs. They made a creditable attempt but gave up at the fall of the eighth wicket, six overs from the end.

Close of play: First day, Sri Lankans 342-7 (S. T. Jayasuriya 60*, A. W. R. Madurasinghe 2*); Second day, Sri Lankans 28-0 (R. S. Mahanama 16*, U. C. Hathurusinghe 11*).

Sri Lankans

R. S. Mahanama c Bramhall b Yates	103	– b Speak	9
U. C. Hathurusinghe c Lloyd b Martin	15	– run out	3
D. S. B. P. Kuruppu c Fitton b Martin	2	– not out	5
*P. A. de Silva c Fairbrother b Yates	95	– not out	1
†H. P. Tillekeratne lbw b Folley	44		
M. S. Atapattu c and b Yates	6		
S. T. Jayasuriya not out	105		
G. P. Wickremansinghe b Yates	0		
A. W. R. Madurasinghe not out	28		
B 3, l-b 3, n-b 2	8	L-b 5	

1/31 2/35 3/203 4/224 5/248   (7 wkts dec.) 406   1/75 2/179   (2 wkts dec.) 19
6/274 7/277

K. I. W. Wijegunawardene and P. K. Wijetunge did not bat.

Bowling: *First Innings*—Martin 23–2–84–2; Austin 9.5–3–23–0; Crawley 8–1–9–0; Folle 35.1–4–126–1; Fitton 19–4–64–0; Yates 38–9–94–4. *Second Innings*—Martin 12–4–34–4 Crawley 6–2–16–0; Yates 8–0–39–0; Fitton 7–1–18–0; Folley 7–0–25–0; Fairbroth 7–0–29–0; Speak 5–0–26–1; Lloyd 1–0–7–0.

Lancashire

G. D. Lloyd st Tillekeratne b Wijetunge	96	– st Kuruppu b Madurasinghe	3
N. J. Speak b Madurasinghe	43	– c Tillekeratne b Madurasinghe	5
S. P. Titchard lbw b Madurasinghe	11	– c de Silva b Madurasinghe	
*N. H. Fairbrother c Mahanama b Wijetunge	6	– c Kuruppu b Wijetunge	2
M. A. Crawley c de Silva b Wijetunge	42	– b de Silva	4
I. D. Austin c Wijetunge b Madurasinghe	3	– (7) c Wijegunawardene b de Silva	2
J. D. Fitton c Hathurusinghe b Madurasinghe	13	– (6) c and b Wijetunge	
G. Yates c de Silva b Jayasuriya	42	– not out	1
I. Folley not out	47	– run out	
†S. Bramhall c Tillekeratne b Wijetunge	0	– not out	
P. J. Martin c de Silva b Madurasinghe	2		
B 3, l-b 4, n-b 1	8	B 6, l-b 8, n-b 1	1

1/115 2/143 3/155 4/160 5/178   313   1/51 2/61 3/113 4/130   (8 wkts) 22
6/204 7/221 8/298 9/303   5/141 6/191 7/207 8/225

Bowling: *First Innings*—Wickremansinghe 3–0–11–0; Wijegunawardene 3–1–16–0 Wijetunge 38–6–133–4; Madurasinghe 37.3–7–108–5; de Silva 2–0–7–0; Jayasuriya 5–0–14–1 Atapattu 3–0–17–0. *Second Innings*—Wickremansinghe 1–0–11–0; Wijegunawarden 1–0–5–0; Wijetunge 23–6–83–2; Madurasinghe 26–3–89–3; de Silva 6–0–25–2; Jayasuriy 1–1–0–0.

Umpires: J. C. Balderstone and R. A. White.

HAMPSHIRE v SRI LANKANS

At Southampton, September 12, 13, 14. Drawn. Toss: Hampshire. The Sri Lankan captain, d Silva, put paid to Hampshire's hopes of becoming the only county to beat his side in a three day match. After the Sri Lankans had struggled against the left-arm spin of Maru in their firs innings and been made to follow on, de Silva, 59 not out overnight, kept Hampshire at ba throughout the final day to finish unbeaten with 221. He batted in all for 443 minutes, facin 399 deliveries, hit three sixes and 38 fours, and shared a partnership of 263 in 74 overs wit Tillekeratne for the fourth wicket. Hampshire's innings had been dominated by Terry, wh hit eighteen fours in a typically applied century, and enlivened by flourishes from Ayling an Aymes.

Close of play: First day, Sri Lankans 4-0 (R. S. Mahanama 2*, U. C. Hathurusinghe 1*) Second day, Sri Lankans 213-3 (P. A. de Silva 59*, H. P. Tillekeratne 60*).

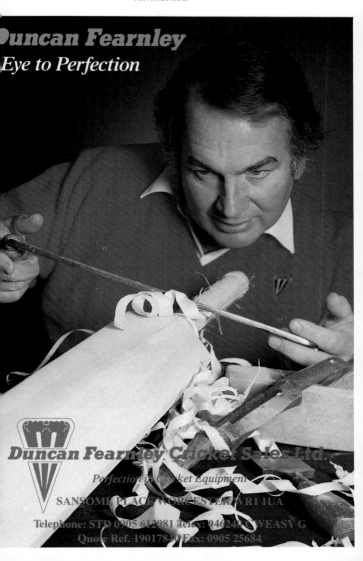

Duncan Fearnley
Eye to Perfection

Duncan Fearnley Cricket Sales Ltd.
Perfection in Cricket Equipment
SANSOME PLACE WORCESTER WR1 1UA
Telephone: STD 0905 612981 Telex: 946240 GIVEASY G
Quote Ref. 19017840 Fax: 0905 25684

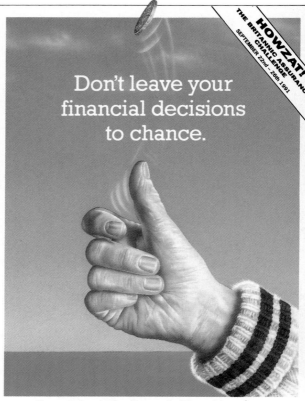

Hampshire

V. P. Terry c Wijegunawardene b Madurasinghe	.120	†A. N. Aymes not out	62
T. C. Middleton c Kuruppu b Ramanayake	22	R. J. Maru c Tillekeratne b Hathurusinghe	6
M. C. J. Nicholas c Mahanama b Ramanayake	0	S. D. Udal c de Silva b Ramanayake	14
R. Ayling c Wijegunawardene b Madurasinghe	59	C. A. Connor not out	29
D. I. Gower c and b Madurasinghe	0	L-b 5, w 2, n-b 14	21
R. M. F. Cox b Wijegunawardene	34		

P. J. Bakker did not bat.

1/45 2/45 3/151   (8 wkts dec.) 367
4/151 5/242 6/260
7/290 8/325

Bowling: Labrooy 12–1–53–0; Ramanayake 26–2–106–3; Madurasinghe 30–4–99–3; Wijegunawardene 21–2–75–1; Hathurusinghe 7–2–29–1.

Sri Lankans

R. S. Mahanama c Aymes b Bakker	32	– lbw b Udal	56
J. C. Hathurusinghe c Maru b Connor	1	– c Nicholas b Bakker	5
D. S. B. P. Kuruppu lbw b Maru	24	– c Gower b Maru	21
P. A. de Silva lbw b Bakker	2	– not out	221
H. P. Tillekeratne st Aymes b Maru	10	– b Maru	100
S. T. Jayasuriya c Middleton b Maru	18	– c Aymes b Udal	54
M. S. Atapattu c Gower b Udal	9	– st Aymes b Udal	0
G. F. Labrooy c Connor b Udal	5	– st Aymes b Udal	18
C. P. H. Ramanayake not out	5	– not out	9
A. W. R. Madurasinghe c Cox b Maru	4		
†J. I. W. Wijegunawardene c Cox b Maru	0		
L-b 1, n-b 7	8	B 5, l-b 6, w 3, n-b 8	22

1/4 2/53 3/55 4/76 5/88   118   1/7 2/84 3/94   (7 wkts dec.) 506
6/103 7/108 8/109 9/118   4/357 5/457
6/459 7/491

Bowling: *First Innings*—Bakker 13–1–36–2; Connor 10–2–32–1; Ayling 7–4–9–0; Maru 1.5–4–25–5; Udal 7–2–15–2. *Second Innings*—Bakker 17–0–87–1; Connor 10–2–63–0; Maru 40–20–119–2; Udal 40–9–139–4; Ayling 16–4–38–0; Nicholas 4–0–29–0; Middleton 4–0–19–0; Cox 1–0–1–0.

Umpires: K. E. Palmer and R. C. Tolchard.

THE UNIBIND ICC TROPHY, 1990

By DAVID HARDY

The fourth tournament for the ICC Trophy, following the 1979, 1982 and 1986 events, which were all held in England, was for the first time staged in one of the Associate Member countries competing for it, The Netherlands. For the first time, too, a sponsor's name was attached to the event, that of the Dutch book-binding firm, Unibind. It was indeed a new departure, which had demanded three years of thorough preparation by the ICC Management Committee – under the chairmanship of Gibraltarian Joe Buzaglo, himself a participant in the 1986 tournament – and the Royal Dutch Cricket Association committee, led by the former national wicket-keeper and national association chairman, Henk van Eck.

This was also the first ICC Trophy not to be played on grass pitches, which theoretically should have given an advantage to those countries, such as the host country and Denmark, who habitually play on matting or artificial surfaces. With no grass pitches in The Netherlands, the organising committee was faced with the choice, in the interests of standardisation, of choosing venues with coconut matting wickets, laid over a gravel base, or artificial grass. The former surface was chosen and ten clubs were selected to stage the 58 matches. The majority were located in the west of the country, the heart of Dutch cricket: three in The Hague, two in the Amsterdam area, two in the Rotterdam area and one in Haarlem. The other two venues were at Nijmegen and Deventer, in the east but no more than two hours' drive from the Bel Air Hotel in The Hague, the nerve centre of the tournament for three weeks. Both semi-finals and the final were scheduled for the beautiful HCC ground in The Hague.

It was hoped that all eighteen Associate Members would participate, but at the eleventh hour West Africa pulled out. The only differences from 1986 were the participation this time of Singapore and the expansion of the East Africa team to embrace East and Central Africa (representing Malawi, Tanzania, Uganda and Zambia). However, the arrangement of the qualifying groups was certainly different from the previous tournament. The seventeen teams initially played in four qualifying groups: three of four teams (Groups A, B and C) and one of five (Group D). The first two teams from each group then went forward to two second-round groups (E and F), the first two teams of which qualified for the knockout semi-finals. In order to ensure that all teams played roughly the same number of matches over the three weeks, two additional groups (G and H) were formed by the teams which did not qualify for Groups E and F.

A curiosity of the playing conditions was that group matches not completed because of the weather had to be replayed in their entirety the following day. (In fact, the weather was so kind that only one group match was so affected.) However, this regulation did not apply to the semi-finals or final. These, it was ruled, would be resumed at the score when the game was interrupted, as happened in the Zimbabwe-Bangladesh semi-final. In the event of teams finishing level in groups, run-rate was decisive. Papua New Guinea, although aware of this, failed to realise that in the event of a team being dismissed the run-rate would be decided by the total divided by 60 vers, and not by the actual overs batted. In their last Group E match, chasing the USA's 190, they were all out for 123 in 25.2 overs and failed in the end by 0.28 to reach the semi-finals.

It was thought by many that The Netherlands, with the advantage of playing on home grounds, would never have a better chance of qualifying for the World Cup. They failed by just 25 runs to beat Zimbabwe in 1986; this time, surely, they could go one better. Zimbabwe returned in 1990, however, as favourites with the nucleus of their 1986 team. Moreover, their captain, David Houghton, as the professional for Quick CC of The Hague, had ample experience of Dutch conditions. The Netherlands had two English county cricketers to call on, Paul-Jan Bakker of Hampshire and Roland Lefebvre of Somerset, and selected three foreign-born players – Rupert Gomes, the Trinidadian who played in their 1986 team, Sri Lankan Flavian Aponso, and Nolan Clarke, the 41-year-old prolific six-hitter from Barbados, who a few days before the start of the tournament had broken the all-time Dutch record by scoring 265 not out in a league match. Holland's best all-rounder, Ron Elferink, unfortunately missed the tournament through injury.

The final was duly a repeat of the 1986 Lord's contest. But in front of thousands of enthusiastic Dutch supporters, The Netherlands performed less creditably than in 1986 and lost comfortably to a polished, professional Zimbabwe team. For Zimbabwe, who had never lost an ICC match, the Flower brothers, Andy (who also kept wicket excellently) and Grant, were outstanding with the bat, Andy finishing with the best average of the tournament, 77.75, and Grant third in the list with 63.25. The Zimbabwean pace attack of Eddo Brandes, Malcolm Jarvis, Kevin Duers and Ali Shah, supported by the 43-year-old off-spinner, John Traicos, the meanest bowler in the tournament (1.81 runs per over), was too good for everyone. Houghton himself had scored just 4 runs in three innings before the semi-finals, in which his masterly 91 rescued his side when they were 37 for four against Bangladesh. The Netherlands, despite having the heaviest run-scorer of the tournament in Clarke (523 runs) and the "player of the tournament" in Lefebvre (315 runs at 45 and fourteen wickets at 9.43), failed to achieve what they dearly wanted, principally through a careless batting display in the final.

Although Kenya and Bangladesh reached the semi-finals, their places could have been filled by two of several teams. Kenya, curiously, won only two of their six group matches, qualifying from Group B in the first round with a run-rate 0.14 better than Fiji's, and from Group E in the second round by virtue of that 0.28 runs per over superiority over Papua New Guinea. Bangladesh won all three matches in the initial phase, beating Kenya along the way, and finished level with The Netherlands in Group F in the second stage with two wins out of three. Another 0.07 runs per over from Bangladesh would, in fact, have pitted Zimbabwe and The Netherlands, clearly the two best teams, against each other in the semi-finals. Kenya, with many locally born players in the party, including four Odumbe brothers (the most successful was Maurice with 289 runs at 48.17) and two Tikolos, showed a refreshing advance since 1986. Bangladesh, the only ICC Associate Member with a Test ground, possessed an accomplished opening batsman in Nurul Abedin (235 runs at 47) and an outstanding wicket-keeper in Nasir Nasu, who recorded 22 dismissals.

Canada were the only team to beat The Netherlands before the final, but their batting was too inconsistent. Denmark, with Ole Mortensen, the Derbyshire professional, could not emulate their 1986 performance of reaching the semi-finals and once again lost the "European championship final" against The Netherlands in a decisive Group F match. The other two teams to reach the second stage, Papua New Guinea and USA, were eased out of a semi-final place by Kenya on run-rate.

Of the weaker nations, Fiji emerged as an improved force, pulling off the surprise of the first-round matches by beating Bermuda on the first day of the tournament. Hong Kong had little chance to progress from the five-team Group D – J. Marsden was, however, one of only four batsmen in the tournament to score more than 300 runs – and Singapore were similarly outclassed in Group A. Neither Malaysia nor East and Central Africa managed a win in the first round. Argentina failed as well, but Israel and Gibraltar, the two nations with the smallest reservoir of clubs, both went home happy after winning a qualifying match. Israel, with largely home-grown players, beat Argentina (Israel's star player in that match, with the good cricketing name of Alan Moss, scored 42 and took five for 37), while Gibraltar beat East and Central Africa to register their second-ever win in the ICC Trophy.

The organisation of the tournament, whereby the non-qualifiers for the second stage played in Groups G and H, gave the lesser teams full value for their long trip to The Netherlands, and contributed considerably to the now traditional, extremely sociable atmosphere amongst the players and officials of the Associate Members. The decision to move the tournament away from England proved a great success, and it was hoped that this success would be repeated when the Associate Member countries came together for the 1994 ICC Trophy.

GROUP A

At KZKC, The Hague, June 4. Canada won by eight wickets. Singapore 108 (57 overs) (M. Prashad four for 21); Canada 110 for two (30.5 overs) (G. Budhoo 41 not out, F. Kirmani 31 not out).

At HBS, The Hague, June 4. Zimbabwe won by nine wickets. Malaysia 80 (38.4 overs) (A. J. Traicos four for 10); Zimbabwe 81 for one (23.4 overs) (A. Flower 56 not out).

At Koninklijke UD, Deventer, June 6. Canada won by eight wickets. Malaysia 148 (57.5 overs) (A. Stephens 56; B. Seebaran four for 34, T. Gardner three for 21); Canada 153 for two (39 overs) (P. Prashad 52 not out, I. Lyburd 41, F. Kirmani 33).

At Quick, Nijmegen, June 6. Zimbabwe won by ten wickets. Singapore 108 (50.1 overs) (M. P. Jarvis four for 21, E. A. Brandes three for 30); Zimbabwe 109 for no wkt (24.5 overs) (G. W. Flower 53 not out, G. A. Paterson 52 not out).

At VRA, Amstelveen, June 10. Singapore won by four wickets. Malaysia 147 (51.1 overs) (R. Chander 34; T. Seal three for 16, S. Muruthi three for 26); Singapore 151 for six (58.2 overs) (B. Bala 55 not out).

At Rood en Wit, Haarlem, June 10. Zimbabwe won by 68 runs. Zimbabwe 215 (59.4 overs) (G. W. Flower 70, A. H. Shah 39; D. Joseph three for 27, T. Gardner three for 47); Canada 147 (51.4 overs) (A. Dornellas 33, M. Prashad 32 not out; A. J. Traicos three for 16, A. H. Shah three for 37).

	Played	Won	Lost	Points	Run-rate
Zimbabwe	3	3	0	12	3.79
Canada	3	2	1	8	3.18
Singapore	3	1	2	4	2.06
Malaysia	3	0	3	0	2.08

GROUP B

At VRA, Amstelveen, June 4. Bangladesh won by three wickets. Kenya 189 for nine (60 overs) (Maurice Odumbe 41, A. Njoroge 33 not out, I. Tariq Iqbal 31; Minhaz-ul-Abedin three for 29); Bangladesh 190 for seven (58.1 overs) (C. A. Hossain 40, M. A. Khan 39 not out).

At Hermes DVS, Schiedam, June 4. Fiji won by 58 runs. Fiji 206 for nine (60 overs) (S. Campbell 55, J. Sorovakatini 37; K. Lightbourne three for 38); Bermuda 148 (43 overs).

At HBS, The Hague, June 6. Kenya won by four wickets. Fiji 168 for eight (50 overs) (C. Browne 66, A. Browne 36; Martin Odumbe three for 21, B. Odumbe three for 24); Kenya 169 for six (46.2 overs) (A. Njoroge 43 not out, D. McDonald 35, Maurice Odumbe 31; N. Maxwell three for 20).

At KZKC, The Hague, June 6. Bangladesh won by 36 runs. Bangladesh 175 (56.5 overs) (Minhaz-ul-Abedin 47, M. Islam 30; A. Edwards three for 22); Bermuda 139 (53.5 overs) (R. Hill 49; Minhaz-ul-Abedin three for 23).

At VOC, Rotterdam, June 10. Bangladesh won by three wickets. Fiji 189 (59.5 overs) (J. Sorovakatini 43, C. Browne 36, N. Maxwell 36; M. E. Hoque Moni three for 26); Bangladesh 193 for seven (58.4 overs) (M. A. Khan 42 not out; S. Campbell three for 45).

At ACC, Amstelveen, June 10. Bermuda won by 66 runs. Bermuda 280 (58.3 overs) (W. Smith 57, T. Smith 54, O. Jones 44; A. Njoroge three for 58); Kenya 214 for nine (60 overs) (T. Tikolo 44, Maurice Odumbe 41).

	Played	Won	Lost	Points	Run-rate
Bangladesh	3	3	0	12	3.17
Kenya	3	1	2	4	3.45
Fiji	3	1	2	4	3.31
Bermuda	3	1	2	4	3.15

GROUP C

At Rood en Wit, Haarlem, June 4. USA won by 95 runs. USA 198 for seven (50 overs) (Z. Amin 53, S. Shivnarine 43, T. Mills 31 not out); Gibraltar 103 (42 overs) (T. Buzaglo 35; K. Khan four for 11, Z. Amin four for 29).

At Hermes DVS, Schiedam, June 6. Denmark won by 103 runs. Denmark 197 for nine (60 overs) (S. Mikkelsen 54 not out, O. Stoustrup 39); East and Central Africa 94 (43.5 overs) (O. H. Mortensen four for 30).

At Koninklijke UD, Deventer, June 8. Denmark won by seven wickets. Gibraltar 128 (46.5 overs) (B. Chinappa 31, A. Raikes 30; O. H. Mortensen four for 27, J. Bredo three for 22, S. Henriksen three for 32); Denmark 129 for three (36 overs) (T. Jensen 36 not out).

At Quick, Nijmegen, June 8. No result; match declared null and replayed on June 11. USA 404 for nine (60 overs) (E. Peart 101, H. Blackman 100, R. R. Winter 44 not out, N. Lashkari 34, S. Shivnarine 32; F. Sarigat four for 76); East and Central Africa 41 for two (20 overs).

At HBS, The Hague, June 10. Gibraltar won by eight wickets. East and Central Africa 123 (42.4 overs) (H. Patadia 55; R. Brooks four for 18, B. Chinappa three for 17); Gibraltar 124 for two (31.3 overs) (T. Buzaglo 40 not out, R. Buzaglo 39).

At Quick, Nijmegen, June 11. USA won by five wickets. East and Central Africa 184 (59.3 overs) (P. Desai 51, H. Bagas 34, Y. Wanakabulo 34; R. Benjamin five for 27, K. Khan three for 41); USA 186 for five (39.5 overs) (H. Blackman 63, S. Smith 45; B. Bouri four for 44).

At ACC, Amstelveen, June 12. USA won by 12 runs. USA 224 for eight (60 overs) (E. Peart 59, K. Khan 38, S. Shivnarine 32; N. Bindsley four for 53); Denmark 212 (58.5 overs) (J. Jensen 57, P. Jensen 48, O. H. Mortensen 35 not out; Z. Amin three for 34).

	Played	Won	Lost	Points	Run-rate
USA	3	3	0	12	4.08
Denmark	3	2	1	8	3.45
Gibraltar	3	1	2	4	2.52
East and Central Africa	3	0	3	0	2.23

GROUP D

At Quick, Nijmegen, June 4. Papua New Guinea won by 167 runs. Papua New Guinea 265 for seven (60 overs) (T. Ao 88, T. Raka 59 not out, V. Pala 36; H. Pereyra three for 29) Argentina 98 (44.3 overs) (G. Ravu three for 16, T. Raka three for 28).

At ACC, Amstelveen, June 4. The Netherlands won by 338 runs. The Netherlands 402 for four (60 overs) (R. Gomes 169 not out, N. E. Clarke 154, R. P. Lefebvre 46); Israel 64 (38.1 overs) (S. W. Lubbers four for 13).

At HCC, The Hague, June 6. Israel won by one wicket. Argentina 127 (54.2 overs) (C. Nino 35; A. Moss five for 37, M. Jacob three for 29); Israel 129 for nine (51 overs) (A. Moss 42, S. Perlman 31; D. Annand three for 29, H. Pereyra three for 37).

At VOC, Rotterdam, June 6. The Netherlands won by seven wickets. Hong Kong 178 for seven (60 overs) (K. Kumar 43, M. Sabine 40; R. P. Lefebvre three for 24); The Netherlands 184 for three (25.3 overs) (N. E. Clarke 116 not out, R. Gomes 40).

At Rood en Wit, Haarlem, June 8. Papua New Guinea won by 36 runs. Papua New Guinea 220 for seven (60 overs) (R. Ila 56, C. Amini 50; G. Davies three for 28); Hong Kong 184 (56.5 overs) (D. A. Jones 71, N. Perera 43, J. Marsden 31; K. Loi five for 34).

At KZKC, The Hague, June 8. The Netherlands won by 223 runs. The Netherlands 302 for seven (60 overs) (R. P. Lefebvre 109 not out, N. E. Clarke 61, R. van Oosterom 43, G. J. A. F. Aponso 38); Argentina 79 (40.4 overs) (F. Jansen three for 13).

At Hermes DVS, Schiedam, June 10. Papua New Guinea won by 57 runs. Papua New Guinea 190 (48.4 overs) (T. Ao 59, W. Maha 35; C. Callendar three for 36); Israel 133 for nine (60 overs) (S. Perlman 49; C. Amini three for 21).

At Koninklijke UD, Deventer, June 10. Hong Kong won by 63 runs. Hong Kong 230 for nine (60 overs) (N. Stearns 57, D. A. Jones 30; A. Morris four for 38); Argentina 167 (54.3 overs) (T. Ferguson 57; D. Paull five for 27, S. Tariq four for 34).

At Rood en Wit, Haarlem, June 12. The Netherlands won by 160 runs. The Netherlands 237 (59.5 overs) (T. de Leede 50, S. W. Lubbers 46, N. E. Clarke 40); Papua New Guinea 77 (38.1 overs) (A. van Troost three for 11).

At VRA, Amstelveen, June 12. Hong Kong won by 144 runs. Hong Kong 323 for four (60 overs) (J. Marsden 150, M. Sabine 60 not out, K. Kumar 58); Israel 179 (50 overs) (S. Erulkar 46, C. Callendar 37, A. Moss 31; D. N. Brettell four for 53).

	Played	Won	Lost	Points	Run-rate
The Netherlands	4	4	0	16	5.49
Papua New Guinea	4	3	1	12	3.27
Hong Kong	4	2	2	8	3.81
Israel	4	1	3	4	2.29
Argentina	4	0	4	0	1.96

GROUP E

At Rood en Wit, Haarlem, June 14. Zimbabwe won by nine wickets. Papua New Guinea 133 (47.3 overs) (K. Ila 34; K. G. Duers three for 19, J. P. Brent three for 40); Zimbabwe 134 for one (35.4 overs) (A. Flower 80 not out, G. W. Flower 49 not out).

At ACC, Amstelveen, June 14. Kenya won by six wickets. USA 162 (58.5 overs) (S. Shivnarine 30; Maurice Odumbe three for 36); Kenya 163 for four (42 overs) (Maurice Odumbe 79 not out).

At Quick, Nijmegen, June 16. Zimbabwe won by seven wickets. USA 131 (59.3 overs) (K. Khan 32; E. A. Brandes five for 22, K. G. Duers three for 23); Zimbabwe 132 for three (46 overs) (G. W. Flower 52 not out, A. Flower 32).

At HBS, The Hague, June 16. Papua New Guinea won by 37 runs. Papua New Guinea 230 (59.4 overs) (C. Amini 55; E. Odumbe three for 42); Kenya 193 (57.2 overs) (Maurice Odumbe 64; T. Raka three for 29, G. Ravu three for 37, K. Loi three for 37).

At VRA, Amstelveen, June 18. USA won by 67 runs. USA 190 (51.2 overs) (K. Khan 52; V. Pala three for 31); Papua New Guinea 123 (25.2 overs) (W. Maha 34; E. Daley four for 35, R. R. Winter three for 30).

At ACC, Amstelveen, June 18. Zimbabwe won by 133 runs. Zimbabwe 259 for nine (60 overs) (A. H. Shah 69, G. A. Briant 48, A. Flower 44, A. J. Pycroft 34; M. Suji three for 47); Kenya 126 for six (60 overs) (I. Tariq Iqbal 36, S. Gupta 30 not out; E. A. Brandes three for 39).

	Played	Won	Lost	Points	Run-rate
Zimbabwe	3	3	0	12	3.72
Kenya	3	1	2	4	2.98
Papua New Guinea	3	1	2	4	2.70
USA	3	1	2	4	2.68

GROUP F

At VOC, Rotterdam, June 14. Bangladesh won by three wickets. Denmark 233 for nine (60 overs) (A. From Hansen 57, J. Jensen 50, Aftab Ahmed 34; M. J. Alam three for 27); Bangladesh 235 for seven (59.4 overs) (Nurul Abedin 85, M. A. Khan 50, Minhaz-ul-Abedin 37; S. Sorensen three for 32).

At Koninklijke UD, Deventer, June 14. Canada won by 21 runs. Canada 199 (57.2 overs) (D. Singh 64, T. Gardner 46, A. Dornellas 36; E. Dulfer five for 38, A. van Troost three for 25); The Netherlands 178 for eight (60 overs) (T. Gardner three for 40).

At KZKC, The Hague, June 16. Canada won by six wickets. Canada 142 (54 overs) (M. Prashad 39, T. Gardner 37; O. H. Mortensen three for 15, S. Sorensen three for 32); Denmark 143 for four (50.5 overs) (P. Jensen 32).

At VRA, Amstelveen, June 16. The Netherlands won by 161 runs. The Netherlands 309 for seven (60 overs) (N. E. Clarke 83, R. P. Lefebvre 75, T. de Leede 46, C. Ruskamp 38); Bangladesh 148 (47.4 overs) (Minhaz-ul-Abedin 38; R. P. Lefebvre three for 16, G. J. A. F. Aponso three for 26).

At Rood en Wit, Haarlem, June 18. Bangladesh won by 117 runs. Bangladesh 265 for six (60 overs) (Nurul Abedin 105, Faruq Ahmed 56); Canada 148 (44.4 overs) (I. Lyburd 60).

At Hermes DVS, Schiedam, June 18. The Netherlands won by 54 runs. The Netherlands 176 (59.3 overs) (G. J. A. F. Aponso 54, R. P. Lefebvre 35; S. Sorensen four for 43, S. Mikkelsen three for 15); Denmark 122 (53.4 overs) (O. Stoustrup 31, S. Mikkelsen 30).

	Played	Won	Lost	Points	Run-rate
The Netherlands	3	2	1	8	3.68
Bangladesh	3	2	1	8	3.62
Denmark	3	1	2	4	2.93
Canada	3	1	2	4	2.72

GROUP G

At VRA, Amstelveen, June 14. Singapore won by seven wickets. Israel 111 (34.5 overs) (T. Seal three for 20, Srimal three for 28); Singapore 112 for three (30.2 overs) (B. Bala 38, B. Muruga 37 not out).

At Quick, Nijmegen, June 15. Bermuda won by 180 runs. Bermuda 320 for nine (60 overs) (R. Hill 100, A. Douglas 63 not out, T. Smith 48, A. R. Manders 40; R. Brooks four for 42); Gibraltar 140 (49.3 overs) (B. Chinappa 53; G. Brangman three for 18, K. Lightbourne three for 40).

At Hermes DVS, Schiedam, June 16. Gibraltar won by six wickets. Singapore 144 (54.5 overs) (B. Bala 60 not out; A. Raikes four for 30); Gibraltar 146 for four (45.3 overs) (B. Chinappa 51 not out).

At VOC, Rotterdam, June 18. Gibraltar won by five wickets. Israel 269 for nine (60 overs) (H. Awaskar 66, S. Erulkar 54); Gibraltar 270 for five (54.4 overs) (C. Robinson 79, A. Raikes 43 not out, R. Buzaglo 42).

At KZKC, The Hague, June 18. Bermuda won by 208 runs. Bermuda 291 for seven (60 overs) (N. Gibbons 68 not out, D. Lewis 48, A. Amory 41, A. N. Manders 41); Singapore 83 (49.1 overs) (R. Leverock four for 14).

At VOC, Rotterdam, June 19. Bermuda won by seven wickets. Israel 84 (26.3 overs) (G. Brangman four for 9); Bermuda 85 for three (14.3 overs) (A. N. Manders 52 not out).

	Played	Won	Lost	Points	Run-rate
Bermuda	3	3	0	12	5.19
Gibraltar	3	2	1	8	3.48
Singapore	3	1	2	4	2.26
Israel	3	0	3	0	2.58

GROUP H

At KZKC, The Hague, June 14. Fiji won by 68 runs. Fiji 288 for eight (60 overs) (J. Sorovakatini 63, C. Browne 52; L. Alonso three for 48, D. Forrester three for 66); Argentina 220 (56.4 overs) (M. Morris 61, G. Kirschbaum 32; A. Tawatatau three for 26).

At Hermes DVS, Schiedam, June 14. East and Central Africa won by 49 runs. East and Central Africa 180 for eight (50 overs) (B. Bouri 41, S. Walusimbi 38 not out); Malaysia 131 (44.4 overs) (S. W. Hong 33; B. Bouri three for 15, S. Lakha three for 19).

At HCC, The Hague, June 15. Argentina won by three wickets. East and Central Africa 184 (59.2 overs) (G. R. Shariff 42); Argentina 188 for seven (54.5 overs) (M. Ryan 76 not out).

At Hermes DVS, Schiedam, June 15. Hong Kong won by three wickets. Malaysia 168 (60 overs) (S. Bell 61; G. Davies three for 27); Hong Kong 169 for seven (58.2 overs) (N. Stearns 34; A. Stephens three for 28).

At VOC, Rotterdam, June 16. Fiji won by six wickets. Hong Kong 182 (60 overs) (K. Kumar 46, N. Stearns 32, J. Marsden 30; N. Maxwell four for 30); Fiji 185 for four (37.3 overs) (C. Browne 65, J. Sorovakatini 57, N. Maxwell 41 not out).

At Koninklijke UD, Deventer, June 16. Malaysia won by 155 runs. Malaysia 246 for nine (60 overs) (A. Stephens 102, M. Saat Jalil 53); Argentina 91 (42.4 overs) (C. Nino 30; S. Muniandy four for 17, R. Chander three for 23).

At HBS, The Hague, June 18. Hong Kong won by three wickets. East and Central Africa 203 (50 overs) (G. R. Shariff 42, H. Patadia 34, H. Tejani 33; S. Tariq four for 46, D. N. Brettell three for 33); Hong Kong 204 for seven (58.2 overs) (J. Marsden 38, D. N. Brettell 32 not out, N. Stearns 32).

At Quick, Nijmegen, June 18. Fiji won by eight wickets. Malaysia 146 (57.2 overs) (R. Chander 31; K. Batina three for 15, J. Mateyawa three for 30); Fiji 147 for two (27.4 overs) N. Maxwell 84, S. Campbell 34).

At ACC, Amstelveen, June 19. Fiji won by 95 runs. Fiji 214 for nine (50 overs) (J. Sorovakatini 42; S. Lakha three for 35, S. Naik three for 44); East and Central Africa 119 (32 overs) (F. Sarigat 30; J. Mateyawa three for 12, A. Waqa three for 34).

	Played	Won	Lost	Points	Run-rate
Fiji	4	4	0	16	4.77
Hong Kong	4	3	1	12	3.33
East and Central Africa	4	1	3	4	3.12
Malaysia	4	1	3	4	3.00
Argentina	4	1	3	4	2.85

Note: Argentina and Hong Kong did not play each other in Group H. However, for the purpose of the table, the result of their Group D game on June 10 was included in the above figures.

SEMI-FINALS

KENYA v THE NETHERLANDS

At HCC, The Hague, June 20. The Netherlands won by five wickets. Toss: Kenya.
   Man of the Match: T. de Leede.

Kenya

I. Tariq Iqbal c Ruskamp b Bakker	14	E. Odumbe c Ruskamp b Bakker	1
O. Chudasama lbw b Bakker	6	*T. Tikolo c Gomes b Bakker	8
S. Gupta run out	1	A. Njoroge not out	1
Maurice Odumbe b Lefebvre	21	B 4, l-b 4, w 13	21
L. Tikolo b Bakker	0		
A. V. Karim c Clarke b Lefebvre	53	1/9 2/17 3/35 (59.4 overs)	202
†M. Kanji c van Oosterom b Lefebvre	52	4/36 5/52 6/167	
Martin Odumbe c de Leede b Bakker	24	7/168 8/175 9/199	

Bowling: van Troost 12–2–49–0; Bakker 11.4–2–41–6; Lefebvre 12–2–39–3; Dulfer 11–1–38–0; Aponso 7–3–9–0; Lubbers 6–0–18–0.

The Netherlands

G. J. A. F. Aponso c Karim b E. Odumbe	9	T. de Leede not out	56
†C. Ruskamp c Maurice Odumbe b Karim	37	*S. W. Lubbers not out	26
R. Gomes c Kanji b E. Odumbe	4	B 1, l-b 1, w 18, n-b 1	21
N. E. Clarke b E. Odumbe	32	1/9 2/15 3/62 (5 wkts, 56.2 overs)	205
R. P. Lefebvre lbw b Maurice Odumbe	20	4/108 5/120	

R. van Oosterom, P. J. Bakker, A. van Troost and E. Dulfer did not bat.

Bowling: Martin Odumbe 8–0–29–0; E. Odumbe 11.2–2–39–3; Njoroge 9–0–45–0; Karim 12–0–33–1; L. Tikolo 10–2–34–0; Maurice Odumbe 6–2–23–1.

Umpires: S. A. Ahad (Bangladesh) and J. D. Robinson (Zimbabwe).

BANGLADESH v ZIMBABWE

At HCC, The Hague, June 21, 22. Zimbabwe won by 84 runs. Toss: Bangladesh.
   Man of the Match: D. L. Houghton.

Zimbabwe

G. W. Flower c Chowdhury b Nawsher	7		G. A. Briant st Nasir Nasu		
A. H. Shah c Faruq Ahmed b Nawsher	5			b Hoque Moni .	0
†A. Flower run out	1		E. A. Brandes not out		66
*D. L. Houghton c Minhaz-ul-Abedin			A. J. Traicos not out		1
b Chowdhury .	91				
G. A. Paterson c Hoque Moni			L-b 7, w 10, n-b 10		27
b Nawsher .	4				
K. J. Arnott c Nurul Abedin			1/7 2/21 3/23 4/37	(7 wkts, 60 overs)	231
b Hoque Moni .	29		5/134 6/135 7/196		
K. G. Duers and M. P. Jarvis did not bat.					

Bowling: Nawsher 12–2–47–3; Alam 12–0–42–0; Chowdhury 10–0–51–1; M. A. Hossain 12–1–37–0; Hoque Moni 12–1–35–2; Minhaz-ul-Abedin 2–0–12–0.

Bangladesh

M. A. Hossain c and b Jarvis	9		M. J. Alam b Jarvis		5
Nurul Abedin c Jarvis b Duers	9		†Nasir Nasu not out		3
*C. A. Hossain b Duers	4		G. M. Nawsher b Brandes		0
Faruq Ahmed c Houghton b Duers	6		L-b 8, w 8, n-b 2		18
A. Karim c A. Flower b Duers	6				
Minhaz-ul-Abedin c and b Jarvis	57		1/13 2/23 3/31	(53.1 overs)	147
M. E. Hoque Moni run out	28		4/32 5/45 6/128		
G. Chowdhury c A. Flower b Jarvis	2		7/137 8/137 9/147		

Bowling: Jarvis 9–2–22–4; Duers 12–2–25–4; Traicos 12–2–32–0; Brandes 8.1–1–36–1; Shah 12–2–24–0.

Umpires: W. Molenaar (The Netherlands) and A. Sarkar (Kenya).

FINAL

THE NETHERLANDS v ZIMBABWE

At HCC, The Hague, June 23. Zimbabwe won by six wickets. Toss: The Netherlands. Aponso and Ruskamp provided a solid start for The Netherlands. But an irresponsible innings from Clarke, who holed out on the boundary off Shah, having already hit him for two sixes in the same over – and all this just before lunch – sowed seeds of panic in the Dutch batting. Gomes, Lefebvre, de Leede and van Oosterom all played careless shots before they had settled, and it was left to the captain, Lubbers, to give the home team some sort of chance with a masterly 47 (he was run out in the last over). However, a total of 197 was never going to be enough against the experienced Zimbabwe batting. Lefebvre captured two early wickets (and finished with two for 12 in eleven overs), but Bakker could make no impression and the Dutch attack looked unbalanced with three off-spinners. Andy Flower played a superbly controlled innings and was well supported by Pycroft in a match-winning third-wicket stand of 93. Houghton, on his 33rd birthday, hurried his side to victory with a whirlwind 28, including four sixes.

Man of the Match: A. Flower.

The Netherlands

G. J. A. F. Aponso c A. Flower b Shah	36		P. J. Bakker c A. Flower b Brandes		7
†C. Ruskamp c A. Flower b Brandes	21		A. van Troost not out		9
R. Gomes c Jarvis b Traicos	16		E. Dulfer not out		0
N. E. Clarke c Paterson b Shah	14		B 2, l-b 4, w 19, n-b 3		28
R. P. Lefebvre c Houghton b Shah	8				
T. de Leede c Jarvis b Duers	9		1/49 2/77 3/100	(9 wkts, 60 overs)	197
*S. W. Lubbers run out	47		4/100 5/117 6/125		
R. van Oosterom c Arnott b Shah	2		7/139 8/166 9/195		

Bowling: Jarvis 12–2–32–0; Duers 12–1–39–1; Traicos 12–2–19–1; Shah 12–2–56–4; Brandes 12–1–45–2.

Zimbabwe

G. A. Paterson c Aponso b Lefebvre	.. 20	A. H. Shah not out	 11
G. W. Flower b Lefebvre	 10		
†A. Flower not out	 69	L-b 8, w 7	 15
A. J. Pycroft c Ruskamp b van Troost	. 45		—
*D. L. Houghton c Lefebvre		1/25 2/41 3/134	(4 wkts, 54.2 overs) 198
	b van Troost . 28	4/180	

K. J. Arnott, E. A. Brandes, A. J. Traicos, K. G. Duers and M. P. Jarvis did not bat.

Bowling: van Troost 12–1–43–2; Bakker 10.2–2–35–0; Lefebvre 11–3–12–2; Dulfer 12–1–52–0; Aponso 5–0–23–0; Lubbers 2–0–10–0; de Leede 2–0–15–0.

Umpires: J. W. Holder (England) and R. G. Singh (Canada).

PREVIOUS ICC TROPHY FINALS

1979   SRI LANKA beat Canada by 60 runs at Worcester.
1982   ZIMBABWE beat Bermuda by five wickets at Leicester.
1986   ZIMBABWE beat The Netherlands by 25 runs at Lord's.

FUTURE TOURS

1991	West Indians to England Sri Lankans to England	1993-94	England to West Indies* Indians to Pakistan New Zealanders to Australia

1991-92	Indians* and West Indians to
	    Australia
	Sri Lankans to Pakistan
	England to New Zealand
	World Cup in Australia and
	    New Zealand
	Sri Lankans to India
			Sri Lankans to Australia
			Pakistanis to New Zealand
			Indians to Sri Lanka
			Australians to Pakistan*

		1994	Indians to England* New Zealanders to England
1992	Pakistanis to England Australians to Sri Lanka*	1994-95	England to Australia West Indians to India* Pakistanis to India West Indians to New Zealand Australians to West Indies*
1992-93	West Indians to Australia England to India and *Sri Lanka Pakistanis to Australia* Australians to New Zealand Indians to West Indies Pakistanis to West Indies		
		1995-96	Pakistanis and West Indians to Australia* Sri Lankans to India England to New Zealand New Zealanders to West Indies
1993	Australians to England New Zealanders to Sri Lanka*		

Signifies unconfirmed.

Note: The following tours were scheduled for 1990-91: New Zealanders to Pakistan, West Indians to Pakistan, Sri Lankans to India, England to Australia and New Zealand, New Zealanders to Australia, Pakistanis to India (cancelled), Sri Lankans to New Zealand, Australians to West Indies.

THE MARYLEBONE CRICKET CLUB, 1990

Members' concern at the delay in the completion of the Compton and Edrich
Stands was voiced at the 203rd Annual General Meeting of MCC, held in the
Club's Indoor Cricket School on May 2, 1990, with the President, The Hon.
Sir Denys Roberts, in the chair. In January the Secretary of the Club had
written to members advising of the delay, and the President in his statement

members expressed regret that this should have been necessary. The
committee had originally hoped the stands would be officially opened on the
first day of the Lord's Test match between England and New Zealand in
June; as it transpired, work on the stands had not been completed by the end
of the 1990 season.

The President also drew to the members' attention the Club's good fortune
in its staff, some 90 of whom were full-time employees. These were supported
by more than 300 part-time assistants during the summer, many of whom
received less than the full market-rate for their services, yet provided them
cheerfully and willingly because they loved Lord's and what it represented.
He warned of the need for more accommodation for MCC and TCCB staff at
Lord's, adding that in due course members may have to be consulted on
further expansion.

In presenting the Club's accounts, the chairman of the finance sub-
committee, Sir Anthony Tuke, said that in the past seven years the club had
spent £3 million on improvements to the ground, in addition to which some
£750,000 had been spent on safety work to comply with current legislation. In
this respect, the public address system had been completely rewired and
lightning conductors had been fitted to the Pavilion within the previous year;
and further expenditure was expected following the publication of Lord
Justice Taylor's report on the Hillsborough disaster. Maintenance costs in
1989 had run at approximately the same level as in 1988, but with income
showing an increase, and taking into account major contributions to the
National Coaching Scheme, The Cricket Foundation and ICC, the Club had
an excess of income over expenditure against a deficit the previous year. The
surplus for the year, after taxation, was £240,000 compared with a surplus of
£508,000 in 1988. Members were informed that the Club had signed a four-
year Deed of Covenant for £50,000 per annum in favour of The Cricket
Foundation, a trust fund for the development of youth cricket.

Following Sir Anthony's decision to retire as chairman of finance on
September 30, 1990, the meeting approved the appointment of D. L. Hudd as
his successor. Similarly J. J. Warr was appointed a Trustee to succeed F. G.
Mann when he retired in accordance with Rule 23 on September 30.
Following a ballot, there being five nominations and four vacancies, J. R. T.
Barclay, Sir Ian MacLaurin, S. G. Metcalfe and M. O. C. Sturt were elected
to join the committee on October 1, 1990, to replace C. A. Fry, D. L. Hudd,
N. E. J. Pocock and D. R. W. Silk, all of whom were to retire by rotation as
elected members on September 30.

The President named The Rt Hon. The Lord Griffiths, a Lord of Appeal in
Ordinary, to succeed him on October 1. As W. H. Griffiths, he was in the
Charterhouse XI in 1940 and, after wartime service in the Welsh Guards,
went up to Cambridge and opened the bowling at Lord's in 1946, 1947 and
1948. During these years he also played eight times for Glamorgan.

The membership of the Club on December 31, 1989 was 19,264, made up
of 17,048 full members, 1,970 associate members and 246 honorary members.
These comprised the following: 10,375 full and 1,594 associate town members, 2,275 full and 248 associate country members, 3,451 at the over-65
rate, 75 full and 83 associate members at the under-25 rate, 279 full and 20
associate members at the special schoolmasters' rate, 540 full and 25 associate
members on the abroad list, 7 life vice-presidents, 53 life members, 16 60-
year life members, 41 honorary England cricketers and 182 honorary life

members. In 1989, 603 vacancies occurred, owing to 262 deaths, 248 resignations and 93 lapsed memberships.

At a Special General Meeting immediately following the Annual General Meeting, members approved by postal vote or in person the updated and revised Rules of the Club.

MCC v WORCESTERSHIRE

At Lord's, April 17, 18, 19, 20. Drawn. Toss: Worcestershire. England's series in the West Indies had finished only the previous day – a day ahead of schedule at that – and so the opening match of the Lord's season offered an opportunity to a selection of players hoping to catch the selectors' eye. But if either captain was thinking of ways to conjure a result, his plans were ruined by the weather, which cut the third day to 28.1 overs and prevented any play at all on the fourth. Throughout, conditions were cold; neither the weather nor the closeness of the pitch to the Mound and Tavern boundary favoured the bowlers, but with the ball moving about, the batsmen did not have everything their own way. Parker, dropped at slip by Botham off Newport after reaching his fifty, was prevented by his earlier benefactor from starting his season with a century, while the left-handed Benson played and missed a number of times, as well as giving further evidence of his judgement of line. On the second day, Cowans lent some humour, as well as runs, to the end of MCC's innings by hitting two sixes and six fours in 23 balls. Curtis and Lord gave the champion county a solid start, but on the stroke of tea the left-hander's middle stump was plucked out by Lawrence, one of few joyous moments for the Gloucestershire fast bowler. He was no-balled 27 times for over-stepping, recalling the problem he had encountered on the England A team's tour of Zimbabwe. Hick, who had chosen to winter there and take a rest from first-class cricket, enjoyed a less traumatic return to English cricket, even if, on occasions, his strokeplay looked in need of some fine tuning.

Close of play: First day, MCC 285-5 (D. A. Reeve 39*, W. K. Hegg 36*); Second day, Worcestershire 181-3 (G. A. Hick 53*); Third day, Worcestershire 289-7 (P. A. Neale 22*, P. J. Newport 1*).

MCC

M. D. Moxon c Rhodes b McEwan	12	S. L. Watkin c Hick b McEwan	14
M. R. Benson c Newport b Radford	52	N. G. Cowans not out	46
*P. W. G. Parker b Botham	93	P. C. R. Tufnell b Botham	12
M. A. Atherton lbw b Botham	19		
J. E. Morris lbw b Botham	15	L-b 11, w 3, n-b 8	22
D. A. Reeve c Hick b Radford	39		
†W. K. Hegg c Rhodes b Radford	57	1/13 2/151 3/184 4/191	385
D. V. Lawrence c McEwan b Radford	4	5/216 6/285 7/299 8/319 9/349	

Bowling: Radford 34-7-116-4; McEwan 31-9-101-2; Botham 20-4-68-4; Newport 18-0-85-0; Illingworth 1-0-4-0.

Worcestershire

T. S. Curtis lbw b Watkin	81	†S. J. Rhodes c Hegg b Watkin	19
G. J. Lord b Lawrence	20	P. J. Newport not out	1
G. A. Hick c Parker b Lawrence	72		
R. K. Illingworth c Atherton b Watkin	6	B 4, l-b 5, w 1, n-b 27	37
I. T. Botham c Hegg b Cowans	19		
*P. A. Neale not out	22	1/81 2/165 3/181 4/213	(7 wkts) 289
D. B. D'Oliveira b Watkin	12	5/237 6/258 7/288	

S. M. McEwan and N. V. Radford did not bat.

Bowling: Lawrence 25.1-1-105-2; Cowans 18-5-39-1; Reeve 13-3-40-0; Watkin 29-7-83-4; Tufnell 7-2-13-0.

Umpires: B. Dudleston and K. J. Lyons.

†At Lord's, May 2. Drawn. Toss: MCC. MCC 248 for five dec. (R. T. Virgin 42, I. J. F. Hutchinson 31, R. O. Butcher 80, J. R. T. Barclay 31 not out; M. J. Thursfield three for 34); MCC Young Cricketers 162 for six (T. K. Chadwick 45, M. N. Lathwell 70; J. R. T. Barclay four for 52).

At Lord's, May 7. MCC beat NEW ZEALANDERS by six wickets (See New Zealand tour section).

At Oxford, May 30, 31, June 1. MCC drew with OXFORD UNIVERSITY (See Oxford University section).

At Cambridge, June 11, 12, 13. MCC drew with CAMBRIDGE UNIVERSITY (See Cambridge University section).

At Durham, June 14, 15. MCC lost to DURHAM UNIVERSITY by six wickets (See Other Matches, 1990).

At Coleraine, June 16, 17, 18. MCC lost to IRELAND by 6 runs (See Other Matches, 1990).

†MCC v MCC SCHOOLS

At Lord's, July 18. MCC Schools won by two wickets. Toss: MCC Schools. A disciplined 54 not out by Walton, of Leeds Grammar School, helped MCC Schools to victory over the parent club, Walton hitting the winning runs from the penultimate ball of the final over. However, just as important in the thrust for victory was a fighting 73 from Wasim Khan, of Mason Sixth Form College in Warwick, who added 94 for the second wicket with Fulton, of Judd School. MCC, put in by Richards, lost Downton at 15, but Nurton and Goldsmith steadied the innings, and Goldsmith and Bainbridge established it with a third-wicket partnership of 104. Goldsmith, from the Chobham club, reached his century in 173 minutes and hit thirteen boundaries, and when he was caught at cover in the 60th over, a third wicket for the well-flighted leg-spin of Hodgson, MCC declared.

MCC

P. R. Downton lbw b Laudat	10	*R. D. V. Knight not out	0
M. D. Nurton c Richards b Hodgson	17	B 4, l-b 9, w 2, n-b 1	16
A. J. Goldsmith b Laney b Hodgson	103		
P. Bainbridge b Hodgson	60	1/15 2/89 3/193 4/206 (4 wkts dec.) 206	

G. J. Toogood, M. Hart, †D. J. Goldsmith, S. Welch, A. T. Crouch and C. Hodgkins did not bat.

Bowling: Weston 8–0–28–0; Laudat 7–0–19–1; Walton 8–2–17–0; Richards 22–6–64–0; Hodgson 14.1–1–65–3.

MCC Schools

Wasim Khan (*Josiah Mason SFC*) b Welch	73	*A. C. Richards (*Forest*) b Bainbridge	8
G. Archer (*Stafford CFE*) c and b Hodgkins	7	S. V. Laudat (*Oxford CFE*) run out	0
D. P. Fulton (*Judd*) lbw b Crouch	39	†M. A. Khan (*Aylesbury CFE*) run out	2
J. Laney (*St John's, Marlborough*) c A. J. Goldsmith b Crouch	12	W. P. C. Weston (*Durham*) not out	0
T. C. Walton (*Leeds GS*) not out	54	B 4, l-b 6, w 1, n-b 1	12
R. Murray (*Brigshaw*) c Nurton b Crouch	2	1/26 2/120 3/132 4/159 (8 wkts) 209	
		5/177 6/195 7/195 8/205	

J. Hodgson (*Ranelagh*) did not bat.

Bowling: Toogood 8–3–19–0; Hodgkins 6–2–20–1; Welch 12–3–52–1; Crouch 21–5–62–3; Bainbridge 10.5–1–46–1.

Umpires: E. G. Burston and A. R. Smith.

†At Lord's, August 22, 23. Scotland won by seven wickets. Toss: MCC. MCC 198 (G. D. Mendis 57; C. L. Parfitt six for 57) and 218 for six dec. (S. C. Wundke 101 not out; C. L. Parfitt three for 71); Scotland 190 for eight dec. (D. J. Haggo 33; M. R. Whitney three for 14, G. Stead three for 68) and 227 for three (I. L. Philip 83, A. C. Storie 37, G. Salmond 56 not out, A. B. Russell 38 not out).

At Swansea, August 27, 28. MCC drew with WALES (See Other Matches, 1990).

MCC HONORARY ENGLAND CRICKETERS

C. J. Barnett	T. W. Graveney, OBE	G. Pullar
H. Larwood	G. A. R. Lock	F. J. Titmus, MBE
D. C. S. Compton, CBE	D. A. Allen	D. J. Brown
D. V. P. Wright	R. W. Barber	M. H. Denness
T. G. Evans, CBE	E. R. Dexter	J. M. Brearley, OBE
C. Washbrook	P. H. Parfitt	R. W. Taylor, MBE
A. V. Bedser, CBE	F. H. Tyson	R. G. D. Willis, MBE
P. B. H. May, CBE	M. C. Cowdrey, CBE	J. H. Edrich, MBE
W. Watson	J. T. Murray, MBE	A. P. E. Knott
P. E. Richardson	J. M. Parks	C. M. Old
T. E. Bailey	D. B. Close, CBE	J. A. Snow
M. J. K. Smith, OBE	B. L. D'Oliveira, OBE	D. L. Amiss, MBE
J. B. Statham, CBE	R. Illingworth, CBE	K. W. R. Fletcher, OBE
F. S. Trueman, OBE		

STATUS OF MATCHES IN THE UK

(a) Automatic First-Class Matches

The following matches of three or more days' duration should automatically be considered first-class:

  (i) County Championship matches.
  (ii) Official representative tourist matches from Full Member Countries, unless specifically excluded.
  (iii) MCC v any First-Class County.
  (iv) Oxford v Cambridge and either University against First-Class Counties.
  (v) Scotland v Ireland.

(b) Excluded from First-Class Status

The following matches of three or more days' duration should not normally be accorded first-class status:

  (i) County "friendly" matches.
  (ii) Matches played by Scotland or Ireland, other than their annual match against each other.
  (iii) Unofficial tourist matches, unless circumstances are exceptional.
  (iv) MCC v Oxford/Cambridge.
  (v) Matches involving privately raised teams, unless included officially in a touring team's itinerary.

(c) Consideration of Doubtful Status

Matches played by unofficial touring teams of exceptional ability can be considered in advance and decisions taken accordingly.

Certain other matches comprising 22 recognised first-class cricketers might also be considered in advance.

OTHER MATCHES AT LORD'S, 1990

†ETON v HARROW

June 9. Eton won by seven wickets. Toss: Eton. Eton ended the sequence of drawn games since their 1985 victory, winning the 155th match between the two schools with four balls to spare. Although it was their batsmen who provided the victory by successfully chasing a target of 220 in 153 minutes, Eton owed as much to their bowlers who, assisted by some excellent fielding, held Harrow to 219 for eight from 237 minutes' batting. Aldous and Holyoake occupied 32.3 overs while putting on 77 for Harrow's first wicket, and the other major partnership, 57 between Guillebaud and Hewens for the fifth wicket, took almost 21 overs. Whittington employed flight and accuracy effectively in a long and tidy stint of slow left-arm bowling, and when Chetwood, their captain and off-spinner, strained a calf muscle, Eton were well served by Ssennyamantono just as Harrow were looking to accelerate. In reply, Eton first put down a good foundation, then set off in serious pursuit. Eastwood (95 balls) and Sellar added 50 for the second wicket in 38 minutes, and as Eton went into the final twenty overs, needing 121, Sellar (64 balls) and Hagen put on 70 in 46 minutes. Finally, Hagen (68 balls) and Strickland hit off the remaining 54 runs in the last half-hour, with the latter's unbeaten 23 coming from just twenty deliveries.

Harrow

S. H. Aldous c Eastwood b Whittington	26	†H. D. Duncan not out		1
M. A. Holyoake b Whittington	47	R. E. Sexton not out		2
C. E. Williams c Strickland b Lewis	11			
S. M. Guillebaud lbw b Ssennyamantono	34	B 7, l-b 6, w 6, n-b 6		25
*M. E. D. Jarrett c Sellar b Lewis	10			
E. M. S. Hewens b Lewis	43	1/77 2/98 3/98	(8 wkts dec.)	219
J. L. Pool lbw b Whittington	1	4/111 5/168 6/173		
F. S. J. Yates b Ssennyamantono	19	7/214 8/214		

W. J. D. Hewitt did not bat.

Bowling: Lewis 17–5–50–3; Ulvert 7–4–7–0; Ssennyamantono 17–2–46–2; Chetwood 10–1–25–0; Whittington 25–4–78–3.

Eton

T. A. J. Jenkins c Hewitt b Hewens	19	S. C. E. Strickland not out		23
P. M. Eastwood c Duncan b Hewitt	53	B 3, l-b 8, w 4, n-b 1		16
W. R. G. Sellar c Guillebaud b Pool	57			
N. R. J. Hagen not out	53	1/47 2/97 3/167	(3 wkts)	221

*H. J. P. Chetwood, J. M. S. Whittington, †T. J. Stanley, B. K. Ssennyamantono, C. N. Ulvert and G. H. B. Lewis did not bat.

Bowling: Pool 10.2–1–40–1; Hewitt 12–1–52–1; Sexton 10–1–41–0; Hewens 4–0–26–1; Williams 5–0–19–0; Jarrett 7–0–32–0.

Umpires: P. Adams and D. J. Dennis.

ETON v HARROW, RESULTS AND HUNDREDS

Of the 155 matches played Eton have won 51, Harrow 44 and 60 have been drawn. This is the generally published record, but Harrow men object strongly to the first game in 1805 being treated as a regular contest between the two schools, contending that it is no more correct to count that one than the fixture of 1857 which has been rejected.

The matches played during the war years 1915-18 and 1940-45 are not reckoned as belonging to the regular series.

Results since 1950:

1950	Drawn	1971	Drawn
1951	Drawn	1972	Drawn
1952	Harrow won by seven wickets	1973	Drawn
1953	Eton won by ten wickets	1974	Harrow won by eight wickets
1954	Harrow won by nine wickets	1975	Harrow won by an innings and 151 runs
1955	Eton won by 38 runs	1976	Drawn
1956	Drawn	1977	Eton won by six wickets
1957	Drawn	1978	Drawn
1958	Drawn	1979	Drawn
1959	Drawn	1980	Drawn
1960	Harrow won by 124 runs	1981	Drawn
1961	Harrow won by an innings and 12 runs	1982	Drawn
1962	Drawn	1983	Drawn
1963	Drawn	1984	Drawn
1964	Eton won by eight wickets	1985	Eton won by 3 runs
1965	Harrow won by 48 runs	1986	Drawn
1966	Drawn	1987	Drawn
1967	Drawn	1988	Drawn
1968	Harrow won by seven wickets	1989	Drawn
1969	Drawn	1990	Eton won by seven wickets
1970	Eton won by 97 runs		

Forty-five three-figure innings have been played in matches between these two schools. Those since 1918:

161*	M. K. Fosh	1975 Harrow	106	D. M. Smith	1966 Eton
159	E. W. Dawson	1923 Eton	104	R. Pulbrook	1932 Harrow
158	I. S. Akers-Douglas	1928 Eton	103	L. G. Crawley	1921 Harrow
153	N. S. Hotchkin	1931 Eton	103	T. Hare	1947 Eton
151	R. M. Tindall	1976 Harrow	102*	P. H. Stewart-Brown	1923 Harrow
135	J. C. Atkinson-Clark	1930 Eton	102	R. V. C. Robins	1953 Eton
115	E. Crutchley	1939 Harrow	100	R. H. Cobbold	1923 Eton
112	A. W. Allen	1931 Eton	100*	P. V. F. Cazalet	1926 Eton
112*	T. M. H. James	1978 Harrow	100	A. N. A. Boyd	1934 Eton
111	R. A. A. Holt	1937 Harrow	100*	P. M. Studd	1935 Harrow
109	K. F. H. Hale	1929 Eton	100	S. D. D. Sainsbury	1947 Eton
109	N. S. Hotchkin	1932 Eton	100	M. J. J. Faber	1968 Eton
107	W. N. Coles	1946 Eton			

* *Signifies not out.*

In 1904, D. C. Boles of Eton, making 183, set a record for the match, beating the 152 obtained for Eton in 1841 by Emilius Bayley, afterwards the Rev. Sir John Robert Laurie Emilius Bayley Laurie. M. C. Bird, Harrow, in 1907, scored 100 not out and 131, the only batsman who has made two 100s in the match. N. S. Hotchkin, Eton, played the following innings: 1931, 153; 1932, 109 and 96; 1933, 88 and 12.

June 21, 22, 23, 25, 26. Second Cornhill Test. ENGLAND drew with NEW ZEALAND (See New Zealand tour section).

OXFORD UNIVERSITY v CAMBRIDGE UNIVERSITY

July 4, 5, 6. Drawn. Toss: Cambridge University. With no play possible on the first day owing to rain, and the second limited to 42 overs because of interruptions from the weather, not even the decision of the captains to forfeit innings could prevent the match being drawn. Cambridge, commencing their innings almost half an hour after lunch on the final day, needed to score 270 in 61 overs for victory, but at tea, 85 without loss from 26 overs, they had already fallen behind the run-rate. Heap was bowled by Crawley ten minutes after the resumption; and when James gave the former Oxford captain his second wicket, having batted 2 hours 25 minutes (125 balls) for 56, and Turner was run out soon afterwards, the prospect of Cambridge then scoring 159 from the last twenty overs was negligible. Crawley was moving the ball disconcertingly in the air and off the seam at medium pace, but time was not on Oxford's side either, and in the end the match was called off with ten overs remaining. In the morning, Oxford had gone for runs positively and entertainingly, putting on 153 in the session. Crawley's solid half-century was the springboard for van der Merwe's assault which, with eight fours and a six among the workmen on the Nursery End stands, took him to 50 from 45 balls.

Close of play: First day, No play; Second day, Oxford University 108-4 (M. A. Crawley 5*, D. M. Curtis 0*).

Oxford University

D. A. Hagan (*Trinity, Leamington Spa and Linacre*) c James b Jenkins	....	8
*R. E. Morris (*Dyffryn Conwy, Llanrwst and Oriel*) c Turner b Jenkins	....	21
P. D. Lunn (*Abingdon and New*) b Shufflebotham	....	35
G. J. Turner (*St Stithian's, Cape Town U. and St Anne's*) c Jenkins b Shufflebotham		36
M. A. Crawley (*Manchester GS and Keble*) c Johnson b Buzza	....	55
D. M. Curtis (*Falcon Coll., Harare, Cape Town U. and St Anne's*) run out	....	27
W. M. van der Merwe (*Grey, OFS U., Cape Town U. and St Anne's*) st Turner b Buzza		50
P. S. Gerrans (*Daramalau Coll., Aust. Nat. U. and Worcester*) c James b Shufflebotham	.	16
S. D. Weale (*Westminster City and Keble*) not out	....	4
I. M. Henderson (*Laxton and Pembroke*) not out	....	0
B 3, l-b 12, n-b 2		17

1/13 2/41 3/95 4/108 5/175 6/238 7/263 8/265   (8 wkts dec.) 269

†R. W. D. Trevelyan (*Marlborough and Pembroke*) did not bat.

Bowling: Johnson 16-1-48-0; Jenkins 20-2-68-2; Pyman 18-7-63-0; Shufflebotham 19-5-60-3; Buzza 8-1-15-2.

Oxford University forfeited their second innings.

Cambridge University

Cambridge University forfeited their first innings.

S. P. James (*Monmouth and Hughes Hall*) c Hagan b Crawley	....	56
R. Heap (*Ipswich and Magdalene*) b Crawley	....	37
†R. J. Turner (*Millfield and Magdalene*) run out	....	7
*J. C. M. Atkinson (*Millfield and Downing*) b Crawley	....	7
M. J. Lowrey (*Radley and Homerton*) not out	....	18
M. J. Morris (*Cherwell and Pembroke*) not out	....	9
B 3, l-b 7, n-b 2		12

1/87 2/110 3/111 4/118   (4 wkts) 146

R. A. Pyman (*Harrow and Pembroke*), D. H. Shufflebotham (*Neath GS and Magdalene*), R. H. J. Jenkins (*Oundle and Downing*), A. J. Buzza (*Redruth CS and Hughes Hall*) and S. W. Johnson (*Royal GS, Newcastle and Magdalene*) did not bat.

Bowling: van der Merwe 14-2-23-0; Henderson 5-0-21-0; Gerrans 13-0-37-0; Crawley 17-4-46-3; Lunn 2-1-9-0.

Umpires: D. J. Constant and K. E. Palmer.

OXFORD v CAMBRIDGE, RESULTS AND HUNDREDS

The University match dates back to 1827. Altogether there have been 145 official matches, Cambridge winning 54 and Oxford 46, with 45 drawn. The 1988 match was abandoned without a ball bowled. Results since 1950:

1950	Drawn	1971	Drawn
1951	Oxford won by 21 runs	1972	Cambridge won by an innings and
1952	Drawn		25 runs
1953	Cambridge won by two wickets	1973	Drawn
1954	Drawn	1974	Drawn
1955	Drawn	1975	Drawn
1956	Drawn	1976	Oxford won by ten wickets
1957	Cambridge won by an innings	1977	Drawn
	and 186 runs	1978	Drawn
1958	Cambridge won by 99 runs	1979	Cambridge won by an innings and
1959	Oxford won by 85 runs		52 runs
1960	Drawn	1980	Drawn
1961	Drawn	1981	Drawn
1962	Drawn	1982	Cambridge won by seven wickets
1963	Drawn	1983	Drawn
1964	Drawn	1984	Oxford won by five wickets
1965	Drawn	1985	Drawn
1966	Oxford won by an innings and 9 runs	1986	Cambridge won by five wickets
1967	Drawn	1987	Drawn
1968	Drawn	1988	Abandoned
1969	Drawn	1989	Drawn
1970	Drawn	1990	Drawn

Ninety-three three-figure innings have been played in the University matches. For those scored before 1919 see 1940 *Wisden*. Those subsequent to 1919 include the seven highest:

238* Nawab of Pataudi, sen.	1931 Oxford	121 J. N. Grover	1937 Oxford
211 G. Goonesena	1957 Cam.	119 J. M. Brearley	1964 Cam.
201* M. J. K. Smith	1954 Oxford	118 H. Ashton	1921 Cam.
201 A. Ratcliffe	1931 Cam.	118 D. R. W. Silk	1954 Cam.
200 Majid Khan	1970 Cam.	117 M. J. K. Smith	1956 Oxford
193 D. C. H. Townsend	1934 Oxford	116* D. R. W. Silk	1953 Cam.
174 P. A. C. Bail	1986 Cam.	116 M. C. Cowdrey	1953 Oxford
170 M. Howell	1919 Oxford	115 A. W. Allen	1934 Cam.
167 B. W. Hone	1932 Oxford	114* D. R. Owen-Thomas	1972 Cam.
158 P. M. Roebuck	1975 Cam.	114 J. F. Pretlove	1955 Cam.
157 D. R. Wilcox	1932 Cam.	113* J. M. Brearley	1962 Cam.
155 F. S. Goldstein	1968 Oxford	113 E. R. T. Holmes	1927 Oxford
149 J. T. Morgan	1929 Cam.	112* E. D. Fursdon	1975 Oxford
149 G. J. Toogood	1985 Oxford	111* G. W. Cook	1957 Cam.
146 R. O'Brien	1956 Cam.	109 C. H. Taylor	1923 Oxford
146 D. R. Owen-Thomas	1971 Cam.	109 G. J. Toogood	1984 Oxford
145* H. E. Webb	1948 Oxford	108 F. G. H. Chalk	1934 Oxford
145 D. P. Toft	1967 Oxford	106 Nawab of Pataudi, sen.	1929 Oxford
142 M. P. Donnelly	1946 Oxford	105 E. J. Craig	1961 Cam.
140 M. A. Crawley	1987 Oxford	104* D. A. Thorne	1986 Oxford
139 R. J. Boyd-Moss	1983 Cam.	104 H. J. Enthoven	1924 Cam.
136 E. T. Killick	1930 Cam.	104 M. J. K. Smith	1955 Oxford
135 H. A. Pawson	1947 Oxford	103* A. R. Lewis	1962 Cam.
131 Nawab of Pataudi, jun.	1960 Oxford	103* D. R. Pringle	1979 Cam.
129 H. J. Enthoven	1925 Cam.	102* A. P. F. Chapman	1922 Cam.
128* A. J. T. Miller	1984 Oxford	101* R. W. V. Robins	1928 Cam.
127 D. S. Sheppard	1952 Cam.	101 N. W. D. Yardley	1937 Cam.
124 A. K. Judd	1927 Cam.	100* M. Manasseh	1964 Oxford
124 A. Ratcliffe	1932 Cam.	100 P. J. Dickinson	1939 Cam.
124 R. J. Boyd-Moss	1983 Cam.	100 N. J. Cosh	1967 Cam.
122 P. A. Gibb	1938 Cam.	100 R. J. Boyd-Moss	1982 Cam.

 * *Signifies not out.*

Highest Totals

503	Oxford	1900	432-9	Cambridge	1936
457	Oxford	1947	431	Cambridge	1932
453-8	Oxford	1931	425	Cambridge	1938

Lowest Totals

32	Oxford	1878	42	Oxford	1890
39	Cambridge	1858	47	Cambridge	1838

Notes: A. P. F. Chapman and M. P. Donnelly enjoy the following distinction: Chapman scored a century at Lord's in the University match (102*, 1922); for Gentlemen v Players (160, 1922), (108, 1926); and for England v Australia (121, 1930). Donnelly scored a century at Lord's in the University match (142, 1946); for Gentlemen v Players (162*, 1947); and for New Zealand v England (206, 1949).

A. Ratcliffe's 201 for Cambridge in 1931 remained a record for the match for only one day, being beaten by the Nawab of Pataudi's 238* for Oxford next day.

M. J. K. Smith (Oxford) and R. J. Boyd-Moss (Cambridge) are the only players who have scored three hundreds. Smith scored 201* in 1954, 104 in 1955, and 117 in 1956; Boyd-Moss scored 100 in 1982 and 139 and 124 in 1983. His aggregate of 489 surpassed Smith's previous record of 477.

The following players have scored two hundreds: W. Yardley (Cambridge) 100 in 1870 and 130 in 1872; H. J. Enthoven (Cambridge) 104 in 1924 and 129 in 1925; Nawab of Pataudi (Oxford) 106 in 1929 and 238* in 1931; A. Ratcliffe (Cambridge) 201 in 1931 and 124 in 1932; D. R. W. Silk (Cambridge) 116* in 1953 and 118 in 1954; J. M. Brearley (Cambridge) 113* in 1962 and 119 in 1964; D. R. Owen-Thomas (Cambridge) 146 in 1971 and 114* in 1972; G. J. Toogood (Oxford) 109 in 1984 and 149 in 1985.

F. C. Cobden, in the Oxford v Cambridge match in 1870, performed the hat-trick by taking the last three wickets and won an extraordinary game for Cambridge by 2 runs. The feat is without parallel in first-class cricket. Other hat-tricks, all for Cambridge, have been credited to A. G. Steel (1879), P. H. Morton (1880), J. F. Ireland (1911), and R. G. H. Lowe (1926).

S. E. Butler, in the 1871 match, took all the wickets in the Cambridge first innings. The feat is unique in University matches. He bowled 24.1 overs. In the follow-on he took five wickets for 57, giving him match figures of fifteen for 95 runs.

The best all-round performances in the history of the match have come from P. R. Le Couteur, who scored 160 and took eleven Cambridge wickets for 66 runs in 1910, and G. J. Toogood, who in 1985 scored 149 and took ten Cambridge wickets for 93.

D. W. Jarrett (Oxford 1975, Cambridge 1976), S. M. Wookey (Cambridge 1975-76, Oxford 1978) and G. Pathmanathan (Oxford 1975-78, Cambridge 1983) are alone in gaining cricket Blues for both Universities.

July 14. Benson and Hedges Cup final. LANCASHIRE beat WORCESTERSHIRE by 69 runs (See Benson and Hedges Cup section).

July 18. MCC SCHOOLS beat MCC by two wickets (See MCC section).

†MCC SCHOOLS v NATIONAL ASSOCIATION OF YOUNG CRICKETERS

July 19. Drawn. Toss: National Association of Young Cricketers. MCC Schools fell 35 runs short of achieving a double on their annual visit to Lord's, having beaten MCC the previous day. The Schools had enjoyed a fair run of success in this match in recent years, through such outstanding young players as Hugh Morris, Roseberry, Atherton and Ramprakash, and while the 1990 crop was not quite of that class, Wasim Khan, Fulton and Walton all showed promise over the two days at Lord's. When Archer of Stafford CFE was claimed by NAYC to

open their batting, although in the original Schools selection, Snape of Denstone came in as
his replacement. However, Archer was soon despatched by his former team-mate, Weston
after NAYC won the toss and elected to bat. Williams and Simmonite, both of
Lancashire, added 48 for the second wicket, and Dessaur and Shephard 54 for the sixth, but in
batting for 62 overs, NAYC left time for only 48 overs for the Schools' innings. Hodgson again
flighted the ball well and deserved his four wickets. Needing 4.5 runs an over for victory
MCC Schools were greatly dependent on Wasim Khan. He made an attacking 61, with
support from Laney, but as wickets began to fall and the overs ran out, a draw became
inevitable.

National Association of Young Cricketers

G. Archer (*Staffs.*) b Weston 3	G. F. Shephard (*Warwicks.*) not out ... 32
A. Williams (*Lancs.*) c Fulton b Hodgson 64	†I. Gill (*Yorks.*) c Snape b Hodgson ... 0
P. C. P. Simmonite (*Lancs.*)	A. Hollioake (*Surrey*) not out 16
c M. A. Khan b Walton . 35	B 6, l-b 4, w 2, n-b 2 14
A. R. Cornford (*Sussex*) b Walton 4	
*R. Bates (*Lincs.*) b Hodgson 10	1/4 2/52 3/60 4/104 (7 wkts dec.) 219
W. A. Dessaur (*Notts.*) c and b Hodgson 37	5/135 6/189 7/195

L. Slater (*Staffs.*) and J. Mann (*Hunts. and Peterborough*) did not bat.

Bowling: Weston 11–2–32–1; Laudat 6–0–21–0; Walton 13–1–56–2; Richards 16–4–53–0;
Hodgson 16–5–43–4.

MCC Schools

Wasim Khan (*Josiah Mason SFC*)	R. Murray (*Brigshaw*) c Simmonite
st Gill b Mann . 61	b Shephard . 11
D. P. Fulton (*Judd*) c Gill b Hollioake . 13	*A. C. Richards (*Forest*) not out 14
J. N. Snape (*Denstone*) c Gill b Mann . 9	S. V. Laudat (*Oxford CFE*) not out 4
J. Laney (*St John's, Marlborough*)	B 3, l-b 6, w 2 11
c Archer b Dessaur . 46	
T. C. Walton (*Leeds GS*) c Bates	1/55 2/66 3/99 4/133 (6 wkts) 181
b Dessaur . 12	5/152 6/158

†M. A. Khan (*Aylesbury CFE*), W. P. C. Weston (*Durham*) and J. Hodgson (*Ranelagh*) did not
bat.

Bowling: Slater 5–0–25–0; Hollioake 10–1–33–1; Mann 13–1–44–2; Bates 3–1–16–0;
Shephard 11–5–27–1; Dessaur 6–0–27–2.

Umpires: K. Hopley and J. F. Jarvis.

The National Cricket Association selected the following to play for NCA Young Cricketers
against Combined Services: Wasim Khan (Warwicks.), A. Williams (Lancs.), T. C. Walton
(Yorks.), P. C. P. Simmonite (Lancs.), J. Laney (Wilts.), *A. C. Richards (Essex), G. F.
Shephard (Warwicks.), †M. A. Khan (Oxon.), W. P. C. Weston (Worcs.), A. Hollioake
(Surrey) and J. Mann (Hunts. and Peterborough).

†July 20. NCA Young Cricketers won by eight wickets. Toss: Combined Services.
Combined Services 231 (2nd Lt R. J. Greatorex 31, Capt. P. J. Presland 88, Extras 32;
W. P. C. Weston three for 41, T. C. Walton three for 48); NCA Young Cricketers 233 for two
(Wasim Khan 80, A. Williams 75, T. C. Walton 67 not out).

July 26, 27, 28, 30, 31. First Cornhill Test. ENGLAND beat INDIA by 247 runs (See Indian
tour section).

August 8. ENGLAND YOUNG CRICKETERS beat PAKISTAN YOUNG CRICKETERS by 76 runs (See Pakistan Young Cricketers tour section).

August 19, 20. Holt Cup Knockout final. BUCKINGHAMSHIRE beat LINCOLNSHIRE by 16 runs (See Minor Counties section).

†BLACKPOOL v CHEAM

Cockspur Cup Final

August 24. Blackpool won by three wickets. Toss: Cheam. After successive washouts at headquarters in the two previous years, the final of the National Club Championship, the last under the sponsorship of Cockspur Rum, was played in glorious weather. Indeed, it was so hot that drinks were taken after the first 45 minutes. Neither Blackpool, the north section champions, nor Cheam, the south champions, had won the title before, although Blackpool had been finalists fifteen years earlier, and both were strongly supported. Cheam chose to bat, and after the openers were back in the Pavilion, Butcher, eighteen-year-old son of Glamorgan's captain, enlivened proceedings with two sixes, one of them taking Cheam past 100 in the 29th over. Falconer, the captain, held the innings together, but from 173 for four Cheam lost wickets in the pursuit of runs. Blackpool saw Lawton run out in the first over by Butcher, and were in deeper trouble when Pickles was bowled with the score 10. However, Hesketh, playing almost a lone hand, lifted his side to victory. He and Ashton added 70 for the sixth wicket to rescue Blackpool from a parlous position at 95 for five and leave them needing 40 from the last six overs. The Cheam seam bowlers gave little away, but Hesketh kept the runs coming until 6 were required from the final over. He scored them off the first two balls.

Man of the Match: R. J. Falconer.

Cheam

G. R. E. Martin b Cole	17	C. M. Cornell run out	6
N. B. Driscoll c Mathers b Cole	20	S. F. Travers not out	4
A. W. Smith st Mathers b Lawton	35	B 1, l-b 9, w 4, n-b 1	15
M. A. Butcher c Sanders b Cresswell	27		
*R. J. Falconer b Rayton	53	1/32 2/64 3/97 (8 wkts, 45 overs) 193	
†M. A. Rowland c and b Cresswell	13	4/121 5/173 6/183	
P. M. James b Rayton	3	7/187 8/193	

D. J. Allen and D. J. Morgan did not bat.

Bowling: Cross 9–2–24–0; Rayton 9–1–32–2; Cole 9–1–27–2; Lawton 9–0–51–1; Cresswell 9–0–49–2.

Blackpool

M. Pickles b Travers	8	*†D. Mathers b Travers	9
S. Lawton run out	0	D. Rayton not out	7
A. Hesketh not out	86	L-b 7, w 2, n-b 1	10
D. Horn c Driscoll b Cornell	15		
G. Sanders run out	23	1/2 2/10 3/45 (7 wkts, 44.2 overs) 194	
P. Cole b Allen	8	4/84 5/95	
M. Ashton lbw b Butcher	28	6/165 7/178	

D. Cresswell and G. Cross did not bat.

Bowling: Butcher 8.2–0–37–1; Travers 9–1–32–2; Allen 9–2–27–1; Cornell 9–1–30–1; Morgan 3–0–26–0; Smith 5–0–29–0; Falconer 1–0–6–0.

Umpires: A. Tayler and B. Wilson.

NATIONAL CLUB CHAMPIONSHIP WINNERS 1969-90

1969 HAMPSTEAD beat Pocklington Pixies by 14 runs.
1970 CHELTENHAM beat Stockport by three wickets.
1971 BLACKHEATH beat Ealing by eight wickets.
1972 SCARBOROUGH beat Brentham by six wickets.
1973 WOLVERHAMPTON beat The Mote by five wickets.
1974 SUNBURY beat Tunbridge Wells by seven wickets.
1975 YORK beat Blackpool by six wickets.
1976 SCARBOROUGH beat Dulwich by five wickets.
1977 SOUTHGATE beat Bowdon by six wickets.
1978 CHELTENHAM beat Bishop's Stortford by 15 runs.
1979 SCARBOROUGH beat Reading by two wickets.
1980 MOSELEY beat Gosport Borough by nine wickets.
1981 SCARBOROUGH beat Blackheath by 57 runs.
1982 SCARBOROUGH beat Finchley by 4 runs.
1983 SHREWSBURY beat Hastings and St Leonards Priory by 2 runs.
1984 OLD HILL beat Bishop's Stortford by five wickets.
1985 OLD HILL beat Reading by nine wickets.
1986 STOURBRIDGE beat Weston-super-Mare by four wickets.
1987 OLD HILL beat Teddington by five wickets.
1988 ENFIELD beat Wolverhampton by nine wickets.
1989 TEDDINGTON beat Old Hill by 11 runs.
1990 BLACKPOOL beat Cheam by three wickets.

From 1969 to 1975, the Championship was contested for the D. H. Robins Trophy, from 1976 to 1982 for the John Haig Trophy, from 1983 to 1986 for the William Younger Cup, and from 1987 to 1990 for the Cockspur Cup.

†DUNSTALL v GOATACRE

National Village Championship Final

August 25. Goatacre won by 50 runs. Toss: Goatacre. Iles, grandson of the Wiltshire village club's founder, played one of the finest innings seen at Lord's for many a day, and by virtually monopolising this nineteenth village final he gave Goatacre their second title. The first was in 1988, when the match was washed out at Lord's and replayed elsewhere. This August Saturday, though, was a glorious day and Iles was its worthy hero. Having won the toss and decided to bat, he saw Leavey out to the first ball of the morning, Spencer at 23 and the punishing Turner at 100 before he joined Hunt. After that it was all Iles. His hundred took only 45 minutes and included seven sixes – four in succession off Shipton – and six fours in 39 balls received. He added two more sixes and a four in his total of 123 (49 balls) and came to the Pavilion to a standing ovation from MCC members and the supporters of both clubs. Iles's hundred was the first, and Goatacre's total the highest, in a village championship final. Dunstall, a tiny Staffordshire village, who had done their share of giant-killing *en route* to Lord's, faced a near-impossible target but stuck bravely to the task. Wallbank, the captain, and Shilton opened with 67, but after 40 overs Dunstall were still 50 runs behind with two wickets in hand. Iles employed two bowlers, and at the end Ali struck the bowling with gusto. Without a sponsor, the *Cricketer* shouldered the entire responsibility for the organisation, and in doing so they made possible a day of spectacular cricket.

Man of the Match: K. M. Iles.

Goatacre

P. J. Leavey b Shipton	0	†J. Wilkins not out	3
M. A. Hunt b Crossland	39		
A. J. Spencer c Higgott b Shipton	12	L-b 12, w 10, n-b 3	25
J. B. Turner c Crossland b Scrimshaw	53		
*K. M. Iles c Boulton b Shipton	123	1/0 2/23 3/100 (5 wkts, 40 overs) 267	
A. Dawson not out	12	4/220 5/260	

P. D. Rose, J. I. N. Angell, J. C. Haines and P. Dolman did not bat.

Bowling: Shipton 9-0-83-3; Crossland 9-1-54-1; Scrimshaw 9-2-35-1; Boulton 5-0-17-0; Ali 6-0-41-0; Wallbank 2-0-25-0.

▶unstall

. M. Shilton c Leavey b Rose 35	A. Ali not out 31
▶. H. Wallbank c Haines b Angell 51	S. N. J. Scrimshaw not out 7
. J. Cooper b Turner 1	
. K. A. Shilton b Angell 23	B 1, l-b 3, w 6, n-b 3 13
. D. Boulton run out 21	
. E. Crossland b Angell 2	1/67 2/73 3/114 (8 wkts, 40 overs) 217
. J. Ingles b Dawson 24	4/125 5/141 6/143
A. Higgott c Dawson b Angell 9	7/163 8/188

. K. Shipton did not bat.

Bowling: Dawson 6–0–41–1; Spencer 5–0–16–0; Rose 7–0–37–1; Turner 4–1–8–1; Dolman ▶0–41–0; Angell 6–0–18–4; Iles 2–0–15–0; Haines 3–0–31–0; Leavey 1–0–6–0.

Umpires: P. S. G. Stevens and W. A. U. Wickremasinghe.

VILLAGE CHAMPIONSHIP WINNERS 1972-90

▶972 TROON (Cornwall) beat Astwood Bank (Worcestershire) by seven wickets.
▶973 TROON (Cornwall) beat Gowerton (Glamorgan) by 12 runs.
▶974 BOMARSUND (Northumberland) beat Collingham (Nottinghamshire) by three wickets.
▶975 GOWERTON (Glamorgan) beat Isleham (Cambridgeshire) by six wickets.
▶976 TROON (Cornwall) beat Sessay (Yorkshire) by 18 runs.
▶977 COOKLEY (Worcestershire) beat Lindal Moor (Cumbria) by 28 runs.
▶978 LINTON PARK (Kent) beat Toft (Cheshire) by four wickets.
▶979 EAST BIERLEY (Yorkshire) beat Ynysygerwn (Glamorgan) by 92 runs.
▶980 MARCHWIEL (Clwyd) beat Longparish (Hampshire) by 79 runs.
▶981 ST FAGANS (Glamorgan) beat Broad Oak (Yorkshire) by 22 runs.
▶982 ST FAGANS (Glamorgan) beat Collingham (Nottinghamshire) by six wickets.
▶983 QUARNDON (Derbyshire) beat Troon (Cornwall) by eight wickets.
▶984 MARCHWIEL (Clwyd) beat Hursley Park (Hampshire) by 8 runs.
▶985 FREUCHIE (Fife) beat Rowledge (Surrey) by virtue of fewer wickets lost with the scores level.
▶986 FORGE VALLEY (Yorkshire) beat Ynysygerwn (Glamorgan) by 5 runs.
▶987 LONGPARISH (Hampshire) beat Treeton Welfare (Yorkshire) by 76 runs.
▶988 GOATACRE (Wiltshire) beat Himley (West Midlands) by four wickets.
▶989 TOFT (Cheshire) beat Hambledon (Hampshire) by six wickets.
▶990 GOATACRE (Wiltshire) beat Dunstall (Staffordshire) by 50 runs.

From 1972 to 1977, the Village Championship was sponsored by John Haig Ltd, in 1978 and ▶990 *by the* Cricketer, *from 1979 to 1984 by Samuel Whitbread and Co. Ltd, and 1986 to 1989* ▶ *Hydro Fertilizers. There was no sponsor in 1985.*

▶eptember 1. NatWest Bank Trophy final. LANCASHIRE beat NORTHAMPTONSHIRE by seven wickets (See NatWest Bank Trophy section).

BRITANNIC ASSURANCE
COUNTY CHAMPIONSHIP, 1990

Middlesex won the County Championship outright for the tenth time, having also shared the title twice, and for the fourth time in eleven seasons. That they deserved to win the pennant is not open to dispute. Middlesex won more games than any other county – two more than their nearest rivals, Essex and Hampshire – and suffered their only defeat on a pitch at Derby which cost the home county 25 points after an inspection by the TCCB. Only runners-up Essex and fifteenth-placed Somerset recorded as many batting bonus points and while a number of counties had more bowling points, Middlesex could point to the fact that, in eight of their ten victories, they bowled out their opponents in the second innings. Only once, discounting their rain-affected match at Manchester, did they win as a result of being set a target, beating Somerset at Uxbridge by scoring 371 in 69 overs. Middlesex went to the top of the table in June after successive away wins over Leicestershire, Lancashire and Northamptonshire and, but for a ten-day period when they had no game, they were never dislodged. Under Mike Gatting's enterprising captaincy they played positive cricket, fielded well-balanced sides and, in Desmond Haynes, had the Britannic Assurance Player of the Year.

Boosted by three wins in May, Nottinghamshire led the field as the three-day part of the competition settled down in June. But they came back after a fortnight's absence from Championship cricket to find themselves pushed down into fourth place. After that, there was only a win over Yorkshire at Scarborough as they rode the snakes rather than the ladders. Warwickshire top of the table between Nottinghamshire's brief tenure and Middlesex's long

BRITANNIC ASSURANCE CHAMPIONSHIP

					Bonus points		
Win = 16 points	Played	Won	Lost	Drawn	Batting	Bowling	Points
1 – Middlesex (3)	22	10	1	11	73	55	288
2 – Essex (2)	22	8	2	12	73	56	257
3 – Hampshire (6)	22	8	4	10	67	48	243
4 – Worcestershire (1) ...	22	7	1	14	70	58	240
5 – Warwickshire (8)	22	7	7	8	55	64	231
6 – Lancashire (4)	22	6	3	13	65	56	217
7 – Leicestershire (13) ...	22	6	7	9	61	53	210
8 – Glamorgan (17)	22	5	6	11	64	48	192
9 – Surrey (12)	22	4	3	15	54	64	190†
10 – Yorkshire (16)	22	5	9	8	52	55	187
11 – Northamptonshire (5).	22	4	9	9	61	60	185
12 – Derbyshire (6)	22	6	7	9	58	52	181*
13 { Gloucestershire (9) ...	22	4	7	11	51	58	173
13 { Nottinghamshire (11) .	22	4	8	10	51	58	173
15 – Somerset (14)	22	3	4	15	73	45	166
16 – Kent (15)	22	3	6	13	69	35	152
17 – Sussex (10)	22	3	9	10	51	44	143

1989 positions are shown in brackets.

　　* *Derbyshire had 25 points deducted during the season as a penalty for a sub-standard pitch at Derby.*

　　† *The total for Surrey includes 8 points for levelling the scores in a drawn game.*

ne, filled second or third place throughout August, despite three successive
efeats, and a late victory over Glamorgan ensured they held enough points
or fifth-place prizemoney. Hampshire's third place was well earned, for they
vere rarely out of the top four from mid-May.

Worcestershire and Essex, winners and runners-up in 1989, were both slow
o start in 1990 yet finished strongly to suggest they would again be among
he challengers in 1991. Five of the defending champions' seven wins came in
August, and September to lift them from thirteenth to fourth, and with four
ictories in their six four-day fixtures, Worcestershire reinforced the view
aat they are ideally suited to the extended game. Essex, who finished in the
op three for the third year running, once more found their challenge for the
tle governed by the "if" factor: if Essex picked up points here and
Middlesex dropped them elsewhere, it was suggested, Essex would be
hampions. Three successive wins in July had taken them from fourteenth to
eventh, and within a month they were hard on Middlesex's heels. However,
Northamptonshire arrested their momentum, as they had the previous
eason, and after winning at Derby by an innings in two days, Essex failed to
vin in any of their last four games.

Lancashire could have been, should have been, contenders. Like Middle-
ex, they had a balanced side, if lacking the new champions' resources in spin
owling, but along the way they were sidetracked by the glamour and the big
noney of the Lord's finals. A ten-wicket defeat by Worcestershire at Kidder-
iinster early in August removed them from the top three for only the second
me since June, and this time they did not come back. They finished just out
f the money, still to prove themselves capable of staying over the distance.

Yorkshire and Glamorgan, with five wins apiece, had every reason to be
atisfied with their seasons, climbing to the middle of the table from sixteenth
nd seventeenth respectively in 1989. While the Welsh county benefited
om the influence of their new overseas player, Viv Richards, Yorkshire's
nprovement was all their own work, despite the gathering murmurings that
ne county should look beyond its Ridings for a saviour. The presence of
obby Simpson, the Australian manager, at Grace Road may have had
omething to do with Leicestershire's move up six places to seventh, while
eighbours Derbyshire would have finished a place behind them but for the
eduction of 25 points for that unsatisfactory pitch in the Middlesex match.
nstead, they were twelfth, one place behind the enigmatic Northampton-
iire, whose talented line-up only occasionally played to its potential.

Activities off the field, as much as those on it, occupied the attentions of
Gloucestershire and Kent as they struggled in the lower reaches. Gloucester-
hire spent most of the season alternating with Sussex between sixteenth and
eventeenth, only to escape in the last month with convincing wins over
Northamptonshire and Sussex which showed what they could have been
apable of. Sussex, on the other hand, rarely looked more than ordinary. They
ad been rooted at the bottom of the table for more than a month when
Middlesex beat them with a day and an innings in hand to clinch the
hampionship.

REGULATIONS FOR BRITANNIC ASSURANCE CHAMPIONSHIP

(As applied in 1990)

1. Prizemoney

First (Middlesex)	£40,0(
Second (Essex)	£20,0(
Third (Hampshire)	£11,5(
Fourth (Worcestershire)	£5,7!
Fifth (Warwickshire)	£3,0(
Winner of each match	£2
Championship Player of the Year (D. L. Haynes)	£1,0(
County of the Month	£1,0(
Player of the Month	£3(

2. Scoring of Points

(a) For a win, sixteen points, plus any points scored in the first innings.

(b) In a tie, each side to score eight points, plus any points scored in the first innings.

(c) If the scores are equal in a drawn match, the side batting in the fourth innings to sco eight points, plus any points scored in the first innings.

(d) **First-innings points** (awarded only for performances *in the first 100 overs* of each fir innings and retained whatever the result of the match).

    (i) A maximum of four batting points to be available as under:
        150 to 199 runs – 1 point; 200 to 249 runs – 2 points; 250 to 299 runs – 3 point
        300 runs or over – 4 points.

    (ii) A maximum of four bowling points to be available as under:
        3 to 4 wickets taken – 1 point; 5 to 6 wickets taken – 2 points; 7 to 8 wicke
        taken – 3 points; 9 to 10 wickets taken – 4 points.

(e) If play starts when less than eight hours' playing time remains and a one-innin, match is played, no first-innings points shall be scored. The side winning on the o innings to score twelve points.

(f) A county which is adjudged to have prepared a pitch unsuitable for first-class crick shall be liable to have 25 points deducted from its aggregate of points.

(g) The side which has the highest aggregate of points gained at the end of the season sha be the Champion County. Should any sides in the Championship table be equal points the side with most wins will have priority.

3. Hours of Play

1st, 2nd [3rd] days ...	11.00 a.m. to 6.30 p.m. or after 110 overs, whichever is the late (For Sunday play, the home county may decide to play from noon to 7.30 p.m.)
Final day	11.00 a.m. to 6.00 p.m. or after 102 overs, whichever is the late

Note: The hours of play, including intervals, were brought forward by half an hour f matches in September.

(a) If play is suspended (including any interval between innings) the minimum number overs to be bowled in a day to be reduced by one over for each $3\frac{1}{2}$ minutes or pa thereof of such suspension or suspensions in aggregate.

(b) If at 5.00 p.m. on the final day, nineteen overs or less remain to be bowled, th umpires shall indicate that play shall continue until a minimum of a further twen overs has been bowled, or until 6.00 p.m., whichever is the later. Play may cease on t final day at any time between 5.30 p.m. and 6.00 p.m. by mutual agreement of t captains. Should an innings end between 4.50 p.m. and 5.00 p.m., the time at the e of the ten-minute interval to replace 5.00 p.m.

(c) The captains may agree or, in the event of disagreement, the umpires may decide to play 30 minutes (or minimum ten overs) extra time at the end of the first and/or second day's play (and/or the third day of four) if, in their opinion, it would bring about a definite result on that day. In the event of the possibility of a finish disappearing before the full period has expired, the whole period must be played out. Any time so claimed does not affect the timing for cessation of play on the final day.

(d) If an innings ends during the course of an over, that part shall count as a full over so far as the minimum number of overs per day is concerned.

(e) If play is suspended for the day in the middle of an over, that over must be completed next day in addition to the minimum overs required that day.

tervals

unch: 1.15 p.m. to 1.55 p.m. (1st, 2nd [3rd] days), 2.15 p.m. to 2.55 p.m. on Sundays when play commences at 12 noon
1.00 p.m. to 1.40 p.m. (final day)

ea: 4.10 p.m. to 4.30 p.m. (1st, 2nd [3rd] days), 5.10 p.m. to 5.30 p.m. on Sundays when play commences at 12 noon; or when 40 overs remain to be bowled, whichever is the later.
3.40 p.m. to 4.00 p.m. (final day), or when 40 overs remain to be bowled, whichever is the later.

Substitutes

Law 2.1 will apply, but in addition:

A substitute shall be allowed as of right in the event of a cricketer currently playing in a Championship match being required to join the England team for a Test match (or one-day international). Such a substitute may be permitted to bat or bowl in that match, subject to the approval of the TCCB. The player who is substituted may not take further part in the match, even though he might not be required by England. If batting at the time, the player substituted shall be retired "not out" and his substitute may be permitted to bat later in that innings subject to the approval of the TCCB.

The opposing captain shall have no right of objection to any player acting as substitute in the field, nor as to where he shall field. However, no substitute may act as wicket-keeper.

No substitute may take the field until the player for whom he is to substitute has been absent from the field for five consecutive complete overs, with the exception that if a fieldsman sustains an obvious, serious injury, a substitute shall be allowed immediately. If a player leaves the field during an over, the remainder of that over shall not count in the calculation of five complete overs.

Fieldsman Leaving the Field

No fieldsman shall leave the field or return during a session of play without the consent of the umpire at the bowler's end. The umpire's consent is also necessary at the start of play or when his side returns to the field after an interval.

If a member of the fielding side does not take the field at the start of play, leaves the field, or fails to return after an interval and is absent longer than fifteen minutes, he shall not bowl in that innings after his return until he has been on the field for at least the length of playing time for which he was absent; nor shall he be permitted to bat unless or until, in the aggregate, he has returned to the field and/or his side's innings has been in progress for at least the length of playing time for which he was absent or, if earlier, when his side has lost five wickets. The restrictions shall not apply if he has been absent for exceptional and acceptable reasons (other than injury or illness) and consent for a substitute has been granted by the opposing captain.

New ball

The captain of the fielding side shall have the choice of taking the new ball after 100 overs have been bowled with the old one.

Covering of Pitches and Bowler's Run-up

The whole pitch shall be covered:

(a) The night before a match and, if necessary, until the first ball is bowled.

(b) On each night of a match and, if necessary, throughout Sunday.

(*c*) In the event of play being suspended because of bad light or rain, during the hours o
play.

The bowler's run-up shall be covered to a distance of at least ten yards, with a width o
four yards.

8. Declarations

Law 14 will apply, but, in addition, a captain may also forfeit his first innings, subject to th
provisions set out in Law 14.2. If, owing to weather conditions, the match has not starte
when fewer than eight hours of playing time remain, the first innings of each side sha
automatically be forfeited and a one-innings match played.

CHAMPION COUNTY SINCE 1864

Note: The earliest county champions were decided usually by the fewest matches lost, but i
1888 an unofficial points system was introduced. In 1890, the Championship was constitute
officially. From 1977 to 1983 it was sponsored by Schweppes, and since 1984 by Britanni
Assurance.

1864	Surrey	1901	Yorkshire	1951	Warwickshire
1865	Nottinghamshire	1902	Yorkshire	1952	Surrey
1866	Middlesex	1903	Middlesex	1953	Surrey
1867	Yorkshire	1904	Lancashire	1954	Surrey
1868	Nottinghamshire	1905	Yorkshire	1955	Surrey
1869	{ Nottinghamshire / Yorkshire	1906	Kent	1956	Surrey
		1907	Nottinghamshire	1957	Surrey
1870	Yorkshire	1908	Yorkshire	1958	Surrey
1871	Nottinghamshire	1909	Kent	1959	Yorkshire
1872	Nottinghamshire	1910	Kent	1960	Yorkshire
1873	{ Gloucestershire / Nottinghamshire	1911	Warwickshire	1961	Hampshire
		1912	Yorkshire	1962	Yorkshire
1874	Gloucestershire	1913	Kent	1963	Yorkshire
1875	Nottinghamshire	1914	Surrey	1964	Worcestershire
1876	Gloucestershire	1919	Yorkshire	1965	Worcestershire
1877	Gloucestershire	1920	Middlesex	1966	Yorkshire
1878	Undecided	1921	Middlesex	1967	Yorkshire
1879	{ Nottinghamshire / Lancashire	1922	Yorkshire	1968	Yorkshire
		1923	Yorkshire	1969	Glamorgan
1880	Nottinghamshire	1924	Yorkshire	1970	Kent
1881	Lancashire	1925	Yorkshire	1971	Surrey
1882	{ Nottinghamshire / Lancashire	1926	Lancashire	1972	Warwickshire
		1927	Lancashire	1973	Hampshire
1883	Nottinghamshire	1928	Lancashire	1974	Worcestershire
1884	Nottinghamshire	1929	Nottinghamshire	1975	Leicestershire
1885	Nottinghamshire	1930	Lancashire	1976	Middlesex
1886	Nottinghamshire	1931	Yorkshire	1977	{ Middlesex / Kent
1887	Surrey	1932	Yorkshire		
1888	Surrey	1933	Yorkshire	1978	Kent
1889	{ Surrey / Lancashire / Nottinghamshire	1934	Lancashire	1979	Essex
		1935	Yorkshire	1980	Middlesex
		1936	Derbyshire	1981	Nottinghamshire
1890	Surrey	1937	Yorkshire	1982	Middlesex
1891	Surrey	1938	Yorkshire	1983	Essex
1892	Surrey	1939	Yorkshire	1984	Essex
1893	Yorkshire	1946	Yorkshire	1985	Middlesex
1894	Surrey	1947	Middlesex	1986	Essex
1895	Surrey	1948	Glamorgan	1987	Nottinghamshire
1896	Yorkshire	1949	{ Middlesex / Yorkshire	1988	Worcestershire
1897	Lancashire			1989	Worcestershire
1898	Yorkshire	1950	{ Lancashire / Surrey	1990	Middlesex
1899	Surrey				
1900	Yorkshire				

Notes: The title has been won outright as follows: Yorkshire 31 times, Surrey 18, Nottinghamshire 14, Middlesex 10, Lancashire 8, Kent 6, Worcestershire 5, Essex 4, Gloucestershire 3, Warwickshire 3, Glamorgan 2, Hampshire 2, Derbyshire 1, Leicestershire 1.

Eight times the title has been shared as follows: Nottinghamshire 5, Lancashire 4, Middlesex 2, Surrey 2, Yorkshire 2, Gloucestershire 1, Kent 1.

The earliest date the Championship has been won in any season since it was expanded in 1895 was August 12, 1910, by Kent.

BRITANNIC ASSURANCE CHAMPIONSHIP
STATISTICS FOR 1990

	For			Against		
County	Runs	Wickets	Avge	Runs	Wickets	Avge
Derbyshire	9,475	280	33.83	9,960	289	34.46
Essex	11,341	232	48.88	10,907	283	38.54
Glamorgan	10,792	276	39.10	10,858	230	47.20
Gloucestershire	9,643	273	35.32	9,942	277	35.89
Hampshire	9,985	228	43.79	10,035	282	35.58
Kent	11,700	326	35.88	10,630	248	42.86
Lancashire	9,725	220	44.20	10,465	269	38.90
Leicestershire	10,380	308	33.70	9,901	265	37.36
Middlesex	10,905	270	40.38	10,486	306	34.26
Northamptonshire ..	10,742	284	37.82	11,018	286	38.52
Nottinghamshire	11,298	336	33.62	10,953	265	41.33
Somerset	11,277	217	51.96	11,609	264	43.97
Surrey	10,307	220	46.85	11,102	300	37.00
Sussex	10,673	330	32.34	10,735	230	46.67
Warwickshire	9,944	299	33.25	9,709	280	34.67
Worcestershire	11,070	240	46.12	10,513	309	34.02
Yorkshire	10,103	293	34.48	10,537	249	42.31
	179,360	4,632	38.72	179,360	4,632	38.72

COUNTY CHAMPIONSHIP – MATCH RESULTS, 1864-1990

County	Years of Play	Played	Won	Lost	Tied	Drawn
Derbyshire	1871-87; 1895-1990	2,112	517	769	1	825
Essex	1895-1990	2,075	585	596	5	889
Glamorgan	1921-1990	1,609	346	554	0	709
Gloucestershire ..	1870-1990	2,350	694	867	2	787
Hampshire	1864-85; 1895-1990	2,184	572	752	4	856
Kent	1864-1990	2,472	895	751	4	822
Lancashire	1865-1990	2,550	951	517	3	1,079
Leicestershire ...	1895-1990	2,042	441	761	1	839
Middlesex	1864-1990	2,252	842	570	5	835
Northamptonshire	1905-1990	1,809	429	643	3	734
Nottinghamshire .	1864-1990	2,381	723	624	0	1,034
Somerset	1882-85; 1891-1990	2,082	485	851	3	743
Surrey	1864-1990	2,629	1,042	574	4	1,009
Sussex	1864-1990	2,521	702	870	5	944
Warwickshire ...	1895-1990	2,056	535	603	1	917
Worcestershire ..	1899-1990	1,997	493	703	1	800
Yorkshire	1864-1990	2,650	1,194	441	2	1,013
Cambridgeshire ..	1864-69; 1871	19	8	8	0	3
		18,895	11,454	11,454	22	7,419

Notes: Matches abandoned without a ball bowled are wholly excluded.

Counties participated in the years shown, except that there were no matches in the years 1915-18 and 1940-45; Hampshire did not play inter-county matches in 1868-69, 1871-74 and 1879; Worcestershire did not take part in the Championship in 1919.

COUNTY CHAMPIONSHIP – FINAL POSITIONS, 1890-1990

	Derbyshire	Essex	Glamorgan	Gloucestershire	Hampshire	Kent	Lancashire	Leicestershire	Middlesex	Northamptonshire	Nottinghamshire	Somerset	Surrey	Sussex	Warwickshire	Worcestershire	Yorkshire
1890	—	—	—	6	—	3	2	—	7	—	5	—	1	8	—	—	3
1891	—	—	—	9	—	5	2	—	3	—	4	5	1	7	—	—	8
1892	—	—	—	7	—	7	4	—	5	—	2	3	1	9	—	—	6
1893	—	—	—	9	—	4	2	—	3	—	6	8	5	7	—	—	1
1894	—	—	—	9	—	4	4	—	3	—	7	6	1	8	—	—	2
1895	5	9	—	4	10	14	2	12	6	—	12	8	1	11	6	—	3
1896	7	5	—	10	8	9	2	13	3	—	6	11	4	14	12	—	1
1897	14	3	—	5	9	12	1	13	8	—	10	11	2	6	7	—	4
1898	9	5	—	3	12	7	6	13	2	—	8	13	4	9	9	—	1
1899	15	6	—	9	10	8	4	13	2	—	10	13	1	5	7	12	3
1900	13	10	—	7	15	3	2	14	7	—	5	11	7	3	6	12	1
1901	15	10	—	14	7	7	3	12	2	—	9	12	6	4	5	11	1
1902	10	13	—	14	15	7	5	11	12	—	3	7	4	2	6	9	1
1903	12	8	—	13	14	8	4	14	1	—	5	10	11	2	7	6	3
1904	10	14	—	9	15	3	1	7	4	—	5	12	11	6	7	13	2
1905	14	12	—	8	16	6	2	5	11	13	10	15	4	3	7	8	1
1906	16	7	—	9	8	1	4	15	11	11	5	11	3	10	6	14	2
1907	16	7	—	10	12	8	6	11	5	15	1	14	4	13	9	2	2
1908	14	11	—	10	9	2	7	13	4	15	8	16	3	5	12	6	1
1909	15	14	—	16	8	1	2	13	6	7	10	11	5	4	12	8	3
1910	15	11	—	12	6	1	4	10	3	9	5	16	2	7	14	13	8
1911	14	6	—	12	11	2	4	15	3	10	8	16	5	13	1	9	7
1912	12	15	—	11	6	3	4	13	5	2	8	14	7	10	9	16	1
1913	13	15	—	9	10	1	8	14	6	4	5	16	3	7	11	12	2
1914	12	8	—	16	5	3	11	13	2	9	10	15	1	6	7	14	4
1919	9	14	—	8	7	2	5	9	13	12	3	5	4	11	15	—	1
1920	16	9	—	8	11	5	2	13	1	14	7	10	3	6	12	15	4
1921	12	15	17	7	6	4	5	11	1	13	8	10	2	9	16	14	3
1922	11	8	16	13	6	4	5	14	7	15	2	10	3	9	12	17	1
1923	10	13	16	11	7	5	3	14	8	17	2	9	4	6	12	15	1
1924	17	15	13	6	12	5	4	11	2	16	6	8	3	10	9	14	1
1925	14	7	17	10	9	5	3	12	6	11	4	15	2	13	8	16	1
1926	11	9	8	15	7	3	1	13	6	16	4	14	5	10	12	17	2
1927	5	8	15	12	13	4	1	7	9	16	2	14	6	10	11	17	3
1928	10	16	15	5	12	2	1	9	8	13	3	14	6	7	11	17	4
1929	7	12	17	4	11	8	2	9	6	13	1	15	10	4	14	16	2
1930	9	6	11	2	13	5	1	12	16	17	4	13	8	7	15	10	3
1931	7	10	15	2	12	3	6	16	11	17	5	13	8	4	9	14	1
1932	10	14	15	13	8	3	6	12	10	16	4	7	5	2	9	17	1
1933	6	4	16	10	14	3	5	17	12	13	8	11	9	2	7	15	1
1934	3	8	13	7	14	5	1	12	10	17	9	15	11	2	4	16	5
1935	2	9	13	15	16	10	4	6	3	17	5	14	11	7	8	12	1
1936	1	9	16	4	10	8	11	15	2	17	5	7	6	14	13	12	3
1937	3	6	7	4	14	12	9	16	2	17	10	13	8	5	11	15	1
1938	5	6	16	10	14	9	4	15	2	17	12	7	3	8	13	11	1
1939	9	4	13	3	15	5	6	17	2	16	12	14	8	10	11	7	1
1946	15	8	6	5	10	6	3	11	2	16	13	4	11	17	14	8	1
1947	5	11	9	2	16	4	3	14	1	17	11	11	6	9	15	7	7
1948	6	13	1	8	9	15	5	11	3	17	14	12	2	16	7	10	4
1949	15	9	8	7	16	13	11	17	1	6	11	9	5	13	4	3	1

	Derbyshire	Essex	Glamorgan	Gloucestershire	Hampshire	Kent	Lancashire	Leicestershire	Middlesex	Northamptonshire	Nottinghamshire	Somerset	Surrey	Sussex	Warwickshire	Worcestershire	Yorkshire
1950	5	17	11	7	12	9	1	16	14	10	15	7	1	13	4	6	3
1951	11	8	5	12	9	16	3	15	7	13	17	14	6	10	1	4	2
1952	4	10	7	9	12	15	3	6	5	8	16	17	1	13	10	14	2
1953	6	12	10	6	14	16	3	3	5	11	8	17	1	2	9	15	12
1954	3	15	4	13	14	11	10	16	7	7	5	17	1	9	6	11	2
1955	8	14	16	12	3	13	9	6	5	7	11	17	1	4	9	15	2
1956	11	11	13	3	6	16	2	17	5	4	8	15	1	9	14	9	7
1957	4	5	9	12	13	14	6	17	7	2	15	8	1	9	11	16	3
1958	6	6	15	14	2	8	7	12	10	4	17	3	1	13	16	9	11
1959	7	9	6	2	8	13	5	16	10	11	17	12	3	15	4	14	1
1960	5	6	11	8	12	10	2	17	3	9	16	14	7	4	15	13	1
1961	7	6	14	5	1	11	13	9	3	16	17	10	15	8	12	4	2
1962	7	9	14	4	10	11	16	17	13	8	15	6	5	12	3	2	1
1963	17	12	2	8	10	13	15	16	6	7	9	3	11	4	4	14	1
1964	12	10	11	17	12	7	14	16	6	3	15	8	4	9	2	1	5
1965	9	15	3	10	12	5	13	14	6	2	17	7	8	16	11	1	4
1966	9	16	14	15	11	4	12	8	12	5	17	3	7	10	6	2	1
1967	6	15	14	17	12	2	11	2	7	9	15	8	4	13	10	5	1
1968	8	14	3	16	5	2	6	9	10	13	4	12	15	17	11	7	1
1969	16	6	1	2	5	10	15	14	11	9	8	17	3	7	4	12	13
1970	7	12	2	17	10	1	3	15	16	14	11	13	5	9	7	6	4
1971	17	10	16	8	9	4	3	5	6	14	12	7	1	11	2	15	13
1972	17	5	13	3	9	2	15	6	8	4	14	11	12	16	1	7	10
1973	16	8	11	5	1	4	12	9	13	3	17	10	2	15	7	6	14
1974	17	12	16	14	2	10	8	4	6	3	15	5	7	13	9	1	11
1975	15	7	9	16	3	5	4	1	11	8	13	12	6	17	14	10	2
1976	15	6	17	3	12	14	16	4	1	2	13	7	9	10	5	11	8
1977	7	6	14	3	11	1	16	5	1	9	17	4	14	8	10	13	12
1978	14	2	13	10	8	1	12	6	3	17	7	5	16	9	11	15	4
1979	16	1	17	10	12	5	13	6	14	11	9	8	3	4	15	2	7
1980	9	8	13	7	17	16	15	10	1	12	3	5	2	4	14	11	6
1981	12	5	14	13	7	9	16	8	4	15	1	3	6	2	17	11	10
1982	11	7	16	15	3	13	12	2	1	9	4	6	5	8	17	14	10
1983	9	1	15	12	3	7	12	4	2	6	14	10	8	11	5	16	17
1984	12	1	13	17	15	5	16	4	3	11	2	7	8	6	9	10	14
1985	13	4	12	3	2	9	14	16	1	10	8	17	6	7	15	5	11
1986	11	1	17	2	6	8	15	7	12	9	4	16	3	14	12	5	10
1987	6	12	13	10	5	14	2	3	16	7	1	11	4	17	15	9	8
1988	14	3	17	10	15	2	9	8	7	12	5	11	4	16	6	1	13
1989	6	2	17	9	6	15	4	13	3	5	11	14	12	10	8	1	16
1990	12	2	8	13	3	16	6	7	1	11	13	15	9	17	5	4	10

Note: From 1969 onwards, positions have been given in accordance with the Championship regulations which state that "Should *any* sides in the table be equal on points the side with most wins will have priority".

DERBYSHIRE

President: The Duke of Devonshire
Chairman: C. N. Middleton
Chairman, Cricket Committee: B. Holling
Chief Executive: R. J. Lark
County Ground, Nottingham Road, Derby
DE2 6DA (Telephone: 0332-383211)
Captain: K. J. Barnett
Coach: P. E. Russell

Winning the Refuge Assurance League gave Derbyshire their first
success for nine years and, significantly, they avoided the mistakes which
had made their victory in the 1981 NatWest Bank Trophy final an end
rather than a beginning. The team which won at Lord's under Barry
Wood started to break up in a matter of days and, against a background
of the smallest membership among the first-class counties, Derbyshire
spent most of the 1980s in patient rebuilding. Three people were chiefly
responsible for recreating a team: Kim Barnett, 22 when he was
appointed captain in 1983, coach Philip Russell, and Guy Willatt, a
former captain, who stepped down as cricket committee chairman before
the 1990 season. His successor, Brian Holling, was insistent that the
credit belonged, at committee level, to Willatt.

After completing their Sunday League season with an exciting victory
over Essex, Derbyshire announced an intelligent retained list, designed
to keep a nucleus of eight players on long-term contracts to the end of
1994. They also demonstrated their ambition by announcing a £10
million redevelopment of the County Ground at Derby, and by engaging
India's captain, Mohammad Azharuddin, as their overseas player for
1991 on the assumption that Ian Bishop would be on tour with the West
Indians. Adrian Kuiper, as disappointing in the Britannic Assurance
Championship as he was successful in one-day cricket, decided not to
return from South Africa.

In the other one-day competitions, Derbyshire wasted good positions,
thus failing to reach the knockout stages of the Benson and Hedges Cup
and allowing Lancashire to escape in the NatWest Trophy. They lost the
final of the Refuge Assurance Cup on a depressingly sluggish pitch at
Edgbaston.

In addition to his forthright captaincy, Barnett set a Derbyshire record
when he passed Denis Smith's total of 30 hundreds for the county, a
mark which had stood for 40 years. There were 21 first-class hundreds
in the season, another Derbyshire record, but there was also an under-
lying inconsistency, despite important individual improvements. Bruce
Roberts had a better year, and in his first full summer Chris Adams was
close to 1,000 runs. Adams also proved himself to be a fine fielder, as he
showed a wider audience when he acted as England's substitute against
India at Old Trafford. In addition, Bishop, who scored a maiden century
against Yorkshire at Scarborough, suggested he had sufficient quality to
emerge as a genuine all-rounder.

The Championship batting, however, relied to an unhealthy extent on Barnett, John Morris and Peter Bowler. Spectacular collapses were never far away and certain opponents, notably Essex and Hampshire, could be forgiven for wondering how Derbyshire ever won a game. Bowler completed three notably consistent seasons, and there was much pleasure in the county when Morris, considered unlucky to miss a tour in 1989-90, made his England début against India. Only at The Oval did he have the chance to play a long innings, and failure to do so meant an anxious wait before he was chosen to tour Australia.

Devon Malcolm's selection was in less doubt. He was an unknown quantity when he went to the West Indies, but he was England's leading wicket-taker there and in the home series against New Zealand. Although fatigue was setting in during the second half of the summer, he had by then established himself as fast enough to unsettle the best batsmen in the world. For a variety of reasons – including international calls, the county's system of rotating their fast bowlers, and despair about slow pitches at Derby – Malcolm and Bishop played together in only six Championship games. Yet even when the odds were loaded heavily in favour of batsmen, Bishop, capped in 1990 along with Simon Base, compelled respect and he took his wickets at less than 20 each.

Concern about the pitches culminated in the deduction of 25 points for an unacceptable surface in the Championship match against Middlesex in August. The loss of the points pushed Derbyshire from eighth to twelfth in the final table and knocked on the head any last, lingering hopes of the title or prizemoney. While Derbyshire accepted the decision, they expressed concern about the circumstances leading to it. In May, a Derby pitch which had provided a satisfactory game against Nottinghamshire was reported, not because of its behaviour but because it was too green. Having been ordered to shave the pitches, Derbyshire followed instructions with a sense of impending disaster. They relaid two strips in the autumn, a long-term rather than an immediate solution.

Derbyshire hope that some of their younger players will develop. Andrew Brown, taken back on the staff, scored a maiden century against Northamptonshire, but ended that innings with a broken hand. Dominic Cork, picked as a bowler for England Young Cricketers, saved the series against their Pakistani counterparts with a century as night-watchman, and Tim O'Gorman should be available regularly after a year at Law School. However, Geoff Miller, having made major contributions to two Championship victories and to the balance of the Sunday team on his return after three years with Essex, left when offered a match contract for 1991, rather than a longer-term one.

The memories of 1990 will be of Sunday games, especially the successful pursuits of steep targets at Taunton, where Morris scored four centuries in three competitions, and against Kent at Chesterfield. Kuiper's savage hitting gave Derbyshire a good start and an exciting climax, while Barnett fell only 1 run short of his 1986 record of 700 Sunday runs. It was on Sundays that Ole Mortensen, always the most reliable of Derbyshire's bowlers, Base and Allan Warner were at their most influential. Derbyshire earned their moments of good fortune and believed that more success was on the way. – Gerald Mortimer.

DERBYSHIRE 1990

[Bill Smith]

Back row: F. A. Griffith, A. M. Brown, D. G. Cork, T. J. G. O'Gorman, C. J. Adams, S. C. Goldsmith, K. M. Krikken. Middle row: B. Roberts, A. E. Warner, S. J. Base, P. D. Bowler, M. Jean-Jacques, S. W. Tacey (scorer). Front row: O. H. Mortensen, J. E. Morris, R. J. Lark (chief executive), K. J. Barnett (captain), P. E. Russell (coach), G. Miller, B. J. M. Maher. Inset: D. F. Malcolm, I. R. Bishop, A. P. Kuiper.

DERBYSHIRE RESULTS

All first-class matches – Played 24: Won 7, Lost 8, Drawn 9.

County Championship matches – Played 22: Won 6, Lost 7, Drawn 9.

Bonus points – Batting 58, Bowling 52.

*Competition placings – Britannic Assurance County Championship, 12th;
NatWest Bank Trophy, 2nd round; Benson and Hedges Cup, 3rd in Group B;
Refuge Assurance League, winners; Refuge Assurance Cup, finalists.*

BRITANNIC ASSURANCE CHAMPIONSHIP AVERAGES

BATTING

	Birthplace	M	I	NO	R	HI	Avge
‡J. E. Morris	Crewe	16	26	4	1,353	157*	61.50
‡K. J. Barnett	Stoke-on-Trent	22	36	5	1,572	141	50.70
‡P. D. Bowler.......	Plymouth	21	37	4	1,408	210	42.66
T. J. G. O'Gorman .	Woking	6	11	1	393	100	39.30
A. M. Brown	Heanor	7	11	1	379	139*	37.90
‡B. Roberts.........	Lusaka, N. Rhodesia	22	35	7	1,038	124*	37.07
‡G. Miller	Chesterfield	13	13	7	208	47*	34.66
‡I. R. Bishop	Port-of-Spain, Trinidad	12	15	4	326	103*	29.63
C. J. Adams	Whitwell	21	32	3	800	101	27.58
‡S. J. Base	Maidstone	13	13	2	215	58	19.54
A. P. Kuiper.......	Johannesburg, SA	10	15	0	288	48	19.20
K. M. Krikken	Bolton	21	28	2	426	77*	16.38
S. C. Goldsmith	Ashford, Kent	11	16	1	216	34	14.40
M. Jean-Jacques ...	Soufrière, Dominica	10	11	4	80	25	11.42
‡D. E. Malcolm	Kingston, Jamaica	9	6	2	44	20*	11.00
‡O. H. Mortensen ..	Vejle, Denmark	11	11	9	20	5*	10.00
‡A. E. Warner	Birmingham	14	19	2	160	59	9.41

Also batted: D. G. Cork (*Newcastle-under-Lyme*) (1 match) 7; F. A. Griffith (*Whipps Cross, London*) (1 match) 1; Z. A. Sadiq (*Nairobi, Kenya*) (1 match) 0.

* *Signifies not out.* ‡ *Denotes county cap.*

The following played a total of twenty three-figure innings for Derbyshire in County Championship matches – J. E. Morris 6, K. J. Barnett 5, P. D. Bowler 3, B. Roberts 2, C. J. Adams 1, I. R. Bishop 1, A. M. Brown 1, T. J. G. O'Gorman 1.

BOWLING

	O	M	R	W	BB	5W/i	Avge
I. R. Bishop..........	395.3	91	1,087	59	6-71	3	18.42
O. H. Mortensen	301.2	88	764	32	4-22	0	23.87
D. E. Malcolm........	277.4	44	947	30	4-63	0	31.56
K. J. Barnett	267.1	42	720	19	3-49	0	37.89
S. J. Base	414.3	68	1,402	35	6-105	2	40.05
A. E. Warner.........	393.3	67	1,330	33	3-56	0	40.30
G. Miller	427.2	94	1,285	31	6-45	1	41.45
M. Jean-Jacques	261.2	33	983	19	6-60	1	51.73

Also bowled: C. J. Adams 8-0-36-1; P. D. Bowler 8-0-56-1; D. G. Cork 24-6-70-0; S. C. Goldsmith 112-19-347-7; F. A. Griffith 11-2-20-1; A. P. Kuiper 108.3-25-325-9; J. E. Morris 20-0-123-1; B. Roberts 7-0-26-0.

Wicket-keepers: K. M. Krikken 58 ct, 3 st; P. D. Bowler 4 ct.

Leading Fielders: B. Roberts 23, C. J. Adams 22.

At Cambridge, April 18, 19, 20. DERBYSHIRE beat CAMBRIDGE UNIVERSITY by 243 runs.

At Nottingham, April 26, 27, 28, 30. DERBYSHIRE drew with NOTTINGHAMSHIRE.

At Northampton, May 3, 4. DERBYSHIRE beat NORTHAMPTONSHIRE by an innings and 51 runs.

DERBYSHIRE v LANCASHIRE

At Derby, May 15, 16, 17, 18. Lancashire won by 60 runs. Lancashire 21 pts, Derbyshire 3 pts. Toss: Lancashire. A lifeless pitch contributed to some dull cricket, but the match ended satisfactorily for Lancashire when Miller was lbw to DeFreitas to give them victory with five balls to spare. Lancashire batted until tea on the second day, having lost 87 minutes because of a thunderstorm on the first, and only DeFreitas, with 79 from 107 balls, interrupted the pattern of steady accumulation. Although Barnett also showed that it was possible to play strokes, Lancashire's policy was justified by Atherton's excellent leg-spin bowling. He took five for 95, the best figures of his career, and Lancashire led by 136. Their second declaration set Derbyshire to score 309 off what proved to be 87 overs but, after a bright start by Barnett and Morris, only Bowler played an innings of substance. Hughes, a bowling recluse in recent seasons, was much the most effective of the spinners.
  Close of play: First day, Lancashire 223-2 (M. A. Atherton 69*, N. H. Fairbrother 23*); Second day, Derbyshire 105-2 (S. J. Base 9*, M. Jean-Jacques 0*); Third day, Lancashire 81-2 (M. A. Atherton 28*, N. H. Fairbrother 22*).

Lancashire

G. D. Mendis c Roberts b Miller	90	– c and b Jean-Jacques 4
G. Fowler b Barnett	25	– c Roberts b Jean-Jacques 23
M. A. Atherton b Barnett	93	– run out 51
N. H. Fairbrother c Kuiper b Jean-Jacques	63	– not out 65
T. E. Jesty not out	55	– not out 15
P. A. J. DeFreitas st Krikken b Barnett	79	
B 17, l-b 18, w 1, n-b 4	40	B 3, l-b 11 14

1/79 2/171 3/267 4/325 5/445   (5 wkts dec.) 445   1/10 2/45 3/141   (3 wkts dec.) 172

J. D. Fitton, *D. P. Hughes, P. J. W. Allott, †W. K. Hegg and P. J. Martin did not bat.

Bonus points – Lancashire 2 (Score at 100 overs: 225-2).

Bowling: *First Innings*—Base 39-8-67-0; Jean-Jacques 34-5-112-1; Miller 59-17-111-1; Goldsmith 11-2-39-0; Barnett 33.3-4-81-3. *Second Innings*—Jean-Jacques 19-2-55-2; Base 8-1-30-0; Miller 19-5-45-0; Barnett 8-0-28-0.

Derbyshire

*K. J. Barnett c Hegg b Fitton	69	– c Allott b Fitton 33
J. E. Morris c Hegg b Atherton	27	– b Fitton 52
S. J. Base c Fitton b Atherton	54	– (9) not out 16
M. Jean-Jacques b Martin	18	– (10) c Jesty b Hughes 2
A. P. Kuiper c Fowler b Fitton	13	– (3) b Atherton 13
C. J. Adams c Fairbrother b Atherton	9	– (5) lbw b Hughes 36
B. Roberts lbw b Atherton	8	– (6) b Atherton 0
S. C. Goldsmith b Atherton	24	– (7) c Mendis b Hughes 4
P. D. Bowler c Mendis b DeFreitas	24	– (4) c Fairbrother b Fitton 54
†K. M. Krikken b Allott	11	– (8) b Hughes 26
G. Miller not out	3	– lbw b DeFreitas 1
B 4, l-b 8, n-b 2	14	B 4, l-b 6, n-b 1 11

1/93 2/105 3/155 4/183 5/206   309   1/64 2/99 3/103 4/154 5/155   248
6/216 7/255 8/275 9/301   6/160 7/223 8/229 9/243

Bonus points – Derbyshire 3, Lancashire 3 (Score at 100 overs: 275-8).

Bowling: *First Innings*—DeFreitas 24.3-4-70-1; Allott 13-3-40-1; Fitton 36-10-82-2; Atherton 38-11-95-5; Martin 8-4-10-1. *Second Innings*—DeFreitas 7.1-1-36-1; Allott 7-0-26-0; Fitton 24-4-69-3; Atherton 24-5-82-2; Hughes 44-12-25-4.

Umpires: H. D. Bird and R. Palmer.

At Taunton, May 19, 21, 22. DERBYSHIRE beat SOMERSET by 146 runs.

DERBYSHIRE v YORKSHIRE

At Chesterfield, May 23, 24, 25. Derbyshire won by 144 runs. Derbyshire 24 pts, Yorkshire 8 pts. Toss: Derbyshire. A Derbyshire collapse, in which six first-innings wickets fell for the addition of 9 runs, was redeemed by Miller and Base in a last-wicket partnership of 107, 25 short of the county record, also against Yorkshire, set in 1986. Base scored his second half-century, and the stand was one of the crucial phases in an entertaining match. Byas and the hard-hitting Hartley, who added 140 for the seventh wicket in 24 overs, were largely responsible for Yorkshire's lead, but any slight advantage disappeared as Barnett attacked fiercely. The Derbyshire captain and Roberts scored centuries in a partnership of 249, Derbyshire's highest against Yorkshire. Barnett scored 100 from 104 balls with fifteen fours, and went on to 141 from 150 balls. Roberts reached his century from 131 balls, with sixteen fours. Yorkshire, set 307 in 72 overs, were unpicked by Miller's high-class off-spin. Back after three years with Essex, Miller returned his best figures since 1987.

Close of play: First day, Yorkshire 33-0 (M. D. Moxon 9*, A. A. Metcalfe 19*); Second day, Derbyshire 148-1 (K. J. Barnett 93*, B. Roberts 43*).

Derbyshire

*K. J. Barnett c Byas b Fletcher	38	– c Blakey b Hartley	141
J. E. Morris c Byas b Hartley	60	– c Blakey b Fletcher	5
B. Roberts c Byas b Jarvis	49	– not out	124
P. D. Bowler lbw b Fletcher	29		
C. J. Adams run out	12	– c Metcalfe b Byas	10
S. C. Goldsmith c Byas b Hartley	0	– c Moxon b Byas	8
†K. M. Krikken c Bairstow b Hartley	0		
G. Miller not out	47		
I. R. Bishop c Berry b Fletcher	0		
A. E. Warner c Moxon b Jarvis	1	– (4) c Blakey b Hartley	10
S. J. Base c Hartley b Berry	58	– (7) c Robinson b Byas	7
L-b 16, w 1, n-b 6	23	B 1, l-b 9, w 3, n-b 3	16

1/44 2/119 3/180 4/201 5/201   **317**   1/10 2/259 3/272   (6 wkts dec.) **321**
6/201 7/207 8/207 9/210   4/292 5/308 6/321

Bonus points – Derbyshire 4, Yorkshire 4.

Bowling: *First Innings*—Jarvis 29–5–88–2; Hartley 23–4–80–3; Fletcher 24–9–57–3; Byas 8–3–28–0; Berry 13.4–1–48–1. *Second Innings*—Jarvis 12–0–59–0; Fletcher 14–1–100–1; Hartley 14–0–74–2; Berry 9–2–23–0; Byas 11–1–55–3.

Yorkshire

*M. D. Moxon b Warner	45	– c Krikken b Warner	15
A. A. Metcalfe c Krikken b Bishop	32	– c Roberts b Bishop	5
R. J. Blakey c Bowler b Goldsmith	9	– c Goldsmith b Miller	25
S. A. Kellett b Barnett	22	– lbw b Miller	55
P. E. Robinson c Roberts b Base	12	– lbw b Miller	1
†D. L. Bairstow lbw b Base	19	– b Miller	21
D. Byas c Krikken b Bishop	67	– c Goldsmith b Bishop	6
P. J. Hartley c Goldsmith b Warner	75	– c Bowler b Miller	11
P. W. Jarvis c Base b Bishop	15	– c Adams b Bishop	8
P. J. Berry not out	6	– not out	4
S. D. Fletcher c Bowler b Bishop	2	– b Miller	0
L-b 12, w 3, n-b 13	28	L-b 2, w 2, n-b 7	11

1/64 2/80 3/118 4/131 5/143   **332**   1/16 2/26 3/78 4/82 5/114   **162**
6/157 7/297 8/308 9/319   6/135 7/141 8/158 9/158

Bonus points – Yorkshire 4, Derbyshire 4.

Bowling: *First Innings*—Bishop 21.2–6–62–4; Base 15–0–72–2; Warner 22–1–90–2; Barnett 9–1–37–1; Goldsmith 7–1–21–1; Miller 11–2–38–0. *Second Innings*—Bishop 18–3–42–3; Warner 10–4–32–1; Base 7–1–29–0; Miller 20.3–6–45–6; Barnett 6–1–12–0.

Umpires: P. J. Eele and A. A. Jones.

DERBYSHIRE v NOTTINGHAMSHIRE

At Derby, May 26, 27, 28. Drawn. Derbyshire 7 pts, Nottinghamshire 6 pts. Toss: Derbyshire. Mortensen gained least reward in Nottinghamshire's first innings, although he was the outstanding bowler. Only Robinson held the visitors together. However, Derbyshire also lost their way after a fine 103 by Morris, whose century came from 193 balls and included seventeen fours. Krikken's 31 was the next highest score. Cooper's consistent accuracy was rewarded by five wickets, limiting Derbyshire's lead to 52, and on the final day Nottingham-shire were steered to safety by French's maiden century. He was struck on the helmet three times but batted with courage and application to achieve three figures from 154 balls, hitting a six and seventeen fours. Randall also batted with determination, and Robinson's declaration was little more than a gesture. The evident ill-feeling in the match reflected no credit on the teams, who ended it as joint leaders of the Championship.

Close of play: First day, Derbyshire 71-2 (J. E. Morris 20*, B. Roberts 12*); Second day, Nottinghamshire 143-4 (D. W. Randall 39*, M. Saxelby 14*).

Nottinghamshire

B. C. Broad c Adams b Warner	45	– lbw b Mortensen	50
D. J. R. Martindale lbw b Mortensen	12	– c Krikken b Malcolm	2
*R. T. Robinson c Adams b Malcolm	69	– lbw b Bishop	15
P. Johnson c Mortensen b Bishop	20	– c Roberts b Malcolm	2
D. W. Randall c Krikken b Bishop	12	– c Roberts b Mortensen	88
M. Saxelby c Krikken b Warner	6	– c Roberts b Bishop	14
†B. N. French c Krikken b Malcolm	9	– not out	105
G. W. Mike c Krikken b Warner	11	– b Barnett	7
K. E. Cooper c Warner b Bishop	16	– not out	35
R. A. Pick not out	1		
J. A. Afford c Roberts b Malcolm	0		
B 4, l-b 12, w 3, n-b 2	21	B 12, l-b 21, w 12, n-b 6	51

1/53 2/77 3/120 4/134 5/147   222   1/10 2/46 3/55   (7 wkts dec.) 369
6/162 7/179 8/216 9/222   4/99 5/145
                                                      6/234 7/287

Bonus points – Nottinghamshire 2, Derbyshire 4.

Bowling: *First Innings*—Bishop 18-3-60-3; Malcolm 16.2-2-46-3; Warner 23-4-64-3; Mortensen 24-12-36-1. *Second Innings*—Bishop 24-7-57-2; Malcolm 31-3-106-2; Warner 20-3-72-0; Mortensen 19-5-73-2; Barnett 6-0-28-1.

Derbyshire

*K. J. Barnett c Randall b Cooper	29	– not out	46
P. D. Bowler c Randall b Pick	8	– (4) c French b Cooper	23
J. E. Morris c French b Saxelby	103	– (2) c and b Cooper	7
B. Roberts b Pick	15	– (5) c French b Afford	7
C. J. Adams c Randall b Mike	14	– (6) not out	4
S. C. Goldsmith c French b Cooper	30		
†K. M. Krikken b Cooper	31		
I. R. Bishop lbw b Cooper	8		
A. E. Warner run out	8	– (3) c Mike b Pick	1
O. H. Mortensen not out	0		
D. E. Malcolm b Cooper	12		
L-b 4, w 1, n-b 11	16	B 4, l-b 3, n-b 8	15

1/32 2/42 3/97 4/141 5/191   274   1/8 2/21 3/73 4/91   (4 wkts) 103
6/235 7/243 8/258 9/262

Bonus points – Derbyshire 3, Nottinghamshire 4.

Bowling: *First Innings*—Pick 24-3-97-2; Cooper 25-6-72-5; Mike 14-2-59-1; Afford 18-9-21-0; Saxelby 3-0-21-1. *Second Innings*—Pick 11-1-38-1; Cooper 12-4-36-2; Afford 11-7-13-1; Mike 4-1-9-0.

Umpires: P. J. Eele and A. A. Jones.

at Derby, June 2, 3, 4. DERBYSHIRE lost to NEW ZEALANDERS by 82 runs (See New Zealand tour section).

at The Oval, June 6, 7, 8. DERBYSHIRE drew with SURREY.

DERBYSHIRE v WARWICKSHIRE

at Derby, June 16, 18, 19. Warwickshire won by two wickets. Warwickshire 16 pts, Derbyshire 4 pts. Toss: Warwickshire. The pitch was so obviously bland that Reeve, Warwickshire's captain, sent for Moody, a batsman, to replace Donald, a bowler, as the county's overseas player. Barnett and Bowler scored centuries in Derbyshire's highest opening stand against Warwickshire, and there was a chance of the first four in the order reaching three figures, something not achieved in Championship cricket since Middlesex did it in 1923. Rain prevented play until five o'clock on the second day, after which Morris completed his century but Roberts fell 14 runs short. It was only the fourth time in Derbyshire's history that three or more players had scored centuries in an innings. After negotiations and a forfeiture, Warwickshire were set 350 in what would have been 83 overs. Moody, in his first Championship innings, batted magnificently to win a game in which the opposition had lost only four wickets, reaching his hundred with two consecutive sixes off Miller. When caught at third man, he had made 168 from 173 balls with six sixes and nineteen fours. Ostler then saw Warwickshire to victory with an over to spare.

Close of play: First day, Derbyshire 408-2 (J. E. Morris 70*, B. Roberts 70*); Second day, Warwickshire 25-0 (A. J. Moles 11*, J. D. Ratcliffe 14*).

Derbyshire

*K. J. Barnett c Small b Munton	131	C. J. Adams not out	6
P. D. Bowler b Reeve b Moody	120	B 5, l-b 8, w 2, n-b 3	18
J. E. Morris not out	103		
B. Roberts c Reeve b Twose	86	1/249 2/281 3/437	(4 wkts dec.) 475
A. P. Kuiper c Reeve b Munton	11	4/452	

†K. M. Krikken, G. Miller, S. J. Base, D. E. Malcolm and A. E. Warner did not bat.

Bonus points – Derbyshire 4 (Score at 100 overs: 340-2).

Bowling: Small 14-3-44-0; Munton 29.2-4-105-2; Pierson 37-9-84-0; Twose 17-1-82-1; Moody 7-0-43-1; Asif Din 19-1-85-0; Moles 7-2-19-0.

Derbyshire forfeited their second innings.

Warwickshire

A. J. Moles not out	70	c Krikken b Malcolm	4
J. D. Ratcliffe c and b Bowler	38	c Roberts b Base	25
Asif Din not out	17	c Miller b Base	30
T. M. Moody (did not bat)		c Base b Malcolm	168
†G. W. Humpage (did not bat)		b Barnett	34
*D. A. Reeve (did not bat)		c Krikken b Malcolm	25
R. G. Twose (did not bat)		lbw b Malcolm	1
D. P. Ostler (did not bat)		not out	42
G. C. Small (did not bat)		run out	8
T. A. Munton (did not bat)		not out	0
L-b 1	1	L-b 8, w 3, n-b 5	16

1/74	(1 wkt dec.) 126	1/9 2/54 3/80 4/152 (8 wkts) 353
		5/261 6/271 7/334 8/349

A. R. K. Pierson did not bat.

Bowling: *First Innings*—Miller 7-4-11-0; Warner 3-1-9-0; Barnett 4-2-5-0; Morris 5-0-52-0; Bowler 6-0-48-1. *Second Innings*—Malcolm 19-1-63-4; Warner 17-4-66-0; Base 18-2-88-2; Kuiper 6-1-18-0; Miller 12-0-71-0; Barnett 10-1-39-1.

Umpires: J. H. Hampshire and A. G. T. Whitehead.

At Leicester, June 20, 21, 22. DERBYSHIRE lost to LEICESTERSHIRE by 140 runs.

DERBYSHIRE v GLOUCESTERSHIRE

At Derby, June 30, July 2, 3. Drawn. Derbyshire 4 pts, Gloucestershire 4 pts. Toss: Derbyshire. Barnett scored his 30th century for Derbyshire to equal the record set by Denis Smith in 1950. It was the first of three hundreds in consecutive Championship innings by Barnett, followed by an unbeaten 90 against Lancashire. There was no substance in either first innings, good bowling and poor batting combining as the first twenty wickets fell for 186. On a first day in which 56 overs were lost, Derbyshire collapsed against Walsh and Lawrence, and then Malcolm and Bishop made inroads into the Gloucestershire innings. With help from Mortensen, they completed the rout next day. Derbyshire batted freely in the second innings and Barnett reached his century from 181 balls, hitting twelve fours. It was his 387th innings for Derbyshire, whereas Smith batted 711 times for the county. Umpire Holder intervened as an argument followed the bowling of a beamer by Walsh to Bowler. Gloucestershire were set 305 in 70 overs but, despite a good start by Wright and Hodgson, they found the chase too demanding and concentrated on saving the game.

Close of play: First day, Gloucestershire 39-4 (P. Bainbridge 3*, K. M. Curran 3*); Second day, Derbyshire 233-3 (B. Roberts 10*, C. J. Adams 5*).

Derbyshire

*K. J. Barnett b Lawrence	7	– c Curran b Walsh	107
P. D. Bowler b Walsh	5	– lbw b Walsh	23
J. E. Morris c Athey b Walsh	9	– c Athey b Lloyds	66
B. Roberts c Barnes b Lawrence	2	– b Barnes	59
C. J. Adams b Barnes	7	– lbw b Barnes	48
S. C. Goldsmith lbw b Lawrence	5	– not out	7
†K. M. Krikken c Lloyds b Barnes	9	– c Russell b Curran	1
M. Jean-Jacques b Lawrence	7	– not out	3
I. R. Bishop b Walsh	10		
D. E. Malcolm not out	0		
O. H. Mortensen b Walsh	4		
N-b 7	7	B 3, l-b 13, w 1, n-b 15	32

1/11 2/13 3/23 4/26 5/31   72   1/74 2/202 3/213   (6 wkts dec.) 346
6/44 7/49 8/68 9/68   4/328 5/337 6/338

Bonus points – Gloucestershire 4.

Bowling: *First Innings*—Walsh 14-2-32-4; Lawrence 10-1-27-4; Curran 3-1-3-0; Barnes 6-2-10-2. *Second Innings*—Walsh 26.4-2-86-2; Lawrence 3-0-20-0; Curran 20.2-2-75-1; Lloyds 29-6-74-1; Barnes 23-2-75-2.

Gloucestershire

G. D. Hodgson c Morris b Bishop	13	– c Krikken b Bishop	52
*A. J. Wright c Morris b Malcolm	3	– c Krikken b Jean-Jacques	44
I. P. Butcher c Krikken b Malcolm	0	– (8) not out	0
C. W. J. Athey lbw b Bishop	12	– (3) b Bishop	21
P. Bainbridge lbw b Bishop	6	– (4) lbw b Barnett	40
K. M. Curran b Bishop	24	– (5) c Morris b Jean-Jacques	3
J. W. Lloyds not out	28	– (6) not out	25
†R. C. Russell b Mortensen	2	– (7) c Krikken b Barnett	15
C. A. Walsh b Mortensen	1		
D. V. Lawrence c Krikken b Mortensen	8		
S. N. Barnes lbw b Mortensen	6		
B 3, l-b 5, w 3	11	B 1, l-b 3	4

1/7 2/7 3/33 4/34 5/43   114   1/81 2/116 3/137   (6 wkts) 204
6/71 7/74 8/78 9/96   4/146 5/170 6/198

Bonus points – Derbyshire 4.

Bowling: *First Innings*—Bishop 19–4–38–4; Malcolm 18–5–46–2; Mortensen 15–7–22–4.
Second Innings—Bishop 14–1–44–2; Malcolm 17–4–49–0; Mortensen 17–2–52–0; Jean-
acques 8–0–26–2; Barnett 11–6–19–2; Morris 1–0–10–0.

Umpires: J. W. Holder and B. Leadbeater.

At Hove, July 4, 5, 6. DERBYSHIRE beat SUSSEX by 18 runs.

At Liverpool, July 7, 9, 10. DERBYSHIRE drew with LANCASHIRE.

At Chesterfield, July 16. DERBYSHIRE lost to INDIANS by two wickets (See Indian tour
section).

At Colchester, July 18, 19, 20. DERBYSHIRE lost to ESSEX by nine wickets.

At Portsmouth, July 21, 23, 24. DERBYSHIRE lost to HAMPSHIRE by 48 runs.

DERBYSHIRE v WORCESTERSHIRE

At Derby, July 25, 26, 27. Drawn. Derbyshire 2 pts, Worcestershire 7 pts. Toss: Worcestershire. Hick arrived with 592 runs since his last dismissal and needed a further 118 to pass the
first-class record set by K. C. Ibrahim in India in 1947-48. He made 53 before falling to a
spectacular slip catch by Adams. On an uncertain pitch, Worcestershire concentrated on
building a big total, and Derbyshire's bowling was stretched when Mortensen withdrew with a
calf injury, even though Base filled the breach with his best return of the season. Worcestershire's decision to bat into the second day was justified when they were able to enforce the
follow-on. Derbyshire's batting lacked resolution against Illingworth and Lampitt, who shared
the wickets. However, Adams and Brown batted well in the second innings as Derbyshire
fought to save the game, and rain, coming ten minutes before the start of the last hour, denied
an intriguing finish. Illingworth's sustained effort was reflected in match figures of
91–50–111–8.

Close of play: First day, Worcestershire 332-9 (S. R. Lampitt 10*, N. V. Radford 5*);
Second day, Derbyshire 39-1 (A. M. Brown 11*, T. J. G. O'Gorman 8*).

Worcestershire

T. S. Curtis c Krikken b Base	17	P. J. Newport c Barnett b Base		2
C. M. Tolley lbw b Base	16	S. R. Lampitt not out		16
G. A. Hick c Adams b Warner	53	N. V. Radford c Krikken b Base		14
D. B. D'Oliveira b Warner	87			
I. T. Botham c Brown b Barnett	27	B 12, l-b 15, w 5, n-b 13		45
*P. A. Neale c Roberts b Warner	65			
†S. J. Rhodes c Krikken b Base	0	1/35 2/44 3/136 4/173		348
R. K. Illingworth c Adams b Base	6	5/275 6/277 7/295 8/310 9/323		

Bonus points – Worcestershire 3, Derbyshire 1 (Score at 100 overs: 269-4).

Bowling: Mortensen 3–2–4–0; Base 39.3–3–105–6; Kuiper 19–8–42–0; Barnett 32–8–61–1;
Warner 30–5–109–3.

Derbyshire

P. D. Bowler c Botham b Illingworth	36	– c Rhodes b Newport	18
A. M. Brown lbw b Illingworth	32	– c Rhodes b Hick	42
T. J. G. O'Gorman c Radford b Illingworth	0	– c Neale b Lampitt	9
C. J. Adams c Rhodes b Illingworth	32	– st Rhodes b Illingworth	63
A. P. Kuiper c Hick b Lampitt	38	– b Hick	41
B. Roberts c Hick b Lampitt	18	– c Rhodes b Illingworth	0
*K. J. Barnett b Lampitt	9	– c Rhodes b Illingworth	23
†K. M. Krikken lbw b Lampitt	4	– c Neale b Newport	13
A. E. Warner lbw b Lampitt	4	– not out	5
S. J. Base b Illingworth	14	– not out	0
O. H. Mortensen not out	0		
L-b 2, n-b 3	5	B 9, l-b 12	21

1/61 2/61 3/76 4/121 5/147   192   1/24 2/50 3/119 4/181   (8 wkts) 235
6/164 7/171 8/175 9/192   5/181 6/201 7/229 8/235

Bonus points – Derbyshire 1, Worcestershire 4.

Bowling: *First Innings*—Newport 8–1–23–0; Radford 5–0–23–0; Botham 7–2–12–0; Illingworth 38–19–59–5; Hick 14–2–39–0; Lampitt 19.4–6–34–5. *Second Innings*—Newport 7–1–29–2; Radford 4–2–10–0; Illingworth 53–31–52–3; Hick 25–9–45–2; Lampitt 19–3–52–1; Botham 6–1–26–0.

Umpires: P. J. Eele and K. J. Lyons.

DERBYSHIRE v KENT

At Chesterfield, August 4, 6, 7. Derbyshire won by ten wickets. Derbyshire 24 pts, Kent 5 pts. Toss: Kent. Bishop gave Derbyshire an early advantage by dismissing the openers in his first two overs and went on to take six wickets. The support, however, was poor and Ward, who had missed two months of the season with an ankle injury, played powerful and attractive strokes in a career-best 124 from 152 balls, with a six and twenty fours. Bowler scored his first double-century, the county's highest against Kent, and Derbyshire passed 500 for the first time since 1952, against Nottinghamshire at Ilkeston. Kent were weakened by injuries to Ellison and de Villiers as Bowler shared three century partnerships, reached 200 from 353 balls with a five and 25 fours, and batted for 412 minutes. Roberts took full advantage of the situation to hit an unbeaten 100 from 117 balls (four sixes, ten fours). Kent's top batting showed little resolution in the second innings as Jean-Jacques produced his best figures for four years, but Ellison organised more determined resistance. Derbyshire awarded caps to Bishop and Base on the second morning.
Close of play: First day, Derbyshire 110-0 (K. J. Barnett 49*, P. D. Bowler 57*); Second day, Derbyshire 514-5 (B. Roberts 100*, K. M. Krikken 27*).

Kent

S. G. Hinks c Krikken b Bishop	0	– c Roberts b Jean-Jacques	9
*M. R. Benson c Morris b Bishop	0	– b Malcolm	15
N. R. Taylor c Krikken b Base	18	– c Bowler b Jean-Jacques	12
G. R. Cowdrey c Krikken b Malcolm	6	– c Bowler b Jean-Jacques	21
T. R. Ward lbw b Base	124	– c Krikken b Base	5
†S. A. Marsh c Adams b Bishop	38	– c Krikken b Base	4
R. M. Ellison c Roberts b Base	41	– c Krikken b Jean-Jacques	62
R. P. Davis c Krikken b Bishop	41	– c Brown b Malcolm	26
P. S. de Villiers c Roberts b Bishop	5	– c Base b Bishop	30
M. M. Patel c Roberts b Bishop	7	– not out	25
A. P. Igglesden not out	1	– b Jean-Jacques	2
L-b 3, w 5, n-b 14	22	B 4, l-b 4, w 1, n-b 12	21

1/2 2/3 3/15 4/40 5/133   303   1/29 2/35 3/46 4/58 5/70   232
6/231 7/245 8/259 9/293   6/89 7/134 8/187 9/214

Bonus points – Kent 4, Derbyshire 4.

Bowling: *First Innings*—Bishop 22.1–3–71–6; Malcolm 18–7–58–1; Base 21–3–85–3; Jean-Jacques 21–2–84–0; Barnett 2–1–2–0. *Second Innings*—Bishop 15–4–45–1; Malcolm 17–0–57–2; Jean-Jacques 20.4–5–60–6; Base 19–3–59–1; Barnett 1–0–3–0.

Derbyshire

K. J. Barnett c Davis b de Villiers	64 – not out	10
P. D. Bowler c Cowdrey b Patel	210 – not out	13
J. E. Morris c de Villiers b Davis	32	
A. M. Brown lbw b Igglesden	6	
C. J. Adams c Taylor b Patel	52	
B. Roberts not out	100	
K. M. Krikken not out	27	
B 2, l-b 20, w 1	23	W 1 1

1/138 2/179 3/191 4/304 5/449   (5 wkts dec.) 514   (no wkt) 24

J. R. Bishop, M. Jean-Jacques, S. J. Base and D. E. Malcolm did not bat.

Bonus points – Derbyshire 4, Kent 1 (Score at 100 overs: 376-4).

Bowling: First Innings—de Villiers 21–3–75–1; Igglesden 25–4–113–1; Ellison 6–0–26–0; Davis 39–8–152–1; Patel 27–6–97–2; Hinks 7–0–29–0. Second Innings—Marsh 3.4–0–16–0; Taylor 3–0–8–0.

Umpires: J. H. Hampshire and B. Hassan.

DERBYSHIRE v NORTHAMPTONSHIRE

At Chesterfield, August 8, 9, 10. Drawn. Derbyshire 6 pts, Northamptonshire 7 pts. Toss: Northamptonshire. Brown, released by Derbyshire in 1987 and re-engaged for 1990, held an uneven innings together with his maiden century. After spending eight increasingly fretful overs on 99, he reached three figures in 306 minutes from 294 balls. On the second day, he was hit on the left hand by a ball from Ambrose and forced to retire with a broken knuckle, which put him out for the rest of the season. Northamptonshire replied enterprisingly, and Capel, off 9 balls, hit a remarkable century which included eight sixes, a five and eight fours. Larkins declared behind and, after Northamptonshire's bowling changes had encouraged free scoring, Barnett set them 269 in what became 51 overs. Everything depended on Bailey, although Capel (50 from 40 balls) again batted excitingly. Bailey hit four sixes and fourteen fours in a fine display as an ultimately entertaining match ended in a draw, Northamptonshire finishing 9 runs short of victory with two wickets standing.

Close of play: First day, Derbyshire 282-7 (A. M. Brown 122*, G. Miller 11*); Second day, Derbyshire 6-0 (K. J. Barnett 2*, P. D. Bowler 4*).

Derbyshire

K. J. Barnett b Robinson	20 – c Ripley b Robinson	3
P. D. Bowler c Ripley b Robinson	22 – b Hughes	40
A. M. Brown retired hurt	139	
T. J. G. O'Gorman c Ripley b Hughes	19 – (3) c Bailey b Felton	82
C. J. Adams c Larkins b Robinson	5 – (4) c Fordham b Bailey	12
B. Roberts c Felton b Ambrose	34 – (5) not out	56
K. M. Krikken c Capel b Ambrose	0 – (6) b Robinson b Cook	24
J. R. Bishop b Williams	34 – (7) c and b Cook	0
G. Miller b Hughes	36 – (8) not out	6
A. E. Warner run out	24	
O. H. Mortensen not out	0	
L-b 9, n-b 6	15	L-b 10, n-b 1 11

1/45 2/46 3/99 4/118 5/181   348   1/9 2/73 3/109   (6 wkts dec.) 234
6/181 7/248 8/344 9/348   4/153 5/204 6/206

Bonus points – Derbyshire 3, Northamptonshire 3 (Score at 100 overs: 251-7).

In the first innings A. M. Brown retired hurt at 320.

Bowling: First Innings—Ambrose 33–8–90–2; Robinson 26–9–96–3; Williams 35–19–41–1; Hughes 15–2–57–2; Cook 19–2–55–0. Second Innings—Ambrose 9–2–20–0; Robinson 9–1–24–1; Hughes 8–1–36–1; Bailey 17–4–44–1; Larkins 4–0–24–0; Felton 6–0–48–1; Cook 6–1–19–2; Williams 3–0–9–0.

Northamptonshire

A. Fordham c and b Miller	74	– c Krikken b Bishop	4
N. A. Felton c O'Gorman b Mortensen	5	– c Warner b Miller	42
*W. Larkins c sub b Mortensen	16	– c O'Gorman b Miller	5
R. J. Bailey run out	79	– not out	134
D. J. Capel not out	103	– c Krikken b Warner	50
R. G. Williams lbw b Bishop	9	– c Adams b Warner	4
†D. Ripley c Barnett b Warner	12	– hit wkt b Bishop	0
J. G. Hughes b Warner	0	– (9) run out	0
N. G. B. Cook not out	0	– (8) run out	4
C. E. L. Ambrose (did not bat)		– not out	0
L-b 13, n-b 3	16	B 1, l-b 6	7

1/16 2/38 3/185 4/186 5/221   (7 wkts dec.) 314   1/4 2/18 3/91 4/188   (8 wkts) 250
6/310 7/310   5/211 6/211 7/235 8/246

M. A. Robinson did not bat.

Bonus points – Northamptonshire 4, Derbyshire 3.

Bowling: *First Innings*—Bishop 15–6–27–1; Mortensen 13–1–43–2; Warner 21–4–68–2; Miller 19.2–2–108–1; Barnett 12–2–32–0; Roberts 5–0–23–0. *Second Innings*—Bishop 13.5–2–43–2; Mortensen 13–2–42–0; Miller 12–0–62–2; Warner 12–0–96–2.

Umpires: H. D. Bird and B. Hassan.

DERBYSHIRE v MIDDLESEX

At Derby, August 18, 20, 21. Derbyshire won by 171 runs. Derbyshire 22 pts, Middlesex 6 pts. Toss: Derbyshire. Derbyshire became the first county to beat Middlesex in the 1990 Championship, but it was obvious from the first day that the pitch was unsatisfactory. The umpires reported it and, after inspection by Donald Carr (chairman of the TCCB Pitches Committee), Tim Lamb (TCCB Cricket Secretary), Doug Lucas (Northamptonshire) and Old Trafford groundsman Peter Marron, the deputy Inspector of Pitches, Derbyshire had 2 points deducted. "The pitch was clearly unsuitable for first-class cricket", said the TCCB. There was, however, some interesting cricket. After Morris and O'Gorman batted well for Derbyshire, Gatting compiled a magnificent century from 217 balls, hitting fifteen fours in his innings. His display was the more commendable because weekend rain had forced its way under the covers, and Derbyshire's chairman, Chris Middleton, wrote to Middlesex thanking Gatting for his attitude in an embarrassing situation for the home county. Roberts and Miller suggested that sensible application would bring its rewards, but Middlesex, set 271 in a minimum of 54 overs, responded feebly. Base wrecked their innings and bowled well, perhaps too well for Derbyshire's ultimate good.

Close of play: First day, Middlesex 68-3 (M. W. Gatting 31*, D. L. Haynes 8*); Second day, Derbyshire 116-3 (T. J. G. O'Gorman 10*, A. P. Kuiper 20*).

Derbyshire

*K. J. Barnett c Downton b Fraser	3	– c Gatting b Emburey	7
P. D. Bowler b Emburey	38	– c Gatting b Emburey	5
J. E. Morris b Emburey	67	– c Roseberry b Tufnell	12
T. J. G. O'Gorman c Brown b Emburey	55	– c Brown b Fraser	2
A. P. Kuiper b Fraser	0	– c Downton b Emburey	36
B. Roberts c Haynes b Williams	27	– not out	48
†K. M. Krikken c Brown b Emburey	3	– c Roseberry b Emburey	0
G. Miller lbw b Cowans	1	– not out	32
M. Jean-Jacques not out	17		
S. J. Base lbw b Emburey	0		
O. H. Mortensen c Brown b Fraser	1		
B 10, l-b 24, w 1, n-b 2	37	L-b 16, n-b 9	25

1/4 2/112 3/119 4/126 5/176   249   1/36 2/70 3/91   (6 wkts dec.) 230
6/203 7/204 8/236 9/236   4/131 5/137 6/143

Bonus points – Derbyshire 2, Middlesex 4.

Bowling: *First Innings*—Fraser 19.1–4–49–3; Williams 16–2–56–1; Cowans 12–3–40–1; Tufnell 16–6–38–0; Emburey 18–4–32–5. *Second Innings*—Fraser 19–5–46–1; Williams 0–1–39–0; Emburey 36–8–71–4; Cowans 4–0–14–0; Tufnell 16–3–29–1; Ramprakash 0–15–0.

Middlesex

A. A. Roseberry c Bowler b Mortensen	7	– (2) b Base	2
I. F. Williams lbw b Base	5	– (8) c Bowler b Miller	3
M. W. Gatting not out	119	– (5) c Kuiper b Base	4
M. R. Ramprakash lbw b Base	1	– (3) lbw b Base	8
D. L. Haynes b Mortensen	12	– (1) c Kuiper b Mortensen	8
K. R. Brown c Krikken b Base	7	– (4) c Kuiper b Mortensen	12
P. R. Downton c and b Mortensen	4	– (6) c Barnett b Base	3
J. E. Emburey b Miller	14	– (7) c Bowler b Jean-Jacques	12
A. R. C. Fraser b Base	8	– st Krikken b Miller	26
C. R. Tufnell c O'Gorman b Miller	10	– lbw b Miller	5
N. G. Cowans c Jean-Jacques b Miller	0	– not out	5
B 10, l-b 7, n-b 5	22	B 8, l-b 2, n-b 1	11

1/13 2/17 3/28 4/79 5/89	209	1/4 2/18 3/22 4/28 5/37	99
6/97 7/155 8/166 9/205		6/38 7/41 8/88 9/94	

Bonus points – Middlesex 2, Derbyshire 4.

Bowling: *First Innings*—Base 27–4–92–3; Mortensen 22–11–29–4; Miller 14.5–3–31–3; Jean-Jacques 15–2–40–0. *Second Innings*—Mortensen 10–4–21–1; Base 14–3–28–5; Miller 5–3–21–3; Jean-Jacques 5–0–19–1.

Umpires: J. C. Balderstone and P. B. Wight.

DERBYSHIRE v ESSEX

At Derby, August 23, 24. Essex won by an innings and 94 runs. Essex 24 pts, Derbyshire 3 pts. Toss: Derbyshire. For the second time in five weeks, Derbyshire were totally outplayed by Essex. After the deduction of 25 points earlier in the week, more grass was left on to hold the Derby pitch together, but it was woefully inadequate batting, rather than the green tinge, which caused the collapse against Foster and Ilott. Only Bishop gave evidence of sound technique as Ilott returned the best figures of his career to date. Prichard, who completed his fourth century of the season from 201 balls with eleven fours, and Waugh shared a stand of 126 in 38 overs, and although Essex did not make the most of their position, a lead of 221 was more than adequate. The impressive Ilott dismissed Barnett cheaply for a second time and, despite some hectic counter-attacking by Adams and Goldsmith, Derbyshire collapsed again. They batted for fewer than 80 overs in the match and nothing impeded Essex as they emphasised their challenge for the Championship.

Close of play: First day, Essex 207-3 (P. J. Prichard 65*, M. C. Ilott 2*).

Derbyshire

K. J. Barnett lbw b Ilott	4	– b Ilott	3
D. Bowler c Waugh b Ilott	11	– b Foster	5
J. G. O'Gorman c Garnham b Foster	1	– c Garnham b Foster	4
J. Adams c Garnham b Foster	0	– c Garnham b Andrew	41
B. Roberts b Ilott	13	– c and b Foster	7
C. Goldsmith c Shahid b Foster	11	– lbw b Andrew	32
K. M. Krikken b Ilott	2	– c Waugh b Ilott	14
G. Miller c Garnham b Foster	19	– absent ill	
R. Bishop not out	39	– (8) lbw b Andrew	17
A. E. Warner c Garnham b Foster	4	– (9) lbw b Andrew	0
M. Jean-Jacques lbw b Ilott	0	– (10) not out	0
L-b 6	6	L-b 4	4

1/5 2/16 3/16 4/17 5/41	110	1/8 2/12 3/12 4/22 5/84	127
6/41 7/47 8/91 9/101		6/99 7/125 8/125 9/127	

Bonus points – Essex 4.

Bowling: *First Innings*—Foster 16–6–39–5; Ilott 18.4–8–34–5; Andrew 6–2–18–0; Pring 3–0–13–0. *Second Innings*—Ilott 10.4–3–34–2; Foster 11–1–57–3; Andrew 11–2–30–4; Child 3–2–2–0.

Essex

N. Shahid c Krikken b Warner	55	N. A. Foster c Adams b Bishop		2
J. P. Stephenson c Adams b Warner	11	J. H. Childs c Krikken b Bishop		
P. J. Prichard run out	103	S. J. W. Andrew not out		
M. E. Waugh c Barnett b Jean-Jacques	61			
M. C. Ilott c Adams b Bishop	6	L-b 6, w 3, n-b 11		2
N. Hussain c Adams b Goldsmith	28			
†M. A. Garnham c Roberts b Warner	8	1/59 2/79 3/205 4/234		
*D. R. Pringle b Goldsmith	0	5/274 6/284 7/284 8/294 9/316		33

Bonus points – Essex 4, Derbyshire 3 (Score at 100 overs: 306-8).

Bowling: Bishop 23.5–7–57–3; Warner 24–7–56–3; Jean-Jacques 24–3–105–1; Goldsmith 33–6–105–2; Barnett 1–0–2–0.

Umpires: D. J. Constant and R. Julian.

At Cardiff, August 29, 30, 31. DERBYSHIRE drew with GLAMORGAN.

At Scarborough, September 7, 8, 9, 10. DERBYSHIRE lost to YORKSHIRE by four wickets

DERBYSHIRE v LEICESTERSHIRE

At Derby, September 18, 19, 20, 21. Drawn. Derbyshire 6 pts, Leicestershire 6 pts. Toss Derbyshire. After a good start, Leicestershire lost their last nine wickets while adding 60 on a bleakly cold first day which set the tone for a cheerless match. Briers and Whitaker added 13 in 39 overs before Bishop took four for 3 in 21 balls, Briers falling 1 run short of his sixth century of the season. Mortensen finished the innings with three for 1 in fourteen balls. Fewer than two hours of play were possible on the second day, but on the third O'Gorman, who spent much of the summer at Law School, reached 100 from 185 balls, with thirteen fours. It was Derbyshire's 21st first-class century of the season, a county record, but there was little assistance for O'Gorman as Lewis took five for 4 in 36 balls. Briers was 4 short of 2,000 runs when Leicestershire collapsed to 9 for three before the close, leaving themselves to bat through for survival on the final day.

Close of play: First day, Derbyshire 19-1 (T. J. G. O'Gorman 9*, K. M. Krikken 1*). Second day, Derbyshire 124-3 (T. J. G. O'Gorman 64*, C. J. Adams 29*). Third day, Leicestershire 9-3 (J. J. Whitaker 0*, L. Potter 0*).

Leicestershire

T. J. Boon c Barnett b Base	15	lbw b Base		
*N. E. Briers b Bishop	99	b Bishop		
J. J. Whitaker c Barnett b Base	65	c Barnett b Bishop		2
P. Willey b Bishop	1	b Base		
L. Potter c Krikken b Bishop	2	lbw b Barnett		6
C. C. Lewis lbw b Bishop	0	(7) c Adams b Base		5
P. N. Hepworth not out	14	(6) not out		5
†P. A. Nixon c Roberts b Bishop	17			
C. J. Hawkes c Krikken b Mortensen	3	(8) not out		
J. P. Agnew c Krikken b Mortensen	6			
A. D. Mullally lbw b Mortensen	0			
B 5, l-b 10, w 2, n-b 8	25	B 1, l-b 9, n-b 1		1

1/54 2/187 3/196 4/197 5/197	247	1/9 2/9 3/9 4/48	(6 wkts) 21
6/200 7/221 8/233 9/247		5/136 6/209	

Bonus points – Leicestershire 2, Derbyshire 4.

Bowling: *First Innings*—Bishop 26–8–62–5; Mortensen 22.3–8–40–3; Base 18–6–51–2; Cork 10–1–39–0; Goldsmith 14–2–40–0. *Second Innings*—Bishop 14–4–39–2; Base 18–7–51–3; Cork 14.5–31–0; Mortensen 12–2–43–0; Adams 3–0–12–0; Barnett 20–6–30–1.

Derbyshire

*K. J. Barnett b Lewis	4	I. R. Bishop c Nixon b Lewis	3
T. J. G. O'Gorman c Hawkes		S. J. Base b Lewis	2
b Mullally	100	D. G. Cork c Briers b Mullally	7
†K. M. Krikken b Mullally	1	O. H. Mortensen not out	5
B. Roberts b Agnew	15	L-b 12, n-b 5	17
C. J. Adams b Lewis	54		
Z. A. Sadiq b Lewis	0	1/18 2/19 3/77 4/175 5/181	208
S. C. Goldsmith b Lewis	0	6/181 7/189 8/195 9/195	

Bonus points – Derbyshire 2, Leicestershire 4.

Bowling: Lewis 24–4–58–6; Mullally 20–7–56–3; Agnew 10–1–42–1; Hawkes 14–3–40–0.

Umpires: H. D. Bird and R. A. White.

OVERS BOWLED AND RUNS SCORED IN THE BRITANNIC ASSURANCE CHAMPIONSHIP, 1990

	Over-rate per hour			Run-rate per 100 balls		
	1st half	*2nd half*	*Total*	*1st half*	*2nd half*	*Total*
Derbyshire (12)	18.0979	17.8088*	17.9533	53.6269	53.5073	53.5702
Essex (2)	18.2686	18.2253	18.2453	62.4260	65.2450	63.8246
Glamorgan (8)	18.3779	18.3022	18.3408	54.2284	60.1199	57.2519
Gloucestershire (13=)	17.7610*	18.1417	17.9718	49.7259	51.6533	50.9107
Hampshire (3)	18.0425	18.1264	18.0887	56.4806	54.3076	55.2756
Kent (16)	18.2448	18.5674	18.4175	49.7421	57.0352	53.6008
Lancashire (6)	18.1837	18.1257	18.1550	54.3865	58.7860	56.4164
Leicestershire (7)	17.8532*	18.0865	17.9879	50.6758	51.2370	50.9597
Middlesex (1)	18.9109	18.2565	18.5390	54.6164	61.1399	58.0269
Northamptonshire (11)	17.8331*	18.1644	18.0078	54.6617	62.5912	58.9522
Nottinghamshire (13=)	18.1004	18.0883	18.0944	57.6759	51.1340	54.1506
Somerset (15)	18.1044	18.1669	18.1359	59.5397	57.8061	58.5453
Surrey (9)	17.4340†	17.9146*	17.6866	54.4643	57.8941	56.2931
Sussex (17)	18.0586	18.0742	18.0668	54.2411	48.3362	51.1698
Warwickshire (5)	18.1984	17.6749*	17.9211	55.8116	54.9363	55.3335
Worcestershire (4)	18.2891	18.4505	18.3768	54.9120	55.5606	55.2643
Yorkshire (10)	18.1824	18.1315	18.1537	51.6132	55.9143	53.9978
1990	average rate		18.1260			55.5025
1989	average rate		18.3621			50.6788
1988	average rate		18.9202			49.9340
1987	average rate		18.64			51.79
1986	average rate		18.49			52.22
1985	average rate		18.43			52.61

1990 Championship positions are shown in brackets.
* £2,000 fine.   † £3,000 fine.

ESSEX

President: T. N. Pearce
Chairman: D. J. Insole
Chairman, Cricket Committee: G. J. Saville
Secretary/General Manager: P. J. Edwards
County Ground, New Writtle Street,
Chelmsford CM2 0PG
(Telephone: 0245-252420)
Captain: G. A. Gooch

In finishing runners-up in the Britannic Assurance Championship for the second successive year, Essex again ended the season nursing acute pangs of disappointment. Yet their achievement represented something of a success, for in the second week of July they were only three places off the foot of the table. A surge in August, during which they won four matches, saw them emerge as title contenders; but failure to win any of their four final games, when dropped catches cost them dearly, kept them in second place behind Middlesex. In the limited-overs competitions, however, Essex were never seen as a potent force. Defeat in the opening four games of the Refuge Assurance League soon relegated them to "also-rans", and they failed to make home advantage count in the quest to reach a Lord's final. Nottinghamshire beat them by six wickets in their Benson and Hedges Cup quarter-final, while in the second round of the NatWest Bank Trophy, Hampshire won because they lost fewer wickets in equalling the Essex total of 307 for six.

It was through no fault of Graham Gooch that Essex failed to land any of the domestic honours. His deeds at Test level, highlighted by his 333 at Lord's, are well chronicled elsewhere, and he also maintained a phenomenal level of consistency for his county. In the eleven first-class matches in which he batted for them, he never once failed to record at least 50, and only a broken thumb, suffered while fielding against Kent in the penultimate fixture, cost him the opportunity of becoming the first batsman since W. E. Alley in 1961 to register 3,000 runs in a season. No doubt he was satisfied with a golden harvest of 2,746 for a first-class average of 101.70 and a total of eighteen hundreds in all forms of cricket.

Mark Waugh, with an elegant ease bordering on arrogance, displayed a rich talent, and even when confronted with the occasional pitch giving encouragement to bowlers, he showed an ability to gather runs fluently. He contributed eight Championship centuries, including double-hundreds against Gloucestershire and Yorkshire, and an aggregate in excess of 2,000 runs. That landmark was one which narrowly eluded John Stephenson, who showed great character in overcoming a wretched start to the season. By early June he had scored just 265 runs in twelve innings, but in twelve of his remaining eighteen first-class games he collected eleven half-centuries and four centuries, including a career-best 202 not out against Somerset. Paul Prichard was another to record a personal best, scoring 245 in only the second Championship match of the summer, against Leicestershire, on a sweltering Chelmsford day. With Gooch he shared a record-breaking second-wicket partnership of 403, the highest stand for any Essex wicket, and Essex's eventual 761 for six declared was the biggest total in the county's history. Neil Foster reached three figures for the first time before Gooch called off the assault on the Leicestershire bowlers.

Nasser Hussain, on the other hand, could not look back on the summer with any real degree of satisfaction. His inspired form the previous season had earned him a place in the England team to the West Indies, but while there he had fractured his wrist. That injury kept him out of first-class cricket until June 30, and his lack of form on his return, combined with an erosion of confidence, was such that he passed 50 only twice in thirteen Championship matches before, in the final game of the season, scoring 197 against Surrey. By then, however, his hopes of regaining a place in the England side had long disappeared, although selection for the A tour provided an opportunity for him to rediscover his touch.

Foster was easily the pick of the bowlers. There were fears at the outset that his knees would not stand up to the rigours of a gruelling summer, especially on hard grounds. But he swept those aside by displaying remarkable resilience and stamina to send down more than 800 overs in the Championship and emerge as the country's leading wicket-taker with 94 victims, six times claiming five or more wickets in an innings. Unfortunately, the attack lacked anyone with the same degree of penetration at the other end. Derek Pringle missed several matches with a troublesome back, while Steve Andrew, despite the occasional match-winning performance, struggled for consistency. There were no rich pickings for the spinners, having to bowl on unhelpful pitches. John Childs, although missing only the opening game, managed just 27 first-class wickets at an average of 58.88, and Peter Such's eleven matches produced a mere twenty dismissals.

Probably the most pleasing aspect was the performance of the younger players. Nadeem Shahid grasped the opportunity to prove himself a fluent batsman and was rewarded with just over 1,000 runs, including a maiden century against Lancashire at Colchester. In addition, he demonstrated a fearlessness in the bat-pad position, where he held several fine catches. Mark Ilott, a left-arm seam bowler, impressed sufficiently to suggest that Essex have quickly found a successor to John Lever, while twenty-year-old Jonathan Lewis, brought into the side for the final fixture against Surrey, marked his first-class début with an unbeaten 116 in his only innings.

One familiar face which will be missing in the months ahead is that of Brian Hardie, the Scot whose ready quip and smile were features of the county circuit for almost two decades. Although his style often defied the coaching manuals, there was never any doubt as to the success of his methods, or to his fierce determination and tremendous value to the side. Following a playing career which brought him 18,103 first-class runs, and well over 400 catches in all competitions, many of them at short leg, he left to take up a post as coach at Brentwood School. Another departure was that of Ray East, the county's youth development officer, an appointment now entrusted to Alan Lilley. East also moved to a school, in Ipswich, and Essex will be pleased that he and Hardie have pursued careers from which the county will undoubtedly benefit in the years ahead. – Nigel Fuller.

ESSEX 1990

[Bill Smith]

Back row: M. A. Garnham, P. M. Such, M. E. Waugh, K. O. Thomas, A. C. Seymour, A. G. J. Fraser, J. J. B. Lewis, K. A. Butler, N. Shahid. Middle row: R. Cole (physiotherapist), D. J. P. Boden, T. D. Topley, J. P. Stephenson, A. W. Lilley, A. T. Van-Lint, N. V. Knight, M. C. Ilott, S. J. W. Andrew. Front row: P. J. Prichard, J. H. Childs, D. E. East, D. R. Pringle, G. A. Gooch (captain), K. W. R. Fletcher, N. A. Foster, B. R. Hardie, N. Hussain.

ESSEX RESULTS

All first-class matches – Played 24: Won 9, Lost 2, Drawn 13.

County Championship matches – Played 22: Won 8, Lost 2, Drawn 12.

Bonus points – Batting 73, Bowling 56.

Competition placings – Britannic Assurance County Championship, 2nd;
NatWest Bank Trophy, 2nd round; Benson and Hedges Cup, q-f;
Refuge Assurance League, 12th.

BRITANNIC ASSURANCE CHAMPIONSHIP AVERAGES

BATTING

	Birthplace	*M*	*I*	*NO*	*R*	*HI*	*Avge*
‡G. A. Gooch	*Leytonstone*	11	18	2	1,586	215	99.12
‡M. E. Waugh	*Sydney, Australia*	21	32	6	2,009	207*	77.26
‡B. R. Hardie	*Stenhousemuir*	11	15	5	650	125	65.00
‡J. P. Stephenson	*Stebbing*	22	37	7	1,525	202*	50.83
N. Shahid	*Karachi, Pakistan*	18	27	7	964	125	48.20
‡P. J. Prichard	*Billericay*	20	30	3	1,276	245	47.25
‡N. Hussain	*Madras, India*	14	21	2	714	197	37.57
‡M. A. Garnham ...	*Johannesburg, SA*	22	26	7	589	84*	31.00
‡D. R. Pringle	*Nairobi, Kenya*	15	13	2	318	84	28.90
‡N. A. Foster	*Colchester*	22	22	2	530	101	26.50
P. M. Such	*Helensburgh*	10	5	3	44	27	22.00
‡T. D. Topley	*Canterbury*	7	4	1	55	23	18.33
M. C. Ilott	*Watford*	8	10	2	123	42*	15.37
S. J. W. Andrew ...	*London*	16	15	7	119	35	14.87
‡J. H. Childs	*Plymouth*	21	16	5	123	26	11.18

Also batted: J. J. B. Lewis (*Isleworth*) (1 match) 116*; ‡A. W. Lilley (*Ilford*) (1 match) 1; A. C. Seymour (*Royston*) (2 matches) 10*, 0, 4*.

* Signifies not out.   *‡ Denotes county cap.*

The following played a total of 27 three-figure innings for Essex in County Championship matches – M. E. Waugh 8, G. A. Gooch 7, P. J. Prichard 4, B. R. Hardie 2, J. P. Stephenson 2, N. A. Foster 1, N. Hussain 1, J. J. B. Lewis 1, N. Shahid 1.

BOWLING

	O	*M*	*R*	*W*	*BB*	*5W/i*	*Avge*
N. A. Foster	819.2	175	2,502	94	6-32	6	26.61
D. R. Pringle	325.3	82	927	29	5-66	1	31.96
T. D. Topley	178	26	557	16	4-67	0	34.81
P. M. Such	252.3	58	682	18	3-34	0	37.88
M. C. Ilott	289.1	60	951	25	5-34	1	38.04
S. J. W. Andrew	449	67	1,763	43	5-55	1	41.00
J. H. Childs	595.1	189	1,435	25	4-56	0	57.40
M. E. Waugh	183	33	731	12	5-37	1	60.91

Also bowled: G. A. Gooch 35–8–125–0; B. R. Hardie 1–0–16–0; N. Hussain 4–1–29–0; A. W. Lilley 1–0–7–0; P. J. Prichard 1.4–0–11–0; N. Shahid 106.2–18–413–7; J. P. Stephenson 96–22–383–3.

Wicket-keeper: M. A. Garnham 45 ct, 1 st.

Leading Fielders: N. Shahid 22, M. E. Waugh 18.

At Lord's, April 26, 27, 28, 30. ESSEX drew with MIDDLESEX.

ESSEX v LEICESTERSHIRE

At Chelmsford, May 3, 4, 5, 7. Drawn. Essex 5 pts, Leicestershire 3 pts. Toss: Leicestershire. Gooch and Prichard, the latter recording the highest score of his career, both hit double-hundreds and shared in a second-wicket stand of 403. This was the highest for any wicket by an Essex pair and helped take the county to the highest score in their history, beating their 692 against Somerset at Taunton in 1895. Gooch struck 28 fours and a six in his 215 and Prichard 31 fours and two 6s in his 245. Later Foster raced to his maiden century from just 79 balls, five of which he hit for six. Earlier Lewis had taken full advantage of the docile pitch to collect his first century, and there were five sixes among his 21 boundaries in a stay of six hours. Briers joined the list of century-makers when Leicestershire batted a second time, and with Briers and Boon putting on their second century opening partnership, Leicestershire had no difficulty in saving the match after trailing by 241 on first innings.

Close of play: First day, Leicestershire 323-6 (C. C. Lewis 57*, M. I. Gidley 2*); Second day, Essex 158-1 (G. A. Gooch 73*, P. J. Prichard 38*); Third day, Essex 712-5 (B. R. Hardie 52*, N. A. Foster 83*).

Leicestershire

T. J. Boon lbw b Such	90	– c Waugh b Childs	89
*N. E. Briers c Garnham b Such	65	– c Garnham b Such	104
J. J. Whitaker c and b Such	31	– b Stephenson	15
L. Potter c Prichard b Waugh	62	– not out	16
J. D. R. Benson c Shahid b Foster	8	– not out	10
C. C. Lewis not out	189		
†P. Whitticase lbw b Waugh	0		
M. I. Gidley c and b Shahid	9		
J. P. Agnew lbw b Shahid	37		
G. J. F. Ferris c Waugh b Foster	11		
A. D. Mullally b Foster	3		
B 1, l-b 9, w 4, n-b 1	15	B 5, l-b 3, w 1, n-b 6	15

1/145 2/178 3/197 4/214   520   1/170 2/205 3/236   (3 wkts) 249
5/303 6/309 7/458 8/460 9/498

Bonus points – Leicestershire 3, Essex 1 (Score at 100 overs: 294-4).

In the first innings M. I. Gidley, when 9, retired hurt at 371 and resumed at 458.

Bowling: *First Innings*—Foster 41–8–102–3; Andrew 20–3–72–0; Waugh 23–5–76–2; Childs 41–14–88–0; Such 43–7–118–3; Shahid 13–1–54–2. *Second Innings*—Foster 8–2–30–0; Andrew 9–1–31–0; Childs 33–10–93–1; Shahid 11–3–42–0; Such 19–9–29–1; Stephenson 9–5–16–1.

Essex

*G. A. Gooch c Whitticase b Lewis	215	N. A. Foster run out	101
J. P. Stephenson c Lewis b Mullally	35		
P. J. Prichard c Briers b Mullally	245	B 9, l-b 20, w 3, n-b 16	48
M. E. Waugh b Lewis	43		
B. R. Hardie not out	74	1/82 2/485 3/551 (6 wkts dec.) 761
†M. A. Garnham b Lewis	0	4/587 5/589 6/761

N. Shahid, J. H. Childs, S. J. W. Andrew and P. M. Such did not bat.

Bonus points – Essex 4 (Score at 100 overs: 435-1).

Bowling: Mullally 31–3–124–2; Agnew 35.5–4–170–0; Ferris 23–2–100–0; Lewis 28–3–115–3; Potter 14–0–91–0; Gidley 25–3–121–0; Benson 2–0–11–0.

Umpires: K. E. Palmer and D. R. Shepherd.

†ESSEX v ZIMBABWEANS

At Chelmsford, May 14. Essex won by 71 runs. Toss: Essex. Having dropped himself down the order, Gooch watched his early batsmen struggle to 83 for four before he emerged in the 27th over of this 55-over contest to stamp his authority on the innings. He did so with a century off only 78 balls, his batting contrasting with Stephenson's laboured effort of 163 deliveries. Only Pycroft provided prolonged resistance when the Zimbabweans replied, but he could not prevent Essex from winning with ease.

Essex

J. P. Stephenson c Arnott b Jarvis 105	P. J. Prichard not out	3
A. C. Seymour lbw b Brandes 6	N. A. Foster not out	4
A. W. Lilley run out 12	L-b 12, n-b 4	16
M. E. Waugh b Duers 0		—
*M. A. Garnham c Robertson b Duers . 14	1/7 2/49 3/50 (6 wkts, 55 overs)	265
†G. A. Gooch c Briant b Jarvis 105	4/83 5/258 6/258	

T. D. Topley, J. H. Childs and S. J. W. Andrew did not bat.

Bowling: Brandes 11–2–58–1; Jarvis 10–2–44–2; Shah 6–0–20–0; Duers 11–0–52–2; Traicos 11–0–45–0; Brent 6–0–34–0.

Zimbabweans

K. J. Arnott c Garnham b Andrew 6	M. P. Jarvis c Waugh b Foster 5
A. H. Shah c Garnham b Andrew 0	A. J. Traicos not out 8
*W. R. James b Andrew 27	K. G. Duers b Foster 1
*A. J. Pycroft c Prichard b Stephenson . 62	L-b 8, w 12, n-b 6 26
C. M. Robertson c Seymour b Andrew . 3		—
G. A. Briant b Childs 17	1/1 2/21 3/46 (51.1 overs) 194
A. P. Brent lbw b Stephenson 32	4/60 5/95 6/170
E. A. Brandes c Prichard b Stephenson . 7	7/173 8/180 9/184

Bowling: Foster 8.1–2–19–2; Andrew 11–1–36–4; Gooch 7–1–17–0; Topley 5–0–29–0; Childs 11–1–37–1; Waugh 5–0–22–0; Stephenson 4–0–26–3.

Umpires: P. J. Eele and A. G. T. Whitehead.

At Cambridge, May 16, 17, 18. ESSEX beat CAMBRIDGE UNIVERSITY by 120 runs.

At Worcester, May 19, 21, 22. ESSEX beat WORCESTERSHIRE by ten wickets.

At Southampton, May 23, 24, 25. ESSEX drew with HAMPSHIRE.

ESSEX v MIDDLESEX

At Ilford, June 2, 4, 5. Drawn. Essex 3 pts, Middlesex 8 pts. Toss: Middlesex. Essex had to wait until after tea on the opening day for their first success, by which time Roseberry had registered a career-best 135, which featured 23 fours and a six. The immaculate Haynes continued to accumulate his runs with superb timing on either side of the wicket, and he never looked in the slightest trouble while gathering 33 fours in a day-long effort which also produced a career best. His unbeaten 220 at the close was only the second double-hundred of his distinguished career. Essex never recovered from the early loss of Gooch, despite the fighting qualities of Hardie, but the Essex and England captain was at his imperious best as Essex easily saved the match after being asked to follow on 185 behind. Gooch hit nineteen boundaries, including two sixes, and following his departure, Prichard and Waugh further frustrated the visitors.

Close of play: First day, Middlesex 442-2 (D. L. Haynes 220*, M. R. Ramprakash 30*); Second day, Essex 91-1 (G. A. Gooch 57*, N. A. Foster 2*).

Middlesex

D. L. Haynes not out 220	
M. A. Roseberry c Prichard b Foster ..135	
*M. W. Gatting b Pringle 34	
M. R. Ramprakash not out 30	
B 4, l-b 11, w 3, n-b 5 23	

1/306 2/369   (2 wkts dec.) 442

K. R. Brown, †P. R. Downton, N. F. Williams, J. E. Emburey, S. P. Hughes, M. J. Thursfield and P. C. R. Tufnell did not bat.

Bonus points – Middlesex 4 (Score at 100 overs: 377-2).

Bowling: Foster 18-6-60-1; Pringle 22-8-66-1; Andrew 14-3-61-0; Gooch 9-2-36-0; Childs 17-1-58-0; Stephenson 10-2-36-0; Such 9-2-41-0; Waugh 15-2-69-0.

Essex

*G. A. Gooch c Downton b Hughes 0	– c Brown b Tufnell 120	
J. P. Stephenson c Downton b Williams 16	– c Brown b Tufnell 31	
P. J. Prichard c Downton b Thursfield 7	– (4) not out 56	
M. E. Waugh c Haynes b Emburey 39	– (5) not out 59	
B. R. Hardie c Downton b Hughes 74		
†M. A. Garnham lbw b Emburey 36		
D. R. Pringle c Downton b Emburey 8		
N. A. Foster c Brown b Emburey 0	– (3) c Gatting b Williams 13	
S. J. W. Andrew c Roseberry b Emburey 15		
J. H. Childs not out 10		
P. M. Such b Williams 27		
L-b 17, n-b 8 25	B 8, l-b 8, n-b 10 26	

1/2 2/19 3/31 4/83 5/153   257   1/88 2/112 3/201   (3 wkts) 305
6/168 7/170 8/205 9/213

Bonus points – Essex 3, Middlesex 4.

Bowling: *First Innings*—Williams 19.5-4-58-2; Hughes 14-2-43-2; Thursfield 8-2-24-1; Tufnell 27-7-54-0; Emburey 24-7-61-5. *Second Innings*—Hughes 12-2-58-0; Williams 18-4-57-1; Thursfield 9-2-21-0; Emburey 32-9-80-0; Tufnell 33-12-73-2.

Umpires: B. Leadbeater and B. J. Meyer.

ESSEX v GLOUCESTERSHIRE

At Ilford, June 6, 7, 8. Drawn. Essex 6 pts, Gloucestershire 4 pts. Toss: Essex. Rain was the only winner, restricting the final day's play to fewer than 90 minutes. When Seymour, deputising for Gooch, was forced to retire with a broken hand after being struck by Walsh, Waugh took full advantage of an easy-paced pitch to post his first double-hundred. His 204 contained 92 in boundaries and spanned 291 minutes and 267 deliveries. Hardie, whose second century of the season was a subdued affair, containing just half-a-dozen boundaries, gave the Australian fine support as they added 242 for the third wicket. Essex's overnight declaration left Gloucestershire with a draw as the height of their ambitions. A dour 92 from Wright, plus a more aggressive half-century by Bainbridge, ensured that the follow-on was avoided, but in the end the weather had the final say.

Close of play: First day, Essex 425-4 (B. R. Hardie 110*, M. A. Garnham 20*); Second day, Gloucestershire 289-6 (J. W. Lloyds 29*, G. A. Tedstone 9*).

Essex

P. Stephenson b Lawrence	1	– (2) not out	35
A. C. Seymour retired hurt	4		
J. Prichard c Curran b Bainbridge	45		
M. E. Waugh b Graveney	204		
R. Hardie not out	110	– (1) c Tedstone b Walsh	13
N. Shahid c Lawrence b Curran	15	– (3) not out	14
M. A. Garnham not out	20		
B 8, l-b 6, w 1, n-b 11	26	L-b 1, w 3, n-b 1	5

1/2 2/105 3/347 4/388   (4 wkts. dec.) 425   1/23   (1 wkt) 67

D. R. Pringle, N. A. Foster, J. H. Childs and P. M. Such did not bat.

Bonus points – Essex 4, Gloucestershire 1 (Score at 100 overs: 411-4).

In the first innings A. C. Seymour retired hurt at 16.

Bowling: *First Innings*—Walsh 16–2–60–0; Lawrence 11–0–57–1; Curran 19–2–93–1; Graveney 27–2–101–1; Bainbridge 18–2–65–1; Lloyds 11–1–35–0. *Second Innings*—Bainbridge 4–0–11–0; Athey 7–1–25–0; Lawrence 6–1–17–0; Walsh 9–6–8–1; Lloyds 2–1–4–0; Tedstone 2–1–1–0.

Gloucestershire

A. J. Wright b Foster	92	†G. A. Tedstone c Garnham b Foster	13
G. D. Hodgson c sub b Foster	27	D. A. Graveney not out	0
P. Butcher c Waugh b Foster	5	B 6, l-b 4, n-b 10	20
C. W. J. Athey run out	9		
P. Bainbridge run out	64	1/58 2/88 3/111 (7 wkts. dec.) 298	
K. M. Curran c Garnham b Childs	39	4/170 5/235	
M. W. Lloyds not out	29	6/264 7/298	

C. A. Walsh and D. V. Lawrence did not bat.

Bonus points – Gloucestershire 3, Essex 2 (Score at 100 overs: 283-6).

Bowling: Foster 32.4–5–104–4; Pringle 18–3–52–0; Childs 32–16–48–1; Such 9–2–34–0; Waugh 7–3–17–0; Stephenson 7–1–33–0.

Umpires: B. Leadbeater and B. J. Meyer.

At Birmingham, June 9, 11, 12. ESSEX lost to WARWICKSHIRE by five wickets.

At Bath, June 16, 18, 19. ESSEX drew with SOMERSET.

At Chelmsford, June 30, July 1, 2. ESSEX drew with NEW ZEALANDERS (See New Zealand tour section).

At Maidstone, July 4, 5, 6. ESSEX beat KENT by four wickets.

ESSEX v DERBYSHIRE

At Colchester, July 18, 19, 20. Essex won by nine wickets. Essex 24 pts, Derbyshire 7 pts. Toss: Derbyshire. The match swung decisively in Essex's favour after tea on the second day as Derbyshire set out to clear a first-innings deficit of 98. Foster removed Barnett and Brown in his opening over and, underlining the virtue of line and length on a pitch affording generous bounce, went on to take six for 49 as the visitors surrendered meekly. Only brave resistance from Krikken took the match into the third day, when just 45 minutes were needed. Roberts batted spiritedly in Derbyshire's first innings, while Waugh, with his fifth Championship century of the summer, one containing sixteen fours and two sixes, displayed great authority and excellent timing in the Essex reply. Hussain also batted attractively while he and Waugh shared the only three-figure partnership of the match.

Close of play: First day, Essex 62-1 (B. R. Hardie 15*, N. Shahid 29*); Second day, Esse
5-0 (B. R. Hardie 4*, J. P. Stephenson 0*).

Derbyshire

*K. J. Barnett c Stephenson b Foster	38	– c Shahid b Foster	
P. D. Bowler b Childs	33	– b Foster	
A. M. Brown c Garnham b Foster	3	– c Garnham b Foster	
B. Roberts c Shahid b Andrew	56	– c Hardie b Andrew	2
C. J. Adams c Hussain b Andrew	33	– lbw b Foster	
S. C. Goldsmith c Hardie b Such	11	– lbw b Foster	2
†K. M. Krikken c Hardie b Andrew	4	– b Childs	4
I. R. Bishop lbw b Foster	26	– c Such b Foster	
A. E. Warner c Shahid b Such	0	– lbw b Andrew	
G. Miller not out	24	– not out	18
S. J. Base c Garnham b Andrew	26	– b Such	
B 1, l-b 8, n-b 5	14	L-b 2, w 4, n-b 2	8

1/67 2/71 3/85 4/170 5/176   268   1/1 2/1 3/26 4/34 5/53   14
6/188 7/198 8/203 9/231   6/66 7/84 8/94 9/132

Bonus points – Derbyshire 3, Essex 4.

Bowling: *First Innings*—Foster 24-4-75-3; Andrew 15.5-4-60-4; Childs 19-7-57-1
Pringle 6-1-31-0; Such 17-3-36-2. *Second Innings*—Foster 15-2-49-6; Andrew 9-2-49-2
Pringle 8-1-31-0; Childs 7-4-7-1; Such 2-0-7-1.

Essex

B. R. Hardie c Brown b Warner	24	– not out	4
J. P. Stephenson c Krikken b Bishop	1	– c Krikken b Bishop	
N. Shahid c Krikken b Goldsmith	42	– not out	
M. E. Waugh c Krikken b Miller	126		
N. Hussain c Krikken b Bishop	60		
†M. A. Garnham c Krikken b Bishop	16		
*D. R. Pringle b Miller	30		
N. A. Foster b Barnett	32		
J. H. Childs c Base b Barnett	2		
S. J. W. Andrew c Roberts b Miller	1		
P. M. Such not out	0		
L-b 9, w 6, n-b 17	32	L-b 1, w 1	2

1/5 2/72 3/109 4/237 5/267   366   1/32   (1 wkt) 5
6/310 7/359 8/363 9/366

Bonus points – Essex 4, Derbyshire 4.

Bowling: *First Innings*—Bishop 23-7-41-3; Warner 24-2-76-1; Base 17-2-90-0; Mille
25-0-113-3; Goldsmith 7-0-25-1; Barnett 4-0-12-2. *Second Innings*—Bishop 5-2-21-1; Base
4.3-0-29-0.

Umpires: P. J. Eele and N. T. Plews.

ESSEX v LANCASHIRE

At Colchester, July 21, 23, 24. Essex won by six wickets. Essex 24 pts, Lancashire 8 pts. Toss
Lancashire. Gooch led Essex to a spectacular victory with an over to spare after they had been
set the daunting task of making 348 in 54 overs. He scored 177 from 152 balls, 21 of which he
despatched to the boundary, to inspire his county's third successive Championship win. On a
benign pitch, Stephenson and Waugh provided the chief support with brisk half-centuries
Atherton and Fairbrother, who included three sixes among his nineteen boundaries, had hi

nbeaten hundreds in a stand of 220 to set up Lancashire's declaration. Hegg rescued ancashire on the first day with 100 not out off 150 deliveries, while for Essex 21-year-old hahid played with maturity and style in making 125, his maiden first-class century, which cluded 21 fours. Having moved from fifteenth place in the Championship to seventh in two ames, Essex could look back on their week at Colchester with considerable satisfaction.

Close of play: First day, Essex 24-0 (G. A. Gooch 3*, J. P. Stephenson 20*); Second day, ancashire 104-2 (M. A. Atherton 20*, N. H. Fairbrother 51*).

ancashire

. D. Mendis c Shahid b Andrew	9	– lbw b Childs 20
. Fowler b Foster	12	– c Pringle b Foster 9
1. A. Atherton c Shahid b Pringle	11	– not out 108
1. H. Fairbrother c Gooch b Pringle	24	– not out 109
. E. Jesty c Garnham b Childs	66	
1. Watkinson c Garnham b Pringle	45	
Vasim Akram b Pringle	0	
. A. J. DeFreitas c Foster b Such	41	
W. K. Hegg not out	100	
D. P. Hughes run out	57	
. J. W. Allott not out	10	
B 4, l-b 6, w 1, n-b 9	20	B 1, l-b 2, n-b 3 6

/24 2/24 3/38 4/70 5/161   (9 wkts dec.) 395   1/24 2/32   (2 wkts dec.) 252
/162 7/190 8/262 9/375

Bonus points – Lancashire 4, Essex 4 (Score at 100 overs: 389-9).

Bowling: *First Innings*—Foster 20-1-98-1; Andrew 20-2-81-1; Pringle 17-3-47-4; Such 6-4-57-1; Stephenson 2-0-11-0; Childs 19.4-3-63-1; Shahid 6-2-28-0. *Second Innings*—oster 11-3-30-1; Andrew 7-0-51-0; Childs 23-7-45-1; Such 15-3-24-0; Pringle 8-0-38-0; hahid 10-0-46-0; Hussain 2-0-15-0.

ssex

G. A. Gooch c Hegg b DeFreitas	17	– lbw b Atherton 177
. P. Stephenson run out	21	– c Watkinson b Atherton 60
. Shahid c and b Atherton	125	– run out 26
1. E. Waugh c Hegg b DeFreitas	0	– c sub b Atherton 58
1. Hussain c Hegg b Atherton	40	– not out 9
M. A. Garnham lbw b Allott	17	
. R. Pringle c Mendis b Hughes	45	– (6) not out 6
1. A. Foster c and b Atherton	4	
H. Childs not out	13	
. J. W. Andrew b Hughes	0	
. M. Such not out	13	
L-b 2, n-b 3	5	B 3, l-b 7, w 2, n-b 3 15

/39 2/39 3/39 4/130 5/158   (9 wkts dec.) 300   1/158 2/214   (4 wkts) 351
/268 7/270 8/274 9/276   3/331 4/336

Bonus points – Essex 4, Lancashire 4.

Bowling: *First Innings*—Wasim Akram 3-0-19-0; DeFreitas 22.1-4-68-2; Allott 7-2-76-1; Watkinson 6-0-19-0; Atherton 22-3-73-3; Hughes 14-4-43-2. *Second Innings*—•eFreitas 12-0-69-0; Allott 12-1-59-0; Watkinson 10-0-64-0; Hughes 5-0-43-0; Atherton 4-0-106-3.

Umpires: P. J. Eele and N. T. Plews.

t Leicester, July 25, 26, 27. ESSEX drew with LEICESTERSHIRE.

ESSEX v SUSSEX

At Chelmsford, July 28, 30, 31. Drawn. Essex 7 pts, Sussex 6 pts. Toss: Essex. In a thrilling finish, both sides were tantalisingly close to victory after Essex had been set to score 302 in minimum of 43 overs. They finished 4 runs short with their last pair together, a fine 89 from 67 balls by Shahid providing the inspiration for their challenge. In contrast, dour half centuries from Hall were the sheet-anchor for both Sussex innings, and Gould's 122-ball 73 on the opening day, containing twelve fours, was more pleasing to the eye. Waugh also hit twelve fours, as well as a six, as he flowed to his sixth Championship century of the summer from 120 deliveries. Essex then declared, 101 adrift, but Sussex consumed 72.5 overs in adding a further 200 and were able to set a demanding target.

Close of play: First day, Sussex 274-8 (A. I. C. Dodemaide 37*, B. T. P. Donelan 9*). Second day, Sussex 46-1 (J. W. Hall 9*, P. Moores 20*).

Sussex

D. M. Smith c Pringle b Andrew	3	– b Andrew	1?	
J. W. Hall c Pringle b Childs	62	– c Garnham b Topley	5(	
*P. W. G. Parker lbw b Foster	20	– (9) c Andrew b Childs	1⁴	
A. P. Wells c Garnham b Topley	19	– lbw b Pringle	1⁴	
I. J. Gould c Waugh b Topley	73	– c and b Childs	⁴	
C. M. Wells c Stephenson b Topley	0	– lbw b Topley	2?	
A. I. C. Dodemaide not out	79	– not out	3⁴	
†P. Moores c Stephenson b Childs	27	– (3) c Topley b Childs	2⁴	
A. C. S. Pigott c Garnham b Andrew	0	– (8) c Prichard b Childs	⁴	
B. T. P. Donelan b Childs	31	– not out	1?	
R. A. Bunting not out	11			
B 4, l-b 9, n-b 13	26	N-b 10	1(	

1/3 2/47 3/78 4/190 5/190   (9 wkts dec.) 351   1/26 2/69 3/101   (8 wkts dec.) 20(
6/207 7/247 8/254 9/337   4/102 5/131 6/143
                                                     7/145 8/171

Bonus points – Sussex 4, Essex 4 (Score at 100 overs: 337-9).

Bowling: *First Innings*—Foster 26-2-102-1; Andrew 25-4-108-2; Topley 14-2-36-3; Pringle 10-2-29-0; Waugh 2-0-12-0; Childs 25-11-51-3. *Second Innings*—Foster 11-3-23-0; Andrew 13-0-60-1; Childs 30-13-56-4; Shahid 3.5-0-15-0; Pringle 4-2-12-1; Topley 10-1-34-2; Waugh 1-1-0-0.

Essex

N. Shahid c Moores b Bunting	55	– b Donelan	8⁹	
J. P. Stephenson c A. P. Wells b Pigott	14	– c Gould b Pigott	4?	
P. J. Prichard lbw b Bunting	11	– (4) b Donelan	2?	
M. E. Waugh not out	103	– (3) b Pigott	1?	
N. Hussain lbw b Dodemaide	21	– c Moores b Pigott	2?	
†M. A. Garnham run out	8	– (7) c Dodemaide b Bunting	2(	
*D. R. Pringle lbw b C. M. Wells	21	– (6) c Smith b Donelan	3?	
N. A. Foster not out	2	– c Pigott b Bunting	3(	
T. D. Topley (did not bat)		– not out	⁴	
J. H. Childs (did not bat)		– run out	⁴	
S. J. W. Andrew (did not bat)		– not out	⁴	
B 10, l-b 2, w 1, n-b 2	15	B 9, l-b 5	1⁴	

1/37 2/65 3/100 4/171   (6 wkts dec.) 250   1/137 2/137 3/168   (9 wkts) 29?
5/196 6/244   4/176 5/226 6/236
                                               7/282 8/292 9/294

Bonus points – Essex 3, Sussex 2.

Bowling: *First Innings*—Pigott 16-2-67-1; Dodemaide 13-2-41-1; Bunting 12-1-53-2; Donelan 4-0-33-0; C. M. Wells 14.3-2-44-1. *Second Innings*—Pigott 14-1-79-3; Dodemaide 8-1-46-0; Bunting 8-2-36-2; C. M. Wells 4-0-37-0; Donelan 11-0-86-3.

Umpires: D. O. Oslear and K. E. Palmer.

ESSEX v NOTTINGHAMSHIRE

At Southend, August 4, 6, 7. Essex won by ten wickets. Essex 24 pts, Nottinghamshire 4 pts. Toss: Nottinghamshire. Any fears over the pitch at Southchurch Park, scene of so much controversy twelve months earlier when Essex received a 25-point penalty, which cost them the Championship, were swept aside as Gooch and his men gained an easy victory after scoring 400 in the second innings of the match. A resolute half-century by Evans saw Nottinghamshire achieve respectability in the first innings, and Broad and Johnson batted attractively in their second. However, none was able to score with the freedom of Gooch, whose first-innings 87 arrived from 99 deliveries with a dozen boundaries. With Prichard and Hussain also compiling stylish fifties, Essex forged a substantial lead, which Nottinghamshire cleared with difficulty. They did succeed in keeping Essex in the field until after tea, but Gooch and Stephenson knocked off the 99 needed for victory with nearly seven overs to spare.

Close of play: First day, Essex 140-2 (P. J. Prichard 0*, M. C. Ilott 4*); Second day, Nottinghamshire 80-3 (B. C. Broad 44*).

Nottinghamshire

Batsman	First Innings		Second Innings	
B. C. Broad c Stephenson b Ilott	19	– c Garnham b Ilott	84
P. R. Pollard c Waugh b Foster	12	– c Gooch b Foster	10
R. T. Robinson c Waugh b Pringle	6	– c and b Childs	26
P. Johnson run out	34	– (5) b Childs	60
D. W. Randall c Pringle b Ilott	34	– (6) not out	36
F. D. Stephenson c Prichard b Foster	2	– (7) c Prichard b Childs	4
K. P. Evans c Gooch b Foster	51	– (8) c sub b Foster	31
B. N. French run out	25	– (4) b Such	0
E. E. Hemmings lbw b Foster	32	– c Childs b Ilott	12
K. E. Cooper not out	10	– b Childs	4
J. A. Afford lbw b Such	1	– lbw b Ilott	0
B 1, l-b 1, n-b 3	5	L-b 3	3

1/26 2/38 3/38 4/90 5/100   **231**   1/19 2/73 3/80 4/175 5/183   **270**
6/126 7/158 8/219 9/222   6/194 7/235 8/255 9/270

Bonus points – Nottinghamshire 2, Essex 4.

Bowling: *First Innings*—Foster 25–5–73–4; Ilott 15–2–63–2; Pringle 15–2–74–1; Gooch 0–4–0–0; Childs 8–3–10–0; Such 4.3–1–5–1. *Second Innings*—Foster 30–12–59–2; Ilott 9.5–9–48–3; Such 20–4–56–1; Childs 41–13–104–4.

Essex

Batsman	First Innings		Second Innings	
G. A. Gooch c Johnson b Hemmings	87	– not out	65
J. P. Stephenson b Hemmings	46	– not out	32
P. J. Prichard b Hemmings	60		
M. C. Ilott b Cooper	37		
M. E. Waugh c Robinson b Hemmings	30		
N. Hussain c French b Stephenson	64		
M. A. Garnham c French b Hemmings	22		
N. A. Foster b Evans	22		
D. R. Pringle c French b Evans	15		
J. H. Childs c French b Stephenson	2		
P. M. Such not out	2		
B 3, l-b 8, w 1, n-b 4	16	B 1, n-b 2	3

1/135 2/135 3/190 4/261 5/266   **403**   **(no wkt) 100**
6/336 7/379 8/383 9/401

Bonus points – Essex 4, Nottinghamshire 2 (Score at 100 overs: 328-5).

Bowling: *First Innings*—Stephenson 27.2–2–105–2; Cooper 17–3–76–1; Evans 15–3–53–2; Hemmings 39–15–99–5; Afford 25–7–59–0. *Second Innings*—Stephenson 6–0–30–0; Hemmings 5–0–32–0; Afford 4–0–18–0; Cooper 3.1–1–19–0.

Umpires: J. C. Balderstone and J. H. Harris.

ESSEX v GLAMORGAN

At Southend, August 8, 9, 10. Drawn. Essex 7 pts, Glamorgan 7 pts. Toss: Glamorgan. An exciting finish ended with Essex, despite 94 in 73 balls by Prichard, 8 runs short of a victory target of 333 in 55 overs. The feature of the match was the batting of Richards, who hit a hundred in each innings for the second time in his career, the previous occasion being for the West Indians against Tasmania in 1975-76. His first-innings 111, containing three sixes and thirteen fours, came off 136 deliveries and was followed by an unbeaten 118 from as many balls in the second. His chief support on that occasion came from Cottey, the pair sharing an unbroken partnership of 206 for the fourth wicket. Dale enjoyed a substantial fifth-wicket stand of 160 with Richards on the opening day while putting together a career-best 92. Garnham, Waugh and Stephenson were others to take advantage of a good pitch, helping Essex get within 31 runs on first innings before Foster, captaining them for the first time in the absence of Gooch and Pringle, declared.

Close of play: First day, Essex 10-1 (J. P. Stephenson 1*, M. C. Ilott 8*); Second day, Glamorgan 85-0 (A. R. Butcher 59*, H. Morris 24*).

Glamorgan

*A. R. Butcher c Foster b Ilott	0	– c Garnham b Andrew 5
H. Morris c Childs b Foster	9	– b Such 2
P. A. Cottey c Garnham b Foster	51	– not out 8
M. P. Maynard c Childs b Such	46	– c Shahid b Andrew ....
I. V. A. Richards c Stephenson b Ilott	111	– not out 11
A. Dale c Waugh b Andrew	92	
R. D. B. Croft c Hussain b Foster	6	
†C. P. Metson not out	15	
S. L. Watkin c Foster b Andrew	7	
S. Bastien not out	3	
L-b 11, w 1, n-b 4	16	L-b 9, n-b 2 1

1/5 2/15 3/103 4/121 5/281   (8 wkts dec.) 356   1/86 2/94 3/95   (3 wkts dec.) 30
6/297 7/337 8/345

M. Frost did not bat.

Bonus points – Glamorgan 4, Essex 3 (Score at 100 overs: 346-8).

Bowling: *First Innings*—Foster 23-6-71-3; Ilott 17-4-62-2; Andrew 16-1-66-2; Childs 19-4-69-0; Such 20-7-43-1; Waugh 3-0-11-0; Shahid 4-1-23-0. *Second Innings*—Foster 7-0-46-0; Ilott 6-0-22-0; Andrew 18-1-67-2; Such 21-4-73-1; Childs 9-2-35-0; Waugh 6-1-40-0; Prichard 1-0-9-0.

Essex

N. Shahid hit wkt b Bastien	1	– c Cottey b Bastien 4
J. P. Stephenson b Watkin	63	– c Metson b Bastien 6
M. C. Ilott c Metson b Frost	9	– (8) b Watkin 1
P. J. Prichard c Metson b Bastien	34	– (3) c Metson b Richards 9
M. E. Waugh c Richards b Watkin	66	– (4) lbw b Frost 1
N. Hussain lbw b Frost	33	– (5) c Morris b Richards 2
†M. A. Garnham not out	84	– (6) b Watkin 1
*N. A. Foster c Cottey b Watkin	18	– (7) run out 1
J. H. Childs not out	8	– (10) not out ....
S. J. W. Andrew (did not bat)		– (9) not out 1
B 4, l-b 3, n-b 2	9	B 4, l-b 6, w 1, n-b 1 1

1/1 2/20 3/66 4/178 5/181   (7 wkts dec.) 325   1/97 2/154 3/200 4/252 (8 wkts) 32
6/230 7/311   5/257 6/292 7/294 8/317

P. M. Such did not bat.

Bonus points – Essex 4, Glamorgan 3.

Bowling: *First Innings*—Watkin 22-2-72-3; Bastien 20-6-60-2; Frost 20-4-73-2; Croft 12-0-63-0; Dale 3-0-18-0; Richards 11-3-32-0. *Second Innings*—Watkin 18-0-102-2; Bastien 14-0-75-2; Croft 5-0-24-0; Frost 8-1-51-1; Richards 10-0-63-2.

Umpires: J. C. Balderstone and J. H. Harris.

t Middlesbrough, August 11, 13. ESSEX beat YORKSHIRE by an innings and 11 runs.

ESSEX v SURREY

t Chelmsford, August 18, 20, 21. Essex won by 283 runs. Essex 22 pts, Surrey 4 pts. Toss: urrey. Foster emerged as the match-winner as Essex added momentum to their title hallenge. His 58 was the major contribution in the first innings and he went on to exploit a helmsford pitch containing pace and bounce to collect match figures of eleven for 76. Only tewart, hitting eight boundaries in his half-century, offered any real resistance as Surrey were owled out for their lowest score of the season in the first innings. The lively Andrew inflicted he early damage. Gooch, Waugh and Shahid all batted attractively on the second afternoon, nd Essex's declaration at their overnight score left their opponents to score 404 for victory on he final day. Surrey never looked like making a fight of it and lost their last six wickets for 30 uns after lunch.

Close of play: First day, Surrey 17-1 (A. J. Stewart 3*, N. M. Kendrick 4*); Second day, ssex 281-5 (M. E. Waugh 79*, N. Shahid 55*).

ssex

G. A. Gooch c Greig b Waqar Younis	9	– c Clinton b Robinson	53
P. Stephenson c Greig b Waqar Younis	7	– b Murphy	36
. J. Prichard c Medlycott b Murphy	27	– c Ward b Greig	42
1. E. Waugh c Ward b Waqar Younis	0	– not out	79
4. Hussain b Murphy	29	– c Kendrick b Greig	8
4. Shahid lbw b Murphy	27	– (7) not out	55
M. A. Garnham c Thorpe b Murphy	32		
4. A. Foster c Medlycott b Murphy	58	– (6) c Ward b Greig	0
4. C. Ilott lbw b Robinson	7		
H. Childs run out	4		
J. W. Andrew not out	9		
B 12, 1-b 14, w 1	27	B 4, 1-b 2, w 2	8
	236	(5 wkts dec.)	281

'9 2/28 3/28 4/79 5/82   236   1/80 2/98 3/168   (5 wkts dec.) 281
'142 7/156 8/209 9/218   4/186 5/186

Bonus points – Essex 2, Surrey 4.

Bowling: *First Innings*—Waqar Younis 18.3–4–51–3; Murphy 26.1–4–67–5; Robinson 4.3–5–49–1; Greig 4–0–16–0; Medlycott 3–0–27–0. *Second Innings*—Waqar Younis 4–2–64–0; Murphy 18–0–73–1; Robinson 15–4–39–1; Greig 15–0–60–3; Kendrick 8–0–39–0.

Surrey

4. S. Clinton c Gooch b Ilott	10	– c Garnham b Andrew	32
4. J. Stewart lbw b Andrew	53	– c Ilott b Foster	11
4. M. Kendrick b Andrew	12	– (9) c Hussain b Ilott	3
4. P. Thorpe c Garnham b Andrew	0	– (3) c Garnham b Foster	0
D. M. Ward c Shahid b Andrew	0	– (4) c Shahid b Andrew	11
4. A. Lynch b Foster	4	– (5) b Childs	25
D. Robinson hit wkt b Foster	0	– (6) b Foster	18
4. A. Greig c Garnham b Foster	0	– (7) c Gooch b Foster	4
4. T. Medlycott c Hussain b Foster	20	– (8) not out	11
Vaqar Younis not out	11	– b Foster	1
. J. Murphy b Foster	1	– c Waugh b Foster	0
L-b 2, n-b 1	3	L-b 4	4
	114		120

'13 2/47 3/57 4/70 5/78   114   1/27 2/27 3/58 4/59 5/99   120
'78 7/78 8/96 9/110   6/101 7/112 8/115 9/120

Bonus points – Essex 4.

Bowling: *First Innings*—Foster 19.2–4–44–5; Ilott 17–5–41–1; Andrew 11–3–27–4. *Second innings*—Foster 18–6–32–6; Ilott 14–2–40–1; Andrew 9–2–34–2; Childs 6–2–10–1.

Umpires: H. D. Bird and J. H. Hampshire.

At Derby, August 23, 24. ESSEX beat DERBYSHIRE by an innings and 94 runs.

At Northampton, August 29, 30, 31. ESSEX drew with NORTHAMPTONSHIRE.

ESSEX v NORTHAMPTONSHIRE

At Chelmsford, September 7, 8, 9, 10. Northamptonshire won by 276 runs. Northamptonshire 21 pts, Essex 6 pts. Toss: Essex. Northamptonshire hurried to victory before lunch on the final day after Essex, resuming at 134 for four in pursuit of a target of 589, never threatened to stave off their second Championship defeat of the summer. Only Stephenson, with a gritty 7 spread over nearly three hours, put up prolonged resistance. The course of the match was decided by the visitors' second innings, in which they improved on their highest-ever score made only nine days earlier against Essex at Northampton. Fordham showed the way on Saturday, batting for four hours twenty minutes and hitting a six and twenty fours while sharing century partnerships with Felton and Bailey. Bailey, with a six and nine fours, Lamb (26 fours) and Penberthy then drove home the advantage as the Essex bowlers toiled on a pitch which had become increasingly bland. A series of rash strokes contributed to Northamptonshire's downfall in the first innings as Waugh returned career-best figures with his medium-paced, swinging deliveries. In reply, however, Essex also collapsed ignominiously, following a stylish, commanding innings from Gooch, who hit fifteen fours before becoming Robinson's first victim. Earlier in the day the Northamptonshire fast bowler had made history with his eleventh successive scoreless innings in first-class matches.

Close of play: First day, Essex 185-5 (N. Hussain 12*, M. A. Garnham 3*); Second day, Northamptonshire 330-3 (R. J. Bailey 76*, A. J. Lamb 13*); Third day, Essex 134-4 (J. P. Stephenson 49*, N. Hussain 0*).

Northamptonshire

A. Fordham c Garnham b Andrew	23	– c Foster b Ilott 15
N. A. Felton c Waugh b Foster	25	– b Foster 5
W. Larkins c Prichard b Ilott	37	– c Hussain b Foster 0
R. J. Bailey c Garnham b Waugh	28	– lbw b Foster 10
*A. J. Lamb c and b Waugh	22	– c sub b Childs 16
A. L. Penberthy c Foster b Waugh	0	– c Hussain b Andrew 8
R. G. Williams lbw b Waugh	0	– not out 1
†D. Ripley c Shahid b Waugh	18	
C. E. L. Ambrose lbw b Foster	9	
J. G. Thomas c and b Foster	15	
M. A. Robinson not out	0	
L-b 6, w 1, n-b 12	19	B 10, l-b 29, w 2, n-b 13 54

1/42 2/53 3/117 4/121 5/122   **196**   1/157 2/175 3/286   (6 wkts dec.) 636
6/122 7/151 8/176 9/196   4/434 5/584 6/636

Bonus points – Northamptonshire 1, Essex 4.

Bowling: *First Innings*—Foster 19.2–4–67–3; Ilott 11–3–28–1; Andrew 9–0–58–1; Waugh 12–3–37–5. *Second Innings*—Foster 29–7–79–3; Ilott 26–4–120–1; Childs 37–5–119–1; Andrew 23–1–132–1; Waugh 24–4–87–0; Stephenson 2–0–17–0; Gooch 18–5–43–0.

Essex

G. A. Gooch c Penberthy b Robinson	92	– c Felton b Robinson	40
P. Stephenson c Thomas b Ambrose	0	– b Ambrose	76
J. Prichard c Ripley b Ambrose	7	– c Williams b Penberthy	5
N. Shahid b Thomas	26	– (7) c Thomas b Williams	43
M. E. Waugh c Bailey b Ambrose	44	– (4) c Lamb b Ambrose	36
N. Hussain b Robinson	17	– c Ripley b Thomas	24
M. A. Garnham c and b Ambrose	34	– (8) c Penberthy b Robinson	10
J. A. Foster c Larkins b Thomas	11	– (9) b Robinson	12
A. C. Ilott c Felton b Robinson	0	– (5) c Thomas b Ambrose	0
H. Childs c Williams b Thomas	4	– not out	21
J. W. Andrew not out	1	– c Thomas b Williams	35
L-b 6, w 1, n-b 1	8	L-b 8, n-b 2	10

1/3 2/29 3/81 4/170 5/170   244   1/83 2/94 3/134 4/134 5/173   312
6/192 7/221 8/225 9/238   6/199 7/221 8/256 9/263

Bonus points – Essex 2, Northamptonshire 4.

Bowling: *First Innings*—Ambrose 23.4–3–67–4; Robinson 22–5–73–3; Penberthy 9–1–34–0; Thomas 13–0–64–3. *Second Innings*—Ambrose 19–6–52–3; Thomas 11–0–72–1; Robinson 15–2–89–3; Penberthy 6–0–27–1; Williams 12.1–2–64–2.

Umpires: B. J. Meyer and R. Palmer.

ESSEX v KENT

At Chelmsford, September 12, 13, 14, 15. Drawn. Essex 6 pts, Kent 6 pts. Toss: Essex. Ellison was the key figure in denying Essex the victory they needed to remain in contention for the Championship. He resisted for nearly three and a quarter hours while scoring an unbeaten 44 in the first innings, and his 68 not out in the second was spread over more than four hours. On the final day Ellison received stubborn match-saving support from Davis after Kent had gone to lunch less than 200 runs ahead with only three wickets remaining. Missed catches cost Essex dearly, and they were handicapped by the absence of Gooch, who broke his left thumb in two places attempting to catch Ward in the first hour of the match. Essex were also frustrated by Taylor, who compiled two half-centuries but failed by 21 runs to complete his 2,000 runs for the season. Waugh, with his eighth Championship hundred of the summer, provided the most entertaining batting of the match, his 169 containing 98 in boundaries and taking him past 2,000 runs. Prichard, with whom he put on 239 for the third wicket, also stroked the ball around elegantly.

Close of play: First day, Kent 358-6 (S. A. Marsh 69*, R. M. Ellison 13*); Second day, Essex 335-3 (M. E. Waugh 152*, N. Hussain 32*); Third day, Kent 185-4 (N. R. Taylor 54*, M. V. Fleming 18*).

Kent

B. G. Hinks c and b Childs	43	– b Andrew	16
T. R. Ward c Garnham b Foster	79	– c Hussain b Ilott	7
V. J. Wells c Waugh b Andrew	34	– lbw b Ilott	46
G. R. Cowdrey c Hussain b Childs	0	– c Garnham b Waugh	33
*N. R. Taylor c Garnham b Foster	56	– c Garnham b Foster	86
M. V. Fleming c Foster b Ilott	36	– c Hussain b Childs	36
†S. A. Marsh b Foster	70	– b Foster	47
R. M. Ellison not out	44	– not out	68
D. J. M. Kelleher c Garnham b Ilott	1	– lbw b Foster	6
R. P. Davis c Shahid b Foster	0	– b Foster	52
T. N. Wren c Foster b Shahid	16	– c sub b Foster	0
B 5, l-b 5, w 6, n-b 14	30	B 7, l-b 10, w 1, n-b 9	27

1/115 2/155 3/156 4/187 5/253   409   1/8 2/38 3/97 4/129 5/221   424
6/271 7/363 8/366 9/366   6/251 7/293 8/309 9/424

Bonus points – Kent 4, Essex 2 (Score at 100 overs: 323-6).

Bowling: *First Innings*—Foster 37–8–108–3; Ilott 31–7–73–3; Andrew 21–0–99–1; Waug
5–1–21–0; Childs 37–14–79–2; Stephenson 4–0–18–0; Shahid 2.3–1–1–1. *Second Innings*—
Foster 41.3–9–94–5; Ilott 26–4–72–2; Andrew 24–3–78–1; Childs 31–10–60–1; Shahi
17–5–43–0; Waugh 14–4–37–1; Hussain 2–1–14–0; Stephenson 3–1–9–0.

Essex

J. P. Stephenson c Marsh b Ellison	11		
N. Shahid b Ellison	20 – (1) c Ellison b Kelleher		
P. J. Prichard c Marsh b Fleming	102		
M. E. Waugh c Davis b Wren	169		
N. Hussain c Marsh b Wren	45		
†M. A. Garnham c Marsh b Kelleher	33		
N. A. Foster b Fleming	14		
M. C. Ilott not out	42 – (2) not out		
J. H. Childs c Taylor b Ellison	26		
S. J. W. Andrew c and b Ellison	11 – (3) not out		
L-b 8, w 8, n-b 19	35	W 1, n-b 1	

1/26 2/41 3/280 4/357 5/375 (9 wkts dec.) 508 1/2   (1 wkt) 1
6/398 7/429 8/495 9/508

*G. A. Gooch did not bat.

Bonus points – Essex 4, Kent 2 (Score at 100 overs: 415-6).

Bowling: *First Innings*—Wren 28–1–135–2; Ellison 24.4–2–76–4; Fleming 25–1–87–2; Wel
3–0–22–0; Kelleher 12–1–68–1; Davis 26–3–112–0. *Second Innings*—Kelleher 1–0–10–1.

Umpires: J. C. Balderstone and A. G. T. Whitehead.

At The Oval, September 18, 19, 20, 21. ESSEX drew with SURREY.

UMPIRES FOR 1991

FIRST-CLASS UMPIRES

G. I. Burgess, the former Somerset all-rounder, and R. C. Tolchard, who played for Devo
and whose brothers, J.G. and R.W., played for Leicestershire, have been promoted from th
Reserve list to join the first-class list for 1991. The full list is: J. C. Balderstone, H. D. Bir
J. D. Bond, G. I. Burgess, D. J. Constant, B. Dudleston, J. H. Hampshire, J. H. Harri
B. Hassan, J. W. Holder, A. A. Jones, R. Julian, M. J. Kitchen, B. Leadbeater, K. J. Lyon
B. J. Meyer, D. O. Oslear, K. E. Palmer, R. Palmer, N. T. Plews, D. R. Shepherd, R.
Tolchard, R. A. White, A. G. T. Whitehead and P. B. Wight. *Reserves:* Dr D. Fawkne
Corbett, M. J. Harris, V. A. Holder, H. J. Rhodes and G. A. Stickley.

Note: The panel of umpires for the Test matches and one-day internationals was n
available at the time *Wisden* went to press.

MINOR COUNTIES UMPIRES

P. Adams, N. P. Atkins, R. Bell, K. Bray, P. Brown, C. J. Chapman, R. K. Curtis, Dr I
Fawkner-Corbett, J. B. Foulkes, P. Gray, D. J. Halfyard, M. A. Johnson, B. Knight, G.
McLean, T. G. A. Morley, D. Norton, M. K. Reed, K. S. Shenton, C. Smith, C. T. Spence
G. A. Stickley, J. Stobart, R. Walker, T. V. Wilkins and T. G. Wilson. *Reserves:* D.
Burden, K. Coburn, H. Cohen, H. W. Cook, R. M. Davison, R. F. Elliott, R. E. Elvidg
A. G. Forster, R. F. Harriott, S. W. Kuhlmann, M. P. Moran, W. Morgan, B. J. Orton, C.
Puckett, J. M. Tythcott, J. Waite, T. J. White, B. H. Willey and R. Wood.

GLAMORGAN

Patron: HRH The Prince of Wales
President: His Honour Rowe Harding
Chairman: A. R. Lewis
Chairman, Cricket Committee: A. R. Lewis
Chief Executive: 1990 – P. G. Carling
Secretary: 1990 – A. P. Dilloway
1991 – G. Stone
Sophia Gardens, Cardiff CF1 9XR
(Telephone: 0222-343478)
Captain: A. R. Butcher
Senior Coach: A. Jones

It was not a coincidence that the arrival of Viv Richards in Wales led to Glamorgan's most successful season for twenty years, with the club rising from bottom place in the Britannic Assurance Championship, where they had languished for two years, to eighth position. They also reached the quarter-finals of the Benson and Hedges Cup and NatWest Bank Trophy, and the only major disappointment was in the Sunday League, in which they fell away after a promising start. Richards provided inspiration from the moment he helped his adopted county win their first Benson and Hedges tie by trapping Reeve of Warwickshire leg-before with the game's final delivery.

The encouraging early-season form was maintained in the Championship, and they gained a resounding victory at Bristol in the third game of the season. It was achieved without any substantial contribution from Richards, and with Matthew Maynard and Geoff Holmes absent in the second innings, having suffered fractured fingers. However, Richards had already tuned up with a hundred against Leicestershire, and another soon followed against Sussex at Hove. His presence brought out the best in others, notably Maynard, who looked a far more disciplined batsman than in previous years. At Northampton in June, the pair hammered the home attack for 227 in 41 overs, which enabled Glamorgan to win with six wickets and nine overs in hand; and in the following game Richards played one of the greatest innings seen at Southampton. Glamorgan, set 364 by Hampshire, looked to be out of contention at 139 for five, but Richards, in partnership with Cowley, initiated a remarkable recovery and Glamorgan won with two deliveries to spare. The West Indies captain's imperious 164 not out included five sixes and seventeen fours.

Richards hit seven Championship hundreds, but even his outstanding deeds were overshadowed by those of Alan Butcher and Hugh Morris, both of whom exceeded 2,000 runs for the season and broke a number of Glamorgan batting records. The two left-handers proved themselves the most consistent opening pair in the country, sharing ten century partnerships, and allied to Butcher's prolific batting was his positive and thoughtful captaincy. For the second successive season he reached 1,000 runs before any other English-born player, and he fully deserved the accolade of becoming one of *Wisden's* Five Cricketers of the Year. Welsh anger at Morris's omission from the team for Australia was tempered by his appointment as captain of the England A team selected to tour Pakistan. Morris had an outstanding season. His ten hundreds beat by two the previous Glamorgan record, set by Javed Miandad in 1981, and his aggregate of 2,276 runs surpassed by 193 another of Miandad's county records.

Maynard played a number of entertaining innings, scoring 1,501 runs and this gifted, naturally talented batsman would be capable of even better things if he could curb his impetuosity. Tony Cottey passed 1,000 runs for the first time in his career, fluctuating between No. 3 and No. 6 while Nigel Cowley, in his first season with Glamorgan, played some useful innings in the middle order before his injury in August. There were, however, some disappointments. Holmes, suffering from a troublesome eye infection, played only occasionally, and Ian Smith's form, despite an unbeaten century against Lancashire, fell away. The former Young England player has yet to confirm his early promise.

Steve Watkin was again Glamorgan's willing workhorse, bowling 76 overs in the first-class games, and while his wickets were more expensive than the previous year, he was again the county's leading wicket-taker. The averages, however, were headed by Steve Bastien, a product of Haringey Cricket College, who grasped the opportunity of an extended run in the first team from the end of July and, bowling at a brisk medium pace, finished with 39 wickets at a shade over 30. He took five for 31 as Nottinghamshire were dismissed between lunch and tea on the final day and he closed his season at Worcester with a match return of nine wickets. Mark Frost, discarded by Surrey, made an immediate impact when he bowled Graeme Hick for 0 in a Benson and Hedges match early in the season, and he ended with 59 first-class wickets at 34.69. There was less joy, though, for Stephen Barwick, who was injured for much of the season and played in only three Championship games. His control over lengthy spells on unresponsive pitches, and his ability to switch from seam to off-cutters, were assets the county could ill afford to lose in a batsman's summer.

The emergence of Glamorgan's younger brigade epitomised the club's policy of promoting Welsh-born players. ASW Holdings, the county's main sponsors, have ensured that any aspiring young cricketer in the Principality is given every opportunity, and through the efforts of Alan Jones, the chief coach, promising young talent has been emerging. Robert Croft, in his first full season, struck 672 runs at 44.80, including an innings of 91 not out when Glamorgan failed by only 2 runs to reach an improbable 495 to beat Worcestershire at Abergavenny. He also emerged as an off-spinner of considerable promise, prompting Bishan Bedi to single him out as the best young spinner he had seen during India's tour. Although Steve James scored almost 1,000 runs in the short Cambridge season, he failed to maintain his form on his return to Glamorgan in July. None the less, he has the ability to succeed, and with Adrian Dale he should be available full-time in 1991. Once again Colin Metson's wicket-keeping was of the highest class; yet in spite of his being rated by most umpires and players as the best in the country, he was denied a tour with the England teams because of his modest batting.

A disappointing feature was the comprehensive defeat sustained in each of the final three games, when Richards was absent owing to a virus. However, Glamorgan's players have to realise that life without him has to go on, and the confidence which he instilled in them must be renewed and the resurgence continued. – Edward Bevan.

421

GLAMORGAN 1990

[*Bill Smith*

Back row: M. Davies, R. N. Pook, S. Bastien, R. Nancarrow, M. Frost, H. A. G. Anthony, K. A. Somaia, P. A. Cottey, R. D. B. Croft. *Middle row*: D. Conway (*physiotherapist*), M. J. Cann, N. G. Cowley, S. J. Dennis, I. Smith, M. L. Roberts, D. J. Shepherd (*assistant coach*), G. Lewis (*scorer*). *Front row*: J. F. Steele, C. P. Metson, G. C. Holmes, H. Morris, P. G. Carling (*chief executive*), A. R. Butcher (*captain*), S. R. Barwick, M. P. Maynard, J. Derrick, A. Jones (*senior coach*). *Insets*: I. V. A. Richards, S. L. Watkin, S. P. James, D. L. Hemp.

GLAMORGAN RESULTS

All first-class matches – Played 26: Won 5, Lost 6, Drawn 15.

County Championship matches – Played 22: Won 5, Lost 6, Drawn 11.

Bonus points – Batting 64, Bowling 48.

Competition placings – Britannic Assurance County Championship, 8th;
NatWest Bank Trophy, q-f; Benson and Hedges Cup, q-f;
Refuge Assurance League, 15th equal.

BRITANNIC ASSURANCE CHAMPIONSHIP AVERAGES

BATTING

	Birthplace	M	I	NO	R	HI	Avge
‡I. V. A. Richards ...	St John's, Antigua	18	28	5	1,425	164*	61.95
‡A. R. Butcher	Croydon	21	39	5	2,044	151*	60.11
‡H. Morris	Cardiff	22	41	4	1,914	160*	51.72
‡M. P. Maynard	Oldham	19	34	5	1,306	125*	45.0
R. D. B. Croft	Morriston	14	23	10	570	91*	43.84
N. G. Cowley	Shaftesbury	13	16	4	523	76	43.58
I. Smith	Chopwell	6	8	1	293	112*	41.85
‡G. C. Holmes	Newcastle-upon-Tyne	7	10	3	260	125*	37.14
P. A. Cottey	Swansea	17	30	5	816	125	32.64
M. J. Cann	Cardiff	5	8	0	180	64	22.50
A. Dale	Germiston, SA	7	11	0	179	92	16.27
‡C. P. Metson	Goffs Oak	22	26	4	302	34	13.72
‡S. L. Watkin	Maesteg	22	22	7	170	25*	11.33
S. Bastien	Stepney, London	10	9	3	47	12	7.81
M. Frost	Barking	18	17	7	40	12	4.0
S. J. Dennis	Scarborough	12	8	1	23	6	3.28
S. P. James	Lydney	3	6	0	10	7	1.66

Also batted: H. A. G. Anthony (*Urlings Village, Antigua*) (2 matches) 39, 0, 13; ‡S. R.
Barwick (*Neath*) (3 matches) 0*, 2*; M. L. Roberts (*Mullion*) (1 match) 13.

* Signifies not out.   ‡ Denotes county cap.

The following played a total of 27 three-figure innings for Glamorgan in County
Championship matches – H. Morris 8, I. V. A. Richards 7, A. R. Butcher 6, P. A. Cottey 2
M. P. Maynard 2, G. C. Holmes 1, I. Smith 1.

BOWLING

	O	M	R	W	BB	5W/i	Avge
S. Bastien	274.5	47	1,075	35	6-75	2	30.71
M. Frost	509.1	63	1,919	56	5-40	2	34.2
S. L. Watkin	731.1	118	2,489	61	5-100	1	40.8
S. J. Dennis	283	53	957	20	5-76	1	47.85
R. D. B. Croft	357.1	76	1,126	23	3-10	0	48.95
N. G. Cowley	296.3	58	851	11	3-84	0	77.36

Also bowled: H. A. G. Anthony 62–13–207–5; S. R. Barwick 124.4–27–396–5; A. R.
Butcher 25.3–2–153–1; M. J. Cann 35–3–162–1; P. A. Cottey 18–0–116–1; A. Dale
51–8–187–0; G. C. Holmes 21–3–85–1; M. P. Maynard 20–1–150–0; H. Morris 6–0–62–0
I. V. A. Richards 137–26–426–5; I. Smith 33–3–157–1.

Wicket-keeper: C. P. Metson 58 ct.

Leading Fielder: M. P. Maynard 13.

At Oxford, April 14, 16, 17. GLAMORGAN drew with OXFORD UNIVERSITY.

GLAMORGAN v LEICESTERSHIRE

At Cardiff, April 26, 27, 28, 30. Leicestershire won by nine wickets. Leicestershire 24 pts, Glamorgan 3 pts. Toss: Glamorgan. Despite Richards's first century for Glamorgan in their second innings, Leicestershire always looked to have control of a match which began with the weather allowing only 36 overs on the first day. Consistent batting in their first innings and some hostile bowling by Lewis, who took ten wickets in a match for the first time, enabled the visitors to collect maximum points. After Glamorgan's capitulation in the first innings, Richards and Maynard gave them hope with a partnership of 186 when they followed on, but Maynard was run out late on the third day to open the way for Leicestershire. With only 106 needed for victory, Boon led the way with his second half-century of the match.

Close of play: First day, Leicestershire 113-2 (T. J. Boon 52*, L. Potter 4*); Second day, Glamorgan 68-4 (H. Morris 25*, M. J. Cann 6*); Third day, Glamorgan 283-4 (I. V. A. Richards 118*, M. J. Cann 7*).

Leicestershire

T. J. Boon c Holmes b Dennis	72	– not out		61
*N. E. Briers c Maynard b Frost	21	– c Maynard b Watkin		10
J. J. Whitaker b Dennis	32	– not out		31
L. Potter lbw b Frost	50			
J. D. R. Benson lbw b Frost	9			
C. C. Lewis lbw b Dennis	39			
†P. Whitticase c Metson b Dennis	11			
M. I. Gidley c Dennis b Croft	73			
G. J. F. Ferris lbw b Frost	24			
J. P. Agnew c Metson b Dennis	0			
A. D. Mullally not out	16			
L-b 9, w 3, n-b 2	14	L-b 4, n-b 3		7

1/57 2/109 3/135 4/150 5/230   361   1/26   (1 wkt) 109
6/230 7/252 8/320 9/322

Bonus points – Leicestershire 4, Glamorgan 3 (Score at 100 overs: 302-7).

Bowling: *First Innings*—Watkin 30-3-94-0; Frost 33-3-117-4; Dennis 37-15-76-5; Croft 9.3-0-42-1; Richards 5-2-9-0; Holmes 5-2-14-0. *Second Innings*—Watkin 10.4-0-60-1; Frost 7-0-26-0; Dennis 3-0-16-0; Croft 3-2-3-0.

Glamorgan

*A. R. Butcher b Lewis	10	– c Agnew b Ferris		4
H. Morris c Whitticase b Lewis	33	– c Whitticase b Agnew		32
G. C. Holmes lbw b Ferris	14	– c Gidley b Mullally		11
M. P. Maynard c Gidley b Ferris	6	– run out		92
I. V. A. Richards b Lewis	3	– lbw b Lewis		119
M. J. Cann c Whitticase b Lewis	11	– c Potter b Ferris		17
R. D. B. Croft c Whitticase b Ferris	5	– not out		27
†C. P. Metson c Boon b Lewis	8	– c Benson b Lewis		5
S. J. Dennis c Whitticase b Lewis	3	– c Whitticase b Lewis		2
S. L. Watkin not out	21	– c Briers b Lewis		5
M. Frost c Boon b Ferris	1	– lbw b Agnew		0
L-b 5, n-b 7	12	L-b 7, w 3, n-b 15		25

1/14 2/34 3/45 4/48 5/86   127   1/7 2/51 3/53 4/239   339
6/87 7/101 8/101 9/116   5/287 6/309 7/320
                                   8/330 9/336

Bonus points – Leicestershire 4.

Bowling: *First Innings*—Lewis 24-7-55-6; Ferris 11.2-1-44-4; Mullally 4-2-10-0; Gidley 2-1-1-0; Agnew 10-5-12-0. *Second Innings*—Lewis 25-3-64-4; Ferris 16-3-57-2; Mullally 24-6-67-1; Agnew 23.5-3-92-2; Gidley 14-7-31-0; Potter 5-2-21-0.

Umpires: M. J. Kitchen and B. Leadbeater.

GLAMORGAN v SOMERSET

At Cardiff, May 3, 4, 5, 6. Drawn. Glamorgan 3 pts, Somerset 5 pts. Toss: Somerset. A match which produced an aggregate of 1,430 runs for the loss of seventeen wickets will be remembered for Cook's mammoth innings of 313 not out, his first triple-hundred. Taking advantage of a benign pitch under a cloudless sky, Cook batted for eight and a half hours, struck 43 fours, and was only 9 runs short of I. V. A. Richards's Somerset record of 322 – achieved against Warwickshire in 1985 – when his captain, Tavaré, declared. His innings was the highest recorded in Wales and also the highest against Glamorgan. Four Glamorgan batsmen hit half-centuries, with Holmes going on to an unbeaten 125, as Glamorgan comfortably avoided the follow-on, and when Somerset batted again, Hayhurst, the former Lancashire all-rounder, scored a century on his Championship début for his new county. Tavaré set Glamorgan the stiff task of scoring 368 at almost 5 an over, but they gave up the chase once Maynard and Richards were dismissed.

Close of play: First day, Somerset 361-2 (S. J. Cook 96*, C. J. Tavaré 33*); Second day, Glamorgan 198-3 (G. C. Holmes 23*, I. Smith 23*); Third day, Somerset 138-1 (A. N. Hayhurst 66*, R. J. Harden 64*).

Somerset

S. J. Cook not out 313		
P. M. Roebuck lbw b Dennis 69		
J. J. E. Hardy b Holmes................ 7	– (2) lbw b Dennis	0
*C. J. Tavaré not out 120		
A. N. Hayhurst (did not bat)	– (1) not out	110
R. J. Harden (did not bat)	– (3) c Richards b Smith	64
†N. D. Burns (did not bat)	– (4) c sub b Barwick	28
I. G. Swallow (did not bat)	– (5) not out	31
B 8, l-b 16, n-b 2 26	L-b 6, w 1, n-b 4	11

1/210 2/250   (2 wkts dec.) 535   1/4 2/138 3/181   (3 wkts dec.) 244

G. D. Rose, R. P. Lefebvre and A. N. Jones did not bat.

Bonus points – Somerset 4 (Score at 100 overs: 306-2).

Bowling: *First Innings*—Watkin 27-6-84-0; Dennis 27-3-125-1; Barwick 29-7-107-0; Cowley 41-5-88-0; Smith 3-0-19-0; Richards 9-1-22-0; Holmes 12-1-44-1; Cann 6-1-22-0. *Second Innings*—Barwick 16-1-56-1; Dennis 7-1-16-1; Smith 11-1-43-1; Richards 22-2-68-0; Cann 15-2-44-0; Maynard 3-0-11-0.

Glamorgan

M. J. Cann c Harden b Jones 64	– c Swallow b Hayhurst	54
H. Morris c Hardy b Jones 52	– b Lefebvre	19
G. C. Holmes not out 125	– c Burns b Lefebvre	44
M. P. Maynard c Roebuck b Swallow 19	– c Cook b Lefebvre	64
I. Smith c Jones b Swallow 56	– (6) c Cook b Roebuck	16
I. V. A. Richards c Burns b Rose 16	– (5) c Swallow b Roebuck	16
N. G. Cowley run out 43	– not out	8
†C. P. Metson (did not bat)	– not out	4
B 6, l-b 22, w 4, n-b 5 37	B 3, l-b 7, w 3, n-b 1	14

1/120 2/127 3/159 4/270   (6 wkts dec.) 412   1/61 2/80 3/188   (6 wkts) 239
5/296 6/412   4/205 5/218 6/227

S. J. Dennis, *S. R. Barwick and S. L. Watkin did not bat.

Bonus points – Glamorgan 3, Somerset 1 (Score at 100 overs: 263-3).

Bowling: *First Innings*—Jones 18-1-80-2; Rose 22-6-50-1; Swallow 45-11-117-2; Lefebvre 26-8-45-0; Hayhurst 16-2-37-0; Roebuck 20-6-33-0; Harden 7-1-21-0; Tavaré 0.3-0-1-0. *Second Innings*—Jones 9-4-23-0; Lefebvre 17-2-52-3; Hayhurst 8-0-39-1; Swallow 21-6-57-0; Roebuck 14.3-5-34-2.

Umpires: P. J. Eele and J. W. Holder.

At Bristol, May 15, 16, 17. GLAMORGAN beat GLOUCESTERSHIRE by 145 runs.

t Hove, May 19, 21, 22. GLAMORGAN drew with SUSSEX.

GLAMORGAN v KENT

.t Swansea, May 23, 24, 25. Kent won by 6 runs. Kent 19 pts, Glamorgan 4 pts. Toss: Kent.
he game provided an exciting finish, with Kent winning in the penultimate over after
enson, deputising for Chris Cowdrey, had kept proceedings open by feeding some easy runs
▪ revive Glamorgan's interest. Kent had laboured in the first innings, Taylor taking 351
ʌinutes to score 106 (eleven fours) and sharing a partnership of 161 for the second wicket with
ʌe more enterprising Hinks, whose 107 contained sixteen boundaries. After Kent had batted
ʌ during the second morning, Glamorgan's openers scored briskly, putting on 255 without
eing parted before Butcher declared 73 runs behind in the final session. Butcher hit twenty
ʌurs in his 151, which included a century between lunch and tea, and there were ten in
ʌorris's first Championship hundred of the season. Kent's declaration, helped along by
ottey and Cann, left Glamorgan to score 321 from a minimum of 63 overs, and the match
ʌppeared to be heading for a draw before Cowley and Smith plundered 122 in 56 minutes,
ith encouragement from some friendly bowling. When Cowley went at 267, Smith took
ʌlamorgan to within 13 runs of victory before he was run out by de Villiers with three overs
ʌmaining. Glamorgan's hopes finally evaporated when the South African fast bowler had
ʌatkin caught at long-off and, next ball, trapped Dennis leg-before to give Kent an unlikely
ʌctory.

Close of play: First day, Kent 291-3 (N. R. Taylor 101*, G. R. Cowdrey 46*); Second day,
ʌent 46-1 (M. R. Benson 40*, R. P. Davis 2*).

ʌent

. G. Hinks b Watkin	107	– c Morris b Dennis	4
M. R. Benson lbw b Watkin	17	– c Morris b Dennis	96
٭. R. Taylor lbw b Watkin	106		
. R. Ward c Cann b Watkin	3	– b Cowley	7
٭. R. Cowdrey not out	68	– not out	80
٭. V. Fleming not out	10	– not out	45
. P. Davis (did not bat)		– (3) run out	12
B 6, l-b 7, w 3, n-b 1	17	B 1, l-b 2	3

٭/33 2/194 3/210 4/297   (4 wkts dec.) 328   1/23 2/92 3/112   (4 wkts dec.) 247
                                                          4/132

S. A. Marsh, M. A. Ealham, C. Penn and P. S. de Villiers did not bat.

Bonus points – Kent 3, Glamorgan 1 (Score at 100 overs: 263-3).

Bowling: *First Innings*—Watkin 28–5–77–4; Dennis 11–0–39–0; Barwick 28.2–9–72–0;
ʌichards 13–4–34–0; Cowley 33–7–75–0; Cann 1–0–1–0; Butcher 3–1–17–0. *Second Innings*—
ʌatkin 10–1–27–0; Dennis 12–0–53–2; Cowley 22–4–67–1; Barwick 8–3–18–0; Cann
-0–56–0; Cottey 3–0–23–0.

ʌlamorgan

A. R. Butcher not out	151	– b Davis	50
٭. Morris not out	100	– c and b Davis	29
V. A. Richards (did not bat)		– c Cowdrey b Davis	21
٭. J. Cann (did not bat)		– c Fleming b Davis	10
. A. Cottey (did not bat)		– c sub b Ward	21
Smith (did not bat)		– run out	66
. G. Cowley (did not bat)		– b de Villiers	76
C. P. Metson (did not bat)		– b de Villiers	21
J. Dennis (did not bat)		– lbw b de Villiers	6
L. Watkin (did not bat)		– c Davis b de Villiers	1
R. Barwick (did not bat)		– not out	0
L-b 2, n-b 2	4	B 8, l-b 1, n-b 4	13

                         (no wkt dec.) 255   1/60 2/87 3/108 4/139 5/145   314
                                                       6/267 7/297 8/308 9/314

Bonus points – Glamorgan 3.

Bowling: *First Innings*—de Villiers 17–5–39–0; Penn 14–5–44–0; Fleming 16–1–48–0;
Ealham 12.2–2–48–0; Davis 24–4–74–0. *Second Innings*—de Villiers 15.3–3–69–4; Penn
7–0–39–0; Davis 25–5–97–4; Ward 9–0–52–1; Benson 3–0–28–0; Fleming 3–0–20–0.

Umpires: J. H. Harris and P. B. Wight.

GLAMORGAN v LANCASHIRE

At Colwyn Bay, May 26, 28, 29. Drawn. Glamorgan 5 pts, Lancashire 8 pts. Toss
Glamorgan. Glamorgan returned to Colwyn Bay after an absence of sixteen years, with the
team flying from Swansea airport instead of undergoing a tiring 190-mile road journey. On the
other hand, the attractive venue on the North Wales coast was an ideal one for Lancashire's
supporters, many of whom were only an hour's drive away. Two days of glorious sunshine
were followed by a miserable final day when Glamorgan, through the efforts of Butcher and
Smith, fought back after being in danger of an innings defeat. Lancashire were indebted to
Mendis, Fairbrother and Hegg, who enabled them to declare at 399 for seven with a lead of
194 and almost a day and a half remaining. The home county were vulnerable at 29 for three
in their second innings but Smith, whose aggressive century included two sixes and nine fours
and Butcher, batting at No. 4, staved off defeat. When the rain set in, Glamorgan had a
slender lead of 9 runs with the new ball due in eighteen overs. Their first innings also owed
much to Butcher, while Anthony's spectacular 39 from 32 balls, including two sixes and five
fours, on his Championship début prompted resistance from the lower order.

Close of play: First day, Lancashire 187-3 (G. D. Mendis 80*, T. E. Jesty 7*); Second day,
Glamorgan 97-3 (A. R. Butcher 31*, I. Smith 41*).

Glamorgan

M. J. Cann c Hughes b DeFreitas	4	– c Hegg b DeFreitas		7
H. Morris lbw b Patterson	3	– lbw b Patterson		1
P. A. Cottey c Hegg b Allott	8	– c Mendis b DeFreitas		13
*A. R. Butcher c Hegg b Patterson	46	– not out		66
I. Smith c Atherton b DeFreitas	10	– not out		112
M. L. Roberts c Jesty b Allott	13			
N. G. Cowley c Allott b Patterson	4			
H. A. G. Anthony c Fairbrother b DeFreitas	39			
†C. P. Metson c and b Allott	34			
S. L. Watkin not out	25			
M. Frost c Hegg b Allott	0			
B 9, l-b 4, n-b 6	19	L-b 3, n-b 1		4

1/5 2/11 3/26 4/39 5/60	205	1/5 2/22 3/29 (3 wkts) 203
6/68 7/114 8/139 9/205		

Bonus points – Glamorgan 2, Lancashire 4.

Bowling: *First Innings*—Patterson 19–4–88–3; DeFreitas 24–7–53–3; Allott 15–8–23–4;
Fitton 4–1–17–0; Atherton 5–1–11–0. *Second Innings*—Patterson 17–5–41–1; DeFreitas
22–6–61–2; Allott 20–6–54–0; Fitton 15–6–25–0; Atherton 8–5–19–0.

Lancashire

G. D. Mendis c Metson b Watkin	90	*D. P. Hughes b Cowley		3
G. Fowler c Butcher b Watkin	22	J. D. Fitton not out		2
M. A. Atherton lbw b Cowley	15	B 4, l-b 11, n-b 6		21
N. H. Fairbrother c and b Cowley	60			
T. E. Jesty b Anthony	30	1/60 2/92 3/169 (7 wkts dec.) 399		
P. A. J. DeFreitas lbw b Anthony	21	4/210 5/237		
†W. K. Hegg not out	82	6/252 7/345		

B. P. Patterson and P. J. W. Allott did not bat.

Bonus points – Lancashire 4, Glamorgan 3.

Bowling: Frost 21–3–81–0; Anthony 20–2–99–2; Watkin 25–4–84–2; Cowley 28–8–84–3;
Butcher 3–1–17–0; Smith 3–0–19–0.

Umpires: J. H. Harris and P. B. Wight.

At Oxford, June 2, 4, 5. GLAMORGAN drew with OXFORD UNIVERSITY.

At Northampton, June 9, 11, 12. GLAMORGAN beat NORTHAMPTONSHIRE by six wickets.

At Southampton, June 16, 18, 19. GLAMORGAN beat HAMPSHIRE by four wickets.

At Bath, June 20, 21, 22. GLAMORGAN drew with SOMERSET.

GLAMORGAN v YORKSHIRE

At Cardiff, June 23, 25, 26. Yorkshire won by five wickets. Yorkshire 19 pts, Glamorgan 4 pts. Toss: Yorkshire. Yorkshire, having won their previous game following a generous declaration by the opposing captain, repeated the exercise after Butcher had set them a target of 271 in 72 overs. Although four wickets fell for 102, a partnership of 121 between the aggressive Byas and Blakey ensured Yorkshire of a second successive victory with 6.1 overs to spare. Morris's second Championship century of the season was the counterpoint to Maynard's 54 from 80 balls, and with Richards hitting 38 off 47 balls, Glamorgan were able to declare on Saturday evening with four batting points. However, rain allowed only 36 overs on the second day. Butcher's second declaration was based on Yorkshire's poor batting displays earlier in the season, but Blakey, who had scored only 30 runs in his eight previous Championship innings, and Byas corrected this impression. Robinson then returned after a blow on the chin from Watkin to see Yorkshire home.

Close of play: First day, Yorkshire 8-0 (M. D. Moxon 4*, A. A. Metcalfe 4*); Second day, Yorkshire 152-3 (K. Sharp 53*, P. E. Robinson 53*).

Glamorgan

A. R. Butcher c Kellett b Carrick	50	– c Robinson b Hartley	17
H. Morris c Blakey b Hartley	102	– c Blakey b Moxon	28
P. A. Cottey c Kellett b Hartley	18	– not out	36
M. P. Maynard c and b Hartley	54	– not out	26
V. A. Richards b Gough	38		
I. C. Holmes not out	30		
C. P. Metson b Gough	14		
W 1, n-b 2	3	L-b 1, n-b 5	6

1/107 2/196 3/209 4/255   (6 wkts dec.) 309   1/31 2/75   (2 wkts dec.) 113
5/276 6/309

M. Frost, S. J. Dennis, S. L. Watkin and S. Bastien did not bat.

Bonus points – Glamorgan 4, Yorkshire 2.

In the first innings P. A. Cottey, when 0, retired hurt at 112 and resumed at 255.

Bowling: *First Innings*—Jarvis 20–3–83–0; Hartley 24–7–51–3; Moxon 13–4–36–0; Gough 14–2–72–2; Carrick 22–6–67–1. *Second Innings*—Hartley 10–1–35–1; Gough 7–0–44–0; Moxon 5–0–10–1; Byas 8–4–23–0.

Yorkshire

*M. D. Moxon c Cottey b Dennis	27	– b Frost	1(
A. A. Metcalfe c Morris b Bastien	5	– c Dennis b Watkin	37
S. A. Kellett b Bastien	2	– c Butcher b Bastien	8
K. Sharp not out	53	– b Dennis	24
P. E. Robinson not out	53	– not out	2▮
†R. J. Blakey (did not bat)	–	– not out	7▮
D. Byas (did not bat)	–	– c Metson b Frost	79
B 4, l-b 4, w 4	12	B 9, l-b 8, w 2, n-b 2	2▮

1/12 2/18 3/76   (3 wkts dec.) 152   1/28 2/40 3/70   (5 wkts) 27▮
                                              4/102 5/223

P. J. Hartley, P. Carrick, P. W. Jarvis and D. Gough did not bat.

Bonus points – Yorkshire 1, Glamorgan 1.

In the second innings P. E. Robinson, when 11, retired hurt at 102-3 and resumed at 223.

Bowling: *First Innings*—Frost 13–2–23–0; Watkin 13–2–38–0; Bastien 11–1–49–2; Denni▮ 7–0–34–1. *Second Innings*—Frost 15.5–1–64–2; Bastien 16–0–67–1; Watkin 14–1–46–1 Dennis 15–2–58–1; Richards 5–0–19–0.

Umpires: D. J. Constant and R. Julian.

GLAMORGAN v SURREY

At Cardiff, June 30, July 2, 3. Drawn. Glamorgan 3 pts, Surrey 5 pts. Toss: Surrey. Surrey seeking their first Championship win of the season, were content to hold out for a draw on th final afternoon, having been asked to score 277 in 60 overs. On a truncated first day of 4 overs, Morris and Butcher again laid the foundation of a substantial total with an openin partnership of 136 – their seventh century partnership of the summer in all matches. In th course of it, the 36-year-old Butcher, for the second successive season, became the firs England-qualified player to reach 1,000 runs. However, Glamorgan failed by 1 run to achiev maximum batting points, losing their last two wickets in the 100th over. Surrey declared 14 runs behind, and while at first glance Butcher's target-setting declaration appeared generous Surrey had only nine fit players. Alikhan had broken a bone in his foot while fielding on th first day and Darren Bicknell was suffering from an infected hand, although he was prepare to bat in an emergency. At 68 for four Surrey were in trouble, but Greig, with a defian innings of 25 which occupied the same number of overs, saved his team from defeat. Crof Glamorgan's twenty-year-old off-spinner, bowled an admirable spell of 24 overs, taking career-best three for 46.
Close of play: First day, Glamorgan 148-1 (H. Morris 62*, P. A. Cottey 4*); Second day Surrey 150-1 dec.

Glamorgan

*A. R. Butcher c and b Medlycott	67	– c sub b Feltham	2
H. Morris lbw b M. P. Bicknell	62	– c sub b Gray	
P. A. Cottey c Ward b M. P. Bicknell	19	– not out	3▮
M. P. Maynard c Ward b Feltham	22	– c Thorpe b Feltham	
I. V. A. Richards lbw b Feltham	0	– lbw b M. P. Bicknell	1
A. Dale lbw b M. P. Bicknell	25	– lbw b M. P. Bicknell	
R. D. B. Croft c Lynch b Medlycott	35	– not out	2
†C. P. Metson st Ward b Medlycott	21		
S. J. Dennis c Gray b M. P. Bicknell	2		
S. L. Watkin not out	3		
M. Frost c Clinton b Medlycott	0		
B 10, l-b 9, w 4, n-b 20	43	B 4, l-b 7, n-b 9	2

1/136 2/148 3/188 4/192 5/192   299   1/37 2/37 3/45   (5 wkts dec.) 12
6/252 7/291 8/296 9/299   4/70 5/84

Bonus points – Glamorgan 3, Surrey 4.

Bowling: *First Innings*—Gray 21–5–42–0; M. P. Bicknell 28–4–87–4; Feltham 21–5–60– Medlycott 26.5–3–77–4; Greig 3–1–14–0. *Second Innings*—Gray 11–2–29–1; M. P. Bickne 10–0–36–2; Feltham 7–1–32–2; Medlycott 7–3–19–0.

Surrey

D. J. Bicknell not out	59		
G. S. Clinton b Watkin	41	– c Morris b Croft	22
G. P. Thorpe not out	40	– c Watkin b Croft	4
K. T. Medlycott (did not bat)		– (1) lbw b Frost	4
†D. M. Ward (did not bat)		– (4) c Butcher b Frost	29
M. A. Lynch (did not bat)		– (5) c Metson b Watkin	7
*I. A. Greig (did not bat)		– (6) c Dale b Croft	25
M. A. Feltham (did not bat)		– (7) not out	30
M. P. Bicknell (did not bat)		– (8) not out	0
L-b 9, n-b 1	10	B 6, l-b 6, w 2, n-b 4	18

1/90	(1 wkt dec.) 150	1/6 2/20 3/68 4/68 (6 wkts) 139
		5/84 6/117

R. I. Alikhan and A. H. Gray did not bat.

Bonus points – Surrey 1.

Bowling: *First Innings*—Frost 13–2–48–0; Watkin 14–3–36–1; Croft 20.1–6–46–0; Dennis 8–1–11–0. *Second Innings*—Frost 14–2–33–2; Watkin 17–3–33–1; Croft 24–7–46–3; Dennis 2–0–5–0; Richards 2–1–10–0.

Umpires: R. A. White and A. G. T. Whitehead.

GLAMORGAN v GLOUCESTERSHIRE

At Swansea, July 4, 5, 6. Drawn. Glamorgan 4 pts, Gloucestershire 3 pts. Toss: Glamorgan. The rain, which had prevented any play on the first day, relented on Thursday but returned again on the final afternoon as Gloucestershire were making a spirited effort to achieve their first Championship win after a dismal start to the season. Glamorgan took advantage of an inexperienced Gloucestershire attack, which was without the injured Walsh and Lawrence, to obtain maximum batting points. Croft, with 68, again confirmed his all-round potential, while Maynard, Richards and Cowley all batted consistently. Predictably the two captains forfeited an innings, and Gloucestershire were left with a maximum of 102 overs in which to reach their target. Butcher, brother of the Glamorgan captain, and Athey consolidated with a useful third-wicket partnership, and when play was eventually abandoned in mid-afternoon, the game was interestingly poised.

Close of play: First day, No play; Second day, Glamorgan 334-8 dec.

Glamorgan

*A. R. Butcher b Bell	19	†C. P. Metson b Barnes	30
H. Morris c Williams b Curran	21	S. L. Watkin not out	19
P. A. Cottey lbw b Curran	12	S. J. Dennis not out	4
M. P. Maynard c and b Curran	63	B 5, l-b 7, n-b 1	13
I. V. A. Richards run out	41		
R. D. B. Croft b Curran	68	1/39 2/45 3/55 4/134 (8 wkts dec.) 334
N. G. Cowley b Lloyds	44	5/182 6/262 7/302 8/314

M. Frost did not bat.

Bonus points – Glamorgan 4, Gloucestershire 3 (Score at 100 overs: 306-7).

Bowling: Curran 30–4–92–4; Barnes 21–4–47–1; Bell 27–3–76–1; Bainbridge 3–0–17–0; Alleyne 2–0–14–0; Lloyds 25–6–76–1.

Glamorgan forfeited their second innings.

Gloucestershire

Gloucestershire forfeited their first innings.

G. D. Hodgson lbw b Watkin	23
*A. J. Wright lbw b Dennis	19
I. P. Butcher not out	25
C. W. J. Athey not out	35
L-b 2, w 2, n-b 2	6

1/44 2/44   (2 wkts) 108

P. Bainbridge, K. M. Curran, M. W. Alleyne, †R. C. J. Williams, J. W. Lloyds, R. M. Bell and S. N. Barnes did not bat.

Bowling: Frost 8–1–31–0; Dennis 12–4–23–1; Watkin 6–1–23–1; Croft 8–2–23–0; Cowley 5–2–6–0.

Umpires: R. A. White and A. G. T. Whitehead.

At Hinckley, July 7, 8, 9. GLAMORGAN drew with LEICESTERSHIRE.

GLAMORGAN v WORCESTERSHIRE

At Abergavenny, July 21, 23, 24. Drawn. Glamorgan 5 pts, Worcestershire 6 pts. Toss: Glamorgan. A remarkable game in which a number of records were broken ended with Glamorgan failing by just 2 runs to score 495 for victory. On a perfect pitch and a parched outfield, 1,641 runs were scored, a record aggregate for a three-day county match and only 9 runs less than the record established for a Championship match by Surrey and Lancashire, over four days, earlier in the season. Hick, the first to hit a double-century and century in a match since 1984, became at 24 the youngest batsman to score 50 first-class hundreds, that record having previously been held by Sir Donald Bradman, when 26. He hit five sixes and 38 fours in the course of his unbeaten 252, and his 79-minute hundred in the second innings, off 71 balls (four sixes, eleven fours), was the fastest so far in the 1990 Championship, in addition to being his 50th. Hick's two innings took his aggregate of runs without being dismissed to 592, beating E. D. Weekes's record for first-class cricket in England (575 runs in 1950). Cottey hit sixteen fours in his unbeaten hundred, and when Glamorgan declared in arrears. Next day they were given 88 overs in which to reach their mammoth target. Butcher and Morris began with 256, their ninth century stand of the summer and the best for Glamorgan against Worcestershire, but the loss of four wickets for 32 runs was a setback. Richards struck 43 from only eighteen deliveries, and when Glamorgan required 169 from twenty overs, Neale kept them interested by using occasional bowlers, who were plundered for 69 in six overs. Cowley and Croft put on 124 in fifteen overs, and at the start of the last over 15 runs were needed. Croft hit a six from the fourth ball, but with 3 required from the final delivery, Illingworth conceded no more than a leg-bye. During the game, sixteen sixes and 249 fours were struck on one of the smallest yet loveliest grounds on the County Championship circuit.

Close of play: First day, Glamorgan 50-0 (A. R. Butcher 16*, H. Morris 31*); Second day, Worcestershire 215-1 (T. S. Curtis 81*, G. A. Hick 48*).

Worcestershire

T. S. Curtis b Watkin	23	– not out	111
P. Bent c Cowley b Croft	69	– c Metson b Watkin	79
G. A. Hick not out	252	– not out	100
D. B. D'Oliveira c Maynard b Cowley	121		
I. T. Botham c Morris b Bastien	29		
B 9, l-b 10, n-b 1	20	L-b 9, w 4, n-b 4	17

1/53 2/157 3/421 4/514   (4 wkts dec.) 514   1/132   (1 wkt dec.) 307

*P. A. Neale, †S. J. Rhodes, R. K. Illingworth, P. J. Newport, S. R. Lampitt and N. V Radford did not bat.

Bonus points – Worcestershire 4, Glamorgan 1.

Bowling: *First Innings*—Frost 18–0–109–0; Watkin 23–3–93–1; Bastien 15.2–2–90–1; Croft 2–0–71–1; Cowley 22–3–101–1; Richards 7–0–31–0. *Second Innings*—Watkin 19–1–109–1; Frost 11–0–38–0; Cowley 1–0–1–0; Bastien 12.3–2–61–0; Croft 10–0–61–0; Butcher 4–0–28–0.

Glamorgan

A. R. Butcher b Lampitt	79 – c Neale b Illingworth	130
H. Morris lbw b Botham	57 – c Lampitt b Newport	119
P. A. Cottey not out	100 – (5) c D'Oliveira b Newport	1
M. P. Maynard c Lampitt b Botham	15 – (3) c Hick b Newport	1
V. A. Richards c Rhodes b Radford	41 – (4) c and b Illingworth	43
R. D. B. Croft c D'Oliveira b Illingworth	28 – (7) not out	91
N. G. Cowley not out	2 – (6) c Rhodes b Botham	63
C. P. Metson (did not bat)	– not out	12
L-b 1, n-b 4	5	B 10, l-b 21, n-b 2	33

1/140 2/144 3/178 4/248 5/317 (5 wkts dec.) 327   1/256 2/257 3/272 4/288 (6 wkts) 493
                                                                        5/326 6/450

S. Bastien, S. L. Watkin and M. Frost did not bat.

Bonus points – Glamorgan 4, Worcestershire 2.

Bowling: *First Innings*—Newport 15–0–72–0; Radford 15–1–79–1; Illingworth 15.1–2–80–1; Lampitt 11–2–40–1; Botham 12–1–55–2; Hick 1–1–0–0. *Second Innings*—Newport 19–4–87–3; Radford 12–1–67–0; Lampitt 3–1–14–0; Hick 12–3–61–0; Botham 2–2–40–1; Illingworth 24–2–124–2; Curtis 3–0–30–0; D'Oliveira 3–0–39–0.

Umpires: D. R. Shepherd and D. S. Thompsett.

GLAMORGAN v WARWICKSHIRE

At Swansea, July 25, 26, 27. Glamorgan won by five wickets. Glamorgan 20 pts, Warwickshire 7 pts. Toss: Warwickshire. Glamorgan achieved their fourth Championship win of the season and their first in Wales, and once again they were involved in a game producing an assault on the record books. Moody, Warwickshire's Australian all-rounder, hit the fastest first-class hundred ever in terms of time, reaching 100 in 26 minutes from only 36 balls with his seventh six. He also hit eleven fours, and went to 50 in eleven minutes from sixteen balls. The record, however, was achieved in farcical proceedings. Maynard and Cottey, who were bowling to hasten the declaration, tossed up a succession of donkey-drops which were struck for four or six. Warwickshire had amassed 443 for the loss of three wickets in the first day, with Moles hitting his highest score in Championship cricket. Glamorgan declared 70 runs behind after Morris had made his fifth century of the season and Croft had played another cultured innings. Rain prevented any play for the first hour of the final day, and after the easy runs had been taken, Glamorgan were set 283 to win from 55 overs. Butcher gave them a splendid start with his fifth hundred of the summer, and after Maynard had struck a breezy 56, Richards, hitting an unbeaten 65 from 43 deliveries, took his team to victory with 2 balls remaining.

Close of play: First day, Warwickshire 443-3 (A. J. Moles 224*, P. A. Smith 14*); Second day, Warwickshire 16-2 (A. J. Moles 9*, T. A. Munton 0*).

Warwickshire

A. J. Moles not out	224 – not out	83
T. A. Lloyd c Watkin b Croft	101 – c Maynard b Bastien	0
Asif Din c Metson b Watkin	47 – lbw b Bastien	6
T. M. Moody c Dennis b Cowley	40 – (5) not out	103
P. A. Smith not out	14		
T. A. Munton (did not bat)	– (4) c Butcher b Cottey	14
L-b 12, w 2, n-b 3	17	L-b 6	6

1/220 2/327 3/394 (3 wkts dec.) 443   1/4 2/15 3/81 (3 wkts dec.) 212

D. A. Reeve, †K. J. Piper, G. C. Small, J. E. Benjamin and A. R. K. Pierson did not bat.

Bonus points – Warwickshire 4 (Score at 100 overs: 381-2).

Bowling: *First Innings*—Watkin 22–2–94–1; Dennis 25–3–91–0; Bastien 17–1–81–0; Cowle 30–2–111–1; Croft 16–2–54–1. *Second Innings*—Watkin 8–1–36–0; Bastien 6–1–11–2; Crof 7–4–12–0; Cowley 4–2–9–0; Maynard 6–0–89–0; Cottey 6–0–49–1.

Glamorgan

*A. R. Butcher c Piper b Munton	33	– c Piper b Pierson ....11(
H. Morris c Reeve b Pierson	106	– c Munton b Small .... 1!
P. A. Cottey lbw b Pierson	50	– run out .... ;
M. P. Maynard b Pierson	27	– c Piper b Asif Din .... 5(
I. V. A. Richards c and b Munton	11	– not out 6
R. D. B. Croft not out	74	– (7) not out 1:
N. G. Cowley c Moody b Pierson	30	– (6) c Moody b Pierson .... 1(
†C. P. Metson st Piper b Pierson	7	
S. L. Watkin not out	10	
B 6, l-b 14, w 2, n-b 3	25	L-b 3, w 1, n-b 3 ....

1/47 2/163 3/201 4/218 5/267   (7 wkts dec.) 373   1/42 2/70 3/167   (5 wkts) 28.
6/347 7/355   4/206 5/232

S. Bastien and S. J. Dennis did not bat.

Bonus points – Glamorgan 4, Warwickshire 3.

Bowling: *First Innings*—Small 12–3–47–0; Munton 17–2–65–2; Benjamin 10–1–45–0; Smi 3–0–17–0; Pierson 35–6–101–5; Asif Din 13–2–50–0; Reeve 7–2–28–0. *Second Innings*—Sma 12.4–2–62–1; Munton 15–1–77–0; Pierson 15–2–78–2; Benjamin 6–2–24–0; Asif Di 6–0–39–1.

Umpires: D. R. Shepherd and D. S. Thompsett.

At Lord's, August 4, 6, 7. GLAMORGAN drew with MIDDLESEX.

At Southend, August 8, 9, 10. GLAMORGAN drew with ESSEX.

At Worksop, August 11, 13, 14. GLAMORGAN beat NOTTINGHAMSHIRE by 238 run

At Swansea, August 18, 19, 20. GLAMORGAN drew with INDIANS (See Indian tou section).

At Ebbw Vale, August 22, 23, 24. GLAMORGAN drew with SRI LANKANS (See S Lankan tour section).

GLAMORGAN v DERBYSHIRE

At Cardiff, August 29, 30, 31. Drawn. Glamorgan 8 pts, Derbyshire 4 pts. Toss: Derbyshir Rain permitted only 25.4 overs on the first day and prevented any play on the final day un 3.30 p.m. Derbyshire made early inroads and reduced Glamorgan to 90 for four on th opening day, but another outstanding contribution from Morris, with useful support from th middle-order and tail-end batsmen, enabled Glamorgan to obtain maximum batting poin Morris's 160 not out, a career-best score, contained twenty fours and was his tenth first-cla hundred of the summer. Derbyshire collapsed dramatically in the 31 remaining overs of th second day, losing five wickets for only 5 runs in six overs as they failed to cope with Frost seam bowling and the spin of young Croft. The latter claimed his three wickets in the space fifteen balls at a cost of 1 run. However, on the final afternoon Barnett, who had come in

No. 7, and Warner played more purposefully. They added 73 in fifteen overs, with Warner hitting an attractive 59 from 44 deliveries. After Derbyshire were dismissed there was enough time for Morris to score the 16 he needed to reach 2,000 runs for the season, but when 4 he was unaccountably out to a long-hop from his Derbyshire namesake, a very occasional bowler.

Close of play: First day, Glamorgan 90-4 (H. Morris 47*, A. Dale 2*); Second day, Derbyshire 97-7 (K. J. Barnett 2*, A. E. Warner 3*).

Glamorgan

*A. R. Butcher b Base	4	– not out		13
H. Morris not out	160	– c Mortensen b Morris		4
P. A. Cottey c Adams b Malcolm	8	– b Adams		3
M. P. Maynard c Barnett b Warner	20	– not out		11
I. V. A. Richards c Roberts b Mortensen	0			
A. Dale lbw b Mortensen	16			
R. D. B. Croft c and b Barnett	31			
†C. P. Metson c Bowler b Barnett	22			
S. L. Watkin c Krikken b Warner	8			
S. Bastien not out	9			
L-b 10, w 3, n-b 10	23	B 4, l-b 1, w 1, n-b 4		10

1/6 2/40 3/79 4/80 5/123   (8 wkts dec.) 301   1/8 2/30   (2 wkts) 41
6/206 7/262 8/285

M. Frost did not bat.

Bonus points – Glamorgan 4, Derbyshire 3.

Bowling: *First Innings*—Malcolm 16-4-61-1; Base 18-3-73-1; Mortensen 18-6-48-2; Warner 16-2-53-2; Barnett 21.4-2-56-2. *Second Innings*—Base 2-0-14-0; Morris 4-0-17-1; Adams 2-0-5-1.

Derbyshire

P. D. Bowler b Croft	28	A. E. Warner b Watkin		59
C. J. Adams c Butcher b Watkin	14	D. E. Malcolm b Frost		2
J. E. Morris b Croft	40	O. H. Mortensen not out		1
B. Roberts lbw b Frost	5			
S. J. Base c Morris b Croft	0	B 4, l-b 5		9
A. P. Kuiper b Frost	0			
*K. J. Barnett c Metson b Watkin	30			188
†K. M. Krikken lbw b Frost	0	1/23 2/81 3/92 4/92 5/92		
		6/92 7/94 8/167 9/170		

Bonus points – Derbyshire 1, Glamorgan 4.

Bowling: Watkin 14.4-0-39-3; Bastien 7-0-41-0; Frost 18-3-80-4; Croft 10-4-10-3; Dale 2-0-9-0.

Umpires: A. A. Jones and R. Palmer.

GLAMORGAN v HAMPSHIRE

At Pontypridd, September 7, 8, 9. Hampshire won by eight wickets. Hampshire 24 pts, Glamorgan 6 pts. Toss: Glamorgan. Hampshire outplayed Glamorgan to secure an emphatic victory shortly after lunch on the third of the scheduled four days. Without Richards, who withdrew at the last minute because of flu, Glamorgan struggled after Morris and Butcher had given them their customary good start. Maynard put together a disciplined half-century, but Marshall demolished the middle- and lower-order batting, taking five for 23 in a spell of twelve overs. Marshall also contributed with the bat, striking a rapid 51, but Hampshire were themselves struggling at 160 for seven before Aymes, with a career-best 75 not out, and in partnership with Tremlett and Udal, changed the course of the match. Hampshire's last three wickets added an invaluable 153 runs to give them a lead of 103. Glamorgan's opening pair again laid the foundation with a partnership of 77, but the later batsmen wilted as Marshall emulated his first-innings onslaught. On the third morning seven wickets fell for 53 runs in 21.4 overs, Marshall finishing with six for 47 and a match aggregate of eleven for 92.

Close of play: First day, Hampshire 92-3 (R. A. Smith 33*, R. J. Maru 4*); Second day, Glamorgan 116-3 (M. P. Maynard 26*, P. A. Cottey 5*).

Glamorgan

*A. R. Butcher b Udal	58	– c Terry b Tremlett	33
H. Morris lbw b Udal	29	– lbw b Tremlett	45
P. A. Cottey lbw b Maru	13	– (5) c Aymes b Marshall	23
M. P. Maynard c Maru b Marshall	50	– c Terry b Marshall	27
A. Dale c R. A. Smith b Maru	14	– (6) c Aymes b Marshall	0
S. P. James c Gower b Maru	1	– (3) run out	2
R. D. B. Croft not out	27	– c Terry b Marshall	10
†C. P. Metson b Marshall	0	– c R. A. Smith b Marshall	15
S. L. Watkin c R. A. Smith b Marshall	5	– b Udal	3
S. Bastien c Maru b Marshall	2	– c Gower b Marshall	0
M. Frost c Aymes b Marshall	0	– not out	4
B 6, l-b 1, w 1, n-b 3	11	B 1, l-b 7, w 1, n-b 1	10

1/63 2/95 3/118 4/168 5/174   210   1/77 2/79 3/84 4/119 5/121   172
6/174 7/174 8/194 9/200   6/150 7/151 8/156 9/157

Bonus points – Glamorgan 2, Hampshire 4.

Bowling: *First Innings*—Bakker 17–4–51–0; Marshall 22.4–6–45–5; Tremlett 8–2–29–0; Udal 19–5–56–2; Maru 15–8–22–3. *Second Innings*—Bakker 11–0–46–0; Marshall 22.4–8–47–6; Udal 17–7–34–1; Maru 8–4–22–0; Tremlett 7–3–15–2.

Hampshire

V. P. Terry c Dale b Croft	36	– b Frost	8
C. L. Smith lbw b Frost	1	– not out	25
D. I. Gower c Metson b Watkin	17	– c Cottey b Frost	23
R. A. Smith b Watkin	42	– not out	14
R. J. Maru lbw b Bastien	5		
M. D. Marshall c Croft b Frost	51		
*M. C. J. Nicholas run out	5		
†A. N. Aymes not out	75		
T. M. Tremlett c Maynard b Croft	23		
S. D. Udal c Metson b Bastien	28		
P. J. Bakker c James b Bastien	12		
B 4, l-b 11, n-b 3	18	B 1, n-b 1	2

1/15 2/48 3/87 4/101 5/105   313   1/11 2/52   (2 wkts) 72
6/158 7/160 8/230 9/295

Bonus points – Hampshire 4, Glamorgan 4.

Bowling: *First Innings*—Frost 19–3–59–2; Watkin 22–3–100–2; Bastien 23.4–5–70–3; Croft 26–8–69–2. *Second Innings*—Watkin 6–1–18–0; Frost 6–1–25–2; Croft 5.2–1–28–0.

Umpires: R. Julian and K. E. Palmer.

At Birmingham, September 12, 13, 14, 15. GLAMORGAN lost to WARWICKSHIRE by 170 runs.

At Worcester, September 18, 19, 20, 21. GLAMORGAN lost to WORCESTERSHIRE by 261 runs.

GLOUCESTERSHIRE

Patron: HRH The Princess of Wales
President: F. J. Twisleton
Chairman: R. W. Rossiter
Chairman, Cricket Committee: D. A. Allen
Secretary: P. G. M. August
    Phoenix County Ground, Nevil Road, Bristol
    BS7 9EJ (Telephone: 0272-245216)
Captain: A. J. Wright
Senior Coach: E. J. Barlow
Youth Coach: G. G. M. Wiltshire

Gloucestershire finished the season in such good style, winning four of their last nine Championship matches, that in normal circumstances it would have been possible to look forward to 1991 with a degree of optimism. Unhappily, however, the season again ended on a note of discord, following the decision to dispense with the services of Kevin Curran, one of the best all-rounders in the county game. The first official announcement, after some weeks of rumour, said that Curran was leaving by "mutual consent". But a day or two later, Dickie Rossiter, the club chairman, revealed that the decision had been taken because Curran was perceived to be a disruptive influence. Eddie Barlow, coming to the end of his first season of a three-year contract as chief coach, said: "It was a difficult decision, but one we felt had to be made in the interests of the club."

Curran certainly presented impressive playing credentials to potential employers in the two remaining games of the season, with scores of 144 not out, 78 and 101 not out, as well as capturing nine wickets. In the same two games David Graveney, who had said earlier in the season that he would be ending his long association with the county, took fifteen wickets. Then, at the end of September, Phil Bainbridge announced his retirement to concentrate on his business interests.

These three departures, allied to the near certainty that Courtney Walsh would be touring with the West Indians in 1991, left a daunting task of rebuilding facing Barlow and the captain, Tony Wright, who had joined forces at the start of the summer. They had made no promises of early success, but with the talent available they must have hoped for a good season. Things soon began to go wrong; there were defeats in three different competitions in the first eight days. They finished bottom of their group in the Benson and Hedges Cup, without a win; and with no Championship wins either, they were soon bottom of the table. The weather was unkind for much of June, the Gloucester week being badly affected by rain, and Wright was quite unable to win the toss. Following defeat at Worcester, when both Walsh and David Lawrence were absent through injury, Gloucestershire arrived at Cheltenham in a parlous state, adrift at the foot of the Championship table with no more than 49 points to show from twelve matches.

However, the players seemed to take heart from the more intimate atmosphere of the College ground and its pitches, which encouraged strokemaking and the quick bowlers. The elusive first victory came when

Northamptonshire were routed in their second innings by some high-class fast bowling from Walsh, whose return of eight for 58 proved to be the best in the Championship during the season. After that, although weaknesses were still apparent, the team began to play with much more confidence, and there was a string of outstanding personal performances. Bill Athey's two centuries against Warwickshire were largely responsible for another win, Jack Russell played two fine innings against Nottinghamshire, and Lawrence achieved his first hat-trick in the same match. Mark Alleyne played a truly remarkable innings in the return game against Northamptonshire, his 256 being the highest for the county since 1939, and Dean Hodgson made his first Championship hundred, with 109 against Worcestershire at Bristol.

The ignominy of bottom place was safely avoided and Alleyne, having been overlooked earlier in the season, was awarded his county cap for playing a full part in the revival. Hodgson could also look back with satisfaction, having scored 1,320 first-class runs in his first full season, a deserved reward for his perseverance and the hard work he had put into improving his game. It has to be said, however, that he and Wright were among the weaker opening pairs around the counties. Wright passed 50 only five times in Championship games, and fears that the captaincy might affect his own form proved to be only too well founded. Gloucestershire's low total of batting points, when conditions were more in favour of batsmen than for many years, must be put down, to a large extent, to the lack of a reliable opening partnership. A total of fifteen Championship centuries, although three more than in 1989, was below par, and Athey would assuredly have scored more heavily had his primary task been more one of consolidation than damage limitation.

The middle order was much stronger when Russell was not required by England; he scored his first two centuries in the Championship with the confidence of a player his country has come to rely on. In fact, Russell was missed more for his batting than his peerless wicket-keeping, for Gloucestershire's discovery of the season was his new deputy, Richard "Reggie" Williams, a club cricketer who, with limited Second Eleven experience, made the transition to the first-class game in splendid style. He not only pulled off some spectacular dismissals but also showed promise as a batsman. Little, however, was seen of Martyn Ball, who had looked so promising in 1989, and Graveney gave as one of the reasons for his own departure a desire not to stand in the young off-spinner's path.

There were fewer Championship hundreds – eleven – scored against Gloucestershire than any other county, which reflected well on an attack which was handicapped by Graveney's absence for a lengthy period, while he recovered from a hand operation, and was not as well supported in the field as in previous years. The team showed improved form in the Refuge Assurance League, without being able to mount a prolonged challenge for a place in the top four, while the NatWest Bank Trophy campaign ended in a defeat of record proportions at Old Trafford in the quarter-finals.

The announcement that Andy Babington, from Sussex, and Jonathan Hardy, from Somerset, would be joining the staff for 1991 hardly assuaged understandable anxieties among members and supporters about the immediate outlook. All were keenly interested to see what Barlow, never a man to shirk a challenge, had come up with in the winter months. – *Geoffrey Wheeler.*

GLOUCESTERSHIRE 1990

[*Bill Smith*]

Back row: G. A. Tedstone, E. T. Milburn, S. N. Barnes, K. B. S. Jarvis, G. D. Hodgson, N. M. A. Pritchard, R. C. J. Williams. *Middle row*: G. G. M. Wiltshire (*youth coach*), K. M. Curran, P. W. Romaines, I. P. Butcher, J. W. Lloyds, M. W. Alleyne, M. W. Pooley, M. C. J. Ball. *Front row*: A. W. Stovold, P. Bainbridge, A. J. Wright (*captain*), E. J. Barlow (*senior coach*), C. W. J. Athey, D. A. Graveney. *Insets*: D. V. Lawrence, C. A. Walsh, R. C. Russell.

GLOUCESTERSHIRE RESULTS

All first-class matches – Played 25: Won 5, Lost 7, Drawn 13.

County Championship matches – Played 22: Won 4, Lost 7, Drawn 11.

Bonus points – Batting 51, Bowling 58.

*Competition placings – Britannic Assurance County Championship, 13th equal;
NatWest Bank Trophy, q-f; Benson and Hedges Cup, 5th in Group A;
Refuge Assurance League, 8th equal.*

BRITANNIC ASSURANCE CHAMPIONSHIP AVERAGES

BATTING

	Birthplace	M	I	NO	R	HI	Avge
‡C. W. J. Athey	Middlesbrough	21	32	6	1,384	131	53.23
‡K. M. Curran	Rusape, S. Rhodesia	22	32	8	1,261	144*	52.54
‡M. W. Alleyne	Tottenham, London	11	17	0	763	256	44.88
‡P. Bainbridge	Stoke-on-Trent	18	25	2	1,019	152	44.30
‡R. C. Russell	Stroud	11	16	1	651	120	43.40
‡J. W. Lloyds	Penang, Malaya	21	29	10	704	93	37.05
G. D. Hodgson	Carlisle	21	34	2	1,059	109	33.09
‡P. W. Romaines ...	Bishop Auckland	5	7	1	177	61	29.50
‡C. A. Walsh	Kingston, Jamaica	19	19	3	464	63*	29.00
I. P. Butcher	Farnborough, Kent	9	13	3	280	102	28.00
‡A. W. Stovold	Bristol	2	4	0	104	74	26.00
‡A. J. Wright	Stevenage	22	36	3	809	112	24.51
R. C. J. Williams ..	Bristol	7	7	3	82	44*	20.50
‡D. A. Graveney	Bristol	12	12	4	100	46*	12.50
M. C. J. Ball	Bristol	3	5	0	39	15	7.80
‡D. V. Lawrence	Gloucester	20	21	3	124	29	6.88
S. N. Barnes	Bath	7	7	1	11	6	1.83

Also batted: R. M. Bell (*St Mary's, Isles of Scilly*) (2 matches) 0, 0*; K. B. S. Jarvis (*Dartford*) (1 match) 0*, 1*; E. T. Milburn (*Nuneaton*) (1 match) 0, 3*; P. A. Owen (*Regina, Canada*) (3 matches) 1, 1; G. A. Tedstone (*Southport*) (4 matches) 13, 6, 23.

* Signifies not out.   ‡ Denotes county cap.

The following played a total of fifteen three-figure innings for Gloucestershire in County Championship matches – C. W. J. Athey 3, K. M. Curran 3, M. W. Alleyne 2, P. Bainbridge 2, R. C. Russell 2, I. P. Butcher 1, G. D. Hodgson 1, A. J. Wright 1.

BOWLING

	O	M	R	W	BB	5W/i	Avge
M. W. Alleyne	77	23	254	11	3-23	0	23.09
C. A. Walsh	584.1	98	1,961	70	8-58	3	28.01
K. M. Curran	561.3	105	1,839	60	5-63	1	30.65
D. V. Lawrence	418.3	45	1,679	50	5-51	2	33.58
D. A. Graveney	462.4	125	1,145	29	5-45	3	39.48
J. W. Lloyds	314.5	52	1,175	24	4-11	0	48.95

Also bowled: C. W. J. Athey 36.5-9-104-2; P. Bainbridge 137.4-24-426-9; M. C. J. Ball 34-7-114-0; S. N. Barnes 138-25-388-8; R. M. Bell 44-7-114-3; K. B. S. Jarvis 12-1-61-1; E. T. Milburn 7-1-34-0; P. A. Owen 57-7-239-4; G. A. Tedstone 2-1-1-0; A. J. Wright 0.5-0-7-0

Wicket-keepers: R. C. Russell 27 ct; R. C. J. Williams 22 ct, 4 st; G. A. Tedstone 3 ct.

Leading Fielders: A. J. Wright 21, C. W. J. Athey 18, K. M. Curran 15, J. W. Lloyds 15.

At Taunton, April 26, 27, 28, 29. GLOUCESTERSHIRE lost to SOMERSET by ten wickets.

GLOUCESTERSHIRE v GLAMORGAN

At Bristol, May 15, 16, 17. Glamorgan won by 145 runs. Glamorgan 23 pts, Gloucestershire 4 pts. Toss: Glamorgan. Glamorgan overcame the handicap of losing two leading batsmen with broken fingers on the first day to gain a thoroughly deserved victory with more than a day to spare. Maynard batted splendidly, hitting ten fours in his 55, before he retired hurt following a blow from a ball from Lawrence – Holmes was the other casualty, a victim of Walsh – and Butcher grafted for some five and a half hours to ensure a reasonable total. The Gloucestershire bowlers fell into the trap of pitching too short, whereas on the second day Glamorgan's attack, with Frost outstanding, showed the merit of bowling to a fuller length. They also benefited from some slipshod batting. Although Butcher and Cowley again played well in Glamorgan's second innings, Gloucestershire were left with nearly two days in which to get 291. Once more, however, they batted poorly, losing three wickets in four balls with the score at 29. Two of these went to the eager Frost, who completed a match haul of ten wickets for the first time.

Close of play: First day, Gloucestershire 0-0 (M. C. J. Ball 0*, A. J. Wright 0*); Second day, Glamorgan 137-4 (N. G. Cowley 50*, C. P. Metson 0*).

Glamorgan

*A. R. Butcher c Wright b Alleyne	83	– c Wright b Lloyds	53
H. Morris c Athey b Walsh	7	– c Russell b Lawrence	1
G. C. Holmes c Lawrence b Walsh	12	– absent injured	
M. P. Maynard retired hurt	55	– absent injured	
I. V. A. Richards c and b Bainbridge	32	– (3) lbw b Walsh	1
I. Smith c Russell b Curran	19	– (4) c Athey b Lawrence	14
N. G. Cowley not out	51	– (5) c Athey b Walsh	61
†C. P. Metson lbw b Alleyne	0	– (6) b Walsh	4
S. J. Dennis c Ball b Alleyne	6	– (7) b Walsh	0
S. L. Watkin c Athey b Walsh	1	– (8) c Curran b Walsh	10
M. Frost lbw b Walsh	1	– (9) not out	4
B 1, l-b 7, w 2, n-b 14	24	B 4, l-b 5, n-b 13	22
	291		**170**

1/20 2/47 3/170 4/203 5/253 6/253 7/275 8/283 9/291 **291**

1/4 2/11 3/51 4/136 5/153 6/156 7/157 8/170 **170**

Bonus points – Glamorgan 3, Gloucestershire 3 (Score at 100 overs: 290-8).

In the first innings M. P. Maynard retired hurt at 120.

Bowling: *First Innings*—Walsh 22.4–4–62–4; Lawrence 17–0–65–0; Bainbridge 17–7–36–1; Curran 16–5–39–1; Ball 12–3–34–0; Alleyne 16–5–47–3. *Second Innings*—Walsh 17.2–3–48–5; Lawrence 10–0–40–2; Curran 13–0–35–0; Bainbridge 3–1–12–0; Alleyne 4–3–9–0; Ball 3–2–4–0; Athey 3–2–4–0; Lloyds 5–3–9–1.

Gloucestershire

M. C. J. Ball c Richards b Frost	5	– (10) lbw b Cowley	15
*A. J. Wright b Frost	3	– (1) lbw b Frost	5
A. W. Stovold c Metson b Frost	7	– (2) c Metson b Watkin	19
P. Bainbridge b Watkin	35	– (3) b Frost	1
C. W. J. Athey c Smith b Dennis	8	– (4) b Frost	0
K. M. Curran c Metson b Watkin	47	– (5) c Richards b Watkin	44
J. W. Lloyds c Metson b Frost	9	– (6) c Metson b Frost	14
M. W. Alleyne b Frost	0	– c Metson b Frost	6
†R. C. Russell c Metson b Dennis	33	– (7) b Dennis	0
C. A. Walsh not out	19	– (9) b Watkin	31
D. V. Lawrence lbw b Cowley	1	– not out	1
B 1, l-b 2, n-b 1	4	L-b 5, w 2, n-b 2	9
	171		**145**

1/3 2/11 3/28 4/43 5/75 6/98 7/98 8/134 9/168 **171**

1/17 2/29 3/29 4/29 5/50 6/51 7/61 8/124 9/129 **145**

Bonus points – Gloucestershire 1, Glamorgan 4.

Bowling: *First Innings*—Frost 14–4–42–5; Watkin 18–5–55–2; Dennis 15–5–46–2; Cowley 14.3–6–25–1. *Second Innings*—Frost 14–2–40–5; Watkin 13–3–51–3; Dennis 11–3–35–1; Cowley 5.5–2–14–1.

Umpires: J. D. Bond and K. E. Palmer.

GLOUCESTERSHIRE v ZIMBABWEANS

At Bristol, May 19, 21, 22. Drawn. Toss: Gloucestershire. Curran and Lawrence had to pull out all the stops to deny the touring side a notable victory after they had needed no more than 106 runs from what proved to be 21 overs. It would have been Zimbabwe's first first-class win over a county side in England. Gloucestershire's first-innings declaration, after Hodgson had completed a maiden century in just over four hours, was not reciprocated by the visitors, who decided to let an innings dominated by Shah's seven-hour 185 run its course. Shah, missed three times off Lawrence, ground down the attack during a partnership of 178 in 50 overs with Briant. Providing some extrovert moments amid periods of solid defence, he hit 24 fours and had one five. Gloucestershire, looking forward to second-innings batting practice, were undermined by the artful Traicos and finished off by Brandes, but not quite quickly enough for the Zimbabweans to press home their advantage.

Close of play: First day, Zimbabweans 45-0 (W. R. James 24*, A. H. Shah 21*); Second day, Zimbabweans 366-7 (E. A. Brandes 10*, A. J. Traicos 1*).

Gloucestershire

I. P. Butcher c Robertson b Brent	78	– (6)	not out	26
G. D. Hodgson c Traicos b Brent	126	– (7)	c James b Traicos	6
M. W. Alleyne b Shah	37	– (4)	b Traicos	54
*C. W. J. Athey not out	8	– (9)	lbw b Brandes	2
P. Bainbridge not out	4	– (1)	b Traicos	23
J. W. Lloyds (did not bat)		– (2)	b Jarvis	31
K. M. Curran (did not bat)		– (3)	c Briant b Jarvis	6
†G. A. Tedstone (did not bat)		– (5)	c Traicos b Dolphin	23
D. A. Graveney (did not bat)		– (8)	b Brandes	7
D. V. Lawrence (did not bat)		–	b Brandes	0
S. N. Barnes (did not bat)		–	b Brandes	0
B 4, l-b 8, n-b 2	14		B 10, l-b 15, n-b 3	28

1/170 2/255 3/255 (3 wkts dec.) 267
1/52 2/60 3/90 4/138 5/158 206
6/175 7/188 8/198 9/202

Bowling: *First Innings*—Brandes 12–3–32–0; Jarvis 9–1–40–0; Butchart 7–1–23–0; Dolphin 13–2–58–0; Traicos 17–8–30–0; Shah 15–4–44–1; Brent 13–2–28–2. *Second Innings*—Brandes 10.2–3–35–4; Jarvis 21–6–61–2; Traicos 25–10–43–3; Dolphin 16–7–29–1; Brent 5–3–13–0.

Zimbabweans

W. R. James c Graveney b Lawrence	36	–	lbw b Curran	23
A. H. Shah c Alleyne b Graveney	185			
C. M. Robertson c Tedstone b Curran	6	– (2)	c Tedstone b Lawrence	6
*A. J. Pycroft st Tedstone b Graveney	9	–	retired hurt	15
†G. A. Briant c Graveney b Curran	69			
J. P. Brent b Alleyne	23	– (3)	not out	27
I. P. Butchart lbw b Curran	6	– (5)	run out	5
E. A. Brandes lbw b Lawrence	10	– (6)	not out	8
A. J. Traicos lbw b Lawrence	1			
M. P. Jarvis not out	1			
B 10, l-b 12, w 1, n-b 1	24		B 3, l-b 1, n-b 1	5

1/60 2/78 3/103 4/281 5/340 (9 wkts dec.) 368
6/351 7/359 8/366 9/368
1/14 2/36 3/78 (3 wkts) 89

D. F. Dolphin did not bat.

Bowling: *First Innings*—Lawrence 18.1–5–45–3; Barnes 26–8–80–0; Curran 27–4–80–3; Graveney 23–11–44–2; Alleyne 10–2–42–1; Bainbridge 5–0–29–0; Lloyds 5–0–26–0. *Second Innings*—Lawrence 10.4–0–43–1; Curran 10–2–42–1.

Umpires: J. D. Bond and R. Julian.

At Cambridge, May 23, 24, 25. GLOUCESTERSHIRE beat CAMBRIDGE UNIVERSITY by 70 runs.

At Lord's, May 26, 28, 29. GLOUCESTERSHIRE lost to MIDDLESEX by 10 runs.

GLOUCESTERSHIRE v SOMERSET

At Bristol, June 2, 4, 5. Drawn. Gloucestershire 7 pts, Somerset 4 pts. Toss: Somerset. Rain took some three hours out of the third day and put an end to Gloucestershire's already fading hopes of avenging their defeat in the opening match of the season. The bowlers had been on top until Curran and Russell joined together on the second day in a seventh-wicket partnership which produced 229 runs and put Gloucestershire in a useful position. Russell, welcoming the opportunity of batting with time on his side, made his first Championship century, which included seventeen fours and came from 179 balls in 205 minutes. Curran's hundred took half an hour longer. Wright was able to declare with a lead of 156, but Cook and Burns played out the day's remaining overs with comparative ease. On the shortened final day, a draw soon became the inevitable outcome.

Close of play: First day, Gloucestershire 69-2 (I. P. Butcher 17*, C. W. J. Athey 24*); second day, Somerset 53-0 (S. J. Cook 19*, N. D. Burns 28*).

Somerset

S. J. Cook c Wright b Lawrence	40	– lbw b Lawrence	81
P. M. Roebuck c Russell b Walsh	3		
A. N. Hayhurst b Curran	15	– not out	17
C. J. Tavaré b Lloyds b Graveney	30	– not out	1
R. J. Harden c Lawrence b Curran	81		
N. D. Burns c Russell b Graveney	16	– (2) c Athey b Walsh	38
G. D. Rose c Athey b Lawrence	0		
I. G. Swallow lbw b Graveney	10		
N. A. Mallender b Walsh	8		
R. C. Hallett c Athey b Graveney	0		
A. N. Jones not out	0		
B 3, l-b 11, n-b 8	22	L-b 10, n-b 11	21
	225	(2 wkts)	158

1/37 2/58 3/70 4/143 5/174 6/175 7/197 8/215 9/221   1/111 2/148

Bonus points – Somerset 2, Gloucestershire 4.

Bowling: *First Innings*—Walsh 14.5–1–43–2; Lawrence 14–2–65–2; Curran 16–4–41–2; Graveney 27–7–53–4; Athey 1–0–9–0. *Second Innings*—Walsh 17–3–53–1; Lawrence 2–1–41–1; Graveney 18–7–38–0; Curran 4–2–14–0; Athey 0.5–0–2–0.

Gloucestershire

A. J. Wright c Roebuck b Mallender	4	†R. C. Russell c Burns b Rose	120
G. D. Hodgson b Jones	24		
I. P. Butcher c Harden b Hallett	41	B 6, l-b 8, w 2, n-b 4	20
C. W. J. Athey c Cook b Rose	37		
P. Bainbridge c Burns b Rose	29	1/9 2/31 3/134	(7 wkts dec.) 381
K. M. Curran not out	103	4/142 5/149	
J. W. Lloyds c and b Rose	3	6/152 7/381	

D. A. Graveney, C. A. Walsh and D. V. Lawrence did not bat.

Bonus points – Gloucestershire 3, Somerset 2 (Score at 100 overs: 289-6).

C. W. J. Athey, when 27, retired hurt at 76 and resumed at 134.

Bowling: Jones 25–2–96–1; Mallender 26–7–69–1; Rose 24.3–7–78–4; Swallow 19–5–43–0; Hallett 21–3–63–1; Hayhurst 7–1–18–0.

Umpires: J. C. Balderstone and N. T. Plews.

At Ilford, June 6, 7, 8. GLOUCESTERSHIRE drew with ESSEX.

At Manchester, June 9, 11, 12. GLOUCESTERSHIRE lost to LANCASHIRE by five wickets.

At Hove, June 16, 18, 19. GLOUCESTERSHIRE drew with SUSSEX.

GLOUCESTERSHIRE v HAMPSHIRE

At Gloucester, June 20, 21, 22. Drawn. Toss: Hampshire. Although the game began on time only twenty overs were bowled before the forecast rain arrived. Subsequently the ground took such a soaking that no further play was possible. There were hopes of play on the final afternoon, but the umpires found that the wicket surrounds were still too wet.

Close of play: First day, Gloucestershire 54-2 (G. D. Hodgson 22*, C. W. J. Athey 14*) Second day, No play.

Gloucestershire

*A. J. Wright c Connor b Marshall ...	9
G. D. Hodgson not out	22
I. P. Butcher b Connor	4
C. W. J. Athey not out	14
L-b 2, w 1, n-b 2	5

1/19 2/25   (2 wkts) 54

K. M. Curran, M. W. Alleyne, J. W. Lloyds, †G. A. Tedstone, D. A. Graveney, C. A. Walsh and D. V. Lawrence did not bat.

Bowling: Marshall 6–0–20–1; Connor 6–1–17–1; Tremlett 4.1–0–9–0; Shine 3–1–6–0; Maru 1–1–0–0.

Hampshire

V. P. Terry, C. L. Smith, T. C. Middleton, D. I. Gower, *M. C. J. Nicholas, M. D. Marshall †R. J. Parks, R. J. Maru, T. M. Tremlett, C. A. Connor and K. J. Shine.

Umpires: A. A. Jones and D. S. Thompsett.

GLOUCESTERSHIRE v LEICESTERSHIRE

At Gloucester, June 23, 25, 26. Leicestershire won by 111 runs. Leicestershire 20 pts Gloucestershire 3 pts. Toss: Gloucestershire. Agnew literally swung the game in Leicestershire's favour on the third morning when he took full advantage of a fortuitous change in conditions to wreck the start of Gloucestershire's second innings. There was only an hour's play on the first day, when Boon and Briers began an opening partnership of 146 in 42 overs which put their side in a position to dictate terms. Boon went on to his second Championship century of the summer, hitting eighteen fours in a stay of 322 minutes. Following Wright's declaration and Leicestershire's forfeiture of their second innings, Gloucestershire were left with all of the final day in which to score 352. However, the weather, which had been cold and blustery, was now sultry, and Agnew, swinging the Reader ball in alarming fashion, took four wickets in 28 balls at a cost of 6 runs. Gloucestershire could find no way back from 13 for five although as conditions eased Bainbridge rode his luck and the later batsmen, showing commendable determination, kept Leicestershire in the field until 70 minutes after tea.

Close of play: First day, Leicestershire 59-0 (T. J. Boon 27*, N. E. Briers 25*); Second day Gloucestershire 75-0 (G. D. Hodgson 23*, A. J. Wright 51*).

Leicestershire

T. J. Boon b Lloyds	138	†P. A. Nixon not out		24
*N. E. Briers b Lawrence	67	J. P. Agnew not out		46
J. J. Whitaker c Lloyds b Curran	37			
P. Willey c Tedstone b Curran	8	B 1, l-b 11, w 1, n-b 15		28
L. Potter b Walsh	11			
J. D. R. Benson c Graveney b Curran	45	1/146 2/209 3/217	(8 wkts dec.)	426
C. C. Lewis lbw b Lloyds	6	4/267 5/289 6/314		
W. K. M. Benjamin c Athey b Curran	16	7/342 8/361		

A. D. Mullally did not bat.

Bonus points – Leicestershire 4, Gloucestershire 3 (Score at 100 overs: 357-7).

Bowling: Walsh 21–2–97–1; Curran 28–3–100–4; Lawrence 19–1–84–1; Bainbridge 4–4–16–0; Graveney 28–6–96–0; Lloyds 7–1–21–2.

Leicestershire forfeited their second innings.

Gloucestershire

G. D. Hodgson not out	23	– b Agnew		4
*A. J. Wright not out	51	– lbw b Agnew		2
A. P. Butcher (did not bat)		– c Potter b Benjamin		0
C. W. J. Athey (did not bat)		– c Potter b Agnew		5
P. Bainbridge (did not bat)		– c Nixon b Mullally		74
K. M. Curran (did not bat)		– c Nixon b Agnew		0
M. W. Lloyds (did not bat)		– c Whitaker b Benjamin		26
†G. A. Tedstone (did not bat)		– c Benjamin b Lewis		23
D. A. Graveney (did not bat)		– not out		46
C. A. Walsh (did not bat)		– b Mullally		12
D. V. Lawrence (did not bat)		– c Whitaker b Agnew		29
L-b 1	1	B 5, l-b 9, w 3, n-b 2		19

(no wkt dec.)	75	1/6 2/7 3/11 4/13 5/13	240
		6/102 7/135 8/173 9/187	

Bowling: *First Innings*—Willey 7–0–25–0; Potter 7–0–49–0. *Second Innings*—Benjamin 23–11–44–2; Agnew 25.5–10–70–5; Mullally 16–5–37–2; Lewis 17–3–73–1; Willey 2–1–2–0.

Umpires: A. A. Jones and D. S. Thompsett.

At Derby, June 30, July 2, 3. GLOUCESTERSHIRE drew with DERBYSHIRE.

At Swansea, July 4, 5, 6. GLOUCESTERSHIRE drew with GLAMORGAN.

At Worcester, July 7, 9, 10. GLOUCESTERSHIRE lost to WORCESTERSHIRE by 148 runs.

GLOUCESTERSHIRE v YORKSHIRE

At Cheltenham, July 21, 23, 24. Drawn. Gloucestershire 6 pts, Yorkshire 5 pts. Toss: Yorkshire. It was surprising that there were no more than two individual hundreds in a match of 1,244 runs. Gloucestershire's innings of 574 was their highest against Yorkshire, and the total against that county had been exceeded only by Somerset, on two occasions. Metcalfe set the tone with a brilliant century before lunch on the opening day, needing only 108 deliveries to reach three figures as the ball was sent racing over the parched outfield, and he finished with 27 fours and two sixes in his 162 made from 172 balls. Moxon was a very junior partner in an opening stand of 204. Gloucestershire, faced with some good off-spin bowling by young

Batty, batted more soberly until the follow-on had been saved. Bainbridge then cut loose and made his first hundred for a year, hitting a six and 21 fours in all. Wright, bravely, decided to try to force a win rather than declare behind, and after Walsh had slogged four sixes and six fours to reach 63 from 42 balls, Yorkshire went in again facing arrears of 123. They had no trouble saving the game.

Close of play: First day, Gloucestershire 42-0 (G. D. Hodgson 26*, A. J. Wright 15*). Second day, Gloucestershire 458-6 (P. Bainbridge 132*, R. C. Russell 4*).

Yorkshire

*M. D. Moxon b Walsh	66	– c and b Lloyds	18
A. A. Metcalfe c and b Lawrence	162	– c Wright b Lawrence	26
†R. J. Blakey c Russell b Curran	9	– c Curran b Lloyds	94
K. Sharp c Russell b Lawrence	38		
P. E. Robinson lbw b Walsh	49	– (4) not out	70
D. Byas not out	63	– (5) not out	0
P. Carrick c Russell b Curran	17		
C. S. Pickles not out	28		
B 4, l-b 4, w 1, n-b 10	19	L-b 1, w 2, n-b 8	11

1/204 2/224 3/286 4/297　　　(6 wkts dec.) 451　　1/45 2/51 3/213　　(3 wkts dec.) 219
5/362 6/409

P. J. Hartley, J. D. Batty and S. D. Fletcher did not bat.

Bonus points – Yorkshire 4, Gloucestershire 2.

Bowling: *First Innings*—Walsh 22–5–70–2; Lawrence 14–0–94–2; Curran 22–4–84–2; Bainbridge 7–0–37–0; Lloyds 14–1–73–0; Owen 16–1–72–0; Athey 4–0–13–0. *Second Innings*—Walsh 11–1–46–0; Curran 10–4–30–0; Lawrence 8–0–34–1; Lloyds 3–1–61–2 Owen 16–3–47–0.

Gloucestershire

G. D. Hodgson b Batty	65	C. A. Walsh not out	63
*A. J. Wright c Robinson b Batty	78	D. V. Lawrence c Blakey b Fletcher	4
P. W. Romaines c Byas b Fletcher	46	P. A. Owen run out	1
C. W. J. Athey b Batty	68		
P. Bainbridge c Blakey b Hartley	152	B 8, l-b 17, w 1, n-b 7	33
K. M. Curran c Moxon b Hartley	8		
J. W. Lloyds b Batty	38		574
†R. C. Russell b Hartley	16	1/126 2/163 3/227 4/309 5/350	
		6/452 7/489 8/499 9/554	

Bonus points – Gloucestershire 4, Yorkshire 1 (Score at 100 overs: 309-4).

Bowling: Hartley 28–5–111–3; Fletcher 28.1–5–98–2; Carrick 50–16–144–0; Pickles 8–0–45–0; Batty 38–6–137–4; Byas 1–0–14–0.

Umpires: J. H. Hampshire and R. A. White.

GLOUCESTERSHIRE v NORTHAMPTONSHIRE

At Cheltenham, July 25, 26, 27. Gloucestershire won by an innings and 128 runs. Gloucestershire 24 pts, Northamptonshire 3 pts. Toss: Northamptonshire. Although every player in the Gloucestershire side made a valuable contribution to their first Championship victory of the season, it might not have been achieved without the fine bowling of Walsh, who dealt Northamptonshire a series of hammer blows. On the first morning his spell of three for 11 in 25 balls began a collapse that was completed by Curran and Lawrence. Ambrose could strike no such sparks from the pitch when Gloucestershire batted, and Wright's first century of the season was well supported all down the order. Walsh knocked the heart out of the Northamptonshire second innings by the sheer pace and variety of his attack, capturing five wickets for 9 runs in 27 balls. Nevertheless Gloucestershire, unable to finish the match in two days, experienced some anxious hours of waiting on the Friday. Three of the remaining four wickets were taken in the 55 minutes of play possible before lunch, but the defiant Felton refused to be moved. Rain prevented any play until four o'clock when Walsh, fittingly, immediately dismissed Robinson to complete match figures of eleven for 99.

Close of play: First day, Gloucestershire 181-2 (A. J. Wright 94*, C. W. J. Athey 0*); Second day, Northamptonshire 113-6 (N. A. Felton 34*, D. Ripley 25*).

Northamptonshire

A. Fordham c Wright b Curran	13	– c Williams b Walsh	1
*W. Larkins c Williams b Walsh	16	– b Walsh	30
N. A. Felton c Williams b Walsh	6	– not out	82
R. J. Bailey b Curran	36	– c Hodgson b Owen	3
D. J. Capel b Walsh	10	– (6) c Romaines b Walsh	4
R. G. Williams c Williams b Curran	47	– (7) b Walsh	0
†D. Ripley c Williams b Lawrence	6	– (8) b Walsh	31
A. R. Roberts c Lloyds b Curran	0	– (9) b Walsh	0
J. G. Hughes c Williams b Lawrence	1	– (5) hit wkt b Walsh	0
C. E. L. Ambrose c Wright b Lawrence	8	– lbw b Curran	6
M. A. Robinson not out	0	– c Williams b Walsh	0
L-b 1, n-b 6	7	B 8, l-b 4, n-b 8	20
	150		**177**

1/20 2/34 3/39 4/61 5/123   1/40 2/41 3/53 4/60 5/72
6/136 7/140 8/142 9/142   6/72 7/127 8/127 9/141

Bonus points – Northamptonshire 1, Gloucestershire 4.

Bowling: *First Innings*—Walsh 12-0-41-3; Curran 13.4-4-37-4; Lawrence 13.4-1-52-3; Owen 5-0-12-0; Athey 2-1-7-0. *Second Innings*—Walsh 19.2-6-58-8; Curran 16-1-58-1; Lloyds 5-3-16-0; Owen 4-1-13-1; Lawrence 6-2-20-0.

Gloucestershire

G. D. Hodgson c Fordham b Robinson	50	†R. C. J. Williams not out	44
*A. J. Wright c Ripley b Ambrose	112	D. V. Lawrence b Williams	0
P. W. Romaines b Williams	28		
C. W. J. Athey b Bailey	27	L-b 13, w 5, n-b 10	28
P. Bainbridge c Capel b Roberts	34		
K. M. Curran c and b Roberts	86	1/97 2/159 3/203	(9 wkts dec.) 455
J. W. Lloyds c Ripley b Ambrose	34	4/271 5/271 6/315	
C. A. Walsh c Larkins b Robinson	12	7/343 8/454 9/455	

P. A. Owen did not bat.

Bonus points – Gloucestershire 4, Northamptonshire 2 (Score at 100 overs: 310-5).

Bowling: Ambrose 22-7-53-2; Robinson 36-5-119-2; Roberts 39-6-123-2; Hughes 17-4-69-0; Williams 19.2-7-42-2; Bailey 9-1-36-1.

Umpires: J. H. Hampshire and R. A. White.

GLOUCESTERSHIRE v SURREY

At Cheltenham, July 28, 30, 31. Drawn. Gloucestershire 5 pts, Surrey 5 pts. Toss: Surrey. With any one of four results possible off the final ball, the Cheltenham Festival came to a thrilling conclusion. Waqar Younis, Surrey's last man, needing 3 to win the game, swung wildly at Lawrence and edged the ball uppishly. But although Williams, the Gloucestershire wicket-keeper, just got his right hand to it, he could not complete the catch and the batsmen crossed for a single. From Lawrence's previous delivery, Williams had held a fine catch to send back Martin Bicknell and end a ninth-wicket partnership with Medlycott which had taken Surrey to the brink of victory. They had been set a target of 304 in 59 overs. On the opening day, Alleyne batted for five hours for his highest first-class score to date, and in doing so he dashed Greig's hopes of dismissing Gloucestershire cheaply. Bainbridge, who had retired hurt after being hit on the hand by a ball from Younis, returned at the fall of the seventh wicket to see the score past 300. There was an accomplished 83 not out from Darren Bicknell in the Surrey first innings, and he laid a secure foundation for the second-innings run-chase. Explosive batting by Lynch put Surrey in command, but Lawrence, bowling genuinely fast, brought Gloucestershire back into contention.

Close of play: First day, Surrey 9-0 (D. J. Bicknell 1*, G. S. Clinton 8*); Second day, Gloucestershire 44-1 (G. D. Hodgson 25*, C. W. J. Athey 3*).

Gloucestershire

G. D. Hodgson c Medlycott b M. P. Bicknell	54	– c M. P. Bicknell b Medlycott	44
*A. J. Wright c Greig b M. P. Bicknell	2	– c Waqar Younis b M. P. Bicknell	12
P. Bainbridge not out	37		
C. W. J. Athey c Thorpe b M. P. Bicknell	0	– (3) not out	86
M. W. Alleyne c and b Feltham	118	– (4) c Lynch b Greig	15
K. M. Curran lbw b Medlycott	46	– (5) c Feltham b Greig	25
J. W. Lloyds b Medlycott	23	– (6) not out	8
†R. C. J. Williams c Sargeant b Waqar Younis	0		
D. V. Lawrence c Sargeant b Waqar Younis	2		
S. N. Barnes c Thorpe b M. P. Bicknell	2		
P. A. Owen c and b Feltham	1		
B 1, l-b 7, n-b 8	16	B 2, l-b 6, w 4	12

1/14 2/27 3/86 4/169 5/217   301   1/28 2/96 3/129   (4 wkts dec.) 202
6/218 7/222 8/283 9/291   4/183

Bonus points – Gloucestershire 3, Surrey 3 (Score at 100 overs: 284-8).

In the first innings P. Bainbridge, when 3, retired hurt at 23 and resumed at 222.

Bowling: *First Innings*—Waqar Younis 23–4–69–2; M. P. Bicknell 24–4–63–4; Feltham 19.4–2–73–2; Greig 2–0–6–0; Medlycott 35–10–82–2. *Second Innings*—Waqar Younis 13–4–36–0; M. P. Bicknell 3–0–17–1; Medlycott 25.3–7–97–1; Feltham 6–1–17–0; Greig 10–2–27–2.

Surrey

D. J. Bicknell not out	83	– c sub b Lloyds	81
G. S. Clinton c Williams b Lloyds	38	– c Williams b Owen	13
G. P. Thorpe b Lloyds	0	– (4) c Williams b Lawrence	0
D. M. Ward c Hodgson b Barnes	5	– (3) c Williams b Lawrence	45
M. A. Lynch c Lloyds b Owen	33	– b Curran	77
*I. A. Greig st Williams b Owen	1	– c Curran b Lawrence	34
M. A. Feltham c Hodgson b Lloyds	14	– b Lawrence	1
K. T. Medlycott not out	14	– not out	18
†N. F. Sargeant (did not bat)		– c Wright b Curran	1
M. P. Bicknell (did not bat)		– c Williams b Lawrence	7
Waqar Younis (did not bat)		– not out	1
B 3, l-b 7, w 1, n-b 1	12	B 6, l-b 16, n-b 2	24

1/83 2/83 3/90 4/138   (6 wkts dec.) 200   1/45 2/124 3/124   (9 wkts) 302
5/140 6/161   4/194 5/259 6/262
                                                       7/273 8/278 9/301

Bonus points – Surrey 2, Gloucestershire 2.

Bowling: *First Innings*—Lawrence 7–1–28–0; Curran 10–2–26–0; Alleyne 5–1–15–0; Barnes 12–4–19–1; Lloyds 19.3–5–65–3; Owen 9–2–37–2. *Second Innings*—Lawrence 15–3–54–5; Curran 14–1–59–2; Lloyds 15–0–80–1; Owen 7–0–58–1; Barnes 8–1–29–0.

Umpires: J. C. Balderstone and B. Leadbeater.

At Bristol, August 4, 5, 6. GLOUCESTERSHIRE drew with INDIANS (See Indian tour section).

GLOUCESTERSHIRE v WARWICKSHIRE

At Bristol, August 8, 9, 10. Gloucestershire won by 66 runs. Gloucestershire 21 pts, Warwickshire 7 pts. Toss: Warwickshire. Nothing looked less likely at the start of the final day than a win for Gloucestershire, who were still 53 runs behind with two second-innings wickets already gone. However, for the second time in the match, Athey stood firmly in

Warwickshire's path. Romaines was a stout partner in a stand of 155 for the third wicket, and by the time Athey had completed his second century of the game, having played almost a lone hand in the first innings, Gloucestershire were out of danger. Curran benefited from the cheap runs then offered before Wright invited his opponents to attempt a target of 243 in 33 overs. While Asif Din was applying his wristy skills, Warwickshire were in with a chance. But he and Reeve both fell in the same over to Lawrence, and when Warwickshire turned to saving the game, Lloyds swept through the tail. Warwickshire were left regretting their inability to capitalise on Small's fine bowling in Gloucestershire's first innings and on the opening partnership of 131 between Moles and Ratcliffe in their own.

Close of play: First day, Warwickshire 59-0 (A. J. Moles 19*, J. D. Ratcliffe 34*); Second day, Gloucestershire 39-2 (P. W. Romaines 16*, C. W. J. Athey 9*).

Gloucestershire

G. D. Hodgson c Ostler b Munton	8	– b Small	8
*A. J. Wright c Lloyd b Small	4	– c Reeve b Munton	4
P. W. Romaines c Ostler b Munton	1	– c Smith b Pierson	61
C. W. J. Athey not out	108	– c Piper b Lloyd	122
M. W. Alleyne c Ratcliffe b Small	34	– b Pierson	13
K. M. Curran c Ratcliffe b Small	15	– not out	83
†J. W. Lloyds c Piper b Reeve	14	– not out	18
†R. C. J. Williams c Piper b Reeve	2		
C. A. Walsh lbw b Reeve	8		
D. V. Lawrence b Small	7		
S. N. Barnes c Ostler b Small	0		
L-b 10, w 2	12	B 14, l-b 10, n-b 1	25
	213	(5 wkts dec.)	334

1/11 2/13 3/13 4/94 5/114 6/160 7/174 8/184 9/207

1/10 2/24 3/179 4/196 5/254

Bonus points – Gloucestershire 2, Warwickshire 4.

Bowling: *First Innings*—Small 23–5–57–5; Munton 23–5–69–2; Reeve 25–4–46–3; Smith 10–1–31–0. *Second Innings*—Small 16–6–39–1; Munton 22–4–40–1; Pierson 18–4–69–2; Reeve 6–3–9–0; Smith 8–2–26–0; Asif Din 5–2–17–0; Lloyd 9–1–58–1; Moles 6–0–52–0.

Warwickshire

A. J. Moles c Lloyds b Curran	94	– c Athey b Walsh	12
J. D. Ratcliffe b Lloyds	75	– c Athey b Curran	7
*T. A. Lloyd c Williams b Lloyds	11	– (5) c Lloyds b Curran	5
Asif Din b Walsh	0	– (3) c Williams b Lawrence	65
P. A. Smith run out	4	– (4) c Curran b Walsh	21
D. A. Reeve lbw b Walsh	1	– c Williams b Lawrence	20
D. P. Ostler c Romaines b Curran	54	– b Lloyds	23
†K. J. Piper b Wright b Lawrence	0	– (9) b Lloyds	9
G. C. Small c Curran b Alleyne	24	– (8) st Williams b Lloyds	5
A. R. K. Pierson not out	16	– not out	0
T. A. Munton c Hodgson b Curran	2	– c Curran b Lloyds	0
B 3, l-b 17, n-b 4	24	B 1, l-b 6, n-b 2	9
	305		176

1/131 2/147 3/148 4/164 5/171 6/203 7/211 8/257 9/302

1/21 2/23 3/51 4/90 5/139 6/140 7/151 8/171 9/176

Bonus points – Warwickshire 3, Gloucestershire 3 (Score at 100 overs: 258-8).

Bowling: *First Innings*—Walsh 32–10–86–2; Curran 27.1–9–50–3; Lawrence 16–2–56–1; Barnes 15–2–38–0; Lloyds 19–5–51–2; Alleyne 2–1–4–1. *Second Innings*—Walsh 11–0–51–2; Curran 9–0–70–2; Lawrence 6–0–37–2; Lloyds 3.4–0–11–4.

Umpires: D. R. Shepherd and P. B. Wight.

GLOUCESTERSHIRE v KENT

At Bristol, August 11, 13, 14. Drawn. Gloucestershire 4 pts, Kent 6 pts. Toss: Kent. Kent'
domination was disturbed when the weather broke on the third morning, ruling out a
resumption until 40 minutes after lunch. Gloucestershire had finished the second day five
wickets down and still needing 128 to avoid the follow-on. But after the rain, with time
pressing, they declared, Kent forfeited their second innings, and Gloucestershire set off in
pursuit of 278 in 57 overs. Athey, having repaired a poor start to the first innings, batting fo
four and a half hours, was called upon to do the same in the second. Walsh, enjoying hi
promotion to No. 5, hit 55 from 38 balls, including five sixes, but Gloucestershire were never
really on terms with the required rate. When Athey was sixth out at 237, they were out of the
hunt. Davis, who bowled shrewdly for Kent, was well supported in the field. Gloucestershire
on the other hand, dropped too many catches on the opening day when, in splendid batting
conditions, runs flowed freely for Kent and Ward, in particular, played with great purpose.

Close of play: First day, Kent 452-7 (S. A. Marsh 54*, R. P. Davis 2*); Second day
Gloucestershire 221-5 (K. M. Curran 45*, J. W. Lloyds 0*).

Kent

S. G. Hinks c Hodgson b Alleyne	53	R. P. Davis c sub b Curran	2(
*M. R. Benson c Williams b Walsh	65	C. Penn not out	2:
N. R. Taylor c Alleyne b Walsh	22		
G. R. Cowdrey c Walsh b Alleyne	80	B 1, l-b 8, w 1, n-b 9	1!
T. R. Ward c Walsh b Curran	82		
M. V. Fleming c Ashley b Curran	45	1/98 2/145 3/150 (9 wkts dec.) 49!
†S. A. Marsh c Hodgson b Walsh	54	4/293 5/350 6/362
D. J. M. Kelleher c Williams b Walsh	35	7/448 8/454 9/498

M. M. Patel did not bat.

Bonus points – Kent 4, Gloucestershire 2 (Score at 100 overs: 379-6).

Bowling: Walsh 24–2–117–4; Curran 22–4–97–3; Lawrence 14–4–69–0; Barnes 17–1–51–0
Lloyds 30–6–114–0; Alleyne 13–3–41–2.

Kent forfeited their second innings.

Gloucestershire

G. D. Hodgson c Marsh b Penn	2	– c Benson b Davis	1'
*A. J. Wright b Davis	16	– run out	9
P. W. Romaines c Hinks b Penn	8	– c Cowdrey b Davis	21
C. W. J. Athey c Marsh b Fleming	83	– c and b Penn	7!
M. W. Alleyne c Davis b Patel	47	– (6) c Ward b Davis	40
K. M. Curran not out	45	– (7) c and b Davis	13
J. W. Lloyds not out	0	– (8) not out	6
C. A. Walsh (did not bat)		– (5) b Davis	55
D. V. Lawrence (did not bat)		– st Marsh b Davis	0
†R. C. J. Williams (did not bat)		– not out	0
B 2, l-b 7, w 1, n-b 10	20	B 7, l-b 13, n-b 4	24

1/2 2/32 3/33 4/127 5/221		(5 wkts dec.) 221	1/20 2/53 3/56 4/134	(8 wkts) 256	
			5/214 6/237 7/256 8/256		

S. N. Barnes did not bat.

Bonus points – Gloucestershire 2, Kent 2.

Bowling: *First Innings*—Penn 20–5–44–2; Kelleher 20–7–35–0; Davis 19–6–59–1; Pate
17–4–38–1; Fleming 18–5–36–1. *Second Innings*—Penn 13–0–59–1; Kelleher 9–1–18–0; Davi:
22.5–1–111–6; Patel 5–1–30–0; Fleming 7–0–18–0.

Umpires: D. R. Shepherd and P. B. Wight.

At Nottingham, August 18, 20, 21. GLOUCESTERSHIRE drew with NOTTINGHAM
SHIRE.

At Northampton, August 23, 24, 25, 27. GLOUCESTERSHIRE beat NORTHAMPTON-SHIRE by 157 runs.

GLOUCESTERSHIRE v WORCESTERSHIRE

At Bristol, September 7, 8, 9, 10. Drawn. Gloucestershire 5 pts, Worcestershire 5 pts. Toss: Gloucestershire. A slow pitch dictated the course of the match from the outset. The bowlers had a heartbreaking task, although Illingworth bowled impressively on the first day when Hodgson, who reached his maiden Championship century, and Bainbridge, whose own hundred came at a much livelier tempo, put on 182 in 42 overs. That Hick would achieve the 2nd hundred of his career was almost a foregone conclusion, although he took more than four hours over it as Worcestershire carefully removed the threat of the follow-on. Gloucestershire, meanwhile, improved their over-rate by giving Graveney a long bowl. Neale declared 101 behind, but when Athey in a painfully slow mode on the final day, Gloucestershire's declaration was delayed until only 55 overs remained for Worcestershire to score 321. Hit on the helmet by a delivery from Lawrence, Hick recovered to pose a brief threat. When he was brilliantly caught in the deep, Worcestershire were content to coast to the draw.

Close of play: First day, Gloucestershire 376-5 (M. W. Alleyne 47*, R. C. Russell 2*); Second day, Worcestershire 185-1 (T. S. Curtis 81*, G. A. Hick 28*); Third day, Gloucestershire 72-2 (A. J. Wright 48*).

Gloucestershire

G. D. Hodgson c Rhodes b Illingworth	109	– lbw b Newport		22
A. J. Wright b Newport	21	– st Rhodes b Illingworth		72
P. Bainbridge c Rhodes b Illingworth	129	– (4) lbw b Illingworth		39
C. W. J. Athey c Lord b Illingworth	18	– (5) not out		34
M. W. Alleyne c and b Radford	52	– (6) c and b Illingworth		8
K. M. Curran c Rhodes b Illingworth	18	– (7) not out		35
†R. C. Russell c Curtis b D'Oliveira	76			
J. W. Lloyds not out	71			
C. A. Walsh c Curtis b D'Oliveira	18			
D. V. Lawrence not out	6	– (3) lbw b Newport		0
B 1, l-b 22, n-b 10	33	B 2, l-b 3, n-b 4		9

1/52 2/234 3/284 4/323 5/365 (8 wkts dec.) 551   1/67 2/72 3/115 (5 wkts dec.) 219
6/381 7/526 8/544   4/150 5/164

D. A. Graveney did not bat.

Bonus points – Gloucestershire 4, Worcestershire 1 (Score at 100 overs: 358-4).

Bowling: *First Innings*—Dilley 21-3-54-0; Radford 25-6-98-1; Newport 29-7-80-1; Lampitt 25-2-103-0; Illingworth 46-12-121-4; Hick 13-1-49-0; D'Oliveira 2.3-0-23-2. *Second Innings*—Dilley 10-0-43-0; Radford 12-1-45-0; Illingworth 27-7-91-3; Newport 10-3-19-2; Lampitt 4-0-16-0.

Worcestershire

T. S. Curtis lbw b Graveney	96	– lbw b Lawrence		8
G. J. Lord b Lloyds	64	– not out		70
G. A. Hick c Alleyne b Bainbridge	110	– c Wright b Graveney		38
D. B. D'Oliveira c Alleyne b Graveney	5	– b Graveney		0
*P. A. Neale c Alleyne b Bainbridge	95	– b Walsh		3
S. R. Lampitt not out	45	– not out		20
†S. J. Rhodes not out	7			
B 7, l-b 8, w 1, n-b 12	28	L-b 6, n-b 3		9

1/114 2/219 3/245 4/343 5/431 (5 wkts dec.) 450   1/23 2/88 3/88 4/103 (4 wkts) 148

N. V. Radford, P. J. Newport, R. K. Illingworth and G. R. Dilley did not bat.

Bonus points – Worcestershire 4, Gloucestershire 1 (Score at 100 overs: 301-3).

Bowling: *First Innings*—Walsh 28-8-83-0; Lawrence 15-0-55-0; Curran 15-8-25-0; Graveney 53-15-96-2; Lloyds 23-1-97-1; Alleyne 4-1-26-0; Bainbridge 16.4-4-39-2; Athey 4-1-14-0. *Second Innings*—Lawrence 7-0-30-1; Curran 8-1-21-0; Graveney 19-3-58-2; Walsh 10-2-24-1; Lloyds 6-0-9-0.

Umpires: D. R. Shepherd and P. B. Wight.

GLOUCESTERSHIRE v SUSSEX

At Bristol, September 12, 13, 14. Gloucestershire won by an innings and 86 runs. Glouceste
shire 24 pts, Sussex 4 pts. Toss: Gloucestershire. Graveney led Gloucestershire from the fiel
after taking the final Sussex wicket on his last home appearance for the county he had serve
for nineteen seasons. Ironically, Gloucestershire's victory, which ensured that they woul
escape bottom place, where they had spent much of the season, was founded on the efforts o
Graveney, who took ten wickets, and Curran, another departure. Curran's adieu was marke
by the completion of the modern double of 1,000 runs and 50 wickets during the course of th
century which condemned Sussex to defeat. Sussex, who had the worst of the conditions, ha
struggled against keen Gloucestershire bowling on the opening day, but Pigott put them bac
in the match. At 82 for five early on the second day, Gloucestershire had lost their advantage
However, Bainbridge attacked while Curran, after being all but bowled by the first ball h
received from Lawrence, dropped anchor. When Bainbridge went, Curran in unhurrie
fashion – he took four and a half hours (233 balls) to reach his hundred – built a matcl
winning advantage with support from Russell, Lloyds and Walsh. Although Sussex failed t
take the match into the fourth day, Moores played with great spirit to delay the end.

Close of play: First day, Gloucestershire 59-4 (P. Bainbridge 30*, D. V. Lawrence 4*
Second day, Gloucestershire 435-8 (K. M. Curran 133*, C. A. Walsh 46*).

Sussex

N. J. Lenham b Curran	11	– lbw b Walsh	3
D. M. Smith c Lloyds b Graveney	52	– c Curran b Lawrence	
*P. W. G. Parker c Graveney b Curran	0	– c Wright b Graveney	
A. P. Wells c Wright b Curran	5	– c and b Graveney	2
M. P. Speight c and b Graveney	34	– c Athey b Graveney	1
A. I. C. Dodemaide c Curran b Walsh	17	– c Curran b Lawrence	2
†P. Moores c Lloyds b Graveney	0	– b Walsh	7
A. C. S. Pigott c Russell b Graveney	1	– lbw b Lawrence	
I. D. K. Salisbury b Walsh	0	– c Alleyne b Graveney	
B. T. P. Donelan not out	37	– b Graveney	1
R. A. Bunting c Athey b Graveney	4	– not out	
L-b 10, n-b 8	18	B 2, l-b 5, n-b 7	1

1/22 2/53 3/103 4/110 5/110   179   1/7 2/29 3/55 4/83 5/88   20
6/112 7/113 8/140 9/155   6/132 7/136 8/150 9/198

Bonus points – Sussex 1, Gloucestershire 4.

In the first innings N. J. Lenham, when 4, retired hurt at 22-0 and resumed at 140.

Bowling: *First Innings*—Walsh 17-2-45-2; Lawrence 12-4-17-0; Curran 15-6-24-
Bainbridge 6-1-7-0; Athey 4-1-15-0; Alleyne 5-1-16-0; Graveney 23.4-7-45-5. *Secon
Innings*—Lawrence 15-3-59-3; Curran 11-5-20-0; Graveney 37.2-15-59-5; Wals
15-3-46-2; Lloyds 5-1-11-0.

Gloucestershire

G. D. Hodgson c Salisbury b Pigott	1	J. W. Lloyds b Dodemaide	5
*A. J. Wright c Salisbury b Pigott	3	C. A. Walsh b Pigott	6
P. Bainbridge c Moores b Bunting	97	D. A. Graveney c Moores b Pigott	
C. W. J. Athey c Moores b Pigott	4		
M. W. Alleyne c Donelan b Dodemaide	15	B 21, l-b 17, w 1, n-b 4	4
D. V. Lawrence lbw b Salisbury	13		
K. M. Curran not out	144	1/4 2/5 3/19 4/52 5/82	46
†R. C. Russell c Moores b Donelan	31	6/173 7/244 8/331 9/453	

Bonus points – Gloucestershire 4, Sussex 3 (Score at 100 overs: 308-7).

Bowling: Dodemaide 28-6-83-2; Pigott 37.3-7-87-5; Bunting 22-4-67-1; Salisbu
29-6-103-1; Donelan 31-8-89-1.

Umpires: P. J. Eele and K. J. Lyons.

At Southampton, September 18, 19, 20, 21. GLOUCESTERSHIRE lost to HAMPSHIRE b
two wickets.

HAMPSHIRE

President: W. J. Weld
Chairman: D. Rich
Chairman, Cricket Committee: J. R. Gray
Chief Executive: A. F. Baker
  Northlands Road, Southampton SO9 2TY
  (Telephone: 0703-333788)
Captain: M. C. J. Nicholas
Coaches: P. J. Sainsbury and T. M. Tremlett

Optimism was tempered with a strong thread of realism when Hampshire began their season in April. The realism was their knowledge that they were short of one top-quality bowler to make a genuine challenge for the supreme prize, the Britannic Assurance Championship. And when the curtain was lowered in mid-September, the truth of that analysis was borne out. Only a dramatic last-afternoon scramble to the highest fourth-innings winning total in their history, reaching 446 for eight against Gloucestershire, took them into third place. Most, possibly, would have settled for that at the outset.

When the early assessments were being made, Hampshire considered that their best chance of a trophy lay in the one-day competitions. They argued that the recruitment of David Gower's supreme skill would tip the balance and make their batting sufficiently powerful to offset the absence of a bowler to complement Malcolm Marshall. But it was not to be. The Benson and Hedges Cup was a disaster for them: a mauling by Yorkshire, an even heavier defeat by Surrey and a wash-out at Old Trafford. The only victory was over the Combined Universities. The NatWest Bank Trophy, however, offered the possibility of consolation and provided great drama. Leicestershire were beaten by a single run, and Essex by virtue of fewer wickets lost when the scores were tied. After that, Yorkshire were destroyed by Marshall's pace in the quarter-final at Southampton, and for the third summer in succession Hampshire were through to the semi-finals. But even though Gower played his most disciplined innings of the season for Hampshire, and Marshall batted with typical flamboyance, Northamptonshire, despite an embarrassment of dropped catches, emerged as the victors by 1 run.

That left the Refuge Assurance League. Six successive victories, making up for an inconsistent beginning, left them needing to win their final match to finish in fourth place and so qualify for the Refuge Cup. Instead they lost by just 4 runs to Surrey.

Curiously, in a summer when batsmen fed themselves insatiably, 1990 was not a vintage year for a side reckoned to have more talent than most. Only three men scored 1,000 runs for Hampshire in all first-class matches, let alone in the Championship, and two of those were predictable. Chris Smith, despite the distractions of his benefit and the problem of suspect knees, had set himself a pre-season target of 1,800 runs, and achieved it with three matches to spare. His aggregate of 1,886 was 554 more than that of Paul Terry, Hampshire's second-highest scorer. It was the third man to attain four figures who was the major surprise. Tony Middleton's continued presence on the staff had been a question of some debate the previous autumn, and when Gower was signed it seemed inevitable that his chances would be limited. However injuries and England calls decreed otherwise, and the 26-year-old from Winchester made the most of his opportunity. He hit his maiden first class hundred in the opening match, at Canterbury, and went on to finish with five hundreds, a Championship aggregate of 1,216 and a county cap. In addition, he scored five centuries for the Second Eleven. Not a flamboyant character, nor a prodigious striker of the ball, Middleton nevertheless offered a superb temperament, sound technique and neat placement of shot.

Three other batsmen were within touching distance of their thousand for the county. Robin Smith's regular selection for England allowed him just eleven Championship matches, in which he scored 897 runs; Gower's 972 runs in seventeen matches included 684 in fourteen Britannic appearances; and Marshall, whose first-class innings were restricted to the Championship, finished 38 runs short of the milestone. Gower, perhaps not surprisingly, became a cause of frustration among the county's supporters. Occasionally he batted with almost ethereal skill as when hitting his lone Championship century against Sussex, but at other times he fell to shots of seemingly careless disdain.

Almost inevitably, Hampshire's bowlers paled in comparison with Marshall. Some felt the West Indian might freewheel a trifle in what was initially intended to be his farewell season, a decision reversed in September. Instead he missed only four Championship matches, bowled 554 overs – a total surpassed only by the left-arm spinner, Raj Maru, the one ever-present in the side – and took 72 wickets at an impressive 19.18. Four times he took five wickets in an innings, twice ten in a match, and it was his blistering pace and controlled swing which brought Hampshire their most dramatic Britannic victory of the season. Derbyshire were 146 for one in pursuit of 235 runs at Portsmouth, yet finished 49 runs short of their target as Marshall took seven for 47.

While Marshall was Hampshire's player of the season, with Middleton not far behind, possibly the most intriguing performances came from 26-year-old Adrian Aymes, who late in the summer ousted Bob Parks as first-choice wicket-keeper. He laid claims to filling the position on a long-term basis with a combination of effective wicket-keeping and impressive batting that brought him three half-centuries in an aggregate of 317 runs from five matches.

For Mark Nicholas, the captain, it was a traumatic and demanding season. The malaria which he contracted while leading the England A tour of Kenya and Zimbabwe was severely debilitating, and his stamina understandably, was drained. In spite of that, and often against well meaning advice, he missed only two matches. His form with the bat certainly suffered, but it was a fitting reward for his selfless dedication that he was at the crease, having completed his fifth Championship fifty, when Hampshire claimed third place on the last afternoon of the season. For no one, though, was the summer more frustrating than for Kevan James. He began with 104 not out at Canterbury, then fell victim to a serious back condition and played no more. In contrast, Jon Ayling, who had not hit or bowled a ball the previous summer because of a serious knee injury, resumed his career. Although still some way short of his peak of 1988, he did enough to suggest that his future remains bright. – Mike Neasom.

HAMPSHIRE 1990

[Bill Smith]

Back row: R. J. Maru, C. A. Connor, P. J. Bakker, J. R. Ayling, T. M. Tremlett (coach), R. A. Smith, R. J. Scott, R. J. Parks. Front row: M. D. Marshall, C. L. Smith, M. C. J. Nicholas (captain), V. P. Terry, D. I. Gower. Insets: K. D. James, S. D. Udal, J. R. Wood, A. N. Aymes, K. J. Shine, T. C. Middleton.

HAMPSHIRE RESULTS

All first-class matches – Played 25: Won 9, Lost 4, Drawn 12.

County Championship matches – Played 22: Won 8, Lost 4, Drawn 10.

Bonus points – Batting 67, Bowling 48.

Competition placings – Britannic Assurance County Championship, 3rd;
NatWest Bank Trophy, s-f; Benson and Hedges Cup, 4th in Group C;
Refuge Assurance League, 5th.

BRITANNIC ASSURANCE CHAMPIONSHIP AVERAGES

BATTING

	Birthplace	M	I	NO	R	HI	Avge
L. A. Joseph	Georgetown, Guyana	4	4	3	83	43*	83.00
‡T. M. Tremlett	Wellington, Somerset	8	5	3	143	78	71.50
‡R. A. Smith	Durban, SA	11	18	4	897	181	64.07
A. N. Aymes	Southampton	4	7	3	255	75*	63.75
‡C. L. Smith	Durban, SA	20	35	7	1,678	132*	59.92
‡T. C. Middleton ..	Winchester	16	28	3	1,216	127	48.64
R. M. F. Cox	Guildford	3	6	2	186	104*	46.50
‡M. D. Marshall ...	St Michael, Barbados	18	24	3	962	117	45.80
J. R. Ayling	Portsmouth	7	9	2	288	62*	41.14
‡V. P. Terry	Osnabruck, WG	19	31	3	1,084	165	38.71
‡D. I. Gower	Tunbridge Wells	14	21	1	684	145	34.20
‡R. J. Maru	Nairobi, Kenya	22	18	2	513	59	32.06
‡M. C. J. Nicholas ..	London	20	30	8	670	78*	30.45
S. D. Udal	Farnborough, Hants	6	5	2	65	28*	21.66
‡R. J. Parks	Cuckfield	18	19	9	203	36*	20.30
‡C. A. Connor	The Valley, Anguilla	19	9	3	119	46	19.83
‡P. J. Bakker	Vlaardingen, Netherlands	14	9	4	95	20	19.00
R. J. Scott	Bournemouth	6	10	2	144	71	18.00

Also batted: ‡K. D. James (*Lambeth, London*) (1 match) 50, 104*; I. J. Turner (*Denmead*) (4 matches) 1, 0*; J. R. Wood (*Winchester*) (2 matches) 17, 11. K. J. Shine (*Bracknell*) (6 matches) did not bat.

* Signifies not out.   ‡ *Denotes county cap.*

The following played a total of twenty three-figure innings for Hampshire in County Championship matches – T. C. Middleton 5, R. A. Smith 4, C. L. Smith 3, V. P. Terry 3, M. D. Marshall 2, R. M. F. Cox 1, D. I. Gower 1, K. D. James 1.

BOWLING

	O	M	R	W	BB	5W/i	Avge
M. D. Marshall	554.2	142	1,381	72	7-47	4	19.18
P. J. Bakker	371.2	86	1,195	33	5-101	1	36.21
C. A. Connor	462.1	77	1,623	44	5-96	1	36.88
T. M. Tremlett	120.5	30	393	10	3-33	0	39.30
R. J. Maru	720.1	178	2,087	53	6-97	1	39.37
K. J. Shine	129.4	17	501	12	4-52	0	41.75
J. R. Ayling	135.2	35	454	10	2-48	0	45.40
S. D. Udal	191.3	35	746	16	4-144	0	46.62

Also bowled: K. D. James 28–8–74–1; L. A. Joseph 82–12–406–5; T. C. Middleton 1–0–10–0; M. C. J. Nicholas 54.2–7–209–2; R. J. Scott 36.4–5–165–5; C. L. Smith 22–8–76–3; R. A. Smith 0.3–0–5–0; V. P. Terry 1–0–19–0; I. J. Turner 108.2–28–326–7.

Wicket-keepers: R. J. Parks 46 ct, 4 st; A. N. Aymes 7 ct; R. J. Maru 2 ct.

Leading Fielders: R. J. Maru 23, V. P. Terry 21.

At Canterbury, April 26, 27, 28, 30. HAMPSHIRE beat KENT by 6 runs.

At Oxford, May 3, 4, 5. HAMPSHIRE drew with OXFORD UNIVERSITY.

HAMPSHIRE v SUSSEX

At Southampton, May 15, 16, 17. Hampshire won by an innings and 157 runs. Hampshire 24 pts, Sussex 2 pts. Toss: Sussex. Injuries played a decisive part as Hampshire won conclusively with a day to spare. Early in the Sussex first innings, a ball from Marshall struck Smith's hand, reopening the fracture in his left thumb which he suffered in the West Indies, and he took no further part in the match. In their second innings, Alan Wells's right thumb was broken by Marshall and he, too, retired hurt. To round off the Sussex casualty list, late in their vain bid to make Hampshire bat a second time, Hansford was struck on the forearm by Marshall and, although he batted on, was later found to have a fractured bone. The loss of Smith was a key factor in the collapse of the Sussex first innings, which would have been a disaster had it not been for a 76-run partnership between Pigott and Salisbury. Hampshire's innings was dominated by Gower's first century for his new county, a serene 145 containing 22 fours and two sixes. His third-wicket partnership of 256 in 48 overs with Robin Smith, whose 181 in 188 balls had four sixes and 23 fours, laid the basis for an eventual total of 600 for eight declared. In the Sussex second innings, Lenham batted defiantly, hitting eighteen boundaries in a career-best 121, and with Salisbury, the night-watchman, he added 120 for the second wicket. Once they were parted, however, the absence of Smith and the loss of Alan Wells made the outcome a formality.

Close of play: First day, Hampshire 184-2 (D. I. Gower 87*, R. A. Smith 20*); Second day, Sussex 24-1 (N. J. Lenham 11*, I. D. K. Salisbury 3*).

Sussex

N. J. Lenham c Gower b Marshall	0	– b Maru	121
D. M. Smith retired hurt	5	– absent injured	
†P. Moores c Nicholas b Bakker	7	– (2) c C. L. Smith b Bakker	5
A. P. Wells lbw b Bakker	0	– retired hurt	22
M. P. Speight c Gower b Marshall	7	– c Parks b Maru	3
*C. M. Wells c Turner b Connor	22	– c Maru b Turner	25
I. J. Gould c C. L. Smith b Marshall	6	– c Marshall b Turner	1
A. I. C. Dodemaide c Parks b Bakker	10	– not out	37
A. C. S. Pigott c Parks b Turner	50	– c Marshall b Maru	3
I. D. K. Salisbury c Terry b Maru	37	– (3) c Parks b Connor	19
A. R. Hansford not out	3	– (10) b Connor	29
N-b 5	5	B 1, l-b 14, w 2, n-b 9	26
	152		**291**

1/0 2/7 3/7 4/21 5/29   1/20 2/140 3/192 4/207 5/219
6/48 7/66 8/142 9/152   6/222 7/225 8/291

Bonus points – Sussex 1, Hampshire 4.

In the first innings D. M. Smith retired hurt at 15; in the second innings A. P. Wells retired hurt at 190.

Bowling: *First Innings*—Marshall 15-3-26-2; Bakker 20-4-51-4; Connor 12-3-52-1; Turner 5-1-13-1; Maru 7.2-3-10-1. *Second Innings*—Marshall 24-10-66-0; Bakker 16-9-21-1; Turner 27-10-60-2; Connor 21-3-80-2; Maru 22-11-49-3; C. L. Smith 2-2-0-0.

Hampshire

V. P. Terry c Moores b Dodemaide	40	R. J. Maru not out	54
C. L. Smith b Salisbury	35	I. J. Turner st Moores b Salisbury	1
D. I. Gower c A. P. Wells b Dodemaide	145		
R. A. Smith c Moores b C. M. Wells	181	B 1, l-b 8, n-b 2	11
M. D. Marshall c Gould b Hansford	85		
*M. C. J. Nicholas c Gould b Hansford	12		**(8 wkts dec.) 600**
†R. J. Parks c Speight b C. M. Wells	36		

1/68 2/112 3/368
4/453 5/496 6/507
7/593 8/600

C. A. Connor and P. J. Bakker did not bat.

Bonus points – Hampshire 4, Sussex 1 (Score at 100 overs: 458-4).

Bowling: Pigott 20–2–87–0; Dodemaide 37–6–161–2; Salisbury 28.3–2–159–2; Hansford 26–2–102–2; C. M. Wells 25–1–73–2; Lenham 3–1–9–0.

Umpires: J. C. Balderstone and A. A. Jones.

At The Oval, May 19, 21, 22. HAMPSHIRE drew with SURREY.

HAMPSHIRE v ESSEX

At Southampton, May 23, 24, 25. Drawn. Hampshire 4 pts, Essex 4 pts. Toss: Essex. Two major partnerships dictated the pattern of a match played on a benign wicket. First Hardie, leading Essex in the absence of Gooch, and Waugh frustrated Hampshire after Shine had struck two early blows. They put on 203 for the third wicket in 51 overs before Hardie was dismissed for a patient 125 (thirteen fours). Waugh hit a six and sixteen fours in his 125. Essex declared after 100 overs, and next morning Foster quickly removed Terry. This, however, brought Smith in to join Middleton, and they were not parted for 75 overs, when Smith, having hit twenty fours in his 128, edged a catch to the wicket-keeper. They added 237, and Middleton completed his second first-class century, extending a remarkable sequence in which he had scored five successive Second XI Championship centuries since his maiden first-class hundred at Canterbury in the opening Britannic fixture. Hampshire declared 55 runs behind in the hope of breathing life into the game, and when Essex were 126 for six, it seemed that Nicholas's gamble might pay off. Instead, Garnham and Foster added 75 in sixteen overs and Hardie's challenge to score 266 in 58 overs was too steep.

Close of play: First day, Hampshire 20–0 (V. P. Terry 14*, T. C. Middleton 6*); Second day, Essex 78–2 (M. E. Waugh 37*, T. D. Topley 0*).

Essex

*B. R. Hardie b Connor	125	– c Parks b Maru		31
J. P. Stephenson c Parks b Shine	2	– retired hurt		4
P. J. Prichard c Maru b Shine	23	– b Connor		4
M. E. Waugh c Parks b Marshall	125	– c Maru b Shine		39
N. Shahid not out	19	– (6) b Marshall		0
A. C. Seymour not out	10	– (7) c Parks b Marshall		0
T. D. Topley (did not bat)		– (5) c Parks b Shine		23
†M. A. Garnham (did not bat)		– not out		62
N. A. Foster (did not bat)		– b Maru		40
J. H. Childs (did not bat)		– c Connor b Maru		0
S. J. W. Andrew (did not bat)		– c Turner b Maru		0
B 4, l-b 5, n-b 2	11	B 2, l-b 2, w 1, n-b 2		7

1/16 2/67 3/270 4/294   (4 wkts dec.) 315   1/18 2/78 3/81 4/82 5/86   210
                                                      6/126 7/201 8/208 9/210

Bonus points – Essex 4, Hampshire 1.

In the second innings J. P. Stephenson retired hurt at 11.

Bowling: *First Innings*—Marshall 21–3–49–1; Shine 15–1–56–2; Connor 28–6–95–1; Turner 14–2–48–0; Maru 20–5–45–0; Scott 2–0–13–0. *Second Innings*—Marshall 15–5–18–2; Shine 16–6–52–2; Connor 17–1–71–1; Maru 18.3–2–47–4; Turner 9–3–18–0.

Hampshire

V. P. Terry c Stephenson b Foster	14	– c Topley b Andrew		12
T. C. Middleton not out	104	– (3) b Childs		11
C. L. Smith c Garnham b Waugh	128	– (2) st Garnham b Childs		31
†R. J. Parks not out	3			
*M. C. J. Nicholas (did not bat)		– (4) not out		32
M. D. Marshall (did not bat)		– (5) b Foster		9
R. J. Scott (did not bat)		– (6) not out		7
B 4, l-b 3, n-b 4	11			

1/20 2/257   (2 wkts dec.) 260   1/27 2/42 3/59 4/88   (4 wkts) 102

R. J. Maru, I. J. Turner, C. A. Connor and K. J. Shine did not bat.

Bonus points – Hampshire 3.

Bowling: *First Innings*—Foster 19–5–43–1; Andrew 15–5–50–0; Topley 15–3–53–0; Childs 3–6–49–0; Waugh 9–0–33–1; Shahid 5–1–25–0. *Second Innings*—Foster 15–4–33–1; Andrew 3–4–42–1; Childs 17–10–24–2; Topley 2–0–3–0.

Umpires: R. Julian and M. J. Kitchen.

At Leeds, May 26, 28, 29. HAMPSHIRE beat YORKSHIRE by five wickets.

At Leicester, June 2, 4, 5. HAMPSHIRE drew with LEICESTERSHIRE.

HAMPSHIRE v SOMERSET

At Basingstoke, June 6, 7, 8. Drawn. Hampshire 3 pts, Somerset 2 pts. Toss: Hampshire. Somerset's opening batsman, Cook, provided the only memorable moments of a match ruined by persistent rain. Late on the second day, Hampshire declared their first innings at 257 for six after a tea-time conference between Nicholas and Tavaré which aimed to make good the loss of 85 overs. Hampshire's total had been built on a solid but unspectacular innings of 90 by Middleton. The agreement was that Cook would have a chance to score the 59 runs he needed to become the first batsman to reach 1,000 first-class runs for the summer, whereupon Somerset would declare. Cook's pursuit of the target was out of keeping with much of the batting the chilled spectators had earlier suffered. His first 50 was immaculately crafted from 76 deliveries, with Bakker and Joseph the principal sufferers, but he then became circumspect and the remaining 9 runs took 30 deliveries. By the close Hampshire had extended their lead to 202, but on the final morning they found run-scoring difficult. Chris Smith batted with typical determination for his eighth half-century. Somerset were challenged to score 321 in 62 overs, only for the return of the rain to render the equation academic.

Close of play: First day, Hampshire 83-1 (V. P. Terry 50*, T. C. Middleton 6*); Second day, Hampshire 34-2 (C. L. Smith 6*, D. I. Gower 16*).

Hampshire

V. P. Terry lbw b Mallender	64	– lbw b Rose	6
C. L. Smith lbw b Rose	25	– not out	73
T. C. Middleton c Burns b Rose	90	– c Swallow b Rose	1
D. I. Gower lbw b Jones	1	– c and b Swallow	26
M. C. J. Nicholas retired ill	23	– b Swallow	23
R. J. Parks c Mallender b Rose	11	– not out	15
R. A. Joseph lbw b Hayhurst	13		
J. R. Maru not out	17		
T. M. Tremlett not out	3		
B 4, l-b 3, w 2, n-b 1	10	B 4, w 1, n-b 3	8

1/69 2/117 3/118 4/218	(6 wkts dec.) 257	1/6 2/12 3/50	(4 wkts dec.) 152
5/233 6/254		4/99

C. A. Connor and P. J. Bakker did not bat.

Bonus points – Hampshire 3, Somerset 2.

In the first innings M. C. J. Nicholas retired ill at 189.

Bowling: *First Innings*—Jones 20–2–56–1; Mallender 26–7–50–1; Rose 25–1–84–3; Swallow 7–2–24–0; Hayhurst 11–5–12–1; Trump 8–1–24–0. *Second Innings*—Rose 9–4–21–2; Hayhurst 7–2–18–0; Swallow 25–8–54–2; Mallender 5–1–9–0; Trump 9.2–0–46–0.

Somerset

S. J. Cook not out	59	– c Parks b Connor	29
J. J. E. Hardy not out	30	– not out	23
A. N. Hayhurst (did not bat)		– not out	31
		N-b 1	1

(no wkt dec.) 89   1/36   (1 wkt) 84

*C. J. Tavaré, R. J. Harden, †N. D. Burns, G. D. Rose, I. G. Swallow, H. R. J. Trump, N. A. Mallender and A. N. Jones did not bat.

Bowling: *First Innings*—Bakker 4–1–24–0; Joseph 5–1–40–0; Connor 5.2–1–23–0; Mar 4–2–2–0. *Second Innings*—Connor 7–1–20–1; Bakker 6–1–35–0; Middleton 1–0–10–0; Terry 1–0–19–0.

Umpires: D. R. Shepherd and A. G. T. Whitehead.

HAMPSHIRE v GLAMORGAN

At Southampton, June 16, 18, 19. Glamorgan won by four wickets. Glamorgan 19 pts, Hampshire 4 pts. Toss: Hampshire. Richards produced a masterpiece of aggression and timing to steer Glamorgan to a second successive Championship victory, successful negotiations between the captains having overcome the weather's earlier interference. Hampshire's first innings had been dominated by a magnificent 153 from Robin Smith off 15 deliveries. He hit three sixes and 23 fours. Glamorgan were then thwarted by rain, which claimed 86 overs of the second day, and declared 292 behind, which Hampshire quickly extended to 363. A second declaration left Glamorgan with 102 overs to better that, and when they lost half their wickets for 139, Nicholas's boldness seemed likely to be rewarded. However, the former Hampshire all-rounder, Cowley, provided the support Richards needed to play an innings of enormous quality. When the last hour was called with 112 still required, it seemed Richards might have miscalculated, but a four, six and four in Marshall's last over saw Glamorgan home with two balls to spare. Richards faced only 155 deliveries for his 164 and hit five sixes – none of them exploiting a short boundary on the pavilion side – and seventeen fours.
Close of play: First day, Glamorgan 31-1 (H. Morris 20*); Second day, Hampshire 71-0 dec.

Hampshire

V. P. Terry c Metson b Richards	52	– not out	25
C. L. Smith c Metson b Watkin	48	– not out	39
D. I. Gower c Metson b Watkin	41		
R. A. Smith c Metson b Frost	153		
M. D. Marshall c Metson b Dennis	4		
*M. C. J. Nicholas c Cowley b Watkin	30		
†R. J. Parks c Metson b Watkin	0		
R. J. Maru c Maynard b Cowley	9		
T. M. Tremlett not out	14		
L-b 10, w 1, n-b 1	12	L-b 5, w 1, n-b 1	7

1/73 2/127 3/177 4/182 5/336   (8 wkts dec.) 363   (no wkt dec.) 71
6/340 7/341 8/363

C. A. Connor and P. J. Bakker did not bat.

Bonus points – Hampshire 4, Glamorgan 3.

Bowling: *First Innings*—Frost 24–4–107–1; Watkin 30–9–84–4; Dennis 20–5–83–1; Cowley 17.5–6–47–1; Richards 8–3–32–1. *Second Innings*—Smith 8–2–27–0; Maynard 6–1–22–0; Butcher 1.5–0–17–0.

Glamorgan

*A. R. Butcher c Terry b Bakker	7	– c Connor b Maru	51
H. Morris not out	38	– c Maru b Connor	44
M. P. Maynard not out	20	– (4) c Gower b Connor	1
G. C. Holmes (did not bat)		– (3) c Terry b Marshall	14
I. V. A. Richards (did not bat)		– not out	164
. Smith (did not bat)		– c Parks b Marshall	0
N. G. Cowley (did not bat)		– c and b Maru	58
*C. P. Metson (did not bat)		– not out	14
B 1, l-b 1, w 1, n-b 3	6	B 5, l-b 11, n-b 5	21

|/31 | (1 wkt dec.) 71 | 1/90 2/104 3/106 | (6 wkts) 367 |
| | | 4/135 5/139 6/306 | |

S. J. Dennis, S. L. Watkin and M. Frost did not bat.

Bowling: *First Innings*—Marshall 3–1–9–0; Bakker 4–0–14–1; Tremlett 5–2–19–0; Nicholas 4.1–0–27–0. *Second Innings*—Bakker 23–6–54–0; Marshall 22.4–7–63–2; Tremlett 24–7–80–0; Connor 18–1–86–2; Maru 14–2–68–2.

Umpires: J. W. Holder and B. J. Meyer.

At Gloucester, June 20, 21, 22. HAMPSHIRE drew with GLOUCESTERSHIRE.

At Manchester, June 23, 25, 26. HAMPSHIRE drew with LANCASHIRE.

At Southampton, July 4, 5, 6. HAMPSHIRE beat INDIANS by seven wickets (See Indian tour section).

HAMPSHIRE v NOTTINGHAMSHIRE

At Portsmouth, July 18, 19, 20. Hampshire won by eight wickets. Hampshire 24 pts, Nottinghamshire 4 pts. Toss: Hampshire. On a United Services ground known for the encouragement it has offered the faster bowlers, Marshall's pace and control were decisive in sweeping Hampshire to a comfortable victory. The only check on his depredations was provided by a stubborn sixth-wicket partnership of 58 between Saxelby and Stephenson after Nottinghamshire had followed on 191 behind. Once Saxelby was dismissed by Bakker after a patient half-century, Stephenson's aggression, which brought him fourteen boundaries, ensured that Nottinghamshire avoided an innings defeat. Hampshire had claimed maximum batting points in the 100th over, largely through a typically applied innings by Smith, a solid 70 from Nicholas, who at last showed signs of shaking off the effects of his bout of malaria, and some delightful driving by Ayling, a local product.

Close of play: First day, Nottinghamshire 10-1 (P. R. Pollard 2*, K. P. Evans 0*); Second day, Nottinghamshire 177-6 (F. D. Stephenson 32*, B. N. French 1*).

Hampshire

V. P. Terry c Cooper b Stephenson	0		
C. L. Smith c Pollard b Stephenson	85	– not out	46
T. C. Middleton c Evans b Saxelby	37	– (1) b Afford	5
*M. C. J. Nicholas c Robinson b Cooper	70	– (3) c Afford b Cooper	9
M. D. Marshall c Newell b Afford	5	– (4) not out	23
J. R. Wood c French b Evans	11		
J. R. Ayling lbw b Evans	61		
†R. J. Parks c Evans b Cooper	0		
R. J. Maru c Robinson b Evans	19		
C. A. Connor not out	2		
P. J. Bakker not out	1		
L-b 9, w 1	10	L-b 1	1

1/0 2/109 3/149 4/170 5/198   (9 wkts dec.) 301   1/25 2/50   (2 wkts) 84
6/257 7/257 8/285 9/298

Bonus points – Hampshire 4, Nottinghamshire 4.

Bowling: *First Innings*—Stephenson 23–6–78–2; Cooper 24–7–49–2; Evans 21–3–76–3; Afford 21–6–58–1; Saxelby 11–3–31–1. *Second Innings*—Stephenson 8–1–26–0; Cooper 8–3–15–1; Afford 9–3–38–1; Saxelby 1–0–4–0.

Nottinghamshire

B. C. Broad b Maru	8	– c Parks b Connor	13
P. R. Pollard b Bakker	21	– c Wood b Maru	21
K. P. Evans c Terry b Marshall	8	– (9) c Parks b Marshall	7
M. Newell run out	13	– (3) c Parks b Marshall	34
*R. T. Robinson c Maru b Connor	3	– (4) c Marshall b Ayling	7
P. Johnson c Terry b Maru	34	– (5) b Maru	8
M. Saxelby b Connor	0	– (6) c Smith b Bakker	51
F. D. Stephenson lbw b Marshall	10	– (7) not out	88
†B. N. French lbw b Marshall	0	– (8) lbw b Marshall	21
K. E. Cooper b Marshall	6	– c Maru b Marshall	7
J. A. Afford not out	0	– c Parks b Marshall	1
B 4, l-b 2, w 1	7	B 4, l-b 7, w 2, n-b 3	16

1/10 2/41 3/47 4/55 5/63   110   1/27 2/43 3/54 4/63 5/118   274
6/63 7/99 8/104 9/110   6/176 7/216 8/228 9/259

Bonus points – Hampshire 4.

Bowling: *First Innings*—Bakker 9–4–28–1; Marshall 16.1–4–30–4; Maru 8–6–5–2; Ayling 7–3–12–0; Connor 7–2–29–2. *Second Innings*—Bakker 18–3–57–1; Marshall 21.1–4–64–5; Connor 14–3–41–1; Maru 30–6–87–2; Ayling 9–4–14–1.

Umpires: J. C. Balderstone and D. J. Constant.

HAMPSHIRE v DERBYSHIRE

At Portsmouth, July 21, 23, 24. Hampshire won by 48 runs. Hampshire 22 pts, Derbyshire 8 pts. Toss: Hampshire. Among Marshall's many astonishing pieces of fast bowling for Hampshire, few could have bettered that which fashioned this improbable victory. On the opening day, stretched to 7.33 p.m. by Derbyshire's slow over-rate, Hampshire had been dismissed for 307, an innings illuminated by a delightful 45-ball 48 from Gower at his most elegant. Derbyshire had closed at 83 for one, and on Monday Morris's aggressive, unbeaten 157 off 226 deliveries (one six, 28 fours) allowed Barnett to declare at 300 for six after 83.2 overs. As the Derbyshire pace and seam attack dismissed Hampshire for a second time, the only real resistance came from Middleton and Marshall in a fourth-wicket partnership of 94 which Mortensen broke just before the close. The pitch was still playing well on the final day, and when Barnett raced to 63 in under an hour, Derbyshire's target of 235 seemed comfortably attainable. It still seemed so when they lost their second wicket, Bowler, to Marshall at 140, but the great West Indian then gave such a master-class in control and swing that in 16.3 overs Derbyshire lost their remaining wickets for 46 runs. Marshall finished with seven for 47.

Close of play: First day, Derbyshire 83-1 (P. D. Bowler 45*, J. E. Morris 13*); Second day, Hampshire 173-5 (T. C. Middleton 54*, M. C. J. Nicholas 1*).

Hampshire

T. C. Middleton c Barnett b Malcolm	6	– c Krikken b Warner 59
C. L. Smith b Malcolm	57	– c Krikken b Mortensen 2
D. I. Gower run out	48	– b Bishop 3
R. A. Smith c Morris b Mortensen	2	– c Brown b Bishop 37
M. D. Marshall c Adams b Bishop	32	– c Barnett b Mortensen 60
*M. C. J. Nicholas c Krikken b Warner	7	– (7) c Krikken b Warner 15
J. R. Ayling c Krikken b Mortensen	31	– (8) c Morris b Malcolm 5
R. J. Maru c Krikken b Bishop	44	– (6) c Krikken b Mortensen 0
†R. J. Parks run out	0	– not out 8
C. A. Connor b Bishop	46	– c Barnett b Malcolm 6
P. J. Bakker not out	16	– c Krikken b Warner 10
B 4, l-b 11, w 2, n-b 1	18	B 6, l-b 9, w 2, n-b 5 22

1/11 2/85 3/93 4/150 5/159	307	1/2 2/15 3/78 4/172 5/172 227
6/167 7/207 8/208 9/267		6/196 7/199 8/201 9/212

Bonus points – Hampshire 4, Derbyshire 4.

Bowling: *First Innings*—Bishop 23.2–6–72–3; Malcolm 19–1–90–2; Mortensen 18–6–64–2; Warner 16–2–63–1; Roberts 2–0–3–0. *Second Innings*—Bishop 15–4–32–1; Mortensen 17–3–47–3; Malcolm 15–2–39–2; Warner 22.4–4–75–3; Barnett 4–0–19–0.

Derbyshire

P. D. Bowler c Parks b Ayling	58	– (2) b Marshall 56
A. M. Brown lbw b Connor	24	– (3) b Connor 15
J. E. Morris not out	157	– (4) c and b Marshall 10
B. Roberts c Parks b Marshall	7	– (5) c Parks b Marshall 0
C. J. Adams c Parks b Marshall	4	– (6) c Parks b Marshall 1
†K. M. Krikken c Nicholas b Bakker	0	– (7) lbw b Marshall 0
*K. J. Barnett b Marshall	13	– (1) c Parks b Ayling 63
I. R. Bishop not out	27	– b Connor 31
A. E. Warner (did not bat)		– c Parks b Marshall 0
O. E. Malcolm (did not bat)		– b Marshall 0
O. H. Mortensen (did not bat)		– not out 0
B 6, n-b 4	10	L-b 10 10

1/46 2/153 3/179 4/195	(6 wkts dec.) 300	1/91 2/140 3/150 4/150 5/151 186
5/200 6/230		6/151 7/156 8/160 9/186

Bonus points – Derbyshire 4, Hampshire 2.

Bowling: *First Innings*—Bakker 13–1–45–1; Marshall 21–7–60–3; Connor 15–7–58–1; Maru 22–5–70–0; Ayling 12.2–1–61–1. *Second Innings*—Bakker 3–0–40–0; Marshall 15–4–47–7; Maru 12–2–33–0; Connor 12.1–2–49–2; Ayling 6–1–23–1.

Umpires: J. C. Balderstone and D. J. Constant.

At Arundel, July 25, 26, 27. HAMPSHIRE drew with SUSSEX.

At Birmingham, July 28, 30, 31. HAMPSHIRE lost to WARWICKSHIRE by six wickets.

HAMPSHIRE v NORTHAMPTONSHIRE

At Bournemouth, August 4, 6. Hampshire won by an innings and 22 runs. Hampshire 24 pts, Northamptonshire 1 pts. Toss: Hampshire. Northamptonshire, without the pace of Ambrose and the all-round competitiveness of Capel, were swept to defeat in two days on a slow Dean Park pitch. Hampshire's Terry and Middleton built an opening partnership of 292 in 87 overs – the highest stand on the ground – before Middleton became the first of three wickets for off-spinner Williams. He had faced 268 deliveries and hit fifteen fours. Although Robin Smith failed, Hampshire collected maximum points before Terry was stumped, having batted for almost six hours and hit two sixes and twenty fours. Fordham's dogged half-century provided the only resistance to Hampshire's attack, in which left-arm spinner Maru was as effective as Marshall, and Northamptonshire were required to follow on 219 behind. In their second innings Felton played with great composure and, in a lively partnership with Davis, which produced 95 runs in thirteen overs, lent comparative respectability to Northamptonshire's effort. He was ninth out, falling to a spectacular one-handed catch by Ayling at mid-off just 1 run short of a richly deserved century.

Close of play: First day, Northamptonshire 11-1 (A. Fordham 6*).

Hampshire

V. P. Terry st Ripley b Williams	165	*M. C. J. Nicholas not out	19
T. C. Middleton b Williams	123	B 6, l-b 10, w 2, n-b 7	25
R. A. Smith lbw b Williams	0		
D. I. Gower not out	28	1/292 2/294 3/331 (3 wkts dec.)	360

M. D. Marshall, J. R. Ayling, R. J. Maru, †R. J. Parks, C. A. Connor and P. J. Bakker did not bat.

Bonus points – Hampshire 4, Northamptonshire 1 (Score at 100 overs: 335-3).

Bowling: Davis 21–3–61–0; Robinson 20–0–60–0; Cook 24–5–73–0; Hughes 14–5–47–0; Williams 19–1–82–3; Bailey 6–1–21–0.

Northamptonshire

A. Fordham c Parks b Marshall	58	– c Parks b Marshall	1	
W. Larkins c Bakker b Maru	5	– lbw b Marshall	1	
N. A. Felton c and b Connor	24	– c Ayling b Bakker	99	
R. J. Bailey c Parks b Connor	5	– lbw b Marshall	6	
*A. J. Lamb c Parks b Maru	9	– lbw b Bakker	15	
R. G. Williams b Maru	16	– c Gower b Maru	13	
†D. Ripley c Terry b Marshall	0	– c Parks b Ayling	5	
J. G. Hughes c Maru b Marshall	0	– c Parks b Ayling	2	
N. G. B. Cook not out	2	– (10) not out	7	
W. W. Davis c Gower b Maru	13	– (9) c Smith b Maru	47	
M. A. Robinson b Marshall	0	– b Bakker	0	
L-b 5, n-b 2	7	L-b 1	1	

1/11 2/62 3/78 4/95 5/121	141	1/1 2/8 3/24 4/43 5/57	197
6/121 7/125 8/125 9/140		6/70 7/72 8/167 9/197	

Bonus points – Hampshire 4.

Bowling: *First Innings*—Bakker 9–0–26–0; Marshall 17–4–37–4; Maru 12–3–37–4; Connor 7–0–21–2; Ayling 3–1–15–0. *Second Innings*—Bakker 9.2–0–38–3; Marshall 10–4–24–3; Connor 10–2–22–0; Maru 17–3–64–2; Ayling 6–0–48–2.

Umpires: B. J. Meyer and D. O. Oslear.

HAMPSHIRE v MIDDLESEX

At Bournemouth, August 8, 9, 10. Drawn. Hampshire 4 pts, Middlesex 5 pts. Toss: Middlesex. Having won the toss, Gatting gambled on all bowling Hampshire out twice, delaying his declaration until shortly before lunch on the second day. Tufnell raised his captain's hopes by taking five consecutive wickets to reduce Hampshire to 199 for six, but

Ayling and Maru frustrated the game-plan with a stubborn seventh-wicket partnership which virtually ensured that the follow-on would be avoided. Once that was achieved, the match was consigned to a stalemate. Middlesex had scored only 255 for five in 100 overs and owed their eventual healthy total to a typically improvised and entertaining century by Emburey, whose 11 not out off 127 balls included four sixes and twelve fours.

Close of play: First day, Middlesex 288-5 (P. R. Downton 27*, J. E. Emburey 19*); Second day, Hampshire 183-4 (C. L. Smith 27*, M. C. J. Nicholas 2*).

Middlesex

D. L. Haynes c Scott b Bakker	75	– c Parks b Bakker	0
M. A. Roseberry c Maru b Marshall	84	– c Terry b Bakker	6
*M. W. Gatting b Bakker	3	– (5) c Parks b Maru	35
M. R. Ramprakash c Parks b Marshall	47	– (3) lbw b Marshall	0
K. R. Brown c Maru b Bakker	23	– (4) lbw b Marshall	12
†P. R. Downton c Parks b Bakker	38	– c Smith b Scott	38
J. E. Emburey not out	111	– st Parks b Smith	36
S. P. Hughes c Scott b Bakker	6	– b Smith	0
P. C. R. Tufnell not out	28	– c Parks b Smith	12
N. R. Taylor (did not bat)		– lbw b Scott	0
N. G. Cowans (did not bat)		– not out	4
L-b 12, w 1, n-b 2	15	B 2, 1-b 2, n-b 4	8

1/139 2/143 3/179 4/219 5/253   (7 wkts dec.) 430   1/0 2/1 3/11 4/23 5/72   151
6/320 7/370   6/126 7/134 8/143 9/147

Bonus points – Middlesex 3, Hampshire 2 (Score at 100 overs: 255-5).

Bowling: *First Innings*—Bakker 35-8-101-5; Marshall 25-5-54-2; Maru 40-5-153-0; Connor 3-0-15-0; Ayling 25-5-63-0; Smith 1-1-0-0; Scott 7-1-24-0; Nicholas 1-0-8-0. *Second Innings*—Bakker 6-1-19-2; Marshall 11-2-28-2; Ayling 5-1-12-0; Maru 9-3-40-1; Smith 10-2-35-3; Nicholas 6-2-8-0; Scott 2-1-5-2.

Hampshire

T. C. Middleton run out	31	†R. J. Parks lbw b Taylor	4
R. J. Scott c and b Tufnell	71	C. A. Connor c Gatting b Taylor	2
C. L. Smith c Emburey b Tufnell	31	P. J. Bakker not out	7
V. P. Terry c Hughes b Tufnell	31		
M. D. Marshall lbw b Tufnell	9	B 4, 1-b 6, n-b 9	19
*M. C. J. Nicholas c Brown b Tufnell	7		
J. R. Ayling c Taylor b Tufnell	41	1/104 2/104 3/163 4/179 5/187	296
R. J. Maru c Ramprakash b Taylor	43	6/199 7/271 8/281 9/285	

Bonus points – Hampshire 2, Middlesex 2 (Score at 100 overs: 239-6).

Bowling: Cowans 17-5-49-0; Hughes 18-4-51-0; Taylor 14-5-44-3; Emburey 34-8-63-0; Tufnell 38-11-79-6.

Umpires: B. J. Meyer and D. O. Oslear.

At Worcester, August 11, 13, 14. HAMPSHIRE drew with WORCESTERSHIRE.

At Taunton, August 18, 19, 20, 21. HAMPSHIRE lost to SOMERSET by five wickets.

HAMPSHIRE v SURREY

At Southampton, August 23, 24, 25, 27. Surrey won by nine wickets. Surrey 23 pts, Hampshire 2 pts. Toss: Hampshire. Hampshire's first encounter with Surrey's new fast bowler, Waqar Younis, was a painful one, the young Pakistani Test cricketer wrecking their first innings with six wickets for 66. He took three wickets in four balls as they plunged from a promising 72 without loss to 143 for eight. Nicholas and fast bowlers Connor and Bakker then added a defiant 54. For Surrey, Ward played an innings of majestic authority, hitting three sixes and 24 fours in his 191, and the visitors built a lead of 320. Chris Smith's fourth century of the season ensured the match would go beyond the weekend, and on Monday Aymes, who kept wicket in preference to Parks, and Maru prevented an innings defeat. Surrey, needing 74 for victory, scored the runs at almost 10 an over.

Close of play: First day, Surrey 106-1 (R. I. Alikhan 30*, A. J. Stewart 34*); Second day, Surrey 467-7 (D. M. Ward 175*, M. P. Bicknell 28*); Third day, Hampshire 263-6 (A. N. Aymes 19*, R. J. Maru 1*).

Hampshire

T. C. Middleton b Waqar Younis	25	– b Feltham	33
C. L. Smith b Waqar Younis	43	– c Greig b Bicknell	111
*M. C. J. Nicholas c Lynch b Bicknell	70	– b Waqar Younis	19
V. P. Terry c Waqar Younis b Bicknell	8	– lbw b Bicknell	6
M. D. Marshall lbw b Feltham	6	– c Stewart b Medlycott	31
R. M. F. Cox c Stewart b Feltham	0	– lbw b Feltham	22
†A. N. Aymes lbw b Waqar Younis	6	– lbw b Feltham	48
R. J. Maru c Lynch b Waqar Younis	0	– c Lynch b Waqar Younis	36
S. D. Udal b Waqar Younis	0	– not out	28
C. A. Connor b Waqar Younis	12	– c Bicknell b Feltham	20
P. J. Bakker not out	12	– b Feltham	10
B 6, w 2, n-b 7	15	B 9, l-b 5, w 3, n-b 11	28

1/72 2/77 3/104 4/115 5/115   **197**   1/106 2/156 3/184 4/190 5/227   **393**
6/143 7/143 8/143 9/158   6/251 7/330 8/335 9/369

Bonus points – Hampshire 1, Surrey 4.

Bowling: *First Innings*—Waqar Younis 21–5–66–6; Bicknell 18–4–46–2; Feltham 17–1–64–2; Greig 8–2–15–0. *Second Innings*—Waqar Younis 36–4–132–2; Bicknell 32–9–75–2; Feltham 30.5–2–109–5; Medlycott 25–4–63–1.

Surrey

R. I. Alikhan b Connor	72	– lbw b Bakker	0
G. S. Clinton c and b Maru	21		
†A. J. Stewart c Nicholas b Maru	72	– not out	27
D. M. Ward c Nicholas b Connor	191		
M. A. Lynch c Nicholas b Maru	13		
*I. A. Greig c Terry b Bakker	11	– (2) not out	45
M. A. Feltham c Marshall b Udal	30		
K. T. Medlycott run out	15		
M. P. Bicknell c Udal b Connor	40		
N. M. Kendrick c Middleton b Connor	7		
Waqar Younis not out	13		
B 1, l-b 16, n-b 15	32	B 2, l-b 1	3

1/42 2/175 3/217 4/238 5/273   **517**   1/0   **(1 wkt) 75**
6/374 7/408 8/494 9/502

Bonus points – Surrey 3, Hampshire 1 (Score at 100 overs: 262-4).

Bowling: *First Innings*—Bakker 25–8–65–1; Marshall 32–12–64–0; Maru 54–13–129–3; Connor 27.3–3–112–4; Udal 21–6–87–1; Nicholas 12–2–43–0. *Second Innings*—Bakker 3–1–18–1; Connor 3–0–29–0; Udal 1–0–9–0; Nicholas 0.3–0–16–0.

Umpires: J. D. Bond and A. A. Jones.

HAMPSHIRE v KENT

At Bournemouth, August 29, 30, 31. Drawn. Hampshire 4 pts, Kent 6 pts. Toss: Hampshire. Kent's last pair played out the final fourteen deliveries to deny Hampshire victory. Yet the first two days had been the visitors'. On a slow pitch they had reduced Hampshire to 108 for five before being baulked by Aymes and Tremlett's 102-run partnership. Then, after Hinks had fallen to the first ball of Kent's innings, Ward and Wells regained the initiative with a partnership of 131, and Kent waited until Ward was dismissed for an impressive 175 before declaring. His boundaries, three sixes and 27 fours, included a six and four fours in one over from Joseph. Middleton produced another of his invaluable innings of patience and technique for Hampshire, and Robin Smith hit a six and twelve fours in a rapid 74 to enable Nicholas to set a target of 249 in two and threequarter hours, or a minimum of 35 overs. Despite Fleming's belligerent 76, with 50 in boundaries, a draw always seemed the most likely outcome until Bakker induced the sudden collapse which left Patel and Merrick to survive the last overs.

Close of play: First day, Hampshire 215-6 (T. M. Tremlett 42*, R. J. Maru 5*); Second day, Hampshire 56-0 (T. C. Middleton 25*, C. L. Smith 25*).

Hampshire

T. C. Middleton lbw b Kelleher	4	– c Taylor b Patel	104
C. L. Smith c Davis b Merrick	32	– c Marsh b Fleming	53
D. I. Gower c Marsh b Wells	44	– c Davis b Wells	3
R. A. Smith c Patel b Davis	9	– c sub b Davis	74
*M. C. J. Nicholas c Fleming b Wells	1	– not out	42
†A. N. Aymes c Davis b Merrick	70	– not out	10
T. M. Tremlett c Davis b Fleming	78		
R. J. Maru c Cowdrey b Fleming	34		
L. A. Joseph not out	2		
L-b 4, w 1, n-b 3	8	B 1, l-b 9, n-b 1	11

1/14 2/71 3/80 4/85 5/108   (8 wkts dec.) 282   1/137 2/156 3/192   (4 wkts dec.) 297
6/210 7/275 8/282   4/266

S. D. Udal and P. J. Bakker did not bat.

Bonus points – Hampshire 2, Kent 2 (Score at 100 overs: 216-6).

Bowling: *First Innings*—Merrick 28–8–62–2; Kelleher 16–4–54–1; Davis 14–4–31–1; Wells 13–3–29–2; Fleming 30.5–9–75–2; Patel 16–4–27–0. *Second Innings*—Merrick 5.2–3–8–0; Kelleher 6–2–14–0; Davis 30.5–2–127–1; Patel 29.4–6–112–1; Ward 1–1–0–0; Wells 8–4–8–1; Fleming 6–0–18–1.

Kent

S. G. Hinks c C. L. Smith b Bakker	0	– run out	27
T. R. Ward c R. A. Smith b Tremlett	175	– c C. L. Smith b Joseph	8
V. J. Wells c Middleton b Maru	58	– lbw b Udal	9
G. R. Cowdrey c and b Maru	47	– c sub b Udal	41
†S. A. Marsh c Bakker b Joseph	3	– (7) b Bakker	34
M. V. Fleming not out	45	– b Udal	76
*N. R. Taylor (did not bat)		– (5) lbw b Tremlett	0
D. J. M. Kelleher (did not bat)		– c Nicholas b Bakker	9
R. P. Davis (did not bat)		– lbw b Bakker	0
M. M. Patel (did not bat)		– not out	0
T. A. Merrick (did not bat)		– not out	0
L-b 3	3	B 1, l-b 5, n-b 1	7

1/0 2/131 3/215 4/227 5/331   (5 wkts dec.) 331   1/18 2/49 3/55   (9 wkts) 211
                                                    4/55 5/145 6/173
                                                    7/202 8/210 9/211

Bonus points – Kent 4, Hampshire 2.

Bowling: *First Innings*—Bakker 14–1–73–1; Joseph 10–1–76–1; Tremlett 7.4–1–46–1; Maru 18.3–6–48–2; Udal 16–2–80–0; R. A. Smith 0.3–0–5–0. *Second Innings*—Bakker 11–3–24–3; Joseph 12–1–67–1; Tremlett 6–0–44–1; Udal 18–4–70–3.

Umpires: J. H. Harris and B. Hassan.

At Pontypridd, September 7, 8, 9. HAMPSHIRE beat GLAMORGAN by eight wickets.

At Southampton, September 12, 13, 14. HAMPSHIRE drew with SRI LANKANS (See Sri Lankan tour section).

HAMPSHIRE v GLOUCESTERSHIRE

At Southampton, September 18, 19, 20, 21. Hampshire won by two wickets. Hampshire 21 pts, Gloucestershire 7 pts. Toss: Gloucestershire. Hampshire closed their season spectacularly by chasing a target of 445 throughout the final day and achieving it with an over to spare. In doing so they eclipsed their previous-highest winning fourth-innings total by 36 runs. The first three days had belonged to Gloucestershire, and in particular to Curran. He topscored in their first innings with 78, and then returned five for 63 to earn his county a first-innings lead of 94. Only another determined display by Aymes prevented Gloucestershire from gaining a greater advantage. Finally, Curran marked his last appearance for the West Country county by hitting an unbeaten century after going in at No. 7, facing 219 balls and hitting thirteen fours. Hampshire's chances of reaching their daunting target wavered when Gower threw away his wicket, but Robin Smith and Middleton gave the innings its base with a partnership of 155 in 30 overs. Smith and Marshall maintained the momentum with 68 in ten overs, and when Smith was brilliantly caught down the leg side by Russell off Walsh, having hit a six and 23 fours in his 124 off 113 balls, Hampshire required 133 from 35 overs. However, the next three wickets managed just 50 in seventeen overs, and it fell to Nicholas to play the decisive innings. His half-century, allied to Maru's 42, ended on a triumphant note a season in which the Hampshire captain had laboured against ill health.

Close of play: First day, Hampshire 2-0 (V. P. Terry 0*, T. C. Middleton 0*); Second day, Gloucestershire 98-3 (G. D. Hodgson 40*, D. A. Graveney 1*); Third day, Hampshire 5-0 (V. P. Terry 5*, T. C. Middleton 0*).

Gloucestershire

G. D. Hodgson c Aymes b Bakker	58	– c and b Maru		76
*A. J. Wright c Terry b Marshall	19	– c Aymes b Maru		19
P. Bainbridge c Aymes b Connor	16	– c Nicholas b Maru		30
M. W. Alleyne c Aymes b Bakker	18	– (6) c Gower b Maru		33
K. M. Curran c Bakker b Maru	78	– (7) not out		101
†R. C. Russell b Ayling	23	– (8) c Smith b Connor		24
J. W. Lloyds b Maru	0	– (9) c Smith b Maru		24
E. T. Milburn c Middleton b Maru	0	– (10) not out		3
C. A. Walsh c Terry b Ayling	20			
D. V. Lawrence b Marshall	18	– (4) lbw b Maru		0
D. A. Graveney not out	1	– (5) c Marshall b Ayling		20
L-b 5, n-b 7	12	B 6, l-b 6, n-b 8		20

1/35 2/62 3/114 4/121 5/172   263   1/39 2/93 3/93   (8 wkts dec.) 350
6/177 7/177 8/210 9/239   4/135 5/172 6/228
                                7/278 8/333

Bonus points – Gloucestershire 3, Hampshire 4.

Bowling: *First Innings*—Marshall 21-4-54-2; Bakker 21-8-51-2; Connor 17-4-56-1; Ayling 16-5-57-2; Maru 14-4-40-3. *Second Innings*—Marshall 27-7-70-0; Bakker 18-4-61-0; Connor 24-5-55-1; Maru 53.4-18-97-6; Ayling 21-6-55-1.

Hampshire

V. P. Terry c Alleyne b Curran	1	– c Russell b Graveney	46
T. C. Middleton c Russell b Curran	5	– c Russell b Curran	82
D. I. Gower c Lawrence b Curran	14	– b Graveney	4
R. A. Smith b Walsh	8	– c Russell b Walsh	124
M. D. Marshall c Russell b Lawrence	21	– c Walsh b Graveney	46
*M. C. J. Nicholas c Wright b Lawrence	4	– not out	54
J. R. Ayling b Walsh	28	– c Wright b Graveney	10
†A. N. Aymes not out	44	– c Russell b Graveney	2
R. J. Maru c Lloyds b Curran	20	– run out	42
C. A. Connor b Walsh	2	– not out	0
P. J. Bakker c and b Curran	7		
B 4, l-b 8, n-b 8	15	B 5, l-b 16, n-b 15	36

1/3 2/24 3/33 4/40 5/51
6/64 7/128 8/155 9/158   169   1/80 2/89 3/244 4/312   (8 wkts) 446
5/339 6/358 7/362 8/442

Bonus points – Hampshire 1, Gloucestershire 4.

Bowling: *First Innings*—Walsh 18–3–51–3; Lawrence 9–2–30–2; Curran 17.2–3–63–5; Milburn 4–1–10–0; Graveney 9–5–8–0. *Second Innings*—Curran 18–2–86–1; Walsh 25–4–93–1; Lawrence 19–1–64–0; Graveney 35–5–140–5; Milburn 3–0–24–0; Bainbridge 4–0–18–0.

Umpires: J. H. Harris and R. Palmer.

YOUNG CRICKETER OF THE YEAR

(*Elected by the Cricket Writers Club*)

1950	R. Tattersall	1971	J. Whitehouse
1951	P. B. H. May	1972	D. R. Owen-Thomas
1952	F. S. Trueman	1973	M. Hendrick
1953	M. C. Cowdrey	1974	P. H. Edmonds
1954	P. J. Loader	1975	A. Kennedy
1955	K. F. Barrington	1976	G. Miller
1956	B. Taylor	1977	I. T. Botham
1957	M. J. Stewart	1978	D. I. Gower
1958	A. C. D. Ingleby-Mackenzie	1979	P. W. G. Parker
1959	G. Pullar	1980	G. R. Dilley
1960	D. A. Allen	1981	M. W. Gatting
1961	P. H. Parfitt	1982	N. G. Cowans
1962	P. J. Sharpe	1983	N. A. Foster
1963	G. Boycott	1984	R. J. Bailey
1964	J. M. Brearley	1985	D. V. Lawrence
1965	A. P. E. Knott	1986	{ A. A. Metcalfe
1966	D. L. Underwood		{ J. J. Whitaker
1967	A. W. Greig	1987	R. J. Blakey
1968	R. M. H. Cottam	1988	M. P. Maynard
1969	A. Ward	1989	N. Hussain
1970	C. M. Old	1990	M. A. Atherton

An additional award, in memory of Norman Preston, Editor of *Wisden* from 1952 to 1980, was made to C. W. J. Athey in 1980.

KENT

Patron: HRH The Duke of Kent
President: 1990 – D. G. Clark
            1991 – P. G. Foster
Chairman: P. H. Edgley
Chairman, Cricket Committee:
     A. J. P. Woodhouse
Secretary: 1990 – D. B. Dalby
            1991 – S. T. W. Anderson
     St Lawrence Ground, Old Dover Road,
     Canterbury CT1 3NZ
     (Telephone: 0227-456886)
Captain: 1990 – C. S. Cowdrey
            1991 – M. R. Benson
Cricket Administrator: B. W. Luckhurst

Once again Kent flattered to deceive. It is beginning to sound like the old gramophone record with the worn needle, but the facts have to be relayed – and they add up to yet another disappointing season. Take into account all the injury problems, often to key players; it was still a poor summer, which for the second year in succession ended with the county involved in a struggle to avoid finishing last in the Britannic Assurance Championship. That possibility continued until the final game of the season, when Kent, their programme finished, had to hope that Middlesex would beat Sussex to keep them off the bottom rung. They did, and so it was sixteenth place in the table for Kent; a bitter pill, none the less, for supporters, team and club officials to swallow.

It was not only the Championship that proved disappointing. The side failed to qualify for the Benson and Hedges Cup quarter-finals, fell at the second hurdle in the NatWest Bank Trophy, and, after a promising start, could improve only one position on the previous season's eleventh in the Refuge Assurance League. They had led the Sunday League from early in the summer until late June, encouraging themselves and Kent's success-starved members to think that they could finish in the top four and so qualify for the Refuge Assurance Cup play-offs. The way they subsequently faded was disconcerting, particularly as it was felt that this was the competition which presented them with their best chance of success.

As the season was drifting towards another unsuccessful conclusion, Kent were shocked by the sudden resignation of the captain, Christopher Cowdrey. His decision was made known just before the start of the game against Leicestershire at Dartford on August 8. Ironically, it was a game which Kent then won, on a pitch reported by the umpires on the third day. The surface was not dangerous, but the spin bowlers had been delighted to find their cause assisted from before lunch on the opening day. Cowdrey, unavailable because of injury at that stage, indicated that he would continue until the end of the season and remain as a player for the following summer, as he was contracted to. It must have been a hard decision for the son of a former captain, M. C. Cowdrey, but he had clearly had enough. His own form was suffering, and he was finding it difficult to motivate his side. He played in only thirteen of Kent's 24 first-class games, and while he achieved a batting average of 40.72, his bowling at first-class level fell away and was confined to just 61 overs.

Mark Benson and Neil Taylor performed the captain's duties when Cowdrey was not available, Taylor taking over when Benson was out of action at the end of the season with a broken thumb. Benson had led Kent to that important victory over Leicestershire at Dartford, which provided the escape route from the bottom rung, and his first-innings century represented easily the most accomplished batting of the match. He now succeeds Cowdrey as captain and will need the best possible support from his dressing- and committee-rooms if Kent are to see a revival of their fortunes soon.

In 1990, during a summer dominated by good batting pitches, the Kent bowlers struggled more than most in the Championship, finishing with the fewest bonus points of all the counties. Tony Merrick, newly signed from Warwickshire, and Alan Igglesden were heralded as a fast-bowling duo which could bring better days to Kent cricket. Unfortunately, they were in harness only twice in the Championship, injury reducing Igglesden's first-class appearances to fourteen and Merrick's to seven. As a result, Fanie de Villiers, brought over from South Africa as an additional fast bowler, found himself playing rather more cricket than he might have expected. Chris Penn played in only seven first-class games and Richard Ellison in fifteen as injury and loss of form took their toll, and Ellison's all-round ability was sorely missed by a struggling side.

Fortunately Richard Davis, with his left-arm spin, prospered in his best season yet, taking 73 first-class wickets and scoring more than 500 very useful runs to help shore up a batting order that did not always perform as soundly in the middle as it promised on paper. Midway through the season Davis was joined by another left-arm spinner, twenty-year-old Minal Patel, whose potential came to the fore in the win at Dartford, where he and Davis took all twenty Leicestershire wickets.

Towards the end of the summer, Kent were without seven first-team players, including both their overseas fast bowlers, and with so many injuries there were chances for young players. Vince Wells, with bat and ball, finally revealed some form, and Matthew Fleming, who was awarded his county cap, consolidated his all-round promise by scoring 980 runs and taking 22 wickets. Trevor Ward had a good season with the bat once he had recovered from an early-season injury, and there were more than 900 runs from the bat of wicket-keeper Steven Marsh. None of the side's leading batsmen was in the mood to waste the opportunities provided by the good pitches, and four of them cruised past the thousand mark. Taylor, only 21 runs short of 2,000, and the left-handed Simon Hinks had their best seasons, as did Graham Cowdrey, who benefited from having a regular place in the side.

The county retained all their players for 1991, except for de Villiers, and if fitness could be guaranteed, team selection might cause some headaches for the new captain; but ones he would probably welcome. To put Kent on the upward path will require much dedication from all concerned, on the field and off. At the end of the year, David Dalby retired as secretary and was succeeded by Stuart Anderson, a former army brigadier. Like the players, he will be aware that the club and the supporters will be looking for better results in 1991. – Dudley Moore.

KENT 1990

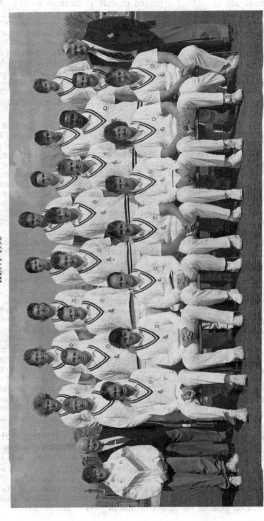

[Bill Smith]

Back row: J. I. Longley, V. J. Wells, M. C. Dobson, N. J. Llong, T. N. Wren, M. A. Ealham, M. M. Patel, G. J. Kersey. Middle row: F. Errington (physiotherapist), J. Foley (scorer), M. V. Fleming, T. R. Ward, C. Penn, R. P. Davis, A. P. Igglesden, D. J. M. Kelleher, T. A. Merrick, A. G. E. Ealham (coach), J. C. T. Page (director of coaching). Front row: S. G. Hinks, S. A. Marsh, M. R. Benson, C. S. Cowdrey (captain), N. R. Taylor, R. M. Ellison, G. R. Cowdrey.

KENT RESULTS

All first-class matches – Played 24; Won 4, Lost 7, Drawn 13.

County Championship matches – Played 22; Won 3, Lost 6, Drawn 13.

Bonus points – Batting 69, Bowling 35.

Competition placings – Britannic Assurance County Championship, 16th;
NatWest Bank Trophy, 2nd round; Benson and Hedges Cup, 3rd in Group A;
Refuge Assurance League, 10th equal.

BRITANNIC ASSURANCE CHAMPIONSHIP AVERAGES

BATTING

	Birthplace	M	I	NO	R	HI	Avge
‡N. R. Taylor	Orpington	20	35	4	1,752	204	56.51
‡G. R. Cowdrey	Farnborough, Kent	20	36	5	1,471	135	47.45
‡M. R. Benson	Shoreham	14	23	1	1,029	159	46.77
‡M. V. Fleming	Macclesfield	17	30	5	940	102	37.60
‡R. M. Ellison	Ashford, Kent	13	18	6	444	81	37.00
‡S. G. Hinks	Northfleet	22	41	0	1,484	234	36.19
‡C. S. Cowdrey	Farnborough, Kent	11	21	4	599	107*	35.23
‡S. A. Marsh	Westminster, London	22	34	8	867	114*	33.34
‡T. R. Ward	Farningham	15	28	1	863	175	31.96
V. J. Wells	Dartford	8	15	0	352	58	23.46
P. S. de Villiers	Vereeniging, SA	12	15	3	264	37	22.00
‡R. P. Davis	Margate	22	32	3	504	59	17.37
‡C. Penn	Dover	6	6	2	66	23*	16.50
M. M. Patel	Bombay, India	9	12	5	104	41*	14.85
‡A. P. Igglesden	Farnborough, Kent	13	17	9	105	24	13.12
D. J. M. Kelleher	Southwark, London	5	8	0	101	44	12.62
T. A. Merrick	St John's, Antigua	5	7	2	60	35	12.00
T. N. Wren	Folkestone	5	5	2	23	16	7.66

Also batted: M. C. Dobson (*Canterbury*) (1 match) 0, 6; M. A. Ealham (*Willesborough*) (2 matches) 0, 13*.

* *Signifies not out.*   ‡ *Denotes county cap.*

The following played a total of 23 three-figure innings for Kent in County Championship matches – M. R. Benson 5, N. R. Taylor 5, S. G. Hinks 4, G. R. Cowdrey 3, C. S. Cowdrey 2, T. R. Ward 2, M. V. Fleming 1, S. A. Marsh 1.

BOWLING

	O	M	R	W	BB	5W/i	Avge
V. J. Wells	85	19	257	12	5-43	1	21.41
T. A. Merrick	146.2	31	376	13	4-66	0	28.92
A. P. Igglesden	306	42	1,093	30	4-79	0	36.43
P. S. de Villiers	304.5	58	992	25	6-70	1	39.68
R. P. Davis	839.1	202	2,648	65	6-59	4	40.73
M. M. Patel	297.5	72	836	20	6-57	2	41.80
R. M. Ellison	260.5	45	869	19	4-76	0	45.73
M. V. Fleming	360.5	81	994	18	3-65	0	55.22

Also bowled: M. R. Benson 8-2-46-1; C. S. Cowdrey 57-12-173-4; G. R. Cowdrey 3.3-0-32-0; M. C. Dobson 3.1-1-7-0; M. A. Ealham 34.2-5-120-3; S. G. Hinks 15-2-60-2; D. J. M. Kelleher 112.5-20-398-7; S. A. Marsh 8.4-0-36-2; C. Penn 158-33-535-9; N. R. Taylor 21-5-57-1; T. R. Ward 53-6-225-4; T. N. Wren 122-14-489-6.

Wicket-keeper: S. A. Marsh 46 ct, 4 st.

Leading Fielder: R. P. Davis 24.

KENT v HAMPSHIRE

At Canterbury, April 26, 27, 28, 30. Hampshire won by 6 runs. Hampshire 21 pts, Kent 4 pts. Toss: Hampshire. Only 37 overs were bowled on the first day, and from then on Hampshire's batsmen dominated. Terry reached 102 out of 176 in 242 minutes with a six and fifteen fours, and shared an opening stand of 183 off 75 overs with Middleton, whose maiden first-class century, containing nine fours, took him 345 minutes. After losing Taylor in Joseph's first Championship over, Kent were launched on the road to recovery by a century stand for the fourth wicket from the Cowdrey brothers. Hampshire responded to their declaration by gathering quick runs, James following his first-innings half-century with a hundred in which he hit sixteen fours as well as the six with which he achieved three figures. Set a victory target of 278 in 65 overs, Kent developed the run-chase through a third-wicket partnership of 162 between Hinks and Chris Cowdrey, but when the captain ran out at 222, with ten overs remaining, the innings lost its impetus. The last five wickets tumbled for 18 runs, leaving Hampshire the winners with five balls to spare.

Close of play: First day, Hampshire 76-0 (V. P. Terry 39*, T. C. Middleton 34*); Second day, Kent 29-1 (S. G. Hinks 14*, T. R. Ward 12*); Third day, Hampshire 55-1 (V. P. Terry 16*, K. D. James 14*).

Hampshire

*V. P. Terry c Ward b Fleming	107	– c Hinks b Merrick	17
T. C. Middleton lbw b Penn	127	– b Fleming	23
K. D. James b Penn	50	– not out	104
C. L. Smith c and b Davis	16	– c C. S. Cowdrey b Hinks	52
R. J. Scott lbw b Penn	0	– not out	1
J. R. Wood c Ellison b Merrick	17		
†R. J. Parks not out	19		
L. A. Joseph not out	25		
B 1, l-b 14, w 1, n-b 2	18	B 1, w 1, n-b 1	3

1/183 2/289 3/300 4/300   (6 wkts dec.) 379   1/32 2/57 3/179   (3 wkts dec.) 200
5/325 6/337

R. J. Maru, C. A. Connor and K. J. Shine did not bat.

Bonus points – Hampshire 3 (Score at 100 overs: 252-1).

Bowling: *First Innings*—Merrick 29–4–83–1; Penn 28–8–79–3; Fleming 20–3–50–1; Ellison 22–6–43–0; Davis 31–8–96–1; C. S. Cowdrey 2–0–13–0. *Second Innings*—Merrick 13–3–24–1; Penn 6–2–6–0; Fleming 7–3–23–1; Ellison 4–1–12–0; Davis 21–3–63–0; Ward 10–3–41–0; C. S. Cowdrey 5–2–14–0; Hinks 3–1–16–1.

Kent

S. G. Hinks c Middleton b Shine	31	– c Maru b James	82
N. R. Taylor c Terry b Joseph	0	– c Terry b Shine	6
T. R. Ward c Parks b Connor	21	– c Middleton b Connor	11
*C. S. Cowdrey b Connor	79	– c Connor b Scott	107
G. R. Cowdrey b Scott	87	– st Parks b Scott	30
†S. A. Marsh not out	61	– b Shine	4
M. V. Fleming not out	6	– b Maru	20
R. M. Ellison (did not bat)		– c Smith b Connor	0
T. A. Merrick (did not bat)		– b Connor	0
C. Penn (did not bat)		– not out	0
R. P. Davis (did not bat)		– run out	1
B 3, l-b 5, w 6, n-b 3	17	L-b 8, w 1, n-b 1	10

1/2 2/45 3/74 4/197 5/290   (5 wkts dec.) 302   1/11 2/25 3/187 4/222 5/237   271
6/253 7/258 8/258 9/270

Bonus points – Kent 4, Hampshire 2.

Bowling: *First Innings*—Shine 19–4–70–1; Joseph 17–3–76–1; Connor 19–5–38–2; James 17–6–31–0; Maru 17–2–64–0; Scott 5–1–15–1. *Second Innings*—Shine 13–1–48–2; Connor 12.1–2–44–3; Maru 20–5–87–1; James 11–2–43–1; Scott 8–1–41–2.

Umpires: J. W. Holder and K. J. Lyons.

KENT v SUSSEX

At Folkestone, May 3, 4, 5, 7. Kent won by five wickets. Kent 20 pts, Sussex 4 pts. Toss: Sussex. Superb batting by Parker dominated the opening day. Hitting fourteen fours, he scored his century in 246 minutes, but Sussex's hopes of a really big score when they resumed on the second day were dashed by Igglesden, who took three of the last four wickets to fall. Benson's third first-class century against Sussex, his native county, was reached in 234 minutes with thirteen boundaries, and with Fleming making a maiden first-class fifty and Ellison 81, Kent obtained a lead of 109. On the final day Sussex fared badly against the left-arm spin of Davis, whose career-best figures included a spell of three wickets in twelve balls without conceding a run and prompted the award of his county cap. Kent, with 21 overs in which to score 81 to win, made a nervous start and later lost three more wickets in sight of their target. Dodemaide made life as difficult as he could for them, taking four of the five wickets, but Kent won with two overs to spare.

Close of play: First day, Sussex 277-6 (C. M. Wells 7*, I. D. K. Salisbury 2*); Second day, Kent 192-1 (M. R. Benson 105*, N. R. Taylor 29*); Third day, Kent 465-9 (R. M. Ellison 81*, A. P. Igglesden 2*).

Sussex

N. J. Lenham c Fleming b de Villiers	63	– c Ward b Igglesden	18
P. Moores c Marsh b Igglesden	0	– c Benson b Davis	46
P. W. G. Parker c Ward b Davis	107	– c Ward b Davis	19
A. P. Wells b Ellison	69	– lbw b Davis	13
M. P. Speight b Davis	12	– lbw b Davis	22
C. M. Wells c Ward b Igglesden	14	– c Marsh b Davis	0
I. J. Gould c Marsh b Ellison	0	– c de Villiers b Ward	33
I. D. K. Salisbury not out	30	– (10) not out	5
A. I. C. Dodemaide c Cowdrey b Igglesden	9	– (8) c and b Davis	13
J. A. North b Igglesden	9	– (9) b de Villiers	6
A. R. Hansford c Marsh b Ellison	19	– lbw b de Villiers	2
B 5, l-b 16, w 1, n-b 2	24	B 6, l-b 6	12
	356		**189**

1/4 2/133 3/225 4/257 5/269 356   1/35 2/64 3/102 4/105 5/105 189
6/274 7/286 8/296 9/318   6/160 7/160 8/175 9/187

Bonus points – Sussex 3, Kent 1 (Score at 100 overs: 268-4).

Bowling: *First Innings*—de Villiers 29-4-84-1; Igglesden 31-9-86-4; Ellison 24.4-8-70-3; Davis 42-14-75-2; Fleming 14-8-20-0. *Second Innings*—Igglesden 17-1-44-1; de Villiers 12.1-4-37-2; Ellison 6-4-10-0; Davis 26-10-59-6; Fleming 11-5-21-0; Ward 2-0-6-1.

Kent

S. G. Hinks c North b C. M. Wells	48	– c Moores b Dodemaide	4
M. R. Benson c Speight b Dodemaide	109	– c Moores b Dodemaide	13
N. R. Taylor c Speight b Hansford	57	– (4) c Speight b Dodemaide	20
T. R. Ward c Moores b Hansford	13	– (5) lbw b Dodemaide	0
C. S. Cowdrey lbw b Dodemaide	24	– (6) not out	0
S. A. Marsh b Dodemaide	10	– (7) not out	4
M. V. Fleming c Moores b Hansford	53	– (3) b Salisbury	39
P. S. de Villiers c Dodemaide b C. M. Wells	37		
R. M. Ellison b Dodemaide	81		
R. P. Davis run out	3		
A. P. Igglesden not out	2		
B 2, l-b 19, w 1, n-b 6	28	L-b 4	4
	465		**(5 wkts) 84**

1/115 2/210 3/236 4/265 5/268 465   1/4 2/23 3/79   (5 wkts) 84
6/297 7/348 8/412 9/436   4/79 5/80

Bonus points – Kent 3, Sussex 1 (Score at 100 overs: 253-3).

Bowling: *First Innings*—Dodemaide 43.1-10-105-4; Hansford 35-11-91-3; C. M. Wells 30-9-67-2; Salisbury 60-15-135-0; North 15-6-30-0; Gould 2-0-8-0; Lenham 2-1-8-0. *Second Innings*—Dodemaide 7-1-29-4; Hansford 7-0-31-0; Salisbury 5-1-20-1.

Umpires: D. J. Constant and N. T. Plews.

At Lord's, May 15, 16, 17. KENT lost to MIDDLESEX by eight wickets.

At Swansea, May 23, 24, 25. KENT beat GLAMORGAN by 6 runs.

KENT v NOTTINGHAMSHIRE

At Tunbridge Wells, June 2, 4, 5. Drawn. Kent 4 pts, Nottinghamshire 8 pts. Toss: Nottinghamshire. Broad's first double-century and an exciting, vastly entertaining innings by Randall were the highlights on the Saturday. Broad's early dominance was reflected by his reaching 100 (out of 129) off 123 balls with an over to spare before lunch. Randall scored his 178 out o a fourth-wicket stand of 285 in 51 overs with Broad, hitting three sixes and thirteen fours during his 191-minute stay (162 balls). Broad's unbeaten 227 was made off 296 balls in 33⁹ minutes and contained two sixes and 23 fours. Kent lost half their side for 72 before Marsh came to their rescue with 114 not out, made in 217 minutes with a six and twelve fours, but no even his century and his ninth-wicket stand of 94 with Merrick could save Kent from following on. They made another disastrous start, but this time Fleming was the saviour with a maiden first-class century in 175 minutes (one six, thirteen fours) to thwart some good fas bowling by Stephenson. Needing 75 to win off nine overs, Nottinghamshire abandoned th chase with four overs left.

Close of play: First day, Nottinghamshire 477-6 dec.; Second day, Kent 37-2 (N. R. Taylo 16*, R. P. Davis 6*).

Nottinghamshire

B. C. Broad not out	227	– c Marsh b Merrick ....
D. J. R. Martindale lbw b Davis	23	
*R. T. Robinson b Davis	2	– (5) not out ....
P. Johnson c Wells b Davis	25	– (3) c Davis b Merrick ....
D. W. Randall c Benson b Merrick	178	– (2) c Marsh b Merrick 6
†B. N. French c Marsh b Igglesden	0	
F. D. Stephenson c Fleming b Igglesden	4	– (4) not out ....
B 5, l-b 12, w 1	18	L-b 3, w 2 5

1/115 2/121 3/177 4/462   (6 wkts dec.) 477   1/3 2/11 3/16   (3 wkts) 17
5/467 6/477

E. E. Hemmings, K. E. Cooper, R. A. Pick and J. A. Afford did not bat.

Bonus points – Nottinghamshire 4, Kent 1 (Score at 100 overs: 421-3).

Bowling: *First Innings*—Merrick 23–2–60–1; Igglesden 20.3–2–62–2; Penn 19–1–105–0 Davis 37–3–155–3; Fleming 10–0–78–0. *Second Innings*—Merrick 3–0–10–3; Igglesden 2–0–4–0.

Kent

S. G. Hinks b Stephenson	6	– c Afford b Pick 14
*M. R. Benson c French b Cooper	34	– lbw b Stephenson 1
N. R. Taylor c Stephenson b Pick	1	– c Martindale b Hemmings ... 21
G. R. Cowdrey c French b Stephenson	27	– (5) c French b Stephenson 51
V. J. Wells c French b Pick	2	– (6) c Hemmings b Stephenson .. 20
M. V. Fleming c Broad b Cooper	1	– (7) b Stephenson 102
†S. A. Marsh not out	114	– (8) c French b Stephenson 4
R. P. Davis lbw b Afford	9	– (4) c French b Pick 13
C. Penn b Pick	23	– b Pick 17
T. A. Merrick c Martindale b Afford	35	– c Martindale b Stephenson ... 15
A. P. Igglesden c Johnson b Afford	0	– not out 1
B 2, l-b 17, n-b 4	23	B 4, l-b 4, w 1, n-b 8 17

1/19 2/20 3/52 4/65 5/72   275   1/4 2/28 3/50 4/50 5/104   276
6/103 7/129 8/171 9/265   6/142 7/185 8/210 9/258

Bonus points – Kent 3, Nottinghamshire 4.

Bowling: *First Innings*—Pick 22–7–57–3; Stephenson 24–5–77–2; Cooper 20–9–40–2; Hemmings 12–2–52–0; Afford 13–4–30–3. *Second Innings*—Pick 28–6–91–3; Stephenson 21–3–84–6; Hemmings 18–12–15–1; Afford 10–3–21–0; Cooper 18–1–57–0.

Umpires: D. O. Oslear and R. Palmer.

KENT v YORKSHIRE

At Tunbridge Wells, June 6, 7, 8. Drawn. Kent 4 pts, Yorkshire 2 pts. Toss: Kent. The weather ruined this game, virtually washing out the first and last days. On the second, an unbeaten 124 in 342 minutes (eight fours) by Taylor took Kent to maximum batting points, Benson having earlier hit 51 out of 75 off 70 balls. With two early declarations on the last morning, the stage was set for Yorkshire to chase 301 in a minimum of 95 overs, but the weather had the final say. The only result of the negotiations was that Metcalfe, the Yorkshire opener, found himself dismissed twice in the space of 44 minutes.

Close of play: First day, Kent 53-1 (M. R. Benson 37*, N. R. Taylor 2*); Second day, Kent 333-5 (N. R. Taylor 124*, S. A. Marsh 41*).

Kent

S. G. Hinks c Bairstow b Jarvis	6	†S. A. Marsh not out	41
*M. R. Benson c Metcalfe b Hartley	57		
N. R. Taylor not out	124	B 4, l-b 12	16
J. R. Cowdrey c Kellett b Moxon	67		
V. J. Wells c Bairstow b Hartley	4	1/42 2/84 3/230 (5 wkts dec.) 333	
M. V. Fleming c Kellett b Hartley	18	4/243 5/277	

R. M. Ellison, P. S. de Villiers, R. P. Davis and A. P. Igglesden did not bat.

Bonus points – Kent 4, Yorkshire 2 (Score at 100 overs: 303-5).

Bowling: Jarvis 8–4–16–1; Hartley 36–8–105–3; Gough 23–3–94–0; Carrick 25–9–40–0; White 10–0–33–0; Moxon 10–2–29–1.

Kent forfeited their second innings.

Yorkshire

*M. D. Moxon not out	24	– not out	6
A. A. Metcalfe c Davis b Benson	0	– c Marsh b de Villiers	14
R. J. Blakey not out	9	– not out	1
		L-b 2	2
1/1 (1 wkt dec.) 33		1/21 (1 wkt) 23	

S. A. Kellett, P. E. Robinson, †D. L. Bairstow, P. Carrick, C. White, P. J. Hartley, P. W. Jarvis and D. Gough did not bat.

Bowling: *First Innings*—Benson 2–0–14–1; Cowdrey 1.3–0–19–0. *Second Innings*—de Villiers 4.1–0–10–1; Igglesden 4–1–11–0.

Umpires: D. O. Oslear and R. Palmer.

KENT v SOMERSET

At Canterbury, June 9, 11, 12. Drawn. Kent 4 pts, Somerset 8 pts. Toss: Somerset. Tavaré, the former Kent captain and now leading Somerset, made a happy return to the St Lawrence Ground, reaching his half-century out of 71 off 64 balls and hitting eleven fours before being caught on the second morning, 18 runs short of his century. Rain had delayed the start on the opening day until after lunch. Kent, 114 for five after 49 overs, found themselves 130 for eight on the final morning when Rose took three wickets in four balls. However, Ellison and the tailenders managed something of a recovery, and when Cowdrey declared well in arrears,

Tavaré's response was to set Kent a target of 270 in a minimum of 45 overs. With Hinks and Benson scoring 121 for the first wicket, and Benson's 116 coming from 115 balls with twelve fours and a six, they were in with a chance. But when they lost five wickets for 26 runs, four of them to Rose in seventeen balls, they were forced to hold on to draw the game.

Close of play: First day, Somerset 200-2 (A. N. Hayhurst 36*, C. J. Tavaré 77*); Second day, Kent 121-5 (M. V. Fleming 31*, S. A. Marsh 3*).

Somerset

S. J. Cook c and b Davis	36		
J. J. E. Hardy c Marsh b Hinks	42	– not out	47
A. N. Hayhurst lbw b Igglesden	55	– c Benson b Igglesden	9
*C. J. Tavaré c Hinks b Igglesden	82		
R. J. Harden not out	52	– (4) not out	50
†N. D. Burns c Ellison b Davis	31	– (1) run out	40
G. D. Rose not out	8		
L-b 15, w 1	16	L-b 3, w 1	4

1/85 2/85 3/211 4/230 5/299 (5 wkts dec.) 322   1/50 2/59 (2 wkts dec.) 150

J. C. Hallett, N. A. Mallender, A. N. Jones and I. G. Swallow did not bat.

Bonus points – Somerset 4, Kent 2.

Bowling: *First Innings*—Igglesden 20-2-85-2; de Villiers 23-7-51-0; Ellison 25-2-101-0; Hinks 5-1-15-1; Davis 19-7-50-2; Fleming 4-0-5-0. *Second Innings*—de Villiers 2-0-7-0; Igglesden 7-1-42-1; C. S. Cowdrey 4-2-9-0; Ellison 7-0-38-0; Taylor 6-1-29-0; Davis 5-0-18-0; Benson 3-2-4-0.

Kent

S. G. Hinks lbw b Hallett	30	– b Swallow	55
M. R. Benson b Jones	0	– c Burns b Rose	116
N. R. Taylor c Hardy b Mallender	9	– c Hardy b Swallow	5
G. R. Cowdrey b Hayhurst	42	– c Cook b Mallender	10
*C. S. Cowdrey b Hallett	0	– b Rose	14
M. V. Fleming c Swallow b Rose	37	– b Rose	6
†S. A. Marsh c Burns b Rose	5	– c Tavaré b Hallett	8
R. M. Ellison not out	31	– not out	6
R. P. Davis lbw b Rose	0	– (10) not out	8
P. S. de Villiers c Burns b Rose	15	– (9) lbw b Rose	0
A. P. Igglesden not out	19		
B 1, l-b 11, w 1, n-b 2	15	L-b 4	4

1/1 2/12 3/61 4/61 5/114 (9 wkts dec.) 203   1/121 2/135 3/162 (8 wkts) 232
6/129 7/130 8/130 9/153   4/198 5/209 6/210
7/222 8/224

Bonus points – Kent 2, Somerset 4.

Bowling: *First Innings*—Jones 8.4-1-24-1; Mallender 19-6-32-1; Rose 19-4-59-4; Hallett 12.2-4-40-2; Hayhurst 14-1-36-1. *Second Innings*—Mallender 10-2-34-1; Rose 10.5-0-55-4; Hayhurst 8-0-48-0; Hallett 7-0-32-1; Swallow 9-1-59-2.

Umpires: D. J. Constant and B. J. Meyer.

At Cambridge, June 20, 21, 22. KENT beat CAMBRIDGE UNIVERSITY by 92 runs.

At Birmingham, June 23, 25, 26. KENT drew with WARWICKSHIRE.

KENT v LANCASHIRE

At Maidstone, June 30, July 2, 3. Lancashire won by three wickets. Lancashire 22 pts, Kent 5 pts. Toss: Kent. After losing half their side for 72 runs in 32 overs, Kent were boosted by the resistance of Graham Cowdrey, but it was Ellison and Davis who rescued them when they were 126 for eight. Lancashire lost Fowler and their night-watchman on Saturday evening, but on Monday Jesty played superbly in a stand of 168 off 50 overs with Atherton, hitting sixteen fours in his highest innings for Lancashire. Atherton, who hit ten boundaries, reached his century amid a collapse in which eight wickets fell for 75 in 23 overs. Batting a second time, Kent found that Atherton's leg-spin presented problems, and they left Lancashire needing to score 190 at less than 3 runs an over for victory. Atherton and Fairbrother established the innings with a stand of 60 in eighteen overs for the third wicket, and then Watkinson really stamped his side's authority on the game, racing to 66 off 60 balls with two sixes and ten fours. The left-arm spin of Davis again caused Lancashire some concern before they won with 14.5 overs in hand.

Close of play: First day, Lancashire 16-2 (M. A. Atherton 5*, T. E. Jesty 7*); Second day, Kent 109-4 (C. S. Cowdrey 15*, R. P. Davis 6*).

Kent

S. G. Hinks c Atherton b DeFreitas	29	– c Fowler b Atherton	49
M. C. Dobson run out	0	– b Allott	6
V. J. Wells lbw b Wasim Akram	9	– lbw b Watkinson	11
G. R. Cowdrey c Fowler b Allott	40	– b Atherton	14
*C. S. Cowdrey b Watkinson	6	– c Hegg b DeFreitas	28
†S. A. Marsh run out	11	– (7) c and b DeFreitas	8
D. J. M. Kelleher b Wasim Akram	0	– (9) lbw b Wasim Akram	0
R. M. Ellison c Hegg b DeFreitas	41	– not out	12
P. S. de Villiers b Allott	0	– (10) lbw b Atherton	33
R. P. Davis c Allott b Wasim Akram	59	– (6) c Hegg b Wasim Akram	19
A. P. Igglesden not out	16	– c Fowler b Atherton	0
L-b 14, n-b 12	26	B 5, l-b 12, w 1, n-b 3	21
	237		**201**

1/11 2/34 3/45 4/54 5/72   1/38 2/53 3/83 4/98 5/139
6/76 7/125 8/126 9/194   6/152 7/154 8/154 9/201

Bonus points – Kent 2, Lancashire 4.

Bowling: *First Innings*—Wasim Akram 22-6-86-3; Allott 23-10-55-2; DeFreitas 19-6-43-2; Watkinson 18-6-38-1; Atherton 1-0-1-0. *Second Innings*—Wasim Akram 21-6-58-2; DeFreitas 23-7-55-2; Allott 9-5-16-1; Watkinson 11-3-32-1; Atherton 10.3-3-23-4.

Lancashire

G. Fowler c and b de Villiers	3	– c sub b de Villiers	13
M. A. Atherton lbw b Kelleher	101	– c Marsh b Davis	44
J. D. Fitton c Kelleher b Igglesden	0		
T. E. Jesty b C. S. Cowdrey	98	– (3) b Ellison	4
N. H. Fairbrother c G. R. Cowdrey b Davis	6	– (4) c Marsh b de Villiers	47
M. Watkinson b Davis	0	– (5) c Marsh b Davis	66
Wasim Akram st Marsh b C. S. Cowdrey	1	– (6) c and b Davis	9
P. A. J. DeFreitas c and b de Villiers	6	– (7) not out	7
†W. K. Hegg not out	20	– (8) lbw b Davis	0
*D. P. Hughes c C. S. Cowdrey b Davis	1	– (9) not out	0
P. J. W. Allott b Davis			
B 2, l-b 8, w 1, n-b 2	13	L-b 2, w 1	3
	249	(7 wkts)	**193**

1/5 2/6 3/174 4/185 5/185   1/28 2/37 3/97 4/151
6/188 7/210 8/247 9/249   5/174 6/189 7/189

Bonus points – Lancashire 2, Kent 4.

Bowling: *First Innings*—Igglesden 8–2–29–1; de Villiers 19–6–73–2; Davis 23–7–49–4; Kelleher 8–2–30–1; Ellison 8–1–38–0; C. S. Cowdrey 12–3–20–2. *Second Innings*—de Villiers 11–0–58–2; Ellison 12–1–41–1; Kelleher 6–1–21–0; Davis 17–6–54–4; Dobson 3.1–1–7–0; C. S. Cowdrey 1–0–10–0.

Umpires: J. C. Balderstone and B. Dudleston.

KENT v ESSEX

At Maidstone, July 4, 5, 6. Essex won by four wickets. Essex 17 pts, Kent 4 pts. Toss: Essex. After the first day had been lost to rain, a good finish was achieved by Kent declaring and then forfeiting their second innings, and Essex forfeiting their first. An excellent stand of 268 off 85 overs by Benson and Graham Cowdrey dominated Kent's innings, with Benson hitting eighteen fours in a stay of 345 minutes and Cowdrey eighteen fours in an innings of 320 minutes. Needing 309 off a minimum of 84 overs, Essex paced their effort well. They looked in trouble when three wickets fell for 16 runs in ten overs, but Hussain and Shahid restored their advantage, adding 98 in 24 overs. Pringle then hit six fours in scoring 40 off 34 balls, and with two reverse sweeps for four in the closing stages he hustled Essex home with three overs to spare.

Close of play: First day, No play; Second day, Kent 269-2 (M. R. Benson 141*, G. R. Cowdrey 104*).

Kent

S. G. Hinks c Topley b Pringle	1	M. V. Fleming not out	0
M. R. Benson lbw b Pringle	159	L-b 8, n-b 15	23
N. R. Taylor c Hardie b Pringle	6		
G. R. Cowdrey run out	116	1/4 2/30 3/298	(4 wkts dec.) 308
*C. S. Cowdrey not out	3	4/308	

†S. A. Marsh, R. M. Ellison, P. S. de Villiers, C. Penn and R. P. Davis did not bat.

Bonus points – Kent 4, Essex 1 (Score at 100 overs: 300-3).

Bowling: Foster 33–2–107–0; Pringle 31–9–54–3; Topley 25–4–60–0; Childs 10–1–41–0; Stephenson 7–1–38–0.

Kent forfeited their second innings.

Essex

Essex forfeited their first innings.

B. R. Hardie c Hinks b de Villiers	12	*D. R. Pringle not out	40
J. P. Stephenson b Davis	67	†M. A. Garnham not out	17
P. J. Prichard c Marsh b Fleming	55	B 2, l-b 6, n-b 3	11
M. E. Waugh c Marsh b Davis	3		
N. Hussain c C. S. Cowdrey b de Villiers	41	1/18 2/124 3/140	(6 wkts) 309
N. Shahid run out	63	4/140 5/238 6/265	

N. A. Foster, T. D. Topley and J. H. Childs did not bat.

Bowling: de Villiers 19–2–84–2; Penn 22–6–68–0; Davis 18–5–76–2; Ellison 12–0–46–0; Fleming 10–1–23–1; C. S. Cowdrey 2–0–4–0.

Umpires: J. C. Balderstone and B. Dudleston.

At Canterbury, July 7, 8, 9. KENT lost to INDIANS by seven wickets (See Indian tour section).

At Northampton, July 18, 19, 20. KENT drew with NORTHAMPTONSHIRE.

At Guildford, July 21, 23, 24. KENT drew with SURREY.

KENT v MIDDLESEX

At Canterbury, July 25, 26, 27. Drawn. Kent 5 pts, Middlesex 4 pts. Toss: Middlesex. A record Kent second-wicket partnership, in which Hinks scored his first double-century, lasted 101 overs and realised 366 runs. That beat the previous best of 352 between W. H. Ashdown and F. E. Woolley, against Essex at Brentwood in 1934. Hinks hit thirty fours in a stay of 441 minutes, while Taylor, who survived a "catch" by Brown at short leg because the ball first touched the fielder's helmet, batted for 346 minutes and hit eighteen fours. Roseberry and Gatting added 109 in 23 overs, and as Middlesex raced to a declaration Ramprakash hit an unbeaten century off 169 balls in 185 minutes with two sixes and twelve fours. Kent promptly lost five wickets for 53 in nineteen overs, but Marsh batted with resolution and Middlesex were left to score 282 to win in a minimum of 58 overs. At 23 for two they were in trouble, with de Villiers bowling well, but Gatting and Ramprakash put them in sight of victory by adding 198 from 37 overs. Gatting made his 101 off 131 balls with fifteen fours, and Ramprakash's second century of the match – his third in consecutive innings – came off 109 balls with four sixes and seven fours. However, de Villiers and Igglesden struck back, and by keeping Ramprakash away from the strike Kent denied Middlesex victory with a good all-round performance in the field.

Close of play: First day, Kent 392-1 (S. G. Hinks 209*, N. R. Taylor 121*); Second day, Kent 30-3 (G. R. Cowdrey 13*, R. P. Davis 0*).

Kent

S. G. Hinks c Farbrace b Hughes	234	– b Cowans	2
*M. R. Benson c Farbrace b Haynes	45	– b Emburey	10
N. R. Taylor not out	152	– (8) c Roseberry b Cowans	3
G. R. Cowdrey (did not bat)		– (3) lbw b Williams	22
T. R. Ward (did not bat)		– (4) c Williams b Emburey	0
†S. A. Marsh (did not bat)		– c Emburey b Williams	61
R. M. Ellison (did not bat)		– c Brown b Tufnell	9
P. S. de Villiers (did not bat)		– (9) c Haynes b Emburey	9
R. P. Davis (did not bat)		– (5) c Farbrace b Cowans	12
M. M. Patel (did not bat)		– not out	1
A. P. Igglesden (did not bat)		– b Williams	1
L-b 6, w 1, n-b 11	18	B 1, l-b 2, n-b 7	10

1/83 2/449 (2 wkts dec.) 449   1/15 2/30 3/30 4/43 5/53   140
                                            6/75 7/86 8/126 9/138

Bonus points – Kent 4 (Score at 100 overs: 344-1).

Bowling: *First Innings*—Williams 15–2–49–0; Cowans 23–5–57–0; Hughes 16.1–1–87–1; Haynes 10–1–47–1; Emburey 28–4–93–0; Tufnell 22–2–69–0; Ramprakash 9–0–41–0. *Second Innings*—Williams 19.5–1–65–3; Cowans 10–2–20–3; Tufnell 14–5–35–1; Emburey 7–4–3–3; Hughes 2–0–14–0.

Middlesex

D. L. Haynes b Igglesden	9	– b de Villiers	0
M. A. Roseberry c Igglesden b Ellison	82	– lbw b de Villiers	14
*M. W. Gatting c Igglesden b Davis	52	– b Igglesden	101
M. R. Ramprakash not out	100	– b de Villiers	125
K. R. Brown not out	57	– c Hinks b Igglesden	5
J. E. Emburey (did not bat)		– c Marsh b de Villiers	0
N. F. Williams (did not bat)		– c Marsh b de Villiers	8
†P. Farbrace (did not bat)		– lbw b de Villiers	3
S. P. Hughes (did not bat)		– not out	6
N. G. Cowans (did not bat)		– not out	2
B 5, l-b 1, n-b 2	8	B 2, l-b 10	12

1/12 2/121 3/155 (3 wkts dec.) 308   1/0 2/23 3/221 4/231 (8 wkts) 276
                                            5/232 6/240 7/250 8/271

P. C. R. Tufnell did not bat.

Bonus points – Middlesex 4, Kent 1.

Bowling: *First Innings*—Igglesden 10–1–53–1; de Villiers 11–1–32–0; Ellison 9–0–37–1 Davis 30–8–104–1; Patel 16.2–4–54–0; Ward 5–0–22–0. *Second Innings*—de Villiers 21–3–70–6; Igglesden 20–0–93–2; Ellison 9–0–45–0; Davis 8–1–56–0.

Umpires: A. A. Jones and R. Julian.

KENT v WORCESTERSHIRE

At Canterbury, July 28, 30, 31. Drawn. Kent 5 pts, Worcestershire 7 pts. Toss: Worcestershire. For the first time in its 148-year history, Canterbury's Festival Week was completed by the end of July, rather than in August. Despite an assured innings from Hick, who reached 50 off 63 balls, Worcestershire were struggling until Neale and Rhodes embarked on their rescue operation with a sixth-wicket stand of 185. Neale reached 100 in 270 minutes with fourteen boundaries. Newport soon had Kent in trouble, taking five quick wickets as half the side went for 46, but Fleming inspired a recovery which was continued by the injured Taylor and the indisposed Cowdrey, both batting lower down the order. Responding to Kent's declaration in arrears, Worcestershire went for and achieved quick runs and left Kent to chase 272 in a minimum of 57 overs. Never really in touch with the target, they required 124 from the last twenty overs and were forced to hang on grimly when the left-arm spin of Illingworth made a telling contribution. During the luncheon interval on the second day the teams had been presented to the Duke of Kent, the home county's patron.

Close of play: First day, Worcestershire 302-5 (P. A. Neale 101*, S. J. Rhodes 85*); Second day, Kent 236-8 (N. R. Taylor 57*, A. P. Igglesden 7*).

Worcestershire

G. J. Lord c Benson b Wren	14	– c and b Ward	81
C. M. Tolley c Taylor b Ellison	4	– lbw b Ellison	0
G. A. Hick c Marsh b Ellison	66	– c and b Wren	22
D. B. D'Oliveira c Marsh b Igglesden	21	– c Davis b Ward	4
I. T. Botham c Marsh b Igglesden	4	– b Davis	46
*P. A. Neale not out	119	– not out	14
†S. J. Rhodes c Igglesden b Wren	94	– not out	0
R. K. Illingworth lbw b Igglesden	15		
P. J. Newport not out	5		
L-b 5, w 3, n-b 1	9	L-b 3	3

1/12 2/40 3/71 4/75 5/132   (7 wkts dec.) 351   1/16 2/82 3/88   (5 wkts dec.) 170
6/317 7/341   4/133 5/162

S. R. Lampitt and N. V. Radford did not bat.

Bonus points – Worcestershire 4, Kent 2 (Score at 100 overs: 305-5).

Bowling: *First Innings*—Igglesden 21–1–97–3; Ellison 21–4–65–2; Wren 24–4–78–2 Fleming 18–3–46–0; Davis 22–8–54–0; Ward 3–1–6–0. *Second Innings*—Igglesden 6–1–23–0 Ellison 5–1–33–1; Wren 2–0–17–1; Davis 11–1–46–1; Ward 9.3–0–48–2.

Kent

S. G. Hinks b Newport	32	– hit wkt b Botham	25
*M. R. Benson c Rhodes b Newport	10	– c Rhodes b Newport	8
†S. A. Marsh c Hick b Newport	0	– (7) lbw b Newport	8
T. R. Ward c D'Oliveira b Newport	1	– (5) c D'Oliveira b Tolley	18
M. V. Fleming b Radford	59	– (6) b Illingworth	42
R. M. Ellison c Hick b Newport	0	– (8) c Radford b Illingworth	1
G. R. Cowdrey lbw b Newport	57	– (4) lbw b Radford	9
N. R. Taylor not out	64	– (3) st Rhodes b Illingworth	73
R. P. Davis c Rhodes b Botham	8	– not out	2
A. P. Igglesden not out	13	– not out	0
L-b 4, w 1, n-b 1	6	B 4, l-b 3, n-b 1	8

1/15 2/17 3/19 4/46 5/46   (8 wkts dec.) 250   1/23 2/33 3/64 4/107   (8 wkts) 194
6/132 7/197 8/218   5/161 6/184 7/189 8/192

T. N. Wren did not bat.

Bonus points – Kent 3, Worcestershire 3.

Bowling: *First Innings*—Newport 27.1–11–73–6; Botham 13–2–44–1; Lampitt 21–7–42–0; Illingworth 7–3–19–0; Radford 10–2–33–1; Tolley 8–1–29–0; Hick 2–0–6–0. *Second Innings*—Newport 14.5–2–27–2; Botham 6–2–29–1; Lampitt 11–1–45–0; Radford 9–2–41–1; Tolley 0–3–25–1; Illingworth 10–3–20–3.

Umpires: A. A. Jones and R. Julian.

At Chesterfield, August 4, 6, 7. KENT lost to DERBYSHIRE by ten wickets.

KENT v LEICESTERSHIRE

At Dartford, August 8, 9, 10. Kent won by seven wickets. Kent 21 pts, Leicestershire 4 pts. Toss: Leicestershire. With the wicket taking spin early on the first day, Kent's left-arm pair, Davis and Patel, were soon causing all kinds of problems for the Leicestershire batsmen. Ironically, given that Kent bowled only fifteen overs of pace, it was the medium pace of Parsons that accounted for Kent, but not before Benson had put together a fine century, batting for 220 minutes and hitting eighteen fours. When Leicestershire batted a second time, Patel and Davis again shared the wickets, causing a search through the record books to discover when two left-arm spinners had last taken all twenty wickets in a match for Kent. The answer was 1912, at Canterbury, when C. Blythe and F. E. Woolley, taking eleven and nine wickets respectively, bowled unchanged throughout the match against Nottinghamshire. Needing 112 to win, Kent cruised home after Hinks had taken 28 off the first two overs from Agnew. Although the pitch was reported to the TCCB by the umpires, no penalty was imposed.

Close of play: First day, Kent 50-0 (S. G. Hinks 8*, M. R. Benson 39*); Second day, Leicestershire 46-1 (N. E. Briers 16*, J. D. R. Benson 2*).

Leicestershire

T. J. Boon c Ward b Davis	18	– lbw b Patel 21
*N. E. Briers c Fleming b Patel	55	– b Davis 35
J. J. Whitaker c Cowdrey b Patel	6	– (7) b Patel 0
P. Willey c Marsh b Davis	61	– c sub b Davis 10
G. J. Parsons st Marsh b Davis	15	– (6) c Marsh b Patel 13
L. Potter c Marsh b Patel	7	– (5) c Marsh b Davis 0
J. D. R. Benson b Davis	9	– (3) c and b Davis 25
†P. A. Nixon lbw b Davis	17	– b Patel 14
J. P. Agnew c Wren b Patel	0	– b Patel 12
A. D. Mullally c Hinks b Davis	7	– b Patel 21
D. J. Millns not out	0	– not out 10
L-b 5, n-b 1	6	B 6, l-b 12, n-b 1 19

1/41 2/68 3/115 4/136 5/149   201   1/36 2/95 3/100 4/100 5/119   180
6/162 7/185 8/190 9/200   6/121 7/121 8/135 9/163

Bonus points – Leicestershire 1, Kent 3 (Score at 100 overs: 193-8).

Bowling: *First Innings*—Igglesden 8–3–19–0; Wren 7–2–18–0; Davis 44.2–18–63–6; Patel 44–13–91–4; Ward 1–0–5–0. *Second Innings*—Fleming 3–0–20–0; Igglesden 2–0–6–0; Davis 39–9–79–4; Patel 37.5–15–57–6.

Kent

S. G. Hinks c Boon b Willey	14	– b Willey	37
*M. R. Benson c Mullins b Potter	107	– b Potter	18
N. R. Taylor b Willey	18	– c Boon b Parsons	32
G. R. Cowdrey c Mullins b Parsons	39	– not out	17
T. R. Ward b Parsons	14	– not out	0
M. V. Fleming c Benson b Parsons	31		
†S. A. Marsh b Mullally	0		
R. P. Davis lbw b Mullally	0		
M. M. Patel b Parsons	17		
T. N. Wren b Parsons	1		
A. P. Igglesden not out	0		
B 19, l-b 6, n-b 4	29	B 5, l-b 3	8

1/62 2/159 3/173 4/213 5/230   270   1/43 2/67 3/106   (3 wkts) 112
6/231 7/231 8/259 9/261

Bonus points – Kent 2, Leicestershire 3 (Score at 100 overs: 231-7).

Bowling: *First Innings*—Agnew 11–3–44–0; Willey 39–12–94–2; Mullally 15–6–31–2; Potter 33–15–45–1; Parsons 15–5–31–5. *Second Innings*—Agnew 2–0–28–0; Willey 12–3–29–1; Potter 15–4–29–1; Parsons 5.5–0–18–1.

Umpires: D. S. Thompsett and A. G. T. Whitehead.

At Bristol, August 11, 13, 14. KENT drew with GLOUCESTERSHIRE.

At Hove, August 18, 20, 21. KENT drew with SUSSEX.

At Leicester, August 23, 24, 25, 27. KENT lost to LEICESTERSHIRE by two wickets.

At Bournemouth, August 29, 30, 31. KENT drew with HAMPSHIRE.

KENT v SURREY

At Canterbury, September 7, 8, 9, 10. Drawn. Kent 4 pts, Surrey 6 pts. Toss: Kent. A match which proved remarkable for personal achievement and county records rarely looked like producing a result. Taylor dominated both Kent innings. On the first day he reached his hundred off 99 balls in 106 minutes between lunch and tea, and he continued to his first double-century, batting for 322 minutes (240 balls) and hitting four sixes and 23 fours. Surrey took a substantial first-innings lead after Ward and Darren Bicknell had made career-best scores in a Surrey record third-wicket partnership of 413, which beat the previous best of 353 in 1919 by A. Ducat and E. G. Hayes against Hampshire at Southampton. Bicknell batted for a minute over eight hours and hit 21 fours, while Ward's more fluent strokes produced three sixes and 37 fours. Their stand was the highest for any wicket by any county against Kent. Ward's 263 was the highest by a Surrey batsman against Kent; and Surrey's 648 was the highest total by a county side against Kent. Follow that? Taylor did. He batted for another 263 minutes, hitting 22 fours in his 142, and apart from A. E. Fagg, who scored a double century in each innings against Essex in 1938, became only the second Kent player after H. T. W. Hardinge (1921) to score a double-hundred and hundred in a match.

Close of play: First day, Kent 367-6 (N. R. Taylor 162*, D. J. M. Kelleher 42*); Second day, Surrey 315-2 (D. J. Bicknell 103*, D. M. Ward 147*); Third day, Kent 67-3 (V. J. Wells 11* R. P. Davis 6*).

Kent

G. Hinks c Lynch b Robinson	16	– c Gray b Robinson	19
R. Ward c Kendrick b Murphy	55	– c and b Gray	10
J. Wells lbw b Gray	50	– b Murphy	11
R. Cowdrey b Gray	8	– c Lynch b Murphy	9
N. R. Taylor c Robinson b Murphy	204	– (6) c Stewart b Gray	142
V. Fleming c Stewart b Greig	9	– (7) b Murphy	80
S. A. Marsh c Kendrick b Murphy	17	– (8) not out	25
J. M. Kelleher c sub b Gray	44	– (9) lbw b Gray	6
P. Davis c Stewart b Murphy	5	– (5) lbw b Robinson	46
M. Patel c Lynch b Murphy	3	– b Gray	0
N. Wren not out	5	– not out	1
B 1, l-b 5, w 1, n-b 2	9	B 6, l-b 17, n-b 6	29

1/62 2/74 3/90 4/252 5/266   425   1/31 2/37 3/52   (9 wkts) 378
6/293 7/385 8/392 9/402   4/68 5/185 6/339
                                           7/345 8/358 9/358

Bonus points – Kent 4, Surrey 2 (Score at 100 overs: 377-6).

Bowling: First Innings—Gray 35–7–80–3; M. P. Bicknell 3.3–1–12–0; Murphy 32.1–6–99–5; Robinson 21–3–95–1; Kendrick 12–1–73–0; Greig 14–0–60–1. *Second Innings*—Gray 42.4–9–83–4; Murphy 33–4–112–3; Robinson 24–5–84–2; Greig 10–0–57–0; Kendrick 5–1–19–0.

Surrey

D. J. Bicknell c and b Wells	186	A. H. Gray c Hinks b Kelleher	11
G. S. Clinton c Marsh b Wren	57	M. P. Bicknell b Kelleher	28
A. J. Stewart b Wells	1	A. J. Murphy run out	1
D. M. Ward c Kelleher b Wells	263		
M. A. Lynch not out	73	B 2, l-b 4, w 1, n-b 5	12
I. A. Greig c and b Wells	0		
P. D. Robinson c Marsh b Fleming	16	1/99 2/100 3/513 4/530	648
N. M. Kendrick c Wells b Kelleher	0	5/531 6/566 7/571 8/607 9/646	

Bonus points – Surrey 4 (Score at 100 overs: 341-2).

Bowling: Kelleher 34.5–2–148–3; Wren 33–3–128–1; Davis 11–1–49–0; Wells 35–4–126–4; Fleming 37–4–127–1; Patel 24–4–64–0.

Umpires: M. J. Kitchen and D. S. Thompsett.

At Chelmsford, September 12, 13, 14, 15. KENT drew with ESSEX.

LANCASHIRE

Patron: HM The Queen
President: A. J. Leggat
Chairman: R. Bennett
Secretary: C. D. Hassell
    County Cricket Ground, Old Trafford,
    Manchester M16 0PX
    (Telephone: 061-848 7021)
Captain: D. P. Hughes
Coach: J. A. Ormrod

Lancashire had a marvellous summer. They became the first county to win both Lord's finals, finished runners-up in the Refuge Assurance League, and were sixth in the Britannic Assurance Championship. The Second Eleven won the 55-overs Bain Clarkson Trophy, but like their seniors they were unable to make their mark in Championship cricket.

Lancashire were virtually invincible in all forms of the limited-over game, losing only four out of 28 matches. The formidable line-up of batting was enough to carry them to victory on most days, and high among the list of Sunday wins was the seven-wicket victory, with eleven balls to spare, when set to score 268 in 39 overs at The Oval. But the most crushing win of the season was their 241-run victory over Gloucestershire in the quarter-finals of the NatWest Bank Trophy. Lancashire's 37 for five was the highest in any limited-overs game between first-class counties. Another record was denied Lancashire when the weather forced their Benson and Hedges Cup tie against Hampshire to be expunged after they had scored 352 for six, following a third-wicket partnership of 244 between Neil Fairbrother and Mike Atherton.

Lancashire stayed in the running for all the trophies right through to the closing stages of the season. They would have won the Refuge Assurance League if Derbyshire had slipped up in their final game with Essex, and they went into the last eight matches of the Championship handily placed in second position behind Middlesex. However, they won only one of those games, and there is no doubt that success in all the competitions up to the beginning of August took its mental and physical toll on the players. Even while Lancashire managed to stay among the leaders in the Championship, their minds always seemed to be rather more on the next important limited-overs match.

The turning-point came at Northampton in the middle of August, a game which ended the day before the NatWest semi-final against Middlesex. Lancashire, at least one game ahead of the other contenders, had to beat Northamptonshire to stay in the race. Atherton was already absent because of the Old Trafford Test match, and five other key players were rested. All five, nevertheless, returned for the Sunday League match the same weekend, and for the NatWest Trophy semi-final. The Championship was effectively surrendered in that game at Northampton as Lancashire continued their triumphant march in the one-day competitions.

By winning the finals of the Benson and Hedges Cup and the NatWest Bank Trophy Lancashire took to four their total of trophies won in the our years of David Hughes's captaincy. His batting and bowling contributions continued to be modest in 1990, but his fielding was as alert as ever and his enthusiasm for the game and for Lancashire cricket never flagged. Not surprisingly, he was asked to captain the county again in 1991 in his 25th season. Fairbrother, who captained the team whenever Hughes was absent, was appointed vice-captain for the first time, a clear pointer to the day when Hughes decides to retire. He had his best-ever season for Lancashire with 1,681 runs and an average of 80.04, blazing his way through the summer with a series of confident, swash-buckling innings to delight spectators all over the country. But the Fairbrothers of Lancashire and of England looked like two different people, one assured and convincing, the other diffident and uncertain. He was dropped by England after five innings against New Zealand had brought him only 59 runs, but his continuing good form for Lancashire earned him a place in England's A team to Pakistan. His 366 against Surrey at The Oval was the third-highest innings in England after fellow-Lancastrian A. C. MacLaren's 424 and G. A. Hick's 405 not out.

Atherton, too, had an outstanding season, playing in all six Tests, in which he scored two centuries, and falling just 76 runs short of 2,000 in his first full season since completing his studies at Cambridge. He scored seven hundreds and twelve fifties to finish ninth in the national averages, and although opening the innings for England, he provided the back-bone that Lancashire have long needed at No. 3. He is unquestionably Lancashire's best batting find since Cyril Washbrook was discovered nearly 60 years ago. Atherton also proved to be Lancashire's best bowler, his leg-spin bringing him 44 wickets at a respectable cost of 27 runs each, including three five-wicket returns.

Gehan Mendis was as reliable as ever, his 1,551 runs taking his total to 7,035 in his five seasons with Lancashire since leaving Sussex. But Graeme Fowler had another eccentric summer. Although failing to reach 1,000 first-class runs despite playing in 21 of the 22 Championship matches, he beat Harry Pilling's record of 625 runs in the Sunday game by scoring 773. Lancashire's persistence with Fowler, and preference for Trevor Jesty in the middle of the order meant that Graham Lloyd's opportunities were limited to eleven Championship games, though he played in all but one of the Refuge games.

Mike Watkinson took 47 first-class wickets to go with his 754 runs, while Phillip DeFreitas had a season of mixed fortune. He took only 40 first-class wickets, with just two five-wicket returns, yet he destroyed the Northamptonshire batting in the NatWest final with an opening spell of 8–4–19–5, and he also scored two first-class hundreds.

All in all, the bowling was disappointing, with no-one taking even 50 first-class wickets: the two overseas players, Patrick Patterson – who was released at the end of the season – and Wasim Akram, managed only 45 between them. Wasim had a frustrating year, beset by injury; playing in just seven Championship matches, he took fifteen expensive wickets and scored 117 runs. However, Warren Hegg enhanced his wicket-keeping reputation to win a place on the England A tour and showed his merit as a batsman with 674 first-class runs. Off-spinner Dexter Fitton had a miserable summer on a succession of perfect pitches, and left-arm spinner Ian Folley, unable to regain the form of 1987, was released at the end of the season. – Brian Bearshaw.

LANCASHIRE 1990

[Bill Smith]

Back row: I. Folley, I. D. Austin, N. J. Speak, B. P. Patterson, P. J. Martin, Wasim Akram, P. A. J. DeFreitas, W. K. Hegg, G. D. Lloyd, J. A. Ormrod (coach).
Front row: S. Bramhall, G. D. Mendis, T. E. Jesty, N. H. Fairbrother, D. P. Hughes (captain), D. I. W. Atherton, G. Fowler, M. Watkinson, I. an M. Atwater (captain)

LANCASHIRE RESULTS

All first-class matches – Played 25: Won 6, Lost 3, Drawn 16.

County Championship matches – Played 22: Won 6, Lost 3, Drawn 13.

Bonus points – Batting 65, Bowling 56.

Competition placings – Britannic Assurance County Championship, 6th;
NatWest Bank Trophy, winners; Benson and Hedges Cup, winners;
Refuge Assurance League, 2nd; Refuge Assurance Cup, s-f.

BRITANNIC ASSURANCE CHAMPIONSHIP AVERAGES

BATTING

	Birthplace	M	I	NO	R	HI	Avge
‡N. H. Fairbrother ..	Warrington	17	24	6	1,544	366	85.77
‡M. A. Atherton	Manchester	12	18	4	1,053	191	75.21
‡G. D. Mendis	Colombo, Ceylon	21	35	6	1,551	180	53.48
‡T. E. Jesty	Gosport	17	24	6	785	98	43.61
‡W. K. Hegg	Whitefield	20	21	6	617	100*	41.13
‡P. A. J. DeFreitas ..	Scotts Head, Dominica	15	17	3	506	100*	36.14
‡M. Watkinson	Westhoughton	18	22	2	706	138	35.30
‡I. D. Austin	Haslingden	11	12	5	238	58	34.00
‡G. Fowler	Accrington	21	35	6	938	126	32.34
G. D. Lloyd	Accrington	11	15	1	434	70	31.00
‡P. J. W. Allott	Altrincham	13	6	2	114	55*	28.50
‡D. P. Hughes	Newton-le-Willows	18	17	7	237	57	23.70
J. D. Fitton	Littleborough	14	11	5	114	25*	19.00
P. J. Martin	Accrington	9	6	3	42	21	14.00
‡Wasim Akram	Lahore, Pakistan	7	10	0	117	32	11.70
N. J. Speak	Manchester	3	4	0	41	30	10.25
‡B. P. Patterson	Portland, Jamaica	10	4	1	5	4*	1.66

Also batted: S. Bramhall (*Warrington*) (1 match) 0*; S. N. V. Waterton (*Dartford*) (1 match) 3; G. Yates (*Ashton-under-Lyne*) (2 matches) 106. J. P. Crawley (*Maldon*) (1 match) did not bat.

* Signifies not out. ‡ Denotes county cap.

The following played a total of seventeen three-figure innings for Lancashire in County Championship matches – M. A. Atherton 4, G. D. Mendis 4, N. H. Fairbrother 3, G. Fowler 2, P. A. J. DeFreitas 1, W. K. Hegg 1, M. Watkinson 1, G. Yates 1.

BOWLING

	O	M	R	W	BB	5W/i	Avge
M. A. Atherton	356.3	85	1,111	42	6-78	3	26.45
M. Watkinson	503.2	120	1,572	47	5-65	3	33.44
B. P. Patterson	281.4	45	1,015	29	4-52	0	35.00
P. A. J. DeFreitas	408.5	96	1,219	33	6-39	1	36.93
P. J. Martin	240.3	46	750	20	4-68	0	37.50
D. P. Hughes	280.4	61	918	24	4-25	0	38.25
Wasim Akram	191	43	594	15	3-76	0	39.60
P. J. W. Allott	266	77	730	18	4-23	0	40.55
I. D. Austin	208.1	64	536	10	3-42	0	53.60
J. D. Fitton	428.4	86	1,365	14	3-69	0	97.50

Also bowled: G. Fowler 4.1–2–33–1; T. E. Jesty 8–3–27–1; G. D. Lloyd 2.1–0–22–0; G. Yates 51–12–117–3.

Wicket-keepers: W. K. Hegg 47 ct, 2 st; S. N. V. Waterton 4 ct; S. Bramhall 1 ct, 1 st.

Leading Fielders: N. H. Fairbrother 18, M. A. Atherton 16, G. D. Mendis 16.

LANCASHIRE v WORCESTERSHIRE

At Manchester, April 26, 27, 28, 30. Drawn. Lancashire 7 pts, Worcestershire 5 pts. Toss: Worcestershire. The combination of a good pitch and two strong contenders for the Championship forced the match to a dull, inconclusive finish. After the first day had been washed out, Lancashire took advantage of what little help the pitch offered bowlers by reducing Worcestershire to 86 for five on the second morning. But D'Oliveira, with his first century in three seasons – a career-best 155 in 257 minutes (205 balls), with two sixes and 24 fours – shared in a stand of 226 in 65 overs with Rhodes. Hick was allowed to reach his century on the final day – he batted for 161 minutes (123 balls) and hit three sixes and ten fours – before Lancashire were set to score 292 in 46 overs, a target they never entertained.

Close of play: First day, No play; Second day, Worcestershire 360-7 (R. K. Illingworth 35*, P. J. Newport 5*); Third day, Worcestershire 22-0 (T. S. Curtis 16*, G. J. Lord 4*).

Worcestershire

T. S. Curtis c DeFreitas b Patterson	7	– b Patterson 37
G. J. Lord c Hegg b Patterson	9	– c Hegg b Jesty 19
G. A. Hick b Watkinson	23	– not out 106
I. T. Botham c Hegg b DeFreitas	17	– not out 50
*P. A. Neale lbw b DeFreitas	10	
D. B. D'Oliveira c Fairbrother b Hughes	155	
†S. J. Rhodes b Hughes	72	
R. K. Illingworth not out	35	
P. J. Newport not out	5	
B 8, l-b 6, n-b 13	27	B 3, l-b 5, w 1, n-b 10 ... 19

1/17 2/25 3/49 4/65 5/86   (7 wkts dec.) 360   1/48 2/114   (2 wkts dec.) 231
6/312 7/341

N. V. Radford and G. R. Dilley did not bat.

Bonus points – Worcestershire 4, Lancashire 3 (Score at 100 overs: 348-7).

Bowling: *First Innings*—Patterson 22.1-5-55-2; DeFreitas 26-11-62-2; Watkinson 21-1-96-1; Atherton 6-0-32-0; Fitton 21-2-79-0; Hughes 8-1-22-2. *Second Innings*—Patterson 10.0-0-27-1; DeFreitas 15-5-51-0; Watkinson 9-3-19-0; Jesty 5-1-20-1; Fitton 14-1-70-0; Atherton 8-0-36-0.

Lancashire

G. D. Mendis b Illingworth	80	– not out 35
G. Fowler c Botham b Illingworth	16	– not out 35
M. A. Atherton b Illingworth	50	
N. H. Fairbrother not out	74	
T. E. Jesty b Illingworth	54	
M. Watkinson not out	0	
L-b 17, w 5, n-b 4	26	B 1, l-b 6, n-b 1 8

1/47 2/155 3/160 4/296   (4 wkts dec.) 300   (no wkt) 78

*D. P. Hughes, †W. K. Hegg, P. A. J. DeFreitas, J. D. Fitton and B. P. Patterson did not bat.

Bonus points – Lancashire 4, Worcestershire 1.

Bowling: *First Innings*—Dilley 16-1-80-0; Radford 19-6-66-0; Newport 19-3-61-0; Illingworth 35.3-17-46-4; Botham 7-1-24-0; Hick 1-0-6-0. *Second Innings*—Dilley 3-0-9-0; Radford 6-0-15-0; Newport 5-2-14-0; Illingworth 6-2-5-0; Hick 12-4-11-0; D'Oliveira 5-1-12-0; Curtis 2-1-5-0.

Umpires: J. C. Balderstone and H. D. Bird.

At The Oval, May 3, 4, 5, 7. LANCASHIRE drew with SURREY.

at Derby, May 15, 16, 17, 18. LANCASHIRE beat DERBYSHIRE by 60 runs.

LANCASHIRE v LEICESTERSHIRE

at Manchester, May 19, 21, 22. Drawn. Lancashire 6 pts, Leicestershire 3 pts. Toss: Leicestershire. A target of 316 in 61 overs proved too stiff for Lancashire after declarations had been necessary to set up a run-chase on another perfect wicket. Leicestershire recovered from losing two wickets to the new ball on the first morning, and Lancashire declared 86 behind after their first double-century opening stand in sixteen years. Fowler's century, containing a six and twelve fours, was his second in successive days, following his 108 in the Refuge League match. Neither Patterson nor DeFreitas bowled on the final morning as Leicestershire headed for the declaration, a fair one on a still-firm, unmarked pitch that had yielded 479 runs for the loss of two wickets – one of them a run-out – in the previous eight hours. Mendis and Fowler took 62 off the first eleven overs, Mendis and Fairbrother quickly put on 70 for the third wicket, but the loss of four batsmen in six overs left Lancashire blocking out the overs.

Close of play: First day, Leicestershire 318-7 (W. K. M. Benjamin 65*, P. A. Nixon 23*); second day, Leicestershire 66-1 (N. E. Briers 26*, J. J. Whitaker 3*).

Leicestershire

T. J. Boon c and b Atherton	84	– run out	30
*N. E. Briers c Hegg b DeFreitas	0	– not out	81
J. J. Whitaker c Mendis b Patterson	8	– not out	107
P. Willey c Hegg b Fitton	43		
L. Potter c and b Atherton	55		
C. C. Lewis c Hegg b Atherton	32		
M. I. Gidley st Hegg b Atherton	2		
W. K. M. Benjamin run out	65		
†P. A. Nixon not out	33		
J. P. Agnew c Fairbrother b Patterson	6		
A. D. Mullally c sub b Patterson	2		
L-b 2, n-b 4	6	B 2, l-b 5, n-b 4	11

1/4 2/17 3/113 4/158 5/227   336   1/49   (1 wkt dec.) 229
6/228 7/251 8/319 9/326

Bonus points – Leicestershire 3, Lancashire 3 (Score at 100 overs: 265-7).

Bowling: *First Innings*—Patterson 21-2-68-3; DeFreitas 26-3-78-1; Martin 19-4-45-0; Fitton 22-8-54-1; Atherton 27-5-89-4. *Second Innings*—Patterson 6-2-27-0; DeFreitas 7-0-23-0; Fitton 24-4-54-0; Atherton 15-3-55-0; Martin 5-0-17-0; Hughes 13-1-46-0.

Lancashire

G. D. Mendis c Boon b Willey	113	– c and b Agnew	82
G. Fowler not out	115	– b Willey	22
M. A. Atherton not out	10	– c Briers b Willey	3
N. H. Fairbrother (did not bat)		– c Mullally b Agnew	46
T. E. Jesty (did not bat)		– b Lewis	0
P. A. J. DeFreitas (did not bat)		– not out	19
†W. K. Hegg (did not bat)		– c and b Lewis	1
*D. P. Hughes (did not bat)		– c sub b Potter	6
J. D. Fitton (did not bat)		– not out	0
L-b 7, w 1, n-b 4	12	B 5, l-b 10, w 4, n-b 3	22

1/231   (1 wkt dec.) 250   1/78 2/88 3/158 4/159   (7 wkts) 201
                                     5/163 6/167 7/189

P. J. Martin and B. P. Patterson did not bat.

Bonus points – Lancashire 3.

Bowling: *First Innings*—Lewis 6-0-21-0; Agnew 18-3-76-0; Mullally 22.2-5-60-0; Willey 19-6-43-1; Gidley 9-0-43-0. *Second Innings*—Mullally 17-1-61-0; Agnew 11-1-43-2; Lewis 17-8-20-2; Willey 11-1-54-2; Potter 4.4-3-8-1.

Umpires: B. Hassan and R. Palmer.

LANCASHIRE v ZIMBABWEANS

At Manchester, May 23, 24, 25. Drawn. Toss: Lancashire. Speak hit fifteen boundaries in a maiden first-class hundred as he and Lloyd shared in two opening century partnerships for a Lancashire team mostly made up of second-team players. P. J. Martin was originally named in Lancashire's team, but withdrew injured at the end of the opening day before taking the field. Irani was allowed to play instead and so made his first-class début. Wasim Akram and Watkinson also withdrew injured, which led to Martin fielding as a substitute. For the tourists, Robertson scored a sparkling century, hitting two sixes and twelve fours, and with Flower he put on 188 for the third wicket. The Zimbabweans declared 50 ahead but later refused to take up Lancashire's challenge to score 261 at about 6 runs an over.

Close of play: First day, Zimbabweans 17-1 (G. W. Flower 4*, D. F. Dolphin 6*); Second day, Lancashire 70-0 (G. D. Lloyd 38*, N. J. Speak 31*).

Lancashire

G. D. Lloyd c Traicos b Butchart	78	– c Flower b Shah	76
N. J. Speak c and b Traicos	138	– c sub b Duers	74
S. P. Titchard c Flower b Duers	15	– b Flower	80
J. P. Crawley run out	1	– not out	76
M. Watkinson c Traicos b Shah	48		
Wasim Akram c James b Duers	18		
I. D. Austin not out	11		
G. Yates not out	2		
L-b 5, w 6, n-b 4	15	B 1, l-b 3	4

1/154 2/188 3/204 4/284   (6 wkts dec.) 326   1/133 2/165 3/310   (3 wkts dec.) 310
5/294 6/320

I. Folley, R. Irani and *†J. Stanworth did not bat.

Bowling: *First Innings*—Dube 11-1-48-0; Duers 23-5-96-2; Traicos 15-0-44-1; Butchart 12-3-48-1; Dolphin 8-1-28-0; Shah 23-7-57-1. *Second Innings*—Dube 4-1-18-0; Duers 20-4-59-1; Traicos 27-4-69-0; Dolphin 2-0-19-0; Flower 13.5-0-68-1; Shah 11-1-46-1; Butchart 5-1-27-0.

Zimbabweans

K. J. Arnott c Stanworth b Wasim Akram	0	– (2) lbw b Irani	2
G. W. Flower c Crawley b Folley	65	– (1) not out	20
D. F. Dolphin c Lloyd b Austin	25		
C. M. Robertson c sub b Yates	125	– not out	0
I. P. Butchart c Speak b Irani	71		
*A. J. Pycroft b Austin	55		
†W. R. James not out	16	– (3) lbw b Folley	52
L-b 4, w 1, n-b 14	19	W 2, n-b 2	4

1/0 2/39 3/227 4/228 5/342   (6 wkts dec.) 376   1/6 2/76   (2 wkts) 78
6/376

A. H. Shah, A. J. Traicos, K. G. Duers and L. E. Dube did not bat.

Bowling: *First Innings*—Wasim Akram 13-1-46-1; Watkinson 5-2-6-0; Irani 15-3-61-1; Austin 19-5-93-2; Yates 28-5-88-1; Folley 27-7-78-1. *Second Innings*—Austin 8-4-10-0; Irani 7-4-12-1; Folley 11-3-30-1; Yates 11-3-26-0.

Umpires: G. I. Burgess and D. O. Oslear.

At Colwyn Bay, May 26, 28, 29. LANCASHIRE drew with GLAMORGAN.

At Horsham, June 2, 4, 5. LANCASHIRE beat SUSSEX by nine wickets.

LANCASHIRE v GLOUCESTERSHIRE

At Manchester, June 9, 11, 12. Lancashire won by five wickets. Lancashire 18 pts, Gloucestershire 3 pts. Toss: Lancashire. After the first day had been washed out, both teams forfeited an innings on the final day to leave Lancashire with a victory target of 322 in at least 90 overs. Fowler gave the innings the right base, batting for four and a half hours and hitting sixteen fours in his 126, and Jesty saw Lancashire home, and to the top of the Championship table, with five overs to spare.

Close of play: First day, No play; Second day, Gloucestershire 280-7 (D. A. Graveney 10*, C. A. Walsh 2*).

Gloucestershire

*A. J. Wright c Hegg b Patterson	15	D. A. Graveney not out	19
G. D. Hodgson c and b Hughes	72	C. A. Walsh not out	33
P. W. Romaines retired hurt	12		
C. W. J. Athey c Hegg b Patterson	33	B 2, l-b 8, n-b 1	11
P. Bainbridge b Austin	72		
K. M. Curran c Allott b Fitton	48		(7 wkts dec.) 321
J. W. Lloyds lbw b Austin	0		
†G. A. Tedstone b Austin	6		

D. V. Lawrence did not bat.

1/26 2/127 3/161 4/236 5/236 6/240 7/273

Bonus points – Gloucestershire 3, Lancashire 2 (Score at 100 overs: 254-6).

P. W. Romaines retired hurt at 52.

Bowling: Patterson 18-4-43-2; Allott 16-2-39-0; Austin 21-3-42-3; Watkinson 12-3-33-0; Fitton 36-7-111-1; Hughes 17.5-5-43-1.

Gloucestershire forfeited their second innings.

Lancashire

Lancashire forfeited their first innings.

G. Fowler c Lloyds b Curran	126	I. D. Austin not out	26
G. D. Mendis c Hodgson b Graveney	23		
N. J. Speak c Tedstone b Lawrence	30	B 5, l-b 14, w 1, n-b 11	31
T. E. Jesty not out	84		
M. Watkinson b Lawrence	4		(5 wkts) 324
†W. K. Hegg lbw b Lawrence	0		

1/94 2/146 3/247 4/277 5/277

*D. P. Hughes, J. D. Fitton, P. J. W. Allott and B. P. Patterson did not bat.

Bowling: Walsh 20-1-66-0; Lawrence 18-2-86-3; Bainbridge 11-1-32-0; Curran 14-0-68-1; Graveney 19-3-39-1; Lloyds 2-0-7-0; Wright 0.5-0-7-0.

Umpires: M. J. Kitchen and K. J. Lyons.

At Oxford, June 16, 18, 19. LANCASHIRE drew with OXFORD UNIVERSITY.

LANCASHIRE v MIDDLESEX

At Manchester, June 20, 21, 22. Middlesex won by five wickets. Middlesex 18 pts, Lancashire 2 pts. Toss: Middlesex. After only 40 overs had been possible on the opening day and 57 on the second, the second successive double forfeiture of innings at Old Trafford left Middlesex with a minimum of 73 overs in which to score 302 for victory. This they did comfortably with fourteen overs to spare after century stands for the first two wickets involving Haynes, Roseberry and Gatting. For Lancashire, Mendis had scored his third century of the season, occupying more than six hours and spread over three days.

Close of play: First day, Lancashire 91-2 (G. D. Mendis 34*, T. E. Jesty 3*); Second day, Lancashire 222-5 (G. D. Mendis 92*, I. D. Austin 2*).

Lancashire

G. D. Mendis b Emburey	114	I. D. Austin not out	45
G. Fowler b Williams	24	J. D. Fitton not out	13
G. D. Lloyd c Emburey b Fraser	21	B 3, l-b 5, n-b 20	28
T. E. Jesty c Emburey b Tufnell	5		
M. Watkinson c Roseberry b Tufnell	37	1/41 2/77 3/104	(6 wkts dec.) 301
†W. K. Hegg c Haynes b Tufnell	14	4/182 5/219 6/262	

*D. P. Hughes, P. J. W. Allott and B. P. Patterson did not bat.

Bonus points – Lancashire 2, Middlesex 2 (Score at 100 overs: 224-5).

Bowling: Williams 15–4–53–1; Fraser 24–5–52–1; Hughes 13–4–32–0; Tufnell 44–12–90–3; Emburey 18–4–35–1; Ramprakash 2–0–17–0; Roseberry 1–0–14–0.

Lancashire forfeited their second innings.

Middlesex

Middlesex forfeited their first innings.

D. L. Haynes c Mendis b Watkinson	49	†P. Farbrace not out	17
M. A. Roseberry hit wkt b Patterson	79		
*M. W. Gatting c Hegg b Watkinson	95	B 8, l-b 11, n-b 9	28
M. R. Ramprakash c Hegg b Watkinson	8		
K. R. Brown not out	21	1/100 2/216 3/255	(5 wkts) 303
J. E. Emburey c Hegg b Watkinson	6	4/258 5/282	

P. C. R. Tufnell, N. F. Williams, S. P. Hughes and A. R. C. Fraser did not bat.

Bowling: Patterson 13–0–74–1; Allott 7–0–32–0; Austin 13.1–1–58–0; Watkinson 13–0–61–4; Fitton 8–0–35–0; Hughes 5–0–24–0.

Umpires: H. D. Bird and P. J. Eele.

LANCASHIRE v HAMPSHIRE

At Manchester, June 23, 25, 26. Drawn. Lancashire 2 pts, Hampshire 4 pts. Toss: Lancashire. Rain and bad light severely hit the third successive match at Old Trafford, producing another contrived finish. Left to score 330 in at least 70 overs, Lancashire, without Atherton, Fairbrother and DeFreitas, who were playing in the Test match at Lord's, gave up hope after losing their top four batsmen for 60 runs. On the second day, Marshall had put the distractions of several stoppages behind him to ensure that Hampshire achieved four batting points.
Close of play: First day, Hampshire 155-3 (D. I. Gower 43*, M. D. Marshall 27*); Second day, Lancashire 58-0 (G. D. Mendis 37*, G. Fowler 15*).

Hampshire

V. P. Terry lbw b Watkinson	15	– c Hegg b Wasim Akram	0
C. L. Smith c Jesty b Wasim Akram	25	– not out	53
T. C. Middleton b Watkinson	20	– not out	34
D. I. Gower c Speak b Wasim Akram	49		
M. D. Marshall c Mendis b Watkinson	86		
*M. C. J. Nicholas not out	58		
†R. J. Parks not out	14		
B 11, l-b 10, w 1, n-b 11	33		

1/32 2/64 3/104 4/168 5/247	(5 wkts dec.) 300	1/0	(1 wkt dec.) 87

R. J. Maru, T. M. Tremlett, C. A. Connor and K. J. Shine did not bat.

Bonus points – Hampshire 4, Lancashire 2.

Bowling: *First Innings*—Wasim Akram 29–3–106–2; Allott 17–8–26–0; Watkinson 22–8–54–3; Fitton 21.4–5–75–0; Austin 10–5–18–0. *Second Innings*—Wasim Akram 4–0–5–1; Allott 5–1–10–0; Watkinson 4–0–10–0; Fitton 11–1–34–0; Austin 8–1–28–0.

Lancashire

G. D. Mendis not out	37	– c Parks b Marshall	23
G. Fowler not out	15	– c Middleton b Maru	17
G. D. Lloyd (did not bat)		– c Tremlett b Maru	6
N. J. Speak (did not bat)		– b Marshall	6
T. E. Jesty (did not bat)		– not out	26
M. Watkinson (did not bat)		– not out	41
L-b 1, n-b 5	6	B 6, l-b 2, n-b 4	12

(no wkt dec.) 58   1/31 2/47 3/50 4/60   (4 wkts) 131

†W. K. Hegg, I. D. Austin, J. D. Fitton, *P. J. W. Allott and Wasim Akram did not bat.

Bowling: *First Innings*—Marshall 5–0–28–0; Shine 5–0–22–0; Connor 1–0–1–0; Tremlett 1–0–6–0. *Second Innings*—Connor 5.2–1–12–0; Maru 20–12–22–2; Marshall 14–2–42–2; Shine 6.4–0–15–0; Tremlett 5–1–13–0; Nicholas 5–0–11–0; Smith 5–3–8–0.

Umpires: H. D. Bird and P. J. Eele.

At Maidstone, June 30, July 2, 3. LANCASHIRE beat KENT by three wickets.

LANCASHIRE v DERBYSHIRE

At Liverpool, July 7, 9, 10. Drawn. Lancashire 4 pts, Derbyshire 6 pts. Toss: Lancashire. After Lancashire had declared at their Saturday night score, Barnett led his side's reply with his third successive Championship hundred to equal a Derbyshire record shared by W. Storer, L. G. Wright and P. N. Kirsten. He hit seventeen fours while putting on 200 with Bowler for the first wicket. Following Barnett's declaration, half an hour before tea and 51 runs behind, Derbyshire retained the ascendancy by taking five wickets before the close. However, Lancashire rallied on the final morning to leave them with a daunting victory target of 326 in 58 overs, which was way beyond them. Barnett, though hitting fifteen fours in his unbeaten 90, declined the chance of pursuing his fourth successive century.

Close of play: First day, Lancashire 301-8 (D. P. Hughes 25*, J. D. Fitton 6*); Second day, Lancashire 129-5 (M. Watkinson 25*, P. A. J. DeFreitas 6*).

Lancashire

G. D. Mendis c Kuiper b Base	7	– b Kuiper	25
G. Fowler c Roberts b Jean-Jacques	19	– (8) c Goldsmith b Jean-Jacques	31
G. D. Lloyd lbw b Kuiper	62	– (5) c Krikken b Kuiper	26
T. E. Jesty c Krikken b Base	27	– c Adams b Base	4
M. Watkinson b Kuiper	4	– (6) c Goldsmith b Jean-Jacques	63
P. A. J. DeFreitas c Goldsmith b Kuiper	16	– (7) c Kuiper b Base	11
†W. K. Hegg lbw b Miller	83	– (3) c Krikken b Kuiper	34
I. D. Austin c Roberts b Miller	29	– (9) not out	27
*D. P. Hughes not out	25	– (10) not out	36
J. D. Fitton not out	6	– (2) b Kuiper	4
L-b 11, w 4, n-b 8	23	L-b 2, w 1, n-b 10	13

1/10 2/53 3/111 4/122 5/138   (8 wkts dec.) 301   1/12 2/58 3/71   (8 wkts dec.) 274
6/146 7/234 8/284   4/84 5/112 6/139
                                                   7/206 8/207

P. J. W. Allott did not bat.

Bonus points – Lancashire 4, Derbyshire 3.

Bowling: *First Innings*—Base 24–2–79–2; Jean-Jacques 25–3–104–1; Goldsmith 6–1–24–0; Kuiper 19–6–42–3; Barnett 1–0–9–0; Miller 18–5–32–2. *Second Innings*—Jean-Jacques 16.3–0–90–2; Kuiper 24–4–69–4; Base 24–5–79–2; Miller 11–4–26–0; Goldsmith 2–0–8–0.

Derbyshire

*K. J. Barnett c Hegg b Watkinson	109	– not out		90
P. D. Bowler not out	115	– (5) c sub b Watkinson		30
J. E. Morris c sub b Hughes	14	– (2) c Hegg b Austin		22
B. Roberts not out	4	– (6) not out		1
A. P. Kuiper (did not bat)		– (3) c Lloyd b DeFreitas		8
S. C. Goldsmith (did not bat)		– (4) lbw b DeFreitas		7
B 2, l-b 4, n-b 2	8	B 8, l-b 3		11

1/200 2/240   (2 wkts dec.) 250   1/55 2/81 3/89 4/152   (4 wkts) 169

C. J. Adams, †K. M. Krikken, M. Jean-Jacques, S. J. Base and G. Miller did not bat.

Bonus points – Derbyshire 3.

Bowling: First Innings—DeFreitas 13–1–44–0; Watkinson 14.2–0–56–1; Austin 12–0–33–0; Fitton 23–5–66–0; Hughes 15–3–45–1. *Second Innings*—DeFreitas 10–2–35–2; Watkinson 13–5–47–1; Austin 7–2–18–1; Fitton 11–3–43–0; Hughes 7–1–15–0.

Umpires: R. Julian and D. O. Oslear.

At Coventry, July 18, 19, 20. LANCASHIRE drew with WARWICKSHIRE.

At Colchester, July 21, 23, 24. LANCASHIRE lost to ESSEX by six wickets.

LANCASHIRE v NOTTINGHAMSHIRE

At Southport, July 25, 26, 27. Lancashire won by seven wickets. Lancashire 24 pts, Nottinghamshire 4 pts. Toss: Lancashire. Mendis ended a lean period in the Championship with his fourth century of the season, hitting a six and 26 fours before he was fourth out at 378. Fairbrother's entertaining 93 contained four sixes and twelve fours, and Watkinson hit five sixes before becoming one of the last six wickets to fall for 20 runs. Nottinghamshire followed on 247 behind, despite a fine innings of 122 off 159 balls (22 fours) from Broad. His only support, however, came from Evans in an eighth-wicket partnership of 84. Nottinghamshire were only 18 runs in arrears with seven wickets standing at the end of the second day, but Lancashire cleaned up the remaining batsmen for 144 runs. Rain delayed Lancashire's response, but a requirement of 127 runs in 34 overs was easily reached with seven overs to spare. Waterton, a wicket-keeper formerly with Kent and Northamptonshire, made his Lancashire début as replacement for Hegg, who was injured, and held four catches on the second day.

Close of play: First day, Lancashire 452; Second day, Nottinghamshire 229-3 (P. Johnson 69*, D. W. Randall 34*).

Lancashire

G. D. Mendis c Robinson b Stephenson	180	– c Evans b Stephenson		21
G. Fowler c Stephenson b Evans	18	– c Robinson b Afford		6
G. D. Lloyd c Johnson b Afford	39	– not out		59
N. H. Fairbrother c Robinson b Cooper	93	– c Johnson b Afford		10
T. E. Jesty c and b Evans	38	– not out		30
M. Watkinson st French b Afford	47			
J. D. Fitton c French b Evans	3			
*D. P. Hughes b Evans	7			
†S. N. V. Waterton c French b Broad b Afford	3			
P. J. W. Allott st French b Afford	5			
P. J. Martin not out	1			
B 2, l-b 5, n-b 11	18	L-b 2, w 1, n-b 1		4

1/54 2/155 3/318 4/378 5/432   452   1/26 2/39 3/53   (3 wkts) 130
6/434 7/441 8/442 9/449

Bonus points – Lancashire 4, Nottinghamshire 2 (Score at 100 overs: 434-5).

Bowling: First Innings—Stephenson 23–4–127–1; Cooper 23–1–94–1; Evans 25–10–57–4; Afford 34.5–5–137–4; Saxelby 3–0–30–0. *Second Innings*—Stephenson 9–0–44–1; Cooper 2–1–11–0; Afford 11–2–58–2; Evans 4.4–1–15–0.

Nottinghamshire

B. C. Broad c Mendis b Allott	122 – lbw b Allott	46
P. R. Pollard lbw b Allott	0 – c Waterton b Martin	27
*R. T. Robinson c Waterton b Martin	0 – c Waterton b Hughes	41
P. Johnson c Mendis b Martin	4 – b Allott	82
D. W. Randall lbw b Allott	0 – c and b Martin	68
M. Saxelby c Waterton b Fitton	13 – c Fairbrother b Martin	8
F. D. Stephenson c Hughes b Fitton	8 – run out	18
†B. N. French lbw b Martin	6 – run out	1
K. P. Evans not out	48 – not out	34
K. E. Cooper b Allott	0 – c Fitton b Watkinson	24
J. A. Afford c Watkinson b Hughes	0 – run out	0
L-b 2, w 1, n-b 1	4	B 1, l-b 18, w 3, n-b 2	24

1/16 2/17 3/37 4/38 5/77		205	1/58 2/98 3/172 4/251 5/284	373
5/97 7/112 8/196 9/202			6/295 7/313 8/314 9/367	

Bonus points – Nottinghamshire 2, Lancashire 4.

Bowling: *First Innings*—Martin 14–1–57–3; Allott 16–5–37–4; Watkinson 7–0–36–0; Fitton 12–1–61–2; Hughes 5–1–12–1. *Second Innings*—Martin 27–2–110–3; Watkinson 34.3–7–129–1; Fitton 6–0–33–0; Allott 14–2–52–2; Hughes 10–3–30–1.

Umpires: J. W. Holder and A. G. T. Whitehead.

LANCASHIRE v SOMERSET

At Manchester, July 28, 30, 31. Drawn. Lancashire 8 pts, Somerset 5 pts. Toss: Lancashire. When the second day ended, Lancashire were in total control. Somerset, in their second innings, were only 35 ahead with five wickets standing after Watkinson had followed his 96 (three sixes, seven fours) by taking four wickets. Lancashire's hopes of a second successive 24-point win could hardly have been higher, but they were thwarted by a remarkable innings from Tavaré, who batted through an uninterrupted final day to add 65 to his overnight 19. He scored 26 in the first session, 25 in the second and 14 in the third, batting for 345 minutes in all and receiving stout support from Rose in a three-hour stand worth 131.

Close of play: First day, Lancashire 95-3 (N. H. Fairbrother 35*, T. E. Jesty 9*); Second day, Somerset 137-5 (C. J. Tavaré 19*, N. D. Burns 0*).

Somerset

S. J. Cook lbw b Martin	49 – c Fairbrother b Watkinson	64
P. M. Roebuck lbw b Watkinson	26 – c Hegg b Patterson	12
A. N. Hayhurst c Hegg b Watkinson	6 – c Hegg b Watkinson	30
*C. J. Tavaré c Fairbrother b Patterson	17 – not out	84
R. J. Harden b Martin	60 – (6) c Jesty b Watkinson	2
†N. D. Burns c Hegg b Patterson	7 – (7) c Fowler b Watkinson	10
G. D. Rose c Mendis b Austin	27 – (8) c Lloyd b Martin	76
R. P. Lefebvre lbw b Austin	0 – (9) lbw b Austin	2
I. G. Swallow c Lloyd b Watkinson	16 – (5) b Watkinson	0
N. A. Mallender not out	3 – c Lloyd b Austin	7
H. R. J. Trump b Patterson	1 – not out	4
B 8, l-b 8, w 1, n-b 8	25	B 13, l-b 12, w 3, n-b 5	33

1/74 2/86 3/96 4/138 5/163		237	1/53 2/108 3/133	(9 wkts dec.) 324
6/206 7/206 8/212 9/230			4/133 5/137 6/166	
			7/297 8/300 9/312	

Bonus points – Somerset 2, Lancashire 4.

Bowling: *First Innings*—Patterson 13.5–2–76–3; Martin 17–5–55–2; Watkinson 18–12–29–3; Fitton 4–0–17–0; Austin 16–8–44–2. *Second Innings*—Patterson 23–7–68–1; Martin 18–4–50–1; Fitton 26–7–65–0; Watkinson 35–7–97–5; Austin 23–14–19–2; Fowler 2–2–0–0.

Lancashire

G. D. Mendis c and b Swallow	29	J. D. Fitton not out	2?
G. Fowler c Burns b Swallow	10	P. J. Martin c Trump b Rose	
G. D. Lloyd lbw b Swallow	0	B. P. Patterson b Mallender	
*N. H. Fairbrother c Burns b Rose	91		
T. E. Jesty b Mallender	30	B 5, l-b 3, w 1, n-b 5	14
M. Watkinson c Cook b Trump	96		
†W. K. Hegg c Rose b Trump	33	1/42 2/42 3/68 4/141 5/212	33?
I. D. Austin c Swallow b Trump	1	6/301 7/302 8/307 9/334	

Bonus points – Lancashire 4, Somerset 3 (Score at 100 overs: 307-7).

Bowling: Mallender 18–5–63–2; Rose 18–0–77–2; Lefebvre 14–5–22–0; Swallow 28–11–88–3; Trump 26–10–58–3; Roebuck 6–0–17–0; Hayhurst 1–0–6–0.

Umpires: J. W. Holder and A. G. T. Whitehead.

At Leeds, August 4, 6, 7. LANCASHIRE drew with YORKSHIRE.

At Kidderminster, August 8, 9, 10. LANCASHIRE lost to WORCESTERSHIRE by ten wickets.

At Northampton, August 11, 13, 14. LANCASHIRE drew with NORTHAMPTONSHIRE

LANCASHIRE v YORKSHIRE

At Manchester, August 18, 19, 20, 21. Drawn. Lancashire 5 pts, Yorkshire 4 pts. Toss: Lancashire. Lancashire took up a strong position on the opening day through Atherton's seventh century of the season, Watkinson's second of his career, and a near-miss by Fairbrother. The free-scoring left-hander faced only 86 balls for his 99, having reached 50 in 29. After the second day had been washed out, and 35 overs had been lost on the third, two declarations on the fourth morning brought Yorkshire into the game and gave them 95 overs in which to score 317 for victory. In the end it was Lancashire who almost squeezed home. Watkinson, who bowled off-breaks and delivered 44 of the 47 overs from the Warwick Road end, captured five wickets in another big-hearted all-round performance. Sharp, whose right thumb was broken in the first innings by a ball from Wasim Akram, defied Lancashire for thirteen overs, and he and Batty held out for the last 32 deliveries to save the match.

Close of play: First day, Lancashire 417-8 (I. D. Austin 11*, D. P. Hughes 14*); Second day, No play; Third day, Yorkshire 190-3 (M. D. Moxon 90*, D. Byas 2*).

Lancashire

G. D. Mendis c Batty b Hartley	13	– (3) not out	15
G. Fowler c Batty b Hartley	7	– not out	50
M. A. Atherton c Byas b Carrick	108		
N. H. Fairbrother c Moxon b Hartley	99		
M. Watkinson c Robinson b Carrick	138		
Wasim Akram c Hartley b Carrick	8	– (1) c Blakey b Jarvis	6
P. A. J. DeFreitas b Batty	4		
†W. K. Hegg c Byas b Carrick	3		
I. D. Austin not out	21		
*D. P. Hughes c Byas b Hartley	16		
P. J. W. Allott st Blakey b Carrick	2		
B 10, l-b 2, n-b 2	14	W 1, n-b 1	2

1/18 2/29 3/164 4/335 5/349   433   1/11   (1 wkt dec.) 73
6/354 7/365 8/392 9/422

Bonus points – Lancashire 4, Yorkshire 3 (Score at 100 overs: 392-8).

Bowling: *First Innings*—Jarvis 20–3–73–0; Hartley 22–1–109–4; Pickles 12–0–57–0; Carrick 40–11–98–5; Batty 22–1–84–1. *Second Innings*—Jarvis 3–2–2–1; Hartley 2.1–0–10–0; Metcalfe 5.4–0–44–0; Pickles 5–1–17–0.

Yorkshire

*M. D. Moxon not out	90	– c Fowler b Atherton	50
A. A. Metcalfe lbw b DeFreitas	2	– c Allott b Watkinson	39
K. Sharp retired hurt	5	– (10) not out	9
P. E. Robinson c Hughes b Watkinson	70	– (3) c Hughes b Watkinson	9
†R. J. Blakey c Allott b Watkinson	1	– (4) c Hegg b Atherton	4
D. Byas not out	2	– (5) c Allott b Atherton	39
P. Carrick (did not bat)		– (6) lbw b Watkinson	57
C. S. Pickles (did not bat)		– (7) c Hegg b Watkinson	16
P. J. Hartley (did not bat)		– (8) lbw b Wasim Akram	0
P. W. Jarvis (did not bat)		– (9) b Watkinson	11
J. D. Batty (did not bat)		– not out	7
B 8, l-b 1, w 2, n-b 9	20	B 10, l-b 6, n-b 9	25

1/3 2/171 3/177	(3 wkts dec.) 190	1/77 2/107 3/109	(9 wkts) 266
		4/116 5/178 6/223	
		7/224 8/237 9/258	

Bonus points – Yorkshire 1, Lancashire 1.

In the first innings K. Sharp retired hurt at 24.

Bowling: *First Innings*—Wasim Akram 16–1–47–0; DeFreitas 12–1–44–1; Austin 4–2–5–0; Allott 4–1–10–0; Atherton 12–3–42–0; Watkinson 10–3–24–2; Hughes 8–5–9–0. *Second Innings*—Wasim Akram 21–8–46–1; DeFreitas 5–0–30–0; Watkinson 44–12–105–5; Atherton 25–6–69–3.

Umpires: R. A. White and A. G. T. Whitehead.

LANCASHIRE v SURREY

At Blackpool, August 29, 30, 31. Drawn. Lancashire 3 pts, Surrey 3 pts. Toss: Lancashire. Lancashire's first Championship match at the Stanley Park ground since 1984 was ruined by rain. There was no play on the first day, and with only 71 overs on the second and 29 on the third, there was never any chance of even a concocted finish. Mendis grafted for 245 minutes after the match got under way half an hour before lunch on the second day. Play could not start until 1.40 p.m. on the final afternoon, and Surrey used the remaining time for batting practice.

Close of play: First day, No play; Second day, Lancashire 261-8 (W. K. Hegg 34*, I. D. Austin 6*).

Lancashire

G. D. Mendis c Lynch b M. P. Bicknell	94	P. A. J. DeFreitas b M. P. Bicknell	13
G. Fowler lbw b Murphy	42	†W. K. Hegg not out	34
G. D. Lloyd lbw b Medlycott	1	I. D. Austin not out	6
N. H. Fairbrother c Stewart b Murphy	8	B 3, l-b 6, w 2, n-b 10	21
T. E. Jesty b Waqar Younis	25		
M. Watkinson lbw b Waqar Younis	0	1/97 2/100 3/112 (8 wkts dec.) 261	
Wasim Akram c D. J. Bicknell		4/170 5/170 6/198	
b Feltham	17	7/217 8/218	

*D. P. Hughes did not bat.

Bonus points – Lancashire 3, Surrey 3.

Bowling: Waqar Younis 18–4–65–2; M. P. Bicknell 18–3–65–2; Feltham 13–4–40–1; Murphy 17–1–73–2; Medlycott 5–1–9–1.

Surrey

D. J. Bicknell lbw b Wasim Akram	...	25
R. I. Alikhan c Hegg b DeFreitas	.....	9
†A. J. Stewart not out	....	23
D. M. Ward not out	....	16
B 1, l-b 2, n-b 6	....	9

1/40 2/48   (2 wkts dec.) 82

M. A. Lynch, *I. A. Greig, M. A. Feltham, K. T. Medlycott, M. P. Bicknell, A. J. Murphy and Waqar Younis did not bat.

Bowling: Wasim Akram 11–2–32–1; DeFreitas 8–4–31–1; Watkinson 6–3–13–0; Austin 4–2–3–0.

Umpires: B. J. Meyer and R. A. White.

At Manchester, September 8, 9, 10. LANCASHIRE drew with SRI LANKANS (See Sri Lankan tour section).

At Nottingham, September 12, 13, 14, 15. LANCASHIRE beat NOTTINGHAMSHIRE by ten wickets.

LANCASHIRE v WARWICKSHIRE

At Manchester, September 18, 19, 20, 21. Drawn. Lancashire 3 pts, Warwickshire 2 pts. Toss: Lancashire. Only 126.3 overs were possible in a game which lost the final day of the season to the weather. Reeve went in to bat when Warwickshire were 79 for five on the second day and overcame the handicap of a bitterly cold, blustery wind to score 121 of the 201 runs added in nearly four hours for the last five wickets. He hit a six and fourteen fours in his unbeaten innings. John Crawley, younger brother of Mark, made his Championship début before going to Cambridge, but did not have an opportunity to bat.

Close of play: First day, Warwickshire 78-4 (T. A. Lloyd 24*, P. A. Smith 0*); Second day, Warwickshire 271-9 (D. A. Reeve 117*, A. A. Donald 3*); Third day, Lancashire 48-0 (G. D. Mendis 22*, M. A. Atherton 22*).

Warwickshire

A. J. Moles c Fairbrother b Watkinson	9		G. C. Small c Hegg b Atherton	....	30
J. D. Ratcliffe c Hegg b Atherton	.....	17	T. A. Munton c Atherton b Watkinson	.	8
Asif Din c DeFreitas b Watkinson	.....	24	A. A. Donald c and b Watkinson	.....	8
*T. A. Lloyd c Atherton b Martin	.....	35			
P. A. Booth c Lloyd b Yates	....	0	L-b 4	....	4
P. A. Smith c Watkinson b Martin	.....	1			
D. A. Reeve not out	121		1/14 2/50 3/73 4/78 5/79		280
†K. J. Piper c Hegg b Watkinson	.....	23	6/92 7/154 8/188 9/231		

Bonus points – Warwickshire 2, Lancashire 3 (Score at 100 overs: 217-8).

Bowling: DeFreitas 4–0–6–0; Martin 29–6–88–2; Watkinson 24.3–6–65–5; Austin 13–8–23–0; Atherton 23–6–52–2; Yates 21–6–42–1.

Lancashire

G. D. Mendis not out	....	22
M. A. Atherton not out	....	22
L-b 4	....	4

(no wkt) 48

J. P. Crawley, *N. H. Fairbrother, G. D. Lloyd, M. Watkinson, P. A. J. DeFreitas, †W. K. Hegg, G. Yates, I. D. Austin and P. J. Martin did not bat.

Bowling: Donald 6–0–24–0; Munton 3–0–16–0; Booth 3–1–4–0.

Umpires: D. J. Constant and B. Leadbeater.

LEICESTERSHIRE

President: C. H. Palmer
Chairman: J. M. Josephs
Chairman, Cricket Committee: P. R. Haywood
Chief Executive: F. M. Turner
  County Cricket Ground, Grace Road,
  Leicester LE2 8AD
  (Telephone: 0533-831880/832128)
Cricket Manager: R. B. Simpson
Captain: N. E. Briers
Coach: 1990 – K. Higgs

After the disappointments of 1989, when Leicestershire were able only to reinforce a reputation for under-achievement, it was essential from the county committee's point of view that something be done to provide fresh impetus, to generate renewed enthusiasm in the dressing-room, and to maintain an air of optimism in an unfavourable commercial climate. Guided by the club's chief executive, Mike Turner, they decided to appoint a manager: someone with both an unquestionable pedigree and a high media profile. The man they sought initially was Ray Illingworth, who had been Leicestershire's captain during the county's most successful era, in the 1970s, but Illingworth resisted several attempts to lure him back to Grace Road.

Undeterred, the county continued to pitch high and were successful in tempting Bobby Simpson, the Australian national coach, to try his hand in the English domestic game. Coming so soon after Simpson had masterminded England's humiliating surrender of the Ashes, the appointment could not have been matched for prestige. Leicestershire also appointed a new captain, the experienced and enthusiastic Nigel Briers, to take over from David Gower, who had resigned to concentrate on rebuilding his international career.

Against the background of these changes, Leicestershire looked sure to embark on the 1990 season with burgeoning hopes, and so they did, despite the further decision by Gower to join Hampshire. To lose their one batsman of true international class was unquestionably a blow to Leicestershire, but it is reasonable to speculate that Gower's temperament may have made it difficult for him to feel comfortable in a dressing-room run by someone with such a high regard for discipline and punctuality as Simpson. The Australian's arrival was not greeted without scepticism among the players, some of whom held the view that a strong captain was as much leadership as a team required. None the less, within a few days of taking up his duties Simpson had introduced a more organised, professional approach to pre-season preparations than had been customary.

Once the new campaign began, however, it was difficult to distinguish the new Leicestershire from the old model. Although they convincingly defeated Glamorgan in their opening Britannic Assurance Championship fixture, they began badly in the Refuge Assurance League and failed again to qualify for the knockout rounds of the Benson and Hedges Cup, in which they had not progressed beyond the group stage since winning the trophy in 1985. Nor did their fortunes in the limited-overs game improve, in spite of predictions to the contrary made by the manager. The Sunday League soon became a hopelessly lost cause, and the 1-run defeat by Hampshire in the first round of the NatWest Bank Trophy merely emphasised all the failings that Simpson needed to put right.

Leicestershire finished next to bottom of the Refuge table, but their form in the Championship was a contradiction. During August, they were strong contenders for a top-five position in the Britannic table, and they won six matches in total, an improvement of two on 1989. Had they been able to press home clear advantages gained in three or four other games, they might have mounted a strong challenge for the title itself. Sometimes, on these occasions, Briers could have been less cautious in his tactics, but culpability largely rested with individuals for performing below their best. A Championship position of seventh, however, was six places up on 1989.

Briers combined captaincy with supervising a benefit campaign, as well as opening the innings, and he appeared to thrive on multiple responsibility. His aggregate in first-class cricket was 1,996, surpassing his previous highest aggregate by 661 and quashing suggestions that his batting would be impaired by such a heavy workload. He scored five centuries, also a personal best, and in a summer less devalued by the sheer weight of runs made, his innings of 176 against Northamptonshire on a bouncy, awkward pitch at Grace Road might have been regarded as one of the outstanding performances.

The much improved nature of pitches, at Grace Road and elsewhere, helped James Whitaker and Tim Boon to set revised marks, Boon passing 1,500 for the first time in his career and Whitaker totalling 1,767 including four hundreds. Chris Lewis, awarded his county cap on the opening day of the campaign, posted his maiden century in spectacular style when he contributed 189 not out to a high-scoring contest at Chelmsford in May. But while producing regular glimpses of his exceptional all-round talent, he made a smaller contribution in terms of runs and wickets than had been hoped for, although a series of minor fitness and health problems did not help his progress.

Jon Agnew was the busiest Leicestershire bowler, shouldering the heaviest workload and returning the most wickets, 59. David Millns signed from Nottinghamshire during the close season, and Gordon Parsons made a late impact, the former demonstrating that he possessed genuine pace about a purple patch which placed him third in the national averages with 31 wickets at 21.35 runs apiece. Alan Mullally, a lanky left-arm seam bowler raised in Perth, Western Australia, but English by birth, had an impressive début season, bowling rather better than a first-class average of 38.05 might suggest. Spin was notable only for the modest contribution made by Peter Willey, Laurie Potter and Martyn Gidley.

The season ended with the county in transition, some would say facing a crisis. Two former England bowlers, Agnew and Les Taylor, retired, Agnew to begin a full-time career in journalism. George Ferris, anticipating that he would be surplus to requirements in 1991, decided to take a contract with a Lancashire League club, only for Winston Benjamin, his fellow-Antiguan, to announce that he was giving up county cricket after a summer disrupted by knee trouble. It left Simpson returning home to Sydney, and Leicestershire to contemplate a winter of major rebuilding. – Jon Culley.

LEICESTERSHIRE 1990

[*Bill Smith*]

Back row: J. P. Agnew, G. J. Parsons, J. D. R. Benson, L. Potter, D. J. Millns, C. C. Lewis, P. A. Nixon, P. N. Hepworth. *Front row*: T. J. Boon, R. B. Simpson (*cricket manager*), N. E. Briers (*captain*), J. J. Whitaker, P. Willey. *Insets*: W. K. M. Benjamin, R. A. Cobb, G. J. F. Ferris, L. B. Taylor, P. Whiticase.

LEICESTERSHIRE RESULTS

All first-class matches – Played 24: Won 6, Lost 7, Drawn 11.

County Championship matches – Played 22: Won 6, Lost 7, Drawn 9.

Bonus points – Batting 61, Bowling 53.

Competition placings – Britannic Assurance County Championship, 7th;
NatWest Bank Trophy, 1st round; Benson and Hedges Cup, 3rd in Group D;
Refuge Assurance League, 15th equal.

BRITANNIC ASSURANCE CHAMPIONSHIP AVERAGES

BATTING

	Birthplace	M	I	NO	R	HI	Avge
‡N. E. Briers	Leicester	22	43	3	1,846	176	46.1
‡J. J. Whitaker	Skipton	22	42	4	1,575	116	41.4
‡C. C. Lewis	Georgetown, Guyana	13	21	5	632	189*	39.5
‡T. J. Boon	Doncaster	22	43	4	1,522	138	39.0
‡W. K. M. Benjamin .	St John's, Antigua	11	13	2	382	101*	34.7
‡L. Potter	Bexleyheath	22	36	5	1,028	109*	33.1
P. N. Hepworth	Ackworth	4	8	2	185	55*	30.8
J. D. R. Benson	Dublin, Ireland	16	24	6	525	86	29.1
‡P. Willey	Sedgefield	20	37	6	892	112	28.7
M. I. Gidley	Leicester	4	5	1	113	73	28.2
P. A. Nixon	Carlisle	17	20	6	379	46	27.0
‡G. J. F. Ferris	Urlings Village, Antigua	5	6	0	104	35	17.3
‡J. P. Agnew	Macclesfield	22	26	5	257	46*	12.2
‡G. J. Parsons	Slough	8	12	2	101	20	10.1
A. D. Mullally	Southend-on-Sea	18	18	6	113	29	9.4
‡P. Whitticase	Solihull	5	7	2	39	11*	7.8
D. J. Millns	Clipstone	8	10	5	23	10*	4.6

Also batted: C. J. Hawkes (*Loughborough*) (1 match) 3, 2*; B. F. Smith (*Corby*) (1 match)
15*. ‡L. B. Taylor (*Earl Shilton*) (1 match) did not bat.

  * *Signifies not out.*   ‡ *Denotes county cap.*

The following played a total of thirteen three-figure innings for Leicestershire in County
Championship matches – N. E. Briers 4, J. J. Whitaker 3, T. J. Boon 2, W. K. M. Benjamin 1,
C. C. Lewis 1, L. Potter 1, P. Willey 1.

BOWLING

	O	M	R	W	BB	5W/i	Avge
D. J. Millns	164.1	20	568	25	6-63	1	22.7
G. J. Parsons	247.5	56	821	31	6-75	2	26.4
C. C. Lewis	411.2	80	1,238	44	6-55	2	28.1
W. K. M. Benjamin ...	260.3	60	769	27	5-73	2	28.4
A. D. Mullally	464.2	116	1,351	37	4-59	0	36.5
J. P. Agnew	612	108	2,196	59	5-54	5	37.2
P. Willey	377.4	101	1,016	20	2-7	0	50.8

Also bowled: J. D. R. Benson 35.5–1–145–1; T. J. Boon 3.5–0–25–0; G. J. F. Ferris
101.2–16–404–9; M. I. Gidley 61–15–228–0; C. J. Hawkes 14–3–40–0; L. Potter
169–39–583–6; L. B. Taylor 9–1–34–0.

Wicket-keepers: P. A. Nixon 44 ct, 1 st; P. Whitticase 13 ct.

Leading Fielder: L. Potter 22.

At Cardiff, April 26, 27, 28, 30. LEICESTERSHIRE beat GLAMORGAN by nine wickets.

At Chelmsford, May 3, 4, 5, 7. LEICESTERSHIRE drew with ESSEX.

LEICESTERSHIRE v NOTTINGHAMSHIRE

At Leicester, May 15, 16, 17. Nottinghamshire won by five wickets. Nottinghamshire 22 pts, Leicestershire 7 pts. Toss: Leicestershire. The match began well for the Leicestershire captain, Briers, who carried his bat for 157, having batted for 6 hours 47 minutes (324 balls) and hit eighteen fours. It was a mark he had bettered only once in his career. In the meantime, Whiticase, Leicestershire's wicket-keeper, had suffered a badly broken finger batting against the quickish medium pace of Pick, whose analysis of seven for 128 was a career best. Boon took over behind the stumps when the visitors batted, which partially accounted for the 71 extras conceded. Nottinghamshire, reduced by Agnew and Lewis to 43 for six in reply, eventually totalled 361, 318 runs having been added in 59 overs in an astonishing recovery led by Randall (197 balls, two sixes, eleven fours) and Hemmings (90 balls, one six, eleven fours). The two put on 163 in 27 overs for the eighth wicket. Leicestershire collapsed in the second innings, losing their last eight wickets for 58 runs, and Nottinghamshire claimed the extra half-hour to win with a day to spare.

Close of play: First day, Leicestershire 301-7 (N. E. Briers 139*); Second day, Leicestershire 33-0 (L. Potter 13*, N. E. Briers 19*).

Leicestershire

T. J. Boon c Randall b Pick	1	– (3) c Randall b Stephenson	27
*N. E. Briers not out	157	– b Pick	22
J. J. Whitaker lbw b Pick	43	– (4) lbw b Pick	13
P. Willey c Robinson b Hemmings	30	– (5) c Randall b Hemmings	1
L. Potter b Pick	24	– (1) c French b Stephenson	50
C. C. Lewis lbw b Pick	1	– c Hemmings b Pick	2
†P. Whiticase retired hurt	2	– absent injured	
M. I. Gidley st French b Afford	8	– (7) not out	21
J. P. Agnew c Afford b Pick	36	– b Stephenson	4
G. J. F. Ferris lbw b Pick	35	– (8) b Hemmings	0
A. D. Mullally c French b Pick	0	– (10) b Stephenson	0
B 2, l-b 6, w 3, n-b 11	22	B 4, l-b 5, w 2, n-b 7	18
	359		**158**

1/3 2/67 3/107 4/171 5/173   6/185 7/301 8/357 9/359

1/55 2/100 3/119 4/120 5/126   6/133 7/134 8/158 9/158

Bonus points – Leicestershire 3, Nottinghamshire 2 (Score at 100 overs: 269-6).

In the first innings P. Whiticase retired hurt at 176.

Bowling: *First Innings*—Stephenson 27-4-98-0; Pick 34.5-5-128-7; Saxelby 10-2-39-0; Hemmings 22-6-58-1; Afford 29-17-28-1. *Second Innings*—Stephenson 20.5-4-33-4; Pick 17-2-56-3; Afford 13-5-27-0; Saxelby 6-0-30-0; Hemmings 12-9-3-2.

Nottinghamshire

B. C. Broad c Boon b Agnew	3	– lbw b Willey	23
D. J. R. Martindale c sub b Lewis	9	– c Whitaker b Mullally	43
*R. T. Robinson lbw b Agnew	0	– lbw b Mullally	8
P. Johnson c sub b Lewis	4	– lbw b Mullally	11
D. W. Randall c Whitaker b Ferris	120	– c Mullally b Willey	11
M. Saxelby b Agnew	11	– not out	18
F. D. Stephenson c Boon b Agnew	0	– not out	13
†B. N. French b Mullally	37		
E. E. Hemmings c Whitaker b Agnew	83		
R. A. Pick b Ferris	22		
J. A. Afford not out	1		
B 33, l-b 26, w 2, n-b 10	71	B 21, l-b 7, n-b 2	30
	361	(5 wkts)	**157**

1/11 2/11 3/21 4/22 5/39   6/43 7/99 8/262 9/358

1/49 2/66 3/98   4/101 5/139

Bonus points – Nottinghamshire 4, Leicestershire 4.

Bowling: *First Innings*—Lewis 22–1–92–2; Agnew 22–4–85–5; Mullally 14–2–65–1; Ferris 11–1–37–2; Gidley 5–1–23–0; Willey 1–1–0–0. *Second Innings*—Lewis 10–2–34–0; Ferris 5–0–19–0; Willey 18–4–40–2; Mullally 17.2–5–27–3; Gidley 6–3–9–0.

Umpires: B. J. Meyer and N. T. Plews.

At Manchester, May 19, 21, 22. LEICESTERSHIRE drew with LANCASHIRE.

At Oxford, May 23, 24, 25. LEICESTERSHIRE drew with OXFORD UNIVERSITY.

LEICESTERSHIRE v SOMERSET

At Leicester, May 26, 28, 29. Drawn. Leicestershire 6 pts, Somerset 5 pts. Toss: Leicestershire. Forceful batting on a pitch of easy pace enabled Leicestershire to dominate the opening day, Boon making 128 in five and a half hours, his first century of the season. Whitaker, with whom he shared a second-wicket stand of 161 in 53 overs, failed by 11 runs to record a third consecutive first-class hundred. Leicestershire declared overnight and conditions appeared as good as could be for Cook, Somerset's prolific opening batsman, to attempt the unlikely task of scoring 230 to total 1,000 first-class runs before the end of May. The chance effectively disappeared when he was caught behind off Mullally for 42, but Somerset comfortably collected full batting points before declaring 52 runs behind. They then picked off both Leicestershire openers in the fifteen overs to the close and enjoyed the best of the final morning, having the home side 66 for five. In doing so, however, they committed themselves to bowling Leicestershire out, which, although Rose bowled well, they could not quite manage. Leicestershire's declaration left Somerset to score 253 in 36 overs, little more than a gesture on a pitch becoming erratic, and they declined the challenge as soon as Cook was caught off the glove in the first over.
Close of play: First day, Leicestershire 352-4 (L. Potter 41*, J. D. R. Benson 29*); Second day, Leicestershire 32-2 (J. J. Whitaker 8*, P. Willey 9*).

Leicestershire

T. J. Boon c Harden b Swallow	128 – lbw b Mallender	10
*N. E. Briers lbw b Hayhurst	39 – c Harden b Jones	5
J. J. Whitaker c Burns b Lefebvre	89 – lbw b Mallender	18
P. Willey c Rose b Lefebvre	15 – lbw b Rose	29
L. Potter not out	41 – c Harden b Rose	2
J. D. R. Benson not out	29 – c Tavaré b Rose	13
†P. A. Nixon (did not bat)	– c Cook b Rose	33
J. P. Agnew (did not bat)	– b Rose	36
G. J. F. Ferris (did not bat)	– lbw b Swallow	33
A. D. Mullally (did not bat)	– not out	12
D. J. Millns (did not bat)	– not out	1
B 4, l-b 3, w 2, n-b 2	11	B 5, l-b 2, n-b 1	8

1/97 2/258 3/272 4/284   (4 wkts dec.) 352   1/11 2/15 3/61   (9 wkts dec.) 200
                                            4/65 5/66 6/103
                                            7/122 8/167 9/193

Bonus points – Leicestershire 4, Somerset 1 (Score at 100 overs: 301-4).

Bowling: *First Innings*—Jones 9–3–34–0; Mallender 19–2–51–0; Rose 17–0–85–0; Lefebvre 24–3–61–2; Hayhurst 14–2–35–1; Swallow 17–2–47–1; Roebuck 10–3–32–0. *Second Innings*—Jones 12–6–26–1; Mallender 21–8–62–2; Swallow 10–3–16–1; Roebuck 4–3–1–0; Rose 20–6–52–5; Lefebvre 10–5–26–0; Hayhurst 4–1–10–0.

Somerset

. J. Cook c Nixon b Mullally	42	– c Benson b Agnew	8
?. M. Roebuck c Potter b Willey	63	– not out	23
‹. N. Hayhurst c Whitaker b Mullally	34	– not out	22
‹C. J. Tavaré c Willey b Millns	88		
‹. J. Harden c Nixon b Millns	44		
N. D. Burns not out	2		
‹. D. Rose not out	3		
B 2, l-b 6, w 1, n-b 15	24	B 1, l-b 3, w 2, n-b 3	9

1/64 2/121 3/170 4/293 5/296   (5 wkts dec.) 300   1/9   (1 wkt) 62

‹. P. Lefebvre, I. G. Swallow, N. A. Mallender and A. N. Jones did not bat.

Bonus points – Somerset 4, Leicestershire 2.

Bowling: *First Innings*—Agnew 24–6–84–0; Ferris 15–4–55–0; Mullally 23–6–57–2; Millns 5.1–1–57–2; Willey 11–5–23–1; Potter 3–1–16–0. *Second Innings*—Agnew 7–3–18–1; Ferris 1–1–15–0; Mullally 4–1–9–0; Willey 4–1–4–0; Potter 7–3–5–0; Benson 4.5–1–7–0.

Umpires: D. J. Constant and B. Dudleston.

LEICESTERSHIRE v HAMPSHIRE

At Leicester, June 2, 4, 5. Drawn. Leicestershire 4 pts, Hampshire 8 pts. Toss: Hampshire. Rain washed out the whole of the last day, to the relief of the home side, who were facing defeat. Gower, the former Leicestershire captain, returned to Grace Road at a time when he needed to reassert his credentials as a current international player, rather than a former one. After a breezy start, though, he was dismissed playing loosely outside off stump, and Hampshire slid to 144 for five. They were rescued superbly by Marshall's second Championship hundred (eighteen fours) in successive matches. Chris Smith came back after retiring with a hand injury, and with him Maru raced to 59 in a seventh-wicket stand which produced 115 runs in 24 overs. Bakker reduced Leicestershire to 7 for two by the close, from which they never properly recovered. By lunch on the second day they were 123 for eight, three of the wickets having fallen to Tremlett, restored to the Hampshire side after postponing his retirement. Lewis shrugged off doubts over his fitness for the First Test against New Zealand by sharing a spirited last-wicket stand of 54 with Mullally, but this failed to save the follow-on. Although Whitaker played well for 62 when Leicestershire batted again, their fortunes did not substantially improve. Had the weather not intervened, they would have begun the final day effectively 18 for five.

Close of play: First day, Leicestershire 7-2 (T. J. Boon 6*, J. J. Whitaker 0*); Second day, Leicestershire 189-5 (J. D. R. Benson 29*, C. C. Lewis 40*).

Hampshire

‹. P. Terry c Nixon b Ferris	7	R. J. Maru c Boon b Agnew	59
‹. L. Smith not out	80	T. M. Tremlett not out	25
‹. I. Gower c Whitaker b Lewis	25	L-b 8, w 1, n-b 16	25
R. A. Smith c Potter b Mullally	1		
‹. D. Marshall b Mullally	112	1/21 2/69 3/73 (7 wkts dec.) 349	
M. C. J. Nicholas b Mullally	13	4/119 5/144	
‹R. J. Parks c Willey b Agnew	2	6/220 7/295	

‹. A. Connor and P. J. Bakker did not bat.

Bonus points – Hampshire 4, Leicestershire 3.

‹. L. Smith, when 37, retired hurt at 69-1 and resumed at 220.

Bowling: Agnew 32–2–115–2; Ferris 16–4–77–1; Lewis 14–2–56–1; Mullally 20–4–68–3; Willey 12–3–25–0.

Leicestershire

T. J. Boon c Connor b Marshall	6	– lbw b Bakker	1
*N. E. Briers c sub b Bakker	0	– c Terry b Connor	20
†P. A. Nixon b Bakker	0		
J. J. Whitaker b Bakker	6	– (3) b Marshall	63
P. Willey c Connor b Marshall	42	– (4) c Terry b Marshall	2
L. Potter b Tremlett	43	– (5) b Marshall	4
J. D. R. Benson lbw b Tremlett	11	– (6) not out	29
C. C. Lewis not out	36	– (7) not out	40
J. P. Agnew c Parks b Tremlett	0		
G. J. F. Ferris c Marshall b Bakker	1		
A. D. Mullally b Connor	29		
L-b 4	4	L-b 3, n-b 2	5

1/2 2/2 3/8 4/26 5/87   178   1/2 2/81 3/111   (5 wkts) 189
6/111 7/111 8/123 9/124   4/111 5/130

Bonus points – Leicestershire 1, Hampshire 4.

Bowling: *First Innings*—Marshall 13–2–44–2; Bakker 15–4–51–4; Connor 10.5–2–46–1; Tremlett 15–4–33–3. *Second Innings*—Bakker 10–2–46–1; Marshall 15–4–44–3; Connor 17–4–54–1; Maru 7–1–26–0; Tremlett 9–4–16–0.

Umpires: J. H. Hampshire and P. B. Wight.

At Northampton, June 6, 7, 8. LEICESTERSHIRE drew with NORTHAMPTONSHIRE.

At Leicester, June 14. LEICESTERSHIRE beat NEW ZEALANDERS by four wickets. (See New Zealand tour section).

LEICESTERSHIRE v MIDDLESEX

At Leicester, June 16, 18, 19. Middlesex won by 103 runs. Middlesex 19 pts, Leicestershire 4 pts. Toss: Middlesex. Having gained momentum from a fine innings by Haynes, Middlesex collapsed from 129 for two to 174 for seven, which would have been 174 for eight had Benson caught Tufnell first ball at short leg. They were rescued by Ramprakash, who batted almost five hours for 87 and shared a valuable partnership of 79 for the eighth wicket with the fortunate Tufnell. Leicestershire's first innings, which began on the first day, could not resume until four o'clock on the second because of rain, which cost 69 overs. This necessitated some careful manoeuvring by the captains. Leicestershire declared 204 behind and then Middlesex, encouraged to a certain extent by friendly bowling, but with Haynes again in majestic form, declared at close of play, leaving Leicestershire to chase 321 from 102 overs on the last day. Boon and Briers gave the home side a useful start, but after an interruption for rain Fraser and Williams made the necessary breakthrough. Emburey and Tufnell then took advantage of the dry, wearing pitch to dismiss Leicestershire with seventeen overs to spare.

Close of play: First day, Leicestershire 38-1 (N. E. Briers 16*, J. J. Whitaker 8*); Second day, Middlesex 116-1 dec.

Middlesex

D. L. Haynes b Benjamin	85	– not out	68
M. A. Roseberry c Lewis b Benjamin	15	– b Lewis	0
*M. W. Gatting lbw b Lewis	4	– not out	41
M. R. Ramprakash not out	87		
K. R. Brown lbw b Benjamin	0		
J. E. Emburey c Nixon b Mullally	16		
†P. Farbrace c Potter b Agnew	5		
N. F. Williams c and b Lewis	1		
P. C. R. Tufnell b Lewis	37		
S. P. Hughes c Benson b Benjamin	4		
A. R. C. Fraser c Potter b Benjamin	12		
B 4, l-b 10, n-b 15	29	L-b 1, n-b 6	7

1/38 2/60 3/129 4/129 5/148   295   1/2   (1 wkt dec.) 116
6/173 7/174 8/253 9/264

Bonus points – Middlesex 3, Leicestershire 4.

Bowling: *First Innings*—Benjamin 24.1–10–73–5; Agnew 15–2–60–1; Mullally 19–6–34–1; Lewis 21–3–98–3; Willey 8–0–14–0; Potter 1–0–2–0. *Second Innings*—Lewis 6–0–11–1; Agnew 11–1–62–0; Potter 5.2–0–42–0.

Leicestershire

T. J. Boon c Farbrace b Hughes	10	– c Brown b Fraser	51
*N. E. Briers c Farbrace b Fraser	23	– c Farbrace b Tufnell	34
J. J. Whitaker not out	42	– lbw b Fraser	0
P. Willey not out	5	– lbw b Williams	11
L. Potter (did not bat)		– c Brown b Emburey	7
J. D. R. Benson (did not bat)		– b Williams	45
C. C. Lewis (did not bat)		– b Tufnell	21
W. K. M. Benjamin (did not bat)		– c Roseberry b Emburey	1
†P. A. Nixon (did not bat)		– c Gatting b Emburey	22
J. P. Agnew (did not bat)		– c Roseberry b Emburey	0
A. D. Mullally (did not bat)		– not out	0
L-b 1, n-b 10	11	L-b 4, n-b 21	25

1/25 2/65   (2 wkts dec.) 91   1/82 2/82 3/113 4/113 5/126   217
6/159 7/162 8/210 9/212

Bowling: *First Innings*—Williams 12–1–34–0; Fraser 13–1–34–1; Emburey 2–1–2–0; Hughes 3–1–5–1; Tufnell 6–2–15–0. *Second Innings*—Fraser 20–2–45–2; Williams 12.4–2–49–2; Hughes 7–1–23–0; Emburey 26–7–57–4; Tufnell 16–5–39–2.

Umpires: B. Hassan and K. E. Palmer.

LEICESTERSHIRE v DERBYSHIRE

At Leicester, June 20, 21, 22. Leicestershire won by 140 runs. Leicestershire 20 pts, Derbyshire 2 pts. Toss: Leicestershire. A century of increasing confidence from Whitaker, his third of the season, provided the mainstay of Leicestershire's batting on a first day restricted by rain to 86 overs. Only 34 overs were possible on the second day, with no play after lunch. However, enterprising batting, first from Benjamin, who raced from 46 overnight to a 141-ball maiden first-class century in sixteen overs, then from Barnett and Bowler, the Derbyshire openers, sustained the possibility of a positive finish on the last day. Benjamin hit three sixes and eleven fours in his unbeaten 101. More rain caused the first session on the third day to be lost, but declarations by both captains left Derbyshire with a target of 271 from 63 overs. This became meaningless when Derbyshire lost both openers without scoring and stumbled to 43 for six in seventeen overs. Only Morris and, to a lesser extent, Krikken defied a fashion for rash or feeble shots as Derbyshire were dismissed for a miserable 130 runs.

Close of play: First day, Leicestershire 244-5 (J. J. Whitaker 115*, W. K. M. Benjamin 46*); Second day, Derbyshire 70-0 (K. J. Barnett 31*, P. D. Bowler 36*).

Leicestershire

T. J. Boon b Warner	8	– not out	5
*N. E. Briers c Krikken b Jean-Jacques	29	– not out	14
J. J. Whitaker b Warner	116		
P. Willey c Miller b Goldsmith	4		
L. Potter lbw b Miller	16		
J. D. R. Benson c Adams b Miller	9		
W. K. M. Benjamin not out	101		
†P. A. Nixon not out	20		
B 3, l-b 5, n-b 9	17	N-b 1	1

1/22 2/67 3/73 4/148   (6 wkts dec.) 320   (no wkt dec.) 20
5/163 6/249

J. P. Agnew, A. D. Mullally and L. B. Taylor did not bat.

Bonus points – Leicestershire 4, Derbyshire 2 (Score at 100 overs: 315-6).

Bowling: *First Innings*—Warner 28.5–8–72–2; Jean-Jacques 21–3–93–1; Goldsmith 13–5–24–1; Barnett 8–0–25–0; Miller 32–10–98–2. *Second Innings*—Bowler 2–0–8–0; Adams 1.2–0–12–0.

Derbyshire

*K. J. Barnett not out	31	– c Potter b Benjamin	0
P. D. Bowler not out	36	– c Potter b Agnew	0
J. E. Morris (did not bat)		– not out	63
B. Roberts (did not bat)		– c Nixon b Agnew	1
A. P. Kuiper (did not bat)		– c and b Agnew	3
C. J. Adams (did not bat)		– c Nixon b Mullally	5
S. C. Goldsmith (did not bat)		– lbw b Mullally	8
†K. M. Krikken (did not bat)		– b Willey	30
G. Miller (did not bat)		– c Nixon b Benjamin	1
M. Jean-Jacques (did not bat)		– lbw b Benjamin	4
A. E. Warner (did not bat)		– c Whitaker b Willey	2
N-b 3	3	B 2, l-b 9, n-b 2	13

(no wkt dec.) 70   1/0 2/0 3/2 4/12 5/29   130
                              6/43 7/110 8/113 9/117

Bowling: *First Innings*—Benjamin 4–0–17–0; Agnew 4–0–25–0; Taylor 4–0–18–0; Mullally 4–2–10–0; Willey 2–2–0–0. *Second Innings*—Benjamin 16–5–35–3; Agnew 9–2–33–3; Mullally 12–3–28–2; Willey 8–4–7–2; Taylor 5–1–16–0.

Umpires: B. Hassan and K. E. Palmer.

At Gloucester, June 23, 25, 26. LEICESTERSHIRE beat GLOUCESTERSHIRE by 111 runs.

At Nottingham, June 30, July 2, 3. LEICESTERSHIRE drew with NOTTINGHAMSHIRE.

LEICESTERSHIRE v GLAMORGAN

At Hinckley, July 7, 8, 9. Drawn. Leicestershire 6 pts, Glamorgan 6 pts. Toss: Glamorgan. Butcher and Morris put on 112 inside 39 overs for the first wicket, their sixth partnership of 100 or more in the Championship in 1990, and Butcher completed his third century of the summer, made off 171 balls, during a 91-run stand with Maynard for the third wicket. With his dismissal, however, the Glamorgan innings tailed off. Nixon, the nineteen-year-old Leicestershire reserve wicket-keeper, held five catches and made one stumping, which equalled the county record for dismissals in an innings, held jointly by P. Corrall and R. W.

Tolchard. The second day's pattern almost repeated that of the first, with Leicestershire's opening pair sharing a century partnership before lunch. Briers and Whitaker added 81 for the second wicket, but both fell short of their centuries and the innings began to lose its way. On the final morning, their bowlers unable to make much headway, Leicestershire resorted to feeding cheap runs to encourage a declaration. The chief beneficiary was Cottey, who struck a maiden Championship century off 166 balls. When Leicestershire set out to score 289 from a minimum of 58 overs, Boon completed his 1,000 runs for the season, as Whitaker had the previous day, and looked in commanding form, but with 137 needed from 21 overs, rain thwarted Leicestershire's bid.

Close of play: First day, Glamorgan 312-9 (R. D. B. Croft 25*, M. Frost 0*); Second day, Glamorgan 33-1 (A. R. Butcher 13*, P. A. Cottey 18*).

Glamorgan

*A. R. Butcher c Nixon b Benjamin	115	– c Mullally b Willey 30
H. Morris c Potter b Agnew	53	– c Nixon b Benjamin 0
P. A. Cottey c Nixon b Agnew	3	– c Smith b Willey 125
M. P. Maynard c Nixon b Agnew	59	– c Potter b Benson 47
I. V. A. Richards c Nixon b Agnew	14	– not out 68
R. D. B. Croft not out	25	– not out 0
N. G. Cowley c Nixon b Agnew	13	
†C. P. Metson c Potter b Willey	2	
S. L. Watkin c and b Potter	2	
S. J. Dennis st Nixon b Potter	0	
M. Frost not out	0	
B 6, l-b 11, w 1, n-b 8	26	L-b 6, w 1 7

1/112 2/127 3/218 4/258 5/261   (9 wkts dec.) 312   1/3 2/71 3/150   (4 wkts dec.) 277
6/292 7/304 8/307 9/309   4/272

Bonus points – Glamorgan 4, Leicestershire 2 (Score at 100 overs: 303-6).

Bowling: *First Innings*—Benjamin 25-6-59-1; Agnew 29-4-89-5; Mullally 29-8-84-0; Willey 19-4-60-1; Benson 1-0-1-0; Potter 2-0-2-2. *Second Innings*—Benjamin 5-0-17-1; Agnew 3-0-8-0; Mullally 10-2-26-0; Willey 16-3-69-2; Benson 17-0-83-1; Potter 7-0-48-0; Boon 3-0-20-0.

Leicestershire

T. J. Boon c Cowley b Watkin	51	– not out 75
*N. E. Briers c Richards b Frost	80	– b Croft 22
J. J. Whitaker c Cowley b Watkin	94	– c Cottey b Cowley 45
P. Willey c and b Frost	4	– not out 0
L. Potter c Butcher b Croft	13	
J. D. R. Benson not out	35	
B. F. Smith not out	15	
B 1, l-b 7, n-b 1	9	L-b 7, n-b 3 10

1/105 2/186 3/196 4/228 5/271   (5 wkts dec.) 301   1/60 2/152   (2 wkts) 152

W. K. M. Benjamin, †P. A. Nixon, J. P. Agnew and A. D. Mullally did not bat.

Bonus points – Leicestershire 4, Glamorgan 2.

Bowling: *First Innings*—Frost 16-5-56-2; Watkin 22.5-6-53-2; Dennis 19-4-79-0; Richards 4-1-13-0; Cowley 18-3-46-0; Croft 13-3-46-1. *Second Innings*—Watkin 10-1-34-0; Dennis 8-1-28-0; Croft 10-2-33-1; Frost 6-0-31-0; Cowley 4.4-0-19-1.

Umpires: J. H. Hampshire and K. J. Lyons.

At Leicester, July 21, 22, 23. LEICESTERSHIRE drew with INDIANS (See Indian tour section).

LEICESTERSHIRE v ESSEX

At Leicester, July 25, 26, 27. Drawn. Leicestershire 7 pts, Essex 5 pts. Toss: Essex. Captained by Pringle in Gooch's absence, Essex chose to bat first in search of a fourth consecutive Championship victory but were dismissed for 197, their lowest total of the season. It might have been lower had Leicestershire not dropped four catches, although the Essex cause was not helped by an injury to Stephenson, who was struck on the helmet by Benjamin and had to play his innings in two parts. With Briers providing stability and Potter and Benjamin lending good support, the home side established a useful first-innings lead of 104. Despite dropping Stephenson at 23 and 66, Leicestershire had Essex in trouble at 176 for six on the final morning. However, bold batting by Pringle, hitting 84 off 80 balls, rescued his side, he and Stephenson (332 minutes) adding 132 in 28 overs before he declared with a lead of 245. Leicestershire began with 59 overs in which to reach their target, but four stoppages for rain reduced this crucially by thirteen overs, more to the disadvantage of Essex, who had taken the first five Leicestershire wickets for 96.

Close of play: First day, Leicestershire 124-3 (N. E. Briers 52*, L. Potter 31*); Second day, Essex 154-4 (J. P. Stephenson 62*, N. Hussain 0*).

Essex

J. P. Stephenson c Nixon b Agnew	7	– not out			131
N. Shahid b Agnew	2	– hit wkt b Agnew			48
P. J. Prichard lbw b Benjamin	2	– c Potter b Agnew			0
M. E. Waugh c Boon b Benjamin	69	– c Willey b Mullally			31
N. Hussain c Nixon b Agnew	9	– (6) c Nixon b Agnew			0
†M. A. Garnham c Benjamin b Parsons	8	– (7) b Mullally			7
*D. R. Pringle c Willey b Benjamin	20	– (8) c Nixon b Mullally			84
N. A. Foster lbw b Benjamin	23	– (9) not out			32
T. D. Topley b Agnew	23	– (5) c Nixon b Mullally			2
J. H. Childs run out	13				
S. J. W. Andrew not out	3				
B 6, l-b 8, w 2, n-b 2	18	B 7, l-b 3, w 1, n-b 3			14

1/10 2/13 3/38 4/58 5/127   197   1/74 2/76 3/150   (7 wkts dec.) 349
6/136 7/159 8/191 9/197   4/154 5/159
                                                6/176 7/308

Bonus points – Essex 1, Leicestershire 4.

In the first innings J. P. Stephenson, when 7, retired hurt at 10-1 and resumed at 197.

Bowling: *First Innings*—Benjamin 21-5-51-4; Agnew 21.3-3-73-4; Mullally 17-6-37-0; Parsons 7-2-22-1. *Second Innings*—Agnew 24-4-106-3; Benjamin 11-1-48-0; Mullally 32-11-131-4; Parsons 18-6-54-0; Willey 2-2-0-0.

Leicestershire

T. J. Boon c Pringle b Andrew	13	– c Waugh b Andrew			20
*N. E. Briers run out	92	– lbw b Foster			1
J. J. Whitaker c Topley b Foster	8	– c Hussain b Foster			34
P. Willey c Shahid b Pringle	7	– c Stephenson b Foster			1
L. Potter c Shahid b Andrew	48	– c Stephenson b Andrew			23
J. D. R. Benson b Pringle	12	– not out			34
W. K. M. Benjamin c Foster b Topley	54	– not out			9
†P. A. Nixon c Garnham b Topley	11				
G. J. Parsons not out	19				
J. P. Agnew c Hussain b Topley	5				
A. D. Mullally b Pringle	0				
B 1, l-b 17, n-b 14	32	B 8, l-b 2, n-b 9			19

1/33 2/51 3/71 4/150 5/178   301   1/11 2/40 3/48   (5 wkts) 141
6/228 7/272 8/277 9/294   4/79 5/96

Bonus points – Leicestershire 3, Essex 4 (Score at 100 overs: 294-9).

Bowling: *First Innings*—Foster 22-3-70-1; Andrew 24-4-62-2; Topley 22-3-69-3; Pringle 20.2-3-51-3; Childs 14-3-31-0. *Second Innings*—Foster 21-9-47-3; Pringle 8-3-19-0; Andrew 9-1-39-2; Topley 3-0-22-0; Waugh 1-0-4-0.

Umpires: D. J. Constant and B. J. Meyer.

At Sheffield, July 28, 30, 31. LEICESTERSHIRE beat YORKSHIRE by eight wickets.

LEICESTERSHIRE v WORCESTERSHIRE

At Leicester, August 4, 6, 7. Worcestershire won by 1 run. Worcestershire 23 pts, Leicestershire 4 pts. Toss: Worcestershire. In sweltering heat, Hick completed his 51st first-class century, which left Derbyshire the only Championship county, apart from his own, against whom he had not made a three-figure score. Although he struck seventeen fours, the innings was not among Hick's most impressive, and he showed a fallibility when hooking which eventually cost him his wicket. Nevertheless, with Curtis overcoming early uncertainty to reach 151 not out, passing the milestone of 10,000 runs for Worcestershire in the process, the visitors declared handsomely placed at 365 for four. The second day was packed with incident. Lampitt, a promising seam bowler, was banished from the attack after warnings from umpire Holder for damaging the pitch with his follow-through stride; Illingworth bowled 41 consecutive overs of testing left-arm spin; and McEwan achieved the first hat-trick of his career to end the Leicestershire innings. Briers's fourth century of the summer, a personal best tally of hundreds, was Leicestershire's salvation. Curtis, captaining Worcestershire in the absence of the injured Neale, left the home side to score 265 in 56 overs, a target they looked sure to reach until, after needing 23 off 27 balls, they lost their last five wickets for 41 runs. Nixon was run out off the final delivery trying to level the scores.

Close of play: First day, Leicestershire 20-0 (T. J. Boon 7*, N. E. Briers 13*); Second day, Worcestershire 22-1 (G. J. Lord 9*, S. R. Lampitt 2*).

Worcestershire

T. S. Curtis not out	151	– lbw b Lewis	6
G. J. Lord lbw b Agnew	19	– b Mullally	35
G. A. Hick c Boon b Agnew	102	– (4) not out	88
D. B. D'Oliveira c Potter b Willey	5	– (5) not out	44
I. T. Botham run out	26		
*P. A. Neale not out	20		
S. R. Lampitt (did not bat)		– (3) b Lewis	6
B 6, l-b 15, n-b 21	42	B 4, l-b 6, w 1, n-b 10	21

1/33 2/226 3/235 4/288 (4 wkts dec.) 365   1/7 2/30 3/105 (3 wkts dec.) 200

†S. J. Rhodes, R. K. Illingworth, P. J. Newport and S. M. McEwan did not bat.

Bonus points – Worcestershire 4, Leicestershire 1.

Bowling: *First Innings*—Benjamin 9-1-31-0; Agnew 18-2-73-2; Lewis 22-2-76-0; Mullally 19.4-6-56-0; Willey 28-5-96-1; Potter 3-0-12-0. *Second Innings*—Lewis 13-2-31-2; Mullally 16-3-78-1; Willey 16-2-59-0; Potter 7-3-22-0.

Leicestershire

T. J. Boon c D'Oliveira b Lampitt	42	– st Rhodes b Illingworth	40
*N. E. Briers c D'Oliveira b Lampitt	111	– c and b Newport	17
J. J. Whitaker c Hick b Illingworth	16	– c sub b Newport	62
P. Willey c Curtis b Illingworth	7	– b Lampitt	79
L. Potter c Newport b Illingworth	20	– c Rhodes b McEwan	27
C. C. Lewis c Neale b Illingworth	27	– c sub b Lampitt	16
D. R. Benson not out	28	– st Rhodes b Illingworth	2
W. K. M. Benjamin c D'Oliveira b Newport	10	– b Illingworth	6
†P. A. Nixon c Hick b McEwan	5	– run out	3
J. P. Agnew b McEwan	0	– run out	1
A. D. Mullally lbw b McEwan	0	– not out	3
B 10, l-b 17, w 4, n-b 4	35	L-b 4, n-b 3	7

1/104 2/162 3/180 4/198 5/248 301   1/35 2/120 3/125 4/178 5/242 263
6/256 7/282 8/301 9/301   6/248 7/250 8/258 9/260

Bonus points – Leicestershire 3, Worcestershire 3 (Score at 100 overs: 291-7).

Bowling: *First Innings*—Newport 26.1–2–84–1; McEwan 20–4–62–3; Illingworth
42–16–85–4; Lampitt 17.5–4–43–2. *Second Innings*—Newport 15–4–56–2; McEwan
13–5–37–1; Lampitt 11–0–68–2; Illingworth 21–5–98–3.

Umpires: J. W. Holder and R. Palmer.

At Dartford, August 8, 9, 10. LEICESTERSHIRE lost to KENT by seven wickets.

At The Oval, August 11, 13, 14. LEICESTERSHIRE lost to SURREY by an innings and
5 runs.

At Birmingham, August 18, 20, 21. LEICESTERSHIRE beat WARWICKSHIRE by six
wickets.

LEICESTERSHIRE v KENT

At Leicester, August 23, 24, 25, 27. Leicestershire won by two wickets. Leicestershire 22 pts,
Kent 3 pts. Toss: Kent. Parsons and Millns, thrust into Leicestershire's front-line attack with
Mullally injured and Lewis on Test duty, combined with Benjamin to dismiss Kent for 169 in
only 52.3 overs. Boon and Briers set up Leicestershire's reply by compiling their seventh
opening stand of 100 or more. They were parted at 133 by Wells, Kent's reserve wicket-
keeper, whose sharpish medium pace in a depleted attack prompted alarms for Leicestershire
when he took three wickets in eighteen balls without conceding a run. He ended with five for
43, a career best. Still, Leicestershire led by 135 on first innings and looked to be in a position
to win comfortably when they had Kent 136 for three. This reckoned without a splendid effort
by Graham Cowdrey, who struck a century in less than three hours and shared with Hinks a
partnership of 258 in 68 overs for the fourth wicket. Hinks went on to reach 163 in 44
minutes with 24 fours, making Leicestershire deeply regret dropping him twice at 14. The
declaration left Leicestershire to score a formidable 347 in 87 overs, but they succeeded with
three balls to spare. Briers and Whitaker (nineteen fours) provided early impetus with a
partnership of 164, and Benjamin hammered a breathtaking 53 off 21 balls, with five sixes
and three fours.

Close of play: First day, Leicestershire 64-0 (T. J. Boon 18*, N. E. Briers 38*); Second day,
Kent 51-1 (S. G. Hinks 14*, R. P. Davis 1*); Third day, Kent 419-5 (M. V. Fleming 14*,
M. M. Patel 0*).

Kent

S. G. Hinks c Nixon b Benjamin	6	– b Millns .... 16?
T. R. Ward c Parsons b Agnew	14	– b Benjamin .... 2?
V. J. Wells c Nixon b Parsons	40	– (4) c Boon b Parsons .... 2?
G. R. Cowdrey b Millns	16	– (5) b Millns .... 13?
M. V. Fleming b Millns	0	– (6) c Briers b Millns .... 1?
*C. S. Cowdrey c Willey b Parsons	15	– (8) c Whitaker b Parsons ...... ?
†S. A. Marsh c Nixon b Parsons	5	– (9) not out .... 3?
R. P. Davis c Hepworth b Benjamin	36	– (3) c Nixon b Agnew .... ?
P. S. de Villiers c Nixon b Millns	21	– (10) not out .... 2?
M. M. Patel not out	3	– (7) c Nixon b Parsons .... ?
A. P. Igglesden b Benjamin	0	
L-b 1, w 1, n-b 11	13	B 11, l-b 12, w 9, n-b 18 .. 5?

1/15 2/26 3/61 4/62 5/98   169   1/48 2/65 3/136   (8 wkts dec.) 4?
6/104 7/109 8/156 9/169   4/394 5/418 6/420
                                                     7/423 8/440

Bonus points – Kent 1, Leicestershire 4.

Bowling: *First Innings*—Benjamin 14.3–2–52–3; Agnew 15–4–39–1; Millns 11–1–37–3;
Parsons 12–3–40–3. *Second Innings*—Benjamin 27–4–70–1; Agnew 23–5–69–1; Millns
30–7–88–3; Parsons 27–8–104–3; Willey 19–5–84–0; Potter 15–4–43–0.

eicestershire

. J. Boon c Marsh b Wells	66	– c Marsh b Fleming	20
N. E. Briers b Wells	62	– c G. R. Cowdrey b Patel	75
. J. Whitaker c Davis b Wells	0	– b Patel	100
. Willey c Davis b de Villiers	14	– c Ward b Davis	25
. Potter lbw b Wells	30	– c Wells b Patel	27
. N. Hepworth lbw b Wells	43	– (8) c sub b Davis	7
J. K. M. Benjamin c de Villiers b Fleming	18	– c Fleming b Patel	53
P. A. Nixon c Marsh b Igglesden	21	– (9) not out	11
. J. Parsons c Hinks b Igglesden	20	– (6) c sub b Patel	2
. P. Agnew b Fleming	6	– not out	3
. J. Millns not out	0		
B 4, l-b 15, w 1, n-b 4	24	B 13, l-b 11	24

1/133 2/139 3/144 4/177 5/190   304   1/30 2/194 3/210 4/250 (8 wkts) 347
6/229 7/272 8/287 9/294   5/258 6/291 7/328 8/338

Bonus points – Leicestershire 2, Kent 2 (Score at 100 overs: 242-6).

Bowling: *First Innings*—de Villiers 24–9–57–1; Igglesden 30–7–84–2; Davis 19–7–47–0; Fleming 18–5–25–2; Patel 10–3–29–0; Wells 18–7–43–5. *Second Innings*—Igglesden 2–0–11–0; de Villiers 7–0–31–0; Fleming 14–4–36–1; Davis 27.3–4–120–2; Patel 27–3–96–5; C. S. Cowdrey 1–1–0–0; Wells 8–1–29–0.

Umpires: B. Dudleston and D. O. Oslear.

LEICESTERSHIRE v SUSSEX

At Leicester, August 29, 30, 31. Sussex won by 29 runs. Sussex 23 pts, Leicestershire 4 pts. Toss: Leicestershire. Sussex took advantage of Leicestershire's decision to field first by achieving full batting bonus points on a placid pitch. Alan Wells, captain of Sussex for the first time, dominated the innings with a carefully constructed 109 not out. A marathon spell of Salisbury's leg-spin was a feature of the second day, but Willey's first Championship century for two years, combined with the doughty support of Potter, enabled Leicestershire to recover from 34 for three and declare just 62 runs in arrears. The final day was a triumph for Wells's tactical leadership. The cavalier approach to batting he prescribed brought Sussex 210 runs from 62 overs, to which he contributed 42 and Speight 53 off 53 balls. Then, as Leicestershire chased 273 in 57 overs to secure a third consecutive win, Wells boldly employed Salisbury as his chief weapon of attack. The policy paid handsome dividends. The home side came to the final twenty overs needing 122 with eight wickets in hand, but Salisbury then took the wickets of Briers, Willey and Potter in three overs, added that of Whitticase and, critically, had Lewis stumped for the second time in the match after the England all-rounder had raced to 54 off 42 balls (one six, nine fours). Salisbury finished with an impressive five for 79 in a Sussex triumph achieved with seventeen balls remaining.

Close of play: First day, Leicestershire 24-2 (J. J. Whitaker 12*, P. Willey 6*); Second day, Sussex 58-1 (J. W. Hall 9*, I. D. K. Salisbury 6*).

Sussex

N. J. Lenham lbw b Parsons	58	– c Whitticase b Parsons	40
. W. Hall lbw b Willey	34	– c Whitticase b Lewis	17
K. Greenfield c sub b Millns	38	– (4) b Willey	20
A. P. Wells not out	109	– (5) c Parsons b Millns	43
M. P. Speight c Potter b Millns	45	– (7) lbw b Millns	53
A. I. C. Dodemaide not out	17	– lbw b Lewis	0
. D. K. Salisbury (did not bat)		– (3) c Potter b Parsons	6
A. North (did not bat)		– c Willey b Millns	0
P. Moores (did not bat)		– c Lewis b Millns	18
A. C. S. Pigott (did not bat)		– not out	6
R. A. Bunting (did not bat)		– c Lewis b Parsons	0
L-b 6, w 1, n-b 6	13	L-b 6, n-b 1	7

1/90 2/98 3/186 4/277   (4 wkts dec.) 314   1/49 2/59 3/82 4/96 5/96   210
6/166 7/166 8/192 9/205

Bonus points – Sussex 4, Leicestershire 1.

Bowling: *First Innings*—Agnew 9–2–35–0; Lewis 23–9–62–0; Millns 16–1–67–2; Parso
17–5–53–1; Willey 27–10–61–1; Potter 8–1–30–0. *Second Innings*—Lewis 14–1–36–2; Mill
11–3–48–4; Parsons 20–2–90–3; Willey 17–9–30–1.

Leicestershire

T. J. Boon lbw b Pigott	6	– run out	
*N. E. Briers c Dodemaide b Pigott	0	– c Moores b Salisbury	7
J. J. Whitaker c Bunting b Pigott	16	– b Dodemaide	4
P. Willey c Wells b North	112	– c Lenham b Salisbury	3
L. Potter b Pigott	51	– c Greenfield b Salisbury	
C. C. Lewis st Moores b Salisbury	20	– st Moores b Salisbury	5
P. N. Hepworth c Moores b Pigott	17	– run out	
†P. Whitticase not out	11	– c Wells b Salisbury	
G. J. Parsons not out	1	– b Pigott	
J. P. Agnew (did not bat)		– not out	
D. J. Millns (did not bat)		– b Pigott	
B 9, l-b 5, w 2, n-b 2	18	L-b 6, n-b 2	

1/1 2/6 3/34 4/135 5/174   (7 wkts dec.) 252   1/34 2/114 3/156 4/160 5/183   24
6/234 7/247   6/187 7/212 8/224 9/240

Bonus points – Leicestershire 3, Sussex 3.

Bowling: *First Innings*—Pigott 17–5–52–5; Dodemaide 20–4–30–0; Bunting 15–7–21–0
North 14–0–48–1; Salisbury 33.4–9–87–1. *Second Innings*—Pigott 10.1–2–41–2; Dodemaid
18–1–64–1; Bunting 5–0–27–0; Salisbury 17–1–79–5; North 4–0–26–0.

Umpires: M. J. Kitchen and A. G. T. Whitehead.

LEICESTERSHIRE v NORTHAMPTONSHIRE

At Leicester, September 12, 13, 14, 15. Northamptonshire won by 171 runs. Northampton
shire 22 pts, Leicestershire 7 pts. Toss: Northamptonshire. Steep bounce at one end enable
Millns, bowling with genuine pace, to return career-best figures, but with Ambrose and Coo
making 84 for the ninth wicket, Northamptonshire still accumulated a useful total. The ta
Ambrose then employed the awkward end to his advantage, taking the first five Leicestershi
wickets. Only a brave and wholly admirable innings from their captain, Briers, who batted fo
five hours for his 176, kept Leicestershire in the game. Briers shared a stand of 101 for th
sixth wicket with the promising Hepworth, but Ambrose came back to return his best figur
for Northamptonshire. Having conceded a lead of 31, Northamptonshire lost Fordham an
Larkins for 2 runs, and when Agnew, on his farewell appearance at Grace Road, remove
Bailey and Felton, they looked in trouble at 66 for four. But as Leicestershire failed to pre
home their advantage, Lamb, Williams and Ripley plundered runs against an attack deprive
of Millns, who had an injured knee. Lamb's declaration gave Leicestershire 75 overs to sco
337, a task which always looked too steep once both openers had fallen for 3 runs. Whitak
made a forceful 92 off 99 balls, but when Ambrose had him caught behind, Leicestershi
subsided rapidly, losing six wickets for 15 runs. Ambrose returned match figures of twelv
for 155.

Close of play: First day, Northamptonshire 342-8 (C. E. L. Ambrose 49*, N. G. B. Coo
25*); Second day, Leicestershire 341-7 (P. Whitticase 9*); Third day, Northamptonshir
300-8 (D. Ripley 58*, N. G. B. Cook 4*).

Northamptonshire

A. Fordham c Whitticase b Millns	85	– c Potter b Millns	0
N. A. Felton c Potter b Lewis	5	– b Agnew	13
W. Larkins b Millns	27	– c Millns b Lewis	0
R. J. Bailey lbw b Parsons	77	– lbw b Agnew	33
*A. J. Lamb c Whitticase b Millns	0	– b Willey	67
A. L. Penberthy c Whitticase b Millns	52	– c Lewis b Parsons	10
R. G. Williams b Millns	1	– b Lewis	89
†D. Ripley c Agnew b Lewis	6	– not out	109
C. E. L. Ambrose not out	55	– c Whitticase b Lewis	0
N. G. B. Cook b Millns	28	– b Agnew	13
M. A. Robinson lbw b Lewis	0	– not out	1
L-b 6, w 1, n-b 8	15	B 11, l-b 9, w 1, n-b 11	32

1/26 2/102 3/128 4/128 5/218   351   1/0 2/2 3/50   (9 wkts dec.) 367
5/230 7/263 8/266 9/350   4/66 5/103 6/172
                                        7/288 8/295 9/363

Bonus points – Northamptonshire 4, Leicestershire 3 (Score at 100 overs: 337-8).

Bowling: *First Innings*—Agnew 26–5–96–0; Lewis 33.3–8–83–3; Parsons 19–2–91–1; Millns 22–3–63–6; Willey 6–0–12–0. *Second Innings*—Millns 11–0–31–1; Lewis 30–6–84–3; Agnew 26–4–69–3; Parsons 20–1–88–1; Willey 20–4–56–1; Potter 4–1–19–0.

Leicestershire

T. J. Boon c Larkins b Ambrose	13	– c Ripley b Robinson	0
*N. E. Briers c and b Bailey	176	– c Fordham b Ambrose	0
J. J. Whitaker c Robinson b Ambrose	28	– c Ripley b Ambrose	92
P. Willey c Bailey b Ambrose	0	– c Larkins b Cook	30
L. Potter b Ambrose	0	– not out	31
C. C. Lewis b Ambrose	1	– c Cook b Ambrose	0
P. N. Hepworth c Penberthy b Williams	49	– lbw b Ambrose	0
†P. Whitticase b Ambrose	11	– b Ambrose	0
G. J. Parsons c Bailey b Ambrose	8	– run out	0
J. P. Agnew c Cook b Penberthy	24	– c Fordham b Williams	6
D. J. Millns not out	1	– absent injured	
B 8, l-b 15, w 1, n-b 2	26	B 6	6

1/36 2/115 3/120 4/213 5/215   382   1/1 2/3 3/98 4/150 5/150   165
6/316 7/341 8/351 9/380   6/158 7/158 8/158 9/165

Bonus points – Leicestershire 4, Northamptonshire 2 (Score at 100 overs: 328-6).

Bowling: *First Innings*—Ambrose 28–5–89–7; Robinson 23–3–117–0; Penberthy 15.5–3–57–1; Cook 37–18–56–0; Williams 6–1–27–1; Bailey 8–2–13–1. *Second Innings*—Ambrose 15–4–66–5; Robinson 8–2–23–1; Penberthy 7–0–26–0; Cook 8–2–37–1; Williams 6–4–7–1.

Umpires: J. D. Bond and B. Leadbeater.

At Derby, September 18, 19, 20, 21. LEICESTERSHIRE drew with DERBYSHIRE.

MIDDLESEX

Patron: HRH The Duke of Edinburgh
President: F. G. Mann
Chairman: M. P. Murray
Chairman, Cricket Committee: R. A. Gale
Secretary: J. Hardstaff
   Lord's Cricket Ground, St John's Wood,
   London NW8 8QN (Telephone: 071-289 1300)
Captain: M. W. Gatting
Coach: D. Bennett

Two unconnected decisions taken in 1989 were decisive factors in Middlesex winning the 1990 Britannic Assurance Championship. Firstly Mike Gatting and John Emburey committed themselves to a tour of South Africa, which carried a five-year suspension from Test cricket and meant that they would be available for their county throughout the season. Gatting especially has been such a focal-point of Middlesex's success in the 1980s that they automatically became favourites for the title, outweighing the claims of recent winners. When it was pointed out to him that supporters would look forward to a Championship or two during their suspension, Gatting asked, "Why not five?"

His self-belief was reinforced by the second decision. This was taken by the TCCB, who, having finally begun to penalise counties for poor pitches, also legislated for a reduced seam on the ball. The policy on pitches and the ball ensured that only attacking bowlers would earn regular reward, and proved advantageous to Middlesex, whose attack was not made up of trundling medium-pacers. Their bowlers knew that, even if they were destined for hard work, some bowlers in other counties were due for even harder toil. Moreover, as the hot summer kept pitches hard and guaranteed long spells for spinners, Middlesex benefited from their policy over two decades of invariably choosing two spinners. Where once Edmonds and Titmus, and then Edmonds and Emburey had held sway, now another left- and right-arm alliance, Tufnell and Emburey, emerged as a match-winner. "They bowled nearly 2,000 overs between them and took plenty of wickets", said a grateful Gatting. "They were comforting alternatives, because the pace-bowling strength was sometimes worryingly near breaking-point with Test calls and injuries."

Even before the season began, the potential of the new-ball attack was jeopardised when it was discovered, in the West Indies, that Ricardo Ellcock needed a back operation. Happily, Neil Williams, who had endured back problems himself, remained active all season, and his sharp pace and out-swing won him an unexpected England call. This brought to seven the number of Test players in the team – in 1981 there were eleven – and Philip Tufnell was given the opportunity to achieve that status when he was chosen to tour Australia. Angus Fraser, recovering from a side injury and then wanted by England, Norman Cowans and Simon Hughes all made a limited impact until they began taking wickets in the last four fixtures.

Although the bowlers varied from match to match, the top five in the batting remained constant. In a particularly rare occurrence in the County Championship, Desmond Haynes, Mike Roseberry, Gatting,

Mark Ramprakash and Keith Brown played in all 22 games. Roseberry could hardly fail to profit from opening with Haynes, and they launched the innings with such commanding strokeplay that the opposition was forced into premature defence. Brown was the near-perfect No. 5, capable of stabilising the innings when it became necessary, or consolidating a thriving start, as he demonstrated when making an unbeaten double-hundred against Nottinghamshire. Middlesex expected much of Haynes when he joined them in 1989, and he fulfilled their expectations in both Championship and limited-overs cricket.

Gatting had averaged 58 in all Championship games in the 1980s, and with the best batting conditions of his career he would surely have backed himself to surpass that mark last summer. His average, however, remained in the late 50s. He had ankle trouble at the start of the season, and never shook off a hamstring problem, but he enjoyed himself in the last eleven days of July, when he amassed 534 runs, including two big centuries, and in August he showed his team what bad-pitch technique is with a brave, unbeaten 119 against Derbyshire. While Gatting's injuries were an occupational hazard, Paul Downton had a career-threatening wound when a bail struck him in the eye during a Sunday League game at Basingstoke. He showed admirable dedication in returning successfully to his twin tasks as wicket-keeper and batsman.

Middlesex went top of the Championship following three consecutive wins in late June. By this time, undisciplined batting in their quarter-final at Taunton had ended their interest in the Benson and Hedges Cup; but the Championship match against Somerset at Uxbridge in July introduced a run of three centuries from Ramprakash. A Middlesex victory there depended on whether Ramprakash could score 12 runs from the final over, and his nerve and skill stood the test. He developed significantly in 1990 and at twenty established himself as Middlesex's No. 4.

A sequence of draws led up to the only defeat, at Derby, on a pitch which cost the hosts 25 points. Yorkshire were again beaten, and between then and their next Championship match Middlesex had a ten-day respite. Even though it allowed Essex to go to the top of the table, the break could not have come at a better time. In the week of the Derby setback, they had been eliminated from the NatWest Bank Trophy in a high-scoring semi-final at Old Trafford and had seen their Refuge Assurance League hopes badly damaged when the no result at Derby followed a surprise defeat by Sussex.

Refreshed, Middlesex found the run-in for the Championship unexpectedly easy. They won twice, Essex lost and then drew twice, and the winning margin was an emphatic 31 points. The title was made certain when Sussex were bowled out twice, the sixth time Middlesex had managed the feat in a batsman's summer.

They had tuned up for the last lap of the Championship by winning their Refuge Cup semi-final at Old Trafford, and when they returned to the top of the table, with one game left, they expressed their confident mood by winning the Refuge Cup final. Of the longer-standing competitions, Gatting has now won the Championship, Benson and Hedges Cup and NatWest Bank Trophy twice each in his eight years as captain, and has gone only two summers without a trophy. It is a record to compare with J. M. Brearley's four Championship and two Gillette Cup titles in his last seven years in charge. – Terry Cooper.

MIDDLESEX 1990

[*Bill Smith*]

Back row: P. Farbrace, M. A. Roseberry, J. C. Pooley, P. N. Weekes, K. R. Brown, A. Habib. *Middle row:* H. P. H. Sharp (*scorer*), D. Bennett (*coach*), M. Keech, J. D. Carr, A. A. Barnett, J. R. Hemstock, I. J. F. Hutchinson, P. C. R. Tufnell, M. R. Ramprakash, J. Davis (*physiotherapist*), C. T. Radley (*assistant coach*), A. Jones (*2nd XI scorer*). *Front row:* S. P. Hughes, N. G. Cowans, P. R. Downton, J. E. Emburey, M. W. Gatting (*captain*), R. O. Butcher, N. F. Williams, D. L. Haynes. *Insets:* A. R. C. Fraser, R. M. Ellcock, T. A. Radford.

MIDDLESEX RESULTS

All first-class matches – Played 24: Won 10, Lost 1, Drawn 13.

County Championship matches – Played 22: Won 10, Lost 1, Drawn 11.

Bonus points – Batting 73, Bowling 55.

Competition placings – Britannic Assurance County Championship, winners;
NatWest Bank Trophy, s-f; Benson and Hedges Cup, q-f;
Refuge Assurance League, 3rd; Refuge Assurance Cup, winners.

BRITANNIC ASSURANCE CHAMPIONSHIP AVERAGES

BATTING

	Birthplace	M	I	NO	R	HI	Avge
‡D. L. Haynes	*Holders Hill, Barbados*	22	37	5	2,036	255*	63.62
‡M. W. Gatting	*Kingsbury*	22	36	7	1,685	170*	58.10
‡K. R. Brown	*Edmonton*	22	33	7	1,416	200*	54.46
‡M. R. Ramprakash .	*Bushey*	22	38	8	1,327	146*	44.23
‡M. A. Roseberry ...	*Houghton-le-Spring*	22	40	3	1,497	135	40.45
‡J. E. Emburey	*Peckham*	22	31	7	698	111*	29.08
‡P. R. Downton	*Farnborough, Kent*	15	23	1	530	63	24.09
‡A. R. C. Fraser	*Billinge*	12	11	2	213	92	23.66
‡P. C. R. Tufnell	*Barnet*	20	20	9	235	37	21.36
‡N. F. Williams	*Hope Well, St Vincent*	19	22	3	390	55*	20.52
‡S. P. Hughes	*Kingston-upon-Thames*	15	17	5	109	23*	9.08
P. Farbrace	*Ash, Kent*	7	7	2	45	17*	9.00
‡N. G. Cowans	*Enfield St Mary, Jamaica*	16	16	6	81	31	8.10

Also batted: C. W. Taylor (*Banbury*) (2 matches) 13, 0*; N. R. Taylor (*Boscombe*) (1 match)
0; P. N. Weekes (*Hackney, London*) (2 matches) 51, 2. M. J. Thursfield (*South Shields*)
(1 match) did not bat.

* *Signifies not out.* ‡ *Denotes county cap.*

The following played a total of 23 three-figure innings for Middlesex in County Championship
matches – D. L. Haynes 6, K. R. Brown 5, M. W. Gatting 4, M. R. Ramprakash 4, M. A.
Roseberry 3, J. E. Emburey 1.

BOWLING

	O	M	R	W	BB	5Wi	Avge
A. R. C. Fraser	436.5	103	1,073	41	6-30	2	26.17
N. F. Williams	469.1	88	1,430	49	7-61	2	29.18
N. G. Cowans	415	115	1,127	36	5-67	1	31.30
J. E. Emburey	902	254	1,911	57	5-32	2	33.52
P. C. R. Tufnell	948.5	254	2,389	65	6-79	2	36.75
S. P. Hughes	333	60	1,121	28	5-101	1	40.03

Also bowled: K. R. Brown 6–2–49–0; P. R. Downton 1.1–0–4–1; M. W. Gatting
45–18–113–7; D. L. Haynes 35–7–113–2; M. R. Ramprakash 34–5–147–2; M. A. Roseberry
11–3–74–1; C. W. Taylor 47.5–7–139–6; N. R. Taylor 14–5–44–3; M. J. Thursfield
17–4–45–1; P. N. Weekes 54–8–183–3.

Wicket-keepers: P. R. Downton 40 ct, 2 st; P. Farbrace 15 ct, 2 st.

Leading Fielders: J. E. Emburey 31, K. R. Brown 27, M. A. Roseberry 21, M. W. Gatting 19.

MIDDLESEX v ESSEX

At Lord's, April 26, 27, 28, 30. Drawn. Middlesex 5 pts, Essex 6 pts. Toss: Essex. There were only 33 overs on the first day and, with two cautious counties, this militated against a win. Brown was the only Middlesex batsman to develop a first innings, staying for six hours, hitting twenty fours and a six, and being rewarded with his county cap when he returned to the dressing-room. Inevitably, Gooch was the more authoritative and faster of the first-innings century-makers. He batted two hours less than Brown and struck nineteen fours and a six. Essex declared 76 behind, whereupon Middlesex doubled their lead by the end of the third day. Although they began the fourth day without Gatting, who injured an ankle in the Sunday League game, Haynes swept them to a declaration with 116 off 185 balls, including 21 boundaries. Essex's target was 313 in a minimum of 55 overs, but only when Gooch was hitting six fours and a six in 41 balls did it look other than hopeless.

Close of play: First day, Middlesex 76-3 (M. W. Gatting 19*, K. R. Brown 8*); Second day, Essex 24-0 (G. A. Gooch 14*, J. P. Stephenson 8*); Third day, Middlesex 82-1 (D. L. Haynes 47*, M. W. Gatting 32*).

Middlesex

D. L. Haynes c Garnham b Foster	24	– c Foster b Shahid	116
M. A. Roseberry c Waugh b Andrew	12	– c Stephenson b Foster	1
*M. W. Gatting b Andrew	41	– retired hurt	32
M. R. Ramprakash c Topley b Pringle	12	– c Garnham b Foster	1
K. R. Brown lbw b Topley	141	– c Waugh b Andrew	12
†P. R. Downton lbw b Topley	47	– not out	42
J. E. Emburey b Andrew	41	– not out	21
N. F. Williams c Garnham b Waugh	26		
N. G. Cowans b Waugh	2		
S. P. Hughes not out	14		
P. C. R. Tufnell not out	7		
L-b 6, n-b 3	9	B 2, l-b 5, n-b 4	11

1/36 2/36 3/61 4/111 5/217   (9 wkts dec.) 376   1/11 2/88   (4 wkts dec.) 236
6/296 7/346 8/349 9/356   3/126 4/210

Bonus points – Middlesex 3, Essex 2 (Score at 100 overs: 277-5).

Bowling: *First Innings*—Foster 30-7-86-1; Pringle 30-10-79-1; Andrew 29-5-93-3; Topley 36-4-79-2; Shahid 1-0-12-0; Waugh 8-1-21-2. *Second Innings*—Foster 17-4-39-2; Pringle 5-3-12-0; Topley 10-2-42-0; Andrew 20-2-79-1; Waugh 3-1-17-0; Shahid 8-0-33-1; Gooch 1-1-0-0; Stephenson 2-0-7-0.

Essex

*G. A. Gooch c Downton b Williams	137	– c Downton b Williams	39
J. P. Stephenson c Downton b Hughes	14	– c Roseberry b Tufnell	59
P. J. Prichard c Downton b Williams	10	– not out	49
M. E. Waugh b Tufnell	34	– run out	0
B. R. Hardie c Emburey b Williams	21	– not out	0
N. Shahid not out	34		
†M. A. Garnham not out	36		
B 1, l-b 6, w 1, n-b 6	14	B 4, l-b 6, n-b 6	16

1/44 2/75 3/146 4/223 5/227   (5 wkts dec.) 300   1/67 2/141 3/141   (3 wkts) 163

D. R. Pringle, T. D. Topley, N. A. Foster and S. J. W. Andrew did not bat.

Bonus points – Essex 4, Middlesex 2.

Bowling: *First Innings*—Williams 18-4-69-3; Cowans 17-3-43-0; Hughes 16-3-60-1; Emburey 19-3-53-0; Tufnell 21.5-5-68-1. *Second Innings*—Cowans 5-1-32-0; Hughes 7-0-29-0; Williams 6-0-26-1; Emburey 16-7-23-0; Tufnell 13-4-35-1; Ramprakash 1-0-8-0.

Umpires: B. Hassan and A. G. T. Whitehead.

At Cambridge, May 3, 4, 5. MIDDLESEX drew with CAMBRIDGE UNIVERSITY.

MIDDLESEX v KENT

At Lord's, May 15, 16, 17. Middlesex won by eight wickets. Middlesex 23 pts, Kent 4 pts. Toss: Middlesex. Williams confirmed his return to match-winning form after back injuries by bowling at a fast-medium pace which at times became genuinely fast. His seven wickets included two bowled, two caught behind and one caught at slip – an illustration of his straightness – and provided his best figures for Middlesex. Middlesex batted as though a long lead were a formality, and several of their batsmen were out to loose strokes. However, the Middlesex bowlers did not allow Kent to escape, despite Taylor's defiance for more than five hours. Gatting enjoyed a purple patch by taking the last four Kent wickets in a seven-ball span and then winning the match with a day to spare with the disdainful, powerful strokeplay that has been his hallmark against county attacks.

Close of play: First day, Middlesex 71-0 (D. L. Haynes 32*, M. A. Roseberry 38*); Second day, Kent 118-3 (N. R. Taylor 55*, C. S. Cowdrey 19*).

Kent

S. G. Hinks b Williams	16	– c Haynes b Fraser	5
M. R. Benson b Cowans	0	– c Emburey b Williams	24
N. R. Taylor c Emburey b Williams	12	– c Emburey b Hughes	91
T. R. Ward b Williams	0	– lbw b Fraser	13
*C. S. Cowdrey c Haynes b Williams	47	– c Gatting b Fraser	44
M. V. Fleming c Downton b Cowans	69	– b Williams	12
†S. A. Marsh c Downton b Williams	15	– b Gatting	38
M. A. Ealham c Downton b Williams	0	– not out	13
C. Penn c Ramprakash b Williams	3	– b Gatting	0
T. A. Merrick c Emburey b Hughes	10	– c Ramprakash b Gatting	0
R. P. Davis not out	6	– lbw b Gatting	0
B 4, l-b 3, n-b 11	18	B 11, l-b 8, n-b 6	25

1/0 2/20 3/20 4/33 5/155   **196**   1/24 2/63 3/83 4/172 5/198   **265**
6/166 7/166 8/174 9/183   6/220 7/265 8/265 9/265

Bonus points – Kent 1, Middlesex 4.

Bowling: *First Innings*—Fraser 17–3–30–0; Cowans 16–6–41–2; Williams 22–4–61–7; Hughes 19.3–5–50–1; Emburey 3–2–7–0. *Second Innings*—Fraser 26–4–79–3; Cowans 11–4–39–0; Williams 20–0–67–2; Hughes 17–4–43–1; Emburey 14–6–16–0; Gatting 2–1–2–4.

Middlesex

D. L. Haynes st Marsh b Cowdrey	36	– lbw b Ealham	25
M. A. Roseberry c Ward b Merrick	50	– c Marsh b Ealham	37
*M. W. Gatting b Merrick	58	– not out	87
M. R. Ramprakash c Ward b Penn	9	– not out	36
K. R. Brown c Taylor b Davis	58		
†P. R. Downton c Marsh b Ealham	19		
N. F. Williams c Taylor b Penn	18		
J. E. Emburey c Marsh b Merrick	3		
S. P. Hughes c Davis b Penn	4		
A. R. C. Fraser lbw b Merrick	0		
N. G. Cowans not out	0		
B 1, l-b 6, n-b 10	17	B 4, l-b 3, n-b 1	8

1/86 2/96 3/145 4/202 5/247   **272**   1/60 2/79   (2 wkts) **193**
6/247 7/267 8/272 9/272

Bonus points – Middlesex 3, Kent 3 (Score at 100 overs: 269-7).

Bowling: *First Innings*—Merrick 26–7–66–4; Penn 22–5–45–3; Fleming 21–7–49–0; Ealham 11–2–39–1; Davis 12–4–25–1; Cowdrey 12–2–41–1. *Second Innings*—Merrick 10–2–44–0; Penn 7–1–46–0; Ealham 11–1–33–2; Cowdrey 2–1–2–0; Fleming 7–1–23–0; Davis 7–2–23–0; Ward 4.3–1–15–0.

Umpires: J. H. Hampshire and M. J. Kitchen.

At Lord's, May 19, 20, 21. MIDDLESEX drew with NEW ZEALANDERS (See New Zealand tour section).

MIDDLESEX v SURREY

At Lord's, May 23, 24, 25. Drawn. Middlesex 7 pts, Surrey 6 pts. Toss: Middlesex. Roseberry underpinned the Middlesex first innings, making his best score, and hit two sixes and seventeen fours in a responsible balance between consolidation and attack. Surrey's batsmen struggled in reply against an attack that presented no unusual menace, and only two batting points were taken before Bicknell and Kendrick batted briskly for an hour. However, when Bicknell and Murphy dismissed both Middlesex openers without scoring before the close, and Bicknell claimed two more wickets early on the third morning, Middlesex were obliged to bat for most of the day to avoid defeat. Brown and Downton supplied the necessary defensive innings.

Close of play: First day, Surrey 17-0 (R. I. Alikhan 10*, P. D. Atkins 7*); Second day, Middlesex 8-2 (J. E. Emburey 8*, M. W. Gatting 0*).

Middlesex

D. L. Haynes c Lynch b Gray	33	– b Bicknell	0
M. A. Roseberry c Greig b Murphy	122	– c Ward b Murphy	0
*M. W. Gatting c Ward b Gray	20	– (4) c Medlycott b Bicknell	13
M. R. Ramprakash c Alikhan b Kendrick	30	– (5) b Medlycott	10
K. R. Brown c Murphy b Medlycott	16	– (6) c and b Medlycott	56
†P. R. Downton b Murphy	3	– (7) st Ward b Kendrick	55
N. F. Williams c Alikhan b Medlycott	40	– (8) c Kendrick b Medlycott	18
J. E. Emburey c Ward b Medlycott	10	– (3) b Bicknell	17
N. G. Cowans c Kendrick b Medlycott	6	– (10) c Bicknell b Kendrick	5
S. P. Hughes c Greig b Bicknell	0	– (9) not out	23
P. C. R. Tufnell not out	14	– b Medlycott	1
B 4, l-b 8, w 1, n-b 3	16	B 16, l-b 8, n-b 2	26
	310		**224**

1/75 2/103 3/165 4/206 5/220   310   1/0 2/4 3/24 4/31 5/85   224
6/241 7/258 8/266 9/275   6/137 7/167 8/201 9/221

Bonus points – Middlesex 4, Surrey 4 (Score at 100 overs: 310-9).

Bowling: *First Innings*—Gray 22–3–68–2; Bicknell 25–7–72–1; Murphy 22–8–50–2; Greig 1–0–5–0; Medlycott 26.1–5–91–4; Kendrick 4–0–12–1. *Second Innings*—Bicknell 25–14–25–3; Murphy 25–7–75–1; Medlycott 32–14–65–4; Greig 3–0–8–0; Kendrick 14–4–25–2; Alikhan 1–0–2–0.

Surrey

R. I. Alikhan b Hughes	20	– not out	0
P. D. Atkins c Gatting b Hughes	23	– not out	0
G. P. Thorpe c Tufnell b Emburey	16		
†D. M. Ward c Downton b Hughes	46		
M. A. Lynch b Tufnell	46		
*I. A. Greig b Williams	44		
K. T. Medlycott c Downton b Williams	0		
M. P. Bicknell not out	26		
N. M. Kendrick not out	52		
L-b 11, n-b 2	13		
	286		**0**

1/42 2/53 3/77 4/124 5/206   (7 wkts dec.) 286   (no wkt)   0
6/206 7/208

A. H. Gray and A. J. Murphy did not bat.

Bonus points – Surrey 2, Middlesex 3 (Score at 100 overs: 227-7).

Bowling: *First Innings*—Williams 22–5–57–2; Cowans 21–8–36–0; Tufnell 14–11–57–1; Emburey 24.1–8–58–1; Hughes 16–2–57–3; Gatting 2–0–6–0; Haynes 1–0–4–0. *Second Innings*—Haynes 3–3–0–0; Tufnell 2–2–0–0.

Umpires: K. J. Lyons and R. A. White.

MIDDLESEX v GLOUCESTERSHIRE

At Lord's, May 26, 28, 29. Middlesex won by 10 runs. Middlesex 21 pts, Gloucestershire 6 pts. Toss: Middlesex. Curran ended Middlesex's promising start with three wickets in nine overs, after which the innings maintained an uneven course. However, Ramprakash showed enterprise, and Emburey hit effectively to ensure full batting points. Williams, who forced Wright to retire after a blow on the elbow, had both Gloucestershire's chief scorers dropped early on, and, having survived, Hodgson and Butcher played watchfully against the Middlesex spinners. Butcher, batting for four hours, hit his county's first Championship hundred of the season, but the innings was so laboured that Gloucestershire had to scramble to record a third batting point. Middlesex lost wickets dangerously before Brown, Downton, Williams and Emburey saw them to a declaration which set 272 in 66 overs. When Gloucestershire were 232 for eight with just four overs remaining, Gatting ordered Brown to concede runs. Curran took 18 off the over and subsequently hit Tufnell for six to make the target 13 off ten balls. But Tufnell then had Graveney caught at slip, and when Lawrence sliced Emburey to cover, Curran was left stranded. Gatting had presented Gloucestershire with a slog or block dilemma, and his tactics brought a win with two balls to spare.

Close of play: First day, Gloucestershire 25-0 (A. J. Wright 15*, G. D. Hodgson 8*); Second day, Middlesex 44-2 (D. L. Haynes 31*, M. R. Ramprakash 0*).

Middlesex

D. L. Haynes c Wright b Curran	24	– c Bainbridge b Lloyds	49
A. Roseberry c Russell b Curran	50	– lbw b Lawrence	1
M. W. Gatting c and b Curran	16	– lbw b Walsh	4
R. Ramprakash c Bainbridge b Graveney	64	– b Lloyds	0
K. R. Brown b Graveney	5	– c Russell b Athey	60
P. R. Downton lbw b Curran	63	– c Russell b Athey	25
N. F. Williams b Lloyds	0	– not out	50
J. E. Emburey not out	38	– not out	30
S. P. Hughes not out	12		
B 1, l-b 14, n-b 14	29	L-b 9, n-b 2	11

1/61 2/94 3/97 4/124 5/210 (7 wkts dec.) 301   1/30 2/39 3/44 (6 wkts dec.) 230
6/211 7/261   4/77 5/136 6/157

N. G. Cowans and P. C. R. Tufnell did not bat.

Bonus points – Middlesex 4, Gloucestershire 3.

Bowling: *First Innings*—Walsh 17-6-59-0; Lawrence 16-4-46-0; Curran 22.4-7-64-4; Graveney 32-7-89-2; Bainbridge 5-2-9-0; Lloyds 5-0-19-1. *Second Innings*—Walsh 7-2-25-1; Lawrence 4-0-13-1; Lloyds 20.2-3-109-2; Graveney 27-6-61-0; Athey 7-2-13-2.

Gloucestershire

A. J. Wright retired hurt	24	– b Cowans	8
G. D. Hodgson c Emburey b Tufnell	65	– b Hughes	25
A. P. Butcher c Roseberry b Emburey	102	– st Downton b Tufnell	31
C. W. J. Athey c Gatting b Tufnell	31	– c Ramprakash b Emburey	69
P. Bainbridge st Downton b Tufnell	2	– (6) c Roseberry b Emburey	22
K. M. Curran not out	9	– (7) not out	53
J. W. Lloyds not out	10	– (5) c Roseberry b Tufnell	19
C. A. Walsh (did not bat)		– b Emburey	16
R. C. Russell (did not bat)		– c and b Tufnell	1
D. A. Graveney (did not bat)		– c Emburey b Tufnell	3
D. V. Lawrence (did not bat)		– c Hughes b Emburey	0
B 1, l-b 10, n-b 6	17	B 9, l-b 4, n-b 1	14

1/155 2/231 3/241 4/241 (4 wkts dec.) 260   1/27 2/33 3/87 4/127 5/169 261
                                             6/194 7/199 8/232 9/260

Bonus points – Gloucestershire 3, Middlesex 1 (Score at 100 overs: 250-4).

In the first innings A. J. Wright retired hurt at 45.

Bowling: *First Innings*—Williams 17–5–32–0; Cowans 16–5–36–0; Emburey 32–10–63–1
Tufnell 27–6–68–3; Hughes 10–2–37–0; Gatting 4–1–13–0. *Second Innings*—William
5–2–10–0; Cowans 9–4–24–1; Hughes 6–3–16–1; Tufnell 22–0–111–4; Emburey 22.4–4–69–4
Brown 1–0–18–0.

Umpires: K. J. Lyons and R. A. White.

At Ilford, June 2, 4, 5. MIDDLESEX drew with ESSEX.

MIDDLESEX v WARWICKSHIRE

At Lord's, June 6, 7, 8. Drawn. Middlesex 2 pts, Warwickshire 8 pts. Toss: Middlesex
Warwickshire outplayed Middlesex all the way, building on a massive double-century star
which involved Moles, Lloyd and Asif Din. Lloyd had batted fluently before aggravating
hamstring injury and retiring during lunch. Moles, 22 at that stage, accelerated in the next tw
sessions and at the close had faced 354 balls and hit two sixes and eleven fours in his 128 no
out. Humpage cut loose towards the end with 73 from 57 balls, including two sixes and nin
fours. In contrast, Middlesex failed to profit from an excellent opening which saw them 14
for one at lunch on the second day. Gatting batted on after being cracked on the back of th
helmet by Donald, but he was dismissed in a collapse so sharp that it needed the last pair t
get Middlesex past the follow-on. Benjamin's attacking bowling brought him his bes
Championship figures. With Moles maintaining his good form, Warwickshire eventually se
Middlesex a target of 273 in 49 overs, but with Haynes out first ball, and Gatting prevente
from batting until No. 7 because he had not fielded, this was never a prospect. B
the time rain washed out the final hour, Warwickshire's bowlers again had Middlesex i
disarray.

Close of play: First day, Warwickshire 372-4 (A. J. Moles 128*, P. A. Smith 0*); Secon
day, Middlesex 243.

Warwickshire

A. J. Moles not out	128	– not out	6!
*T. A. Lloyd retired hurt	70		
Asif Din c Emburey b Tufnell	49	– (2) c Williams b Roseberry	4
A. I. Kallicharran c Emburey b Tufnell	10		
†G. W. Humpage c Gatting b Emburey	73		
D. A. Reeve b Hughes	12	– (3) not out	3
P. A. Smith not out	0		
B 11, l-b 16, w 1, n-b 2	30	B 1, l-b 1, n-b 1	

1/206 2/222 3/351 4/371   (4 wkts dec.) 372   1/94   (1 wkt dec.) 14

N. M. K. Smith, A. A. Donald, J. E. Benjamin and T. A. Munton did not bat.

Bonus points – Warwickshire 4 (Score at 100 overs: 305-2).

In the first innings T. A. Lloyd retired hurt at 106.

Bowling: *First Innings*—Williams 22–2–77–0; Fraser 19–9–18–0; Hughes 16–5–48–1
Gatting 11–3–43–0; Tufnell 28–4–111–2; Emburey 14–3–48–1. *Second Innings*—Frase
8–1–23–0; Hughes 4–1–20–0; Roseberry 6–0–58–1; Ramprakasl
4–0–28–0.

Middlesex

D. L. Haynes c Humpage b Donald	67	– b Donald	0
M. A. Roseberry lbw b Benjamin	64	– retired hurt	19
M. W. Gatting c sub b P. A. Smith	23		
M. R. Ramprakash lbw b Benjamin	0	– (3) c Reeve b Munton	38
K. R. Brown c Reeve b Benjamin	15	– (4) not out	41
P. R. Downton lbw b P. A. Smith	4	– (5) lbw b Munton	11
N. F. Williams c Humpage b Donald	17		
J. E. Emburey c Benjamin b Donald	18	– (6) not out	5
P. C. R. Tufnell not out	11		
S. P. Hughes c sub b Benjamin	2		
A. R. C. Fraser b Benjamin	7		
B 8, l-b 7	15	B 4, l-b 4	8

1/130 2/142 3/142 4/178 5/178   243   1/0 2/90 3/116   (3 wkts) 122
6/191 7/204 8/219 9/221

Bonus points – Middlesex 2, Warwickshire 4.

In the second innings M. A. Roseberry retired hurt at 46.

Bowling: *First Innings*—Donald 25–5–60–3; Benjamin 22.5–5–71–5; Munton 18–7–36–0; P. A. Smith 11–3–46–2; N. M. K. Smith 5–1–15–0. *Second Innings*—Donald 7–3–26–1; Benjamin 7–0–30–0; Munton 8–1–21–2; Reeve 7.4–1–37–0.

Umpires: D. J. Constant and R. Julian.

At Leicester, June 16, 18, 19. MIDDLESEX beat LEICESTERSHIRE by 103 runs.

At Manchester, June 20, 21, 22. MIDDLESEX beat LANCASHIRE by five wickets.

At Luton, June 23, 25, 26. MIDDLESEX beat NORTHAMPTONSHIRE by 79 runs.

MIDDLESEX v WORCESTERSHIRE

At Lord's, June 30, July 2, 3. Drawn. Middlesex 8 pts, Worcestershire 4 pts. Toss: Middlesex. After McEwan had removed Haynes and Gatting when they were in full flow, Illingworth, in 2 consecutive overs, prevented the Middlesex batting from establishing control. Roseberry and Ramprakash both had prolonged passive patches, with Ramprakash remaining on 27 for 7 balls. The first day was shortened by the weather, forcing Middlesex to bat on into the second, but an impressive all-round bowling performance made up for lost time by making Worcestershire follow on. On the final day, the spinners worked tirelessly, but in a situation in which inactivity was a virtue for batsmen, their only reward came when Tufnell gained Hick's wicket. Although Botham went instantly to Fraser, D'Oliveira, who batted just over four and a half hours, and Neale saw that the match was saved.

Close of play: First day, Middlesex 276-7 (N. F. Williams 7*, P. C. R. Tufnell 2*); Second day, Worcestershire 2-1 (P. Bent 1*, S. M. McEwan 1*).

Middlesex

D. L. Haynes b McEwan	40	N. F. Williams not out	49
M. A. Roseberry c Botham b Illingworth	43	P. C. R. Tufnell b Lampitt	3
M. W. Gatting c Rhodes b McEwan	26	A. R. C. Fraser b Botham	27
M. R. Ramprakash c D'Oliveira b Lampitt	69	N. G. Cowans c Hick b Botham	1
K. R. Brown c Rhodes b Illingworth	52	B 4, l-b 10, n-b 1	15
P. Farbrace c Curtis b Illingworth	14		
J. E. Emburey lbw b Lampitt	9		348

1/57 2/85 3/130 4/201 5/225
6/256 7/269 8/281 9/344

Bonus points – Middlesex 4, Worcestershire 3 (Score at 100 overs: 301-8).

Bowling: Botham 18.1–3–71–2; Lampitt 32–1–119–3; McEwan 14–1–51–2; Illingworth 27–12–65–3; Hick 8–1–28–0.

Worcestershire

T. S. Curtis c Emburey b Williams	30 –	lbw b Cowans 0
P. Bent b Cowans	7 –	b Fraser 13
G. A. Hick b Cowans	0 –	(4) c Roseberry b Tufnell 80
D. B. D'Oliveira st Farbrace b Emburey	13 –	(5) not out 87
I. T. Botham c Haynes b Williams	4 –	(6) c Emburey b Fraser 0
*P. A. Neale c Farbrace b Fraser	16 –	(7) not out 41
M. J. Weston c and b Emburey	2	
†S. J. Rhodes c Emburey b Cowans	26	
R. K. Illingworth lbw b Fraser	0	
S. R. Lampitt lbw b Williams	5	
S. M. McEwan not out	27 –	(3) b Fraser 2
B 3, l-b 25, n-b 12	40	B 1, l-b 7, n-b 9 17

1/21 2/21 3/48 4/68   170   1/0 2/11 3/30   (5 wkts dec.) 24?
5/70 6/77 7/95 8/95 9/122   4/153 5/154

Bonus points – Worcestershire 1, Middlesex 4.

Bowling: *First Innings*—Fraser 22–7–40–2; Cowans 10–5–23–3; Williams 17–4–27–3; Emburey 19–9–27–2; Tufnell 14–7–25–0. *Second Innings*—Cowans 15–6–36–1; Fraser 23–6–53–3; Williams 11–3–28–0; Emburey 22–6–52–0; Tufnell 31–12–68–1.

Umpires: R. Palmer and D. R. Shepherd.

MIDDLESEX v YORKSHIRE

At Uxbridge, July 18, 19, 20. Middlesex won by seven wickets. Middlesex 24 pts, Yorkshire 5 pts. Toss: Yorkshire. Middlesex began their annual visit to Uxbridge in a business-like manner. Yorkshire's top batting failed on a pitch which had always rewarded determined effort by bowlers and they never caught up. Byas, clipping ten neat fours and one six, effected a partial repair with help from White and Carrick. When Middlesex batted, Gatting exploited the ground's accessible boundaries to hit 60 of his 86 in fours, and when he was out the stalwart Brown, initially in partnership with Emburey, ensured that Middlesex's lead would be a worthwhile one. Carrick efficiently worked his way through the tail, leaving Brown unbeaten with 109 from 175 balls, including fourteen fours. On the final day William removed Yorkshire's overnight pair in a hostile early burst, after which Emburey and Tufnell found there was just enough turn and bounce in the pitch for their contrasting spin attack. Brown continued to have an influence on the match by taking four catches at short leg, and he was at the crease when Middlesex won before the last hour.

Close of play: First day, Middlesex 48-1 (M. A. Roseberry 16*, M. W. Gatting 9*); Second day, Yorkshire 59-1 (M. D. Moxon 21*, R. J. Blakey 27*).

Yorkshire

*M. D. Moxon c Roseberry b Williams	12 –	c Gatting b Williams ...... 2?
C. A. Chapman c Farbrace b Emburey	20 –	lbw b Emburey .... ?
†R. J. Blakey c Farbrace b Williams	0 –	c Farbrace b Williams ..... 4?
P. E. Robinson c Emburey b Hughes	3 –	c Emburey b Williams 40
D. Byas c Gatting b Emburey	83 –	c Brown b Tufnell .... 1?
C. White c Haynes b Williams	12 –	c Brown b Emburey 0
P. Carrick b Emburey	52 –	c and b Emburey 10
C. S. Pickles c Roseberry b Tufnell	17 –	c Brown b Tufnell 18
P. J. Hartley c Farbrace b Tufnell	11 –	not out 9
D. Gough b Emburey	11 –	c Brown b Tufnell 0
S. D. Fletcher not out	0 –	b Williams 0
B 6, l-b 5, n-b 11	22	B 10, l-b 8, w 1, n-b 7 ... 26

1/31 2/31 3/39 4/56 5/106   243   1/20 2/77 3/84 4/122 5/123   192
6/195 7/204 8/229 9/239   6/140 7/161 8/187 9/191

Bonus points – Yorkshire 2, Middlesex 4.

Bowling: *First Innings*—Williams 19–5–55–3; Cowans 11–3–21–0; Emburey 27–10–51–4; Hughes 9–3–38–1; Tufnell 24–7–67–2. *Second Innings*—Williams 18.5–2–43–4; Cowans 3–1–7–0; Emburey 27–8–62–3; Tufnell 24–7–49–3; Haynes 1–0–4–0; Hughes 5–1–9–0.

Middlesex

D. L. Haynes c Robinson b Hartley	18	– c Hartley b Carrick	26
M. A. Roseberry c Blakey b Gough	36	– c Moxon b Hartley	9
*M. W. Gatting c Carrick b Fletcher	86	– b White	28
M. R. Ramprakash c Chapman b Hartley	9	– not out	15
K. R. Brown not out	109	– not out	12
J. E. Emburey st Blakey b Carrick	45		
N. F. Williams b Pickles	2		
†P. Farbrace c Chapman b Carrick	2		
P. C. R. Tufnell c White b Carrick	10		
S. P. Hughes st Blakey b Carrick	4		
N. G. Cowans c Pickles b Carrick	2		
L-b 7, n-b 10	17	L-b 2, n-b 4	6

1/30 2/104 3/125 4/180 5/266   340   1/13 2/60 3/76   (3 wkts) 96
6/281 7/290 8/318 9/338

Bonus points – Middlesex 4, Yorkshire 3 (Score at 100 overs: 319-8).

Bowling: *First Innings*—Hartley 20–3–76–2; Fletcher 17–7–29–1; Gough 13–5–40–1; Carrick 31–4–99–5; White 12–1–59–0; Pickles 10–3–30–1. *Second Innings*—Hartley 5–0–24–1; Fletcher 4–0–10–0; Carrick 10.3–2–22–1; White 9–0–38–1.

Umpires: J. D. Bond and B. Dudleston.

MIDDLESEX v SOMERSET

At Uxbridge, July 21, 23, 24. Middlesex won by four wickets. Middlesex 20 pts, Somerset 4 pts. Toss: Somerset. Despite their large opening stand, Somerset came nowhere near obtaining full batting points, but they did leave Middlesex without a single bowling point. Cook stroked eight of his first 65 balls for four, but then he and Roebuck and their successors submitted to the trio of spinners, Middlesex having given Weekes, an off-spinner, his Championship début. Cook was 305 balls over his 152, which contained 21 fours, and it needed Rose to galvanise Somerset. On the second morning he struck four fours and four sixes in his 38-ball 57, taking 26 off one over from Weekes. Gatting's belligerence was the focus as Middlesex hurried the match along by taking maximum batting points in the 68th over and immediately declaring. He opened his score with a six, hit three more, made 100 in fours and required only 188 balls for his unbeaten 170. Somerset's second declaration set Middlesex to score 369 in what proved to be 69 overs. Haynes made a crisp century, but the last twenty overs began with 149 wanted and wickets falling. In an attempt to collect more wickets, Tavaré fed Ramprakash with soft bowling. His gamble was seized upon. Ramprakash hit him for three sixes in an over, hit Trump for two more and, with 12 wanted from the last over, stroked three twos and then two fours for a Middlesex victory. His 146 not out had come from 133 balls and, in addition to the five sixes, contained twelve fours.

Close of play: First day, Somerset 340-4 (C. J. Tavaré 53*, N. D. Burns 6*); Second day, Somerset 63-1 (S. J. Cook 29*, R. J. Harden 20*).

Somerset

S. J. Cook c Farbrace b Tufnell	152	– lbw b Ramprakash	85
P. M. Roebuck b Tufnell	70	– b Fraser	9
A. N. Hayhurst c and b Weekes	15		
*C. J. Tavaré c Haynes b Weekes	57	– c Emburey b Tufnell	61
R. J. Harden c Brown b Tufnell	17	– (3) c Farbrace b Emburey	38
†N. D. Burns not out	37	– not out	4
G. D. Rose b Fraser	57	– (5) not out	10
I. G. Swallow not out	11		
L-b 22, n-b 7	29	B 10, l-b 2, n-b 9	21

1/189 2/234 3/274 4/302   (6 wkts dec.) 445   1/27 2/100 3/210   (4 wkts dec.) 228
5/349 6/426   4/218

H. R. J. Trump, A. N. Jones and N. A. Mallender did not bat.

Bonus points – Somerset 3 (Score at 100 overs: 273-2).

Bowling: *First Innings*—Fraser 23–3–66–1; Williams 10–0–45–0; Emburey 35–11–57–0; Tufnell 51–11–140–3; Weekes 28–2–115–2. *Second Innings*—Fraser 6–1–11–1; Williams 5–0–38–0; Emburey 20–4–52–1; Tufnell 24–4–96–1; Ramprakash 5–1–19–1.

Middlesex

D. L. Haynes c Cook b Swallow	41	– c Harden b Mallender 108
M. A. Roseberry c Burns b Mallender	25	– lbw b Rose 7
*M. W. Gatting not out	170	– b Mallender 36
M. R. Ramprakash c Tavaré b Mallender	2	– not out 146
K. R. Brown c and b Trump	46	– c Burns b Mallender 9
J. E. Emburey not out	1	– b Mallender 11
N. F. Williams (did not bat)	–	b Jones 22
†P. Farbrace (did not bat)	–	not out 4
B 6, l-b 4, n-b 10	20	B 10, l-b 14, n-b 4 28

1/67 2/117 3/142 4/296   (4 wkts dec.) 305   1/40 2/110 3/215 4/238   (6 wkts) 371
                                                      5/260 6/353

A. R. C. Fraser, P. N. Weekes and P. C. R. Tufnell did not bat.

Bonus points – Middlesex 4, Somerset 1.

Bowling: *First Innings*—Jones 10–1–47–0; Mallender 11–2–46–2; Trump 20.4–3–91–1; Swallow 19–2–100–1; Rose 7–3–11–0. *Second Innings*—Jones 14–2–69–1; Mallender 16.5–1–60–4; Rose 10–1–43–1; Swallow 12–0–66–0; Trump 15–1–89–0; Tavaré 1–0–20–0.

Umpires: J. D. Bond and B. Dudleston.

At Canterbury, July 25, 26, 27. MIDDLESEX drew with KENT.

At Nottingham, July 28, 30, 31. MIDDLESEX drew with NOTTINGHAMSHIRE.

MIDDLESEX v GLAMORGAN

At Lord's, August 4, 6, 7. Drawn. Middlesex 7 pts, Glamorgan 7 pts. Toss: Middlesex. Only three days after their bowlers had suffered at the hands of Haynes and Gatting in the NatWest Trophy quarter-finals, Glamorgan endured similar treatment. The pair added 171 in 37 overs, and later Brown assisted Haynes while 134 came in 35 overs. Helped by the proximity of the Tavern boundary, most of the batsmen in the match plundered runs. Haynes hit 24 fours in his 244-ball innings. Brown increased his pace dramatically after taking 95 balls over his first fifty; his next fifty came from 54 balls, and in his penultimate over he hit Frost for 20 to finish with three sixes and twelve fours in his 120. Glamorgan had their own century-maker in Morris (fourteen fours), and with Richards gracing one of his favourite settings, they took full batting points, declared and then forced Middlesex to struggle towards a declaration. Only when Butcher and Cottey were scoring 79 in 21 overs did Glamorgan hint that 251 in 53 overs was possible. Fraser captured wickets regularly as Glamorgan went into defensive mode, but Watkin and Frost fended off the last 34 balls to save the match.

Close of play: First day, Glamorgan 10-0 (A. R. Butcher 9*, H. Morris 1*); Second day, Glamorgan 360-9 (N. G. Cowley 52*, M. Frost 4*).

Middlesex

D. L. Haynes b Croft	173		
M. A. Roseberry c Metson b Bastien	0	– (1) b Croft	62
*M. W. Gatting b Bastien	89	– (2) b Watkin	21
M. R. Ramprakash lbw b Watkin	8	– (3) c Metson b Frost	18
K. R. Brown c Metson b Croft	120	– (4) c Morris b Frost	4
†P. R. Downton c Watkin b Croft	4	– (5) c Maynard b Bastien	6
J. E. Emburey c Butcher b Frost	23	– (6) c Metson b Watkin	7
N. F. Williams c Morris b Frost	17	– (7) c Cowley b Bastien	1
A. R. C. Fraser not out	4	– (8) c Metson b Frost	23
P. C. R. Tufnell (did not bat)		– (9) not out	4
N. G. Cowans (did not bat)		– (10) not out	12
L-b 7, n-b 2	9	L-b 4, n-b 1	5

1/0 2/171 3/196 4/330 5/344   (8 wkts dec.) 447   1/33 2/63 3/72   (8 wkts dec.) 163
6/413 7/431 8/447   4/83 5/93 6/98
                                            7/147 8/151

Bonus points – Middlesex 4, Glamorgan 3 (Score at 100 overs: 434-7).

Bowling: *First Innings*—Watkin 24–2–85–1; Bastien 15.2–1–81–2; Frost 19.4–1–110–2; Croft 24–4–100–3; Cowley 9–1–29–0; Richards 6–0–22–0; Butcher 3.4–0–13–0. *Second Innings*—Watkin 15–4–47–2; Bastien 21–4–72–2; Frost 8–0–24–3; Croft 2–0–16–1.

Glamorgan

*A. R. Butcher c Brown b Williams	34	– lbw b Fraser	54
H. Morris c Downton b Cowans	100	– lbw b Williams	4
P. A. Cottey c Gatting b Williams	0	– b Fraser	33
M. P. Maynard c Downton b Tufnell	27	– c Cowans b Tufnell	20
I. V. A. Richards c Haynes b Emburey	80	– b Fraser	9
R. D. B. Croft c Brown b Cowans	15	– b Tufnell	13
N. G. Cowley not out	52	– c Downton b Fraser	8
†C. P. Metson lbw b Williams	4	– c Gatting b Fraser	0
S. L. Watkin c Gatting b Williams	9	– not out	0
S. Bastien c and b Williams	11	– lbw b Fraser	0
M. Frost not out	4	– not out	0
B 9, l-b 11, w 1, n-b 3	24	L-b 2, n-b 3	5

1/71 2/71 3/117 4/255 5/266   (9 wkts dec.) 360   1/7 2/86 3/101   (9 wkts) 146
6/280 7/294 8/324 9/346   4/125 5/125 6/146
                                         7/146 8/146 9/146

Bonus points – Glamorgan 4, Middlesex 3 (Score at 100 overs: 311-7).

Bowling: *First Innings*—Fraser 21–2–76–0; Williams 23–6–59–5; Emburey 32–10–88–1; Cowans 15–2–50–2; Tufnell 24–4–67–1. *Second Innings*—Fraser 14–7–30–6; Williams 7–2–30–1; Cowans 2–1–8–0; Emburey 16–7–28–0; Tufnell 14–5–48–2.

Umpires: D. J. Constant and K. J. Lyons.

At Bournemouth, August 8, 9, 10. MIDDLESEX drew with HAMPSHIRE.

MIDDLESEX v SUSSEX

At Lord's, August 11, 13, 14. Drawn. Middlesex 7 pts, Sussex 4 pts. Toss: Middlesex. For the second consecutive Saturday Haynes played the outstanding innings, recording his second double-century of the summer after scoring his first hundred before lunch, and he batted with easy command into the second day. He faced 353 balls for his unbeaten 255 and hit 30 fours and a six. However, the failure of the other main batsmen to produce a big innings forced Middlesex to take extra time to build their total. Sussex set their sights on saving the follow-on and they managed it in an innings that lurched erratically. Hall and Smith gave a promise of the later defiance when they battled for 40 overs, but at 129 for five, with the ball turning for their three spinners, Middlesex looked winners. Instead, Speight and Dodemaide ground out runs on the second day, and Moores and Pigott emulated them on the third with a partnership of 97 which saw the follow-on saved before lunch. Salisbury prolonged the Sussex innings, and Middlesex's hopes of bowling Sussex out twice were put in perspective when they failed to do so once.

Close of play: First day, Middlesex 385-6 (D. L. Haynes 222*, P. N. Weekes 34*); Second day, Sussex 217-7 (P. Moores 8*, A. C. S. Pigott 7*).

Middlesex

D. L. Haynes not out	255		
M. A. Roseberry b Donelan	22	– (1) lbw b Salisbury	37
*M. W. Gatting b Dodemaide	28		
M. R. Ramprakash c Dodemaide b Salisbury	28	– (2) c C. M. Wells b Donelan	5
K. R. Brown st Moores b Donelan	2		
†P. R. Downton c and b Salisbury	3		
J. E. Emburey c Moores b Salisbury	14		
P. N. Weekes b Pigott	51	– (3) lbw b Donelan	2
N. F. Williams lbw b Dodemaide	9	– (4) not out	55
P. C. R. Tufnell not out	3	– (5) not out	0
B 8, l-b 16, n-b 10	34	B 5, l-b 2, n-b 1	8

1/99 2/188 3/251 4/270 5/279   (8 wkts dec.) 449   1/17 2/27 3/103   (3 wkts) 107
6/331 7/427 8/444

N. G. Cowans did not bat.

Bonus points – Middlesex 4, Sussex 2 (Score at 100 overs: 341-6).

Bowling: *First Innings*—Pigott 23–2–105–1; Dodemaide 32–6–75–2; Donelan 37–5–116–2; Salisbury 31–3–115–3; C. M. Wells 2–0–14–0. *Second Innings*—C. M. Wells 2–0–2–0; Donelan 22–7–38–2; Salisbury 20–4–60–1.

Sussex

N. J. Lenham c Downton b Williams	5		A. C. S. Pigott c Gatting b Tufnell	58
J. W. Hall c Roseberry b Emburey	49		I. D. K. Salisbury not out	40
D. M. Smith c Downton b Weekes	42		B. T. P. Donelan not out	8
A. P. Wells lbw b Emburey	9		B 18, l-b 14, w 3, n-b 13	48
M. P. Speight lbw b Cowans	52			
*C. M. Wells c Brown b Tufnell	1		1/9 2/93 3/113	(9 wkts dec.) 387
A. I. C. Dodemaide c Brown b Tufnell	26		4/126 5/129 6/196	
†P. Moores c Brown b Haynes	49		7/203 8/300 9/363	

Bonus points – Sussex 2, Middlesex 3 (Score at 100 overs: 209-7).

Bowling: Cowans 11–2–30–1; Williams 20–4–69–1; Tufnell 54–20–85–3; Emburey 51–17–85–2; Weekes 26–6–68–1; Haynes 7–1–18–1.

Umpires: B. J. Meyer and A. G. T. Whitehead.

At Derby, August 18, 20, 21. MIDDLESEX lost to DERBYSHIRE by 171 runs.

At Leeds, August 23, 24, 25, 27. MIDDLESEX beat YORKSHIRE by 64 runs.

MIDDLESEX v NOTTINGHAMSHIRE

At Lord's, September 7, 8, 9, 10. Middlesex won by ten wickets. Middlesex 24 pts, Nottinghamshire 3 pts. Toss: Middlesex. Having slipped to second place in the Championship since they last played, Middlesex were in some anxiety when their top three were prised out without making a significant score. Ramprakash and Brown eased all tension with their excellently judged stand of 188 in 58 overs. Ramprakash faced 253 balls and hit 21 fours in his

132. Brown's strokeplay and authority developed on the second morning, and he enabled Middlesex to declare on schedule, having batted for six hours for his maiden double-hundred (309 balls, 23 fours). Nottinghamshire produced two contrasting days of batting. There were occasional pockets of resistance in the first innings, but only when the last two wickets held out for 95 minutes on the third morning did Middlesex realise that a concerted defensive action had begun. Fraser dug out Broad, but for the rest of the day Newell and Robinson batted Middlesex to a standstill. On the last day, however, Fraser ran out Robinson and Cowans, having earlier broken Johnson's finger, finally bowled Newell after the opener had battled for six and a half hours (319 balls). The rest of the innings folded in time for Middlesex to hit off the winning runs after tea and return to the top of the Championship table.

Close of play: First day, Middlesex 358-4 (K. R. Brown 127*, P. R. Downton 12*); Second day, Nottinghamshire 179-8 (B. N. French 10*, R. A. Pick 16*); Third day, Nottinghamshire 185-1 (M. Newell 61*, R. T. Robinson 87*).

Middlesex

D. L. Haynes b Stephenson	29	– not out	44
M. A. Roseberry lbw b Pick	11	– not out	20
*M. W. Gatting c French b Stephenson	30		
M. R. Ramprakash c Martindale b Hemmings	132		
K. R. Brown not out	200		
†P. R. Downton c Stephenson b Cooper	63		
J. E. Emburey not out	22		
B 5, l-b 10, n-b 8	23		

1/38 2/42 3/108 4/296 5/464   (5 wkts dec.) 510   (no wkt) 64

N. F. Williams, A. R. C. Fraser, P. C. R. Tufnell and N. G. Cowans did not bat.

Bonus points – Middlesex 4, Nottinghamshire 1 (Score at 100 overs: 304-4).

Bowling: *First Innings*—Stephenson 33-5-89-2; Cooper 31-3-134-1; Pick 22-3-79-1; Afford 29-10-76-0; Hemmings 29.3-2-117-1. *Second Innings*—Cooper 5-1-10-0; Hemmings 7-0-31-0; Afford 3-1-23-0.

Nottinghamshire

B. C. Broad b Tufnell	38	– b Fraser	20
M. Newell lbw b Williams	6	– b Cowans	80
*R. T. Robinson lbw b Cowans	57	– run out	105
P. Johnson c Williams b Tufnell	2	– retired hurt	12
D. J. R. Martindale c Brown b Tufnell	32	– c Gatting b Fraser	11
F. D. Stephenson c Downton b Cowans	7	– c Downton b Cowans	20
†B. N. French not out	40	– c Downton b Cowans	1
E. E. Hemmings c Tufnell b Williams	3	– c Brown b Emburey	6
K. E. Cooper lbw b Fraser	5	– (10) b Cowans	21
R. A. Pick b Williams	35	– (9) lbw b Emburey	26
J. A. Afford b Tufnell	3	– not out	0
L-b 3, w 1, n-b 3	7	B 9, l-b 10, w 1, n-b 13	33

1/8 2/71 3/87 4/130 5/142   235   1/32 2/211 3/240 4/273 5/277   335
6/144 7/150 8/155 9/220   6/285 7/297 8/335 9/335

Bonus points – Nottinghamshire 2, Middlesex 4 (Score at 100 overs: 229-9).

In the second innings P. Johnson retired hurt at 232.

Bowling: *First Innings*—Fraser 23-5-63-1; Williams 13-4-41-3; Cowans 14-2-26-2; Emburey 25-7-33-0; Tufnell 26.5-6-69-4. *Second Innings*—Fraser 34-9-84-2; Cowans 24-11-46-4; Emburey 43-14-85-2; Tufnell 47-16-93-0; Haynes 2-1-8-0.

Umpires: D. J. Constant and A. G. T. Whitehead.

At The Oval, September 12, 13, 14, 15. MIDDLESEX drew with SURREY.

At Hove, September 18, 19, 20. MIDDLESEX beat SUSSEX by an innings and 57 runs.

NORTHAMPTONSHIRE

Patron: The Earl of Dalkeith
President: W. R. F. Chamberlain
Chairman: L. A. Wilson
Chairman, Cricket Committee: A. P. Arnold
Secretary: S. P. Coverdale
  County Ground, Wantage Road,
  Northampton NN1 4TJ
  (Telephone: 0604-32917)
Captain: A. J. Lamb
Coach: R. M. Carter
Cricket Development Officer: B. L. Reynolds

Northamptonshire retained the unwanted title of the county circuit's principal under-achievers after failing, for the tenth season running, to capture a major honour. By reaching the NatWest Bank Trophy final, they gave themselves a chance to erase at least some of the earlier disappointments, but an emphatic seven-wicket defeat at the hands of Lancashire served only to expose to a wider public many of the shortcomings apparent to regular followers throughout the season.

The Britannic Assurance Championship campaign began promisingly enough, Alan Fordham and Allan Lamb hitting double-centuries in an innings win at Headingley, and ended with victories against Essex, contenders for the title, and Leicestershire in the last two games. The intervening period, however, featured a solitary win in a run-chase against Somerset at Taunton; and much of the cricket played by the team was, at best, mediocre. For the first time since 1951, Northamptonshire did not win a single Championship match at their own headquarters, and although the late rally enabled them to finish eleventh, this was still a drop of six places on 1989. All this, together with another wretched showing to take the Refuge Assurance League wooden spoon, and the early exit from the Benson and Hedges Cup, prompted understandable consternation among supporters. Lamb had already attended a "clear the air" meeting with a group of them in mid-season.

Much discussion centred around the on-field leadership, particularly the lack of continuity brought about by Lamb's frequent absences on international duty. Injuries at various times to the vice-captain, Wayne Larkins, and the senior cricketer, Nick Cook, did not help the situation, and as early as May 12 Northamptonshire were being led by the fourth choice, Robert Bailey, who displayed a level-headed approach during his short spell in charge. By September, Lamb himself was supporting the appointment of a cricket manager to be in attendance with the team.

Few excuses could legitimately be offered for the succession of poor performances, although the club's inability to field the strongest eleven on more than a handful of occasions was a source of intense frustration. All the recognised bowlers were sidelined with fitness problems at some stage, and the back injury suffered by the key all-rounder, David Capel, led to a reappraisal of his long-term role in the side. Physiotherapist Richie Norman was frequently the man most in demand at the County Ground, never more so than during the traumatic and portentous Championship game with Derbyshire in early May. Northamptonshire, batting three men short in the second innings, lost inside two days by an innings, and from that low point the season never completely recovered.

The majority of outstanding individual performances came from the batsmen. Bailey failed by just 13 runs to achieve 2,000 for the county, and his tally of seven hundreds was one short of R. A. Haywood's 69-year-old Northamptonshire record. He blossomed in the second half of the summer, whereas Capel shone most brightly in June and July, his purple patch producing three memorable centuries in a week. Lamb was also at his best, when available, and comfortably headed Northamptonshire's first-class averages.

The new opening partnership of Fordham and Nigel Felton replaced the "old firm" of Larkins and Geoff Cook. Fordham built impressively on the foundations laid during the previous year to score 1,767 runs in his first full season, while Felton, often thriving in adversity, played many valuable innings. They formed an excellent understanding and ran well between the wickets to capitalise on the advantages enjoyed by a left- and right-hand combination. In contrast, Larkins, his newly revived international career jeopardised again by a badly broken finger, which caused a seven-week lay-off, struggled to find consistent form. A timely 207 against Gooch's Essex secured his place on England's winter tour to Australia.

Geoff Cook announced in June his intention to retire at the end of the season, and immediately drifted out of the side. There were occasions when one yearned for Cook's batting experience and determination, and it was pleasing to witness the warm reception afforded him by the Northampton crowd when he and Larkins opened together for the last time in the Refuge game against Gloucestershire.

In a summer heavy with prolific run-scoring around the country, only Curtly Ambrose exceeded 50 wickets for Northamptonshire, saving his best effort – twelve for 155 – until the final Championship fixture at Leicester. The club hope he will return in 1992, after the West Indies tour of England this summer. However, his overseas colleague, Winston Davis, was not retained at the end of a season which had offered him few opportunities, with the consequent decline in his confidence.

Mark Robinson was promoted to take the new ball in the absence of the injured Capel and Greg Thomas, and while his first-class figures did not always do him justice, he could never be faulted for lack of effort. He enjoyed some well-deserved success in the NatWest quarter- and semi-final matches, in which he twice kept his head during the hectic closing overs to secure victory for his side. Like so many others in the squad, Nick Cook fought a year-long battle for full fitness, and neither he nor fellow-spinner Richard Williams could look back on the summer with a great deal of satisfaction. In mitigation, the bowlers did not always receive adequate fielding support. Important catches were missed, and David Ripley was generally a little below his best behind the stumps.

Despite Northamptonshire's immediate problems, the quality of their rising generation offered genuine hope for the future. Tony Penberthy, Wayne Noon, Andy Roberts and John Hughes have all sampled life in the first team, and it should not be long before a trio of talented young batsmen – Russell Warren, Malachy Loye and Richard Montgomerie – do likewise. The kind of cricketing environment they inherit at Northampton, though, depends on the club's response to the tribulations of 1990. – Andrew Radd.

NORTHAMPTONSHIRE 1990

[*Bill Smith*]

Back row: J. W. Govan, J. G. Hughes, A. L. Penberthy, A. Walker, W. W. Davis, D. J. Wild, D. J. Ripley, R. J. Warren, P. J. Berry, A. R. Roberts. *Middle row*: R. Norman (*physiotherapist*), R. R. Montgomerie, M. B. Loye, S. J. Brown, M. A. Robinson, C. E. L. Ambrose, J. G. Thomas, A. Fordham, W. M. Noon, N. A. Felton, R. M. Carter (*coach*). *Front row*: D. J. Capel, G. Cook, W. Larkins, A. J. Lamb (*captain*), N. G. B. Cook, R. J. Bailey, R. G. Williams.

NORTHAMPTONSHIRE RESULTS

All first-class matches – Played 24: Won 4, Lost 9, Drawn 11.

County Championship matches – Played 22: Won 4, Lost 9, Drawn 9.

Bonus points – Batting 61, Bowling 60.

Competition placings – Britannic Assurance County Championship, 11th;
NatWest Bank Trophy, finalists; Benson and Hedges Cup, 5th in Group D;
Refuge Assurance League, 17th.

BRITANNIC ASSURANCE CHAMPIONSHIP AVERAGES

BATTING

	Birthplace	M	I	NO	R	HI	Avge
‡A. J. Lamb	Langebaanweg, SA	10	16	3	1,040	235	80.00
‡R. J. Bailey	Biddulph	22	37	8	1,965	204*	67.75
‡A. Fordham	Bedford	22	38	2	1,653	206*	45.91
‡N. A. Felton	Guildford	20	35	2	1,484	122	44.96
‡D. J. Capel	Northampton	17	27	5	904	113	41.09
‡D. Ripley	Leeds	20	27	6	634	109*	30.19
‡W. Larkins	Roxton	15	25	0	701	207	28.04
‡R. G. Williams	Bangor	16	24	4	482	96	24.10
A. L. Penberthy ...	Troon	11	16	2	334	83	23.85
‡G. Cook	Middlesbrough	8	11	1	200	49	20.00
‡C. E. L. Ambrose ..	Swetes Village, Antigua	14	17	5	203	55*	16.91
‡W. W. Davis	Sion Hill, St Vincent	8	6	0	96	47	16.00
J. G. Thomas	Trebanos	11	11	2	131	48	14.55
‡N. G. B. Cook	Leicester	17	17	7	133	30	13.30
J. G. Hughes	Wellingborough	4	7	0	4	2	0.57
‡M. A. Robinson ..	Hull	17	16	10	3	1*	0.50

Also batted: S. J. Brown (*Cleadon*) (3 matches) 2, 4*; J. W. Govan (*Dunfermline*) (2 matches) 17, 4, 17; W. M. Noon (*Grimsby*) (2 matches) 2, 2; A. R. Roberts (*Kettering*) (2 matches) 5, 0, 0; ‡D. J. Wild (*Northampton*) (1 match) 17, 0.

* *Signifies not out.* ‡ *Denotes county cap.*

The following played a total of 24 three-figure innings for Northamptonshire in County Championship matches – R. J. Bailey 7, N. A. Felton 4, A. Fordham 4, A. J. Lamb 4, D. J. Capel 2, W. Larkins 2, D. Ripley 1.

BOWLING

	O	M	R	W	BB	5W/i	Avge
C. E. L. Ambrose	483.4	124	1,353	58	7-89	5	23.32
D. J. Capel	234	51	711	25	5-74	1	28.44
N. G. B. Cook	507.1	159	1,320	40	5-44	2	33.00
R. G. Williams	417.3	116	1,165	31	4-94	0	37.58
J. G. Thomas	288.2	49	1,098	28	7-75	1	39.21
A. L. Penberthy	196	23	768	19	4-91	0	40.42
M. A. Robinson	520.1	97	1,794	38	3-47	0	47.21
R. J. Bailey	168.2	29	604	11	3-82	0	54.90
W. W. Davis	216.5	26	747	12	3-28	0	62.25

Also bowled: S. J. Brown 52–7–221–4; N. A. Felton 19–1–113–1; A. Fordham 9–0–39–1; J. W. Govan 33–5–120–3; J. G. Hughes 66–12–293–3; W. Larkins 10–1–45–0; A. R. Roberts 63–14–207–3; D. J. Wild 12.5–4–42–0.

Wicket-keepers: D. Ripley 28 ct, 6 st; W. M. Noon 4 ct, 1 st.

Leading Fielders: A. Fordham 22, N. A. Felton 18, R. J. Bailey 16, D. J. Capel 15.

At Cambridge, April 14, 15, 16. NORTHAMPTONSHIRE drew with CAMBRIDGE UNIVERSITY.

At Leeds, April 26, 27, 28, 30. NORTHAMPTONSHIRE beat YORKSHIRE by an innings and 50 runs.

NORTHAMPTONSHIRE v DERBYSHIRE

At Northampton, May 3, 4. Derbyshire won by an innings and 51 runs. Derbyshire 23 pts, Northamptonshire 6 pts. Toss: Northamptonshire. Beset by injuries and faced with hostile fast bowling from Bishop and Malcolm, Northamptonshire capitulated inside two of the scheduled four days to give Derbyshire a most emphatic victory. The home side's problems began on the first morning, when Lamb tore a hamstring and was unable to take any further part in the match. Later in the day Nick Cook suffered a fractured knuckle from a blow on the hand off Malcolm, and Ripley could not take the field on the second day owing to a stomach ailment. With these three absent, Northamptonshire were dismissed in seventeen overs for their lowest first-class total since 1946; only Fordham, last out, offered any serious resistance. First time around Geoff Cook held the innings together during a 170-minute stay, but solid Derbyshire batting earned a lead of 101, which proved more than sufficient. Northamptonshire's substitute fielders included two members of the county's colts team, one of whom, Jonathan Swann, held a good catch to dismiss Griffith.

Close of play: First day, Derbyshire 55-1 (A. M. Brown 15*, C. J. Adams 9*).

Northamptonshire

A. Fordham c Krikken b Bishop	10	– (2) c and b Bishop	32
W. Larkins c Krikken b Malcolm	1	– (1) b Bishop	0
R. J. Bailey c Adams b Griffith	30	– b Malcolm	8
*A. J. Lamb retired hurt	14	– absent injured	
D. J. Capel c Roberts b Jean-Jacques	11	– lbw b Bishop	2
G. Cook run out	44	– (4) b Bishop	3
†D. Ripley c Roberts b Malcolm	17	– absent ill	
J. W. Govan lbw b Goldsmith	17	– (6) c Adams b Malcolm	4
W. W. Davis c Barnett b Malcolm	23	– (7) b Malcolm	0
N. G. B. Cook retired hurt	9	– absent injured	
M. A. Robinson not out	1	– (8) not out	0
B 4, l-b 9, w 6, n-b 6	25	W 1	1
	202		**50**

1/5 2/24 3/62 4/79 5/119   202   1/0 2/9 3/20 4/40 5/48   50
6/161 7/166 8/202   6/48 7/50

Bonus points – Northamptonshire 2, Derbyshire 3.

In the first innings A. J. Lamb retired hurt at 53 and N. G. B. Cook at 186.

Bowling: *First Innings*—Bishop 17–2–48–1; Malcolm 22.4–5–60–3; Jean-Jacques 17–3–39–1; Griffith 11–2–20–1; Goldsmith 11–2–21–1; Barnett 3–2–1–0. *Second Innings*—Bishop 9–2–25–4; Malcolm 8–2–25–3.

Derbyshire

P. D. Bowler lbw b Robinson	24	I. R. Bishop b Davis	19
A. M. Brown c Fordham b Govan	44	M. Jean-Jacques run out	4
C. J. Adams c Larkins b Capel	24	D. E. Malcolm not out	20
*K. J. Barnett c and b Capel	58		
B. Roberts lbw b Robinson	44	B 5, l-b 19, n-b 7	31
S. C. Goldsmith b Robinson	34		
F. A. Griffith c sub b Capel	1	1/37 2/71 3/142 4/183	303
†K. M. Krikken lbw b Capel	0	5/234 6/253 7/253 8/254 9/258	

Bonus points – Derbyshire 4, Northamptonshire 4.

Bowling: Davis 24.3–3–85–1; Capel 27–7–83–4; Robinson 28–8–80–3; Govan 14–5–19–1; Bailey 5–2–12–0.

Umpires: J. H. Harris and R. A. White.

NORTHAMPTONSHIRE v WARWICKSHIRE

At Northampton, May 15, 16, 17, 18. Warwickshire won by an innings and 30 runs. Warwickshire 23 pts, Northamptonshire 4 pts. Toss: Northamptonshire. A match in which controversy was no stranger ended in victory for Warwickshire 35 minutes into the fourth day. After a poor start the visitors, put in to bat by Bailey, recovered magnificently, initially through Kallicharran, who batted carefully for more than three hours, and then Reeve, the vice-captain. Reeve's unbeaten 202 (405 minutes, 355 balls, 4 sixes, 25 fours) was the highest individual innings for Warwickshire against Northamptonshire, beating F. R. Santall's 57-year-old record, and with Small and Donald helping him in century stands for the seventh and eighth wickets, Warwickshire built up an unassailable position. In the course of his innings Reeve, who survived a confident appeal for a catch behind when 103, received three "beamers" in quick succession from Ambrose. The bowler was duly warned by umpire Dudleston, and the following day Northamptonshire issued a statement, condemning such deliveries and promising strong disciplinary action in the event of any repetition. Dudleston was also instrumental in the removal of Robinson from the Northamptonshire attack for running on the pitch. After all these problems, the home team appeared to have little stomach for the fight and twice fell to Munton, who returned the best match figures of his career.

Close of play: First day, Warwickshire 286-6 (D. A. Reeve 82*, G. C. Small 42*); Second day, Northamptonshire 136-6 (G. Cook 32*, D. Ripley 23*); Third day, Northamptonshire 192-7 (D. Ripley 5*, J. G. Thomas 0*).

Warwickshire

A. J. Moles lbw b Thomas	13	A. A. Donald c Felton b Robinson	24	
*T. A. Lloyd c Ripley b Ambrose	21	J. E. Benjamin b Penberthy	14	
Asif Din lbw b Penberthy	3	T. A. Munton not out	1	
A. I. Kallicharran c and b Penberthy	72	B 4, l-b 28, w 7, n-b 8	47	
†G. W. Humpage c Ripley b Thomas	13			
D. A. Reeve not out	202	1/29 2/38 3/47	(9 wkts dec.) 473	
N. M. K. Smith b Penberthy	8	4/75 5/174 6/198		
G. C. Small c Felton b Robinson	55	7/317 8/419 9/458		

Bonus points – Warwickshire 3, Northamptonshire 2 (Score at 100 overs: 276-6).

Bowling: Ambrose 30-8-80-1; Thomas 28-5-84-2; Robinson 35.1-9-91-2; Penberthy 29.5-5-91-4; Wild 12.5-4-42-0; Williams 5-1-38-0; Bailey 8-1-15-0.

Northamptonshire

A. Fordham c Kallicharran b Munton	37	– c Humpage b Munton	18
N. A. Felton c Moles b Small	8	– c Small b Asif Din	75
*R. J. Bailey c Kallicharran b Small	0	– c Humpage b Munton	31
A. L. Penberthy run out	0	– lbw b Reeve	12
G. Cook lbw b Munton	33	– c Humpage b Reeve	13
R. G. Williams c Smith b Donald	8	– b Smith	9
D. J. Wild c Humpage b Small	17	– b Reeve	0
†D. Ripley c Humpage b Munton	36	– c Reeve b Munton	6
J. G. Thomas c Asif Din b Munton	30	– not out	14
C. E. L. Ambrose not out	11	– c Moles b Donald	16
M. A. Robinson c Kallicharran b Munton	1	– lbw b Munton	0
B 17, l-b 8, w 8, n-b 5	38	B 8, l-b 9, w 9, n-b 4	30

1/18 2/18 3/29 4/46 5/58	219	1/43 2/127 3/160 4/169 5/181	224
6/94 7/140 8/184 9/198		6/181 7/187 8/193 9/223	

Bonus points – Northamptonshire 2, Warwickshire 4.

Bowling: *First Innings*—Donald 20-5-51-1; Small 20-3-72-3; Munton 25.1-10-33-5; Benjamin 12-2-16-0; Smith 13-4-17-0; Asif Din 2-1-5-0. *Second Innings*—Munton 19.5-7-44-4; Small 7-1-34-0; Donald 14-2-45-1; Benjamin 9-2-23-0; Reeve 17-7-26-3; Smith 12-7-22-1; Asif Din 4-1-13-1.

Umpires: B. Dudleston and D. O. Oslear.

At Nottingham, May 23, 24, 25. NORTHAMPTONSHIRE lost to NOTTINGHAMSHIRE by eight wickets.

At Birmingham, June 2, 4, 5. NORTHAMPTONSHIRE drew with WARWICKSHIRE.

NORTHAMPTONSHIRE v LEICESTERSHIRE

At Northampton, June 6, 7, 8. Drawn. Northamptonshire 4 pts, Leicestershire 3 pts. Toss: Northamptonshire. Rain, which docked 78 overs from the first two days, prevented any play at all on the third, dashing hopes of a positive outcome which had been raised by Nick Cook's enterprising declaration, 166 runs behind, on the second afternoon. Benson (209 minutes, eleven fours) scored a maiden Championship half-century and received good support from Benjamin in a sixth-wicket stand worth 70 in fourteen overs. Northamptonshire made a purposeful reply, Fordham striking the ball handsomely on his way to 59 off 76 balls before the declaration.

Close of play: First day, Leicestershire 210-6 (J. D. R. Benson 57*, P. A. Nixon 20*); Second day, Leicestershire 46-2 (T. J. Boon 18*, P. Willey 20*).

Leicestershire

T. J. Boon c Capel b Thomas	4	– not out		18
*N. E. Briers b Thomas	6	– b Capel		5
J. J. Whitaker c N. G. B. Cook b Penberthy	35	– c and b Capel		3
P. Willey c Noon b Ambrose	34	– not out		20
L. Potter c Noon b Ambrose	14			
J. D. R. Benson c Capel b Penberthy	86			
W. K. M. Benjamin b Capel	33			
†P. A. Nixon b Ambrose	27			
J. P. Agnew c Noon b Capel	8			
A. D. Mullally not out	1			
D. J. Millns c Capel b Penberthy	1			
B 3, l-b 3, w 3, n-b 3	12			

1/6 2/13 3/81 4/83 5/112   261   1/13 2/17   (2 wkts) 46
6/182 7/223 8/259 9/259

Bonus points – Leicestershire 3, Northamptonshire 4.

Bowling: *First Innings*—Ambrose 23–6–54–3; Thomas 22–5–74–2; Capel 22–7–49–2; N. G. B. Cook 6–1–17–0; Penberthy 15.2–2–61–3. *Second Innings*—Capel 6–3–4–2; Thomas 4–0–12–0; Williams 9–3–19–0; N. G. B. Cook 7–3–11–0.

Northamptonshire

A. Fordham not out	59
N. A. Felton c Benjamin b Mullally	22
G. Cook not out	8
L-b 2, w 2, n-b 2	6

1/44   (1 wkt dec.) 95

R. J. Bailey, D. J. Capel, R. G. Williams, A. L. Penberthy, †W. M. Noon, J. G. Thomas, C. E. L. Ambrose and *N. G. B. Cook did not bat.

Bowling: Benjamin 11–2–33–0; Agnew 7–1–23–0; Mullally 5–0–17–1; Willey 1–0–1–0; Millns 2–0–19–0.

Umpires: J. D. Bond and P. B. Wight.

NORTHAMPTONSHIRE v GLAMORGAN

At Northampton, June 9, 11, 12. Glamorgan won by six wickets. Glamorgan 22 pts, Northamptonshire 8 pts. Toss: Northamptonshire. Batting of the highest calibre from Maynard and Richards guided Glamorgan to a first Championship victory at Northampton since their title-winning year of 1969. Set 307 to win in 72 overs, the visitors lost three wickets for 71 before their fourth-wicket pair took charge, adding 227 in 41 overs and totally dominating the home attack. Maynard batted for 169 minutes (150 balls) and hit a six and nineteen fours; Richards's 109 came off 111 balls in 164 minutes and contained four sixes and twelve fours. Northamptonshire, however, had only themselves to blame. Richards survived two chances before reaching 20, while Maynard was dropped in the slips when 19. The first day belonged to Capel, who unveiled his full range of strokes, hitting three sixes and sixteen fours during his two and a half hours (120 balls) at the crease. His brilliance tended to overshadow Felton's worthy effort which, although not chanceless, laid a solid foundation for which Capel could build. After a century opening stand between Morris and Butcher, Glamorgan ran into trouble against Thomas, who produced a career-best performance against his former county to earn Northamptonshire a lead of 91. With Capel again in sparkling form, the home side made good progress on the final morning after Frost had claimed three wickets in an over that spanned two days.

Close of play: First day, Glamorgan 16-0 (A. R. Butcher 2*, H. Morris 14*); Second day, Northamptonshire 91-2 (A. Fordham 37*, G. Cook 0*).

Northamptonshire

A. Fordham lbw b Frost	27	– lbw b Barwick	45
A. Felton c Richards b Barwick	122	– c Metson b Frost	44
G. Cook lbw b Frost	7	– (4) c Metson b Frost	0
R. J. Bailey c Metson b Barwick	38	– (5) not out	47
D. J. Capel c Metson b Frost	113	– (6) not out	64
A. L. Penberthy c Watkin b Barwick	1		
R. G. Williams c Metson b Frost	34		
W. M. Noon run out	2	– (3) lbw b Frost	2
J. G. Thomas not out	0		
L-b 4, n-b 2	6	B 6, l-b 4, w 3	13

1/50 2/62 3/149 4/267 (8 wkts dec.) 350 1/89 2/91 3/91 (4 wkts dec.) 215
5/283 6/342 7/350 8/350   4/124

C. E. L. Ambrose and *N. G. B. Cook did not bat.

Bonus points – Northamptonshire 4, Glamorgan 3.

Bowling: *First Innings*—Frost 23.2-6-82-4; Watkin 26-2-93-0; Barwick 24-4-76-3; Cowley 12-1-65-0; Richards 11-3-30-0. *Second Innings*—Frost 13-0-58-3; Watkin 13-1-66-0; Barwick 19.2-3-67-1; Cowley 6-0-14-0.

Glamorgan

A. R. Butcher b Williams	43	– st Noon b Williams	36
H. Morris lbw b Thomas	80	– c Noon b Williams	24
P. A. Cottey c Bailey b N. G. B. Cook	11	– lbw b Capel	2
I. V. A. Richards lbw b Thomas	25	– (5) c Fordham b Williams	109
N. G. Cowley lbw b Thomas	0		
C. P. Metson b Thomas	0		
M. P. Maynard lbw b Thomas	74	– (4) not out	125
G. C. Holmes c Bailey b N. G. B. Cook	9	– (6) not out	0
S. L. Watkin b Thomas	3		
S. R. Barwick not out	2		
M. Frost c Capel b Thomas	4		
B 2, l-b 5, n-b 1	8	B 3, l-b 4, w 5, n-b 1	13

1/102 2/131 3/137 4/137 259 1/58 2/61 3/71 (4 wkts) 309
5/145 6/178 7/208 8/248 9/253   4/298

Bonus points – Glamorgan 3, Northamptonshire 4.

Bowling: *First Innings*—Ambrose 20–4–65–0; Thomas 25–7–75–7; Penberthy 5–0–33–0;
Williams 19–5–42–1; Capel 6–0–20–0; N. G. B. Cook 11–2–17–2. *Second Innings*—Ambros
14–4–58–0; Thomas 10–0–68–0; Williams 13–2–51–3; Capel 7–2–17–1; N. G. B. Cool
19.4–1–108–0.

Umpires: J. D. Bond and P. B. Wight (B. Leadbeater deputised for P. B. Wight on 3rd day`

At Northampton, June 16, 17, 18. NORTHAMPTONSHIRE drew with NEW
ZEALANDERS (See New Zealand tour section).

NORTHAMPTONSHIRE v MIDDLESEX

At Luton, June 23, 25, 26. Middlesex won by 79 runs. Middlesex 23 pts, Northamptonshir
3 pts. Toss: Middlesex. The two Middlesex spinners, Emburey and Tufnell, claimed fifteen
wickets between them to clinch victory with 7.5 overs remaining, despite two skilful an
disciplined innings from Bailey. Although rain caused the loss of 26 overs on Saturday
Middlesex took the initiative as Roseberry and Gatting added 130. Roseberry, who hit thre
sixes and eight fours in an innings of 322 minutes, completed his century early on the secon
morning before Williams and Nick Cook took the last seven wickets for 67. It was then clea
that the slow men would hold sway for the rest of the game, and although Bailey managed t
avoid the follow-on for Northamptonshire with a single off the last ball of the day, the hom
side trailed by 144. Haynes and Roseberry then attacked seamers and spinners alike, givin
Gatting the opportunity to set a generous target of 252 in 81 overs. Once the fourth-wicke
stand between Bailey and Capel was broken, however, a Middlesex win always looked likel
Bailey was again last out, having batted for more than seven and a half hours in the matc
with minimal support, no-one else reaching 20 in either innings.
Close of play: First day, Middlesex 252-3 (M. A. Roseberry 98*, K. R. Brown 35*); Secon
day, Northamptonshire 195-9 (R. J. Bailey 68*, M. A. Robinson 0*).

Middlesex

D. L. Haynes c G. Cook b Ambrose	9	– not out	69
M. A. Roseberry c and b N. G. B. Cook	115	– c Fordham b Ambrose	36
*M. W. Gatting c Felton b Ambrose	62	– c Ripley b Ambrose	0
M. R. Ramprakash b Williams	26	– not out	0
K. R. Brown b N. G. B. Cook	69		
†P. Farbrace c Robinson b Williams	0		
J. E. Emburey st Ripley b Williams	13		
N. F. Williams st Ripley b Williams	14		
P. C. R. Tufnell c Williams b N. G. B. Cook	8		
A. R. C. Fraser not out	1		
S. P. Hughes c G. Cook b N. G. B. Cook	1		
B 2, l-b 9, n-b 15	26	W 1, n-b 1	2

1/17 2/147 3/191 4/277 5/278   344   1/107 2/107   (2 wkts dec.) 107
6/302 7/328 8/339 9/342

Bonus points – Middlesex 3, Northamptonshire 2 (Score at 100 overs: 294-5).

Bowling: *First Innings*—Ambrose 18–4–53–2; Thomas 17–3–40–0; Robinson 19–6–46–0
N. G. B. Cook 28.4–4–79–4; Capel 6–0–21–0; Williams 35–6–94–4. *Second Innings*—Ambrose
11–2–38–2; Thomas 6–0–38–0; N. G. B. Cook 4–0–31–0; Robinson 0.3–0–0–0.

Northamptonshire

A. Fordham c Farbrace b Williams	4	– c and b Fraser	7
N. A. Felton lbw b Williams	19	– c Brown b Tufnell	11
G. Cook c Roseberry b Emburey	8	– c Farbrace b Fraser	1
R. J. Bailey c Roseberry b Emburey	73	– b Tufnell	87
D. J. Capel c Gatting b Tufnell	12	– st Farbrace b Tufnell	15
R. G. Williams c Roseberry b Emburey	4	– c Gatting b Emburey	11
D. Ripley run out	17	– c Roseberry b Emburey	5
J. G. Thomas lbw b Emburey	0	– b Emburey	5
N. G. B. Cook c Roseberry b Tufnell	18	– c Brown b Tufnell	0
C. E. L. Ambrose b Tufnell	6	– c and b Tufnell	3
M. A. Robinson not out	0	– not out	0
B 10, l-b 8, w 1, n-b 20	39	B 6, l-b 6, n-b 15	27

1/5 2/34 3/40 4/72 5/86   200   1/7 2/9 3/36 4/94 5/118   172
6/113 7/126 8/178 9/194   6/133 7/150 8/155 9/166

Bonus points – Northamptonshire 1, Middlesex 4 (Score at 100 overs: 198-9).

Bowling: *First Innings*—Williams 9–1–23–2; Fraser 10–1–22–0; Emburey 44.1–17–55–4; Tufnell 38–8–80–3; Ramprakash 1–0–2–0. *Second Innings*—Williams 5–1–12–0; Fraser 6–2–11–2; Emburey 33–5–80–3; Tufnell 30.1–7–57–5.

Umpires: N. T. Plews and R. A. White.

At Taunton, June 30, July 2, 3. NORTHAMPTONSHIRE beat SOMERSET by seven wickets.

At The Oval, July 4, 5, 6. NORTHAMPTONSHIRE lost to SURREY by 147 runs.

NORTHAMPTONSHIRE v YORKSHIRE

At Northampton, July 7, 9, 10. Drawn. Northamptonshire 6 pts, Yorkshire 7 pts. Toss: Yorkshire. Cook played out the last over from Carrick to earn the home side a draw in a match which came to life on the final afternoon. Set 314 for victory in 55 overs, Northamptonshire prospered thanks to an opening partnership of 115 before Felton (170 minutes, one six, ten fours) and Capel added 127 at 7 per over to bring the target down to 62. The charge was halted, however, by the departure of both batsmen in consecutive overs, and with Carrick and Fletcher sharing another five wickets in quick succession, Yorkshire were closer to victory at the end. The first two days saw each side collect maximum batting points, Yorkshire achieving them when Hartley hit the last two balls of the 100th over, from Williams, for six. Overall, though, the most memorable feature of the game was the strokeplay of Capel, whose 83 in the second innings came in just 60 deliveries with two sixes and ten fours.

Close of play: First day, Yorkshire 318; Second day, Yorkshire 62-0 (R. J. Blakey 18*, A. A. Metcalfe 39*).

Yorkshire

R. J. Blakey c Felton b Ambrose	17	– c Bailey b Cook	57
A. A. Metcalfe b Cook	48	– c and b Bailey	79
K. Sharp retired hurt	40		
P. E. Robinson b Cook	58	– not out	76
D. Byas lbw b Cook	28	– c Ripley b Fordham	35
C. A. Chapman c Felton b Williams	5	– (3) c Fordham b Bailey	17
C. White c Felton b Cook	38	– (6) not out	29
P. Carrick c Capel b Robinson	27		
P. J. Hartley c Fordham b Williams	40		
S. D. Fletcher lbw b Cook	0		
J. Houseman not out	0		
B 2, l-b 8, w 1, n-b 6	17	L-b 4, w 1, n-b 4	9

1/50 2/97 3/203 4/204 5/222   318   1/143 2/143 3/187 (4 wkts dec.) 302
6/263 7/318 8/318 9/318   4/260

Bonus points – Yorkshire 4, Northamptonshire 2 (Score at 100 overs: 304-6).

In the first innings K. Sharp retired hurt at 129.

Bowling: *First Innings*—Ambrose 12–0–42–1; Capel 5–0–24–0; Robinson 22–3–67–1; Cook 25–10–44–5; Penberthy 12–2–32–0; Williams 27.2–5–99–2. *Second Innings*—Robinson 12–2–50–0; Capel 6–1–17–0; Cook 14–6–25–1; Williams 4–1–6–0; Penberthy 6–0–29–0; Bailey 24.2–3–81–2; Felton 12–0–65–0; Fordham 5–0–25–1.

Northamptonshire

A. Fordham c Blakey b Hartley	12	– c Metcalfe b Fletcher	59
N. A. Felton c Fletcher b Carrick	66	– b Carrick	106
R. J. Bailey b Hartley	0	– c and b Carrick	6
D. J. Capel c Metcalfe b Fletcher	64	– b Fletcher	83
*W. Larkins c Hartley b Fletcher	15	– c and b Carrick	4
R. G. Williams run out	69	– st Blakey b Carrick	2
A. L. Penberthy c and b Carrick	8	– c and b Fletcher	1
†D. Ripley not out	34	– c Blakey b Fletcher	16
N. G. B. Cook run out	30	– (10) not out	1
C. E. L. Ambrose (did not bat)		– (9) b Fletcher	14
M. A. Robinson (did not bat)		– not out	0
L-b 5, n-b 4	9	B 2, l-b 4, n-b 2	8

1/52 2/52 3/107 4/156 5/169 (8 wkts dec.) 307
6/200 7/257 8/307

1/115 2/125 3/252 (9 wkts) 300
4/264 5/268 6/269
7/271 8/299 9/300

Bonus points – Northamptonshire 4, Yorkshire 3 (Score at 100 overs: 306-7).

Bowling: *First Innings*—Hartley 15.2–2–56–2; Fletcher 17–6–44–2; Houseman 12–1–53–0; Carrick 37–9–91–2; White 10–1–39–0; Byas 9–1–19–0. *Second Innings*—Hartley 11–0–66–0; Fletcher 18–0–94–5; Houseman 6–0–36–0; Carrick 20–1–98–4.

Umpires: J. C. Balderstone and A. A. Jones.

NORTHAMPTONSHIRE v KENT

At Northampton, July 18, 19, 20. Drawn. Northamptonshire 8 pts, Kent 4 pts. Toss: Northamptonshire. Northamptonshire recovered from the early loss of both openers to equal their highest Championship total against Kent, benefiting from two significant middle-order partnerships. First Felton and Capel posted 146 for the third wicket, and then Bailey (228 minutes three sixes, twelve fours) was assisted by Williams in a fifth-wicket stand worth 187 in 51 overs. Capel hit 74 of his 85 runs in boundaries, three sixes among them. Kent's reply owed much to Taylor who, alone of the early batsmen, came to terms with the hostility of Ambrose. The West Indian claimed four for 10 in 24 balls, and despite Taylor's three-and-a-half-hour stay, followed by stubborn efforts from Davis, Patel and Igglesden, Kent followed on 162 behind late on the second day. With the pitch becoming progressively easier, they encountered few problems in saving the match. Davis, promoted to open in the absence of the injured Benson, and Hinks put on 131, and Chris Cowdrey (148 minutes) brightened the closing overs with some attractive strokes as he reached a century containing a six and seventeen fours.

Close of play: First day, Northamptonshire 445-8 (R. J. Bailey 138*, C. E. L. Ambrose 0*); Second day, Kent 21-0 (S. G. Hinks 10*, R. P. Davis 10*).

Northamptonshire

A. Fordham c Marsh b Igglesden	2	N. G. B. Cook c C. S. Cowdrey b Ellison	1
*W. Larkins c Marsh b de Villiers	12	C. E. L. Ambrose not out	0
N. A. Felton b Patel	90		
D. J. Capel c Taylor b Igglesden	85	L-b 12	12
R. J. Bailey not out	138		
R. G. Williams c Ellison b de Villiers	96	1/5 2/29 3/175 (8 wkts dec.) 445
†D. Ripley b Ellison	7	4/207 5/394 6/409
S. J. Brown b Ellison	2	7/419 8/441

M. A. Robinson did not bat.

Bonus points – Northamptonshire 4, Kent 1 (Score at 100 overs: 378-4).

Bowling: de Villiers 20–2–78–2; Igglesden 14–2–41–2; Ellison 21–1–85–3; C. S. Cowdrey 9–0–39–0; Davis 24–4–109–0; Patel 22–4–81–1.

Kent

S. G. Hinks c Capel b Ambrose	5	– b Cook	83
M. R. Benson c Ripley b Ambrose	10		
N. R. Taylor c Fordham b Cook	97	– b Bailey	36
G. R. Cowdrey c Larkins b Ambrose	0	– c Felton b Ambrose	4
*C. S. Cowdrey c Fordham b Ambrose	0	– not out	107
†S. A. Marsh c Felton b Brown	29	– not out	25
R. M. Ellison c Ripley b Robinson	24		
R. P. Davis c Capel b Bailey	43	– (2) c Bailey b Cook	41
P. S. de Villiers c and b Williams	0		
M. M. Patel not out	41		
A. P. Igglesden b Ambrose	24		
L-b 2, w 1, n-b 7	10	B 4, l-b 2, n-b 3	9

1/15 2/42 3/45 4/49 5/94   283   1/131 2/132 3/151   (4 wkts dec.) 305
6/143 7/202 8/203 9/230   4/210

Bonus points – Kent 3, Northamptonshire 4.

Bowling: *First Innings*—Ambrose 19–4–59–5; Brown 15–1–81–1; Robinson 19–3–75–1; Cook 25–17–33–1; Williams 18–7–28–1; Bailey 3–2–5–1. *Second Innings*—Ambrose 18–7–47–1; Robinson 10–2–19–0; Williams 22–8–67–0; Brown 8–2–22–0; Cook 28–13–59–2; Bailey 19–3–71–1; Fordham 4–0–14–0.

Umpires: B. Hassan and B. Leadbeater.

NORTHAMPTONSHIRE v SUSSEX

At Northampton, July 21, 23, 24. Drawn. Northamptonshire 7 pts, Sussex 5 pts. Toss: Sussex. Even on an easy-paced pitch and with a depleted attack, Northamptonshire erred on the side of caution in setting Sussex 389 to win in 64 overs. In the event, some indiscreet batting allowed the home side a glimpse of victory, but a level-headed century from Alan Wells ensured a draw. This, once Northamptonshire had weathered some testing new-ball bowling on the first morning, had always appeared the most likely result. Lamb was at his brutal best, hitting a six and 22 fours in a 158-ball innings of great power and dominating an unbroken fifth-wicket partnership of 105 with Bailey. Sussex responded with an even display in which Parker was outstanding, but events on the last day bordered on the farcical when the visitors, having reduced Northamptonshire to 183 for five – just 210 ahead – opted to feed runs to Bailey. He duly helped himself to the third double-century of his career, featuring five sixes and 27 fours, before Lamb's guarded declaration.

Close of play: First day, Sussex 35-0 (N. J. Lenham 27*, J. W. Hall 7*); Second day, Northamptonshire 110-2 (N. A. Felton 37*, R. J. Bailey 34*).

Northamptonshire

A. Fordham c C. M. Wells b Pigott	9	– c Lenham b Bunting	26
W. Larkins b Pigott	61	– lbw b Pigott	11
N. A. Felton c Moores b Dodemaide	78	– c Speight b Dodemaide	42
*A. J. Lamb not out	135	– (6) b A. P. Wells	1
D. J. Capel c Speight b Bunting	12	– b Lenham	29
R. J. Bailey not out	24	– (4) not out	204
†D. Ripley (did not bat)		– not out	44
B 4, l-b 6	10	B 1, l-b 3	4

1/11 2/136 3/179 4/224   (4 wkts dec.) 329   1/30 2/42 3/118   (5 wkts dec.) 361
                                       4/178 5/183

S. J. Brown, W. W. Davis, N. G. B. Cook and M. A. Robinson did not bat.

Bonus points – Northamptonshire 4, Sussex 1.

Bowling: *First Innings*—Dodemaide 21–4–55–1; Pigott 19–2–83–2; C. M. Wells 20–6–42–0; Bunting 23–6–79–1; Salisbury 7–1–36–0; Lenham 8–3–24–0. *Second Innings*—Dodemaide 12–1–26–1; Pigott 5–0–28–1; Bunting 15–1–68–1; C. M. Wells 4–2–10–0; Lenham 13.5–1–78–1; A. P. Wells 16–4–88–1; Parker 8–0–59–0.

Sussex

N. J. Lenham c Felton b Davis	41	– lbw b Robinson	38
J. W. Hall lbw b Cook	42	– b Brown	7
*P. W. G. Parker lbw b Davis	90	– lbw b Robinson	38
A. P. Wells c Bailey b Brown	21	– not out	102
M. P. Speight c Bailey b Cook	2	– b Bailey	13
C. M. Wells b Cook	42	– c Lamb b Bailey	6
A. I. C. Dodemaide c Ripley b Robinson	26	– c Fordham b Bailey	14
†P. Moores b Cook	10	– c Cook b Robinson	8
A. C. S. Pigott not out	5	– not out	17
I. D. K. Salisbury not out	0		
L-b 9, w 2, n-b 12	23	B 4, l-b 1, n-b 3	8

1/61 2/120 3/163 4/166 5/239   (8 wkts dec.) 302   1/25 2/78 3/89 4/111   (7 wkts) 251
6/264 7/295 8/299   5/131 6/174 7/209

R. A. Bunting did not bat.

Bonus points – Sussex 4, Northamptonshire 3.

Bowling: *First Innings*—Davis 21–5–75–2; Robinson 17.1–3–61–1; Cook 31–9–89–4; Brown 14–3–46–1; Bailey 3–0–22–0. *Second Innings*—Brown 7–0–41–1; Robinson 17–2–68–3; Cook 13–4–21–0; Bailey 20–2–82–3; Larkins 6–1–21–0; Capel 1–0–13–0.

Umpires: B. Hassan and B. Leadbeater.

At Cheltenham, July 25, 26, 27. **NORTHAMPTONSHIRE** lost to **GLOUCESTERSHIRE** by an innings and 128 runs.

At Bournemouth, August 4, 6. **NORTHAMPTONSHIRE** lost to **HAMPSHIRE** by an innings and 22 runs.

At Chesterfield, August 8, 9, 10. **NORTHAMPTONSHIRE** drew with **DERBYSHIRE**.

NORTHAMPTONSHIRE v LANCASHIRE

At Northampton, August 11, 13, 14. Drawn. Northamptonshire 6 pts, Lancashire 5 pts. Toss: Northamptonshire. In fourth place and still in contention for the Championship title, Lancashire chose to rest several players and nearly came unstuck after being set 253 to win. With Davis producing his best spell of the season, they lost wickets at regular intervals and were grateful for Fowler's two and a quarter hours of defence. Northamptonshire enjoyed a highly successful first day as Fordham took complete command, batting for 272 minutes and hitting three sixes and 25 fours. Felton, Larkins and Bailey all lent excellent support. Lloyd batted beautifully for the visitors before throwing away a most promising start when he tried to charge Cook. Nevertheless, progress was generally sound rather than spectacular until DeFreitas launched a thrilling assault, completing a superb hundred off 94 deliveries with four sixes and eleven fours. Hughes declared 88 behind and Northamptonshire, although faltering briefly when three wickets went for 20 on the last morning, were able to issue a realistic challenge after Ripley had cashed in against the occasional bowlers.

Close of play: First day, Lancashire 23-0 (G. D. Mendis 15*, G. Fowler 8*); Second day, Northamptonshire 14-0 (A. Fordham 3*, N. A. Felton 11*).

Northamptonshire

A. Fordham c Bramhall b Patterson	172	– lbw b DeFreitas	24
N. A. Felton c DeFreitas b Hughes	66	– c Hughes b DeFreitas	51
*W. Larkins b Hughes	56		
R. J. Bailey not out	62	– (3) st Bramhall b Hughes	30
D. J. Capel c DeFreitas b Hughes	19	– (4) c Jesty b Hughes	9
R. G. Williams not out	11	– (5) not out	10
†D. Ripley (did not bat)		– (6) c Speak b Fowler	34
S. J. Brown (did not bat)		– (7) not out	4
B 14, l-b 14, n-b 7	35	L-b 2	2

1/179 2/294 3/325 4/365   (4 wkts dec.) 421   1/47 2/94 3/109   (5 wkts dec.) 164
                                               4/114 5/155

W. W. Davis, N. G. B. Cook and M. A. Robinson did not bat.

Bonus points – Northamptonshire 4, Lancashire 1.

Bowling: *First Innings*—Patterson 14–2–54–1; DeFreitas 15–3–59–0; Martin 17–3–64–0; Austin 24–5–73–0; Hughes 30–1–143–3. *Second Innings*—Patterson 6–0–32–0; Martin 5–0–15–0; DeFreitas 11–3–23–2; Hughes 13–4–45–2; Jesty 2–2–0–0; Fowler 2.1–0–33–1; Lloyd 2–0–14–0.

Lancashire

G. D. Mendis b Brown	50	– c Capel b Davis	5
G. Fowler c Felton b Davis	30	– c Williams b Davis	47
G. D. Lloyd st Ripley b Cook	59	– c Ripley b Robinson	8
T. E. Jesty c Capel b Robinson	56	– lbw b Cook	8
N. J. Speak c Cook b Williams	5	– b Capel	0
P. A. J. DeFreitas not out	100	– st Ripley b Cook	15
I. D. Austin run out	5	– c Bailey b Davis	11
*D. P. Hughes not out	1	– not out	1
†S. Bramhall (did not bat)		– not out	0
B 4, l-b 12, w 1, n-b 10	27	L-b 6, w 1, n-b 8	15

1/79 2/84 3/180 4/199   (6 wkts dec.) 333   1/10 2/36 3/58 4/59   (7 wkts) 110
5/294 6/331   5/84 6/95 7/108

P. J. Martin and B. P. Patterson did not bat.

Bonus points – Lancashire 4, Northamptonshire 2.

Bowling: *First Innings*—Davis 25–2–85–1; Robinson 18.2–1–81–1; Cook 21–12–53–1; Capel 6–2–10–0; Brown 8–1–31–1; Williams 19–7–57–1. *Second Innings*—Davis 14.4–2–28–3; Robinson 6–1–19–1; Williams 9–4–16–0; Capel 8–1–22–1; Cook 7–2–19–2.

Umpires: J. H. Harris and D. S. Thompsett.

At Worcester, August 18, 20, 21. NORTHAMPTONSHIRE drew with WORCESTERSHIRE.

NORTHAMPTONSHIRE v GLOUCESTERSHIRE

At Northampton, August 23, 24, 25, 27. Gloucestershire won by 157 runs. Gloucestershire 22 pts, Northamptonshire 5 pts. Toss: Gloucestershire. The batting of Alleyne was the feature of a match which Gloucestershire won with virtually 25 overs to spare, completing their first double over Northamptonshire since 1961. The 22-year-old hit 38 fours and displayed remarkable powers of concentration, as well as a full range of strokes, during his 439-minute stay. He became the county's youngest double-centurion in the Championship – D. N. Moore was nineteen when he scored 206 against Oxford University in 1930 – and his was the highest score recorded by any Gloucestershire batsman since W. R. Hammond's 302 against Glamorgan at Newport in 1939. Northamptonshire were left needing 372 to avoid the follow-on and achieved this task for the loss of six wickets. Bailey (184 minutes, fourteen fours) passed 10,000 first-class runs for his county on his way to a responsible century. The visitors built purposefully on their lead of 119 to set a victory target of 366 in 72 overs, and although Ripley offered late resistance, a four-wicket burst from Walsh decided the outcome. His victims included Capel, who suffered a broken finger when he gloved a catch to silly point.

Close of play: First day, Gloucestershire 271-4 (M. W. Alleyne 132*, K. M. Curran 9*); Second day, Northamptonshire 169-2 (W. Larkins 32*, R. J. Bailey 18*); Third day, Gloucestershire 143-3 (C. W. J. Athey 34*, M. W. Alleyne 30*).

Gloucestershire

G. D. Hodgson c Ripley b Ambrose	4	– lbw b Ambrose 22
*A. J. Wright c Felton b Capel	11	– c Felton b Thomas 4
P. Bainbridge c Ripley b Penberthy	19	– c Felton b Capel 45
C. W. J. Athey lbw b Capel	79	– not out 88
M. W. Alleyne c Cook b Penberthy	256	– lbw b Ambrose 38
K. M. Curran c Ripley b Williams	19	– b Penberthy 19
J. W. Lloyds b Cook	35	– not out 16
†R. C. J. Williams not out	35	
C. A. Walsh c Penberthy b Cook	31	
D. V. Lawrence c Bailey b Penberthy	3	
M. C. J. Ball c and b Cook	4	
B 2, l-b 21, w 1, n-b 1	25	B 5, l-b 9 14

1/10 2/33 3/47 4/246 5/297   521   1/10 2/54 3/75   (5 wkts dec.) 246
6/390 7/472 8/511 9/517   4/163 5/220

Bonus points – Gloucestershire 3, Northamptonshire 1 (Score at 100 overs: 289-4).

Bowling: *First Innings*—Ambrose 27–5–77–1; Thomas 19–6–58–0; Capel 28–5–90–2; Penberthy 20–1–83–3; Cook 28–5–97–3; Williams 33–5–73–1; Bailey 3–0–20–0. *Second Innings*—Ambrose 16–7–35–2; Thomas 13–2–59–1; Penberthy 11–1–51–1; Capel 8–2–16–1; Cook 17–1–58–0; Williams 5–0–13–0.

Northamptonshire

A. Fordham st Williams b Bainbridge	64	– lbw b Lawrence 41
N. A. Felton b Bainbridge	41	– c Lloyds b Walsh 15
*W. Larkins c Williams b Lawrence	36	– b Walsh 1
R. J. Bailey c Hodgson b Lawrence	105	– c Wright b Walsh 4
D. J. Capel b Lawrence	38	– c Ball b Walsh 2
R. G. Williams b Walsh	0	– b Curran 15
A. L. Penberthy c Hodgson b Alleyne	28	– c Williams b Curran 18
†D. Ripley lbw b Curran	34	– not out 41
J. G. Thomas b Curran	0	– b Lloyds 5
C. E. L. Ambrose lbw b Lawrence	10	– st Williams b Lloyds 18
N. G. B. Cook not out	0	– c Wright b Lawrence 11
B 11, l-b 8, w 6, n-b 20	45	B 8, l-b 8, w 4, n-b 17 ... 37

1/99 2/133 3/174 4/318 5/320   402   1/53 2/54 3/63 4/71 5/71   208
6/320 7/385 8/385 9/388   6/101 7/114 8/123 9/179

Bonus points – Northamptonshire 4, Gloucestershire 3 (Score at 100 overs: 385-7).

Bowling: *First Innings*—Walsh 18–3–63–1; Lawrence 24.5–2–90–4; Curran 22–2–68–2; Ball 6–1–35–0; Bainbridge 12–1–38–2; Alleyne 11–4–36–1; Lloyds 12–2–53–0. *Second Innings*—Walsh 19–3–101–4; Curran 7–1–17–2; Lawrence 13.1–1–53–2; Lloyds 8–1–21–2.

Umpires: P. J. Eele and K. E. Palmer.

NORTHAMPTONSHIRE v ESSEX

At Northampton, August 29, 30, 31. Drawn. Northamptonshire 7 pts, Essex 5 pts. Toss: Essex. Anxious for a victory in their quest for Championship honours, Essex were thwarted by another docile Northampton pitch on which 1,285 runs were scored in three innings for the loss of only seventeen wickets. The match began in controversial fashion, with Davis showing blatant dissent at umpire Lyons's decision when his appeal for leg-before against Gooch was turned down in the first over. The West Indian bowler was subsequently fined heavily by the club, and Gooch went on to dominate the home attack for four and a half hours (225 balls), hitting a six and 31 fours. However, this achievement was put in the shade as Northamptonshire beat their 76-year-old county record total in first-class cricket, only to surpass the new figure nine days later at Chelmsford. Larkins, in five and a half hours, survived four chances to register two sixes and 27 fours in his third double-hundred, while both Bailey (three sixes, ten fours) and Lamb (one six, 26 fours) completed centuries before the declaration came with five hours left for play. Any possibility of a result was soon discounted as Gooch (25 fours) passed the three-figure mark for the second time in the match, he and Stephenson becoming only the third pair ever to post a double-hundred opening stand in each innings of a first-class game.

Close of play: First day, Northamptonshire 18-1 (A. Fordham 11*, D. Ripley 5*); Second day, Northamptonshire 515-5 (A. J. Lamb 101*, R. G. Williams 1*).

Essex

*G. A. Gooch c and b Williams	174	– c Lamb b Bailey	126
J. P. Stephenson b Penberthy	76	– c Davis b Thomas	82
P. J. Prichard c Fordham b Williams	22	– not out	29
M. E. Waugh b Davis	1	– b Penberthy	16
N. Hussain not out	30	– b Penberthy	3
†M. A. Garnham lbw b Davis	1	– not out	23
D. R. Pringle lbw b Williams	1		
N. A. Foster c Fordham b Williams	50		
B 5, l-b 12, w 1, n-b 17	35	L-b 14, w 1, n-b 9	24

1/227 2/300 3/301 4/308 5/310   (7 wkts dec.) 390   1/220 2/231 3/254   (4 wkts dec.) 303
6/313 7/390   4/258

M. C. Ilott, P. M. Such and J. H. Childs did not bat.

Bonus points – Essex 4, Northamptonshire 3.

Bowling: *First Innings*—Davis 24-1-76-2; Robinson 14-0-75-0; Thomas 13-2-60-0; Penberthy 20-4-59-1; Williams 26.4-8-99-4; Bailey 1-0-4-0. *Second Innings*—Davis 5-0-37-0; Robinson 15-0-69-0; Thomas 14-3-49-1; Penberthy 14-1-67-2; Bailey 16-4-59-1; Williams 4-1-8-0; Felton 1-1-0-0.

Northamptonshire

A. Fordham lbw b Foster	16	R. G. Williams not out	21
N. A. Felton c Stephenson b Foster	0	A. L. Penberthy not out	15
†D. Ripley c Garnham b Waugh	50	B 14, l-b 21, n-b 6	41
W. Larkins c Waugh b Stephenson	207		
R. J. Bailey lbw b Pringle	108	1/9 2/45 3/94 (6 wkts dec.) 592	
*A. J. Lamb c Prichard b Such	134	4/303 5/514 6/561	

J. G. Thomas, W. W. Davis and M. A. Robinson did not bat.

Bonus points – Northamptonshire 4, Essex 1 (Score at 100 overs: 392-4).

Bowling: Foster 31-6-115-2; Ilott 27-4-115-0; Pringle 14-2-46-1; Waugh 19-1-96-1; Childs 14-4-46-0; Such 15-1-57-1; Stephenson 9-1-40-1; Gooch 6-0-42-0.

Umpires: D. J. Constant and K. J. Lyons.

At Chelmsford, September 7, 8, 9, 10. NORTHAMPTONSHIRE beat ESSEX by 276 runs.

At Leicester, September 12, 13, 14, 15. NORTHAMPTONSHIRE beat LEICESTERSHIRE by 171 runs.

NOTTINGHAMSHIRE

President: 1990 – J. W. Baddiley
Chairman: C. W. Gillott
Chairman, Cricket Committee: R. T. Simpson
General Manager/Secretary: B. Robson
  County Cricket Ground, Trent Bridge,
  Nottingham NG2 6AG
  (Telephone: 0602-821525)
Cricket Manager: 1990 – K. A. Taylor
              1991 – J. D. Birch
  Captain: R. T. Robinson

Nottinghamshire's fortunes underwent such a dramatic about-turn during 1990 that a season for which expectations were so high at one point ended in bitter disappointment. Where only a few months earlier there had been optimism, and talk of building on the 1989 Benson and Hedges Cup success, despondency settled on Trent Bridge. Only a top-four place in the Refuge Assurance League, to qualify for the Refuge Assurance Cup, held back the gloom as Nottinghamshire suffered seven defeats in their last eleven Britannic Assurance Championship games and plummeted to thirteenth, their lowest position for seven years.

At the beginning of June, however, the story had been quite different. Nottinghamshire, with three consecutive wins behind them, sat proudly atop the Championship table and were within one step of carrying their defence of the Benson and Hedges trophy back to Lord's. They were bubbling with confidence after eight wins in their last nine games in all cricket. Even more encouraging, in a summer in which a high proportion of Championship victories would be achieved by teams successfully chasing targets – an aspect of their game for which they had not previously been noted – Nottinghamshire had indicated that they were capable of meeting such challenges.

Yet it was the frailty of the Nottinghamshire batting that was responsible for the complexion of their season changing so drastically. All too often, a lack of application and consistency in the first innings gave their opponents the opportunity to seize the initiative, and only occasionally were Nottinghamshire able to regain it. Paul Pollard, who had made such an impression in 1989, experienced a traumatic time in 1990 and played just fourteen games of first-team cricket, while Derek Randall was hampered by injury all summer: this had an unsettling effect on a batting line-up which, on paper at least, looked particularly strong. Both Chris Broad and Tim Robinson, the captain, were available throughout the season, and Paul Johnson began the season as though determined to prove a point.

Broad, without any doubt, had an outstanding summer. He hit the first double-hundred of his career, 227 not out against Kent at Tunbridge Wells, passed 2,000 runs in a season for the first time, despite playing only in Championship matches, and his nine hundreds equalled the county record shared by W. W. Whysall and M. J. Harris, who accomplished the feat in 1928 and 1971 respectively. Rarely did a bad ball go unpunished; though considering Broad's reputation as a strong leg-side player, it was astonishing how many bowlers fed his strength with inviting deliveries. Robinson also hit a double-hundred, against Yorkshire, and finished the season with a flourish after experiencing a remarkable series of first-innings failures. Including the match in which Nottinghamshire forfeited, he did not reach double figures in nine successive first innings. Happily, the introduction of the Second Eleven captain, John Birch, to help with the running of the side towards the end of the season took a lot of weight off the captain's shoulders, and the benefit was seen in the form Robinson produced late on.

Johnson was anxious to show that he had matured from being merely a promising young player to an established middle-order batsman. For a time he succeeded, especially with his match-winning hundreds against Northamptonshire and Yorkshire. But old habits die hard, and there were too many occasions later in the season when he failed to turn sparkling cameos into more substantial contributions.

Nottinghamshire were no different from many other counties in that their bowlers, having been pampered for so long with "result" pitches, found the going considerably tougher as the balance swung in favour of batsmen. Given the change in conditions, the form of Andy Pick was most pleasing. Had his season been less disrupted by injury, the fast bowler might easily have figured among the country's leading wicket-takers. As it was, he made a good enough impression to earn selection for the England A tour to Pakistan in the winter. Franklyn Stephenson was troubled by fitness problems and never looked like reproducing his bowling form of the previous two summers. But his batting showed signs of greater consistency after a disappointing season in 1989.

An all-rounder who did excel was Kevin Evans. The 26-year-old's development into a reliable performer with bat and ball was rewarded when he was presented with his county cap, an honour also bestowed upon the left-arm spinner, Andy Afford. In Afford's case, the recognition was based on previous success rather than current performances, for his 38 Championship wickets cost him more than 47 runs apiece. With the county's most experienced bowler, Eddie Hemmings, required by England throughout the summer, Kevin Cooper, the other senior bowler, had to carry the heaviest workload – and this in his benefit year.

On the whole, Nottinghamshire could be satisfied with their record in the limited-overs competitions, despite going out in the second round of the NatWest Bank Trophy to the eventual finalists, Northamptonshire. In the Sunday League and especially the Benson and Hedges Cup, the excellent batting of Robinson was the chief reason for their progressing so far, but the side could not rise to the occasion in the semi-finals of the Benson and Hedges and Refuge Assurance cups.

As for resolving what went wrong in the Championship, Nottinghamshire wasted no time in taking steps towards an improvement. Birch was appointed cricket manager as successor to the long-serving Ken Taylor, and the club looked to strengthen the staff with players of proven calibre. Just how much Nottinghamshire owe Taylor for leading them out of the doldrums in his thirteen years as manager is incalculable: they were seventeenth in the Championship when he took over and had never won a limited-overs trophy. All that has changed, and now Birch has to try to retain the club's hard-won status at the forefront of English cricket. – Nick Lucy.

550

NOTTINGHAMSHIRE 1990

[Bill Smith]

Back row: P. Johnson, R. A. Pick, M. Newell, J. A. Afford, K. E. Cooper, D. J. R. Martindale, B. C. Broad. Front row: E. E. Hemmings, R. T. Robinson (captain), B. N. French, F. D. Stephenson. Insets: P. R. Pollard, C. W. Scott, D. W. Randall, K. Saxelby, M. Saxelby, J. D. Birch, K. P. Evans.

NOTTINGHAMSHIRE RESULTS

All first-class matches – Played 25: Won 4, Lost 8, Drawn 13.
County Championship matches – Played 22: Won 4, Lost 8, Drawn 10.
Bonus points – Batting 51, Bowling 58.

Competition placings – Britannic Assurance County Championship, 13th equal;
NatWest Bank Trophy, 2nd round; Benson and Hedges Cup, s-f;
Refuge Assurance League, 4th; Refuge Assurance Cup, s-f.

BRITANNIC ASSURANCE CHAMPIONSHIP AVERAGES

BATTING

	Birthplace	M	I	NO	R	HI	Avge
‡B. C. Broad	*Bristol*	22	43	2	2,226	227*	54.29
‡K. P. Evans	*Calverton*	12	22	8	638	100*	45.57
‡R. T. Robinson	*Sutton-in-Ashfield*	22	43	5	1,693	220*	44.55
‡P. Johnson	*Newark*	19	36	2	1,294	165*	38.05
‡D. W. Randall	*Retford*	15	28	1	987	178	36.55
‡M. Newell	*Blackburn*	12	23	1	653	89*	29.68
D. J. R. Martindale ..	*Harrogate*	14	24	3	559	108*	26.61
‡F. D. Stephenson ...	*St James, Barbados*	19	33	6	715	121	26.48
P. R. Pollard	*Nottingham*	5	10	0	254	72	25.40
M. Saxelby	*Worksop*	7	13	3	232	51	23.20
‡E. E. Hemmings ...	*Leamington Spa*	11	14	4	230	83	23.00
‡R. A. Pick	*Nottingham*	14	15	6	199	35	22.11
‡B. N. French	*Warsop*	22	34	9	506	105*	20.24
G. W. Mike	*Nottingham*	3	5	1	45	18*	11.25
‡K. E. Cooper	*Hucknall*	20	25	5	217	35*	10.85
‡K. Saxelby	*Worksop*	4	6	0	42	20	7.00
‡J. A. Afford	*Crowland*	19	21	7	14	5	1.00

Also batted: R. J. Evans (*Calverton*) (1 match) 11, 4; M. G. Field-Buss (*Mtarfa, Malta*) (1 match) 0, 0.

* *Signifies not out.*   ‡ *Denotes county cap.*

The following played a total of 21 three-figure innings for Nottinghamshire in County Championship matches – B. C. Broad 9, R. T. Robinson 4, P. Johnson 2, D. W. Randall 2, K. P. Evans 1, B. N. French 1, D. J. R. Martindale 1, F. D. Stephenson 1.

BOWLING

	O	M	R	W	BB	5W/i	Avge
R. A. Pick	443.5	70	1,507	48	7-128	1	31.39
F. D. Stephenson	592.4	90	2,047	53	6-84	2	38.62
E. E. Hemmings	443.3	127	1,175	30	5-99	1	39.16
K. P. Evans	292	60	1,085	27	4-57	0	40.18
K. E. Cooper	667.4	141	2,105	51	5-56	3	41.27
J. A. Afford	627	186	1,804	38	4-137	0	47.47

Also bowled: M. G. Field-Buss 10-2-43-0; G. W. Mike 54.2-9-230-2; M. Newell 2.2-0-13-0; K. Saxelby 89-19-309-7; M. Saxelby 56.4-8-260-3.

Wicket-keeper: B. N. French 46 ct, 11 st.

Leading Fielder: D. W. Randall 14.

NOTTINGHAMSHIRE v DERBYSHIRE

At Nottingham, April 26, 27, 28, 30. Drawn. Nottinghamshire 5 pts, Derbyshire 3 pts. Toss: Nottinghamshire. Broad dominated a showery first day, on which there were four breaks for rain, and remained undefeated at the close after giving a sound display. On the second morning however, he looked less comfortable and soon lost his wicket, having faced 349 balls and having hit 22 fours in his highest score. Runs came slowly in Derbyshire's reply. They had managed only 123 in 54 overs by the close, and good bowling by Hemmings and Afford kept the run-rate low on the Saturday. With just 41 runs between the two sides after the first innings, it looked as if Monday's play would be of little consequence, and so it turned out. Robinson set the visitors 267 off a minimum of 52 overs, but once the openers were out, no attempt was made to chase the target.

Close of play: First day, Nottinghamshire 295-4 (B. C. Broad 171*, F. D. Stephenson 2*); Second day, Derbyshire 123-2 (J. E. Morris 45*, A. P. Kuiper 0*); Third day, Nottinghamshire 47-1 (P. R. Pollard 25*, R. T. Robinson 13*).

Nottinghamshire

B. C. Broad c Miller b Base	180	– c Bowler b Base	5
P. R. Pollard c Bowler b Mortensen	40	– lbw b Mortensen	27
*R. T. Robinson b Kuiper	11	– b Barnett	86
P. Johnson c Bowler b Warner	45	– b Barnett	54
D. W. Randall c Brown b Barnett	6	– c and b Barnett	23
F. D. Stephenson c sub b Warner	18	– b Miller	12
†B. N. French c Brown b Mortensen	25	– not out	1
E. E. Hemmings c Adams b Mortensen	15		
K. E. Cooper b Miller	12		
R. A. Pick not out	14		
J. A. Afford c Bowler b Mortensen	2		
B 4, l-b 12, w 4, n-b 13	33	B 5, l-b 7, w 3, n-b 2	17

1/127 2/153 3/266 4/293 5/308   **401**   1/12 2/62 3/180   (6 wkts dec.) **225**
6/323 7/366 8/378 9/384   4/195 5/221 6/225

Bonus points – Nottinghamshire 3, Derbyshire 1 (Score at 100 overs: 282-3).

Bowling: *First Innings*—Mortensen 26.5–6–67–4; Base 28–5–89–1; Warner 30–6–78–2; Kuiper 13–2–60–1; Miller 45–16–84–1; Barnett 2–0–7–1. *Second Innings*—Base 12.3–2–56–1; Warner 4–1–14–0; Miller 18–3–60–1; Barnett 17–2–49–3; Kuiper 7–2–20–0; Mortensen 7–3–14–1.

Derbyshire

†P. D. Bowler c Broad b Pick	20	– lbw b Afford	11
A. M. Brown c Johnson b Cooper	54	– c Cooper b Hemmings	20
J. E. Morris lbw b Cooper	66	– not out	16
A. P. Kuiper c Randall b Afford	25	– c Pollard b Afford	10
C. J. Adams c French b Cooper	3	– not out	11
B. Roberts st French b Hemmings	46		
*K. J. Barnett c Johnson b Hemmings	73		
G. Miller b Hemmings	10		
A. E. Warner lbw b Pick	11		
S. J. Base st French b Afford	34		
O. H. Mortensen not out	5		
L-b 9, n-b 4	13	B 2, l-b 4, n-b 1	7

1/50 2/122 3/170 4/170 5/175   **360**   1/32 2/34 3/53   (3 wkts) **75**
6/280 7/299 8/320 9/326

Bonus points – Derbyshire 2, Nottinghamshire 2 (Score at 100 overs: 224-5).

Bowling: *First Innings*—Stephenson 27–7–92–0; Cooper 35–9–75–3; Pick 25–4–81–2; Hemmings 39–17–64–3; Afford 19.5–8–39–2. *Second Innings*—Stephenson 4–0–9–0; Cooper 6–1–17–0; Afford 22–17–21–2; Hemmings 21–12–22–1.

Umpires: B. J. Meyer and D. O. Oslear.

t Worcester, May 3, 4, 5, 7. NOTTINGHAMSHIRE lost to WORCESTERSHIRE by an
innings and 6 runs.

t Leicester, May 15, 16, 17. NOTTINGHAMSHIRE beat LEICESTERSHIRE by five
wickets.

t Birmingham, May 19, 21, 22. NOTTINGHAMSHIRE beat WARWICKSHIRE by
5 runs.

NOTTINGHAMSHIRE v NORTHAMPTONSHIRE

t Nottingham, May 23, 24, 25. Nottinghamshire won by eight wickets. Nottinghamshire
2 pts, Northamptonshire 8 pts. Toss: Northamptonshire. The Northamptonshire first
nnings occupied the whole of the first day, with Penberthy putting the run-out of Bailey and
n early chance to second slip behind him to remain unbeaten at the close. He and the more
dventurous Ripley added 95 for the seventh wicket, and were instrumental in Northampton-
hire's achieving four batting points. Despite losing Martindale cheaply, Nottinghamshire
eached 150 by lunch on the second morning, but with wickets falling regularly, they only just
btained three batting points. In the evening Fordham and Felton hit up a century
artnership for Northamptonshire's first wicket, and when the declaration came at lunch next
ay Felton, with nine fours and a six in 214 balls, had gone on to his best score for his new
ounty. As Nottinghamshire set out to get 341 in a minimum of 70 overs, Broad was run out
ff the first ball. By tea, however, they were 102 for two off 32 overs, and in the last session
ohnson attacked the bowlers with increasing confidence, reaching 100 in 88 minutes. His
areer-best 165 not out from 120 balls contained 24 fours and a six, and his unbroken
artnership of 249 with Martindale, occupying 35 overs, saw Nottinghamshire to victory with
.2 overs in hand.
Close of play: First day, Northamptonshire 325; Second day, Northamptonshire 117-0 (A.
ordham 60*, N. A. Felton 47*).

Northamptonshire

A. Fordham c Johnson b Pick	21	– c French b Pick	74
N. A. Felton lbw b Pick	11	– not out	119
R. J. Bailey run out	65	– not out	54
G. Cook b Pick	49		
D. J. Capel c Randall b Cooper	4		
A. L. Penberthy not out	67		
G. Thomas c French b Afford	5		
D. Ripley st French b Afford	55		
W. W. Davis b Cooper	4		
A. R. Roberts b Afford	5		
J. W. Govan b Saxelby	17		
L-b 12, n-b 10	22	B 6, l-b 11, n-b 1	18

/24 2/47 3/150 4/157 5/170   325   1/147   (1 wkt dec.) 265
/178 7/273 8/278 9/301

Bonus points – Northamptonshire 4, Nottinghamshire 3 (Score at 100 overs: 300-8).

Bowling: *First Innings*—Stephenson 16-5-23-0; Cooper 25-6-65-2; Pick 19-1-64-3;
Saxelby 13.4-1-71-1; Afford 33-6-90-3. *Second Innings*—Pick 17-4-40-1; Cooper
2-1-59-0; Stephenson 13-0-52-0; Afford 17-4-74-0; Saxelby 5-1-23-0.

Nottinghamshire

B. C. Broad b Govan	49	– run out	(
D. J. R. Martindale c Fordham b Thomas	0	– not out	108
*R. T. Robinson b Capel	30	– lbw b Davis	56
P. Johnson c Thomas b Govan	27	– not out	165
D. W. Randall run out	37		
M. Saxelby b Penberthy	42		
F. D. Stephenson b Roberts	11		
†B. N. French c and b Penberthy	33		
K. E. Cooper c Ripley b Penberthy	4		
R. A. Pick c Penberthy b Davis	3		
J. A. Afford not out	0		
L-b 3, w 2, n-b 9	14	B 4, l-b 4, w 1, n-b 6	15

1/6 2/82 3/94 4/150 5/153   250   1/0 2/95   (2 wkts) 344
6/176 7/233 8/237 9/246

Bonus points – Nottinghamshire 3, Northamptonshire 4.

Bowling: *First Innings*—Davis 13–1–50–1; Thomas 7–1–41–1; Govan 13–0–56–2; Cape
14–2–45–1; Penberthy 6–0–28–3; Roberts 15–8–27–1. *Second Innings*—Davis 14.4–1–63–1;
Thomas 12–1–54–0; Capel 13–1–60–0; Penberthy 10–1–57–0; Roberts 9–0–57–0; Govan
6–0–45–0.

Umpires: J. W. Holder and A. G. T. Whitehead.

At Derby, May 26, 27, 28. NOTTINGHAMSHIRE drew with DERBYSHIRE.

At Tunbridge Wells, June 2, 4, 5. NOTTINGHAMSHIRE drew with KENT.

At Oxford, June 6, 7, 8. NOTTINGHAMSHIRE drew with OXFORD UNIVERSITY.

At Cambridge, June 16, 18, 19. NOTTINGHAMSHIRE drew with CAMBRIDGE
UNIVERSITY.

NOTTINGHAMSHIRE v SURREY

At Nottingham, June 20, 21, 22. Drawn. Nottinghamshire 1 pt, Surrey 8 pts. Toss: Surrey.
The miserable conditions which were a feature of June continued on the first day, when
Nottinghamshire, put in to bat, collapsed to 87 for seven by lunch. Only Randall of the
specialist batsmen remained, and with his dismissal soon after the resumption, adjudged
caught behind much to the batsman's displeasure, went Nottinghamshire's resistance.
Bicknell was the chief destroyer, his five wickets including four for 7 in 24 balls and first-ball
dismissals for Martindale, Field-Buss and Saxelby. Surrey lost two cheap wickets, but by the
time the bad weather ended play they had already moved ahead. Next morning Ward hit 9?
runs before lunch, and his Championship-best 154 not out, coming in 245 minutes and
containing four sixes and nineteen fours, put Surrey in a strong position, despite the loss of
half the second day to rain. Nottinghamshire batted much better on the final day, however,
with Robinson and Johnson adding 141 for the third wicket, and although wickets fell quickly
at the end, Surrey were left with only six overs in which to score 105. It was a challenge they
declined.
Close of play: First day, Surrey 102-2 (R. I. Alikhan 39*, D. M. Ward 28*); Second day,
Surrey 303-3 (D. M. Ward 154*, M. A. Lynch 18*).

Nottinghamshire

. C. Broad c Thorpe b Robinson	30	– b Medlycott	30
. J. R. Martindale lbw b Bicknell	0	– b Medlycott	33
R. T. Robinson lbw b Waqar Younis	5	– lbw b Medlycott	72
. Johnson b Murphy	10	– b Medlycott	78
. W. Randall c Ward b Bicknell	24	– c Ward b Bicknell	26
. D. Stephenson b Waqar Younis	9	– c and b Medlycott	2
B. N. French b Waqar Younis	0	– not out	14
. G. Field-Buss lbw b Bicknell	0	– c Alikhan b Medlycott	0
. E. Cooper c Ward b Bicknell	7	– lbw b Bicknell	1
. Saxelby c Thorpe b Bicknell	0	– lbw b Medlycott	8
. A. Afford not out	0	– lbw b Bicknell	0
B 1, l-b 13, w 1	15	B 26, l-b 14, w 3	43
	100		**307**

/5 2/22 3/54 4/54 5/73   1/76 2/77 3/218 4/263 5/269
/79 7/80 8/97 9/97   6/287 7/292 8/293 9/306

Bonus points – Surrey 4.

Bowling: *First Innings*—Waqar Younis 15-3-29-3; Bicknell 14.2-4-34-5; Murphy –1-9-1; Robinson 4-2-14-1. *Second Innings*—Waqar Younis 22-3-86-0; Bicknell 9.3-6-46-3; Murphy 9-2-34-0; Medlycott 33-4-92-7; Greig 1-0-9-0.

Surrey

. I. Alikhan c Robinson b Stephenson	88	M. A. Lynch not out	18
. S. Clinton lbw b Stephenson	1	B 5, l-b 11, n-b 6	22
. P. Thorpe c Randall b Afford	20		
D. M. Ward not out	154	1/3 2/40 3/262 (3 wkts dec.)	303

I. A. Greig, K. T. Medlycott, J. D. Robinson, M. P. Bicknell, Waqar Younis and A. J. Murphy did not bat.

Bonus points – Surrey 4, Nottinghamshire 1.

Bowling: Stephenson 27.5-7-66-2; Cooper 25-8-52-0; Saxelby 14-5-42-0; Afford 2-3-84-1; Field-Buss 10-2-43-0.

Umpires: J. C. Balderstone and J. H. Hampshire.

NOTTINGHAMSHIRE v LEICESTERSHIRE

At Nottingham, June 30, July 2, 3. Drawn. Nottinghamshire 5 pts, Leicestershire 6 pts. Toss: Leicestershire. The same damp conditions prevailed as in the previous match, and again Nottinghamshire, invited to bat, fell apart. In between two stoppages for rain, aggressive bowling by Benjamin and Agnew reduced them to 109 for six before French joined Stephenson and 77 runs were added for the seventh wicket. Stephenson, batting responsibly but without inhibition, reached his hundred before the close, and on Monday he went on to his highest score for the county, batting in all for 245 minutes and hitting sixteen fours. With Leicestershire's runs coming too slowly, Briers declared in arrears and on the final morning fed Nottinghamshire runs until Robinson set a target of 271 off a minimum of 48 overs. Leicestershire began badly, but some vigorous batting by Whitaker, Potter and Benson left them needing 76 off eleven overs. However, Cooper and Stephenson took four wickets, and Leicestershire's last pair had 21 balls to face to save the match. Owing to a dropped catch, they survived.

Close of play: First day, Nottinghamshire 241-8 (F. D. Stephenson 105*, R. A. Pick 0*); Second day, Nottinghamshire 21-0 (B. C. Broad 14*, M. Newell 6*).

Nottinghamshire

B. C. Broad lbw b Benjamin	40	– not out 11
M. Newell lbw b Benjamin	7	– lbw b Potter 2
*R. T. Robinson lbw b Agnew	0	– not out 6
P. Johnson c Benson b Benjamin	4	
D. J. R. Martindale c Nixon b Benjamin	7	
F. D. Stephenson c Lewis b Willey	121	
E. E. Hemmings c Nixon b Agnew	17	
†B. N. French c Nixon b Mullally	27	
K. E. Cooper c Benson b Benjamin	29	
R. A. Pick c Nixon b Mullally	34	
J. A. Afford not out	0	
L-b 5, w 1	6	B 3, l-b 4 ....

1/13 2/16 3/27 4/47 5/64   292   1/79   (1 wkt dec.) 21
6/109 7/186 8/230 9/292

Bonus points – Nottinghamshire 3, Leicestershire 4.

Bowling: *First Innings*—Benjamin 32–5–109–5; Agnew 27–5–97–2; Lewis 6–1–23–C
Mullally 17–1–43–2; Willey 8.4–3–15–1. *Second Innings*—Lewis 14–5–28–0; Benjami
3–0–12–0; Willey 10–3–24–0; Mullally 7–1–17–0; Potter 18–0–78–1; Benson 11–0–43–0; Boo
0.5–0–5–0.

Leicestershire

T. J. Boon st French b Afford	40	– lbw b Cooper ....
*N. E. Briers c French b Stephenson	30	– c Johnson b Cooper ....
J. J. Whitaker c Cooper b Hemmings	43	– c French b Stephenson 8
P. Willey not out	73	– c Broad b Afford ....
L. Potter lbw b Cooper	0	– (6) c and b Cooper 4
J. D. R. Benson c Afford b Cooper	11	– (7) c French b Cooper 6
C. C. Lewis not out	28	– (5) run out ....
W. K. M. Benjamin (did not bat)		– lbw b Cooper ....
†P. A. Nixon (did not bat)		– lbw b Stephenson ....
J. P. Agnew (did not bat)		– not out ....
A. D. Mullally (did not bat)		– not out ....
B 3, l-b 6, n-b 2	11	B 10, l-b 6, n-b 2 1

1/56 2/94 3/146 4/150 5/170   (5 wkts dec.) 236   1/17 2/20 3/42   (9 wkts) 24
                                                    4/49 5/195 6/230
                                                    7/232 8/232 9/232

Bonus points – Leicestershire 2, Nottinghamshire 2.

In the second innings J. J. Whitaker, when 66, retired hurt at 118 and resumed at 195.

Bowling: *First Innings*—Stephenson 16–4–53–1; Pick 14–1–52–0; Cooper 21–6–47–2
Hemmings 13–3–52–1; Afford 11–4–23–1. *Second Innings*—Stephenson 15–5–36–2; Pic
2–0–12–0; Cooper 15–2–56–5; Afford 15–4–62–1; Hemmings 14–1–60–0.

Umpires: R. Julian and D. S. Thompsett.

At Scarborough, July 4, 5, 6. NOTTINGHAMSHIRE beat YORKSHIRE by five wickets

NOTTINGHAMSHIRE v SUSSEX

At Nottingham, July 7, 9, 10. Drawn. Nottinghamshire 5 pts, Sussex 8 pts. Toss: Nottingham
shire. Pick quickly removed Lenham and Gould when Sussex were put in on an overcast day
Hall, however, batted soundly and was nearing his century when rain arrived to en
Saturday's play. On Monday he went on to reach 125, his innings of 267 minutes containin
eighteen fours, and Sussex collected full batting points. Although the weather was muc

mproved, Nottinghamshire fared poorly, the only landmark being Randall's 20,000th first-ass run for his county, and they narrowly avoided the follow-on. Sussex batted until lunch on ne third day, then set Nottinghamshire 347 off 68 overs. Newell, who batted for 166 minutes, elped Robinson to add 111 for the second wicket; later Evans and French were content to at out time.

Close of play: First day, Sussex 219-5 (J. W. Hall 96*, A. I. C. Dodemaide 25*); Second day, ussex 36-0 (N. J. Lenham 24*, J. W. Hall 11*).

Sussex

. J. Lenham c French b Pick	0	– c French b Pick	27
W. Hall b Cooper	125	– not out	59
J. Gould c Newell b Pick	4		
. P. Wells c French b Evans	23	– (3) c and b Saxelby	25
M. P. Speight lbw b Pick	55	– (4) c Broad b Afford	30
C. M. Wells c Evans b Saxelby	5	– (5) c Saxelby b Afford	44
. I. C. Dodemaide c French b Evans	72	– (6) c and b Pick	7
P. Moores c Johnson b Evans	22	– (7) not out	7
. C. S. Pigott lbw b Cooper	3		
D. K. Salisbury not out	0		
L-b 9, w 1, n-b 3	13	L-b 9, n-b 1	10

/0 2/4 3/48 4/135 5/146 (9 wkts dec.) 322   1/43 2/80 3/136 (5 wkts dec.) 209
/279 7/311 8/320 9/322   4/190 5/197

R. A. Bunting did not bat.

Bonus points – Sussex 4, Nottinghamshire 4.

Bowling: *First Innings*—Pick 21–5–49–3; Saxelby 14–3–44–1; Cooper 19.4–2–79–2; Evans 3–2–69–3; Afford 19–2–72–0. *Second Innings*—Pick 13–1–40–2; Cooper 10–1–37–0; Evans -2–47–0; Afford 9–2–47–2; Saxelby 10–2–29–1.

Nottinghamshire

B. C. Broad c Moores b Pigott	12	– b Dodemaide	34
M. Newell c Salisbury b Pigott	8	– b C. M. Wells	85
R. T. Robinson c Gould b Pigott	6	– c Pigott b C. M. Wells	52
P. Johnson c Salisbury b Dodemaide	68	– c Speight b C. M. Wells	14
D. W. Randall c Moores b C. M. Wells	34	– lbw b Salisbury	9
K. P. Evans c Salisbury b Dodemaide	29	– not out	21
B. N. French c Moores b Dodemaide	5	– not out	17
R. A. Pick not out	0		
K. E. Cooper c Gould b Salisbury	0		
K. Saxelby b Bunting	5		
J. A. Afford b Bunting	0		
L-b 4, w 1	5	L-b 7, w 4, n-b 1	12

/14 2/23 3/34 4/111 5/147   185   1/64 2/175 3/186 (5 wkts) 244
/166 7/166 8/166 9/185   4/201 5/201

Bonus points – Nottinghamshire 1, Sussex 4.

Bowling: *First Innings*—Pigott 14–4–47–3; Dodemaide 15–4–44–3; Bunting 13–3–42–2; C. M. Wells 9–1–20–1; Salisbury 9–2–28–1. *Second Innings*—Pigott 9–2–18–0; Dodemaide 4–4–39–1; Bunting 9–0–46–0; Salisbury 23–6–86–1; C. M. Wells 14–3–48–3.

Umpires: H. D. Bird and K. E. Palmer.

At Portsmouth, July 18, 19, 20. NOTTINGHAMSHIRE lost to HAMPSHIRE by eight wickets.

At Southport, July 25, 26, 27. NOTTINGHAMSHIRE lost to LANCASHIRE by seven wickets.

NOTTINGHAMSHIRE v MIDDLESEX

At Nottingham, July 28, 30, 31. Drawn. Nottinghamshire 7 pts, Middlesex 4 pts. Toss Nottinghamshire. Only Broad and Randall of the Nottinghamshire batsmen took advantage of Robinson's decision to bat first. But while Broad hit fourteen fours in his 140 (264 balls), Randall was more subdued over approximately three hours. Nevertheless, with Middlesex struggling against the seam bowlers on the second day, the home side gathered a substantial lead. Stephenson and Evans hit out before lunch on the last morning, and Robinson's declaration set Middlesex 354 in a minimum of 70 overs. They made a dreadful start, but Gatting was in fine form, and helped first by Ramprakash and then Brown he took the total to 244. At this point Stephenson bowled Brown, and he then bowled so accurately that the remaining batsmen were unable to maintain the scoring-rate. Gatting was unbeaten at the end with 169, having faced 205 balls in four and a quarter hours and hit fifteen fours and a six.

Close of play: First day, Nottinghamshire 336-8 (K. P. Evans 28*, K. E. Cooper 3*); Second day, Nottinghamshire 87-3 (P. R. Pollard 34*, D. W. Randall 17*).

Nottinghamshire

B. C. Broad lbw b Cowans	140	– b Tufnell	2
P. R. Pollard c Brown b Emburey	24	– c Haynes b Tufnell	7
*R. T. Robinson lbw b Cowans	5	– (4) c Downton b Williams	
P. Johnson c Emburey b Cowans	30	– (3) c and b Tufnell	
D. W. Randall b Emburey	70	– b Cowans	5
F. D. Stephenson c Downton b Tufnell	8	– not out	4
K. P. Evans not out	28	– not out	2
†B. N. French c Cowans b Emburey	4		
G. W. Mike c Downton b Tufnell	9		
K. E. Cooper not out	3		
B 2, l-b 10, n-b 3	15	L-b 7, w 4, n-b 1	1

1/58 2/63 3/116 4/254 5/271   (8 wkts dec.) 336   1/57 2/63 3/66   (5 wkts dec.) 24
6/291 7/309 8/331   4/156 5/171

J. A. Afford did not bat.

Bonus points – Nottinghamshire 3, Middlesex 2 (Score at 100 overs: 296-6).

Bowling: *First Innings*—Williams 18–6–34–0; Cowans 22–3–80–3; Taylor 13–1–45–0; Emburey 18–0–61–3; Tufnell 39–5–104–2. *Second Innings*—Williams 15–4–46–1; Cowans 17–1–70–1; Taylor 6–0–15–0; Emburey 8–2–16–0; Tufnell 26–6–86–3.

Middlesex

D. L. Haynes c Pollard b Cooper	21	– c French b Cooper	
M. A. Roseberry c Mike b Evans	74	– c Cooper b Stephenson	
*M. W. Gatting c French b Cooper	6	– not out	169
M. R. Ramprakash lbw b Stephenson	46	– c Randall b Afford	5
K. R. Brown c Johnson b Stephenson	4	– b Stephenson	5
†P. R. Downton b Cooper	16	– (7) b Evans	2
J. E. Emburey c Johnson b Cooper	0	– (8) b Stephenson	1
N. F. Williams lbw b Evans	14	– (9) lbw b Stephenson	
P. C. R. Tufnell c Pollard b Evans	12	– (10) not out	
C. W. Taylor b Cooper	13		
N. G. Cowans not out	11	– (6) lbw b Stephenson	
L-b 5, n-b 1	6	L-b 13, n-b 2	1

1/27 2/39 3/129 4/133 5/164   223   1/0 2/7 3/99 4/244   (8 wkts) 32
6/173 7/178 8/198 9/201   5/244 6/293 7/310 8/318

Bonus points – Middlesex 2, Nottinghamshire 4.

Bowling: *First Innings*—Stephenson 16–6–33–2; Cooper 25–6–108–5; Evans 18–4–54–3; Mike 6–3–12–0; Afford 5–1–11–0. *Second Innings*—Cooper 14–2–41–1; Stephenson 20.5–1–82–5; Evans 12–2–72–1; Afford 14–1–75–1; Mike 9–0–46–0.

Umpires: J. H. Hampshire and M. J. Kitchen.

At Southend, August 4, 6, 7. NOTTINGHAMSHIRE lost to ESSEX by ten wickets.

At Weston-super-Mare, August 8, 9, 10. NOTTINGHAMSHIRE drew with SOMERSET.

NOTTINGHAMSHIRE v GLAMORGAN

At Worksop, August 11, 13, 14. Glamorgan won by 238 runs. Glamorgan 22 pts, Nottinghamshire 7 pts. Toss: Glamorgan. The visiting batsmen enjoyed themselves on the first day. Morris (one six, fourteen fours) and Maynard added 164 for the third wicket, with Maynard needing just 112 balls for his 115 (one six, 21 fours), having hit 46 of his first fifty in boundaries. Then came Richards. The West Indian captain hit 127 off 136 balls, his third consecutive hundred, with fourteen fours and five sixes. Several of his strokes cleared the ground and landed in either the river or the canal. Broad (thirteen fours) and Robinson shared a century stand on Monday, and Martindale and Evans ensured full batting points for Nottinghamshire. However, the final day was one of humiliation for the home team. Unbeaten hundreds by Butcher (twenty fours) and Morris (a six and fourteen fours) left Nottinghamshire needing 351 off a minimum of 65 overs. Their batting fell apart, and though Newell fought against the tide until he was seventh out, the Welshmen strolled to victory with 35 overs to spare.

Close of play: First day, Nottinghamshire 1-0 (R. A. Pick 1*, M. Newell 0*); Second day, Glamorgan 76-0 (A. R. Butcher 41*, H. Morris 32*).

Glamorgan

*A. R. Butcher c Evans b Saxelby	13	– not out 121
H. Morris c French b Afford	110	– not out 102
P. A. Cottey c Broad b Pick	5	
M. P. Maynard b Afford	115	
I. V. A. Richards c Pick b Saxelby	127	
A. Dale c Johnson b Evans	7	
R. D. B. Croft run out	1	
†C. P. Metson c Cooper b Saxelby	29	
S. L. Watkin lbw b Saxelby	0	
S. Bastien not out	10	
M. Frost lbw b Cooper	0	
L-b 6, n-b 4	10	B 4, l-b 6, w 1, n-b 2 13

1/33 2/57 3/221 4/274 5/309   427   (no wkt dec.) 236
6/315 7/399 8/399 9/427

Bonus points – Glamorgan 4, Nottinghamshire 3 (Score at 100 overs: 399-8).

Bowling: *First Innings*—Pick 13–1–65–1; Saxelby 23–4–92–4; Cooper 21.2–4–95–1; Evans 8–3–69–1; Afford 29–4–100–2. *Second Innings*—Pick 13–1–55–0; Saxelby 12–1–47–0; Cooper 1–40–0; Afford 16–4–47–0; Evans 7–1–37–0.

Nottinghamshire

R. A. Pick b Bastien	11	– (9) c Cottey b Bastien 2
M. Newell c Metson b Bastien	10	– c Cottey b Bastien 42
B. C. Broad c Metson b Croft	98	– (1) c Metson b Watkin 10
R. T. Robinson c Metson b Watkin	46	– (3) c Maynard b Frost 8
P. Johnson c Metson b Bastien	44	– (4) c Dale b Frost 12
D. J. R. Martindale not out	35	– (5) c Metson b Bastien 1
K. P. Evans not out	60	– (6) lbw b Bastien 26
B. N. French (did not bat)		– (7) c Maynard b Croft 1
K. E. Cooper (did not bat)		– (8) b Bastien 2
K. Saxelby (did not bat)		– c Dale b Watkin 3
J. A. Afford (did not bat)		– not out 1
L-b 3, w 3, n-b 3	9	L-b 2, w 1, n-b 1 4

1/19 2/39 3/152 4/216 5/216   (5 wkts dec.) 313   1/18 2/28 3/42 4/55 5/99   112
6/100 7/102 8/104 9/107

Bonus points – Nottinghamshire 4, Glamorgan 2.

Bowling: *First Innings*—Watkin 19–2–79–1; Bastien 20–5–71–3; Frost 22–2–79–0; Cro 22–5–65–1; Dale 7–0–16–0. *Second Innings*—Watkin 10–1–45–2; Frost 7–0–32–2; Bastie 10–2–31–5; Croft 3–1–2–1.

Umpires: D. J. Constant and D. O. Oslear.

NOTTINGHAMSHIRE v GLOUCESTERSHIRE

At Nottingham, August 18, 20, 21. Drawn. Nottinghamshire 7 pts, Gloucestershire 6 pts Toss: Gloucestershire. Stephenson and Pick gave the home side an excellent start, sendin back the first four Gloucestershire batsmen for 16, but Russell held the lower order togethe and the total was not as low as expected. On the second day Newell and Robinson increase their partnership to 203, and a large lead seemed in the offing until Lawrence transformed th innings by taking five wickets in fifteen balls, including those of Robinson, Evans an Stephenson with successive deliveries. The captain's 123 lasted 225 balls and included thirtee fours and a six. Nottinghamshire, missing the injured Randall, lost nine wickets for 30 runs i the afternoon session. Gloucestershire again began badly, and again Russell came to th rescue, remaining unbeaten with 103 (233 balls, one six, twelve fours). Left with 42 over Nottinghamshire never looked like scoring 236 for victory, and if Martindale had n defended stoutly, the match might have ended in defeat.

Close of play: First day, Nottinghamshire 109-1 (M. Newell 30*, R. T. Robinson 52*) Second day, Gloucestershire 115-5 (M. W. Alleyne 65*, R. C. Russell 10*).

Gloucestershire

*A. J. Wright lbw b Pick	2	– (2) b Pick	
G. D. Hodgson b Stephenson	4	– (1) c French b Stephenson	
P. Bainbridge b Stephenson	6	– c French b Stephenson	29
C. W. J. Athey lbw b Pick	37	– c Newell b Pick	
M. W. Alleyne lbw b Pick	1	– lbw b Pick	69
K. M. Curran lbw b Stephenson	54	– b Stephenson	
†R. C. Russell b Afford	79	– not out	103
C. A. Walsh lbw b Pick	29	– (9) c Saxelby b Hemmings	1
M. C. J. Ball c Robinson b Hemmings	14	– (8) c Stephenson b Hemmings	
D. V. Lawrence st French b Afford	0	– c Evans b Afford	1
S. N. Barnes not out	0	– b Pick	
L-b 5, w 1, n-b 7	13	B 2, n-b 5	
	239		**25**

1/4 2/6 3/15 4/16 5/104   1/0 2/2 3/2 4/61 5/79   25
6/117 7/161 8/222 9/238   6/121 7/137 8/168 9/231

Bonus points – Gloucestershire 2, Nottinghamshire 4.

Bowling: *First Innings*—Stephenson 18–0–66–3; Pick 18–2–70–4; Evans 13–3–51–0; Affor 13.1–4–28–2; Hemmings 9–3–19–1. *Second Innings*—Stephenson 27–4–94–3; Pic 21.1–10–45–4; Evans 9–1–38–0; Hemmings 29–7–48–2; Afford 17–8–28–1.

Nottinghamshire

B. C. Broad c Russell b Walsh	13	– c Russell b Alleyne	3
M. Newell c Alleyne b Lawrence	78	– c Russell b Walsh	
*R. T. Robinson lbw b Lawrence	123	– c Hodgson b Walsh	1
D. J. R. Martindale lbw b Lawrence	0	– not out	66
M. Saxelby not out	11	– c Walsh b Curran	1
K. P. Evans lbw b Lawrence	0	– (7) c Russell b Curran	
F. D. Stephenson c Alleyne b Lawrence	0	– (6) c Bainbridge b Curran	
†B. N. French b Alleyne	5	– lbw b Lawrence	
E. E. Hemmings b Alleyne	0	– c Curran b Lawrence	
R. A. Pick c and b Alleyne	3	– not out	
J. A. Afford b Walsh	0		
B 4, l-b 10, w 1, n-b 11	26	B 1, l-b 5, w 1, n-b 7	14
	259	(8 wkts)	**15**

1/26 2/229 3/231 4/234 5/234   1/20 2/42 3/85 4/109   (8 wkts) 15
6/234 7/250 8/250 9/258   5/110 6/111 7/140 8/147

Bonus points – Nottinghamshire 3, Gloucestershire 4.

Bowling: *First Innings*—Walsh 23.1–6–44–2; Curran 15–3–36–0; Lawrence 18–1–51–5; Barnes 13–5–39–0; Alleyne 9–3–23–3; Athey 2–1–2–0; Ball 11–1–32–0; Bainbridge 5–0–18–0. *Second Innings*—Walsh 14–0–41–2; Lawrence 10.5–2–41–2; Alleyne 6–1–23–1; Curran 9–0–35–3; Ball 2–0–9–0.

Umpires: J. D. Bond and N. T. Plews.

At Cleethorpes, August 25, 26, 27. NOTTINGHAMSHIRE drew with SRI LANKANS (See Sri Lankan tour section).

NOTTINGHAMSHIRE v WORCESTERSHIRE

At Nottingham, August 29, 30, 31. Drawn. Nottinghamshire 7 pts, Worcestershire 8 pts. Toss: Nottinghamshire. A marvellous third-wicket partnership between Broad and Johnson produced 183 runs at 5 an over on the first day. Broad scored 91 before lunch and hit 23 fours and a six in his 156; Johnson's 98 came off 108 balls with sixteen fours and a six. Bad light ended play early after the visitors had lost Lord. Stephenson took three quick wickets on the second morning, but Curtis soldiered on and, with help from the lower order, full batting points were achieved. Neale then closed the innings, but with the Nottinghamshire batsmen unable to score at a fast rate on Friday morning, and Neale not resorting to joke bowling, Robinson in the end set a demanding target of 266 off a minimum of 49 overs. Hick failed, and with fifteen overs unbowled the players went home.

Close of play: First day, Worcestershire 28-1 (T. S. Curtis 13*, S. M. McEwan 0*); Second day, Nottinghamshire 18-1 (M. Newell 9*, D. J. R. Martindale 0*).

Nottinghamshire

B. C. Broad c Illingworth b Hick	156	– c Hick b Newport	7
M. Newell c Rhodes b Newport	1	– run out	16
D. J. R. Martindale c Newport b Lampitt	37	– c Rhodes b Newport	14
P. Johnson c Neale b Hick	98	– c Neale b McEwan	13
*R. T. Robinson b Lampitt	39	– c Rhodes b Illingworth	45
K. P. Evans c Neale b Illingworth	12	– c Hick b Newport	0
F. D. Stephenson b Newport	25	– c Rhodes b Illingworth	30
†B. N. French b Newport	3	– c Hick b Illingworth	25
E. E. Hemmings not out	12	– not out	6
K. E. Cooper b Newport	7	– not out	1
R. A. Pick not out	4		
B 2, l-b 3, n-b 3	8	L-b 1, w 2, n-b 4	7

1/2 2/107 3/290 4/303 5/336   (9 wkts dec.) 402   1/16 2/41 3/55 4/59 (8 wkts dec.) 164
6/368 7/375 8/382 9/390   5/59 6/106 7/142 8/161

Bonus points – Nottinghamshire 4, Worcestershire 4.

Bowling: *First Innings*—Dilley 12–3–47–0; Newport 18.4–2–75–4; McEwan 14–1–76–0; Lampitt 22–2–90–2; Illingworth 22–5–79–1; Hick 8–0–30–2. *Second Innings*—Newport 23–7–50–3; McEwan 13–4–41–1; Illingworth 18–9–34–3; Lampitt 10–1–38–0.

Worcestershire

T. S. Curtis b Evans	82	– not out	84
G. J. Lord b Pick	13	– c Pick b Hemmings	12
S. M. McEwan b Stephenson	6		
G. A. Hick c French b Stephenson	4	– (3) c Broad b Hemmings	18
D. A. Leatherdale c French b Stephenson	2	– (4) lbw b Cooper	10
*P. A. Neale lbw b Cooper	74	– (5) not out	5
S. R. Lampitt lbw b Hemmings	40		
†S. J. Rhodes not out	50		
R. K. Illingworth not out	15		
L-b 6, n-b 9	15	B 1, l-b 5, n-b 1	7

1/22 2/49 3/53 4/57 5/153   (7 wkts dec.) 301   1/57 2/89 3/119   (3 wkts) 136
6/197 7/251

P. J. Newport and G. R. Dilley did not bat.

Bonus points – Worcestershire 4, Nottinghamshire 3.

Bowling: *First Innings*—Stephenson 21.2–3–72–3; Pick 18–2–72–1; Cooper 16–6–48–1; Hemmings 25–7–54–1; Evans 17–2–49–1. *Second Innings*—Stephenson 12–1–51–0; Pick 3–0–21–0; Cooper 7–0–28–1; Evans 1–0–3–0; Hemmings 12–1–27–2.

Umpires: H. D. Bird and J. D. Bond.

At Lord's, September 7, 8, 9, 10. NOTTINGHAMSHIRE lost to MIDDLESEX by ten wickets.

NOTTINGHAMSHIRE v LANCASHIRE

At Nottingham, September 12, 13, 14, 15. Lancashire won by ten wickets. Lancashire 24 pts, Nottinghamshire 5 pts. Toss: Nottinghamshire. Put in to bat, Lancashire reached 148 for one by lunch, Mendis and Atherton batting well. After the interval Nottinghamshire seemed to gain control, the total slipping to 216 for six, but DeFreitas, Hegg and Yates changed the picture. The second morning was one of embarrassment for the home side as Yates, making his Championship début, completed his maiden first-class hundred off 188 balls, hitting twenty fours, and with Allott added 116 for the last wicket. Martin then removed Newell, Robinson and Randall in quick succession, and although Broad and Evans made useful scores, Lancashire enforced the follow-on early on the third day, during which 56 former Nottinghamshire players attended a reunion on the ground. Broad's 122 second time round, with seventeen fours and off 218 balls, was his ninth century for the county in 1990, equalling the record held by W. W. Whysall (1928) and M. J. Harris (1971). On the final day 9 runs were still required to avoid an innings defeat, and though this was achieved with comfort, Atherton's leg-spin put paid to any prolonged resistance. His six-wicket return was a career best, and Lancashire won the match half an hour before lunch.

Close of play: First day, Lancashire 382-8 (G. Yates 45*, P. J. Martin 21*); Second day, Nottinghamshire 168-7 (B. N. French 10*, G. W. Mike 3*); Third day, Nottinghamshire 288-6 (F. D. Stephenson 15*, B. N. French 12*).

Lancashire

G. D. Mendis b Evans	85	– not out	23
G. Fowler c French b Cooper	1	– not out	20
M. A. Atherton c Randall b Stephenson	81		
*N. H. Fairbrother lbw b Evans	0		
G. D. Lloyd c Mike b Afford	31		
M. Watkinson c Stephenson b Afford	4		
P. A. J. DeFreitas c French b Evans	49		
†W. K. Hegg c French b Afford	48		
G. Yates c Cooper b Mike	106		
P. J. Martin c French b Evans	21		
P. J. W. Allott not out	55		
L-b 7, w 5, n-b 6	18	L-b 7, n-b 1	8

1/8 2/151 3/151 4/194 5/211   499   (no wkt) 51
6/216 7/299 8/320 9/383

Bonus points – Lancashire 4, Nottinghamshire 3 (Score at 100 overs: 363-8).

Bowling: *First Innings*—Stephenson 29–3–131–1; Cooper 30–8–93–1; Mike 17.2–3–80–1; Evans 28–4–95–4; Afford 29–5–93–3. *Second Innings*—Evans 4–1–20–0; Mike 4–0–24–0.

Nottinghamshire

B. C. Broad c Mendis b Watkinson	42	– c Martin b Yates 122
M. Newell c Allott b Martin	0	– c Atherton b DeFreitas 12
*R. T. Robinson c Lloyd b Martin	8	– lbw b Watkinson 23
D. W. Randall lbw b Martin	0	– c Fairbrother b Atherton 24
D. J. R. Martindale c Fairbrother b DeFreitas	22	– c Hegg b Atherton 6
K. P. Evans c Fowler b Watkinson	49	– b Yates 55
F. D. Stephenson c Martin b Watkinson	24	– c Watkinson b Atherton 51
†B. N. French c Fowler b DeFreitas	16	– c Fairbrother b Atherton 19
G. W. Mike not out	18	– c Hegg b Atherton 0
K. E. Cooper c Mendis b DeFreitas	5	– not out 9
J. A. Afford c Atherton b Martin	5	– c Martin b Atherton 0
B 4, l-b 9	13	B 9, l-b 13, w 1, n-b 2 ... 25

1/20 2/34 3/34 4/65 5/97   202   1/20 2/63 3/147 4/161 5/247   346
6/144 7/165 8/181 9/197   6/258 7/323 8/323 9/346

Bonus points – Nottinghamshire 2, Lancashire 4.

Bowling: First Innings—DeFreitas 25–7–63–3; Martin 20.3–4–68–4; Watkinson 16–3–34–3; Allott 14–8–18–0; Yates 2–0–6–0. *Second Innings*—DeFreitas 14–5–33–1; Martin 10–3–30–0; Allott 15–7–41–0; Watkinson 17–1–73–1; Yates 28–6–69–2; Atherton 21.3–4–78–6.

Umpires: J. H. Hampshire and B. J. Meyer.

NOTTINGHAMSHIRE v YORKSHIRE

At Nottingham, September 18, 19, 20, 21. Yorkshire won by four wickets. Yorkshire 21 pts, Nottinghamshire 3 pts. Toss: Nottinghamshire. On the first day, reduced by bad light and showers to 88 overs, Robinson reached his hundred in 213 minutes. Resuming next day, he not only improved his career best but also made the highest individual score for Nottinghamshire against Yorkshire. He hit 28 fours and faced 370 balls for his 220 not out. Stephenson enjoyed himself, hitting 95 off 109 balls as he and his captain put on 197 for the sixth wicket. The pitch was still perfect when Yorkshire batted, and Metcalfe hit 30 fours in his 194, missing his double-hundred when Moxon declared as soon as the follow-on was avoided. The weather remained miserable on the last day, and Robinson generously declared at lunch, leaving Yorkshire to score 324 from a minimum of 66 overs. Stephenson, who strained his side in the first innings, was unable to bowl properly, which further eased Yorkshire's task on such a bland pitch. Moxon and Metcalfe put on 143 for the first wicket, and Metcalfe again reached three figures, as well as completing 2,000 runs for the season, the first to do so for Yorkshire since G. Boycott in 1971. His 107 came from 155 balls and contained thirteen fours. Yorkshire won off the penultimate ball.

Close of play: First day, Nottinghamshire 241-4 (R. T. Robinson 101*, K. P. Evans 29*); Second day, Yorkshire 51-0 (M. D. Moxon 25*, A. A. Metcalfe 26*); Third day, Nottinghamshire 0-0 (B. C. Broad 0*, M. Newell 0*).

Nottinghamshire

B. C. Broad lbw b Hartley	40	– st Blakey b Grayson 43
M. Newell b Hartley	38	– not out 89
*R. T. Robinson not out	220	– not out 36
D. W. Randall lbw b Hartley	10	
D. J. R. Martindale c Byas b Pickles	11	
K. P. Evans b Pickles	43	
F. D. Stephenson c Byas b Jarvis	95	
†B. N. French not out	2	
B 3, l-b 14, w 1, n-b 5	23	B 3, l-b 4 7

1/62 2/109 3/125 4/175   (6 wkts dec.) 482   1/93   (1 wkt dec.) 175
5/272 6/469

E. E. Hemmings, K. E. Cooper and J. A. Afford did not bat.

Bonus points – Nottinghamshire 3, Yorkshire 2 (Score at 100 overs: 284-5).

Bowling: *First Innings*—Jarvis 27–1–106–1; Hartley 35–7–95–3; Pickles 32–9–120–2; White 17–2–66–0; Grayson 28–6–78–0. *Second Innings*—Jarvis 2–0–9–0; Hartley 6–0–23–0; Pickles 7–3–16–0; Grayson 13–4–55–1; White 11–1–65–0.

Yorkshire

*M. D. Moxon c French b Cooper	42	– c Martindale b Stephenson	83
A. A. Metcalfe not out	194	– c and b Evans	107
S. A. Kellett c Evans b Hemmings	27	– (6) c and b Cooper	20
P. E. Robinson not out	62	– (3) lbw b Cooper	5
†R. J. Blakey (did not bat)		– (4) c Afford b Cooper	64
D. Byas (did not bat)		– (5) lbw b Evans	8
A. P. Grayson (did not bat)		– not out	6
C. S. Pickles (did not bat)		– not out	23
L-b 6, n-b 3	9	B 1, l-b 7, n-b 3	11

1/89 2/163   (2 wkts dec.) 334   1/143 2/152 3/246   (6 wkts) 327
                                                             4/260 5/298 6/299

P. J. Hartley, P. W. Jarvis and C. White did not bat.

Bonus points – Yorkshire 3 (Score at 100 overs: 254-2).

Bowling: *First Innings*—Stephenson 0.2–0–4–0; Cooper 27.4–9–70–1; Evans 25.2–9–71–0; Hemmings 27–5–102–1; Afford 35–12–81–0. *Second Innings*—Cooper 29.5–3–128–3; Evans 16–0–79–2; Afford 4–0–33–0; Stephenson 5–0–30–1; Hemmings 11–1–49–0.

Umpires: J. W. Holder and M. J. Kitchen.

THE CRICKETER CUP WINNERS, 1967-1990

1967	REPTON PILGRIMS	beat Radley Rangers by 96 runs.
1968	OLD MALVERNIANS	beat Harrow Wanderers by five wickets.
1969	OLD BRIGHTONIANS	beat Stowe Templars by 156 runs.
1970	OLD WYKEHAMISTS	beat Old Tonbridgians by 94 runs.
1971	OLD TONBRIDGIANS	beat Charterhouse Friars on faster scoring-rate.
1972	OLD TONBRIDGIANS	beat Old Malvernians by 114 runs.
1973	RUGBY METEORS	beat Old Tonbridgians by five wickets.
1974	OLD WYKEHAMISTS	beat Old Alleynians on faster scoring-rate.
1975	OLD MALVERNIANS	beat Harrow Wanderers by 97 runs.
1976	OLD TONBRIDGIANS	beat Old Blundellians by 170 runs.
1977	SHREWSBURY SARACENS	beat Oundle Rovers by nine wickets.
1978	CHARTERHOUSE FRIARS	beat Oundle Rovers by nine wickets.
1979	OLD TONBRIDGIANS	beat Uppingham Rovers by 5 runs.
1980	MARLBOROUGH BLUES	beat Old Wellingtonians by 31 runs.
1981	CHARTERHOUSE FRIARS	beat Old Wykehamists by nine wickets.
1982	OLD WYKEHAMISTS	beat Old Malvernians on faster scoring-rate.
1983	REPTON PILGRIMS	beat Haileybury Hermits by seven wickets.
1984	OLD TONBRIDGIANS	beat Old Malvernians by seven wickets.
1985	OUNDLE ROVERS	beat Repton Pilgrims by three wickets.
1986	OLD MALVERNIANS	beat Downside Wanderers by six wickets.
1987	SHREWSBURY SARACENS	beat Old Cliftonians by 58 runs.
1988	OUNDLE ROVERS	beat Shrewsbury Saracens by 19 runs.
1989	OUNDLE ROVERS	beat Shrewsbury Saracens by 9 runs.
1990	OLD MALVERNIANS	beat Harrow Wanderers by four wickets.

From 1967 to 1983 the final was played at Burton Court, Chelsea. Since then, it has been played at Vincent Square, Westminster.

SOMERSET

President: C. R. M. Atkinson
Chairman: R. Parsons
Chairman, Cricket Committee: R. E. Marshall
Chief Executive: P. W. Anderson
  The County Ground, St James's Street,
  Taunton TA1 1JT
  (Telephone: 0823-272946/253666)
Cricket Manager: 1990 – J. Birkenshaw
Captain: C. J. Tavaré
Coach: P. J. Robinson

In an unusual season memorable mostly for high scores, flat seams, flatter pitches and contrived run-chases, Somerset, despite a number of changes in personnel, finished with a playing record remarkably similar to that of 1989. After a promising start, with a ten-wicket win over Gloucestershire, they endured some sterile periods which produced little reward. Two wins in their last four Championship games helped them do no more than finish one position lower in the Britannic Assurance table than in 1989, and a rise of two places to eighth in the Refuge Assurance League constituted a marginal improvement. A good win over Middlesex at Taunton took them to the semi-finals of the Benson and Hedges Cup for the second year in succession, but no farther, and they again failed to get beyond the second round in the NatWest Bank Trophy, being beaten decisively by Worcestershire. All in all, it added up to a disappointing return.

It was a curious commentary on the Championship system, none the less, that Somerset should be fifteenth, and yet have gained more bonus points than nine counties, and have lost fewer matches than all but six counties. They collected as many batting bonus points as Middlesex and Essex, the champions and runners-up.

In general terms, Somerset's was a happy team. They usually fielded excellently, often played interesting cricket, and they reacted well to adversity. The batting rarely failed, and occasionally it rose to great heights. Jimmy Cook, the prolific South African opener, again played in every match, despite suffering a bruising blow on the arm from a fierce drive by Richard Harden in the Championship game against Northamptonshire at Taunton. Once more he was the first to reach 1,000 runs, getting there at exactly the same stage of the season as the previous year, and the first to 2,000, finishing with 2,608 runs in first-class cricket. Added to that were his new Sunday League record of 902 runs and the excellent work he did as vice-captain. At the age of 37, Cook always gave an enthusiastic display in the field and continued to provide an outstanding example.

Chris Tavaré proved to be a popular captain and enjoyed another fine year with the bat, scoring more than 2,500 runs in all cricket at an average of 53. Harden, returning to his best form, notched just over 2,000 runs at 51.51 in all cricket, while Peter Roebuck, although standing down from some games in his benefit year, averaged 54 in the Championship as a result of a golden mid-season spell.

For some years the No. 3 position in the batting order had caused Somerset problems, but last summer these were solved by one of the new recruits. Andy Hayhurst, released by Lancashire in 1989, scored 1,559 first-class runs for an average of 57.74 and made some useful contributions with bat and ball in the one-day games. Wicket-keeper Neil Burns had a good season, almost getting his thousand runs for the first time, a feat which was accomplished by Graham Rose, the county's most improved player. Given the encouragement to play his powerful strokes, Rose produced some startling innings, particularly in limited-overs games, and he gave evidence of his worth as an all-round cricketer by taking 53 first-class wickets, as well as making himself into a reliable slip fielder. An excellent fitness record allowed him to be one of those ever present for Somerset throughout the season.

Behind such a weight of batting, there were few chances for Ian Swallow, an off-spinner from Yorkshire, and Roland Lefebvre, two cricketers with plenty of all-round ability. Both, however, had to do a lot of bowling in first-class cricket for the first time, and they could look back on some rewarding days. In a season less affected by the radical changes introduced by the TCCB, the willing Lefebvre, the first Dutchman to play regularly for Somerset, would certainly have produced better results. As in the previous two seasons, Adrian Jones and Neil Mallender each took 50 wickets as the opening attack, and Mallender enjoyed more consistent fitness than in some years.

Indeed, with injuries at a minimum and the side more settled, there were not so many opportunities for the younger players. Harvey Trump's development was a shade slower than hoped for, but Ricky Bartlett, the Second Eleven Player of the Year, performed usefully in his eight Sunday League outings and one Championship appearance. Jeremy Hallett, who the year before had been opening the bowling for Millfield School, began the difficult transition to county cricket and represented England Young Cricketers against the visiting Pakistanis, his five wickets in the second innings of the Headingley "Test" setting up the decisive victory for England. Another heavy Second Eleven scorer, Gareth Townsend, had two Championship games towards the end of the season, and though he did little of note in either game, his 77 was an essential ingredient of Somerset's 71-run victory over the Sri Lankan touring team. The released list included Jonathan Hardy and Jonathon Atkinson, neither of whom, unhappily, had quite lived up to the rich promise of his early Somerset days.

For this summer, the county have signed Ken MacLeay, a 32-year-old, English-born all-rounder from Australia, who has strong one-day international credentials. However, there are clearly still some openings, notably for a slow left-arm bowler, and Somerset, with a small population, will continue to look for recruits from other counties, as they have always had to. But with the Second Eleven reaching the final of the Bain Clarkson competition, and junior teams excelling in national competitions, there are also hopes that more places will be filled by local players in the future. – Eric Hill.

SOMERSET 1990

[Bill Smith]

Back row: A. N. Hayhurst, M. W. Cleal, P. J. Rendell, S. M. Priscott. *Middle row*: R. J. Harden, I. Fletcher, D. M. Kutner, R. P. Lefebvre, N. J. Pringle, G. T. J. Townsend, R. J. Bartlett, I. G. Swallow. *Front row*: P. J. Robinson (*coach*), N. A. Mallender, N. D. Burns, S. J. Cook, C. J. Tavaré (*captain*), R. Parsons (*chairman*), J. Birkenshaw (*cricket manager*), T. Gard, A. N. Jones, J. J. E. Hardy, G. D. Rose, P. M. Roebuck. *Inset*: H. R. J. Trump.

SOMERSET RESULTS

All first-class matches – Played 24: Won 3, Lost 5, Drawn 16.

County Championship matches – Played 22: Won 3, Lost 4, Drawn 15.

Bonus points – Batting 73, Bowling 45.

*Competition placings – Britannic Assurance County Championship, 15th;
NatWest Bank Trophy, 2nd round; Benson and Hedges Cup, s-f;
Refuge Assurance League, 8th equal.*

BRITANNIC ASSURANCE CHAMPIONSHIP AVERAGES

BATTING

	Birthplace	M	I	NO	R	HI	Avge
‡S. J. Cook	*Johannesburg, SA*	22	38	6	2,432	313*	76.00
‡A. N. Hayhurst	*Manchester*	21	33	7	1,554	170	59.76
‡R. J. Harden	*Bridgwater*	22	29	7	1,257	104*	57.13
‡P. M. Roebuck	*Oxford*	16	25	5	1,085	201*	54.25
‡C. J. Tavaré	*Orpington*	22	30	4	1,399	219	53.80
‡G. D. Rose	*Tottenham, London*	22	26	9	897	97*	52.76
‡J. J. E. Hardy	*Nakaru, Kenya*	7	13	5	343	91	42.87
‡N. D. Burns	*Chelmsford*	22	31	9	863	166	39.22
‡N. A. Mallender ..	*Kirk Sandall*	19	10	3	177	87*	25.28
‡A. N. Jones	*Woking*	20	9	5	100	41	25.00
I. G. Swallow	*Barnsley*	21	17	7	187	32	18.70
R. P. Lefebvre	*Rotterdam, Netherlands*	16	16	3	214	53	16.46
G. T. J. Townsend .	*Tiverton*	2	4	1	21	15	7.00
H. R. J. Trump	*Taunton*	7	5	1	11	4*	2.75

Also batted: R. J. Bartlett (*Ash Priors*) (1 match) 73, 12; J. C. Hallett (*Yeovil*) (2 matches) 0.

* Signifies not out. ‡ *Denotes county cap.*

The following played a total of nineteen three-figure innings for Somerset in County Championship matches – S. J. Cook 8, A. N. Hayhurst 4, R. J. Harden 2, P. M. Roebuck 2, C. J. Tavaré 2, N. D. Burns 1.

BOWLING

	O	M	R	W	BB	5W/i	Avge
N. A. Mallender	537.2	114	1,555	51	5-46	2	30.49
G. D. Rose	530.4	93	1,807	51	5-52	1	35.43
A. N. Jones	539.4	81	1,990	52	6-75	2	38.26
R. P. Lefebvre	493.1	132	1,258	30	5-30	1	41.93
A. N. Hayhurst	291.2	46	974	17	3-58	0	57.29
I. G. Swallow	642.1	150	2,042	31	3-88	0	65.87

Also bowled: N. D. Burns 0.3–0–8–0; S. J. Cook 8–0–42–2; J. C. Hallett 40.2–7–135–4; R. J. Harden 64–6–254–6; P. M. Roebuck 160.3–37–460–7; C. J. Tavaré 17.2–0–162–0; H. R. J. Trump 164–41–520–9.

Wicket-keeper: N. D. Burns 43 ct, 1 st.

Leading Fielders: R. J. Harden 18, C. J. Tavaré 15.

at Oxford, April 18, 19, 20. SOMERSET drew with OXFORD UNIVERSITY.

SOMERSET v GLOUCESTERSHIRE

at Taunton, April 26, 27, 28, 29. Somerset won by ten wickets. Somerset 24 pts, Gloucestershire 6 pts. Toss: Somerset. Rain reduced the first day to 35.3 overs, but after that the weather was ideal. Lefebvre, in his first Championship match, and Mallender supported their captain's decision to put Gloucestershire in, and on a good pitch only Athey (146 balls), Curran and Walsh made any significant progress. Building on the determined batting of Roebuck and Harden when Somerset replied, Burns hit one six and nineteen fours in a career-best 166 from 252 balls, and Rose splendidly helped him put on a brilliant, decisive 213 in 37 overs for the sixth wicket as the bowling wilted. Although Gloucestershire trailed by 241, Stovold led a crisp response with 74 in 119 balls. However, the Somerset bowlers, and in particular Jones, whittled away at the innings until all that stood between them their team and victory was the former Somerset player, Lloyds. When, finally, he hooked Jones to square leg to bring his defiant, 221-ball innings to an end, Somerset required just 99 runs with 52 overs remaining.

Close of play: First day, Gloucestershire 114-3 (C. W. J. Athey 46*, K. M. Curran 25*); Second day, Somerset 382-5 (N. D. Burns 148*, G. D. Rose 75*); Third day, Gloucestershire 59-5 (J. W. Lloyds 32*, D. V. Lawrence 7*).

Gloucestershire

A. J. Wright c Tavaré b Lefebvre	25	– c Hardy b Rose	37
A. W. Stovold b Mallender	4	– st Burns b Swallow	74
G. D. Hodgson lbw b Lefebvre	8	– lbw b Jones	25
C. W. J. Athey c Rose b Lefebvre	68	– b Jones	39
K. M. Curran c Burns b Lefebvre	41	– c Burns b Rose	13
J. W. Lloyds b Mallender	0	– c Lefebvre b Jones	93
R. C. Russell lbw b Rose	12	– (8) c Tavaré b Jones	18
C. A. Walsh c Burns b Mallender	26	– (9) c Harden b Jones	0
D. V. Lawrence lbw b Mallender	3	– (7) c Lefebvre b Rose	9
D. A. Graveney b Lefebvre	2	– c Rose b Jones	5
B. S. Jarvis not out	0	– not out	1
L-b 6, n-b 2	8	B 1, l-b 21, n-b 3	25
	197		**339**

1/16 2/38 3/39 4/133 5/134 6/148 7/192 8/192 9/197   **197**

1/84 2/141 3/149 4/178 5/228 6/250 7/301 8/305 9/338   **339**

Bonus points – Gloucestershire 1, Somerset 4.

Bowling: *First Innings*—Jones 14-1-68-0; Mallender 19-4-46-4; Rose 15-5-46-1; Lefebvre 15.1-7-30-5; Swallow 1-0-1-0. *Second Innings*—Jones 27.1-5-75-6; Mallender 26-6-55-0; Lefebvre 24-6-66-0; Rose 25-5-64-3; Swallow 34-13-57-1.

Somerset

S. J. Cook c Russell b Walsh	16	– not out	62
P. M. Roebuck c Graveney b Curran	40		
J. J. E. Hardy c Walsh b Lawrence	4	– (2) not out	30
C. J. Tavaré c Lloyds b Jarvis	18		
R. J. Harden c Athey b Walsh	46		
N. D. Burns c Athey b Curran	166		
G. D. Rose c Russell b Walsh	85		
R. P. Lefebvre lbw b Walsh	3		
I. G. Swallow not out	7		
N. A. Mallender c Russell b Walsh	0		
A. N. Jones c Wright b Walsh	9		
B 3, l-b 15, w 4, n-b 22	44	B 4, l-b 1, n-b 2	7
	438	(no wkt)	**99**

1/30 2/38 3/75 4/101 5/196 7/409 7/419 8/419 9/420   **438**

Bonus points – Somerset 4, Gloucestershire 4.

Bowling: *First Innings*—Lawrence 14-1-77-1; Walsh 26.1-2-112-6; Jarvis 12-1-61-1; Curran 18-3-91-2; Graveney 19-3-62-0; Lloyds 5-1-17-0. *Second Innings*—Walsh 5-0-31-0; Curran 2-0-8-0; Graveney 11-4-12-0; Lawrence 2-0-21-0; Lloyds 6.2-0-22-0.

Umpires: K. E. Palmer and N. T. Plews.

At Cardiff, May 3, 4, 5, 6. SOMERSET drew with GLAMORGAN.

At Taunton, May 16, 17, 18. SOMERSET lost to NEW ZEALANDERS by five wicke▮
(See New Zealand tour section).

SOMERSET v DERBYSHIRE

At Taunton, May 19, 21, 22. Derbyshire won by 146 runs. Derbyshire 21 pts, Somerset 5 pt
Toss: Somerset. Barnett, in 152 balls, and Morris, hitting 22 fours in 216 balls, took fu
advantage of an easy pitch and some early wayward bowling. Adams, with a half-century i
147 balls, led the support. After early inroads by Warner, Somerset's response rested wit
Hayhurst (226 balls), Tavaré and Harden before Tavaré declared 100 runs behind. Th
extensive use of occasional bowlers helped Morris to his second century of the match, and h
fourth on the ground in 21 days, and Krikken achieved a career-best 77 not out before th
declaration left Somerset to score 366 in four hours. Malcolm and Mortensen put a Derbyshir
victory on the cards with three wickets, but there was a later rearm-attack from Hardy, wit
91 in 134 balls and Harden, followed by defiance from Rose and Lefebvre. Eventuall
however, Malcolm and Miller assured the win with eleven overs to spare.
Close of play: First day, Derbyshire 372-9 (O. H. Mortensen 2*); Second day, Derbyshir
93-2 (J. E. Morris 59*, K. M. Krikken 3*).

Derbyshire

*K. J. Barnett c Hayhurst b Jones	94			
P. D. Bowler c Harden b Rose	6	– (7) lbw b Swallow	2	
J. E. Morris c Burns b Lefebvre	122	– (1) b Harden	10	
A. P. Kuiper b Jones	5	– (5) c Hayhurst b Cook	1	
C. J. Adams c Roebuck b Swallow	58	– (2) c Burns b Rose	2	
B. Roberts lbw b Jones	37	– (3) lbw b Roebuck		
†K. M. Krikken lbw b Lefebvre	24	– (4) not out	7	
A. E. Warner lbw b Swallow	1	– (6) lbw b Cook		
D. E. Malcolm lbw b Swallow	10			
O. H. Mortensen not out	2	– (8) not out		
B 1, l-b 9, n-b 3	13	N-b 5		

1/18 2/189 3/217 4/237 5/317   (9 wkts dec.) 372   1/52 2/81 3/178   (6 wkts dec.) 26
6/335 7/338 8/360 9/372   4/201 5/204 6/249

G. Miller did not bat.

Bonus points – Derbyshire 4, Somerset 2 (Score at 100 overs: 335-6).

Bowling: *First Innings*—Jones 17–1–85–3; Rose 16–0–75–1; Lefebvre 24.3–6–67–2
Hayhurst 16–5–42–0; Swallow 40–7–89–3; Roebuck 3–2–4–0. *Second Innings*—Jon
4–0–26–0; Rose 5–1–24–1; Lefebvre 3–1–5–0; Swallow 20–4–51–1; Roebuck 12–3–23–
Harden 16–2–60–1; Tavaré 5–0–43–0; Cook 5–0–25–2; Burns 0.3–0–8–0.

Somerset

S. J. Cook c Kuiper b Warner	1	– c Adams b Malcolm		
J. J. E. Hardy c Krikken b Warner	4	– c sub b Malcolm	9	
A. N. Hayhurst c Mortensen b Miller	90	– lbw b Mortensen		
*C. J. Tavaré b Kuiper	64	– c Kuiper b Malcolm		
R. J. Harden not out	69	– c Mortensen b Warner	4	
P. M. Roebuck not out	34	– lbw b Miller		
†N. D. Burns (did not bat)		– c Kuiper b Barnett	1	
G. D. Rose (did not bat)		– c Krikken b Malcolm	3	
R. P. Lefebvre (did not bat)		– st Krikken b Miller	1	
I. G. Swallow (did not bat)		– lbw b Miller		
A. N. Jones (did not bat)		– not out		
B 1, l-b 6, n-b 3	10	B 1, w 1, n-b 2		

1/3 2/25 3/152 4/189   (4 wkts dec.) 272   1/6 2/7 3/25 4/118 5/138   2▮
                                               6/153 7/174 8/201 9/211

Bonus points – Somerset 3, Derbyshire 1.

Bowling: *First Innings*—Malcolm 12.4–4–20–0; Warner 11–3–30–2; Mortensen 10–3–17–0; uiper 12–1–46–1; Miller 19–3–69–1; Barnett 25–3–83–0. *Second Innings*—Mortensen -0–25–1; Malcolm 17–2–88–4; Miller 23.5–5–57–3; Warner 9–1–34–1; Barnett 4–0–14–1.

Umpires: K. E. Palmer and D. S. Thompsett.

SOMERSET v SUSSEX

t Taunton, May 23, 24, 25. Drawn. Somerset 7 pts, Sussex 4 pts. Toss: Somerset. A agnificent innings by Cook, lasting 258 minutes and comprising 197 balls, one six and 30 urs, was well supported by a career-best 170 off 277 balls from Hayhurst (one six, 23 fours). ogether they added 243 in 54 overs for the second wicket and effectively gave Somerset's owlers two days in which to dismiss Sussex twice. They made a useful start, having Sussex 08 for four despite a defiant 166-ball half-century from Lenham. But Colin Wells, after an scape when 7, batted through 185 balls in a determined rearguard action. He hit two sixes nd eleven fours in his 99 not out, and had he not turned down many singles at the end, he ould have had a deserved century. Speight, with 73 from 131 balls, and Gould also profited om escapes. Following on 187 behind, Sussex were again forced on to the defensive by an arly wicket, but the patient Lenham (252 balls, eleven fours) found equally determined artners in Dodemaide and Alan Wells, and by the time Speight had ensured the draw with is second half-century, Somerset had had recourse to ten bowlers.

Close of play: First day, Somerset 500-5 (N. D. Burns 14*, G. D. Rose 4*); Second day, ussex 304-9 (C. M. Wells 92*, A. M. Babington 8*).

omerset

J. Cook c Gould b C. M. Wells	197		†N. D. Burns not out		14
M. Roebuck c Moores b Babington	. 27		G. D. Rose not out		4
N. Hayhurst c Babington			B 1, l-b 3, w 1, n-b 4		9
	b Dodemaide	.170			—
C. J. Tavaré c and b Babington	 28		1/76 2/319 3/364	(5 wkts dec.)	500
J. Harden c and b Pigott	 51		4/477 5/487		

. P. Lefebvre, I. G. Swallow, N. A. Mallender and A. N. Jones did not bat.

Bonus points – Somerset 4, Sussex 1 (Score at 100 overs: 453-3).

Bowling: Pigott 22–2–117–1; Dodemaide 25–2–115–1; Babington 23–2–109–2; C. M. Wells 1–1–72–1; Salisbury 17–4–66–0; Lenham 2–0–17–0.

ussex

. J. Lenham lbw b Roebuck	....	51	– run out	108
W. Hall lbw b Mallender	....	6	– c Tavaré b Jones	 1
I. C. Dodemaide lbw b Rose	....	0	– b Lefebvre	 20
. P. Wells c Burns b Roebuck	....	18	– b Mallender	 23
4. P. Speight c Rose b Lefebvre	....	73	– not out	 83
C. M. Wells not out	....	99	– not out	 6
J. Gould c sub b Rose	....	30		
P. Moores b Rose	....	1		
. C. S. Pigott c Rose b Swallow	....	2		
D. K. Salisbury c Harden b Jones	....	5		
. M. Babington c Burns b Jones	....	8		
B 4, l-b 2, n-b 14	....	20	B 5, l-b 7, w 3	 15

'30 2/30 3/64 4/108 5/206		313	1/4 2/45 3/107	(4 wkts dec.) 256
'268 7/270 8/277 9/291			4/219	

Bonus points – Sussex 3, Somerset 3 (Score at 100 overs: 280-8).

Bowling: *First Innings*—Jones 18.5–1–71–2; Mallender 16–6–21–1; Swallow 24–8–62–1; ose 17–4–52–3; Roebuck 21–4–63–2; Lefebvre 18–4–38–1. *Second Innings*—Jones 8–5–11–1; ose 8–2–21–0; Lefebvre 12–2–33–1; Mallender 13–2–24–1; Swallow 14–4–28–0; Roebuck 2–1–38–0; Harden 11–1–43–0; Hayhurst 5–0–22–0; Tavaré 3–0–12–0; Cook 2–0–12–0.

Umpires: K. E. Palmer and D. S. Thompsett.

At Leicester, May 26, 28, 29. SOMERSET drew with LEICESTERSHIRE.

At Bristol, June 2, 4, 5. SOMERSET drew with GLOUCESTERSHIRE.

At Basingstoke, June 6, 7, 8. SOMERSET drew with HAMPSHIRE.

At Canterbury, June 9, 11, 12. SOMERSET drew with KENT.

SOMERSET v ESSEX

At Bath, June 16, 18, 19. Drawn. Somerset 3 pts, Essex 4 pts. Toss: Essex. Stephenson
maiden double-century, coming from 343 balls and containing three sixes and 24 fours, se
Essex up on a slow pitch. Having shared a century opening stand with Gooch, Stephenso
then added 225 for the second wicket with Prichard, whose appreciation of an escape befo
scoring came in the form of 115 from 188 balls, his third hundred of the summer to date. Rai
took the first 40 overs of the second day, after which Hayhurst, in 175 balls, and Tavaré bui
on a fair start. Somerset declared 200 runs behind, and then fed Essex with easy runs unt
Gooch set a target of 353 in five hours. A thunderstorm ended any prospect of a good finish
  Close of play: First day, Essex 431-3 (J. P. Stephenson 202*, B. R. Hardie 22*); Second day
Somerset 231-2 (A. N. Hayhurst 65*, C. J. Tavaré 78*).

Essex

*G. A. Gooch c Hardy b Swallow	72		
J. P. Stephenson not out	202	– not out	6
P. J. Prichard c Burns b Mallender	115	– c Hayhurst b Harden	
M. E. Waugh c Burns b Mallender	0	– not out	7
B. R. Hardie not out	22		
†M. A. Garnham (did not bat)		– (1) c Hayhurst b Harden	1(
B 1, l-b 14, n-b 5	20	L-b 1, n-b 1	

1/106 2/331 3/331   (3 wkts dec.) 431   1/13 2/17   (2 wkts dec.) 15

D. R. Pringle, T. D. Topley, N. A. Foster, J. H. Childs and P. M. Such did not bat.

Bonus points – Essex 4, Somerset 1 (Score at 100 overs: 349-3).

Bowling: *First Innings*—Jones 17–2–59–0; Mallender 20–2–74–2; Rose 18–1–78–0; Swallo
35–8–140–1; Hayhurst 12–1–39–0; Roebuck 8–2–26–0. *Second Innings*—Hayhurst 2–0–11–(
Harden 9–1–54–2; Tavaré 7.5–0–86–0.

Somerset

S. J. Cook c Childs b Foster	32	– not out	1(
J. J. E. Hardy lbw b Topley	42	– not out	1.
A. N. Hayhurst not out	65		
*C. J. Tavaré not out	78		
B 1, l-b 10, n-b 3	14		

1/52 2/100   (2 wkts dec.) 231   (no wkt) 3:

P. M. Roebuck, R. J. Harden, †N. D. Burns, G. D. Rose, I. G. Swallow, N. A. Mallender an
  A. N. Jones did not bat.

Bonus points – Somerset 2

Bowling: *First Innings*—Pringle 15–6–28–0; Foster 14–2–56–1; Topley 14–1–48–1; Child
16–8–21–0; Such 12–2–29–0; Waugh 6–0–38–0. *Second Innings*—Foster 6.5–2–25–0; Pringl
6–3–7–0.

Umpires: R. Julian and K. J. Lyons.

SOMERSET v GLAMORGAN

\t Bath, June 20, 21, 22. Drawn. Somerset 4 pts, Glamorgan 1 pt. Toss: Somerset. Having ·educed play on the first two days to a total of 45.1 overs, rain then removed 45 minutes at a ·ritical stage on the last day as Glamorgan were pursuing a target of 302 in four hours. On a ·itch generally slow but providing some variations, Cook (163 balls) and Hayhurst put on 86 ·a 31 overs against a searching attack, while on the final day, largely against the occasional ·owlers, Rose (87 balls, six sixes, eight fours) and Burns took 160 off 26 overs. Each side then ··rfeited an innings. Glamorgan lost two early wickets, but Butcher (152 balls) and Maynard ·dded 60 in fourteen overs either side of a thunderstorm. This interruption, followed by the ·ss of Maynard and Richards, put paid to the run-chase, leaving Croft to support his captain ·hrough the final 21 overs.

Close of play: First day, Somerset 95-1 (S. J. Cook 40*, A. N. Hayhurst 38*); Second day, ·omerset 104-1 (S. J. Cook 42*, A. N. Hayhurst 44*).

\;omerset

\;. J. Cook c Metson b Watkin	61		G. D. Rose not out		97
\;. J. E. Hardy lbw b Bastien	10		L-b 7, w 2, n-b 5		14
\;.. N. Hayhurst c Butcher b Watkin	48				—
\;N. D. Burns not out	71		1/22 2/108 3/141	(3 wkts dec.)	301

\;C. J. Tavaré, R. J. Harden, I. G. Swallow, N. A. Mallender, H. R. J. Trump and A. N. Jones did not bat.

Bonus points – Somerset 4, Glamorgan 1.

Bowling: Watkin 26–9–53–2; Bastien 25–9–64–1; Dennis 8–1–20–0; Cowley 1–0–4–0; Croft ·1–12–0; Holmes 4–0–27–0; Morris 3–0–41–0; Butcher 7–0–45–0; Maynard 5–0–28–0.

·omerset forfeited their second innings.

\;lamorgan

·lamorgan forfeited their first innings.

A. R. Butcher not out	83		R. D. B. Croft not out		17
\;. Morris c Harden b Jones	2				
\;. C. Holmes lbw b Mallender	1		L-b 2, n-b 6		8
\;. P. Maynard c Harden b Swallow	33				—
\;V. A. Richards b Swallow	21		1/8 2/27 3/87 4/113	(4 wkts)	165

\;. G. Cowley, †C. P. Metson, S. J. Dennis, S. L. Watkin and S. Bastien did not bat.

Bowling: Jones 7–3–15–1; Mallender 9–1–27–1; Swallow 19–3–63–2; Rose 9–0–35–0; ·rump 4–2–11–0; Harden 3–0–12–0.

Umpires: R. Julian and N. T. Plews.

SOMERSET v NORTHAMPTONSHIRE

\t Taunton, June 30, July 2, 3. Northamptonshire won by seven wickets. Northamptonshire \; pts, Somerset 5 pts. Toss: Somerset. On a pitch which played easily after starting slightly ·amp, the batsmen dominated throughout and it needed three declarations before \;lorthamptonshire were left to score 329 in four hours. Cook and Roebuck opened for ·omerset with more than 100 in each innings, and Lefebvre's maiden first-class fifty in the ·econd came from just 44 balls against the spinners. Cook's retirement in the second innings ·esulted from a blow on the arm from Harden's fierce straight drive. Felton, in 158 balls, hit a ·x and thirteen fours to register a hundred against his former county and received steady ·upport throughout, although night-watchman Thomas's 48 was at the cost of a broken hand. ·n Northamptonshire's second innings, Fordham (169 balls) and Bailey (108 balls) redressed a ·ow start to the run-chase by adding 185 in 34 overs, after which Lamb, with 64 from 51 balls, ·eered his side home with fifteen balls to spare.

Close of play: First day, Northamptonshire 14-1 (N. A. Felton 7*, J. G. Thomas 0*); ·econd day, Somerset 124-0 (S. J. Cook 71*, P. M. Roebuck 42*).

Somerset

S. J. Cook c Fordham b Williams	65	– retired hurt	11
P. M. Roebuck c Ripley b Thomas	60	– lbw b Davis	4
A. N. Hayhurst c Davis b Cook	81	– (7) not out	2
*C. J. Tavaré c Felton b Williams	39		
R. J. Harden b Williams	23	– (3) b Robinson	2
G. D. Rose not out	33	– (4) c sub b Robinson	0
†N. D. Burns b Thomas	0	– (6) c Bailey b Cook	0
R. P. Lefebvre not out	0	– (5) c Bailey b Cook	5
I. G. Swallow (did not bat)		– (8) run out	
L-b 8, w 1, n-b 14	23	L-b 3, n-b 13	1

1/128 2/134 3/254 4/278   (6 wkts dec.) 324   1/126 2/196 3/211   (6 wkts dec.) 30
5/309 6/317   4/254 5/279 6/305

N. A. Mallender and A. N. Jones did not bat.

    Bonus points – Somerset 4, Northamptonshire 1 (Score at 100 overs: 302-4).

In the second innings S. J. Cook retired hurt at 184.

Bowling: *First Innings*—Davis 18–1–45–0; Thomas 20–5–76–2; Cook 25–8–69–1; Robinso
18–1–62–0; Williams 22–6–64–3. *Second Innings*—Davis 14–2–72–1; Robinson 15–1–76–2
Cook 20–3–63–2; Williams 21–5–54–0; Bailey 4–0–37–0.

Northamptonshire

A. Fordham c Tavaré b Mallender	6	– c Burns b Rose	12
N. A. Felton c Rose b Jones	101	– c Rose b Lefebvre	
J. G. Thomas c Roebuck b Rose	48		
R. J. Bailey not out	80	– (3) b Jones	10
*A. J. Lamb c Mallender b Swallow	40	– (4) not out	6
D. J. Capel not out	13	– (5) not out	2
B 1, l-b 5, w 1, n-b 6	13	B 5, l-b 3, n-b 3	1

1/13 2/92 3/215 4/263   (4 wkts dec.) 301   1/26 2/211 3/287   (3 wkts) 33

R. G. Williams, †D. Ripley, W. W. Davis, N. G. B. Cook and M. A. Robinson did not bat

    Bonus points – Northamptonshire 4, Somerset 1.

Bowling: *First Innings*—Jones 14–0–48–1; Mallender 14–1–70–1; Lefebvre 14–4–49–0; Ros
7–1–15–1; Swallow 21–5–84–1; Roebuck 6–2–17–0; Hayhurst 5–0–12–0. *Second Innings*—
Jones 12–2–63–1; Mallender 12–2–33–0; Lefebvre 10–2–41–1; Rose 13–0–77–1; Swallo
13.3–0–76–0; Roebuck 4–0–21–0; Hayhurst 1–0–13–0.

                Umpires: K. J. Lyons and D. O. Oslear.

SOMERSET v WARWICKSHIRE

At Taunton, July 4, 5, 6. Drawn. Somerset 4 pts, Warwickshire 5 pts. Toss: Warwickshire.
gritty, patient first century of the season by Roebuck, who hit thirteen fours in 269 balls whil
carrying his bat for the third time in his career, held the Somerset innings together after the
had been put in on a pitch giving some encouragement to bowlers. Rain reduced the first da
to 54 overs, and the second was marked by gale-force winds, although these did not hampe
Asif Din and Humpage as they shaped a brisk response, which allowed Reeve to make a
enterprising declaration. Next day, in the best batting conditions of the match, and give
some help by the use of occasional bowlers, Cook and Roebuck put on 223 in 54 overs. Coo
hit two sixes and nineteen fours in his 137 from 170 balls, while Roebuck's unbeaten 90 cam
from 160 balls. Warwickshire, chasing a target of 357 in 210 minutes, received a setback whe
Mallender took two wickets in his fourth over, but rain three overs later banished any hopes c
a win for either side by bringing the game to a premature conclusion.
    Close of play: First day, Somerset 173-6 (P. M. Roebuck 75*, N. A. Mallender 0*); Secon
day, Somerset 15-0 (S. J. Cook 10*, P. M. Roebuck 5*).

omerset

J. Cook c Piper b Reeve	35	– c Ostler b Moles	137
M. Roebuck not out	114	– not out	90
N. Hayhurst c Humpage b Reeve	6	– c Reeve b Moles	3
C. J. Tavaré c Piper b Benjamin	23		
J. Harden lbw b Benjamin	9		
N. D. Burns c Piper b Benjamin	0	– (4) not out	3
D. Rose c Piper b Donald	14		
A. Mallender c Piper b Benjamin	0		
P. Lefebvre c Humpage b Reeve	22		
G. Swallow c Reeve b Pierson	32		
N. Jones st Piper b Pierson	0		
L-b 3, w 1, n-b 11	15	B 1, l-b 2, w 1, n-b 1	5

1/77 2/97 3/129 4/146 5/152   270   1/223 2/231   (2 wkts dec.) 238
6/173 7/181 8/226 9/268

Bonus points – Somerset 3, Warwickshire 4.

Bowling: *First Innings*—Donald 23–9–58–1; Benjamin 27–3–86–4; Munton 21–2–65–0; Reeve 20–8–47–3; Pierson 1.5–0–11–2. *Second Innings*—Donald 8–1–27–0; Benjamin 7–1–31–0; Pierson 9–2–23–0; Reeve 5–0–19–0; Munton 6–0–35–0; Asif Din 10–0–41–0; Moles 8–0–56–2; Humpage 2–1–3–0.

Warwickshire

J. Moles c Harden b Jones	14	– c Burns b Mallender	6
D. Ratcliffe lbw b Rose	7	– not out	16
Asif Din c Rose b Lefebvre	45	– lbw b Mallender	0
W. Humpage not out	67	– not out	0
D. A. Reeve b Jones	4		
P. Ostler not out	11		
L-b 2, n-b 2	4	L-b 1, n-b 1	2

1/16 2/46 3/106 4/117   (4 wkts dec.) 152   1/22 2/22   (2 wkts) 24

K. J. Piper, A. A. Donald, J. E. Benjamin, A. R. K. Pierson and T. A. Munton did not bat.

Bonus points – Warwickshire 1, Somerset 1.

Bowling: *First Innings*—Jones 11–3–38–2; Mallender 10.2–2–24–0; Lefebvre 11–5–31–1; Rose 9–0–57–1. *Second Innings*—Jones 6–1–19–0; Mallender 5–4–4–2.

Umpires: K. J. Lyons and D. O. Oslear.

At Worcester, July 18, 19, 20. SOMERSET drew with WORCESTERSHIRE.

At Uxbridge, July 21, 23, 24. SOMERSET lost to MIDDLESEX by four wickets.

At Scarborough, July 25, 26, 27. SOMERSET drew with YORKSHIRE.

At Manchester, July 28, 30, 31. SOMERSET drew with LANCASHIRE.

SOMERSET v SURREY

At Weston-super-Mare, August 4, 6, 7. Drawn. Somerset 6 pts, Surrey 6 pts. Toss: Surrey. After Cook had, for the second season in succession, become the first player to 2,000 first-class runs, Somerset batted productively. The high points were Harden's unbeaten 117-ball century and the mighty innings of Rose, whose 85 from 55 balls contained eight sixes and five fours.

In one over Medlycott was struck for 29 runs. As the pitch continued to play easily, Surre recovered handsomely from 39 for four through a fifth-wicket partnership of 188 betwee Greig (220 balls) and Lynch (155 balls, eighteen fours). Greig declared 139 behind, and Cook seventh first-class century of the summer set up a target of 369 in 250 minutes. Thorpe (13 balls) and Ward, before he was brilliantly caught on the boundary, put on 105 in 28 overs t launch the charge, and Lynch, with a superb 104 from 83 balls, including five sixes and nir fours, propelled Surrey to 325 for five with six overs left. However, Lynch, Medlycott an Stewart all went in four balls, and it fell to the ninth-wicket pair to play out the final 2 deliveries.

Close of play: First day, Somerset 441-8 (R. J. Harden 104*); Second day, Somerset 58- (S. J. Cook 29*, P. M. Roebuck 18*).

Somerset

S. J. Cook c Stewart b Waqar Younis	52	– not out	11
P. M. Roebuck c Lynch b Bicknell	49	– lbw b Kendrick	3
A. N. Hayhurst c Stewart b Waqar Younis	40		
*C. J. Tavaré b Kendrick	38	– (3) b Kendrick	
R. J. Harden not out	104	– (4) not out	5
†N. D. Burns b Waqar Younis	25		
G. D. Rose b Bicknell	85		
R. P. Lefebvre c Stewart b Bicknell	8		
I. G. Swallow c Stewart b Bicknell	11		
B 8, l-b 9, w 3, n-b 9	29	B 1, l-b 10, n-b 4	1

1/99 2/110 3/194 4/194 5/277 (8 wkts dec.) 441   1/110 2/118 (2 wkts dec.) 22
6/401 7/415 8/441

N. A. Mallender and A. N. Jones did not bat.

Bonus points – Somerset 4, Surrey 2 (Score at 100 overs: 392-5).

Bowling: *First Innings*—Waqar Younis 23–2–80–3; Bicknell 23–3–79–4; Feltham 6–0–23–(Medlycott 25–8–100–0; Kendrick 21–3–87–1; Greig 12–0–55–0. *Second Innings*—Waqa Younis 8–1–31–0; Bicknell 8–1–15–0; Kendrick 21–4–73–2; Medlycott 21–3–99–0; Gre 0.1–0–0–0.

Surrey

G. S. Clinton c Roebuck b Jones	8	– (2) c Burns b Jones	1
M. A. Feltham c Harden b Jones	0	– (1) b Jones	
G. P. Thorpe run out	9	– lbw b Swallow	8
†D. M. Ward b Lefebvre	18	– c Lefebvre b Swallow	4
M. A. Lynch b Swallow	97	– b Hayhurst	10
*I. A. Greig not out	123	– lbw b Lefebvre	2
A. J. Stewart not out	24	– (8) lbw b Rose	
K. T. Medlycott (did not bat)		– (7) c sub b Rose	3
M. P. Bicknell (did not bat)		– not out	
N. M. Kendrick (did not bat)		– not out	
B 4, l-b 6, w 4, n-b 9	23	L-b 13, w 1	1

1/1 2/13 3/25 4/39 5/227 (5 wkts dec.) 302   1/0 2/37 3/142 4/179 (8 wkts) 32
5/245 6/325 7/325 8/325

Waqar Younis did not bat.

Bonus points – Surrey 4, Somerset 2.

Bowling: *First Innings*—Jones 16–4–62–2; Mallender 13–2–49–0; Lefebvre 17–4–47–1; Ros 13–1–40–0; Hayhurst 6–2–11–0; Swallow 20.5–3–83–1. *Second Innings*—Jones 9–1–36–2 Mallender 14–1–47–0; Lefebvre 14.5–0–72–1; Rose 9–3–26–2; Hayhurst 13–0–59–1; Swallo 11–0–74–2.

Umpires: P. J. Eele and R. A. White.

SOMERSET v NOTTINGHAMSHIRE

t Weston-super-Mare, August 8, 9, 10. Drawn. Somerset 8 pts, Nottinghamshire 5 pts. Toss: ottinghamshire. In good weather, on a gradually slowing pitch, Trump's spell of three for 4 eight balls arrested a useful start initiated by Robinson (236 balls) and Newell, who added 4 in 41 overs. Stephenson helped his captain add 69, but Mallender swept the tail aside to mplete a fine bowl. Somerset's poor start was redressed by Tavaré (167 balls, sixteen fours) d Hayhurst, who put on 164 in 55 overs for the third wicket. Crisp half-centuries from rns and Rose helped produce a lead of 150. Nottinghamshire also began badly, and when allender reduced them to 96 for five, still 54 behind with 160 minutes remaining, they emed doomed. However, Robinson kept doggedly on, remaining unbeaten for close on five urs (281 balls), and Evans, soon settling, registered his maiden century from 167 balls, a nely and sterling effort in a partnership of 196 which saved the match.

Close of play: First day, Somerset 38-2 (A. N. Hayhurst 21*, C. J. Tavaré 4*); Second day, ottinghamshire 11-1 (M. Newell 3*, K. Saxelby 0*).

Nottinghamshire

C. Broad c Burns b Mallender	4	c Burns b Mallender	7
. Newell c Burns b Trump	59	c Hayhurst b Lefebvre	7
R. T. Robinson b Lefebvre	79	(4) not out	125
Johnson c Mallender b Trump	4	(5) b Mallender	12
. W. Randall b Trump	0	(6) c Burns b Mallender	0
. P. Evans lbw b Mallender	0	(7) not out	100
D. Stephenson b Swallow	34		
3. N. French not out	24		
. E. Cooper c Tavaré b Mallender	7		
. Saxelby lbw b Mallender	6	(3) c Cook b Trump	20
A. Afford lbw b Mallender	0		
B 4, l-b 13, w 3, n-b 1	21	B 10, l-b 6, n-b 5	21

12 2/116 3/120 4/120 5/121 238 1/11 2/19 3/64 (5 wkts dec.) 292
190 7/201 8/220 9/230 4/96 5/96

Bonus points – Nottinghamshire 2, Somerset 4.

Bowling: *First Innings*—Mallender 20.1–6–46–5; Rose 13–4–37–0; Lefebvre 13–6–20–1; ayhurst 8–2–24–0; Swallow 15–6–33–1; Trump 21–5–61–3. *Second Innings*—Mallender 5–6–69–3; Rose 13–4–26–0; Trump 19.5–5–56–1; Lefebvre 13–5–24–1; Hayhurst 4–0–15–0; oebuck 8–1–22–0; Swallow 16–5–46–0; Harden 6–1–13–0; Cook 1–0–5–0.

Somerset

J. Cook lbw b Cooper	6	I. G. Swallow c Johnson b Cooper	27
M. Roebuck c French b Cooper	0	N. A. Mallender not out	17
. N. Hayhurst c and b Saxelby	79	H. R. J. Trump st French b Afford	4
C. J. Tavaré b Stephenson	96		
. J. Harden c Afford b Stephenson	0	B 4, l-b 24, w 1, n-b 14	43
N. D. Burns c and b Afford	56		
. D. Rose b Afford	60	1/1 2/17 3/181 4/185 5/258	388
. P. Lefebvre lbw b Evans	0	6/288 7/289 8/355 9/365	

Bonus points – Somerset 4, Nottinghamshire 3 (Score at 100 overs: 318-7).

Bowling: Stephenson 27–2–89–2; Cooper 20–1–57–3; Saxelby 16–4–55–1; Afford 8–11–102–3; Evans 15–5–57–1.

Umpires: P. J. Eele and R. A. White.

SOMERSET v HAMPSHIRE

t Taunton, August 18, 19, 20, 21. Somerset won by five wickets. Somerset 22 pts, Hampshire pts. Toss: Hampshire. Terry's 224-ball vigil held Hampshire together after a poor start, and e received excellent help from Robin Smith and Marshall, although Ayling and Maru put gether the highest stand of the innings – 105 in 29 overs. Mallender bowled steadily, and was responsible for Ayling's retirement shortly before the close. Only six overs were possible ‹ the second day, owing to bad light and rain, but on the third day Cook gave Somerset a fi start with his eighth hundred of the season (181 balls, sixteen fours). The patient Tavaré, wi 66 from 206 balls, kept them going after a mid-innings slump, getting spirited assistance fr‹ Lefebvre. Terry and Chris Smith put Hampshire on the way to a declaration which set a targ of 302 in 205 minutes (53 overs minimum). Cook again starred, making his 77 from 103 bal and after healthy contributions from Hayhurst, Tavaré (67 balls) and Harden, Rose and Bur were left to score 30 from four overs. Rose, hitting three sixes in his nineteen-ball 33, steer‹ his side home with four balls to spare.

Close of play: First day, Hampshire 359-8 (C. A. Connor 8*, P. J. Bakker 3*); Second da Hampshire 401-9 (J. R. Ayling 62*, C. A. Connor 29*); Third day, Hampshire 21-0 (V. Terry 10*, C. L. Smith 9*).

Hampshire

V. P. Terry c Jones b Rose	96	– c and b Harden	‹
C. L. Smith lbw b Mallender	1	– c and b Harden	8
D. I. Gower c Burns b Jones	14	– c Harden b Lefebvre	2
R. A. Smith c Burns b Mallender	58	– not out	‹
M. D. Marshall lbw b Swallow	58		
*M. C. J. Nicholas lbw b Jones	0	– (5) not out	
J. R. Ayling not out	62		
R. J. Maru c Lefebvre b Mallender	46		
†R. J. Parks lbw b Mallender	1		
C. A. Connor not out	29		
P. J. Bakker b Mallender	20		
L-b 11, n-b 5	16	L-b 4, n-b 2	‹

1/4 2/26 3/129 4/221 5/222   (9 wkts dec.) 401   1/135 2/182 3/182   (3 wkts dec.) 2(
6/242 7/347 8/356 9/401

Bonus points – Hampshire 4, Somerset 2 (Score at 100 overs: 314-6).

In the first innings J. R. Ayling, when 62, retired hurt at 347 and resumed at 401.

Bowling: *First Innings*—Jones 22–3–87–2; Mallender 27–3–102–5; Lefebvre 19–6–59–‹ Rose 15–2–48–1; Hayhurst 12–2–40–0; Swallow 17–7–37–1; Roebuck 4–0–17–0. *Seco‹ Innings*—Jones 9–1–21–0; Mallender 8–1–23–0; Rose 3–2–2–0; Lefebvre 12.4–1–40–‹ Roebuck 8–0–34–0; Hayhurst 6–0–38–0; Harden 8–0–39–2.

Somerset

S. J. Cook c Parks b Maru	114	– lbw b Marshall	7
P. M. Roebuck c Connor b Bakker	0	– c Parks b Nicholas	‹
A. N. Hayhurst c Parks b Connor	28	– st Parks b Maru	‹
*C. J. Tavaré c Parks b Maru	66	– run out	6
R. J. Harden lbw b Marshall	0	– c Gower b Connor	2
†N. D. Burns c and b Maru	1	– (7) not out	
G. D. Rose c C. L. Smith b Marshall	13	– (6) not out	3
R. P. Lefebvre c Parks b Maru	37		
N. A. Mallender b Marshall	17		
A. N. Jones not out	8		
I. G. Swallow not out	0		
L-b 11, n-b 6	17	B 10, l-b 8, w 1, n-b 1	2

1/1 2/65 3/179 4/180 5/181   (9 wkts dec.) 301   1/84 2/147 3/155   (5 wkts) 3(
6/194 7/273 8/284 9/292   4/246 5/272

Bonus points – Somerset 4, Hampshire 4.

Bowling: *First Innings*—Bakker 22–6–58–1; Marshall 16–3–43–3; Connor 17–2–75–1; Ma‹ 37.3–5–103–4; Nicholas 6–2–11–0. *Second Innings*—Marshall 11–2–34–1; Bakker 11–0–53–‹ Maru 24.2–2–123–1; Connor 8–0–45–1; Nicholas 2–0–7–1; C. L. Smith 1–0–2–0; Aylir 3–0–22–0.

Umpires: J. H. Harris and B. Hassan.

Hove, August 23, 24, 25, 27. SOMERSET beat SUSSEX by ten wickets.

Taunton, September 3. SOMERSET beat SRI LANKANS by 71 runs (See Sri Lankan tour section).

Birmingham, September 7, 8, 9, 10. SOMERSET drew with WARWICKSHIRE.

SOMERSET v WORCESTERSHIRE

Taunton, September 12, 13, 14, 15. Worcestershire won by 173 runs. Worcestershire 23 pts, Somerset 5 pts. Toss: Worcestershire. A second-wicket stand of 264 in 68 overs between Hick and Curtis established the Worcestershire innings, and after a second-morning slump the last-wicket pair of Newport and McEwan added an unbroken 88 in seventeen overs. Curtis hit 100 of his 156 (280 balls) in boundaries, while Hick, having reached 2,000 runs with a six off the last ball before lunch, scored 109 in the second session and had 27 fours in his 154 from 195 balls. Cook (165 balls, 24 fours) responded in kind for Somerset, including 100 runs between lunch and tea, and after another morning collapse Harden and Jones put on 70 in eighteen overs for Somerset's last wicket. Newport was warned by stand-in umpire Harris after bowling four bouncers in one over to Jones. Lord, Hick and D'Oliveira added briskly to Worcestershire's lead of 78, and after another quick fall of wickets the target was set at 400 in 80 overs. Radford, getting more out of the slightly wearing pitch, set Somerset back with a spell of three for 16 in 33 balls, and with Newport chipping in they were reduced to 57 for five. Harden defiantly and positively hit seventeen fours in 90 from 111 balls, but safe slip catching took the visitors home with 30 overs to spare.

Close of play: First day, Worcestershire 378-4 (P. A. Neale 31*, S. R. Lampitt 10*); Second day, Somerset 287-2 (R. J. Bartlett 69*, C. J. Tavaré 14*); Third day, Worcestershire 267-4 (. B. D'Oliveira 59*, S. R. Lampitt 2*).

Worcestershire

S. Curtis c Tavaré b Jones	156	– c Swallow b Jones	10		
J. Lord c Tavaré b Jones	6	– lbw b Mallender	80		
A. Hick c Tavaré b Mallender	154	– lbw b Jones	81		
B. D'Oliveira b Jones	14	– c Burns b Jones	60		
A. Neale lbw b Mallender	40	– lbw b Mallender	12		
R. Lampitt lbw b Mallender	16	– c Burns b Jones	10		
J. Rhodes c Harden b Mallender	6	– not out	34		
K. Illingworth c Lefebvre b Jones	8	– b Jones	3		
J. Newport not out	65	– not out	7		
V. Radford c Lefebvre b Hayhurst	14				
M. McEwan not out	30				
L-b 9, n-b 2	11	B 12, l-b 10, n-b 2	24		

1/43 2/307 3/331 4/346 5/386   (9 wkts dec.) 520   1/28 2/166 3/198   (7 wkts dec.) 321
6/398 7/411 8/411 9/432   4/252 5/268
                                                 6/279 7/284

Bonus points – Worcestershire 4, Somerset 1 (Score at 100 overs: 356-4).

Bowling: *First Innings*—Jones 35–6–154–4; Mallender 32–7–100–4; Rose 6–1–15–0; Lefebvre 30–9–67–0; Hayhurst 22–2–87–1; Swallow 24–5–88–0. *Second Innings*—Jones 22–2–76–5; Mallender 24–4–75–2; Hayhurst 8–1–43–0; Rose 9–1–51–0; Swallow 9–0–51–0; Lefebvre 4–2–3–0.

Somerset

A. N. Hayhurst c Rhodes b Lampitt	50	– c Hick b Newport
S. J. Cook c Neale b Illingworth	143	– c Hick b Radford
R. J. Bartlett c D'Oliveira b Newport	73	– c Rhodes b Radford
*C. J. Tavaré c Rhodes b Newport	18	– b Radford
R. J. Harden not out	51	– c D'Oliveira b Radford
†N. D. Burns b Newport	0	– c Hick b Newport
G. D. Rose b Lampitt	29	– lbw b Lampitt
R. P. Lefebvre c Hick b Lampitt	0	– c D'Oliveira b McEwan
I. G. Swallow run out	4	– b Illingworth
N. A. Mallender c Hick b Lampitt	15	– c Hick b Lampitt
A. N. Jones b Illingworth	41	– not out
B 1, l-b 3, w 3, n-b 11	18	L-b 1, w 1, n-b 6

1/132 2/252 3/295 4/296 5/296　　　　　442　　1/23 2/50 3/52 4/56 5/57　　　2
6/345 7/345 8/352 9/372　　　　　　　　　　　6/119 7/172 8/173 9/212

Bonus points – Somerset 4, Worcestershire 3 (Score at 100 overs: 372-8).

Bowling: *First Innings*—Newport 28–4–95–3; McEwan 26–1–116–0; Lampitt 24–3–97–
Radford 18–6–75–0; Illingworth 22.5–5–55–2; Hick 1–1–0–0. *Second Innings*—Newpo
13–1–74–2; Radford 13–2–55–4; Lampitt 10.5–1–43–2; McEwan 8–0–39–1; Illingwor
8–3–10–1; Hick 2–0–4–0.

Umpires: R. Julian and D. R. Shepherd.
(J. H. Harris deputised for D. R. Shepherd on 2nd, 3rd and 4th days).

FIELDING IN 1990

(Qualification: 20 dismissals)

69　S. J. Rhodes (61 ct, 8 st)	30　G. W. Humpage (all ct)
63　K. M. Krikken (60 ct, 3 st)	30　M. A. Lynch
63　P. Moores (53 ct, 10 st)	30　R. J. Maru
59　C. P. Metson (all ct)	27　R. P. Davis
57　B. N. French (46 ct, 11 st)	26　G. A. Hick
54　R. J. Blakey (45 ct, 9 st)	26　D. A. Reeve
54　S. A. Marsh (49 ct, 5 st)	25　C. J. Adams
53　R. J. Parks (49 ct, 4 st)	24　M. A. Atherton
51　W. K. Hegg (49 ct, 2 st)	24　A. J. Stewart
50　M. A. Garnham (48 ct, 2 st)	24　V. P. Terry
50　P. A. Nixon (49 ct, 1 st)	23　L. Potter
46　R. C. Russell (45 ct, 1 st)	23　B. Roberts
45　P. R. Downton (42 ct, 3 st)	23　M. A. Roseberry
44　N. D. Burns (43 ct, 1 st)	23　A. J. Wright
44　K. J. Piper (40 ct, 4 st)	22　A. Fordham
35　D. M. Ward (32 ct, 3 st)	22　N. Shahid
34　D. Ripley (28 ct, 6 st)	21　D. Byas
33　D. B. D'Oliveira	20　N. H. Fairbrother
33　J. E. Emburey	20　M. W. Gatting
31　R. C. J. Williams (27 ct, 4 st)	20　P. E. Robinson
30　K. R. Brown	

SURREY

Patron: HM The Queen
President: 1990 – E. A. Bedser
    1991 – B. Coleman
Chairman: D. H. Newton
Chairman, Cricket Committee: J. A. Fulford
Secretary: D. G. Seward
 The Oval, London SE11 5SS
 (Telephone: 071-582 6660)
Captain: I. A. Greig
County Coach: G. G. Arnold
Assistant County Coach: C. E. Waller

a a year when batsmen reigned supreme, Surrey spent much of the
ummer of 1990 admiring their unexpected and rare gift from the
rient, the teenage Pakistani fast bowler, Waqar Younis. Club coach
eoff Arnold polished the magic lamp provided by the great all-rounder,
nran Khan, the genie Waqar appeared, and, granting three wishes in
ne, he provided a treasure chest of 95 wickets in all cricket.

Imran could hardly have recommended his latest pace protégé to
urrey at a more propitious time. Tony Gray, the West Indian fast
owler, whom they had re-engaged after a year's absence, was
xperiencing fitness problems, and Arnold, himself a fine purveyor of
wing bowling, saw enough of Younis in a brief net trial to thrust him
raight into a Benson and Hedges Cup quarter-final at Old Trafford at a
w hours' notice. That was late May, and Younis was there to stay for
e season. Initially, that is. The Surrey committee prudently recognised
e benefits of such a special talent and granted him a five-year contract.
he compactly built Younis, of the two-way swing and devastating
orker, was Surrey's most effective Championship bowler, with 57
ickets at just under 24 apiece. Of these, 29 were bowled and eight lbw;
e other twenty were all caught behind the wicket, twelve by the wicket-
eeper or first slip. In the Refuge Assurance League, he was top of the
ational averages and the leading wicket-taker with 31 at 12.77.

Indeed, Surrey's season was highlighted by Waqar and Ward, a
ricketing double-act with an entrepreneurial ring which produced its
ost profitable business in the middle. David Ward, hitherto regarded as
useful county professional, became one of ten players in the country to
ass 2,000 runs in a prosperous summer for strokemakers. In his previous
ve years at The Oval, he had made only three hundreds, but now he
ubbed shoulders with such international "heavyweights" as Gooch,
ook, Hick and Haynes. Of his seven hundreds, two were doubles,
cluding a career-best 263 against Kent at Canterbury, and he became
e first Surrey player since J. H. Edrich in 1962, and the thirteenth in
ll, to score 2,000 for the county alone. Greats such as Hayward, Hobbs,
andham and May had achieved the same feat, but in the days when
ore matches were played.

Although the final Britannic Assurance Championship placing of
inth was an improvement of three places on 1989, the Surrey members
oubtless expected better. However, the committee and the backroom

staff were largely content to be patient and await the harvest of the
expansive youth scheme within the next few years. Furthermore, whi
The Oval pitches, with all their excellence and reliability, were a
outstanding example to the rest of English cricket, they were a two-edge
sword for Surrey. They won only three matches at The Oval, albeit goin
undefeated there. Their preference for four-day cricket, therefore, is n
surprising, for it would offer them the opportunity to enjoy more winnir
options; in theory, anyway, if not always in practice.

The second of Surrey's six four-day matches last summer, again
Lancashire, became a record-breaking bonanza which produced a ne
Championship mark of 1,650 runs for nineteen wickets. Ian Greig's 29
was the highest Championship score by a Surrey player at The Oval sin
A. Sandham's 292 not out against Northamptonshire in 1921. The Surr
captain was, however, upstaged by Neil Fairbrother's 366 in
Lancashire total of 863, the second highest in the Championship and t
ninth biggest in all first-class cricket. It set the trend for the glut of ru
getting around the country and left Martin Bicknell, with just one wick
for 305 in the opening two matches, fearing for his Surrey place. But I
allying a deft change of pace to his natural away-swing, Bicknell claim
67 wickets in first-class games and earned a place in England's side
tour Australia, along with team-mate Alec Stewart. Bicknell and Waq
Younis helped Surrey collect 64 bowling bonus points, joint best in t
country, although their total of 54 for batting was of a low order.

Darren Bicknell made five first-class hundreds, all in the Champio
ship, to win selection for the England A tour, for which he was joined I
Keith Medlycott and Graham Thorpe. Left-arm spinner Medlycott had
chequered season after touring the West Indies with the England seni
side early in 1990, while Thorpe, after a splendid first full season in 198
had a lean time as others broke the run bank. However, his phlegmat
temperament and undoubted class once more won the selecto
confidence, whereas Ward, in spite of his feats, went unrecognised.
the coming summer, Surrey will be without one of their other le
handers, Grahame Clinton, who signed off not only by passing 1,0
runs for the seventh time in twelve seasons at The Oval but by achievi
his highest aggregate in seventeen years of first-class cricket.

The one-day game produced nothing special in terms of results. Af
reaching the last eight of the Benson and Hedges Cup, Surrey we
drawn against the eventual winners, Lancashire, while they did n
progress beyond a meeting with Middlesex in round two of the NatW
Bank Trophy. Sixth place in the Refuge Assurance League mirrored th
Sabbath performances of the previous summer. As the season unfolde
the impressive West Side stand was nearing completion, and apart fr
finishing touches, it was ready for spectators, sponsors and scribes duri
the traditional final Test, against India, in late August. – David Field

583

SURREY 1990

[Bill Smith]

Back row: A. W. Smith, M. A. Butcher, A. G. Robson, J. Boiling, G. P. Thorpe, A. Hollioake, N. F. Sargeant. *Middle row*: J. Deary (*physiotherapist*), G. G. Arnold (*county coach*), A. D. Brown, A. J. Murphy, D. M. Ward, D. J. Bicknell, R. I. Alikhan, P. D. Atkins, J. D. Robinson, N. M. Kendrick, C. E. Waller (*assistant county coach*). M. R. L. W. Ayers (*scorer*). *Front row*: C. K. Bullen, M. P. Bicknell, M. A. Lynch, A. J. Stewart, I. A. Greig (*captain*), G. S. Clinton, K. T. Medlycott, A. H. Gray, M. A. Feltham. *Inset*: Waqar Younis.

SURREY RESULTS

All first-class matches – Played 24: Won 4, Lost 3, Drawn 17.

County Championship matches – Played 22: Won 4, Lost 3, Drawn 15.

Bonus points – Batting 54, Bowling 64.

*Competition placings – Britannic Assurance County Championship, 9th;
NatWest Bank Trophy, 2nd round; Benson and Hedges Cup, q-f;
Refuge Assurance League, 6th equal.*

BRITANNIC ASSURANCE CHAMPIONSHIP AVERAGES

BATTING

	Birthplace	M	I	NO	R	HI	Avge
‡D. M. Ward	Croydon	22	31	7	1,843	263	76.7
‡D. J. Bicknell	Guildford	13	20	4	1,199	186	74.9
‡I. A. Greig	Queenstown, SA	22	26	5	1,130	291	53.8
R. I. Alikhan	Westminster	11	16	2	726	138	51.8
‡A. J. Stewart	Merton	12	21	6	709	100*	47.2
‡G. S. Clinton	Sidcup	18	29	4	1,092	146	43.6
‡M. A. Lynch	Georgetown, BG	22	29	4	1,049	104	41.9
‡M. P. Bicknell	Guildford	19	15	7	309	50*	38.6
‡M. A. Feltham	St John's Wood	14	14	3	373	101	33.9
‡Waqar Younis	Vehari, Pakistan	14	9	7	56	14	28.0
G. P. Thorpe	Farnham	16	24	4	537	86	26.8
‡K. T. Medlycott	Whitechapel	20	22	7	389	44	25.9
J. D. Robinson	Epsom	7	9	0	151	72	16.7
N. M. Kendrick ...	Bromley	11	12	4	124	52*	15.5
A. J. Murphy	Manchester	12	6	3	6	4*	2.0

Also batted: P. D. Atkins (*Aylesbury*) (1 match) 23, 0*; ‡A. H. Gray (*Port-of-Spain, Trinidad*) (6 matches) 11, 11; N. F. Sargeant (*Hammersmith*) (2 matches) 1.

* *Signifies not out.*   ‡ *Denotes county cap.*

The following played a total of nineteen three-figure innings for Surrey in County Championship matches – D. M. Ward 6, D. J. Bicknell 5, R. I. Alikhan 2, I. A. Greig 2, G. S. Clinton 1, M. A. Feltham 1, M. A. Lynch 1, A. J. Stewart 1.

BOWLING

	O	M	R	W	BB	5W/i	Avge
Waqar Younis	422	70	1,357	57	7-73	3	23.8
M. P. Bicknell	597.5	137	1,653	60	5-34	1	27.5
M. A. Feltham	334.4	59	1,082	39	6-53	2	27.7
A. H. Gray	212.4	43	556	16	4-83	0	34.7
K. T. Medlycott	617.5	134	2,020	53	7-92	3	38.1
A. J. Murphy	404.2	76	1,367	30	5-67	2	45.5
N. M. Kendrick	273	50	987	17	4-110	0	58.0
I. A. Greig	199.1	19	805	12	3-60	0	67.0

Also bowled: R. I. Alikhan 20-1-83-1; D. J. Bicknell 9-1-20-0; M. A. Lynch 27-5-130-1; J. D. Robinson 118.3-21-393-6; A. J. Stewart 5-0-32-0; G. P. Thorpe 9-1-69-0.

Wicket-keepers: D. M. Ward 25 ct, 2 st; A. J. Stewart 10 ct; N. F. Sargeant 5 ct.

Leading Fielders: M. A. Lynch 29, I. A. Greig 16.

At Hove, April 26, 27, 28, 30. SURREY lost to SUSSEX by five wickets.

SURREY v LANCASHIRE

At The Oval, May 3, 4, 5, 7. Drawn. Surrey 4 pts, Lancashire 6 pts. Toss: Surrey. This record-breaking match will long be remembered and chronicled for its quite phenomenal feats of scoring on a pitch exemplifying the tougher standards laid down by the Test and County Cricket Board. Greig, the Surrey captain, drove an extremely hard tactical bargain by amassing 707 for nine declared in the hope that his bowlers could take twenty wickets for an innings victory. However, it presented Lancashire with a *fait accompli*. Needing 558 to avoid the follow-on, and realising that victory for them was out of the question, they settled down to revel in the sumptuous batting conditions. The home bowling was savaged for a colossal 863, the highest Championship total of the century and second only to Yorkshire's 887 against Warwickshire at Birmingham in 1896. Lancashire's dapper left-hander, Fairbrother, was unstoppable in the run-glut, thrashing 366 to pass by 2 runs the previous best score at The Oval – 364 by Sir Leonard Hutton in the 1938 Test match against Australia. Greig, who, coming in at No. 7, had made the highest Championship innings by a Surrey player since 1926 and by one on the ground since 1921, could hardly have envisaged his career-best 291 off 251 balls being bettered the next day.

Although Surrey enjoyed a bountiful first day, reaching 396 for six, with Lynch falling just short of three figures, there was no reason to suspect such a wholesale assault on the pages of this Almanack. Greig's stand of 205 with Bicknell next day was a Surrey best for the eighth wicket, surpassing their oldest record partnership which had stood since 1898: 204 by T. W. Hayward and L. C. Braund, also against Lancashire at The Oval. In his first Championship hundred for Surrey, Greig hit 145 runs before lunch and was the prime contributor to the 101 runs which came in twelve overs after the interval as Surrey powered on to the highest total conceded by Lancashire. He batted in all for 277 minutes and hit nine sixes and 25 fours.

Lancashire, having responded with 179 for one from 55 overs by the close, took over inexorably on day three. Mendis, 97 overnight, was out soon after reaching his hundred, but Atherton eased to a personal top score of 191 and Fairbrother strode on to 311. By lunch Fairbrother had reached 100 from 102 balls (125 minutes), and in the next two sessions he scored 108 from 109 balls (135 minutes) and 103 from 110 balls (120 minutes), leaving the statisticians with Sunday to wonder if he might beat the English record of 424, set by another famous Lancastrian, A. C. MacLaren. Already the Atherton–Fairbrother alliance of 364 had eclipsed the county's third-wicket record of 306 by E. Paynter and N. Oldfield against Hampshire at Southampton in 1938. Lancashire's captain, Hughes, gave Fairbrother the chance of batting throughout the final day to pass MacLaren, but fatigue had its way. He eventually departed to his 407th ball, having batted for 500 minutes and struck five sixes and 47 fours, the eighth highest number in the list of boundary hits. His 366 was the third highest in the Championship after MacLaren's 424 and G. A. Hick's 405 not out. Surrey reached 80 for one in the remaining time, with Stewart passing 50 for the second time and the aggregate for the match soaring to 1,650 runs, a new mark in Championship cricket and the second highest for a match in England.

Close of play: First day, Surrey 396-6 (I. A. Greig 56*, K. T. Medlycott 33*); Second day, Lancashire 179-1 (G. D. Mendis 97*, M. A. Atherton 56*); Third day, Lancashire 665-3 (N. H. Fairbrother 311*, T. E. Jesty 18*).

Surrey

R. I. Alikhan st Hegg b Fitton	55		
G. S. Clinton c Patterson b DeFreitas	8	– (1) c Watkinson b Atherton	15
A. J. Stewart c Fowler b Patterson	70	– (2) not out	54
M. A. Lynch c and b Watkinson	95	– (3) not out	6
G. P. Thorpe c Atherton b Fitton	27		
†D. M. Ward c Hughes b Fitton	36		
*I. A. Greig c Jesty b Hughes	291		
K. T. Medlycott c Fairbrother b Patterson	33		
M. P. Bicknell c Hegg b Hughes	42		
N. M. Kendrick not out	18		
B 6, l-b 16, n-b 10	32	B 2, l-b 1, n-b 2	5

1/10 2/118 3/187 4/261 5/275   (9 wkts dec.) 707   1/57   (1 wkt) 80
6/316 7/401 8/606 9/707

A. J. Murphy did not bat.

Bonus points – Surrey 4, Lancashire 2 (Score at 100 overs: 335-6).

Bowling: *First Innings*—Patterson 27–4–108–2; DeFreitas 26–4–99–1; Watkinson 23–2–113–1; Fitton 45–6–185–3; Atherton 22–5–75–0; Hughes 22.1–0–105–2. *Second Innings*—DeFreitas 4–0–10–0; Fitton 16–4–42–0; Atherton 13–5–25–1.

Lancashire

G. D. Mendis run out	102	*D. P. Hughes not out	8
G. Fowler run out	20	J. D. Fitton c Stewart b Murphy	3
M. A. Atherton c Greig b Kendrick	191	B. P. Patterson c Greig b Medlycott	0
N. H. Fairbrother c Kendrick b Greig	.366		
T. E. Jesty retired hurt	18	B 8, l-b 15, w 1, n-b 9	33
M. Watkinson b Greig	46		
†W. K. Hegg c Ward b Bicknell	45	1/45 2/184 3/548 4/745 5/774	863
P. A. J. DeFreitas b Murphy	31	6/844 7/848 8/862 9/863	

Bonus points – Lancashire 4 (Score at 100 overs: 401-2).

T. E. Jesty retired hurt at 665.

Bowling: Murphy 44–6–160–2; Bicknell 43–2–175–1; Kendrick 56–10–192–1; Medlycott 50.5–4–177–1; Lynch 5–2–17–0; Greig 19–3–73–2; Thorpe 7–1–46–0.

Umpires: B. Dudleston and A. A. Jones.

At Oxford, May 16, 17, 18. SURREY drew with OXFORD UNIVERSITY.

SURREY v HAMPSHIRE

At The Oval, May 19, 21, 22. Drawn. Surrey 5 pts, Hampshire 5 pts. Toss: Hampshire. Not even three declarations and a target which required Hampshire to score 329 in a minimum of 62 overs could produce a positive conclusion on another top-rate Oval pitch. On the opening day Surrey's Ward, with only the fifth hundred of his five-year career, but his second in successive innings, destroyed the Hampshire change bowlers with an explosive 129 not out off 144 balls (23 fours) and lifted Surrey from 173 for four to 374 for five. Left-arm spinner Maru was his main opponent, bowling an unchanged spell of 36 overs lasting four hours. Next morning the Smith brothers also found the conditions to their liking, Chris making a solid 71 and Robin clubbing fourteen fours in an unbeaten 114 before Hampshire conceded a lead of 124 runs. Stewart then hit the game's third century to set up the final declaration. Hampshire's hopes were high during a stand of 158 between Chris Smith and Gower, Smith making 84 off 117 balls and Gower 69 from 83. But when they lost their top order, Hampshire abandoned the chase and Marshall saw them to a draw with his second solid innings of the match.

Close of play: First day, Surrey 374-5 (D. M. Ward 129*, K. T. Medlycott 30*); Second day, Surrey 59-0 (A. J. Stewart 21*, G. S. Clinton 35*).

Surrey

D. J. Bicknell retired hurt	41		
G. S. Clinton c Maru b Connor	73	– retired hurt	37
A. J. Stewart c Maru b Connor	17	– (1) not out	100
M. A. Lynch c Gower b Marshall	11	– (3) c Gower b Shine	2
G. P. Thorpe c Parks b Marshall	2	– (4) lbw b Maru	18
†D. M. Ward not out	129	– (5) b Turner	23
*I. A. Greig c Terry b Marshall	34	– (6) c Maru b Turner	4
K. T. Medlycott not out	30	– (7) c Parks b Maru	8
M. A. Feltham (did not bat)		– (8) not out	3
B 4, l-b 15, w 2, n-b 16	37	B 2, l-b 4, w 1, n-b 2	9
1/148 2/151 3/166 4/173 5/308	(5 wkts dec.) 374	1/73 2/111 3/154 (5 wkts dec.) 204	
		4/158 5/187	

M. P. Bicknell and A. J. Murphy did not bat.

Bonus points – Surrey 4, Hampshire 2 (Score at 100 overs: 321-5).

In the first innings D. J. Bicknell retired hurt at 117; in the second innings G. S. Clinton retired hurt at 70.

Bowling: *First Innings*—Marshall 20–4–65–3; Shine 16–2–75–0; Connor 25–4–84–2; Turner 13–0–45–0; Maru 36–12–86–0. *Second Innings*—Marshall 7–1–14–0; Shine 9–0–55–1; Connor 5–0–13–0; Maru 21–5–47–2; Turner 14.3–4–60–2; C. L. Smith 1–0–9–0.

Hampshire

V. P. Terry lbw b Murphy	8	– c Medlycott b M. P. Bicknell	0
*C. L. Smith run out	71	– c Medlycott b Murphy	84
D. I. Gower b Feltham	4	– c sub b M. P. Bicknell	69
R. A. Smith not out	114	– c Feltham b M. P. Bicknell	1
T. C. Middleton lbw b Greig	1	– (6) b Medlycott	20
M. D. Marshall not out	47	– (5) not out	51
†R. J. Parks (did not bat)		– not out	5
B 2, l-b 2, n-b 1	5	B 6, l-b 1, w 1	8

1/19 2/26 3/163 4/179   (4 wkts dec.) 250   1/0 2/158 3/161   (5 wkts) 238
                                                          4/167 5/197

R. J. Maru, C. A. Connor, I. J. Turner and K. J. Shine did not bat.

Bonus points – Hampshire 3, Surrey 1.

Bowling: *First Innings*—M. P. Bicknell 15–5–43–0; Murphy 22–6–65–1; Feltham 19–7–51–1; Greig 8–1–40–1; Medlycott 21.1–8–47–0. *Second Innings*—M. P. Bicknell 16–5–39–3; Murphy 12–1–65–1; Feltham 8–0–31–0; Medlycott 20–3–84–1; Lynch 3–0–12–0.

Umpires: P. J. Eele and J. W. Holder.

At Lord's, May 23, 24, 25. SURREY drew with MIDDLESEX.

SURREY v DERBYSHIRE

At The Oval, June 6, 7, 8. Drawn. Surrey 5 pts, Derbyshire 3 pts. Toss: Surrey. Alikhan, after 71 first-class appearances without a hundred, was 18 runs short when a heavy downpour swept in at the start of the last hour, with Surrey needing another 107 in seventeen overs for victory and all their wickets intact. On an opening day when 44 overs were lost to rain, Waqar Younis, the young Pakistani fast bowler, registered a week earlier, claimed the wickets of Barnett, Morris and Kuiper as the ball swung consistently. Bowler, 75 overnight, became his fourth victim first thing next morning, and the visitors had to settle for a total of 275 when Medlycott produced his own four-wicket flourish. Thorpe's first half-century of the season saw Surrey to an expected declaration, although there was little urgency to their batting until Ward arrived to reel off six fours in quick succession. Derbyshire's second innings took on a more familiar look as Barnett and Bowler moved solidly to 144 before the first of the last day's stoppages. This advanced a declaration which left Surrey to make 268 in just over three hours, but the threat of a further interruption was always evident in the slate-grey skies. The pitch had become depressingly slow, as indicated by the lack of a single wicket while 304 runs were scored on the abbreviated final day.

Close of play: First day, Derbyshire 183-5 (P. D. Bowler 75*, K. M. Krikken 7*); Second day, Derbyshire 1-0 (K. J. Barnett 1*, P. D. Bowler 0*).

Derbyshire

*K. J. Barnett c Greig b Waqar Younis	1	– not out	51
P. D. Bowler c Ward b Waqar Younis	75	– not out	85
J. E. Morris lbw b Waqar Younis	25		
B. Roberts c Clinton b Feltham	17		
A. P. Kuiper lbw b Waqar Younis	37		
C. J. Adams lbw b Feltham	3		
†K. M. Krikken c Feltham b Medlycott	35		
M. Jean-Jacques c Greig b Medlycott	25		
A. E. Warner c sub b Medlycott	17		
S. J. Base b Medlycott	0		
G. Miller not out	10		
B 6, l-b 14, w 6, n-b 4	30	B 4, l-b 4	8

1/9 2/57 3/95 4/163 5/168   275   (no wkt dec.) 144
6/186 7/239 8/242 9/242

Bonus points – Derbyshire 3, Surrey 4 (Score at 100 overs: 271-9).

Bowling: *First Innings*—Waqar Younis 30–4–77–4; Bicknell 20–4–64–0; Murphy 22–4–59–0; Feltham 19–7–40–2; Medlycott 10.1–4–14–4; Alikhan 1–0–1–0. *Second Innings*—Waqar Younis 4–0–16–0; Murphy 4–2–7–0; Medlycott 11–2–21–0; Greig 9–1–36–0; Alikhan 5–0–29–0; Lynch 4–0–27–0.

Surrey

R. I. Alikhan c Bowler b Miller	39	– not out 82
K. T. Medlycott run out	6	
G. P. Thorpe not out	58	
†D. M. Ward not out	37	
G. S. Clinton (did not bat)		– (2) not out 70
L-b 3, w 2, n-b 7	12	L-b 6, w 2, n-b 1 9

1/9 2/88   (2 wkts dec.) 152   (no wkt) 161

M. A. Lynch, *I. A. Greig, M. A. Feltham, M. P. Bicknell, Waqar Younis and A. J. Murphy did not bat.

Bonus points – Surrey 1.

Bowling: *First Innings*—Jean-Jacques 14.1–3–47–0; Base 12–1–38–0; Warner 11–2–36–0; Kuiper 7–1–15–0; Miller 8–2–13–1. *Second Innings*—Jean-Jacques 8–0–49–0; Base 9–2–33–0; Warner 9–0–30–0; Kuiper 1.3–0–13–0.

Umpires: J. H. Harris and J. W. Holder.

At Harrogate, June 9, 11, 12. SURREY drew with YORKSHIRE.

SURREY v WORCESTERSHIRE

At The Oval, June 16, 18, 19. Drawn. Surrey 4 pts, Worcestershire 4 pts. Toss: Surrey. A resolute century from Botham, his first for three seasons in the Championship, helped Worcestershire recover from 94 for four. He cast off his attacking instincts and batted for more than four hours (198 balls), hitting two sixes and eleven fours in his 113. The value of his innings was fully realised next morning when the defending county champions were able to declare with maximum batting points. Surrey, for their part, were rewarded with four bowling points, and that proved to be the high point of a second day restricted by rain after lunch to 38 overs. Surrey declared immediately on the third morning, and when Worcestershire closed their second innings, somewhat generously, at 84, the home county were left to score 318 in 77 overs. Worcestershire squandered three chances as Clinton and Stewart added 113 for the second wicket, but when McEwan dismissed Stewart and Thorpe in successive balls, Surrey faltered. With 146 required from the final twenty overs, Neale gambled with the spin of Stemp and Hick, and the strategy almost worked. Surrey lost three wickets for 47 and Medlycott and Bicknell were obliged to play out the final twelve overs encircled by close fielders.

Close of play: First day, Worcestershire 263-7 (P. J. Newport 28*, S. R. Lampitt 0*); Second day, Surrey 67-1 (G. S. Clinton 33*, A. J. Stewart 7*).

Worcestershire

T. S. Curtis c Ward b Bicknell	0	– not out 31
M. J. Weston c Gray b Bicknell	6	– not out 38
G. A. Hick c Ward b Bicknell	59	
D. B. D'Oliveira c Lynch b Bicknell	0	
I. T. Botham c Stewart b Medlycott	113	
*P. A. Neale b Gray	36	
P. J. Newport c Ward b Medlycott	41	
†S. J. Rhodes c Lynch b Medlycott	4	
S. R. Lampitt not out	21	
S. M. McEwan c Bicknell b Medlycott	2	
R. D. Stemp not out	0	
B 5, l-b 11, w 1, n-b 1	18	B 4, l-b 9, w 2 15

1/11 2/16 3/22 4/94 5/187   (9 wkts dec.) 300   (no wkt dec.) 84
6/257 7/263 8/282 9/284

Bonus points – Worcestershire 4, Surrey 4.

Bowling: *First Innings*—Gray 26–8–41–1; Bicknell 22–4–70–4; Murphy 19–4–64–0; Medlycott 29–8–92–4; Greig 4–0–17–0. *Second Innings*—Gray 6–3–8–0; Bicknell 5–0–15–0; Murphy 5–1–12–0; Medlycott 5–1–19–0; Alikhan 1–0–17–0.

Surrey

R. I. Alikhan run out	23	– c Rhodes b Lampitt	21
G. S. Clinton not out	33	– c Lampitt b Newport	80
A. J. Stewart not out	7	– c Rhodes b McEwan	55
G. P. Thorpe (did not bat)		– c D'Oliveira b McEwan	0
†D. M. Ward (did not bat)		– c Curtis b Hick	21
M. A. Lynch (did not bat)		– c Botham b Hick	21
*I. A. Greig (did not bat)		– c Lampitt b Hick	6
K. T. Medlycott (did not bat)		– not out	16
M. P. Bicknell (did not bat)		– not out	15
L-b 2, n-b 2	4	L-b 7, w 1, n-b 1	9

1/46   (1 wkt dec.) 67   1/42 2/155 3/155 4/163   (7 wkts) 244
                                                                 5/199 6/212 7/219

A. H. Gray and A. J. Murphy did not bat.

Bowling: *First Innings*—Newport 9–7–6–0; McEwan 6–2–26–0; Stemp 9–3–13–0; Lampitt 6.2–1–20–0. *Second Innings*—Newport 13–1–35–1; McEwan 17–4–40–2; Lampitt 13–4–40–1; Botham 10.4–2–24–0; Stemp 17–5–78–0; Hick 6–1–20–3.

Umpires: H. D. Bird and J. H. Harris.

At Nottingham, June 20, 21, 22. SURREY drew with NOTTINGHAMSHIRE.

At Cardiff, June 30, July 2, 3. SURREY drew with GLAMORGAN.

SURREY v NORTHAMPTONSHIRE

At The Oval, July 4, 5, 6. Surrey won by 147 runs. Surrey 20 pts. Toss: Northamptonshire. Following the loss of the opening day's play, Surrey won their first Championship match of the season. Two forfeitures on the final day left Northamptonshire needing 348 from 76 overs, but they never came close and Surrey eased home with 12.4 overs in hand. The initial work was done by Darren Bicknell and Clinton who, on the second day after 45 overs had been lost to heavy morning rain, put on 251 without being parted. Next morning, when Surrey batted on for another 23 overs, they stretched their opening stand to 321, the county's highest since J. B. Hobbs and T. W. Hayward compiled 352 against Warwickshire in 1909. Bicknell's 169 was easily a career best. His brother, Martin, quickly made inroads into Northamptonshire's innings, and then Waqar Younis, with his swinging, skidding deliveries, accounted for the middle order. Only Larkins, batting in the unaccustomed position of No. 5 on his return after seven weeks off through injury, stood in their way. Though made in a lost cause, his hundred in 165 minutes, resplendent with two sixes and eighteen fours, was a resounding effort.

Close of play: First day, No play; Second day, Surrey 251-0 (D. J. Bicknell 131*, G. S. Clinton 108*).

Surrey

D. J. Bicknell b Williams	169
G. S. Clinton b Robinson	146
G. P. Thorpe not out	15
†D. M. Ward not out	4
L-b 3, n-b 10	13

1/321 2/331   (2 wkts dec.) 347

M. A. Lynch, *I. A. Greig, J. D. Robinson, M. A. Feltham, K. T. Medlycott, M. P. Bicknell and Waqar Younis did not bat.

Bonus points – Surrey 4.

Bowling: Davis 22–5–70–0; Robinson 20–4–57–1; Hughes 12–0–84–0; Williams 25–8–65–1; Cook 9–2–34–0; Bailey 7–1–34–0.

Surrey forfeited their second innings.

Northamptonshire

Northamptonshire forfeited their first innings.

A. Fordham c Greig b M. P. Bicknell	3	W. W. Davis b Waqar Younis	9
N. A. Felton lbw b M. P. Bicknell	2	N. G. B. Cook b Waqar Younis	0
R. J. Bailey c Ward b Waqar Younis	33	M. A. Robinson not out	0
D. J. Capel b Waqar Younis	19		
*W. Larkins b Waqar Younis	107	B 4, l-b 6, n-b 7	17
R. G. Williams b Waqar Younis	0		—
†D. Ripley b M. P. Bicknell	9	1/3 2/6 3/58 4/83 5/83	200
J. G. Hughes c Ward b M. P. Bicknell	1	6/107 7/153 8/187 9/199	

Bowling: Waqar Younis 18.2–9–36–6; M. P. Bicknell 16–3–58–4; Feltham 13–1–42–0; Medlycott 16–4–54–0.

Umpires: M. J. Kitchen and R. Palmer.

SURREY v WARWICKSHIRE

At The Oval, July 7, 9, 10. Surrey won by 168 runs. Surrey 24 pts, Warwickshire 3 pts. Toss: Warwickshire. Ward's consistent middle-order batting, mirrored in his fourth first-class hundred in eleven innings, gave Surrey an advantage they never conceded. It was driven home by Waqar Younis, whose seven for 73 was the best return of his brief career. Ultimately he finished with match figures of eleven for 128. Ward arrived with Surrey 13 for two; at 47 for three, Warwickshire's decision to put them in was looking a sound one. However, Lynch shed his natural exuberance and joined Ward in a vital stand of 208. He was out 8 runs short of a century after facing 199 balls. Ward's 126 contained three sixes and eleven fours in 220 deliveries. On the second day, Younis scythed through the Warwickshire innings, illustrating his pace by hitting the stumps five times and having an lbw and a caught behind in his impressive tally. Warwickshire were nine wickets down when they avoided the follow-on, Benjamin being dropped in the gully with a single needed, but Surrey purposefully extended their lead to 317 by the close of play. To some extent they were helped by the back strain which prevented Donald from bowling. Next morning Surrey added 45 in 35 minutes and set a target of 363. Apart from Ostler and Benjamin, Warwickshire had no consistent answer to Younis, who was well supported by Feltham.

Close of play: First day, Warwickshire 18-0 (A. J. Moles 5*, J. D. Ratcliffe 11*); Second day, Surrey 191-7 (K. T. Medlycott 9*, M. A. Feltham 1*).

Surrey

D. J. Bicknell c Ratcliffe b Benjamin	1	– lbw b Benjamin	9
G. S. Clinton c Humpage b Munton	18	– b Benjamin	33
G. P. Thorpe c Humpage b Donald	9	– c Piper b Munton	3
†D. M. Ward c Ostler b Reeve	126	– c Benjamin b Munton	15
M. A. Lynch c Piper b Munton	92	– c Piper b Benjamin	46
J. D. Robinson c Piper b Reeve	11	– (7) b Benjamin	27
*I. A. Greig not out	30	– (6) b Munton	34
K. T. Medlycott not out	4	– c sub b Benjamin	23
M. A. Feltham (did not bat)		– not out	22
M. P. Bicknell (did not bat)		– not out	6
B 2, l-b 8, w 1, n-b 1	12	L-b 14, n-b 4	18

1/2 2/13 3/47 4/255   (6 wkts dec.) 303   1/22 2/31 3/55   (8 wkts dec.) 236
5/255 6/293   4/100 5/115 6/173
                                                7/185 8/210

Waqar Younis did not bat.

Bonus points – Surrey 4, Warwickshire 2.

Bowling: *First Innings*—Donald 12–1–31–1; Benjamin 17–4–37–1; Munton 33–4–85–2; Reeve 24–6–64–2; Pierson 7–0–39–0; Asif Din 2–0–6–0; Humpage 5–1–31–0. *Second Innings*—Benjamin 24–2–72–5; Munton 27–3–107–3; Reeve 12–3–43–0.

Warwickshire

A. J. Moles b Waqar Younis	16	– b Waqar Younis	1
J. D. Ratcliffe lbw b Waqar Younis	15	– (7) lbw b M. P. Bicknell	19
Asif Din c Lynch b M. P. Bicknell	22	– (2) c Lynch b Waqar Younis	4
G. W. Humpage b Waqar Younis	0	– c sub b Waqar Younis	4
D. P. Ostler b Waqar Younis	30	– (3) b Medlycott	59
†K. J. Piper c Clinton b M. P. Bicknell	28	– (5) b Feltham	14
*D. A. Reeve c Medlycott b M. P. Bicknell	11	– (6) lbw b Waqar Younis	17
A. R. K. Pierson c Ward b Waqar Younis	0	– not out	10
J. E. Benjamin not out	28	– c M. P. Bicknell b Feltham	41
A. A. Donald b Waqar Younis	0	– c Lynch b Feltham	3
T. A. Munton b Waqar Younis	6	– c Thorpe b Feltham	3
B 3, l-b 11, w 7	21	B 9, l-b 3, w 1, n-b 6	19

1/34 2/44 3/44 4/74 5/124   177   1/9 2/10 3/21 4/56 5/78   194
6/138 7/141 8/143 9/151   6/128 7/128 8/185 9/188

Bonus points – Warwickshire 1, Surrey 4.

Bowling: *First Innings*—Waqar Younis 21.1–2–73–7; M. P. Bicknell 24–7–56–3; Feltham 10–3–15–0; Robinson 2–0–9–0; Medlycott 2–0–10–0. *Second Innings*—Waqar Younis 14–0–55–4; M. P. Bicknell 16–7–32–1; Feltham 15.4–2–59–4; Medlycott 8–0–36–1.

Umpires: D. J. Constant and R. Palmer.

SURREY v SUSSEX

At Guildford, July 18, 19, 20. Sussex won by seven wickets. Sussex 21 pts, Surrey 7 pts. Toss: Surrey. Sussex, languishing near the foot of the Championship table, raced to their second win of the season against Surrey after Lenham had fashioned an aggressive, unbeaten 109 off 127 deliveries. They won with two balls remaining after being asked to make an improbable 254 in a minimum of 43 overs. On the first day, Surrey looked to be establishing control as Darren Bicknell, handicapped by ribs painfully bruised by Pigott, spent five and a half hours (98 overs) compiling a century on a pitch prompting suspicion and caution. Salisbury's leg-breaks spun generously, although a belligerent 52 from Lynch in 75 minutes raised the tenor. Bicknell progressed to 143 on the second day, when Sussex, after a collapse from 76 for one to 80 for five, were spared the follow-on by a more spectacular century from Speight. He reached 100 off 105 balls and had hit six sixes and eight fours when he was caught behind by Greig, Surrey's third wicket-keeper of the innings after Ward had damaged a thumb and Lynch had proved untidy. Sussex trailed by 32, but with Clinton taking 56 overs for his 93, and no easy runs offered, it was three o'clock before Surrey set out their demands. However, the fast-scoring Guildford ground proved to the liking of Lenham and his captain, Parker, and with quick running and attacking batting they upset Greig's calculations in their second-wicket partnership of 90.

Close of play: First day, Surrey 305-6 (D. J. Bicknell 123*, K. T. Medlycott 8*); Second day, Surrey 7-0 (D. J. Bicknell 6*, G. S. Clinton 1*).

Surrey

D. J. Bicknell b Pigott	143	– b Donelan	6
G. S. Clinton c Parker b Dodemaide	1	– b Dodemaide	93
G. P. Thorpe c Speight b C. M. Wells	33	– c and b Salisbury	79
†D. M. Ward b Salisbury	40	– not out	36
M. A. Lynch c Dodemaide b Salisbury	52	– not out	1
*I. A. Greig run out	37		
M. A. Feltham lbw b Dodemaide	0		
K. T. Medlycott c A. P. Wells b Dodemaide	16		
M. P. Bicknell c and b Pigott	8		
N. M. Kendrick c Parker b Dodemaide	2		
Waqar Younis not out	1		
B 2, l-b 9, w 1	12	L-b 4, w 1, n-b 1	6

1/2 2/67 3/152 4/228 5/293　　　　　345　　1/9 2/140 3/220　　(3 wkts dec.) 221
6/296 7/314 8/340 9/343

Bonus points – Surrey 3, Sussex 1 (Score at 100 overs: 250-4).

Bowling: *First Innings*—Pigott 22.3–0–68–2; Dodemaide 27–2–84–4; C. M. Wells 22–10–47–1; Donelan 21–7–42–0; Salisbury 26–4–84–2; Lenham 2–0–9–0. *Second Innings*—Dodemaide 10–3–23–1; Pigott 7–1–26–0; Donelan 22–3–70–1; Salisbury 15–0–77–1; C. M. Wells 6.3–0–21–0.

Sussex

N. J. Lenham run out	46	– not out	109
J. W. Hall c and b Medlycott	16	– c M. P. Bicknell b Medlycott	21
*P. W. G. Parker b Waqar Younis	11	– c Ward b Feltham	64
A. P. Wells c Kendrick b Medlycott	0	– c Kendrick b Medlycott	42
M. P. Speight c Greig b Waqar Younis	108	– not out	0
C. M. Wells c Ward b Waqar Younis	0		
A. I. C. Dodemaide b Medlycott	11		
†P. Moores lbw b Feltham	24		
A. C. S. Pigott c Feltham b Medlycott	33		
I. D. K. Salisbury b Medlycott	21		
B. T. P. Donelan not out	11		
B 19, l-b 9, w 1, n-b 3	32	B 7, l-b 10, n-b 1	18

1/54 2/76 3/76 4/80 5/80　　　　　313　　1/69 2/159 3/251　　(3 wkts) 254
6/111 7/193 8/263 9/290

Bonus points – Sussex 4, Surrey 4.

Bowling: *First Innings*—Waqar Younis 21–4–65–3; M. P. Bicknell 18–5–32–0; Feltham 17–5–44–1; Medlycott 27.1–3–121–5; Kendrick 8–2–23–0. *Second Innings*—Waqar Younis 8–0–45–0; M. P. Bicknell 12.4–3–52–0; Medlycott 14–3–61–2; Kendrick 5–0–43–0; Feltham 4–0–36–1.

Umpires: B. J. Meyer and K. E. Palmer.

SURREY v KENT

At Guildford, July 21, 23, 24. Drawn. Surrey 8 pts, Kent 6 pts. Toss: Surrey. Hinks, Taylor and Graham Cowdrey all flourished on a docile pitch, with Hinks's second Championship hundred of the season the basis of Kent's secure 372. Surrey lost Darren Bicknell on Saturday evening, and on Monday were 181 in arrears with five wickets down before Greig's unbeaten 89 in 112 balls and Feltham's first half-century of the season saw them to a declaration only 28 behind. An interesting finish looked in prospect when Kent lost three top wickets before the close, but Ward's 88 and Graham Cowdrey's 119 not out in 205 minutes thwarted Surrey. When they claimed an eighth wicket with 107 minutes left, and Kent 262 ahead, Surrey still entertained the possibility of a run-chase, but the Cowdrey brothers stayed together for 90 minutes to deny them. The outcome might have been different had Chris, batting with a fractured toe, inflicted by Waqar Younis in the Sunday League game, not been missed at silly point when 2.

Close of play: First day, Surrey 35-1 (G. S. Clinton 20*, G. P. Thorpe 10*); Second day, Kent 62-3 (T. R. Ward 18*, P. S. de Villiers 6*).

Kent

S. G. Hinks c Clinton b Gray	120	– c and b Feltham	1
R. P. Davis c Lynch b Feltham	0	– b Gray	4
N. R. Taylor c Gray b Kendrick	69	– (4) lbw b Gray	26
G. R. Cowdrey c Lynch b Feltham	71	– (6) not out	119
T. R. Ward lbw b Feltham	10	– (3) c Thorpe b Medlycott	88
*C. S. Cowdrey c Greig b Gray	20	– (10) lbw b Medlycott	27
†S. A. Marsh c Sargeant b Kendrick	7	– c Sargeant b Medlycott	11
R. M. Ellison c and b Kendrick	10	– c Sargeant b Medlycott	0
P. S. de Villiers lbw b Kendrick	32	– (5) b Kendrick	28
M. M. Patel c Lynch b Feltham	2	– (9) c Lynch b Medlycott	0
A. P. Igglesden not out	15	– c Ward b Kendrick	6
B 2, l-b 2, n-b 12	16	B 1, l-b 2, w 2, n-b 14	19
	372		**329**

1/4 2/118 3/243 4/257 5/298 6/301 7/314 8/328 9/335

1/4 2/10 3/48 4/125 5/187 6/228 7/234 8/234 9/310

Bonus points – Kent 4, Surrey 4.

Bowling: *First Innings*—Gray 20-4-54-2; Feltham 22-1-86-4; Greig 6-0-36-0; Thorpe 2-0-23-0; Medlycott 7-0-59-0; Kendrick 33.2-8-110-4. *Second Innings*—Gray 24-2-93-2; Feltham 11-1-32-1; Medlycott 41-13-99-5; Kendrick 29.4-7-102-2; Lynch 1-1-0-0.

Surrey

D. J. Bicknell c Patel b Igglesden	4	– not out	9
G. S. Clinton c Marsh b Igglesden	38	– not out	8
G. P. Thorpe lbw b Igglesden	42		
D. M. Ward c Marsh b Igglesden	48		
M. A. Lynch b de Villiers	20		
M. A. Feltham b Ellison	55		
*I. A. Greig not out	89		
K. T. Medlycott b Ellison	28		
B 1, l-b 11, w 4, n-b 4	20		
(7 wkts dec.)	**344**	(no wkt)	**17**

1/4 2/85 3/114 4/148 5/191 6/249 7/344

N. M. Kendrick, A. H. Gray and †N. F. Sargeant did not bat.

Bonus points – Surrey 4, Kent 2 (Score at 100 overs: 310-6).

Bowling: *First Innings*—Igglesden 25-1-88-4; de Villiers 21-5-57-1; Davis 24-3-89-0; Patel 17-3-54-0; Ellison 19.3-4-44-2. *Second Innings*—Davis 6-2-9-0; Patel 5-2-6-0; Ward 1-0-1-0; Taylor 1-0-1-0.

Umpires: B. J. Meyer and K. E. Palmer.

At Cheltenham, July 28, 30, 31. SURREY drew with GLOUCESTERSHIRE.

At The Oval, August 1, 2, 3. SURREY drew with INDIANS (See Indian tour section).

At Weston-super-Mare, August 4, 6, 7. SURREY drew with SOMERSET.

SURREY v LEICESTERSHIRE

At The Oval, August 11, 13, 14. Surrey won by an innings and 5 runs. Surrey 24 pts, Leicestershire 4 pts. Toss: Leicestershire. Feltham's career-best six for 53 triggered Surrey's third win of a disappointing Championship campaign and hastened Leicestershire's third defeat in as many matches. On the opening day, the visiting county did not benefit from taking first use of the pitch, or from a sound start by Boon and Briers, the penetrative Waqar Younis doing the initial damage with four wickets in 26 balls in his second spell. Only Potter and Nixon, adding 93 for the sixth wicket, stood in Surrey's way. With Darren Bicknell providing the foundation over five and a half hours, Surrey built heavily on their advantage in the hope of bowling Leicestershire out a second time. Already without Lewis and Benjamin, the Leicestershire bowling was further weakened when Mullally was forced off with a strained hip. However, Parsons responded well to the extra responsibility and finished with six for 75. Leicestershire again passed 50 without loss, but with Feltham gaining extra lift to go with his swing, the match was over twenty minutes before tea. Boon's 56 from 78 balls was little consolation as the last nine wickets fell for 72.

Close of play: First day, Surrey 58-2 (D. J. Bicknell 14*, N. M. Kendrick 0*); Second day, Leicestershire 32-0 (T. J. Boon 16*, N. E. Briers 13*).

Leicestershire

T. J. Boon b Waqar Younis	32	– c Ward b M. P. Bicknell	56
*N. E. Briers c Greig b M. P. Bicknell	22	– b Waqar Younis	16
J. J. Whitaker b Waqar Younis	20	– b Feltham	23
P. Willey b Waqar Younis	1	– lbw b Feltham	3
L. Potter not out	52	– c Greig b Feltham	19
J. D. R. Benson c Kendrick b Waqar Younis	7	– c Lynch b M. P. Bicknell	5
†P. A. Nixon c and b Medlycott	46	– not out	17
G. J. Parsons run out	14	– lbw b Feltham	7
J. P. Agnew b M. P. Bicknell	4	– b Waqar Younis	3
A. D. Mullally c Ward b M. P. Bicknell	9	– c and b Feltham	8
D. J. Millns b M. P. Bicknell	1	– b Feltham	4
B 15, l-b 12, w 2, n-b 7	36	B 6, l-b 2, w 1, n-b 1	10

1/55 2/80 3/84 4/89 5/99   244   1/53 2/99 3/104 4/107 5/118   171
6/192 7/212 8/225 9/237   6/138 7/146 8/155 9/164

Bonus points – Leicestershire 2, Surrey 4.

Bowling: *First Innings*—Waqar Younis 23-2-72-4; M. P. Bicknell 22-3-42-4; Feltham 15-4-40-0; Medlycott 20-6-44-1; Greig 2-0-16-0; Kendrick 4-1-3-0. *Second Innings*—Waqar Younis 17-3-41-2; M. P. Bicknell 22-3-69-2; Feltham 18.5-4-53-6.

Surrey

D. J. Bicknell c Whitaker b Millns	111	K. T. Medlycott not out 21
G. S. Clinton c Nixon b Parsons 34	M. P. Bicknell c Whitaker b Parsons .. 23
A. J. Stewart c Nixon b Mullally 3	Waqar Younis not out 10
†D. M. Ward c Benson b Parsons 33	B 6, l-b 26, w 1, n-b 9 42
N. M. Kendrick c Potter b Millns 9	
M. A. Lynch c Nixon b Parsons 12	1/14 2/57 3/97 (9 wkts dec.) 420
*I. A. Greig c and b Parsons 84	4/178 5/194 6/274
M. A. Feltham c Whitaker b Parsons .. 38	7/355 8/362 9/400

Bonus points – Surrey 4, Leicestershire 2 (Score at 100 overs: 330-6).

G. S. Clinton, when 2, retired hurt at 6 and resumed at 97.

Bowling: Agnew 30–2–126–0; Mullally 9–3–14–1; Millns 25–1–97–2; Parsons 31–8–75–6;
Villey 18–4–60–0; Potter 6–0–16–0.

Umpires: J. D. Bond and B. Leadbeater.

At Chelmsford, August 18, 20, 21. SURREY lost to ESSEX by 283 runs.

At Southampton, August 23, 24, 25, 27. SURREY beat HAMPSHIRE by nine wickets.

At Blackpool, August 29, 30, 31. SURREY drew with LANCASHIRE.

At The Oval, September 2. SURREY beat SRI LANKANS by 14 runs (See Sri Lankan tour
section).

At Canterbury, September 7, 8, 9, 10. SURREY drew with KENT.

SURREY v MIDDLESEX

At The Oval, September 12, 13, 14, 15. Drawn. Surrey 5 pts, Middlesex 6 pts. Toss: Surrey.
Middlesex, entertaining ambitions of winning the County Championship six days before the
end of the season, received early indications that victory would be a feat in itself on the
country's most reliable batting surface. Alikhan compiled his maiden hundred in his 79th
first-class match, a whimsical innings in which his first 60 runs came in the opening session
and the next 59 took more than five hours. Ward's magnificent season was reflected in a
robust 75 off as many balls in a stand of 102, and he was the only player to master Fraser's
quality fast bowling. On the second day, Feltham stretched Surrey's innings to 480 for nine
with his maiden century (one six, thirteen fours), and by the close Middlesex were in some
difficulty after fierce fast bowling from Waqar Younis. He beat Haynes for pace, had
Roseberry taken at slip and, worse still for Middlesex, hit Gatting below the left elbow first
ball and put him out of the match. Ramprakash passed 50 on the third morning before
departing to the refreshed Waqar Younis, but Downton, Emburey and Fraser saw Middlesex
avoid the follow-on. Fraser's astonishing, career-best 92 included five sixes off Kendrick in
the space of twelve balls as 90 raced up in ten overs before Gatting declared 55 behind. An
earlier closure might have encouraged Greig to be more expansive in his outlook, but with
three bowlers incapacitated the Surrey captain found it beyond his means to set a target.
Bicknell's fifth hundred of the season, containing a six and fourteen fours, and solid lower-
middle-order batting against non-recognised bowling made the draw a certainty.

Close of play: First day, Surrey 302-5 (R. I. Alikhan 116*, J. D. Robinson 15*); Second day,
Middlesex 182-3 (M. R. Ramprakash 46*, P. R. Downton 11*); Third day, Surrey 132-3 (D. J.
Bicknell 61*, A. J. Stewart 33*).

Surrey

D. J. Bicknell c Gatting b Fraser	41	– b Hughes	114
R. I. Alikhan c Haynes b Cowans	119	– c Roseberry b Fraser	13
*A. J. Stewart b Fraser	0	– (5) c Emburey b Tufnell	47
D. M. Ward c Haynes b Tufnell	75	– (6) c Downton b Tufnell	6
M. A. Lynch c Emburey b Fraser	17	– (4) c Downton b Hughes	22
*I. A. Greig c Ramprakash b Emburey	31	– (7) lbw b Hughes	30
J. D. Robinson c Haynes b Emburey	72	– (3) c Ramprakash b Fraser	0
M. A. Feltham c Emburey b Fraser	101	– c Fraser b Ramprakash	58
K. T. Medlycott c Downton b Fraser	5	– b Emburey	44
N. M. Kendrick not out	6	– lbw b Downton	14
Waqar Younis (did not bat)		– not out	4
B 1, l-b 3, n-b 9	13	B 8, l-b 10, w 1, n-b 2	21

1/106 2/108 3/210 4/238 5/282   (9 wkts dec.) 480   1/29 2/29 3/71 4/184 5/194   373
6/320 7/444 8/453 9/480   6/236 7/237 8/344 9/365

Bonus points – Surrey 3, Middlesex 2 (Score at 100 overs: 284-5).

Bowling: *First Innings*—Fraser 32.4–9–95–5; Cowans 24–6–76–1; Hughes 21–1–89–0; Emburey 45–10–96–2; Haynes 4–0–17–0; Tufnell 35–10–103–1. *Second Innings*—Cowans 15–5–49–0; Fraser 20–9–44–2; Tufnell 30–8–90–2; Hughes 16–1–56–3; Emburey 23–5–49–1; Ramprakash 10–4–17–1; Haynes 4–0–13–0; Brown 5–2–31–0; Roseberry 4–3–2–0; Downton 1.1–0–4–1.

Middlesex

D. L. Haynes b Waqar Younis	69	
M. A. Roseberry c Greig b Waqar Younis	28	– (4) not out 27
*M. W. Gatting retired hurt	0	
M. R. Ramprakash c Stewart b Waqar Younis	54	– (3) not out 40
K. R. Brown c Feltham b Kendrick	21	
†P. R. Downton c Waqar Younis b Kendrick	48	
J. E. Emburey c Kendrick b Feltham	66	
A. R. C. Fraser b Feltham	92	
S. P. Hughes c Medlycott b Feltham	15	– (1) c Stewart b Alikhan 4
P. C. R. Tufnell not out	23	
N. G. Cowans (did not bat)		– (2) c Feltham b Lynch 31
B 2, l-b 6, w 1	9	

1/100 2/108 3/145 4/197 5/267   (8 wkts dec.) 425   1/6 2/45   (2 wkts) 102
6/354 7/389 8/425

Bonus points – Middlesex 4, Surrey 2 (Score at 100 overs: 335-5).

In the first innings M. W. Gatting retired hurt at 101.

Bowling: *First Innings*—Waqar Younis 28–4–91–3; Feltham 20.4–4–69–3; Greig 11–1–41–0; Robinson 17–2–59–0; Medlycott 8–1–35–0; Kendrick 30–8–122–2. *Second Innings*—Alikhan 7–1–12–1; Bicknell 7–1–15–0; Lynch 5–0–43–1; Stewart 5–0–32–0.

Umpires: B. Dudleston and B. Hassan.

SURREY v ESSEX

At The Oval, September 18, 19, 20, 21. Drawn. Surrey 2 pts, Essex 7 pts. Toss: Essex. Surrey comfortably preserved their unbeaten record at The Oval after following on, thanks principally to Ward's second double-hundred and seventh three-figure innings of the season. In the course of his 208 from 182 balls, during which he struck three sixes and 33 fours, Ward became the first Surrey batsman to score 2,000 runs in a season for the county since J. H. Edrich in 1962. After Essex had won the toss and batted, Hussain compensated for the absence of Gooch and Waugh, through injury, with a pugnacious hundred. Even so, they had to forego one batting point, despite Waqar Younis managing only one spell because of elbow trouble. Hussain fell 3 runs short of a maiden double-century on the second day after batting for 5 hours 38 minutes, and Lewis, with whom he put on 194 for the sixth wicket, marked his first-class début with an unbeaten hundred. For all the batting excellence of the pitch, Foster buckled Surrey with figures of six for 72 and they followed on 399 behind. By the end of the third day, however, the home county had entrenched themselves defiantly at 177 for one, and the news had come through that Middlesex had won at Hove to secure the Championship, consigning Essex to second place. Alikhan duly progressed to his second hundred in successive matches, batting for almost seven and a half hours, but Ward, hitting powerfully through the line, monopolised the glory as they added 239 for the third wicket.

Close of play: First day, Essex 328-5 (N. Hussain 124*, J. J. B. Lewis 25*); Second day, Surrey 124-8 (M. P. Bicknell 7*, Waqar Younis 4*); Third day, Surrey 177-1 (R. I. Alikhan 61*, A. J. Stewart 50*).

ssex

P. Stephenson c Lynch b Greig	51	M. C. Ilott c Waqar Younis	
. Shahid c Lynch b Greig	42	b Kendrick	5
. J. Prichard c Stewart b Murphy	28	J. H. Childs c Stewart b M. P. Bicknell	0
. Hussain run out	197	S. J. W. Andrew c sub	
. R. Hardie c sub b Kendrick	42	b M. P. Bicknell	18
M. A. Garnham c Lynch b Greig	5	B 4, l-b 11, n-b 1	16
. J. B. Lewis not out	116		
N. A. Foster c D. J. Bicknell		1/96 2/103 3/133 4/262	539
b Murphy	19	5/275 6/469 7/496 8/515 9/519	

Bonus points – Essex 3, Surrey 2 (Score at 100 overs: 291-5).

Bowling: M. P. Bicknell 30.5–8–64–2; Waqar Younis 5–0–21–0; Murphy 41–9–154–2; obinson 14–0–44–0; Greig 42–6–150–3; Kendrick 20–1–64–2; Alikhan 5–0–22–0; D. J. icknell 2–0–5–0.

urrey

. J. Bicknell b Foster	0	– c and b Foster	50
. I. Alikhan lbw b Foster	16	– c Hardie b Shahid	138
. M. Ward c Shahid b Andrew	58	– (4) b Stephenson	208
A. J. Stewart c Shahid b Foster	2	– (3) c Garnham b Foster	51
. A. Lynch c Garnham b Ilott	12	– b Shahid	16
. A. Greig c Garnham b Foster	11	– not out	57
. D. Robinson run out	7	– b Shahid	0
1. P. Bicknell c Hussain b Foster	13	– not out	49
. M. Kendrick lbw b Ilott	1		
Vaqar Younis c Lewis b Foster	14		
. J. Murphy not out	0		
L-b 2, w 1, n-b 3	6	B 9, l-b 20, w 1, n-b 14	44
/0 2/76 3/78 4/80 5/96	140	1/80 2/184 3/423 (6 wkts dec.)	613
/112 7/113 8/120 9/135		4/455 5/511 6/514	

Bonus points – Essex 4.

Bowling: *First Innings*—Foster 17.3–2–72–6; Ilott 16–3–42–2; Andrew 9–4–24–1. *Second nnings*—Foster 29–10–88–2; Ilott 34–2–157–0; Childs 21–3–51–0; Andrew 18–4–65–0; hahid 25–4–91–3; Stephenson 29–7–116–1; Hardie 1–0–16–0.

Umpires: A. A. Jones and P. B. Wight.

HONOURS' LIST, 1990

n 1990, the following were decorated for their services to cricket:

Jew Year's Honours: E. J. Chatfield (New Zealand) MBE, T. Jones (Merseyside cricket) BEM, J. Simmons (Lancashire) MBE.

Queen's Birthday Honours: B. Coleman (Surrey and TCCB committees) OBE, Sir Richard Hadlee (New Zealand) Kt, J. K. Lever (England) MBE, P. J. Mansfield (services to groundsmanship) BEM.

SUSSEX

President: The Marquess of Abergavenny
Chairman: A. M. Caffyn
Secretary: N. Bett
   County Ground, Eaton Road,
   Hove BN3 3AN
   (Telephone: 0273-732161)
Captain: P. W. G. Parker
Coach: N. Gifford

Not surprisingly, Sussex, finishing bottom of the Britannic Assurance Championship for the second time in four years, derived most satisfaction from the performance of their Second Eleven. While the senior side recorded only twelve victories in all cricket during 1990, the second team capped a splendid summer by capturing the Second Eleven Championship for the second time, winning nine of their sixteen games and losing only once. This heartening display went some way toward rescuing a forgettable, depressing season in which Sussex managed only three Championship victories and flopped in limited-overs cricket. Their low point came with a dramatic collapse when they were well placed to beat Glamorgan in the second round of the NatWest Bank Trophy. After that defeat in Cardiff Sussex won only four games in the remaining ten weeks of the season.

Sussex's dive to the depths of the Championship followed the optimism of the previous season, when a final placing of tenth was their best position since they finished seventh in 1985. The coach, Norman Gifford, having completed his second year at Hove, warned that although some supporters would be demanding changes, Sussex might not be able to strengthen the side and might have to go into 1991 with the same players.

The county's major weakness – the lack of a fast bowler to provide back-up for the Tony Pigott-Tony Dodemaide new-ball attack – was in evidence throughout the season. Of Sussex's three Championship victories, only one was achieved by bowling a side out. Nevertheless, Pigott and Dodemaide stuck to an uphill task manfully to take 100 Championship wickets between them, and the Australian all-rounder, in his second season with Sussex, again proved himself a splendid team man. He played in all Championship games and, in addition to his bowling, scored 1,001 runs in first-class cricket. Pigott, leading wicket-taker the previous season, ended with 54 first-class wickets, seven fewer than Dodemaide, and with thirteen years of loyal service behind him he takes a deserved benefit in 1991.

The fine form of Neil Lenham, after his unlucky run of finger injuries, was a major plus for the batting; he passed 1,000 runs for the first time, heading the club's Championship averages with 1,499 at 44.08, and his four hundreds. Batting with a specially designed glove to protect his right index finger, broken no fewer than five times, Lenham displayed a new confidence and was rewarded with his county cap in June. He also led the way for Sussex in the Sunday League, with 444 runs at 40.36, but neither he nor any Sussex player scored a century in the 40-overs competition, in which Sussex finished thirteenth – a drop of two places. A troublesome thumb injury limited David Smith to only eight Championship appearances, and Sussex lost no time in drafting in Jamie Hall, a promising 22-year-old batsman from Chichester. Hall failed to make double figures in his first four innings, but he never looked back after scoring his maiden first-class century against the New Zealanders in his fifth and finished with 1,140 runs from twenty first-class matches.

Martin Speight emerged as a dependable middle-order batsman in his first full season since leaving Durham University, scoring 1,349 Championship runs, including two hundreds, and he was followed closely in the averages by Alan Wells, who like Speight missed only one Championship game. While Wells completed 1,000 first-class runs for the fifth time, his elder brother, Colin, was handicapped by a hernia problem, which required an operation. This restricted his usual haul of runs and limited his success as a bowler. Colin gave way as on-field captain to his brother late in a season which had seen the club captain, Paul Parker, suffering from severe hamstring problems for the second successive year. Parker missed ten Championship matches, yet finished the season just 15 runs short of his first-class 1,000, having hit two hundreds. Ian Gould was another troubled by injury and, dropped midway through the summer, he appeared in only eight first-class games in his benefit season.

The selection of Ian Salisbury for the England A tour in the winter gave Sussex supporters a welcome lift and came as a complete surprise to the gifted twenty-year-old leg-spinner, who had not even received a letter from Lord's asking about his availability. Salisbury, after an early interest in soccer, was fourteen before he started to play cricket, and following a spell on Northamptonshire's books he joined the Lord's groundstaff. He was spotted by Sussex when playing against them for MCC Young Cricketers, and they wasted no time in offering him a contract. Salisbury, who claimed 42 first-class wickets in his second season, was quick to acknowledge the help he had received from Gifford, especially on the way he should bowl on certain pitches, and his tour place emphasised the value of his coach's vast experience. Sussex also have high hopes of Bradleigh Donelan, a promising off-spinner, who took 25 wickets for the first team and 59 for the Second Eleven.

As Sussex turned to Salisbury and Donelan, leg-spinner Andy Clarke was again out of favour, and he played only in limited-overs cricket. Clarke had appeared in just five first-class matches the previous year, after taking 42 Championship wickets in his début season, 1988, and he was not retained at the end of the season. Nor was seam bowler Andy Babington, who promptly joined Gloucestershire.

Sussex had good cause to look back on a successful first Championship fixture at the picturesque Arundel Castle ground, where a crowd of more than 3,500 watched the first day's play against Hampshire and gate receipts topped £11,000. Meanwhile, plans are under way to redevelop completely the Hove County Ground, at an estimated cost of five to seven million pounds. The rebuilding programme will take ten years and will include the construction of a new pavilion, function and conference facilities, and terraced seating to increase the ground capacity to some 6,500. – Jack Arlidge.

SUSSEX 1990

Back row: A. R. Clarke, C. C. Remy, A. R. Hansford, A. M. Babington, K. Greenfield, B. T. P. Donelan. *Middle row:* L. V. Chandler (*scorer*), C. P. Cate (*assistant coach*), A. R. Cornford, I. D. K. Salisbury, P. W. Threlfall, R. A. Bunting, J. W. Hall, A. I. C. Dodemaide, N. J. Lenham, I. C. Waring (*assistant coach*), B. Turner (*physiotherapist*), N. Gifford (*coach*). *Front row:* J. A. North, P. Moores, A. C. S. Pigott, C. M. Wells, P. W. G. Parker (*captain*).

[*Bill Smith*]

SUSSEX RESULTS

All first-class matches – Played 25: Won 3, Lost 11, Drawn 11.

County Championship matches – Played 22: Won 3, Lost 9, Drawn 10.

Bonus points – Batting 51, Bowling 44.

*Competition placings – Britannic Assurance County Championship, 17th;
NatWest Bank Trophy, 2nd round; Benson and Hedges Cup, 4th in Group B;
Refuge Assurance League, 13th.*

BRITANNIC ASSURANCE CHAMPIONSHIP AVERAGES

BATTING

	Birthplace	M	I	NO	R	HI	Avge
‡N. J. Lenham	Worthing	19	35	1	1,499	123	44.08
‡P. W. G. Parker . . .	Bulawayo, S. Rhodesia	12	21	2	778	107	40.94
M. P. Speight	Walsall	21	39	6	1,349	131	40.87
‡A. P. Wells	Newhaven	21	39	6	1,245	144*	37.72
B. T. P. Donelan . . .	Park Royal, London	9	13	6	211	53	30.14
‡C. M. Wells	Newhaven	19	31	4	812	107	30.07
J. W. Hall	Chichester	17	31	1	888	125	29.60
‡A. I. C. Dodemaide .	Melbourne, Australia	22	35	6	854	112	29.44
‡D. M. Smith	Balham, London	8	14	2	324	71	27.00
I. D. K. Salisbury . .	Northampton	18	23	10	313	68	24.07
‡I. J. Gould	Slough	7	11	1	229	73	22.90
‡P. Moores	Macclesfield	22	35	3	680	106*	21.25
‡A. C. S. Pigott	London	20	29	5	451	64*	18.79
K. Greenfield	Brighton	2	4	0	74	38	18.50
A. R. Hansford	Burgess Hill	4	6	1	55	29	11.00
R. A. Bunting	East Winch	13	13	5	85	24*	10.62
J. A. North	Slindon	3	5	1	41	19*	10.25
R. Hanley	Tonbridge	2	4	0	32	28	8.00

Also batted: A. M. Babington (*London*) (2 matches) 20, 8; C. C. Remy (*Castries, St Lucia*) (1 match) 4*.

* *Signifies not out.*   ‡ *Denotes county cap.*

The following played a total of fifteen three-figure innings for Sussex in County Championship matches – N. J. Lenham 4, A. P. Wells 3, P. W. G. Parker 2, M. P. Speight 2, A. I. C. Dodemaide 1, J. W. Hall 1, P. Moores 1, C. M. Wells 1.

BOWLING

	O	M	R	W	BB	5W/i	Avge
A. C. S. Pigott	516.1	88	1,916	51	5-52	3	37.56
A. I. C. Dodemaide . . .	681.1	112	2,206	56	6-106	1	39.39
B. T. P. Donelan	258.4	50	853	19	3-79	0	44.89
I. D. K. Salisbury	535.1	103	1,796	40	5-32	2	44.90
R. A. Bunting	298	55	1,113	21	2-36	0	53.00
C. M. Wells	366	63	1,195	17	3-48	0	70.29

Also bowled: A. M. Babington 43–7–166–2; I. J. Gould 5–0–18–0; K. Greenfield 0.3–0–8–0; A. R. Hansford 123.5–21–425–7; N. J. Lenham 62.5–11–231–2; J. A. North 49.2–10–147–3; P. W. G. Parker 8–0–59–0; C. C. Remy 17–0–91–1; A. P. Wells 29–4–144–1.

Wicket-keeper: P. Moores 46 ct, 10 st.

Leading Fielders: I. D. K. Salisbury 13, M. P. Speight 13.

SUSSEX v SURREY

At Hove, April 26, 27, 28, 30. Sussex won by five wickets. Sussex 21 pts, Surrey 4 pts. Toss: Sussex. Speight, starting his first full season of first-class cricket, and Gould, in his benefit year, put on 122 in thirteen overs to take Sussex to victory with sixteen balls remaining after the Surrey captain, Greig, had set them to score 335 in 220 minutes. Only 40 overs were possible on the first day, but consistent batting, with Bicknell and Stewart establishing the innings with 136 in 44 overs for the second wicket, enabled Surrey to control the game's path. Parker, with eight fours and a five in his only century of the match, declared 125 behind on the third afternoon in expectation of a target, but the easy nature of the pitch persuaded Greig to delay his declaration until after lunch on the final day. However, with Medlycott's left-arm spin proving costly, Sussex began the season with an impressive win.

Close of play: First day, Surrey 118-1 (D. J. Bicknell 36*, A. J. Stewart 31*); Second day, Sussex 29-1 (N. J. Lenham 11*, P. W. G. Parker 12*); Third day, Surrey 64-2 (G. S. Clinton 17*, M. A. Lynch 26*).

Surrey

D. J. Bicknell lbw b Dodemaide	65	– c Speight b Dodemaide	2
G. S. Clinton b Hansford	43	– run out	98
A. J. Stewart c A. P. Wells b Salisbury	77	– c Speight b Hansford	15
M. A. Lynch c Lenham b C. M. Wells	70	– b C. M. Wells	46
G. P. Thorpe c Gould b Salisbury	9	– not out	23
†D. M. Ward c Parker b Pigott	38	– not out	18
*I. A. Greig c Salisbury b Pigott	9		
K. T. Medlycott c Lenham b Salisbury	29		
M. P. Bicknell not out	50		
A. H. Gray run out	11		
A. J. Murphy not out	4		
B 5, l-b 15	20	L-b 6, w 1	7

1/57 2/193 3/201 4/221 5/282   (9 wkts dec.) 425   1/9 2/37 3/110   (4 wkts dec.) 209
6/304 7/355 8/367 9/393   4/180

Bonus points – Surrey 3, Sussex 1 (Score at 100 overs: 274-4).

Bowling: *First Innings*—Pigott 30–8–77–2; Dodemaide 26–3–96–1; C. M. Wells 27–8–59–1; Hansford 25.5–3–84–1; Salisbury 32–7–89–3. *Second Innings*—Pigott 5–1–17–0; Dodemaide 13–3–38–1; Hansford 10–2–41–1; Salisbury 11–0–26–0; C. M. Wells 9–2–16–1; A. P. Wells 9–0–39–0; Lenham 4–0–16–0; Gould 3–0–10–0.

Sussex

N. J. Lenham c Lynch b Murphy	85	– run out	44
†P. Moores b Gray	1	– c Stewart b Medlycott	30
*P. W. G. Parker b Murphy	100	– b Murphy	42
A. P. Wells not out	44	– c Ward b Murphy	16
M. P. Speight not out	50	– not out	75
C. M. Wells (did not bat)		– c Lynch b Medlycott	37
I. J. Gould (did not bat)		– not out	62
B 5, l-b 8, n-b 7	20	B 8, l-b 21, w 1, n-b 1	31

1/9 2/197 3/198   (3 wkts dec.) 300   1/52 2/123 3/130   (5 wkts) 337
                                           4/154 5/215

A. I. C. Dodemaide, A. C. S. Pigott, I. D. K. Salisbury and A. R. Hansford did not bat.

Bonus points – Sussex 4, Surrey 1.

Bowling: *First Innings*—Gray 15–0–58–1; M. P. Bicknell 24–5–71–0; Murphy 19–4–68–2; Medlycott 29–9–67–0; Greig 5–0–19–0; Lynch 2–1–4–0. *Second Innings*—M. P. Bicknell 15–2–59–0; Murphy 17–2–76–2; Greig 10–2–45–0; Medlycott 14.2–1–101–2; Lynch 7–1–27–0.

Umpires: D. J. Constant and D. S. Thompsett.

At Folkestone, May 3, 4, 5, 7. SUSSEX lost to KENT by five wickets.

†SUSSEX v ZIMBABWEANS

At Hove, May 13. Sussex won by 95 runs. Toss: Zimbabweans. Hall celebrated his first-team début with a half-century and a share in a century partnership for the third wicket with Speight. Speight's 76 came off 100 balls and included twelve fours.

Sussex

N. J. Lenham b Jarvis	1	R. A. Bunting lbw b Traicos	6
J. W. Hall c Briant b Brandes	53	P. W. Threlfall not out	17
K. Greenfield b Jarvis	10		
M. P. Speight c Butchart b Traicos	76	B 7, l-b 6, w 3, n-b 5	21
C. C. Remy not out	0		
*P. W. G. Parker lbw b Shah	10	1/1 2/23 3/145 (8 wkts, 55 overs)	233
†P. Moores c Robertson b Brandes	39	4/158 5/177 6/182	
I. D. K. Salisbury run out	0	7/190 8/232	

A. M. Babington did not bat.

C. C. Remy retired hurt at 155 and resumed at 232.

Bowling: Brandes 11–0–39–2; Jarvis 9–3–30–2; Dube 8–0–43–0; Shah 11–1–36–1; Traicos 11–0–42–2; Butchart 5–0–30–0.

Zimbabweans

K. J. Arnott lbw b Threlfall	11	A. J. Traicos b Salisbury	0
G. A. Paterson b Salisbury	18	M. P. Jarvis b Threlfall	4
C. M. Robertson b Threlfall	0	L. E. Dube not out	0
*A. J. Pycroft run out	10	L-b 10, w 7, n-b 3	20
†G. A. Briant run out	7		
A. H. Shah b Salisbury	21	1/32 2/38 3/50 (40.3 overs)	138
I. P. Butchart lbw b Babington	24	4/55 5/106 6/108	
E. A. Brandes c Bunting b Salisbury	23	7/108 8/114 9/127	

Bowling: Babington 9–2–20–1; Threlfall 10–0–40–3; Lenham 7–0–13–0; Bunting 7–1–30–0; Salisbury 7.3–2–25–4.

Umpires: B. Dudleston and P. B. Wight.

At Southampton, May 15, 16, 17, 18. SUSSEX lost to HAMPSHIRE by an innings and 157 runs.

SUSSEX v GLAMORGAN

At Hove, May 19, 21, 22. Drawn. Sussex 3 pts, Glamorgan 8 pts. Toss: Glamorgan. Sussex batted throughout the final day for a draw after being forced to follow on 180 behind. Speight, although batting with a runner because of blood poisoning in his leg, registered his maiden first-class century, hitting twenty fours, while Moores faced 125 deliveries for his second first-class hundred. On another excellent batting pitch, Glamorgan scored at nearly 4 an over on the Saturday, Butcher and Morris giving them a perfect start with 188 in 59 overs. Butcher had seventeen fours and three sixes in his 139, but he was overshadowed by a scintillating innings from Richards, whose hundred came from just 73 balls. In all he faced 87 deliveries, cracking sixteen fours and four sixes, before Glamorgan declared. Sussex lost Hall that evening and on Monday, despite Speight's 60 with ten fours, collapsed against persistent Glamorgan bowling to 157 for nine in 47 overs. Parker, batting at No. 9 because of a torn hamstring, then added 65 for the last wicket with Babington, but Sussex were still 31 short of avoiding the follow-on when Cowley caught and bowled Babington.

Close of play: First day, Sussex 12-1 (N. J. Lenham 3*); Second day, Sussex 120-2 (A. I. C. Dodemaide 26*, M. P. Speight 62*).

Glamorgan

*A. R. Butcher c Moores b Pigott	139	P. A. Cottey not out	 43
H. Morris c Moores b Dodemaide	 73	B 6, l-b 7, n-b 3	 16
M. J. Cann c Moores b Wells	 13		
I. V. A. Richards not out	118	1/188 2/241 3/241	(3 wkts dec.) 402

I. Smith, N. G. Cowley, †C. P. Metson, S. J. Dennis, S. L. Watkin and M. Frost did not bat.

Bonus points – Glamorgan 4, Sussex 1 (Score at 100 overs: 386-3).

Bowling: Pigott 17–1–86–1; Dodemaide 24–4–81–1; Babington 20–5–57–0; Wells 22–2–90–1; Lenham 6–1–18–0; Salisbury 13–2–57–0.

Sussex

N. J. Lenham lbw b Dennis	 34	– c Cowley b Watkin	 18
J. W. Hall lbw b Frost	 8	– c Metson b Dennis	 7
A. I. C. Dodemaide c Cottey b Watkin	 3	– c Richards b Dennis	 45
M. P. Speight c Richards b Frost	 60	– c Cann b Dennis	131
C. M. Wells c and b Watkin	 1	– c Frost b Watkin	 94
I. J. Gould lbw b Frost	 9	– c Morris b Butcher	 11
†P. Moores lbw b Richards	 3	– not out	106
A. C. S. Pigott c Metson b Richards	 8	– c Morris b Cann	 54
*P. W. G. Parker not out	 57		
I. D. K. Salisbury c Metson b Frost	 3	– (9) not out	 10
A. M. Babington c and b Cowley	 20		
B 10, l-b 3, n-b 3	 16	B 4, l-b 4, w 5, n-b 3	 16

1/12 2/29 3/76 4/91 5/118		222	1/15 2/27 3/163 (7 wkts dec.) 492
6/121 7/121 8/138 9/157			4/279 5/295
			6/350 7/443

Bonus points – Sussex 2, Glamorgan 4.

Bowling: *First Innings*—Frost 18–2–62–4; Watkin 19–2–66–2; Dennis 11–2–36–1; Richards 15–4–27–2; Cowley 8.4–1–18–1. *Second Innings*—Frost 24–0–96–0; Watkin 30–4–94–2; Cowley 13–5–28–0; Dennis 25–3–83–3; Richards 9–2–14–0; Smith 8–0–49–0; Cottey 9–0–44–0; Cann 7–0–39–1; Butcher 3–0–16–1; Morris 3–0–21–0.

Umpires: M. J. Kitchen and R. A. White.

At Taunton, May 23, 24, 25. SUSSEX drew with SOMERSET.

At Hove, May 26, 27, 28. SUSSEX lost to NEW ZEALANDERS by seven wickets (See New Zealand tour section).

SUSSEX v LANCASHIRE

At Horsham, June 2, 4, 5. Lancashire won by nine wickets. Lancashire 24 pts, Sussex 6 pts. Toss: Sussex. Devastating fast bowling from DeFreitas, in poor light on the final morning, set up a straightforward victory that brought Lancashire maximum points. Almost as important was the ninth-wicket partnership of 100 in Lancashire's first innings between Fowler and Allott which, in addition to ensuring their third and fourth batting points, gave the visitors a crucial lead of 89 as the pitch began to wear. Fowler had gone in as low as No. 9 because of an injury to his lip, suffered while fielding on the opening day. Sussex, after winning the toss, had been unable to dominate the Lancashire bowling, with Dodemaide lingering some four and a quarter hours while scoring 70. However, Lancashire, apart from Atherton's 76 in 64 overs, and Watkinson's violent 51 from 74 balls, also struggled as Dodemaide exploited the increasingly varied bounce. They were 11 runs behind when their eighth wicket fell, but Allott then joined Fowler and they wrested the initiative. Next day, after DeFreitas had demolished the Sussex top- and middle-order batting, Patterson, bowling at great speed, ripped out the tail with three wickets in four balls.

Close of play: First day, Lancashire 47-1 (M. A. Atherton 12*, J. D. Fitton 25*); Second day, Sussex 57-1 (N. J. Lenham 22*, A. I. C. Dodemaide 13*).

Sussex

N. J. Lenham c Mendis b Watkinson	8	– c Hughes b DeFreitas	24
J. W. Hall c Watkinson b Allott	24	– c Allott b Patterson	15
A. I. C. Dodemaide c Hegg b Watkinson	70	– c Hughes b DeFreitas	14
A. P. Wells c Fairbrother b Fitton	33	– lbw b DeFreitas	0
M. P. Speight c Hughes b Patterson	11	– lbw b DeFreitas	21
*C. M. Wells c Hegg b Patterson	0	– (8) c Atherton b DeFreitas	13
†P. Moores c Fairbrother b Allott	28	– (6) c Mendis b DeFreitas	2
A. C. S. Pigott c Fairbrother b Atherton	14	– (7) c Hegg b Patterson	6
I. D. K. Salisbury c Hughes b Atherton	15	– not out	0
B. T. P. Donelan c Atherton b Watkinson	8	– b Patterson	0
R. A. Bunting not out	10	– c Hegg b Patterson	0
B 3, l-b 9, n-b 2	14	B 1, l-b 2, n-b 10	13

1/21 2/47 3/108 4/127 5/127   235   1/21 2/58 3/58 4/62 5/72   108
6/161 7/197 8/207 9/219   6/87 7/106 8/108 9/108

Bonus points – Sussex 2, Lancashire 4.

Bowling: First Innings—Patterson 17–3–37–2; DeFreitas 13–4–27–0; Watkinson 14–8–26–3; Allott 14·4–30–2; Fitton 19–6–56–1; Atherton 20.1–8–47–2. *Second Innings*—Patterson 18.4–2–52–4; DeFreitas 19–8–39–6; Allott 4–2–10–0; Atherton 3–2–4–0.

Lancashire

G. D. Mendis lbw b Dodemaide	9	– c Moores b Bunting	11
M. A. Atherton c Pigott b Dodemaide	76	– not out	0
J. D. Fitton c Pigott b Dodemaide	25		
N. H. Fairbrother c A. P. Wells b Bunting	22	– (3) not out	10
M. Watkinson c Donelan b Salisbury	51		
P. A. J. DeFreitas c Moores b Pigott	26		
†W. K. Hegg c Dodemaide b Salisbury	10		
*D. P. Hughes c Moores b Dodemaide	0		
G. Fowler not out	54		
P. J. W. Allott b Dodemaide	42		
B. P. Patterson b Dodemaide	0		
B 4, l-b 4, n-b 1	9	L-b 1	1

1/11 2/54 3/111 4/185 5/187   324   1/12   (1 wkt) 22
6/224 7/224 8/224 9/324

Bonus points – Lancashire 4, Sussex 4.

Bowling: First Innings—Pigott 14–2–60–1; Dodemaide 28.4–2–106–6; Salisbury 24–7–46–2; C. M. Wells 7–1–16–0; Bunting 13–1–61–1; Donelan 5–1–27–0. *Second Innings*—Bunting 3–0–20–1; Donelan 2–1–1–0.

Umpires: B. Hassan and D. R. Shepherd.

SUSSEX v GLOUCESTERSHIRE

At Hove, June 16, 18, 19. Drawn. Sussex 4 pts, Gloucestershire 5 pts. Toss: Sussex. Sussex finished 17 runs short of victory with two wickets standing after both captains had reacted positively to the loss of more than five hours' play on the second day. Set 342 to win in at least 84 overs, they needed just 47 from the last eight overs after Colin Wells and Speight had put on 105 in seventeen overs. Instead, disciplined bowling from Walsh and Curran enabled Gloucestershire not only to avoid defeat but to come close to seizing victory. After putting Gloucestershire in, Sussex had reduced them to 177 for six before Athey, whose 131 included 22 fours, and Russell (98 from 140 balls) put on 169. On the second day, Parker, scoring 36 of his 48 in boundaries, had taken his side to 120 for three before rain and bad light drove the players from the field after 31 overs.

Close of play: First day, Sussex 30-0 (N. J. Lenham 15*, J. W. Hall 11*); Second day, Sussex 120-3 (P. W. G. Parker 48*, M. P. Speight 0*).

Gloucestershire

*A. J. Wright c Moores b Dodemaide	17	– not out 45
G. D. Hodgson c Salisbury b Dodemaide	0	– b Remy 33
I. P. Butcher c Speight b C. M. Wells	42	– not out 3
C. W. J. Athey st Moores b Salisbury	131	
P. Bainbridge c Salisbury b C. M. Wells	3	
K. M. Curran c and b Bunting	15	
J. W. Lloyds b Bunting	43	
†R. C. Russell c Moores b Dodemaide	98	
C. A. Walsh c and b Salisbury	9	
D. A. Graveney c Dodemaide b Salisbury	0	
D. V. Lawrence not out	0	
B 4, l-b 9, w 1, n-b 2	16	L-b 6 6

1/3 2/49 3/69 4/73 5/117   374   1/73   (1 wkt dec.) 87
6/177 7/346 8/368 9/368

Bonus points – Gloucestershire 4, Sussex 4.

Bowling: *First Innings*—Dodemaide 22–3–95–3; Bunting 23–6–91–2; C. M. Wells 20–3–59–2; Remy 12–0–54–0; Salisbury 20–6–62–3. *Second Innings*—Dodemaide 3–0–6–0; Bunting 4–0–21–0; Remy 5–0–37–1; A. P. Wells 4–0–17–0.

Sussex

N. J. Lenham c Russell b Lawrence	37	– c Wright b Curran 84
J. W. Hall b Walsh	19	– c Russell b Walsh 17
*P. W. G. Parker not out	48	– c Wright b Lloyds 53
A. P. Wells b Walsh	8	– c Lloyds b Curran 22
M. P. Speight not out	0	– run out 59
C. M. Wells (did not bat)		– c Walsh b Curran 55
†P. Moores (did not bat)		– run out 6
A. I. C. Dodemaide (did not bat)		– c Lawrence b Walsh 11
C. C. Remy (did not bat)		– not out 4
I. D. K. Salisbury (did not bat)		– not out 3
L-b 2, n-b 6	8	L-b 8, n-b 3 11

1/57 2/69 3/117   (3 wkts dec.) 120   1/35 2/132 3/183 4/190   (8 wkts) 325
5/295 6/306 7/314 8/321

R. A. Bunting did not bat.

Bonus point – Gloucestershire 1.

Bowling: *First Innings*—Lawrence 9–3–30–1; Walsh 13–3–40–2; Graveney 4.4–2–9–0; Curran 11–1–33–0; Bainbridge 3–0–6–0. *Second Innings*—Lawrence 10–0–56–0; Walsh 21–1–79–2; Curran 19–3–64–3; Graveney 16–3–48–0; Lloyds 18–2–70–1.

Umpires: J. D. Bond and R. Palmer.

At Worcester, June 20, 21, 22. SUSSEX drew with WORCESTERSHIRE.

SUSSEX v CAMBRIDGE UNIVERSITY

At Hove, June 30, July 2, 3. Cambridge University won by three wickets. Toss: Cambridge University. On the eve of the University Match at Lord's, Cambridge recorded their first victory over a county since 1982, when Lancashire were beaten by seven wickets. Set 256 to win in a minimum of 61 overs, they reached their target with seven balls to spare, thanks principally to James, an opening batsman under contract to Glamorgan. His 102, containing eleven fours, came in only 158 minutes, and as they added 142 in 35 overs for the second wicket, he and Lowrey exploited an inexperienced Sussex attack with attacking flair. James fell with 27 still needed, but a huge six from Heap settled the issue in Cambridge's favour. Sussex fielded seven uncapped players and one, Greenfield, the Second XI captain, went on to a maiden first-class hundred after Wells had hit twenty fours and two sixes in his 137. Remy returned a career-best four for 63 in Cambridge's first innings, when James and Heap both scored worthy half-centuries.

Close of play: First day, Sussex 318-3 (K. Greenfield 92*, P. W. G. Parker 2*); Second day, Cambridge University 248-9 (R. H. J. Jenkins 19*, S. W. Johnson 8*).

Sussex

N. J. Lenham b Shufflebotham	70	– b Pyman	22
J. W. Hall c Heap b Jenkins	3	– c Turner b Buzza	49
K. Greenfield not out	102	– not out	54
A. P. Wells c Shufflebotham b Pyman	137	– not out	27
*P. W. G. Parker not out	10		
B 5, l-b 1, n-b 11	17	B 1, l-b 9, n-b 2	12

1/15 2/124 3/316   (3 wkts dec.) 339   1/40 2/114   (2 wkts dec.) 164

M. P. Speight, C. C. Remy, J. A. North, †P. Moores, B. T. P. Donelan and R. A. Bunting did not bat.

Bowling: *First Innings*—Johnson 12–1–48–0; Jenkins 22.2–5–94–1; Pyman 26–7–60–1; Shufflebotham 12–2–36–1; Buzza 12–2–65–0; Lowrey 4–0–30–0. *Second Innings*—Johnson 6–1–18–0; Jenkins 4–0–18–0; Pyman 14–1–59–1; Shufflebotham 6–1–25–0; Buzza 7.5–1–34–1.

Cambridge University

S. P. James c Wells b Remy	61	– c Speight b North	102
R. Heap b Bunting	63	– (7) not out	20
†R. J. Turner c Moores b Wells	38	– (2) c Moores b Bunting	14
*J. C. M. Atkinson c Parker b Wells	2	– run out	0
M. J. Lowrey lbw b North	6	– (3) lbw b Lenham	72
M. J. Morris c Hall b Remy	12	– (5) lbw b Lenham	7
R. A. Pyman b Remy	0	– (6) run out	8
D. H. Shufflebotham b Remy	0	– b North	6
R. H. J. Jenkins not out	19	– not out	4
A. J. Buzza c Moores b Bunting	10		
S. W. Johnson not out	8		
B 8, l-b 20, w 1	29	B 9, l-b 12, w 1, n-b 3	25

1/88 2/171 3/181 4/185 5/202   (9 wkts dec.) 248   1/28 2/170 3/178 4/206   (7 wkts) 258
6/202 7/202 8/205 9/238   5/223 6/229 7/245

Bowling: *First Innings*—Bunting 27–4–60–2; North 22–5–46–1; Remy 22–6–63–4; Donelan 11–2–26–0; Wells 10–4–25–2. *Second Innings*—Bunting 14–0–54–1; North 11.5–2–43–2; Remy 15–0–70–0; Donelan 12–1–44–0; Lenham 7–1–26–2.

Umpires: J. H. Harris and A. A. Jones.

SUSSEX v DERBYSHIRE

At Hove, July 4, 5, 6. Derbyshire won by 18 runs. Derbyshire 20 pts, Sussex 3 pts. Toss: Sussex. Two forfeitures compensated for the loss of 136 overs, including the whole of the first day, to rain and opened the way for a dramatic finish in which a last-wicket partnership of 89 between two uncapped bowlers, Salisbury and Bunting, took Sussex to within 19 runs of victory. Derbyshire had scored 363 for seven in the 84.1 overs available on the second day, with Barnett hitting 123, including sixteen fours, in three and a half hours. He needed just 39 balls to move from 50 to 100, and when he reached three figures he passed the Derbyshire record of 30 centuries established by opener Denis Smith in a career that went from 1927 to

1952. Adams, with a six and twelve fours in his 91, was the other major contributor. The weather on the final day was excellent as Sussex embarked on the task of scoring 364 to win in 102 overs. Despite 51 from Colin Wells, they were rarely in contention and looked to have lost when their ninth wicket fell at 256. However, Salisbury, hitting nine fours in a career-best 68, and Bunting batted with such confidence that they were within 18 runs of Derbyshire, with more than six overs left, when Salisbury was taken at second slip off the shoulder of the bat to give Bishop his fifth wicket.

Close of play: First day, No play; Second day, Derbyshire 363-7 dec.

Derbyshire

*K. J. Barnett c Salisbury b Pigott	123	M. Jean-Jacques not out	....	0
P. D. Bowler b Bunting	 50	I. R. Bishop not out	....	0
J. E. Morris c Hall b Pigott	 21	L-b 6, w 2	....	8
B. Roberts c Moores b Pigott	 47			—
C. J. Adams st Moores b Salisbury .. 91		1/126 2/185 3/214	(7 wkts dec.) 363
S. C. Goldsmith c Moores b Pigott 11		4/265 5/291	
†K. M. Krikken c Lenham b Salisbury . 3		6/338 7/361	

S. J. Base and O. H. Mortensen did not bat.

Bonus points – Derbyshire 4, Sussex 3.

Bowling: Dodemaide 22.1–1–81–0; Pigott 18–4–69–4; Bunting 20–1–100–1; C. M. Wells 13–1–58–0; Salisbury 11–4–49–2.

Derbyshire forfeited their second innings.

Sussex

Sussex forfeited their first innings.

N. J. Lenham lbw b Mortensen	 12	*P. W. G. Parker c Krikken b Bishop . 35
J. W. Hall c Morris b Bishop	 6	I. D. K. Salisbury c Adams b Bishop .. 68
†P. Moores c Goldsmith b Mortensen .. 13		R. A. Bunting not out	 24
A. P. Wells c sub b Jean-Jacques 18			
M. P. Speight lbw b Base	 43	B 5, l-b 8, w 2, n-b 15 30
C. M. Wells c Morris b Goldsmith 51			
A. I. C. Dodemaide c and b Bishop ... 33	1/16 2/33 3/47 4/68 5/152	345
A. C. S. Pigott c Roberts b Bishop 12	6/166 7/185 8/243 9/256	

Bowling: Bishop 27.1–6–90–5; Mortensen 27–5–77–2; Jean-Jacques 13–3–60–1; Base 20–5–65–1; Goldsmith 8–0–40–1.

Umpires: J. H. Harris and A. A. Jones.

At Nottingham, July 7, 9, 10. SUSSEX drew with NOTTINGHAMSHIRE.

At Guildford, July 18, 19, 20. SUSSEX beat SURREY by seven wickets.

At Northampton, July 21, 23, 24. SUSSEX drew with NORTHAMPTONSHIRE.

SUSSEX v HAMPSHIRE

At Arundel, July 25, 26, 27. Drawn. Sussex 5 pts, Hampshire 6 pts. Toss: Sussex. The first County Championship match at Arundel Castle was blessed with fine weather. And although it petered out into a draw, it was nevertheless a financial success for Sussex, with more than 3,500 spectators present on the first day. The pitch proved slow, which enabled the home side to recover from 28 for three to a declaration on the second day at 383 for nine. Colin Wells's first Championship hundred of the season came from 133 balls and included fifteen fours and

ree sixes, while there were four wickets for the Hampshire off-spinner, Udal, on his
hampionship début. Hampshire batted carefully to secure a third bonus point and then
eclared, 129 behind, at their overnight score. Smith, unbeaten from the start, hit sixteen
urs in his 132. Sussex lost wickets rapidly as they attempted to set a realistic target and
entually declared at lunch, leaving 70 overs for Hampshire to score 274 runs. But once
nith (87 balls) and Marshall had gone, Hampshire struggled to maintain the momentum,
d with ten overs to go they abandoned the chase.

Close of play: First day, Sussex 342-9 (A. C. S. Pigott 30*, B. T. P. Donelan 6*); Second day,
ampshire 254-5 (C. L. Smith 132*, J. R. Ayling 28*).

ussex

. J. Lenham c Maru b Ayling	15	– b Connor	15
W. Hall lbw b Marshall	4	– run out	36
. W. G. Parker b Marshall	0	– b Ayling	18
. P. Wells c Scott b Udal	53	– b Maru	32
. P. Speight c and b Udal	37	– run out	24
. M. Wells c Ayling b Udal	107	– c Cox b Udal	6
. I. C. Dodemaide lbw b Marshall	2	– (8) not out	2
. Moores c Smith b Udal	61		
C. S. Pigott not out	64	– (7) b Udal	5
D. K. Salisbury run out	0		
T. P. Donelan not out	11		
B 1, l-b 21, w 4, n-b 3	29	L-b 4, n-b 2	6

13 2/13 3/28 4/105 5/134   (9 wkts dec.) 383   1/27 2/51 3/90   (7 wkts dec.) 144
137 7/276 8/319 9/324   4/123 5/129
                                        6/141 7/144

Bonus points – Sussex 3, Hampshire 3 (Score at 100 overs: 289-7).

Bowling: *First Innings*—Connor 12–4–20–0; Marshall 16–4–35–3; Ayling 15.4–8–36–1;
laru 32.2–5–105–0; Udal 43–7–144–4; Scott 4–1–21–0. *Second Innings*—Connor 8–1–23–1;
larshall 9–4–18–0; Maru 6–0–51–1; Ayling 6.2–0–36–1; Udal 2–0–12–2.

lampshire

. C. Middleton b Pigott	50	– b Donelan	28
. L. Smith not out	132	– st Moores b Donelan	61
. J. Scott c Dodemaide b Salisbury	13	– st Moores b Donelan	16
M. C. J. Nicholas run out	0	– c Moores b Pigott	1
. D. Marshall c Dodemaide b Salisbury	11	– c Donelan b Salisbury	34
. M. F. Cox c Moores b Dodemaide	9	– (7) not out	35
R. Ayling not out	28	– (6) c Hall b Salisbury	22
R. J. Parks (did not bat)		– not out	15
B 6, l-b 4, n-b 1	11	B 6, n-b 2	8

96 2/131 3/144 4/157 5/192   (5 wkts dec.) 254   1/76 2/93 3/94 4/141   (6 wkts) 220
                                             5/143 6/189

. J. Maru, S. D. Udal and C. A. Connor did not bat.

Bonus points – Hampshire 3, Sussex 2.

Bowling: *First Innings*—Dodemaide 20–9–31–1; Pigott 18–7–43–1; C. M. Wells 5–0–18–0;
onelan 19–5–44–0; Salisbury 36–5–108–2. *Second Innings*—Dodemaide 10–2–23–0; Pigott
-3–12–1; C. M. Wells 11–1–31–0; Salisbury 16–1–69–2; Donelan 19.4–4–79–3.

Umpires: B. Dudleston and B. Leadbeater.

t Chelmsford, July 28, 30, 31. SUSSEX drew with ESSEX.

SUSSEX v WARWICKSHIRE

At Eastbourne, August 4, 6, 7. Warwickshire won by six wickets. Warwickshire 24 pts, Susse
4 pts. Toss: Sussex. A remarkable hat-trick by Paul Smith, wearing odd boots, set up
comfortable victory for Warwickshire. Smith went off to borrow a spare from Munton, whic
was two sizes too big, after his had split. He returned, promptly bowled Dodemaide, an
immediately had Moores caught at short leg and Pigott snapped up by wicket-keeper Piper.
was the second hat-trick of his career and left Warwickshire needing 99 to win. Smith ha
earlier played his part in the first innings as Warwickshire bowled accurately on a lifeles
pitch, and in sweltering heat, to dismiss Sussex cheaply. Then, after Moles and Ratcliffe ha
begun with 113 for the first wicket, Moody ensured Warwickshire of a substantial firs
innings lead by hitting thirteen fours and a six in his 110. Sussex, batting again 196 in arrear
were given some hope of saving the match by Alan Wells's unbeaten 144, his highest score
the season, which included 24 fours and two sixes. Donelan chipped in with a career-best 53
the pair added 112 for the sixth wicket, but the other batting was generally poor. Hanley,
22-year-old making his first-class début on his home ground, showed promise in his 28.

Close of play: First day, Warwickshire 96-0 (A. J. Moles 52*, J. D. Ratcliffe 38*); Secon
day, Sussex 130-5 (A. P. Wells 61*, B. T. P. Donelan 0*).

Sussex

D. M. Smith c Piper b Munton	18	– b G. Smith	1
J. W. Hall b Moody	30	– lbw b Munton	1
R. Hanley lbw b P. A. Smith	2	– c and b Munton	2
A. P. Wells lbw b P. A. Smith	0	– not out	14
M. P. Speight c Piper b G. Smith	22	– b Pierson	1
*C. M. Wells run out	40	– (8) c G. Smith b Reeve	1
†P. Moores lbw b Munton	10	– (10) c Asif Din b P. A. Smith	
A. C. S. Pigott lbw b G. Smith	32	– (11) c Piper b P. A. Smith	
B. T. P. Donelan c Reeve b G. Smith	6	– (7) c Piper b Munton	5
R. A. Bunting not out	1	– (6) c Asif Din b Pierson	
B 4, l-b 3, w 1, n-b 6	14	B 10, l-b 6, w 2, n-b 2	2

1/33 2/48 3/48 4/79 5/79   179   1/9 2/23 3/73 4/120 5/130   29
6/93 7/109 8/162 9/170   6/242 7/277 8/294 9/294

Bonus points – Sussex 1, Warwickshire 4.

Bowling: *First Innings*—Munton 20-7-46-3; G. Smith 15.5-2-36-3; P. A. Smi
13-3-30-2; Reeve 14-5-28-0; Pierson 3-0-8-0; Moody 8-5-7-1; Asif Din 4-1-17-0. *Secon
Innings*—Munton 28-7-63-3; G. Smith 11-1-45-1; P. A. Smith 11.5-2-45-3; Reev
11-1-31-1; Pierson 14-3-65-2; Asif Din 9-5-29-0.

Warwickshire

A. J. Moles b Dodemaide	58	– c Moores b Donelan	3
J. D. Ratcliffe c Moores b Bunting	61	– c Moores b Dodemaide	
T. M. Moody c Hall b Donelan	110		
*T. A. Lloyd b Bunting	1	– (3) c Moores b Donelan	2
P. A. Smith b Dodemaide	2	– (4) lbw b Dodemaide	1
D. A. Reeve c and b Pigott	30	– (5) not out	
Asif Din not out	57	– (6) not out	
†K. J. Piper lbw b Pigott	5		
A. R. K. Pierson b Pigott	9		
G. Smith b Dodemaide	30		
B 1, l-b 11	12	B 4, l-b 3	

1/113 2/131 3/143 4/183 5/271   (9 wkts dec.) 375   1/24 2/73 3/88 4/98   (4 wkts) 10
6/273 7/279 8/297 9/375

T. A. Munton did not bat.

Bonus points – Warwickshire 4, Sussex 3 (Score at 100 overs: 334-8).

Bowling: *First Innings*—Pigott 30–4–101–3; Dodemaide 28.2–6–84–3; Bunting 21–3–89–2; Donelan 12–3–46–1; C. M. Wells 17–5–43–0. *Second Innings*—Pigott 3–0–21–0; Dodemaide 11.2–0–45–2; Bunting 3–0–10–0; Donelan 6–1–19–2.

Umpires: J. D. Bond and M. J. Kitchen.

SUSSEX v YORKSHIRE

At Eastbourne, August 8, 9, 10. Yorkshire won by an innings and 5 runs. Yorkshire 23 pts, Sussex 2 pts. Toss: Yorkshire. Outstanding performances by Moxon and Carrick sentenced Sussex to a crushing innings defeat and brought a sorry end to Eastbourne week, where both Championship matches and the Sunday League game were lost. Moxon, the Yorkshire captain, applied himself superbly in wilting heat to hit his county's highest individual score since Boycott's 233 against Essex in 1971. His unbeaten 218, from 318 balls in exactly six hours, included 28 fours and a six, and he shared century partnerships with Metcalfe and Robinson. When Sussex replied, Smith and Hall put on 60 for the opening wicket before Carrick took charge, ripping out the heart of the innings with his left-arm spin on a turning pitch. Sussex began the final day needing 160 to avoid an innings defeat, with all wickets standing, but once the openers were parted for 62 only Speight, with a defiant 53, offered much resistance. Carrick increased his match return to nine for 86; Jarvis was the best fast bowler on view, taking six wickets; and Blakey gave a fine display behind the stumps to hold nine catches.

Close of play: First day, Sussex 9-0 (D. M. Smith 2*, J. W. Hall 5*); Second day, Sussex 13-0 (D. M. Smith 5*, J. W. Hall 8*).

Yorkshire

*M. D. Moxon not out	218	†R. J. Blakey not out	2
A. A. Metcalfe b Donelan	53	B 12, l-b 6, n-b 8	26
K. Sharp c Moores b C. M. Wells	42		
P. E. Robinson c Hansford b Donelan	59	1/120 2/213 3/375 (3 wkts dec.)	400

D. Byas, P. Carrick, C. S. Pickles, P. J. Hartley, P. W. Jarvis and J. D. Batty did not bat.

Bonus points – Yorkshire 4, Sussex 1 (Score at 100 overs: 378-3).

Bowling: Dodemaide 20–3–57–0; Pigott 21–7–76–0; Hansford 20–3–76–0; C. M. Wells 14–3–76–1; Donelan 28–1–97–2.

Sussex

D. M. Smith c Blakey b Pickles	29	– c Blakey b Pickles	37
J. W. Hall c Blakey b Carrick	32	– c Hartley b Jarvis	38
R. Hanley b Jarvis	2	– c Metcalfe b Pickles	0
A. P. Wells c Blakey b Carrick	42	– c Blakey b Carrick	4
M. P. Speight lbw b Jarvis	14	– c Blakey b Jarvis	53
*C. M. Wells c Blakey b Carrick	0	– b Carrick	15
A. I. C. Dodemaide c Byas b Pickles	40	– lbw b Hartley	0
†P. Moores c Blakey b Carrick	10	– c and b Carrick	2
A. C. S. Pigott not out	29	– lbw b Carrick	0
B. T. P. Donelan c Blakey b Carrick	9	– not out	10
A. R. Hansford b Jarvis	2	– b Jarvis	0
B 14, l-b 4	18	B 9	9

1/60 2/70 3/70 4/85 5/92		227	1/62 2/62 3/69 4/91 5/124 168
6/158 7/181 8/197 9/218			6/131 7/140 8/148 9/160

Bonus points – Sussex 1, Yorkshire 3 (Score at 100 overs: 197-8).

Bowling: *First Innings*—Jarvis 21.4–7–56–3; Hartley 19–7–50–0; Carrick 44–22–49–5; Pickles 15–5–28–2; Batty 9–1–26–0. *Second Innings*—Jarvis 14.1–4–39–3; Hartley 16–2–60–1; Pickles 6–2–23–2; Carrick 20–6–37–4.

Umpires: J. D. Bond and M. J. Kitchen.

At Lord's, August 11, 13, 14. SUSSEX drew with MIDDLESEX.

SUSSEX v KENT

At Hove, August 18, 20, 21. Drawn. Sussex 5 pts, Kent 6 pts. Toss: Sussex. An exciting finish to an absorbing struggle looked likely when Kent asked Sussex to score 312 off at least 71 overs on the final afternoon. The second-wicket pair, Hall and Smith, put on 82 in good time, but Sussex's push for victory was undermined by the Kent left-arm spinner, Davis, in a marathon spell. When Pigott became his sixth victim – his fifth in seven overs – Sussex called off the chase with 65 needed from the last six overs. A rain-affected first day had been dominated by Kent's left-handed opener, Benson, who hit his fifth century of the season, including fourteen fours and a six, before his right thumb was broken by a rising delivery from Dodemaide. He and Taylor added 113 for the second wicket before his injury. Dodemaide and Pigott bowled well without enjoying a great deal of luck. Kent's hopes of bowling their hosts out twice were dashed by the defiance of Lenham, but things might have been different had Wren held a chance at fine leg when Lenham was 11. Sussex declared 150 behind on the second evening, but Pigott checked Kent's bid for quick runs on the final morning by taking four wickets during a hundred-minute spell.

Close of play: First day, Kent 449-7 (S. A. Marsh 70*, P. S. de Villiers 15*); Second day, Kent 31-2 (N. R. Taylor 8*, G. R. Cowdrey 18*).

Kent

S. G. Hinks b Dodemaide	7	– b Dodemaide	4
M. R. Benson retired hurt	115		
N. R. Taylor c Pigott b Dodemaide	61	– (2) not out	70
G. R. Cowdrey b Dodemaide	29	– lbw b Pigott	34
T. R. Ward lbw b Donelan	64	– c Moores b Pigott	12
M. V. Fleming b Pigott	30	– b Pigott	16
*C. S. Cowdrey c Lenham b Donelan	20	– b Pigott	0
†S. A. Marsh not out	70		
R. P. Davis c Speight b Pigott	29	– (3) c Moores b Pigott	0
P. S. de Villiers not out	15	– (8) not out	19
B 3, l-b 3, w 2, n-b 1	9	B 5, l-b 1	6

1/60 2/212 3/227 4/311 5/311   (7 wkts dec.) 449   1/5 2/6 3/54   (6 wkts dec.) 161
6/365 7/418   4/72 5/116 6/116

T. N. Wren did not bat.

Bonus points – Kent 4, Sussex 2 (Score at 100 overs: 393-6).

In the first innings M. R. Benson retired hurt at 173.

Bowling: *First Innings*—Pigott 22–5–93–2; Dodemaide 31–4–123–3; Bunting 22–5–88–0; C. M. Wells 19–5–80–0; Donelan 16–4–59–2. *Second Innings*—Pigott 18–2–77–5; Dodemaide 12.4–2–43–1; Bunting 7–1–28–0; Donelan 3–0–7–0.

Sussex

N. J. Lenham b Fleming	86	– c C. S. Cowdrey b Fleming	20
J. W. Hall b Fleming	24	– c sub b Davis	52
†P. Moores run out	23	– (9) not out	1
A. P. Wells c Ward b Davis	78	– c and b Davis	36
M. P. Speight c C. S. Cowdrey b Fleming	14	– lbw b Davis	1
*C. M. Wells not out	41	– not out	42
D. M. Smith not out	6	– (3) c Ward b Davis	71
A. I. C. Dodemaide (did not bat)		– (7) c de Villiers b Davis	13
A. C. S. Pigott (did not bat)		– (8) c Ward b Davis	10
B 14, l-b 4, w 6, n-b 3	27	B 14, l-b 5	19

1/53 2/129 3/180 4/202 5/293   (5 wkts dec.) 299   1/50 2/132 3/193 4/198   (7 wkts) 265
                                                       5/201 6/221 7/247

R. A. Bunting and B. T. P. Donelan did not bat.

Bonus points – Sussex 3, Kent 2.

Bowling: *First Innings*—de Villiers 14–1–34–0; Wren 21–4–74–0; Fleming 27–10–65–3; C. S. Cowdrey 5–0–16–0; Davis 31–11–89–1; Ward 2–0–3–0. *Second Innings*—de Villiers 14–3–46–0; Wren 7–0–39–0; Davis 31.4–10–97–6; Fleming 14–3–38–1; Ward 5–0–26–0.

Umpires: P. J. Eele and R. Julian.

SUSSEX v SOMERSET

At Hove, August 23, 24, 25, 27. Somerset won by ten wickets. Somerset 23 pts, Sussex 3 pts.
Toss: Somerset. Somerset were always in control after they had dismissed Sussex cheaply on the first day. Their lively seam attack found little resistance, apart from Lenham and the determined Dodemaide, and although Sussex briefly threatened to bowl themselves back into contention, reducing Somerset to 30 for three, Tavaré ensured there was no way back. His career-best 219, a maiden double-hundred, was an innings full of glorious shots which, in 413 deliveries, included 29 fours. Having shared in century stands with Harden and Rose, he equalled the county's ninth-wicket record of 183, set 27 years earlier, in partnership with Mallender, whose Somerset-best 87 was made with the aid of a runner. Tavaré declared 372 ahead first thing on the third morning, and although Lenham and Dodemaide again led a spirited rearguard action, Somerset's victory was never in much doubt. Lenham's 123 featured twenty fours, and Dodemaide took the match into the final day, hitting thirteen fours in his maiden Championship century.

Close of play: First day, Somerset 136-4 (C. J. Tavaré 45*, H. R. J. Trump 0*); Second day, Somerset 525-9 (N. A. Mallender 87*, A. N. Jones 24*); Third day, Sussex 331-8 (A. I. C. Dodemaide 86*, I. D. K. Salisbury 13*).

Sussex

N. J. Lenham c Burns b Lefebvre	45	– c Trump b Hayhurst	123
J. W. Hall c Townsend b Jones	1	– c Townsend b Rose	2
K. Greenfield c Burns b Mallender	5	– c and b Hayhurst	11
A. P. Wells lbw b Mallender	2	– b Rose	14
M. P. Speight c Hayhurst b Jones	2	– c Burns b Jones	11
*C. M. Wells c Burns b Rose	4	– c Burns b Lefebvre	2
A. I. C. Dodemaide not out	57	– c and b Jones	112
†P. Moores c Tavaré b Lefebvre	8	– c Tavaré b Trump	38
A. C. S. Pigott lbw b Rose	2	– c Cook b Harden	23
I. D. K. Salisbury c Burns b Lefebvre	3	– not out	30
R. A. Bunting c Burns b Hayhurst	14	– c Tavaré b Hayhurst	8
L-b 4, w 1, n-b 5	10	L-b 3, n-b 5	8
	153		**382**

1/19 2/43 3/45 4/51 5/68 6/78 7/108 8/111 9/122   1/14 2/69 3/105 4/119 5/148 6/183 7/258 8/290 9/365

Bowling: *First Innings*—Jones 11–2–47–2; Mallender 13–5–31–2; Rose 11–4–22–2; Lefebvre 17–4–46–3; Hayhurst 3.4–2–3–1. *Second Innings*—Jones 34–5–117–2; Rose 26–5–95–2; Hayhurst 23–6–58–3; Lefebvre 24–9–48–1; Trump 23–9–49–1; Harden 4–0–12–1.

Somerset

S. J. Cook c Moores b Pigott	13		
G. T. J. Townsend c Moores b Dodemaide	0	– not out	0
A. N. Hayhurst c Moores b Dodemaide	11		
*C. J. Tavaré c Speight b Pigott	219		
R. J. Harden c Moores b Pigott	59		
H. R. J. Trump c Moores b Dodemaide	0		
†N. D. Burns c C. M. Wells b Bunting	28	– (1) not out	13
G. D. Rose b Dodemaide	54		
R. P. Lefebvre b Pigott	6		
N. A. Mallender not out	87		
A. N. Jones not out	24		
B 8, l-b 9, n-b 7	24		
	525		**13**

1/2 2/20 3/30 4/132 5/137   (9 wkts dec.) 525   (no wkt) 13
6/176 7/292 8/301 9/484

Bonus points – Somerset 3, Sussex 2 (Score at 100 overs: 282-6).

Bowling: *First Innings*—Pigott 37–6–119–4; Dodemaide 36–5–117–4; Bunting 33–8–77–1; C. M. Wells 23–1–111–0; Salisbury 29–9–80–0; Lenham 3–0–4–0. *Second Innings*—Salisbury 1–0–5–0; Greenfield 0.3–0–8–0.

Umpires: J. C. Balderstone and R. A. White.

At Leicester, August 29, 30, 31. SUSSEX beat LEICESTERSHIRE by 29 runs.

At Hove, September 5, 6, 7. SUSSEX drew with SRI LANKANS (See Sri Lankan tour section).

At Bristol, September 12, 13, 14. SUSSEX lost to GLOUCESTERSHIRE by an innings and 86 runs.

SUSSEX v MIDDLESEX

At Hove, September 18, 19, 20. Middlesex won by an innings and 57 runs. Middlesex 24 pts, Sussex 3 pts. Toss: Middlesex. Any hope Sussex had of denying Middlesex the Championship was effectively over on the first of the four scheduled days. Middlesex, inspired by Hughes's nagging accuracy and Gatting's important two-wicket contribution, bowled their hosts out cheaply on a good pitch, despite brave innings from the dependable Smith and Speight. The visitors then batted steadily rather than spectacularly. Haynes and Roseberry provided the perfect platform by putting on 133 for the first wicket, and Brown produced the highlight of the innings with an undefeated 116 which included thirteen boundaries. However, Haynes hardly endeared himself to the spectators with a display of bad temper when he was caught by wicket-keeper Moores after being distracted by a cameraman's movements behind the bowler's arm. Gatting and Emburey both chipped in with useful runs, and Middlesex were 224 ahead when they were dismissed at the end of the second day. The weather, rather than Sussex's batting, was their main worry, but the rain stayed away long enough to ensure a fifth Championship title, plus one shared, in fifteen seasons. Fraser bowled beautifully to take four wickets, and Hughes, who finished with match figures of seven for 89, signalled great celebrations among the large contingent of Middlesex supporters by claiming the last two wickets with successive balls.

Close of play: First day, Middlesex 88-0 (D. L. Haynes 34*, M. A. Roseberry 51*); Second day, Middlesex 411.

Sussex

N. J. Lenham c Emburey b Williams	9	– lbw b Fraser	5
D. M. Smith c Downton b Cowans	32	– lbw b Cowans	10
*P. W. G. Parker c Brown b Hughes	24	– b Cowans	16
A. P. Wells lbw b Gatting	6	– c Downton b Fraser	50
M. P. Speight c Downton b Hughes	33	– b Fraser	12
A. I. C. Dodemaide b Fraser	18	– c Downton b Fraser	16
†P. Moores c sub b Hughes	4	– lbw b Hughes	10
J. A. North lbw b Cowans	7	– not out	19
A. C. S. Pigott c Fraser b Gatting	4	– c sub b Gatting	9
I. D. K. Salisbury not out	18	– b Hughes	0
R. A. Bunting c Emburey b Hughes	11	– lbw b Hughes	0
B 10, l-b 6, n-b 5	21	B 8, l-b 4, w 1, n-b 7	20
	187		**167**

1/19 2/42 3/78 4/103 5/130   1/10 2/17 3/46 4/74 5/119
6/136 7/151 8/151 9/170   6/126 7/158 8/167 9/167

Bonus points – Sussex 1, Middlesex 4.

Bowling: *First Innings*—Fraser 21–4–55–1; Williams 3–1–9–1; Cowans 12–5–19–2; Hughes 17.1–4–34–4; Gatting 18–8–42–2; Emburey 10–5–12–0; Haynes 1–1–0–0. *Second Innings*—Fraser 17–4–47–4; Cowans 16–4–33–2; Hughes 16.5–3–55–3; Gatting 8–5–7–1; Emburey 3–0–13–0.

Middlesex

D. L. Haynes c Moores b Bunting	46	A. R. C. Fraser b Salisbury	13
M. A. Roseberry run out	83	S. P. Hughes lbw b Salisbury	0
*M. W. Gatting c Parker b Lenham	51	N. G. Cowans c Pigott b North	0
M. R. Rampraksh lbw b Bunting	13		
K. R. Brown not out	116	B 1, l-b 12, w 1, n-b 4	18
†P. R. Downton lbw b North	5		
J. E. Emburey c Smith b Dodemaide	48	1/133 2/135 3/168 4/225 5/244	411
N. F. Williams c Wells b Dodemaide	18	6/352 7/389 8/410 9/410	

Bonus points – Middlesex 4, Sussex 2 (Score at 100 overs: 362-6).

Bowling: Dodemaide 28–2–128–2; Pigott 24–4–92–0; Bunting 17–4–49–2; North 16.2–4–43–2; Lenham 19–4–48–1; Salisbury 11–2–38–2.

Umpires: K. E. Palmer and D. S. Thompsett.

I ZINGARI RESULTS, 1990

Matches – 22: Won 9, Lost 4, Drawn 8, Abandoned 1.

April 24	Eton College	Drawn
May 12	Honourable Artillery Company	Won by 128 runs
May 20	Staff College, Camberley	Drawn
May 26	Eton Ramblers	Drawn
May 31	Harrow School	Drawn
June 9	Hurlingham CC	Drawn
June 10	Earl of Carnarvon's XI	Won by 53 runs
June 16	Charterhouse School	Lost by four wickets
June 23	Guards CC	Abandoned
July 7	Bradfield Waifs	Won by 102 runs
July 8	Hagley CC	Won by four wickets
July 14	Green Jackets Club	Drawn
July 15	Rickling Green CC	Lost by two wickets
July 21	Leicester Gentlemen	Won by five wickets
July 22	Sir John Starkey's XI	Won by eight wickets
July 29	Royal Armoured Corps	Won by 60 runs
August 4	R. Leigh-Pemberton's XI	Drawn
August 5	Band of Brothers	Lost by seven wickets
August 11, 12	South Wales Hunts XI	Lost by six wickets
September 2	Captain R. H. Hawkins' XI	Won by 127 runs
September 8	Hampshire Hogs	Drawn
September 9	J. H. Pawle's XI	Won by 102 runs

WARWICKSHIRE

President: The Earl of Aylesford
Chairman: R. J. Evans
Chairman, Cricket Committee: W. N. Houghton
Secretary: D. M. W. Heath
  County Ground, Edgbaston,
  Birmingham B5 7QU
  (Telephone: 021-446 4422)
Cricket Manager/Coach: 1990 – R. M. H. Cottam
Captain: T. A. Lloyd

Given that Warwickshire's 64 bowling bonus points in the Britannic
Assurance Championship were more than those obtained by any county
other than Surrey (64 also), their seemingly satisfactory advance from
eighth to fifth in the final table was, in fact, a slight disappointment. The
summer produced the biggest swing of balance between bat and ball for
many years. Yet only five counties secured fewer batting points than
Warwickshire's 55, and the side suffered from a shortage of runs far too
often to be realistic title contenders.

Even so, a win in their last, rain-ruined game at Old Trafford would
still have earned Warwickshire third place, a remarkable effort considering that injury and a decline in form restricted Allan Donald and
Gladstone Small to only 55 wickets between them at 34 apiece, compared
with 137 at just under 19 in the 1989 Championship. It was fortunate for
the club that this shortfall was more than made up for by the advance of
Tim Munton and the breakthrough made by Joey Benjamin, together
with supportive performances from Dermot Reeve and Paul Smith.

The consistency of the bowlers, however, was not matched by the top
batsmen. Only Andy Moles, with his best-ever aggregate of 1,854 runs,
and the prolific Australian, Tom Moody, took advantage of the most
favourable batting conditions for many summers. Moody's 1,000 runs
were recorded in fewer innings, twelve, than anyone had previously
taken for the county, and his seven hundreds came in his first eight
games. He hit the fastest hundred of the season, off 36 balls against
Glamorgan at Swansea, but his best hundred was a brilliant 168 from 173
balls to win the Championship game at Derby. Nevertheless, it was
ironic that, having been signed on a one-year contract to play in the
limited-overs matches, Moody should help the side into the place money
in the Championship. Warwickshire's performances in the three one-day
competitions were unmitigated disasters.

The county's policy resulted in Donald, one of the most successful
bowlers in limited-overs cricket the previous year, playing only one such
game, because of the legislation governing overseas players, while Moody
played in all but one of the rest. Twice forced, as a result, to chase targets
in excess of 250 in the Benson and Hedges Cup group games, the county
failed to qualify for the knockout stage; and after winning three of their
first four games in the Refuge Assurance League, they managed only
two more wins in the next twelve matches and finished fourteenth as in
1989. In the NatWest Bank Trophy, Yorkshire handed out a ten-wicket
thrashing at Headingley in the second round to underline the difference a
fit and in-form Donald might have made.

The South African fast bowler sustained a back injury halfway through the season, and this enabled Moody to come into the side and score so consistently that it was far from automatic which player would return to Edgbaston in 1991. In the end the committee unanimously decided to honour their contractual obligations to Donald, and Moody eventually signed for Worcestershire. In addition to his 1,163 runs in first-class cricket at an average of 89.46, the big Western Australian scored 581 runs in limited-overs cricket from twenty games. To illustrate his powerful strokeplay, which included the ability to drive in a wide "V" and square cut with great ferocity, he passed 1,000 runs off only 1,200 deliveries.

As well as Donald's back, the side had other injuries to contend with, among them the hamstring problem which kept Andy Lloyd, the captain, out of action for a third of the season. Lloyd's overall form was disappointing, not an unusual occurrence in a player's benefit year, but with Alvin Kallicharran and Geoff Humpage stepping down from the first team midway through their farewell season, much depended on Asif Din. He had a splendid season in one-day cricket, scoring 792 runs in 21 games, but a first-class record of 974 runs for an average of 27.82 was well below both his capabilities and the needs of the team. To some degree the middle order compensated, with Reeve in particular having his best season with the bat, his three first-class hundreds including his maiden double-century. As well as his 1,412 runs at an average of 54.30, he took 33 wickets, held 26 catches, many of them at slip, and led the side in Lloyd's absence.

All-rounder Paul Smith bounced back after a serious knee operation, and although he played in only twelve first-class and ten one-day games, for the second season in succession he averaged more than 30 with the bat and less than 30 with the ball in the Championship to emphasise his importance to the side's balance. Twenty-year-old Keith Piper performed well as wicket-keeper when he took over from Humpage, and in addition to his 43 dismissals he scored 432 useful runs in the Championship, including his maiden first-class hundred. He looked set for a long and successful career. Other youngsters to make their mark were Jason Ratcliffe and Dominic Ostler, both of whom batted well enough to show that a first-class career is within their capabilities.

Even though Humpage was omitted after thirteen games, he still averaged 34.88 to finish fourth in Warwickshire's first-class averages. He announced his retirement to go into business, and left Edgbaston after a distinguished career of seventeen years, having been one of the best wicket-keeper-batsmen of the 1980s. His 29 first-class hundreds enabled him to finish with a county average of 36.41, which has been bettered for Warwickshire by only six players, while his 704 dismissals for the county are exceeded only by E. J. "Tiger" Smith. Kallicharran, one of the best batsmen to play for the county, scored in excess of 18,000 runs at an average of more than 40 for Warwickshire, including 52 of his 87 hundreds.

An unexpected departure was that of the cricket manager and coach, Bob Cottam, who resigned in late October over policy differences with the cricket committee. In spite of this, however, the 1991 season promises much, provided the playing staff steer clear of injuries – and assuming that the bowlers receive better support from the batsmen than they did in 1990. – Jack Bannister.

WARWICKSHIRE 1990

[Bill Smith]

Back row: K. J. Piper, R. G. Twose, N. M. K. Smith, J. E. Benjamin, S. J. Green, G. Welch, I. G. S. Steer. *Middle row*: T. L. Penney, G. Smith, D. P. Ostler, A. R. K. Pierson, T. A. Munton, J. D. Ratcliffe, A. A. Donald, A. J. Moles, P. A. Booth. *Front row*: R. N. Abberley (*coach*), G. C. Small, G. W. Humpage, R. M. H. Cottam (*cricket manager/coach*), T. A. Lloyd (*captain*), A. I. Kallicharran, Asif Din, P. A. Smith. *Insets*: T. M. Moody, D. A. Reeve, P. C. L. Holloway.

WARWICKSHIRE RESULTS

All first-class matches – Played 25: Won 7, Lost 8, Drawn 10.

County Championship matches – Played 22: Won 7, Lost 7, Drawn 8.

Bonus points – Batting 55, Bowling 64.

*Competition placings – Britannic Assurance County Championship, 5th;
NatWest Bank Trophy, 2nd round; Benson and Hedges Cup, 4th in Group A;
Refuge Assurance League, 14th.*

BRITANNIC ASSURANCE CHAMPIONSHIP AVERAGES

BATTING

	Birthplace	M	I	NO	R	HI	Avge
‡T. M. Moody	Adelaide, Australia	7	12	2	866	168	86.60
‡D. A. Reeve	Kowloon, Hong Kong	22	34	11	1,265	202*	55.00
‡A. J. Moles	Solihull	22	42	8	1,669	224*	49.08
‡G. W. Humpage	Birmingham	11	18	3	552	74	36.80
J. E. Benjamin	Christ Church, St Kitts	12	11	6	169	41	33.80
D. P. Ostler	Solihull	9	15	2	432	71	33.23
‡P. A. Smith	Jesmond	12	20	4	520	117	32.50
N. M. K. Smith	Birmingham	7	9	2	214	83*	30.57
J. D. Ratcliffe	Solihull	14	27	3	689	81*	28.70
‡Asif Din	Kampala, Uganda	21	37	3	874	70	25.70
K. J. Piper	Leicester	14	18	1	432	111	25.41
‡A. I. Kallicharran	Paidama, BG	5	8	1	175	72	25.00
‡T. A. Lloyd	Oswestry	15	27	1	646	101	24.84
P. A. Booth	Huddersfield	7	12	0	177	60	14.75
R. G. Twose	Torquay	4	6	0	88	51	14.66
A. R. K. Pierson	Enfield	11	9	5	57	16*	14.25
‡G. C. Small	St George, Barbados	12	18	2	212	55	13.25
‡T. A. Munton	Melton Mowbray	22	23	9	121	29*	8.64
‡A. A. Donald	Bloemfontein, SA	14	18	3	118	24*	7.86

Also batted: G. Smith (*Jarrow*) (1 match) 30.

* Signifies not out. ‡ *Denotes county cap.*

The following played a total of thirteen three-figure innings for Warwickshire in County
Championship matches – T. M. Moody 5, A. J. Moles 3, D. A. Reeve 2, T. A. Lloyd 1,
K. J. Piper 1, P. A. Smith 1.

BOWLING

	O	M	R	W	BB	5W/i	Avge
P. A. Smith	148.5	34	497	20	5-48	1	24.85
T. A. Munton	748.3	174	2,086	75	5-33	2	27.81
D. A. Reeve	319.4	94	782	28	4-42	0	27.92
J. E. Benjamin	322.3	51	1,036	34	5-71	3	30.47
G. C. Small	321.4	78	900	27	6-94	2	33.33
A. A. Donald	355.1	81	988	28	3-28	0	35.28
A. R. K. Pierson	302.4	55	965	25	5-101	1	38.60
P. A. Booth	214.2	70	495	12	4-55	0	41.25

Also bowled: Asif Din 133.2–24–569–6; G. W. Humpage 7–2–34–0; T. A. Lloyd 9–1–58–1;
A. J. Moles 22–2–133–2; T. M. Moody 38–7–145–3; G. Smith 26.5–3–81–4; N. M. K. Smith
09.5–20–350–5; R. G. Twose 26–2–101–2.

Wicket-keepers: K. J. Piper 39 ct, 4 st; G. W. Humpage 22 ct.

Leading Fielder: D. A. Reeve 23.

At Cambridge, April 26, 27, 28. WARWICKSHIRE drew with CAMBRIDGE UNIVERSITY.

WARWICKSHIRE v YORKSHIRE

At Birmingham, May 3, 4, 5. Warwickshire won by seven wickets. Warwickshire 23 pts, Yorkshire 5 pts. Toss: Yorkshire. With Small, Donald and Munton bowling with great penetration on a slow, seaming pitch, Yorkshire had to rely on Sidebottom's 38, top score of the innings, to gain a single batting point. In turn, Sidebottom and Fletcher, in particular, disconcerted Warwickshire on the first evening and second morning, and it took an unbeaten hard-hitting 83 from Smith to rescue them from a parlous position at 162 for eight and put them 92 ahead. Smith hit a six and twelve fours, and in partnership with Donald added 80 for the ninth wicket. Only Robinson, batting for three and threequarter hours, showed the necessary application when Yorkshire batted a second time. Booth, the former Yorkshire left-arm spinner, bowled well for his four wickets on the second evening and left his home county facing defeat inside three of the scheduled four days. Reeve finished with a freakish match analysis of 22–15–8–3.

Close of play: First day, Warwickshire 111-4 (G. W. Humpage 40*, D. A. Reeve 24*). Second day, Yorkshire 139-5 (P. E. Robinson 21*, P. Carrick 13*).

Yorkshire

*M. D. Moxon c Humpage b Small	12	– (5) c Kallicharran b Booth 6
A. A. Metcalfe c Reeve b Donald	33	– b Smith 2
†R. J. Blakey c Booth b Reeve	6	– c Moles b Booth 26
S. A. Kellett lbw b Small	31	– (1) c Humpage b Booth 3
P. E. Robinson run out	1	– (4) lbw b Reeve 59
C. White b Small	1	– c Asif Din b Booth 4
P. Carrick c Reeve b Munton	7	– b Small 4
A. Sidebottom c Asif Din b Munton	38	– c Moles b Munton 10
P. W. Jarvis c Humpage b Small	0	– c Humpage b Reeve 4
D. Gough c Humpage b Donald	4	– not out 4
S. D. Fletcher not out	11	– b Donald 8
B 9, l-b 11, w 2, n-b 1	23	B 17, l-b 12, w 2, n-b 2 .. 33

1/35 2/60 3/74 4/102 5/104   167   1/57 2/61 3/100 4/104 5/120   216
6/105 7/119 8/121 9/139   6/149 7/199 8/213 9/216

Bonus points – Yorkshire 1, Warwickshire 4.

Bowling: *First Innings*—Donald 19-5-56-2; Small 18-5-40-4; Munton 15.5-3-41-2; Reeve 17-12-6-1; Booth 2-1-4-0. *Second Innings*—Donald 17.4-4-41-1; Small 19-9-29-1; Munton 8-3-21-1; Booth 33-9-55-4; Smith 12-2-36-1; Asif Din 2-1-6-0; Reeve 5-3-2-2.

Warwickshire

A. J. Moles lbw b Sidebottom	6	– (2) c Blakey b White 3
*T. A. Lloyd b Fletcher	31	– (1) b Carrick 3
Asif Din c Blakey b Sidebottom	0	– c Blakey b Carrick 2
A. I. Kallicharran lbw b Fletcher	2	– not out 1
†G. W. Humpage lbw b Sidebottom	52	– not out 1
D. A. Reeve c Moxon b Fletcher	29	
N. M. K. Smith not out	83	
P. A. Booth lbw b Jarvis	15	
G. C. Small b Jarvis	0	
A. A. Donald c Sidebottom b Carrick	16	
T. A. Munton lbw b Fletcher	0	
B 10, l-b 6, w 5, n-b 4	25	B 8, l-b 5 13

1/11 2/11 3/38 4/43 5/127   259   1/60 2/96 3/102   (3 wkts) 12
6/134 7/162 8/162 9/242

Bonus points – Warwickshire 3, Yorkshire 4.

Bowling: *First Innings*—Jarvis 16–1–52–2; Sidebottom 18–4–54–3; Fletcher 20.5–6–47–4; Gough 14–1–53–0; Carrick 10–3–31–1; White 2–0–6–0. *Second Innings*—Jarvis 6–2–22–0; Fletcher 4–0–18–0; Carrick 12.2–2–35–2; White 11–2–40–1.

Umpires: R. Palmer and P. B. Wight.

At Northampton, May 15, 16, 17, 18. WARWICKSHIRE beat NORTHAMPTONSHIRE by an innings and 30 runs.

WARWICKSHIRE v NOTTINGHAMSHIRE

At Birmingham, May 19, 21, 22. Nottinghamshire won by 5 runs. Nottinghamshire 24 pts, Warwickshire 5 pts. Toss: Nottinghamshire. A thrilling finale, which brought victory to the visitors, saw Stephenson take the last three wickets in eight deliveries, including two with consecutive balls in the last over. Set to score 304 off a minimum of 64 overs, Warwickshire at one stage were 259 for four, with time on their side. And though in retrospect the run-out of Humpage for 62 from 68 balls was to prove the turning-point, Warwickshire looked certain to win when they needed just 20 from the last four overs with five wickets in hand. However, the run-out of Lloyd, who was batting with a runner, and the first-ball dismissal of Small tipped the scales. Nottinghamshire deserved their win, having batted solidly in both innings and declared twice. Broad hit nineteen fours in his first-innings 119 and his opening partnership of 176 in 63 overs with Martindale provided his side with an excellent start. Humpage, with 74 from 88 balls, gave substance to Warwickshire's reply, and while on the final day Asif Din and Kallicharran seemingly set the home side on course for victory, the bowling of Hemmings and later Stephenson proved conclusive.

Close of play: First day, Warwickshire 17-1 (A. J. Moles 8*, T. A. Munton 5*); Second day, Nottinghamshire 126-2 (R. T. Robinson 38*, P. Johnson 43*).

Nottinghamshire

B. C. Broad b Smith	119	– c Reeve b Benjamin	30
D. J. R. Martindale c Humpage b Munton	73	– lbw b Munton	10
R. T. Robinson c Smith b Small	41	– lbw b Small	47
P. Johnson c sub b Munton	2	– c Benjamin b Munton	73
D. W. Randall c Humpage b Small	5	– lbw b Benjamin	17
M. Saxelby not out	32	– c Asif Din b Smith	13
F. D. Stephenson c Munton b Donald	15	– c Moles b Smith	12
B. N. French not out	1	– not out	25
E. E. Hemmings (did not bat)		– not out	16
L-b 14, n-b 1	15	L-b 5, w 2, n-b 2	9

1/176 2/247 3/247 4/254 (6 wkts dec.) 303   1/30 2/54 3/135 (7 wkts dec.) 252
5/255 6/295   4/176 5/195
                                                    6/197 7/217

K. E. Cooper and R. A. Pick did not bat.

Bonus points – Nottinghamshire 4, Warwickshire 2.

Bowling: *First Innings*—Donald 16–5–38–1; Small 19–3–34–2; Munton 25–5–85–2; Smith 3.5–0–82–1; Benjamin 14–2–41–0; Asif Din 2–1–9–0. *Second Innings*—Small 12–1–39–1; Munton 18–3–57–2; Donald 3–0–5–0; Smith 17–1–76–2; Benjamin 18–1–55–2; Asif Din –0–15–0.

Warwickshire

A. J. Moles b Cooper	13	– lbw b Cooper	35
*T. A. Lloyd lbw b Stephenson	4	– (7) run out	10
T. A. Munton lbw b Cooper	13	– (11) b Stephenson	0
Asif Din c Randall b Hemmings	41	– (2) lbw b Hemmings	61
A. I. Kallicharran st French b Hemmings	20	– (3) c Saxelby b Hemmings	58
†G. W. Humpage c Randall b Pick	74	– (4) run out	62
D. A. Reeve c French b Stephenson	34	– (5) c Saxelby b Hemmings	26
N. M. K. Smith c French b Pick	6	– (6) c Robinson b Stephenson	14
G. C. Small c Randall b Cooper	0	– (8) c French b Pick	0
A. A. Donald not out	24	– (9) not out	9
J. E. Benjamin b Stephenson	14	– (10) b Stephenson	1
B 1, l-b 7, n-b 1	9	B 4, l-b 18	22

1/8 2/28 3/45 4/79 5/134   252   1/88 2/120 3/185 4/253 5/259   298
6/178 7/190 8/198 9/234   6/284 7/285 8/287 9/298

Bonus points – Warwickshire 3, Nottinghamshire 4.

Bowling: *First Innings*—Pick 20–4–46–2; Stephenson 19.3–1–69–3; Hemmings 15–3–46–2
Cooper 23–6–72–3; Saxelby 4–1–11–0. *Second Innings*—Pick 11–0–56–1; Cooper 16–3–43–1
Stephenson 14.4–2–69–3; Hemmings 23–0–108–3.

Umpires: J. H. Hampshire and A. A. Jones.

WARWICKSHIRE v WORCESTERSHIRE

At Birmingham, May 26, 28, 29. Drawn. Warwickshire 6 pts, Worcestershire 5 pts. Toss Warwickshire. Rain on the final afternoon prevented any tangible reward coming from the three earlier declarations. Lloyd, with understandable caution on such a good pitch, had asked Worcestershire to score 244 in a minimum of 46 overs and then challenged them to chase the target by employing his spin bowlers. In Warwickshire's first innings, a second-wicket stand of 151 in 174 minutes between Moles and Asif Din (134 balls) was the major contribution to a batting effort that struggled at times against Botham's swing bowling and the negative tactic of Illingworth, bowling over the wicket into the rough to the right-handers. This line of attack was later emulated by Booth, earning the disapprobation of Botham, one of four wickets for Munton in a six-over spell which left Worcestershire much in need of the entertaining ninth-wicket partnership of 89 in 29 overs between Radford and Dilley. On the last day, a Warwickshire extended their lead of 42 on first innings, Moles hit his second half-century of the game and Booth underlined his increasing value to the side with a career-best 43 as night watchman.

Close of play: First day, Worcestershire 11-0 (T. S. Curtis 4*, M. J. Weston 6*); Second day Warwickshire 20-1 (A. J. Moles 11*, P. A. Booth 0*).

Warwickshire

A. J. Moles c Rhodes b Illingworth	76	– c Rhodes b Illingworth	56
*T. A. Lloyd c Illingworth b Dilley	9	– lbw b Newport	9
Asif Din c D'Oliveira b Botham	70	– (7) c Radford b Illingworth	1
†G. W. Humpage c Curtis b Illingworth	9	– c Weston b Illingworth	12
D. A. Reeve lbw b Botham	21	– not out	49
D. P. Ostler c Rhodes b Lampitt	26	– b Lampitt	14
N. M. K. Smith c Dilley b Lampitt	33	– (8) c D'Oliveira b Lampitt	0
P. A. Booth lbw b Lampitt	3	– (3) c Rhodes b Radford	43
A. A. Donald not out	10	– b Lampitt	0
J. E. Benjamin not out	12	– not out	12
B 2, l-b 16, w 4, n-b 4	26	L-b 4, n-b 1	5

1/18 2/169 3/169 4/193 5/203   (8 wkts dec.) 295   1/16 2/109 3/118   (8 wkts dec.) 201
6/251 7/257 8/281   4/129 5/168 6/169
                                                       7/169 8/169

T. A. Munton did not bat.

Bonus points – Warwickshire 3, Worcestershire 3 (Score at 100 overs: 291-8).

Bowling: *First Innings*—Dilley 10–2–34–1; Radford 12–2–49–0; Newport 11–2–38–0; Botham 22–6–46–2; Lampitt 14–3–44–3; Illingworth 33–9–66–2. *Second Innings*—Dilley 11–3–33–0; Radford 8–1–32–1; Newport 7–1–26–1; Lampitt 10.1–1–39–3; Illingworth 22–4–67–3.

Worcestershire

T. S. Curtis lbw b Benjamin	34	– not out	47
M. J. Weston c Humpage b Donald	6	– c Reeve b Booth	11
*P. A. Neale c Humpage b Donald	29	– not out	39
I. T. Botham b Munton	48		
D. B. D'Oliveira c Humpage b Munton	29		
S. R. Lampitt c Humpage b Munton	0		
P. J. Newport lbw b Munton	9		
†S. J. Rhodes c Reeve b Booth	2		
N. V. Radford not out	43		
G. R. Dilley not out	32		
B 2, l-b 12, w 4, n-b 3	21	L-b 8, n-b 1	9

1/12 2/60 3/87 4/151 5/152   (8 wkts dec.) 253   1/29   (1 wkt) 106
6/153 7/162 8/164

R. K. Illingworth did not bat.

Bonus points – Worcestershire 2, Warwickshire 3 (Score at 100 overs: 213-8).

Bowling: *First Innings*—Donald 21–4–54–2; Benjamin 19–5–52–1; Munton 21.5–6–45–4; Booth 38–18–67–1; Smith 1–1–0–0; Reeve 10–4–21–0. *Second Innings*—Donald 4–2–10–0; Benjamin 3–1–6–0; Munton 2.3–0–12–0; Booth 11–2–36–1; Smith 8–2–34–0.

Umpires: B. Leadbeater and N. T. Plews.

At Birmingham, May 30, 31, June 1. WARWICKSHIRE drew with NEW ZEALANDERS (See New Zealand tour section).

WARWICKSHIRE v NORTHAMPTONSHIRE

At Birmingham, June 2, 4, 5. Drawn. Warwickshire 5 pts, Northamptonshire 8 pts. Toss: Northamptonshire. Rain, which had already cost 30 overs on the opening day, cut 285 minutes from the final day's play, but Northamptonshire made a brave bid for victory in the hour and a half possible that evening. They were thwarted by Pierson and Munton, the last-wicket pair, who came together in the fifteenth of the final twenty overs, with Warwickshire just 16 runs ahead, and made sure that there would be no improbable win to avenge the innings defeat handed out by Warwickshire at Northampton in May. Warwickshire, put in on another slow, seaming pitch, had been on the defensive since Capel, on the first day, had removed Lloyd, Asif Din and Kallicharran at a cost of 5 runs in 31 balls to set himself up for a five-wicket haul. On the second day Capel batted brilliantly for 89 off 85 deliveries, hitting three sixes and twelve fours. For Warwickshire, there was some consolation in the return after injury of Paul Smith, who brought stability to the middle of the order.

Close of play: First day, Northamptonshire 57-2 (R. J. Bailey 14*); Second day, Warwickshire 88-5 (G. W. Humpage 25*, P. A. Smith 25*).

Warwickshire

A. J. Moles lbw b Ambrose	40	– lbw b Ambrose	13
*T. A. Lloyd lbw b Capel	65	– b Thomas	10
Asif Din b Capel	5	– c Fordham b Thomas	9
A. I. Kallicharran b Capel	2	– lbw b Thomas	0
†G. W. Humpage c Fordham b Ambrose	13	– b Ambrose	42
D. A. Reeve c Fordham b Capel	5	– lbw b Ambrose	0
P. A. Smith b Ambrose	23	– run out	41
G. C. Small lbw b Capel	24	– c and b Thomas	0
A. A. Donald c Capel b Ambrose	0	– (10) run out	1
A. R. K. Pierson not out	5	– (9) not out	9
T. A. Munton b Ambrose	0	– not out	10
B 11, l-b 8, w 1	20	L-b 7	7

1/104 2/113 3/123 4/140 5/141	202	1/20 2/30 3/32 4/42 (9 wkts) 142
6/153 7/171 8/171 9/201		5/42 6/115 7/118
		8/122 9/132

Bonus points – Warwickshire 2, Northamptonshire 4.

Bowling: *First Innings*—Ambrose 21–8–53–5; Thomas 6–0–29–0; Capel 21–5–74–5; Penberthy 7–2–27–0. *Second Innings*—Ambrose 25–6–55–3; Thomas 23–6–53–4; Capel 7–3–21–0; N. G. B. Cook 4–4–0–0; Penberthy 2–0–6–0.

Northamptonshire

A. Fordham c Lloyd b Munton	33	C. E. L. Ambrose not out	23
N. A. Felton c Kallicharran b Small	8	†D. Ripley not out	2
R. J. Bailey c Humpage b Munton	40		
*A. J. Lamb run out	48	B 1, l-b 13, w 1	15
D. J. Capel lbw b Smith	89		
G. Cook b Munton	34	1/14 2/57 3/134 (8 wkts dec.) 318
A. L. Penberthy c Humpage b Donald	17	4/134 5/263 6/267
J. G. Thomas c Asif Din b Pierson	9	7/289 8/304

N. G. B. Cook did not bat.

Bonus points – Northamptonshire 4, Warwickshire 3.

Bowling: Donald 23–5–56–1; Small 17–2–44–1; Munton 33–8–92–3; Smith 15–4–63–1; Pierson 8–1–49–1.

Umpires: D. J. Constant and B. Dudleston.

At Lord's, June 6, 7, 8. WARWICKSHIRE drew with MIDDLESEX.

WARWICKSHIRE v ESSEX

At Birmingham, June 9, 11, 12. Warwickshire won by five wickets. Warwickshire 18 pts, Essex 3 pts. Toss: Essex. With six hours lost to rain, mostly on the first day, only agreement between the captains made a result possible. Warwickshire were given a target of 291 in a minimum of 85 overs, which could have become 89 had they not scored the runs with 8.3 overs to spare. A solid 97 by Moles anchored the run-chase and enabled the free-scoring Asif Din (56 balls) and Humpage (46 balls) to make the win possible. The feature of the Essex innings was a splendid 103 off 164 balls by Waugh, his fourth Championship hundred in seven innings and containing a six and nine fours. Stephenson, who contributed just 29 runs to their third-wicket partnership of 134, was altogether more circumspect over his 85, taking 274 balls against a steady attack on a good pitch, while Shahid's unbeaten 75 was a career best.

Close of play: First day, Essex 57-1 (J. P. Stephenson 26*, P. J. Prichard 27*); Second day, Essex 331-5 dec.

Essex

B. R. Hardie lbw b Benjamin 2	†M. A. Garnham not out 26
J. P. Stephenson c Humpage b Benjamin 85	
P. J. Prichard c and b Munton 29	B 6, w 1, n-b 3 10
M. E. Waugh c Humpage b Munton ..103	
A. W. Lilley lbw b Donald 1	1/11 2/60 3/194 (5 wkts dec.) 331
N. Shahid not out 75	4/197 5/244

*D. R. Pringle, N. A. Foster, J. H. Childs and S. J. W. Andrew did not bat.

Bonus points – Essex 3, Warwickshire 2 (Score at 100 overs: 268-5).

Bowling: Donald 25–7–53–1; Benjamin 22–2–79–2; Munton 35–8–72–2; Pierson 26.1–2–86–0; N. M. K. Smith 12–2–35–0.

Essex forfeited their second innings.

Warwickshire

A. J. Moles not out 14	– lbw b Pringle 97
J. D. Ratcliffe not out 27	– run out 22
Asif Din (did not bat)	– run out 42
†G. W. Humpage (did not bat)	– run out 43
*D. A. Reeve (did not bat)	– not out 33
P. A. Smith (did not bat)	– lbw b Pringle 2
N. M. K. Smith (did not bat)	– not out 30
	B 1, l-b 12, w 1, n-b 11 .. 25

(no wkt dec.) 41   1/56 2/148 3/212   (5 wkts) 294
4/245 5/253

A. R. K. Pierson, A. A. Donald, J. E. Benjamin and T. A. Munton did not bat.

Bowling: *First Innings*—Waugh 6–2–7–0; Stephenson 6–2–25–0; Lilley 1–0–7–0; Prichard 0.4–0–2–0. *Second Innings*—Foster 14–2–68–0; Pringle 23–6–72–2; Childs 25.3–7–66–0; Stephenson 3–1–7–0; Andrew 12–1–44–0; Waugh 3–0–24–0.

Umpires: B. Dudleston and R. A. White.

At Derby, June 16, 18, 19. WARWICKSHIRE beat DERBYSHIRE by two wickets.

At Sheffield, June 20, 21, 22. WARWICKSHIRE lost to YORKSHIRE by two wickets.

WARWICKSHIRE v KENT

At Birmingham, June 23, 25, 26. Drawn. Warwickshire 6 pts, Kent 6 pts. Toss: Warwickshire. A declaration from each side was not enough to make up for the three hours lost to rain on the first two days, and a slow pitch also helped defeat their efforts to obtain a positive result. The promising Ostler again impressed as he compiled a career-best 71, the top score in a match which contained five half-centuries. Kent, who collected four bowling bonus points for the first time in 1990, were eventually able to score 233 in just under two and a half hours, but three wickets by Donald in the fourth over of the final twenty ended their interest.
    Close of play: First day, Warwickshire 208-6 (D. P. Ostler 49*, A. R. K. Pierson 0*); Second day, Kent 177-8 (C. S. Cowdrey 38*, A. P. Igglesden 0*).

Warwickshire

A. J. Moles b Merrick	12	– run out	11
J. D. Ratcliffe c Marsh b Ellison	28	– b Davis	43
Asif Din c and b Igglesden	19	– c Davis b Fleming	14
R. G. Twose c C. S. Cowdrey b Ellison	51	– c G. R. Cowdrey b Davis	12
*D. A. Reeve c Marsh b Igglesden	30	– not out	59
D. P. Ostler c and b Davis	71	– b Taylor	8
†K. J. Piper c Wells b C. S. Cowdrey	9	– c Wells b Davis	10
A. R. K. Pierson c Marsh b Igglesden	2	– lbw b Marsh	6
A. A. Donald c Wells b Davis	0	– c Igglesden b Marsh	1
J. E. Benjamin not out	3	– not out	15
T. A. Munton c C. S. Cowdrey b Igglesden	4		
B 4, l-b 7, w 1, n-b 1	13	B 4, l-b 6, w 1	11

1/14 2/51 3/68 4/127 5/166   242   1/17 2/51 3/70   (8 wkts dec.) 190
6/202 7/223 8/224 9/237   4/84 5/105 6/118
                                             7/155 8/173

Bonus points – Warwickshire 2, Kent 4.

Bowling: *First Innings*—Merrick 9-2-19-1; Igglesden 27.3-4-79-4; Fleming 13-7-22-0; Ellison 18-7-36-2; Davis 26-8-70-2; C. S. Cowdrey 2-1-5-1. *Second Innings*—Igglesden 6-0-23-0; Ellison 7-3-23-0; Davis 26-5-61-3; Fleming 7-1-21-1; Taylor 11-4-19-1; G. R. Cowdrey 2-0-13-0; Marsh 5-0-20-2.

Kent

S. G. Hinks lbw b Donald	66	– lbw b Benjamin	15
V. J. Wells c Twose b Benjamin	5	– lbw b Pierson	25
N. R. Taylor lbw b Pierson	25	– b Donald	28
G. R. Cowdrey c Reeve b Munton	20	– not out	22
*C. S. Cowdrey not out	56	– lbw b Donald	0
M. V. Fleming lbw b Reeve	3	– b Donald	0
†S. A. Marsh c Reeve b Benjamin	5		
R. M. Ellison lbw b Benjamin	6	– (7) not out	8
R. P. Davis c Twose b Pierson	5		
A. P. Igglesden c Munton b Asif Din	5		
T. A. Merrick not out	0		
L-b 2, w 2	4	L-b 1, n-b 3	4

1/10 2/47 3/90 4/133 5/136   (9 wkts dec.) 200   1/19 2/68 3/76   (5 wkts) 102
6/154 7/160 8/177 9/192   4/76 5/76

Bonus points – Kent 2, Warwickshire 4.

Bowling: *First Innings*—Donald 14-5-19-1; Benjamin 16-4-31-3; Munton 13-4-46-1; Pierson 21-5-68-2; Reeve 7-3-16-1; Asif Din 1.5-0-18-1. *Second Innings*—Donald 10.5-2-28-3; Benjamin 8-1-34-1; Pierson 14-5-19-1; Asif Din 3-0-14-0; Munton 7-4-6-0.

Umpires: J. D. Bond and K. E. Palmer.

At Taunton, July 4, 5, 6. WARWICKSHIRE drew with SOMERSET.

At The Oval, July 7, 9, 10. WARWICKSHIRE lost to SURREY by 168 runs.

WARWICKSHIRE v LANCASHIRE

At Coventry, July 18, 19, 20. Drawn. Warwickshire 7 pts, Lancashire 7 pts. Toss: Warwickshire. The first first-class match at the Binley Road ground since 1919 was dominated by a staggering performance from the Lancashire left-hander, Fairbrother, who rescued his side from a disastrous position at 116 for six with a brilliant, unbeaten double-century in 299 minutes. He faced 223 balls and hit two sixes and 35 fours with strokeplay that annihilated an otherwise successful Warwickshire attack and made a mockery of his disappointing Test-match batting for England. A pitch with welcome pace had also enabled the home batsmen to strike form, and Reeve and Smith both played well while adding 130 in even time for the sixth wicket on the opening day. In Warwickshire's second innings, not even the impressive Wasim Akram troubled Moles as he scored 100 not out off 276 balls, and Moody was superb, hitting eighteen fours in his 96 off 149 balls. He and Moles put on 158 for the third wicket as Warwickshire looked to set Lancashire a target. It was a stiff one, 299 off only 39 overs, but while Fairbrother was cracking 50 he briefly raised their hopes. Once he was out, a draw was inevitable.

Close of play: First day, Lancashire 12-1 (G. D. Mendis 5*, J. D. Fitton 4*); Second day, Warwickshire 51-2 (A. J. Moles 24*, T. M. Moody 6*).

Warwickshire

A. J. Moles b Wasim Akram	31	– not out	100
*T. A. Lloyd lbw b Allott	1	– b Wasim Akram	8
Asif Din c Mendis b Watkinson	45	– lbw b Wasim Akram	1
T. M. Moody c Hegg b Wasim Akram	30	– c Hegg b Hughes	96
D. P. Ostler lbw b Wasim Akram	3	– c Mendis b Hughes	18
D. A. Reeve run out	78		
P. A. Smith c Hughes b Fitton	82	– (6) not out	7
†K. J. Piper not out	40		
J. E. Benjamin not out	28		
B 13, l-b 18, w 2, n-b 3	36	B 5, l-b 7, n-b 14	26

1/2 2/71 3/105 4/114 5/117 (7 wkts dec.) 374   1/29 2/31 3/189 (4 wkts dec.) 256
6/247 7/332   4/235

A. R. K. Pierson and T. A. Munton did not bat.

Bonus points – Warwickshire 4, Lancashire 3 (Score at 100 overs: 339-7).

Bowling: *First Innings*—Wasim Akram 26-6-76-3; Allott 14-1-45-1; Austin 16-5-48-0; Watkinson 15-3-53-1; Hughes 17-0-73-0; Fitton 15-3-48-1. *Second Innings*—Allott 10-1-31-0; Watkinson 17-3-38-0; Wasim Akram 18-7-51-2; Austin 10-3-19-0; Fitton 15-2-44-0; Hughes 15.4-2-54-2; Jesty 1-0-7-0.

Lancashire

G. D. Mendis c Piper b Munton	5	– (6) not out	20
G. Fowler c Piper b Munton	0	– (1) c sub b Pierson	30
J. D. Fitton c Ostler b Benjamin	10		
T. E. Jesty c Ostler b Benjamin	17	– (5) lbw b Asif Din	6
N. H. Fairbrother not out	203	– (4) b Pierson	50
M. Watkinson lbw b Smith	14	– (2) lbw b Benjamin	5
Wasim Akram c Ostler b Smith	7	– (3) c sub b Pierson	32
†W. K. Hegg c Pierson b Benjamin	9	– (7) not out	20
I. D. Austin lbw b Munton	9		
*D. P. Hughes not out	29		
B 12, l-b 5, w 3, n-b 9	29	B 1, l-b 7, n-b 2	10

1/7 2/12 3/26 4/49 5/107 (8 wkts dec.) 332   1/25 2/44 3/86 (5 wkts) 173
6/116 7/181 8/203   4/107 5/131

P. J. W. Allott did not bat.

Bonus points – Lancashire 4, Warwickshire 3.

Bowling: *First Innings*—Munton 22-7-75-3; Benjamin 21-4-97-3; Pierson 24-8-70-0; Smith 10-2-37-2; Moody 5-0-25-0; Asif Din 4.3-2-11-0. *Second Innings*—Munton 3-0-30-0; Benjamin 7-0-42-1; Pierson 14-1-56-3; Asif Din 10-3-37-1.

Umpires: R. Palmer and R. A. White.

At Swansea, July 25, 26, 27. **WARWICKSHIRE** lost to **GLAMORGAN** by five wickets.

WARWICKSHIRE v HAMPSHIRE

At Birmingham, July 28, 30, 31. Warwickshire won by six wickets. Warwickshire 21 pts, Hampshire 3 pts. Toss: Hampshire. Only nineteen wickets fell on a good batting pitch which provided some turn, albeit slowly, but Warwickshire revived their title challenge with a successful run-chase. Set to score 271 in a minimum of 56 overs, and with Nicholas admirably keeping the game open by his generous use of spin, they won in the final over thanks to a well-paced, unbeaten 101 off 100 balls by Moody. On the opening day, Terry and Maru had put Hampshire on the road to recovery with 118 for the sixth wicket after Reeve, on a humid morning, had reduced them to 81 for four at lunch. Terry marked his return to form, following illness, with 119 not out in 281 minutes. Contrasting innings from Ratcliffe (228 minutes) and Smith (101 balls) were the basis of Warwickshire's first innings, the pair adding 143 in 31 overs before Lloyd declared 54 in arrears to make up for time lost to rain in the morning. Nicholas hit 78 from 73 balls as Hampshire set up the third declaration of the match.

Close of play: First day, Hampshire 287-6 (V. P. Terry 113*, R. J. Parks 29*); Second day, Hampshire 40-0 (T. C. Middleton 21*, C. L. Smith 11*).

Hampshire

T. C. Middleton c Asif Din b Reeve	10	– c Reeve b Asif Din	64
C. L. Smith c Ratcliffe b Reeve	18	– b Smith	29
R. J. Scott lbw b Reeve	4	– c Reeve b Pierson	0
*M. C. J. Nicholas b Munton	16	– not out	78
M. D. Marshall c Reeve b Pierson	26	– c Moody b Pierson	10
V. P. Terry not out	119	– not out	19
R. J. Maru run out	53		
†R. J. Parks c Asif Din b Pierson	33		
S. D. Udal b Pierson	9		
B 4, l-b 7, n-b 8	19	B 11, l-b 1, n-b 4	16

1/28 2/34 3/37 4/80 5/90   (8 wkts dec.) 307   1/82 2/92 3/123   (4 wkts dec.) 216
6/208 7/291 8/307   4/150

C. A. Connor and P. J. Bakker did not bat.

Bonus points – Hampshire 2, Warwickshire 2 (Score at 100 overs: 236-6).

Bowling: *First Innings*—Benjamin 12-3-37-0; Munton 27-9-50-1; Reeve 29-11-58-3; Smith 7-3-11-0; Pierson 30.4-2-73-3; Asif Din 14-0-67-0. *Second Innings*—Munton 8-1-24-0; Benjamin 3-0-7-0; Pierson 25-5-66-2; Asif Din 11-2-62-1; Smith 6-1-16-1; Moody 3-0-23-0; Moles 1-0-6-0.

Warwickshire

A. J. Moles b Connor	24	– b Udal	36
J. D. Ratcliffe not out	81	– st Parks b Maru	46
*T. A. Lloyd c Terry b Connor	1	– b Udal	61
T. M. Moody c Middleton b Maru	48	– not out	101
P. A. Smith not out	85	– c Smith b Maru	5
D. A. Reeve (did not bat)		– not out	12
B 4, l-b 8, n-b 2	14	L-b 8, n-b 5	13

1/32 2/38 3/110   (3 wkts dec.) 253   1/79 2/103 3/234 4/251   (4 wkts) 274

Asif Din, †K. J. Piper, A. R. K. Pierson, J. E. Benjamin and T. A. Munton did not bat.

Bonus points – Warwickshire 3, Hampshire 1.

Bowling: *First Innings*—Bakker 14-6-44-0; Marshall 8-3-17-0; Maru 22-2-67-1; Connor 10-2-23-2; Udal 13-0-66-0; Nicholas 2.4-0-24-0. *Second Innings*—Bakker 4-1-17-0; Marshall 8-1-27-0; Maru 24-1-90-2; Connor 9-0-39-0; Udal 17.3-0-93-2.

Umpires: D. R. Shepherd and R. A. White.

At Eastbourne, August 4, 6, 7. WARWICKSHIRE beat SUSSEX by six wickets.

At Bristol, August 8, 9, 10. WARWICKSHIRE lost to GLOUCESTERSHIRE by 66 runs.

WARWICKSHIRE v LEICESTERSHIRE

At Birmingham, August 18, 20, 21. Leicestershire won by six wickets. Leicestershire 22 pts, Warwickshire 5 pts. Toss: Leicestershire. Warwickshire never recovered from being put in on a slow, seaming pitch and being bowled out for 154. Agnew made the early inroads, and just when wicket-keeper Piper was leading Warwickshire to a relative recovery from 81 for seven, Parsons returned to finish with four well-earned wickets. The loss of 58 overs on Monday, to wet ground conditions in the morning and poor light in the evening, kept the game in Leicestershire's grasp, even though they lost their last seven wickets for 95. On the final day Agnew and Lewis, the latter ending Warwickshire's innings with three wickets in fourteen balls, ensured that Leicestershire needed only 162 to win at less than 4 an over, which they achieved with sixteen balls to spare. Victory would have come sooner but for Moody's seventh hundred in eight first-class matches; his fourth in successive games. His 117, made out of 161 runs scored in three partnerships, came from 151 deliveries and included a six and eighteen fours. In the first innings, when 7, he had set a Warwickshire record by reaching 1,000 runs for the season in twelve innings, five fewer than R. B. Kanhai in 1970.

Close of play: First day, Leicestershire 147-3 (P. Willey 38*, L. Potter 4*); Second day, Warwickshire 38-1 (A. J. Moles 19*, T. A. Lloyd 0*).

Warwickshire

A. J. Moles c Nixon b Agnew	5	– c Willey b Lewis	30
J. D. Ratcliffe c Lewis b Agnew	15	– lbw b Parsons	14
*T. A. Lloyd c Lewis b Agnew	0	– lbw b Agnew	4
T. M. Moody c Willey b Parsons	26	– c Willey b Agnew	117
P. A. Smith b Millns	22	– c Lewis b Agnew	2
D. A. Reeve c Nixon b Millns	1	– c Boon b Agnew	31
Asif Din lbw b Parsons	0	– c Briers b Agnew	1
†K. J. Piper c Agnew b Parsons	36	– b Lewis	11
G. C. Small b Lewis	16	– not out	10
P. A. Booth c sub b Parsons	14	– c Potter b Lewis	10
T. A. Munton not out	0	– b Lewis	0
L-b 12, w 2, n-b 5	19	B 8, l-b 4, n-b 7	19
	154		**249**

1/20 2/20 3/27 4/72 5/73   154   1/38 2/47 3/60 4/71 5/208   249
6/76 7/81 8/122 9/154   6/217 7/222 8/232 9/249

Bonus points – Warwickshire 1, Leicestershire 4.

Bowling: *First Innings*—Agnew 18-5-51-3; Lewis 17-4-48-1; Parsons 10-2-21-4; Millns 10-1-22-2. *Second Innings*—Agnew 21-4-75-5; Lewis 24.5-6-70-4; Parsons 16-3-53-1; Millns 11-2-39-0.

Leicestershire

T. J. Boon c Moles b Reeve	40	– c Lloyd b Munton	5
*N. E. Briers lbw b Reeve	33	– c sub b Reeve	55
J. J. Whitaker b Moody	16	– c Small b Munton	13
P. Willey c Piper b Munton	46	– not out	51
L. Potter c Piper b Small	13	– lbw b Reeve	3
C. C. Lewis c Munton b Smith	38	– not out	25
J. D. R. Benson c Moles b Munton	1		
†P. A. Nixon not out	25		
G. J. Parsons b Reeve	1		
J. P. Agnew c Moody b Reeve	0		
D. J. Millns run out	4		
B 5, l-b 19, w 1	25	L-b 9, w 1	10
	242	(4 wkts)	**162**

1/78 2/101 3/109 4/156 5/170   242   1/17 2/43 3/107 4/121   (4 wkts) 162
6/171 7/224 8/229 9/231

Bonus points – Leicestershire 2, Warwickshire 4.

Bowling: *First Innings*—Small 20–8–34–1; Munton 22–5–74–2; Booth 5–1–7–0; Smith 10–1–25–1; Moody 12–2–36–1; Reeve 20–7–42–4. *Second Innings*—Small 9–2–36–0; Munton 11–2–21–2; Reeve 14–1–51–2; Smith 2–0–11–0; Booth 5.2–0–34–0.

Umpires: J. W. Holder and K. E. Palmer.

At Worcester, August 23, 24, 25, 27. WARWICKSHIRE lost to WORCESTERSHIRE by 323 runs.

At Birmingham, August 29, 30, 31. WARWICKSHIRE lost to SRI LANKANS by eight wickets (See Sri Lankan tour section).

WARWICKSHIRE v SOMERSET

At Birmingham, September 7, 8, 9, 10. Drawn. Warwickshire 6 pts, Somerset 6 pts. Toss: Warwickshire. Two top-order collapses illustrated perfectly why Warwickshire's challenge for Championship honours was not a realistic one. The middle-order batsmen had to work hard to achieve recoveries, rather than use their talents to build on a solid platform. On the first day, Piper underlined his potential by reaching 50 for the first time and going on to a maiden first-class hundred by the close, having hit fifteen boundaries, and half-centuries from Reeve and Booth helped the young wicket-keeper add 112 for the sixth and eighth wickets. Somerset, batting solidly, established a lead of 37, Smith finishing the innings with a career-best return of five for 48. But with Warwickshire batting for 118 overs in their second innings, the visitors were left with a minimum of 50 overs in which to score 254 to win. When three wickets fell, their thoughts turned to saving the match. Warwickshire's second recovery had been underpinned by Smith, who with 75 completed a good all-round match, and Reeve, who remained unbeaten for four and a half hours.

Close of play: First day, Warwickshire 321-7 (K. J. Piper 100*, P. A. Booth 59*); Second day, Somerset 264-5 (N. D. Burns 42*, G. D. Rose 33*); Third day, Warwickshire 152-4 (P. A. Smith 60*, D. A. Reeve 22*).

Warwickshire

A. J. Moles c Rose b Jones	2	– c Burns b Jones	44
J. D. Ratcliffe lbw b Jones	6	– lbw b Hayhurst	20
Asif Din lbw b Hayhurst	55	– c Tavaré b Hayhurst	0
D. P. Ostler lbw b Hayhurst	11	– c Hayhurst b Lefebvre	1
P. A. Smith c Harden b Hayhurst	4	– lbw b Jones	75
*D. A. Reeve run out	58	– not out	81
†K. J. Piper b Rose	111	– c Townsend b Jones	0
G. C. Small lbw b Lefebvre	7	– b Lefebvre	10
P. A. Booth c Swallow b Rose	60	– c Rose b Jones	15
A. A. Donald b Rose	7	– b Lefebvre	1
T. A. Munton not out	0	– not out	29
B 4, l-b 9, w 4, n-b 2	19	L-b 6, w 4, n-b 4	14

1/10 2/17 3/56 4/60 5/91   340   1/43 2/45 3/52   (9 wkts dec.) 290
6/203 7/215 8/327 9/335   4/75 5/178 6/178
                                 7/192 8/210 9/215

Bonus points – Warwickshire 4, Somerset 3 (Score at 100 overs: 318-7).

Bowling: *First Innings*—Jones 27–2–110–2; Rose 19.2–3–49–3; Hayhurst 21–1–82–3; Lefebvre 21–6–44–1; Swallow 12–4–26–0; Trump 9–3–16–0. *Second Innings*—Jones 33–8–72–4; Rose 12–2–54–0; Hayhurst 26–8–68–2; Lefebvre 26–7–48–3; Swallow 12–4–23–0; Trump 9–2–19–0.

Somerset

S. J. Cook c Moles b Smith	52	– c Moles b Munton	27
G. T. J. Townsend c Piper b Munton	15	– c Piper b Small	6
A. N. Hayhurst c Ostler b Munton	57	– not out	56
*C. J. Tavaré lbw b Donald	10	– c Reeve b Munton	2
R. J. Harden lbw b Munton	32		
†N. D. Burns b Smith	88	– (5) b Booth	28
G. D. Rose c Ratcliffe b Munton	41	– (6) not out	14
R. P. Lefebvre b Smith	27		
I. G. Swallow not out	14		
H. R. J. Trump b Smith	2		
A. N. Jones c Booth b Smith	8		
B 7, l-b 19, w 3, n-b 2	31	B 4, l-b 1	5

1/57 2/84 3/102 4/176 5/185   377   1/12 2/43 3/57 4/114   (4 wkts) 138
6/278 7/340 8/351 9/359

Bonus points – Somerset 3, Warwickshire 2 (Score at 100 overs: 271-5).

Bowling: *First Innings*—Donald 27–5–91–1; Small 24–5–58–0; Munton 33–11–66–4; Smith 16.1–5–48–5; Reeve 12–2–26–0; Booth 23–4–57–0; Asif Din 2–1–5–0. *Second Innings*—Donald 10–2–36–0; Small 6–0–18–1; Munton 9–5–7–2; Booth 8–0–37–1; Asif Din 4–0–18–0; Smith 3.5–0–17–0.

Umpires: J. H. Hampshire and D. O. Oslear.

WARWICKSHIRE v GLAMORGAN

At Birmingham, September 12, 13, 14, 15. Warwickshire won by 170 runs. Warwickshire 24 pts, Glamorgan 5 pts. Toss: Glamorgan. Maximum points kept alive Warwickshire's hopes of finishing in the first three in the Championship. There were splendid batting performances from Smith, Lloyd and Reeve in the first innings, while Piper's 65, and his seventh-wicket partnership with Reeve, steadied the home side's second innings when good bowling by Watkin and Frost had threatened to let Glamorgan into the game. Smith's first-innings 117, in 211 minutes, underlined how much his all-round talents had been missed earlier in the season, owing to a knee injury. He hit a six and eighteen fours and shared a fourth-wicket stand of 187 in 53 overs with his captain. Glamorgan's first innings began well, with Butcher and Morris putting up a hundred for the tenth time in 1990, but then fell away surprisingly. Morris passed Javed Miandad's Glamorgan record of 2,083 runs in a season, while Butcher reached 2,000 runs for the first time. But once Smith dismissed them both, only Cottey resisted the keen home attack. Lloyd's decision not to enforce the follow-on seemed curious at the time, but his bowlers proved him right by dismissing Glamorgan a second time with half a day to spare. Donald, ripping through the lower order, showed that, in form and fully fit, he was still one of the most penetrative fast bowlers in the game, which was why the Warwickshire committee had decided to retain him and release Moody as their overseas player.

Close of play: First day, Warwickshire 351-9 (D. A. Reeve 37*, T. A. Munton 1*); Second day, Warwickshire 13-2 (P. A. Booth 5*, Asif Din 0*); Third day, Glamorgan 67-3 (M. P. Maynard 36*, P. A. Cottey 7*).

Warwickshire

A. J. Moles c Metson b Frost	0	– c Dale b Croft	8
J. D. Ratcliffe b Anthony	41	– lbw b Frost	0
Asif Din lbw b Watkin	40	– (4) b Frost	34
*T. A. Lloyd c Metson b Frost	78	– (5) lbw b Watkin	39
P. A. Smith c Dale b Watkin	117	– (6) lbw b Watkin	0
D. A. Reeve not out	68	– (7) c Croft b Watkin	45
†K. J. Piper c Metson b Anthony	8	– (8) b Croft	65
G. C. Small c Metson b Watkin	2	– (9) c Maynard b Croft	4
P. A. Booth c Metson b Watkin	0	– (3) c Metson b Watkin	10
A. A. Donald b Watkin	7	– b Anthony	3
T. A. Munton c Metson b Frost	23	– not out	1
L-b 8, w 3, n-b 10	21	B 1, l-b 5	6

1/1 2/78 3/94 4/281 5/296   405   1/1 2/13 3/26 4/91 5/91   215
6/327 7/342 8/342 9/350   6/102 7/191 8/196 9/207

Bonus points – Warwickshire 4, Glamorgan 2 (Score at 100 overs: 327-6).

Bowling: *First Innings*—Anthony 26–9–70–2; Frost 23.2–4–78–3; Watkin 36–9–100–5; Dale 14–1–64–0; Croft 28–3–85–0. *Second Innings*—Frost 17–2–49–2; Anthony 16–2–38–1; Croft 35.1–13–64–3; Watkin 19–4–48–4; Dale 4–1–10–0.

Glamorgan

*A. R. Butcher c Asif Din b Smith	71	– c Ratcliffe b Munton	3
H. Morris c Lloyd b Smith	73	– lbw b Munton	20
S. P. James lbw b Smith	0	– lbw b Munton	0
M. P. Maynard st Piper b Booth	8	– lbw b Munton	79
P. A. Cottey c Lloyd b Munton	52	– c Moles b Booth	22
A. Dale c Piper b Donald	5	– c Piper b Munton	9
R. D. B. Croft lbw b Donald	0	– c Piper b Donald	12
H. A. G. Anthony st Piper b Booth	0	– c Piper b Booth	13
†C. P. Metson c Piper b Munton	2	– lbw b Donald	4
S. L. Watkin b Munton	0	– not out	15
M. Frost not out	6	– c Reeve b Donald	12
B 6, l-b 6, n-b 1	13	B 6, l-b 3, n-b 1	10

1/141 2/146 3/151 4/161 5/168   251   1/13 2/13 3/27 4/101 5/124   199
6/168 7/169 8/214 9/214   6/151 7/154 8/158 9/170

Bonus points – Glamorgan 3, Warwickshire 4.

Bowling: *First Innings*—Small 10–0–44–0; Munton 13.3–1–44–3; Donald 14–4–51–2; Booth 25–11–44–2; Reeve 3–0–13–0; Smith 13–4–43–3. *Second Innings*—Donald 10.4–2–33–3; Munton 18–3–64–5; Small 9–3–14–0; Smith 9–3–31–0; Booth 18–8–48–2.

Umpires: N. T. Plews and P. B. Wight.

At Manchester, September 18, 19, 20, 21. WARWICKSHIRE drew with LANCASHIRE.

COUNTY CAPS AWARDED IN 1990

Derbyshire	S. J. Base, I. R. Bishop.
Essex	M. A. Garnham.
Glamorgan	I. V. A. Richards.
Gloucestershire	M. W. Alleyne.
Hampshire	D. I. Gower, T. C. Middleton.
Kent	R. P. Davis, M. V. Fleming.
Lancashire	I. D. Austin.
Leicestershire	C. C. Lewis.
Middlesex	K. R. Brown, M. R. Ramprakash, M. A. Roseberry, P. C. R. Tufnell.
Northamptonshire	C. E. L. Ambrose, N. A. Felton, A. Fordham, M. A. Robinson.
Nottinghamshire	J. A. Afford, K. P. Evans.
Somerset	A. N. Hayhurst.
Surrey	D. J. Bicknell, C. K. Bullen, M. A. Feltham, Waqar Younis, D. M. Ward.
Sussex	N. J. Lenham.
Warwickshire	T. M. Moody.
Worcestershire	G. J. Lord.

No cap was awarded by Yorkshire.

WORCESTERSHIRE

Patron: The Duke of Westminster
President: G. H. Chesterton
Chairman: C. D. Fearnley
Chairman, Cricket Committee: M. G. Jones
Secretary: The Revd Michael Vockins
   County Ground, New Road, Worcester
   WR2 4QQ (Telephone: 0905-748474)
Captain: P. A. Neale
Coach: B. L. D'Oliveira

Few counties can have suffered quite as much from injuries in one season as Worcestershire did in 1990: not one of their first-team squad avoided some period of inactivity. The catalogue of casualties contained five players needing surgery, while Curtis, Hick, Illingworth and Rhodes were among five others out at some stage with broken fingers or thumbs. By mid-July, when the injury crisis was at its worst, the Britannic Assurance champions of 1988 and 1989 were second from bottom after ten matches. Yet by winning five of their last twelve Championship fixtures they managed to finish with a share of the prizemoney, only three points behind third-placed Hampshire. Most impressive was the fact that in all but one of their nineteen Championship victories in 1989 and 1990, Worcestershire bowled out their opponents in both innings.

There was also the disappointment of their failure, at the third attempt, to win a Benson and Hedges Cup final. Defeat by Lancashire sent them away from Lord's for the sixth time without a trophy and meant that Worcestershire and Glamorgan remained the only counties not to have won a final there. In the other competitions, Northamptonshire beat them by 4 runs in a thrilling finish to their quarter-final of the NatWest Bank Trophy, while a record of only seven wins in the Refuge Assurance League left them in tenth place, after being Sunday champions in 1987 and 1988 and runners-up in 1989.

Worcestershire, however, wasted little time in setting out their stall for 1991 and, barring a similar series of setbacks through injuries, there seemed little to suggest they would not be a side to reckon with. No sooner had Warwickshire announced that they were retaining Allan Donald as their overseas player, in preference to Tom Moody, than Worcestershire had signed up the record-breaking Australian as their overseas player for 1991, when Graeme Hick became eligible for England.

As for Hick, second to Gooch in the national averages with 2,347 runs at 90.26, he hit eight hundreds to increase his career count to 54, and his unbeaten century in the second innings at Abergavenny made him the youngest player, at 24 years and 62 days, to compile 50 first-class hundreds. The previous record had been held by Sir Donald Bradman, who was 26 years and eight days old when he reached the landmark. When Hick had scored 147 of his unbeaten 252 in the first innings of that game, he became the youngest player to complete 10,000 first-class runs for the county, in his 179th innings, and he was the first Worcestershire player to record a hundred and double-hundred in the same match. By its end he had scored 592 runs without being dismissed, a record for cricket in England, and he needed another 118 to beat K. C. Ibrahim's world record of 709 for Bombay in 1947-48. In his next match, however, he was dismissed for 53 at Derby by the former Worcestershire seam bowler, Allan Warner.

Tim Curtis, the Worcestershire supporters' Player of the Year, was second to Hick with a career-best aggregate of 1,731 runs which included 197 not out against Warwickshire, his highest innings. He was the first to reach 1,000 runs in one-day cricket during the summer and finished with a county-best 784 runs in the Sunday League. In addition, he proved a most capable deputy when Phil Neale went into hospital in August for an operation on his left thigh.

The Dick Lygon award for the best team man went to Curtis's opening partner, Gordon Lord. The left-hander, emerging from a three-month spell in the second team, during which his future with the county was in doubt, hit a century against Lancashire and followed it with 190 against Hampshire in the next game. He sealed a new contract, and won his county cap, by scoring 127 and 57 in the final match of the season to complete 1,000 runs for the first time. Damian D'Oliveira also enjoyed his most successful season, finishing with 1,263 runs, including a career-best 155 against Lancashire, and 33 catches in the Championship.

Ian Botham's appearances were restricted first by an early-season knee operation and towards the end by a hamstring strain. His 138 not out against Gloucestershire was a personal best in the Benson and Hedges Cup, while his 113 against Surrey was his first Championship hundred since July 1987. Graham Dilley, who in July underwent the fourth operation in two years on his right knee, made only ten Championship appearances, and did not play in the Sunday League, and Neal Radford was out of action for six weeks after an operation on a torn stomach muscle. Radford returned for the Benson and Hedges final, whereas Martin Weston had delayed surgery on his right knee until after Lord's, having hit an unbeaten 99 in the semi-final victory over holders Nottinghamshire to win his first Gold Award.

Richard Illingworth, Steve Rhodes and Phil Newport were named for the winter's England A team. Illingworth had his best wicket-taking season to date with 75 first-class wickets, as well as hitting his third first-class century, while Rhodes's 61 catches and eight stumpings put him on top of the wicket-keepers' list, and he twice went close to achieving an elusive maiden first-class hundred. Newport had a similar experience, following a career-best 98 against the New Zealanders with 96 against Essex, and he showed a welcome recovery after his misfortunes in 1989 to finish with 63 wickets.

Stuart Lampitt and Steve McEwan, meanwhile, further enhanced their reputations. Only Illingworth and Newport bowled more overs than Lampitt, and McEwan, against Leicestershire, became the first Worcestershire bowler since H. L. Alleyne in 1981 to take a hat-trick in the Championship. David Leatherdale's appearances were reserved in the main for the one-day competitions, while the injury position provided opportunities for all-rounder Chris Tolley, left-arm spinner Richard Stemp, reserve wicket-keeper Stuart Bevins and off-spinner Steve Herzberg to experience first-team cricket. – Chris Moore.

WORCESTERSHIRE 1990

[Bill Smith]

Back row: R. P. Gofton, R. D. Stemp, G. J. Lord, G. R. Haynes, D. A. Leatherdale. *Middle row*: S. R. Bevins, S. M. McEwan, I. T. Botham, G. R. Dilley, B. L. D'Oliveira (*coach*), S. R. Lampitt, P. Bent, W. P. C. Weston, M. S. Scott. *Front row*: P. J. Newport, S. J. Rhodes, N. V. Radford, T. S. Curtis, P. A. Neale (*captain*), D. B. D'Oliveira, G. A. Hick, R. K. Illingworth, M. J. Weston.

WORCESTERSHIRE RESULTS

All first-class matches – Played 24: Won 7, Lost 2, Drawn 15.

County Championship matches – Played 22: Won 7, Lost 1, Drawn 14.

Bonus points – Batting 70, Bowling 58.

*Competition placings – Britannic Assurance County Championship, 4th;
NatWest Bank Trophy, q-f; Benson and Hedges Cup, finalists;
Refuge Assurance League, 10th equal.*

BRITANNIC ASSURANCE CHAMPIONSHIP AVERAGES

BATTING

	Birthplace	M	I	NO	R	HI	Avge
‡G. A. Hick	Salisbury, Rhodesia	19	33	8	2,273	252*	90.92
‡T. S. Curtis	Chislehurst	21	38	8	1,650	197*	55.00
‡G. J. Lord	Birmingham	12	23	2	983	190	46.80
‡P. A. Neale	Scunthorpe	19	29	9	934	122	46.70
‡S. J. Rhodes	Bradford	21	24	10	653	96	46.64
‡G. R. Dilley	Dartford	10	8	4	185	45*	46.25
‡D. B. D'Oliveira ...	Cape Town, SA	21	32	2	1,179	155	39.30
‡I. T. Botham	Heswall	12	17	1	576	113	36.00
‡R. K. Illingworth ...	Bradford	20	19	6	452	117	34.76
‡P. J. Newport	High Wycombe	19	15	5	318	96	31.80
P. Bent	Worcester	6	10	0	315	79	31.50
D. A. Leatherdale ..	Bradford	4	6	0	154	70	25.66
‡S. M. McEwan	Worcester	13	10	3	163	54	23.28
‡N. V. Radford	Luanshya, N. Rhodesia	10	6	1	104	43*	20.80
‡S. R. Lampitt	Wolverhampton	21	22	5	286	45*	16.82
C. M. Tolley	Kidderminster	6	6	1	79	29	15.80
‡M. J. Weston	Worcester	5	8	1	80	38*	11.42

Also batted: S. R. Bevins (*Solihull*) (1 match) 6*; R. D. Stemp (*Erdington*) (2 matches)
3*, 0*.

* *Signifies not out.* ‡ *Denotes county cap.*

The following played a total of 21 three-figure innings for Worcestershire in County
Championship matches – G. A. Hick 8, T. S. Curtis 4, G. J. Lord 3, D. B. D'Oliveira 2,
P. A. Neale 2, I. T. Botham 1, R. K. Illingworth 1.

BOWLING

	O	M	R	W	BB	5W/i	Avge
R. K. Illingworth	804.5	261	1,946	71	5-59	1	27.40
S. M. McEwan	310	61	970	32	3-31	0	30.31
S. R. Lampitt	539.3	96	1,794	57	5-34	2	31.47
P. J. Newport	563.2	104	1,806	57	6-73	3	31.68
I. T. Botham	174.4	34	546	17	4-65	0	32.11
G. A. Hick	208.5	41	645	20	5-37	1	32.25
G. R. Dilley	224.2	30	818	24	5-62	2	34.08
N. V. Radford	245	38	999	14	4-55	0	71.35

Also bowled: T. S. Curtis 5.3–1–43–0; D. B. D'Oliveira 11.3–1–80–2; R. D. Stemp
45–14–123–1; C. M. Tolley 88–14–326–5; M. J. Weston 7–1–23–0.

Wicket-keepers: S. J. Rhodes 59 ct, 8 st; S. R. Bevins 3 ct.

Leading Fielders: D. B. D'Oliveira 33, G. A. Hick 24.

At Lord's, April 17, 18, 19, 20. WORCESTERSHIRE drew with MCC.

At Manchester, April 26, 27, 28, 30. WORCESTERSHIRE drew with LANCASHIRE.

WORCESTERSHIRE v NOTTINGHAMSHIRE

At Worcester, May 3, 4, 5, 7. Worcestershire won by an innings and 6 runs. Worcestershire 23 pts, Nottinghamshire 2 pts. Toss: Worcestershire. Even without the injured Botham, Radford and Rhodes, Worcestershire secured their first Championship win of the season with more than two sessions to spare. Following on 347 in arrears, Nottinghamshire were indebted to a fifth-wicket stand of 187 between Randall and Johnson which took play into the fourth day. But on the last morning the visitors lost their remaining wickets in 75 minutes, with Dilley's swing bringing him four for 16 in 8.2 overs. Hick had reached another milestone on the first day, in passing 13,000 runs in his 150th first-class game before departing to a low delivery from Stephenson when only 3 short of his 48th century. Neale, with twenty boundaries in his 122, then added 220 for the sixth wicket with Illingworth, who batted four hours for his 117. By the close on the second day, Nottinghamshire were 110 for nine, with Newport having taken four for 32 in sixteen overs, his first Championship wickets since suffering an Achilles' tendon injury in the First Test of the Ashes series the previous year.

Close of play: First day, Worcestershire 292-5 (P. A. Neale 72*, R. K. Illingworth 35*); Second day, Nottinghamshire 110-9 (E. E. Hemmings 7*, R. A. Pick 20*); Third day, Nottinghamshire 302-4 (P. Johnson 77*, D. W. Randall 86*).

Worcestershire

T. S. Curtis c French b Cooper	46	G. R. Dilley b Hemmings		8
G. J. Lord b Pick	12	†S. R. Bevins not out		6
G. A. Hick b Stephenson	97	S. M. McEwan lbw b Pick		0
D. B. D'Oliveira c Evans b Pick	9			
P. A. Neale b Hemmings	122	B 10, l-b 9, w 2, n-b 7		28
R. Lampitt st French b Hemmings	1			
R. K. Illingworth b Stephenson	117	1/24 2/133 3/154 4/193 5/206		481
P. J. Newport c Newell b Pick	35	6/426 7/432 8/451 9/481		

Bonus points – Worcestershire 3, Nottinghamshire 2 (Score at 100 overs: 265-5).

Bowling: Stephenson 35–4–112–2; Cooper 37–11–113–1; Pick 36.5–5–119–4; Hemmings 41–21–117–3; Newell 1–0–1–0.

Nottinghamshire

B. C. Broad c Newport b Dilley		2 – c Hick b Dilley	16
M. Newell c Curtis b Lampitt		6 – c Curtis b Lampitt	30
R. J. Evans c Lampitt b Newport		11 – (4) lbw b McEwan	4
R. T. Robinson c Bevins b Newport		15 – (3) c Lampitt b McEwan	48
P. Johnson c Dilley b Newport		3 – lbw b McEwan	83
D. W. Randall b Lampitt		6 – c Bevins b Dilley	87
†B. N. French b Newport		10 – (8) c Bevins b Dilley	0
F. D. Stephenson lbw b McEwan		13 – (7) not out	12
E. E. Hemmings lbw b Lampitt		24 – retired hurt	4
K. E. Cooper c and b McEwan		1 – b Dilley	1
R. A. Pick not out		27 – b Dilley	0
B 8, l-b 3, w 4, n-b 1		16	B 15, l-b 26, w 11, n-b 4 .	56
1/3 2/24 3/24 4/27 5/36		134	1/22 2/99 3/121 4/122 5/309	341
6/49 7/77 8/77 9/79			6/309 7/309 8/341 9/341	

Bonus points – Worcestershire 4.

In the second innings E. E. Hemmings retired hurt at 327.

Bowling: *First Innings*—Dilley 8–2–13–1; McEwan 13–2–26–2; Newport 18–4–44–4; Illingworth 1–1–0–0; Lampitt 11.2–2–40–3. *Second Innings*—Dilley 23.2–4–62–5; McEwan 3–5–57–3; Newport 16–3–42–0; Illingworth 30–15–47–0; Lampitt 19–6–60–1; Hick 1–1–32–0.

Umpires: B. Leadbeater and K. J. Lyons.

At Worcester, May 12, 13, 14. WORCESTERSHIRE lost to NEW ZEALANDERS by six wickets (See New Zealand tour section).

WORCESTERSHIRE v ESSEX

At Worcester, May 19, 21, 22. Essex won by ten wickets. Essex 24 pts, Worcestershire 4 pts. Toss: Essex. Worcestershire, outplayed in all departments, suffered their first defeat in eleven Championship games, and Neale, their captain, admitted afterwards that he doubted his team would ever bowl as badly as on the first day. Gooch needed just 126 balls for his third Championship century in four innings and hit 22 boundaries in his 121. Waugh's unbeaten 166, including 27 fours, was his highest score to date for Essex, who declared when they had amassed 447 for four in 100 overs. Despite 89 runs from night-watchman Illingworth, Worcestershire were forced to follow on, only to be reduced to 32 for five in the first eleven overs from Foster and Pringle. Six dropped catches and a ninth-wicket partnership of 120 between Newport and Dilley saved them from an innings defeat in two days, but Essex were left needing only 45 for victory. Newport fell just short of his maiden first-class century for the second time in ten days.

Close of play: First day, Worcestershire 26-1 (T. S. Curtis 9*, R. K. Illingworth 15*). Second day, Worcestershire 165-8 (P. J. Newport 71*, G. R. Dilley 18*).

Essex

*G. A. Gooch c Rhodes b Newport	121	– not out	42
J. P. Stephenson c Curtis b Radford	4	– not out	6
P. J. Prichard run out	45		
M. E. Waugh not out	166		
B. R. Hardie c D'Oliveira b Botham	59		
N. Shahid not out	35		
L-b 7, n-b 10	17		

1/37 2/135 3/226 3/392　　　　(4 wkts dec.) 447　　　　(no wkt) 48

D. R. Pringle, †M. A. Garnham, N. A. Foster, T. D. Topley and J. H. Childs did not bat.

Bonus points – Essex 4, Worcestershire 1.

Bowling: *First Innings*—Dilley 10–1–76–0; Radford 16–1–95–1; Newport 19–2–88–1; Lampitt 15–5–55–0; Botham 19–2–58–1; Illingworth 14–3–45–0; Weston 7–1–23–0. *Second Innings*—Dilley 5–1–33–0; Newport 5–1–7–0; Curtis 0.3–0–8–0.

Worcestershire

T. S. Curtis c Shahid b Pringle	48	– lbw b Foster	2
M. J. Weston c Gooch b Foster	0	– c Gooch b Foster	14
R. K. Illingworth b Pringle	89	– (7) c Gooch b Topley	9
*P. A. Neale b Pringle	9	– (3) c Hardie b Pringle	4
I. T. Botham c Foster b Topley	53	– (4) lbw b Pringle	5
D. B. D'Oliveira c Hardie b Topley	32	– (5) c Stephenson b Pringle	25
S. R. Lampitt lbw b Topley	0	– (6) c Stephenson b Foster	1
†S. J. Rhodes b Foster	1	– (11) not out	5
P. J. Newport c Waugh b Topley	18	– (8) c and b Pringle	96
N. V. Radford b Foster	10	– (9) lbw b Pringle	10
G. R. Dilley not out	0	– (10) c Garnham b Foster	40
L-b 6, w 2, n-b 5	13	L-b 4, n-b 3	7

1/5 2/104 3/152 4/163 5/223　　　273　　1/12 2/19 3/21 4/25 5/32　　　218
6/223 7/226 8/254 9/267　　　　　　　　6/58 7/66 8/82 9/202

Bonus points – Worcestershire 3, Essex 4.

Bowling: *First Innings*—Foster 22.1–5–70–3; Pringle 21–2–67–3; Topley 19–5–67–4; Waugh 13–4–63–0. *Second Innings*—Foster 23–5–64–4; Pringle 24.1–6–66–5; Topley 8–1–44–1; Childs 8–6–9–0; Waugh 3–0–21–0; Stephenson 3–1–10–0.

Umpires: B. Dudleston and P. B. Wight.

At Birmingham, May 26, 28, 29. WORCESTERSHIRE drew with WARWICKSHIRE.

WORCESTERSHIRE v YORKSHIRE

At Worcester, June 2, 4, 5. Drawn. Worcestershire 7 pts, Yorkshire 6 pts. Toss: Yorkshire. Worcestershire were left with mixed feelings as the final day's play was lost to the weather. Yorkshire had begun badly, sliding from 44 without loss to 45 for four, but injuries deprived Worcestershire of the bowling of Botham and Newport in the second innings; they were already without Dilley, Radford and Illingworth. Botham made light of a hamstring strain on the second morning, when he reached 86, his highest score in the County Championship for three years, and shared a fifth-wicket stand of 125 in 32 overs with night-watchman McEwan, who contributed a career-best 54. Yorkshire wiped out their deficit of 66 in the evening session, notable mostly for newcomer Stemp's first first-class wicket.

Close of play: First day, Worcestershire 108-4 (I. T. Botham 11*, S. M. McEwan 0*); Second day, Yorkshire 106-2 (A. A. Metcalfe 56*, S. A. Kellett 4*).

Yorkshire

*M. D. Moxon c Botham b Lampitt	23	– c D'Oliveira b McEwan	28
A. A. Metcalfe c Rhodes b Lampitt	20	– not out	56
R. J. Blakey lbw b Botham	0	– c McEwan b Stemp	8
S. A. Kellett c Rhodes b Lampitt	0	– not out	4
P. E. Robinson c Rhodes b Botham	28		
†D. L. Bairstow c D'Oliveira b Lampitt	61		
P. Carrick c D'Oliveira b Botham	2		
C. S. Pickles c D'Oliveira b Newport	30		
P. J. Hartley b Lampitt	36		
P. W. Jarvis c Stemp b Botham	17		
S. D. Fletcher not out	0		
L-b 1, n-b 4	5	B 2, l-b 3, w 3, n-b 2	10

1/44 2/45 3/45 4/45 5/85   222   1/78 2/95   (2 wkts) 106
6/87 7/127 8/197 9/216

Bonus points – Yorkshire 2, Worcestershire 4.

Bowling: *First Innings*—Newport 17–2–55–1; McEwan 13–3–47–0; Botham 16.5–3–65–4; Lampitt 20–5–54–5. *Second Innings*—McEwan 15–4–35–1; Lampitt 17–6–34–0; Stemp 19–6–32–1.

Worcestershire

T. S. Curtis lbw b Fletcher	13	†S. J. Rhodes c Bairstow b Hartley	13
P. Bent c Blakey b Jarvis	39	S. R. Lampitt b Hartley	10
*P. A. Neale c Jarvis b Fletcher	1	R. D. Stemp not out	3
D. B. D'Oliveira c Hartley b Pickles	41		
I. T. Botham lbw b Carrick	86	L-b 6, n-b 2	8
S. M. McEwan c Bairstow b Jarvis	54		
M. J. Weston lbw b Jarvis	3	1/19 2/27 3/95 4/108 5/233	288
P. J. Newport c Bairstow b Carrick	17	6/245 7/246 8/266 9/276	

Bonus points – Worcestershire 3, Yorkshire 4 (Score at 100 overs: 288-9).

Bowling: Jarvis 25–5–59–3; Hartley 20.1–4–92–2; Fletcher 11–2–31–2; Carrick 36–12–70–2; Pickles 8–3–30–1.

Umpires: J. H. Harris and K. J. Lyons.

At The Oval, June 16, 18, 19. WORCESTERSHIRE drew with SURREY.

WORCESTERSHIRE v SUSSEX

At Worcester, June 20, 21, 22. Drawn. Worcestershire 1 pt, Sussex 3 pts. Toss: Sussex. Rain restricted play on the first two days to 40 overs and both sides forfeited an innings in a bid to fashion a finish. Sussex began the final day at 85 without loss, and their declaration left Worcestershire a target of 291 from a minimum of 53 overs after Hall, with 72, and Lenham had put on 126 for the first wicket. Worcestershire were on course as Botham and D'Oliveira added 122 in eighteen overs for the fourth wicket. But fortunes changed dramatically after Botham, having completed his fifth half-century in eight Championship innings, holed out next ball from leg-spinner Salisbury, who went on to take four wickets in thirteen deliveries and finished with career-best figures of five for 32. It was left to Rhodes and Illingworth to play out the last three overs to deny Sussex the spoils.

Close of play: First day, Sussex 55-0 (N. J. Lenham 27*, J. W. Hall 23*); Second day, Sussex 85-0 (N. J. Lenham 42*, J. W. Hall 36*).

Sussex

N. J. Lenham b Illingworth	66	M. P. Speight not out		60
J. W. Hall lbw b Botham	72	L-b 8, w 2, n-b 9		19
*P. W. G. Parker c Hick b Botham	14			
A. P. Wells not out	59	1/126 2/155 3/183	(3 wkts dec.)	290

C. M. Wells, A. I. C. Dodemaide, A. C. S. Pigott, †P. Moores, R. A. Bunting and I. D. K. Salisbury did not bat.

Bonus points – Sussex 3, Worcestershire 1.

Bowling: Newport 22-3-64-0; McEwan 6-2-12-0; Lampitt 14-2-55-0; Botham 15-4-32-2; Illingworth 23-6-82-1; Hick 6-0-37-0.

Sussex forfeited their second innings.

Worcestershire

Worcestershire forfeited their first innings.

T. S. Curtis c Parker b Bunting	27	†S. J. Rhodes not out		9
P. Bent b Bunting	5	S. R. Lampitt c and b Salisbury		3
G. A. Hick c Moores b Pigott	28	R. K. Illingworth not out		0
D. B. D'Oliveira st Moores b Salisbury	79	L-b 6, w 1, n-b 1		8
I. T. Botham c A. P. Wells b Salisbury	50			
*P. A. Neale c Pigott b Salisbury	8	1/21 2/43 3/71 4/193 5/197	(8 wkts)	219
P. J. Newport st Moores b Salisbury	2	6/207 7/210 8/217		

S. M. McEwan did not bat.

Bowling: Dodemaide 14.5-6-32-0; Pigott 15-2-68-1; Bunting 10-2-40-2; C. M. Wells 5-0-41-0; Salisbury 10-2-32-5.

Umpires: D. J. Constant and J. W. Holder.

At Lord's, June 30, July 2, 3. WORCESTERSHIRE drew with MIDDLESEX.

WORCESTERSHIRE v GLOUCESTERSHIRE

At Worcester, July 7, 9, 10. Worcestershire won by 148 runs. Worcestershire 22 pts, Gloucestershire 5 pts. Toss: Worcestershire. Hick, dismissed without scoring on the opening morning, had the final say with bat and ball to seal what was only Worcestershire's second win in their nine Championship matches to date. His 79 off 45 balls, as the home batsmen plundered 165 runs from the final morning session, left Gloucestershire a target of 276 from a minimum of 75 overs on a worn wicket conducive to spin. After Dilley, playing his first match for five weeks, had sent back the top three Gloucestershire batsmen, Hick followed up his best bowling figures of five for 37 in the first innings with four for 43, returning nine for 80 in the match. The previous day only Hodgson, with 77, had offered prolonged resistance against Hick and Illingworth, and Gloucestershire trailed by 99; in the visitors' second innings their last five wickets went for 7 runs.

Close of play: First day, Worcestershire 265-7 (R. K. Illingworth 41*, C. M. Tolley 26*); second day, Worcestershire 11-0 (T. S. Curtis 4*, P. Bent 6*).

Worcestershire

. S. Curtis lbw b Curran	4	– b Graveney	21
. Bent c Athey b Barnes	44	– b Curran	22
. A. Hick c Williams b Bell	0	– b Bainbridge	79
. B. D'Oliveira c Williams b Bell	69	– b Bainbridge	26
T. Botham c Wright b Barnes	2	– c Barnes b Bainbridge	16
P. A. Neale c Wright b Curran	14	– not out	3
S. J. Rhodes b Graveney	55		
. K. Illingworth run out	50		
. M. Tolley b Curran	29		
R. Lampitt not out	20		
. R. Dilley not out	17		
B 1, l-b 11, w 1, n-b 2	15	L-b 6, n-b 3	9

/16 2/17 3/60 4/62 5/94   (9 wkts dec.) 319   1/46 2/46 3/126   (5 wkts dec.) 176
/168 7/214 8/274 9/279   4/173 5/176

Bonus points – Worcestershire 2, Gloucestershire 3 (Score at 100 overs: 225-7).

Bowling: *First Innings*—Curran 33–6–76–3; Barnes 22–4–74–2; Bell 17–4–38–2; Graveney 5–24–64–1; Bainbridge 13–1–42–0; Lloyds 2–0–13–0. *Second Innings*—Curran 12–2–37–1; arnes 1–0–6–0; Graveney 11–1–67–1; Lloyds 3–0–37–0; Bainbridge 3–0–23–3.

Gloucestershire

. D. Hodgson lbw b Hick	77	– c D'Oliveira b Dilley	22
A. J. Wright lbw b Botham	13	– (3) lbw b Dilley	5
P. Butcher b Dilley	27	– (2) c D'Oliveira b Dilley	0
. W. J. Athey c D'Oliveira b Hick	15	– c Botham b Illingworth	32
. Bainbridge not out	31	– c Botham b Illingworth	7
. M. Curran b Illingworth	7	– b Hick	19
W. Lloyds c Rhodes b Hick	28	– st Rhodes b Hick	40
. A. Graveney c and b Illingworth	1	– b Hick	0
R. C. J. Williams c Curtis b Illingworth	0	– st Rhodes b Hick	1
N. Barnes b Hick	0	– c D'Oliveira b Illingworth	0
. M. Bell c Curtis b Hick	0	– not out	0
B 10, l-b 7, w 3, n-b 1	21	B 1	1

/44 2/96 3/133 4/140 5/155   220   1/15 2/26 3/27 4/49 5/80   127
/208 7/215 8/215 9/218   6/120 7/121 8/126 9/127

Bonus points – Gloucestershire 2, Worcestershire 4.

Bowling: *First Innings*—Dilley 9–1–26–1; Lampitt 11–0–38–0; Tolley 3–1–7–0; Botham 0–3–20–1; Illingworth 32–10–75–3; Hick 16.3–5–37–5. *Second Innings*—Dilley 7–2–16–3; olley 2–0–20–0; Illingworth 18–4–47–3; Hick 14.3–1–43–4.

Umpires: P. J. Eele and P. B. Wight.

WORCESTERSHIRE v SOMERSET

t Worcester, July 18, 19, 20. Drawn. Worcestershire 4 pts, Somerset 5 pts. Toss: Somerset. here was never any possibility of either side forcing victory on the most benign of pitches nd in searing heat. The first two days produced 764 runs while only six wickets fell. Memories of the way Worcestershire, through Hick, had scored 300 in 57 overs to win the orresponding game the year before ensured that Tavaré would be less generous in his eclaration. In the event, Worcestershire never seriously contemplated the challenge of 340 in 0 overs, calling a halt with twelve of the final twenty remaining. Roebuck dominated the first ay in reaching the second double-hundred of his career, a chanceless innings bearing witness o his concentration. He completed his hundred in 187 balls and scored 26 boundaries in all, sharing a second-wicket stand of 258 in 79 overs with Hayhurst. Somerset's 66-year-old recor of 290 for the second wicket was under threat before Hayhurst was needlessly run out, havir reached his century in 240 balls, with one six and thirteen fours. Inevitably, the second da belonged to Hick, whose unbeaten 171, including 29 fours and one six, was his fifth Cham pionship century against Somerset in six seasons. In seventeen first-class innings against then he had scored a total of 1,389, at an average of 126.27. Hick added 139 in 46 overs wit D'Oliveira and 148 in 32 overs with Neale before Worcestershire declared 98 runs behind. A the close the following day he was unbeaten again with 69.

Close of play: First day, Somerset 398-3 (P. M. Roebuck 201*, R. J. Harden 0*); Secon day, Somerset 66-0 (S. J. Cook 37*, P. M. Roebuck 28*).

Somerset

S. J. Cook c and b Tolley	6	– c Neale b Tolley	3
P. M. Roebuck not out	201	– lbw b Lampitt	6
A. N. Hayhurst run out	119	– (5) c Rhodes b Tolley	1
*C. J. Tavaré c and b Newport	54	– b Lampitt	1
R. J. Harden not out	0	– (3) c Rhodes b Lampitt	2
†N. D. Burns (did not bat)		– not out	2
G. D. Rose (did not bat)		– not out	4
B 5, l-b 7, w 1, n-b 5	18	B 2, l-b 4, n-b 2	

1/9 2/267 3/398   (3 wkts dec.) 398   1/85 2/137 3/144   (5 wkts dec.) 24
                                                4/152 5/189

R. P. Lefebvre, I. G. Swallow, N. A. Mallender and A. N. Jones did not bat.

Bonus points – Somerset 4 (Score at 100 overs: 324-2).

Bowling: *First Innings*—Newport 19–1–70–1; Tolley 24–4–84–1; Radford 18–0–78–C Lampitt 16–2–70–0; Illingworth 30–8–72–0; Hick 3–0–12–0. *Second Innings*—Newpo 11–2–46–0; Tolley 18–2–66–2; Lampitt 13.2–1–46–3; Radford 12–0–49–0; Illingwor 7–1–28–0.

Worcestershire

T. S. Curtis lbw b Mallender	6	– lbw b Mallender	2
P. Bent c Rose b Jones	1	– c and b Lefebvre	3
G. A. Hick not out	171	– not out	6
D. B. D'Oliveira c sub b Swallow	55	– c and b Swallow	2
*P. A. Neale not out	49	– not out	2
B 7, l-b 10, w 1	18	L-b 4, n-b 2	

1/3 2/13 3/152   (3 wkts dec.) 300   1/40 2/94 3/127   (3 wkts) 18

C. M. Tolley, †S. J. Rhodes, R. K. Illingworth, P. J. Newport, S. R. Lampitt and N. \ Radford did not bat.

Bonus points – Worcestershire 4, Somerset 1.

Bowling: *First Innings*—Jones 8–3–17–1; Mallender 13–5–35–1; Rose 13–1–49–0; Lefebvr 17–4–49–0; Swallow 23–5–84–1; Roebuck 5–1–20–0; Hayhurst 5.4–0–29–0. *Second Innings*— Jones 5–0–25–0; Mallender 5–1–13–1; Rose 10–1–29–0; Lefebvre 11–2–33–1; Swallo 15–0–69–1; Roebuck 2–1–8–0.

Umpires: A. A. Jones and D. S. Thompsett.

At Abergavenny, July 21, 23, 24. WORCESTERSHIRE drew with GLAMORGAN.

At Derby, July 25, 26, 27. WORCESTERSHIRE drew with DERBYSHIRE.

At Canterbury, July 28, 30, 31. WORCESTERSHIRE drew with KENT.

Leicester, August 4, 6, 7. WORCESTERSHIRE beat LEICESTERSHIRE by 1 run.

WORCESTERSHIRE v LANCASHIRE

Kidderminster, August 8, 9, 10. Worcestershire won by ten wickets. Worcestershire 24 pts, Lancashire 2 pts. Toss: Worcestershire. Worcestershire completed their fourth Championship win of the season, and their second of the week under the captaincy of Curtis, deputising for the injured Neale. Curtis and Lord, scoring his first Championship century for two seasons, provided the platform for their formidable first-innings total of 451 for six declared. Hick passed 50 for the tenth time in eleven Championship innings, adding 90 in 24 overs with D'Oliveira, and there was little respite for the Lancashire attack as Leatherdale hit his highest score of 70. Newport pressed home Worcestershire's advantage with five wickets for 59 as the visitors were dismissed for 160 in 47.1 overs, their last three wickets falling to Illingworth in deliveries. Following on 291 behind, they fared little better, slumping to 162 for six at the end of the second day. Fairbrother, batting down the order after being hit on the jaw by McEwan in the first innings, added 123 in 31 overs with Austin in a defiant eighth-wicket stand. But it still left Worcestershire needing just 7 runs for victory, which they achieved with almost two sessions to spare.

Close of play: First day, Worcestershire 395-4 (D. A. Leatherdale 68*, C. M. Tolley 15*); second day, Lancashire 162-6 (T. E. Jesty 50*, I. D. Austin 1*).

Worcestershire

T. S. Curtis lbw b Austin	56	– not out	4
G. J. Lord c Martin b Hughes	101	– not out	0
G. A. Hick c Lloyd b Hughes	67		
D. B. D'Oliveira run out	59		
D. A. Leatherdale c Fairbrother b Hughes	70		
C. M. Tolley not out	28		
S. J. Rhodes b Austin	22		
R. K. Illingworth not out	19		
B 10, l-b 9, n-b 10	29	W 4	4
1/52 2/189 3/279 4/336 (6 wkts dec.)	451	(no wkt)	8
5/398 6/424			

J. Newport, S. R. Lampitt and S. M. McEwan did not bat.

Bonus points – Worcestershire 4, Lancashire 1 (Score at 100 overs: 335-3).

Bowling: *First Innings*—Wasim Akram 20-4-68-0; Martin 17-7-39-0; Watkinson 16-3-85-0; Austin 27-5-105-2; Hughes 42-12-135-3. *Second Innings*—Lloyd 0.1-0-8-0.

Lancashire

D. Mendis b Newport	15	– c D'Oliveira b Lampitt	36
G. Fowler c Rhodes b Newport	9	– lbw b Lampitt	18
D. Lloyd b McEwan	2	– b Tolley	14
N. H. Fairbrother c Rhodes b Newport	22	– (9) not out	64
T. E. Jesty b Lampitt	35	– (4) b Illingworth	54
M. Watkinson lbw b Newport	4	– (5) c Rhodes b Lampitt	7
Wasim Akram c Hick b Newport	14	– (6) c D'Oliveira b McEwan	23
W. K. Hegg b Lord b Illingworth	47	– (7) lbw b McEwan	5
I. D. Austin c D'Oliveira b Illingworth	0	– (8) c Lampitt b Hick	58
D. P. Hughes lbw b Illingworth	2	– c Leatherdale b Hick	1
P. J. Martin not out	1	– b Illingworth	0
L-b 5, w 2, n-b 2	9	B 12, l-b 4, n-b 1	17
1/9 2/23 3/35 4/51 5/55	160	1/41 2/68 3/72 4/99 5/133	297
6/89 7/144 8/149 9/151		6/157 7/167 8/290 9/296	

Bonus points – Lancashire 1, Worcestershire 4.

Bowling: *First Innings*—Newport 18-1-59-5; McEwan 10-1-31-1; Tolley 9-1-41-0; Lampitt 6-1-16-1; Illingworth 4.1-0-8-3. *Second Innings*—Newport 10-0-48-0; McEwan 13-3-25-2; Lampitt 16-4-58-3; Tolley 10-2-39-1; Illingworth 25.3-3-92-2; Hick 6-2-19-2.

Umpires: B. Dudleston and K. E. Palmer.

WORCESTERSHIRE v HAMPSHIRE

At Worcester, August 11, 13, 14. Drawn. Worcestershire 5 pts, Hampshire 5 pts. Tos̄
Worcestershire. Worcestershire failed by two wickets to force a third successive Cha͏̄
pionship victory, which would have kept alive their aspirations of retaining the title. S
a target of 266 in 61 overs, Hampshire were rescued by an unbeaten 43 from Joseph, after th͏
had started the final twenty overs precariously placed at 126 for five. Worcestershire had r͏
up 413 for six against the visitors' second-string attack on the opening day. Lord struck
fours and two sixes in his five-and-a-half-hour innings before being caught 9 runs short of ʰ
career-best 199. He put on 167 with Curtis for the first wicket and 164 in 35 overs with Hi͏
and completed his second Championship hundred in four days, in 159 balls. Hampshir͏
target of 300 to avoid the follow-on looked a long way off when Newport reduced them to ͏
for two. But Middleton, with his fourth Championship century of the season, and Cox, wʰ
reached his maiden hundred in 133 balls during his second first-class game, added 161 for tʰ
fifth wicket, steering Hampshire to 302 for four at the close on the second day.

Close of play: First day, Worcestershire 413-6 (S. J. Rhodes 8*, R. K. Illingworth 1͏⁴
Second day, Hampshire 302-4 (T. C. Middleton 117*, R. M. F. Cox 104*).

Worcestershire

*T. S. Curtis c Scott b Joseph	71	– not out		͏
G. J. Lord c Middleton b Udal	190	– c Joseph b Maru		͏
G. A. Hick c Parks b Joseph	72	– not out		͏
D. B. D'Oliveira lbw b Tremlett	30			
D. A. Leatherdale c Maru b Tremlett	13			
C. M. Tolley c Parks b Tremlett	2			
†S. J. Rhodes not out	33			
R. K. Illingworth not out	9			
B 7, l-b 15, w 1, n-b 6	29	B 2, l-b 5, n-b 4		͏

1/167 2/331 3/375 4/388 5/403   (6 wkts dec.) 449   1/40   (1 wkt dec.) 1͏
6/404

P. J. Newport, S. R. Lampitt and S. M. McEwan did not bat.

Bonus points – Worcestershire 4, Hampshire 1 (Score at 100 overs: 388-3).

Bowling: *First Innings*—Joseph 30–4–128–2; Scott 7–0–38–0; Tremlett 23–4–61–3; Ma͏
29–5–92–0; Udal 24–4–95–1; Nicholas 4–0–13–0. *Second Innings*—Joseph 8–2–19–0; Tremlͤ
6–2–22–0; Maru 3–0–13–1; Nicholas 5–0–27–0; Smith 2–0–22–0; Scott 1.4–0–8–0.

Hampshire

R. J. Scott c Rhodes b Newport	17	– c D'Oliveira b McEwan		͏
C. L. Smith c Rhodes b Newport	5	– c Leatherdale b McEwan		͏
T. C. Middleton not out	117	– c D'Oliveira b McEwan		͏
V. P. Terry c Rhodes b Illingworth	40	– c D'Oliveira b Illingworth		͏
*M. C. J. Nicholas lbw b Lampitt	6	– c and b Lampitt		͏
R. M. F. Cox not out	104	– run out		͏
L. A. Joseph (did not bat)		– not out		͏
R. J. Maru (did not bat)		– c Tolley b Illingworth		͏
†R. J. Parks (did not bat)		– c Hick b Illingworth		͏
S. D. Udal (did not bat)		– not out		͏
L-b 6, w 1, n-b 6	13	L-b 3, w 2, n-b 4		͏

1/9 2/26 3/120 4/141   (4 wkts dec.) 302   1/20 2/27 3/34 4/101   (8 wkts) 1͏
5/120 6/130 7/167 8/179

T. M. Tremlett did not bat.

Bonus points – Hampshire 4, Worcestershire 1.

Bowling: *First Innings*—Newport 16–6–23–2; McEwan 12–1–40–0; Lampitt 18–2–39–͏;
Illingworth 32–6–99–1; Tolley 4–0–15–0; Hick 17–1–74–0; D'Oliveira 1–0–6–0. *Secon͏
Innings*—Newport 18–2–61–0; McEwan 11–1–38–3; Illingworth 21–8–44–3; Lampͤ
9–0–29–1; Hick 1.5–0–5–0.

Umpires: B. Dudleston and K. E. Palmer.

WORCESTERSHIRE v NORTHAMPTONSHIRE

t Worcester, August 18, 20, 21. Drawn. Worcestershire 6 pts, Northamptonshire 6 pts. Toss: orthamptonshire. The most absorbing contest of the season at New Road, dominated by the inners, ended with Rhodes and Newport batting out the last eleven overs to stave off defeat. ith the ball turning appreciably and lifting from the Diglis End, Cook and Illingworth iished with respective match figures of nine for 137 and seven for 92. In his first appearance r six weeks, after a fourth knee operation, Dilley quickly accounted for Felton, and ordham and Lamb were the only Northamptonshire batsmen to make significant con- ibutions on the opening day. Curtis anchored Worcestershire's reply, staying 64 overs for s 48, while Rhodes and Dilley added 35 for the last wicket to reduce the deficit to 9. orcestershire looked to have regained the initiative when the visitors were 78 for four on the al morning, but Bailey's defiant 66 enabled Northamptonshire to set a demanding target of 1 in 51 overs. Cook ran through the middle order with four wickets in seven overs, including ick's after his thirteenth half-century in fifteen innings, but Worcestershire's eighth-wicket air held firm to the finish.

Close of play: First day, Worcestershire 39-1 (T. S. Curtis 11*, S. M. McEwan 10*); Second ay, Northamptonshire 77-2 (W. Larkins 26*, R. J. Bailey 11*).

lorthamptonshire

. Fordham c Hick b Lampitt	81	– c Rhodes b Newport 19
. A. Felton c Rhodes b Dilley	10	– c Rhodes b McEwan 11
. Larkins c D'Oliveira b Newport	27	– c Rhodes b Illingworth 26
. J. Bailey c McEwan b Lampitt	7	– run out 66
. J. Capel st Rhodes b Illingworth	12	– lbw b Dilley 0
A. J. Lamb c Illingworth b McEwan	63	– c Rhodes b Illingworth 28
L. Penberthy c Rhodes b Hick	1	– c Lampitt b Hick 21
). Ripley c Hick b Illingworth	14	– not out 26
E. L. Ambrose b Illingworth	12	– b Illingworth 12
. G. B. Cook b Illingworth	2	– not out 7
. A. Robinson not out	0	
B 1, l-b 5, w 1, n-b 6	13	B 2, l-b 12, n-b 1 15

27 2/114 3/132 4/132 5/167   242   1/19 2/51 3/77   (8 wkts dec.) 231
182 7/223 8/233 9/241   4/78 5/121 6/184
                              7/190 8/221

Bonus points – Northamptonshire 2, Worcestershire 4.

Bowling: *First Innings*—Dilley 16–3–36–1; Newport 17–2–67–1; McEwan 11–1–39–1; ampitt 17–7–44–2; Illingworth 17.4–6–29–4; Hick 7–0–21–1. *Second Innings*—Dilley ⌐0–48–1; McEwan 5–2–11–1; Illingworth 38–12–63–3; Newport 6–1–11–1; Hick ⌐8–66–1; Lampitt 4–0–18–0.

Vorcestershire

. S. Curtis lbw b Ambrose	48	– lbw b Ambrose 12
. J. Lord c Ripley b Capel	17	– lbw b Robinson 6
M. McEwan b Cook	14	
. A. Hick c Ripley b Cook	34	– (3) st Ripley b Cook 50
. B. D'Oliveira c Penberthy b Cook	0	– (4) c and b Robinson 21
. A. Leatherdale c Capel b Cook	52	– (5) c Felton b Cook 7
R. Lampitt lbw b Ambrose	0	– (6) c Lamb b Cook 16
s. J. Rhodes not out	44	– (7) not out 28
K. Illingworth lbw b Robinson	9	– (8) lbw b Cook 0
J. Newport c Larkins b Robinson	1	– (9) not out 8
. R. Dilley b Cook	8	
L-b 2, n-b 4	6	B 4, l-b 2, n-b 3 9

25 2/44 3/88 4/92 5/153   233   1/19 2/20 3/70 4/85   (7 wkts) 157
153 7/171 8/196 9/198   5/111 6/132 7/132

Bonus points – Worcestershire 2, Northamptonshire 4 (Score at 100 overs: 233-9).

Bowling: *First Innings*—Ambrose 26–7–53–2; Robinson 22–3–63–2; Capel 4–0–13–1; Coo 40.1–17–80–5; Bailey 8–1–22–0. *Second Innings*—Ambrose 11–3–28–1; Robinson 13–4–40–2 Cook 19.4–3–57–4; Bailey 7–2–26–0.

Umpires: D. J. Constant and B. Leadbeater.

WORCESTERSHIRE v WARWICKSHIRE

At Worcester, August 23, 24, 25, 27. Worcestershire won by 323 runs. Worcestershire 23 pt Warwickshire 6 pts. Toss: Worcestershire. Rarely can a side have made a more complet recovery to win by such a large margin. Neale's decision to bat first, on a relaid pitch not use before, was in question when Small took five wickets for 13 in 25 balls, reducing the home sid to 57 for five on the first morning. Rhodes and Neale held up the slide by adding 88 in 2 overs, but Warwickshire regained the initiative the following day when they reached 101 fc 1, only to lose their last nine wickets for 121 and trail by 43 on first innings. Thereaft Worcestershire assumed total control. Curtis's unbeaten 197 was his highest first-class scor and his third century of the summer. He occupied the crease for seven and a quarter hour hitting two sixes and 25 fours. Needing 420 for their first Championship win over thei neighbours for ten years, Warwickshire were bowled out in just 29.3 overs for 96, Newpor taking five for 37 in 14.3 overs.

Close of play: First day, Worcestershire 228-9 (G. R. Dilley 11*, S. M. McEwan 0*); Secon day, Worcestershire 47-0 (T. S. Curtis 25*, G. J. Lord 13*); Third day, Worcestershire 376- (T. S. Curtis 197*, S. J. Rhodes 30*).

Worcestershire

T. S. Curtis c Lloyd b Small	27	– not out	.19
G. J. Lord lbw b Small	7	– c Piper b Munton	2
G. A. Hick c Piper b Small	14	– b Reeve	4
D. B. D'Oliveira c Piper b Small	0	– c Moles b Booth	3
*P. A. Neale c Twose b Reeve	46	– c Piper b Twose	1
S. R. Lampitt c Piper b Small	0	– c and b Munton	
†S. J. Rhodes b Reeve	96	– not out	3
R. K. Illingworth lbw b Munton	13		
P. J. Newport c Piper b Munton	7		
G. R. Dilley c Lloyd b Small	35		
S. M. McEwan not out	12		
L-b 7, w 1	8	B 8, l-b 20, w 2, n-b 1	3

1/35 2/40 3/40 4/57 5/57   265   1/78 2/155 3/204   (5 wkts dec.) 37
6/145 7/169 8/183 9/217   4/258 5/273

Bonus points – Worcestershire 3, Warwickshire 4.

Bowling: *First Innings*—Small 29–5–94–6; Munton 27–6–84–2; Reeve 23–3–60–2; Mood 3–0–11–0; Booth 7–5–9–0. *Second Innings*—Small 25–12–61–0; Munton 27–9–66–2; Reev 25–8–85–1; Booth 36–10–93–1; Smith 6–0–33–0; Twose 5–1–10–1.

Warwickshire

A. J. Moles c Neale b Dilley	59	– b Dilley	
J. D. Ratcliffe c Lampitt b Newport	29	– lbw b Newport	
*T. A. Lloyd c Neale b Lampitt	12	– lbw b Newport	
T. M. Moody c Rhodes b McEwan	21	– c Rhodes b Dilley	
R. G. Twose b Newport	9	– lbw b Dilley	
D. A. Reeve c D'Oliveira b Lampitt	27	– b McEwan	2
N. M. K. Smith c D'Oliveira b Newport	20	– b Newport	
†K. J. Piper b Dilley	14	– c Rhodes b Newport	
G. C. Small not out	5	– c Illingworth b Newport	1
P. A. Booth c Rhodes b Lampitt	2	– c Rhodes b McEwan	
T. A. Munton c Curtis b Lampitt	1	– not out	
B 1, l-b 7, w 2, n-b 13	23	L-b 3, w 1, n-b 5	

1/66 2/101 3/123 4/146 5/150   222   1/14 2/16 3/16 4/19 5/45   9
6/182 7/209 8/212 9/214   6/71 7/71 8/82 9/88

Bonus points – Warwickshire 2, Worcestershire 4.

Bowling: *First Innings*—Dilley 16–2–56–2; Newport 19–5–60–3; McEwan 14–2–49–1; Illingworth 1–0–2–0; Lampitt 14–1–47–4. *Second Innings*—Dilley 10–0–45–3; Newport 4.3–4–37–5; McEwan 5–2–11–2.

Umpires: J. H. Harris and B. Hassan.

At Nottingham, August 29, 30, 31. WORCESTERSHIRE drew with NOTTINGHAM-SHIRE.

At Bristol, September 7, 8, 9, 10. WORCESTERSHIRE drew with GLOUCESTERSHIRE.

At Taunton, September 12, 13, 14, 15. WORCESTERSHIRE beat SOMERSET by 173 runs.

WORCESTERSHIRE v GLAMORGAN

At Worcester, September 18, 19, 20, 21. Worcestershire won by 261 runs. Worcestershire 24 pts, Glamorgan 6 pts. Toss: Worcestershire. Worcestershire, who two months earlier had been next to bottom in the County Championship table, fashioned their fifth win in their last twelve games to finish fourth. Hick signed off with his eighth hundred of the summer on his way to passing 15,000 first-class runs, hitting sixteen fours and one six in an unbeaten 138 off 55 balls. But Lord could feel no less satisfied. His 127 on the third day was rated one of the most entertaining innings of the year at New Road, and he was later awarded his county cap. By adding 57 runs in the second innings he completed 1,000 runs in a season for the first time. For the visitors, a spell of three for 0 in seven balls had helped Bastien to return his best bowling figures, six for 75, in the first innings. On the final day, when Glamorgan were chasing 477 for victory, Morris made his twentieth first-class score of 50 or more and brought his total runs for the season to 2,276, a record for his county. Butcher helped him delay the inevitable, but Dilley bowled Morris and took the last two wickets to finish with five for 72.

Close of play: First day, Glamorgan 14-0 (S. P. James 6*, H. Morris 8*); Second day, Worcestershire 10-0 (T. S. Curtis 4*, G. J. Lord 6*); Third day, Glamorgan 27-2 (H. Morris 9*, M. P. Maynard 2*).

Worcestershire

T. S. Curtis lbw b Frost	16	– c James b Watkin	60
G. J. Lord c Maynard b Bastien	127	– c Maynard b Croft	57
G. A. Hick c Metson b Watkin	6	– not out	138
D. B. D'Oliveira c Metson b Bastien	22	– b Bastien	12
*P. A. Neale b Bastien	4	– c Morris b Bastien	17
S. R. Lampitt lbw b Bastien	34	– c Metson b Watkin	18
†S. J. Rhodes c Cottey b Bastien	0	– c Maynard b Bastien	22
R. K. Illingworth c Metson b Watkin	48	– not out	7
N. V. Radford lbw b Watkin	13		
G. R. Dilley not out	45		
S. M. McEwan b Bastien	11		
B 4, l-b 4, n-b 1	9	L-b 12	12

1/24 2/43 3/95 4/107 5/212   335   1/117 2/138 3/168   (6 wkts dec.) 343
6/212 7/213 8/239 9/307   4/198 5/248 6/314

Bonus points – Worcestershire 4, Glamorgan 4 (Score at 100 overs: 313-9).

Bowling: *First Innings*—Frost 23–2–71–1; Watkin 31–7–124–3; Bastien 24–8–75–6; Croft 20–5–41–0; Dale 10–5–16–0. *Second Innings*—Frost 12–3–44–0; Watkin 20–5–47–2; Bastien 17–0–76–3; Dale 11–1–54–0; Croft 28–3–110–1.

Glamorgan

S. P. James lbw b Dilley		7 – c D'Oliveira b Dilley	0
H. Morris c Rhodes b McEwan	71	– b Dilley	50
P. A. Cottey c Rhodes b Lampitt	19	– c Curtis b Dilley	3
M. P. Maynard b Radford	4	– c Rhodes b McEwan	35
*A. R. Butcher c Hick b McEwan	21	– c Lord b Illingworth	61
A. Dale lbw b McEwan	7	– c Rhodes b McEwan	0
R. D. B. Croft not out	26	– c Neale b Lampitt	27
†C. P. Metson c Rhodes b Lampitt	10	– lbw b Lampitt	4
S. L. Watkin c McEwan b Radford	19	– b Dilley	4
S. Bastien c Rhodes b Radford	0	– c Lord b Dilley	12
M. Frost lbw b Radford	0	– not out	4
B 5, l-b 6, n-b 7	18	L-b 8, w 1, n-b 6	15

1/20 2/86 3/91 4/123 5/142   202   1/1 2/18 3/68 4/102 5/107   215
6/145 7/177 8/198 9/200   6/152 7/156 8/191 9/199

Bonus points – Glamorgan 2, Worcestershire 4.

Bowling: *First Innings*—Dilley 13–1–35–1; Radford 20–4–58–4; McEwan 18–6–31–3; Lampitt 22–7–52–2; Illingworth 14–7–15–0. *Second Innings*—Dilley 14–1–72–5; Radford 11–1–31–0; McEwan 9–4–30–2; Lampitt 12–2–52–2; Illingworth 9–5–22–1.

Umpires: P. J. Eele and R. Julian.

NATIONAL POWER AWARDS, 1990

The National Power Awards, of £1,000 each, went to the leading run-scorer, wicket-taker and six-hitter in first-class matches during the English season. A special bonus of £10,000 was available to be shared by batsmen scoring 2,500 runs and bowlers taking 125 wickets, while those players hitting twenty or more sixes received £10 per six. G. A. Gooch, the leading run-scorer, received an additional £1,000 for being the first to reach a bonus target. As part of their sponsorship, National Power presented the winners' counties with a similar sum to that won by the players. The Awards were run with the cooperation of *Wisden Cricket Monthly*.

Batting Awards
£7,000   G. A. Gooch (Essex)   2,746 runs.   £5,000   S. J. Cook (Somerset)   2,608 runs.

Bowling Award
£1,000   N. A. Foster (Essex)   94 wickets.

Six-hit Awards
£1,400   I. V. A. Richards (Glamorgan) . . . 40 sixes.

The following received £10 per six:

N. H. Fairbrother (Lancashire)	32	D. M. Ward (Surrey)	23
G. D. Rose (Somerset)	30	C. A. Walsh (Gloucestershire)	22
G. A. Hick (Worcestershire)	28	M. A. Roseberry (Middlesex)	21
D. J. Capel (Northamptonshire)	27	M. E. Waugh (Essex)	21
R. J. Bailey (Northamptonshire)	25	I. A. Greig (Surrey)	20
T. M. Moody (Warwickshire)	23		

YORKSHIRE

Patron: HRH The Duchess of Kent
President: 1990 – Sir Leonard Hutton
1991 – Sir Lawrence Byford
Chairman: B. Walsh
Chairman, Cricket Committee: D. B. Close
Secretary: J. Lister
Headingley Cricket Ground, Leeds LS6 3BU
(Telephone: 0532-787394)
Cricket Manager: S. Oldham
Captain: M. D. Moxon

Yorkshire cricket was a mass of contradictions at the end of yet another worrying season. On the one hand, leading officials took public comfort from an overall statistical improvement reflected in the county's rise from sixteenth to tenth in the Britannic Assurance Championship and from eleventh to sixth in the Refuge Assurance League, arguing that important strides had been made in the right direction. In contrast, however, other members of the committee were so concerned at the poor quality of the cricket that they echoed the dressing-room plea from the previous year for outside assistance. And the loss of around 1,000 members caused the overseas-player issue to be debated once more. The outcome was that in November, by 18-1, the committee voted to relax the county's "Yorkshire born" policy and make eligible those cricketers who, although not born in Yorkshire, had grown up there.

Martyn Moxon and manager Steve Oldham, the new partnership in charge of the team, adopted some positive attitudes, and Yorkshire were always ready to run the risk of defeat in pursuit of victory. But as the season developed, all concerned became rather too keen to set up a last-afternoon run-chase, forgetting, it appeared, that the object in the Championship should be to bowl out the opposition twice. Yorkshire managed this just once – against bottom-of-the-table Sussex – yet conceded all twenty wickets themselves on eight occasions.

The bowling proved dreadfully poor, and for the first time in a full Championship season no-one took 50 wickets. Peter Hartley, with 48, was the most successful, but his form remained erratic. Arnie Sidebottom was restricted to two Championship games and sixteen appearances in the national one-day competitions by a knee injury for which he twice had surgery, while Paul Jarvis, the other seamer capable of upsetting batsmen on good pitches, rarely hit an effective rhythm. Jarvis suffered the indignity of being dropped at the end of May, for the Hampshire game, and he subsequently missed most of July with a stress fracture of the shin. Even so, it was disappointing and significant that he did not take five wickets in any first-class innings.

Stuart Fletcher fell out of favour for the second successive year and was not offered an extension of his contract, due to expire at the end of 1991, and Darren Gough did little to justify the high hopes held for him. The absence of Sidebottom gave Chris Pickles another chance to press his claims, but while he showed an unfailing enthusiasm, his tidy medium pace never threatened to take wickets on a match-winning basis. His brightest moments concerned his batting. Phil Carrick headed the bowling averages and, after a rather shaky start, enjoyed one of his better summers. However, off-spinner Jeremy Batty, when brought into the side, lacked the control to avoid fairly heavy punishment, and it was an indictment of Yorkshire's failure to encourage younger exponents of an almost lost art that at 38 Carrick was Yorkshire's only reliable spinner.

The county expressed great faith in the Academy venture at Bradford and in a scheme to develop fast bowlers with the aid of specialised athletic coaching, but neither of these ventures looked like solving the immediate problem. Certainly there is no-one with an excess of pace at the Academy, which no doubt was why a keen interest was displayed in the plans of Yorkshire exiles with other first-class counties.

Overall, the batting was patchy and could not be relied on under pressure. Moxon scored steadily without quite fulfilling his potential, and Ashley Metcalfe had the satisfaction of becoming the first batsman since Geoff Boycott in 1971 to score 2,000 first-class runs. Richard Blakey, however, endured a miserable sequence early on, averaging only 17.46 in the Championship at the end of June. Although he scored fluently in the Sunday League, he continued to be hesitant at the higher level and eventually dropped down the order. This was a sensible move, for he was establishing himself as first-choice wicket-keeper in succession to David Bairstow, who featured briefly in his testimonial year before being informed that his services would no longer be required.

Moxon, Metcalfe and Phil Robinson all compiled career-best first-class aggregates, the last-mentioned managing just one Championship century while maintaining a steady consistency. But miserable luck with injuries meant that Kevin Sharp had little opportunity to approach his benefit season in style, though he took some advantage of favourable conditions when he did get to the middle. Given that Yorkshire's prospects were not helped by a collective inability to hold reasonable chances, notably at slip, it was an indication of how things went for them that their most reliable catcher, David Byas, suffered a lean time with the bat. Indeed, with Simon Kellett emerging as a leading candidate for regular inclusion, the tall left-hander's future became distinctly clouded.

Another player to make an interesting mark was Craig White, a young all-rounder born in Morley, near Leeds, who learned his cricket in Australia. Arriving to join the Academy, he immediately impressed Oldham sufficiently to be included in the senior squad. In the event, he did little either as a batsman or with his off-spin, but he looked very much the part and Yorkshire were convinced that, after another winter in Australia, he would figure prominently in their plans.

The team made a disastrous start, losing their first four Championship fixtures and four of the opening five games in the Sunday League. Losing to the Combined Universities – at Headingley – put them out of the Benson and Hedges Cup at the qualifying stages for the third time in a row. They followed on in three out of four Championship matches in late July and August, but four generous declarations subsequently enabled them to pick up useful points, and they also won seven of their last nine Sunday games to finish with a much needed flourish. In the NatWest Bank Trophy, Yorkshire became the first side to reach the last eight without losing a wicket, only to collapse miserably against Hampshire at Southampton. The consequent defeat merely reinforced the doubts about their temperament. – John Callaghan.

651

YORKSHIRE 1990

[Bill Smith]

Back row: D. Gough, P. J. Berry, M. K. Bore (Academy coach), C. Shaw, D. Byas, C. S. Pickles, S. A. Kellett, N. G. Nicholson, I. J. Houseman. Middle row: W. P. Morton (physiotherapist), R. J. Blakey, P. W. Jarvis, S. D. Fletcher, P. J. Hartley, P. E. Robinson, S. N. Hartley, J. D. Batty, A. P. Grayson, M. J. Doidge. Front row: A. Sidebottom, D. L. Bairstow, D. E. V. Padgett (coach), S. Oldham (cricket manager), M. D. Moxon (captain), A. A. Metcalfe, P. Carrick, K. Sharp.

YORKSHIRE RESULTS

All first-class matches – Played 24: Won 5, Lost 9, Drawn 10.

County Championship matches – Played 22: Won 5, Lost 9, Drawn 8.

Bonus points – Batting 52, Bowling 55.

Competition placings – Britannic Assurance County Championship, 10th; NatWest Bank Trophy, q-f; Benson and Hedges Cup, 3rd in Group C; Refuge Assurance League, 6th equal.

BRITANNIC ASSURANCE CHAMPIONSHIP AVERAGES

BATTING

	Birthplace	*M*	*I*	*NO*	*R*	*HI*	*Avge*
‡A. A. Metcalfe	*Horsforth*	21	40	3	1,854	194*	50.10
‡K. Sharp	*Leeds*	8	12	5	316	53*	45.14
A. P. Grayson	*Ripon*	4	7	4	135	44*	45.00
‡P. E. Robinson	*Keighley*	22	38	7	1,389	150*	44.80
‡M. D. Moxon	*Barnsley*	19	36	5	1,353	218*	43.64
S. A. Kellett	*Mirfield*	14	25	2	699	75*	30.39
C. S. Pickles	*Mirfield*	15	21	7	424	57*	30.28
‡D. L. Bairstow	*Bradford*	5	6	0	179	61	29.83
‡R. J. Blakey	*Huddersfield*	22	39	7	928	111	29.00
D. Byas	*Kilham*	17	27	3	693	83	28.87
‡A. Sidebottom	*Barnsley*	2	4	0	104	38	26.00
‡P. Carrick	*Armley*	18	22	2	515	64	25.75
‡P. W. Jarvis	*Redcar*	15	16	4	212	43*	17.66
‡P. J. Hartley	*Keighley*	16	14	1	215	75	16.53
C. White	*Morley Hall*	8	9	1	106	38	13.25
C. A. Chapman	*Bradford*	2	4	0	47	20	11.75
D. Gough	*Barnsley*	13	16	5	116	24	10.54
J. D. Batty	*Bradford*	7	5	2	30	21	10.00
‡S. D. Fletcher	*Keighley*	10	13	3	39	19	3.90
P. J. Berry	*Saltburn*	2	4	4	45	31*	–

Also batted: I. J. Houseman (*Harrogate*) (2 matches) 0*.

* *Signifies not out.*   ‡ *Denotes county cap.*

The following played a total of ten three-figure innings for Yorkshire in County Championship matches – A. A. Metcalfe 6, M. D. Moxon 2, R. J. Blakey 1, P. E. Robinson 1.

BOWLING

	O	*M*	*R*	*W*	*BB*	*5W/i*	*Avge*
P. Carrick	601	173	1,570	46	5-49	3	34.13
S. D. Fletcher	268.5	58	936	27	5-94	1	34.66
P. J. Hartley	481.1	79	1,754	48	6-57	2	36.54
P. W. Jarvis	405.2	68	1,393	37	4-53	0	37.64
D. Gough	256.4	43	984	24	4-68	0	41.00
C. S. Pickles	296.1	59	1,107	25	3-56	0	44.28
J. D. Batty	195	29	722	12	4-76	0	60.16

Also bowled: P. J. Berry 44.3–4–172–2; D. Byas 69–14–253–3; A. P. Grayson 63–13–227–1; I. J. Houseman 30–6–129–0; A. A. Metcalfe 9.1–0–88–0; M. D. Moxon 57–9–175–3; P. E. Robinson 3.3–0–28–1; A. Sidebottom 44–9–121–4; C. White 122–12–519–9.

Wicket-keepers: R. J. Blakey 34 ct, 8 st; D. L. Bairstow 9 ct; C. White 1 ct.

Leading Fielders: D. Byas 19, P. E. Robinson 18.

YORKSHIRE v NORTHAMPTONSHIRE

At Leeds, April 26, 27, 28, 30. Northamptonshire won by an innings and 50 runs. Northamptonshire 24 pts, Yorkshire 1 pt. Toss: Northamptonshire. Put in on a pitch from which Ambrose made the occasional delivery lift sharply, Yorkshire collapsed. And though their bowlers claimed two early wickets in their turn, Fordham and Lamb took complete command, adding 393 in 100 overs, the highest partnership for any Northamptonshire wicket. The previous best was 376 for the sixth wicket between R. Subba Row and A. Lightfoot at The Oval in 1958. Lamb made his runs in 342 minutes, from 301 balls, hitting three sixes and 31 fours. Fordham's career-best, unbeaten 206 took 446 minutes, and in 378 deliveries he hit a six as well as 28 fours. Both batsmen took full advantage as Yorkshire stood back and waited for the declaration. Lamb's 235, his best for the county, was the highest innings by a Northamptonshire batsman against Yorkshire, and the total of 498 for three was the biggest for the county at Yorkshire's expense. Yorkshire did slightly better at the second attempt, Kellett completing his maiden first-class half-century as he resisted for 142 balls and hit five fours. Thomas, however, took three wickets without cost in eleven balls on the final morning to expose the middle order. Blakey, who came in at No. 10, had fallen ill during Northamptonshire's innings and White had taken over as wicket-keeper, subsequently catching Lamb.

Close of play: First day, Yorkshire 119-5 (C. White 9*, P. Carrick 10*); Second day, Northamptonshire 241-2 (A. Fordham 87*, A. J. Lamb 126*); Third day, Yorkshire 125-2 (S. A. Kellett 55*, P. E. Robinson 14*).

Yorkshire

S. A. Kellett c Fordham b Ambrose	0	–	lbw b Thomas	63
*A. A. Metcalfe c Fordham b Robinson	38	–	lbw b Capel	45
†R. J. Blakey b Ambrose	25	–	(10) b Robinson	0
P. E. Robinson c Ripley b Ambrose	30	–	b Thomas	22
C. White c Thomas b Ambrose	9	–	(3) lbw b Ambrose	9
D. Byas b Robinson	0	–	(5) c Ripley b Thomas	0
P. Carrick b Capel	37	–	(6) c Lamb b Robinson	23
A. Sidebottom c Fordham b Ambrose	16	–	(7) c Ripley b Capel	31
P. W. Jarvis b Capel	29	–	(8) c Ripley b Robinson	0
P. J. Berry not out	4	–	(9) not out	31
S. D. Fletcher c Robinson b Thomas	1	–	b Capel	19
B 4, l-b 5	9		B 4, l-b 2, w 1	7
	198			**250**

1/0 2/44 3/98 4/98 5/98   1/69 2/93 3/136 4/138 5/141
6/124 7/144 8/188 9/197   6/191 7/191 8/201 9/201

Bonus points – Yorkshire 1, Northamptonshire 4.

Bowling: *First Innings*—Ambrose 22-9-49-5; Thomas 12.2-2-45-1; Capel 16-4-40-2; Robinson 22-12-47-2; N. G. B. Cook 5-2-8-0. *Second Innings*—Ambrose 21-5-70-1; Thomas 13-1-47-3; Capel 23-6-72-3; Robinson 20-5-47-3; N. G. B. Cook 7-2-8-0.

Northamptonshire

W. Larkins b Jarvis	0	D. J. Capel not out	21
A. Fordham not out	206	B 3, l-b 16, n-b 1	20
R. J. Bailey c Byas b Sidebottom	16		
*A. J. Lamb c White b Berry	235	1/0 2/41 3/434 (3 wkts dec.)	498

G. Cook, †D. Ripley, J. G. Thomas, C. E. L. Ambrose, N. G. B. Cook and M. A. Robinson did not bat.

Bonus points – Northamptonshire 4 (Score at 100 overs: 337-2).

Bowling: Jarvis 23-3-90-1; Sidebottom 26-5-67-1; Fletcher 28-6-109-0; Byas 8-2-33-0; Carrick 23-4-89-0; Berry 21.5-1-101-1.

Umpires: J. H. Hampshire and D. R. Shepherd.

At Birmingham, May 3, 4, 5. YORKSHIRE lost to WARWICKSHIRE by seven wickets.

YORKSHIRE v ZIMBABWEANS

At Leeds, May 16, 17, 18. Drawn. Toss: Zimbabweans. Moxon, making his runs from 211 balls and hitting twenty boundaries, had the satisfaction of recording Yorkshire's first century of the season in the course of a patchy batting performance on a slow pitch. Once Metcalfe had fallen to a superb catch, the innings fell apart in the face of steady seam bowling. Pickles, however, saved Yorkshire's potential embarrassment by hammering eleven fours in a 45-ball half-century. After a long delay because of rain on the second day, Hartley had the visitors in trouble, gaining extra pace and bounce, and although Brandes followed his useful bowling with a determined defensive display, they were spared the indignity of the follow-on only because Moxon wanted to give some of his batsmen practice. Kellett had the unusual experience of being "retired out" by the umpires when he made way for White during this exercise. The Zimbabweans were finally set a victory target of 299, but, more realistically, Yorkshire left themselves with 67 overs in which to try to win the game. Brent frustrated them as he battled through the last 28 overs after Gough, taking three wickets in five balls, had initiated a collapse to 84 for five.

Close of play: First day, Zimbabweans 8-1 (A. H. Shah 2*, W. R. James 6*); Second day, Yorkshire 7-0 (S. A. Kellett 2*, A. A. Metcalfe 5*).

Yorkshire

*M. D. Moxon c Pycroft b Shah	.130	
A. A. Metcalfe c Brandes b Duers	49	– c Pycroft b Butchart ... 30
†R. J. Blakey c James b Brandes	5	– not out ... 58
S. A. Kellett lbw b Brandes	0	– (1) retired out ... 39
P. E. Robinson b Flower	13	
C. White c and b Flower	9	– (4) not out ... 12
D. Byas c Flower b Shah	3	
A. P. Grayson c James b Brandes	10	
C. S. Pickles not out	54	
P. J. Hartley b Duers	3	
D. Gough not out	7	
B 6, l-b 8, w 1	15	B 5, l-b 1, n-b 2 ... 8

1/93 2/126 3/126 4/188 5/218   (9 wkts dec.) 298   1/57 2/93   (2 wkts dec.) 147
6/220 7/225 8/261 9/290

Bowling: First Innings—Brandes 21–5–75–3; Dube 4–1–19–0; Butchart 7–1–19–0; Duers 18–5–63–2; Shah 26–7–46–2; Brent 6–1–29–0; Flower 16–4–33–2. *Second Innings*—Brandes 6–1–23–0; Dube 6–1–22–0; Duers 13–3–48–0; Butchart 10–1–39–1; Brent 2–0–9–0.

Zimbabweans

G. W. Flower c Robinson b Hartley	0	– c Hartley b Gough ... 12
A. H. Shah c Blakey b Hartley	10	– lbw b Gough ... 20
†W. R. James b Hartley	16	– lbw b Gough ... 0
*A. J. Pycroft lbw b Byas	18	– (6) b White ... 23
C. M. Robertson lbw b White	18	– c Kellett b White ... 15
G. A. Briant c Byas b Pickles	5	– (4) c Moxon b Pickles ... 35
J. P. Brent b White	17	– not out ... 34
I. P. Butchart c White b Pickles	18	– not out ... 15
E. A. Brandes b Gough	22	
K. G. Duers not out	11	
L. E. Dube c Robinson b Hartley	1	
B 2, l-b 8, w 1	11	L-b 5 ... 5

1/0 2/20 3/31 4/59 5/64   147   1/28 2/32 3/33   (6 wkts) 159
6/74 7/85 8/114 9/146   4/82 5/84 6/134

Bowling: First Innings—Hartley 9.5–1–27–4; Gough 10–1–21–1; Pickles 17–6–29–2; Byas 12–4–40–1; White 8–2–12–2; Grayson 4–2–8–0. *Second Innings*—Pickles 12–7–27–1; Gough 13–5–32–3; Byas 7–1–20–0; White 22–7–40–2; Grayson 13–4–35–0.

Umpires: B. Leadbeater and K. J. Lyons.

At Chesterfield, May 23, 24, 25. YORKSHIRE lost to DERBYSHIRE by 144 runs.

YORKSHIRE v HAMPSHIRE

At Leeds, May 26, 28, 29. Hampshire won by five wickets. Hampshire 23 pts, Yorkshire 7 pts. Toss: Yorkshire. Yorkshire batted carefully on an easy-paced pitch, Robinson leading the way with 60 from 147 balls. Maru bowled his slow left-arm spin accurately, until he was called on to keep wicket for the rest of the match when Parks injured a finger in the 76th over, and Shine gained reward for keeping a full length, but Yorkshire plundered 21 from the last two overs to gain the maximum batting points. Marshall held the Hampshire reply together with a workmanlike century, batting for almost four hours as he received 193 deliveries and hit one six and eighteen fours. The declaration by Nicholas, with a lead of 37, appeared to have left the game in no-man's-land, but Connor, finding some uneven bounce, suddenly broke the back of the Yorkshire second innings, taking three for 8 in the space of nineteen balls. Carrick and Pickles, the latter launching a furious counter-attack to make 57 from 65 balls with ten fours, rescued the situation, and Hampshire were left to make 215 from 47 overs. Yorkshire did not help themselves by setting defensive fields, which often allowed a single from every ball, and Robinson, at slip, missed Chris Smith on 30 and 34. Smith's 58 came from 88 deliveries and set the stage for his brother, Robin, to win the game with an unbeaten 51 from only 39 balls. Hampshire had seven balls to spare at the end.

Close of play: First day, Hampshire 28-0 (V. P. Terry 11*, C. L. Smith 14*); Second day, Yorkshire 83-1 (A. A. Metcalfe 35*, R. J. Blakey 15*).

Yorkshire

S. A. Kellett c Gower b Connor	56	– c sub b Turner 26
*A. A. Metcalfe c Maru b Connor	22	– c C. L. Smith b Connor 35
R. J. Blakey c Parks b Shine	17	– b Connor 20
P. E. Robinson lbw b Shine	60	– b Connor 24
D. Byas b Shine	29	– c Maru b Connor 0
†D. L. Bairstow c Connor b Turner	37	– lbw b Marshall 9
P. Carrick c Maru b Marshall	23	– c Gower b Marshall 32
P. J. Hartley c Terry b Shine	3	– c Terry b Nicholas 5
C. S. Pickles not out	13	– not out 57
D. Gough not out	7	– c Shine b Marshall 8
S. D. Fletcher (did not bat)		– c Gower b Connor 6
L-b 19, w 1, n-b 13	33	B 10, l-b 11, w 1, n-b 7 .. 29
	300	**251**

1/56 2/93 3/130 4/200 5/225 (8 wkts dec.) 300 1/45 2/84 3/100 4/100 5/113 251
5/259 7/279 8/288   6/138 7/153 8/186 9/230

Bonus points – Yorkshire 4, Hampshire 3.

Bowling: *First Innings*—Marshall 22-7-44-1; Shine 19-2-52-4; Maru 21-9-43-0; Connor 21-2-79-2; Turner 16.5-3-63-1. *Second Innings*—Shine 8-0-50-0; Marshall 22-5-51-3; Connor 27.5-3-96-5; Turner 9-5-19-1; Nicholas 6-1-14-1.

Hampshire

V. P. Terry lbw b Pickles	23	– b Fletcher 18
C. L. Smith c Kellett b Hartley	28	– c Bairstow b Gough 58
D. I. Gower lbw b Hartley	64	– c Robinson b Gough 33
R. A. Smith b Pickles	15	– not out 51
M. D. Marshall c Blakey b Carrick	117	– b Gough 28
*M. C. J. Nicholas lbw b Fletcher	0	– c Gough b Hartley 15
R. J. Maru c Bairstow b Gough	24		
†R. J. Parks not out	36	– (7) not out 1
I. J. Turner not out	0		
B 3, l-b 19, w 1, n-b 6	29	L-b 11 11
	337	**215**

1/53 2/61 3/99 4/178 (7 wkts dec.) 337 1/37 2/103 3/113 (5 wkts) 215
5/182 6/281 7/337   4/181 5/206

C. A. Connor and K. J. Shine did not bat.

Bonus points – Hampshire 4, Yorkshire 3.

Bowling: *First Innings*—Hartley 23–6–68–2; Fletcher 20–5–57–1; Carrick 15.4–6–46–1; Pickles 14–1–64–2; Gough 13–3–67–1; Byas 7–1–13–0. *Second Innings*—Hartley 15–3–52–1; Fletcher 14–1–66–1; Pickles 4–0–25–0; Gough 12.5–1–61–3.

Umpires: D. O. Oslear and A. G. T. Whitehead.

At Worcester, June 2, 4, 5. YORKSHIRE drew with WORCESTERSHIRE.

At Tunbridge Wells, June 6, 7, 8. YORKSHIRE drew with KENT.

YORKSHIRE v SURREY

At Harrogate, June 9, 11, 12. Drawn. Yorkshire 3 pts, Surrey 12 pts. Toss: Surrey. Surrey received eight extra points as the side batting last in a drawn game in which the scores finished level. The two captains came to an agreement after the first day had been washed out by rain. Bicknell put Yorkshire under pressure on a good pitch which had enough pace to interest the quicker bowlers, his first fifteen overs bringing him two wickets for 9 runs. Robinson, with 85 from 211 balls, began the recovery, and Carrick, with nine boundaries, also played well in an eighth-wicket stand worth 131 from 37 overs. Surrey were finally set a target of 281 in what became 73 overs and were hurried along by Ward, whose 71 needed only 96 balls as he hit eleven fours. Greig was even more forceful, racing to 72 from 71 deliveries with nine fours. He survived a difficult chance when 2 to backward short leg off White, who took career-best figures of five for 74 with his off-spin. In a hectic finish, Bicknell was run out attempting a bye to wicket-keeper Bairstow, whose throw from the final ball missed the stumps as Waqar Younis scrambled home for the bye which levelled the scores.

Close of play: First day, No play; Second day, Yorkshire 200-7 (P. E. Robinson 71*, P. Carrick 36*).

Yorkshire

*M. D. Moxon lbw b Waqar Younis	10	– not out	23
A. A. Metcalfe c Lynch b Bicknell	6	– c Lynch b Medlycott	1
R. J. Blakey b Waqar Younis	1	– not out	2
S. A. Kellett lbw b Feltham	24		
P. E. Robinson c Lynch b Medlycott	85		
†D. L. Bairstow c Ward b Bicknell	32		
C. White b Waqar Younis	2		
C. S. Pickles c and b Bicknell	0		
P. Carrick c Bicknell b Medlycott	64		
P. W. Jarvis b Feltham	7		
D. Gough not out	1		
B 7, l-b 8, w 7	22		

1/14 2/19 3/29 4/55 5/101   254   1/9   (1 wkt dec.) 26
6/110 7/114 8/245 9/252

Bonus points – Yorkshire 3, Surrey 4.

Bowling: *First Innings*—Waqar Younis 24–6–56–3; Bicknell 25–11–40–3; Feltham 18–4–45–2; Murphy 13–4–45–0; Medlycott 16–0–53–2. *Second Innings*—Medlycott 3.4–2–5–1; Feltham 3–0–21–0.

Surrey

Surrey forfeited their first innings.

R. I. Alikhan lbw b Pickles	31	M. P. Bicknell run out	0
G. S. Clinton c Robinson b White	5	Waqar Younis not out	1
G. P. Thorpe c Blakey b White	44	A. J. Murphy not out	0
†D. M. Ward c Blakey b Pickles	71		
M. A. Lynch c Bairstow b Jarvis	11	B 6, l-b 6, w 6	18
*I. A. Greig c Pickles b White	72		
K. T. Medlycott b White	6	1/41 2/45 3/147 4/166 5/183 (9 wkts) 280	
M. A. Feltham c Jarvis b White	21	6/204 7/270 8/270 9/279	

Bowling: Jarvis 17–4–60–1; Gough 6–1–24–0; Pickles 12–2–45–2; White 18–2–74–5; Carrick 20–6–65–0.

Umpires: J. C. Balderstone and D. S. Thompsett.

YORKSHIRE v WARWICKSHIRE

At Sheffield, June 20, 21, 22. Yorkshire won by two wickets. Yorkshire 20 pts, Warwickshire 4 pts. Toss: Yorkshire. Rain on all three days encouraged a series of declarations to set up a positive finish. Warwickshire were in trouble at 118 for six, but Ostler and Piper both achieved career-best first-class scores in a partnership worth 81 in 27 overs. Ostler played particularly well, his 61 coming from 114 balls and including ten fours. Hartley's return of six for 57 was also his best at this level. Only Metcalfe played with any assurance in the first innings for Yorkshire, who survived with a good deal of luck a very hostile spell from Donald. In contrast, Moles and Reeve scored readily in Warwickshire's second innings before the declaration set a target of 243 in 55 overs. Yorkshire took some time to get the run-chase under way, Moxon being in for 39 overs for his 46. Kellett, however, played extremely well. Although he needed some fortune after completing his half-century, being missed twice in the 50s off reasonably straightforward chances, he finished unbeaten with 75 from 83 deliveries, having hit two sixes and three fours. Benjamin bowled a long and persistent spell, but Robinson's 28 from seventeen balls turned the game Yorkshire's way, and when Jarvis hit his second ball for six over cover, they had scrambled home with two balls to spare. The match was contested in a very good spirit, both Moles and Moxon walking without hesitation for the thinnest of edges.

Close of play: First day, Warwickshire 207-7 (K. J. Piper 31*, A. A. Donald 2*); Second day, Yorkshire 123-5 (K. Sharp 22*, P. Carrick 1*).

Warwickshire

A. J. Moles c Blakey b Hartley	21	– not out	60
J. D. Ratcliffe b Gough	9	– run out	16
Asif Din lbw b Hartley	0	– lbw b Jarvis	0
G. W. Humpage lbw b Gough	23	– b Jarvis	12
*D. A. Reeve lbw b Moxon	30	– not out	42
R. G. Twose c Blakey b Hartley	15		
D. P. Ostler c Carrick b Gough	61		
†K. J. Piper c Moxon b Hartley	49		
A. A. Donald c Blakey b Hartley	4		
J. E. Benjamin c Moxon b Hartley	1		
T. A. Munton not out	1		
L-b 8, w 2, n-b 7	17	L-b 2, w 1, n-b 1	4

1/33 2/33 3/33 4/88 5/97	231	1/36 2/38 3/52 (3 wkts dec.) 134
6/118 7/199 8/212 9/222		

Bonus points – Warwickshire 2, Yorkshire 4.

Bowling: *First Innings*—Jarvis 22–6–52–0; Hartley 21.3–3–57–6; Gough 18–5–36–3; Pickles 9–5–33–0; Moxon 8–2–16–1; Carrick 13–5–29–0. *Second Innings*—Jarvis 8–0–43–2; Hartley 6–1–21–0; Pickles 9.3–0–34–0; Gough 8–0–34–0.

Yorkshire

*M. D. Moxon c Ratcliffe b Donald	3	– c Piper b Benjamin	46
A. A. Metcalfe c and b Munton	53	– c Moles b Benjamin	45
S. A. Kellett c Benjamin b Asif Din	15	– not out	75
†R. J. Blakey b Munton	1	– (5) c Piper b Benjamin	8
P. E. Robinson c Piper b Benjamin	14	– (6) c Humpage b Benjamin	28
K. Sharp not out	22	– (4) c Humpage b Munton	8
P. Carrick not out	1	– (8) run out	3
P. J. Hartley (did not bat)		– (7) b Donald	13
C. S. Pickles (did not bat)		– b Benjamin	1
P. W. Jarvis (did not bat)		– not out	7
L-b 8, n-b 3	11	B 3, l-b 5, n-b 1	9

1/14 2/64 3/75 4/88 5/105   (5 wkts dec.) 123   1/70 2/135 3/148 4/161   (8 wkts) 243
                                                                                            5/197 6/219 7/234 8/235

D. Gough did not bat.

Bonus points – Warwickshire 2.

Bowling: *First Innings*—Donald 12–3–30–1; Benjamin 16–4–37–1; Munton 18.3–6–34–2; Twose 4–0–9–0; Asif Din 3–1–5–1. *Second Innings*—Donald 13–0–65–1; Benjamin 20.4–2–83–5; Munton 15–1–63–1; Reeve 6–0–24–0.

Umpires: B. Leadbeater and D. O. Oslear.

At Cardiff, June 23, 25, 26. YORKSHIRE beat GLAMORGAN by five wickets.

At Leeds, June 30, July 1, 2. YORKSHIRE drew with INDIANS (See Indian tour section).

YORKSHIRE v NOTTINGHAMSHIRE

At Scarborough, July 4, 5, 6. Nottinghamshire won by five wickets. Nottinghamshire 17 pts, Yorkshire 4 pts. Toss: Nottinghamshire. After the first day had been lost to rain, both sides forfeited an innings. Yorkshire, put in on a typical Scarborough pitch which heavily favoured the batsmen, scored readily. Moxon, enjoying most of the strike for long spells, registered the county's first Championship hundred of the season, reaching three figures in less than three hours, having hit fifteen fours. His 123 came out of an opening stand of 175 in 52 overs with Metcalfe, who also batted well. Nottinghamshire were clearly happy to wait on events and had little trouble in meeting a target of 352 in 94 overs, although only once before had a bigger total been made in the last innings to beat Yorkshire – by Gloucestershire, who compiled 392 for four at Bristol in 1948. Yorkshire, fielding a weakened attack, paid a heavy price for missing Broad, who was 15 when Byas put him down at slip off Hartley. The left-hander completed his fifth century of the season from 165 balls, while Johnson made his 149 at a run a ball, hitting 21 fours. The Broad-Johnson partnership, which put on 187 in 37 overs, effectively settled the contest, and Nottinghamshire won with five wickets and 6.3 overs to spare.

Close of play: First day, No play; Second day, Yorkshire 304-3 (P. E. Robinson 47*, R. J. Blakey 26*).

Yorkshire

*M. D. Moxon c Robinson b Evans	123	†R. J. Blakey not out	46
A. A. Metcalfe c Pick b Evans	75	L-b 13, n-b 4	17
K. Sharp c Robinson b Afford	17		
P. E. Robinson not out	73	1/175 2/223 3/223	(3 wkts dec.) 351

D. Byas, C. White, P. Carrick, P. J. Hartley, D. Gough and I. J. Houseman did not bat.

Bonus points – Yorkshire 4, Nottinghamshire 1 (Score at 100 overs: 325-3).

Bowling: Stephenson 6–1–23–0; Cooper 25–5–69–0; Pick 20–2–74–0; Evans 22–4–73–2; Afford 29–7–87–1; Newell 1.2–0–12–0.

Yorkshire forfeited their second innings.

Nottinghamshire

Nottinghamshire forfeited their first innings.

B. C. Broad c Robinson b White 126	K. P. Evans not out 12
M. Newell b Hartley 0	
*R. T. Robinson c Sharp b Carrick ... 43	B 8, l-b 2, n-b 6 16
P. Johnson c and b White 149	
D. J. R. Martindale b Carrick 4	1/15 2/111 3/298 (5 wkts) 354
F. D. Stephenson not out 4	4/334 5/334

†B. N. French, K. E. Cooper, R. A. Pick and J. A. Afford did not bat.

Bowling: Hartley 18–2–75–1; Houseman 12–5–40–0; Carrick 23.3–4–69–2; Gough 8–0–46–0; White 22–3–99–2; Byas 4–0–15–0.

Umpires: H. D. Bird and R. Julian.

At Northampton, July 7, 9, 10. YORKSHIRE drew with NORTHAMPTONSHIRE.

At Uxbridge, July 18, 19, 20. YORKSHIRE lost to MIDDLESEX by seven wickets.

At Cheltenham, July 21, 23, 24. YORKSHIRE drew with GLOUCESTERSHIRE.

YORKSHIRE v SOMERSET

At Scarborough, July 25, 26, 27. Drawn. Yorkshire 6 pts, Somerset 6 pts. Toss: Somerset. Yorkshire, still with a much weakened attack, made an impressive start on a pitch offering the bowlers no hint of assistance. However, Hayhurst and Harden then shared in a partnership of 174 in 48 overs for the fourth wicket. Harden's 101 came from 145 balls and included fifteen fours; Hayhurst made his 170 from 285 deliveries with one six and 29 fours. Metcalfe, with 102 from 214 balls as he collected fourteen boundaries, led a solid Yorkshire reply, while Swallow bowled a good spell of off-spin, without luck, against his former county. Somerset recovered from a minor second-innings collapse through some robust hitting from Burns, which ended when Robinson claimed his first wicket in county cricket as Yorkshire assisted in the timing of the declaration. The target was 320 in what became 65 overs and Blakey, hitting two sixes and fifteen fours in 111 from only 155 deliveries, kept Yorkshire in touch. With Blakey and Kellett adding 116 in 28 overs, Yorkshire needed 152 from the last twenty overs, which became 85 from ten. Rose bowled an accurate spell for Somerset, and in an exciting finish Grayson tried to hit the last ball – a yorker from Mallender – for the necessary six. Instead he managed only 2.

Close of play: First day, Yorkshire 25-0 (M. D. Moxon 14*, A. A. Metcalfe 10*); Second day, Somerset 49-1 (S. J. Cook 30*, A. N. Hayhurst 11*).

Somerset

S. J. Cook b Fletcher 21	– c Blakey b Gough 53
P. M. Roebuck b Pickles 11	– c Byas b Fletcher 8
A. N. Hayhurst c Blakey b Gough 170	– c Byas b Pickles 24
*C. J. Tavaré c Robinson b Gough 14	– b Gough 0
R. J. Harden c Pickles b Batty 101	– b Pickles 24
†N. D. Burns c Moxon b Pickles 33	– c Metcalfe b Robinson 72
G. D. Rose c Batty b Gough 35	– c Blakey b Pickles 0
R. P. Lefebvre not out 3	– not out 25
I. G. Swallow not out 3	– not out 12
B 1, l-b 6, w 1, n-b 2 10	L-b 2, n-b 1 3

1/33 2/33 3/77 4/251 5/302	(7 wkts dec.) 401	1/21 2/85 3/85	(7 wkts dec.) 221
6/376 7/396		4/85 5/126	
		6/126 7/206	

A. N. Jones and N. A. Mallender did not bat.

Bonus points – Somerset 4, Yorkshire 2 (Score at 100 overs: 367-5).

Bowling: *First Innings*—Fletcher 22.5–6–47–1; Gough 15–3–77–3; Pickles 20–1–82–2; Batty 22–3–83–1; Moxon 6–0–24–0; Grayson 17–2–66–0; Byas 2–0–15–0. *Second Innings*—Fletcher 5–1–12–1; Gough 13–3–47–2; Pickles 15–1–56–3; Batty 8–2–41–0; Grayson 4–1–23–0; Byas 5–2–14–0; Moxon 3–1–6–0; Metcalfe 1.3–0–10–0; Robinson 1–0–10–1.

Yorkshire

*M. D. Moxon c Burns b Mallender	23	– lbw b Jones	4
A. A. Metcalfe c Jones b Roebuck	102	– b Rose	23
†R. J. Blakey c Hayhurst b Swallow	29	– c Swallow b Roebuck	111
S. A. Kellett c Roebuck b Swallow	15	– c Cook b Rose	57
P. E. Robinson c Burns b Rose	31	– c Lefebvre b Hayhurst	44
D. Byas b Jones	36	– b Hayhurst	32
A. P. Grayson not out	44	– (8) not out	16
C. S. Pickles not out	9	– (7) b Mallender	1
D. Gough (did not bat)		– not out	7
B 1, l-b 5, n-b 8	14	B 8, l-b 13	21

1/36 2/118 3/159 4/202 5/210   (6 wkts dec.) 303   1/4 2/57 3/173 4/244   (7 wkts) 316
6/277   5/274 6/280 7/298

J. D. Batty and S. D. Fletcher did not bat.

Bonus points – Yorkshire 4, Somerset 2.

Bowling: *First Innings*: Jones 18–1–78–1; Mallender 11–2–42–1; Lefebvre 15–2–40–0; Rose 15–2–41–1; Swallow 25.5–6–71–2; Roebuck 11–3–25–1. *Second Innings*—Jones 12–1–54–1; Mallender 15–0–69–1; Lefebvre 16–5–52–0; Rose 10–2–41–2; Swallow 7–2–35–0; Roebuck 2–0–25–1; Hayhurst 3–0–19–2.

Umpires: M. J. Kitchen and P. B. Wight.

YORKSHIRE v LEICESTERSHIRE

At Sheffield, July 28, 30, 31. Leicestershire won by eight wickets. Leicestershire 24 pts, Yorkshire 5 pts. Toss: Leicestershire. Boon, missed by Hartley from a hard return chance when 6, and Briers provided the visitors with a sound platform on a good pitch with plenty of pace. Potter also took full advantage of an inexperienced attack, his unbeaten 109 coming from 192 balls with two sixes and eight fours. Only Hartley, the sole capped bowler, threatened the Leicestershire batsmen's security. When Yorkshire replied, Agnew swept through some feeble resistance to his best figures of the season. Despite an unbeaten 36 by Grayson, who displayed a sound batting technique in his second Championship match, Yorkshire had to follow on for the first time in four years. They did little better at the second attempt, until Byas and Kellett put on 83 in 36 overs for the fifth wicket. Even so, only a late flourish from Pickles stretched Yorkshire's innings into the third afternoon. Wicket-keeper Nixon equalled the Leicestershire record for catches in a match with eight, and Mullally bowled accurately for his career-best four for 59.

Close of play: First day, Yorkshire 18-1 (M. D. Moxon 12*, S. A. Kellett 5*); Second day, Yorkshire 116-4 (S. A. Kellett 53*, D. Byas 23*).

Leicestershire

T. J. Boon lbw b Hartley	76	– c Moxon b Pickles	11
*N. E. Briers c Batty b Hartley	45	– b Hartley	21
J. J. Whitaker c Byas b Hartley	23	– not out	38
P. Willey c Blakey b Hartley	47	– not out	18
L. Potter not out	109		
J. D. R. Benson lbw b Hartley	0		
W. K. M. Benjamin c Kellett b Batty	16		
†P. A. Nixon b Batty	33		
J. P. Agnew not out	4		
B 1, l-b 10, w 2, n-b 10	23	N-b 2	2

1/121 2/152 3/161 4/271 5/271   (7 wkts dec.) 376   1/27 2/35   (2 wkts) 90
6/294 7/372

G. J. Parsons and A. D. Mullally did not bat.

Bonus points – Leicestershire 4, Yorkshire 3.

Bowling: *First Innings*—Hartley 26–2–106–5; Gough 15–3–53–0; Pickles 20–7–65–0; Batty 32–4–124–2; Moxon 5–0–12–0; Grayson 1–0–5–0. *Second Innings*—Hartley 7–1–20–1; Gough 7–1–34–0; Pickles 4–0–9–1; Byas 4–0–20–0; Moxon 2–0–7–0.

Yorkshire

*M. D. Moxon c Nixon b Benjamin	21	– b Mullally	17
A. A. Metcalfe c Benson b Agnew	1	– c Benson b Agnew	1
S. A. Kellett c Nixon b Mullally	47	– (4) c Nixon b Mullally	54
†R. J. Blakey c Nixon b Agnew	36	– (3) c Nixon b Mullally	12
P. E. Robinson c Potter b Mullally	7	– c Nixon b Mullally	4
P. Byas run out	5	– b Willey	81
A. P. Grayson not out	36	– c Nixon b Parsons	11
C. S. Pickles lbw b Agnew	14	– not out	56
P. J. Hartley c Nixon b Agnew	0	– c Willey b Agnew	7
D. Gough lbw b Agnew	24	– c Briers b Agnew	2
J. D. Batty b Benjamin	2	– run out	0
B 1, l-b 2, w 1, n-b 3	7	B 7, l-b 7, n-b 3	17

1/6 2/34 3/107 4/107 5/118   **200**   1/1 2/33 3/38 4/50 5/133   **262**
5/130 7/158 8/158 9/193   6/156 7/218 8/247 9/249

Bonus points – Yorkshire 2, Leicestershire 4.

Bowling: *First Innings*—Benjamin 19.5–3–78–2; Agnew 21–4–54–5; Parsons 7–2–20–0; Mullally 15–2–45–2. *Second Innings*—Agnew 22–4–54–3; Benjamin 15–5–40–0; Parsons 23–7–61–1; Mullally 25–9–59–4; Willey 16–4–29–1; Potter 4–2–5–0.

Umpires: K. J. Lyons and P. B. Wight.

YORKSHIRE v LANCASHIRE

At Leeds, August 4, 6, 7. Drawn. Yorkshire 5 pts, Lancashire 8 pts. Toss: Lancashire. A solid batting performance on an easy-paced pitch put Lancashire in control of the match. Mendis, Fowler and Atherton made sure of a substantial total, and DeFreitas added impetus with 66 from 85 balls, hitting three sixes and six fours. Carrick bowled his 36 overs straight through, with breaks for only lunch and tea, and gained some slow turn. Despite the absence of DeFreitas, who had bruised his left big toe while batting, Lancashire brought about a remarkable Yorkshire collapse. Atherton's leg-spin claimed five for 26, his best bowling figures to date, and only a vigorous effort by the tail prevented total disaster. When Yorkshire followed on, Metcalfe, whose 146 came from 325 balls and included sixteen fours, organised a revival, to which Pickles added substance after another middle-order failure. Lancashire were left needing 148 in thirteen overs. They made a brave effort as Lloyd struck a superb 70 from 38 balls, hitting four sixes and two fours, and adding 74 in six overs with Atherton. Yorkshire had eight men on the boundary, and while this tactic allowed a number of twos, the target proved just too stiff. As wickets fell Lancashire, who had bowled their overs slowly throughout, settled for a draw.

Close of play: First day, Yorkshire 26-1 (A. A. Metcalfe 12*, D. Gough 0*); Second day, Yorkshire 90-0 (M. D. Moxon 32*, A. A. Metcalfe 50*).

Lancashire

G. D. Mendis c Metcalfe b Gough	54	– lbw b Fletcher	10
G. Fowler c Moxon b Carrick	43	– c Moxon b Fletcher	6
M. A. Atherton c Kellett b Jarvis	64	– (6) st Blakey b Fletcher	25
N. H. Fairbrother c Fletcher b Carrick	7	– c Blakey b Jarvis	7
G. D. Lloyd c Blakey b Pickles	36	– (3) c Pickles b Jarvis	70
M. Watkinson b Jarvis	33	– (5) run out	1
P. A. J. DeFreitas st Blakey b Carrick	66	– b Jarvis	2
†W. K. Hegg st Blakey b Carrick	29	– not out	0
*D. P. Hughes b Jarvis	14		
P. J. Martin not out	10		
B. P. Patterson not out	4		
L-b 10, n-b 1	11	B 1, l-b 11	12

1/94 2/116 3/123 4/195 5/230   (9 wkts dec.) **369**   1/15 2/26 3/49 4/55   (7 wkts) **133**
6/253 7/328 8/349 9/355   5/129 6/131 7/133

Bonus points – Lancashire 4, Yorkshire 4.

Bowling: *First Innings*—Jarvis 21–2–91–3; Fletcher 15–3–55–0; Pickles 16–4–69–1; Gough 12–3–37–1; Carrick 36–10–107–4. *Second Innings*—Jarvis 6.4–0–59–3; Fletcher 6–0–62–3.

Yorkshire

*M. D. Moxon c Fowler b Atherton	14	– b Patterson	39
A. A. Metcalfe c Atherton b Patterson	31	– c Atherton b Watkinson	146
D. Gough lbw b Patterson	3	– (10) c Fowler b Atherton	13
†R. J. Blakey c Fairbrother b Atherton	22	– (3) b Watkinson	3
S. A. Kellett b Watkinson	25	– (8) run out	15
P. E. Robinson c Atherton b Watkinson	2	– (4) b Martin	11
D. Byas c Hughes b Atherton	0	– (5) c Hegg b Martin	9
P. Carrick not out	34	– (6) b Martin	5
C. S. Pickles b Martin	21	– (7) c Fowler b Watkinson	39
P. W. Jarvis c Fowler b Atherton	27	– (9) not out	20
S. D. Fletcher c Hegg b Atherton	0	– c Patterson b Atherton	0
B 1, l-b 1, n-b 7	9	B 3, l-b 11, n-b 14	28

1/23 2/41 3/50 4/94 5/98   188
6/100 7/100 8/154 9/188

1/115 2/118 3/155 4/167 5/197   328
6/262 7/283 8/296 9/328

Bonus points – Yorkshire 1, Lancashire 4.

Bowling: *First Innings*—Patterson 18–3–77–2; Martin 16–2–54–1; Atherton 11–5–26–5; Watkinson 11–4–29–2. *Second Innings*—Patterson 18–0–88–1; Watkinson 38–14–94–3; Atherton 27.2–5–71–2; Hughes 9–6–6–0; Martin 18–1–48–3; DeFreitas 2–0–7–0.

Umpires: B. Leadbeater and N. T. Plews.

At Eastbourne, August 8, 9, 10. YORKSHIRE beat SUSSEX by an innings and 5 runs.

YORKSHIRE v ESSEX

At Middlesbrough, August 11, 13. Essex won by an innings and 11 runs. Essex 24 pts, Yorkshire 4 pts. Toss: Yorkshire. Nothing went right for Yorkshire from the moment Moxon elected to field first. The pitch, which looked slightly green and hard, did not play as expected. Still, Essex would have been in trouble had Waugh not struck a career-best 207 not out, the highest score on the ground since first-class cricket was introduced there in 1956. The Australian batted for 346 minutes, faced 288 balls and hit four sixes and 26 fours. He shared two crucial partnerships, 123 with Stephenson and 92 with Garnham. Although Metcalfe and Sharp gave Yorkshire a solid start with a second-wicket stand worth 91 in 27 overs, they were forced to follow on for the third time in four matches. There was some uneven bounce, and Such achieved slow turn with his off-spin, but the conditions did not explain why Yorkshire lost nineteen wickets for 239 runs in 67 overs. The failure of Moxon, who received two balls which lifted sharply, appeared to unsettle his colleagues, and Essex held some fine catches as Foster, Pringle and Andrew made the most of Yorkshire's uncertainty. With Essex claiming the extra half-hour, the match ended on the second day.

Close of play: First day, Essex 308-8 (M. E. Waugh 178*, J. H. Childs 0*).

Essex

N. Shahid c Robinson b Jarvis	3	S. J. W. Andrew c Robinson b Carrick	0
J. P. Stephenson b Gough	62	J. H. Childs c Byas b Jarvis	11
P. J. Prichard b Jarvis	1	P. M. Such b Jarvis	2
M. E. Waugh not out	207		
N. Hussain c Blakey b Pickles	6	L-b 5, w 1, n-b 1	7
†M. A. Garnham c Robinson b Gough	35		
*D. R. Pringle c Byas b Pickles	9	1/20 2/22 3/145 4/160 5/252 351
N. A. Foster c Robinson b Carrick	8	6/279 7/306 8/308 9/343	

Bonus points – Essex 4, Yorkshire 3 (Score at 100 overs: 343-8).

Bowling: Jarvis 23.5–4–53–4; Hartley 20–2–71–0; Pickles 20–5–68–2; Gough 14–1–54–2; Carrick 22–6–88–2; Moxon 3–0–12–0.

Yorkshire

*M. D. Moxon c Stephenson b Foster	1	– c Waugh b Pringle	27
A. A. Metcalfe c Shahid b Pringle	60	– c Garnham b Andrew	0
K. Sharp b Such	42	– c Pringle b Foster	16
P. E. Robinson b Pringle	3	– c Stephenson b Andrew	39
†R. J. Blakey c Prichard b Pringle	5	– c Garnham b Andrew	26
D. Byas lbw b Foster	7	– c Shahid b Childs	6
P. Carrick b Such	19	– c Shahid b Andrew	3
C. S. Pickles c Hussain b Such	20	– c Shahid b Such	19
P. J. Hartley lbw b Foster	0	– c Garnham b Andrew	5
P. W. Jarvis not out	8	– b Such	0
D. Gough lbw b Foster	1	– not out	0
L-b	14	B 8, l-b 9, n-b 2	19
	180		**160**

1/10 2/101 3/104 4/119 5/120 6/143 7/151 8/151 9/171

1/2 2/30 3/57 4/109 5/124 6/126 7/154 8/160 9/160

Bonus points – Yorkshire 1, Essex 4.

Bowling: *First Innings*—Foster 16–3–63–4; Andrew 6–1–28–0; Pringle 11–6–15–3; Childs 5–0–26–0; Such 19–6–34–3. *Second Innings*—Foster 6–0–14–1; Andrew 13.1–2–55–5; Such 11–3–39–2; Pringle 6–1–18–1; Childs 4–0–17–1.

Umpires: B. Hassan and A. A. Jones.

At Manchester, August 18, 19, 20, 21. YORKSHIRE drew with LANCASHIRE.

YORKSHIRE v MIDDLESEX

At Leeds, August 23, 24, 25, 27. Middlesex won by 64 runs. Middlesex 23 pts, Yorkshire 5 pts. Toss: Middlesex. Haynes, who achieved 2,000 first-class runs for the season when 30, plundered a weakened Yorkshire attack on an easy-paced pitch, making his first 51 runs out of a total of 61 and going on to hit a hundred before lunch. His 131 took only 145 balls and included 26 boundaries. Gatting, despite a hamstring strain, made sure that the tempo did not slacken while Gough was rewarded for his persistence with career-best bowling figures of four for 68. Moxon held the Yorkshire reply together, but Hughes, during a long spell, took three for 8 in 22 balls. The pressure was kept up by the accurate Tufnell. Moxon's 95, which included one six and fourteen fours, came from 206 deliveries, and there was some spirited resistance from the bottom half of the order. Haynes and Roseberry tightened Middlesex's grip with an opening partnership of 104, while Emburey hammered a brisk 51 from 84 balls. Yorkshire had little chance of making the 331 needed for victory and Cowans, claiming two wickets for no runs in less than two overs, soon had them in trouble. Robinson battled defiantly in a lost cause, but the inexperienced Taylor, bowling an effective line, cut through the middle order and took five wickets in an innings for the first time.

Close of play: First day, Middlesex 377; Second day, Yorkshire 229-6 (P. Carrick 33*, C. S. Pickles 7*); Third day, Yorkshire 13-0 (M. D. Moxon 5*, A. A. Metcalfe 7*).

Middlesex

D. L. Haynes lbw b Pickles	131	– b Batty	57
M. A. Roseberry c Blakey b Gough	2	– c Grayson b Gough	80
M. R. Ramprakash c Blakey b Jarvis	29	– c Robinson b Batty	29
K. R. Brown c Byas b Jarvis	56	– c Pickles b Batty	0
*M. W. Gatting c Robinson b Carrick	91	– (7) lbw b Gough	10
†P. R. Downton b Pickles	12	– (5) b Jarvis	1
J. E. Emburey lbw b Gough	0	– (6) c Metcalfe b Jarvis	51
S. P. Hughes c Moxon b Jarvis	4	– (9) not out	10
P. C. R. Tufnell c Grayson b Gough	37	– (8) c Robinson b Batty	5
C. W. Taylor not out	0		
N. G. Cowans c Metcalfe b Gough	0		
B 1, l-b 14	15	B 5, l-b 2, w 1	8
	377	(8 wkts dec.)	**251**

1/10 2/116 3/182 4/270 5/304 6/305 7/328 8/373 9/377

1/104 2/156 3/158 4/159 5/190 6/208 7/219 8/251

Bonus points – Middlesex 4, Yorkshire 3 (Score at 100 overs: 355-7).

Bowling: *First Innings*—Jarvis 23–4–74–3; Gough 17.5–2–68–4; Pickles 20–2–80–2; Moxon 2–0–23–0; Byas 2–0–14–0; Carrick 29–8–61–1; Batty 13–3–42–0. *Second Innings*—Jarvis 16–3–51–2; Gough 19–6–43–2; Carrick 14–5–35–0; Pickles 9–1–39–0; Batty 23–4–76–4.

Yorkshire

*M. D. Moxon c Downton b Tufnell	95	– c Hughes b Cowans	7
A. A. Metcalfe c Downton b Hughes	26	– lbw b Cowans	26
A. P. Grayson b Hughes	4	– c sub b Cowans	18
P. E. Robinson c Downton b Hughes	0	– c Downton b Taylor	72
†R. J. Blakey c and b Tufnell	14	– c Emburey b Taylor	16
D. Byas c Emburey b Hughes	36	– lbw b Cowans	12
P. Carrick c Emburey b Hughes	34	– c Downton b Taylor	20
C. S. Pickles c and b Cowans	37	– c Emburey b Taylor	1
P. W. Jarvis b Cowans	14	– not out	43
D. Gough lbw b Hughes	21	– lbw b Cowans	9
J. D. Batty not out	0	– c Downton b Taylor	21
B 1, l-b 9, w 1, n-b 6	17	B 10, l-b 8, w 1, n-b 2	21

1/63 2/73 3/81 4/108 5/158   298   1/34 2/34 3/60 4/97 5/125   266
6/206 7/238 8/266 9/294   6/172 7/176 8/192 9/233

Bonus points – Yorkshire 2, Middlesex 3 (Score at 100 overs: 244-7).

Bowling: *First Innings*—Cowans 22–6–55–2; Hughes 28.2–5–101–5; Taylor 14–2–46–1; Emburey 19–6–43–0; Tufnell 26–9–41–2; Haynes 2–0–2–0. *Second Innings*—Cowans 21–6–67–5; Hughes 23–2–66–0; Emburey 12–2–32–0; Tufnell 21–5–50–0; Taylor 14.5–4–33–5.

Umpires: J. W. Holder and D. S. Thompsett.

At Scarborough, September 1. YORKSHIRE lost to MICHAEL PARKINSON'S WORLD XI by 7 runs (See Other Matches, 1990).

At Scarborough, September 6. YORKSHIRE beat THE YORKSHIREMEN by eight wickets (See Other Matches, 1990).

YORKSHIRE v DERBYSHIRE

At Scarborough, September 7, 8, 9, 10. Yorkshire won by four wickets. Yorkshire 22 pts, Derbyshire 4 pts. Toss: Derbyshire. Much of the first day was washed out by rain, but next day Derbyshire scored freely in ideal batting conditions, with Yorkshire conceding three centuries in an innings for the first time since 1986 against Nottinghamshire at Worksop. Bishop struck some lusty blows in reaching his maiden hundred from 99 deliveries. Derbyshire were equally vulnerable in the field as Metcalfe and Robinson shared a partnership of 293 in 70 overs – the best for the county's third wicket since 1939. Yorkshire declared 98 behind and were content to sit back and wait for a target, helping the visitors along with some gentle bowling which O'Gorman and Roberts cheerfully despatched in a stand worth 109 in 23 overs. Yorkshire required 300 in 59 overs, and Moxon gave them a splendid start with 94 from 122 balls, hitting a six and eleven fours. Blakey maintained the momentum with an unbeaten 91 from 88 deliveries, putting on 70 in eleven overs with Carrick for the sixth wicket. For Derbyshire, Bishop and Malcolm bowled too short on a slow pitch and were inevitably expensive, although Yorkshire had only one ball to spare in the end. Carrick became the eighth Yorkshire player to complete the double of 9,000 first-class runs and 900 wickets for the county.

Close of play: First day, Derbyshire 114-2 (J. E. Morris 88*, C. J. Adams 0*); Second day, Yorkshire 8-0 (M. D. Moxon 6*, A. A. Metcalfe 1*); Third day, Derbyshire 13-0 (J. E. Morris 8*, P. D. Bowler 1*).

Derbyshire

P. D. Bowler c Blakey b Jarvis	4	– (2) c Blakey b Jarvis	13
J. E. Morris c and b Carrick	109	– (1) c Byas b Hartley	36
T. J. G. O'Gorman b Pickles	21	– not out	82
C. J. Adams c Metcalfe b Carrick	101	– c Robinson b Hartley	17
B. Roberts b Pickles	31	– not out	44
*K. J. Barnett c Robinson b Carrick	47		
†K. M. Krikken c Pickles b Carrick	35		
I. R. Bishop not out	103		
A. E. Warner not out	10		
L-b 13, n-b 1	14	B 2, l-b 5, n-b 2	9

1/4 2/95 3/158 4/229 5/323   (7 wkts dec.) 475   1/47 2/61 3/92   (3 wkts dec.) 201
5/326 7/411

D. E. Malcolm and G. Miller did not bat.

Bonus points – Derbyshire 4, Yorkshire 2 (Score at 100 overs: 337-6).

Bowling: *First Innings*—Jarvis 29–1–124–1; Hartley 23–2–109–0; Pickles 20.4–4–72–2; Carrick 39–14–90–4; Batty 17–3–67–0. *Second Innings*—Jarvis 12–4–32–1; Hartley 15–6–58–2; Batty 11–2–42–0; Carrick 8–2–10–0; Robinson 2.3–0–18–0; Metcalfe 2–0–34–0.

Yorkshire

*M. D. Moxon b Bishop	14	– c Adams b Miller	94
A. A. Metcalfe not out	150	– lbw b Warner	32
S. A. Kellett b Warner	22	– b Warner	2
P. E. Robinson not out	150	– run out	14
†R. J. Blakey (did not bat)		– not out	91
D. Byas (did not bat)		– c Krikken b Malcolm	13
P. Carrick (did not bat)		– b Bishop	31
C. S. Pickles (did not bat)		– not out	4
B 9, l-b 18, w 7, n-b 7	41	B 9, l-b 7, n-b 3	19

1/34 2/84   (2 wkts dec.) 377   1/83 2/109 3/148   (6 wkts) 300
4/178 5/225 6/295

P. J. Hartley, P. W. Jarvis and J. D. Batty did not bat.

Bonus points – Yorkshire 4 (Score at 100 overs: 372-2).

Bowling: *First Innings*—Bishop 15–3–50–1; Malcolm 15–1–56–0; Warner 14–3–43–1; Miller 25–2–92–0; Barnett 21–1–58–0; Morris 9–0–44–0; Adams 1.4–0–7–0. *Second Innings*—Bishop 16.5–1–61–1; Malcolm 16–1–83–1; Warner 16–0–64–2; Barnett 1–0–8–0; Miller 9–0–68–1.

Umpires: H. D. Bird and J. D. Bond.

At Nottingham, September 18, 19, 20, 21. YORKSHIRE beat NOTTINGHAMSHIRE by four wickets.

OXFORD UNIVERSITY 1990

[Bill Smith]

Back row: L. J. Lenham (*coach*), R. W. D. Trevelyan, P. S. Gerrans, W. M. van der Merwe, G. J. Turner, P. D. Lunn, D. M. Curtis, M. J. Russell.
Front row: I. M. Henderson, S. D. Weale, R. E. Morris (*captain*), D. A. Hagan, M. A. Crawley.

THE UNIVERSITIES IN 1990

OXFORD

President: M. J. K. Smith (St Edmund Hall)
Hon. Treasurer: Dr S. R. Porter (Nuffield College)

Captain: R. E. Morris (Dyffryn Conwy, Llanrwst and Oriel)
Secretary: S. A. Almaer (Ilford County HS and St Catherine's)

Captain for 1991: G. J. Turner (St Stithian's, University of Cape Town and St Anne's)
Secretary: M. J. Russell (Medina HS, Isle of Wight, and Pembroke)

The season heralded the revival, long overdue, of Oxford University as respected opponents in English first-class cricket. The excellent pitches prepared at The Parks by head groundsman Richard Sula and the controversial new ball played their part, but there were other factors, too. Not the least were the willingness of St Anne's to admit sportsmen of high academic ability, the return of several old Blues as post-graduates, and the use of a full-time coach, Les Lenham, who instilled a more positive and professional attitude. It was at his suggestion that all players wore sweaters resembling those awarded to Blues, and although some spectators regretted the loss of a multicoloured array, the uniformity was accepted by the team.

The 1990 captain, Russell Morris, had eight Blues at his disposal, four of them post-graduates, while the new intake included Willem van der Merwe and Graeme Turner, both of whom had played for Western Province in South Africa. This provided Morris with a well-balanced side little affected by the demands of examiners.

Thanks to their strongest batting for many years, Oxford were unbeaten by a first-class side, a feat they had not achieved since the Second World War. The line-up was headed by the 1989 captain, Mark Crawley, who enjoyed an outstanding season with an average of more than 94 in his games at The Parks, where he hit the University's two centuries – against Glamorgan and Leicestershire – and 91 not out against Lancashire. Mike Kilborn's 83 against Glamorgan and 95 against Lancashire were his highest first-class scores, Morris's 96 against Surrey was his best in senior cricket, and van der Merwe, a powerful left-hander, gave the counties the sort of punishment more often inflicted on university bowlers. One result of this strength was that Morris began to bat when he won the toss, a shock to opponents accustomed to batting first. Their score of 289 for seven declared in the opening match was Oxford's highest in first-class games in The Parks for five years, and they passed 300 on three occasions. An average of 35 runs scored for each wicket lost, against 17 the previous year, underlined the improvement.

The bowling was more hostile and varied than in 1989. The new ball was shared by van der Merwe, Iain Henderson and Phil Gerrans, backed by Crawley who, having taken just one wicket in the previous two seasons, emerged as the leading wicket-taker with seventeen. The bulk of the slow bowling was shared by the off-spinners, Turner and Henry Davies, and Simon Weale (slow left-arm). With conditions so much in favour of batsmen, the almost identical haul of wickets to that of 1989, at a similar cost, was a real achievement. There was also an improvement in the Oxford out-cricket, though wicket-keeping remained weak.

In 1991 Turner, the new captain, will be without Crawley, van der Merwe (winner of the Gold Award in the Benson and Hedges match against Yorkshire), and Henderson, who have completed their studies. However, several Freshmen with outstanding credentials will be in residence, and there are high hopes that the renaissance will continue. – Paton Fenton.

OXFORD UNIVERSITY RESULTS

First-class matches – Played 9: Drawn 9.

FIRST-CLASS AVERAGES

BATTING AND FIELDING

	Birthplace	M	I	NO	R	HI	Avge	Ct/St
M. A. Crawley	Newton-le-Willows	9	10	3	620	105*	88.57	8
W. M. van der Merwe	Rustenburg, SA	7	7	3	272	84	68.00	4
M. J. Kilborn	Gunnedah, Australia	5	6	1	279	95	55.80	4
I. M. Henderson	Glapthorn	6	4	3	46	44	46.00	2
R. E. Morris	St Asaph	8	10	1	370	96	41.11	1
P. D. Lunn	Oxford	8	10	4	184	44*	30.66	1
G. J. Turner	Bulawayo, Rhodesia	8	10	0	258	59	25.80	4
D. M. Curtis	Salisbury, Rhodesia	4	4	0	89	43	22.25	0
H. R. Davies		4	4	2	36	24	18.00	0
D. A. Hagan	Wide Open	9	12	0	175	47	14.58	2
P. S. Gerrans	Melbourne, Australia	8	7	0	95	39	13.57	3
S. D. Weale	Knightsbridge	5	4	2	24	13	12.00	0

Also batted: S. A. Almaer (*Wanstead*) (1 match) 4 (2 ct); S. Chauhan (*Delhi, India*) (3 matches) 25, 4; J. E. McGrady (*Ryton, Co. Durham*) (6 matches) 14, 1 (2 st); M. J. Russell (*Lincoln*) (4 matches) 4, 4, 2 (1 ct); R. W. D. Trevelyan (*Folkestone*) (3 matches) 0 (2 ct); A. L. C. Winchester (1 match) 0*.

* *Signifies not out.*

M. A. Crawley played the two three-figure innings for Oxford University.

BOWLING

	O	M	R	W	BB	Avge
M. A. Crawley	190.2	30	673	17	6-92	39.58
G. J. Turner	177.2	36	680	10	3-100	68.00
P. S. Gerrans	181	31	618	9	3-86	68.66
I. M. Henderson	105.2	9	469	6	3-102	78.16

Also bowled: S. Chauhan 15–1–58–1; D. M. Curtis 1–0–8–0; H. R. Davies 54–6–261–3; P. D. Lunn 23–4–92–2; W. M. van der Merwe 112–23–341–3; S. D. Weale 50–8–251–1; A. L. C. Winchester 13–0–81–0.

OXFORD UNIVERSITY v GLAMORGAN

At Oxford, April 14, 16, 17. Drawn. Toss: Oxford University. Glamorgan responded to the invitation to bat with two century stands in succession. Morris put on 123 with Butcher and then 103 with Holmes, completing his own hundred in 298 minutes and striking fifteen fours. Crawley, bowling at a steady medium pace, took six of the seven wickets which fell before the county's declaration at 352, and before the second day was over he had begun the game's next hundred partnership, in company with Kilborn. He next added 74 with Hagan, who returned at the fall of the third wicket after being hit on the hand by the first ball of the innings. Crawley's unbeaten century, which took nearly five and a half hours, contained ten fours and helped his team to their highest first-class score in The Parks for five years. When Oxford declared Glamorgan made 55 without loss in the remaining half-hour of play.

Close of play: First day, Glamorgan 188-1 (H. Morris 73*, G. C. Holmes 36*); Second day, Oxford University 90-2 (M. J. Kilborn 45*, M. A. Crawley 16*).

Glamorgan

*A. R. Butcher c Lunn b Crawley	60		
H. Morris c and b Crawley	103		
G. C. Holmes c van der Merwe b Turner	62		
M. P. Maynard b Crawley	40	– (2) not out	32
I. Smith c van der Merwe b Crawley	17	– (1) not out	18
H. A. G. Anthony c Gerrans b Crawley	19		
N. G. Cowley c and b Crawley	13		
†M. L. Roberts not out	5		
B 9, l-b 9, w 5, n-b 10	33	L-b 2, n-b 3	5

1/123 2/226 3/278 4/301 5/325 (7 wkts dec.) 352
6/337 7/352

(no wkt) 55

S. J. Dennis, M. Frost and S. R. Barwick did not bat.

Bowling: *First Innings*—van der Merwe 15-3-43-0; Henderson 9-2-36-0; Gerrans 27-7-80-0; Crawley 27.3-4-92-6; Turner 16-3-52-1; Weale 10-3-31-0. *Second Innings*—Henderson 4-1-8-0; van der Merwe 2-0-24-0; Turner 2-0-21-0.

Oxford University

D. A. Hagan c Holmes b Cowley	47	P. S. Gerrans b Anthony	0
*R. E. Morris c Cowley b Dennis	16	S. D. Weale not out	7
M. J. Kilborn c Roberts b Holmes	83	B 2, l-b 9, w 2, n-b 9	22
G. J. Turner lbw b Barwick	5		
M. A. Crawley not out	103	1/41 2/54 3/165 (7 wkts dec.) 289
P. D. Lunn lbw b Dennis	5	4/239 5/262
W. M. van der Merwe lbw b Anthony	1	6/263 7/263

I. M. Henderson and †J. E. McGrady did not bat.

D. A. Hagan, when 0, retired hurt at 0 and resumed at 165.

Bowling: Anthony 20.4-5-72-2; Frost 20-5-33-0; Cowley 20-6-49-1; Barwick 15-6-16-1; Dennis 24-6-51-2; Smith 6-0-24-0; Holmes 8-2-33-1.

Umpires: J. D. Bond and A. G. T. Whitehead.

OXFORD UNIVERSITY v SOMERSET

At Oxford, April 18, 19, 20. Drawn. Toss: Oxford University. Rain restricted play to fewer than five hours on the last two days of this match, which had begun promisingly for Oxford when they took three wickets for 1 run, reducing Somerset to 58 for three. But their bowlers' success was put in perspective by former Blue Tavaré and Harden, who put on 188 for the next wicket. Replying to a total of 328 for six declared, Oxford also lost three early wickets, for 14 runs, before their former captains, Kilborn and Crawley, came to the rescue with a stand of 69. Lunn and van der Merwe increased the score to 144 in the time left by rain.

Close of play: First day, Oxford University 6-0 (D. A. Hagan 0*, S. A. Almaer 4*); Second day, Oxford University 60-3 (M. J. Kilborn 27*, M. A. Crawley 18*).

Somerset

S. J. Cook lbw b Gerrans	28	†N. D. Burns not out	28
P. M. Roebuck c Crawley		G. D. Rose c Crawley b Turner	32
b van der Merwe	26	B 10, l-b 8, w 3, n-b 11	32
J. J. E. Hardy c Almaer b Gerrans	0		
*C. J. Tavaré c Almaer b Henderson	83	1/57 2/57 3/58	(6 wkts dec.) 328
R. J. Harden c and b Henderson	99	4/246 5/277 6/328	

R. P. Lefebvre, I. G. Swallow, N. A. Mallender and A. N. Jones did not bat.

Bowling: van der Merwe 17–5–44–1; Henderson 17–1–92–2; Gerrans 24–8–56–2; Turner 11.2–4–41–1; Crawley 13–0–63–0; Weale 4–1–14–0.

Oxford University

D. A. Hagan c Roebuck b Jones	7	W. M. van der Merwe not out	18
S. A. Almaer b Rose	4		
M. J. Kilborn c and b Swallow	37	B 2, l-b 15, w 1, n-b 8	26
G. J. Turner b Jones	0		
*M. A. Crawley b Lefebvre	33	1/8 2/14 3/14	(5 wkts) 144
P. D. Lunn not out	19	4/83 5/95	

S. D. Weale, I. M. Henderson, †J. E. McGrady and P. S. Gerrans did not bat.

Bowling: Jones 16–8–17–2; Mallender 16–2–30–0; Rose 14–2–37–1; Lefebvre 13–5–23–1; Swallow 13–6–12–1; Roebuck 5–2–8–0.

Umpires: J. D. Bond and A. G. T. Whitehead.

†At Oxford, April 24, 25. Drawn. Berkshire 205 for nine dec. (M. L. Simmons 67; G. J. Turner five for 57) and 218 for six dec. (J. Barrett 77, D. J. M. Mercer 100 not out); Oxford University 209 for five dec. (W. M. van der Merwe 90 not out, G. J. Turner 81) and 179 for seven (M. J. Russell 57 not out).

OXFORD UNIVERSITY v HAMPSHIRE

At Oxford, May 3, 4, 5. Drawn. Toss: Hampshire. Oxford's bowling was ravaged as Terry and Chris Smith ran up 264 for the first wicket. After reaching a hundred which included fourteen fours, Smith threw caution to the wind and thrashed five sixes and three fours in fifteen balls before being stumped for 148. Terry hit two sixes and twelve fours in his 112, and Gower and Robin Smith kept up the pace with 108 from 22 overs for the third wicket. Hampshire passed 400 before declaring, but Oxford replied with 324, their highest total against a first-class county since 1982, when they made 332 for five declared against Northamptonshire, and their first first-class score over 300 for five years. The captain, Morris, completed his first half-century of the season, and Turner his maiden fifty for the University. The latter's fellow South African, van der Merwe, then took full advantage of an attack which had been reduced to a seamer and two slow left-arm bowlers, hitting two sixes and thirteen fours in his 84. Such was the authority of his batting that Russell contributed only 4 as they added 46 for the seventh wicket. Hampshire's second innings was dominated by an unbeaten 69 from their West Indian bowler, Joseph.

Close of play: First day, Hampshire 437-4 (M. C. J. Nicholas 37*, R. J. Parks 5*); Second day, Oxford University 225-6 (W. M. van der Merwe 38*, M. J. Russell 0*).

Hampshire

V. P. Terry c and b Turner	112		
C. L. Smith st McGrady b Turner	148		
D. I. Gower c and b Crawley	 72	– (1) c van der Merwe b Turner	.. 46
R. A. Smith c van der Merwe b Lunn	 44		
*M. C. J. Nicholas not out	 37	– (2) c Kilborn b Davies	 47
†R. J. Parks not out	 5	– (3) c Kilborn b Davies	 8
R. J. Maru (did not bat)	....	– (4) b Davies	 1
L. A. Joseph (did not bat)	....	– (5) not out	 69
I. J. Turner (did not bat)	....	– (6) c Russell b Turner	 14
K. J. Shine (did not bat)	....	– (7) not out	 24
B 9, l-b 4, n-b 6	 19	B 1, l-b 4, n-b 1	 6

1/264 2/275 3/383 4/427	(4 wkts dec.) 437	1/57 2/82 3/86 4/125 5/164	(5 wkts dec.) 215

C. A. Connor did not bat.

Bowling: *First Innings*—van der Merwe 22-5-77-0; Winchester 10-0-50-0; Crawley 20-1-100-1; Turner 32-4-148-2; Lunn 13-2-49-1. *Second Innings*—van der Merwe 6-2-9-0; Winchester 3-0-31-0; Crawley 3-0-16-0; Turner 23-5-61-2; Davies 23-4-93-3.

Oxford University

D. A. Hagan c R. A. Smith b Maru	... 14	M. J. Russell b Shine	 4
*R. E. Morris c Parks b Shine	 61	H. R. Davies c Nicholas b C. L. Smith.	24
M. J. Kilborn c C. L. Smith b Turner	. 17	†J. E. McGrady c Gower b Maru	 14
G. J. Turner c and b C. L. Smith	 59	A. L. C. Winchester not out	 0
M. A. Crawley c and b Maru	 9	B 4, l-b 12, n-b 6	 22
P. D. Lunn c Maru b Turner	 16		
W. M. van der Merwe c C. L. Smith b Maru .	84	1/39 2/80 3/104 4/142 5/171 6/197 7/243 8/302 9/324	324

Bowling: Shine 27-13-51-2; Joseph 10-2-28-0; Maru 46.3-16-89-4; Turner 40-11-98-2; Nicholas 7-2-21-0; C. L. Smith 6-1-21-2.

Umpires: H. D. Bird and R. Julian.

†At Oxford, May 14, 15. Oxfordshire won by three wickets. Oxford University 201 for three dec. (R. E. Morris 111) and 184 for two dec. (R. E. Morris 78, P. D. Lunn 55 not out); Oxfordshire 137 for four dec. and 249 for seven (D. Woods 75).

OXFORD UNIVERSITY v SURREY

At Oxford, May 16, 17, 18. Drawn. Toss: Oxford University. For the first time in several years Oxford elected to bat after winning the toss, and Morris's decision proved justified. He provided the backbone of his team's innings of 322 for eight, batting for four and a quarter hours and missing a maiden first-class century by only 4 runs. After his dismissal, Crawley and Lunn put on 84 for the fifth wicket, and Lunn stayed to see Oxford to the declaration. Surrey's batsmen all scored freely, and when Lynch and Thorpe had added an unbeaten 123, Greig declared 100 runs behind. In Oxford's second innings, opening bowler Henderson hit a career-best 44 after going in as night-watchman when Hagan was injured, and Morris, Kilborn and Crawley all made useful contributions before Oxford's second declaration set Surrey to score 308 in 100 minutes plus twenty overs. Ward and Darren Bicknell put them in sight of victory with an opening partnership of 256, of which Ward made a magnificent 181 in 152 minutes, passing his previous highest score of 145, against the same opponents in 1989, and scoring 100 of his runs in fours, as well as hitting two sixes. Late in the innings, however, Oxford held three vital catches and Surrey finished 3 runs short.

Close of play: First day, Oxford University 258-4 (M. A. Crawley 54*, P. D. Lunn 21*); Second day, Oxford University 15-0 (R. E. Morris 0*, I. M. Henderson 4*).

Oxford University

D. A. Hagan c Thorpe b Greig	17	– c Ward b Medlycott	12
*R. E. Morris c Ward b M. P. Bicknell	96	– c Stewart b Kendrick	31
M. J. Kilborn c Ward b Thorpe	11	– (7) not out	36
G. J. Turner c Clinton b Kendrick	34	– b Medlycott	3
M. A. Crawley c Lynch b M. P. Bicknell	60	– c Ward b Kendrick	47
P. D. Lunn not out	44	– st Ward b Kendrick	20
H. R. Davies lbw b M. P. Bicknell	2	– (8) not out	1
P. S. Gerrans b Robinson	0		
S. D. Weale c Ward b M. P. Bicknell	13		
I. M. Henderson (did not bat)		– (3) c Ward b Medlycott	44
B 9, l-b 15, w 16, n-b 5	45	B 7, l-b 5, n-b 1	13

1/33 2/81 3/158 4/187 5/271   (8 wkts dec.) 322   1/55 2/62 3/72   (6 wkts dec.) 207
6/280 7/285 8/322   4/141 5/151 6/196

†J. E. McGrady did not bat.

In the second innings D. A. Hagan, when 11, retired hurt at 11 and resumed at 62.

Bowling: *First Innings*—M. P. Bicknell 35.2–11–80–4; Robinson 26–7–69–1; Greig 12–1–38–1; Thorpe 14–6–30–1; Medlycott 33–13–61–0; Kendrick 10–3–20–1. *Second Innings*—M. P. Bicknell 7–1–18–0; Robinson 2–0–14–0; Greig 5–1–15–0; Medlycott 25–7–69–3; Kendrick 25–4–79–3.

Surrey

D. J. Bicknell b Crawley	33	– b Gerrans	63
G. S. Clinton c and b Turner	29		
A. J. Stewart c Crawley b Gerrans	24		
M. A. Lynch not out	81		
G. P. Thorpe not out	46	– (7) not out	2
†D. M. Ward (did not bat)		– (2) c Turner b Crawley	181
J. D. Robinson (did not bat)		– (3) c and b Crawley	24
*I. A. Greig (did not bat)		– (4) c Crawley b Gerrans	17
K. T. Medlycott (did not bat)		– (5) c Kilborn b Gerrans	4
M. P. Bicknell (did not bat)		– (6) not out	1
B 1, l-b 3, w 5	9	B 4, l-b 5, w 1, n-b 3	13

1/64 2/64 3/99   (3 wkts dec.) 222   1/256 2/256 3/278   (5 wkts) 305
                                           4/289 5/302

N. M. Kendrick did not bat.

Bowling: *First Innings*—Henderson 9–1–24–0; Gerrans 13–1–50–1; Crawley 19–5–29–1; Turner 16–4–54–1; Davies 7–1–25–0; Weale 5–0–36–0. *Second Innings*—Henderson 4–1–23–0; Gerrans 15–1–86–3; Turner 10–2–53–0; Crawley 13–0–83–2; Weale 6–0–51–0.

Umpires: P. J. Eele and V. A. Holder.

OXFORD UNIVERSITY v LEICESTERSHIRE

At Oxford, May 23, 24, 25. Drawn. Toss: Oxford University. Oxford's decision to bat first backfired spectacularly when Hagan, Morris and Curtis were dismissed for 1 run, but Turner and Crawley halted the collapse with a stand of 105. When both fell in the fifties, the visitors faced further resistance from van der Merwe and Chauhan. The last wicket gave Millns his best bowling figures, on his first-class début for Leicestershire. It was then the University bowlers' turn to suffer, at the hands of Benson and Willey, who put on 165 before Benson was out 6 short of a century. Willey continued, making his highest score for Leicestershire in a third-wicket partnership of 191 with Whitaker, who was unbeaten on 124 when his captain declared at the overnight score, leaving Oxford needing 268 to avoid an innings defeat. Their cause seemed lost when four wickets fell for 71, but Leicestershire were punished by the later batsmen. After the Zimbabwean, Curtis, had batted nearly two hours for his 19, Crawley put on 67 with Gerrans and an unbeaten 81 with van der Merwe. He had hit sixteen fours in his 105 not out when Briers settled for a draw with ten overs remaining.

Close of play: First day, Leicestershire 17-0 (J. D. R. Benson 8*, P. Willey 7*); Second day, Leicestershire 447-3 (J. J. Whitaker 124*, P. A. Nixon 16*).

Oxford University

D. A. Hagan b Millns	0	– c Parsons b Ferris	6
R. E. Morris lbw b Ferris	0	– c Whitaker b Ferris	11
D. M. Curtis lbw b Millns	0	– c Benson b Willey	19
G. J. Turner c Ferris b Willey	51	– lbw b Gidley	9
M. A. Crawley c Nixon b Millns	50	– not out	105
P. S. Gerrans c Nixon b Millns	0	– lbw b Millns	22
I. Chauhan c Boon b Parsons	25	– not out	39
R. J. J. Russell c Benson b Parsons	4		
R. R. Davies not out	9		
J. E. McGrady lbw b Millns	1		
B 6, l-b 4, w 5	15	L-b 7, n-b 1	8

1/0 2/0 3/1 4/106 5/107   179   1/16 2/17 3/33   (5 wkts) 219
6/114 7/154 8/165 9/170   4/71 5/138

Bowling: *First Innings*—Millns 22.3–8–47–5; Ferris 20–6–45–1; Parsons 24–11–34–3; Gidley 14–4–27–0; Willey 5–4–4–1; Benson 4–2–12–0. *Second Innings*—Millns 20–8–47–1; Ferris 17–7–33–2; Parsons 15–6–35–0; Gidley 19–8–54–1; Willey 22–9–29–1; Boon 3–0–14–0.

Leicestershire

J. D. R. Benson b van der Merwe	94	†P. A. Nixon not out	16
P. Willey b Chauhan	177	B 12, l-b 10, w 5, n-b 5	32
B. F. Smith lbw b Crawley	4		
J. J. Whitaker not out	124	1/165 2/189 3/380 (3 wkts dec.) 447

T. J. Boon, *N. E. Briers, G. J. Parsons, M. I. Gidley, D. J. Millns and G. J. F. Ferris did not bat.

Bowling: van der Merwe 16–1–52–1; Gerrans 19–3–73–0; Crawley 19–4–50–1; Turner 11–3–72–0; Davies 20–1–112–0; Chauhan 15–1–58–1; Curtis 1–0–8–0.

Umpires: R. Palmer and H. J. Rhodes.

†At Oxford, May 26, 28, 29. Oxford University won by two wickets with three balls to spare. Free Foresters 276 (E. D. Fursdon 65 not out, C. J. C. Rowe 59) and 244 for six dec. (J. R. Kilbee 59 retired; D. M. Curtis four for 53); Oxford University 241 for six dec. (R. E. Morris 62) and 280 for eight (R. E. Morris 102, D. A. Hagan 63; C. J. C. Rowe four for 71).

†At Oxford, May 30, 31, June 1. Drawn. Toss: Oxford University. Oxford University 229 for nine dec. (R. E. Morris 40, P. D. Lunn 80) and 323 for eight dec. (R. E. Morris 30, M. J. Russell 51, P. D. Lunn 52, W. M. van der Merwe 59, S. D. Weale 33, I. M. Henderson 33 not out); MCC 279 for seven dec. (S. G. Plumb 34, S. C. Wundke 54, R. M. Wight 40 not out, M. Hart 48 not out; I. M. Henderson three for 77, W. M. van der Merwe four for 67) and 76 for no wkt (D. C. Briance 38 not out).

OXFORD UNIVERSITY v GLAMORGAN

At Oxford, June 2, 4, 5. Drawn. Toss: Oxford University. Paying their second visit of the season to The Parks, Glamorgan made another score of more than 300 after Oxford's gamble of putting them in on a rain-affected pitch had not paid off. Cottey completed a maiden century after adding 104 with Holmes. Oxford lost four wickets for 77, but Crawley, who had hit an unbeaten 103 on the county's first visit, put on 75 in ten overs with Gerrans, and Curtis hit a career-best 43. Although leading by 170, Glamorgan did not enforce the follow-on; but any hopes of a result were spoiled by rain, which restricted play on the third day to 5.2 overs before lunch.

Close of play: First day, Glamorgan 388-7 (J. Derrick 28*, M. Davies 5*); Second day Glamorgan 10-0 (M. J. Cann 0*, G. C. Holmes 8*).

Glamorgan

M. J. Cann c Gerrans b Henderson	19	– c Trevelyan b Henderson	7
P. A. Cottey run out	156		
G. C. Holmes b Henderson	39	– (2) not out	12
M. P. Maynard c Turner b Gerrans	59		
R. N. Pook lbw b Gerrans	0	– (3) not out	0
†M. L. Roberts c Trevelyan b Henderson	14		
H. A. G. Anthony c Gerrans b Crawley	30		
J. Derrick not out	28		
M. Davies not out	5		
B 6, l-b 14, w 2, n-b 16	38	L-b 3, n-b 2	5

1/37 2/141 3/233 4/233 5/284   (7 wkts dec.) 388   1/21   (1 wkt) 24
6/343 7/369

S. Bastien and *S. R. Barwick did not bat.

Bowling: *First Innings*—Henderson 28-1-102-3; Gerrans 26-3-94-2; Crawley 26-6-94-1; Turner 19-4-78-0. *Second Innings*—Gerrans 5-3-4-0; Henderson 4.2-0-17-1.

Oxford University

D. A. Hagan c Cottey b Barwick	43	S. Chauhan run out	
*R. E. Morris c Roberts b Bastien	0	I. M. Henderson not out	
P. D. Lunn c Roberts b Bastien	11	†R. W. D. Trevelyan c Roberts b Bastien	
G. J. Turner b Bastien	13		
M. A. Crawley c Davies b Anthony	67		
P. S. Gerrans c Roberts b Barwick	18		
D. M. Curtis lbw b Holmes	43	L-b 8, w 3, n-b 5	16
M. J. Russell c Roberts b Barwick	2	1/2 2/31 3/66 4/77 5/152	218

6/187 7/204 8/212 9/217

Bowling: Anthony 18-7-29-1; Bastien 20.2-3-51-4; Barwick 19-10-29-3; Derrick 9-2-58-0; Davies 8-1-16-0; Pook 8-3-19-0; Holmes 7-4-8-1.

Umpires: P. J. Eele and A. A. Jones.

OXFORD UNIVERSITY v NOTTINGHAMSHIRE

At Oxford, June 6, 7, 8. Drawn. Toss: Nottinghamshire. An unusual feature of this match was that Nottinghamshire used twelve players. Wicket-keeper Scott had been omitted because of illness, and Newell, their opening batsman, was to have kept wicket in his place. However, at the end of the first day, when he was 20 not out, Newell was summoned to Trent Bridge to act as twelfth man for England in the Test match against New Zealand. After calls to the TCCB, Scott, now recovered, was reinstated, although the TCCB's Playing Conditions for first-class matches made provision for the introduction of a substitute player only in the case of County Championship matches, and Lenham, the Oxford coach, was rightly critical of the whole incident. In the play between showers – only five and a half hours were possible on the first two days and the third was washed out – Johnson hit an unbeaten 112, containing a six and thirteen fours, and the Oxford captain, Morris, was 73 not out in his team's reply.

Close of play: First day, Nottinghamshire 84-2 (M. Newell 20*, P. Johnson 42*); Second day, Oxford University 118-1 (R. E. Morris 73*, P. D. Lunn 22*).

Nottinghamshire

†M. Newell retired not out	20	K. P. Evans not out	43
D. J. R. Martindale c Morris b Crawley	15		
R. J. Evans c sub b Gerrans	1	B 4, l-b 3, n-b 1	8
*P. Johnson not out	112		
D. R. Laing b van der Merwe	2	1/27 2/32 3/92 (3 wkts dec.) 201	

G. W. Mike, M. G. Field-Buss, R. A. Pick, K. Saxelby, †C. W. Scott and J. A. Afford did not bat.

Bowling: van der Merwe 20–5–69–1; Gerrans 19–4–58–1; Crawley 15.5–4–36–1; Davies –0–31–0.

Oxford University

D. A. Hagan c Mike b K. P. Evans ...	15
R. E. Morris not out	73
P. D. Lunn not out	22
B 2, l-b 5, w 1	8

/33   (1 wkt dec.) 118

D. M. Curtis, M. J. Russell, M. A. Crawley, W. M. van der Merwe, H. R. Davies, S. Chauhan, P. S. Gerrans and †R. W. D. Trevelyan did not bat.

Bowling: Pick 3–0–20–0; Saxelby 2–0–10–0; Mike 6–1–33–0; K. P. Evans 6–4–13–1; Afford 8–4–9–0; Laing 5–1–21–0; Field-Buss 2.1–1–5–0.

Umpires: K. J. Lyons and H. J. Rhodes.

†At Oxford, June 13, 14, 15. Drawn. Oxford University 279 for nine dec. (J. Morris 103) and 325 for five dec. (D. A. Hagan 167 not out, P. D. Lunn 82, R. E. Morris 57); Combined Services 376 (Sgt G. S. Lumb 94, 2nd Lt R. J. Greatorex 83) and 207 for six.

OXFORD UNIVERSITY v LANCASHIRE

At Oxford, June 16, 18, 19. Drawn. Toss: Oxford University. Oxford produced their best batting of the season, and their biggest total against a first-class county since their 413 for nine against Warwickshire in 1969. After Gallian, an eighteen-year-old Australian, dismissed Hagan with his first ball in first-class cricket, Kilborn came in to make his highest score, 95, sharing stands which put on a total of 254 runs with Morris, Turner and Crawley. Later Crawley added 86 in twelve overs with van der Merwe, whose unbeaten 56 came from 35 balls, but Oxford's declaration at their overnight score, after rain had delayed the start on the second morning, deprived him of the chance of a hundred against his native county – who were playing his younger brother. Lancashire's reply was even more spectacular, with their three England players, appearing between the Trent Bridge and Lord's Tests, all hitting centuries. Atherton struck nineteen fours and a six in his 117, acting-captain Fairbrother made 105, and on the third day DeFreitas raced to the fastest hundred of the season to date, from 69 balls in 79 minutes. His seven sixes and eleven fours included four sixes and a four in one over from Turner.

Close of play: First day, Oxford University 366-5 (M. A. Crawley 91*, W. M. van der Merwe 56*); Second day, Lancashire 260-2 (N. H. Fairbrother 52*, P. A. J. DeFreitas 12*).

Oxford University

D. A. Hagan c Atherton b Gallian	1	– c Stanworth b Folley	5
R. E. Morris lbw b DeFreitas	61		
M. J. Kilborn c DeFreitas b Atherton	95		
G. J. Turner run out	48		
M. A. Crawley not out	91		
P. D. Lunn c Stanworth b Folley	3	– (3) not out	9
W. M. van der Merwe not out	56		
P. S. Gerrans (did not bat)		– (2) c DeFreitas b Folley	39
S. D. Weale (did not bat)		– (4) lbw b Atherton	0
C. M. Henderson (did not bat)		– (5) not out	1
B 1, l-b 5, w 1, n-b 4	11	B 1, l-b 9	10

/3 2/118 3/189 4/257 5/280   (5 wkts dec.) 366   1/28 2/58 3/58   (3 wkts) 64

*J. E. McGrady did not bat.

Bowling: *First Innings*—DeFreitas 17–3–39–1; Gallian 18–8–50–1; Folley 24–1–120–1; Yates 27–7–52–0; Atherton 31–5–99–1. *Second Innings*—DeFreitas 4–1–7–0; Gallian 8–0–15–0; Atherton 8–5–10–1; Folley 10–3–18–2; Yates 4–2–4–0.

Lancashire

N. J. Speak c Hagan b Turner 61	G. D. Lloyd not out 78
M. A. Atherton c Henderson b Weale .117	J. E. R. Gallian not out 17
*N. H. Fairbrother c Kilborn b Turner.105	
P. A. J. DeFreitas st McGrady	B 12, l-b 3, w 2, n-b 13 30
b Turner .102	
S. P. Titchard b Crawley 22	1/115 2/248 3/383 (6 wkts dec.) 558
J. P. Crawley b Lunn 26	4/416 5/446 6/474

G. Yates, I. Folley and †J. Stanworth did not bat.

Bowling: Henderson 25–2–146–0; Gerrans 20–1–80–0; Crawley 17–2–64–1; Turner 27–7–100–3; Weale 25–4–119–1; Lunn 8–1–34–1.

Umpires: G. I. Burgess and N. T. Plews.

†At Oxford, June 20, 21, 22. Drawn. Wiltshire 325 for five dec. (S. Perrin 117 not out) and second innings forfeited; Oxford University first innings forfeited and 283 for seven (P. D. Lunn 125 not out, R. E. Morris 55; N. Prigent four for 63).

At Lord's, July 4, 5, 6. OXFORD UNIVERSITY drew with CAMBRIDGE UNIVERSITY (See Other Matches at Lord's, 1990).

CAMBRIDGE

President: Lord Butterfield (Downing)

Captain: J. C. M. Atkinson (Millfield and Downing)
Secretary: R. A. Pyman (Harrow and Pembroke)

Captain for 1991: R. J. Turner (Millfield and Magdalene)
Secretary: M. J. Morris (Cherwell, Oxford, Pembroke and Downing)

A glorious finish to the term, when the combined Oxford & Cambridge side beat the New Zealanders, followed immediately by Cambridge's victory over Sussex at Hove – their first win against a county since 1982 – disguised what was, on the whole, a disappointing season at Fenner's.

Much had been expected of the side Jonathon Atkinson was to lead, for there was considerable experience in batting and bowling. Yet for most of the season, one of the driest at Fenner's in living memory, little happened to realise those hopes. The highlights were provided more often than not by Steve James, the Glamorgan batsman, who had given notice of his considerable ability when heading the Cambridge averages the previous season. In eleven matches, including Oxford & Cambridge Universities against the tourists, he scored 921 runs. Only the rain that ruined the University Match at Lord's denied him the chance to become the first Cambridge batsman since J. M. Brearley to score 1,000 first-class runs in a university season, although he did reach the milestone on his return to Glamorgan. Of his four centuries, all scored in the later half of the term, the unbeaten match-winning 131 against the New Zealanders was his best, and was followed by a hundred that proved to be the corner-stone of the victory at Hove. In the same innings he shared in one of only two century partnerships made by the University, putting on 142 with Mark Lowrey as Cambridge chased 256 in 148 minutes plus twenty overs.

CAMBRIDGE UNIVERSITY 1990

[Bill Smith]

Back row: G. J. Saville (*coach*), D. H. Shufflebotham, R. H. J. Jenkins, S. W. Johnson, A. J. Buzza, M. J. Morris, M. J. Lowrey, G. B. A. Dyer. *Front row*: S. P. James, R. A. Pyman, J. C. M. Atkinson (*captain*), R. Heap, R. J. Turner.

James was the only hundred-maker, though Lowrey, a Freshman, showed skills that should stand the University in good stead. He was one of only three other batsmen who passed 50, despite the considerable improvement in the Fenner's pitches. Much work had been carried out on the square during the winter, and the result was a little more bounce and pace to encourage batsmen and bowlers alike.

Alan Buzza was again the top bowler, earning 23 wickets, including five against the New Zealanders, with his left-arm spin, although he was never as effective as he had been the previous season, when bowling at the opposite end to Mike Atherton's leg-spin. Lowrey, an off-spinner, headed Cambridge's averages with ten wickets, while Rory Jenkins, a strongly built Freshman, used the new ball willingly and, along with Richard Pyman, finished with fifteen wickets.

The biggest disappointment was the failure of Atkinson, the captain, to realise fully his potential. He showed what he was capable of in his two half-centuries but innings of sustained application were all too infrequent. He led his side cheerfully, although he often appeared content to let things drift, waiting for declarations by the visitors.

Despite going into the University Match as the underdogs, Cambridge arrived at Lord's in confident mood. But in a match ruined again by rain, they revealed their limitations, failing to grasp the opportunity provided when both captains forfeited an innings and they were required to score 270 to win in a minimum of 61 overs. – David Hallett.

CAMBRIDGE UNIVERSITY RESULTS

First-class matches – Played 10: Won 1, Lost 4, Drawn 5.

FIRST-CLASS AVERAGES

BATTING AND FIELDING

	Birthplace	M	I	NO	R	HI	Avge	Ct/St
S. P. James	Lydney	10	19	1	723	116	40.16	7
J. P. Arscott	Tooting	2	4	1	75	43*	25.00	0/2
M. J. Lowrey	Hampstead	10	18	2	363	72	22.68	1
R. Heap	Leeds	10	19	2	376	63	22.11	3
J. C. M. Atkinson	Butleigh	10	19	2	360	72	21.17	6
R. J. Turner	Malvern	8	14	0	287	38	20.50	6/4
D. H. Shufflebotham	Neath	8	9	3	121	29	20.16	1
G. B. A. Dyer	Glasgow	4	8	2	107	23	17.83	0
S. W. Johnson	Newcastle-upon-Tyne	6	6	4	35	14*	17.50	2
M. J. Morris	Melbourne, Australia	10	17	3	206	45	14.71	4
R. A. Pyman	Changi, Singapore	9	12	1	94	23*	8.54	2
R. H. J. Jenkins	Leicester	9	12	5	58	19*	8.28	1
A. J. Buzza	Beverley	9	11	2	49	21	5.44	2

Also batted: A. M. Hooper (*Perivale*) (2 matches) 0, 0, 5 (1 ct); G. M. Hutchinson (*Welshpool*) (2 matches) 29, 2; G. A. Pointer (*Lewisham*) (1 match) 7, 9.

* *Signifies not out.*

S. P. James played the three three-figure innings for Cambridge University.

BOWLING

	O	M	R	W	BB	Avge
M. J. Lowrey	151.2	33	483	10	2-13	48.30
A. J. Buzza	257	42	955	18	4-108	53.05
R. A. Pyman	285.4	76	870	15	2-29	58.00
R. H. J. Jenkins	281.4	41	959	15	5-100	63.93
D. H. Shufflebotham	139	20	538	6	3-60	89.66

Also bowled: J. C. M. Atkinson 23–3–101–1; S. W. Johnson 113–14–452–3; G. A. Pointer 17–3–67–0.

†At Cambridge, April 11. Middlesex won by 68 runs. Middlesex 187 for eight (50 overs); Cambridge University 119 for five (50 overs) (R. Heap 54).

†At Cambridge, April 12. Cambridge University won on faster scoring-rate in a rain-affected match. Loughborough University 216 for five (55 overs) (N. V. Knight 113 not out, C. M. Tolley 53); Cambridge University 138 for four (33 overs).

CAMBRIDGE UNIVERSITY v NORTHAMPTONSHIRE

At Cambridge, April 14, 15, 16. Drawn. Toss: Cambridge University. From the outset the University bowlers toiled as the county made steady progress on a cold, occasionally showery opening day. With Geoff Cook taking 164 balls to reach 50, the best batting came from the left-handed Penberthy, who completed his fifty by the close and on the second day went on to his maiden hundred and the first century of the season, hitting thirteen fours and a six in 196 deliveries. Later in the day the young all-rounder came back to wrap up the Cambridge innings with an impressive spell of medium-pace bowling. Nick Cook, captaining Northamptonshire in the absence of Lamb and Larkins – playing in the Test match in Antigua, along with county team-mates Bailey, Capel and Ambrose – chose not to enforce the follow-on and eventually set Cambridge a target of 281 in four and a half hours. This time, however, the University batted more confidently and, helped by an interruption for rain, had no trouble saving the match.

Close of play: First day, Northamptonshire 228-4 (A. L. Penberthy 56*, D. Ripley 11*); Second day, Northamptonshire 26-1 (A. Fordham 23*).

Northamptonshire

G. Cook c James b Johnson	87		
A. Fordham c Morris b Johnson	17	– (1) c Johnson b Pyman	54
N. A. Felton b Pyman	26	– (2) lbw b Jenkins	3
D. J. Wild c Hooper b Lowrey	20	– (3) c Turner b Lowrey	43
A. L. Penberthy not out	101		
†D. Ripley lbw b Pyman	22		
J. G. Thomas not out	13	– (6) c James b Lowrey	8
J. W. Govan (did not bat)		– (4) lbw b Pyman	3
*N. G. B. Cook (did not bat)		– (5) not out	0
L-b 6, n-b 5	11		

1/37 2/79 3/110 4/197 5/254   (5 wkts dec.) 297   1/26 2/88 3/103   (5 wkts dec.) 111
                                                   4/103 5/111

S. J. Brown and M. A. Robinson did not bat.

Bowling: *First Innings*—Johnson 21–2–86–2; Jenkins 23.5–2–59–0; Pyman 36–12–62–2; Shufflebotham 5–0–26–0; Lowrey 24–7–58–1. *Second Innings*—Johnson 4–0–17–0; Jenkins 11–1–52–1; Pyman 12–6–29–2; Lowrey 4.1–1–13–2.

Cambridge University

S. P. James lbw b Thomas	39	– lbw b Brown	6
R. Heap c Felton b Govan	18	– c Thomas b Wild	37
M. J. Lowrey run out	8	– not out	23
*J. C. M. Atkinson c N. G. B. Cook b Robinson	2	– not out	47
M. J. Morris b Brown	5		
A. M. Hooper c Thomas b Robinson	0		
R. A. Pyman b Govan	4		
†R. J. Turner c Brown b Penberthy	21		
D. H. Shufflebotham not out	16		
R. H. J. Jenkins lbw b Penberthy	0		
S. W. Johnson c Brown b Penberthy	0		
B 1, l-b 13, w 1	15	L-b 3	3

1/54 2/66 3/74 4/74 5/75   128   1/28 2/46   (2 wkts) 116
6/88 7/90 8/123 9/126

Bowling: *First Innings*—Brown 12–6–18–1; Thomas 10–1–47–1; Govan 11–7–12–2; Robinson 16–6–24–2; N. G. B. Cook 2–1–2–0; Penberthy 8.4–5–11–3. *Second Innings*—Brown 9–4–11–1; Thomas 7–1–26–0; Wild 9–2–32–1; N. G. B. Cook 2–2–0–0; Robinson 6–0–18–0; Govan 3–2–10–0; Penberthy 3–1–12–0; Fordham 1–0–4–0.

Umpires: B. Hassan and R. Julian.

CAMBRIDGE UNIVERSITY v DERBYSHIRE

At Cambridge, April 18, 19, 20. Derbyshire won by 243 runs. Toss: Cambridge University. Derbyshire were in control from the start, when they were asked to bat and enjoyed some gentle practice. Adams completed a maiden century in 206 minutes, hitting twelve fours from 187 deliveries, and the South African, Kuiper, marked his first appearance for the county with a half-century. The visitors tightened their grip on the match on the second day as Cambridge limped to three figures; then Barnett, lending variety to the attack with his leg-spinners, took the last three wickets in eight balls without conceding a run. However, he declined to enforce the follow-on, and after some more Derbyshire batsmen had taken practice he declared a second time, leaving the University a target of 354. That was quite beyond Cambridge, as was batting throughout the final day to save the game; only two batsmen reached double figures. Barnett added another four wickets and Miller, back with his home county after three years with Essex, took three for 14.

Close of play: First day, Cambridge University 16-0 (S. P. James 11*, R. Heap 3*); Second day, Cambridge University 3-1 (S. P. James 3*, M. J. Lowrey 0*).

Derbyshire

*K. J. Barnett c Atkinson b Buzza	62		
T. J. G. O'Gorman c Heap b Pyman	55		
C. J. Adams not out	111		
A. P. Kuiper lbw b Pyman	51		
B. Roberts b Buzza	12	– (1) c Lowrey b Buzza	33
A. M. Brown not out	34	– (2) lbw b Atkinson	51
S. C. Goldsmith (did not bat)		– (3) not out	25
G. Miller (did not bat)		– (4) not out	13
M. Jean-Jacques (did not bat)			
B 3, l-b 4	7	L-b 2, w 3	5

1/78 2/156 3/241 4/268   (4 wkts dec.) 332   1/86 2/86   (2 wkts dec.) 127

†B. J. M. Maher and O. H. Mortensen did not bat.

Bowling: *First Innings*—Jenkins 13–3–47–0; Pointer 8–0–35–0; Pyman 28–3–94–2; Buzza 32–5–117–2; Lowrey 9–1–32–0. *Second Innings*—Jenkins 8–2–37–0; Pointer 9–3–32–0; Atkinson 7–1–27–1; Buzza 10–2–27–1; Pyman 4.3–2–2–0.

Cambridge University

S. P. James b Jean-Jacques	21	– c Adams b Kuiper	7
R. Heap lbw b Mortensen	4	– c Brown b Miller	0
M. J. Lowrey c Adams b Mortensen	4	– lbw b Jean-Jacques	1
*J. C. M. Atkinson lbw b Miller	36	– b Roberts	23
M. J. Morris c Miller b Jean-Jacques	2	– c Miller b Barnett	45
A. M. Hooper lbw b Mortensen	0	– b Barnett	5
R. A. Pyman c O'Gorman b Roberts	5	– b Miller	2
†R. J. Turner c Miller b Barnett	18	– c Goldsmith b Barnett	0
G. A. Pointer lbw b Barnett	7	– b Barnett	9
A. J. Buzza c Goldsmith b Barnett	0	– not out	9
R. H. J. Jenkins not out	0	– lbw b Miller	1
L-b 5, w 3, n-b 1	9	B 5, l-b 3	8
	106		110

1/22 2/32 3/32 4/36 5/39   1/1 2/8 3/8 4/70 5/82
5/58 7/90 8/105 9/105   6/89 7/89 8/92 9/103

Bowling: *First Innings*—Mortensen 15–3–21–3; Jean-Jacques 14–4–31–2; Miller 10–4–9–1; Barnett 8.2–5–9–3; Goldsmith 7–2–15–0; Roberts 6–2–16–1. *Second Innings*—Miller 23.4–16–14–3; Barnett 18–7–28–4; Kuiper 7–2–16–1; Jean-Jacques 10–3–23–1; Goldsmith 9–1–21–0; Roberts 3–3–0–1.

Umpires: B. Hassan and R. Julian.

CAMBRIDGE UNIVERSITY v WARWICKSHIRE

At Cambridge, April 26, 27, 28. Drawn. Toss: Cambridge University. Warwickshire's batsmen picked up three centuries, and Moody celebrated his county début by giving a foretaste of feats to follow. On a first day reduced by rain to two and a half hours, the tall Australian needed only 125 balls to reach his hundred, hitting ten fours and six sixes; next day he went on to 147, from 147 balls, with 100 of his runs coming in boundaries (six sixes, sixteen fours). Reeve was even faster, scoring a hundred before lunch from 109 deliveries with three sixes and ten fours. When Cambridge batted, Atkinson, aided by the tail, limited the damage done by Benjamin, who finished with five wickets for the first time. Then, as Reeve opted to bat again, it was the turn of the Cambridge bowlers to suffer once more. Asif Din rode his luck somewhat with a flourish of strokes which brought him three sixes and thirteen fours, and he reached his hundred in 76 minutes from 70 balls. Cambridge ignored a target of 359 but batted with sufficient determination to save the game.

Close of play: First day, Warwickshire 168-2 (T. M. Moody 105*, A. I. Kallicharran 42*); Second day, Warwickshire 10-0 (A. J. Moles 5*, Asif Din 5*).

Warwickshire

A. J. Moles c Atkinson b Johnson	1	– lbw b Shufflebotham	29
T. M. Moody b Buzza	147		
†G. W. Humpage c Turner b Pyman	17	– not out	4
A. I. Kallicharran c James b Buzza	43		
*D. A. Reeve not out	102		
Asif Din c Turner b Buzza	0	– (2) not out	100
K. J. Piper run out	10		
N. M. K. Smith b Buzza	47		
P. A. Booth not out	3		
L-b 2, n-b 6	8	L-b 8, n-b 2	10
	(7 wkts. dec.) 378		(1 wkt dec.) 143

1/2 2/41 3/188 4/214 5/214   (7 wkts. dec.) 378   1/105   (1 wkt dec.) 143
6/231 7/366

T. A. Munton and J. E. Benjamin did not bat.

Bowling: *First Innings*—Johnson 9–2–43–1; Pyman 20–4–109–1; Shufflebotham 17–1–76–0; Buzza 22–1–108–4; Atkinson 8–1–40–0. *Second Innings*—Johnson 6–0–41–0; Pyman 5–1–43–0; Buzza 1–0–4–0; Shufflebotham 5–0–29–1; Lowrey 3.1–0–18–0.

Cambridge University

S. P. James c Humpage b Benjamin	19	– (7) c Smith b Munton	8
R. Heap lbw b Benjamin	0	– (1) c Humpage b Munton	17
M. J. Lowrey b Benjamin	1	– c Smith b Reeve	24
*J. C. M. Atkinson c Reeve b Smith	41	– c Reeve b Asif Din	17
M. J. Morris lbw b Benjamin	0	– lbw b Reeve	19
G. B. A. Dyer b Asif Din	19	– not out	20
†R. J. Turner c Booth b Asif Din	12	– (2) lbw b Reeve	28
R. A. Pyman run out	21	– not out	23
D. H. Shufflebotham c Reeve b Asif Din	24		
A. J. Buzza b Benjamin	1		
S. W. Johnson not out	14		
L-b 10, w 1	11	B 13, l-b 9, n-b 3	25

1/2 2/6 3/44 4/44 5/72   163   1/19 2/74 3/95 4/101   (6 wkts) 181
6/95 7/106 8/135 9/142   5/122 6/133

Bowling: First Innings—Munton 8–3–17–0; Benjamin 18–8–29–5; Moody 8–1–33–0; Smith 10–4–25–1; Asif Din 10.5–3–17–3; Booth 8–1–23–0; Reeve 6–3–9–0. *Second Innings*—Benjamin 12–5–12–0; Munton 16–4–40–2; Smith 10–2–18–0; Asif Din 15–3–49–1; Reeve 19–7–34–3; Moody 10–7–6–0.

Umpires: B. Dudleston and P. J. Eele.

CAMBRIDGE UNIVERSITY v MIDDLESEX

At Cambridge, May 3, 4, 5. Drawn. Toss: Middlesex. Ramprakash dominated the first day, putting on 90 with Roseberry and 98 with Brown, to complete his hundred in 206 minutes, having faced 176 deliveries and hit nine fours and two sixes. A half-century by James, recapturing his form of the previous year, failed to take the University past the follow-on target, but once again the visiting county preferred to give their other batsmen some practice. Jenkins claimed the first five-wicket haul of the season by a Cambridge bowler as Middlesex increased their lead to 362, then left the University with four hours' batting. In this time the Middlesex players also had some bowling practice; every man was given at least two overs, except wicket-keeper Farbrace, a recent recruit from Kent, who had earlier made his highest first-class score.

Close of play: First day, Cambridge University 15-0 (S. P. James 5*, R. Heap 9*); Second day, Middlesex 112-4 (P. Farbrace 52*, N. F. Williams 8*).

Middlesex

M. A. Roseberry st Turner b Buzza	85	– (9) not out	2
J. C. Pooley b Pyman	8	– b Jenkins	13
*M. W. Gatting c Morris b Buzza	19		
M. R. Ramprakash not out	118	– (8) not out	13
K. R. Brown b Jenkins	42		
R. O. Butcher not out	29	– (1) c Buzza b Jenkins	32
†P. Farbrace (did not bat)		– (3) c Pyman b Buzza	79
S. P. Hughes (did not bat)		– (4) b Jenkins	2
J. E. Emburey (did not bat)		– (5) lbw b Jenkins	4
N. F. Williams (did not bat)		– (6) c Turner b Jenkins	20
P. C. R. Tufnell (did not bat)		– (7) c James b Buzza	36
L-b 7, w 5, n-b 7	19	L-b 2, n-b 1	3

1/26 2/76 3/166 4/264   (4 wkts dec.) 320   1/35 2/52 3/58   (7 wkts dec.) 204
                                         4/70 5/132
                                         6/183 7/200

Bowling: First Innings—Jenkins 20–1–96–1; Pyman 20–8–54–1; Shufflebotham 14–3–50–0; Buzza 26–5–55–2; Lowrey 16–1–58–0. *Second Innings*—Jenkins 26–3–100–5; Pyman 7–2–31–0; Buzza 11.1–2–25–2; Lowrey 9–2–29–0; Shufflebotham 9–1–17–0.

Cambridge University

S. P. James c Butcher b Hughes	54	– c Roseberry b Tufnell	46
R. Heap c Emburey b Williams	15	– b Tufnell	23
M. J. Lowrey c Brown b Williams	6	– (5) c Emburey b Tufnell	12
*J. C. M. Atkinson c Farbrace b Hughes	6	– c Butcher b Brown	17
M. J. Morris lbw b Emburey	9	– (6) not out	32
G. B. A. Dyer c Farbrace b Williams	23	– (7) not out	9
†R. J. Turner c Tufnell b Emburey	26	– (3) c Pooley b Roseberry	34
R. A. Pyman c Brown b Emburey	10		
D. H. Shufflebotham c Brown b Tufnell	1		
A. J. Buzza c Gatting b Emburey	0		
R. H. J. Jenkins not out	0		
B 4, l-b 5, w 3	12	B 4, l-b 17, w 6	27

1/24 2/30 3/38 4/61 5/95   162   1/43 2/91 3/126   (5 wkts) 200
6/135 7/153 8/162 9/162   4/138 5/157

Bowling: *First Innings*—Williams 18–5–35–3; Hughes 20–5–30–2; Emburey 26.3–13–33–4; Tufnell 17–6–36–1; Gatting 8–3–19–0. *Second Innings*—Williams 2–0–5–0; Hughes 4–2–11–0; Tufnell 27–11–57–3; Emburey 14–8–13–0; Ramprakash 7–2–17–0; Brown 10–2–16–1; Roseberry 12–2–41–1; Gatting 3–0–6–0; Pooley 2–0–11–0; Butcher 2–0–2–0.

Umpires: V. A. Holder and M. J. Kitchen.

†At Cambridge, May 13. Cambridge University won by 11 runs. Cambridge University 289 for four dec. (R. A. Pyman 110 not out, S. P. James 102); Cryptics 278 (R. Sethi 68; A. J. Buzza five for 103).

†At Cambridge, May 15. Cambridgeshire won by six wickets. Cambridge University 189 (A. Akhtar five for 42); Cambridgeshire 190 for four (N. T. Gadsby 80, N. J. Adams 67).

CAMBRIDGE UNIVERSITY v ESSEX

At Cambridge, May 16, 17, 18. Essex won by 120 runs. Toss: Essex. Fifties from Heap and Atkinson enabled Cambridge to pass 200 for the first time in the season, in reply to Essex's 319 for five declared. It was also the first time they had compelled a visiting team to bat again, but it was not enough to save the game. Earlier Prichard had batted freely, hitting fifteen fours and a six in his 117-ball hundred, while Stephenson compiled a less fluent half-century. In the county's second innings, the promising Seymour, making a career-best 89, and the experienced Hardie put on 155 for the first wicket before Pringle declared, setting his former university 274 to win at almost a run a minute. Any thoughts of victory were quickly dispelled when Ilott took the first four wickets at a personal cost of 10 runs, and Buzza's dismissal later gave him five in an innings for the first time. Only Lowrey stood in Essex's way. Batting for 206 minutes, and reaching his maiden half-century in a ninth-wicket stand with Jenkins worth 50 in 71 minutes, he was so close to staving off defeat that just 8.5 overs remained when he was last out.

Close of play: First day, Cambridge University 23-2 (R. Heap 6*, A. J. Buzza 4*); Second day, Essex 102-0 (A. C. Seymour 62*, B. R. Hardie 31*).

Essex

J. P. Stephenson c Buzza b Lowrey	58		
A. C. Seymour lbw b Jenkins	28	– (1) b Pyman	89
P. J. Prichard c Heap b Pyman	116		
*M. A. Garnham c James b Jenkins	26		
B. R. Hardie not out	22	– (2) not out	56
D. R. Pringle c Morris b Pyman	58		
T. D. Topley (did not bat)		– (3) lbw b Pyman	0
L-b 7, n-b 4	11	B 5, l-b 4, w 1	10

1/36 2/197 3/235 4/239 5/319   (5 wkts dec.) 319   1/155 2/155   (2 wkts dec.) 155

M. C. Ilott, J. H. Childs, S. J. W. Andrew and P. M. Such did not bat.

Bowling: *First Innings*—Johnson 8–0–59–0; Jenkins 25–7–68–2; Pyman 22.1–7–46–2; Buzza 21–2–90–0; Atkinson 2–0–23–0; Lowrey 9–1–26–1. *Second Innings*—Jenkins 14–3–48–0; Johnson 4–1–23–0; Pyman 16–5–36–2; Lowrey 6–0–22–0; Buzza 5–1–17–0.

Cambridge University

S. P. James c Topley b Andrew	5	– lbw b Ilott		12
R. Heap c Seymour b Pringle	50	– lbw b Ilott		2
R. A. Pyman c Stephenson b Andrew	0	– b Ilott		10
A. J. Buzza b Ilott	21	– (9) c Hardie b Ilott		0
*J. C. M. Atkinson run out	51	– (4) c Pringle b Ilott		0
M. J. Lowrey c Hardie b Pringle	6	– (5) lbw b Such		69
M. J. Morris c Prichard b Pringle	2	– (6) c Garnham b Andrew		1
G. B. A. Dyer c Hardie b Topley	17	– (7) c Pringle b Topley		14
†J. P. Arscott lbw b Childs	9	– (8) c Hardie b Pringle		10
R. H. J. Jenkins c Garnham b Topley	6	– lbw b Such		11
S. W. Johnson not out	10	– not out		2
B 7, l-b 5, w 2, n-b 10	24	B 4, l-b 8, w 3, n-b 7		22

1/13 2/17 3/53 4/137 5/146   201   1/13 2/23 3/24 4/30 5/32   153
6/148 7/153 8/173 9/188   6/76 7/97 8/100 9/150

Bowling: *First Innings*—Andrew 20–3–39–2; Ilott 17–3–42–1; Childs 16–7–39–1; Topley 12–4–25–2; Such 12–4–27–0; Pringle 9–2–16–3; Stephenson 2–1–1–0. *Second Innings*—Andrew 12–1–34–1; Ilott 16–2–43–5; Topley 11–2–29–1; Childs 16–9–18–0; Such 8.1–5–6–2; Pringle 9–3–11–1.

Umpires: G. I. Burgess and J. W. Holder.

CAMBRIDGE UNIVERSITY v GLOUCESTERSHIRE

At Cambridge, May 23, 24, 25. Gloucestershire won by 70 runs. Toss: Gloucestershire. Again the Cambridge bowling struggled on a flat pitch, with four of the first five county batsmen hitting half-centuries, but a first hundred of the season from James led a solid reply by the University batsmen. The Cambridge opener reached three figures in 282 minutes (233 balls) with eleven fours, and shared a 75-minute century partnership for the third wicket with his captain, Atkinson, who struck twelve fours and a six in his 72. When Atkinson eventually declared at 314 for eight, the University's total was their highest against a first-class county since 1982, when they made 380 for six against Middlesex. Gloucestershire had little difficulty in setting a target of 270 in 153 minutes plus twenty overs, but Cambridge made a disastrous start. They were quickly 13 for three, and although they kept up with the required rate, they continued to lose batsmen steadily. Barnes, the Gloucestershire opening bowler, gained four wickets for the second time in the match.

Close of play: First day, Cambridge University 38-1 (S. P. James 18*, A. J. Buzza 6*). Second day, Gloucestershire 73-0 (A. J. Wright 33*, P. W. Romaines 38*).

Gloucestershire

*A. J. Wright st Arscott b Buzza	44	– run out		58
G. D. Hodgson lbw b Shufflebotham	51	– (4) not out		39
I. P. Butcher c Atkinson b Lowrey	79	– (5) b Jenkins		8
P. Bainbridge st Arscott b Lowrey	61			
J. W. Lloyds not out	73	– (6) not out		2
P. W. Romaines not out	15	– (2) c Atkinson b Buzza		95
†G. A. Tedstone (did not bat)		– (3) c Morris b Buzza		23
B 7, l-b 11, w 2, n-b 10	30	L-b 3, w 1, n-b 1		5

1/107 2/107 3/198 4/312   (4 wkts dec.) 353   1/103 2/179 3/198   (4 wkts dec.) 230
                                                             4/220

M. W. Pooley, S. N. Barnes, M. C. J. Ball and K. B. S. Jarvis did not bat.

Bowling: *First Innings*—Jenkins 20–3–61–0; Johnson 14–1–44–0; Shufflebotham 17–2–65–1; Buzza 27–6–97–1; Atkinson 4–1–9–0; Lowrey 14–2–59–2. *Second Innings*—Jenkins 23.3–3–68–1; Johnson 13–5–20–0; Shufflebotham 11–3–37–0; Buzza 20–1–91–2; Lowrey 2–0–6–0.

Cambridge University

S. P. James c Tedstone b Pooley	116	– lbw b Jarvis	6
R. Heap c Butcher b Barnes	11	– c Wright b Barnes	0
A. J. Buzza c Ball b Pooley	6	– (9) b Barnes	1
*J. C. M. Atkinson c Hodgson b Ball	72	– b Ball	34
M. J. Lowrey c Tedstone b Bainbridge	20	– run out	45
M. J. Morris c Butcher b Barnes	18	– lbw b Bainbridge	17
G. B. A. Dyer c Ball b Barnes	1	– (3) c Tedstone b Jarvis	4
*J. P. Arscott c Lloyds b Barnes	13	– (7) not out	43
D. H. Shufflebotham not out	25	– (8) c Tedstone b Barnes	29
R. H. J. Jenkins not out	3	– c Butcher b Barnes	1
S. W. Johnson (did not bat)		– c Wright b Ball	1
B 12, l-b 9, n-b 8	29	B 6, l-b 7, w 1, n-b 4	18

1/23 2/38 3/146 4/190 5/226   (8 wkts dec.) 314   1/7 2/12 3/13 4/81 5/116   199
6/241 7/257 8/304   6/121 7/173 8/184 9/186

Bowling: *First Innings*—Barnes 24–9–65–4; Jarvis 15–2–50–0; Ball 15–4–50–1; Pooley 3–1–51–2; Bainbridge 12–3–33–1; Lloyds 22–5–44–0. *Second Innings*—Barnes 14–2–51–4; Jarvis 7–0–31–2; Pooley 3–0–16–0; Ball 13–4–37–2; Lloyds 11–2–24–0; Bainbridge 8–3–27–1.

Umpires: D. R. Shepherd and R. C. Tolchard.

†At Cambridge, June 10. Cambridge University won by 72 runs. Cambridge University 176 (A. R. Wingfield Digby five for 41); Free Foresters 104 (R. A. Pyman five for 32).

†At Cambridge, June 11, 12, 13. Drawn. Toss: MCC. MCC 317 for five dec. (J. F. Short 105, A. J. Goldsmith 32, R. J. Robinson 45, P. J. Mir 104) and 21 for three; Cambridge University 134 (R. J. Turner 53; P. J. Mir three for 18, M. Halliday three for 21) and 391 for nine dec. (S. P. James 99, J. C. M. Atkinson 56, R. A. Pyman 65, R. H. J. Jenkins 50 not out; M. J. Robinson three for 50).

†At Cambridge, June 14. Cambridge University won by eight wickets. Club Cricket Conference Under-25 96; Cambridge University 97 for two.

CAMBRIDGE UNIVERSITY v NOTTINGHAMSHIRE

At Cambridge, June 16, 18, 19. Drawn. Toss: Nottinghamshire. A second-innings century by James, who hit fifteen fours to reach three figures from 199 balls in 211 minutes, meant Cambridge were never in danger of defeat, but nor was there ever any prospect of victory. On the opening day, Martindale hit nineteen fours in his career-best 138, from 243 deliveries in 274 minutes, and dominated a 183-run partnership with Newell for Nottinghamshire's second wicket. However, with almost two hours lost to rain on the second day, and prevented by Hutchinson, a Freshman in his first match, from making Cambridge follow on, Nottinghamshire needed runs quickly if they were to press for victory. In the event, they batted until lunch, leaving the University 180 minutes plus twenty overs to chase 340. As James and Heap occupied 33 overs while putting on 63 for the first wicket, Nottinghamshire's prospects began to recede.

Close of play: First day, Cambridge University 9-2 (R. H. J. Jenkins 0*); Second day, Nottinghamshire 46-0 (P. Johnson 35*, M. Saxelby 10*).

Nottinghamshire

P. R. Pollard lbw b Jenkins	13		
D. J. R. Martindale st Turner b Lowrey	138		
M. Newell c Atkinson b Jenkins	60		
*P. Johnson lbw b Pyman	4	– (1) run out	49
M. Saxelby not out	30	– (2) c Atkinson b Lowrey	73
R. J. Evans not out	21	– (4) not out	0
†C. W. Scott (did not bat)	–	(3) not out	67
B 2, l-b 2, n-b 6	10	B 4, l-b 3, n-b 2	9

1/29 2/212 3/220 4/226   (4 wkts dec.) 276   1/79 2/172   (2 wkts dec.) 198

K. P. Evans, R. A. Pick, J. A. Afford and M. G. Field-Buss did not bat.

Bowling: *First Innings*—Jenkins 21–1–51–2; Pyman 21–3–72–1; Shufflebotham 11–2–38–0; Lowrey 20–6–55–1; Buzza 18–5–54–0; Atkinson 2–0–2–0. *Second Innings*—Jenkins 11–0–49–0; Pyman 9–0–50–0; Buzza 10–1–50–0; Shufflebotham 5–0–37–0; Lowrey 3–0–5–1.

Cambridge University

S. P. James b Pick	1	– not out	104
R. Heap c K. P. Evans b Field-Buss	4	– lbw b K. P. Evans	31
R. H. J. Jenkins lbw b K. P. Evans	12		
†R. J. Turner c K. P. Evans b Afford	32	– (3) c Scott b K. P. Evans	0
*J. C. M. Atkinson c K. P. Evans b Afford	0	– (4) c Pick b Afford	5
M. J. Lowrey c Pick b K. P. Evans	19	– (5) b Newell	25
M. J. Morris b K. P. Evans	4	– (6) not out	0
G. M. Hutchinson b K. P. Evans	29		
R. A. Pyman b Field-Buss	11		
D. H. Shufflebotham not out	4		
A. J. Buzza b Field-Buss	0		
B 4, l-b 13, n-b 2	19	B 3, l-b 4, w 1, n-b 1	9

1/5 2/9 3/43 4/44 5/57   135   1/63 2/67 3/80 4/173   (4 wkts) 174
6/75 7/88 8/112 9/130

Bowling: *First Innings*—Pick 13–6–31–1; K. P. Evans 23–8–50–4; Afford 14–8–13–2; Field-Buss 15.4–9–14–3; Saxelby 5–1–10–0. *Second Innings*—Pick 5–1–12–0; K. P. Evans 15–6–27–2; Field-Buss 21–4–37–0; Afford 17–6–44–1; Newell 5–2–22–1; R. J. Evans 6–1–24–0; Johnson 1–0–1–0.

Umpires: B. Leadbeater and R. A. White.

†At Cambridge, June 17. Cambridge University won by two wickets. Quidnuncs 184 for seven dec. (D. J. Fell 67); Cambridge University 186 for eight.

CAMBRIDGE UNIVERSITY v KENT

At Cambridge, June 20, 21, 22. Kent won by 92 runs. Toss: Cambridge University. The captains' willingness to achieve a result defeated the weather. Contrasting hundreds from Taylor, hitting fifteen fours from 276 deliveries in 283 minutes, and Chris Cowdrey, with three fours and seven sixes from 104 balls in 137 minutes, had enabled Kent to pass 300 with only three wickets down, but rain and bad light ruled out most of the second day. Cambridge declared their first innings at 57 for two and Kent forfeited their second, to leave the University needing 273 on the final day's play. A half-century by James and solid support from Turner saw them to 122 for one by early afternoon. But Merrick then took three wickets in eleven balls and Davis's left-arm spin brought him career-best figures of six for 40 as Cambridge lost nine wickets for 58 runs.

Close of play: First day, Kent 329-3 (C. S. Cowdrey 102*, M. V. Fleming 19*); Second day, Cambridge University 57-2 (R. Heap 27*, J. C. M. Atkinson 0*).

Kent

1. G. Hinks lbw b Lowrey	42	M. V. Fleming not out	19	
N. R. Taylor c Pyman b Buzza	120	B 1, l-b 5, w 5, n-b 1	12	
G. R. Cowdrey st Turner b Lowrey	34		—	
C. S. Cowdrey not out	102	1/91 2/144 3/225	(3 wkts dec.) 329	

S. A. Marsh, R. M. Ellison, R. P. Davis, T. A. Merrick, N. J. Llong and A. P. Igglesden did not bat.

Bowling: Jenkins 19–5–43–0; Pyman 26–8–60–0; Shufflebotham 8–0–42–0; Buzza 26–7–106–1; Lowrey 28–12–72–2.

Kent forfeited their second innings.

Cambridge University

S. P. James c Marsh b Igglesden	3	– b Merrick	57
R. Heap not out	27	– b Davis	17
R. J. Turner b Fleming	22	– c and b Merrick	35
J. C. M. Atkinson not out	0	– b Merrick	0
M. J. Lowrey (did not bat)		– b Davis	4
M. J. Morris (did not bat)		– b Davis	24
G. M. Hutchinson (did not bat)		– c and b Davis	2
R. A. Pyman (did not bat)		– c G. R. Cowdrey b Davis	0
D. H. Shufflebotham (did not bat)		– c Marsh b Igglesden	16
R. H. J. Jenkins (did not bat)		– c Llong b Davis	1
A. J. Buzza (did not bat)		– not out	1
L-b 5	5	B 12, l-b 8, w 1, n-b 2	23
	—		—
1/3 2/53	(2 wkts dec.) 57	1/27 2/122 3/122 4/125 5/129	180
		6/137 7/141 8/172 9/175	

Bowling: *First Innings*—Merrick 7–5–7–0; Igglesden 6–2–12–1; Fleming 5.3–1–13–1; Ellison 5–0–20–0. *Second Innings*—Merrick 10–6–13–3; Igglesden 14–3–45–1; Davis 8.1–15–40–6; Ellison 7–3–24–0; Llong 7–1–24–0; Fleming 9–5–14–0.

Umpires: G. I. Burgess and B. J. Meyer.

†At Portsmouth, June 23, 24, 25. Cambridge University won by one wicket. Combined Services 314 for three dec. (SAC A. Jones 105 not out, 2nd Lt R. J. Greatorex 79, Cpl G. J. P. Richards 55 not out) and 239 for five dec. (SAC A. Jones 92, Capt. P. S. Germain 57 not out); Cambridge University 206 for six dec. (R. Heap 62) and 349 for nine (G. M. Hutchinson 75, M. J. Lowrey 68, R. A. Pyman 63; Sgt M. W. Ings five for 101).

At Hove, June 30, July 2, 3. CAMBRIDGE UNIVERSITY beat SUSSEX by three wickets.

At Lord's, July 4, 5, 6. CAMBRIDGE UNIVERSITY drew with OXFORD UNIVERSITY (See Other Matches at Lord's, 1990).

OXFORD AND CAMBRIDGE BLUES

From 1946 to 1990, and some others

A full list of Blues from 1837 may be found in all *Wisdens* published between 1923 and 1939. Between 1948 and 1972 the list was confined to all those who had won Blues after 1880, plus some of "special interest for personal or family reasons". Between 1972 and 1982 the list was restricted to those who had won Blues since 1919. Such adjustments have been necessary owing to the exigencies of space.

OXFORD

Aamer Hameed (Central Model HS and Punjab U.) 1979

Abell, G. E. B. (Marlborough) 1924, 1926-27

Allan, J. M. (Edinburgh Academy) 1953-56

Allerton, J. W. O. (Stowe) 1969

Allison, D. F. (Greenmore Coll.) 1970

Almaer, S. A. (Ilford County HS) 1988-89

Altham, H. S. (Repton) 1911-12

Arenhold, J. A. (Diocesan Coll., SA) 1954

Baig, A. A. (Aliya and Osmania U., India) 1959-62

Baig, M. A. (Osmania U., India) 1962-64

Bailey, J. A. (Christ's Hospital) (Capt. in 1958) 1956-58

Barber, A. T. (Shrewsbury) (Capt. in 1929) 1927-29

Barker, A. H. (Charterhouse) 1964-65, 1967

Bartlett, J. H. (Chichester) 1946, 1951

Beech, A. R. (John XXIII Coll., Perth and Univ. of Western Australia) 1987

Bettington, R. H. B. (The King's School, Parramatta) (Capt. in 1923) 1920-23

Bird, W. S. (Malvern) (Capt. in 1906) 1904-06

Birrell, H. B. (St Andrews, SA) 1953-54

Blake, P. D. S. (Eton) (Capt. in 1952) 1950-52

Bloy, N. C. F. (Dover) 1946-47

Boobbyer, B. (Uppingham) 1949-52

Bosanquet, B. J. T. (Eton) 1898-1900

Botton, N. D. (King Edward's, Bath) 1974

Bowman, R. C. (Fettes) 1957

Brettell, D. N. (Cheltenham) 1977

Bristowe, W. R. (Charterhouse) 1984-85

Brooks, R. A. (Quintin and Bristol U.) 1967

Brown, M. E. O. (Diocesan Coll. and Univ. of Cape Town) 1988

Burchnall, R. L. (Winchester) 1970-71

Burki, J. (St Mary's, Rawalpindi and Punjab U.) 1958-60

Burton, M. St J. W. (Umtali HS, Rhodesia and Rhodes U.) (Capt. in 1970) 1969-71

Bury, T. E. O. (Charterhouse) 1980

Bush, J. E. (Magdalen Coll. Sch.) 1952

Campbell, A. N. (Berkhamsted) 1970

Campbell, I. P. (Canford) 1949-50

Campbell, I. P. F. (Repton) (Capt. in 1913) 1911-13

Cantlay, C. P. T. (Radley) 1975

Carr, D. B. (Repton) (Capt. in 1950) 1949-51

Carr, J. D. (Repton) 1983-85

Carroll, P. R. (Newington Coll. and Sydney U.) 1971

Chalk, F. G. H. (Uppingham) (Capt. in 1934) 1931-34

Chesterton, G. H. (Malvern) 1949

Claughton, J. A. (King Edward's, Birmingham) (Capt. in 1978) 1976-79

Clements, S. M. (Ipswich) (Capt. in 1979) 1976, 1979

Clube, S. V. M. (St John's, Leatherhead) 1956

Cope, J. E. B. (St John's, Leatherhead) 1986-87

Corlett, S. C. (Worksop) 1971-72

Corran, A. J. (Gresham's) 1958-60

Coutts, I. D. F. (Dulwich) 1952

Cowan, R. S. (Lewes Priory CS) 1980-82

Cowdrey, M. C. (Tonbridge) (Capt. in 1954) 1952-54

Coxon, A. J. (Harrow CS) 1952

Crawley, A. M. (Harrow) 1927-30

Crawley, M. A. (Manchester GS) (Capt. in 1989) 1987-90

Crutchley, G. E. V. (Harrow) 1912

Cullinan, M. R. (Hilton Coll., SA) 1983-84

Curtis, D. M. (Falcon Coll., Harare and Cape Town U.) 1990

Curtis, I. J. (Whitgift) 1980, 1982

Cushing, V. G. B. (KCS Wimbledon) 1973

Cuthbertson, J. L. (Rugby) 1962-63

Davidson, W. W. (Brighton) 1947-48

Davis, F. J. (Blundell's) 1963

Dawson, T. A. J. (Mill Hill) 1986

Delisle, G. P. S. (Stonyhurst) 1955-56

de Saram, F. C. (Royal Coll., Colombo) 1934-35

Divecha, R. V. (Podar HS and Bombay U.) 1950-51

Dixon, E. J. H. (St Edward's, Oxford) (Capt. in 1939) 1937-39

Donnelly, M. P. (New Plymouth BHS and Canterbury U., NZ) (Capt. in 1947) 1946-47

Dowding, A. L. (St Peter's, Adelaide) (Capt. in 1953) 1952-53

Drybrough, C. D. (Highgate) (Capt. in 1961-62) 1960-62

Duff, A. R. (Radley) 1960-61

Dyer, A. W. (Mill Hill) 1965-66

Dyson, E. M. (QEGS, Wakefield) 1958

Eagar, M. A. (Rugby) 1956-59

Easter, J. N. C. (St Edward's, Oxford) 1967-68

Edbrooke, R. M. (Queen Elizabeth's Hospital) 1984

Edwards, P. G. (Canford) 1987-89

Ellis, R. G. P. (Haileybury) (Capt. in 1982) 1981-83

Elviss, R. W. (Leeds GS) 1966-67

Ezekowitz, R. A. B. (Westville BHS, Durban and Cape Town U., SA) 1980-81

Faber, M. J. J. (Eton) 1972

Fane, F. L. (Charterhouse) 1897-98

Fasken, D. K. (Wellington) 1953-55

Fellows-Smith, J. P. (Durban HS, SA) 1953-55

Fillary, E. W. J. (St Lawrence) 1963-65

Findlay, A. W. (Eton) (Capt. in 1903) 1901-03

Firth, T. (Stockport GS) 1987

Fisher, P. B. (St Ignatius, Enfield) 1975-78

Foster, G. N. (Malvern) 1905-08

Foster, H. K. (Malvern) 1894-96

Foster, R. E. (Malvern) (Capt. in 1900) 1897-1900

Franks, J. G. (Stamford) 1984-85

Fry, C. A. (Repton) 1959-61

Fry, C. B. (Repton) (Capt. in 1894) 1892-95

Fursdon, E. D. (Sherborne) 1974-75

Gamble, N. W. (Stockport GS) 1967

Garofall, A. R. (Latymer Upper) 1967-68

Gerrans, P. S. (Daramalau Coll. and Aust. Nat. U.) 1990

Gibbs, P. J. K. (Hanley GS) 1964-66

Gibson, I. (Manchester GS) 1955-58

Gilliat, R. M. C. (Charterhouse) (Capt. in 1966) 1964-67

Gilligan, F. W. (Dulwich) (Capt. in 1920) 1919-20

Glover, T. R. (Lancaster RGS) (Capt. in 1975) 1973-75

Goldstein, F. S. (Falcon Coll., Bulawayo) (Capt. in 1968-69) 1966-69

Green, D. M. (Manchester GS) 1959-61

Grover, J. N. (Winchester) (Capt. in 1938) 1936-38

Groves, M. G. M. (Diocesan Coll., SA) 1964-66

Guest, M. R. J. (Rugby) 1964-66

Guise, J. L. (Winchester) (Capt. in 1925) 1924-25

Gurr, D. R. (Aylesbury GS) 1976-77

Hagan, D. A. (Trinity, Leamington Spa) 1986, 1988-90

Halliday, S. J. (Downside) 1980

Hamblin, C. B. (King's, Canterbury) 1971-73

Hamilton, A. C. (Charterhouse) 1975

Hampton, A. N. S. (Reading) 1989

Harris, C. R. (Buckingham RLS) 1964

Harris, Hon. G. R. C. (Lord Harris) (Eton) 1871-72, 1874

Hayes, K. A. (QEGS, Blackburn) (Capt. in 1984) 1981-84

Heal, M. G. (St Brendan's, Bristol) 1970, 1972

Heard, H. (QE Hosp.) 1969-70

Henderson, D. (St Edward's, Oxford) 1950

Henderson, I. M. (Laxton) 1987, 1989-90

Henley, D. F. (Harrow) 1947

Heseltine, P. J. (Holgate GS) 1983

Hester, E. D. (Thornleigh Salesian Coll.) 1989

Hiller, R. B. (Bec) 1966

Hobbs, J. A. D. (Liverpool Coll.) 1957

Hofmeyr, M. B. (Pretoria, SA) (Capt. in 1951) 1949-51

Holmes, E. R. T. (Malvern) (Capt. in 1927) 1925-27

Hone, B. W. (Adelaide U.) (Capt. in 1933) 1931-33

Howell, M. (Repton) (Capt. in 1919) 1914, 1919

Huxford, P. N. (Richard Hale) 1981

Imran Khan (Aitchison Coll., Lahore and Worcester RGS) (Capt. in 1974) 1973-75

Jack, T. B. (Aquinas Coll. and Univ. of WA) 1988

Jakobson, T. R. (Charterhouse) 1961

Jardine, D. R. (Winchester) 1920-21, 1923

Jardine, M. R. (Fettes) (Capt. in 1891) 1889-92

Jarrett, D. W. (Wellington) 1975

Johns, R. L. (St Albans and Keele U.) 1970

Jones, A. K. C. (Solihull) (Capt. in 1973) 1971-73

Jones, P. C. H. (Milton HS, Rhodesia and Rhodes U.) (Capt. in 1972) 1971-72

Jose, A. D. (Adelaide U.) 1950-51

Jowett, D. C. P. R. (Sherborne) 1952-55

Jowett, R. L. (Bradford GS) 1957-59

Kamm, A. (Charterhouse) 1954

Kardar, A. H. (Islamia Coll. and Punjab U.) 1947-49

Kayum, D. A. (Selhurst GS and Chatham House GS) 1977-78

Keighley, W. G. (Eton) 1947-48

Kentish, E. S. M. (Cornwall Coll., Jamaica) 1956

Khan, A. J. (Aitchison Coll., Lahore and Punjab U.) 1968-69

Kilborn, M. J. (Farrer Agric. HS and Univ. of NSW) (Capt. in 1988) 1986-88

Kingsley, P. G. T. (Winchester) (Capt. in 1930) 1928-30

Kinkead-Weekes, R. C. (Eton) 1972

Knight, D. J. (Malvern) 1914, 1919

Knight, J. M. (Oundle) 1979

Knott, C. H. (Tonbridge) (Capt. in 1924) 1922-24

Knott, F. H. (Tonbridge) (Capt. in 1914) 1912-14

Knox, F. P. (Dulwich) (Capt. in 1901) 1899-1901

Lamb, Hon. T. M. (Shrewsbury) 1973-74

Lawrence, M. P. (Manchester GS) 1984-86

Lee, R. J. (Church of England GS and Sydney U.) 1972-74

Legge, G. B. (Malvern) (Capt. in 1926) 1925-26

L'Estrange, M. G. (St Aloysius Coll. and Sydney U.) 1977, 1979

Leveson Gower, H. D. G. (Winchester) (Capt. in 1896) 1893-96

Lewis, D. J. (Cape Town U.) 1951

Lloyd, M. F. D. (Magdalen Coll. Sch.) 1974

Luddington, R. S. (KCS, Wimbledon) 1982

Lunn, P. D. (Abingdon) 1989-90

McCanlis, M. A. (Cranleigh) (Capt. in 1928) 1926-28

Macindoe, D. H. (Eton) (Capt. in 1946) 1937-39, 1946

McKinna, G. H. (Manchester GS) 1953

MacLarnon, P. C. (Loughborough U.) 1985

Majendie, N. L. (Winchester) 1962-63

Mallett, A. W. H. (Dulwich) 1947-48

Mallett, N. V. H. (St Andrew's Coll. and Cape Town U.) 1981

Manasseh, M. (Epsom) 1964

Marie, G. V. (Western Australia U. and Reading U.) (Capt. in 1979, but injury prevented him playing v Cambridge) 1978

Marks, V. J. (Blundell's) (Capt. in 1976-77) 1975-78

Marsden, R. (Merchant Taylors', Northwood) 1982

Marshall, J. C. (Rugby) 1953

Marsham, C. D. B. (Private) (Capt. in 1857-58) 1854-58

Marsham, C. H. B. (Eton) (Capt. in 1902) 1900-02

Marsham, C. J. B. (Private) 1851

Marsham, R. H. B. (Private) 1856

Marsland, G. P. (Rossall) 1954

Martin, J. D. (Magdalen Coll. Sch.) (Capt. in 1965) 1962-63, 1965

Maudsley, R. H. (Malvern) 1946-47

May, B. (Prince Edward's, Salisbury and Cape Town U.) (Capt. in 1971) 1970-72

Mee, A. A. G. (Merchant Taylors', Northwood) 1986

Melville, A. (Michaelhouse, SA) (Capt. in 1931-32) 1930-33

Melville, C. D. M. (Michaelhouse, SA) 1957

Metcalfe, S. G. (Leeds GS) 1956

Millener, D. J. (Auckland GS and Auckland U.) 1969-70

Miller, A. J. T. (Haileybury) (Capt. in 1985) 1983-85

Minns, R. E. F. (King's, Canterbury) 1962-63

Mitchell, W. M. (Dulwich) 1951-52

Mitchell-Innes, N. S. (Sedbergh) (Capt. in 1936) 1934-37

Moore, D. N. (Shrewsbury) (Capt. in 1931, when he did not play v Cambridge owing to illness) 1930

Morgan, A. H. (Hastings GS) 1969

Morrill, N. D. (Sandown GS and Millfield) 1979

Morris, R. E. (Dyffryn Conwy, Llanrwst) (Capt. in 1990) 1987, 1989-90

Moulding, R. P. (Haberdashers' Aske's) (Capt. in 1981) 1978-83

Mountford, P. N. G. (Bromsgrove) 1963

Neate, F. W. (St Paul's) 1961-62

Newton-Thompson, J. O. (Diocesan Coll., SA) 1946

Niven, R. A. (Berkhamsted) 1968-69, 1973

Nuttall, J. D. (Pocklington) 1988-89

O'Brien, T. C. (St Charles' College, Notting Hill) 1884-85

Orders, J. O. D. (Winchester) 1978-81

Owen-Smith, H. G. (Diocesan College, SA) 1931-33

Palairet, L. C. H. (Repton) (Capt. in 1892-93) 1890-93

Pataudi, Nawab of (Chief's College, Lahore) 1929-31

Pataudi, Nawab of (Winchester) (Capt. in 1961, when he did not play v Cambridge owing to a car accident, and 1963) 1960, 1963

Pathmanathan, G. (Royal Coll., Colombo and Sri Lanka U.) 1975-78

Paver, R. G. L. (Fort Victoria HS and Rhodes U.) 1973-74

Pawson, A. C. (Winchester) 1903

Pawson, A. G. (Winchester) (Capt. in 1910) 1908-11

Pawson, H. A. (Winchester) (Capt. in 1948) 1947-48

Pearce, J. P. (Ampleforth) 1979

Peebles, I. A. R. (Glasgow Academy) 1930

Petchey, M. D. (Latymer Upper) 1983

Phillips, J. B. M. (King's, Canterbury) 1955

Piachaud, J. D. (St Thomas's, Colombo) 1958-61

Pithey, D. B. (Plumtree HS and Cape Town U.) 1961-62

Porter, S. R. (Peers School) 1973

Potter, I. C. (King's, Canterbury) 1961-62

Potts, H. J. (Stand GS) 1950

Price, V. R. (Bishop's Stortford) (Capt. in 1921) 1919-22
Pycroft, J. (Bath) 1836

Quinlan, J. D. (Sherborne) 1985

Rawlinson, H. T. (Eton) 1983-84
Raybould, J. G. (Leeds GS) 1959
Reynolds, G. D. (Wellington Coll.) 1988-89
Ridge, S. P. (Dr Challenor's GS) 1982
Ridley, G. N. S. (Milton HS, Rhodesia) (Capt. in 1967) 1965-68
Ridley, R. M. (Clifton) 1968-70
Robertson-Glasgow, R. C. (Charterhouse) 1920-23
Robinson, G. A. (Preston Cath. Coll.) 1971
Robinson, H. B. O. (North Shore Coll., Vancouver) 1947-48
Rogers, J. J. (Sedbergh) 1979-81
Ross, C. J. (Wanganui CS and Wellington U., NZ) (Capt. in 1980) 1978-80
Rudd, C. R. D. (Eton) 1949
Rumbold, J. S. (St Andrew's Coll., NZ) 1946
Rutnagur, R. S. (Westminster) 1985-86
Rydon, R. A. (Sherborne) 1986

Sabine, P. N. B. (Marlborough) 1963
Sale, R. (Repton) 1910
Sale, R. (Repton) 1939, 1946
Salvi, N. V. (Rossall) 1986
Sanderson, J. F. W. (Westminster) 1980
Sardesai, R. D. (St Xavier's Coll., Bombay and Univ. of Bombay) 1987
Saunders, C. J. (Lancing) 1964
Savage, R. Le Q. (Marlborough) 1976-78
Sayer, D. M. (Maidstone GS) 1958-60
Scott, M. D. (Winchester) 1957
Singleton, A. P. (Shrewsbury) (Capt. in 1937) 1934-37
Siviter, K. (Liverpool) 1976
Smith, A. C. (King Edward's, Birmingham) (Capt. in 1959-60) 1958-60
Smith, G. O. (Charterhouse) 1895-96
Smith, M. J. K. (Stamford) (Capt. in 1956) 1954-56
Stallibrass, M. J. D. (Lancing) 1974
Stevens, G. T. S. (UCS) (Capt. in 1922) 1920-23
Sutcliffe, S. P. (King George V GS, Southport) 1980-81
Sutton, M. A. (Ampleforth) 1946
Sygrove, M. R. (Lutterworth GS) 1988

Tavaré, C. J. (Sevenoaks) 1975-77
Taylor, C. H. (Westminster) 1923-26
Taylor, T. J. (Stockport GS) 1981-82
Thackeray, P. R. (St Edward's, Oxford and Exeter U.) 1974
Thomas, R. J. A. (Radley) 1965
Thorne, D. A. (Bablake) (Capt. in 1986) 1984-86
Toft, D. P. (Tonbridge) 1966-67

Toogood, G. J. (N. Bromsgrove HS) (Capt. in 1983) 1982-85
Tooley, C. D. M. (St Dunstan's) (Capt. in 1987) 1985-87
Topham, R. D. N. (Shrewsbury and Australian National U., Canberra) 1976
Travers, B. H. (Sydney U.) 1946, 1948
Trevelyan, R. W. D. (Marlborough) 1990
Turner, G. J. (St Stithian's and Cape Town U.) 1990
Twining, R. H. (Eton) (Capt. in 1912) 1910-13

van der Bijl, P. G. (Diocesan Coll., SA) 1932
van der Merwe, W. M. (Grey, OFS U. and Cape Town U.) 1990
Van Ryneveld, C. B. (Diocesan Coll., SA) (Capt. in 1949) 1948-50
Varey, J. G. (Birkenhead) 1982-83

Wagstaffe, M. C. (Rossall and Exeter U.) 1972
Walford, M. M. (Rugby) 1936, 1938
Walker, D. F. (Uppingham) (Capt. in 1935) 1933-35
Waller, G. de W. (Hurstpierpoint) 1974
Walsh, D. R. (Marlborough) 1967-69
Walshe, A. P. (Milton HS, Rhodesia) 1953, 1955-56
Walton, A. C. (Radley) (Capt. in 1957) 1955-57
Ward, J. M. (Newcastle-under-Lyme HS) 1971-73
Warner, P. F. (Rugby) 1895-96
Watson, A. G. M. (St Lawrence) 1965-66, 1968
Weale, S. D. (Westminster City) 1987-88, 1990
Webb, H. E. (Winchester) 1948
Webbe, A. J. (Harrow) (Capt. in 1877-78) 1875-78
Wellings, E. M. (Cheltenham) 1929, 1931
Westley, S. A. (Lancaster RGS) 1968-69
Wheatley, G. A. (Uppingham) 1946
Whitcombe, P. A. (Winchester) 1947-49
Whitcombe, P. J. (Worcester RGS) 1951-52
Wiley, W. G. A. (Diocesan Coll., SA) 1952
Williams, C. C. P. (Westminster) (Capt. in 1955) 1953-55
Wilson, P. R. B. (Milton HS, Rhodesia and Cape Town U.) 1968, 1970
Wilson, R. W. (Warwick) 1957
Wingfield Digby, A. R. (Sherborne) 1971, 1975-77
Winn, C. E. (KCS, Wimbledon) 1948-51
Woodcock, R. G. (Worcester RGS) 1957-58
Wookey, S. M. (Malvern and Cambridge U.) 1978
Wordsworth, Chas. (Harrow) (Capt. both years, first Oxford Capt.) 1827, 1829
Worsley, D. R. (Bolton) (Capt. in 1964) 1961-64
Wrigley, M. H. (Harrow) 1949

CAMBRIDGE

Acfield, D. L. (Brentwood) 1967-68
Aers, D. R. (Tonbridge) 1967
Ahluwalia, M. S. (Latymer Upper) 1986
Aird, R. (Eton) 1923
Alban, M. T. (Sedbergh) 1989
Alexander, F. C. M. (Wolmer's Coll., Jamaica) 1952-53
Allbrook, M. E. (Tonbridge) 1975-78
Allen, G. O. (Eton) 1922-23
Allom, M. J. C. (Wellington) 1927-28
Andrew, C. R. (Barnard Castle) (Capt. in 1985) 1984-85
Ashton, C. T. (Winchester) (Capt. in 1923) 1921-23
Ashton, G. (Winchester) (Capt. in 1921) 1919-21
Ashton, H. (Winchester) (Capt. in 1922) 1920-22
Atherton, M. A. (Capt. in 1988-89) (Manchester GS) 1987-89
Atkins, G. (Dr Challenor's GS) 1960
Atkinson, J. C. M. (Millfield) (Capt. in 1990) 1988-90
Aworth, C. J. (Tiffin) (Capt. in 1975) 1973-75

Bail, P. A. C. (Millfield) 1986-88
Bailey, T. E. (Dulwich) 1947-48
Baker, R. K. (Brentwood) 1973-74
Bannister, C. S. (Caterham) 1976
Barber, R. W. (Ruthin) 1956-57
Barford, M. T. (Eastbourne) 1970-71
Barrington, W. E. J. (Lancing) 1982
Bartlett, H. T. (Dulwich) (Capt. in 1936) 1934-36
Bate, R. (Haberdashers' Aske's) 1988
Beaumont, D. J. (West Bridgford GS and Bramshill Coll.) 1978
Benke, A. F. (Cheltenham) 1962
Bennett, B. W. P. (Welbeck and RMA Sandhurst) 1979
Bennett, C. T. (Harrow) (Capt. in 1925) 1923, 1925
Bernard, J. R. (Clifton) 1958-60
Bhatia, A. N. (Doon School, India) 1969
Bligh, Hon. Ivo F. W. (Lord Darnley) (Eton) (Capt. in 1881) 1878-81
Blofeld, H. C. (Eton) 1959
Bodkin, P. E. (Bradfield) (Capt. in 1946) 1946
Boyd-Moss, R. J. (Bedford) 1980-83
Brearley, J. M. (City of London) (Capt. in 1963-64) 1961-64
Breddy, M. N. (Cheltenham GS) 1984
Brodie, J. B. (Union HS, SA) 1960
Brodrick, P. D. (Royal GS, Newcastle) 1961
Bromley, R. C. (Christ's Coll. and Canterbury U., NZ) 1970
Brooker, M. E. W. (Lancaster RGS and Burnley GS) 1976

Brown, A. D. (Clacton HS) 1986
Brown, F. R. (The Leys) 1930-31
Browne, D. W. (Stamford) 1986
Burnett, A. C. (Lancing) 1949
Burnley, I. D. (Queen Elizabeth, Darlington) 1984
Bush, D. J. (King Edward VI, Fiveways) 1989
Bushby, M. H. (Dulwich) (Capt. in 1954) 1952-54
Buzza, A. J. (Redruth CS) 1989-90

Calthorpe, Hon. F. S. G. (Repton) 1912-14, 1919
Cameron, J. H. (Taunton) 1935-37
Cangley, B. G. M. (Felsted) 1947
Carling, P. G. (Kingston GS) 1968, 1970
Chambers, R. E. J. (Forest) 1966
Chapman, A. P. F. (Oakham and Uppingham) 1920-22
Close, P. A. (Haileybury) 1965
Cobden, F. C. (Harrow) 1870-72
Cockett, J. A. (Aldenham) 1951
Coghlan, T. B. L. (Rugby) 1960
Conradi, E. R. (Oundle) 1946
Cook, G. W. (Dulwich) 1957-58
Cooper, N. H. C. (St Brendan's, Bristol and East Anglia U.) 1979
Cosh, N. J. (Dulwich) 1966-68
Cotterell, T. A. (Downside) 1983-85
Cottrell, G. A. (Kingston GS) (Capt. in 1968) 1966-68
Cottrell, P. R. (Chislehurst and Sidcup GS) 1979
Coverdale, S. P. (St Peter's, York) 1974-77
Craig, E. J. (Charterhouse) 1961-63
Crawford, N. C. (Shrewsbury) 1979-80
Crawley, E. (Harrow) 1887-89
Crawley, L. G. (Harrow) 1923-25
Croft, P. D. (Gresham's) 1955
Crookes, D. V. (Michaelhouse, SA) 1953
Curtis, T. S. (Worcester RGS) 1983

Daniell, J. (Clifton) 1899-1901
Daniels, D. M. (Rutlish) 1964-65
Datta, P. B. (Asutosh Coll., Calcutta) 1947
Davies, A. G. (Birkenhead) 1984-85
Davies, J. G. W. (Tonbridge) 1933-34
Davidson, J. E. (Penglais) 1985-86
Dawson, E. W. (Eton) (Capt. in 1927) 1924-27
Day, S. H. (Malvern) (Capt. in 1901) 1899-1902
Dewes, A. R. (Dulwich) 1978
Dewes, J. G. (Aldenham) 1948-50
Dexter, E. R. (Radley) (Capt. in 1958) 1956-58
Dickinson, D. C. (Clifton) 1953
Doggart, A. G. (Bishop's Stortford) 1921-22
Doggart, G. H. G. (Winchester) (Capt. in 1950) 1948-50

Doggart, S. J. G. (Winchester) 1980-83
Douglas-Pennant, S. (Eton) 1959
Duleepsinhji, K. S. (Cheltenham) 1925-26, 1928

Edmonds, P. H. (Gilbert Rennie HS, Lusaka, Skinner's and Cranbrook) (Capt. in 1973) 1971-73
Edwards, T. D. W. (Sherborne) 1981
Elgood, B. C. (Bradfield) 1948
Ellison, C. C. (Tonbridge) 1982-83, 1985-86
Enthoven, H. J. (Harrow) (Capt. in 1926) 1923-26
Estcourt, N. S. D. (Plumtree, Southern Rhodesia) 1954

Falcon, M. (Harrow) (Capt. in 1910) 1908-11
Farnes, K. (Royal Liberty School, Romford) 1931-33
Fell, D. J. (John Lyon) 1985-87
Fenton, N. C. W. (Rugby) 1988
Field, M. N. (Bablake) 1974
Fitzgerald, J. F. (St Brendan's, Bristol) 1968
Ford, A. F. J. (Repton) 1878-81
Ford, F. G. J. (Repton) (Capt. in 1889) 1887-90
Ford, W. J. (Repton) 1873
Fosh, M. K. (Harrow) 1977-78

Gardiner, S. J. (St Andrew's, Bloemfontein) 1978
Garlick, P. L. (Sherborne) 1984
Gibb, P. A. (St Edward's, Oxford) 1935-38
Gibson, C. H. (Eton) 1920-21
Gilligan, A. E. R. (Dulwich) 1919-20
Goldie, C. F. E. (St Paul's) 1981-82
Golding, A. K. (Colchester GS) 1986
Goodfellow, A. (Marlborough) 1961-62
Goonesena, G. (Royal Coll., Colombo) (Capt. in 1957) 1954-57
Gorman, S. R. (St Peter's, York) 1985, 1987
Grace, W. G., jun. (Clifton) 1895-96
Grant, G. C. (Trinidad) 1929-30
Grant, R. S. (Trinidad) 1933
Green, D. J. (Burton GS) (Capt. in 1959) 1957-59
Greig, I. A. (Queen's Coll., SA) (Capt. in 1979) 1977-79
Grierson, H. (Bedford GS) 1911
Grimes, A. D. H. (Tonbridge) 1984
Griffith, M. G. (Marlborough) 1963-65
Griffith, S. C. (Dulwich) 1935
Griffiths, W. H. (Charterhouse) 1946-48

Hadley, R. J. (Sanfields CS) 1971-73
Hall, J. E. (Ardingly) 1969
Hall, P. J. (Geelong) 1949
Harvey, J. R. W. (Marlborough) 1965
Hawke, Hon. M. B. (Eton) (Capt. in 1885) 1882-83, 1885
Hayes, P. J. (Brighton) 1974-75, 1977
Hays, D. L. (Highgate) 1966, 1968
Hayward, W. I. D. (St Peter's Coll., Adelaide) 1950-51, 1953

Haywood, D. C. (Nottingham HS) 1968
Hazelrigg, A. G. (Eton) (Capt. in 1932) 1930-32
Heap, R. (Ipswich) 1989-90
Heath, S. D. (King Edward's, Birmingham) 1988
Henderson, S. P. (Downside and Durham U.) (Capt. in 1983) 1982-83
Hewitt, S. G. P. (Bradford GS) 1983
Hignell, A. J. (Denstone) (Capt. in 1977-78) 1975-78
Hobson, B. S. (Taunton) 1946
Hodgson, K. I. (Oundle) 1981-83
Hodson, R. P. (QEGS, Wakefield) 1972-73
Holliday, D. C. (Oundle) 1979-81
Hooper, A. M. (Latymer Upper) 1987
Howat, M. G. (Abingdon) 1977, 1980
Howland, C. B. (Dulwich) (Capt. in 1960) 1958-60
Hughes, G. (Cardiff HS) 1965
Human, J. H. (Repton) (Capt. in 1934) 1932-34
Hurd, A. (Chigwell) 1958-60
Hutton, R. A. (Repton) 1962-64
Huxter, R. J. A. (Magdalen Coll. Sch.) 1981

Insole, D. J. (Monoux, Walthamstow) (Capt. in 1949) 1947-49

Jackson, E. J. W. (Winchester) 1974-76
Jackson, F. S. (Harrow) (Capt. in 1892-93) 1890-93
Jahangir Khan (Lahore), 1933-36
James, R. M. (St John's, Leatherhead) 1956-58
James, S. P. (Monmouth) 1989-90
Jameson, T. E. N. (Taunton and Durham U.) 1970
Jarrett, D. W. (Wellington and Oxford U.) 1976
Jefferson, R. I. (Winchester) 1961
Jenkins, R. H. J. (Oundle) 1990
Jenner, Herbert (Eton) (Capt. in 1827, First Cambridge Capt.) 1827
Jessop, G. L. (Cheltenham GS) (Capt. in 1899) 1896-99
Johnson, P. D. (Nottingham HS) 1970-72
Johnson, S. W. (Royal GS, Newcastle) 1990
Jones, A. O. (Bedford Modern) 1893
Jorden, A. M. (Monmouth) (Capt. in 1969-70) 1968-70

Kelland, P. A. (Repton) 1950
Kemp-Welch, G. D. (Charterhouse) (Capt. in 1931) 1929-31
Kendall, M. P. (Gillingham GS) 1972
Kenny, C. J. M. (Ampleforth) 1952
Kerslake, R. C. (Kingswood) 1963-64
Killick, E. T. (St Paul's) 1928-30
Kirby, D. (St Peter's, York) (Capt. in 1961) 1959-61
Kirkman, M. C. (Dulwich) 1963
Knight, R. D. V. (Dulwich) 1967-70
Knightley-Smith, W. (Highgate) 1953

Lacey, F. E. (Sherborne) 1882
Lacy-Scott, D. G. (Marlborough) 1946
Lea, A. E. (High Arcal GS) 1984-86
Lewis, A. R. (Neath GS) (Capt. in 1962) 1960-62
Lewis, L. K. (Taunton) 1953
Littlewood, D. J. (Enfield GS) 1978
Lowrey, M. J. (Radley) 1990
Lowry, T. C. (Christ's College, NZ) (Capt. in 1924) 1923-24
Lumsden, V. R. (Munro College, Jamaica) 1953-55
Lyttelton, 4th Lord (Eton) 1838
Lyttelton, Hon. Alfred (Eton) (Capt. in 1879) 1876-79
Lyttelton, Hon. C. F. (Eton) 1908-09
Lyttelton, Hon. C. G. (Lord Cobham) (Eton) 1861-64
Lyttelton, Hon. Edward (Eton) (Capt. in 1878) 1875-78
Lyttelton, Hon. G. W. S. (Eton) 1866-67

McAdam, K. P. W. J. (Prince of Wales, Nairobi and Millfield) 1965-66
MacBryan, J. C. W. (Exeter) 1920
McCarthy, C. N. (Maritzburg Coll., SA) 1952
McDowall, J. I. (Rugby) 1969
MacGregor, G. (Uppingham) (Capt. in 1891) 1888-91
McLachlan, A. A. (St Peter's, Adelaide) 1964-65
McLachlan, I. M. (St Peter's, Adelaide) 1957-58
Majid Khan (Aitchison Coll., Lahore and Punjab U.) (Capt. in 1971-72) 1970-72
Malalasekera, V. P. (Royal Coll., Colombo) 1966-67
Mann, E. W. (Harrow) (Capt. in 1905) 1903-05
Mann, F. G. (Eton) 1938-39
Mann, F. T. (Malvern) 1909-11
Marlar, R. G. (Harrow) (Capt. in 1953) 1951-53
Marriott, C. S. (St Columba's) 1920-21
Mathews, K. P. A. (Felsted) 1951
May, P. B. H. (Charterhouse) 1950-52
Melluish, M. E. L. (Rossall) (Capt. in 1956) 1954-56
Meyer, R. J. O. (Haileybury) 1924-26
Middleton, M. R. (Harrow) 1987
Miller, M. E. (Prince Henry GS, Hohne, WG) 1963
Mills, J. M. (Oundle) (Capt. in 1948) 1946-48
Mills, J. P. C. (Oundle) (Capt. in 1982) 1979-82
Mischler, N. M. (St Paul's) 1946-47
Mitchell, F. (St Peter's, York) (Capt. in 1896) 1894-97
Morgan, J. T. (Charterhouse) (Capt. in 1930) 1928-30
Morgan, M. N. (Marlborough) 1954

Morris, M. J. (Cherwell) 1990
Morris, R. J. (Blundell's) 1949
Morrison, J. S. F. (Charterhouse) (Capt. in 1919) 1912, 1914, 1919
Moses, G. H. (Ystalyfera GS) 1974
Moylan, A. C. D. (Clifton) 1977
Mubarak, A. M. (Royal Coll., Colombo and Sri Lanka U.) 1978-80
Murray, D. L. (Queen's RC, Trinidad) (Capt. in 1966) 1965-66
Murrills, T. J. (The Leys) (Capt. in 1976) 1973-74, 1976

Nevin, M. R. S. (Winchester) 1969
Norris, D. W. W. (Harrow) 1967-68
Noyes, S. J. (Royal GS, High Wycombe) 1988

O'Brien, R. P. (Wellington) 1955-56
Odendaal, A. (Queen's Coll. and Stellenbosch U., SA) 1980
Owen-Thomas, D. R. (KCS, Wimbledon) 1969-72

Palfreman, A. B. (Nottingham HS) 1966
Palmer, R. W. M. (Bedford) 1982
Parker, G. W. (Crypt, Gloucester) (Capt. in 1935) 1934-35
Parker, P. W. G. (Collyer's GS) 1976-78
Parsons, A. B. D. (Brighton) 1954-55
Pathmanathan, G. (Royal Coll., Colombo, Sri Lanka U. and Oxford U.) 1983
Paull, R. K. (Millfield) 1967
Payne, M. W. (Wellington) (Capt. in 1907) 1904-07
Pearman, H. (King Alfred's and St Andrew's U.) 1969
Pearson, A. J. G. (Downside) 1961-63
Peck, I. G. (Bedford) (Capt. in 1980-81) 1980-81
Pepper, J. (The Leys) 1946-48
Perry, J. N. (Ampleforth) 1987-88
Pieris, P. I. (St Thomas's, Colombo) 1957-58
Pointer, G. A. (St Dunstan's) 1987-88
Pollock, A. J. (Shrewsbury) (Capt. in 1984) 1982-84
Ponniah, C. E. M. (St Thomas's, Colombo) 1967-69
Ponsonby, Hon. F. G. B. (Lord Bessborough) (Harrow) 1836
Popplewell, N. F. M. (Radley) 1977-79
Popplewell, O. B. (Charterhouse) 1949-51
Pretlove, J. F. (Alleyn's) 1954-56
Price, D. G. (Haberdashers' Aske's) (Capt. in 1986-87) 1984-87
Prideaux, R. M. (Tonbridge) 1958-60
Pringle, D. R. (Felsted) (Capt. in 1982, when he did not play v Oxford owing to Test selection) 1979-81
Pritchard, G. C. (King's, Canterbury) 1964
Pryer, B. J. K. (City of London) 1948
Pyemont, C. P. (Marlborough) 1967
Pyman, R. A. (Harrow) 1989-90

Ranjitsinhji, K. S. (Rajkumar Coll., India) 1893

Ratcliffe, A. (Rydal) 1930-32

Reddy, N. S. K. (Doon School, India) 1959-61

Rimell, A. G. J. (Charterhouse) 1949-50

Robins, R. W. V. (Highgate) 1926-28

Roebuck, P. G. P. (Millfield) 1984-85

Roebuck, P. M. (Millfield) 1975-77

Roopnaraine, R. (Queen's RC, BG) 1965-66

Rose, M. H. (Pocklington) 1963-64

Ross, N. P. G. (Marlborough) 1969

Roundell, J. (Winchester) 1973

Russell, D. P. (West Park GS, St Helens) 1974-75

Russell, S. G. (Tiffin) (Capt. in 1967) 1965-67

Russom, N. (Huish's GS) 1980-81

Scott, A. M. G. (Seaford Head) 1985-87

Seabrook, F. J. (Haileybury) (Capt. in 1928) 1926-28

Seager, C. P. (Peterhouse, Rhodesia) 1971

Selvey, M. W. W. (Battersea GS and Manchester U.) 1971

Sheppard, D. S. (Sherborne) (Capt. in 1952) 1950-52

Short, R. L. (Denstone) 1969

Shufflebotham, D. H. (Neath GS) 1989-90

Shuttleworth, G. M. (Blackburn GS) 1946-48

Silk, D. R. W. (Christ's Hospital) (Capt. in 1955) 1953-55

Singh, S. (Khalsa Coll. and Punjab U.) 1955-56

Sinker, N. D. (Winchester) 1966

Slack, J. K. E. (UCS) 1954

Smith, C. S. (William Hulme's GS) 1954-57

Smith, D. J. (Stockport GS) 1955-56

Smyth, R. I. (Sedbergh) 1973-75

Snowden, W. (Merchant Taylors', Crosby) (Capt. in 1974) 1972-75

Spencer, J. (Brighton and Hove GS) 1970-72

Steele, H. K. (King's Coll., NZ) 1971-72

Stevenson, M. H. (Rydal) 1949-52

Studd, C. T. (Eton) (Capt. in 1883) 1880-83

Studd, G. B. (Eton) (Capt. in 1882) 1879-82

Studd, J. E. K. (Eton) (Capt. in 1884) 1881-84

Studd, P. M. (Harrow) (Capt. in 1939) 1937-39

Studd, R. A. (Eton) 1895

Subba Row, R. (Whitgift) 1951-53

Surridge, D. (Richard Hale and Southampton U.) 1979

Swift, B. T. (St Peter's, Adelaide) 1957

Taylor, C. R. V. (Birkenhead) 1971-73

Thomson, R. H. (Bexhill) 1961-62

Thwaites, I. G. (Eastbourne) 1964

Tindall, M. (Harrow) (Capt. in 1937) 1935-37

Tordoff, G. G. (Normanton GS) 1952

Trapnell, B. M. W. (UCS) 1946

Tremellen, J. M. (Bradfield) 1987-88

Turnbull, M. J. (Downside) (Capt. in 1929) 1926, 1928-29

Turner, R. J. (Millfield) 1988-90

Urquhart, J. R. (King Edward VI School, Chelmsford) 1948

Valentine, B. H. (Repton) 1929

Varey, D. W. (Birkenhead) 1982-83

Wait, O. J. (Dulwich) 1949, 1951

Warr, J. J. (Ealing County GS) (Capt. in 1951) 1949-52

Watts, H. E. (Downside) 1947

Webster, W. H. (Highgate) 1932

Weedon, M. J. H. (Harrow) 1962

Wells, T. U. (King's Coll., NZ) 1950

Wheatley, O. S. (King Edward's, Birmingham) 1957-58

Wheelhouse, A. (Nottingham HS) 1959

White, R. C. (Hilton Coll., SA) (Capt. in 1965) 1962-65

Wilcox, D. R. (Dulwich) (Capt. in 1933) 1931-33

Wilenkin, B. C. G. (Harrow) 1956

Wilkin, C. L. A. (St Kitts GS) 1970

Willard, M. J. L. (Judd) 1959-61

Willatt, G. L. (Repton) (Capt. in 1947) 1946-47

Willatt, J. M. G. (Repton) 1989

Windows, A. R. (Clifton) 1962-64

Wood, G. E. C. (Cheltenham) (Capt. in 1920) 1914, 1919-20

Wookey, S. M. (Malvern) 1975-76

Wooller, W. (Rydal) 1935-36

Wright, S. (Mill Hill) 1973

Yardley, N. W. D. (St Peter's, York) (Capt. in 1938) 1935-38

Young, R. A. (Repton) (Capt. in 1908) 1905-08

OTHER MATCHES, 1990

TILCON TROPHY

†SURREY v WARWICKSHIRE

At Harrogate, June 13. Warwickshire won by two wickets. Toss: Warwickshire. Warwickshire were permitted to include three overseas players – Donald of South Africa, Moody of Australia and Penney of Zimbabwe.

Man of the Match: T. M. Moody.

Surrey

G. S. Clinton c Asif Din b Moody	 32	M. P. Bicknell c Donald b Moody	 10
M. A. Feltham c Moody b Donald	 10	A. H. Gray not out	 9
A. J. Stewart c Reeve b Benjamin	 20	A. J. Murphy not out	 6
†D. M. Ward c Asif Din b Moody	 40	B 5, l-b 10, w 8	 23
G. P. Thorpe c Reeve b Smith	 0		
*I. A. Greig run out	 39	1/16 2/47 3/75	(9 wkts, 55 overs) 212
K. T. Medlycott c Benjamin b Munton .	1	4/77 5/127 6/132	
C. K. Bullen run out	 22	7/173 8/193 9/197	

Bowling: Donald 11–0–41–1; Benjamin 11–2–25–1; Munton 11–1–36–1; Moody 11–3–49–3; Smith 11–2–46–1.

Warwickshire

A. J. Moles c and b Medlycott	 51	A. A. Donald c Medlycott b Bicknell	.. 0
Asif Din c Ward b Gray	 0	J. E. Benjamin not out	 7
T. M. Moody lbw b Feltham	 31		
†G. W. Humpage b Gray	 2	B 6, l-b 1, w 7	 14
*D. A. Reeve c and b Murphy	 13		
T. L. Penney b Bicknell	 36	1/15 2/58 3/62	(8 wkts, 54 overs) 213
R. G. Twose not out	 36	4/78 5/121 6/159	
N. M. K. Smith c Ward b Bicknell	 23	7/197 8/197	

T. A. Munton did not bat.

Bowling: Gray 11–1–55–2; Bicknell 9–0–48–3; Feltham 3–0–16–1; Murphy 9–0–23–1; Medlycott 11–0–40–1; Bullen 11–1–24–0.

Umpires: J. C. Balderstone and D. S. Thompsett.

†YORKSHIRE v SUSSEX

At Harrogate, June 14. Yorkshire won by seven wickets. Toss: Yorkshire.

Man of the Match: A. A. Metcalfe.

Sussex

N. J. Lenham c Jarvis b Carrick	 52	I. D. K. Salisbury not out	 14
K. Greenfield c Robinson b Jarvis	 10	B. T. P. Donelan c White b Pickles	.. 4
*P. W. G. Parker c Bairstow b Jarvis ..	0	R. A. Bunting not out	 5
A. P. Wells c Byas b Moxon	 5	L-b 7	 7
M. P. Speight c White b Carrick	 30		
C. C. Remy c Robinson b White	 3	1/19 2/19 3/27	(9 wkts, 55 overs) 176
†P. Moores c Moxon b Pickles	 40	4/68 5/81 6/135	
J. A. North c Byas b Carrick	 6	7/151 8/157 9/162	

Bowling: Jarvis 11–4–29–2; Pickles 11–2–26–2; Moxon 11–4–26–1; White 9–1–42–1; Carrick 11–1–39–3; Byas 2–0–7–0.

Yorkshire

M. D. Moxon c Wells b Lenham	22	P. E. Robinson not out	24	
A. A. Metcalfe c Parker b Remy	64	B 2, l-b 6, w 4	12	
R. J. Blakey run out	21			
K. Sharp not out	37	1/56 2/111 3/119	(3 wkts, 53.3 overs) 180	

D. L. Bairstow, D. Byas, P. Carrick, C. White, C. S. Pickles and P. W. Jarvis did not bat.

Bowling: Remy 11–2–38–1; Bunting 10.3–1–28–0; Donelan 11–2–25–0; Salisbury 1–1–44–0; Lenham 5–2–16–1; North 4–0–17–0; Parker 1–0–4–0.

Umpires: J. C. Balderstone and D. S. Thompsett.

FINAL

†YORKSHIRE v WARWICKSHIRE

At Harrogate, June 15. Warwickshire won by 4 runs. Toss: Warwickshire. Moles faced 139 balls, seven of which he hit for four.
Man of the Match: A. J. Moles.

Warwickshire

A. J. Moles not out	102	T. L. Penney not out	64	
Asif Din c Metcalfe b Pickles	10			
T. M. Moody c Moxon b Carrick	67	B 4, l-b 6, w 4	14	
G. W. Humpage c Bairstow b Carrick	11			
D. A. Reeve lbw b Carrick	2	1/20 2/126 3/142	(5 wkts, 55 overs) 272	
R. G. Twose b Pickles	2	4/152 5/156		

N. M. K. Smith, A. A. Donald, J. E. Benjamin and T. A. Munton did not bat.

Bowling: Jarvis 11–1–53–0; Pickles 11–1–51–2; Fletcher 10–0–59–0; Carrick 11–1–41–3; Byas 11–0–55–0; Moxon 1–0–3–0.

Yorkshire

M. D. Moxon c Smith b Asif Din	77	D. Byas not out	4	
A. A. Metcalfe c Moody b Asif Din	76	P. Carrick not out	7	
R. J. Blakey run out	54	B 4, l-b 2, w 5, n-b 1	12	
K. Sharp c Reeve b Smith	34			
P. E. Robinson c Moody b Smith	3	1/133 2/194 3/240	(6 wkts, 55 overs) 268	
D. L. Bairstow c Reeve b Donald	1	4/254 5/254 6/257		

C. S. Pickles, S. D. Fletcher and P. W. Jarvis did not bat.

Bowling: Donald 11–0–53–1; Benjamin 11–2–35–0; Munton 11–0–49–0; Smith 10–0–52–2; Moody 2–0–15–0; Asif Din 10–0–58–2.

Umpires: J. C. Balderstone and D. S. Thompsett.

†At Durham, June 14, 15. Durham University won by six wickets. Toss: Durham University. MCC 207 for nine dec. (S. P. Henderson 41, S. C. Wundke 95; R. H. Macdonald three for 59, J. R. C. Dakin four for 67) and 214 for three dec. (M. F. Richardson 68 not out, R. M. O. Cooke 120; J. Boiling three for 64); Durham University 193 for five dec. (R. S. M. Morris 58, B. G. Evans 47, J. S. Hodgson 47 not out) and 231 for four (R. S. M. Morris 110 not out, B. G. Evans 59, J. I. Longley 31).

†At Coleraine, June 16, 17, 18. Ireland won by 6 runs. Toss: Ireland. Ireland 275 for eight dec. (A. R. Dunlop 69, S. J. S. Warke 81, Extras 34; W. G. Merry three for 54) and 99 (M. P. Rea 32, D. A. Lewis 34; M. J. Thursfield five for 15); MCC 243 (A. J. Goldsmith 76, T. Smith 58, M. J. Thursfield 32; P. McCrum three for 57, G. D. Harrison three for 46) and 125 (G. D. Mendis 49, G. J. Toogood 30; G. D. Harrison three for 13, P. O'Reilly three for 36).

CALLERS-PEGASUS FESTIVAL

†ENGLAND XI v REST OF THE WORLD XI

At Jesmond, August 2. England XI won by nine wickets. Toss: England XI. After some fin containing work by the England XI seam bowlers, Broad anchored the reply with h unbeaten 84 from 156 balls, hitting a six and ten fours. Gooch (72 balls) had thirteen fours i his 62, and Morris (91 balls) the same number plus a six in his most entertaining 87 not ou
Man of the Match: T. A. Munton.

Rest of the World XI

*C. G. Greenidge lbw b Munton	27	†A. C. Parore c Munton b Cowans	....	
S. J. Cook c Hussain b Munton	39	W. K. M. Benjamin b Munton	....	
M. D. Crowe lbw b Munton	16	I. R. Bishop not out	....	
T. M. Moody c Stephenson b Hemmings	27	B 4, l-b 6, w 7, n-b 3	....	2
M. J. Greatbatch c Hussain b Cowans	57			
A. I. C. Dodemaide b Barnett	36	1/54 2/80 3/91	(9 wkts, 55 overs)	26
P. R. Sleep not out	35	4/121 5/193 6/240		
F. D. Stephenson c Munton b Cowans	0	7/240 8/252 9/259		

Bowling: Cowans 10-0-44-3; Igglesden 10-0-44-0; Munton 11-1-38-4; Stephenso 4-0-20-0; Hemmings 11-1-50-1; Barnett 9-0-58-1.

England XI

*G. A. Gooch c Sleep b Stephenson	62
B. C. Broad not out	84
J. E. Morris not out	87
L-b 13, w 18, n-b 3	34
1/107	(1 wkt, 52.4 overs) 267

J. P. Stephenson, N. Hussain, K. J. Barnett, †B. N. French, N. G. Cowans, E. E. Hemming A. P. Igglesden and T. A. Munton did not bat.

Bowling: Bishop 11-1-40-0; Stephenson 9.4-1-41-1; Benjamin 11-1-40-0; Dodemaid 10-1-67-0; Sleep 6-0-38-0; Moody 5-0-28-0.

Umpires: S. Levison and G. I. McLean.

†ENGLAND XI v REST OF THE WORLD XI

At Jesmond, August 3. Rest of the World XI won by ten wickets. Toss: Rest of the World X This match brought to an end the sponsorship of the Jesmond matches by Callers-Pegasu under whose patronage the event had attracted 119 of the world's leading players in the pa decade. Crowe hit six sixes and thirteen fours in his unbeaten 112, finishing the match wi three successive sixes, while Cook had eleven fours in his 70 not out.
Man of the Match: P. R. Sleep.

England XI

B. C. Broad b Sleep	55	N. G. Cowans c Crowe b Sleep	....	
J. P. Stephenson b Benjamin	7	A. P. Igglesden c Benjamin b Greenidge		
J. E. Morris c Parore b Dodemaide	5	T. A. Munton not out	....	
N. Hussain b Moody	26	B 4, l-b 6, w 4	....	
*A. J. Lamb c Dodemaide b Sleep	20			
K. J. Barnett b Moody	10	1/27 2/36 3/82	(50.2 overs) 17	
†B. N. French c Moody b Greenidge	30	4/118 5/126 6/137		
E. E. Hemmings c Parore b Sleep	7	7/138 8/146 9/179		

Bowling: Benjamin 5-1-21-1; Bishop 4-0-7-0; Dodemaide 7-1-32-1; Stephenso 6-2-17-0; Sleep 10-0-34-4; Moody 8-1-23-2; Crowe 6-0-26-0; Greatbatch 4-0-9-(Greenidge 0.2-0-0-2.

Rest of the World XI

C. J. Cook not out	70
M. D. Crowe not out	112
L-b 2, w 1	3

(no wkt, 25.4 overs) 185

C. G. Greenidge, T. M. Moody, M. J. Greatbatch, A. I. C. Dodemaide, †A. C. Parore, F. D. Stephenson, P. R. Sleep, W. K. M. Benjamin and I. R. Bishop did not bat.

Bowling: Cowans 5–1–22–0; Munton 7–0–33–0; Hemmings 6–0–53–0; Igglesden 3–1–26–0; Barnett 2–0–10–0; Stephenson 2–0–21–0; Hussain 0.4–0–18–0.

Umpires: S. Levison and G. I. McLean.

SCOTLAND v IRELAND

At Myreside, Edinburgh, August 11, 12, 13. Drawn. Toss: Ireland. With Scotland extending their first innings into the third morning, and rain in prospect if only once in evidence, there was little possibility of a result other than the draw. Play had commenced at 10.30 a.m., and stumps were drawn shortly after three o'clock as soon as Warke, with his ninth four, reached 100 (140 minutes, 145 balls). He had been missed at silly point before scoring and again, by the wicket-keeper, when 17. The game's other century-maker, Philip, also benefited from fielding lapses, enjoying three lives as he and Patterson put on 147 for Scotland's first wicket in three and a quarter hours. Philip batted for 216 minutes (175 balls) for his hundred, hitting a six and eight fours, only to become the second of Harrison's nine wickets four balls later. The Irish off-spinner bowled 27 overs unchanged on the second afternoon to take his first five wickets for 72 runs; that evening and the following morning he took a further four for 26 in 12.2 overs to record the best innings figures of the 1990 first-class season.

Close of play: First day, Scotland 22-0 (I. L. Phillip 11*, B. M. W. Patterson 11*); Second day, Scotland 333-8 (A. Bee 7*, J. D. Moir 5*).

Ireland

M. F. Cohen b McKnight	60	– (2) b Mahmood	15
M. P. Rea st Haggo b Russell	22	– (3) not out	21
A. R. Dunlop c and b Mahmood	56		
S. J. S. Warke c Storie b Mahmood	4	– (1) not out	100
D. A. Lewis c Patterson b McKnight	6		
*J. T. Patterson c Patterson b Henry	84		
G. D. Harrison c Patterson b Mahmood	1		
P. B. Jackson st Haggo b Moir	59		
J. Nelson c Moir b McKnight	0		
†McCrum c McKnight b Henry	0		
A. N. Nelson not out	23		
B 6, l-b 4, w 2	12	B 2	2

1/44 2/129 3/137 4/155 5/156 327 1/51 (1 wkt) 138
6/179 7/289 8/291 9/292

Bowling: *First Innings*—Moir 26.3–8–76–1; Bee 19–7–53–0; Russell 6–1–23–1; Henry 18–0–54–2; Mahmood 18–5–63–3; McKnight 16–5–48–3. *Second Innings*—Bee 9–4–20–0; Mahmood 13–4–40–1; Henry 14.4–3–52–0; McKnight 7–0–24–0.

Scotland

I. L. Philip b Harrison	100	A. Bee not out	29
B. M. W. Patterson b Harrison	60	J. D. Moir c Dunlop b Harrison	12
A. C. Storie b Harrison	32	M. Mahmood c Patterson b Harrison	3
*R. G. Swan c sub b Harrison	9		
O. Henry st Jackson b Harrison	23	L-b 8, w 2, n-b 7	17
G. Russell c N. Nelson b A. N. Nelson	47		
†D. J. Haggo lbw b Harrison	34	1/147 2/175 3/193 4/209 5/241	366
C. T. McKnight c Warke b Harrison	0	6/316 7/316 8/324 9/353	

Bowling: McCrum 12–3–28–0; A. N. Nelson 33–8–74–1; N. Nelson 15–0–51–0; Harrison 43.2–11–113–9; Lewis 11–0–55–0; Dunlop 10–0–37–0.

Umpires: J. Breslin and D. N. Herd.

†At Swansea, August 27, 28. Drawn. Toss: MCC. MCC 166 for seven dec. (D. B. Storer 47, K. G. G. Brooks 42; B. J. Lloyd three for 44) and 197 (A. Needham 32, D. B. Storer 33, K. G. G. Brooks 50; B. J. Lloyd five for 43); Wales 181 for five dec. (S. Evans 56, A. Harris 45 not out) and 165 for seven (J. Bishop 66, Extras 30; M. Hart four for 22).

At Scarborough, August 29, 30, 31. MICHAEL PARKINSON'S WORLD XI drew with INDIANS (See Indian tour section).

†At Scarborough, September 1. Michael Parkinson's World XI won by 7 runs. Toss: Michael Parkinson's World XI. Michael Parkinson's World XI 278 for eight (50 overs) (J. E. Morris 60, C. L. Hooper 62, N. Hussain 30, B. C. Lara 34; P. J. Hartley three for 68); Yorkshire 271 for eight (50 overs) (S. A. Kellett 57, P. E. Robinson 114).

SCARBOROUGH FESTIVAL TROPHY

†HAMPSHIRE v WORCESTERSHIRE

At Scarborough, September 2. Hampshire won by 81 runs. Toss: Worcestershire. Terry faced 155 balls and hit six boundaries.
Man of the Match: V. P. Terry.

Hampshire

V. P. Terry st Rhodes b Illingworth	95	†A. N. Aymes not out	11
T. C. Middleton b Botham	39	S. D. Udal not out	0
R. A. Smith b Botham	6	B 4, l-b 17, w 6	27
*M. C. J. Nicholas b Hick	6		
R. M. F. Cox c and b Hick	43	1/96 2/107 3/135 (6 wkts, 50 overs) 249
J. R. Ayling c Botham b Illingworth	22	4/208 5/226 6/247

T. M. Tremlett, C. A. Connor and P. J. Bakker did not bat.

Bowling: McEwan 8–0–35–0; Weston 6–1–18–0; Radford 9–0–40–0; Illingworth 10–0–62–2; Botham 7–0–30–2; Hick 10–0–43–2.

Worcestershire

T. S. Curtis c Smith b Tremlett	16	R. K. Illingworth b Nicholas	29
G. J. Lord b Bakker	1	N. V. Radford not out	39
D. A. Leatherdale c Terry b Connor	5	S. M. McEwan b Nicholas	0
I. T. Botham b Connor	1	B 2, l-b 9, w 4	15
G. A. Hick b Udal	20		
*P. A. Neale run out	1	1/8 2/13 3/16 (45 overs) 168
M. J. Weston lbw b Nicholas	19	4/45 5/46 6/46
†S. J. Rhodes c Terry b Tremlett	22	7/82 8/97 9/166

Bowling: Connor 6–2–14–2; Bakker 7–0–21–1; Tremlett 10–1–24–2; Udal 9–0–42–1; Ayling 6–0–28–0; Nicholas 7–0–28–3.

Umpires: B. Leadbeater and D. O. Oslear.

†YORKSHIRE v ESSEX

At Scarborough, September 3. Essex won by 82 runs. Toss: Essex.
Man of the Match: P. J. Prichard.

Essex

*J. P. Stephenson st Bairstow b Carrick	57	T. D. Topley not out		0
N. Shahid lbw b Jarvis	16	M. C. Ilott not out		6
M. E. Waugh b Jarvis	0	L-b 3, w 8, n-b 3		14
P. J. Prichard c Hartley b Pickles	86			
N. Hussain c Byas b Pickles	31	1/20 2/20 3/163	(7 wkts, 50 overs)	247
*M. A. Garnham c and b Pickles	37	4/178 5/239		
A. G. J. Fraser run out	0	6/239 7/241		

S. J. W. Andrew and P. M. Such did not bat.

Bowling: Jarvis 10–1–48–2; Hartley 10–0–52–0; Pickles 9–0–40–3; Batty 9–0–40–0; Carrick 10–0–54–1; Byas 2–0–10–0.

Yorkshire

*M. D. Moxon c Garnham b Andrew	4	P. J. Hartley c Topley b Shahid		16
S. A. Kellett b Such	28	P. W. Jarvis b Stephenson		3
R. J. Blakey c Garnham b Andrew	0	J. D. Batty not out		5
P. E. Robinson c Prichard b Topley	26	B 1, w 5, n-b 6		12
D. Byas c Waugh b Such	22			
†D. L. Bairstow b Stephenson	36	1/6 2/6 3/50	(47.2 overs)	165
P. Carrick b Stephenson	12	4/73 5/112 6/132		
C. S. Pickles b Waugh	1	7/135 8/141 9/147		

Bowling: Andrew 4–0–35–2; Ilott 7–4–11–0; Topley 6–0–15–1; Such 10–0–32–2; Fraser 4–0–16–0; Stephenson 10–0–42–3; Waugh 6–0–9–1; Shahid 0.2–0–4–1.

Umpires: B. Leadbeater and D. O. Oslear.

FINAL

†HAMPSHIRE v ESSEX

At Scarborough, September 4. Hampshire won by five wickets. Toss: Essex.
Man of the Match: M. C. J. Nicholas.

Essex

*J. P. Stephenson c Smith b Ayling	18	M. C. Ilott b Nicholas		17
N. Shahid c Middleton b Connor	10	S. J. W. Andrew b Nicholas		0
M. E. Waugh c Connor b Turner	30	P. M. Such not out		6
P. J. Prichard st Aymes b Udal	21	B 2, l-b 3, w 12, n-b 2		19
N. Hussain c Nicholas b Tremlett	39			
†M. A. Garnham c Turner b Nicholas	4	1/19 2/33 3/72	(49.5 overs)	165
A. G. J. Fraser run out	0	4/89 5/106 6/109		
T. D. Topley b Turner	1	7/118 8/144 9/144		

Bowling: Connor 7–0–21–1; Tremlett 7.5–2–16–1; Udal 10–0–25–1; Ayling 7–0–26–1; Turner 8–0–44–2; Nicholas 10–1–28–3.

Hampshire

*M. C. J. Nicholas run out	57	†A. N. Aymes not out		1
T. C. Middleton c sub b Fraser	53			
R. M. F. Cox b Stephenson	4	L-b 3, w 7, n-b 1		11
J. R. Ayling c and b Fraser	25			
R. A. Smith not out	14	1/96 2/101 3/140	(5 wkts, 45.1 overs)	166
V. P. Terry c Ilott b Topley	1	4/163 5/164		

T. M. Tremlett, S. D. Udal, C. A. Connor and I. J. Turner did not bat.

Bowling: Topley 7–1–19–1; Ilott 7–1–20–0; Such 10–1–22–0; Andrew 5–0–29–0; Shahi
2–0–6–0; Stephenson 7–0–31–1; Waugh 4–0–11–0; Fraser 3–0–24–2; Prichard 0.1–0–1–0.

Umpires: B. Leadbeater and D. O. Oslear.

SEEBOARD TROPHY

†SUSSEX v KENT

At Hove, September 2. Kent won by 45 runs. Toss: Kent.
Man of the Match: M. V. Fleming.

Kent

T. R. Ward c Greenfield b Donelan	... 67	M. A. Ealham c Moores b Salisbury	... 4
V. J. Wells b Threlfall	... 18	M. M. Patel c Salisbury b Dodemaide	. 1
J. I. Longley c Moores b Dodemaide	.. 3	T. N. Wren not out	...
G. R. Cowdrey st Moores b Salisbury	. 43		
*N. R. Taylor c Smith b Lenham	 30	B 1, l-b 3, w 3	... 7
M. V. Fleming st Moores b Salisbury	. 6		
†S. A. Marsh st Moores b Donelan	 52	1/20 2/29 3/133	(48.1 overs) 233
D. J. M. Kelleher c Greenfield		4/133 5/143 6/220	
b Donelan	. 2	7/223 8/229 9/233	

Bowling: Dodemaide 9–2–20–2; Threlfall 10–0–55–1; Remy 4–0–32–0; Donelan
10–2–34–3; Salisbury 10–0–59–3; Lenham 5.1–0–29–1.

Sussex

N. J. Lenham b Fleming	... 47	I. D. K. Salisbury c Marsh b Fleming	. 0
D. M. Smith lbw b Wren	... 14	B. T. P. Donelan c Wells b Wren	 10
K. Greenfield c and b Taylor	... 34	P. W. Threlfall not out	... 0
*A. P. Wells run out	... 5	L-b 6, w 3, n-b 2	... 11
I. J. Gould c Longley b Ward	... 9		
A. I. C. Dodemaide c Marsh b Fleming	40	1/51 2/75 3/89	(45.4 overs) 188
C. C. Remy c Ealham b Fleming	 16	4/113 5/133 6/162	
†P. Moores run out	... 2	7/165 8/167 9/184	

Bowling: Wren 7–1–18–2; Kelleher 2–0–19–0; Patel 10–0–48–0; Ward 10–0–23–1; Fleming
7.4–0–30–4; Ealham 3–0–14–0; Taylor 6–0–30–1.

Umpires: D. J. Constant and A. G. T. Whitehead.

†SURREY v WARWICKSHIRE

At Hove, September 3. Surrey won by four wickets. Toss: Surrey.
Man of the Match: M. A. Lynch.

Warwickshire

Asif Din c D. J. Bicknell b Greig	 51	R. G. Twose not out	... 8
†K. J. Piper lbw b Bullen	... 44	A. A. Donald not out	... 16
D. P. Ostler c Lynch b Bullen	... 6		
S. J. Green b Waqar Younis	... 21	B 2, l-b 17, w 2	... 21
P. A. Smith c Stewart b Waqar Younis	. 6		
*D. A. Reeve lbw b Waqar Younis	 42	1/86 2/104 3/133	(7 wkts, 50 overs) 228
N. M. K. Smith c Stewart		4/134 5/161	
b M. P. Bicknell	. 13	6/202 7/204	

G. Smith and T. A. Munton did not bat.

Bowling: M. P. Bicknell 10–1–38–1; Murphy 10–0–47–0; Greig 6–0–26–1; Thorpe
4–0–21–0; Waqar Younis 10–1–31–3; Bullen 10–0–46–2.

Surrey

D. J. Bicknell c Twose b Reeve	33	*I. A. Greig run out	2
S. S. Clinton c Piper b Munton	8	C. K. Bullen not out	11
G. P. Thorpe c Twose b Donald	30	L-b 9, w 7, n-b 2	18
A. J. Stewart c N. M. K. Smith b Reeve	36		
D. M. Ward c Piper b G. Smith	27	1/24 2/68 3/104 (6 wkts, 49.1 overs) 230	
A. A. Lynch not out	65	4/133 5/165 6/168	

A. J. Murphy, M. P. Bicknell and Waqar Younis did not bat.

Bowling: Donald 10–3–24–1; Munton 10–0–64–1; G. Smith 9.1–2–38–1; Reeve 10–0–53–2; P. A. Smith 10–0–42–0.

Umpires: D. J. Constant and A. G. T. Whitehead.

FINAL

†KENT v SURREY

At Hove, September 4. Kent won by 35 runs. Toss: Kent. Ealham's return of eight for 49 included a spell of seven for 24 in 4.4 overs. Wells hit eleven fours in his 107.
Man of the Match: M. A. Ealham.

Kent

T. R. Ward b Robinson	41	D. J. M. Kelleher not out	20
V. J. Wells run out	107		
N. I. Longley lbw b Waqar Younis	0		
G. R. Cowdrey b Murphy	78	B 4, l-b 10, w 8	22
N. R. Taylor b Greig	25		
M. V. Fleming not out	43	1/78 2/79 3/223 (6 wkts, 50 overs) 338	
*S. A. Marsh c D. J. Bicknell b M. P. Bicknell	2	4/256 5/277 6/286	

M. A. Ealham, M. M. Patel and T. N. Wren did not bat.

Bowling: M. P. Bicknell 10–1–43–1; Murphy 10–1–71–1; Waqar Younis 10–1–57–1; Robinson 10–1–54–1; Bullen 4–0–49–0; Greig 6–0–50–1.

Surrey

D. J. Bicknell c Marsh b Ealham	2	M. P. Bicknell b Ealham	2
D. D. Robinson b Ealham	98	Waqar Younis not out	13
G. P. Thorpe c Marsh b Patel	78	A. J. Murphy c and b Ealham	2
*A. J. Stewart c Wren b Ealham	52	L-b 3, w 14, n-b 3	20
D. M. Ward b Wren	26		
M. A. Lynch b Ealham	0	1/18 2/166 3/244 (48.4 overs) 303	
*I. A. Greig c Cowdrey b Ealham	4	4/255 5/256 6/266	
C. K. Bullen c Fleming b Ealham	6	7/281 8/286 9/301	

Bowling: Wren 10–0–49–1; Ealham 9.4–0–49–8; Patel 8–0–50–1; Ward 4–0–20–0; Fleming 7–0–64–0; Kelleher 10–0–68–0.

Umpires: D. J. Constant and A. G. T. Whitehead.

†At Scarborough, September 6. Yorkshire won by eight wickets. Toss: The Yorkshiremen. The Yorkshiremen 229 for five (50 overs) (T. J. Boon 82, S. J. Rhodes 66 not out); Yorkshire 235 for two (37.5 overs) (A. A. Metcalfe 65, D. Byas 59, R. J. Blakey 69 not out).

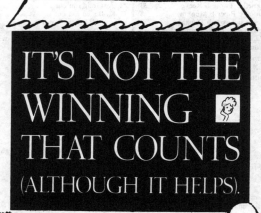

NATWEST BANK TROPHY, 1990

Lancashire, by defeating Northamptonshire convincingly by seven wickets on the first day of September, not only won the NatWest Bank Trophy for the first time but became the only county to win both Lord's finals in the same season. It was their fifth victory in eight finals of the 60-overs competition, putting them ahead of Middlesex and Sussex, each with four wins.

In addition to the NatWest Bank Trophy, held for a year, Lancashire won £24,000 in prizemoney, while Northamptonshire received £12,000. The losing semi-finalists, Hampshire and Middlesex, each received £6,000, and the losing quarter-finalists, Glamorgan, Gloucestershire, Worcestershire and Yorkshire, £3,000 each. The total prizemoney for the competition in 1990, including the Man of the Match awards, was £64,500, an increase of £6,000 over 1989.

Phillip DeFreitas, nominated as Man of the Match in the final by Fred Trueman for his match-winning bowling in the morning session, received a cheque for £550. The awards in the earlier rounds were: first round, £100 each; second round, £125 each; quarter-finals, £200 each; semi-finals, £275 each. Graham Gooch (Essex) and Chris Smith (Hampshire) each won an award in 1990 to increase their total in the competition to seven, a mark also reached by Imran Khan (Worcestershire and Sussex), Peter Willey (Northamptonshire and Leicestershire) and Barry Wood (Lancashire and Cheshire). Only Clive Lloyd, the former Lancashire captain, with eight awards, had been named Man of the Match more times.

FIRST ROUND

BUCKINGHAMSHIRE v NOTTINGHAMSHIRE

At Marlow, June 27. Nottinghamshire won by 192 runs. Toss: Buckinghamshire. Broad's century, his first in the competition, came off 149 balls, and his 115 included a six and fifteen fours. Nottinghamshire's total was their highest in limited-overs competition.
Man of the Match: B. C. Broad.

Nottinghamshire

B. C. Broad b Black	115	K. E. Cooper c Percy b Barry	10
M. Newell b Scriven	35	R. A. Pick not out	4
F. D. Stephenson c Harwood b Burrow	29	J. A. Afford not out	2
*R. T. Robinson c and b Percy	30	B 4, l-b 10, w 6, n-b 2	22
P. Johnson c Harwood b Lynch	14		
M. Saxelby c Lynch b Black	41	1/97 2/140 3/187 (9 wkts, 60 overs) 312	
†B. N. French c Black b Barry	7	4/206 5/277 6/288	
E. E. Hemmings b Barry	3	7/293 8/305 9/308	

Bowling: Barry 12–2–49–3; Black 11–2–52–2; Burrow 12–1–42–1; Scriven 12–0–73–1; Lynch 7–0–52–1; Percy 6–0–30–1.

Buckinghamshire

A. R. Harwood c French b Cooper	13	S. G. Lynch c Newell b Hemmings	46
M. J. Roberts retired hurt	17	T. J. Barry c Saxelby b Hemmings	5
T. Butler c Johnson b Cooper	5	†D. J. Goldsmith not out	0
S. Burrow c Hemmings b Pick	19	L-b 2, w 2	4
T. J. A. Scriven c Robinson b Cooper	1		
*N. G. Hames c French b Hemmings	4	1/32 2/42 3/44 (40.3 overs) 120	
B. S. Percy b Pick	0	4/55 5/56 6/63	
G. R. Black lbw b Pick	6	7/70 8/95 9/120	

M. J. Roberts retired hurt at 30.

Bowling: Stephenson 5–2–12–0; Pick 9–2–22–3; Cooper 8–3–16–3; Afford 11–6–26–0; Hemmings 7.3–2–42–3.

Umpires: P. J. Eele and D. S. Thompsett.

DERBYSHIRE v SHROPSHIRE

At Chesterfield, June 27. Derbyshire won by seven wickets. Toss: Derbyshire. The start of play was delayed by 40 minutes while the match balls were brought to the ground from the county ground at Derby, and the lunch interval was reduced by ten minutes. The third-wicket partnership of 117 between Morris and Kuiper was a record for Derbyshire in the competition.

Man of the Match: J. E. Morris.

Shropshire

*J. Foster lbw b Kuiper	20	A. B. Byram not out	20
J. B. R. Jones c Bowler b Warner	26	B. K. Shantry not out	4
J. Abrahams b Mortensen	47		
T. Parton lbw b Mortensen	2	L-b 11, w 18	29
M. R. Davies c Bowler b Warner	20		—
†J. R. Weaver lbw b Mortensen	0	1/33 2/97 3/112 (8 wkts, 60 overs) 184	
P. B. Wormald b Warner	16	4/114 5/114 6/147	
D. B. K. Page b Warner	0	7/149 8/169	

A. S. Barnard did not bat.

Bowling: Malcolm 12–3–31–0; Mortensen 11–2–29–3; Warner 12–1–39–4; Goldsmith 5–0–23–0; Miller 10–0–31–0; Kuiper 10–0–20–1.

Derbyshire

*K. J. Barnett c Weaver b Shantry	1	B. Roberts not out	14
†P. D. Bowler c Weaver b Shantry	14	L-b 6, w 5, n-b 3	14
J. E. Morris not out	94		—
A. P. Kuiper c Parton b Wormald	49	1/9 2/45 3/162 (3 wkts, 38.1 overs) 186	

C. J. Adams, S. C. Goldsmith, A. E. Warner, G. Miller, D. E. Malcolm and O. H. Mortensen did not bat.

Bowling: Page 5–0–24–0; Shantry 10–1–47–2; Barnard 6–1–19–0; Wormald 5.1–1–24–1; Byram 6–0–35–0; Abrahams 6–0–31–0.

Umpires: J. D. Bond and J. W. Holder.

DEVON v SOMERSET

At Torquay, June 27. Somerset won by 346 runs. Toss: Devon. In a match of record breaking, not only was Somerset's total the highest in a major limited-overs competition in England, but their margin of victory was also the largest. Both these records were previously held by Worcestershire, who scored 404 for three when beating Devon by 299 runs in the first round of the NatWest Bank Trophy at Worcester in 1987. Rose, while scoring 110 from 40 balls, hit the fastest hundred in the 60-overs competition, reaching his century from 36 balls and hitting seven sixes and ten fours. Tavaré's unbeaten 162, the highest innings for Somerset in the competition, came off 130 balls and contained four sixes and 26 fours. When Devon replied, Lefebvre also recorded best figures for the county as he equalled the third-best return in the Gillette Cup/NatWest Bank Trophy.

Man of the Match: C. J. Tavaré.

Somerset

S. J. Cook run out	42
P. M. Roebuck c and b Woodman	43
A. N. Hayhurst c Pugh b Folland	51
*C. J. Tavaré not out	162
G. D. Rose c Pugh b Dawson	110
W 5	5

1/79 2/88 3/224 (4 wkts, 60 overs) 413
4/413

R. J. Harden, †N. D. Burns, I. G. Swallow, R. P. Lefebvre, N. A. Mallender and A. N. Jones did not bat.

Bowling: Donohue 12–2–101–0; Woodman 12–3–50–1; Tierney 11–2–62–0; Yeabsley 12–0–77–0; Rice 6–0–34–0; Dawson 4–0–37–1; Folland 3–0–52–1.

Devon

*J. H. Edwards lbw b Jones	4	J. K. Tierney b Lefebvre	0
K. G. Rice b Mallender	0	M. C. Woodman b Lefebvre	1
N. A. Folland c Burns b Mallender	0	R. S. Yeabsley lbw b Lefebvre	2
A. J. Pugh b Lefebvre	12	L-b 5, w 9	14
P. A. Brown lbw b Lefebvre	12		
†R. C. Turpin c Rose b Lefebvre	4	1/4 2/4 3/11	(30.3 overs) 67
R. I. Dawson lbw b Lefebvre	0	4/35 5/41 6/41	
K. Donohue not out	18	7/44 8/44 9/63	

Bowling: Jones 6–1–20–1; Mallender 6–3–4–2; Rose 5–1–11–0; Lefebvre 9.3–6–15–7; Swallow 4–0–12–0.

Umpires: D. J. Halfyard and R. Julian.

ESSEX v SCOTLAND

At Chelmsford, June 27. Essex won by nine wickets. Toss: Scotland. Gooch's unbeaten 103, which featured eighteen fours, was scored from 109 deliveries.

Man of the Match: G. A. Gooch.

Scotland

†I. L. Philip c Waugh b Andrew	1	J. D. Moir not out	4
C. G. Greenidge b Foster	15	A. Bee run out	14
B. M. W. Patterson b Andrew	19	C. L. Parfitt b Pringle	0
*R. G. Swan c Pringle b Childs	26	B 2, l-b 15, w 9	26
A. B. Russell run out	37		
O. Henry c Hardie b Pringle	53	1/5 2/33 3/37	(59.3 overs) 200
W. Morton c Garnham b Foster	5	4/82 5/164 6/170	
P. G. Duthie lbw b Foster	0	7/176 8/180 9/199	

Bowling: Andrew 12–2–34–2; Foster 12–4–26–3; Topley 7–0–32–0; Pringle 11.3–2–30–2; Childs 12–1–44–1; Waugh 5–1–17–0.

Essex

*G. A. Gooch not out	103
B. R. Hardie b Bee	31
P. J. Prichard not out	37
B 2, l-b 17, w 11, n-b 1	31

1/105   (1 wkt, 42.4 overs) 202

M. E. Waugh, D. R. Pringle, J. P. Stephenson, †M. A. Garnham, N. A. Foster, T. D. Topley, J. H. Childs and S. J. W. Andrew did not bat.

Bowling: Moir 10–3–34–0; Duthie 8–0–37–0; Parfitt 9.4–3–29–0; Bee 10–4–27–1; Henry 3–0–21–0; Morton 2–0–35–0.

Umpires: J. H. Hampshire and H. J. Rhodes.

GLAMORGAN v DORSET

At Swansea, June 27, 28. Glamorgan won by 34 runs. Toss: Dorset. Dorset's total was the highest by a Minor County in the competition, beating by 5 runs Oxfordshire's 256 against Warwickshire at Birmingham in 1983. Morris (188 balls, sixteen fours) and Richards (80 balls, six sixes, eleven fours) provided the first instance for Glamorgan of two players scoring hundreds in a limited-overs game. Close of play: Glamorgan 207-2 (51 overs) (H. Morris 91*, I. V. A. Richards 64*).

Man of the Match: I. V. A. Richards.

Glamorgan

*A. R. Butcher st Fitzgerald b Stone .. 41	A. Dale not out ....
H. Morris c Calway b Merriman 116	L-b 2, w 4 ....
M. P. Maynard st Fitzgerald b Stone .. 8	
I. V. A. Richards c Hall b Merriman ..118	1/76 2/90 3/266 (4 wkts, 60 overs) 29?
P. A. Cottey not out 2	4/288

N. G. Cowley, †C. P. Metson, S. J. Dennis, S. L. Watkin and M. Frost did not bat.

Bowling: Taylor 10–0–55–0; Shackleton 12–1–44–0; Hall 6–2–26–0; Stone 12–2–44–2 Wingfield Digby 12–0–60–0; Calway 4–0–29–0; Merriman 3–0–32–2; Graham-Brown 1–0–3–0.

Dorset

R. P. Merriman c Cottey b Frost 25	N. R. Taylor run out ....
G. D. Reynolds c Dennis b Watkin 60	*A. R. Wingfield Digby not out ...... 2?
J. M. H. Graham-Brown c Metson b Richards . 58	†S. M. Fitzgerald not out ....
	B 2, l-b 11, w 4 .... 1?
G. S. Calway c Butcher b Frost 32	
V. B. Lewis b Watkin 0	1/35 2/127 3/165 (8 wkts, 60 overs) 26?
C. Stone b Richards 25	4/166 5/211 6/215
J. R. Hall c Metson b Frost 12	7/225 8/252

J. H. Shackleton did not bat.

Bowling: Frost 12–3–50–3; Watkin 12–0–56–2; Cowley 12–2–31–0; Dennis 6–0–28–0; Dale 6–1–28–0; Richards 12–0–55–2.

Umpires: D. J. Dennis and A. A. Jones.

GLOUCESTERSHIRE v LINCOLNSHIRE

At Gloucester, June 27. Gloucestershire won by 195 runs. Toss: Gloucestershire. Gloucestershire's total fell just 2 runs short of their highest in the competition: 327 for seven against Berkshire at Reading in 1966.
Man of the Match: A. J. Wright.

Gloucestershire

G. D. Hodgson c McKeown b Airey .. 42	J. W. Lloyds not out .... 7?
*A. J. Wright st Priestley b Marshall .. 92	L-b 13, w 5, n-b 4 .... 2?
P. Bainbridge lbw b Marshall 13	
C. W. J. Athey not out 81	1/113 2/142 3/173 (4 wkts, 60 overs) 32?
K. M. Curran b Pont 2	4/178

M. W. Alleyne, †R. C. Russell, C. A. Walsh, D. A. Graveney and D. V. Lawrence did not bat.

Bowling: Pont 12–0–52–1; French 12–1–42–0; McKeown 12–1–84–0; Airey 10–0–60–1 Marshall 12–0–63–2; Love 2–0–11–0.

Lincolnshire

*†N. Priestley c Graveney b Alleyne .. 54	J. R. Airey st Russell b Alleyne ....
D. B. Storer lbw b Walsh 0	P. D. McKeown not out ....
J. D. Love b Walsh 1	D. Marshall b Lloyds ....
N. J. C. Gandon b Alleyne 31	B 5, l-b 6, w 7, n-b 2 .... 2?
I. L. Pont b Graveney 1	
R. T. Bates b Graveney 5	1/6 2/17 3/79 (49 overs) 13?
S. N. Warman lbw b Alleyne 3	4/80 5/98 6/108
N. French c Wright b Alleyne 7	7/112 8/112 9/117

Bowling: Walsh 7–1–16–2; Curran 8–3–11–0; Lawrence 5–0–15–0; Bainbridge 6–0–15–0 Graveney 12–0–26–2; Alleyne 10–2–30–5; Lloyds 1–0–6–1.

Umpires: J. H. Harris and C. T. Spencer.

HERTFORDSHIRE v WARWICKSHIRE

At St Albans, June 27. Warwickshire won by 128 runs. Toss: Hertfordshire.
Man of the Match: Asif Din.

Warwickshire

A. J. Moles b Surridge	60	G. C. Small c Surridge b Merry	0
Asif Din c Evans b Needham	66	J. E. Benjamin not out	1
T. M. Moody c T. S. Smith b Needham	58		
A. I. Kallicharran c MacLaurin b Surridge	41	B 5, l-b 22, w 3	30
†G. W. Humpage b Surridge	43		
*D. A. Reeve not out	36	1/133 2/147 3/229 (7 wkts, 60 overs) 336	
R. G. Twose c Vartan b Merry	1	4/292 5/304	
		6/321 7/321	

A. R. K. Pierson and T. A. Munton did not bat.

Bowling: Harris 12–0–67–0; Surridge 12–0–61–3; T. S. Smith 12–1–57–0; Merry 11–0–62–2; Needham 12–0–50–2; D. M. Smith 1–0–12–0.

Hertfordshire

B. G. Evans b Munton	27	W. G. Merry c Moody b Asif Din	11
N. P. G. Wright run out	17	G. A. R. Harris c Moles b Asif Din	0
†R. N. R. Vartan c Moody b Munton	10	*D. Surridge not out	3
A. Needham c Benjamin b Asif Din	35	B 4, l-b 12, w 13	29
N. R. C. MacLaurin c Moles b Munton	21		
I. Fletcher c and b Asif Din	1	1/52 2/65 3/74 (53.1 overs) 208	
D. M. Smith st Humpage b Moody	39	4/106 5/125 6/134	
T. S. Smith c Twose b Asif Din	15	7/163 8/189 9/189	

Bowling: Small 6–0–21–0; Benjamin 6–1–9–0; Reeve 8–1–20–0; Munton 12–1–46–3; Pierson 12–1–49–0; Asif Din 8–2–40–5; Moody 1.1–0–7–1.

Umpires: V. A. Holder and A. G. T. Whitehead.

IRELAND v SUSSEX

At Downpatrick, June 27. Sussex won by nine wickets. Toss: Ireland. Dodemaide's figures were the best for Sussex in the 60-overs competition.
Man of the Match: A. I. C. Dodemaide.

Ireland

A. R. Dunlop b Dodemaide	1	†P. B. Jackson b Dodemaide	0
R. Lamba b Dodemaide	5	A. N. Nelson b Dodemaide	3
M. P. Rea c Moores b Pigott	5	A. Johnston b Dodemaide	0
*S. J. S. Warke c Speight b Dodemaide	22	B 3, l-b 3, w 7	13
D. A. Lewis b C. M. Wells	1		
S. G. Smyth c Clarke b Lenham	15	1/1 2/10 3/18 (49 overs) 72	
G. D. Harrison c Moores b Lenham	3	4/19 5/47 6/58	
P. McCrum not out	4	7/61 8/64 9/72	

Bowling: Pigott 8–1–14–1; Dodemaide 11–7–9–6; C. M. Wells 9–6–6–1; Salisbury 5–2–19–0; Clarke 10–7–6–0; Lenham 6–0–12–2.

Sussex

N. J. Lenham not out	41
I. J. Gould c Lamba b Nelson	26
*P. W. G. Parker not out	4
W 2	2

1/58 (1 wkt, 15.1 overs) 73

A. P. Wells, M. P. Speight, C. M. Wells, A. I. C. Dodemaide, †P. Moores, A. C. S. Pigott, I. D. K. Salisbury and A. R. Clarke did not bat.

Bowling: McCrum 3–0–16–0; Johnston 4–0–21–0; Nelson 5–0–27–1; Harrison 3.1–0–9–0.

Umpires: J. C. Balderstone and B. Dudleston.

LANCASHIRE v DURHAM

At Manchester, June 27. Lancashire won by eight wickets. Toss: Lancashire.
Man of the Match: N. H. Fairbrother.

Durham

G. K. Brown lbw b Wasim Akram	42	P. G. Newman lbw b Allott	0
J. D. Glendenen b Allott	14	†A. R. Fothergill b Austin	2
P. Burn c Wasim Akram b Atherton ..	26	I. Young b Wasim Akram	0
P. V. Simmons c Hegg b Austin	14	L-b 11, w 1, n-b 3	15
J. F. Sykes lbw b DeFreitas	4		
A. S. Patel not out	31	1/17 2/76 3/108	(55.2 overs) 164
*N. A. Riddell b Austin	16	4/114 5/116 6/157	
S. Greensword lbw b Allott	0	7/160 8/160 9/163	

Bowling: Allott 10–4–24–3; DeFreitas 10–2–22–1; Wasim Akram 9.2–1–19–2; Watkinson 12–1–45–0; Austin 12–0–36–3; Atherton 2–1–7–1.

Lancashire

G. D. Mendis not out	62
G. Fowler b Newman	31
M. A. Atherton c Burn b Sykes	4
N. H. Fairbrother not out	50
B 5, l-b 4, w 8, n-b 1	18

1/70 2/90   (2 wkts, 34.1 overs) 165

M. Watkinson, *D. P. Hughes, P. A. J. DeFreitas, Wasim Akram, I. D. Austin, †W. K. Hegg and P. J. W. Allott did not bat.

Bowling: Newman 10–0–30–1; Young 6.1–0–47–0; Simmons 4–0–28–0; Sykes 6–0–16–1; Greensword 6–1–23–0; Patel 2–0–12–0.

Umpires: D. B. Harrison and B. Leadbeater.

LEICESTERSHIRE v HAMPSHIRE

At Leicester, June 27. Hampshire won by 1 run. Toss: Leicestershire. Having required 49 runs from the last ten overs, Leicestershire began the final over still needing 9 for victory. Connor conceded just 6 off the first five balls, and off the sixth Nixon was run out attempting a second run.
Man of the Match: P. Willey.

Hampshire

V. P. Terry c Lewis b Willey	21	†R. J. Parks not out	14
C. L. Smith c Willey b Benjamin	52	R. J. Maru not out	6
R. A. Smith c Nixon b Lewis	35	L-b 4, w 8, n-b 4	16
D. I. Gower c Willey b Mullally	28		
M. D. Marshall c Briers b Agnew	6	1/65 2/91 3/129	(7 wkts, 60 overs) 226
*M. C. J. Nicholas b Mullally	19	4/151 5/151	
J. R. Ayling b Agnew	29	6/188 7/213	

C. A. Connor and P. J. Bakker did not bat.

Bowling: Benjamin 12–4–34–1; Agnew 12–1–44–2; Lewis 12–1–35–1; Willey 12–2–54–1; Mullally 12–0–55–2.

Leicestershire

T. J. Boon c Parks b Maru	19	W. K. M. Benjamin c Gower b Ayling	.	7
*N. E. Briers b Bakker	8	†P. A. Nixon run out		12
J. J. Whitaker c R. A. Smith b Maru	24	B 1, l-b 12, w 6, n-b 2		21
P. Willey not out	72			—
C. C. Lewis lbw b Maru	32	1/16 2/55 3/56 (8 wkts, 60 overs)		225
L. Potter run out	19	4/118 5/157 6/185		
J. D. R. Benson c Nicholas b Ayling	11	7/195 8/225		

J. P. Agnew and A. D. Mullally did not bat.

Bowling: Marshall 12–2–32–0; Bakker 12–0–51–1; Connor 12–1–49–0; Ayling 12–3–34–2; Maru 12–1–46–3.

Umpires: H. D. Bird and B. Hassan.

MIDDLESEX v BERKSHIRE

At Lord's, June 27. Middlesex won by four wickets. Toss: Middlesex. Berkshire reached 200 for the first time since they began competing in the 60-overs competition in 1965.
Man of the Match: M. W. Gatting.

Berkshire

G. E. Loveday c Roseberry b Gatting	36	P. J. Oxley not out	33
M. G. Lickley lbw b Cowans	12	M. G. Stear not out	5
*M. L. Simmons c Haynes b Cowans	30	L-b 9, w 8, n-b 12	29
G. T. Headley c Butcher b Emburey	13		—
D. Shaw run out	36	1/24 2/68 3/99 (6 wkts, 60 overs)	204
B. S. Jackson c Farbrace b Fraser	10	4/114 5/135 6/178	

†M. E. Stevens, J. H. Jones and D. J. B. Hartley did not bat.

Bowling: Cowans 10–3–25–2; Williams 12–1–67–0; Fraser 12–0–37–1; Gatting 6–0–31–1; Haynes 8–3–18–0; Emburey 12–2–17–1.

Middlesex

D. L. Haynes b Headley	50	†P. Farbrace b Hartley	17
M. A. Roseberry lbw b Jones	3	J. E. Emburey not out	4
*M. W. Gatting not out	79	B 2, l-b 6, w 5, n-b 1	14
M. R. Ramprakash run out	3		—
K. R. Brown lbw b Stear	16	1/3 2/100 3/117 (6 wkts, 50.3 overs)	208
R. O. Butcher c Jackson b Hartley	22	4/149 5/186 6/204	

N. F. Williams, A. R. C. Fraser and N. G. Cowans did not bat.

Bowling: Jones 9–2–32–1; Jackson 10–1–46–0; Headley 12–1–35–1; Stear 9–0–39–1; Lickley 1–0–13–0; Hartley 9.3–1–35–2.

Umpires: J. A. Jameson and K. E. Palmer.

NORTHAMPTONSHIRE v STAFFORDSHIRE

At Northampton, June 27. Northamptonshire won by 216 runs. Toss: Staffordshire. Northamptonshire's total was their highest in the Gillette Cup/NatWest Bank Trophy, while Fordham, who hit a six and fifteen fours in 130 from 143 balls, equalled G. Cook's county record for the competition. Lamb, scoring 68 not out from 35 balls, hit four sixes and three fours.
Man of the Match: A. Fordham.

Northamptonshire

A. Fordham c Cartledge b Blank	130
N. A. Felton c Humphries b Blank	 70
R. J. Bailey not out	 72
*A. J. Lamb not out	 68
L-b 14, w 6	 20

1/166 2/242		(2 wkts, 60 overs) 360

D. J. Capel, R. G. Williams, †D. Ripley, J. G. Thomas, C. E. L. Ambrose, N. G. B. Cook and M. A. Robinson did not bat.

Bowling: Taylor 12–0–92–0; Grant 12–2–56–0; Blank 12–0–74–2; Dyer 8–0–49–0; Dutton 12–1–52–0; Cartledge 4–0–23–0.

Staffordshire

S. J. Dean c Williams b Ambrose	 8	J. P. Taylor c Capel b Bailey	 5
D. Cartledge run out	 19	D. C. Blank not out	 1
J. P. Addison c Thomas b Robinson	... 10	L-b 1, w 6, n-b 3	 10
P. R. Oliver lbw b Thomas	 28		
*N. J. Archer b Williams	 26	1/29 2/30 3/66	(7 wkts, 60 overs) 144
A. J. Dutton c Lamb b Cook	 32	4/73 5/133	
†M. I. Humphries not out	 5	6/133 7/142	

R. J. Dyer and R. J. Grant did not bat.

Bowling: Ambrose 10–2–15–1; Thomas 10–2–21–1; Cook 12–4–31–1; Robinson 12–1–39–1; Williams 12–3–32–1; Fordham 2–1–3–0; Bailey 2–1–2–1.

Umpires: D. Fawkner-Corbett and N. T. Plews.

OXFORDSHIRE v KENT

At Christ Church, Oxford, June 27. Kent won by 102 runs. Toss: Oxfordshire. Wells, promoted to open because of injuries to senior players, batted throughout the Kent innings, facing 160 deliveries and reaching his maiden century for the county off the final ball. He then kept wicket as Oxfordshire were bowled out for 132.

Man of the Match: V. J. Wells.

Kent

S. G. Hinks c Garner b Hartley	 43	P. S. de Villiers st Waterton b Evans	.. 10
†V. J. Wells not out	100	A. P. Igglesden not out	 12
N. R. Taylor retired hurt	 13		
G. R. Cowdrey c Hartley b Curtis	... 3	B 2, l-b 9, w 8	 19
*C. S. Cowdrey c Jobson b Evans	 6		
M. V. Fleming b Evans	 7	1/70 2/110 3/124	(6 wkts, 60 overs) 234
D. J. M. Kelleher c Evans b Curtis	... 21	4/140 5/188 6/206	

M. M. Patel and R. P. Davis did not bat.

N. R. Taylor retired hurt at 95.

Bowling: Hale 4–0–15–0; Arnold 12–3–48–0; Savin 12–0–35–0; Hartley 8–1–26–1; Curtis 12–0–53–2; Evans 12–1–46–3.

Oxfordshire

G. C. Ford b Davis	26	D. A. Hale lbw b Kelleher	6
†S. N. V. Waterton c c C. S. Cowdrey		K. A. Arnold b Kelleher	2
b Igglesden	0	I. J. Curtis not out	0
J. S. Hartley lbw b Igglesden	7		
T. A. Lester lbw b Kelleher	13	B 4, l-b 11, w 5	20
*P. J. Garner lbw b Patel	4		
P. M. Jobson b Patel	7	1/8 2/22 3/41 (49 overs) 132	
G. P. Savin lbw b Fleming	23	4/58 5/66 6/66	
R. A. Evans b Fleming	24	7/119 8/120 9/131	

Bowling: de Villiers 7–3–28–0; Igglesden 6–1–13–2; Kelleher 9–3–16–3; Patel 12–6–29–2; Davis 12–3–27–1; Fleming 3–1–4–2.

Umpires: D. J. Constant and S. Cook.

SUFFOLK v WORCESTERSHIRE

At Bury St Edmunds, June 27. Worcestershire won by eight wickets. Toss: Worcestershire. *Man of the Match:* S. R. Lampitt.

Suffolk

M. S. A. McEvoy c Illingworth		†A. D. Brown b Lampitt	4
b Lampitt	55	*M. D. Bailey b Botham	0
C. Gladwin c and b Lampitt	5	R. C. Green lbw b Lampitt	0
J. W. Edrich c Rhodes b D'Oliveira	52		
P. J. Caley not out	39	L-b 3, w 3, n-b 2	8
S. M. Clements c Weston b D'Oliveira	11		
M. J. Peck b Botham	0	1/10 2/117 3/121 (59.4 overs) 177	
I. D. Graham lbw b Lampitt	3	4/138 5/146 6/163	
A. K. Golding c Neale b Botham	0	7/164 8/169 9/176	

Bowling: Botham 12–2–44–3; Lampitt 11.4–1–22–5; Illingworth 12–5–26–0; Hick 12–2–30–0; D'Oliveira 5–0–17–2; McEwan 3–0–15–0; Weston 4–0–20–0.

Worcestershire

T. S. Curtis b Golding	16
M. J. Weston c and b Golding	40
G. A. Hick not out	78
D. B. D'Oliveira not out	33
B 2, l-b 2, w 7, n-b 3	14

1/38 2/97   (2 wkts, 48 overs) 181

I. T. Botham, *P. A. Neale, D. A. Leatherdale, †S. J. Rhodes, S. R. Lampitt, R. K. Illingworth and S. M. McEwan did not bat.

Bowling: Green 11–1–38–0; Graham 9–1–37–0; Golding 12–4–29–2; Bailey 6–0–18–0; Caley 9–0–49–0; Gladwin 1–0–6–0.

Umpires: D. O. Oslear and R. A. White.

WILTSHIRE v SURREY

At Trowbridge, June 27. Surrey won by nine wickets. Toss: Surrey. Bullen, called on to open the innings after Stewart had twisted an ankle while fielding, hit two sixes and sixteen fours in his unbeaten 93.
Man of the Match: C. K. Bullen.

Wiltshire

*B. H. White c Lynch b Waqar Younis	0	A. Mildenhall run out		3
P. A. C. Bail run out	66	S. J. Malone not out		5
D. R. Turner c Ward b Bullen	18	M. Holland not out		0
K. N. Foyle b Waqar Younis	16		B 3, l-b 9, w 4	16
S. Williams b Murphy	11			
D. P. Simpkins c Thorpe b Bicknell	18	1/0 2/55 3/102	(9 wkts, 60 overs)	166
J. Thompson run out	7	4/116 5/131 6/148		
†N. Shardlow b Waqar Younis	6	7/158 8/159 9/161		

Bowling: Waqar Younis 12–3–23–3; Bicknell 12–3–16–1; Murphy 12–1–46–1; Medlycott 12–1–27–0; Bullen 12–1–42–1.

Surrey

G. S. Clinton c Shardlow b Mildenhall	50		
C. K. Bullen not out	93		
G. P. Thorpe not out	15		
L-b 5, w 6, n-b 1	12		

1/111   (1 wkt, 36.1 overs) 170

A. J. Stewart, †D. M. Ward, M. A. Lynch, *I. A. Greig, K. T. Medlycott, M. P. Bicknell, Waqar Younis and A. J. Murphy did not bat.

Bowling: Malone 9.1–0–54–0; Thompson 8–0–40–0; Simpkins 6–2–29–0; Mildenhall 8–2–32–1; Holland 5–2–10–0.

Umpires: K. J. Lyons and R. C. Tolchard.

YORKSHIRE v NORFOLK

At Leeds, June 27. Yorkshire won by ten wickets. Toss: Yorkshire.
Man of the Match: P. Carrick.

Norfolk

*S. G. Plumb c Byas b Hartley	20	R. Kingshott b Gough		9
F. L. Q. Handley c Sharp b Hartley	0	†D. E. Mattocks lbw b Hartley		2
D. M. Stamp lbw b Moxon	18	M. T. Ellis not out		0
R. J. Finney c Blakey b Moxon	25		B 5, l-b 1, w 5, n-b 4	15
S. B. Dixon c Sharp b Gough	1			
D. R. Thomas b Carrick	5	1/7 2/29 3/55	(47.5 overs)	104
N. S. Taylor b Carrick	0	4/72 5/81 6/81		
J. C. M. Lewis c Blakey b Carrick	9	7/81 8/92 9/103		

Bowling: Hartley 8.5–1–28–3; Sidebottom 10–1–21–0; Moxon 7–2–19–2; Gough 10–2–22–2; Carrick 12–9–8–3.

Yorkshire

*M. D. Moxon not out	56
A. A. Metcalfe not out	46
L-b 1, w 3	4

(no wkt, 20.2 overs) 106

S. A. Kellett, K. Sharp, P. E. Robinson, †R. J. Blakey, D. Byas, P. Carrick, P. J. Hartley, A. Sidebottom and D. Gough did not bat.

Bowling: Lewis 8–2–37–0; Taylor 4–0–32–0; Kingshott 6–2–24–0; Ellis 2.2–0–12–0.

Umpires: B. J. Meyer and T. G. Wilson.

SECOND ROUND

DERBYSHIRE v LANCASHIRE

At Derby, July 11. Lancashire won by three wickets. Toss: Lancashire. Derbyshire established a good position when Barnett and Morris shared a partnership of 105 for the second wicket. However, Morris suffered from a lapse of concentration before lunch, when he drove Atherton to extra cover, and the later batting collapsed spectacularly as DeFreitas and Wasim Akram took the last five wickets in ten balls. Lancashire were well in control until Malcolm and Goldsmith took three wickets in two overs, and Austin and Hegg had to bat carefully to steer Lancashire through with four balls to spare.

Man of the Match: M. A. Atherton.

Derbyshire

*K. J. Barnett b Wasim Akram	59	A. E. Warner not out	1
†P. D. Bowler b Wasim Akram	2	D. E. Malcolm b Wasim Akram	0
J. E. Morris c Fairbrother b Atherton	74	O. H. Mortensen b Wasim Akram	0
A. P. Kuiper c Atherton b Austin	25		
B. Roberts b DeFreitas	31	L-b 12, w 12, n-b 4	28
C. J. Adams c Hegg b Austin	0		
S. C. Goldsmith c Watkinson		1/18 2/123 3/161	(56.5 overs) 241
b DeFreitas	21	4/180 5/180 6/239	
G. Miller b DeFreitas	0	7/239 8/240 9/241	

Bowling: Wasim Akram 10.5–0–34–4; DeFreitas 11–4–34–3; Watkinson 5–0–31–0; Martin 5–0–28–0; Austin 10–0–46–2; Atherton 12–0–37–1; Hughes 3–0–19–0.

Lancashire

G. D. Mendis c Bowler b Mortensen	42	I. D. Austin not out	13
M. A. Atherton b Miller	55	†W. K. Hegg not out	13
G. D. Lloyd c Adams b Warner	36	B 6, l-b 14, w 6, n-b 3	29
N. H. Fairbrother c Miller b Malcolm	39		
M. Watkinson b Malcolm	5	1/64 2/134 3/184	(7 wkts, 59.2 overs) 242
Wasim Akram b Goldsmith	9	4/194 5/209	
P. A. J. DeFreitas c Roberts b Malcolm	1	6/214 7/215	

*D. P. Hughes and P. J. Martin did not bat.

Bowling: Malcolm 12–1–54–3; Mortensen 12–4–22–1; Warner 12–1–45–1; Miller 12–1–56–1; Kuiper 6–1–25–0; Goldsmith 5.2–0–20–1.

Umpires: M. J. Kitchen and K. E. Palmer.

ESSEX v HAMPSHIRE

At Chelmsford, July 11. Hampshire won, having lost fewer wickets with the scores level. Toss: Hampshire. Nicholas and Ayling took 6 runs off the first five balls of the last over, whereupon the Hampshire captain played the sixth defensively rather than risk losing a wicket going for the winning run. A start of 14 off the first ten overs by Chris Smith and Terry scarcely hinted at their partnership of 173 which launched Hampshire towards the highest total in the competition by a team batting second and winning. When 75 were needed from eleven overs following Gower's dismissal, Robin Smith's powerful fifty was as vital as his brother's century. Had Chris Smith been run out when 79, Gooch's eleventh hundred of the summer might not have been in vain. Gooch batted for 227 minutes without giving a chance, putting on 93 for the first wicket with Stephenson and 97 in sixteen overs with Waugh.

Man of the Match: C. L. Smith.

Essex

*G. A. Gooch b Connor	144	N. Hussain not out	2
J. P. Stephenson run out	44	†M. A. Garnham not out	1
P. J. Prichard c Gower b Marshall	21	B 5, l-b 3, w 3, n-b 4	15
M. E. Waugh c Parks b Marshall	47		
D. R. Pringle c Nicholas b Bakker	33	1/93 2/143 3/240 (6 wkts, 60 overs) 307	
N. A. Foster c Gower b Connor	0	4/304 5/304 6/304	

T. D. Topley, J. H. Childs and M. C. Ilott did not bat.

Bowling: Marshall 12–0–45–2; Bakker 12–3–60–1; Connor 12–0–71–2; Ayling 12–0–57–0; Maru 12–0–66–0.

Hampshire

V. P. Terry c Gooch b Ilott	76	J. R. Ayling not out	10
C. L. Smith c Gooch b Stephenson	106		
D. I. Gower c Topley b Foster	19	L-b 13, w 6	19
R. A. Smith c Topley b Pringle	59		
M. D. Marshall b Pringle	9	1/173 2/195 3/233 (5 wkts, 60 overs) 307	
*M. C. J. Nicholas not out	9	4/253 5/289	

†R. J. Parks, R. J. Maru, C. A. Connor and P. J. Bakker did not bat.

Bowling: Foster 12–4–35–1; Ilott 9–0–45–1; Pringle 12–1–64–2; Topley 11–0–66–0; Childs 12–0–60–0; Stephenson 4–0–24–1.

Umpires: J. D. Bond and J. H. Harris.

GLAMORGAN v SUSSEX

At Cardiff, July 11. Glamorgan won by 34 runs. Toss: Sussex. Put in on a slow pitch, Glamorgan had Richards to thank for a winning total. He and Cowley took 77 off the last seven overs, and his unbeaten 74 from 50 balls included two straight sixes as Dodemaide went for 21 runs in the final over. Morris, in contrast, anchored the innings with 58 in 44 overs. While Wells and Parker were adding 128 in 21 overs, Sussex were in control. When Wells was caught, having hit two sixes and eight fours in his 85, their target was 55 from ten overs. Instead, they lost their remaining seven wickets for 20 runs in 38 deliveries.

Man of the Match: I. V. A. Richards.

Glamorgan

*A. R. Butcher c Pigott b Dodemaide	30	N. G. Cowley not out	32
H. Morris c Salisbury b Dodemaide	58		
P. A. Cottey lbw b Clarke	27	B 2, l-b 12, w 2	16
M. P. Maynard c Speight b Lenham	24		
I. V. A. Richards not out	74	1/33 2/97 3/144 (5 wkts, 60 overs) 283	
I. Smith st Moores b Clarke	22	4/160 5/206	

†C. P. Metson, S. J. Dennis, S. L. Watkin and M. Frost did not bat.

Bowling: Clarke 12–0–53–2; Pigott 11–1–56–0; Dodemaide 12–1–70–2; Remy 10–1–30–0; Salisbury 12–1–47–0; Lenham 3–0–13–1.

Sussex

N. J. Lenham lbw b Smith	47	C. C. Remy b Watkin	1
J. W. Hall run out	0	I. D. K. Salisbury not out	2
*P. W. G. Parker b Richards	83	A. R. Clarke lbw b Watkin	0
A. P. Wells c Smith b Cowley	85	B 1, l-b 18, w 5, n-b 1	25
M. P. Speight c Butcher b Cowley	4		
A. I. C. Dodemaide lbw b Richards	1	1/2 2/101 3/229 (55.5 overs) 249	
A. C. S. Pigott b Watkin	1	4/233 5/236 6/243	
†P. Moores run out	0	7/243 8/247 9/249	

Bowling: Cowley 12–0–71–2; Frost 10–1–34–0; Watkin 11.5–5–18–3; Dennis 8–0–44–0; Richards 10–0–43–2; Smith 4–0–20–1.

Umpires: P. J. Eele and R. Palmer.

GLOUCESTERSHIRE v KENT

At Bristol, July 11. Gloucestershire won by six wickets. Toss: Kent. High-class fast bowling by Walsh quickly made Chris Cowdrey regret his decision to bat. And when Kent hinted at a recovery through Graham Cowdrey and Ward, his three quick wickets after lunch cut the heart out of the innings. Although Ellison and the tailenders nudged the score up to 181, this never seemed enough on what was basically a good batting pitch. Kent's new-ball bowlers were handled comfortably by Wright and Hodgson, and Bainbridge produced some crisp strokes to see Gloucestershire home with nearly twelve overs to spare.

Man of the Match: C. A. Walsh.

Kent

M. R. Benson c Russell b Walsh	7	P. S. de Villiers b Curran	14
S. G. Hinks c Graveney b Curran	15	R. P. Davis c Russell b Walsh	12
N. R. Taylor b Walsh	0	A. P. Igglesden not out	2
G. R. Cowdrey c Bainbridge b Alleyne	37	L-b 9, w 4, n-b 2	15
T. R. Ward lbw b Walsh	47		
*C. S. Cowdrey b Walsh	5	1/11 2/13 3/30 (9 wkts, 60 overs)	181
†S. A. Marsh b Walsh	0	4/93 5/120 6/123	
R. M. Ellison not out	27	7/124 8/156 9/175	

Bowling: Walsh 12–3–21–6; Curran 12–2–30–2; Barnes 6–0–29–0; Bainbridge 11.1–1–38–0; Graveney 6.5–0–21–0; Alleyne 12–2–33–1.

Gloucestershire

G. D. Hodgson c Davis b de Villiers	39	J. W. Lloyds not out	4
*A. J. Wright c Ellison b Davis	45	L-b 3, w 11, n-b 1	15
P. Bainbridge not out	56		
C. W. J. Athey c Marsh b Ellison	22	1/88 2/94 3/175 (4 wkts, 48.3 overs)	182
K. M. Curran c Taylor b G. R. Cowdrey	1	4/178	

M. W. Alleyne, †R. C. Russell, C. A. Walsh, D. A. Graveney and S. N. Barnes did not bat.

Bowling: de Villiers 9–1–29–1; Igglesden 8–0–34–0; Ellison 12–6–18–1; C. S. Cowdrey 5–0–29–0; Davis 9–0–33–1; Hinks 3–0–23–0; G. R. Cowdrey 2.3–0–13–1.

Umpires: B. Hassan and K. J. Lyons.

MIDDLESEX v SURREY

At Uxbridge, July 11. Middlesex won by five wickets. Toss: Middlesex. Though no Surrey batsman did excessive damage, their total was nevertheless more than Middlesex had previously scored in the 60-overs competition. Middlesex were especially pleased to have run out Lynch, who had noted the square-leg boundary with two consecutive sixes off Emburey in his 59 from 74 balls. With Haynes out in the first over and Gatting injured, Middlesex needed major innings from Roseberry, Ramprakash and Brown, who obliged gloriously. Roseberry laid the foundation with Ramprakash, who then added 126 in 26 overs with Brown. Ramprakash faced 142 balls for his 104, but it was necessary for Brown to go even faster. His winning hit, with two balls left, brought his century from just 113 balls.

Man of the Match: K. R. Brown.

Surrey

D. J. Bicknell b Cowans	12	C. K. Bullen not out	20
G. S. Clinton lbw b Fraser	33	M. P. Bicknell not out	4
*A. J. Stewart c Farbrace b Fraser	48		
M. A. Lynch run out	59	B 1, l-b 19, w 16, n-b 6	42
†D. M. Ward c Brown b Haynes	11		
G. P. Thorpe c Cowans b Fraser	16	1/18 2/113 3/114 (8 wkts, 60 overs)	288
M. A. Feltham c Farbrace b Fraser	5	4/175 5/215 6/221	
K. T. Medlycott c Farbrace b Cowans	38	7/221 8/274	

Waqar Younis did not bat.

Bowling: Cowans 11–2–45–2; Williams 11–2–42–0; Haynes 12–0–41–1; Gatting 2–0–20–0; Fraser 12–1–44–4; Emburey 12–0–76–0.

Middlesex

D. L. Haynes c Ward b Waqar Younis .	0	*M. W. Gatting c Ward b Feltham	3
M. A. Roseberry c M. P. Bicknell		J. E. Emburey not out	15
b Waqar Younis .	48		
M. R. Ramprakash c Ward		B 8, l-b 6, w 1, n-b 2	17
b M. P. Bicknell .	104		
K. R. Brown not out	103	1/0 2/94 3/220 (5 wkts, 59.4 overs) 291	
R. O. Butcher c Stewart b Medlycott . .	1	4/223 5/241	

†P. Farbrace, N. F. Williams, A. R. C. Fraser and N. G. Cowans did not bat.

Bowling: Waqar Younis 12–2–39–2; M. P. Bicknell 12–0–63–1; Feltham 11.4–0–65–1; Medlycott 12–0–64–1; Bullen 12–0–46–0.

Umpires: N. T. Plews and D. S. Thompsett.

NORTHAMPTONSHIRE v NOTTINGHAMSHIRE

At Northampton, July 11. Northamptonshire won by 24 runs. Toss: Nottinghamshire. A magnificent innings from Capel, whose 101 runs came off as many balls with five sixes and seven fours, paved the way for a Northamptonshire total far more formidable than had looked likely when they lost their first three wickets for 72. Lamb, for once content to play the secondary role, helped Capel add 154 in 30 overs. Nottinghamshire were unlucky in that two of their key batsmen, Broad (ricked neck) and Johnson (hit on the head by Ambrose) were forced to retire hurt. Although both later returned, the innings lost its momentum for a time. Randall and French regained the initiative in a brisk 64-run stand, but Randall became a third victim of Bailey's occasional off-spin, and with Evans and Cooper succumbing to suicidal run-outs, French was left with too much to do.

Man of the Match: D. J. Capel.

Northamptonshire

A. Fordham c French b Cooper	23	R. G. Williams not out	9
N. A. Felton b Hemmings	32	†D. Ripley not out	1
R. J. Bailey c French b Evans	7	B 1, l-b 14, w 3, n-b 1	19
*A. J. Lamb c Evans b Stephenson	61		
D. J. Capel b Evans	101	1/33 2/66 3/72 (6 wkts, 60 overs) 274	
W. Larkins c French b Stephenson	21	4/226 5/258 6/264	

C. E. L. Ambrose, N. G. B. Cook and M. A. Robinson did not bat.

Bowling: Stephenson 12–1–40–2; Cooper 12–0–49–1; Pick 12–1–64–0; Evans 12–3–53–2; Hemmings 12–2–53–1.

Nottinghamshire

B. C. Broad c Robinson b Williams	13	E. E. Hemmings c and b Cook	0
M. Newell run out	4	K. E. Cooper run out	0
*R. T. Robinson b Bailey	61	R. A. Pick not out	5
P. Johnson b Robinson	48	L-b 3, w 10, n-b 11	24
D. W. Randall c Ambrose b Bailey	56		
F. D. Stephenson c Ambrose b Bailey	4	1/24 2/119 3/149 (57.1 overs) 250	
†B. N. French c Fordham b Ambrose	35	4/163 5/171 6/235	
K. P. Evans run out	0	7/239 8/240 9/240	

B. C. Broad, when 13, retired hurt at 22 and resumed at 117; P. Johnson, when 41, retired hurt at 117 and resumed at 149.

Bowling: Ambrose 10.1–1–30–1; Robinson 11–0–46–1; Cook 12–1–42–1; Capel 6–0–43–0; Williams 8–1–39–1; Bailey 10–1–47–3.

Umpires: J. H. Hampshire and P. B. Wight.

SOMERSET v WORCESTERSHIRE

At Taunton, July 11. Worcestershire won by seven wickets. Toss: Somerset. Accurate bowling by Illingworth and Lampitt slowed Somerset after a brisk start, with Hayhurst and Tavaré needing 28 overs to add 100. And although 76 runs came from the last ten overs, with Tavaré (122 balls) helped notably by Burns, in splendid weather and good conditions for run-scoring a total of 283 hardly looked sufficient. Curtis and Weston, who batted for 147 balls for 98 despite receiving a nasty blow under the heart, put on 188 in 41 overs. Lefebvre then took two quick wickets, but Curtis, reaching 100 in 124 balls, and D'Oliveira ensured Worcestershire won with sixteen balls to spare.

Man of the Match: T. S. Curtis.

Somerset

S. J. Cook lbw b Lampitt	45	†N. D. Burns not out	25
P. M. Roebuck b Lampitt	20		
A. N. Hayhurst c Lampitt b Newport	46	B 6, l-b 7, w 6, n-b 1	20
*C. J. Tavaré not out	99		—
G. D. Rose c Neale b Botham	16	1/64 2/71 3/171 (5 wkts, 60 overs) 283	
R. J. Harden b Botham	12	4/200 5/230	

R. P. Lefebvre, I. G. Swallow, N. A. Mallender and A. N. Jones did not bat.

Bowling: Botham 12-0-65-2; Newport 10-0-54-1; Lampitt 12-1-48-2; Illingworth 12-3-22-0; Tolley 6-0-32-0; Hick 8-0-49-0.

Worcestershire

T. S. Curtis c Swallow b Rose	112	I. T. Botham not out	0
M. J. Weston c Cook b Lefebvre	98	L-b 12, w 7, n-b 2	21
G. A. Hick c Burns b Lefebvre	2		—
D. B. D'Oliveira not out	51	1/188 2/195 3/279 (3 wkts, 57.2 overs) 284	

*P. A. Neale, †S. J. Rhodes, R. K. Illingworth, P. J. Newport, S. R. Lampitt and C. M. Tolley did not bat.

Bowling: Jones 10-0-64-0; Mallender 10-2-29-0; Lefebvre 12-0-46-2; Rose 9-0-40-1; Hayhurst 2-0-14-0; Swallow 9-0-57-0; Roebuck 5.2-0-22-0.

Umpires: B. Dudleston and D. R. Shepherd.

YORKSHIRE v WARWICKSHIRE

At Leeds, July 11. Yorkshire won by ten wickets. Toss: Yorkshire. Warwickshire were always struggling against accurate bowling on a good one-day pitch. Gough claimed two wickets for 1 run in six balls to upset them after a reasonable start, and Carrick won a significant duel with the free-scoring Moody. Asif Din, missed when 22 off Hartley, made his 58 from 80 balls, while Smith's 52 came from 46 deliveries. When Yorkshire batted, Moxon and Metcalfe took complete control, the latter racing to his half-century off 63 balls. The Warwickshire bowlers had no answer as the Yorkshire pair established a new record opening stand for the competition. Moxon's 107 came from 168 balls (nine fours) and Metcalfe's 127 from 165 (fifteen fours).

Man of the Match: M. D. Moxon.

Warwickshire

A. J. Moles c Blakey b Gough	27	G. C. Small b Hartley	8
*T. A. Lloyd c Byas b Sidebottom	15	J. E. Benjamin not out	2
T. M. Moody c Metcalfe b Carrick	51	T. A. Munton not out	1
†G. W. Humpage c Sidebottom b Gough	2	L-b 9, w 7, n-b 5	21
D. A. Reeve c Robinson b Carrick	0		—
D. P. Ostler c Blakey b Carrick	4	1/33 2/79 3/95 (9 wkts, 60 overs) 241	
Asif Din c Gough b Byas	58	4/86 5/97 6/138	
N. M. K. Smith c Robinson b Hartley	52	7/211 8/236 9/236	

Umpires: B. Dudleston and D. R. Shepherd.

Bowling: Hartley 12–0–62–2; Sidebottom 12–4–20–1; Fletcher 12–1–56–0; Carrick 12–0–26–3; Gough 9–1–45–2; Byas 3–0–23–1.

Yorkshire

```
*M. D. Moxon not out .............107
A. A. Metcalfe not out .............127
         L-b 3, w 3, n-b 2 ........... 8
                                    ___
```

(no wkt, 55 overs) 242

S. A. Kellett, P. E. Robinson, †R. J. Blakey, D. Byas, P. Carrick, P. J. Hartley, A. Sidebottom, D. Gough and S. D. Fletcher did not bat.

Bowling: Benjamin 8–1–40–0; Small 9–1–37–0; Reeve 12–1–42–0; Munton 6–0–31–0; Smith 8–0–41–0; Moody 9–0–34–0; Asif Din 3–0–14–0.

Umpires: H. D. Bird and R. A. White.

QUARTER-FINALS

HAMPSHIRE v YORKSHIRE

At Southampton, August 1. Hampshire won by 111 runs. Toss: Yorkshire. Hampshire's often underrated attack bowled them to an unexpected victory. After Hampshire had been restricted to 229 for nine, with Nicholas's vigilant 50 providing the backbone, Yorkshire were clear favourites for a place in the semi-finals. Yet within seven overs their hopes lay in ruins. Moxon was needlessly run out in the first over, and Metcalfe and Kellett fell in Marshall's fourth over with the total 9. After that, only Hartley and Carrick delayed the inevitable with a stand of 34 for the seventh wicket. Hartley hit two sixes and six fours in his lively half-century.
Man of the Match: P. J. Hartley.

Hampshire

V. P. Terry c Byas b Hartley 16	R. J. Maru c Blakey b Fletcher 22	
C. L. Smith c Blakey b Hartley 30	C. A. Connor c Blakey b Fletcher 13	
D. I. Gower c Moxon b Hartley 26	P. J. Bakker not out 3	
R. A. Smith c Byas b Sidebottom 27	L-b 3, w 1 4	
M. D. Marshall c Sidebottom b Hartley 4		
*M. C. J. Nicholas b Hartley 50	1/28 2/63 3/76 (9 wkts, 60 overs) 229	
J. R. Ayling st Blakey b Carrick 7	4/80 5/121 6/154	
†R. J. Parks not out 27	7/168 8/199 9/223	

Bowling: Jarvis 12–1–58–0; Sidebottom 12–3–35–1; Hartley 12–2–46–5; Fletcher 12–0–53–2; Carrick 12–0–34–1.

Yorkshire

*M. D. Moxon run out 1	P. W. Jarvis c Connor b Marshall 6	
A. A. Metcalfe c Maru b Marshall 2	A. Sidebottom c Parks b Marshall 1	
†R. J. Blakey b Ayling 21	S. D. Fletcher not out 6	
S. A. Kellett b Marshall 0	L-b 1, w 2, n-b 1 4	
P. E. Robinson c Terry b Connor 7		
D. Byas b Maru 4	1/1 2/9 3/9 (39 overs) 118	
P. Carrick c R. A. Smith b Ayling 14	4/34 5/34 6/40	
P. J. Hartley c C. L. Smith b Ayling .. 52	7/74 8/105 9/107	

Bowling: Marshall 8–1–17–4; Bakker 7–1–12–0; Connor 6–2–10–1; Ayling 9–2–30–3; Maru 9–0–48–1.

Umpires: R. Julian and R. Palmer.

LANCASHIRE v GLOUCESTERSHIRE

At Manchester, August 1. Lancashire won by 241 runs. Toss: Gloucestershire. Lancashire followed the highest total in any limited-overs game between first-class counties with the highest victory margin. It was Watkinson's 29th birthday and he celebrated with the biggest innings (90 from 58 balls) and the best bowling return in the match. Gloucestershire were never in the game after Mendis and Fowler had given Lancashire a 124-run start at 5 runs an over. Watkinson hit six fours and four sixes, and he and Fairbrother put on 169 in twenty overs.

Man of the Match: M. Watkinson.

Lancashire

G. D. Mendis run out	88	Wasim Akram not out	5
G. Fowler c Russell b Lawrence	52	L-b 5, w 20, n-b 1	26
M. A. Atherton c and b Barnes	25		
N. H. Fairbrother b Walsh	86	1/124 2/176 3/180 (5 wkts, 60 overs)	372
M. Watkinson c Wright b Walsh	90	4/349 5/372	

*D. P. Hughes, P. A. J. DeFreitas, I. D. Austin, †W. K. Hegg and P. J. Martin did not bat.

Bowling: Walsh 12–0–69–2; Curran 12–2–63–0; Barnes 12–1–64–1; Lawrence 9–0–62–1; Alleyne 7–0–51–0; Lloyds 5–0–44–0; Athey 3–0–14–0.

Gloucestershire

*A. J. Wright c Atherton b DeFreitas	4	C. A. Walsh c Hegg b Watkinson	7
G. D. Hodgson c and b Atherton	52	D. V. Lawrence not out	0
P. W. Romaines b Austin	20	S. N. Barnes b Wasim Akram	0
C. W. J. Athey c and b Wasim Akram	8	B 4, w 12	16
†R. C. Russell c and b Atherton	12		
K. M. Curran c Hegg b Watkinson	1	1/21 2/59 3/90 (30 overs)	131
J. W. Lloyds c Hegg b Watkinson	2	4/106 5/107 6/113	
M. W. Alleyne not out	9	7/115 8/123 9/131	

Bowling: Martin 3–0–25–0; DeFreitas 5–1–22–1; Austin 7–0–22–1; Wasim Akram 6–0–29–3; Watkinson 5–0–14–3; Atherton 4–0–15–2.

Umpires: B. Leadbeater and K. J. Lyons.

MIDDLESEX v GLAMORGAN

At Lord's, August 1. Middlesex won by nine wickets. Toss: Glamorgan. This was an unusual limited-overs match, with spin bowlers playing an attacking role on a pitch which assisted them extravagantly. As the Middlesex spin attack was superior to Glamorgan's, there was an inevitability about the result once it became clear that nobody would emulate Butcher's fighting effort. The Glamorgan captain reached his century in the penultimate over and hit ten fours in an innings of 177 balls. Cowley and Croft demanded a degree of watchfulness, but none of the three Middlesex batsmen was anything but forceful as they progressed comfortably towards their target.

Man of the Match: A. R. Butcher.

Glamorgan

*A. R. Butcher not out	104	†C. P. Metson c Gatting b Emburey	9
H. Morris b Tufnell	26	S. L. Watkin not out	6
M. P. Maynard c Cowans b Emburey	1	B 10, l-b 7, w 1, n-b 6	24
I. V. A. Richards c Gatting b Emburey	9		
A. Dale c Emburey b Tufnell	3	1/49 2/50 3/76 (7 wkts, 60 overs)	213
R. D. B. Croft run out	26	4/86 5/150	
N. G. Cowley b Cowans	5	6/162 7/187	

S. J. Dennis and M. Frost did not bat.

Bowling: Cowans 12–2–48–1; Fraser 12–2–47–0; Williams 8–0–38–0; Emburey 12–5–27–3; Tufnell 12–2–22–2; Ramprakash 4–1–14–0.

Middlesex

D. L. Haynes not out	....	75
M. A. Roseberry lbw b Dale	....	48
*M. W. Gatting not out	....	70
L-b 15, w 8	....	23

1/84　　　　　　(1 wkt, 50.1 overs) 216

M. R. Ramprakash, K. R. Brown, †P. R. Downton, J. E. Emburey, N. F. Williams, P. C. R. Tufnell, A. R. C. Fraser and N. G. Cowans did not bat.

Bowling: Frost 9–1–39–0; Watkin 11.1–1–28–0; Dennis 5–0–27–0; Cowley 8–1–33–0; Croft 10–0–44–0; Dale 3–0–14–1; Richards 4–0–16–0.

Umpires: A. A. Jones and D. O. Oslear.

NORTHAMPTONSHIRE v WORCESTERSHIRE

At Northampton, August 1. Northamptonshire won by 4 runs. Toss: Worcestershire. Robinson was Northamptonshire's hero in an absorbing match of fluctuating fortunes, and although Botham was preferred for the Man of the Match award, the young fast bowler enjoyed the greater satisfaction of seeing his side into the semi-finals. Botham (80 balls, four sixes, five fours) had put Worcestershire into a winning position, adding 85 in fourteen overs with Neale and, when Neale and Rhodes departed in quick succession to Williams, exacting revenge by hitting the off-spinner for three sixes in an over. However, with Botham frustratingly losing the strike, Robinson tilted the match back in Northamptonshire's favour by bowling Radford and Newport, and the task of scoring 10 off his final over proved beyond Botham and the last man, Lampitt. Earlier, Northamptonshire's innings had been given a solid foundation by Fordham (143 balls, eleven fours), Larkins and Capel, but Newport bowled impressively at the end as the last five wickets tumbled in three overs.

Man of the Match: I. T. Botham.

Northamptonshire

A. Fordham lbw b Lampitt	....	96	C. E. L. Ambrose lbw b Newport	.....	0
N. A. Felton c Curtis b Newport	.....	12	N. G. B. Cook run out	....	1
W. Larkins b Illingworth	....	52	M. A. Robinson not out	....	0
*A. J. Lamb c Rhodes b Illingworth	...	0	L-b 11, w 1	....	12
D. J. Capel c Rhodes b Newport	.....	53			
R. J. Bailey c Weston b Botham	.....	29	1/46 2/138 3/140	(59.1 overs) 263
R. G. Williams b Newport	....	6	4/205 5/231 6/251	
†D. Ripley run out	....	2	7/259 8/261 9/263	

Bowling: Newport 12–0–46–4; Radford 4–0–23–0; Botham 7.1–0–42–1; Lampitt 12–0–58–1; Illingworth 12–1–44–2; Hick 12–0–39–0.

Worcestershire

T. S. Curtis b Cook	....	30	N. V. Radford b Robinson	....	0
M. J. Weston c Fordham b Robinson	..	14	P. J. Newport b Robinson	....	0
G. A. Hick c Cook b Williams	....	49	S. R. Lampitt not out	....	3
D. B. D'Oliveira b Cook	....	2	B 2, l-b 14, w 7	....	23
I. T. Botham not out	....	86			
*P. A. Neale c Larkins b Williams	....	43	1/28 2/56 3/72	(9 wkts, 60 overs) 259
†S. J. Rhodes c and b Williams	....	2	4/107 5/192 6/195	
R. K. Illingworth b Ambrose	....	7	7/243 8/244 9/246	

Bowling: Ambrose 12–3–39–1; Robinson 12–1–33–3; Capel 12–0–51–0; Cook 12–2–34–2; Williams 12–0–86–3.

Umpires: J. C. Balderstone and M. J. Kitchen.

SEMI-FINALS

HAMPSHIRE v NORTHAMPTONSHIRE

At Southampton, August 15. Northamptonshire won by 1 run. Toss: Hampshire. Twelve months after missing out on their first appearance in a 60-overs final by 4 runs, Hampshire came even closer. This time they needed 2 off the final delivery, from Robinson to Bakker, and managed only a single. After choosing to field first, Hampshire did well to contain Northamptonshire to 284, even though they had lost their early initiative when Lamb and Capel hit 66 in eleven overs for the fourth wicket. Their reply began badly, with Chris Smith falling in the fourth over, and when Hampshire were 55 for three, Northamptonshire were clear favourites. However, Gower, playing his most disciplined innings of the summer for Hampshire, and Marshall, profiting from missed catches, then added 141 in 26 overs to take them to the threshold of victory. Gower, having hit eleven fours in his 86, was caught in the deep, and when Marshall (one six, six fours) drove a return catch to Cook, the pendulum swung back towards Northamptonshire.

Man of the Match: M. D. Marshall.

Northamptonshire

A. Fordham c Ayling b Bakker	1		C. E. L. Ambrose st Parks b Ayling	22
N. A. Felton c Gower b Connor	31		N. G. B. Cook not out	6
W. Larkins c Parks b Ayling	48		M. A. Robinson b Connor	0
*A. J. Lamb c C. L. Smith b Maru	58		L-b 6, w 9, n-b 1	16
D. J. Capel c Nicholas b Maru	43			
R. J. Bailey c Parks b Connor	8		1/6 2/70 3/111	(60 overs) 284
R. G. Williams b Connor	44		4/177 5/205 6/205	
†D. Ripley c Maru b Marshall	7		7/230 8/272 9/284	

Bowling: Marshall 12–3–37–1; Bakker 12–2–41–1; Connor 12–1–73–4; Ayling 12–0–76–2; Maru 12–0–51–2.

Hampshire

V. P. Terry c Robinson b Cook	24		R. J. Maru c Capel b Robinson	14
C. L. Smith c Felton b Robinson	0		C. A. Connor not out	3
R. A. Smith c Ripley b Capel	20		P. J. Bakker run out	2
D. I. Gower c Capel b Williams	86		L-b 12, w 4	16
M. D. Marshall c and b Cook	77			
*M. C. J. Nicholas c Lamb b Cook	29		1/6 2/37 3/55	(60 overs) 283
I. R. Ayling c Williams b Robinson	8		4/196 5/246 6/253	
†R. J. Parks c Felton b Ambrose	4		7/259 8/269 9/280	

Bowling: Ambrose 12–4–29–1; Robinson 12–1–62–3; Cook 12–3–52–3; Capel 12–1–67–1; Williams 12–1–61–1.

Umpires: K. J. Lyons and A. G. T. Whitehead.

LANCASHIRE v MIDDLESEX

At Manchester, August 15, 16, 17. Lancashire won by five wickets. Toss: Lancashire. Only 49 overs were possible on the opening day, when in front of a near-capacity crowd of 18,000 Middlesex reached 199 for two (D. L. Haynes 95*, M. R. Ramprakash 17*). The second day was rained out, and it was still raining on the third morning when play should have started. Happily, all suggestions of bowling at stumps to get a result, or replaying the match the following week, were abandoned when the game resumed at 1.45 p.m. Middlesex added 97 runs in the remaining eleven overs to reach their highest total in the competition, with Haynes batting through the innings, facing 177 balls and hitting eleven fours. Mendis responded with his first century for Lancashire in limited-overs games, and he received sound support from Atherton, followed by sharp acceleration from Fairbrother (48 in 42 balls) and Watkinson (43 in 40 balls, including three huge sixes). As word of the match's progress spread through Manchester, the crowd of about 500 at the start built to 5,000 by the end.

Man of the Match: G. D. Mendis.

Middlesex

D. L. Haynes not out	149	†P. R. Downton not out	
M. A. Roseberry lbw b Allott	16	B 6, l-b 11, w 8, n-b 3	2
*M. W. Gatting b Watkinson	53		
M. R. Ramprakash run out	45	1/23 2/147	(4 wkts, 60 overs) 29
K. R. Brown c Hegg b Wasim Akram	1	3/269 4/271	

J. E. Emburey, N. F. Williams, A. R. C. Fraser, S. P. Hughes and N. G. Cowans did not ba

Bowling: Allott 12–3–40–1; DeFreitas 12–0–52–0; Wasim Akram 12–2–65–1; Watkinso 12–1–62–1; Austin 12–1–60–0.

Lancashire

G. D. Mendis not out	121	P. A. J. DeFreitas not out	
G. Fowler b Cowans	8		
M. A. Atherton b Hughes	34	B 1, l-b 21, w 3, n-b 4	2
N. H. Fairbrother c Downton b Hughes	48		
M. Watkinson c Downton b Fraser	43	1/23 2/83 3/185	(5 wkts, 55.5 overs) 29
Wasim Akram b Fraser	14	4/269 5/293	

†W. K. Hegg, I. D. Austin, *D. P. Hughes and P. J. W. Allott did not bat.

Bowling: Cowans 12–1–40–1; Fraser 11.5–0–43–2; Williams 10–0–72–0; Hughe 12–0–68–2; Emburey 10–0–54–0.

Umpires: D. J. Constant and B. J. Meyer.

FINAL

LANCASHIRE v NORTHAMPTONSHIRE

At Lord's, September 1. Lancashire won by seven wickets. Toss: Lancashire. DeFreitas, wi wickets in the second, sixth, eighth, twelfth and fourteenth overs of the morning, determine the course of the final in an opening spell of 8–4–19–5. Only Hughes's good fortune in winnir the toss and being able to put Northamptonshire in on a pitch containing some moisture cou be said to be more influential. In seaming the ball both ways, DeFreitas exposed technic weaknesses in the Northamptonshire top-order batting. Capel and Ambrose showed wh could be achieved by getting properly forward on the front foot whenever possible; both we unlucky in being run out at the non-striker's end by deflections from the bowler, Allott ar Wasim Akram being the respective agents. The irony was that it was Ambrose's straight dri which brought Capel's dismissal.

To have a chance of winning, Northamptonshire needed to keep Lancashire's batsm under pressure from the start. Fowler was soon caught off a leading edge; Mendis was caug behind off a thin one to leave Lancashire 28 for two in the sixteenth over. Ambrose shou have caught Fairbrother at mid-on off Cook when he was 6. He didn't, and the left-hande provided the batting entertainment of the day. His cavalier innings of 81 from 68 ba included two sixes and nine fours, and he walked off to a standing ovation. Watkinson, hittir two sixes while scoring 24 from eighteen balls, and the steady Atherton then took Lancashi to the victory which made them the first county to win both Lord's finals in the same season

Man of the Match: P. A. J. DeFreitas.

Attendance: 13,500 (excl. members); *receipts* £330,000.

Northamptonshire

A. Fordham lbw b DeFreitas	5	N. G. B. Cook b Austin	
N. A. Felton c Allott b DeFreitas	4	M. A. Robinson not out	
W. Larkins c Hegg b DeFreitas	7		
*A. J. Lamb lbw b DeFreitas	8	B 1, l-b 10, w 9, n-b 2	2
R. J. Bailey c Hegg b DeFreitas	7		
D. J. Capel run out	36	1/8 (2) 2/19 (1) 3/20 (3)	(60 overs) 17
R. G. Williams b Watkinson	9	4/38 (5) 5/39 (4) 6/56 (7)	
†D. Ripley b Watkinson	13	7/87 (8) 8/126 (6)	
C. E. L. Ambrose run out	48	9/166 (9) 10/171 (10)	

Bowling: Allott 12–3–29–0; DeFreitas 12–5–26–5; Wasim Akram 12–0–35–0; Watkinso 12–1–29–2; Austin 12–4–41–1.

ancashire

. D. Mendis c Ripley b Capel	14
. Fowler c Cook b Robinson	7
. A. Atherton not out	38
. H. Fairbrother c Ambrose b Williams	81
. Watkinson not out	24
L-b 4, w 2, n-b 3	9

16 (2) 2/28 (1)   (3 wkts, 45.4 overs) 173
142 (4)

Ͻ. P. Hughes, Wasim Akram, P. A. J. DeFreitas, †W. K. Hegg, I. D. Austin and P. J. W. Allott did not bat.

Bowling: Ambrose 10–1–23–0; Robinson 9–2–26–1; Cook 10.4–2–50–0; Capel 9–0–44–1; 'illiams 7–0–26–1.

Umpires: J. W. Holder and D. R. Shepherd.

NATWEST BANK TROPHY RECORDS

(Including Gillette Cup, 1963-80)

atting

ighest individual scores: 206, A. I. Kallicharran, Warwickshire v Oxfordshire, Birmingham, 1984; 177, C. G. Greenidge, Hampshire v Glamorgan, Southampton, 1975; 172 not out, G. A. Hick, Worcestershire v Devon, Worcester, 1987; 165 not out, V. P. Terry, Hampshire v Berkshire, Southampton, 1985; 162 not out, C. J. Tavaré, Somerset v Devon, Torquay, 1990; 159, C. L. Smith, Hampshire v Cheshire, Chester, 1989; 158, G. D. Barlow, Middlesex v Lancashire, Lord's, 1984; 158, Zaheer Abbas, Gloucestershire v Leicestershire, Leicester, 1983; 156, D. I. Gower, Leicestershire v Derbyshire, Leicester, 1984; 155, J. J. Whitaker, Leicestershire v Wiltshire, Swindon, 1984; 154 not out, H. Morris, Glamorgan v Staffordshire, Cardiff, 1989; 154, P. Willey, Leicestershire v Hampshire, Leicester, 1987; 153, A. Hill, Derbyshire v Cornwall, Derby, 1986. (93 hundreds were scored in the Gillette Cup; 98 hundreds have been scored in the NatWest Bank Trophy.)

ost runs: 1,950, D. L. Amiss.

astest hundred: G. D. Rose off 36 balls, Somerset v Devon, Torquay, 1990.

ost hundreds: 6, C. L. Smith; 5, D. I. Gower and G. M. Turner.

ighest innings totals (off 60 overs): 413 for four, Somerset v Devon, Torquay, 1990; 404 for three, Worcestershire v Devon, Worcester, 1987; 392 for five, Warwickshire v Oxfordshire, Birmingham, 1984; 386 for five, Essex v Wiltshire, Chelmsford, 1988; 372 for five, Lancashire v Gloucestershire, Manchester, 1990; 371 for four, Hampshire v Glamorgan, Southampton, 1975; 365 for three, Derbyshire v Cornwall, Derby, 1986; 360 for two, Northamptonshire v Staffordshire, Northampton, 1990; 359 for four, Kent v Dorset, Canterbury, 1989; 354 for seven, Leicestershire v Wiltshire, Swindon, 1984; 349 for six, Lancashire v Gloucestershire, Bristol, 1984; 341 for six, Leicestershire v Hampshire, Leicester, 1987; 339 for four, Hampshire v Berkshire, Southampton, 1985; 336 for five, Worcestershire v Cumberland, Worcester, 1988; 336 for seven, Warwickshire v Hertfordshire, St Albans, 1990; 330 for four, Somerset v Glamorgan, Cardiff, 1978. *In the final:* 317 for four, Yorkshire v Surrey, 1965.

ighest innings total by a minor county: 261 for eight (60 overs), Dorset v Glamorgan, Swansea, 1990.

ghest innings by a side batting first and losing: 307 for six (60 overs), Essex v Hampshire, Chelmsford, 1990. *In the final:* 242 for eight (60 overs), Lancashire v Sussex, 1986.

Highest totals by a side batting second: 326 for nine (60 overs), Hampshire v Leicestershire, Leicester, 1987; 307 for five (60 overs), Hampshire v Essex, Chelmsford, 1990; 306 for six (59.3 overs), Gloucestershire v Leicestershire, Leicester, 1983; 298 (59 overs), Lancashire v Worcestershire, Manchester, 1985; 297 for four (57.1 overs), Somerset v Warwickshire, Taunton, 1978; 296 for four (58 overs), Kent v Surrey, Canterbury, 1985; 290 for seven (59. overs), Yorkshire v Worcestershire, Leeds, 1982; 287 for six (59 overs), Warwickshire v Glamorgan, Birmingham, 1976; 287 (60 overs), Essex v Somerset, Taunton, 1978; 282 for nine (60 overs), Leicestershire v Gloucestershire, Leicester, 1975. *In the final:* 279 for five (60 overs), Nottinghamshire v Essex, 1985.

Highest total by a side batting second and winning: 307 for five (60 overs), Hampshire v Essex, Chelmsford, 1990. *In the final:* 243 for three (58.2 overs), Sussex v Lancashire, 1986.

Highest total by a side batting second and losing: 326 for nine (60 overs), Hampshire v Leicestershire, Leicester, 1987.

Lowest innings in the final at Lord's: 118 (60 overs), Lancashire v Kent, 1974.

Lowest completed innings totals: 39 (26.4 overs), Ireland v Sussex, Hove, 1985; 41 (20 overs), Cambridgeshire v Buckinghamshire, Cambridge, 1972; 41 (19.4 overs), Middlesex v Essex, Westcliff, 1972; 41 (36.1 overs), Shropshire v Essex, Wellington, 1974.

Lowest total by a side batting first and winning: 98 (56.2 overs), Worcestershire v Durham, Chester-le-Street, 1968.

Shortest innings: 10.1 overs (60 for one), Worcestershire v Lancashire, Worcester, 1963.

Matches re-arranged on a reduced number of overs are excluded from the above.

Record partnerships for each wicket

242* for 1st	M. D. Moxon and A. A. Metcalfe, Yorkshire v Warwickshire at Leeds	199
286 for 2nd	I. S. Anderson and A. Hill, Derbyshire v Cornwall at Derby	198
209 for 3rd	P. Willey and D. I. Gower, Leicestershire v Ireland at Leicester	198
234* for 4th	D. Lloyd and C. H. Lloyd, Lancashire v Gloucestershire at Manchester	197
166 for 5th	M. A. Lynch and G. R. J. Roope, Surrey v Durham at The Oval ..	198
105 for 6th	G. S. Sobers and R. A. White, Nottinghamshire v Worcestershire at Worcester	197
160* for 7th	C. J. Richards and I. R. Payne, Surrey v Lincolnshire at Sleaford ..	198
83 for 8th	S. N. V. Waterton and D. A. Hale, Oxfordshire v Gloucestershire at Oxford	198
87 for 9th	M. A. Nash and A. E. Cordle, Glamorgan v Lincolnshire at Swansea	197
81 for 10th	S. Turner and R. E. East, Essex v Yorkshire at Leeds	198

Bowling

Most wickets: 81, G. G. Arnold; 79, J. Simmons.

Hat-tricks (7): J. D. F. Larter, Northamptonshire v Sussex, Northampton, 1963; D. A. D. Sydenham, Surrey v Cheshire, Hoylake, 1964; R. N. S. Hobbs, Essex v Middlesex, Lord's, 1968; N. M. McVicker, Warwickshire v Lincolnshire, Birmingham, 1971; G. S. le Roux, Sussex v Ireland, Hove, 1985; M. Jean-Jacques, Derbyshire v Nottinghamshire, Derby, 1987; J. F. M. O'Brien, Cheshire v Derbyshire, Chester, 1988.

Four wickets in five balls: D. A. D. Sydenham, Surrey v Cheshire, Hoylake, 1964.

Best bowling (12 overs unless stated): eight for 21 (10.1 overs), M. A. Holding, Derbyshire v Sussex, Hove, 1988; eight for 31 (11.1 overs), D. L. Underwood, Kent v Scotland, Edinburgh, 1987; seven for 15, A. L. Dixon, Kent v Surrey, The Oval, 1967; seven for 1 (9.3 overs), R. P. Lefebvre, Somerset v Devon, Torquay, 1990; seven for 30, P. J. Sainsbury, Hampshire v Norfolk, Southampton, 1965; seven for 32, S. P. Davis, Durham v Lancashire, Chester-le-Street, 1983; seven for 33, R. D. Jackman, Surrey v Yorkshire, Harrogate, 1970; seven for 37, N. A. Mallender, Northamptonshire v Worcestershire, Northampton, 1984.

Most economical analysis: 12–9–3–1, J. Simmons, Lancashire v Suffolk, Bury St Edmunds, 1985.

Most expensive analysis: 12–0–106–2, D. A. Gallop, Oxfordshire v Warwickshire, Birmingham, 1984.

Wicket-keeping and Fielding

Most dismissals: 66, R. W. Taylor; 65, A. P. E. Knott.

Most dismissals in an innings: 6 (5 ct, 1 st), R. W. Taylor, Derbyshire v Essex, Derby, 1981; 6 (4 ct, 2 st), T. Davies, Glamorgan v Staffordshire, Stone, 1986.

Most catches by a fielder: 25, J. Simmons; 24, G. Cook and P. J. Sharpe.

Most catches by a fielder in an innings: 4 – A. S. Brown, Gloucestershire v Middlesex, Bristol, 1963; G. Cook, Northamptonshire v Glamorgan, Northampton, 1972; C. G. Greenidge, Hampshire v Cheshire, Southampton, 1981; D. C. Jackson, Durham v Northamptonshire, Darlington, 1984; T. S. Smith, Hertfordshire v Somerset, St Albans, 1984; H. Morris, Glamorgan v Scotland, Edinburgh, 1988.

Results

Largest victories in runs: Somerset by 346 runs v Devon, Torquay, 1990; Worcestershire by 299 runs v Devon, Worcester, 1987; Essex by 291 runs v Wiltshire, Chelmsford, 1988; Sussex by 244 runs v Ireland, Hove, 1985; Lancashire by 241 runs v Gloucestershire, Manchester, 1990; Warwickshire by 227 runs v Oxfordshire, Birmingham, 1984; Essex by 226 runs v Oxfordshire, Chelmsford, 1985; Northamptonshire by 216 runs v Staffordshire, Northampton, 1990; Leicestershire by 214 runs v Staffordshire, Longton, 1975; Hampshire by 209 runs v Dorset, Southampton, 1987; Derbyshire by 204 runs v Cornwall, Derby, 1986; Warwickshire by 201 runs v Buckinghamshire, Birmingham, 1987; Sussex by 200 runs v Durham, Hove, 1964. *In the final:* 175 runs, Yorkshire v Surrey, Lord's, 1965.

Victories by ten wickets (9): Northamptonshire v Leicestershire, Leicester, 1964; Warwickshire v Cambridgeshire, Birmingham, 1965; Sussex v Derbyshire, Hove, 1968; Hampshire v Nottinghamshire, Southampton, 1977; Middlesex v Worcestershire, Worcester, 1980; Yorkshire v Cheshire, Birkenhead, 1985; Yorkshire v Berkshire, Finchampstead, 1988; Yorkshire v Norfolk, Leeds, 1990; Yorkshire v Warwickshire, Leeds, 1990.

Earliest finishes: both at 2.20 p.m. Worcestershire beat Lancashire by nine wickets at Worcester, 1963; Essex beat Middlesex by eight wickets at Westcliff, 1972.

Scores level (9): Nottinghamshire 215, Somerset 215 for nine at Taunton, 1964; Surrey 196, Sussex 196 for eight at The Oval, 1970; Somerset 287 for six, Essex 287 at Taunton, 1978; Surrey 195 for seven, Essex 195 at Chelmsford, 1980; Essex 149, Derbyshire 149 for eight at Derby, 1981; Northamptonshire 235 for nine, Derbyshire 235 for six in the final at Lord's, 1981; Middlesex 222 for nine, Somerset 222 for eight at Lord's, 1983; Hampshire 224 for eight, Essex 224 for seven at Southampton, 1985; Essex 307 for six, Hampshire 307 for five at Chelmsford, 1990. Under the rules the side which lost fewer wickets won.

Wins by a minor county over a first-class county (7): Durham v Yorkshire (by five wickets), Harrogate, 1973; Lincolnshire v Glamorgan (by six wickets), Swansea, 1974; Hertfordshire v Essex (by 33 runs), 2nd round, Hitchin, 1976; Shropshire v Yorkshire (by 37 runs), Telford, 1984; Durham v Derbyshire (by seven wickets), Derby, 1985; Buckinghamshire v Somerset (by 7 runs), High Wycombe, 1987; Cheshire v Northamptonshire (by one wicket), Chester, 1988.

WINNERS

Gillette Cup

1963   SUSSEX beat Worcestershire by 14 runs.
1964   SUSSEX beat Warwickshire by eight wickets.
1965   YORKSHIRE beat Surrey by 175 runs.
1966   WARWICKSHIRE beat Worcestershire by five wickets.
1967   KENT beat Somerset by 32 runs.
1968   WARWICKSHIRE beat Sussex by four wickets.
1969   YORKSHIRE beat Derbyshire by 69 runs.
1970   LANCASHIRE beat Sussex by six wickets.
1971   LANCASHIRE beat Kent by 24 runs.
1972   LANCASHIRE beat Warwickshire by four wickets.
1973   GLOUCESTERSHIRE beat Sussex by 40 runs.
1974   KENT beat Lancashire by four wickets.
1975   LANCASHIRE beat Middlesex by seven wickets.
1976   NORTHAMPTONSHIRE beat Lancashire by four wickets.
1977   MIDDLESEX beat Glamorgan by five wickets.
1978   SUSSEX beat Somerset by five wickets.
1979   SOMERSET beat Northamptonshire by 45 runs.
1980   MIDDLESEX beat Surrey by seven wickets.

NatWest Bank Trophy

1981   DERBYSHIRE beat Northamptonshire by losing fewer wickets with the scores level
1982   SURREY beat Warwickshire by nine wickets.
1983   SOMERSET beat Kent by 24 runs.
1984   MIDDLESEX beat Kent by four wickets.
1985   ESSEX beat Nottinghamshire by 1 run.
1986   SUSSEX beat Lancashire by seven wickets.
1987   NOTTINGHAMSHIRE beat Northamptonshire by three wickets.
1988   MIDDLESEX beat Worcestershire by three wickets.
1989   WARWICKSHIRE beat Middlesex by four wickets.
1990   LANCASHIRE beat Northamptonshire by seven wickets.

BENSON AND HEDGES CUP, 1990

ancashire, playing in their ninth Lord's final, emerged as convincing inners of the Benson and Hedges Cup, which they had won previously in 84. Their victory also proved to be the first leg of a historic double, for September they returned to take the NatWest Bank Trophy, becoming e first county to win both Lord's finals in the same season. For their ponents, Worcestershire, it was their sixth final at Lord's and for the sixth ne they left runners-up. This was their third defeat in the final of the enson and Hedges Cup.

The total prizemoney for the competition in 1990 was £96,900, an increase £6,000 from 1989. Of this, Lancashire won £24,000 and Worcestershire 2,000. Nottinghamshire and Somerset, the losing semi-finalists, each ceived £6,000, while the losing quarter-finalists, Essex, Glamorgan, liddlesex and Surrey, received £3,000 each. In addition, the winners of each oup match won £750. The prizemoney for the Gold Award winners was 25 in the group matches, £200 in the quarter-finals, £275 in the semi-finals nd £550 in the final.

Benson and Hedges increased their total sponsorship to the TCCB in 1990 v £39,070 to £521,031, and following the final at Lord's on July 14 it was nnounced that the company had signed a new five-year contract with the oard for the 1991 to 1995 seasons.

FINAL GROUP TABLE

	Played	Won	Lost	No Result	Pts	Run-rate
roup A						
ORCESTERSHIRE	4	3	1	0	6	72.77
LAMORGAN	4	3	1	0	6	69.46
ent	4	2	1	1	5	71.71
arwickshire	4	1	3	0	2	63.58
loucestershire	4	0	3	1	1	67.77
roup B						
OMERSET	4	3	1	0	6	85.46
IIDDLESEX	4	3	1	0	6	74.86
erbyshire	4	2	2	0	4	77.34
ssex	4	2	2	0	4	78.94
linor Counties	4	0	4	0	0	66.43
roup C						
ANCASHIRE	4	3	0	1	7	67.84
URREY	4	2	2	0	4	75.30
orkshire	4	2	2	0	4	62.08
ampshire	4	1	2	1	3	75.45
ombined Universities	4	1	3	0	2	61.91
roup D						
SSEX	4	3	0	1	7	82.35
OTTINGHAMSHIRE	4	3	1	0	6	63.44
eicestershire	4	1	2	1	3	62.33
cotland	4	1	3	0	2	66.66
lorthamptonshire	4	1	3	0	2	60.60

The top two teams in each group qualified for the quarter-finals.

Where two or more teams finished with the same number of points, the position in the group was ased on run-rate.

GROUP A

GLOUCESTERSHIRE v WORCESTERSHIRE

At Bristol, April 24. Worcestershire won by three wickets. Toss: Gloucestershire. In his fi three-figure innings since July 1987, Botham faced 145 balls, of which he hit six for six a nine for four.

Gold Award: I. T. Botham.

Gloucestershire

*A. J. Wright c Newport b Botham	... 97	M. W. Alleyne not out	
A. W. Stovold c D'Oliveira b Dilley	... 8	P. Bainbridge not out	
G. D. Hodgson c Botham b Illingworth	1	L-b 6, w 3, n-b 2	
C. W. J. Athey c Neale b Radford	 49		
K. M. Curran c Rhodes b Dilley	 55	1/34 2/37 3/148 (6 wkts, 55 overs) 2	
†R. C. Russell c Hick b Dilley	 10	4/185 5/206 6/250	

D. A. Graveney, E. T. Milburn and D. V. Lawrence did not bat.

Bowling: Dilley 11–0–43–3; Radford 11–1–45–1; Newport 7–0–23–0; Illingwon 10–0–43–1; Hick 5–0–25–0; Botham 11–0–69–1.

Worcestershire

T. S. Curtis c Lawrence b Curran	 2	R. K. Illingworth c Alleyne b Curran	..
G. J. Lord c Athey b Graveney	 26	P. J. Newport not out	
G. A. Hick c Lawrence b Milburn	 2	B 1, l-b 7, w 14, n-b 6	
I. T. Botham not out	138		
*P. A. Neale c and b Curran	 30	1/3 2/20 3/87 (7 wkts, 54.1 overs) 2	
D. B. D'Oliveira b Lawrence	 2	4/184 5/187	
†S. J. Rhodes run out	 1	6/190 7/220	

N. V. Radford and G. R. Dilley did not bat.

Bowling: Curran 11–0–53–3; Lawrence 11–3–36–1; Milburn 5–1–23–1; Bainbrid 8–0–37–0; Graveney 11–0–40–1; Alleyne 8.1–0–59–0.

Umpires: A. A. Jones and M. J. Kitchen.

WARWICKSHIRE v GLAMORGAN

At Birmingham, April 24. Glamorgan won by 3 runs. Toss: Warwickshire.

Gold Award: M. P. Maynard.

Glamorgan

*A. R. Butcher c Humpage b Munton	. 11	S. J. Dennis c Lloyd b Small	....
H. Morris c Humpage b Small	 1	S. L. Watkin not out	....
G. C. Holmes c Asif Din b Munton	... 11		
M. P. Maynard c Lloyd b Small	 77	B 4, l-b 20, w 4, n-b 2	
I. V. A. Richards b Booth	 21		
P. A. Cottey lbw b Booth	 2	1/2 2/21 3/28 (9 wkts, 55 overs)	
N. G. Cowley b Donald	 19	4/97 5/111 6/139	
†C. P. Metson c Booth b Small	 20	7/175 8/182 9/196	

S. R. Barwick did not bat.

Bowling: Donald 11–1–42–1; Small 11–2–22–4; Munton 7–0–28–2; Reeve 10–0–26 Smith 5–0–15–0; Booth 11–1–39–2.

Warwickshire

T. A. Lloyd c Richards b Barwick	... 10	G. C. Small run out	....	1
A. J. Moles run out	 52	P. A. Booth not out	....	13
Asif Din b Cowley	 50	L-b 5, w 7	....	12
A. I. Kallicharran c Holmes b Richards	13			
P. A. Smith lbw b Richards	 13	1/20 2/117 3/123	(8 wkts, 55 overs) 193	
G. W. Humpage c Butcher b Barwick	. 15	4/143 5/162 6/164		
D. A. Reeve lbw b Richards	 14	7/165 8/193		

A. A. Donald and T. A. Munton did not bat.

Bowling: Watkin 11–2–35–0; Dennis 6–0–20–0; Barwick 11–0–44–2; Richards 11–1–38–3; Cowley 11–0–23–1; Holmes 5–0–28–0.

Umpires: B. Hassan and B. Leadbeater.

GLAMORGAN v GLOUCESTERSHIRE

At Cardiff, May 1. Glamorgan won by 9 runs. Toss: Glamorgan.
Gold Award: A. R. Butcher.

Glamorgan

*A. R. Butcher c Russell b Curran	 95	S. J. Dennis not out	....	2
H. Morris lbw b Curran	 23	S. R. Barwick b Walsh	....	1
M. P. Maynard b Graveney b Alleyne	. 33			
I. V. A. Richards c Russell b Alleyne	.. 28	L-b 10, w 1, n-b 2	....	13
G. C. Holmes c Russell b Walsh	 9			
P. Smith c Russell b Alleyne	 0	1/65 2/115 3/157	(9 wkts, 55 overs) 219	
N. G. Cowley lbw b Alleyne	 1	4/172 5/173 6/181		
†C. P. Metson c Athey b Curran	 14	7/215 8/215 9/219		

M. Frost did not bat.

Bowling: Jarvis 10–1–32–0; Walsh 11–1–32–2; Curran 9–1–29–3; Graveney 11–1–55–0; Bainbridge 3–0–19–0; Alleyne 11–1–42–4.

Gloucestershire

*A. J. Wright c Holmes b Barwick	 10	C. A. Walsh lbw b Cowley	....	1
A. W. Stovold b Frost	 1	D. A. Graveney not out	....	12
P. Bainbridge b Dennis	 55			
C. W. J. Athey b Holmes	 20	B 4, l-b 9, w 1, n-b 1	....	15
K. M. Curran b Holmes	 14			
J. W. Lloyds lbw b Richards	 6	1/5 2/17 3/65	(8 wkts, 55 overs) 210	
M. W. Alleyne b Frost	 30	4/87 5/104 6/129		
†R. C. Russell not out	 46	7/159 8/164		

K. B. S. Jarvis did not bat.

Bowling: Frost 8–4–14–2; Barwick 9–1–37–1; Dennis 10–2–38–1; Cowley 11–0–40–1; Holmes 8–0–27–2; Richards 9–0–41–1.

Umpires: P. J. Eele and R. Julian.

WORCESTERSHIRE v KENT

At Worcester, May 1. Worcestershire won by 27 runs. Toss: Kent. Rhodes suffered a broken thumb when he was hit by a ball from Merrick but nevertheless kept wicket in Kent's innings.
Gold Award: T. R. Ward.

Worcestershire

T. S. Curtis lbw b Ealham	11	P. J. Newport c Ward b Ealham	2
†S. J. Rhodes c G. R. Cowdrey b Ealham	8	N. V. Radford not out	
G. A. Hick c Marsh b Ealham	41		
I. T. Botham c Ellison b C. S. Cowdrey	37	L-b 8, w 4, n-b 7	1
*P. A. Neale c Hinks b C. S. Cowdrey	13		
D. B. D'Oliveira c Marsh b Davis	7	1/19 2/32 3/91　　(8 wkts, 55 overs) 20	
S. R. Lampitt c Ward b Fleming	6	4/117 5/130 6/134	
R. K. Illingworth not out	36	7/147 8/203	

G. R. Dilley did not bat.

Bowling: Merrick 11–0–46–0; Ellison 6–2–14–0; Ealham 11–1–57–4; Fleming 9–1–27–1 Davis 11–1–36–1; C. S. Cowdrey 7–1–19–2.

Kent

S. G. Hinks c Hick b Dilley	1	M. A. Ealham c Hick b Dilley	
N. R. Taylor c D'Oliveira b Dilley	8	T. A. Merrick b Newport	1
T. R. Ward c Hick b Newport	94	R. P. Davis not out	
*C. S. Cowdrey c Hick b Newport	6	L-b 5, w 6, n-b 6	1
G. R. Cowdrey c Rhodes b Newport	0		
†S. A. Marsh run out	17	1/11 2/12 3/40　　　　(49 overs) 18	
R. M. Ellison lbw b Dilley	12	4/46 5/86 6/120	
M. V. Fleming c Radford b Lampitt	6	7/132 8/141 9/176	

Bowling: Dilley 9–1–48–4; Radford 7–3–13–0; Newport 8–0–25–4; Lampitt 11–1–47–1 Illingworth 8–1–23–0; Botham 6–2–19–0.

Umpires: M. J. Kitchen and R. A. White.

KENT v WARWICKSHIRE

At Canterbury, May 8. Kent won by 70 runs. Toss: Kent. Hinks kept wicket after tea in place of the injured Marsh.

Gold Award: C. S. Cowdrey.

Kent

S. G. Hinks c Humpage b Small	2	T. A. Merrick not out	
M. R. Benson c Reeve b Smith	85	A. P. Igglesden not out	
N. R. Taylor b Small	90		
T. R. Ward lbw b Small	1	B 2, l-b 4, w 6, n-b 1	1
*C. S. Cowdrey c Humpage b Reeve	64		
M. V. Fleming c Twose b Small	0	1/14 2/142 3/147　　(8 wkts, 55 overs) 26	
†S. A. Marsh c and b Munton	9	4/235 5/235 6/259	
M. A. Ealham run out	0	7/263 8/264	

R. P. Davis did not bat.

Bowling: Small 11–0–38–4; Munton 10–2–39–1; Moody 9–1–50–0; Reeve 9–0–52–1; Smith 10–0–43–1; Booth 4–0–33–0; Twose 2–0–4–0.

Warwickshire

*T. A. Lloyd lbw b Cowdrey	72	P. A. Booth c Merrick b Cowdrey	
Asif Din c Marsh b Ealham	9	G. C. Small lbw b Merrick	2
T. M. Moody c Ealham b Davis	33	T. A. Munton not out	
A. I. Kallicharran c sub b Ealham	11	B 6, l-b 8, w 2	1
†G. W. Humpage lbw b Merrick	1		
D. A. Reeve c Hinks b Cowdrey	12	1/26 2/78 3/111　　　　(44.4 overs) 19	
R. G. Twose run out	2	4/120 5/150 6/152	
N. M. K. Smith c sub b Davis	11	7/153 8/163 9/186	

Bowling: Merrick 8.4–2–30–2; Igglesden 5–0–31–0; Ealham 8–0–37–2; Davis 11–0–40–2 Fleming 6–1–14–0; Cowdrey 6–1–29–3.

Umpires: D. J. Constant and N. T. Plews.

WORCESTERSHIRE v GLAMORGAN

At Worcester, May 8. Glamorgan won by 16 runs. Toss: Glamorgan.
Gold Award: M. Frost.

Glamorgan

A. R. Butcher b Hick	57	†C. P. Metson not out		14
H. Morris c D'Oliveira b Lampitt	57	S. L. Watkin not out		1
M. P. Maynard b Radford	36	L-b 18, w 4, n-b 3		25
V. A. Richards c and b Radford	25			
I. C. Holmes c and b Newport	8	1/121 2/134 3/176	(7 wkts, 55 overs)	255
Smith c Radford b Dilley	21	4/185 5/223		
N. G. Cowley c Lampitt b Dilley	11	6/229 7/248		

M. Frost and S. R. Barwick did not bat.

Bowling: Dilley 11–3–45–2; Radford 11–0–52–2; Lampitt 6–0–43–1; Newport 11–1–28–1; Illingworth 8–0–33–0; Hick 8–0–36–1.

Worcestershire

T. S. Curtis c Metson b Cowley	36	N. V. Radford c Holmes b Barwick		40
G. J. Lord c Morris b Frost	0	G. R. Dilley not out		5
G. A. Hick b Frost	0	†S. R. Bevins not out		0
D. B. D'Oliveira c Smith b Frost	57	L-b 10, w 9		19
P. A. Neale b Barwick	31			
S. R. Lampitt c Metson b Barwick	41	1/15 2/17 3/77	(9 wkts, 55 overs)	239
R. K. Illingworth c Morris b Frost	6	4/112 5/152 6/170		
P. J. Newport c Butcher b Barwick	4	7/175 8/229 9/239		

Bowling: Barwick 11–0–67–4; Watkin 11–1–45–0; Frost 11–3–25–4; Cowley 11–0–33–1; Richards 11–0–59–0.

Umpires: H. D. Bird and P. B. Wight.

WARWICKSHIRE v WORCESTERSHIRE

At Birmingham, May 10. Worcestershire won by 32 runs. Toss: Worcestershire.
Gold Award: G. A. Hick.

Worcestershire

T. S. Curtis c Lloyd b Benjamin	97	S. R. Lampitt not out		1
M. J. Weston b Reeve	36			
G. A. Hick c Twose b Small	64	L-b 13, w 5		18
N. V. Radford run out	31			
D. B. D'Oliveira c Benjamin b Small	3	1/78 2/206 3/217	(5 wkts, 55 overs)	255
P. A. Neale not out	5	4/239 5/250		

R. K. Illingworth, P. J. Newport, G. R. Dilley and †S. R. Bevins did not bat.

Bowling: Small 11–1–36–2; Benjamin 11–4–40–1; Moody 5–0–29–0; Munton 11–0–35–0; Reeve 11–1–70–1; Smith 5–0–20–0; Twose 1–0–12–0.

Warwickshire

T. A. Lloyd b Radford	8	G. C. Small c Radford b Illingworth		5
Asif Din c Bevins b Hick	37	J. E. Benjamin run out		20
T. M. Moody lbw b Hick	41	T. A. Munton c Lampitt b Dilley		0
A. I. Kallicharran c Neale b Lampitt	32	L-b 12, w 7, n-b 2		21
†G. W. Humpage st Bevins b Hick	6			
D. A. Reeve c Bevins b Radford	6	1/16 2/87 3/109	(51.5 overs)	223
R. G. Twose c Weston b Radford	17	4/120 5/136 6/151		
N. M. K. Smith not out	30	7/166 8/173 9/219		

Bowling: Dilley 8.5–0–36–1; Radford 9–1–41–3; Newport 3–0–21–0; Illingworth 9–0–42–; Hick 11–0–36–3; Lampitt 11–0–35–1.

Umpires: D. O. Oslear and D. S. Thompsett.

KENT v GLOUCESTERSHIRE

At Canterbury, May 10, 11. No result. Toss: Kent. This match, of thirteen overs a side, w: begun after rain from before lunch on the second day until after tea had forced th abandonment of the game which started on the first day. Further rain, however, prevented : result. In the original 55-overs match Gloucestershire, 180 for three overnight after 42.2 over: made 268 for seven (A. J. Wright 134 off 176 balls including fourteen fours, A. W. Stovold 4' and Kent were 49 for two from nineteen overs when rain stopped play. Wright's hundre which ceased to count when the match became void, was his first in limited-ove competition.

Kent

S. G. Hinks c Bainbridge b Jarvis		3
T. R. Ward not out		60
*C. S. Cowdrey not out		67
L-b 2, w 3, n-b 3		8

1/7   (1 wkt, 10 overs) 138

M. R. Benson, N. R. Taylor, †S. A. Marsh, M. V. Fleming, R. P. Davis, M. A. Ealham, T. / Merrick and C. Penn did not bat.

Bowling: Bainbridge 2–0–21–0; Jarvis 2–0–30–1; Ball 2–0–28–0; Alleyne 1–0–22–0; Curra: 2–0–23–0; Walsh 1–0–12–0.

Gloucestershire

*A. J. Wright, A. W. Stovold, P. Bainbridge, C. W. J. Athey, K. M. Curran, M. W. Alleyn †R. C. Russell, J. W. Lloyds, M. C. J. Ball, C. A. Walsh and K. B. S. Jarvis.

Umpires: B. Dudleston and J. H. Harris.

GLAMORGAN v KENT

At Swansea, May 12. Kent won by 18 runs. Toss: Kent.
Gold Award: M. R. Benson.

Kent

S. G. Hinks c Morris b Frost	1	P. S. de Villiers run out		
M. R. Benson c Richards b Frost	118	C. Penn not out		
N. R. Taylor c Metson b Dennis	19			
T. R. Ward c Morris b Cowley	36	B 1, l-b 5, w 4		1
G. R. Cowdrey c Cowley b Frost	12			
*C. S. Cowdrey c Morris b Watkin	35	1/8 2/48 3/103	(8 wkts, 55 overs) 26	
†S. A. Marsh c Morris b Holmes	9	4/135 5/195 6/215		
M. A. Ealham not out	17	7/243 8/243		

R. P. Davis did not bat.

Bowling: Frost 11–1–56–3; Dennis 9–1–37–1; Watkin 11–2–51–1; Cowley 9–0–55–1 Richards 11–0–30–0; Holmes 4–0–30–1.

Glamorgan

A. R. Butcher b de Villiers	6	†C. P. Metson b Penn	23
H. Morris run out	16	S. J. Dennis c de Villiers b C. S. Cowdrey	1
J. C. Holmes c G. R. Cowdrey		S. L. Watkin b Penn	6
b C. S. Cowdrey	62	M. Frost not out	1
M. P. Maynard c Davis b de Villiers	84	B 3, w 4, n-b 1	8
V. A. Richards c sub b Ealham	27		
I. Smith c Hinks b Ealham	9	1/8 2/36 3/161	(53.5 overs) 247
R. G. Cowley c G. R. Cowdrey		4/202 5/204 6/214	
b C. S. Cowdrey	4	7/219 8/228 9/246	

Bowling: de Villiers 10–0–37–2; Penn 10.5–1–40–2; Davis 8–0–45–0; Ealham 11–0–47–2; C. S. Cowdrey 9–0–52–3; G. R. Cowdrey 5–0–23–0.

Umpires: J. C. Balderstone and K. J. Lyons.

GLOUCESTERSHIRE v WARWICKSHIRE

At Bristol, May 12. Warwickshire won by six wickets. Toss: Warwickshire.
Gold Award: C. W. J. Athey.

Gloucestershire

A. J. Wright c Small b Reeve	15	†R. C. Russell c Humpage b Benjamin	20
A. W. Stovold c Humpage b Benjamin	5	J. W. Lloyds not out	53
I. Bainbridge c Humpage b Reeve	10	L-b 7, w 3	10
C. W. J. Athey not out	83		
K. M. Curran c Humpage b Munton	0	1/14 2/31 3/34	(6 wkts, 55 overs) 207
M. W. Alleyne c Smith b Small	11	4/36 5/69 6/99	

M. C. J. Ball, C. A. Walsh and K. B. S. Jarvis did not bat.

Bowling: Small 11–1–27–1; Benjamin 11–2–32–2; Reeve 11–3–27–2; Munton 11–1–41–1; Moody 11–0–73–0.

Warwickshire

A. J. Moles run out	57	*D. A. Reeve not out	29
Asif Din c Alleyne b Curran	27	B 4, l-b 14, w 7, n-b 3	28
T. M. Moody c Alleyne b Bainbridge	16		
A. I. Kallicharran c and b Bainbridge	21	1/77 2/109 3/141	(4 wkts, 49.4 overs) 208
G. W. Humpage not out	30	4/141	

R. G. Twose, N. M. K. Smith, G. C. Small, J. E. Benjamin and T. A. Munton did not bat.

Bowling: Walsh 11–1–30–0; Jarvis 5–0–25–0; Curran 10–1–36–1; Alleyne 4.4–0–28–0; Ball 9–0–40–0; Bainbridge 11–3–31–2.

Umpires: A. A. Jones and B. Leadbeater.

GROUP B

DERBYSHIRE v SUSSEX

At Derby, April 24. Sussex won by five wickets. Toss: Sussex. The opening partnership of 169 in 44 overs between Barnett and Bowler was a record for Derbyshire's first wicket in the Benson and Hedges Cup.
Gold Award: M. P. Speight.

Derbyshire

*K. J. Barnett run out	94	C. J. Adams not out	
†P. D. Bowler st Moores b Lenham	61	L-b 8, w 11, n-b 1	2
J. E. Morris b Dodemaide	23		—
A. P. Kuiper not out	41	1/169 2/169 3/206 (4 wkts, 55 overs) 24	
T. J. G. O'Gorman b Pigott	8	4/238	

B. Roberts, G. Miller, A. E. Warner, O. H. Mortensen and S. J. Base did not bat.

Bowling: Pigott 11–2–38–1; Dodemaide 11–3–37–1; C. M. Wells 11–0–44–0; Hansfor 11–0–58–0; Salisbury 6–0–32–0; Lenham 5–0–32–1.

Sussex

N. J. Lenham c Bowler b Warner	22	A. C. S. Pigott not out	3
*P. W. G. Parker c Mortensen b Base	8		
A. P. Wells c and b Warner	53	B 1, l-b 7, w 5, n-b 2	
M. P. Speight c Adams b Mortensen	71		—
C. M. Wells not out	36	1/17 2/59 3/142 (5 wkts, 53.4 overs) 25	
I. J. Gould c Miller b Warner	7	4/167 5/178	

A. I. C. Dodemaide, †P. Moores, A. R. Hansford and I. D. K. Salisbury did not bat.

Bowling: Base 10–3–46–1; Mortensen 11–1–43–1; Kuiper 10.4–0–64–0; Warner 11–0–47–3 Miller 11–0–42–0.

Umpires: D. O. Oslear and D. R. Shepherd.

MIDDLESEX v MINOR COUNTIES

At Lord's, April 24. Middlesex won by four wickets. Toss: Minor Counties.
Gold Award: D. L. Haynes.

Minor Counties

M. J. Roberts c Emburey b Tufnell	57	S. Greensword b Emburey	
†S. N. V. Waterton c Haynes b Hemstock	6	R. A. Evans not out	
G. K. Brown lbw b Emburey	32	L-b 10, w 13, n-b 1	2
N. A. Folland not out	53		—
*S. G. Plumb c Downton b Williams	5	1/16 2/96 3/125 (6 wkts, 55 overs) 18	
T. A. Lester b Hemstock	4	4/145 5/160 6/176	

N. R. Taylor, R. C. Green and A. J. Mack did not bat.

Bowling: Hemstock 10–1–37–2; Williams 11–2–27–1; Haynes 5–0–19–0; Weekes 7–1–27–0 Tufnell 11–0–42–1; Emburey 11–0–27–2.

Middlesex

D. L. Haynes c Waterton b Taylor	80	*J. E. Emburey b Green	
M. A. Roseberry b Taylor	4	N. F. Williams not out	
M. R. Ramprakash c Brown b Mack	2	L-b 5, w 2, n-b 3	1
K. R. Brown b Mack	56		—
R. O. Butcher c Roberts b Evans	23	1/16 2/37 3/129 (6 wkts, 49.5 overs) 19	
†P. R. Downton not out	17	4/157 5/188 6/188	

P. N. Weekes, P. C. R. Tufnell and J. R. Hemstock did not bat.

Bowling: Taylor 11–2–26–2; Green 10.5–1–49–1; Mack 11–2–47–2; Greensword 7–2–30–0 Evans 10–1–36–1.

Umpires: J. W. Holder and K. J. Lyons.

MINOR COUNTIES v SUSSEX

At Marlow, May 1. Sussex won by five wickets. Toss: Sussex. Minor Counties' total was the highest by a non-county side in the Benson and Hedges Cup, while Roberts's 121 was the highest score by a Minor Counties batsman. Playing in only his second match for the side, he faced 151 balls, hitting one six and twelve fours.

Gold Award: M. J. Roberts.

Minor Counties

M. J. Roberts c Dodemaide b Clarke	..	121
D. K. Brown c Speight b Lenham	....	46
N. A. Folland not out	....	78
Sharp not out	....	11
B 4, l-b 7, w 6	....	17

1/118 2/252   (2 wkts, 55 overs) 273

S. G. Plumb, T. A. Lester, S. Greensword, †A. R. Fothergill, N. R. Taylor, R. C. Green and A. J. Mack did not bat.

Bowling: Pigott 9–2–38–0; Dodemaide 11–0–52–0; C. M. Wells 9–1–30–0; Clarke 11–1–53–1; Hansford 11–0–70–0; Gould 3–0–16–0; Lenham 1–0–3–1.

Sussex

N. J. Lenham b Mack	....	37	I. J. Gould not out	....	15
P. Moores c Brown b Greensword	....	41			
P. W. G. Parker not out	....	86	L-b 17, w 3, n-b 2	....	22
M. P. Wells c Fothergill b Mack	.....	0			
M. P. Speight run out	....	40	1/70 2/106 3/106	(5 wkts, 51.4 overs) 274	
C. M. Wells c Taylor b Green	....	33	4/177 5/232		

I. C. Dodemaide, A. C. S. Pigott, A. R. Clarke and A. R. Hansford did not bat.

Bowling: Taylor 9–1–37–0; Green 10.4–0–51–1; Mack 11–2–36–2; Greensword 9–0–53–1; Plumb 9–0–54–0; Sharp 3–0–26–0.

Umpires: J. W. Holder and A. A. Jones.

SOMERSET v DERBYSHIRE

At Taunton, May 1. Somerset won by 7 runs. Toss: Somerset. The match aggregate of 613 runs passed by 12 the previous record, set at the same ground in 1982, while Derbyshire's total was their highest in the competition and the highest by a side batting second and losing. The second-wicket partnership of 210 between Bowler (158 balls, three fours) and Morris (119 balls, fourteen fours) was a record for any Derbyshire wicket in the competition, and Morris's score of 123 was also a Derbyshire record. Hardy faced 147 balls and hit nine fours in his 109 for Somerset.

Gold Award: G. D. Rose.

Somerset

S. J. Cook st Bowler b Miller	....	66	R. J. Harden not out	....	3
J. E. Hardy b Mortensen	....	109	L-b 12, w 9	....	21
G. D. Rose c Morris b Base	....	64			
C. J. Tavaré not out	....	47	1/126 2/234 3/298	(3 wkts, 55 overs) 310	

P. M. Roebuck, A. N. Hayhurst, †N. D. Burns, R. P. Lefebvre, I. G. Swallow and J. C. Hallett did not bat.

Bowling: Malcolm 11–1–54–0; Base 11–1–54–1; Mortensen 10–0–55–1; Miller 11–0–46–1; Kuiper 11–0–80–0; Barnett 1–0–9–0.

Derbyshire

*K. J. Barnett c Hardy b Rose	0	S. J. Base not out		
†P. D. Bowler b Hayhurst	109	D. E. Malcolm not out		
J. E. Morris c Harden b Hallett	123	L-b 13, w 4, n-b 1		
A. P. Kuiper run out	22			
C. J. Adams b Lefebvre	8	1/0 2/210 3/250	(7 wkts, 55 overs) 3(	
B. Roberts c Hardy b Hayhurst	4	4/270 5/275		
S. C. Goldsmith c Cook b Rose	4	6/285 7/291		

G. Miller and O. H. Mortensen did not bat.

Bowling: Rose 11–0–58–2; Hallett 9–0–52–1; Lefebvre 11–1–55–1; Swallow 11–0–45–(
Roebuck 8–0–57–0; Hayhurst 5–0–23–2.

Umpires: B. Leadbeater and R. Palmer.

SOMERSET v MINOR COUNTIES

At Taunton, May 8. Somerset won by six wickets. Toss: Minor Counties.
Gold Award: A. N. Hayhurst.

Minor Counties

G. K. Brown c Tavaré b Rose	4	D. R. Thomas not out	4
M. J. Roberts lbw b Jones	7	†A. R. Fothergill not out	4
N. A. Folland lbw b Hayhurst	16	B 5, l-b 11, w 16	:
*S. G. Plumb st Burns b Swallow	63		
T. A. Lester c Burns b Lefebvre	14	1/9 2/17 3/51	(6 wkts, 55 overs) 24
S. Greensword c Cook b Swallow	10	4/77 5/102 6/160	

N. R. Taylor, R. C. Green and A. J. Mack did not bat.

Bowling: Jones 11–1–63–1; Rose 11–2–31–1; Hallett 2–0–18–0; Lefebvre 11–0–44–
Hayhurst 11–0–36–1; Swallow 9–0–32–2.

Somerset

S. J. Cook b Mack	27	G. D. Rose not out	:
P. M. Roebuck c Fothergill b Taylor	13	L-b 6, w 6, n-b 5	
A. N. Hayhurst lbw b Taylor	76		
*C. J. Tavaré c Fothergill b Mack	29	1/41 2/45 3/107	(4 wkts, 51.4 overs) 24
R. J. Harden not out	53	4/192	

†N. D. Burns, R. P. Lefebvre, A. N. Jones, I. G. Swallow and J. C. Hallett did not bat.

Bowling: Taylor 11–2–50–2; Green 10.4–0–57–0; Mack 9–0–22–2; Thomas 5–0–29–(
Greensword 7–0–34–0; Plumb 9–0–43–0.

Umpires: B. Hassan and K. E. Palmer.

SUSSEX v MIDDLESEX

At Hove, May 8. Middlesex won on faster scoring-rate over the first 30 overs, having tied th
scores with the same number of wickets lost. After 30 overs, Sussex had been 99 for three an
Middlesex 125 for two. Toss: Middlesex. Haynes faced a total of 155 balls, hitting thirtee
fours.
Gold Award: D. L. Haynes.

Sussex

N. J. Lenham c Emburey b Williams	3	I. J. Gould not out	12
P. Moores b Haynes	76		
P. W. G. Parker c Downton b Gatting	7	B 1, l-b 2, w 1, n-b 4	8
A. P. Wells c Ramprakash b Williams	74		
M. P. Speight c Roseberry b Hughes	43	1/39 2/64 3/98 (6 wkts, 55 overs) 282
C. M. Wells c Butcher b Emburey	59	4/197 5/249 6/282

A. I. C. Dodemaide, J. A. North, A. R. Hansford and A. R. Clarke did not bat.

Bowling: Cowans 11–0–66–0; Williams 10–1–45–2; Gatting 8–0–41–1; Hughes 11–0–47–1; Emburey 11–0–57–1; Haynes 4–0–23–1.

Middlesex

D. L. Haynes c A. P. Wells b Hansford	131	†P. R. Downton not out	15
M. A. Roseberry c Gould b C. M. Wells	1	J. E. Emburey not out	4
M. W. Gatting c Parker b Hansford	54		
M. R. Ramprakash c Moores b Dodemaide	44	B 1, l-b 11, w 2, n-b 2	16
K. R. Brown b North	12	1/14 2/110 3/210 (6 wkts, 55 overs) 282
K. O. Butcher b Dodemaide	5	4/229 5/254 6/269

N. F. Williams, S. P. Hughes and N. G. Cowans did not bat.

Bowling: Dodemaide 11–0–36–2; C. M. Wells 11–2–45–1; North 8–0–48–1; Hansford 1–0–55–2; Clarke 11–0–70–0; Lenham 3–0–16–0.

Umpires: J. D. Bond and J. H. Hampshire.

MIDDLESEX v SOMERSET

At Lord's, May 10, 11. Middlesex won by 8 runs. Toss: Somerset. Close of play: Middlesex 283-6 (48 overs) (P. R. Downton 2*, J. E. Emburey 1*).
Gold Award: M. W. Gatting.

Middlesex

D. L. Haynes lbw b Mallender	28	N. F. Williams not out	22
M. A. Roseberry b Mallender	30	N. G. Cowans not out	10
M. W. Gatting run out	66		
M. R. Ramprakash c Burns b Hayhurst	4	B 6, l-b 15, w 5	26
K. R. Brown b Hayhurst	31		
K. O. Butcher run out	3	1/56 2/95 3/115 (8 wkts, 55 overs) 247
P. R. Downton c Mallender b Jones	15	4/160 5/175 6/181
J. E. Emburey c Roebuck b Rose	12	7/205 8/226

S. P. Hughes did not bat.

Bowling: Jones 11–0–49–1; Rose 11–4–47–1; Mallender 11–2–32–2; Lefebvre 11–1–46–0; Swallow 1–0–9–0; Hayhurst 10–0–43–2.

Somerset

S. J. Cook c Downton b Cowans	6	R. P. Lefebvre run out	37
P. M. Roebuck c Butcher b Hughes	8	A. N. Jones c Brown b Gatting	7
A. N. Hayhurst c Emburey b Gatting	20	N. A. Mallender not out	3
C. J. Tavaré c Downton b Gatting	93	L-b 11, w 13	24
R. J. Harden c Haynes b Williams	5		
N. D. Burns c Butcher b Cowans	21	1/13 2/17 3/78 (54.2 overs) 239
G. D. Rose c sub b Williams	15	4/108 5/153 6/178
I. G. Swallow b Emburey	0	7/178 8/197 9/226

Bowling: Hughes 11–0–39–1; Cowans 11–0–35–2; Williams 11–0–52–2; Emburey 10.2–2–37–1; Gatting 11–0–65–3.

Umpires: J. D. Bond and J. H. Hampshire.

MINOR COUNTIES v DERBYSHIRE

At Wellington, May 10. Derbyshire won by 43 runs. Toss: Minor Counties.
Gold Award: S. C. Goldsmith.

Derbyshire

*K. J. Barnett b Taylor	8	A. E. Warner c Sharp b Mack	1
†P. D. Bowler c Folland b Thomas	16	D. E. Malcolm b Taylor	
J. E. Morris lbw b Mack	6	O. H. Mortensen not out	
A. P. Kuiper c Fothergill b Taylor	16	L-b 6, w 3, n-b 5	1
C. J. Adams c Fothergill b Greensword	44		
B. Roberts c Plumb b Greensword	46	1/9 2/15 3/42 (9 wkts, 55 overs) 21
S. J. Base lbw b Greensword	0	4/74 5/131 6/134
S. C. Goldsmith not out	45	7/165 8/192 9/207

Bowling: Taylor 10–0–52–3; Mack 10–1–49–2; Green 8–1–26–0; Thomas 11–3–24–1
Greensword 11–0–38–3; Plumb 5–0–23–0.

Minor Counties

M. J. Roberts lbw b Goldsmith	31	N. R. Taylor b Warner	
G. K. Brown c Barnett b Warner	16	R. C. Green not out	
N. A. Folland c Bowler b Goldsmith	25	A. J. Mack b Base	
S. Sharp b Goldsmith	0	L-b 16, w 7, n-b 5	2
*S. G. Plumb c Kuiper b Malcolm	16		
S. Greensword b Base	28	1/43 2/79 3/79 (50.4 overs) 17
D. R. Thomas b Warner	14	4/99 5/115 6/146
†A. R. Fothergill b Base	3	7/151 8/164 9/164

Bowling: Mortensen 8–3–15–0; Malcolm 8–1–22–1; Warner 11–1–31–3; Base 8.4–0–33–3
Kuiper 5–0–20–0; Goldsmith 10–0–38–3.

Umpires: P. J. Eele and K. E. Palmer.

DERBYSHIRE v MIDDLESEX

At Derby, May 12. Derbyshire won by 8 runs. Toss: Derbyshire. The partnership of 15
between Bowler and Kuiper was a Derbyshire record for the third wicket in all limited-over
cricket. Kuiper's hundred came off 120 balls, with twelve fours.
Gold Award: A. P. Kuiper.

Derbyshire

*K. J. Barnett c Downton b Williams	22	B. Roberts not out	
†P. D. Bowler c Haynes b Hughes	77		
J. E. Morris c Downton b Williams	0	L-b 1, w 4, n-b 3	
A. P. Kuiper not out	106	1/29 2/29 3/187 (5 wkts, 55 overs) 25
C. J. Adams b Williams	26	4/227 5/236
A. E. Warner b Emburey	7	

S. C. Goldsmith, S. J. Base, D. E. Malcolm and O. H. Mortensen did not bat.

Bowling: Williams 11–3–37–3; Cowans 11–2–48–0; Tufnell 7–0–36–0; Hughes 11–0–64–1
Emburey 9–0–41–1; Gatting 6–0–24–0.

Middlesex

D. L. Haynes c Mortensen b Kuiper	64	S. P. Hughes b Base	2
M. R. Ramprakash c Bowler b Malcolm	7	N. G. Cowans b Malcolm	1
*M. W. Gatting b Malcolm	6	P. C. R. Tufnell not out	
K. R. Brown b Kuiper	34	B 1, l-b 7, w 4, n-b 1	1
R. O. Butcher c Barnett b Warner	9		
†P. R. Downton c Adams b Base	40	1/16 2/26 3/89 (54.2 overs) 24
J. E. Emburey c Roberts b Kuiper	1	4/110 5/138 6/141
N. F. Williams b Warner	28	7/186 8/204 9/230

Bowling: Malcolm 11–0–55–3; Mortensen 11–5–18–0; Base 10.2–0–43–2; Kuiper 11–0–71–3; Warner 11–1–48–2.

Umpires: H. D. Bird and R. Palmer.

SUSSEX v SOMERSET

At Hove, May 12. Somerset won by 107 runs. Toss: Somerset. Somerset's total was their highest in the competition, while Cook's innings was a record for Somerset and the second-highest by any batsman in the Benson and Hedges Cup. His hundred came off 113 balls and in all he faced 158 deliveries, hitting one six and 22 fours. C. M. Wells hit two sixes and eleven fours off 100 balls.

Gold Award: S. J. Cook.

Somerset

S. J. Cook c Smith b Dodemaide	177	†N. D. Burns not out	6
P. M. Roebuck b Pigott	91		
G. D. Rose b Salisbury	14	B 1, l-b 6, n-b 1	8
*C. J. Tavaré b Pigott	5		—
R. J. Harden b Dodemaide	15	1/194 2/222 3/280 (5 wkts, 55 overs) 321	
A. N. Hayhurst not out	5	4/309 5/310	

R. P. Lefebvre, A. N. Jones, I. G. Swallow and N. A. Mallender did not bat.

Bowling: Pigott 11–1–33–2; Dodemaide 11–1–68–2; C. M. Wells 11–0–71–0; Hansford 11–0–82–0; Salisbury 11–0–60–1.

Sussex

D. M. Smith c Burns b Jones	3	A. C. S. Pigott b Lefebvre	12
P. Moores c Mallender b Rose	13	I. D. K. Salisbury lbw b Lefebvre	2
P. W. G. Parker lbw b Jones	1	A. R. Hansford not out	2
A. P. Wells c Tavaré b Swallow	23	B 1, l-b 4, w 8	13
M. P. Speight b Rose	6		—
*C. M. Wells c Mallender b Rose	101	1/17 2/20 3/23 (46.2 overs) 214	
†J. Gould c Swallow b Hayhurst	6	4/40 5/87 6/96	
A. I. C. Dodemaide c Cook b Rose	32	7/194 8/206 9/211	

Bowling: Jones 7–2–22–2; Rose 9–0–37–4; Lefebvre 9.2–0–39–2; Mallender 6–0–14–0; Hayhurst 8–0–42–1; Swallow 7–0–55–1.

Umpires: B. Dudleston and P. B. Wight.

GROUP C

The Combined Universities' squad of twelve named for the competition was: M. A. Crawley (Oxford) *(captain)*, J. C. M. Atkinson (Cambridge), J. Boiling (Durham), A. Dale (Swansea), K. P. James (Cambridge), N. V. Knight (Loughborough), J. I. Longley (Durham), T. M. Orrell (Salford), A. M. Smith (Exeter), C. M. Tolley (Loughborough), R. J. Turner (Cambridge) and W. M. van der Merwe (Oxford).

HAMPSHIRE v YORKSHIRE

At Southampton, April 24. Yorkshire won by seven wickets. Toss: Yorkshire.

Gold Award: P. E. Robinson.

Hampshire

*V. P. Terry c Metcalfe b Byas	15	J. R. Ayling b Fletcher		14
R. J. Scott c Metcalfe b Carrick	47	†R. J. Parks not out		6
K. D. James run out	2	L-b 7, w 4		11
C. L. Smith b Fletcher	44			—
M. D. Marshall run out	24		(6 wkts, 55 overs)	206
J. R. Wood not out	43	1/28 2/41 3/106		
		4/121 5/149 6/189		

R. J. Maru, C. A. Connor and K. J. Shine did not bat.

Bowling: Jarvis 11–2–48–0; Sidebottom 11–4–37–0; Fletcher 11–0–42–2; Byas 6–1–13–1; Carrick 11–1–31–1; Berry 5–0–28–0.

Yorkshire

*M. D. Moxon c Parks b James	11	C. White not out		17
A. A. Metcalfe c Parks b Ayling	36	L-b 4, n-b 1		5
†R. J. Blakey b Connor	66			—
P. E. Robinson not out	73	1/37 2/49 3/179	(3 wkts, 53.2 overs)	208

D. Byas, P. Carrick, A. Sidebottom, P. W. Jarvis, S. D. Fletcher and P. J. Berry did not bat.

Bowling: Marshall 10–0–28–0; Shine 9.2–1–53–0; Connor 11–1–25–1; James 11–3–34–1; Ayling 7–0–41–1; Maru 5–0–23–0.

Umpires: A. G. T. Whitehead and P. B. Wight.

LANCASHIRE v SURREY

At Manchester, April 24. Lancashire won by 76 runs. Toss: Surrey.
Gold Award: N. H. Fairbrother.

Lancashire

G. D. Mendis c and b Bullen	40	I. D. Austin not out		8
G. Fowler c and b M. P. Bicknell	9			
M. A. Atherton c M. P. Bicknell b Bullen	44			
N. H. Fairbrother not out	95	L-b 4, w 4, n-b 2		10
M. Watkinson b Thorpe	23			—
P. A. J. DeFreitas c Lynch		1/10 2/71 3/124	(5 wkts, 55 overs)	242
b M. P. Bicknell	20	4/188 5/231		

*D. P. Hughes, P. J. W. Allott, †W. K. Hegg and B. P. Patterson did not bat.

Bowling: Gray 11–1–52–0; M. P. Bicknell 11–4–48–2; Feltham 6–0–28–0; Greig 11–0–45–0; Bullen 11–1–35–2; Thorpe 5–0–30–1.

Surrey

D. J. Bicknell c Hegg b Patterson	9	C. K. Bullen not out		17
G. S. Clinton c Hegg b Austin	40	M. P. Bicknell not out		27
A. J. Stewart c Hegg b Atherton	31			
M. A. Lynch b Austin	0	L-b 4, w 3, n-b 4		11
G. P. Thorpe c Hegg b Austin	8			—
†D. M. Ward st Hegg b Atherton	18	1/11 2/78 3/78	(8 wkts, 55 overs)	166
*I. A. Greig c and b Atherton	1	4/89 5/100 6/101		
M. A. Feltham b Austin	4	7/117 8/121		

A. H. Gray did not bat.

Bowling: Patterson 8–2–6–1; Allott 10–1–35–0; DeFreitas 9–0–33–0; Watkinson 6–0–31–0; Atherton 11–1–32–3; Austin 11–3–25–4.

Umpires: J. C. Balderstone and B. J. Meyer.

COMBINED UNIVERSITIES v LANCASHIRE

At Cambridge, May 1. Lancashire won by 22 runs. Toss: Combined Universities.
Gold Award: C. M. Tolley.

Lancashire

G. D. Mendis c James b van der Merwe	6	I. D. Austin not out 61
G. Fowler c Turner b van der Merwe ..	18	
M. A. Atherton not out	69	L-b 8, w 7 15
N. H. Fairbrother c Turner b Dale	25	——
M. Watkinson lbw b Crawley	3	1/23 2/26 3/65 (5 wkts, 55 overs) 209
P. A. J. DeFreitas c and b Boiling	12	4/74 5/96

*D. P. Hughes, †W. K. Hegg, P. J. W. Allott and B. P. Patterson did not bat.

Bowling: van der Merwe 10–4–42–2; Tolley 8–1–26–0; Crawley 11–3–18–1; Dale 8–1–21–1;
Boiling 8–0–37–1; Smith 10–0–57–0.

Combined Universities

S. P. James c Allott b Patterson	0	W. M. van der Merwe b DeFreitas	10
N. V. Knight c Hegg b Austin	9	†R. J. Turner not out	12
*M. A. Crawley c Fairbrother		A. M. Smith not out	4
b Watkinson .	46	B 1, l-b 8, w 4	13
C. M. Tolley lbw b Allott	77	——
J. I. Longley run out	4	1/0 2/22 3/114 (8 wkts, 55 overs) 187
J. C. M. Atkinson c Hughes b Allott ..	10	4/126 5/154 6/159
A. Dale c Mendis b Watkinson	2	7/161 8/180

J. Boiling did not bat.

Bowling: Patterson 11–3–24–1; Allott 11–3–23–2; Austin 11–1–42–1; DeFreitas 11–0–38–1;
Watkinson 11–0–51–2.

Umpires: D. J. Constant and K. J. Lyons.

SURREY v HAMPSHIRE

At The Oval, May 1. Surrey won by 87 runs. Toss: Hampshire. Surrey's total, their highest
and the third-highest by any county in the competition, was also the highest in a Benson and
Hedges Cup match involving two first-class counties. Darren Bicknell faced 137 balls, hitting
twelve fours, for his 119; Robin Smith hit four sixes and fourteen fours in 132 off 118 balls.
Gold Award: D. J. Bicknell.

Surrey

D. J. Bicknell c Gower b Shine	119	*I. A. Greig not out	9
G. S. Clinton c Terry b James	9	
A. J. Stewart c Parks b Shine	76	L-b 8, w 6, n-b 8	22
M. A. Lynch c Terry b Shine	8	——
G. P. Thorpe not out	50	1/20 2/164 3/174 (5 wkts, 55 overs) 331
†D. M. Ward c Parks b Shine	38	4/262 5/322

K. T. Medlycott, M. A. Feltham, M. P. Bicknell and A. J. Murphy did not bat.

Bowling: Marshall 11–1–52–0; Shine 10–0–68–4; James 5–0–36–1; Connor 11–0–71–0;
Maru 7–0–40–0; Scott 11–0–56–0.

Hampshire

*V. P. Terry st Ward b Medlycott	24	R. J. Maru c and b Greig	9
D. I. Gower c and b M. P. Bicknell ...	6	C. A. Connor c Ward b Murphy	3
R. A. Smith c Greig b Murphy	132	K. J. Shine run out	0
C. L. Smith c Ward b Greig	3	L-b 5, w 2	7
K. D. James b Medlycott	2	——
R. J. Scott run out	7	1/9 2/68 3/75 (46.2 overs) 244
M. D. Marshall c Ward b M. P. Bicknell	31	4/82 5/101 6/161
†R. J. Parks not out	20	7/222 8/233 9/239

Bowling: M. P. Bicknell 8–1–48–2; Murphy 9–3–36–2; Feltham 3–0–24–0; Medlycot
11–0–44–2; Greig 6.2–0–35–2; Lynch 9–0–52–0.

Umpires: N. T. Plews and D. S. Thompsett.

LANCASHIRE v HAMPSHIRE

At Manchester, May 8, 9. No result. Toss: Hampshire. After rain and bad light had
interrupted Hampshire's reply to Lancashire's 352 for six on the second day, the umpires ruled
that there was not sufficient time to complete the match under the playing conditions and
another of eighteen overs a side was started. However, torrential rain and bad light again
intervened and at 7.15 p.m. this game, too, was called off.

Lancashire

G. D. Mendis c Parks b Connor	9	I. D. Austin not out	9
G. Fowler c Nicholas b Connor	1		
N. H. Fairbrother c Terry b Ayling	8	L-b 1, w 1, n-b 1	3
M. A. Atherton c C. L. Smith b Ayling	2		
M. Watkinson st Parks b Maru	40	1/4 2/20 3/22 (5 wkts, 18 overs)	147
P. A. J. DeFreitas not out	75	4/23 5/106	

*D. P. Hughes, P. J. W. Allott, †W. K. Hegg and B. P. Patterson did not bat.

Bowling: Marshall 4–0–45–0; Shine 4–0–13–0; Connor 3–0–26–2; Ayling 3–0–22–2; Maru
4–0–40–1.

Hampshire

V. P. Terry c Fairbrother b DeFreitas . 7
D. I. Gower not out 44
R. A. Smith not out 45
W 2, n-b 1 3

1/24   (1 wkt, 12 overs) 99

C. L. Smith, *M. C. J. Nicholas, K. J. Shine, M. D. Marshall, J. R. Ayling, †R. J. Parks, R. J.
Maru and C. A. Connor did not bat.

Bowling: Patterson 2–0–10–0; Allott 3–0–29–0; DeFreitas 2–0–14–1; Austin 3–0–26–0;
Watkinson 2–0–20–0.

Umpires: D. O. Oslear and D. S. Thompsett.

In the original match, which was subsequently declared void, Lancashire's total would have
been a record for the competition and a county record in limited-overs cricket. Fairbrother's
145, off 119 balls and containing three sixes and eleven fours, was a limited-overs record for
Lancashire, and his third-wicket partnership of 244 with Atherton was a county record for any
wicket in limited-overs competition. Because the match was abandoned, however, and a new
one started, none of these records stood. Just as unsatisfactory was Hampshire's slow over-
rate, with eight overs still to be bowled when the allotted playing time for 55 overs had
elapsed. On the first day, at the close of which Lancashire were 142 for two off 27 overs (M. A.
Atherton 43*, N. H. Fairbrother 82*), some six hours had been lost to the weather.

Lancashire

G. D. Mendis c R. A. Smith b Shine	4	I. D. Austin b Maru	2
G. Fowler c Nicholas b Shine	1	†W. K. Hegg not out	1
M. A. Atherton b Shine	100	L-b 14, w 6, n-b 4	24
N. H. Fairbrother c Shine b Ayling	145		
M. Watkinson not out	40	1/3 2/16 3/260 (6 wkts, 55 overs)	352
P. A. J. DeFreitas c Parks b Connor	35	4/276 5/344 6/347	

*D. P. Hughes, P. J. W. Allott and B. P. Patterson did not bat.

Bowling: Marshall 11–1–48–0; Shine 11–0–73–3; Connor 11–0–72–1; Ayling 11–0–75–1;
Maru 11–1–70–1.

Hampshire

V. P. Terry c Allott b Patterson	......	16
C. L. Smith not out	....	16
R. A. Smith not out	....	1
N-b 2	....	2

/32   (1 wkt, 7 overs) 35

D. I. Gower, *M. C. J. Nicholas, K. J. Shine, M. D. Marshall, J. R. Ayling, †R. J. Parks, R. J. Maru and C. A. Connor did not bat.

Bowling: Patterson 4–0–23–1; Allott 3–1–12–0.

Umpires: D. O. Oslear and D. S. Thompsett.

YORKSHIRE v COMBINED UNIVERSITIES

At Leeds, May 8, 9. Combined Universities won by two wickets. Toss: Combined Universities. Close of play: Yorkshire 197-8 (55 overs).
Gold Award: W. M. van der Merwe.

Yorkshire

*M. D. Moxon run out	....	4	P. J. Hartley c Orrell b van der Merwe	.	0
A. A. Metcalfe c Boiling b Crawley	...	11	P. W. Jarvis not out	....	2
*R. J. Blakey run out	....	65			
S. A. Kellett c Boiling b Smith	....	29	L-b 9, w 2	....	11
P. E. Robinson c Tolley b van der Merwe		57			
C. White run out	....	1	1/14 2/17 3/76	(8 wkts, 55 overs)	197
P. Carrick c James b Smith	....	8	4/166 5/167 6/180		
A. Sidebottom not out	....	9	7/190 8/190		

S. D. Fletcher did not bat.

Bowling: van der Merwe 11–3–34–2; Tolley 11–3–38–0; Crawley 11–2–21–1; Dale 8–1–38–0; Smith 11–0–46–2; Boiling 3–0–11–0.

Combined Universities

S. P. James b Sidebottom	....	63	†R. J. Turner not out	....	12
*M. A. Crawley c Blakey b Jarvis	....	9	A. M. Smith not out	....	4
A. Dale c Sidebottom b Hartley	......	16			
C. M. Tolley c Sidebottom b Hartley	..	6	B 1, l-b 11, w 3, n-b 3	....	18
M. C. M. Atkinson lbw b Hartley	......	16			
J. I. Longley c Blakey b Jarvis	....	14	1/17 2/50 3/65	(8 wkts, 53.5 overs)	200
T. M. Orrell run out	....	15	4/85 5/121 6/145		
W. M. van der Merwe run out	....	27	7/176 8/195		

J. Boiling did not bat.

Bowling: Jarvis 10–0–29–2; Sidebottom 11–1–41–1; Fletcher 10.5–1–44–0; Hartley 11–2–34–3; Carrick 11–0–40–0.

Umpires: J. C. Balderstone and B. J. Meyer.

COMBINED UNIVERSITIES v SURREY

At Oxford, May 10. Surrey won by six wickets. Toss: Surrey.
Gold Award: A. J. Stewart.

Combined Universities

*M. A. Crawley c Lynch b M. P. Bicknell .	9	J. I. Longley st Ward b Medlycott 9
S. P. James b Medlycott	59	T. M. Orrell c Ward b M. P. Bicknell . 0
A. Dale c Clinton b Greig	40	†R. J. Turner not out 25
J. C. M. Atkinson c M. P. Bicknell b Bullen .	9	A. M. Smith not out 15
C. M. Tolley run out	14	B 8, l-b 11, w 10, n-b 5 34
W. M. van der Merwe c Stewart b Medlycott .	14	1/17 2/120 3/133 (8 wkts, 55 overs) 228
J. Boiling did not bat.		4/144 5/162 6/178
		7/179 8/179

Bowling: Gray 10–1–20–0; M. P. Bicknell 11–2–27–2; Greig 10–0–51–1; Thorpe 2–0–15–0; Bullen 11–1–48–1; Medlycott 11–0–48–3.

Surrey

D. J. Bicknell st Turner b Crawley	32	†D. M. Ward not out 33
G. S. Clinton lbw b van der Merwe ...	61	L-b 3, w 4, n-b 3 10
A. J. Stewart not out	84	
M. A. Lynch lbw b van der Merwe ...	1	1/56 2/137 3/149 (4 wkts, 53.4 overs) 229
G. P. Thorpe run out	8	4/165

*I. A. Greig, K. T. Medlycott, C. K. Bullen, M. P. Bicknell and A. H. Gray did not bat.

Bowling: van der Merwe 10.4–0–50–2; Tolley 11–2–43–0; Crawley 11–1–34–1; Boiling 11–1–33–0; Smith 8–0–53–0; Dale 2–0–13–0.

Umpires: B. Hassan and A. G. T. Whitehead.

YORKSHIRE v LANCASHIRE

At Leeds, May 10. Lancashire won by five wickets. Toss: Yorkshire.
Gold Award: M. Watkinson.

Yorkshire

*M. D. Moxon c Hegg b Allott	9	P. J. Hartley c Fowler b Watkinson ... 1
S. A. Kellett lbw b DeFreitas	22	P. W. Jarvis b Patterson 42
R. J. Blakey b Austin	2	S. D. Fletcher not out 15
A. A. Metcalfe lbw b DeFreitas	28	L-b 5, w 3 8
P. E. Robinson c Allott b DeFreitas ..	0	
†D. L. Bairstow c Hegg b Watkinson ..	9	1/22 2/31 3/35 (53.1 overs) 141
P. Carrick b Watkinson	3	4/35 5/49 6/68
A. Sidebottom run out	2	7/77 8/80 9/88

Bowling: Allott 11–2–22–1; Patterson 10.1–4–33–1; Austin 11–6–14–1; DeFreitas 10–1–36–3; Watkinson 11–1–31–3.

Lancashire

G. D. Mendis run out	25	I. D. Austin not out 0
G. Fowler c Jarvis b Fletcher	36	
M. A. Atherton lbw b Sidebottom	3	B 1, l-b 5, w 6, n-b 3 15
N. H. Fairbrother lbw b Fletcher	12	
M. Watkinson not out	43	1/49 2/68 3/86 (5 wkts, 36.1 overs) 144
P. A. J. DeFreitas b Jarvis	10	4/88 5/138

*D. P. Hughes, †W. K. Hegg, P. J. W. Allott and B. P. Patterson did not bat.

Bowling: Jarvis 11–1–51–1; Sidebottom 7.1–0–35–1; Fletcher 9–3–23–2; Hartley 9–1–29–0.

Umpires: B. J. Meyer and R. A. White.

HAMPSHIRE v COMBINED UNIVERSITIES

At Southampton, May 12. Hampshire won by 99 runs. Toss: Hampshire. The opening partnership of 252 in 165 minutes between Terry and Chris Smith was a record for the first wicket in all limited-overs cricket in England. Terry faced 146 balls for his 134, hitting one six and ten fours, while Smith's unbeaten 154 came off 170 balls, fifteen of which produced fours.

Gold Award: C. L. Smith.

Hampshire

V. P. Terry c van der Merwe b Smith	.134
C. L. Smith not out	154
D. I. Gower c Smith b van der Merwe	0
R. A. Smith not out	8
L-b 1	1

/252 2/252   (2 wkts, 55 overs) **297**

*M. C. J. Nicholas, †R. J. Parks, L. A. Joseph, R. J. Maru, C. A. Connor, K. J. Shine and P. J. Bakker did not bat.

Bowling: Smith 11-2-49-1; van der Merwe 11-0-53-1; Crawley 11-1-40-0; Boiling 11-0-71-0; Dale 3-0-21-0; Tolley 8-0-62-0.

Combined Universities

S. P. James b Maru	46	†R. J. Turner b Maru	0
N. V. Knight c Parks b Bakker	16	A. M. Smith not out	7
A. Dale c Maru b Connor	2	J. Boiling lbw b Nicholas	2
C. M. Tolley c C. L. Smith b Connor	74	L-b 16, w 4	20
*M. A. Crawley b Maru	26		
J. C. M. Atkinson lbw b Connor	0	1/33 2/38 3/104	(52 overs) 198
J. I. Longley run out	1	4/171 5/172 6/179	
W. M. van der Merwe run out	4	7/184 8/184 9/190	

Bowling: Shine 9-0-33-0; Bakker 10-3-21-1; Joseph 11-1-38-0; Connor 9-0-40-3; Maru 11-2-46-3; C. L. Smith 1-0-2-0; Nicholas 1-0-2-1.

Umpires: R. Julian and D. R. Shepherd.

SURREY v YORKSHIRE

At The Oval, May 12. Yorkshire won by six wickets. Toss: Yorkshire.

Gold Award: R. J. Blakey.

Surrey

D. J. Bicknell lbw b Sidebottom	55	*I. A. Greig c White b Jarvis	15
G. S. Clinton run out	30	J. D. Robinson not out	2
A. J. Stewart b Fletcher	76	B 5, l-b 8, w 9, n-b 2	24
M. A. Lynch c Bairstow b Jarvis	0		
G. P. Thorpe lbw b White	14	1/71 2/116 3/117	(6 wkts, 55 overs) 262
†D. M. Ward not out	46	4/157 5/222 6/242	

K. T. Medlycott, M. P. Bicknell and A. J. Murphy did not bat.

Bowling: Jarvis 11-0-58-2; Sidebottom 11-2-43-1; Fletcher 11-0-53-1; Gough 6-0-27-0; Byas 7-0-37-0; White 9-0-31-1.

Yorkshire

S. A. Kellett b Robinson	45	†D. L. Bairstow not out	1
*A. A. Metcalfe c Medlycott b Robinson	38		
R. J. Blakey c D. J. Bicknell b M. P. Bicknell	79	B 6, l-b 10, w 2, n-b 3	21
D. Byas c Robinson b M. P. Bicknell	36	1/82 2/104 3/178	(4 wkts, 53.5 overs) 263
P. E. Robinson not out	43	4/258	

C. White, A. Sidebottom, D. Gough, P. W. Jarvis and S. D. Fletcher did not bat.

Bowling: M. P. Bicknell 10.5–0–53–2; Murphy 9–1–41–0; Greig 9–0–45–0; Robinson 11–0–41–2; Medlycott 11–0–53–0; Lynch 3–0–14–0.

Umpires: J. H. Harris and D. O. Oslear.

GROUP D

ESSEX v NOTTINGHAMSHIRE

At Chelmsford, April 24. Essex won by four wickets. Toss: Essex. Johnson faced 125 balls, hitting twelve fours and reaching his hundred with a six. Gooch scored his century off 132 balls, with nine fours. Randall took his total of runs in the competition to 2,339, becoming the second most prolific batsman after Gooch.

Gold Award: G. A. Gooch.

Nottinghamshire

B. C. Broad b Topley	22	F. D. Stephenson not out	22
P. R. Pollard c Garnham b Pringle	5	B 1, l-b 3, w 2, n-b 1	7
*R. T. Robinson c Childs b Waugh	56		
P. Johnson not out	104	1/8 2/51 3/103 (4 wkts, 55 overs)	241
D. W. Randall c Garnham b Foster	25	4/194	

†B. N. French, E. E. Hemmings, R. A. Pick, K. E. Cooper and J. A. Afford did not bat.

Bowling: Foster 11–0–46–1; Pringle 11–0–57–1; Gooch 11–2–51–0; Topley 6–1–16–1; Childs 10–0–42–0; Waugh 6–0–25–1.

Essex

*G. A. Gooch c Hemmings b Stephenson	102	A. W. Lilley b Pick	2
B. R. Hardie c Robinson b Cooper	20	†M. A. Garnham not out	12
P. J. Prichard run out	17	L-b 7, w 4, n-b 2	13
M. E. Waugh c Johnson b Afford	16		
D. R. Pringle not out	55	1/48 2/80 3/131 (6 wkts, 52 overs)	242
J. P. Stephenson b Hemmings	0	4/207 5/210 6/229	

N. A. Foster, T. D. Topley and J. H. Childs did not bat.

Bowling: Stephenson 11–1–49–1; Cooper 10–2–37–1; Pick 9–0–37–1; Hemmings 11–0–49–1; Afford 11–1–63–1.

Umpires: B. Dudleston and D. S. Thompsett.

LEICESTERSHIRE v NORTHAMPTONSHIRE

At Leicester, April 24. Northamptonshire won by 5 runs. Toss: Leicestershire.

Gold Award: R. J. Bailey.

Northamptonshire

G. Cook run out	6	†D. Ripley not out	
W. Larkins c Lewis b Taylor	46		
R. J. Bailey not out	92	B 1, l-b 11, w 1, n-b 1	14
*A. J. Lamb b Mullally	34		
D. J. Capel b Lewis	33	1/14 2/81 3/155 (5 wkts, 55 overs)	226
D. J. Wild c Whitticase b Lewis	0	4/218 5/218	

J. G. Thomas, C. E. L. Ambrose, N. G. B. Cook and M. A. Robinson did not bat.

Bowling: Lewis 11–2–42–2; Mullally 10–2–47–1; Taylor 9–1–32–1; Agnew 11–1–49–0; Willey 11–0–36–0; Potter 3–0–8–0.

Leicestershire

~. J. Boon c G. Cook b Thomas		84
N. E. Briers b Ambrose		7
. J. Whitaker b Capel		46
~. Willey b Ambrose		49
~. Potter c N. G. B. Cook b Ambrose		6
~. C. Lewis run out		5
. D. R. Benson b Thomas		1

†P. Whitticase not out 7

L-b 13, w 2, n-b 1 16

1/9 2/138 3/171   (7 wkts, 55 overs) 221
4/195 5/206
6/211 7/221

. P. Agnew, A. D. Mullally and L. B. Taylor did not bat.

Bowling: Ambrose 11–4–19–3; Capel 11–1–38–1; Thomas 11–0–59–2; Robinson 1–0–47–0; N. G. B. Cook 11–1–45–0.

Umpires: P. J. Eele and R. Palmer.

NOTTINGHAMSHIRE v LEICESTERSHIRE

At Nottingham, May 1. Nottinghamshire won by four wickets. Toss: Nottinghamshire.
Gold Award: K. E. Cooper.

Leicestershire

~. J. Boon c French b Cooper		4
N. E. Briers c Randall b Pick		10
. J. Whitaker c Johnson b Cooper		7
~. Potter c French b Cooper		0
D. R. Benson c Cooper b Pick		43
~. C. Lewis b Afford		23
P. Whitticase c Broad b Pick		45
1. I. Gidley not out		20

W. K. M. Benjamin c Cooper
     b Stephenson . 2
J. P. Agnew not out 1
     B 2, l-b 1, w 6 9

1/10 2/19 3/23   (8 wkts, 55 overs) 164
4/23 5/79 6/103
7/157 8/163

~. B. Taylor did not bat.

Bowling: Stephenson 11–1–39–1; Cooper 11–2–25–3; Pick 11–0–50–3; Hemmings 11–5–10–0; Afford 11–3–37–1.

Nottinghamshire

~. C. Broad run out		49
4. Newell lbw b Agnew		13
~. Johnson c Lewis b Potter		39
D. W. Randall c Whitaker b Taylor		6
~. D. Stephenson c Whitticase		
b Benjamin		10
B. N. French not out		14

E. E. Hemmings b Benjamin 5
*R. T. Robinson not out 25

     B 1, w 2, n-b 4 7

1/46 2/66 3/83   (6 wkts, 46.4 overs) 168
4/119 5/126 6/136

~. E. Cooper, R. A. Pick and J. A. Afford did not bat.

Bowling: Benjamin 9–3–29–2; Lewis 9–2–28–0; Agnew 6–0–34–1; Taylor 9.4–0–34–1; Gidley 5–0–16–0; Potter 8–1–26–1.

Umpires: H. D. Bird and D. R. Shepherd.

SCOTLAND v ESSEX

At Glasgow, May 1. Essex won by 83 runs. Toss: Essex. Pringle's 77 came off 38 balls, with four sixes and six fours, while Prichard faced 131 balls for his first hundred in the competition and hit one six and thirteen fours.
Gold Award: P. J. Prichard.

Essex

*G. A. Gooch run out	2	J. P. Stephenson not out	4
B. R. Hardie c Henry b Parfitt	34		
P. J. Prichard run out	107	B 1, l-b 7, w 5, n-b 5	18
M. E. Waugh b Bee	62		
D. R. Pringle not out	77	1/2 2/105 3/185	(5 wkts, 55 overs) 309
†M. A. Garnham run out	5	4/250 5/304	

T. D. Topley, N. A. Foster, J. H. Childs and A. W. Lilley did not bat.

Bowling: Moir 11–2–50–0; Cowan 11–0–80–0; Bee 10–0–67–1; Parfitt 11–1–41–1; Henry 10–1–54–0; Russell 2–0–9–0.

Scotland

I. L. Philip c Garnham b Pringle	29	†D. J. Haggo not out	18
C. G. Greenidge b Childs	50	J. D. Moir lbw b Stephenson	5
O. Henry c Childs b Foster	24	C. L. Parfitt not out	1
B. M. W. Patterson b Gooch	42	B 4, l-b 13, w 11, n-b 2	30
*R. G. Swan b Childs	11		
A. B. Russell b Foster	9	1/93 2/101 3/131	(9 wkts, 55 overs) 226
A. Bee lbw b Childs	0	4/179 5/188 6/188	
D. Cowan b Stephenson	7	7/195 8/213 9/223	

Bowling: Foster 11–1–44–2; Pringle 8–3–28–1; Topley 11–0–35–0; Gooch 9–0–44–1; Childs 11–1–37–3; Stephenson 3–0–14–2; Lilley 2–0–7–0.

Umpires: B. Hassan and A. G. T. Whitehead.

NORTHAMPTONSHIRE v ESSEX

At Northampton, May 8. Essex won by eight wickets to qualify for the quarter-finals. Toss Essex.

Gold Award: G. A. Gooch.

Northamptonshire

*W. Larkins lbw b Pringle	20	J. W. Govan c Gooch b Foster	1
A. Fordham c Topley b Foster	9	C. E. L. Ambrose run out	12
G. Cook b Childs	28	M. A. Robinson not out	0
R. J. Bailey c Prichard b Stephenson	29	L-b 10, w 6	16
D. J. Capel c Waugh b Stephenson	12		
D. J. Wild b Stephenson	0	1/17 2/43 3/79	(53.3 overs) 167
†D. Ripley c Garnham b Foster	27	4/100 5/107 6/108	
J. G. Thomas c Waugh b Pringle	3	7/116 8/146 9/161	

Bowling: Foster 10–2–18–3; Ilott 9–1–39–0; Topley 11–1–25–0; Pringle 10.3–1–28–2; Childs 6–0–25–1; Stephenson 7–0–22–3.

Essex

*G. A. Gooch not out	94	
B. R. Hardie c Larkins b Robinson	27	
P. J. Prichard b Larkins b Ambrose	26	
M. E. Waugh not out	8	
B 1, l-b 2, w 5, n-b 5	13	

1/82 2/151　　　　　(2 wkts, 38.3 overs) 168

J. P. Stephenson, †M. A. Garnham, D. R. Pringle, T. D. Topley, N. A. Foster, J. H. Childs and M. C. Ilott did not bat.

Bowling: Ambrose 11–0–35–1; Capel 6–0–24–0; Robinson 7.3–0–35–1; Thomas 8–0–48–0; Govan 1–0–3–0; Wild 5–2–20–0.

Umpires: J. H. Harris and R. A. White.

SCOTLAND v NOTTINGHAMSHIRE

At Glasgow, May 8, 9. Nottinghamshire won by four wickets. Toss: Nottinghamshire. Close of play: Scotland 115-4 (37 overs) (R. G. Swan 42*, O. Henry 14*). Parfitt's return of four for 16 was the best by any bowler for Scotland in the competition.
Gold Award: R. T. Robinson.

Scotland

I. L. Philip lbw b Pick	16	D. R. Brown b Stephenson	24
C. G. Greenidge c Cooper b Stephenson	1	†D. J. Haggo not out	2
B. M. W. Patterson run out	22	B 1, l-b 10, w 9, n-b 1	21
*R. G. Swan c Pick b Saxelby	53		
M. J. Smith lbw b Saxelby	7	1/7 2/46 3/46 (6 wkts, 55 overs) 208	
O. Henry not out	62	4/61 5/151 6/204	

D. Cowan, J. D. Moir and C. L. Parfitt did not bat.

Bowling: Stephenson 11–0–49–2; Cooper 11–1–33–0; Pick 11–0–45–1; Saxelby 11–3–39–2; Afford 11–2–31–0.

Nottinghamshire

B. C. Broad b Cowan	14	†B. N. French c Brown b Parfitt	25
P. R. Pollard c Greenidge b Moir	5	K. E. Cooper not out	11
*R. T. Robinson not out	70	B 3, l-b 5, w 14	22
P. Johnson b Parfitt	52		
D. W. Randall lbw b Parfitt	7	1/20 2/20 3/95 (6 wkts, 54.2 overs) 211	
F. D. Stephenson b Parfitt	5	4/114 5/133 6/173	

R. A. Pick, J. A. Afford and K. Saxelby did not bat.

Bowling: Cowan 10.2–0–51–1; Moir 11–2–43–1; Brown 11–0–43–0; Henry 1–0–5–0; Smith 10–0–45–0; Parfitt 11–3–16–4.

Umpires: B. Leadbeater and K. J. Lyons.

ESSEX v LEICESTERSHIRE

At Chelmsford, May 10, 11. No result. Toss: Essex. When rain interrupted play after only four overs on the second day, the match was abandoned and a game of nineteen overs a side scheduled. The captains tossed and Essex elected to bat, but continuing drizzle led to the new game being called off at 5.35 without a ball having been bowled. In the void game, Leicestershire, 153 for four from 41 overs overnight after being put in, were 162 for four, L. Potter 46 not out, when rain drove the players from the field.

Essex

*G. A. Gooch, J. P. Stephenson, M. E. Waugh, P. J. Prichard, B. R. Hardie, A. W. Lilley, D. R. Pringle, †M. A. Garnham, N. A. Foster, T. D. Topley and M. C. Ilott.

Leicestershire

*N. E. Briers, T. J. Boon, J. J. Whitaker, L. Potter, C. C. Lewis, †P. Whitticase, G. J. Parsons, M. I. Gidley, J. P. Agnew, A. D. Mullally and L. B. Taylor.

Umpires: D. J. Constant and N. T. Plews.

NORTHAMPTONSHIRE v SCOTLAND

At Northampton, May 10. Scotland won by 2 runs. Toss: Northamptonshire. Scotland's highest total in the Benson and Hedges Cup brought them their second victory in the competition. The first was against Lancashire at Perth in 1986. Larkins hit one six and thirteen fours, and Philip struck two sixes and seven fours as he compiled the highest innings by a Scotland player in the competition.
Gold Award: I. L. Philip.

Scotland

†I. L. Philip lbw b Ambrose	95	D. Cowan not out	4
C. G. Greenidge lbw b Capel	32	J. D. Moir not out	3
B. M. W. Patterson b Govan	8		
*R. G. Swan c Ripley b Ambrose	44	B 2, l-b 7, w 12	21
A. C. Storie c Larkins b Robinson	8		
A. B. Russell b Robinson	0	1/54 2/81 3/166 (8 wkts, 55 overs)	231
D. R. Brown b Capel	16	4/195 5/195 6/213	
A. Bee b Ambrose	0	7/213 8/221	

C. L. Parfitt did not bat.

Bowling: Ambrose 11–3–26–3; Thomas 9–0–52–0; Robinson 10–0–47–2; Capel 11–0–29–2; Govan 11–2–55–1; Wild 3–0–13–0.

Northamptonshire

*W. Larkins c Bee b Moir	111	J. W. Govan run out	30
A. Fordham lbw b Moir	0	C. E. L. Ambrose not out	11
G. Cook lbw b Cowan	6	M. A. Robinson not out	0
R. J. Bailey b Cowan	1	B 1, l-b 7, w 4, n-b 2	14
D. J. Capel b Brown	0		
D. J. Wild c Parfitt b Brown	15	(9 wkts, 55 overs)	229
†D. Ripley b Brown	9	1/11 2/55 3/57	
J. G. Thomas c Patterson b Cowan	32	4/76 5/105 6/137	
		7/159 8/212 9/226	

Bowling: Moir 11–0–51–2; Bee 11–1–58–0; Parfitt 11–1–26–0; Cowan 11–1–36–3; Brown 11–2–50–3.

Umpires: H. D. Bird and P. B. Wight.

LEICESTERSHIRE v SCOTLAND

At Leicester, May 12. Leicestershire won by seven wickets. Toss: Leicestershire.
Gold Award: N. E. Briers.

Scotland

†I. L. Philip c Whitticase b Agnew	29	A. Bee b Taylor	3
C. G. Greenidge c Whitticase b Taylor	34	J. D. Moir not out	7
B. M. W. Patterson c Lewis b Agnew	4	L-b 4, w 8, n-b 2	14
*R. G. Swan c Potter b Agnew	40		
A. C. Storie b Mullally	19	1/43 2/70 3/72 (8 wkts, 55 overs)	215
O. Henry run out	48	4/128 5/134 6/184	
D. R. Brown c Potter b Taylor	17	7/189 8/215	

D. Cowan and C. L. Parfitt did not bat.

Bowling: Lewis 11–0–49–0; Parsons 4–1–26–0; Agnew 11–3–20–3; Taylor 11–0–65–3; Mullally 11–3–28–1; Gidley 7–1–23–0.

Leicestershire

T. J. Boon run out	39	C. C. Lewis not out	20
*N. E. Briers not out	93	B 1, l-b 2, w 7, n-b 1	11
J. J. Whitaker c Henry b Moir	46		
L. Potter c Philip b Cowan	10	1/75 2/159 3/182 (3 wkts, 51.3 overs)	219

†P. Whitticase, M. I. Gidley, G. J. Parsons, J. P. Agnew, A. D. Mullally and L. B. Taylor did not bat.

Bowling: Bee 3–0–21–0; Moir 11–3–35–1; Brown 8.3–0–47–0; Cowan 7–0–45–1; Parfitt 11–1–39–0; Henry 11–1–29–0.

Umpires: J. D. Bond and K. E. Palmer.

NOTTINGHAMSHIRE v NORTHAMPTONSHIRE

At Nottingham, May 12. Nottinghamshire won by three wickets. Toss: Nottinghamshire. Robinson hit two sixes and eight fours in his unbeaten 106.

Gold Award: R. T. Robinson.

Northamptonshire

A. Fordham c Johnson b Pick	67	C. E. L. Ambrose not out	11
N. A. Felton c Pollard b Hemmings	16	A. Walker b Stephenson	5
*R. J. Bailey st French b Afford	18	M. A. Robinson b Pick	1
R. G. Williams b Stephenson	17	B 8, w 17	25
A. L. Penberthy run out	10		
†D. Ripley c French b Cooper	7	1/64 2/113 3/114 (54.4 overs) 178	
J. G. Thomas c French b Stephenson	0	4/137 5/146 6/146	
J. W. Govan b Cooper	1	7/156 8/157 9/166	

Bowling: Cooper 11–1–41–2; Stephenson 11–1–33–3; Pick 10.4–1–47–2; Hemmings 11–2–30–1; Afford 11–3–19–1.

Nottinghamshire

B. C. Broad c Bailey b Thomas	8	E. E. Hemmings c Ambrose b Robinson	6
P. R. Pollard c Ambrose b Thomas	5	K. E. Cooper not out	8
*R. T. Robinson not out	106	L-b 2, w 8	10
P. Johnson lbw b Thomas	9		
F. D. Stephenson c Ambrose b Thomas	2	1/11 2/16 3/34 (7 wkts, 54.1 overs) 180	
D. W. Randall c Thomas b Ambrose	2	4/40 5/54	
†B. N. French c Ripley b Ambrose	24	6/127 7/159	

R. A. Pick and J. A. Afford did not bat.

Bowling: Ambrose 11–2–20–2; Walker 11–1–39–0; Thomas 11–0–45–4; Robinson 10.1–1–47–1; Govan 11–2–27–0.

Umpires: J. W. Holder and M. J. Kitchen.

QUARTER-FINALS

ESSEX v NOTTINGHAMSHIRE

At Chelmsford, May 30. Nottinghamshire won by six wickets. Toss: Nottinghamshire. Johnson, having taken six overs to score a run, put Nottinghamshire on the way to a comfortable win with 50 off 66 balls in a partnership of 92 from 21 overs with his captain, Robinson. Essex had never managed to break free of Nottinghamshire's control in the field after being put in. At lunch they were 134 for five after 37 overs, and the loss of Gooch in the afternoon prevented the final flourish that might have inconvenienced their visitors.

Gold Award: P. Johnson.

Essex

*G. A. Gooch c French b Cooper	87	N. A. Foster run out	8
B. R. Hardie b Pick	0	T. D. Topley not out	10
P. J. Prichard lbw b Afford	25		
M. E. Waugh st French b Hemmings	4	L-b 8, w 5, n-b 2	15
D. R. Pringle b Afford	19		
J. P. Stephenson c and b Hemmings	4	1/2 2/65 3/84 (8 wkts, 55 overs) 216	
A. W. Lilley b Stephenson	23	4/117 5/132 6/169	
†M. A. Garnham not out	21	7/172 8/184	

J. H. Childs did not bat.

Bowling: Pick 11–0–60–1; Cooper 11–4–34–1; Afford 11–0–47–2; Stephenson 11–1–34–1; Hemmings 11–1–33–2.

Nottinghamshire

B. C. Broad c Garnham b Gooch	38	F. D. Stephenson not out	25
D. W. Randall c Hardie b Childs	16	L-b 11, w 7	18
*R. T. Robinson not out	72		
P. Johnson c and b Stephenson	50	1/51 2/73 3/165 (4 wkts, 52.1 overs) 219	
M. Saxelby st Garnham b Stephenson	0	4/165	

†B. N. French, E. E. Hemmings, K. E. Cooper, R. A. Pick and J. A. Afford did not bat.

Bowling: Foster 11–3–37–0; Pringle 9.1–0–35–0; Gooch 8–1–27–1; Childs 11–2–40–1; Topley 3–0–25–0; Stephenson 10–0–44–2.

Umpires: J. C. Balderstone and D. J. Constant.

LANCASHIRE v SURREY

At Manchester, May 30. Lancashire won by 46 runs. Toss: Surrey. A record second-wicket partnership of 172 for Lancashire between Fowler and Atherton was followed by a 36-ball innings from Fairbrother, who took his total of runs in four innings against Surrey to 573. It also earned him his second Gold Award against Surrey in five weeks, following the qualifying group game in which he scored 95 not out. Surrey, too, were boosted by a second-wicket partnership, 123 between Clinton and Stewart, but once they were separated by Watkinson, Surrey collapsed. The last eight wickets fell in nine overs for 48 runs.

Gold Award: N. H. Fairbrother.

Lancashire

G. D. Mendis c and b Bicknell	9	P. A. J. DeFreitas run out	0
G. Fowler c Bullen b Waqar Younis	96	†W. K. Hegg not out	10
M. A. Atherton c Lynch b Murphy	74	B 4, l-b 8, w 6, n-b 5	23
N. H. Fairbrother not out	61		
M. Watkinson c Lynch b Murphy	4	1/26 2/198 3/203 (6 wkts, 55 overs) 279	
Wasim Akram c Lynch b Waqar Younis	2	4/235 5/246 6/249	

*D. P. Hughes, I. D. Austin and P. J. W. Allott did not bat.

Bowling: Bicknell 11–2–61–1; Waqar Younis 11–0–55–2; Bullen 11–2–37–0; Murphy 11–1–61–2; Medlycott 11–0–53–0.

Surrey

M. A. Lynch c Fowler b Allott	24	M. P. Bicknell c Allott b Watkinson	8
G. S. Clinton c Atherton b DeFreitas	77	Waqar Younis c Mendis b Watkinson	4
A. J. Stewart b Watkinson	67	A. J. Murphy not out	0
†D. M. Ward b Austin	10	B 1, l-b 5, w 7, n-b 1	14
*I. A. Greig b DeFreitas	9		
G. P. Thorpe c Fairbrother b Allott	9	1/37 2/160 3/185 (51.4 overs) 233	
K. T. Medlycott b DeFreitas	1	4/190 5/203 6/207	
C. K. Bullen b Watkinson	10	7/208 8/219 9/233	

Bowling: DeFreitas 11–2–40–3; Allott 11–3–25–2; Wasim Akram 9–0–39–0; Watkinson 10.4–1–58–4; Atherton 3–0–20–0; Austin 7–0–45–1.

Umpires: J. H. Harris and A. G. T. Whitehead.

SOMERSET v MIDDLESEX

At Taunton, May 30. Somerset won by 22 runs. Toss: Middlesex. On an unexpectedly slow pitch, in cloudy weather, Somerset never really came to terms with tight bowling and keen fielding. Of seven players to reach double figures, only Tavaré (82 balls) and Harden put together a partnership, adding 50 in eleven overs. After a racing start, the Middlesex innings plotted a similar course. Some good catches, excellent holding spells by Lefebvre and Swallow, and sharp fielding – which brought two run-outs – gradually whittled away the batting. Mallender, Jones and Roebuck took the last six wickets for 39 runs in twelve overs.

Gold Award: A. N. Jones.

Somerset

S. J. Cook c Downton b Williams	4	I. G. Swallow c Emburey b Hughes	18
P. M. Roebuck b Cowans	17	A. N. Jones b Williams	3
A. N. Hayhurst b Hughes	17	N. A. Mallender not out	6
*C. J. Tavaré c Gatting b Hughes	49	L-b 5, w 6, n-b 3	14
R. J. Harden c Downton b Emburey	23		
†N. D. Burns c Haynes b Cowans	12	1/9 2/35 3/53 (53.5 overs) 183	
G. D. Rose b Emburey	12	4/103 5/123 6/142	
R. P. Lefebvre c Downton b Williams	8	7/146 8/154 9/160	

Bowling: Williams 11–1–40–3; Cowans 11–3–22–2; Hughes 10.5–0–37–3; Gatting 8–1–28–0; Emburey 10–1–36–2; Haynes 3–0–15–0.

Middlesex

D. L. Haynes c Roebuck b Jones	23	J. E. Emburey not out	6
M. A. Roseberry run out	38	S. P. Hughes b Roebuck	2
*M. W. Gatting b Lefebvre	16	N. G. Cowans b Jones	1
M. R. Ramprakash lbw b Mallender	21	L-b 2, w 1, n-b 2	5
K. R. Brown run out	8		
R. O. Butcher c Roebuck b Jones	22	1/34 2/60 3/87 (51.5 overs) 161	
†P. R. Downton lbw b Jones	15	4/100 5/122 6/144	
N. F. Williams lbw b Roebuck	4	7/150 8/153 9/158	

Bowling: Mallender 9–1–25–1; Jones 8.5–0–41–4; Lefebvre 8–1–15–1; Rose 3–0–23–0; Swallow 11–2–26–0; Hayhurst 6–0–16–0; Roebuck 6–0–13–2.

Umpires: K. J. Lyons and B. J. Meyer.

WORCESTERSHIRE v GLAMORGAN

At Worcester, May 30. Worcestershire won by seven wickets. Toss: Glamorgan. Glamorgan, losing nine wickets for 72, squandered a good base laid down by Morris and Holmes in a second-wicket partnership of 89. Both had been dropped by Botham at slip, Morris when 18 and Holmes when 7, but Botham made amends by dismissing Holmes and Maynard in the first four balls of his second spell. His first five overs had conceded just 8 runs. Morris was eighth out, his 106 coming from 137 balls with twelve fours. Worcestershire's batting was much more of a team performance, built around Curtis's unbeaten 76 off 150 balls.

Gold Award: H. Morris.

Glamorgan

H. Morris c D'Oliveira b Newport	106	S. L. Watkin c Rhodes b Radford	5
*A. R. Butcher c D'Oliveira b Dilley	16	S. R. Barwick not out	13
G. C. Holmes c Rhodes b Botham	19	M. Frost c Curtis b Radford	3
M. P. Maynard c Rhodes b Botham	0	L-b 7, w 5, n-b 5	17
I. V. A. Richards lbw b Radford	3		
I. Smith b Radford	2	1/30 2/119 3/119 (54.3 overs) 191	
N. G. Cowley c Newport b Weston	0	4/132 5/138 6/139	
†C. P. Metson c Lampitt b Newport	7	7/158 8/168 9/181	

Bowling: Dilley 11–0–39–1; Radford 10.3–4–26–4; Newport 11–3–34–2; Botham 11–3–29–2; Lampitt 5–0–35–0; Weston 6–1–21–1.

Worcestershire

T. S. Curtis not out	76	D. B. D'Oliveira not out	12
M. J. Weston lbw b Barwick	25	L-b 6, w 3, n-b 1	10
*P. A. Neale lbw b Watkin	50		
I. T. Botham b Richards	22	1/48 2/146 3/176 (3 wkts, 52.2 overs) 195	

D. A. Leatherdale, S. R. Lampitt, P. J. Newport, †S. J. Rhodes, N. V. Radford and G. R. Dilley did not bat.

Bowling: Frost 9.2–0–51–0; Watkin 11–2–32–1; Barwick 10–2–45–1; Cowley 11–2–22–0; Richards 9–0–32–1; Holmes 2–0–7–0.

Umpires: R. Julian and K. E. Palmer.

SEMI-FINALS

LANCASHIRE v SOMERSET

At Manchester, June 13. Lancashire won by six wickets. Toss: Lancashire. Fairbrother, Gold Award winner in Lancashire's quarter-final, received his second award in succession after a devastating round of strokeplay against the moving ball, which, including three sixes and eight fours, produced 78 runs off 53 balls. He and the undefeated Atherton added 111 in just eighteen overs for the third wicket to set Lancashire up for victory with ten overs to spare. Somerset, put in under cloud cover that helped the bowlers in the morning, made a solid start but were never given the freedom to accelerate by Lancashire's accurate bowling, backed by keen fielding.

Gold Award: N. H. Fairbrother.

Somerset

S. J. Cook c Hegg b Austin	49	I. G. Swallow b Wasim Akram	8
J. J. E. Hardy c Allott b Wasim Akram	19	N. A. Mallender run out	3
A. N. Hayhurst c Hegg b Wasim Akram	1	A. N. Jones not out	1
*C. J. Tavaré c Hughes b Austin	10	B 5, l-b 12, w 6, n-b 4	27
R. J. Harden c Hegg b DeFreitas	16		
†N. D. Burns c Hughes b Watkinson	21	1/50 2/55 3/81 (9 wkts, 55 overs) 212	
G. D. Rose run out	32	4/109 5/113 6/163	
R. P. Lefebvre not out	25	7/174 8/202 9/207	

Bowling: Allott 11–2–34–0; DeFreitas 11–0–51–1; Wasim Akram 11–0–29–3; Watkinson 11–1–33–1; Austin 11–0–48–2.

Lancashire

G. D. Mendis c and b Swallow	37	Wasim Akram not out	8
G. Fowler b Jones	14	L-b 4, w 5, n-b 1	10
M. A. Atherton not out	56		
N. H. Fairbrother c Burns b Rose	78	1/34 2/74 3/185 (4 wkts, 44.5 overs) 214	
M. Watkinson c Harden b Rose	11	4/203	

*D. P. Hughes, P. A. J. DeFreitas, I. D. Austin, †W. K. Hegg and P. J. W. Allott did not bat.

Bowling: Jones 9–0–48–1; Mallender 9–3–31–0; Rose 10–0–44–2; Lefebvre 8–1–31–0; Swallow 6.5–1–40–1; Hayhurst 2–0–16–0.

Umpires: B. Dudleston and J. W. Holder.

NOTTINGHAMSHIRE v WORCESTERSHIRE

At Nottingham, June 13. Worcestershire won by nine wickets. Toss: Worcestershire. Put in to bat, Nottinghamshire made a poor start against the moving ball, and only when Stephenson joined Randall did the runs begin to flow. Stephenson's attack on McEwan's last over produced 21 runs but left him 2 runs short of his century, his 98 having come from 92 balls. As the pitch eased in the late afternoon – it was that used for the Test match – Worcestershire, despite poor light, had no difficulty in winning. Curtis and Weston put on 141 by the 35th over, and Weston became the second player in the match to miss out narrowly on a hundred when Hick's seventh four sent Worcestershire to Lord's.

Gold Award: M. J. Weston.

Nottinghamshire

B. C. Broad c Lampitt b Botham	32	†B. N. French run out	4
D. J. R. Martindale b McEwan	0	E. E. Hemmings not out	12
*R. T. Robinson c D'Oliveira b Lampitt	26	L-b 9, w 5, n-b 1	15
P. Johnson c Hick b Botham	4		
D. W. Randall c Rhodes b McEwan	39	1/5 2/56 3/65 (6 wkts, 55 overs) 230	
F. D. Stephenson not out	98	4/70 5/162 6/171	

K. E. Cooper, R. A. Pick and J. A. Afford did not bat.

Bowling: Newport 11–3–28–0; McEwan 11–0–53–2; Lampitt 11–0–47–1; Botham 11–2–43–2; Stemp 8–1–38–0; Hick 3–0–12–0.

Worcestershire

*T. S. Curtis b Stephenson	....	61
M. J. Weston not out	....	99
G. A. Hick not out	....	57
L-b 10, w 3, n-b 2	....	15

1/141   (1 wkt, 53.2 overs) 232

I. T. Botham, S. R. Lampitt, D. B. D'Oliveira, †S. J. Rhodes, P. J. Newport, R. D. Stemp, S. M. McEwan and D. A. Leatherdale did not bat.

Bowling: Pick 11–1–45–0; Cooper 10.2–1–29–0; Stephenson 11–0–45–1; Afford 11–0–43–0; Hemmings 10–0–60–0.

Umpires: D. O. Oslear and R. Palmer.

FINAL

LANCASHIRE v WORCESTERSHIRE

At Lord's, July 14. Lancashire won by 69 runs. Toss: Worcestershire. Thoughts that Lancashire's 241 would not be enough on a dry pitch on a hot midsummer's day had been dispelled by tea, when Worcestershire were 56 for three after 25 overs. The turning point had been the introduction of Wasim Akram to the attack after thirteen overs. His second ball was too fast for Curtis, prompting an involuntary flick as the ball lifted and left him. In Akram's third over, a similar delivery but with not so much movement off the pitch found Hick's defence wanting and Hegg, diving to his right, held his second catch. Botham's reputation meant that Worcestershire always had a chance, but Watkinson, bowling unchanged, permitted few liberties and punished indiscretions. Moreover Hughes, captaining Lancashire with a deft touch, could always recall Akram. Botham batted for 92 minutes and hit three fours before, in the 42nd over, he tried to pull a ball from DeFreitas and was bowled when it did not bounce as much as he expected.

Earlier in the day, Akram had helped wrest the match from Worcestershire's grip, adding 55 in eight overs with DeFreitas after Lancashire had been 136 for five in the 42nd over. The left-arm all-rounder hit two sixes in one over off Radford, scarcely more than a waft depositing the ball over square leg and then a full swing of the bat threatening the top balcony of the Pavilion. His 28 came from 21 balls, and towards the end Hegg improvised a splendid 31 not out off seventeen balls. Like Akram he could have won the Gold Award, for he also kept with great panache; instead R. B. Simpson, the adjudicator, chose Watkinson, whose 50 from 79 balls and partnership of 88 with Atherton provided the platform for the strokeplay that followed.

Gold Award: M. Watkinson.   *Attendance:* 14,618 (excl. members); *receipts* £369,799.

Lancashire

G. D. Mendis c Neale b Botham	 19	†W. K. Hegg not out	....	31
G. Fowler c Neale b Newport	 11	*D. P. Hughes not out	....	1
M. A. Atherton run out	 40	L-b 4, n-b 1	....	5
N. H. Fairbrother b Lampitt	 11			
M. Watkinson c and b Botham	 50	1/25 (2) 2/33 (1) (8 wkts, 55 overs) 241		
Wasim Akram c Radford b Newport	.. 28	3/47 (4) 4/135 (3)		
P. A. J. DeFreitas b Lampitt	 28	5/136 (5) 6/191 (6)		
I. D. Austin run out	 17	7/199 (7) 8/231 (8)		

P. J. W. Allott did not bat.

Bowling: Newport 11–1–47–2; Botham 11–0–49–2; Lampitt 11–3–43–2; Radford 8–1–41–0; Illingworth 11–0–41–0; Hick 3–0–16–0.

Worcestershire

T. S. Curtis c Hegg c Wasim Akram	..	16	P. J. Newport b Wasim Akram 3
M. J. Weston b Watkinson	....	19	S. R. Lampitt b Austin 4
G. A. Hick c Hegg b Wasim Akram	..	1	
D. B. D'Oliveira b Watkinson	....	23	L-b 9, w 8, n-b 4 21
I. T. Botham b DeFreitas	....	38	
*P. A. Neale c Hegg b Austin	....	0	1/27 (1) 2/38 (3) 3/41 (2) (54 overs) 172
†S. J. Rhodes lbw b Allott	....	5	4/82 (4) 5/87 (6) 6/112 (7)
N. V. Radford not out	....	26	7/114 (5) 8/154 (9)
R. K. Illingworth lbw b DeFreitas	....	16	9/164 (10) 10/172 (11)

Bowling: Allott 10–1–22–1; DeFreitas 11–2–30–2; Wasim Akram 11–0–30–3; Watkinson 11–0–37–2; Austin 11–1–44–2.

Umpires: J. H. Hampshire and N. T. Plews.

BENSON AND HEDGES CUP RECORDS

Highest individual scores: 198 not out, G. A. Gooch, Essex v Sussex, Hove, 1982; 177, S. J. Cook, Somerset v Sussex, Hove, 1990; 173 not out, C. G. Greenidge, Hampshire v Minor Counties (South), Amersham, 1973; 158 not out, B. F. Davison, Leicestershire v Warwickshire, Coventry, 1972; 155 not out, M. D. Crowe, Somerset v Hampshire, Southampton, 1987; 155 not out, R. A. Smith, Hampshire v Glamorgan, Southampton, 1989; 154 not out, M. J. Procter, Gloucestershire v Somerset, Taunton, 1972; 154 not out, C. L. Smith, Hampshire v Combined Universities, Southampton, 1990. (188 hundreds have been scored in the competition. The most hundreds in one season is 20 in 1990.)

Fastest hundred: M. A. Nash in 62 minutes, Glamorgan v Hampshire at Swansea, 1976.

Highest totals in 55 overs: 350 for three, Essex v Oxford & Cambridge Univs, Chelmsford, 1979; 333 for four, Essex v Oxford & Cambridge Univs, Chelmsford, 1985; 331 for five, Surrey v Hampshire, The Oval, 1990; 327 for four, Leicestershire v Warwickshire, Coventry, 1972; 327 for two, Essex v Sussex, Hove, 1982; 321 for one, Hampshire v Minor Counties (South), Amersham, 1973; 321 for five, Somerset v Sussex, Hove, 1990. *In the final:* 290 for six, Essex v Surrey, 1979.

Highest total by a side batting second and winning: 291 for five (53.5 overs), Warwickshire v Lancashire (288 for nine), Manchester, 1981. *In the final:* 244 for six (55 overs), Yorkshire v Northamptonshire (244 for seven), 1987; 244 for seven (55 overs), Nottinghamshire v Essex (243 for seven), 1989.

Highest total by a side batting second and losing: 303 for seven (55 overs) Derbyshire v Somerset (310 for three), Taunton, 1990. *In the final:* 255 (51.4 overs), Surrey v Essex (290 for six), 1979.

Highest match aggregate: 613 for ten wickets, Somerset (310-3) v Derbyshire (303-7), Taunton, 1990.

Lowest totals: 56 in 26.2 overs, Leicestershire v Minor Counties, Wellington, 1982; 59 in 34 overs, Oxford & Cambridge Univs v Glamorgan, Cambridge, 1983; 60 in 26 overs, Sussex v Middlesex, Hove, 1978; 62 in 26.5 overs, Gloucestershire v Hampshire, Bristol, 1975. *In the final:* 117 in 46.3 overs, Derbyshire v Hampshire, 1988.

Shortest completed innings: 21.4 overs (156), Surrey v Sussex, Hove, 1988.

Record partnership for each wicket

252 for 1st	V. P. Terry and C. L. Smith, Hampshire v Combined Universities at Southampton		1990
285* for 2nd	C. G. Greenidge and D. R. Turner, Hampshire v Minor Counties (South) at Amersham		1973
269* for 3rd	P. M. Roebuck and M. D. Crowe, Somerset v Hampshire at Southampton		1987
184* for 4th	D. Lloyd and B. W. Reidy, Lancashire v Derbyshire at Chesterfield		1980
160 for 5th	A. J. Lamb and D. J. Capel, Northamptonshire v Leicestershire at Northampton		1986
121 for 6th	P. A. Neale and S. J. Rhodes, Worcestershire v Yorkshire at Worcester		1988
149* for 7th	J. D. Love and C. M. Old, Yorkshire v Scotland at Bradford		1981
109 for 8th	R. E. East and N. Smith, Essex v Northamptonshire at Chelmsford		1977
83 for 9th	P. G. Newman and M. A. Holding, Derbyshire v Nottinghamshire at Nottingham		1985
80* for 10th	D. L. Bairstow and M. Johnson, Yorkshire v Derbyshire at Derby		1981

Best bowling: Seven for 12, W. W. Daniel, Middlesex v Minor Counties (East), Ipswich, 1978; seven for 22, J. R. Thomson, Middlesex v Hampshire, Lord's, 1981; seven for 32, R. G. D. Willis, Warwickshire v Yorkshire, Birmingham, 1981. *In the final:* Five for 13, S. T. Jefferies, Hampshire v Derbyshire, 1988.

Hat-tricks (10): G. D. McKenzie, Leicestershire v Worcestershire, Worcester, 1972; K. Higgs, Leicestershire v Surrey in the final, Lord's, 1974; A. A. Jones, Middlesex v Essex, Lord's, 1977; M. J. Procter, Gloucestershire v Hampshire, Southampton, 1977; W. Larkins, Northamptonshire v Oxford & Cambridge Univs, Northampton, 1980; E. A. Moseley, Glamorgan v Kent, Cardiff, 1981; G. C. Small, Warwickshire v Leicestershire, Leicester, 1984; N. A. Mallender, Somerset v Combined Univs, Taunton, 1987; W. K. M. Benjamin, Leicestershire v Nottinghamshire, Leicester, 1987; A. R. C. Fraser, Middlesex v Sussex, Lord's, 1988.

Largest victories in runs: Essex by 214 runs v Combined Universities, Chelmsford, 1979; Sussex by 186 runs v Cambridge University, Hove, 1974.

Victories by ten wickets (14): By Derbyshire, Essex (twice), Glamorgan, Hampshire, Kent, Lancashire, Leicestershire, Northamptonshire, Somerset, Warwickshire, Worcestershire, Yorkshire (twice).

WINNERS 1972-90

1972	LEICESTERSHIRE beat Yorkshire by five wickets.	
1973	KENT beat Worcestershire by 39 runs.	
1974	SURREY beat Leicestershire by 27 runs.	
1975	LEICESTERSHIRE beat Middlesex by five wickets.	
1976	KENT beat Worcestershire by 43 runs.	
1977	GLOUCESTERSHIRE beat Kent by 64 runs.	
1978	KENT beat Derbyshire by six wickets.	
1979	ESSEX beat Surrey by 35 runs.	
1980	NORTHAMPTONSHIRE beat Essex by 6 runs.	
1981	SOMERSET beat Surrey by seven wickets.	
1982	SOMERSET beat Nottinghamshire by nine wickets.	
1983	MIDDLESEX beat Essex by 4 runs.	
1984	LANCASHIRE beat Warwickshire by six wickets.	
1985	LEICESTERSHIRE beat Essex by five wickets.	
1986	MIDDLESEX beat Kent by 2 runs.	
1987	YORKSHIRE beat Northamptonshire, having taken more wickets with the scores tied.	
1988	HAMPSHIRE beat Derbyshire by seven wickets.	
1989	NOTTINGHAMSHIRE beat Essex by three wickets.	
1990	LANCASHIRE beat Worcestershire by 69 runs.	

WINS BY UNIVERSITIES

1973 OXFORD beat Northamptonshire at Northampton by two wickets.
1975 { OXFORD & CAMBRIDGE beat Worcestershire at Cambridge by 66 runs.
       OXFORD & CAMBRIDGE beat Northamptonshire at Oxford by three wickets.
1976 OXFORD & CAMBRIDGE beat Yorkshire at Barnsley by seven wickets.
1984 OXFORD & CAMBRIDGE beat Gloucestershire at Bristol by 27 runs.
1989 { COMBINED UNIVERSITIES beat Surrey at Cambridge by 9 runs.
       COMBINED UNIVERSITIES beat Worcestershire at Worcester by five wickets.
1990 COMBINED UNIVERSITIES beat Yorkshire at Leeds by two wickets.

WINS BY MINOR COUNTIES AND SCOTLAND

1980 MINOR COUNTIES beat Gloucestershire at Chippenham by 3 runs.
1981 MINOR COUNTIES beat Hampshire at Southampton by 3 runs.
1982 MINOR COUNTIES beat Leicestershire at Wellington by 131 runs.
1986 SCOTLAND beat Lancashire at Perth by 3 runs.
1987 MINOR COUNTIES beat Glamorgan at Oxford (Christ Church) by seven wickets.
1990 SCOTLAND beat Northamptonshire at Northampton by 2 runs.

REFUGE ASSURANCE LEAGUE, 1990

Derbyshire, putting behind them defeat in two days in the County Championship by Essex on the preceding Thursday and Friday, and also the fact that they had not beaten Essex in any competition since 1982, beat them by five wickets at Derby on the last day of the Sunday League season to win the Refuge Assurance Trophy. It was only their third trophy in 120 years, following the County Championship in 1936 and the NatWest Bank Trophy in 1981, and they became the eleventh county to win the Sunday title.

Having begun with four victories in their first five games, Derbyshire had shared the early lead with Kent and Middlesex and, with games in hand, had returned to the top of the table, alongside Middlesex, in mid-July. So closely contested was the competition that if Derbyshire had not taken all four points from their last game, Lancashire would have won the title on away wins by beating Warwickshire. Had Derbyshire and Lancashire both lost on August 26, and Middlesex beaten Yorkshire, Middlesex would have been champions on run-rate. Instead Middlesex, who won nine of their first ten games, lost at Scarborough, their fourth defeat in six games, one of which failed to produce a result.

Lancashire, who began the season by losing to Middlesex, could reflect on two matches lost to the weather. Victory in either would have won them the trophy. Their only other defeats were at the hands of Gloucestershire, when Michael Atherton, Neil Fairbrother and Phillip DeFreitas were away on England duty, and Derbyshire, when they were without the first two.

Continued over

REFUGE ASSURANCE LEAGUE

	P	W	L	T	NR	Pts	Away Wins	Run-Rate
1 – Derbyshire (5)	16	12	3	0	1	50	6	87.354
2 – Lancashire (1)	15	11	3	0	2	48	7	100.186
3 – Middlesex (9)	16	10	5	0	1	42	5	95.400
4 – Nottinghamshire (4)	16	10	5	0	1	42	4	89.312
5 – Hampshire (6)	16	9	5	0	2	40	4	88.827
6 { Yorkshire (11)	15	9	6	0	1	38	4	83.607
{ Surrey (6)	15	9	6	0	1	38	3	90.393
8 { Somerset (10)	16	8	8	0	0	32	4	91.254
{ Gloucestershire (16)	16	7	7	0	2	32	2	87.807
10 { Worcestershire (2)	16	7	8	0	1	30	4	84.964
{ Kent (11)	15	7	8	0	1	30	3	85.949
12 – Essex (3)	15	6	9	0	1	26	3	90.560
13 – Sussex (11)	14	5	9	0	2	24	2	85.906
14 – Warwickshire (14)	16	5	10	0	1	22	2	80.694
15 { Glamorgan (16)	15	4	11	0	1	18	2	84.208
{ Leicestershire (14)	16	4	11	0	1	18	1	76.590
17 – Northamptonshire (6) ..	16	3	12	0	1	14	1	86.406

1989 positions in brackets.

When two or more counties finish with an equal number of points for any of the first four places, the positions are decided by a) most wins, b) most away wins, c) runs per 100 balls.

No play was possible in the following four matches: June 3 – Sussex v Lancashire at Horsham; June 24 – Glamorgan v Yorkshire at Newport; August 19 – Essex v Surrey at Chelmsford, Kent v Sussex at Canterbury.

Derbyshire, it should be added, were without Devon Malcolm and John Morris, with the England team at The Oval, for the crucial match against Essex.

Kent's position in the final table hides the fact that in mid-season they were the front-runners alongside Derbyshire and Middlesex, boasting seven wins from eight games. But defeat by Warwickshire on June 24 began a downhill run that produced just two more points from eight games. Surrey and Yorkshire, on the other hand, operated in a reverse fashion. Yorkshire taking 30 points from their last nine games, and Surrey 26 from their last eight, could look back from joint sixth to early-season occupation of the bottom rungs. Essex, third in 1989, also made a poor start, losing their first four games. Nottinghamshire, inconsistent in midsummer, found winning form in the last fortnight of July to finish fourth in the table and qualify for the Refuge Assurance Cup.

Derbyshire's captain, Kim Barnett, led from the front, scoring 699 runs at 43.68, but he was the only Derbyshire batsman to reach 500. With Simon Base and Adrian Kuiper their leading wicket-takers with nineteen apiece, theirs was very much a team effort. In contrast, Middlesex and Nottinghamshire each had three batsmen with more than 500 runs: Desmond Haynes (632), Mark Ramprakash (615) and Mike Roseberry (575); Paul Johnson (666), Chris Broad (558) and Tim Robinson (514). Graeme Fowler and Graham Lloyd topped Lancashire's batting with 773, a county record, and 512 runs respectively.

The season's leading batsman, however, was the prolific Somerset opener, Jimmy Cook, who with 902 runs at 64.42 set a new aggregate for a Sunday League season, comfortably passing C. E. B. Rice's record of 814 in 1977. Tim Curtis of Worcestershire was the next highest with 784 runs at 60.30. The top wicket-taker was the young Pakistani fast bowler, Waqar Younis, who in his first season of county cricket claimed 31 wickets at 12.77 in twelve games for Surrey, including a best of five for 26 against Kent at The Oval. His strike-rate was a wicket every sixteen balls. After him came Middlesex's John Emburey with 30 at 19.60 apiece. Peter Bowler held 22 catches and made one stumping in thirteen games as Derbyshire's wicket-keeper, while the Gloucestershire captain, Tony Wright (13), and Hampshire's Paul Terry (11) held the most catches, other than those by the wicket-keepers.

After a season when it was 22 yards, the limit on the bowler's run-up in League matches returned to 15 yards in 1990.

DISTRIBUTION OF PRIZEMONEY

Team awards

  £24,000 and Refuge Assurance Trophy: DERBYSHIRE.
  £12,000 to runners-up: LANCASHIRE.
  £6,000 for third place: MIDDLESEX.
  £3,000 for fourth place: NOTTINGHAMSHIRE.
  £275 each match to the winner – shared if tied or no result.

Individual awards

  £300 for highest innings: G. D. Rose (Somerset), 148 v Glamorgan at Neath.
  £300 for best bowling: shared by P. W. Jarvis (Yorkshire), five for 18 v Derbyshire at Leeds, and D. V. Lawrence (Gloucestershire) five for 18 v Somerset at Bristol.

DERBYSHIRE

At Hove, April 22. DERBYSHIRE beat SUSSEX by six wickets.

DERBYSHIRE v WORCESTERSHIRE

At Derby, April 29. Derbyshire won by 35 runs. Toss: Worcestershire.

Derbyshire

*K. J. Barnett st Rhodes b Illingworth	66	A. E. Warner run out	5
*P. D. Bowler lbw b Illingworth	40	D. E. Malcolm not out	0
J. E. Morris run out	3	L-b 5, w 8	13
A. P. Kuiper c Leatherdale b Newport	17		
C. J. Adams b Illingworth	26	1/97 2/117 3/117 (7 wkts, 40 overs) 193	
B. Roberts b Radford	9	4/162 5/166	
G. Miller not out	14	6/178 7/189	

S. J. Base and O. H. Mortensen did not bat.

Bowling: Newport 8–0–30–1; Botham 8–0–27–0; Radford 6–0–26–1; Illingworth 8–0–41–3; McEwan 8–0–42–0; Hick 2–0–22–0.

Worcestershire

T. S. Curtis c Morris b Mortensen	7	R. K. Illingworth c Bowler b Base	8
I. T. Botham c Bowler b Mortensen	15	P. J. Newport not out	12
G. A. Hick c Adams b Kuiper	46	S. M. McEwan b Base	5
D. B. D'Oliveira c Adams b Base	10	L-b 6, w 5	11
*P. A. Neale c Warner b Base	40		
D. A. Leatherdale lbw b Warner	2	1/11 2/40 3/57 (37.5 overs) 158	
†S. J. Rhodes c Roberts b Miller	2	4/95 5/98 6/105	
N. V. Radford c Adams b Miller	0	7/105 8/141 9/144	

Bowling: Malcolm 7–0–32–0; Mortensen 8–3–15–2; Warner 8–0–28–1; Base 5.5–0–32–4; Kuiper 4–0–23–1; Miller 5–2–22–2.

Umpires: J. H. Hampshire and B. J. Meyer.

At Northampton, May 6. DERBYSHIRE beat NORTHAMPTONSHIRE by four wickets.

At Leeds, May 13. DERBYSHIRE lost to YORKSHIRE by six wickets.

At Taunton, May 20. DERBYSHIRE beat SOMERSET by seven wickets.

DERBYSHIRE v NOTTINGHAMSHIRE

At Derby, June 10. Nottinghamshire won by four wickets. Toss: Nottinghamshire. Following a brief stoppage for bad light, Nottinghamshire were set a revised target of 216 off 38 overs. Robinson's 116 came off 110 balls and contained two sixes and five fours.

Derbyshire

*K. J. Barnett c French b Evans	63	S. C. Goldsmith not out	₄
†P. D. Bowler b M. Saxelby	45		
J. E. Morris c Evans b K. Saxelby	32	L-b 13, w 2	1₅
A. P. Kuiper c French b Stephenson	46		—
B. Roberts not out	26	1/112 2/116 3/189 (5 wkts, 40 overs) 22₇	
C. J. Adams b Stephenson	0	4/214 5/216	

A. E. Warner, G. Miller, M. Jean-Jacques and S. J. Base did not bat.

Bowling: K. Saxelby 8–0–53–1; Cooper 8–1–29–0; Stephenson 8–0–43–2; Evans 8–0–39–1; Afford 3–0–26–0; M. Saxelby 5–0–24–1.

Nottinghamshire

B. C. Broad c Bowler b Jean-Jacques	11	†B. N. French not out	1₇
D. W. Randall c Kuiper b Warner	21	K. E. Cooper not out	₉
P. Johnson c Bowler b Base	0		
*R. T. Robinson run out	116	L-b 7, w 6	1₃
M. Saxelby c Kuiper b Jean-Jacques	34		—
F. D. Stephenson c Kuiper		1/23 2/25 3/50 (6 wkts, 38 overs) 21₉	
b Jean-Jacques	6	4/151 5/158 6/214	

K. Saxelby, K. P. Evans and J. A. Afford did not bat.

Bowling: Jean-Jacques 8–0–47–3; Base 8–0–52–1; Warner 6–0–39–1; Miller 8–0–34–0; Barnett 8–0–40–0.

Umpires: J. W. Holder and N. T. Plews.

DERBYSHIRE v WARWICKSHIRE

At Derby, June 17. Derbyshire won by 1 run. Toss: Warwickshire. Small, needing to hit the last ball for six to win the match, could manage only a four.

Derbyshire

*K. J. Barnett c Asif Din b Pierson	19	A. E. Warner c Munton b Smith	₆
†P. D. Bowler c Pierson b Twose	0	D. E. Malcolm c Moles b Moody	₀
J. E. Morris c Ostler b Twose	4	S. J. Base not out	₀
A. P. Kuiper c Ostler b Pierson	37	L-b 15, w 4, n-b 1	2₀
B. Roberts lbw b Small	9		—
C. J. Adams run out	58	1/2 2/10 3/36 4/58 (8 wkts, 40 overs) 20₃	
S. C. Goldsmith b Smith	50	5/77 6/184 7/191 8/191	

G. Miller did not bat.

Bowling: Munton 8–0–25–0; Twose 8–2–11–2; Pierson 8–0–24–2; Small 8–1–53–1; Smith 4–0–37–2; Moody 4–0–38–1.

Warwickshire

A. J. Moles b Malcolm	81	R. G. Twose c Bowler b Kuiper	₉
Asif Din c Bowler b Base	11	G. C. Small not out	₄
T. M. Moody run out	45	B 2, l-b 9, w 3	1₄
†G. W. Humpage c Bowler b Kuiper	0		—
*D. A. Reeve b Base	31	1/27 2/129 3/130 (6 wkts, 40 overs) 20₂	
D. P. Ostler not out	7	4/181 5/181 6/198	

G. Smith, A. R. K. Pierson and T. A. Munton did not bat.

Bowling: Base 8–1–32–2; Malcolm 8–0–33–1; Miller 8–0–38–0; Warner 8–0–35–0; Kuiper 8–0–53–2.

Umpires: J. H. Hampshire and A. G. T. Whitehead.

At The Oval, June 24. DERBYSHIRE beat SURREY by three wickets.

DERBYSHIRE v GLOUCESTERSHIRE

At Derby, July 1. Derbyshire won by six wickets. Toss: Derbyshire. With no play possible until 3.30, the match was reduced to 27 overs a side.

Gloucestershire

R. C. Russell c Roberts b Mortensen .	5	G. D. Hodgson not out	5
C. W. J. Athey c Bowler b Mortensen .	17	C. A. Walsh not out	15
A. J. Wright c Goldsmith b Mortensen	17		
P. Bainbridge run out	21	B 5, l-b 10, w 4	19
K. M. Curran run out	4		
M. W. Romaines run out	2	1/12 2/42 3/48 (8 wkts, 27 overs) 133	
J. W. Lloyds c and b Kuiper	21	4/55 5/59 6/89	
M. W. Alleyne lbw b Base	7	7/105 8/106	

D. V. Lawrence did not bat.

Bowling: Malcolm 5-0-16-0; Mortensen 6-0-16-3; Miller 5-0-26-0; Base 6-0-25-1; Kuiper 5-1-35-1.

Derbyshire

*K. J. Barnett c Hodgson b Lloyds	57	C. J. Adams not out	2
†P. D. Bowler c Lawrence b Curran ...	5	B 1, l-b 4, w 3	8
J. E. Morris run out	57		
A. P. Kuiper c Hodgson b Lloyds	0	1/18 2/125 3/125 (4 wkts, 26.3 overs) 134	
B. Roberts not out	5	4/125	

S. C. Goldsmith, S. J. Base, G. Miller, D. E. Malcolm and O. H. Mortensen did not bat.

Bowling: Walsh 6-0-19-0; Lawrence 2-0-18-0; Curran 6-0-20-1; Bainbridge 5-0-27-0; Alleyne 5-0-32-0; Lloyds 2.3-0-13-2.

Umpires: J. W. Holder and B. Leadbeater.

At Manchester, July 8. DERBYSHIRE beat LANCASHIRE by 5 runs.

DERBYSHIRE v LEICESTERSHIRE

At Knypersley, July 15. Derbyshire won by 118 runs. Toss: Derbyshire. Derbyshire's victory took them back to first place in the League, equal with Middlesex but with a game in hand.

Derbyshire

*K. J. Barnett c Nixon b Mullally	39	S. C. Goldsmith not out	4
†P. D. Bowler c Nixon b Benjamin	4		
J. E. Morris c Nixon b Lewis	21	L-b 13, w 10, n-b 3	26
A. P. Kuiper c Benjamin b Agnew	42		
B. Roberts not out	77	1/16 2/66 3/71 (5 wkts, 40 overs) 222	
C. J. Adams b Benjamin	9	4/158 5/206	

D. E. Malcolm, S. J. Base, A. E. Warner and O. H. Mortensen did not bat.

Bowling: Benjamin 8-0-32-2; Agnew 8-1-52-1; Lewis 8-0-43-1; Mullally 8-1-37-1; Willey 8-0-45-0.

Leicestershire

T. J. Boon c Bowler b Base 2	†P. A. Nixon c Adams b Warner 4
*N. E. Briers lbw b Warner 29	J. P. Agnew b Malcolm 0
J. J. Whitaker c Roberts b Malcolm . . . 12	A. D. Mullally not out 5
P. Willey c Bowler b Malcolm 24	L-b 4, w 5, n-b 1 10
C. C. Lewis run out 0	
L. Potter b Barnett 6	1/6 2/33 3/55 (28 overs) 104
J. D. R. Benson c Morris b Warner . . . 1	4/58 5/79 6/81
W. K. M. Benjamin b Malcolm 11	7/83 8/98 9/98

Bowling: Base 5–0–20–1; Mortensen 6–0–18–0; Malcolm 6–0–21–4; Warner 5–0–18–3 Goldsmith 3–0–14–0; Barnett 3–0–9–1.

Umpires: D. O. Oslear and R. A. White.

At Portsmouth, July 22. DERBYSHIRE lost to HAMPSHIRE by 189 runs.

At Swansea, July 29. DERBYSHIRE beat GLAMORGAN by six wickets.

DERBYSHIRE v KENT

At Chesterfield, August 5. Derbyshire won by six wickets. Toss: Derbyshire. Barnett's 127 came off 101 balls and contained two sixes and thirteen fours.

Kent

S. G. Hinks c Morris b Miller 50	M. V. Fleming not out 15
M. R. Benson run out 4	L-b 6, w 7 13
N. R. Taylor c Roberts b Kuiper 78	
T. R. Ward c Warner b Kuiper 80	1/8 2/80 3/210 (4 wkts, 40 overs) 276
G. R. Cowdrey not out 36	4/249

*C. S. Cowdrey, †S. A. Marsh, T. A. Merrick, R. P. Davis and A. P. Igglesden did not bat

Bowling: Warner 8–0–59–0; Mortensen 8–2–23–0; Malcolm 8–0–55–0; Miller 8–0–59–1 Kuiper 8–0–74–2.

Derbyshire

*K. J. Barnett run out 127	B. Roberts not out 11
†P. D. Bowler b Fleming 54	B 4, l-b 2, w 1 7
J. E. Morris c C. S. Cowdrey b Igglesden 45	
A. P. Kuiper not out 22	1/146 2/232 (4 wkts, 38.2 overs) 277
T. J. G. O'Gorman b Davis 11	3/234 4/259

C. J. Adams, A. E. Warner, G. Miller, O. H. Mortensen and D. E. Malcolm did not bat.

Bowling: Igglesden 7.2–0–54–1; Merrick 7–0–43–0; C. S. Cowdrey 8–0–50–0; Fleming 8–0–60–1; Davis 8–0–64–1.

Umpires: J. H. Hampshire and B. Hassan.

DERBYSHIRE v MIDDLESEX

At Derby, August 19. No result. Toss: Middlesex. Rain, which had reduced the match to fourteen overs a side, ended play before a result could be achieved.

Derbyshire

*K. J. Barnett c Haynes b Williams	5	T. J. G. O'Gorman not out	0
*P. D. Bowler b Fraser	50	B 3, n-b 1	4
J. E. Morris c Roseberry b Cowans	48		
A. P. Kuiper lbw b Emburey	18	1/29 2/100 3/116 (5 wkts, 14 overs) 128	
C. J. Adams run out	3	4/128 5/128	

B. Roberts, A. E. Warner, S. J. Base, D. E. Malcolm and O. H. Mortensen did not bat.

Bowling: Cowans 2–0–26–1; Williams 3–0–27–1; Hughes 3–0–18–0; Emburey 3–0–30–1; Fraser 3–0–24–1.

Middlesex

D. L. Haynes not out	48		
M. A. Roseberry c Bowler b Warner	0		
*M. W. Gatting run out	7		
M. R. Ramprakash not out	26		
L-b 1, w 2, n-b 1	4		

1/1 2/10 (2 wkts, 9.2 overs) 85

K. R. Brown, †P. R. Downton, J. E. Emburey, N. F. Williams, S. P. Hughes, A. R. C. Fraser and N. G. Cowans did not bat.

Bowling: Warner 3–0–20–1; Mortensen 3–0–22–0; Malcolm 2–0–17–0; Kuiper 1–0–15–0; Base 0.2–0–10–0.

Umpires: J. C. Balderstone and P. B. Wight.

DERBYSHIRE v ESSEX

At Derby, August 26. Derbyshire won by five wickets. Toss: Essex. Derbyshire won the Refuge Assurance League when they beat Essex for the first time in any competition since 1982. Kuiper's half-century came off 31 balls and included a six and six fours.

Essex

*B. R. Hardie b Warner	76	N. Shahid not out	9
J. P. Stephenson c Barnett b Mortensen	3	B 1, l-b 11, w 7	19
M. E. Waugh c Adams b Kuiper	59		
P. J. Prichard c Mortensen b Kuiper	25	1/7 2/133 3/177 (4 wkts, 40 overs) 203	
N. Hussain not out	12	4/185	

P. M. Such, †M. A. Garnham, J. H. Childs, M. C. Ilott and S. J. W. Andrew did not bat.

Bowling: Mortensen 8–2–10–1; Warner 8–0–36–1; Base 8–0–33–0; Jean-Jacques 6–0–47–0; Goldsmith 4–0–25–0; Kuiper 6–0–40–2.

Derbyshire

*K. J. Barnett c Garnham b Ilott	7	S. C. Goldsmith not out	5
†P. D. Bowler c Stephenson b Childs	43		
B. Roberts lbw b Waugh	45	B 1, l-b 6, w 5	12
A. P. Kuiper c Prichard b Waugh	56		
T. J. G. O'Gorman c Such b Ilott	12	1/19 2/98 3/116 (5 wkts, 39.3 overs) 207	
C. J. Adams not out	27	4/168 5/179	

M. Jean-Jacques, A. E. Warner, S. J. Base and O. H. Mortensen did not bat.

Bowling: Andrew 8–0–53–0; Ilott 7.3–0–41–2; Such 8–0–28–0; Childs 8–0–38–1; Waugh 8–0–40–2.

Umpires: D. J. Constant and R. Julian.

ESSEX

ESSEX v KENT

At Chelmsford, April 22. Kent won by 27 runs. Toss: Essex. In the Kent innings, Foster captured his four wickets in eight balls while conceding just 1 run.

Kent

S. G. Hinks b Childs	50	M. V. Fleming not out		24
N. R. Taylor c Pringle b Childs	58	†S. A. Marsh not out		27
T. R. Ward c Garnham b Foster	13	B 1, l-b 14, w 8, n-b 3		26
*C. S. Cowdrey b Foster	11			
G. R. Cowdrey c Garnham b Foster	6	1/98 2/122 3/145	(6 wkts, 40 overs)	215
R. M. Ellison b Foster	0	4/153 5/153 6/154		

M. A. Ealham, C. Penn and T. A. Merrick did not bat.

Bowling: Foster 8–1–21–4; Topley 8–0–38–0; Waugh 5–0–32–0; Gooch 5–0–28–0; Pringle 8–0–43–0; Childs 6–0–38–2.

Essex

*G. A. Gooch c Ealham b Merrick	3	N. A. Foster c Ellison b Merrick		6
B. R. Hardie run out	56	T. D. Topley not out		3
M. E. Waugh c Taylor b Fleming	50	J. H. Childs b Penn		2
P. J. Prichard c Ealham b Ellison	18	L-b 8, w 2		10
D. R. Pringle b Ellison	15			
J. P. Stephenson b Penn	5	1/5 2/116 3/121	(39 overs)	188
A. W. Lilley b Merrick	10	4/151 5/152 6/159		
†M. A. Garnham b Merrick	10	7/171 8/181 9/183		

Bowling: Penn 8–1–30–2; Merrick 7–0–24–4; Ealham 8–0–29–0; Fleming 8–0–43–1; C. S. Cowdrey 1–0–9–0; Ellison 7–0–45–2.

Umpires: D. O. Oslear and N. T. Plews.

At Lord's, April 29. ESSEX lost to MIDDLESEX by 12 runs.

At Leicester, May 6. ESSEX lost to LEICESTERSHIRE by five wickets.

ESSEX v GLOUCESTERSHIRE

At Chelmsford, May 13. Gloucestershire won by seven wickets. Toss: Gloucestershire. For their first victory of the season in any competition, Gloucestershire were indebted to Athey, whose century came off 132 balls.

Essex

*G. A. Gooch lbw b Bainbridge	56	†M. A. Garnham not out		24
B. R. Hardie st Russell b Alleyne	42	N. A. Foster not out		11
M. E. Waugh b Bainbridge	1	B 1, l-b 6, w 5		12
P. J. Prichard c Wright b Alleyne	21			
D. R. Pringle c Romaines b Alleyne	21	1/94 2/97 3/120	(6 wkts, 40 overs)	211
J. P. Stephenson run out	23	4/144 5/153 6/182		

T. D. Topley, J. H. Childs and M. C. Ilott did not bat.

Bowling: Walsh 8–0–42–0; Jarvis 6–0–30–0; Curran 8–0–43–0; Alleyne 6–1–25–3; Bainbridge 8–0–46–2; Ball 4–0–18–0.

loucestershire

R. C. Russell c Topley b Foster	62	K. M. Curran not out	5
W. J. Athey not out	101	L-b 9, w 5, n-b 3	17
W. Lloyds c and b Foster	10		—
A. J. Wright c Prichard b Pringle	20	1/137 2/158 3/208 (3 wkts, 39.1 overs) 215

W. Romaines, P. Bainbridge, M. W. Alleyne, C. A. Walsh, K. B. S. Jarvis and M. C. J. Ball did not bat.

Bowling: Ilott 8–0–34–0; Foster 8–0–22–2; Pringle 7.1–0–49–1; Topley 8–0–51–0; Childs 0–35–0; Stephenson 2–0–15–0.

Umpires: P. J. Eele and A. G. T. Whitehead.

At Worcester, May 20. ESSEX beat WORCESTERSHIRE by two wickets.

ESSEX v GLAMORGAN

At Ilford, June 3. Essex won by six wickets. Toss: Essex. The match was reduced to fifteen overs a side after rain had delayed the start until 5.05 p.m. Prichard won it for Essex with a four off the last ball.

Glamorgan

M. P. Maynard b Topley	75	S. J. Dennis b Waugh	3
H. Morris c and b Pringle	18	S. L. Watkin not out	1
V. A. Richards c and b Topley	0	W 4, n-b 6	10
Smith c Gooch b Pringle	8		—
A. R. Butcher c Stephenson b Foster	1	1/95 2/95 3/104 (7 wkts, 15 overs) 131
G. C. Holmes not out	14	4/111 5/115	
C. P. Metson b Waugh	1	6/119 7/123	

R. Barwick and M. Frost did not bat.

Bowling: Andrew 3–0–38–0; Foster 3–0–33–1; Topley 3–0–23–2; Waugh 3–0–19–2; Pringle 3–0–18–2.

ssex

G. A. Gooch run out	58	N. A. Foster not out	0
R. Hardie c Butcher b Barwick	30	L-b 2, w 1	3
M. E. Waugh b Frost	12		—
J. Prichard not out	23	1/75 2/97 3/106 (4 wkts, 15 overs) 135
D. R. Pringle run out	9	4/129	

P. Stephenson, A. W. Lilley, †M. A. Garnham, T. D. Topley and S. J. W. Andrew did not bat.

Bowling: Frost 3–0–26–1; Watkin 3–0–19–0; Dennis 3–0–23–0; Richards 3–0–31–0; Barwick 3–0–34–1.

Umpires: B. Leadbeater and B. J. Meyer.

At Birmingham, June 10. ESSEX beat WARWICKSHIRE by seven wickets.

At Bath, June 17. ESSEX beat SOMERSET by 101 runs.

At Southampton, July 8. ESSEX lost to HAMPSHIRE by seven wickets.

ESSEX v NORTHAMPTONSHIRE

At Chelmsford, July 15. Essex won by six wickets. Toss: Essex. Fourteen deliveries were h
out of the ground during the match, including three in succession by Bailey off Topley.

Northamptonshire

A. Fordham run out	74	†D. Ripley not out	
W. Larkins c Gooch b Foster	6		
D. J. Capel c Garnham b Ilott	56	L-b 7, w 5	
*A. J. Lamb c Prichard b Pringle	34		
R. J. Bailey c Hussain b Topley	26	1/15 2/141 3/147	(7 wkts, 40 overs) 2
D. J. Wild c and b Pringle	20	4/188 5/226	
W. W. Davis c Ilott b Waugh	2	6/227 7/233	

N. G. B. Cook, M. A. Robinson and S. J. Brown did not bat.

Bowling: Foster 8–1–36–1; Ilott 8–0–17–1; Topley 5–0–34–1; Childs 6–0–38–0; Pring
8–0–59–2; Waugh 5–0–42–1.

Essex

*G. A. Gooch run out	0	†M. A. Garnham not out	
J. P. Stephenson c Fordham b Wild	66	L-b 7, w 1	
M. E. Waugh b Cook	53		
N. Hussain b Bailey	22	1/0 2/111 3/139	(4 wkts, 38.2 overs) 2
D. R. Pringle not out	61	4/158	

P. J. Prichard, N. A. Foster, T. D. Topley, J. H. Childs and M. C. Ilott did not bat.

Bowling: Robinson 7–1–46–0; Davis 8–0–38–0; Cook 8–0–42–1; Brown 5.2–0–39–0; Wi
5–0–36–1; Bailey 5–0–31–1.

Umpires: M. J. Kitchen and D. S. Thompsett.

ESSEX v LANCASHIRE

At Colchester, July 22. Lancashire won by two wickets. Toss: Lancashire. Stephenson, who
week earlier had scored his maiden Sunday League fifty, made 109 off 122 balls, including o
six and six fours. He put on 214 for the second wicket with Waugh, who struck a total
twelve fours and reached his hundred off 79 balls. Atherton's hundred, also his first in t
competition, featured one six and ten fours.

Essex

*G. A. Gooch lbw b Allott	1	B. R. Hardie not out	
J. P. Stephenson c Hughes b Austin	109		
M. E. Waugh b DeFreitas	111	L-b 2, w 3, n-b 2	
D. R. Pringle run out	1		
N. Hussain b Wasim Akram	12	1/8 2/222 3/225	(5 wkts, 40 overs) 2
N. A. Foster not out	4	4/234 5/245	

N. Shahid, †M. A. Garnham, M. C. Ilott and J. H. Childs did not bat.

Bowling: DeFreitas 8–0–38–1; Allott 8–0–40–1; Watkinson 8–0–47–0; Wasim Akra
8–0–53–1; Austin 8–0–67–1.

Lancashire

G. Fowler c Hardie b Ilott	5	†W. K. Hegg not out	
M. A. Atherton b Pringle	111	*D. P. Hughes not out	
G. D. Lloyd c Shahid b Pringle	30		
N. H. Fairbrother run out	23	L-b 10, w 6	
M. Watkinson c Garnham b Foster	1		
Wasim Akram b Ilott	3	1/9 2/84 3/145	(8 wkts, 39.5 overs) 2
P. A. J. DeFreitas c Pringle b Foster	18	4/156 5/169 6/198	
I. D. Austin c Hussain b Pringle	10	7/212 8/221	

P. J. W. Allott did not bat.

Bowling: Foster 8–0–42–2; Ilott 8–0–44–2; Gooch 3–0–24–0; Childs 8–0–37–0; Pringle 5–0–47–3; Waugh 5–0–45–0.

Umpires: P. J. Eele and N. T. Plews.

ESSEX v SUSSEX

t Chelmsford, July 29. Essex won by two wickets. Toss: Sussex. Essex, needing 8 runs off the st over with four wickets in hand, lost Garnham and Topley to Hansford in five balls. hilds, however, drove the final delivery past the bowler for four to win the match.

Sussex

. M. Smith b Topley	0	A. C. S. Pigott lbw b Pringle	30
J. Gould c and b Such	56	†P. Moores not out	2
P. W. G. Parker c Such b Topley	72	B 2, l-b 7, w 3, n-b 6	18
. P. Wells c Foster b Such	6		
. M. Wells c Hussain b Childs	28	1/8 2/103 3/124 (6 wkts, 39 overs) 238	
. I. C. Dodemaide not out	26	4/172 5/187 6/233	

. A. Bunting, A. R. Hansford and B. T. P. Donelan did not bat.

Bowling: Foster 8–0–43–0; Topley 8–0–43–2; Childs 8–2–47–1; Such 8–0–43–2; Pringle -0–53–1.

Essex

. R. Hardie run out	44	T. D. Topley b Hansford	0
. Shahid c Parker b Pigott	31	J. H. Childs not out	4
4. E. Waugh b Pigott	28		
. J. Prichard run out	64		
D. R. Pringle c Moores b Donelan	15	L-b 4, w 6, n-b 2	12
. Hussain not out	32		
. A. Foster c Smith b Dodemaide	5	1/76 2/93 3/130 (8 wkts, 39 overs) 241	
M. A. Garnham c Dodemaide		4/171 5/214 6/225	
b Hansford	6	7/234 8/237	

. M. Such did not bat.

Bowling: Dodemaide 8–0–51–1; C. M. Wells 6–1–27–0; Hansford 8–0–62–2; Donelan -0–43–1; Pigott 8–0–42–2; Bunting 1–0–12–0.

Umpires: D. O. Oslear and K. E. Palmer.

ESSEX v NOTTINGHAMSHIRE

t Southend, August 5. Nottinghamshire won by six wickets. Toss: Nottinghamshire. Gooch aced just 106 balls for his 136, which contained fifteen fours. Newell's unbeaten hundred, vhich anchored Nottinghamshire to victory, was his first in the competition.

Essex

G. A. Gooch c Johnson b Cooper	136	T. D. Topley b Evans	2
. P. Stephenson c Randall b Hemmings	50	M. C. Ilott run out	3
4. E. Waugh c Newell b Hemmings	7	J. H. Childs not out	1
. J. Prichard c Johnson b Stephenson	4	L-b 6, w 1, n-b 1	8
J. Hussain c French b Mike	5		
J. Shahid c Mike b Stephenson	8	1/147 2/158 3/178 (38.4 overs) 239	
J. A. Foster c Newell b Stephenson	10	4/192 5/212 6/221	
M. A. Garnham b Evans	5	7/229 8/233 9/238	

Bowling: Cooper 8–0–49–1; Stephenson 8–0–28–3; Evans 7.4–0–52–2; Mike 7–0–68–1; Hemmings 8–0–36–2.

Nottinghamshire

B. C. Broad b Gooch	35	F. D. Stephenson not out	2
M. Newell not out	109	L-b 7, w 1, n-b 1	
P. Johnson c Hussain b Topley	48		
*R. T. Robinson c and b Foster	4	1/61 2/154 3/160 (4 wkts, 38.3 overs) 24	
D. W. Randall run out	9	4/184	

K. P. Evans, †B. N. French, E. E. Hemmings, K. E. Cooper and G. W. Mike did not bat

Bowling: Ilott 7.3–0–41–0; Foster 8–0–50–1; Gooch 8–0–34–1; Childs 6–0–43–0; Topley 7–0–45–1; Waugh 2–0–20–0.

Umpires: J. C. Balderstone and J. H. Harris.

At Middlesbrough, August 12. ESSEX lost to YORKSHIRE by 59 runs.

ESSEX v SURREY

At Chelmsford, August 19. No result.

At Derby, August 26. ESSEX lost to DERBYSHIRE by five wickets.

GLAMORGAN

At Bristol, April 22. GLAMORGAN beat GLOUCESTERSHIRE by 5 runs.

GLAMORGAN v LEICESTERSHIRE

At Cardiff, April 29. Glamorgan won by 32 runs. Toss: Leicestershire.

Glamorgan

A. Dale b Benjamin	3	S. J. Dennis run out	
H. Morris c Boon b Benjamin	13	M. Frost not out	
M. P. Maynard c Whitticase b Taylor	22	S. R. Barwick not out	
I. V. A. Richards b Taylor	59	L-b 8, w 5, n-b 2	
*A. R. Butcher c Potter b Agnew	17		
I. Smith run out	35	1/15 2/39 3/43 (9 wkts, 40 overs) 18	
N. G. Cowley c Whitticase b Taylor	0	4/90 5/131 6/131	
†C. P. Metson c Briers b Mullally	11	7/165 8/180 9/182	

Bowling: Parsons 8–0–53–0; Benjamin 8–1–26–2; Taylor 8–0–34–3; Agnew 8–1–20–1; Mullally 8–0–41–1.

Leicestershire

T. J. Boon c Smith b Frost	2	J. P. Agnew c Barwick b Frost	
*N. E. Briers c Richards b Cowley	37	A. D. Mullally c and b Richards	
J. J. Whitaker c Morris b Frost	72	L. B. Taylor not out	
L. Potter lbw b Cowley	6	L-b 6, w 2	
J. D. R. Benson c Richards b Barwick	3		
†P. Whitticase run out	2	1/2 2/79 3/87 (38.1 overs) 15	
W. K. M. Benjamin c Morris b Dale	5	4/96 5/114 6/121	
G. J. Parsons c Richards b Barwick	12	7/138 8/142 9/145	

Bowling: Frost 8–0–30–3; Dennis 6–0–13–0; Barwick 6.1–0–30–2; Cowley 8–0–26–2; Dale 4–0–22–1; Richards 6–1–23–1.

Umpires: M. J. Kitchen and B. Leadbeater.

GLAMORGAN v KENT

t Llanelli, May 13. Kent won by two wickets. Toss: Glamorgan. Needing to score 20 runs
om the last over, bowled by Watkin, Kent made 23 from five deliveries. Ealham hit the first
or six, a single followed, and then Penn hit two sixes and a four to win the match with a ball
 spare. Glamorgan's innings had also finished with a flourish when Smith hit Chris Cowdrey
or 20 in the final over.

Glamorgan

. Morris c Marsh b Penn	0	I. Smith not out	39
. C. Holmes c Merrick b Fleming	57	N. G. Cowley not out	0
I. P. Maynard c G. R. Cowdrey		B 5, l-b 2, w 4	11
b Fleming	20		
V. A. Richards c Ealham b Fleming	55	1/1 2/41 3/132 (5 wkts, 40 overs)	220
A. R. Butcher c Taylor b C. S. Cowdrey	38	4/132 5/200	

C. P. Metson, S. J. Dennis, S. L. Watkin and M. Frost did not bat.

Bowling: Penn 8–0–51–1; Merrick 8–1–32–0; Davis 4–0–27–0; Fleming 7–0–30–3; Ealham
-1–37–0; C. S. Cowdrey 6–0–36–1.

Kent

. G. Hinks c Metson b Watkin	74	T. A. Merrick b Frost	8
. R. Taylor c Metson b Richards	27	C. Penn not out	20
. R. Ward b Richards	0		
C. S. Cowdrey c Holmes b Cowley	3	B 1, l-b 15, w 10	26
. R. Cowdrey c Dennis b Holmes	5		
I. V. Fleming run out	18	1/65 2/65 3/77 (8 wkts, 39.5 overs)	224
S. A. Marsh b Frost	14	4/124 5/131 6/162	
I. A. Ealham not out	29	7/164 8/177	

. P. Davis did not bat.

Bowling: Watkin 7.5–1–48–1; Richards 8–0–28–2; Dennis 8–0–28–0; Frost 8–0–45–2;
owley 3–0–27–1; Holmes 5–0–32–1.

Umpires: J. C. Balderstone and K. J. Lyons.

t Hove, May 20. GLAMORGAN lost to SUSSEX by six wickets.

GLAMORGAN v LANCASHIRE

t Colwyn Bay, May 27. Lancashire won by four wickets. Toss: Lancashire. Maynard, whose
artnership with Richards produced 143 runs in eighteen overs, hit eleven fours in his 102-ball
entury. But even Glamorgan's third-wicket pair were overshadowed by the hitting of Wasim
kram in Lancashire's innings. He hit three sixes and four fours in reaching his half-century
ff 31 balls.

Glamorgan

I. Morris c Austin b DeFreitas	6	†C. P. Metson not out	5
A. R. Butcher b Wasim Akram	38	N. G. Cowley b Austin	1
I. P. Maynard c Austin		L-b 5, w 3, n-b 1	9
b Wasim Akram	100		
V. A. Richards c Fairbrother b Austin	77	1/26 2/73 3/216 (6 wkts, 40 overs)	242
Smith b Hughes	6	4/224 5/227 6/242	

. J. Dennis, J. Derrick, S. R. Barwick and M. Frost did not bat.

Bowling: Allott 8–1–28–0; DeFreitas 8–0–42–1; Atherton 7–0–66–0; Wasim Akram
-0–46–2; Austin 8–0–51–2; Hughes 1–0–4–1.

Lancashire

G. Fowler c Metson b Dennis	2	P. A. J. DeFreitas not out	3
M. A. Atherton c Maynard b Richards	74	I. D. Austin not out	1
G. D. Lloyd c Metson b Frost	3	B 5, l-b 7, w 8	2
N. H. Fairbrother run out	27		
T. E. Jesty c Butcher b Barwick	25	1/5 2/20 3/113 (6 wkts, 37.5 overs)	24
Wasim Akram c Cowley b Frost	50	4/114 5/183 6/211	

†W. K. Hegg, *D. P. Hughes and P. J. W. Allott did not bat.

Bowling: Frost 8–0–39–2; Dennis 8–0–38–1; Barwick 8–1–54–1; Derrick 3–0–26–0; Richards 6.5–0–42–1; Cowley 4–0–35–0.

Umpires: J. H. Harris and P. B. Wight.

At Ilford, June 3. GLAMORGAN lost to ESSEX by six wickets.

At Northampton, June 10. GLAMORGAN lost to NORTHAMPTONSHIRE by 10 runs.

At Bournemouth, June 17. GLAMORGAN lost to HAMPSHIRE by 64 runs.

GLAMORGAN v YORKSHIRE

At Newport, June 24. No result. There was no play in the last county match scheduled for the Newport ground, on which it was planned to build a school.

GLAMORGAN v SURREY

At Cardiff, July 1. Glamorgan won by eight wickets. Toss: Glamorgan. The first game having been interrupted by rain after eight deliveries, a second match of ten overs a side was started at 4.57 p.m. In the abandoned match, Surrey were 4 for one, having been put in.

Surrey

M. A. Feltham c and b Watkin	12	G. P. Thorpe not out	1
†D. M. Ward c Butcher b Watkin	5	L-b 2, w 1	
M. A. Lynch c Cottey b Frost	38		
*I. A. Greig c Richards b Dennis	23	1/18 2/21 3/73 (5 wkts, 10 overs)	9
D. J. Bicknell c Richards b Frost	6	4/86 5/98	

G. S. Clinton, C. K. Bullen, Waqar Younis, M. P. Bicknell and A. J. Murphy did not bat.

Bowling: Derrick 1–0–12–0; Watkin 2–0–18–2; Dale 2–0–16–0; Richards 1–0–14–0; Dennis 2–0–14–1; Frost 2–0–22–2.

Glamorgan

H. Morris b Waqar Younis	48
M. P. Maynard b Bullen	11
I. V. A. Richards not out	34
*A. R. Butcher not out	0
B 2, l-b 2, w 2	6

1/29 2/94   (2 wkts, 9.5 overs) 99

P. A. Cottey, A. Dale, J. Derrick, †C. P. Metson, S. J. Dennis, S. L. Watkin and M. Frost did not bat.

Bowling: Murphy 2–0–9–0; M. P. Bicknell 2–0–16–0; Feltham 2–0–25–0; Bullen 2–0–28–1; Waqar Younis 1.5–0–17–1.

Umpires: R. A. White and A. G. T. Whitehead.

At Birmingham, July 15. GLAMORGAN beat WARWICKSHIRE by seven wickets.

GLAMORGAN v SOMERSET

At Neath, July 22. Somerset won by 220 runs. Toss: Somerset. Somerset's total passed by 50 runs the previous Sunday League record, achieved by Essex, also against Glamorgan, at Southend in 1983. Their margin of victory was also a record, being 30 runs greater than Kent's 90-run victory over Northamptonshire at Brackley in 1973. Rose, who a month earlier had struck the fastest century in the NatWest Bank Trophy, also set new Sunday League records with the fastest century – off 46 balls – and the fastest fifty – off sixteen. When 54 he was well held by Butcher on the mid-wicket boundary, but in completing the catch the Glamorgan captain stepped on the boundary edge. Rose went on to make 148 off only 69 balls, including eight sixes and seventeen fours, and in nineteen overs he and Cook put on 223 for the third wicket, another record for the competition. Cook, during his highest Refuge League innings 110 balls, two sixes, fifteen fours), passed I. V. A. Richards's Somerset record, set in 1975, of 779 runs in a Sunday League season.

Somerset

S. J. Cook not out	136	R. J. Harden not out	32
R. J. Bartlett c Dale b Cowley	11	L-b 5, w 17, n-b 1	23
*C. J. Tavaré c Maynard b Dale	10		
G. D. Rose c Smith b Richards	148	1/35 2/62 3/285 (3 wkts, 40 overs)	360

†N. D. Burns, A. N. Hayhurst, R. P. Lefebvre, I. G. Swallow, N. A. Mallender and J. C. Hallett did not bat.

Bowling: Watkin 8-0-71-0; Frost 8-0-46-0; Dennis 8-0-67-0; Cowley 5-0-44-1; Dale 8-0-28-1; Richards 7-0-76-1; Maynard 1-0-23-0.

Glamorgan

M. P. Maynard c Swallow b Mallender	0	S. L. Watkin b Lefebvre	28
H. Morris c Lefebvre b Rose	3	S. J. Dennis run out	5
I. V. A. Richards b Hallett	36	M. Frost not out	2
I. Smith run out	6	L-b 6, w 2	8
*A. R. Butcher c Tavaré b Hayhurst	18		
A. Dale c Tavaré b Hallett	14	1/0 2/6 3/19 (28.5 overs)	140
N. G. Cowley c Harden b Hallett	10	4/50 5/81 6/85	
†C. P. Metson b Hayhurst	10	7/96 8/108 9/127	

Bowling: Mallender 5-0-19-1; Rose 5-1-24-1; Hallett 8-0-41-3; Lefebvre 5.5-0-26-1; Hayhurst 5-0-24-2.

Umpires: D. R. Shepherd and D. S. Thompsett.

GLAMORGAN v DERBYSHIRE

At Swansea, July 29. Derbyshire won by six wickets. Toss: Derbyshire. The game was reduced to 34 overs a side after rain interrupted Glamorgan's innings for 50 minutes. At the time they were 55 for one off fifteen overs.

Glamorgan

H. Morris c Bowler b Mortensen	16	†C. P. Metson st Bowler b Kuiper	9
M. P. Maynard b Warner	30	S. L. Watkin not out	2
I. V. A. Richards c Bowler b Warner	22	L-b 3, w 8, n-b 2	13
*A. R. Butcher c Barnett b Base	28		
G. C. Holmes c Base b Kuiper	21	1/41 2/62 3/80 (6 wkts, 34 overs)	154
A. Dale not out	13	4/125 5/143 6/152	

S. Bastien, S. J. Dennis and M. Frost did not bat.

Bowling: Base 8-0-40-1; Mortensen 8-0-17-1; Jean-Jacques 8-0-35-0; Goldsmith 1-0-6-0; Kuiper 4-0-27-2; Warner 5-0-26-2.

Derbyshire

*K. J. Barnett c Metson b Bastien	 14	C. J. Adams not out	 9
†P. D. Bowler not out	 52	L-b 10, w 4	 14
B. Roberts lbw b Watkin	 23		—
A. P. Kuiper b Watkin	 12	1/19 2/55 3/80	(4 wkts, 32.4 overs) 156
T. J. G. O'Gorman c and b Richards	.. 32	4/141	

S. C. Goldsmith, S. J. Base, A. E. Warner, O. H. Mortensen and M. Jean-Jacques did not bat.

Bowling: Frost 7–2–26–0; Bastien 4–0–21–1; Watkin 8–0–29–2; Dennis 6.4–0–26–0; Dale 3–0–17–0; Richards 4–0–27–1.

Umpires: B. Dudleston and B. Hassan.

At Lord's, August 5. GLAMORGAN lost to MIDDLESEX by 84 runs.

At Nottingham, August 12. GLAMORGAN lost to NOTTINGHAMSHIRE by eight wickets.

GLAMORGAN v WORCESTERSHIRE

At Swansea, August 26. Worcestershire won by 34 runs. Toss: Glamorgan. Curtis's 95 took him to a total of 784 runs in the Sunday League season, a record for Worcestershire. The previous record of 668, scored by Younis Ahmed in 1979, had been passed two weeks earlier by Hick, who finished the season with 751.

Worcestershire

T. S. Curtis c Richards b Dale	 95	P. J. Newport st Metson b Dale	 0
G. J. Lord lbw b Watkin	 7	S. R. Lampitt run out	 6
G. A. Hick st Metson b Croft	 31		
D. B. D'Oliveira b Richards	 14	L-b 15, w 11	 26
I. T. Botham b Dale	 4		
*P. A. Neale c Croft b Watkin	 7	1/17 2/97 3/126	(9 wkts, 40 overs) 214
†S. J. Rhodes not out	 23	4/153 5/172 6/188	
R. K. Illingworth run out	 1	7/206 8/207 9/214	

S. M. McEwan did not bat.

Bowling: Frost 6–0–32–0; Watkin 7–1–33–2; Dennis 8–0–42–0; Croft 8–0–39–1; Richards 3–0–18–1; Dale 8–0–35–3.

Glamorgan

H. Morris c Illingworth b Newport	 7	S. L. Watkin b Lampitt	 0
M. P. Maynard c and b Lampitt	 36	S. J. Dennis c Neale b Newport	 14
I. V. A. Richards c and b Newport	... 3	M. Frost not out	 1
*A. R. Butcher c and b Illingworth	 30	L-b 9, w 14, n-b 1	 24
P. A. Cottey st Rhodes b Illingworth	.. 8		
A. Dale c D'Oliveira b Hick	 34	1/17 2/23 3/85	(37.2 overs) 180
R. D. B. Croft c Hick b McEwan	 13	4/87 5/107 6/137	
†C. P. Metson run out	 10	7/162 8/162 9/164	

Bowling: McEwan 8–0–52–1; Newport 6.2–1–19–3; Lampitt 7–0–28–2; Illingworth 8–1–19–2; Hick 8–0–53–1.

Umpires: R. Palmer and A. G. T. Whitehead.

GLOUCESTERSHIRE

GLOUCESTERSHIRE v GLAMORGAN

At Bristol, April 22. Glamorgan won by 5 runs. Toss: Gloucestershire.

Glamorgan

G. C. Holmes c Russell b Curran 8	†C. P. Metson not out	0
H. Morris st Russell b Graveney 46		
A. Dale c Wright b Alleyne 42	L-b 5, w 2, n-b 3	10
M. P. Maynard c Athey b Alleyne 11		
*A. R. Butcher b Lawrence 8	1/10 2/82 3/114 (7 wkts, 40 overs) 188	
I. Smith b Lawrence 46	4/116 5/133	
N. G. Cowley c Russell b Lawrence ... 17	6/180 7/188	

S. J. Dennis, S. L. Watkin and S. R. Barwick did not bat.

Bowling: Curran 8–0–22–1; Jarvis 8–1–45–0; Milburn 2–0–11–0; Lawrence 7–0–40–3; Graveney 8–1–20–1; Alleyne 7–0–45–2.

Gloucestershire

*A. J. Wright c Maynard b Cowley ... 30	E. T. Milburn not out	5
C. W. J. Athey c Butcher b Dale 15		
G. D. Hodgson c Dale b Cowley 28	L-b 6, w 1	7
K. M. Curran run out 37		
P. W. Romaines c Holmes b Watkin ... 22	1/33 2/58 3/84 (7 wkts, 40 overs) 183	
M. W. Alleyne c Maynard b Dennis ... 11	4/134 5/145	
†R. C. Russell c Watkin b Barwick ... 28	6/151 7/183	

D. A. Graveney, D. V. Lawrence and K. B. S. Jarvis did not bat.

Bowling: Dennis 8–1–35–1; Watkin 8–2–24–1; Barwick 8–2–24–1; Dale 6–0–41–1; Cowley 8–1–36–2; Smith 2–0–17–0.

Umpires: B. Hassan and R. Palmer.

At Southampton, May 6. HAMPSHIRE v GLOUCESTERSHIRE. No result.

At Chelmsford, May 13. GLOUCESTERSHIRE beat ESSEX by seven wickets.

GLOUCESTERSHIRE v WARWICKSHIRE

At Moreton-in-Marsh, May 20. Gloucestershire won by 48 runs. Toss: Gloucestershire.

Gloucestershire

†R. C. Russell c Humpage b Munton .. 7	P. W. Romaines c Humpage b Munton. 5	
C. W. J. Athey lbw b Benjamin 4	M. W. Alleyne not out 13	
*A. J. Wright b Munton 40	L-b 15, w 2 17	
K. M. Curran c Smith b Munton 75		
J. W. Lloyds c Twose b Munton 0	1/13 2/21 3/127 (6 wkts, 40 overs) 202	
P. Bainbridge not out 41	4/127 5/159 6/176	

M. W. Pooley, C. A. Walsh and M. C. J. Ball did not bat.

Bowling: Benjamin 8–1–21–1; Munton 8–1–23–5; Moody 8–1–33–0; Small 8–0–50–0; Twose 2–0–14–0; Smith 6–0–46–0.

Warwickshire

Asif Din c Athey b Walsh	59	G. C. Small lbw b Pooley	1
A. I. Kallicharran c Wright b Pooley	0	J. E. Benjamin c Russell b Alleyne	1
T. M. Moody b Walsh	1	T. A. Munton lbw b Curran	3
†G. W. Humpage c Wright b Alleyne	11	B 3, l-b 5, w 14, n-b 1	23
*T. A. Lloyd c and b Bainbridge	13		
N. M. K. Smith c Alleyne b Ball	5	1/1 2/6 3/39 (34.2 overs)	154
R. G. Twose b Alleyne	13	4/71 5/83 6/116	
D. P. Ostler not out	24	7/127 8/132 9/141	

Bowling: Walsh 6-1-14-2; Pooley 7-0-29-2; Curran 5.2-0-22-1; Alleyne 7-0-40-3; Bainbridge 5-0-24-1; Ball 4-0-17-1.

Umpires: J. D. Bond and R. Julian.

At Lord's, May 27. GLOUCESTERSHIRE lost to MIDDLESEX by seven wickets.

GLOUCESTERSHIRE v SOMERSET

At Bristol, June 3. Gloucestershire won by eight wickets. Toss: Gloucestershire. Lawrence's return of five for 18 included a spell of four for 4 in seventeen balls.

Somerset

S. J. Cook c Walsh b Lawrence	10	I. G. Swallow c Wright b Bainbridge	19
P. M. Roebuck b Curran	4	N. A. Mallender b Bainbridge	24
A. N. Hayhurst c Russell b Lawrence	4	J. C. Hallett not out	4
*C. J. Tavaré c Wright b Lawrence	4	B 1, l-b 4, w 6, n-b 1	12
R. J. Harden c Wright b Lawrence	3		
†N. D. Burns c Lloyds b Walsh	20	1/12 2/21 3/21 (39.3 overs)	118
G. D. Rose c Bainbridge b Lawrence	14	4/25 5/32 6/61	
M. W. Cleal c Wright b Alleyne	0	7/63 8/69 9/103	

Bowling: Walsh 8-1-14-1; Curran 8-0-22-1; Lawrence 8-1-18-5; Barnes 5-0-26-0; Alleyne 8-0-26-1; Bainbridge 2.3-0-7-2.

Gloucestershire

†R. C. Russell b Cleal	13
C. W. J. Athey not out	53
*A. J. Wright c Rose b Hayhurst	17
K. M. Curran not out	29
L-b 5, w 2	7

1/39 2/67   (2 wkts, 25.5 overs) 119

P. Bainbridge, J. W. Lloyds, P. W. Romaines, M. W. Alleyne, C. A. Walsh, D. V. Lawrence and S. N. Barnes did not bat.

Bowling: Mallender 8-0-25-0; Hallett 5.5-1-28-0; Rose 5-0-34-0; Cleal 3-0-14-1; Hayhurst 4-0-13-1.

Umpires: J. C. Balderstone and N. T. Plews.

At Manchester, June 10. GLOUCESTERSHIRE beat LANCASHIRE by two wickets.

GLOUCESTERSHIRE v LEICESTERSHIRE

At Gloucester, June 24. Leicestershire won on scoring-rate. Toss: Gloucestershire. Two stoppages for rain reduced Gloucestershire's target first to 173 from 37 overs, and then to 159 from 34 overs.

Leicestershire

T. J. Boon c Wright b Bainbridge	15	J. D. R. Benson not out	8
*N. E. Briers not out	90		
J. J. Whitaker c Lloyds b Alleyne	31	B 7, w 2, n-b 1	10
P. Willey c Lloyds b Lawrence	1		
C. C. Lewis c Hodgson b Curran	30	1/26 2/95 3/98 (5 wkts, 40 overs) 187
L. Potter b Curran	2	4/153 5/166

†P. A. Nixon, W. K. M. Benjamin, J. P. Agnew and A. D. Mullally did not bat.

Bowling: Curran 8–0–38–2; Walsh 8–1–38–0; Bainbridge 8–0–21–1; Lawrence 8–0–47–1; Alleyne 8–0–36–1.

Gloucestershire

*A. J. Wright c Nixon b Agnew	0	G. D. Hodgson lbw b Mullally	12
J. W. Lloyds c Nixon b Benjamin	10	†G. A. Tedstone c Willey b Mullally	25
P. Bainbridge b Benjamin	20	D. V. Lawrence not out	1
K. M. Curran c Willey b Lewis	14	B 4, l-b 4, w 7	15
C. W. J. Athey b Willey	15		
P. W. Romaines c Briers b Benjamin	13	1/0 2/27 3/32 (31 overs) 139
M. W. Alleyne run out	14	4/53 5/83 6/85
C. A. Walsh b Willey	0	7/85 8/102 9/134

Bowling: Agnew 6–0–22–1; Benjamin 7–0–36–3; Lewis 8–0–41–1; Mullally 7–0–20–2; Willey 3–0–12–2.

Umpires: A. A. Jones and D. S. Thompsett.

At Derby, July 1. GLOUCESTERSHIRE lost to DERBYSHIRE by six wickets.

At Worcester, July 8. GLOUCESTERSHIRE lost to WORCESTERSHIRE by eight wickets.

GLOUCESTERSHIRE v SUSSEX

At Swindon, July 15. Gloucestershire won by one wicket. Toss: Gloucestershire. With Gloucestershire needing 9 runs off the last over, Clarke's third-ball dismissal of Hodgson was followed by a leg-bye and five wides which levelled the scores. Lloyds then hit his final delivery for four to win the match.

Sussex

N. J. Lenham run out	65	†P. Moores not out	4
*P. W. G. Parker b Curran	7	C. C. Remy run out	2
A. P. Wells c Russell b Barnes	17	A. R. Clarke b Walsh	0
M. P. Speight c Romaines b Barnes	60	B 4, l-b 5, w 1, n-b 2	12
C. M. Wells b Bainbridge	9		
A. I. C. Dodemaide c Alleyne b Curran	23	1/26 2/60 3/136 (34.5 overs) 210
A. C. S. Pigott run out	10	4/163 5/175 6/198
J. A. North run out	1	7/199 8/205 9/210

Bowling: Walsh 5.5–0–33–1; Curran 5–0–21–2; Bainbridge 8–0–52–1; Barnes 8–0–46–2; Alleyne 8–0–49–0.

Gloucestershire

†R. C. Russell c Moores b Dodemaide .	2	C. A. Walsh c North b Lenham	......	11
C. W. J. Athey c C. M. Wells b Pigott .	23	G. D. Hodgson st Moores b Clarke	....	1
*A. J. Wright c Remy b Dodemaide	... 3	S. N. Barnes not out	....	0
K. M. Curran b Pigott	 52	B 1, l-b 4, w 12	....	17
P. Bainbridge c Speight b Pigott	 0			
P. W. Romaines c Parker b Lenham	.. 47	1/10 2/16 3/32	(9 wkts, 40 overs)	214
J. W. Lloyds not out	 38	4/32 5/130 6/146		
M. W. Alleyne st Moores b Clarke	 20	7/179 8/202 9/204		

Bowling: Dodemaide 8–0–22–2; C. M. Wells 8–0–17–0; Pigott 8–2–35–3; Remy 2–0–23–0; Clarke 7–0–58–2; Lenham 7–0–54–2.

Umpires: D. J. Constant and R. Palmer.

GLOUCESTERSHIRE v YORKSHIRE

At Cheltenham, July 22. Yorkshire won by seven wickets. Toss: Yorkshire.

Gloucestershire

*A. J. Wright c Sharp b Carrick	 57	†R. C. Russell c Sharp b Moxon	......	12
C. W. J. Athey c Blakey b Moxon	... 80	M. W. Alleyne not out	....	14
J. W. Lloyds c Metcalfe b Carrick	 0	L-b 7, w 3, n-b 2	....	12
P. Bainbridge c and b Moxon	 11			
K. M. Curran not out	 31	1/104 2/123 3/145	(6 wkts, 40 overs)	226
P. W. Romaines run out	 9	4/165 5/183 6/203		

C. A. Walsh, R. M. Bell and S. N. Barnes did not bat.

Bowling: Hartley 5–0–36–0; Sidebottom 8–1–27–0; Fletcher 8–0–36–0; Carrick 8–0–47–2; Pickles 4–0–21–0; Moxon 7–0–52–3.

Yorkshire

*M. D. Moxon run out	 68	K. Sharp not out	....	9
A. A. Metcalfe c Russell b Curran	 0	L-b 4, w 11, n-b 2	....	17
†R. J. Blakey not out	 100			
P. E. Robinson c Romaines b Alleyne	.. 33	1/1 2/132 3/204	(3 wkts, 35.5 overs)	227

D. Byas, P. J. Hartley, P. Carrick, C. S. Pickles, A. Sidebottom and S. D. Fletcher did not bat.

Bowling: Curran 8–0–31–1; Walsh 6–0–16–0; Bell 4–0–38–0; Barnes 6–0–53–0; Alleyne 5.5–0–38–1; Lloyds 6–0–47–0.

Umpires: J. H. Hampshire and R. A. White.

GLOUCESTERSHIRE v SURREY

At Cheltenham, July 29. Gloucestershire won by five wickets. Toss: Gloucestershire. Athey struck a six and twelve fours in his 113.

Surrey

A. J. Stewart c Williams b Barnes	 3	†N. F. Sargeant c Romaines b Walsh	..	22
M. A. Feltham c Hodgson b Barnes	... 47	M. P. Bicknell not out	....	4
G. P. Thorpe c Wright b Barnes	 11	Waqar Younis not out	....	0
D. M. Ward c Wright b Milburn	 51	B 1, l-b 4, w 3, n-b 2	....	10
M. A. Lynch c Williams b Walsh	 3			
*I. A. Greig c Walsh b Alleyne	 14	1/10 2/49 3/70	(9 wkts, 40 overs)	192
K. T. Medlycott c Williams b Milburn .	2	4/85 5/113 6/118		
C. K. Bullen c Barnes b Curran	 25	7/157 8/176 9/191		

Bowling: Barnes 8–1–39–3; Walsh 8–0–29–2; Curran 8–0–50–1; Alleyne 8–1–35–1; Milburn 8–0–34–2.

Gloucestershire

G. D. Hodgson c Ward b Medlycott	28	M. W. Alleyne not out	1
C. W. J. Athey c Ward b Waqar Younis	113		
*A. J. Wright c Ward b Bullen	21	L-b 2, w 3	5
K. M. Curran c and b Medlycott	23		
P. W. Romaines c and b Medlycott	0	1/71 2/118 3/185 (5 wkts, 39.5 overs)	196
J. W. Lloyds not out	5	4/185 5/190	

C. A. Walsh, †R. C. J. Williams, E. T. Milburn and S. N. Barnes did not bat.

Bowling: Bicknell 8-0-24-0; Feltham 8-0-44-0; Medlycott 8-0-47-3; Bullen 8-1-41-1; Waqar Younis 7.5-0-38-1.

Umpires: J. C. Balderstone and B. Leadbeater.

GLOUCESTERSHIRE v KENT

At Bristol, August 12. Gloucestershire won by six wickets. Toss: Gloucestershire.

Kent

S. G. Hinks b Barnes	13	P. S. de Villiers run out	4
N. R. Taylor c Athey b Alleyne	37	C. Penn c Williams b Walsh	0
T. R. Ward c Alleyne b Barnes	3	R. P. Davis not out	0
G. R. Cowdrey lbw b Walsh	24	L-b 3, w 1	4
M. V. Fleming c Alleyne b Bainbridge	10		
†S. A. Marsh c Athey b Curran	24	1/18 2/22 3/75 (39.2 overs)	148
*C. S. Cowdrey run out	27	4/90 5/96 6/137	
D. J. M. Kelleher b Walsh	2	7/140 8/148 9/148	

Bowling: Barnes 8-0-25-2; Walsh 7.2-0-28-3; Curran 8-2-24-1; Alleyne 8-0-33-1; Milburn 4-0-24-0; Bainbridge 4-0-11-1.

Gloucestershire

G. D. Hodgson b Fleming	27	M. W. Alleyne not out	39
C. W. J. Athey c and b Kelleher	3	L-b 4, w 1, n-b 1	6
P. Bainbridge not out	59		
K. M. Curran b Fleming	12	1/20 2/65 3/86 (4 wkts, 35.5 overs)	149
*A. J. Wright run out	3	4/89	

P. W. Romaines, C. A. Walsh, E. T. Milburn, †R. C. J. Williams and S. N. Barnes did not bat.

Bowling: Kelleher 8-2-20-1; de Villiers 6.5-2-25-0; C. S. Cowdrey 3-0-20-0; Fleming 8-1-20-2; Penn 7-0-44-0; Davis 3-0-16-0.

Umpires: D. R. Shepherd and P. B. Wight.

At Nottingham, August 19. NOTTINGHAMSHIRE v GLOUCESTERSHIRE. No result.

At Northampton, August 26. GLOUCESTERSHIRE lost to NORTHAMPTONSHIRE by 2 runs.

HAMPSHIRE

At Canterbury, April 29. HAMPSHIRE lost to KENT by 53 runs.

HAMPSHIRE v GLOUCESTERSHIRE

At Southampton, May 6. No result, the match having been ended by a thunderstorm during tea. Toss: Gloucestershire.

Hampshire

V. P. Terry c Lloyds b Walsh	6	M. D. Marshall not out		6
D. I. Gower c Lloyds b Walsh	0	J. R. Ayling not out		2
R. A. Smith c Ball b Bainbridge	85	B 1, l-b 3, w 3, n-b 2		9
C. L. Smith run out	89			
*M. C. J. Nicholas lbw b Bainbridge	15	1/1 2/20 3/165	(6 wkts, 40 overs)	224
R. J. Scott c Ball b Walsh	12	4/201 5/209 6/221		

†R. J. Parks, R. J. Maru and C. A. Connor did not bat.

Bowling: Walsh 8–1–30–3; Curran 8–0–41–0; Alleyne 7–0–41–0; Milburn 4–0–25–0; Ball 6–0–31–0; Bainbridge 7–0–52–2.

Gloucestershire

*A. J. Wright, P. W. Romaines, P. Bainbridge, C. W. J. Athey, J. W. Lloyds, M. W. Alleyne, †R. C. Russell, E. T. Milburn, C. A. Walsh, M. C. J. Ball and K. M. Curran.

Umpires: H. D. Bird and D. S. Thompsett.

At Taunton, May 13. HAMPSHIRE lost to SOMERSET by five wickets.

At Leeds, May 27. HAMPSHIRE beat YORKSHIRE by 36 runs.

At Leicester, June 3. HAMPSHIRE beat LEICESTERSHIRE by five wickets.

HAMPSHIRE v MIDDLESEX

At Basingstoke, June 10. Middlesex won by seven wickets. Toss: Middlesex. Downton, keeping wicket for Middlesex, was hit in the left eye by a bail when Emburey bowled Wood, and was later admitted to hospital.

Hampshire

R. J. Scott c Haynes b Hughes	0	R. J. Maru c Gatting b Hughes		9
V. P. Terry c Downton b Williams	4	C. A. Connor b Hughes		3
D. I. Gower c Hughes b Fraser	23	P. J. Bakker not out		0
M. D. Marshall c Butcher b Hughes	46	L-b 6, w 6, n-b 4		16
J. R. Wood b Emburey	18			
*M. C. J. Nicholas b Emburey	1	1/2 2/12 3/47	(39.5 overs)	140
J. R. Ayling c Brown b Williams	9	4/101 5/102 6/112		
†R. J. Parks b Fraser	11	7/118 8/134 9/137		

Bowling: Hughes 6.5–1–19–4; Williams 8–0–29–2; Fraser 8–1–26–2; Gatting 3–0–20–0; Haynes 6–1–21–0; Emburey 8–2–19–2.

Middlesex

D. L. Haynes b Ayling	19	K. R. Brown not out	13
M. A. Roseberry b Connor	17	B 5, l-b 5, w 5, n-b 1	16
*M. W. Gatting c and b Maru	27		
M. R. Ramprakash not out	52	1/41 2/41 3/93 (3 wkts, 37.5 overs)	144

R. O. Butcher, †P. R. Downton, N. F. Williams, J. E. Emburey, S. P. Hughes and A. R. C. Fraser did not bat.

Bowling: Marshall 8–0–19–0; Bakker 4–0–23–0; Connor 8–1–18–1; Ayling 7–0–27–1; Maru 7.5–0–40–1; Scott 3–0–7–0.

Umpires: K. E. Palmer and R. Palmer.

HAMPSHIRE v GLAMORGAN

At Bournemouth, June 17. Hampshire won by 64 runs in a match reduced to 37 overs a side. Toss: Glamorgan. Robin Smith's century came off 89 balls, and in all he faced 104 balls, hitting two sixes and thirteen fours. Butcher, when 48, passed 5,000 runs in the Sunday League.

Hampshire

V. P. Terry lbw b Watkin	2	J. R. Ayling not out	5
R. J. Scott c Dennis b Cowley	61	R. J. Maru not out	4
R. A. Smith c Maynard b Frost	122	B 1, l-b 14, w 7	22
D. I. Gower lbw b Richards	1		
M. D. Marshall c Metson b Watkin	1	1/6 2/165 3/181 (6 wkts, 37 overs)	234
*M. C. J. Nicholas b Frost	16	4/184 5/215 6/228	

†R. J. Parks, C. A. Connor and P. J. Bakker did not bat.

Bowling: Frost 8–0–49–2; Watkin 8–0–46–2; Dennis 8–0–43–0; Cowley 8–0–43–1; Richards 5–0–38–1.

Glamorgan

*A. R. Butcher c Nicholas b Ayling	52	J. Derrick c sub b Bakker	19
H. Morris c Smith b Bakker	7	S. J. Dennis not out	1
M. P. Maynard c Nicholas b Maru	34	L-b 8, w 2	10
I. V. A. Richards c Terry b Maru	8		
I. Smith c Terry b Maru	2	1/12 2/82 3/98 (7 wkts, 37 overs)	170
N. G. Cowley b Bakker	7	4/104 5/113	
†C. P. Metson not out	30	6/116 7/166	

S. L. Watkin and M. Frost did not bat.

Bowling: Connor 6–0–26–0; Bakker 8–1–33–3; Marshall 5–0–23–0; Ayling 8–0–39–1; Maru 8–0–38–3; Nicholas 2–0–3–0.

Umpires: J. W. Holder and B. J. Meyer.

At Manchester, June 24. LANCASHIRE v HAMPSHIRE. No result.

At Hove, July 1. HAMPSHIRE lost to SUSSEX on scoring-rate.

HAMPSHIRE v ESSEX

At Southampton, July 8. Hampshire won by seven wickets. Toss: Essex.

Essex

B. R. Hardie c Parks b Marshall	4	T. D. Topley c Terry b Bakker	2
J. P. Stephenson c Gower b Tremlett	28	M. C. Ilott not out	1
M. E. Waugh c Gower b Ayling	17		
P. J. Prichard c Parks b Maru	12	B 1, l-b 8, w 4	13
*D. R. Pringle c Gower b Tremlett	63		
N. Hussain b Ayling	12	1/7 2/49 3/53 (8 wkts, 40 overs) 196	
†M. A. Garnham not out	40	4/75 5/120 6/161	
N. A. Foster c Gower b Marshall	4	7/179 8/186	

J. H. Childs did not bat.

Bowling: Bakker 8–2–30–1; Marshall 8–0–33–2; Ayling 8–0–40–2; Tremlett 8–1–43–2; Maru 8–0–41–1.

Hampshire

V. P. Terry c Hardie b Foster	52	C. L. Smith not out	22
R. J. Scott lbw b Foster	7	B 2, l-b 4, w 2, n-b 2	10
*D. I. Gower c Childs b Topley	66		
M. D. Marshall not out	43	1/23 2/130 3/132 (3 wkts, 39 overs) 200	

J. R. Ayling, T. C. Middleton, †R. J. Parks, T. M. Tremlett, R. J. Maru and P. J. Bakker did not bat.

Bowling: Foster 8–0–43–2; Ilott 7–1–34–0; Childs 8–2–36–0; Topley 8–0–32–1; Pringle 7–0–42–0; Waugh 1–0–7–0.

Umpires: B. Hassan and D. R. Shepherd.

HAMPSHIRE v NOTTINGHAMSHIRE

At Southampton, July 15. Hampshire won by 7 runs. Toss: Nottinghamshire.

Hampshire

V. P. Terry c Robinson b Cooper	3	*M. C. J. Nicholas not out	46
R. J. Scott b Saxelby	55	L-b 5, w 7, n-b 1	13
R. A. Smith c Newell b Afford	77		
D. I. Gower not out	66	1/15 2/134 3/154 (4 wkts, 40 overs) 267	
M. D. Marshall run out	7	4/162	

J. R. Ayling, †R. J. Parks, R. J. Maru, C. A. Connor and P. J. Bakker did not bat.

Bowling: Cooper 8–0–44–1; Stephenson 8–1–43–0; Hemmings 7–0–36–0; Mike 4–0–26–0; Afford 8–0–74–1; Saxelby 5–0–39–1.

Nottinghamshire

B. C. Broad b Connor	86	M. Newell not out	11
P. Johnson c Parks b Marshall	9	E. E. Hemmings not out	32
*R. T. Robinson b Maru	44		
M. Saxelby b Ayling	24	B 5, l-b 9, w 3, n-b 3	20
F. D. Stephenson c Nicholas b Ayling	14		
G. W. Mike c Scott b Ayling	10	1/34 2/142 3/155 (8 wkts, 40 overs) 260	
†B. N. French c Terry b Ayling	9	4/182 5/196 6/205	
K. E. Cooper b Marshall	1	7/213 8/214	

J. A. Afford did not bat.

Bowling: Bakker 7–0–52–0; Marshall 8–0–36–2; Connor 7–0–49–1; Ayling 8–0–37–4; Maru 5–0–38–1; Scott 5–0–34–0.

Umpires: J. H. Harris and A. G. T. Whitehead.

HAMPSHIRE v DERBYSHIRE

At Portsmouth, July 22. Hampshire won by 189 runs. Toss: Derbyshire. Derbyshire's total was their lowest in the Sunday League, while the margin of 189 runs was Hampshire's largest and Derbyshire's worst in the competition.

Hampshire

*M. C. J. Nicholas c Malcolm		C. L. Smith run out	30
b Mortensen .	4	J. R. Ayling not out	0
R. J. Scott c Roberts b Malcolm	76	L-b 4, w 5	9
R. A. Smith c Kuiper b Malcolm	83		
D. I. Gower not out	47	1/8 2/155 3/178 (5 wkts, 38 overs) 250	
M. D. Marshall run out	1	4/180 5/245	

†R. J. Parks, R. J. Maru, C. A. Connor and P. J. Bakker did not bat.

Bowling: Base 7-0-37-0; Mortensen 7-0-35-1; Malcolm 8-0-50-2; Miller 8-0-54-0; Goldsmith 4-0-42-0; Kuiper 4-0-28-0.

Derbyshire

*K. J. Barnett c Nicholas b Bakker	5	D. E. Malcolm b Connor	9
J. E. Morris c Parks b Marshall	1	O. H. Mortensen not out	2
B. Roberts c Parks b Connor	10	G. Miller absent injured	
A. P. Kuiper c C. L. Smith b Bakker	1	L-b 3, w 3	6
C. J. Adams c Parks b Connor	21		
S. C. Goldsmith c C. L. Smith b Bakker	4	1/6 2/6 3/14 (19.1 overs) 61	
†K. M. Krikken b Connor	0	4/22 5/37 6/38	
S. J. Base b Ayling	2	7/42 8/50 9/61	

Bowling: Bakker 6-1-31-3; Marshall 4-2-4-1; Connor 5.1-0-11-4; Ayling 3-0-9-1; Scott 1-0-3-0.

Umpires: J. C. Balderstone and D. J. Constant.

At Birmingham, July 29. HAMPSHIRE beat WARWICKSHIRE by three wickets.

HAMPSHIRE v NORTHAMPTONSHIRE

At Bournemouth, August 5. Hampshire won by six wickets. Toss: Northamptonshire.

Northamptonshire

A. Fordham c Scott b Marshall	63	D. J. Wild not out	16
W. Larkins c Scott b Bakker	7	B 1, l-b 2, w 2, n-b 5	10
R. J. Bailey c Marshall b Maru	33		
*A. J. Lamb b Connor	45	1/19 2/109 3/111 (4 wkts, 40 overs) 208	
R. G. Williams not out	34	4/180	

J. W. Govan, †D. Ripley, N. G. B. Cook, M. A. Robinson and S. J. Brown did not bat.

Bowling: Bakker 7-0-36-1; Marshall 8-1-33-1; Connor 8-0-51-1; Ayling 8-0-44-0; Maru 8-0-28-1; Scott 1-0-13-0.

Hampshire

V. P. Terry c Robinson b Brown	84	*M. C. J. Nicholas not out	0
R. J. Scott c Ripley b Brown	70	L-b 9, w 2, n-b 1	12
R. A. Smith c and b Cook	9		
D. I. Gower c Bailey b Cook	18	1/127 2/140 (4 wkts, 37.5 overs) 210	
M. D. Marshall not out	17	3/188 4/200	

J. R. Ayling, †R. J. Parks, R. J. Maru, C. A. Connor and P. J. Bakker did not bat.

Bowling: Robinson 7-1-21-0; Brown 6.5-0-37-2; Wild 4-0-23-0; Cook 8-1-42-2; Govan 3-0-23-0; Larkins 4-0-26-0; Williams 5-0-29-0.

Umpires: B. J. Meyer and D. O. Oslear.

At Worcester, August 12. HAMPSHIRE beat WORCESTERSHIRE by 20 runs.

HAMPSHIRE v SURREY

At Southampton, August 26. Surrey won by 4 runs. Toss: Hampshire. Hampshire, needing to win to qualify for the Refuge Assurance Cup, were well placed at 192 for one before losing Middleton, Marshall, Smith, Ayling and Nicholas in the space of twelve deliveries. In dismissing Marshall, Waqar Younis passed I. A. Greig's Surrey record of 28 wickets in a season in 1988. Surrey's winning total was built around a century off 71 balls by Ward.

Surrey

A. J. Stewart c Nicholas b Connor	 36	*I. A. Greig not out	....	1
A. D. Brown b Tremlett	 24			
G. P. Thorpe lbw b Tremlett	 26	B 1, l-b 3, w 4, n-b 3	....	11
†D. M. Ward not out	102			
M. A. Lynch b Maru	 26	1/44 2/69 3/103	(5 wkts, 39 overs)	248
J. D. Robinson c Middleton b Maru	... 7	4/154 5/186		

K. T. Medlycott, C. K. Bullen, A. J. Murphy and Waqar Younis did not bat.

Bowling: Bakker 5–0–35–0; Marshall 8–0–50–0; Tremlett 8–0–33–2; Connor 7–0–45–1; Maru 5–0–31–2; Ayling 5–0–50–0.

Hampshire

V. P. Terry run out	 56	T. M. Tremlett c Brown b Greig	......	2
T. C. Middleton run out	 72	C. A. Connor not out	....	
*M. C. J. Nicholas b Waqar Younis	... 59	P. J. Bakker not out	....	2
M. D. Marshall lbw b Waqar Younis	.. 0	B 4, l-b 8, w 4	....	16
C. L. Smith c Stewart b Murphy	 0			
J. R. Ayling run out	 3	1/100 2/192 3/192	(9 wkts, 38 overs)	244
†R. J. Parks b Waqar Younis	 10	4/193 5/196 6/200		
R. J. Maru c Stewart b Murphy	 1	7/203 8/223 9/235		

Bowling: Murphy 8–0–41–2; Robinson 5–0–22–0; Greig 5–0–37–1; Medlycott 7–0–49–0; Bullen 5–0–43–0; Waqar Younis 8–0–40–3.

Umpires: J. D. Bond and A. A. Jones.

KENT

At Chelmsford, April 22. KENT beat ESSEX by 27 runs.

KENT v HAMPSHIRE

At Canterbury, April 29. Kent won by 53 runs. Toss: Kent.

Kent

S. G. Hinks c Terry b James	 1	M. V. Fleming not out	....	2
N. R. Taylor st Parks b Scott	 95	R. M. Ellison not out	....	
T. R. Ward c Connor b Maru	 24	L-b 3, w 3	....	
*C. S. Cowdrey c Connor b Tremlett	.. 18			
G. R. Cowdrey st Parks b Scott	 22	1/3 2/51 3/87	(6 wkts, 40 overs)	215
†S. A. Marsh c Terry b Connor	 15	4/134 5/173 6/186		

M. A. Ealham, R. P. Davis and T. A. Merrick did not bat.

Bowling: James 8–0–33–1; Connor 8–2–49–1; Tremlett 5–0–22–1; Maru 6–0–29–1; Marshall 8–0–41–0; Scott 5–0–36–2.

Hampshire

*V. P. Terry b Ellison	9	T. M. Tremlett c C. S. Cowdrey	
R. J. Scott lbw b Merrick	0	b Fleming	18
R. A. Smith c C. S. Cowdrey b Fleming	22	R. J. Maru not out	12
D. I. Gower c Fleming b Davis	32	L-b 6, w 2, n-b 1	9
C. L. Smith not out	47		
K. D. James c Marsh b Davis	4	1/12 2/12 3/61 (8 wkts, 40 overs) 160	
M. D. Marshall c Fleming b Davis	3	4/71 5/78 6/93	
†R. J. Parks b Davis	4	7/98 8/133	
C. A. Connor did not bat.			

Bowling: Ellison 8–0–23–1; Merrick 8–0–32–1; Ealham 8–0–35–0; Davis 8–0–25–4; Fleming 8–0–39–2.

Umpires: J. W. Holder and K. J. Lyons.

KENT v MIDDLESEX

At Folkestone, May 6. Middlesex won by six wickets. Toss: Middlesex.

Kent

S. G. Hinks run out	86	R. M. Ellison not out	11
N. R. Taylor b Emburey	28	T. A. Merrick not out	1
T. R. Ward lbw b Taylor	24	L-b 8	8
*C. S. Cowdrey c Roseberry b Cowans	20		
G. R. Cowdrey st Downton b Gatting	28	1/72 2/129 3/155 (6 wkts, 40 overs) 224	
†S. A. Marsh st Downton b Emburey	18	4/170 5/202 6/222	
R. P. Davis, M. A. Ealham and C. Penn did not bat.			

Bowling: Williams 7–0–51–0; Cowans 8–2–29–1; Taylor 8–0–47–1; Emburey 8–1–36–2; Gatting 7–0–41–1; Haynes 2–0–12–0.

Middlesex

D. L. Haynes c G. R. Cowdrey b Davis	67	†P. R. Downton not out	9
M. A. Roseberry lbw b Ealham	52	L-b 15, w 3	18
M. R. Ramprakash c Ealham b Ellison	32		
K. R. Brown c Marsh b Ward	20	1/112 2/134 (4 wkts, 37.5 overs) 225	
R. O. Butcher not out	27	3/180 4/204	

*M. W. Gatting, J. E. Emburey, N. F. Williams, N. R. Taylor and N. G. Cowans did not bat.

Bowling: Penn 3–0–22–0; Merrick 7.5–0–39–0; Ellison 7–0–32–1; Davis 8–0–29–1; Ealham 7–0–47–1; C. S. Cowdrey 3–0–24–0; Ward 2–0–17–1.

Umpires: D. J. Constant and N. T. Plews.

At Llanelli, May 13. KENT beat GLAMORGAN by two wickets.

KENT v YORKSHIRE

At Canterbury, May 20. Kent won by 69 runs. Toss: Kent. Merrick took three wickets in five balls for no runs, and later forced Yorkshire's White to retire from a blow to the face.

Kent

S. G. Hinks b Fletcher	89	†S. A. Marsh not out	2
N. R. Taylor c Gough b White	35		
T. R. Ward c Gough b White	37	B 1, l-b 11, w 8	20
*C. S. Cowdrey c sub b Gough	18		
G. R. Cowdrey not out	31	1/74 2/156 3/195 (5 wkts, 40 overs) 245	
M. V. Fleming b Fletcher	13	4/196 5/229	

M. A. Ealham, C. Penn, R. P. Davis and T. A. Merrick did not bat.

Bowling: Pickles 8–0–42–0; Jarvis 8–0–37–0; Fletcher 8–1–32–2; Gough 8–0–54–1; White 6–0–49–2; Byas 2–0–19–0.

Yorkshire

*M. D. Moxon c Davis b Fleming	43	P. W. Jarvis c Marsh b Merrick	1
A. A. Metcalfe b Davis	32	D. Gough b Penn	4
R. J. Blakey b Davis	9	S. D. Fletcher not out	1
D. Byas c Ward b Ealham	25	B 4, l-b 8, w 2	14
P. E. Robinson c Taylor b Ealham	17		
†D. L. Bairstow c Marsh b Merrick	10	1/59 2/75 3/105 (36.3 overs) 176	
C. White retired hurt	20	4/122 5/135 6/152	
C. S. Pickles c C. S. Cowdrey b Merrick	0	7/152 8/156 9/176	

C. White retired hurt at 170-8.

Bowling: Penn 6.3–0–28–1; Merrick 7–0–22–3; Fleming 8–1–47–1; Ealham 4–0–25–2; Davis 8–0–30–2; C. S. Cowdrey 3–0–12–0.

Umpires: P. J. Eele and J. W. Holder.

At Northampton, May 27. KENT beat NORTHAMPTONSHIRE by 55 runs.

KENT v SOMERSET

At Canterbury, June 10. Kent won by six wickets. Toss: Kent.

Somerset

S. J. Cook c c C. S. Cowdrey b Fleming	50	M. W. Cleal run out	0
P. M. Roebuck c Benson		I. G. Swallow not out	0
b C. S. Cowdrey	29		
G. D. Rose b Merrick	29	L-b 6, w 2	8
*C. J. Tavaré c Benson b C. S. Cowdrey	11		
R. J. Harden not out	21	1/80 2/89 3/125 (7 wkts, 40 overs) 165	
†N. D. Burns b Igglesden	14	4/127 5/156	
A. N. Hayhurst b Merrick	3	6/163 7/163	

N. A. Mallender and A. N. Jones did not bat.

Bowling: Igglesden 8–0–27–1; Merrick 8–2–26–2; Fleming 8–0–27–1; Ealham 8–0–42–0; Davis 3–0–17–0; C. S. Cowdrey 5–0–20–2.

Kent

S. G. Hinks c Cook b Mallender	1	M. V. Fleming not out	11
M. R. Benson c Roebuck b Rose	55	B 1, l-b 6, w 4	11
N. R. Taylor c Cook b Jones	59		
*C. S. Cowdrey not out	26	1/1 2/121 3/127 (4 wkts, 37.5 overs) 169	
G. R. Cowdrey c Cook b Jones	6	4/150	

†S. A. Marsh, M. A. Ealham, A. P. Igglesden, T. A. Merrick and R. P. Davis did not bat.

Bowling: Jones 8–0–25–2; Mallender 7.5–0–29–1; Rose 8–0–29–1; Cleal 2–0–9–0; Hayhurst 5–0–34–0; Swallow 3–0–12–0; Roebuck 4–0–24–0.

Umpires: D. J. Constant and B. J. Meyer.

KENT v NOTTINGHAMSHIRE

At Canterbury, June 17. Kent won by 24 runs. Toss: Kent. Igglesden hurried his side to victory by taking three wickets in five balls.

Kent

. G. Hinks c Saxelby b Stephenson	... 12	T. A. Merrick not out	....	12
A. A. Ealham c Evans b Stephenson	.. 2	A. P. Igglesden run out	....	0
N. R. Taylor c and b Hemmings	... 28	R. P. Davis not out	....	0
C. S. Cowdrey c Broad b Saxelby	.. 13	L-b 6, w 6, n-b 3	....	15
G. R. Cowdrey c Broad b Stephenson	. 46			
A. V. Fleming b Saxelby	 21	1/10 2/17 3/54	(9 wkts, 40 overs)	178
S. A. Marsh run out	 20	4/73 5/124 6/148		
R. M. Ellison b Stephenson	 9	7/154 8/171 9/171		

Bowling: Stephenson 8–0–28–4; Cooper 8–1–33–0; Saxelby 8–0–48–2; Evans 7–1–34–0; Afford 4–1–12–0; Hemmings 5–0–17–1.

Nottinghamshire

B. C. Broad c Marsh b Igglesden	 8	E. E. Hemmings c Ealham b Igglesden	.	15
D. W. Randall run out	 49	K. E. Cooper c Taylor b Igglesden	...	1
P. Johnson c Marsh b Merrick	 3	J. A. Afford not out		0
R. T. Robinson b Fleming	 3	L-b 7, w 4	....	11
M. Saxelby c G. R. Cowdrey b Davis	.. 25			
B. N. French c and b Davis	 0	1/20 2/23 3/28	(38.3 overs)	154
*. D. Stephenson lbw b C. S. Cowdrey	. 9	4/93 5/93 6/97		
K. P. Evans c Ellison b Igglesden	 30	7/111 8/144 9/154		

Bowling: Igglesden 6.3–1–24–4; Merrick 7–0–26–1; Fleming 8–0–21–1; Ellison 2–0–18–0; Ealham 3–0–18–0; Davis 8–0–25–2; C. S. Cowdrey 4–0–15–1.

Umpires: B. Leadbeater and R. A. White.

At Birmingham, June 24. KENT lost to WARWICKSHIRE by three wickets.

KENT v LANCASHIRE

At Maidstone, July 1. Lancashire won by 77 runs. Toss: Kent. Lloyd, on his 21st birthday, completed his first Sunday League hundred in the final over, having faced 88 balls, of which twelve went for four. He had been dropped by Fleming off Ellison when 10.

Lancashire

G. Fowler c Wells b C. S. Cowdrey	... 59	M. Watkinson not out	....	33
M. A. Atherton c Marsh b Fleming	... 13	L-b 3, w 6	....	9
G. D. Lloyd not out	100			
N. H. Fairbrother c Ealham b de Villiers	45	1/33 2/112 3/201	(3 wkts, 40 overs)	259

Wasim Akram, *D. P. Hughes, I. D. Austin, P. A. J. DeFreitas, †W. K. Hegg and P. J. W. Allott did not bat.

Bowling: Igglesden 8–0–39–0; de Villiers 8–0–53–1; Ellison 4–0–24–0; Fleming 8–0–51–1; Ealham 3–0–21–0; Davis 5–0–33–0; C. S. Cowdrey 4–0–35–1.

Kent

S. G. Hinks b Allott	 17	P. S. de Villiers c Watkinson b DeFreitas		1
M. A. Ealham lbw b Allott	 3	R. P. Davis b Austin	....	14
V. J. Wells c Fowler b DeFreitas	 13	A. P. Igglesden not out	....	0
C. S. Cowdrey b Watkinson	 33			
G. R. Cowdrey c Hegg b Allott	 0	B 2, l-b 9, w 1	....	12
M. V. Fleming c Fairbrother b Wasim Akram	. 8	1/11 2/34 3/36	(37.1 overs)	182
*S. A. Marsh c Hughes b Watkinson	.. 38	4/38 5/69 6/90		
R. M. Ellison b Wasim Akram	 43	7/148 8/151 9/182		

Bowling: Allott 7–1–28–3; DeFreitas 8–0–48–2; Watkinson 8–0–37–2; Wasim Akram 7.1–0–31–2; Austin 7–0–27–1.

Umpires: J. C. Balderstone and B. Dudleston.

At The Oval, July 22. KENT lost to SURREY by five wickets.

KENT v WORCESTERSHIRE

At Canterbury, July 29. Worcestershire won by five wickets. Toss: Worcestershire.

Kent

S. G. Hinks c Botham b Lampitt	51	R. M. Ellison not out	6
M. R. Benson lbw b Newport	24	T. A. Merrick c Rhodes b Botham	1
V. J. Wells c Radford b Botham	16		
T. R. Ward c Lampitt b Botham	45	L-b 5, w 3, n-b 1	9
*C. S. Cowdrey c D'Oliveira b Illingworth	4	1/34 2/85 3/113 (8 wkts, 40 overs) 184	
M. V. Fleming b Illingworth	8	4/123 5/141 6/159	
†S. A. Marsh b Illingworth	7	7/165 8/184	

R. P. Davis and A. P. Igglesden did not bat.

Bowling: Weston 6–0–26–0; Newport 8–1–18–1; Botham 7–0–54–3; Radford 3–0–24–0; Lampitt 8–0–38–1; Illingworth 8–1–19–3.

Worcestershire

I. T. Botham b Davis	45	†S. J. Rhodes not out	6
M. J. Weston c Merrick b Fleming	6		
G. A. Hick b Davis	25	B 2, l-b 13, w 1	16
D. B. D'Oliveira c Merrick b Ellison	35		
*P. A. Neale c Marsh b Merrick	39	1/31 2/83 3/84 (5 wkts, 38 overs) 185	
D. A. Leatherdale not out	20	4/148 5/178	

N. V. Radford, P. J. Newport, R. K. Illingworth and S. R. Lampitt did not bat.

Bowling: Igglesden 7–1–26–0; Merrick 7–0–38–1; Fleming 8–0–32–1; Ellison 8–0–37–1; Davis 5–0–30–2; Cowdrey 3–0–9–0.

Umpires: A. A. Jones and R. Julian.

At Chesterfield, August 5. KENT lost to DERBYSHIRE by six wickets.

At Bristol, August 12. KENT lost to GLOUCESTERSHIRE by six wickets.

KENT v SUSSEX

At Canterbury, August 19. No result.

At Leicester, August 26. KENT lost to LEICESTERSHIRE by six wickets.

LANCASHIRE

LANCASHIRE v MIDDLESEX

At Manchester, April 22. Middlesex won by eight wickets. Toss: Middlesex. Haynes reached his hundred off 97 balls, with three sixes and eight fours, while Fowler's century had come off 118 balls, including ten fours. The Middlesex opening partnership of 176 between Haynes and Roseberry was a record for any wicket against Lancashire in the Sunday League.

Lancashire

G. Fowler lbw b Williams	101	I. D. Austin not out	8
M. A. Atherton b Emburey	63		
N. H. Fairbrother run out	1	L-b 6, w 5, n-b 1	12
G. D. Lloyd run out	7		
M. Watkinson c Emburey b Williams	7	1/141 2/148 3/181 (7 wkts, 40 overs) 215	
P. A. J. DeFreitas c Brown b Williams	6	4/187 5/190	
T. E. Jesty lbw b Williams	10	6/196 7/215	

D. P. Hughes, P. J. W. Allott and †W. K. Hegg did not bat.

Bowling: Williams 8–0–49–4; Hemstock 8–0–43–0; Emburey 8–1–35–1; Carr 4–0–20–0; Weekes 4–0–21–0; Haynes 7.2–0–34–0; Ramprakash 1–0–7–0.

Middlesex

D. L. Haynes not out	107
M. A. Roseberry lbw b Watkinson	73
M. R. Ramprakash run out	22
K. R. Brown not out	2
L-b 9, w 4, n-b 2	15

1/176 2/213   (2 wkts, 38.2 overs) 219

R. Hemstock, *M. W. Gatting, †P. R. Downton, J. E. Emburey, P. N. Weekes, J. D. Carr and N. F. Williams did not bat.

Bowling: DeFreitas 8–0–35–0; Allott 8–1–20–0; Austin 6–0–45–0; Watkinson 7.2–0–50–1; Jesty 2–0–16–0; Atherton 4–0–24–0; Hughes 3–0–20–0.

Umpires: J. H. Hampshire and R. A. White.

At Nottingham, April 29. LANCASHIRE beat NOTTINGHAMSHIRE by five wickets.

At The Oval, May 6. LANCASHIRE beat SURREY by seven wickets.

LANCASHIRE v LEICESTERSHIRE

At Manchester, May 20. Lancashire won by 23 runs. Toss: Leicestershire. Fowler faced 110 balls for his 108, hitting one six and twelve fours.

Lancashire

G. Fowler c Boon b Taylor	108	†W. K. Hegg lbw b Lewis	0
M. A. Atherton b Willey	33	*D. P. Hughes not out	0
N. H. Fairbrother c and b Willey	27		
G. D. Lloyd c Nixon b Lewis	10	L-b 9, w 5	14
T. E. Jesty b Lewis	19		
Wasim Akram b Benson	5	1/117 2/157 3/173 (9 wkts, 39 overs) 225	
P. A. J. DeFreitas b Lewis	7	4/186 5/200 6/212	
I. D. Austin c Whitaker b Agnew	2	7/217 8/224 9/225	

P. J. W. Allott did not bat.

Bowling: Benjamin 5–0–23–0; Lewis 8–1–34–4; Agnew 7–0–39–1; Taylor 8–0–65–1; Willey 8–0–39–2; Benson 3–0–16–1.

Leicestershire

T. J. Boon c Hegg b Austin	46	J. D. R. Benson b DeFreitas	2
*N. E. Briers run out	26	†P. A. Nixon not out	1
J. J. Whitaker c Allott b Austin	34	B 1, l-b 10, w 2, n-b 1	14
P. Willey c Atherton b Austin	18		
C. C. Lewis c Hughes b DeFreitas	10	1/66 2/94 3/131 (6 wkts, 39 overs)	202
L. Potter not out	32	4/143 5/145 6/197	

W. K. M. Benjamin, J. P. Agnew and L. B. Taylor did not bat.

Bowling: DeFreitas 7–0–40–2; Allott 8–0–46–0; Atherton 8–0–40–0; Wasim Akram 8–0–32–0; Austin 8–0–33–3.

Umpires: B. Hassan and R. Palmer.

At Colwyn Bay, May 27. LANCASHIRE beat GLAMORGAN by four wickets.

At Horsham, June 3. SUSSEX v LANCASHIRE. No result.

LANCASHIRE v GLOUCESTERSHIRE

At Manchester, June 10. Gloucestershire won by two wickets. Toss: Gloucestershire.

Lancashire

G. D. Mendis c and b Lawrence	32	†W. K. Hegg not out	2
G. Fowler run out	6	I. D. Austin not out	1
G. D. Lloyd run out	85	B 2, l-b 11, w 9	22
T. E. Jesty c Lawrence b Alleyne	22		
M. Watkinson c Bainbridge b Alleyne	23	1/22 2/68 3/109 (6 wkts, 40 overs)	230
Wasim Akram b Walsh	37	4/162 5/220 6/229	

*D. P. Hughes, J. D. Fitton and P. J. W. Allott did not bat.

Bowling: Walsh 8–0–46–1; Curran 8–0–52–0; Bainbridge 8–0–39–0; Lawrence 8–0–38–1 Alleyne 8–0–42–2.

Gloucestershire

I. P. Butcher c Fowler b Watkinson	13	C. A. Walsh b Wasim Akram	12
C. W. J. Athey c Hegg b Watkinson	6	†G. A. Tedstone not out	1
*A. J. Wright c Mendis b Watkinson	68		
K. M. Curran c Hegg b Wasim Akram	7	L-b 14, w 7, n-b 1	22
P. Bainbridge b Wasim Akram	39		
J. W. Lloyds lbw b Wasim Akram	0	1/15 2/30 3/49 (8 wkts, 39.4 overs)	231
P. W. Romaines not out	45	4/139 5/139 6/166	
M. W. Alleyne st Hegg b Fitton	18	7/188 8/225	

D. V. Lawrence did not bat.

Bowling: Watkinson 8–0–22–3; Allott 8–0–46–0; Wasim Akram 8–0–39–4; Fitton 8–0–53–1; Austin 7.4–0–57–0.

Umpires: M. J. Kitchen and K. J. Lyons.

LANCASHIRE v HAMPSHIRE

At Manchester, June 24. No result. Toss: Hampshire. The match, already reduced to 23 overs a side, was abandoned after only one over.

Lancashire

G. D. Mendis not out 1
G. Fowler not out 1
    W 1 1

     (no wkt, 1 over) 3

G. D. Lloyd, T. E. Jesty, M. Watkinson, Wasim Akram, I. D. Austin, *D. P. Hughes, J. D. Fitton, †J. Stanworth and P. J. W. Allott did not bat.

Bowling: Marshall 1–0–3–0.

Hampshire

V. P. Terry, R. J. Scott, C. L. Smith, D. I. Gower, M. D. Marshall, *M. C. J. Nicholas, J. R. Ayling, R. J. Maru, †R. J. Parks, C. A. Connor and T. M. Tremlett.

Umpires: H. D. Bird and P. J. Eele.

At Maidstone, July 1. LANCASHIRE beat KENT by 77 runs.

LANCASHIRE v DERBYSHIRE

At Manchester, July 8. Derbyshire won by 5 runs. Toss: Lancashire.

Derbyshire

*K. J. Barnett c Wasim Akram		C. J. Adams b Wasim Akram 14	
b Watkinson . 85		S. C. Goldsmith not out 7	
†P. D. Bowler c Allott b Watkinson ... 40		L-b 8, w 3, n-b 2 13	
J. E. Morris c Lloyd b DeFreitas 55			
A. P. Kuiper c Allott b DeFreitas 7		1/108 2/175 3/198 (6 wkts, 40 overs) 249	
B. Roberts b Allott 28		4/198 5/230 6/249	

S. J. Base, G. Miller, A. E. Warner and O. H. Mortensen did not bat.

Bowling: Allott 8–0–34–1; DeFreitas 8–0–53–2; Watkinson 8–0–42–2; Wasim Akram 8–0–59–1; Austin 8–0–53–0.

Lancashire

G. D. Mendis c Barnett b Kuiper 71		I. D. Austin c Bowler b Kuiper 3	
G. D. Lloyd c Bowler b Base 1		*D. P. Hughes not out 21	
†W. K. Hegg run out 10		P. J. W. Allott run out 12	
T. E. Jesty b Miller 20		B 1, l-b 12, w 4 17	
G. Fowler lbw b Warner 57			
M. Watkinson c and b Base 8		1/6 2/30 3/81 (39.5 overs) 244	
Wasim Akram c Adams b Kuiper 7		4/134 5/147 6/158	
P. A. J. DeFreitas c Kuiper b Base ... 17		7/189 8/203 9/207	

Bowling: Mortensen 8–1–25–0; Base 7.5–0–49–3; Miller 8–0–50–1; Warner 8–0–57–1; Kuiper 8–0–50–3.

Umpires: R. Julian and D. O. Oslear.

LANCASHIRE v WORCESTERSHIRE

At Manchester, July 15. Lancashire won by seven wickets. Toss: Lancashire.

Worcestershire

*T. S. Curtis lbw b Watkinson	32	P. J. Newport not out	16
M. J. Weston c Fowler b Watkinson	31	S. R. Lampitt c DeFreitas b Austin	0
G. A. Hick b Wasim Akram	42	C. M. Tolley not out	1
D. B. D'Oliveira c Hegg b Watkinson	3	L-b 8, w 6	14
D. A. Leatherdale c Hughes b Watkinson	4		
†S. J. Rhodes b Austin	12	1/68 2/68 3/80 (8 wkts, 40 overs) 157
N. V. Radford c Atherton		4/92 5/117 6/125
b Wasim Akram	2	7/148 8/149

S. M. McEwan did not bat.

Bowling: Allott 8-0-31-0; DeFreitas 8-1-28-0; Watkinson 8-0-30-4; Wasim Akram 8-0-34-2; Austin 8-1-26-2.

Lancashire

G. Fowler c Curtis b Lampitt	33	M. Watkinson not out	15
M. A. Atherton c Rhodes b Tolley	1	L-b 5, w 4, n-b 1	10
G. D. Lloyd not out	65		
N. H. Fairbrother run out	36	1/4 2/71 3/125 (3 wkts, 30.1 overs) 160

Wasim Akram, †W. K. Hegg, *D. P. Hughes, P. A. J. DeFreitas, I. D. Austin and P. J. W. Allott did not bat.

Bowling: Newport 7-0-31-0; Tolley 6-0-20-1; Radford 4-0-24-0; Lampitt 7.1-0-34-1; McEwan 3-0-23-0; Hick 2-0-17-0; Leatherdale 1-0-6-0.

Umpires: B. Hassan and J. W. Holder.

At Colchester, July 22. LANCASHIRE beat ESSEX by two wickets.

LANCASHIRE v SOMERSET

At Manchester, July 29. Lancashire won by six wickets. Toss: Somerset.

Somerset

S. J. Cook c Martin b Wasim Akram	41	R. P. Lefebvre not out	14
R. J. Bartlett c Lloyd b Watkinson	55	I. G. Swallow not out	7
*C. J. Tavaré c Mendis b Austin	17	L-b 2, w 4, n-b 5	11
R. J. Harden b Wasim Akram	32		
G. D. Rose b Austin	1	1/73 2/110 3/122 (7 wkts, 40 overs) 203
†N. D. Burns b Watkinson	8	4/124 5/140
A. N. Hayhurst c Fowler b Austin	17	6/174 7/188

N. A. Mallender and J. C. Hallett did not bat.

Bowling: DeFreitas 8-0-36-0; Martin 8-0-38-0; Wasim Akram 8-0-36-2; Watkinson 8-0-57-2; Austin 8-1-34-3.

Lancashire

G. Fowler c Rose b Swallow	60	M. Watkinson not out	11
G. D. Mendis c Burns b Mallender	7	L-b 7, w 3, n-b 2	12
G. D. Lloyd c Hayhurst b Rose	57		
*N. H. Fairbrother c Rose b Hallett	47	1/12 2/103 3/171 (4 wkts, 37.4 overs) 207
T. E. Jesty not out	13	4/186

Wasim Akram, P. A. J. DeFreitas, I. D. Austin, †W. K. Hegg and P. J. Martin did not bat.

Bowling: Mallender 8-1-37-1; Rose 8-0-24-1; Hallett 4.4-0-31-1; Hayhurst 4-0-23-0; Swallow 7-0-41-1; Lefebvre 6-0-44-0.

Umpires: J. W. Holder and A. G. T. Whitehead.

At Scarborough, August 5. LANCASHIRE beat YORKSHIRE by 78 runs.

At Northampton, August 12. LANCASHIRE beat NORTHAMPTONSHIRE by seven wickets.

LANCASHIRE v WARWICKSHIRE

At Manchester, August 26. Lancashire won by 49 runs. Toss: Warwickshire. Fowler's tenth Sunday League fifty in 1990 increased his Lancashire record aggregate for a Sunday League season to 773 runs at 55.21.

Lancashire

G. D. Mendis lbw b Munton	9	†W. K. Hegg not out		10
G. Fowler b Smith	69	I. D. Austin not out		2
G. D. Lloyd b Asif Din b Twose	31	B 1, l-b 7, w 6, n-b 1		15
N. H. Fairbrother c Asif Din b Twose	20			
M. Watkinson b Smith	22	1/17 2/100 3/138	(7 wkts, 39 overs)	241
Wasim Akram b Reeve	31	4/143 5/172		
P. A. J. DeFreitas c Moody b Benjamin	32	6/226 7/231		

*D. P. Hughes and P. J. W. Allott did not bat.

Bowling: Small 0.3–0–3–0; Moody 3.3–0–32–0; Munton 7–0–45–1; Benjamin 8–0–41–1; Reeve 6–0–31–1; Twose 6–0–38–2; Smith 8–2–43–2.

Warwickshire

A. J. Moles b DeFreitas	70	J. E. Benjamin c Austin b Watkinson		24
Asif Din c Hegg b Allott	1	T. A. Munton not out		4
T. M. Moody b Allott	17	G. C. Small absent injured		
*T. A. Lloyd b Wasim Akram	16	B 1, l-b 8, w 4, n-b 1		14
D. A. Reeve lbw b Watkinson	0			
R. G. Twose c Fowler b Watkinson	6	1/3 2/45 3/78	(35.4 overs)	192
N. M. K. Smith c Lloyd b Watkinson	10	4/79 5/99 6/116		
†K. J. Piper b Watkinson	30	7/136 8/178 9/192		

Bowling: DeFreitas 8–0–34–1; Allott 8–0–51–2; Wasim Akram 6–0–21–1; Watkinson 7.4–0–46–5; Austin 6–0–31–0.

Umpires: J. H. Harris and B. Hassan.

LEICESTERSHIRE

LEICESTERSHIRE v NORTHAMPTONSHIRE

At Leicester, April 22. Northamptonshire won by six wickets. Toss: Northamptonshire. Robinson's figures were the most economical for Northamptonshire since Sarfraz Nawaz's 8–4–7–2 against Worcestershire at Worcester in 1977.

Leicestershire

T. J. Boon b Capel	9	J. P. Agnew b Brown		1
*N. E. Briers c Lamb b Cook	10	A. D. Mullally not out		0
J. J. Whitaker c Ripley b Robinson	32	L. B. Taylor lbw b Brown		0
P. Willey c Bailey b Cook	5	L-b 9, w 6, n-b 2		17
J. D. R. Benson b Thomas	8			
C. C. Lewis b Thomas	9	1/20 2/35 3/43	(38 overs)	139
†P. Whitticase c Lamb b Thomas	38	4/66 5/80 6/97		
M. I. Gidley c Capel b Brown	10	7/134 8/137 9/138		

Bowling: Capel 6–2–18–1; Brown 6–0–26–3; Robinson 8–4–8–1; Cook 8–1–31–2; Thomas 7–1–27–3; Penberthy 3–0–20–0.

Northamptonshire

W. Larkins c Whitticase b Lewis	17	A. L. Penberthy not out	0
R. J. Bailey c Lewis b Gidley	70	W 5	5
*A. J. Lamb c Whitaker b Lewis	4		
D. J. Capel not out	47	1/39 2/53 3/138 (4 wkts, 37.1 overs)	143
D. J. Wild lbw b Lewis	0	4/139	

†D. Ripley, J. G. Thomas, N. G. B. Cook, M. A. Robinson and S. J. Brown did not bat.

Bowling: Taylor 7–1–34–0; Mullally 6–0–33–0; Lewis 8–0–18–3; Agnew 8–1–25–0; Gidley 6.1–0–28–1; Willey 2–0–5–0.

Umpires: J. W. Holder and B. J. Meyer.

At Cardiff, April 29. LEICESTERSHIRE lost to GLAMORGAN by 32 runs.

LEICESTERSHIRE v ESSEX

At Leicester, May 6. Leicestershire won by five wickets. Toss: Essex. Gooch became the eighth to pass 6,000 runs in the Sunday League. In Leicestershire's reply, Lewis's 93 not out came off 58 balls and contained four sixes and six fours.

Essex

*G. A. Gooch c Nixon b Mullally	65	A. W. Lilley c Boon b Agnew	2
B. R. Hardie c Potter b Mullally	2	T. D. Topley not out	1
M. E. Waugh st Nixon b Benson	84	B 1, l-b 4, w 5, n-b 1	11
P. J. Prichard c Boon b Gidley	8		
J. P. Stephenson not out	38	1/5 2/131 3/140 (7 wkts, 40 overs)	223
N. A. Foster c Potter b Agnew	8	4/186 5/197	
†M. A. Garnham c Briers b Lewis	4	6/214 7/220	

M. C. Ilott and J. H. Childs did not bat.

Bowling: Lewis 8–0–42–1; Mullally 8–0–32–2; Agnew 8–0–39–2; Taylor 8–0–41–0; Gidley 6–0–51–1; Benson 2–0–13–1.

Leicestershire

T. J. Boon b Ilott	56	M. I. Gidley not out	6
*N. E. Briers c Garnham b Foster	5		
J. J. Whitaker c Topley b Gooch	44	L-b 3, w 2	5
C. C. Lewis not out	93		
L. Potter run out	4	1/14 2/80 3/131 (5 wkts, 38.3 overs)	225
J. D. R. Benson b Ilott	12	4/157 5/186	

†P. A. Nixon, A. D. Mullally, J. P. Agnew and L. B. Taylor did not bat.

Bowling: Foster 7.3–0–37–1; Ilott 8–0–41–2; Topley 8–0–49–0; Childs 8–0–29–0; Gooch 7–0–66–1.

Umpires: K. E. Palmer and D. R. Shepherd.

At Manchester, May 20. LEICESTERSHIRE lost to LANCASHIRE by 23 runs.

LEICESTERSHIRE v SOMERSET

At Leicester, May 27. Somerset won by three wickets. Toss: Somerset.

Leicestershire

T. J. Boon c Burns b Cleal	18	†P. A. Nixon not out		9
*N. E. Briers c Lefebvre b Rose	6			
J. J. Whitaker c Tavaré b Rose	83	L-b 5		5
P. Willey c Cook b Rose	52			
L. Potter run out	1	1/17 2/31 3/156	(5 wkts, 40 overs)	191
J. D. R. Benson not out	17	4/163 5/166		

J. P. Agnew, G. J. F. Ferris, A. D. Mullally and D. J. Millns did not bat.

Bowling: Rose 8–0–36–3; Cleal 5–0–27–1; Lefebvre 8–0–42–0; Mallender 8–0–28–0; Swallow 5–0–20–0; Hayhurst 6–0–33–0.

Somerset

S. J. Cook b Millns	60	R. P. Lefebvre lbw b Willey		0
P. M. Roebuck b Ferris	28	M. W. Cleal not out		8
A. N. Hayhurst lbw b Ferris	1	B 1, l-b 4, w 11		16
*C. J. Tavaré b Agnew	26			
R. J. Harden not out	31	1/54 2/62 3/124	(7 wkts, 38.3 overs)	193
†N. D. Burns b Willey	3	4/126 5/131		
G. D. Rose c Briers b Millns	20	6/166 7/169		

N. A. Mallender and I. G. Swallow did not bat.

Bowling: Agnew 7–2–20–1; Millns 8–1–71–2; Mullally 7.3–1–36–0; Ferris 8–1–28–2; Willey 8–0–33–2.

Umpires: D. J. Constant and B. Dudleston.

LEICESTERSHIRE v HAMPSHIRE

At Leicester, June 3. Hampshire won by five wickets. Toss: Hampshire.

Leicestershire

T. J. Boon c Parks b Ayling	6	G. J. F. Ferris lbw b Marshall		6
*N. E. Briers run out	9	A. D. Mullally not out		10
J. J. Whitaker lbw b Connor	0			
P. Willey not out	68	B 5, l-b 2, w 12, n-b 3		22
L. Potter lbw b Tremlett	23			
J. D. R. Benson c Maru b Tremlett	7	1/13 2/13 3/17	(8 wkts, 40 overs)	166
†P. A. Nixon c Maru b Ayling	10	4/75 5/86 6/114		
J. P. Agnew b Connor	5	7/129 8/138		

L. B. Taylor did not bat.

Bowling: Marshall 8–1–23–1; Connor 8–1–35–2; Ayling 8–1–28–2; Tremlett 8–1–28–2; Maru 2–0–14–0; Scott 6–0–31–0.

Hampshire

V. P. Terry c Briers b Agnew	2	J. R. Ayling not out		23
R. J. Scott b Mullally	4			
R. A. Smith c Nixon b Mullally	0	L-b 4, w 9, n-b 2		15
D. I. Gower c Nixon b Taylor	53			
M. D. Marshall c Mullally b Benson	44	1/8 2/8 3/8	(5 wkts, 38.2 overs)	169
*M. C. J. Nicholas not out	28	4/104 5/118		

†R. J. Parks, C. A. Connor, T. M. Tremlett and R. J. Maru did not bat.

Bowling: Agnew 7.2–1–35–1; Mullally 8–0–27–2; Taylor 8–1–35–1; Ferris 5–0–27–0; Willey 8–0–25–0; Benson 2–0–16–1.

Umpires: J. H. Hampshire and P. B. Wight.

LEICESTERSHIRE v SUSSEX

At Leicester, June 10. Leicestershire won by seven wickets. Toss: Leicestershire.

Sussex

N. J. Lenham c Benson b Willey	 32	C. C. Remy not out	....	12
I. J. Gould c Potter b Agnew	 8	†P. Moores not out	....	17
*P. W. G. Parker c Nixon b Lewis	 2	L-b 6, w 5, n-b 5	....	16
A. P. Wells c Willey b Lewis	 2			
M. P. Speight c Lewis b Mullally	 21	1/8 2/21 3/26	(7 wkts, 40 overs)	152
C. M. Wells c Nixon b Lewis	 16	4/70 5/86		
A. I. C. Dodemaide c Briers b Benjamin	26	6/95 7/126		

A. R. Clarke and I. D. K. Salisbury did not bat.

Bowling: Benjamin 8–3–13–1; Agnew 8–1–25–1; Lewis 8–0–36–3; Mullally 8–0–28–1; Willey 8–0–44–1.

Leicestershire

T. J. Boon c Lenham b Dodemaide	... 29	C. C. Lewis not out	....	25
*N. E. Briers c Speight b Salisbury	 31	B 4, l-b 7, w 1, n-b 2	....	14
J. J. Whitaker not out	 53			
P. Willey c Moores b Salisbury	 4	1/65 2/87 3/91	(3 wkts, 37.4 overs)	156

L. Potter, J. D. R. Benson, †P. A. Nixon, W. K. M. Benjamin, J. P. Agnew and A. D. Mullally did not bat.

Bowling: C. M. Wells 7–0–30–0; Dodemaide 8–3–20–1; Remy 6.4–0–34–0; Clarke 8–0–40–0; Salisbury 8–1–21–2.

Umpires: P. J. Eele and D. O. Oslear.

LEICESTERSHIRE v MIDDLESEX

At Leicester, June 17. Middlesex won by 16 runs. Toss: Leicestershire. Gatting's 124 not out, his highest in the Sunday League, came off 93 balls and contained one six and seventeen fours.

Middlesex

D. L. Haynes c and b Lewis	 49	J. E. Emburey not out	....	5
M. A. Roseberry lbw b Agnew	 18	B 1, l-b 6, w 3, n-b 1	....	11
*M. W. Gatting not out	124			
M. R. Ramprakash c and b Willey	... 22	1/34 2/88 3/125	(5 wkts, 40 overs)	259
K. R. Brown c Nixon b Willey	 8	4/164 5/226		
R. O. Butcher lbw b Agnew	 22			

†P. Farbrace, N. F. Williams, S. P. Hughes and A. R. C. Fraser did not bat.

Bowling: Benjamin 8–0–59–0; Agnew 8–3–35–2; Lewis 8–0–64–1; Mullally 8–0–36–0; Willey 8–0–58–2.

Leicestershire

T. J. Boon st Farbrace b Emburey	 84	J. D. R. Benson not out	....	36
*N. E. Briers c Farbrace b Hughes	 46	W. K. M. Benjamin not out	....	2
J. J. Whitaker c Gatting b Haynes	 4	L-b 3, w 3, n-b 4	....	10
C. C. Lewis c Roseberry b Fraser	 14			
P. Willey c Butcher b Williams	 39	1/119 2/128 3/148	(6 wkts, 40 overs)	243
L. Potter c and b Williams	 8	4/168 5/191 6/227		

†P. A. Nixon, J. P. Agnew and A. D. Mullally did not bat.

Bowling: Fraser 8–0–34–1; Williams 8–1–55–2; Haynes 5–0–29–1; Gatting 3–0–18–0; Hughes 8–0–52–1; Emburey 8–0–52–1.

Umpires: B. Hassan and K. E. Palmer.

At Gloucester, June 24. LEICESTERSHIRE beat GLOUCESTERSHIRE on faster scoring-rate.

At Nottingham, July 1. LEICESTERSHIRE lost to NOTTINGHAMSHIRE by eight wickets.

At Knypersley, July 15. LEICESTERSHIRE lost to DERBYSHIRE by 118 runs.

At Sheffield, July 29. LEICESTERSHIRE lost to YORKSHIRE by eight wickets.

LEICESTERSHIRE v WORCESTERSHIRE

At Leicester, August 5. Worcestershire won by seven wickets. Toss: Worcestershire. Hick, having hit thirteen fours, missed his century when, with the scores level, a short-pitched delivery from Lewis flew over his head and was called a wide by umpire Palmer.

Leicestershire

T. J. Boon c Lampitt b Weston	16	†P. A. Nixon c Rhodes b McEwan	0	
*N. E. Briers b Newport	42	G. J. Parsons not out	19	
B. F. Smith c Curtis b McEwan	10	L-b 14, w 9	23	
C. C. Lewis c Neale b Lampitt	13			
J. D. R. Benson b Illingworth	15	1/34 2/49 3/81	(7 wkts, 40 overs) 185	
L. Potter c Lampitt b McEwan	33	4/100 5/132		
M. I. Gidley not out	14	6/156 7/157		

D. J. Millns and A. D. Mullally did not bat.

Bowling: Newport 8–0–36–1; Weston 8–0–27–1; McEwan 8–0–38–3; Lampitt 8–1–38–1; Illingworth 8–0–32–1.

Worcestershire

I. T. Botham c Lewis b Millns	1	*P. A. Neale not out	34	
T. S. Curtis b Mullally	19	B 1, l-b 1, w 7, n-b 1	10	
G. A. Hick not out	98			
D. B. D'Oliveira b Lewis	24	1/3 2/74 3/121	(3 wkts, 36.3 overs) 186	

†S. J. Rhodes, M. J. Weston, P. J. Newport, R. K. Illingworth, S. R. Lampitt and S. M. McEwan did not bat.

Bowling: Lewis 7.3–0–34–1; Millns 5–1–22–1; Parsons 5–0–27–0; Mullally 7–0–35–1; Gidley 8–0–40–0; Benson 4–0–26–0.

Umpires: J. W. Holder and R. Palmer.

At The Oval, August 12. LEICESTERSHIRE lost to SURREY by 69 runs.

At Birmingham, August 19. WARWICKSHIRE v LEICESTERSHIRE. No result.

LEICESTERSHIRE v KENT

At Leicester, August 26. Leicestershire won by six wickets. Toss: Leicestershire.

Kent

S. G. Hinks c and b Benson	60	†S. A. Marsh not out	18
N. R. Taylor c Whitaker b Parsons	52	V. J. Wells not out	7
T. R. Ward c Whitaker b Parsons	0	L-b 5, w 9	14
G. R. Cowdrey c Benson b Millns	43		
*C. S. Cowdrey c Nixon b Millns	6	1/110 2/117 3/122 (6 wkts, 39 overs) 209
M. V. Fleming b Benson	9	4/164 5/175 6/188	

D. J. M. Kelleher, R. P. Davis and T. N. Wren did not bat.

Bowling: Benjamin 7-0-40-0; Parsons 8-0-37-2; Lewis 8-0-23-0; Millns 8-0-47-2; Gidley 3-0-24-0; Benson 5-0-33-2.

Leicestershire

T. J. Boon run out	97	J. D. R. Benson not out	1
*N. E. Briers c Hinks b Wren	16	L-b 4, w 7, n-b 1	12
B. F. Smith lbw b Davis	6		
J. J. Whitaker c and b Fleming	20	1/42 2/55 3/109 (4 wkts, 38.5 overs) 210
C. C. Lewis not out	58	4/202	

W. K. M. Benjamin, †P. A. Nixon, G. J. Parsons, D. J. Millns and M. I. Gidley did not bat.

Bowling: Kelleher 7.5-0-50-0; Wren 6-0-31-1; Davis 8-1-29-1; Ward 8-0-44-0; Fleming 8-0-47-1; Wells 1-0-5-0.

Umpires: B. Dudleston and D. O. Oslear.

MIDDLESEX

At Manchester, April 22. MIDDLESEX beat LANCASHIRE by eight wickets.

MIDDLESEX v ESSEX

At Lord's, April 29. Middlesex won by 12 runs. Toss: Essex.

Middlesex

D. L. Haynes b Pringle	31	†P. R. Downton c Garnham b Pringle	6
M. A. Roseberry c Foster b Pringle	16	J. E. Emburey not out	10
*M. W. Gatting c Garnham b Pringle	7	L-b 12, w 2, n-b 2	16
M. R. Ramprakash c Waugh b Topley	40		
K. R. Brown c Garnham b Topley	50	1/42 2/58 3/59 (6 wkts, 40 overs) 220
R. O. Butcher not out	44	4/145 5/156 6/202	

N. F. Williams, S. P. Hughes and N. G. Cowans did not bat.

Bowling: Foster 8-0-51-0; Topley 8-0-37-2; Pringle 8-3-27-4; Gooch 8-0-44-0; Waugh 4-0-25-0; Childs 4-0-24-0.

Essex

*G. A. Gooch c Downton b Williams	3	N. A. Foster c Roseberry b Cowans	19
B. R. Hardie c and b Emburey	16	T. D. Topley c Downton b Cowans	10
M. E. Waugh c Brown b Williams	44	J. H. Childs not out	3
P. J. Prichard run out	35	L-b 11, w 4, n-b 4	19
D. R. Pringle b Hughes	18		
J. P. Stephenson st Downton b Emburey	5	1/4 2/54 3/91 (39.5 overs) 208
A. W. Lilley c Butcher b Emburey	10	4/129 5/133 6/140	
†M. A. Garnham run out	26	7/157 8/185 9/200	

Bowling: Hughes 8-1-37-1; Williams 8-0-33-2; Cowans 8-1-40-2; Emburey 7.5-1-49-3; Gatting 8-0-38-0.

Umpires: B. Hassan and A. G. T. Whitehead.

At Folkestone, May 6. MIDDLESEX beat KENT by six wickets.

MIDDLESEX v NOTTINGHAMSHIRE

At Lord's, May 13. Nottinghamshire won by 12 runs. Toss: Middlesex. Johnson reached his first Sunday League hundred off 97 balls with fifteen boundaries.

Nottinghamshire

B. C. Broad c Emburey b Cowans	 72	F. D. Stephenson not out	5
*R. T. Robinson run out	 6	L-b 13, w 5	18
P. Johnson c Ramprakash b Williams	..100		
D. W. Randall not out	 30	1/15 2/183 3/192 (4 wkts, 40 overs) 251	
M. Saxelby c Taylor b Haynes	 20	4/244	

†B. N. French, E. E. Hemmings, K. E. Cooper, K. Saxelby and J. A. Afford did not bat.

Bowling: Taylor 8–0–34–0; Williams 8–1–30–1; Cowans 8–1–52–1; Emburey 8–0–53–0; Gatting 5–0–52–0; Haynes 3–0–17–1.

Middlesex

D. L. Haynes lbw b Stephenson	 10	J. E. Emburey st French b Hemmings .	4
M. A. Roseberry lbw b Hemmings	 80	N. G. Cowans c Afford b K. Saxelby ..	27
*M. W. Gatting c Hemmings		N. R. Taylor not out	4
	b Stephenson . 0		
M. R. Ramprakash st French b Afford .	17	B 4, l-b 8, w 7, n-b 2	21
K. R. Brown lbw b Hemmings	 56		
R. O. Butcher c Randall b Hemmings .	7	1/24 2/25 3/80 (37.5 overs) 239	
†P. R. Downton b Hemmings	 10	4/171 5/180 6/187	
N. F. Williams c and b Stephenson	... 3	7/199 8/207 9/208	

Bowling: Stephenson 7–0–29–3; Cooper 8–0–40–0; K. Saxelby 4.5–0–51–1; Afford 6–0–41–1; M. Saxelby 4–0–33–0; Hemmings 8–0–33–5.

Umpires: J. H. Harris and D. O. Oslear.

MIDDLESEX v GLOUCESTERSHIRE

At Lord's, May 27. Middlesex won by seven wickets. Toss: Gloucestershire. When Emburey dismissed Alleyne, he passed T. E. Jesty's total of 248 wickets in the Sunday League to become the seventh most successful bowler in the competition.

Gloucestershire

†R. C. Russell b Cowans	 17	C. A. Walsh b Williams	1
C. W. J. Athey c Gatting b Emburey .	29	D. V. Lawrence b Hughes	1
*A. J. Wright run out	 58	M. C. J. Ball run out	1
K. M. Curran c Roseberry b Gatting .	13	L-b 9, w 6	15
P. Bainbridge b Gatting	 18		
J. W. Lloyds not out	 36	1/29 2/80 3/115 (40 overs) 201	
P. W. Romaines c Downton b Cowans .	11	4/137 5/152 6/179	
M. W. Alleyne b Emburey	 1	7/186 8/195 9/198	

Bowling: Cowans 8–2–27–2; Hughes 8–0–43–1; Gatting 8–0–48–2; Williams 8–0–44–1; Emburey 8–1–30–2.

Middlesex

D. L. Haynes lbw b Alleyne	 50	K. R. Brown not out	39
M. A. Roseberry b Lawrence	 0	L-b 10, w 11	21
*M. W. Gatting c Wright b Walsh	 5		
M. R. Ramprakash not out	 88	1/4 2/17 3/105 (3 wkts, 37.4 overs) 203	

R. O. Butcher, †P. R. Downton, J. E. Emburey, N. F. Williams, S. P. Hughes and N. G. Cowans did not bat.

Bowling: Walsh 7.4–2–22–1; Lawrence 8–0–39–1; Curran 7–0–37–0; Bainbridge 7–0–40–0 Ball 2–0–20–0; Alleyne 6–0–35–1.

Umpires: K. J. Lyons and R. A. White.

MIDDLESEX v WARWICKSHIRE

At Lord's, June 3. Middlesex won by nine wickets in a match reduced by rain to seventeen overs a side. Toss: Middlesex.

Warwickshire

T. M. Moody b Taylor	17	N. M. K. Smith c Williams b Emburey	1(
P. A. Smith b Williams	2	*T. A. Lloyd not out	(
A. I. Kallicharran not out	41	L-b 3, w 7	1(
†G. W. Humpage c Haynes b Hughes	13		
D. A. Reeve c Ramprakash b Emburey	5	1/13 2/29 3/53 (6 wkts, 17 overs) 11$	
Asif Din run out	17	4/62 5/91 6/112	

G. C. Small, J. E. Benjamin and T. A. Munton did not bat.

Bowling: Taylor 4–0–16–1; Williams 4–0–22–1; Gatting 1–0–13–0; Hughes 3–0–32–1 Emburey 3–0–21–2; Haynes 2–0–8–0.

Middlesex

D. L. Haynes c Asif Din b Benjamin	50
M. A. Roseberry not out	51
*M. W. Gatting not out	6
W 3, n-b 6	9

1/107 (1 wkt, 13 overs) 116

M. R. Ramprakash, K. R. Brown, †P. R. Downton, N. F. Williams, J. E. Emburey, S. P Hughes, R. O. Butcher and N. R. Taylor did not bat.

Bowling: Munton 3–0–19–0; Benjamin 3–0–31–1; Small 2–0–28–0; N. M. K. Smith 3–0–26–0; P. A. Smith 2–0–12–0.

Umpires: P. J. Eele and A. A. Jones.

At Basingstoke, June 10. MIDDLESEX beat HAMPSHIRE by seven wickets.

At Leicester, June 17. MIDDLESEX beat LEICESTERSHIRE by 16 runs.

At Luton, June 24. MIDDLESEX beat NORTHAMPTONSHIRE by nine wickets.

MIDDLESEX v WORCESTERSHIRE

At Lord's, July 1. Middlesex won by 99 runs. Toss: Worcestershire. Both Middlesex's total of 290 for six and Ramprakash's unbeaten 147, his maiden hundred in the competition, were records for the county in the Sunday League. Ramprakash, who put on 132 in 51 minutes for the third wicket with Roseberry, scored his runs from only 90 balls, hitting eight sixes and ten fours.

Middlesex

D. L. Haynes c Neale b Lampitt	11	†P. Farbrace b Lampitt 3
M. A. Roseberry lbw b Botham	73	J. E. Emburey not out 8
*M. W. Gatting b Lampitt	9	L-b 19, w 5 24
M. R. Ramprakash not out	147	
K. R. Brown c and b Lampitt	14	1/43 2/64 3/196 (6 wkts, 40 overs) 290
R. O. Butcher c and b Lampitt	1	4/230 5/232 6/238

N. F. Williams, A. R. C. Fraser and N. G. Cowans did not bat.

Bowling: Botham 8-1-42-1; Weston 4-0-30-0; Illingworth 8-1-28-0; Lampitt 8-1-67-5; McEwan 3-0-33-0; Hick 3-0-31-0; Leatherdale 6-0-40-0.

Worcestershire

T. S. Curtis st Farbrace b Gatting	16	R. K. Illingworth not out 16
M. J. Weston c Williams b Gatting	7	S. R. Lampitt not out 25
G. A. Hick c Haynes b Cowans	45	
I. T. Botham c Williams b Emburey	35	L-b 14, w 1, n-b 1 16
D. B. D'Oliveira c Williams b Cowans	2	
*P. A. Neale c Williams b Emburey	13	1/28 2/33 3/86 (8 wkts, 40 overs) 191
D. A. Leatherdale b Emburey	0	4/98 5/125 6/126
†S. J. Rhodes st Farbrace b Emburey	16	7/137 8/152

S. M. McEwan did not bat.

Bowling: Fraser 5-1-15-0; Williams 4-0-17-0; Haynes 4-0-21-0; Gatting 8-0-29-2; Emburey 8-1-39-4; Cowans 8-0-43-2; Ramprakash 2-0-9-0; Brown 1-0-4-0.

Umpires: R. Palmer and D. R. Shepherd.

MIDDLESEX v SOMERSET

At Lord's, July 8. Somerset won by 24 runs. Toss: Middlesex. Tavaré and Harden put on 105 in twelve overs for the third wicket.

Somerset

S. J. Cook b Williams	58
R. J. Bartlett c Gatting b Emburey	54
*C. J. Tavaré not out	72
R. J. Harden not out	41
B 2, l-b 7, w 11, n-b 3	23
1/116 2/143 (2 wkts, 40 overs)	248

A. N. Hayhurst, G. D. Rose, †N. D. Burns, R. P. Lefebvre, I. G. Swallow, J. C. Hallett and N. A. Mallender did not bat.

Bowling: Williams 8-0-39-1; Fraser 8-0-49-0; Haynes 7-0-41-0; Gatting 2-0-11-0; Cowans 7-0-59-0; Emburey 8-1-40-1.

Middlesex

D. L. Haynes c Harden b Mallender	82	J. E. Emburey c and b Rose 32
M. A. Roseberry b Mallender	16	A. R. C. Fraser b Lefebvre 6
*M. W. Gatting b Hayhurst	24	N. G. Cowans not out 0
M. R. Ramprakash b Hayhurst	9	B 4, l-b 12 16
K. R. Brown c Harden b Mallender	15	
R. O. Butcher c Lefebvre b Swallow	12	1/32 2/87 3/107 (39.3 overs) 224
†P. Farbrace b Mallender	0	4/141 5/166 6/166
N. F. Williams c Bartlett b Swallow	12	7/170 8/190 9/204

Bowling: Rose 5.3–0–42–1; Mallender 8–1–32–4; Lefebvre 7–0–37–1; Hallett 5–0–23–0; Hayhurst 6–0–30–2; Swallow 8–0–44–2.

Umpires: J. H. Harris and D. S. Thompsett.

At The Oval, July 15. MIDDLESEX lost to SURREY by 68 runs.

MIDDLESEX v GLAMORGAN

At Lord's, August 5. Middlesex won by 84 runs. Toss: Middlesex. When Embury dismissed Dennis, he passed J. N. Shepherd to become the sixth most successful bowler in the Sunday League.

Middlesex

D. L. Haynes c Cottey b Dale	37	N. F. Williams not out	9
M. A. Roseberry c Frost b Butcher	68		
*M. W. Gatting b Dennis	99	B 2, l-b 14	16
M. R. Ramprakash b Watkin	47		
K. R. Brown run out	5	1/61 2/154 3/264 (5 wkts, 40 overs) 287	
J. E. Embury not out	6	4/270 5/272	

†P. R. Downton, P. C. R. Tufnell, A. R. C. Fraser and N. G. Cowans did not bat.

Bowling: Watkin 8–1–67–1; Frost 5–0–40–0; Dennis 7–0–54–1; Dale 8–0–38–1; Croft 8–0–52–0; Butcher 4–0–20–1.

Glamorgan

M. P. Maynard b Fraser	59	S. L. Watkin b Embury	1
H. Morris c Haynes b Williams	11	S. J. Dennis b Embury	0
I. V. A. Richards b Embury	35	M. Frost c Roseberry b Ramprakash	6
*A. R. Butcher st Downton b Embury	52	B 1, l-b 1, w 1	3
P. A. Cottey b Fraser	28		
R. D. B. Croft b Fraser	6	1/30 2/83 3/136 (39.3 overs) 203	
A. Dale c Ramprakash b Fraser	0	4/176 5/194 6/194	
†C. P. Metson not out	2	7/195 8/196 9/196	

Bowling: Williams 6–0–33–1; Cowans 8–0–46–0; Tufnell 8–0–45–0; Embury 8–2–32–4; Fraser 8–0–28–4; Haynes 1–0–12–0; Ramprakash 0.3–0–5–1.

Umpires: D. J. Constant and K. J. Lyons.

MIDDLESEX v SUSSEX

At Lord's, August 12. Sussex won by seven wickets. Toss: Middlesex.

Middlesex

D. L. Haynes b C. M. Wells	7	N. F. Williams not out	11
M. A. Roseberry run out	4	P. C. R. Tufnell not out	0
*M. W. Gatting run out	5	L-b 4, w 4	8
M. R. Ramprakash b Pigott	11		
K. R. Brown c Pigott b Hansford	68	1/9 2/15 3/27 (7 wkts, 40 overs) 164	
†P. R. Downton b Donelan	23	4/31 5/93	
J. E. Embury c Hanley b Dodemaide	27	6/149 7/162	

N. R. Taylor and N. G. Cowans did not bat.

Bowling: Dodemaide 8–1–24–1; C. M. Wells 8–0–28–1; Pigott 8–0–20–1; Donelan 8–2–23–1; Hansford 5–0–46–1; Salisbury 3–0–19–0.

Sussex

N. J. Lenham b Tufnell	78	A. I. C. Dodemaide not out	19
*C. M. Wells c Emburey b Taylor	10	L-b 2, w 6, n-b 4	12
A. P. Wells c Gatting b Williams	30		
M. P. Speight not out	16	1/36 2/129 3/135 (3 wkts, 34.5 overs) 165	

R. Hanley, †P. Moores, A. C. S. Pigott, B. T. P. Donelan, A. R. Hansford and I. D. K. Salisbury did not bat.

Bowling: Taylor 6.5–0–38–1; Williams 8–0–32–1; Cowans 8–0–23–0; Tufnell 7–0–40–1; Emburey 5–0–30–0.

Umpires: B. J. Meyer and A. G. T. Whitehead.

At Derby, August 19. DERBYSHIRE v MIDDLESEX. No result.

At Scarborough, August 26. MIDDLESEX lost to YORKSHIRE by 44 runs.

NORTHAMPTONSHIRE

At Leicester, April 22. NORTHAMPTONSHIRE beat LEICESTERSHIRE by six wickets.

At Birmingham, April 29. NORTHAMPTONSHIRE lost to WARWICKSHIRE by seven wickets.

NORTHAMPTONSHIRE v DERBYSHIRE

At Northampton, May 6. Derbyshire won by four wickets. Toss: Derbyshire.

Northamptonshire

*W. Larkins c Adams b Malcolm	13	J. W. Govan c Adams b Malcolm	5
A. Fordham c Kuiper b Malcolm	0	W. W. Davis not out	4
R. J. Bailey c Bowler b Kuiper	29	B 1, l-b 6, w 6	13
D. J. Capel c Bowler b Warner	39		
N. A. Felton run out	19	1/2 2/13 3/76 (8 wkts, 40 overs) 180	
D. J. Wild not out	48	4/88 5/123 6/126	
†W. M. Noon run out	1	7/155 8/175	
J. G. Thomas c Barnett b Warner	9		

M. A. Robinson did not bat.

Bowling: Mortensen 8–1–19–0; Malcolm 8–1–34–3; Base 8–0–40–0; Warner 8–0–34–2; Kuiper 8–0–46–1.

Derbyshire

*K. J. Barnett b Robinson	23	S. C. Goldsmith run out	13
†P. D. Bowler b Thomas	30	A. E. Warner not out	13
I. E. Morris b Govan	12	L-b 4, w 3, n-b 1	8
A. P. Kuiper not out	62		
C. J. Adams b Robinson	5	1/57 2/57 3/79 (6 wkts, 38.5 overs) 181	
B. Roberts c Govan b Capel	15	4/92 5/122 6/152	

S. J. Base, O. H. Mortensen and D. E. Malcolm did not bat.

Bowling: Capel 7.5–0–46–1; Davis 7–1–42–0; Thomas 8–1–39–1; Robinson 8–1–23–2; Govan 8–0–27–1.

Umpires: J. H. Harris and R. A. White.

NORTHAMPTONSHIRE v KENT

At Northampton, May 27. Kent won by 55 runs. Toss: Kent. Kent's total of 287 for three was the highest by any county in the Sunday League against Northamptonshire, who suffered their ninth successive defeat of the season in all competitions. Graham Cowdrey hit 70 off 39 balls and shared in an unbroken fourth-wicket partnership of 115 in ten overs with his brother, Chris, whose 45 came off 27 balls.

Kent

S. G. Hinks c Penberthy b Capel	11	G. R. Cowdrey not out		70
N. R. Taylor c Capel b Robinson	73	B 1, l-b 10, w 6		17
T. R. Ward c Felton b Penberthy	71			
*C. S. Cowdrey not out	45	1/17 2/137 3/172	(3 wkts, 40 overs)	287

†S. A. Marsh, M. V. Fleming, M. A. Ealham, C. Penn, R. P. Davis and T. A. Merrick did not bat.

Bowling: Davis 8–1–49–0; Capel 8–1–40–1; Thomas 8–1–46–0; Govan 4–0–28–0; Robinson 8–0–73–1; Penberthy 4–0–40–1.

Northamptonshire

A. Fordham run out	28	J. W. Govan not out		9
N. A. Felton c Marsh b C. S. Cowdrey	64	W. W. Davis c c C. S. Cowdrey b Penn	.	19
*A. J. Lamb c Penn b C. S. Cowdrey	27	M. A. Robinson b Merrick		0
R. J. Bailey lbw b Fleming	11			
D. J. Capel c Davis b C. S. Cowdrey	38	B 2, l-b 16, w 5		23
A. L. Penberthy c Ealham				
b C. S. Cowdrey	6	1/67 2/116 3/135	(37.4 overs)	232
J. G. Thomas c C. S. Cowdrey b Merrick	1	4/145 5/161 6/178		
†D. Ripley c Taylor b Merrick	6	7/189 8/196 9/223		

Bowling: Penn 7–1–33–1; Merrick 7.4–0–37–3; Ealham 5–0–33–0; Davis 4–0–29–0; Fleming 6–0–25–1; C. S. Cowdrey 8–0–57–4.

Umpires: B. J. Meyer and D. S. Thompsett.

At The Oval, June 3. NORTHAMPTONSHIRE lost to SURREY by four wickets.

NORTHAMPTONSHIRE v GLAMORGAN

At Northampton, June 10. Northamptonshire won by 10 runs. Toss: Northamptonshire. Capel, playing in his 100th Sunday League match, reached his first hundred in the competition off 88 deliveries. In all he faced 100 balls, hit three sixes and ten fours, and shared with Bailey in a third-wicket partnership of 191 in 29 overs. Richards, when 33, reached 5,000 runs in the Sunday League.

Northamptonshire

A. Fordham c Metson b Frost	0	†W. M. Noon c Morris b Dennis		11
N. A. Felton c Cowley b Watkin	21	J. G. Thomas not out		0
R. J. Bailey b Frost	71	B 2, l-b 6, w 7		15
D. J. Capel c Morris b Frost	121			
D. J. Wild c Metson b Frost	4	1/0 2/27 3/218	(6 wkts, 40 overs)	244
R. G. Williams not out	1	4/228 5/232 6/243		

*N. G. B. Cook, W. W. Davis and M. A. Robinson did not bat.

Bowling: Frost 8–1–30–4; Watkin 8–0–37–1; Cowley 7–0–43–0; Dennis 8–0–63–1; Richards 7–0–45–0; Holmes 2–0–18–0.

Glamorgan

*A. R. Butcher b Williams	40	N. G. Cowley not out	2
H. Morris lbw b Cook	40		
M. P. Maynard c Williams b Cook	13	B 1, l-b 10, w 5	16
I. V. A. Richards c Cook b Robinson	45		
G. C. Holmes not out	50	1/77 2/102 3/105	(5 wkts, 40 overs) 234
P. A. Cottey c Noon b Davis	28	4/172 5/218	

†C. P. Metson, S. J. Dennis, S. L. Watkin and M. Frost did not bat.

Bowling: Capel 6–0–34–0; Davis 8–1–39–1; Thomas 8–0–42–0; Williams 8–0–34–1; Cook 6–1–40–2; Robinson 4–0–34–1.

Umpires: J. D. Bond and P. B. Wight.

NORTHAMPTONSHIRE v MIDDLESEX

At Luton, June 24. Middlesex won by nine wickets. Toss: Middlesex.

Northamptonshire

A. Fordham c Hughes b Williams	4	W. W. Davis c Ramprakash b Hughes	7
N. A. Felton c Haynes b Gatting	10	*N. G. B. Cook b Emburey	1
R. J. Bailey c Butcher b Emburey	60	M. A. Robinson not out	0
D. J. Capel st Farbrace b Emburey	46	L-b 1, w 3, n-b 5	9
D. J. Wild run out	8		
R. G. Williams run out	1	1/8 2/32 3/113	(37.2 overs) 151
†D. Ripley st Farbrace b Emburey	3	4/127 5/131 6/137	
J. G. Thomas c Ramprakash b Fraser	2	7/140 8/143 9/151	

Bowling: Fraser 7–2–16–1; Williams 8–1–39–1; Gatting 8–1–34–1; Hughes 7–0–35–1; Emburey 7.2–0–26–4.

Middlesex

*M. W. Gatting not out	76
M. A. Roseberry run out	50
M. R. Ramprakash not out	8
L-b 7, w 8, n-b 4	19

1/112   (1 wkt, 27.4 overs) 153

D. L. Haynes, K. R. Brown, R. O. Butcher, J. E. Emburey, †P. Farbrace, N. F. Williams, S. P. Hughes and A. R. C. Fraser did not bat.

Bowling: Davis 5–0–19–0; Capel 4–0–31–0; Thomas 2–0–20–0; Robinson 7–0–32–0; Cook 3–0–13–0; Wild 4.4–0–31–0; Williams 2–2–0–0.

Umpires: N. T. Plews and R. A. White.

At Taunton, July 1. NORTHAMPTONSHIRE lost to SOMERSET by seven wickets.

NORTHAMPTONSHIRE v YORKSHIRE

At Tring, July 8. Yorkshire won by 61 runs. Toss: Northamptonshire.

Yorkshire

S. A. Kellett run out	10	D. Byas not out	18
*A. A. Metcalfe lbw b Wild	55	B 5, l-b 7, w 4, n-b 1	17
†R. J. Blakey st Ripley b Wild	42		
P. E. Robinson not out	58	1/18 2/113 3/118	(4 wkts, 40 overs) 251
P. J. Hartley b Davis	51	4/200	

C. White, C. A. Chapman, P. Carrick, A. Sidebottom and S. D. Fletcher did not bat.

Bowling: Davis 8–1–38–1; Capel 8–0–26–0; Cook 8–0–60–0; Robinson 6–0–53–0; Williams 4–0–36–0; Wild 6–0–26–2.

Northamptonshire

A. Fordham b Sidebottom	28	†D. Ripley c Chapman b Hartley	17
*W. Larkins c Hartley b Sidebottom	12	N. G. B. Cook b White	1
R. J. Bailey b Hartley	18	M. A. Robinson not out	0
D. J. Capel c Robinson b Carrick	25	B 1, l-b 2, w 1, n-b 2	6
N. A. Felton st Blakey b Carrick	9		—
D. J. Wild c Fletcher b White	19	1/40 2/53 3/72 (37.1 overs)	190
R. G. Williams b Hartley	35	4/94 5/97 6/124	
W. W. Davis c Carrick b Byas	20	7/146 8/187 9/190	

Bowling: Sidebottom 8–1–21–2; Hartley 7–0–37–3; Fletcher 5–0–34–0; Carrick 8–2–22–2; White 7.1–0–56–2; Byas 2–0–17–1.

Umpires: J. C. Balderstone and A. A. Jones.

At Chelmsford, July 15. NORTHAMPTONSHIRE lost to ESSEX by six wickets.

NORTHAMPTONSHIRE v SUSSEX

At Wellingborough School, July 22. Sussex won by 21 runs. Toss: Northamptonshire. Capel reached his hundred off 77 balls, and hit four sixes and eleven fours in his 115.

Sussex

N. J. Lenham c Larkins b Robinson	25	J. A. North not out	15
I. J. Gould c Bailey b Cook	55	†P. Moores not out	6
*P. W. G. Parker lbw b Williams	34		
A. P. Wells lbw b Cook	2	B 1, l-b 14, w 6, n-b 1	22
M. P. Speight b Cook	32		—
C. M. Wells c Williams b Davis	6	1/55 2/113 3/121 (8 wkts, 40 overs)	253
A. I. C. Dodemaide c and b Davis	19	4/127 5/140 6/177	
A. C. S. Pigott c Cook b Robinson	37	7/226 8/239	

I. D. K. Salisbury did not bat.

Bowling: Davis 8–1–32–2; Brown 8–0–48–0; Robinson 8–0–59–2; Williams 8–0–63–1; Cook 8–1–36–3.

Northamptonshire

A. Fordham lbw b North	21	S. J. Brown not out	3
W. Larkins lbw b Dodemaide	7	N. G. B. Cook not out	0
*A. J. Lamb c Parker b Pigott	17		
D. J. Capel c Salisbury b Lenham	115	L-b 2, w 7	9
R. J. Bailey c Speight b Pigott	4		—
R. G. Williams c Gould b North	6	1/22 2/39 3/61 (8 wkts, 40 overs)	232
†D. Ripley c C. M. Wells b Pigott	26	4/67 5/88 6/149	
W. W. Davis b Lenham	24	7/204 8/231	

M. A. Robinson did not bat.

Bowling: C. M. Wells 8–0–28–0; Dodemaide 8–0–38–1; Pigott 8–0–60–3; North 8–0–45–2; Lenham 8–0–59–2.

Umpires: B. Hassan and B. Leadbeater.

At Nottingham, July 29. NORTHAMPTONSHIRE lost to NOTTINGHAMSHIRE by 5 runs.

At Bournemouth, August 5. NORTHAMPTONSHIRE lost to HAMPSHIRE by six wickets.

NORTHAMPTONSHIRE v LANCASHIRE

At Northampton, August 12. Lancashire won by seven wickets as Northamptonshire recorded their eighth successive defeat. Toss: Lancashire. Larkins faced a total of 97 balls, needing only for his second fifty, and hit twelve fours. Fowler began Lancashire's reply needing 3 runs to pass H. Pilling's Lancashire record, set in 1970, of 625 runs in a Sunday League season.

Northamptonshire

. Fordham c Mendis b Watkinson	44	R. G. Williams not out		1
. A. Felton run out	8	†D. Ripley not out		6
W. Larkins c Lloyd b DeFreitas	104	B 2, l-b 6, w 1		9
. J. Bailey c Allott b DeFreitas	47			
. J. Capel c Allott b DeFreitas	4	1/13 2/71 3/203	(6 wkts, 40 overs)	223
. J. Wild c Lloyd b DeFreitas	0	4/214 5/214 6/215		

. G. B. Cook, S. J. Brown and M. A. Robinson did not bat.

Bowling: Allott 6–1–19–0; DeFreitas 8–1–22–4; Watkinson 6–0–32–1; Wasim Akram 8–0–50–0; Hughes 6–0–49–0; Austin 6–0–43–0.

Lancashire

. D. Mendis c Felton b Wild	37	M. Watkinson not out		6
. Fowler c Cook b Robinson	81	L-b 10, w 5		15
. D. Lloyd c Ripley b Wild	0			
. H. Fairbrother not out	86	1/67 2/68 3/209	(3 wkts, 36.5 overs)	225

Wasim Akram, P. A. J. DeFreitas, I. D. Austin, †W. K. Hegg, *D. P. Hughes and P. J. W. Allott did not bat.

Bowling: Brown 4.5–0–21–0; Robinson 7–0–56–1; Cook 6–0–42–0; Wild 8–0–31–2; Williams 8–0–45–0; Bailey 3–0–20–0.

Umpires: J. H. Harris and D. S. Thompsett.

At Worcester, August 19. WORCESTERSHIRE v NORTHAMPTONSHIRE. No result.

NORTHAMPTONSHIRE v GLOUCESTERSHIRE

At Northampton, August 26. Northamptonshire won by 2 runs. Toss: Gloucestershire. Larkins faced 77 balls, hitting seven sixes and seven fours.

Northamptonshire

. Cook b Curran	16	†W. M. Noon c and b Curran		0
W. Larkins c Alleyne b Milburn	109	J. G. Thomas c and b Walsh		4
. Fordham c Wright b Bainbridge	50	N. G. B. Cook not out		0
. J. Bailey c Milburn b Alleyne	20	B 1, l-b 5, w 4, n-b 1		11
. J. Capel c Barnes b Alleyne	16			
. A. Felton b Walsh	24	1/28 2/111 3/200	(40 overs)	274
. J. Wild b Walsh	15	4/201 5/225 6/245		
. W. Davis c Barnes b Curran	9	7/268 8/268 9/273		

Bowling: Barnes 6–0–22–0; Walsh 8–0–36–3; Curran 8–0–45–3; Milburn 5–0–54–1; Alleyne 8–0–49–2; Bainbridge 6–0–62–1.

Gloucestershire

C. W. J. Athey c and b Thomas	22	G. D. Hodgson not out ....
M. W. Alleyne c N. G. B. Cook b Wild	38	E. T. Milburn not out ....
P. Bainbridge c Felton b Wild	2	L-b 10, w 6, n-b 1 ....
K. M. Curran c Capel b Thomas	92	
*A. J. Wright b Capel	50	1/44 2/58 3/105 (7 wkts, 40 overs) 2
P. W. Romaines b Davis	31	4/208 5/245
C. A. Walsh b Davis	14	6/265 7/266

†R. C. J. Williams and S. N. Barnes did not bat.

Bowling: Thomas 8-0-43-2; Davis 8-0-40-2; Capel 8-0-62-1; Wild 8-0-58-2; N. G. Cook 8-0-59-0.

Umpires: P. J. Eele and K. E. Palmer.

NOTTINGHAMSHIRE

NOTTINGHAMSHIRE v YORKSHIRE

At Nottingham, April 22. Nottinghamshire won by five wickets. Toss: Nottinghamshire.

Yorkshire

*M. D. Moxon lbw b Pick	37	A. Sidebottom c French b Stephenson .
A. A. Metcalfe lbw b Saxelby	11	P. W. Jarvis not out ....
†R. J. Blakey b Hemmings	30	L-b 9, w 6, n-b 1 ....
P. E. Robinson c Robinson b Hemmings	4	
D. Byas c French b Saxelby	7	1/38 2/61 3/76 (7 wkts, 40 overs) l
C. White not out	26	4/96 5/102
P. Carrick run out	1	6/104 7/107

D. Gough and S. D. Fletcher did not bat.

Bowling: Stephenson 8-2-28-1; Cooper 8-2-24-0; Saxelby 8-0-49-2; Hemmin 8-0-28-2; Pick 8-0-23-1.

Nottinghamshire

B. C. Broad c Blakey b Jarvis	4	†B. N. French not out ....
P. R. Pollard b Jarvis	3	
*R. T. Robinson lbw b Sidebottom	1	
P. Johnson c Blakey b Carrick	39	B 1, l-b 3 ....
D. W. Randall not out	54	1/8 2/9 3/9 (5 wkts, 39.1 overs) l
F. D. Stephenson c Blakey b Gough	42	4/67 5/129

E. E. Hemmings, K. E. Cooper, R. A. Pick and K. Saxelby did not bat.

Bowling: Jarvis 8-1-26-2; Sidebottom 8-3-22-1; Fletcher 7.1-0-31-0; Gough 5-0-29 Carrick 6-0-27-1; Byas 5-0-23-0.

Umpires: J. D. Bond and B. Leadbeater.

NOTTINGHAMSHIRE v LANCASHIRE

At Nottingham, April 29. Lancashire won by five wickets. Toss: Lancashire.

Nottinghamshire

B. C. Broad lbw b Allott	13	E. E. Hemmings c Fowler b DeFreitas .
P. R. Pollard lbw b DeFreitas	8	K. E. Cooper c Jesty b DeFreitas .....
*R. T. Robinson c Fairbrother b Atherton	61	R. A. Pick not out ....
P. Johnson c Atherton b Jesty	15	B 1, l-b 6, w 7, n-b 1 ....
D. W. Randall b Austin	14	
F. D. Stephenson c Fowler b Allott	23	1/14 2/28 3/54 (39.3 overs) l
†B. N. French c Watkinson b Atherton	11	4/107 5/128 6/148
K. P. Evans st Hegg b Atherton	0	7/149 8/162 9/186

Bowling: Allott 8–0–29–2; DeFreitas 7.3–0–36–3; Watkinson 7–0–41–0; Jesty 2–0–9–1; ‥ustin 8–0–38–1; Atherton 7–0–33–3.

‥ancashire

. Fowler c Robinson b Hemmings ... 52	P. A. J. DeFreitas not out 7
‥. A. Atherton c Robinson b Pick 5	
. D. Lloyd b Hemmings 47	B 1, l-b 10, w 4, n-b 1 16
. H. Fairbrother c French b Evans .. 19	‒‒
. E. Jesty c Broad b Stephenson 15	1/14 2/100 3/126　(5 wkts, 38.4 overs) 194
‥. Watkinson not out 33	4/139 5/166

D. Austin, *D. P. Hughes, †W. K. Hegg and P. J. W. Allott did not bat.

Bowling: Cooper 8–0–32–0; Pick 8–0–43–1; Evans 7–0–42–1; Stephenson 7.4–1–48–1; ‥emmings 8–2–18–2.

Umpires: D. O. Oslear and D. R. Shepherd.

‥t Worcester, May 6. NOTTINGHAMSHIRE lost to WORCESTERSHIRE by 61 runs.

‥t Lord's, May 13. NOTTINGHAMSHIRE beat MIDDLESEX by 12 runs.

NOTTINGHAMSHIRE v SURREY

‥t Nottingham, May 20. Nottinghamshire won by eight wickets. Toss: Nottinghamshire. ‥road's 106 not out, his highest in the Sunday League, came off 125 balls and contained a six ‥d eight fours.

‥urrey

. S. Clinton c Broad b Afford 40	C. K. Bullen not out 23
. J. Stewart lbw b K. Saxelby 10	M. P. Bicknell not out 11
‥. A. Lynch b Hemmings 20	
. P. Thorpe c Afford b Hemmings ... 0	
‥. M. Ward c Afford b M. Saxelby .. 34	B 1, l-b 9, w 5 15
‥. A. Greig b Hemmings 12	‒‒
. T. Medlycott c M. Saxelby	1/32 2/64　(8 wkts, 40 overs) 181
b Hemmings . 2	3/68 4/84
‥. A. Feltham c Hemmings	5/107 6/130
b K. Saxelby . 14	7/132 8/154

. J. Murphy did not bat.

Bowling: Stephenson 8–1–21–0; Cooper 6–0–19–0; K. Saxelby 6–0–44–2; Afford 8–1–24–1; ‥emmings 8–0–48–4; M. Saxelby 4–0–15–1.

‥ottinghamshire

. C. Broad not out 106	
‥. T. Robinson c Ward b Bicknell ... 2	
‥ Johnson b Bicknell 63	
‥. W. Randall not out 9	
L-b 3, w 2 5	

‥5 2/144　(2 wkts, 38.1 overs) 185

‥. Saxelby, F. D. Stephenson, †B. N. French, E. E. Hemmings, K. E. Cooper, J. A. Afford and K. Saxelby did not bat.

Bowling: Bicknell 8–1–23–2; Murphy 8–0–41–0; Feltham 8–1–34–0; Medlycott 4–0–35–0; ‥ullen 8–0–36–0; Lynch 2–0–9–0; Stewart 0.1–0–4–0.

Umpires: J. H. Hampshire and A. A. Jones.

At Derby, June 10. NOTTINGHAMSHIRE beat DERBYSHIRE by four wickets.

At Canterbury, June 17. NOTTINGHAMSHIRE lost to KENT by 24 runs.

At Bath, June 24. NOTTINGHAMSHIRE lost to SOMERSET by 29 runs.

NOTTINGHAMSHIRE v LEICESTERSHIRE

At Nottingham, July 1. Nottinghamshire won by eight wickets. Toss: Nottinghamshire. Th match was reduced to 38 overs a side after rain had delayed the start.

Leicestershire

T. J. Boon c French b Evans	13	J. P. Agnew c M. Saxelby b Stephenson
*N. E. Briers c and b K. Saxelby	33	A. D. Mullally run out
J. J. Whitaker c Cooper b Evans	4	
P. Willey b Evans	41	L-b 3, w 1
C. C. Lewis c and b Stephenson	36	
J. D. R. Benson b Stephenson	2	1/28 2/38 3/72 (9 wkts, 38 overs) 15
G. J. Parsons not out	11	4/127 5/131 6/136
†P. A. Nixon b Evans	6	7/145 8/148 9/155

L. B. Taylor did not bat.

Bowling: Stephenson 8–1–21–3; Cooper 8–2–21–0; Evans 8–0–30–4; Hemmings 7–0–33–0 K. Saxelby 5–0–27–1; M. Saxelby 2–0–20–0.

Nottinghamshire

B. C. Broad c Whitaker b Mullally	57
M. Newell not out	60
P. Johnson c Nixon b Taylor	35
*R. T. Robinson not out	0
L-b 4, w 1	5

1/104 2/144   (2 wkts, 31.4 overs) 157

M. Saxelby, F. D. Stephenson, †B. N. French, K. P. Evans, E. E. Hemmings, K. Saxelby an K. E. Cooper did not bat.

Bowling: Agnew 5–0–25–0; Mullally 6.4–1–25–1; Lewis 5–1–27–0; Taylor 7–0–35–1; Wille 2–0–17–0; Parsons 6–1–24–0.

Umpires: R. Julian and D. S. Thompsett.

NOTTINGHAMSHIRE v SUSSEX

At Nottingham, July 8. Nottinghamshire won by 8 runs. Toss: Sussex. Johnson's centu came off only 71 balls, with eight fours.

Nottinghamshire

B. C. Broad c Salisbury b Pigott	61	K. P. Evans not out
M. Newell c Moores b Lenham	15	
P. Johnson lbw b Clarke	104	B 1, l-b 10, w 5
F. D. Stephenson b Pigott	32	
G. W. Mike lbw b Pigott	13	1/51 2/128 3/202 (5 wkts, 40 overs) 26
*R. T. Robinson not out	15	4/224 5/245

†B. N. French, K. E. Cooper, K. Saxelby and J. A. Afford did not bat.

Bowling: C. M. Wells 8–0–45–0; Dodemaide 6–0–46–0; Clarke 7–0–37–1; Lenha 8–0–36–1; Pigott 8–0–55–3; Salisbury 3–0–33–0.

ussex

. J. Lenham b Afford	60	C. C. Remy run out		1
J. Gould c French b Cooper	6	I. D. K. Salisbury b Stephenson		0
P. Wells run out	98	A. R. Clarke not out		0
. P. Speight run out	2	L-b 12, w 2		14
С. M. Wells b Mike	25			
I. C. Dodemaide lbw b Mike	22	1/34 2/93 3/98	(39.2 overs)	255
C. S. Pigott c Johnson b Mike	17	4/150 5/201 6/229		
?. Moores run out	10	7/251 8/254 9/254		

Bowling: Saxelby 6–0–49–0; Cooper 4–0–18–1; Stephenson 7.2–0–48–1; Afford 6–0–40–1; vans 8–0–46–0; Mike 8–0–42–3.

Umpires: H. D. Bird and K. E. Palmer.

t Southampton, July 15. NOTTINGHAMSHIRE lost to HAMPSHIRE by 7 runs.

t Birmingham, July 22. NOTTINGHAMSHIRE beat WARWICKSHIRE by 10 runs.

NOTTINGHAMSHIRE v NORTHAMPTONSHIRE

: Nottingham, July 29. Nottinghamshire won by 5 runs. Toss: Northamptonshire.

ottinghamshire

C. Broad lbw b Capel	38	K. P. Evans not out		28
. Newell lbw b Capel	16			
Johnson c Capel b Larkins	29	L-b 4, w 6		10
₹. T. Robinson not out	74			
. Saxelby b Larkins	5	1/50 2/70 3/115	(5 wkts, 40 overs)	202
D. Stephenson b Williams	2	4/125 5/136		

₹. N. French, K. E. Cooper, G. W. Mike and J. A. Afford did not bat.

Bowling: Robinson 6–0–34–0; Hughes 4–0–16–0; Capel 8–0–34–2; Cook 5–0–21–0; Wild 0–24–0; Larkins 6–0–34–2; Williams 6–0–35–1.

orthamptonshire

Fordham c Robinson b Mike	59	†D. Ripley run out		0
V. Larkins b Afford	58	J. G. Hughes not out		1
J. Capel run out	4	L-b 9, w 7		16
J. Bailey b Cooper	4			
A. Felton not out	33	1/113 2/123 3/136	(7 wkts, 40 overs)	197
G. Williams c Newell b Mike	20	4/138 5/190		
J. Wild b Evans	2	6/195 7/196		

. G. B. Cook and M. A. Robinson did not bat.

Bowling: Cooper 8–0–62–1; Stephenson 8–2–19–0; Evans 8–0–42–1; Mike 8–0–41–2; ford 8–0–24–1.

Umpires: J. H. Hampshire and M. J. Kitchen.

At Southend, August 5. NOTTINGHAMSHIRE beat ESSEX by six wickets.

NOTTINGHAMSHIRE v GLAMORGAN

At Nottingham, August 12. Nottinghamshire won by eight wickets. Toss: Nottinghamshi‖ Robinson celebrated the birth of his second son in the morning with an unbeaten centu‖ reaching three figures off 111 balls. His innings of 107 not out contained twelve fours.

Glamorgan

M. P. Maynard lbw b Cooper	7	R. D. B. Croft c Robinson b Stephenson
H. Morris c Evans b Mike	9	†C. P. Metson not out ....
I. V. A. Richards c and b Afford	54	B 1, l-b 4, w 2, n-b 1 ....
*A. R. Butcher c French b Mike	11	
P. A. Cottey not out	50	1/15 2/28 3/85 (6 wkts, 40 overs) 1
A. Dale c Saxelby b Afford	7	4/87 5/101 6/151

S. L. Watkin, S. J. Dennis and M. Frost did not bat.

Bowling: Cooper 8–1–25–1; Stephenson 8–1–40–1; Evans 8–0–47–0; Mike 8–1–38‖ Afford 8–0–39–2.

Nottinghamshire

B. C. Broad b Richards	26
*R. T. Robinson not out	107
P. Johnson c Metson b Richards	23
M. Saxelby not out	28
L-b 4, w 10	14

1/95 2/154   (2 wkts, 37 overs) 198

M. Newell, F. D. Stephenson, †B. N. French, K. P. Evans, G. W. Mike, K. E. Cooper a‖ J. A. Afford did not bat.

Bowling: Watkin 7–0–27–0; Frost 8–0–48–0; Croft 8–0–40–0; Dennis 5–0–32–0; Richa‖ 8–0–32–2; Dale 1–0–15–0.

Umpires: D. J. Constant and D. O. Oslear.

NOTTINGHAMSHIRE v GLOUCESTERSHIRE

At Nottingham, August 19. No result. Toss: Nottinghamshire. Rain ended the match, whi‖ had already been reduced to twenty overs a side.

Gloucestershire

C. W. J. Athey lbw b Cooper	2	*A. J. Wright not out ....
K. M. Curran b Cooper	15	P. W. Romaines not out ....
P. Bainbridge c French b Mike	2	L-b 6, w 2, n-b 2 ....
†R. C. Russell c French b Mike	45	
M. W. Alleyne c Stephenson b Mike	19	1/6 2/11 3/45 (6 wkts, 20 overs) ‖
C. A. Walsh c Saxelby b Stephenson	23	4/79 5/109 6/120

G. D. Hodgson, D. V. Lawrence and E. T. Milburn did not bat.

Bowling: Mike 4–0–30–3; Cooper 4–0–21–2; Evans 4–0–27–0; Stephenson 4–0–30‖ Hemmings 3–0–30–0; Saxelby 1–0–10–0.

Nottinghamshire

. C. Broad c Athey b Alleyne	22
R. T. Robinson c Hodgson b Lawrence	6
. Johnson not out	25
. Saxelby not out	24
B 1, l-b 2, w 3	6

18 2/37   (2 wkts, 11.4 overs) 83

. Newell, F. D. Stephenson, †B. N. French, K. P. Evans, E. E. Hemmings, G. W. Mike and K. E. Cooper did not bat.

Bowling: Lawrence 4-0-23-1; Curran 2-0-11-0; Alleyne 2-0-12-1; Walsh 2-0-15-0; Milburn 1-0-15-0; Bainbridge 0.4-0-4-0.

Umpires: J. D. Bond and N. T. Plews.

SOMERSET

SOMERSET v WORCESTERSHIRE

At Taunton, April 22. Worcestershire won by 33 runs. Toss: Somerset. Curtis, whose 124 came from 143 balls, and Hick added 150 for Worcestershire's second wicket in just eighteen overs. The six dismissals by Rhodes were a record for Worcestershire in all one-day competitions.

Worcestershire

. S. Curtis c Cook b Roebuck	124
T. Botham st Burns b Swallow	24
. A. Hick not out	78
. B. D'Oliveira not out	0
L-b 6, w 5	11

/86 2/236   (2 wkts, 40 overs) 237

P. A. Neale, M. J. Weston, †S. J. Rhodes, R. K. Illingworth, P. J. Newport, N. V. Radford and S. M. McEwan did not bat.

Bowling: Jones 8-0-40-0; Mallender 8-1-26-0; Rose 8-0-54-0; Swallow 7-0-47-1; Lefebvre 8-0-54-0; Roebuck 1-0-10-1.

Somerset

. J. Cook c Rhodes b Newport	18	A. N. Jones st Rhodes b Illingworth	10
. M. Roebuck c Rhodes b McEwan	39	I. G. Swallow not out	6
. J. Bartlett c Rhodes b Newport	2		
C. J. Tavaré c Rhodes b Botham	3	L-b 11, w 6, n-b 3	20
. J. Harden c Rhodes b Botham	35		
N. D. Burns run out	19	1/30 2/35 3/45 (8 wkts, 40 overs) 204
. D. Rose not out	41	4/102 5/121 6/139	
. P. Lefebvre c and b Illingworth	11	7/175 8/197	

. A. Mallender did not bat.

Bowling: Newport 8-1-17-2; Weston 3-0-22-0; Botham 8-0-39-2; McEwan 8-0-49-1; Radford 5-0-20-0; Illingworth 8-0-46-2.

Umpires: K. E. Palmer and D. R. Shepherd.

SOMERSET v HAMPSHIRE

At Taunton, May 13. Somerset won by five wickets. Toss: Hampshire. Cook faced 87 ball
hitting three sixes and fifteen fours in his second three-figure innings of the weekend. H
second fifty came off just 23 balls.

Hampshire

D. I. Gower c Tavaré b Jones	12	*M. C. J. Nicholas not out	3
V. P. Terry not out	113	B 1, l-b 6, w 5	
R. A. Smith c Hayhurst b Cleal	51		
C. L. Smith b Lefebvre	25	1/23 2/125 3/181 (3 wkts, 40 overs) 24	

J. R. Ayling, M. D. Marshall, †R. J. Parks, R. J. Maru, C. A. Connor and P. J. Bakk
did not bat.

Bowling: Jones 6–1–40–1; Rose 8–0–49–0; Lefebvre 8–0–50–1; Hayhurst 8–0–35–
Swallow 4–0–24–0; Cleal 6–0–41–1.

Somerset

S. J. Cook c R. A. Smith b Bakker	132	†N. D. Burns not out	1
P. M. Roebuck b Bakker	1		
A. N. Hayhurst c and b Maru	38	B 4, l-b 2, w 1, n-b 2	
G. D. Rose c Terry b Marshall	32		
*C. J. Tavaré c Parks b Marshall	9	1/2 2/130 3/195 (5 wkts, 37 overs) 24	
R. J. Harden not out	13	4/211 5/220	

R. P. Lefebvre, A. N. Jones, I. G. Swallow and M. W. Cleal did not bat.

Bowling: Marshall 8–0–53–2; Bakker 6–1–42–2; Connor 8–0–48–0; Ayling 5–0–38–0; Ma
8–0–38–1; Nicholas 2–0–22–0.

Umpires: A. A. Jones and B. Leadbeater.

SOMERSET v DERBYSHIRE

At Taunton, May 20. Derbyshire won by seven wickets. Toss: Derbyshire. The first-wick
partnership of 232 between Barnett and Morris was a Derbyshire record for any wicket in th
Sunday League and was also the highest opening partnership for the county in one-da
competitions. Barnett reached his hundred off 105 balls, while Morris's 134, a record f
Derbyshire in the Sunday League, came off 116 balls and contained two sixes and eleve
fours. This was Morris's third of four hundreds against Somerset in the month. The previo
day he had scored 122 in the County Championship, and he went on to make his secon
the match on the third day. On May 1 he had hit 123 in the Benson and Hedges Cup.
Somerset's innings Cook, when 7, became the first batsman to score 1,000 runs in a
competitive matches in the season.

Somerset

S. J. Cook b Malcolm	53	R. P. Lefebvre not out	
P. M. Roebuck b Barnett	85	M. W. Cleal not out	
A. N. Hayhurst lbw b Miller	13	L-b 2, w 4	
G. D. Rose c Goldsmith b Kuiper	5		
*C. J. Tavaré run out	7	1/91 2/119 3/124 (7 wkts, 40 overs) 2	
R. J. Harden c Barnett b Malcolm	30	4/135 5/183	
†N. D. Burns run out	30	6/210 7/230	

I. G. Swallow and A. N. Jones did not bat.

Bowling: Mortensen 8–0–42–0; Miller 8–0–37–1; Warner 2–0–26–0; Malcolm 8–0–48–
Kuiper 8–0–48–1; Barnett 6–0–55–1.

Derbyshire

*K. J. Barnett b Lefebvre	100	C. J. Adams not out	0
J. E. Morris b Rose	134	L-b 3, w 2	5
A. P. Kuiper not out	21		
A. E. Warner c Harden b Jones	4	1/232 2/240 3/258 (3 wkts, 40 overs) 264	

B. Roberts, S. C. Goldsmith, G. Miller, D. E. Malcolm, O. H. Mortensen and †K. M. Krikken did not bat.

Bowling: Jones 6–0–38–1; Rose 8–0–45–1; Hayhurst 8–0–47–0; Lefebvre 8–0–44–1; Swallow 5–0–38–0; Cleal 3–0–27–0; Roebuck 2–0–22–0.

Umpires: K. E. Palmer and D. S. Thompsett.

At Leicester, May 27. SOMERSET beat LEICESTERSHIRE by three wickets.

At Bristol, June 3. SOMERSET lost to GLOUCESTERSHIRE by eight wickets.

At Canterbury, June 10. SOMERSET lost to KENT by six wickets.

SOMERSET v ESSEX

At Bath, June 17. Essex won by 101 runs. Toss: Somerset.

Essex

*G. A. Gooch b Hayhurst	34	N. A. Foster not out	39
B. R. Hardie b Mallender	7	†M. A. Garnham not out	12
M. E. Waugh b Rose	3	B 5, l-b 2, w 3	10
P. J. Prichard c and b Rose	64		
D. R. Pringle b Mallender	37	1/32 2/38 3/79 (7 wkts, 40 overs) 217	
J. P. Stephenson b Rose	1	4/149 5/150	
A. W. Lilley c Bartlett b Jones	10	6/159 7/179	

T. D. Topley and J. H. Childs did not bat.

Bowling: Jones 7–0–47–1; Mallender 8–0–30–2; Rose 8–0–33–3; Swallow 5–0–32–0; Hayhurst 7–0–41–1; Roebuck 5–0–27–0.

Somerset

S. J. Cook lbw b Pringle	23	I. G. Swallow c Gooch b Topley	3
P. M. Roebuck c Hardie b Foster	0	A. N. Jones b Stephenson	0
R. J. Bartlett run out	16	N. A. Mallender not out	7
*C. J. Tavaré b Childs	5	L-b 6, w 3	9
R. J. Harden run out	13		
A. N. Hayhurst run out	20	1/3 2/33 3/48 (34.5 overs) 116	
G. D. Rose b Topley	20	4/48 5/80 6/104	
†N. D. Burns b Foster	0	7/104 8/106 9/108	

Bowling: Topley 7.5–1–22–2; Foster 6–0–16–2; Childs 8–2–14–1; Pringle 6–0–23–1; Waugh 6–1–32–0; Stephenson 1–0–3–1.

Umpires: R. Julian and K. J. Lyons.

SOMERSET v NOTTINGHAMSHIRE

At Bath, June 24. Somerset won by 29 runs. Toss: Nottinghamshire.

Somerset

S. J. Cook lbw b Stephenson	3	M. W. Cleal not out	12
R. J. Bartlett run out	50	I. G. Swallow not out	3
*C. J. Tavaré b Cooper	86	B 4, l-b 14, w 8	26
†N. D. Burns b K. Saxelby	10		
G. D. Rose b Stephenson	45	1/11 2/120 3/145 (7 wkts, 40 overs) 245	
R. J. Harden c Cooper b Evans	2	4/202 5/218	
A. N. Hayhurst run out	8	6/224 7/236	

J. C. Hallett and N. A. Mallender did not bat.

Bowling: Cooper 8–0–32–1; Stephenson 8–0–34–2; K. Saxelby 8–0–51–1; Evans 6–0–40–1; Afford 4–0–25–0; M. Saxelby 6–0–45–0.

Nottinghamshire

B. C. Broad c Burns b Mallender	18	K. E. Cooper b Hayhurst	9
M. Newell c Cleal b Hayhurst	85	K. Saxelby not out	6
P. Johnson c Burns b Hallett	1		
*R. T. Robinson c Tavaré b Swallow	12	B 4, l-b 5, w 4	13
M. Saxelby c Burns b Rose	19		
F. D. Stephenson c Rose b Hallett	34	1/26 2/27 3/60 (8 wkts, 40 overs) 216	
†B. N. French c Bartlett b Rose	1	4/93 5/155 6/170	
K. P. Evans not out	18	7/180 8/207	

J. A. Afford did not bat.

Bowling: Mallender 8–0–34–1; Hallett 8–0–39–2; Swallow 8–0–35–1; Cleal 4–0–17–0; Rose 8–0–61–2; Hayhurst 4–0–21–2.

Umpires: K. J. Lyons and R. Palmer.

SOMERSET v NORTHAMPTONSHIRE

At Taunton, July 1. Somerset won by seven wickets. Toss: Somerset.

Northamptonshire

A. Fordham b Lefebvre	53	W. W. Davis b Lefebvre	3
N. A. Felton b Swallow	41	S. J. Brown c Burns b Rose	0
R. J. Bailey run out	6	N. G. B. Cook c Burns b Lefebvre	5
*A. J. Lamb c Lefebvre b Hayhurst	41	L-b 6, w 4	10
D. J. Capel c and b Mallender	11		
R. G. Williams c Burns b Lefebvre	1	1/75 2/89 3/118 (40 overs) 193	
J. G. Thomas not out	19	4/154 5/158 6/163	
†D. Ripley c Burns b Rose	3	7/170 8/178 9/183	

Bowling: Mallender 8–1–24–1; Hallett 3–0–27–0; Lefebvre 8–0–35–4; Rose 6–0–40–2; Swallow 8–1–19–1; Hayhurst 7–1–42–1.

Somerset

S. J. Cook run out	88	G. D. Rose not out	22
N. J. Pringle c Ripley b Thomas	1	L-b 3, w 2	5
*C. J. Tavaré c Felton b Williams	56		
R. J. Harden not out	22	1/10 2/124 3/161 (3 wkts, 37.4 overs) 194	

A. N. Hayhurst, †N. D. Burns, I. G. Swallow, R. P. Lefebvre, N. A. Mallender and J. C. Hallett did not bat.

Bowling: Davis 6.4–0–25–0; Thomas 7–0–38–1; Cook 8–0–42–0; Brown 8–0–55–0; Williams 8–0–31–1.

Umpires: K. J. Lyons and D. O. Oslear.

At Lord's, July 8. SOMERSET beat MIDDLESEX by 24 runs.

At Scarborough, July 15. SOMERSET lost to YORKSHIRE by 16 runs.

At Neath, July 22. SOMERSET beat GLAMORGAN by 220 runs.

At Manchester, July 29. SOMERSET lost to LANCASHIRE by six wickets.

SOMERSET v SURREY

At Weston-super-Mare, August 5. Surrey won by six wickets. Toss: Surrey.

Somerset

S. J. Cook c Stewart b Feltham	21	I. G. Swallow not out	8
*C. J. Tavaré c Brown b Waqar Younis	41	N. A. Mallender not out	10
R. J. Harden b Bicknell	53		
J. C. M. Atkinson b Waqar Younis	8	B 7, l-b 4, w 6	17
G. D. Rose run out	3		
R. P. Lefebvre lbw b Feltham	10	1/41 2/98 3/113 (8 wkts, 40 overs) 199	
†N. D. Burns c Brown b Waqar Younis	26	4/119 5/144 6/161	
A. N. Hayhurst b Bicknell	2	7/177 8/179	

A. N. Jones did not bat.

Bowling: Bicknell 8–1–38–2; Feltham 8–0–40–2; Bullen 8–0–37–0; Medlycott 8–0–34–0; Waqar Younis 8–0–39–3.

Surrey

M. A. Feltham b Rose	24	*I. A. Greig not out	27
A. D. Brown c Hayhurst b Jones	32	L-b 8, w 11	19
G. P. Thorpe run out	42		
†D. M. Ward c Burns b Hayhurst	27	1/37 2/76 3/120 (4 wkts, 38.2 overs) 203	
M. A. Lynch not out	32	4/150	

A. J. Stewart, K. T. Medlycott, C. K. Bullen, M. P. Bicknell and Waqar Younis did not bat.

Bowling: Mallender 8–0–44–0; Rose 7–0–41–1; Lefebvre 3.2–0–19–0; Jones 8–0–33–1; Swallow 5–1–28–0; Hayhurst 7–0–30–1.

Umpires: P. J. Eele and R. A. White.

SOMERSET v WARWICKSHIRE

At Weston-super-Mare, August 12. Somerset won by seven wickets. Toss: Warwickshire. Cook's unbeaten 112, scored off 100 balls with ten fours, took him to 857 runs for the season with one possible innings to play. He thus surpassed C. E. B. Rice's record for the competition of 814 runs in 1977. Asif Din faced 109 balls, twelve of which he hit for four.

Warwickshire

A. J. Moles c Cook b Lefebvre	37	D. A. Reeve not out	18
Asif Din c Tavaré b Mallender	113		
S. J. Green b Roebuck	25	B 1, l-b 4, w 6	11
P. A. Smith c Pringle b Rose	33		
N. M. K. Smith c Cook b Roebuck	21	1/70 2/130 3/200 (5 wkts, 40 overs) 270	
*T. A. Lloyd not out	12	4/237 5/240	

†G. W. Humpage, R. G. Twose, J. E. Benjamin and T. A. Munton did not bat.

Bowling: Mallender 8–0–57–1; Rose 8–0–41–1; Hallett 2–0–16–0; Trump 7–0–43–0; Lefebvre 8–0–60–1; Roebuck 7–1–48–2.

Somerset

S. J. Cook not out 112	R. J. Harden not out	41
P. M. Roebuck c Humpage b Benjamin 9		
*C. J. Tavaré b P. A. Smith 54	B 2, l-b 8, w 8	18
G. D. Rose c Benjamin		—
b N. M. K. Smith . 37	1/16 2/114 3/176 (3 wkts, 37.4 overs) 271	

N. J. Pringle, †N. D. Burns, R. P. Lefebvre, N. A. Mallender, H. R. J. Trump and J. C. Hallett did not bat.

Bowling: Munton 7.4–0–42–0; Benjamin 8–0–46–1; Reeve 7–0–55–0; P. A. Smith 5–0–38–1; N. M. K. Smith 8–0–59–1; Twose 2–0–21–0.

Umpires: R. Julian and K. J. Lyons.

At Hove, August 26. SOMERSET beat SUSSEX by 60 runs.

SURREY

At Hove, April 29. SURREY lost to SUSSEX by three wickets.

SURREY v LANCASHIRE

At The Oval, May 6. Lancashire won by seven wickets. Toss: Lancashire. Lancashire's total was their highest in the Sunday League. Stewart faced 101 balls, hitting four sixes and seven fours.

Surrey

G. S. Clinton c Fairbrother	*I. A. Greig not out	21
b DeFreitas . 26		
A. J. Stewart c Atherton b DeFreitas ..125	B 1, l-b 6, w 1, n-b 1	9
M. A. Lynch c Mendis b Watkinson .. 58		—
G. P. Thorpe c Allott b DeFreitas 11	1/75 2/190 3/213 (4 wkts, 39 overs) 267	
†D. M. Ward not out 17	4/232	

K. T. Medlycott, M. A. Feltham, C. K. Bullen, M. P. Bicknell and A. J. Murphy did not bat.

Bowling: Patterson 8–0–55–0; Allott 8–0–40–0; DeFreitas 8–0–48–3; Austin 7–0–56–0; Watkinson 8–0–61–1.

Lancashire

G. D. Mendis c and b Medlycott 45	M. Watkinson not out	3
†G. Fowler c and b Bicknell 84	L-b 4, w 5	9
M. A. Atherton not out 76		—
N. H. Fairbrother c Stewart b Bicknell 51	1/79 2/194 3/265 (3 wkts, 37.1 overs) 268	

G. D. Lloyd, P. A. J. DeFreitas, *D. P. Hughes, I. D. Austin, P. J. W. Allott and B. P. Patterson did not bat.

Bowling: Bicknell 7–0–48–2; Murphy 7.1–0–63–0; Bullen 8–0–46–0; Medlycott 8–0–39–1; Lynch 4–0–40–0; Feltham 3–0–28–0.

Umpires: B. Dudleston and A. A. Jones.

At Nottingham, May 20. SURREY lost to NOTTINGHAMSHIRE by eight wickets.

SURREY v NORTHAMPTONSHIRE

At The Oval, June 3. Surrey won by four wickets. Toss: Surrey. The match was reduced to nineteen overs a side after a heavy rainstorm delayed the start until 4.40 p.m. Surrey's victory was their first of the season in the Sunday League.

Northamptonshire

A. Fordham c and b Bicknell	7	A. L. Penberthy c Bullen	
N. A. Felton c Waqar Younis b Feltham	10	b Waqar Younis	4
*A. J. Lamb b Murphy	0	W. W. Davis c Bicknell b Murphy	9
R. J. Bailey lbw b Bullen	20	N. G. B. Cook not out	7
D. J. Capel c and b Feltham	0	B 2, l-b 4, w 6, n-b 1	13
D. J. Wild c Greig b Bullen	10		
†W. M. Noon c Feltham		1/11 2/14 3/43	(18.4 overs) 101
b Waqar Younis	21	4/46 5/50 6/72	
J. G. Thomas c and b Bullen	0	7/72 8/84 9/84	

Bowling: Bicknell 4-0-21-1; Murphy 3.4-0-15-2; Feltham 3-0-23-2; Bullen 4-0-13-3; Waqar Younis 4-1-23-2.

Surrey

A. J. Stewart c Penberthy b Thomas	20	M. A. Feltham not out	1
M. A. Lynch c Davis b Wild	37	C. K. Bullen not out	1
G. P. Thorpe c Noon b Wild	2	L-b 8, w 2, n-b 1	11
†D. M. Ward c Fordham b Wild	7		
*I. A. Greig c Cook b Thomas	19	1/32 2/56 3/72	(6 wkts, 18.1 overs) 102
J. D. Robinson c Capel b Thomas	4	4/77 5/100 6/101	

M. P. Bicknell, Waqar Younis and A. J. Murphy did not bat.

Bowling: Davis 3.1-0-13-0; Capel 4-0-22-0; Thomas 4-0-21-3; Penberthy 3-0-19-0; Cook 1-0-11-0; Wild 3-0-8-3.

Umpires: D. O. Oslear and R. Palmer.

At Hull, June 10. SURREY beat YORKSHIRE by six wickets.

SURREY v WORCESTERSHIRE

At The Oval, June 17. Surrey won by seven wickets. Toss: Surrey.

Worcestershire

T. S. Curtis c Ward b Bicknell	0	S. R. Lampitt b Waqar Younis	11
M. J. Weston c Ward b Murphy	5	S. M. McEwan b Waqar Younis	0
G. A. Hick c Stewart b Murphy	16	R. D. Stemp not out	3
I. T. Botham b Waqar Younis	27		
D. B. D'Oliveira c and b Medlycott	53	B 2, l-b 10, w 8, n-b 1	21
*P. A. Neale run out	3		
P. J. Newport c Waqar Younis		1/0 2/23 3/23	(9 wkts, 40 overs) 177
b Medlycott	3	4/81 5/90 6/103	
†S. J. Rhodes not out	35	7/131 8/164 9/166	

Bowling: Bicknell 6-0-19-1; Murphy 7-0-38-2; Feltham 3-0-19-0; Bullen 8-1-29-0; Waqar Younis 8-0-27-3; Medlycott 8-0-33-2.

Surrey

A. J. Stewart lbw b Newport	0	M. A. Lynch not out	21
M. A. Feltham c Stemp b Hick	56	L-b 6, w 15	21
G. P. Thorpe c and b Hick	55		—
†D. M. Ward not out	27	1/0 2/120 3/133 (3 wkts, 38.5 overs) 180	

*I. A. Greig, K. T. Medlycott, C. K. Bullen, M. P. Bicknell, Waqar Younis and A. J. Murphy did not bat.

Bowling: Newport 8–2–31–1; Weston 3–0–15–0; McEwan 4–0–15–0; Botham 7–0–32–0; Stemp 8–0–37–0; Lampitt 2–0–15–0; Hick 6.5–1–29–2.

Umpires: H. D. Bird and J. H. Harris.

SURREY v DERBYSHIRE

At The Oval, June 24. Derbyshire won by three wickets. Toss: Derbyshire.

Surrey

G. S. Clinton c Bowler b Kuiper	45	K. T. Medlycott not out	4
M. A. Feltham lbw b Miller	42		
G. P. Thorpe c and b Kuiper	27	L-b 5, w 6	11
†D. M. Ward b Jean-Jacques	25		—
M. A. Lynch c Miller b Jean-Jacques	48	1/64 2/113 3/130 (5 wkts, 40 overs) 210	
*I. A. Greig not out	8	4/167 5/204	

C. K. Bullen, A. G. Robson, Waqar Younis and A. J. Murphy did not bat.

Bowling: Jean-Jacques 8–0–51–2; Mortensen 8–0–27–0; Warner 8–0–56–0; Miller 8–0–39–1; Kuiper 8–0–32–2.

Derbyshire

*K. J. Barnett c Ward b Murphy	0	G. Miller c Ward b Robson	2
†P. D. Bowler run out	50	A. E. Warner not out	11
J. E. Morris b Waqar Younis	45	B 5, l-b 14, w 3, n-b 3	25
A. P. Kuiper c Bullen b Medlycott	34		—
B. Roberts b Waqar Younis	13	1/0 2/77 3/136 (7 wkts, 38.3 overs) 213	
C. J. Adams b Waqar Younis	19	4/143 5/173	
S. C. Goldsmith not out	14	6/178 7/186	

O. H. Mortensen and M. Jean-Jacques did not bat.

Bowling: Murphy 7–0–26–1; Robson 7.3–0–37–1; Feltham 3–0–15–0; Bullen 8–0–38–0; Waqar Younis 7–0–41–3; Medlycott 6–0–37–1.

Umpires: J. H. Harris and B. J. Meyer.

At Cardiff, July 1. SURREY lost to GLAMORGAN by eight wickets.

SURREY v WARWICKSHIRE

At The Oval, July 8. Surrey won by 15 runs. Toss: Warwickshire. The match was reduced to 37 overs a side following a delay during the twelfth over of Surrey's innings. This occurred when Feltham was treated for a blow on the hand, suffered in the previous over.

Surrey

D. J. Bicknell c Piper b Twose 0	M. P. Bicknell b Benjamin 0
M. A. Feltham b Reeve 61	N. M. Kendrick not out 2
G. P. Thorpe c Moody b Munton 35	Waqar Younis not out 1
†D. M. Ward c and b Reeve 0	B 1, l-b 6, w 4 11
M. A. Lynch c Reeve b P. A. Smith ... 25	
*I. A. Greig c Humpage b Reeve 43	1/0 2/90 3/93 (9 wkts, 37 overs) 205
K. T. Medlycott run out 27	4/114 5/142 6/191
C. K. Bullen c and b Reeve 0	7/192 8/193 9/200

Bowling: Twose 4-0-29-1; Benjamin 8-0-38-1; Moody 3-0-27-0; N. M. K. Smith 6-0-35-0; Munton 6-1-25-1; Reeve 8-0-36-4; P. A. Smith 2-1-8-1.

Warwickshire

*T. A. Lloyd run out 5	†K. J. Piper b Waqar Younis 2
P. A. Smith c Waqar Younis b Feltham 9	J. E. Benjamin not out 8
T. M. Moody b M. P. Bicknell 3	T. A. Munton not out 6
G. W. Humpage b Medlycott 33	B 4, l-b 3, w 10 17
D. A. Reeve st Ward b Medlycott 25	
N. M. K. Smith c Greig b Medlycott .. 12	1/8 2/11 3/27 (9 wkts, 37 overs) 190
R. G. Twose c and b Feltham 40	4/76 5/90 6/91
D. P. Ostler run out 30	7/162 8/172 9/175

Bowling: M. P. Bicknell 8-0-34-1; Feltham 8-1-23-2; Bullen 4-0-22-0; Waqar Younis 8-0-41-1; Medlycott 6-0-43-3; Kendrick 3-0-20-0.

Umpires: D. J. Constant (replaced by G. G. Arnold, who stood at square leg) and R. Palmer.

SURREY v MIDDLESEX

At The Oval, July 15. Surrey won by 68 runs. Toss: Middlesex. Waqar Younis took his four wickets for 3 runs in a spell of twelve balls.

Surrey

D. J. Bicknell b Emburey 75	A. D. Brown run out 2
M. A. Feltham c Brown b Williams ... 4	K. T. Medlycott not out 0
G. P. Thorpe c Gatting b Haynes 41	L-b 6, w 10, n-b 1 17
†D. M. Ward c Haynes b Cowans 60	
M. A. Lynch lbw b Emburey 25	1/6 2/77 3/182 (6 wkts, 40 overs) 228
*I. A. Greig not out 4	4/215 5/222 6/224

C. K. Bullen, M. P. Bicknell and Waqar Younis did not bat.

Bowling: Cowans 8-0-46-1; Williams 8-1-42-1; Emburey 8-1-39-2; Brown 2-0-16-0; Fraser 8-0-40-0; Haynes 6-0-39-1.

Middlesex

D. L. Haynes c Ward b M. P. Bicknell. 4	N. F. Williams lbw b Waqar Younis .. 1
M. A. Roseberry b Medlycott 48	A. R. C. Fraser not out 4
*M. W. Gatting b M. P. Bicknell 2	N. G. Cowans c and b M. P. Bicknell . 0
M. R. Ramprakash c Thorpe	
b Waqar Younis . 60	L-b 3, w 5, n-b 1 9
K. R. Brown c Greig b Medlycott 12	
R. O. Butcher b Waqar Younis 3	1/4 2/18 3/99 (33.2 overs) 160
J. E. Emburey c Bullen b M. P. Bicknell 15	4/125 5/134 6/136
†P. Farbrace b Waqar Younis 2	7/142 8/156 9/160

Bowling: M. P. Bicknell 4.2-0-14-4; Feltham 4-0-23-0; Greig 3-0-16-0; Bullen 8-0-38-0; Waqar Younis 6-0-27-4; Medlycott 8-0-39-2.

Umpires: P. J. Eele and D. R. Shepherd.

SURREY v KENT

At The Oval, July 22. Surrey won by five wickets. Toss: Surrey.

Kent

S. G. Hinks run out 41	P. S. de Villiers b Waqar Younis 6
N. R. Taylor c Ward b Medlycott 26	R. P. Davis c Sargeant b Feltham 0
T. R. Ward b Waqar Younis 14	A. P. Igglesden not out 3
*C. S. Cowdrey c Sargeant	
b Waqar Younis . 7	L-b 6, w 8 14
G. R. Cowdrey c Sargeant b Medlycott . 14	
M. V. Fleming b Waqar Younis 4	1/54 2/80 3/93 (37.4 overs) 164
†S. A. Marsh c Bullen b Waqar Younis 35	4/98 5/107 6/122
R. M. Ellison c Robinson b Bullen 0	7/123 8/153 9/157

Bowling: Feltham 7–0–26–1; Robinson 3–0–19–0; Medlycott 8–0–40–2; Greig 4–0–22–0; Bullen 8–0–25–1; Waqar Younis 7.4–0–26–5.

Surrey

D. J. Bicknell b Davis 26	*I. A. Greig not out 0
M. A. Feltham b de Villiers 9	
G. P. Thorpe not out 69	L-b 11, w 6 17
D. M. Ward b Fleming 4	
M. A. Lynch lbw b Ward 26	1/16 2/53 3/64 (5 wkts, 37.1 overs) 167
J. D. Robinson c Igglesden b Ellison .. 16	4/118 5/162

K. T. Medlycott, C. K. Bullen, †N. F. Sargeant and Waqar Younis did not bat.

Bowling: Igglesden 8–0–29–0; de Villiers 6.1–1–26–1; Davis 8–0–30–1; Ellison 8–0–33–1; Fleming 3–0–21–1; Ward 4–0–17–1.

Umpires: B. J. Meyer and K. E. Palmer.

At Cheltenham, July 29. SURREY lost to GLOUCESTERSHIRE by five wickets.

At Weston-super-Mare, August 5. SURREY beat SOMERSET by six wickets.

SURREY v LEICESTERSHIRE

At The Oval, August 12. Surrey won by 69 runs. Toss: Surrey. Surrey's total of 278 for seven was the highest conceded by Leicestershire in the Sunday League.

Surrey

M. A. Feltham c Nixon b Parsons 0	K. T. Medlycott not out 44
A. D. Brown c Mullally b Gidley 56	C. K. Bullen not out 12
G. P. Thorpe c Millns b Mullally 85	B 2, l-b 3, w 3, n-b 5 13
†D. M. Ward b Gidley 6	
M. A. Lynch c Millns b Gidley 23	1/0 2/112 3/121 (7 wkts, 40 overs) 278
*I. A. Greig c Boon b Benson 26	4/163 5/185
J. D. Robinson c Benson b Millns 13	6/213 7/216

M. P. Bicknell and Waqar Younis did not bat.

Bowling: Parsons 8–0–70–1; Millns 8–0–47–1; Mullally 8–0–57–1; Gidley 8–0–45–3; Benson 8–1–54–1.

Leicestershire

J. Whitaker c Bullen b Bicknell	8	M. I. Gidley not out	5
N. E. Briers c Bullen b Bicknell	5	A. D. Mullally c Bicknell b Feltham	5
F. Smith c Bullen b Bicknell	10	D. J. Millns b Waqar Younis	0
J. Boon c Thorpe b Bullen	59	B 5, l-b 10, w 10	25
Potter run out	6		
D. R. Benson c Brown b Bicknell	67	1/15 2/26 3/29 (40 overs)	209
J. Parsons c sub b Waqar Younis	18	4/45 5/160 6/193	
P. A. Nixon b Waqar Younis	1	7/196 8/196 9/208	

Bowling: Bicknell 8–0–26–4; Feltham 7–0–29–1; Bullen 8–0–35–1; Medlycott 6–0–39–0; Waqar Younis 8–0–43–3; Robinson 3–0–22–0.

Umpires: J. D. Bond and B. Leadbeater.

At Chelmsford, August 19. ESSEX v SURREY. No result.

At Southampton, August 26. SURREY beat HAMPSHIRE by 4 runs.

SUSSEX

SUSSEX v DERBYSHIRE

At Hove, April 22. Derbyshire won by six wickets. Toss: Derbyshire.

Sussex

N. J. Lenham c Bowler b Base	0	†P. Moores c Bowler b Base	0
P. W. G. Parker lbw b Mortensen	0	A. R. Hansford not out	5
A. P. Wells c Kuiper b Malcolm	57		
M. P. Speight c Bowler b Base	77	L-b 17, w 2, n-b 4	23
C. M. Wells c Mortensen b Kuiper	8		
J. Gould b Kuiper	0	1/1 2/3 3/140 (8 wkts, 40 overs)	205
*C. S. Pigott c Bowler b Base	11	4/153 5/160 6/164	
I. C. Dodemaide not out	24	7/183 8/183	

D. K. Salisbury did not bat.

Bowling: Mortensen 8–0–23–1; Base 8–0–28–4; Miller 6–0–38–0; Malcolm 8–0–47–1; Kuiper 6–0–30–2; Barnett 4–0–22–0.

Derbyshire

*K. J. Barnett c Moores b Pigott	60	C. J. Adams not out	30
P. D. Bowler c and b Salisbury	51	L-b 6, w 2, n-b 2	10
J. E. Morris run out	5		
A. P. Kuiper not out	53	1/117 2/125 (4 wkts, 38.5 overs)	209
J. G. O'Gorman lbw b Pigott	0	3/128 4/128	

B. Roberts, G. Miller, D. E. Malcolm, S. J. Base and O. H. Mortensen did not bat.

Bowling: C. M. Wells 7.5–1–41–0; Dodemaide 8–0–38–0; Salisbury 8–1–29–1; Hansford 8–0–35–0; Pigott 8–0–60–2.

Umpires: A. G. T. Whitehead and P. B. Wight.

SUSSEX v SURREY

At Hove, April 29. Sussex won by three wickets. Toss: Surrey.

Surrey

D. J. Bicknell c Moores b Clarke	 21	C. K. Bullen b Hansford	....
A. J. Stewart b Salisbury	 64	M. P. Bicknell not out	....
M. A. Lynch lbw b Clarke	 9		
G. P. Thorpe run out	 53	L-b 6, w 1	....
†D. M. Ward b Salisbury	 7		
*I. A. Greig c Moores b Salisbury	 2	1/50 2/64 3/131	(8 wkts, 40 overs) 1
K. T. Medlycott b Hansford	 17	4/141 5/145 6/169	
M. A. Feltham not out	 7	7/183 8/187	

A. J. Murphy did not bat.

Bowling: C. M. Wells 8–1–34–0; Dodemaide 8–0–43–0; Clarke 8–0–23–2; Hansfo 8–0–48–2; Salisbury 8–0–40–3.

Sussex

N. J. Lenham run out	 12	†P. Moores b Lynch	....
I. J. Gould run out	 9	A. R. Clarke not out	....
A. P. Wells not out	 86	B 8, l-b 14, w 1	....
M. P. Speight c Ward b Feltham	 18		
C. M. Wells b Bullen	 5	1/31 2/51 3/89	(7 wkts, 39.4 overs) 1
*P. W. G. Parker b Murphy	 28	4/107 5/165	
A. I. C. Dodemaide b Lynch	 17	6/190 7/190	

I. D. K. Salisbury and A. R. Hansford did not bat.

Bowling: M. P. Bicknell 7–0–33–0; Murphy 7.4–0–41–1; Bullen 8–0–40–1; Medlyco 8–0–30–0; Feltham 8–0–30–1; Lynch 1–0–2–2.

Umpires: D. J. Constant and D. S. Thompsett.

SUSSEX v GLAMORGAN

At Hove, May 20. Sussex won by six wickets. Toss: Sussex.

Glamorgan

H. Morris c Pigott b Salisbury	 68	†M. L. Roberts not out	....
P. A. Cottey lbw b Clarke	 36	L-b 9, w 3	....
I. V. A. Richards c Pigott b Salisbury	. 31		
*A. R. Butcher c Dodemaide b Salisbury	6	1/76 2/126 3/140	(4 wkts, 40 overs) 1
I. Smith not out	 33	4/156	

N. G. Cowley, M. Frost, S. J. Dennis, S. R. Barwick and S. L. Watkin did not bat.

Bowling: Wells 8–0–21–0; Babington 4–0–21–0; Pigott 8–1–32–0; Clarke 8–0–47– Dodemaide 7–0–32–0; Salisbury 5–0–36–3.

Sussex

N. J. Lenham b Richards	 62	A. C. S. Pigott not out	....
I. J. Gould c Butcher b Dennis	 41	L-b 5, w 3, n-b 1	....
M. P. Speight b Richards	 26		
C. M. Wells c Butcher b Richards	 14	1/71 2/120 3/150	(4 wkts, 38.4 overs) 2
A. I. C. Dodemaide not out	 25	4/153	

†P. Moores, *P. W. G. Parker, A. R. Clarke, I. D. K. Salisbury and A. M. Babington d not bat.

Bowling: Watkin 6–0–28–0; Frost 7.4–0–51–0; Dennis 8–0–25–1; Cowley 3–0–15– Barwick 7–0–40–0; Richards 7–0–37–3.

Umpires: M. J. Kitchen and R. A. White.

SUSSEX v LANCASHIRE

At Horsham, June 3. No result. This was the first Sunday League game of the season to be abandoned without a ball bowled.

At Leicester, June 10. SUSSEX lost to LEICESTERSHIRE by seven wickets.

SUSSEX v YORKSHIRE

At Hove, June 17. Yorkshire won by 40 runs. Toss: Sussex.

Yorkshire

K. Sharp b Pigott	34	P. Carrick not out	24
A. Metcalfe c Moores b C. M. Wells	16	P. J. Hartley not out	5
J. Blakey c Moores b Lenham	23	L-b 6, w 4	10
Byas c Parker b Remy	26		—
M. D. Moxon c Dodemaide b Remy	39	1/33 2/77 3/79 (7 wkts, 40 overs) 192	
E. Robinson c Moores b Dodemaide	1	4/132 5/133	
D. L. Bairstow c A. P. Wells b Pigott	14	6/157 7/175	

S. Pickles and P. W. Jarvis did not bat.

Bowling: C. M. Wells 8–1–17–1; Remy 8–0–45–2; Dodemaide 8–2–32–1; Salisbury 0–36–0; Pigott 8–0–35–2; Lenham 4–0–21–1.

Sussex

N. J. Lenham c Robinson b Jarvis	16	†P. Moores c Byas b Jarvis	8
I. J. Gould run out	0	C. C. Remy c Moxon b Hartley	7
*P. W. G. Parker lbw b Moxon	36	I. D. K. Salisbury not out	3
A. P. Wells c Blakey b Moxon	6	B 4, l-b 6, w 1	11
M. P. Speight b Moxon	24		—
A. M. Wells c and b Carrick	2	1/1 2/24 3/38 (36.5 overs) 152	
I. C. Dodemaide c Pickles b Carrick	20	4/76 5/83 6/93	
A. C. S. Pigott st Bairstow b Carrick	19	7/122 8/131 9/143	

Bowling: Pickles 7–0–24–0; Jarvis 5–0–19–2; Hartley 6.5–0–26–1; Moxon 8–0–29–3; Byas 4–0–16–0; Carrick 8–2–28–3.

Umpires: J. D. Bond and R. Palmer.

At Worcester, June 24. SUSSEX lost to WORCESTERSHIRE by 2 runs.

SUSSEX v HAMPSHIRE

At Hove, July 1. Sussex won on scoring-rate. Toss: Hampshire. Rain, which delayed the start for 30 minutes, caused the match to be reduced to 36 overs a side, although Hampshire managed to bowl only 33. When Hampshire were 78 for two off sixteen overs in reply, rain again intervened and they were set a revised target of 208 off 28 overs.

Sussex

N. J. Lenham c Connor b Maru	72	A. I. C. Dodemaide not out	1
I. J. Gould c R. A. Smith b Nicholas	68		
*P. W. G. Parker c Nicholas b Bakker	12	B 1, l-b 13, w 9, n-b 2	25
A. P. Wells not out	44		—
M. P. Speight c R. A. Smith b Ayling	21	1/135 2/172 3/176 (5 wkts, 33 overs) 244	
A. M. Wells b Marshall	1	4/217 5/228	

A. C. S. Pigott, †P. Moores, C. C. Remy and A. R. Clarke did not bat.

Bowling: Marshall 7–0–50–1; Bakker 7–0–48–1; Connor 5–0–18–0; Ayling 7–0–52–1; Maru 7–0–39–1; Nicholas 2–0–23–1.

Hampshire

V. P. Terry c Lenham b C. M. Wells ..	25	R. J. Maru c Clarke b Dodemaide	....
M. D. Marshall c Lenham b C. M. Wells	19	C. A. Connor c Lenham b Pigott	.....
R. A. Smith b Dodemaide	24	P. J. Bakker st Moores b Clarke	......
D. I. Gower c Speight b Pigott	10	L-b 3, w 4	
C. L. Smith c Moores b Pigott	3		
*M. C. J. Nicholas b Dodemaide	27	1/37 2/53 3/79	(27.3 overs) 1!
J. R. Ayling not out	17	4/82 5/88 6/114	
†R. J. Parks c C. M. Wells b Pigott ...	4	7/119 8/123 9/133	

Bowling: C. M. Wells 7–0–30–2; Dodemaide 8–0–50–3; Clarke 5.3–0–26–1; Pigo 7–0–42–4.

Umpires: J. H. Harris and A. A. Jones.

At Nottingham, July 8. SUSSEX lost to NOTTINGHAMSHIRE by 8 runs.

At Swindon, July 15. SUSSEX lost to GLOUCESTERSHIRE by one wicket.

At Wellingborough School, July 22. SUSSEX beat NORTHAMPTONSHIRE by 21 runs.

At Chelmsford, July 29. SUSSEX lost to ESSEX by two wickets.

SUSSEX v WARWICKSHIRE

At Eastbourne, August 5. Warwickshire won by 2 runs. Toss: Sussex.

Warwickshire

A. J. Moles c Moores b Dodemaide ...	3	R. G. Twose not out	
Asif Din c Smith b Dodemaide	6	†K. J. Piper not out	
T. M. Moody b Pigott	64	L-b 4, w 1	
D. A. Reeve lbw b Clarke	22		
P. A. Smith c Hansford b Pigott	11	1/7 2/9 3/65	(7 wkts, 40 overs) 17
*T. A. Lloyd c Remy b Clarke	48	4/82 5/144	
N. M. K. Smith st Moores b Hansford	16	6/174 7/174	

G. Smith and T. A. Munton did not bat.

Bowling: Pigott 8–0–46–2; Dodemaide 8–1–21–2; C. M. Wells 8–1–17–0; Hansfor 8–1–49–1; Clarke 8–0–42–2.

Sussex

M. P. Speight b Munton	20	A. C. S. Pigott not out	2
D. M. Smith b Moody	18	†P. Moores b Munton	
A. P. Wells c Piper b Munton	0	A. R. Hansford c Asif Din b P. A. Smith	
*C. M. Wells c N. M. K. Smith		A. R. Clarke not out	
b P. A. Smith .	64	B 1, l-b 6, w 2	
R. Hanley b N. M. K. Smith	11		
C. C. Remy b N. M. K. Smith	11	1/30 2/30 3/53	(9 wkts, 40 overs) 17
A. I. C. Dodemaide c N. M. K. Smith		4/101 5/121 6/134	
b P. A. Smith .	3	7/134 8/146 9/155	

Bowling: Munton 8–1–36–3; G. Smith 2–0–8–0; Reeve 8–1–20–0; Moody 7–0–31–1 N. M. K. Smith 7–0–41–2; P. A. Smith 8–0–34–3.

Umpires: J. D. Bond and M. J. Kitchen.

Lord's, August 12. SUSSEX beat MIDDLESEX by seven wickets.

Canterbury, August 19. KENT v SUSSEX. No result.

SUSSEX v SOMERSET

Hove, August 26. Somerset won by 60 runs. Toss: Sussex. Cook took his record number of ns for a Sunday League season to 902.

omerset

J. Cook c Pigott b Lenham	45	A. N. Jones c Lenham b Dodemaide	2
J. Bartlett c Moores b Dodemaide	2	H. R. J. Trump b Dodemaide	0
. J. Tavaré b C. M. Wells	12	J. C. Hallett not out	3
J. Harden c Moores b C. M. Wells	0	B 1, l-b 1, w 14	16
D. Rose c Gould b Pigott	7		
N. Hayhurst not out	70	1/14 2/38 3/38 (9 wkts, 40 overs) 222	
N. D. Burns c and b Dodemaide	58	4/61 5/99 6/182	
P. Lefebvre b Pigott	7	7/193 8/197 9/198	

Bowling: Dodemaide 8–0–40–4; C. M. Wells 7–1–28–2; Pigott 8–0–39–2; Salisbury 0–32–0; Donelan 6–0–37–0; Lenham 5–0–44–1.

ussex

J. Lenham c Burns b Jones	19	†P. Moores b Hayhurst	1
J. Gould b Jones	5	I. D. K. Salisbury run out	7
P. Wells c Jones b Trump	31	B. T. P. Donelan b Lefebvre	4
P. Speight c Burns b Hayhurst	21	B 1, l-b 11, w 10, n-b 2	24
. M. Wells c Jones b Hayhurst	3		
Greenfield b Hayhurst	2	1/12 2/37 3/79 (35.4 overs) 162	
I. C. Dodemaide not out	31	4/85 5/91 6/98	
C. S. Pigott c Hayhurst b Trump	14	7/120 8/122 9/145	

Bowling: Jones 7–0–31–2; Rose 5–0–12–0; Hallett 4–1–18–0; Lefebvre 4.4–0–22–1; ayhurst 8–0–37–4; Trump 7–0–30–2.

Umpires: J. C. Balderstone and R. A. White.

WARWICKSHIRE

WARWICKSHIRE v NORTHAMPTONSHIRE

t Birmingham, April 29. Warwickshire won by seven wickets. Toss: Warwickshire.

orthamptonshire

. J. Bailey c Reeve b N. M. K. Smith	58	†D. Ripley not out	3
. Larkins c N. M. K. Smith b Munton	0		
A. J. Lamb b Moody	70	L-b 9, w 7	16
. J. Capel c Small b Moody	20		
. Fordham not out	29	1/0 2/128 3/145 (5 wkts, 40 overs) 196	
. J. Wild c sub b Reeve	0	4/177 5/177	

G. Thomas, N. G. B. Cook, C. E. L. Ambrose and M. A. Robinson did not bat.

Bowling: Small 8–1–27–0; Munton 6–1–22–1; Reeve 8–1–45–1; N. M. K. Smith 7–0–34–1; A. Smith 3–0–17–0; Moody 8–0–42–2.

Warwickshire

Asif Din st wkt b Capel	23	D. A. Reeve not out		...
A. I. Kallicharran b Robinson	76	L-b 4, w 2		...
T. M. Moody b Cook	56			—
†G. W. Humpage not out	22	1/39 2/153 3/171	(3 wkts, 37.3 overs)	2⟨⟩

*T. A. Lloyd, P. A. Smith, G. C. Small, N. M. K. Smith, R. G. Twose and T. A. Munt⟨⟩ did not bat.

Bowling: Ambrose 7–1–31–0; Robinson 7.3–0–53–1; Capel 8–0–35–1; Thomas 7–0–37– Cook 8–0–40–1.

Umpires: J. C. Balderstone and H. D. Bird.

WARWICKSHIRE v YORKSHIRE

At Birmingham, May 6. Warwickshire won by eight wickets. Toss: Yorkshire.

Yorkshire

S. A. Kellett b Reeve	21	P. Carrick c Munton b Reeve		...
*A. A. Metcalfe b Moody	56	P. J. Hartley not out		...
†R. J. Blakey b Reeve	9	L-b 8, w 7		...
P. E. Robinson c Reeve b Booth	22			—
D. Byas run out	7	1/47 2/62 3/96	(6 wkts, 40 overs)	1
C. White not out	30	4/116 5/129 6/171		

P. W. Jarvis, S. D. Fletcher and D. Gough did not bat.

Bowling: Small 8–0–41–0; Munton 8–2–23–0; Reeve 8–1–29–3; Booth 8–0–46–1; Moo 8–0–38–1.

Warwickshire

A. I. Kallicharran c Fletcher b Carrick	65		
Asif Din b Byas	40		
T. M. Moody not out	51		
†G. W. Humpage not out	16		
L-b 13, w 3, n-b 1	17		

1/73 2/140 (2 wkts, 37.1 overs) 189

D. A. Reeve, *T. A. Lloyd, P. A. Booth, G. C. Small, R. G. Twose, N. M. K. Smith a T. A. Munton did not bat.

Bowling: Jarvis 8–1–21–0; Fletcher 5.1–0–27–0; Hartley 4–0–16–0; Gough 3–0–20– Carrick 7–0–39–1; Byas 5–0–27–1; White 5–0–26–0.

Umpires: R. Palmer and P. B. Wight.

At Moreton-in-Marsh, May 20. WARWICKSHIRE lost to GLOUCESTERSHIRE by runs.

At Worcester, May 27. WARWICKSHIRE beat WORCESTERSHIRE by six wickets.

At Lord's, June 3. WARWICKSHIRE lost to MIDDLESEX by nine wickets.

WARWICKSHIRE v ESSEX

At Birmingham, June 10. Essex won by seven wickets. Toss: Essex.

Warwickshire

Asif Din lbw b Foster	4	J. E. Benjamin not out		10
T. M. Moody c Shahid b Childs	54	G. Smith b Pringle		5
P. A. Smith lbw b Topley	2	T. A. Munton not out		2
G. W. Humpage c Stephenson b Pringle	5	L-b 7, w 3, n-b 3		13
R. G. Twose st Garnham b Stephenson	4			
D. A. Reeve b Foster	28	1/19 2/29 3/43	(9 wkts, 40 overs)	155
A. P. Ostler b Waugh	18	4/64 5/82 6/118		
N. M. K. Smith c Stephenson b Pringle	10	7/135 8/137 9/153		

Bowling: Topley 8–1–27–1; Foster 8–0–35–2; Childs 8–0–19–1; Pringle 8–1–29–3; Stephenson 3–0–20–1; Waugh 5–0–18–1.

Essex

B. R. Hardie b G. Smith	54	A. W. Lilley not out		9
J. J. Prichard lbw b Benjamin	8	L-b 4, w 3, n-b 3		10
M. E. Waugh b G. Smith	60			
D. R. Pringle not out	17	1/19 2/121 3/149	(3 wkts, 35.3 overs)	158

P. Stephenson, N. Shahid, †M. A. Garnham, N. A. Foster, T. D. Topley and J. H. Childs did not bat.

Bowling: Munton 8–1–23–0; Benjamin 6–1–18–1; Moody 4–1–18–0; Reeve 3–0–12–0; N. M. K. Smith 6.3–0–40–0; G. Smith 5–0–20–2; P. A. Smith 1–0–6–0; Asif Din 2–0–17–0.

Umpires: B. Dudleston and R. A. White.

At Derby, June 17. WARWICKSHIRE lost to DERBYSHIRE by 1 run.

WARWICKSHIRE v KENT

At Birmingham, June 24. Warwickshire won by three wickets. Toss: Warwickshire. Kallicharran's innings brought him his 5,000th run in the Sunday League.

Kent

S. G. Hinks c Moody b Munton	6	P. S. de Villiers b Benjamin		10
M. A. Ealham b Twose	25	R. P. Davis not out		2
V. R. Taylor st Piper b Pierson	18	A. P. Igglesden c Piper b Reeve		1
C. S. Cowdrey b Benjamin	46	B 6, l-b 3, w 4, n-b 3		16
G. R. Cowdrey run out	16			
M. V. Fleming lbw b Moody	2	1/11 2/45 3/68	(39.1 overs)	159
S. A. Marsh run out	9	4/89 5/95 6/128		
R. M. Ellison run out	8	7/137 8/152 9/158		

Bowling: Munton 6–0–9–1; Twose 8–1–35–1; Benjamin 8–0–29–2; Pierson 5–2–18–1; Moody 6–0–27–1; Reeve 6.1–0–32–1.

Warwickshire

A. J. Moles c Ealham b C. S. Cowdrey	24	†K. J. Piper run out		4
A. I. Kallicharran c Ealham b C. S. Cowdrey	23	J. E. Benjamin not out		14
T. M. Moody c and b Davis	29	B 4, l-b 6, w 4		14
D. A. Reeve b C. S. Cowdrey	25			
Asif Din not out	19	1/46 2/58 3/107	(7 wkts, 39 overs)	160
R. G. Twose c Igglesden b Davis	5	4/115 5/122		
A. P. Ostler c Davis b de Villiers	3	6/127 7/137		

A. R. K. Pierson and T. A. Munton did not bat.

Bowling: Igglesden 8–0–37–0; de Villiers 7–1–17–1; Fleming 8–0–39–0; Ellison 8–0–27–0 C. S. Cowdrey 4–0–19–3; Davis 4–0–11–2.

Umpires: J. D. Bond and K. E. Palmer.

At The Oval, July 8. WARWICKSHIRE lost to SURREY by 15 runs.

WARWICKSHIRE v GLAMORGAN

At Birmingham, July 15. Glamorgan won by seven wickets. Toss: Warwickshire.

Warwickshire

*T. A. Lloyd c Dale b Watkin	12	J. E. Benjamin b Watkin	
Asif Din run out	46	A. R. K. Pierson c Metson b Watkin	
T. M. Moody b Dale	4	T. A. Munton not out	
G. W. Humpage c Watkin b Cowley	11	B 1, l-b 6, w 5	1
D. P. Ostler b Cowley	15		—
D. A. Reeve b Watkin	28	1/19 2/32 3/63	(39.4 overs) 14
†K. J. Piper b Richards	1	4/93 5/95 6/97	
G. C. Small b Watkin	4	7/118 8/130 9/133	

Bowling: Frost 6–0–21–0; Watkin 7.4–0–23–5; Dale 8–0–29–1; Dennis 6–0–24–0; Cowley 8–1–17–2; Richards 4–0–20–1.

Glamorgan

M. P. Maynard not out	61	*A. R. Butcher not out	
H. Morris b Benjamin	19	B 1, l-b 4, w 10	1
I. V. A. Richards c Pierson b Reeve	31		—
I. Smith c Moody b Pierson	10	1/45 2/92 3/125	(3 wkts, 34 overs) 14

A. Dale, N. G. Cowley, †C. P. Metson, S. J. Dennis, S. L. Watkin and M. Frost did not bat

Bowling: Small 8–1–17–0; Munton 6–2–14–0; Benjamin 6–1–34–1; Reeve 6–0–28–1 Pierson 7–1–38–1; Moody 1–0–6–0.

Umpires: A. A. Jones and B. J. Meyer.

WARWICKSHIRE v NOTTINGHAMSHIRE

At Birmingham, July 22. Nottinghamshire won by 10 runs. Toss: Nottinghamshire. Johnso reached his third Sunday League hundred of the season off 82 balls, with three sixes an twelve fours, but then added only 14 from the next nineteen balls he received.

Nottinghamshire

B. C. Broad c Piper b Munton	1	K. P. Evans run out	
P. R. Pollard b Benjamin	3	E. E. Hemmings not out	
P. Johnson c Munton b Twose	114		
*R. T. Robinson c Moody b Twose	63	L-b 6, w 3	
F. D. Stephenson b Munton	4		—
M. Newell run out	6	1/1 2/7 3/176	(8 wkts, 40 overs) 24
G. W. Mike run out	4	4/186 5/196 6/199	
†B. N. French not out	34	7/222 8/239	

K. E. Cooper did not bat.

Bowling: Benjamin 8–0–20–1; Munton 8–2–45–2; Pierson 3–0–27–0; Reeve 7–0–43–0 Small 4–0–29–0; Smith 2–0–21–0; Twose 8–0–50–2.

Warwickshire

*T. A. Lloyd c Pollard b Evans	63	J. E. Benjamin not out	3
Asif Din lbw b Hemmings	43		
T. M. Moody lbw b Mike	7	L-b 7, w 14, n-b 4	25
P. A. Smith st French b Hemmings	19		
D. A. Reeve run out	41	1/99 2/115 3/133 (5 wkts, 40 overs) 231	
R. G. Twose not out	30	4/154 5/224	

†K. J. Piper, G. C. Small, A. R. K. Pierson and T. A. Munton did not bat.

Bowling: Cooper 8–0–50–0; Stephenson 8–0–29–0; Mike 8–0–54–1; Evans 8–0–57–1; Hemmings 8–1–34–2.

Umpires: J. D. Bond and B. Dudleston.

WARWICKSHIRE v HAMPSHIRE

At Birmingham, July 29. Hampshire won by three wickets. Toss: Hampshire.

Warwickshire

A. J. Moles c Parks b Marshall	14	R. G. Twose b Udal	5
*T. A. Lloyd lbw b Bakker	4	N. M. K. Smith not out	38
T. M. Moody b Marshall	5	L-b 6, w 2, n-b 1	9
P. A. Smith c Parks b Ayling	26		
D. A. Reeve b Bakker	1	1/6 2/23 3/24 (6 wkts, 40 overs) 179	
Asif Din not out	77	4/25 5/74 6/102	

†K. J. Piper, J. E. Benjamin and T. A. Munton did not bat.

Bowling: Marshall 8–0–36–2; Bakker 7–1–33–2; Connor 8–0–45–0; Ayling 8–0–27–1; Udal 8–0–20–1; Maru 1–0–12–0.

Hampshire

V. P. Terry c Munton b N. M. K. Smith	53	†R. J. Parks not out	23
R. J. Scott st Piper b N. M. K. Smith	47	S. D. Udal not out	2
*M. C. J. Nicholas b Benjamin	0	B 1, l-b 5, w 2	8
M. D. Marshall run out	24		
C. L. Smith run out	0	1/88 2/89 3/127 (7 wkts, 39.4 overs) 183	
J. R. Ayling c Lloyd b Munton	25	4/127 5/139	
R. J. Maru st Piper b N. M. K. Smith	1	6/149 7/165	

C. A. Connor and P. J. Bakker did not bat.

Bowling: Twose 7.4–0–47–0; Munton 8–1–29–1; Benjamin 8–1–29–1; Reeve 8–0–36–0; N. M. K. Smith 8–0–36–3.

Umpires: D. R. Shepherd and R. A. White.

At Eastbourne, August 5. WARWICKSHIRE beat SUSSEX by 2 runs.

At Weston-super-Mare, August 12. WARWICKSHIRE lost to SOMERSET by seven wickets.

WARWICKSHIRE v LEICESTERSHIRE

At Birmingham, August 19. No result, rain having stopped play. Toss: Warwickshire.

Leicestershire

T. J. Boon b Small	5	M. I. Gidley not out	2
*N. E. Briers b Munton	2		
B. F. Smith st Piper b Booth	29	B 1, l-b 10, w 8	19
C. C. Lewis lbw b Small	43		
J. D. R. Benson b Small	14	1/5 2/15 3/81 (5 wkts, 28.1 overs) 121	
L. Potter not out	7	4/109 5/118	

G. J. Parsons, †P. A. Nixon, A. D. Mullally and D. J. Millns did not bat.

Bowling: Small 8–0–20–3; Munton 6.1–1–8–1; Moody 3–0–23–0; Booth 5–0–33–1; P. A. Smith 6–0–26–0.

Warwickshire

A. J. Moles, Asif Din, T. M. Moody, P. A. Smith, S. J. Green, *T. A. Lloyd, N. M. K. Smith, †K. J. Piper, P. A. Booth, G. C. Small and T. A. Munton.

Umpires: J. W. Holder and K. E. Palmer.

At Manchester, August 26. WARWICKSHIRE lost to LANCASHIRE by 49 runs.

WORCESTERSHIRE

At Taunton, April 22. WORCESTERSHIRE beat SOMERSET by 33 runs.

At Derby, April 29. WORCESTERSHIRE lost to DERBYSHIRE by 35 runs.

WORCESTERSHIRE v NOTTINGHAMSHIRE

At Worcester, May 6. Worcestershire won by 61 runs. Toss: Nottinghamshire. Hick faced 105 balls and hit two sixes and eight fours in his highest score in the Sunday League.

Worcestershire

T. S. Curtis lbw b Pick	73	S. R. Lampitt not out	4
R. K. Illingworth c French b Cooper	3	L-b 6, w 3, n-b 1	10
G. A. Hick not out	114		
D. B. D'Oliveira b Stephenson	6	1/19 2/161 3/182 (4 wkts, 40 overs) 221	
*P. A. Neale b Saxelby	11	4/217	

D. A. Leatherdale, †S. R. Bevins, P. J. Newport, N. V. Radford and S. M. McEwan did not bat.

Bowling: Stephenson 8–1–41–1; Cooper 8–1–32–1; Saxelby 8–0–54–1; Pick 8–0–47–1; Hemmings 8–0–41–0.

Nottinghamshire

B. C. Broad c Bevins b Newport	0	K. E. Cooper c Hick b Newport	4
*R. T. Robinson run out	0	R. A. Pick b Lampitt	12
P. R. Pollard c Leatherdale b Lampitt	13	K. Saxelby not out	6
P. Johnson c Bevins b McEwan	58	L-b 13, w 6	19
D. W. Randall c Hick b Radford	12		
F. D. Stephenson c Bevins b McEwan	3	1/0 2/1 3/35 (39.2 overs) 160	
†B. N. French c Illingworth b Newport	9	4/66 5/76 6/99	
E. E. Hemmings st Bevins b Illingworth	24	7/115 8/129 9/138	

Bowling: Newport 8–0–37–3; McEwan 8–0–32–2; Lampitt 7.2–0–22–2; Radford 8–0–30–1; Illingworth 8–0–26–1.

Umpires: B. Leadbeater and K. J. Lyons.

WORCESTERSHIRE v ESSEX

At Worcester, May 20. Essex won by two wickets. Toss: Worcestershire. Essex achieved their first Sunday League victory of the season in their fifth match.

Worcestershire

T. S. Curtis c Prichard b Topley	34	*P. A. Neale run out	1
M. J. Weston b Pringle	90	B 2, l-b 11, w 5	18
†. T. Botham c Garnham b Foster	5		
D. B. D'Oliveira c Hardie b Pringle	41	1/78 2/116 3/164 (5 wkts, 40 overs) 215	
N. V. Radford not out	26	4/209 5/215	

S. R. Lampitt, †S. J. Rhodes, P. J. Newport, R. K. Illingworth and S. M. McEwan did not bat.

Bowling: Foster 8–1–38–1; Ilott 8–0–28–0; Gooch 6–0–35–0; Topley 8–0–39–1; Pringle 8–0–48–2; Childs 2–0–14–0.

Essex

*G. A. Gooch b Weston	30	T. D. Topley lbw b Botham	0
B. R. Hardie c Newport b Illingworth	54	J. H. Childs not out	5
M. E. Waugh c and b Weston	4		
P. J. Prichard c Neale b Botham	47	L-b 12, w 2	14
D. R. Pringle not out	48		
J. P. Stephenson c McEwan b Botham	9	1/50 2/55 3/148 (8 wkts, 39.3 overs) 216	
†M. A. Garnham c Weston b Botham	5	4/148 5/172 6/181	
N. A. Foster run out	0	7/181 8/188	

M. C. Ilott did not bat.

Bowling: Newport 6–0–33–0; Weston 8–0–33–2; Radford 7–0–39–0; Illingworth 8–0–41–1; Lampitt 4.3–0–33–0; Botham 6–1–25–4.

Umpires: B. Dudleston and P. B. Wight.

WORCESTERSHIRE v WARWICKSHIRE

At Worcester, May 27. Warwickshire won by six wickets. Toss: Worcestershire. Warwickshire's win was their first at New Road in 22 seasons of the Sunday League.

Worcestershire

T. S. Curtis run out	61	N. V. Radford c Munton b Small	4
M. J. Weston c Humpage b Reeve	15	P. J. Newport run out	8
†. T. Botham c Ostler b Smith	29	L-b 13, w 7	20
D. B. D'Oliveira b Smith	3		
*P. A. Neale run out	23	1/42 2/111 3/115 (8 wkts, 40 overs) 182	
D. A. Leatherdale run out	3	4/135 5/139 6/163	
S. R. Lampitt not out	16	7/169 8/182	

†S. J. Rhodes and S. M. McEwan did not bat.

Bowling: Munton 8–0–36–0; Benjamin 8–0–27–0; Reeve 8–2–45–1; Smith 8–1–39–2; Small 8–0–22–1.

Warwickshire

Asif Din not out	86	†G. W. Humpage not out	40
*T. A. Lloyd c Rhodes b Weston	0	B 2, l-b 2, w 7, n-b 3	14
T. M. Moody c Rhodes b Radford	29		
A. I. Kallicharran lbw b McEwan	5	1/2 2/45 3/67 (4 wkts, 39.4 overs) 185	
D. A. Reeve c Botham b Lampitt	11	4/104	

N. M. K. Smith, D. P. Ostler, J. E. Benjamin, G. C. Small and T. A. Munton did not bat.

Bowling: Newport 8–2–20–0; Weston 3–0–12–1; Radford 8–0–34–1; Botham 6–0–43–0; McEwan 6.4–0–39–1; Lampitt 8–0–33–1.

Umpires: B. Leadbeater and N. T. Plews.

WORCESTERSHIRE v YORKSHIRE

At Worcester, June 3. Yorkshire won by 16 runs. Toss: Worcestershire.

Yorkshire

K. Sharp run out	71	P. J. Hartley run out		7
*A. A. Metcalfe c D'Oliveira b Newport	0	P. Carrick not out		0
R. J. Blakey c Rhodes b McEwan	79	L-b 8, w 8		16
P. E. Robinson c Rhodes b McEwan	13			
D. Byas b Lampitt	14	1/4 2/161 3/177	(7 wkts, 37 overs)	205
†D. L. Bairstow not out	5	4/193 5/193		
C. S. Pickles c Rhodes b McEwan	0	6/193 7/204		

P. W. Jarvis and S. D. Fletcher did not bat.

Bowling: Newport 8–0–32–1; Weston 8–0–36–0; Botham 1–0–4–0; McEwan 8–0–44–3; Lampitt 8–0–53–1; Stemp 4–0–28–0.

Worcestershire

T. S. Curtis b Hartley	76	S. R. Lampitt c Hartley b Jarvis		8
M. J. Weston c Jarvis b Hartley	4	R. D. Stemp b Fletcher		1
*P. A. Neale c Sharp b Hartley	18	S. M. McEwan not out		18
D. B. D'Oliveira c Jarvis b Carrick	1	L-b 6		6
D. A. Leatherdale c Blakey b Pickles	35			
†S. J. Rhodes c Metcalfe b Jarvis	2	1/6 2/34 3/37	(36.1 overs)	189
I. T. Botham c Jarvis b Hartley	12	4/105 5/109 6/137		
P. J. Newport c Carrick b Hartley	8	7/152 8/164 9/165		

Bowling: Jarvis 7.1–0–26–2; Hartley 8–0–38–5; Carrick 8–0–34–1; Fletcher 7–0–42–1; Pickles 6–0–43–1.

Umpires: J. H. Harris and K. J. Lyons.

At The Oval, June 17. WORCESTERSHIRE lost to SURREY by seven wickets.

WORCESTERSHIRE v SUSSEX

At Worcester, June 24. Worcestershire won by 2 runs. Toss: Sussex.

Worcestershire

T. S. Curtis c and b Pigott	58	†S. J. Rhodes c and b Dodemaide		0
I. T. Botham b C. M. Wells	19	S. R. Lampitt not out		0
G. A. Hick c Pigott b Dodemaide	75	L-b 12, w 3		15
D. B. D'Oliveira b Clarke	16			
*P. A. Neale c Pigott b Lenham	8	1/46 2/153 3/177	(8 wkts, 40 overs)	200
D. A. Leatherdale run out	6	4/182 5/195 6/200		
P. J. Newport c Salisbury b Dodemaide	3	7/200 8/200		

R. K. Illingworth and S. M. McEwan did not bat.

Bowling: C. M. Wells 8–0–21–1; Dodemaide 8–0–27–3; Clarke 8–0–42–1; Pigott 8–0–43–1; Salisbury 7–0–50–0; Lenham 1–0–5–1.

Sussex

*P. W. G. Parker lbw b McEwan	42	N. J. Lenham not out		3
I. J. Gould b Lampitt	12	I. D. K. Salisbury c Rhodes b Lampitt		0
A. P. Wells c Illingworth b Newport	34	A. R. Clarke not out		1
M. P. Speight lbw b Illingworth	15	L-b 11, w 5, n-b 5		21
C. M. Wells c Neale b Botham	29			
A. C. S. Pigott b Botham	4	1/48 2/83 3/111	(9 wkts, 40 overs)	198
A. I. C. Dodemaide run out	24	4/130 5/155 6/155		
†P. Moores c and b Botham	13	7/171 8/196 9/197		

Bowling: Newport 8–0–33–1; McEwan 8–0–55–1; Botham 8–0–40–3; Lampitt 8–1–24–2; Illingworth 8–0–35–1.

Umpires: B. Hassan and A. G. T. Whitehead.

At Lord's, July 1. WORCESTERSHIRE lost to MIDDLESEX by 99 runs.

WORCESTERSHIRE v GLOUCESTERSHIRE

At Worcester, July 8. Worcestershire won by eight wickets. Toss: Worcestershire.

Gloucestershire

G. D. Hodgson c Leatherdale b Weston 10	J. W. Lloyds b Botham 2
C. W. J. Athey c Leatherdale b Lampitt 63	M. W. Alleyne not out 8
*A. J. Wright c Leatherdale b Tolley .. 24	L-b 9, w 6 15
K. M. Curran c Curtis b Botham 56	
P. Bainbridge lbw b Lampitt 15	1/19 2/53 3/155 (6 wkts, 40 overs) 220
P. W. Romaines not out 27	4/171 5/198 6/205

†R. C. J. Williams, C. A. Walsh and D. A. Graveney did not bat.

Bowling: Weston 7–0–26–1; Tolley 8–0–26–1; Botham 8–0–40–2; Lampitt 6–0–56–2; Hick 4–0–23–0; Herzberg 5–0–28–0; Leatherdale 2–0–12–0.

Worcestershire

T. S. Curtis not out 93
M. J. Weston b Walsh 4
G. A. Hick c Williams b Alleyne 67
I. T. Botham not out 41
    L-b 8, w 7, n-b 1 16

1/20 2/146   (2 wkts, 38.4 overs) 221

*P. A. Neale, D. B. D'Oliveira, †S. J. Rhodes, D. A. Leatherdale, S. R. Lampitt, C. M. Tolley and S. Herzberg did not bat.

Bowling: Curran 7.4–0–39–0; Walsh 7–0–28–1; Bainbridge 5–0–25–0; Graveney 8–0–42–0; Alleyne 7–0–51–1; Lloyds 4–0–28–0.

Umpires: P. J. Eele and P. B. Wight.

At Manchester, July 15. WORCESTERSHIRE lost to LANCASHIRE by seven wickets.

At Canterbury, July 29. WORCESTERSHIRE beat KENT by five wickets.

At Leicester, August 5. WORCESTERSHIRE beat LEICESTERSHIRE by seven wickets.

WORCESTERSHIRE v HAMPSHIRE

At Worcester, August 12. Hampshire won by 20 runs. Toss: Worcestershire. Hick took his total of Sunday League runs for the season to 694, passing Younis Ahmed's Worcestershire record of 668 scored in 1979.

Hampshire

V. P. Terry run out	17	†R. J. Parks b Hick	4
R. J. Scott c McEwan b Hick	53	R. M. F. Cox not out	2
*M. C. J. Nicholas c Illingworth			
b McEwan	17	B 4, l-b 2, w 2	8
C. L. Smith c Lampitt b Hick	21		—
M. D. Marshall c Newport b Lampitt	38	1/42 2/81 3/115 (6 wkts, 40 overs) 207
J. R. Ayling not out	47	4/115 5/191 6/200	

R. J. Maru, T. M. Tremlett and S. D. Udal did not bat.

Bowling: Newport 6–1–33–0; Weston 8–0–32–0; Illingworth 8–0–24–0; McEwan 3–0–15–1; Hick 8–0–47–3; Lampitt 7–0–50–1.

Worcestershire

*T. S. Curtis b Tremlett	13	P. J. Newport run out	7
G. J. Lord c Terry b Tremlett	17	S. R. Lampitt b Scott	8
G. A. Hick c Terry b Scott	88	S. M. McEwan not out	3
D. A. Leatherdale lbw b Tremlett	0	L-b 10, n-b 1	11
M. J. Weston c Terry b Udal	6		—
C. M. Tolley c Terry b Udal	1	1/32 2/35 3/35 (39.4 overs) 187
†S. J. Rhodes c Udal b Ayling	26	4/44 5/46 6/125	
R. K. Illingworth b Marshall	7	7/165 8/171 9/184	

Bowling: Marshall 8–0–22–1; Tremlett 8–0–22–3; Ayling 8–0–43–1; Udal 7–0–36–2; Maru 7–0–46–0; Scott 1.4–0–8–2.

Umpires: B. Dudleston and K. E. Palmer.

WORCESTERSHIRE v NORTHAMPTONSHIRE

At Worcester, August 19. No result. Toss: Northamptonshire. Rain ended the match, which had already been reduced to 35 overs a side. D'Oliveira's 58 came off 38 balls, including two sixes and two fours in one over bowled by Davis.

Worcestershire

*T. S. Curtis not out	83	M. J. Weston not out	3
G. J. Lord c Ripley b Penberthy	78	L-b 11, w 3, n-b 3	17
G. A. Hick c Penberthy b Cook	26		—
D. B. D'Oliveira c Wild b Robinson	58	1/116 2/151 3/248 (4 wkts, 35 overs) 265
D. A. Leatherdale b Robinson	0	4/251	

†S. J. Rhodes, R. K. Illingworth, P. J. Newport, S. R. Lampitt and S. M. McEwan did not bat.

Bowling: Davis 8–0–58–0; Robinson 5–0–36–2; Larkins 3–0–20–0; Capel 5–0–35–0; Cook 8–0–54–1; Penberthy 5–0–45–1; Wild 1–0–6–0.

Northamptonshire

A. Fordham c McEwan b Weston	21	R. J. Bailey not out	0
W. Larkins c Curtis b Newport	1	W 2	2
*A. J. Lamb c Leatherdale b Newport	10		—
D. J. Capel not out	1	1/7 2/33 3/35 (3 wkts, 8.4 overs) 35

D. J. Wild, A. L. Penberthy, †D. Ripley, N. G. B. Cook, W. W. Davis and M. A. Robinson did not bat.

Bowling: Newport 4.4–0–15–2; Weston 4–0–20–1.

Umpires: D. J. Constant and B. Leadbeater.

At Swansea, August 26. WORCESTERSHIRE beat GLAMORGAN by 34 runs.

YORKSHIRE

At Nottingham, April 22. YORKSHIRE lost to NOTTINGHAMSHIRE by five wickets.

At Birmingham, May 6. YORKSHIRE lost to WARWICKSHIRE by eight wickets.

YORKSHIRE v DERBYSHIRE

At Leeds, May 13. Yorkshire won by six wickets. Toss: Yorkshire. Jarvis took three of the last four Derbyshire wickets in his seventh over, a maiden.

Derbyshire

*K. J. Barnett c White b Byas	29	S. J. Base b Fletcher	0
P. D. Bowler c Bairstow b Sidebottom	5	D. E. Malcolm b Jarvis	0
B. Roberts c Sidebottom b Jarvis	53	O. H. Mortensen not out	0
A. P. Kuiper c Blakey b Jarvis	5	L-b 11, w 5, n-b 2	18
C. J. Adams c Bairstow b Byas	7		
S. C. Goldsmith c Byas b Sidebottom	7	1/14 2/71 3/79　　　(38.1 overs) 143	
†K. M. Krikken b Jarvis	14	4/106 5/121 6/122	
A. E. Warner c Kellett b Jarvis	5	7/143 8/143 9/143	

Bowling: Sidebottom 8-0-18-2; Jarvis 7-1-18-5; Fletcher 7.1-0-37-1; Gough 8-0-26-0; Byas 8-0-33-2.

Yorkshire

S. A. Kellett run out	32	†D. L. Bairstow not out	1
*A. A. Metcalfe b Base	41	B 1, l-b 9, w 11	21
R. J. Blakey c Krikken b Base	1		
D. Byas not out	30	1/71 2/78 3/85　　(4 wkts, 39 overs) 147	
P. E. Robinson c Krikken b Barnett	21	4/140	

C. White, A. Sidebottom, P. W. Jarvis, D. Gough and S. D. Fletcher did not bat.

Bowling: Mortensen 8-0-26-0; Malcolm 8-1-28-0; Warner 8-0-28-0; Base 8-2-33-2; Goldsmith 3-0-10-0; Barnett 4-0-12-1.

Umpires: H. D. Bird and R. Palmer.

At Canterbury, May 20. YORKSHIRE lost to KENT by 69 runs.

YORKSHIRE v HAMPSHIRE

At Leeds, May 27. Hampshire won by 36 runs. Toss: Yorkshire.

Hampshire

V. P. Terry b Byas	56	†A. N. Aymes not out	15
D. I. Gower c Byas b Hartley	12	T. M. Tremlett not out	2
R. A. Smith b Hartley	44	L-b 14, w 8, n-b 1	23
M. D. Marshall b Byas	10		
R. J. Scott c Robinson b Carrick	1	1/34 2/113 3/129　　(7 wkts, 40 overs) 184	
*M. C. J. Nicholas c Blakey b Byas	8	4/131 5/146	
J. R. Ayling b Fletcher	13	6/149 7/180	

C. A. Connor and R. J. Maru did not bat.

Bowling: Fletcher 8-0-34-1; Pickles 8-0-30-0; Hartley 8-1-24-2; Carrick 8-1-39-1; Gough 2-0-17-0; Byas 6-0-26-3.

Yorkshire

C. S. Pickles c Maru b Marshall	6	P. J. Hartley b Connor	14
*A. A. Metcalfe b Connor	0	D. Gough not out	17
S. A. Kellett run out	7	S. D. Fletcher c Nicholas b Connor	6
R. J. Blakey c Gower b Tremlett	22	B 1, l-b 10, n-b 2	13
P. E. Robinson c Maru b Scott	26		
D. Byas lbw b Tremlett	2	1/7 2/7 3/23	(39 overs) 148
†D. L. Bairstow c Smith b Scott	21	4/49 5/55 6/71	
P. Carrick c Nicholas b Ayling	14	7/100 8/116 9/125	

Bowling: Connor 8–1–31–3; Marshall 7–1–32–1; Tremlett 8–0–19–2; Ayling 8–2–16–1; Scott 8–0–39–2.

Umpires: D. O. Oslear and A. G. T. Whitehead.

At Worcester, June 3. YORKSHIRE beat WORCESTERSHIRE by 16 runs.

YORKSHIRE v SURREY

At Hull, June 10. Surrey won by six wickets. Toss: Surrey.

Yorkshire

K. Sharp c Ward b Bicknell	0	P. J. Hartley b Waqar Younis	8
A. A. Metcalfe lbw b Feltham	16	P. W. Jarvis c Bicknell b Murphy	3
R. J. Blakey b Medlycott	38	A. Sidebottom not out	3
P. E. Robinson b Medlycott	22	L-b 10, w 5	15
*M. D. Moxon c Ward b Medlycott	9		
D. Byas b Waqar Younis	2	1/0 2/39 3/78	(9 wkts, 40 overs) 144
†D. L. Bairstow not out	21	4/91 5/92 6/102	
P. Carrick b Murphy	7	7/114 8/131 9/136	

Bowling: Bicknell 6–1–20–1; Murphy 8–1–29–2; Feltham 4–0–10–1; Bullen 6–0–21–0; Medlycott 8–1–20–3; Waqar Younis 8–0–34–2.

Surrey

G. S. Clinton c Metcalfe b Byas	28	*I. A. Greig not out	2
M. A. Feltham c Sharp b Sidebottom	16	B 3, l-b 13, w 3, n-b 4	23
G. P. Thorpe not out	46		
†D. M. Ward b Hartley	22	1/39 2/68 3/112	(4 wkts, 37.5 overs) 145
M. A. Lynch c Metcalfe b Jarvis	8	4/131	

C. K. Bullen, K. T. Medlycott, M. P. Bicknell, Waqar Younis and A. J. Murphy did not bat.

Bowling: Jarvis 8–1–19–1; Sidebottom 8–1–29–1; Hartley 8–2–22–1; Byas 6–0–22–1; Carrick 4–0–22–0; Moxon 3.5–0–15–0.

Umpires: J. C. Balderstone and D. S. Thompsett.

At Hove, June 17. YORKSHIRE beat SUSSEX by 40 runs.

At Newport, June 24. GLAMORGAN v YORKSHIRE. No result.

At Tring, July 8. YORKSHIRE beat NORTHAMPTONSHIRE by 61 runs.

YORKSHIRE v SOMERSET

At Scarborough, July 15. Yorkshire won by 16 runs. Toss: Somerset. Moxon's 105, his first Sunday League century, came off 124 balls with nine fours.

Yorkshire

M. D. Moxon c Tavaré b Mallender . .	105	C. S. Pickles not out	1
A. A. Metcalfe c Harden b Hallett	14		
R. J. Blakey c Harden b Rose	52	B 1, l-b 4, w 2	7
P. J. Bartlett c Burns b Lefebvre	27		
S. E. Robinson b Hayhurst	15	1/46 2/157 3/198 (5 wkts, 40 overs) 227	
D. Byas not out	6	4/217 5/226	

C. White, P. Carrick, A. Sidebottom and S. D. Fletcher did not bat.

Bowling: Mallender 8–0–51–1; Rose 8–0–45–1; Lefebvre 8–0–35–1; Hallett 5–0–23–1; Hayhurst 7–0–43–1; Swallow 4–0–25–0.

Somerset

S. J. Cook c Blakey b Carrick	52	I. G. Swallow c Carrick b Fletcher	31
R. J. Bartlett c Robinson b Pickles	21	N. A. Mallender b Hartley	3
C. J. Tavaré c and b Pickles	8	J. C. Hallett not out	0
R. J. Harden c White b Pickles	28	L-b 16, n-b 1	17
G. D. Rose c Moxon b White	6		
N. D. Burns run out	1	1/55 2/69 3/95 (39.4 overs) 211	
A. N. Hayhurst b Pickles	16	4/110 5/119 6/147	
R. P. Lefebvre b Fletcher	28	7/147 8/194 9/205	

Bowling: Hartley 7–0–42–1; Sidebottom 5–0–25–0; Fletcher 7.4–0–40–2; Pickles 6–0–36–4; Carrick 8–0–18–1; White 6–0–34–1.

Umpires: H. D. Bird and J. D. Bond.

At Cheltenham, July 22. **YORKSHIRE** beat **GLOUCESTERSHIRE** by seven wickets.

YORKSHIRE v LEICESTERSHIRE

At Sheffield, July 29. Yorkshire won by eight wickets. Toss: Leicestershire.

Leicestershire

T. J. Boon c Carrick b Hartley	88	W. K. M. Benjamin c Blakey b Jarvis .	3
N. E. Briers st Blakey b Carrick	37	†P. A. Nixon not out	8
J. J. Whitaker c Metcalfe b Carrick	25	B 6, l-b 12, w 3	21
P. Willey b Jarvis	7		
L. Potter c Sharp b Hartley	0	1/104 2/165 3/177 (6 wkts, 40 overs) 207	
J. D. R. Benson not out	18	4/177 5/177 6/183	

G. J. Parsons, J. P. Agnew and A. D. Mullally did not bat.

Bowling: Jarvis 8–0–25–2; Pickles 3–0–21–0; Fletcher 7–0–40–0; Hartley 8–0–42–2; Carrick 8–0–29–2; Moxon 6–0–32–0.

Yorkshire

```
*M. D. Moxon c Whitaker b Potter .... 73
A. A. Metcalfe c Willey b Parsons .... 71
†R. J. Blakey not out ............... 30
K. Sharp not out ................... 26
    L-b 4, w 3, n-b 1 .......... 8
```

1/134 2/155   (2 wkts, 35.5 overs) 208

P. E. Robinson, D. Byas, P. J. Hartley, P. Carrick, C. S. Pickles, P. W. Jarvis and S. D. Fletcher did not bat.

Bowling: Benjamin 6–1–35–0; Agnew 7.5–0–33–0; Mullally 7–0–24–0; Parsons 5–0–36–1; Willey 3–0–25–0; Potter 7–0–51–1.

Umpires: K. J. Lyons and P. B. Wight.

YORKSHIRE v LANCASHIRE

At Scarborough, August 5. Lancashire won by 78 runs. Toss: Yorkshire.

Lancashire

```
G. Fowler c Sidebottom b Fletcher .... 55
M. A. Atherton b Fletcher ........... 53
G. D. Lloyd c and b Fletcher ........ 76
N. H. Fairbrother lbw b Fletcher .... 3
M. Watkinson run out ............... 31
Wasim Akram not out .............. 35
```
```
†W. K. Hegg not out ...............
    L-b 6, n-b 3 ..............
                                    —
1/106 2/115 3/127    (5 wkts, 40 overs) 26.
4/210 5/253
```

P. J. Martin, I. D. Austin, *D. P. Hughes and P. J. W. Allott did not bat.

Bowling: Jarvis 8–0–69–0; Sidebottom 8–0–33–0; Hartley 8–1–44–0; Carrick 8–0–48–0; Fletcher 8–0–63–4.

Yorkshire

```
*M. D. Moxon c Watkinson b Allott .. 31
A. A. Metcalfe c Fairbrother b Allott .. 6
†R. J. Blakey c Hegg b Wasim Akram . 35
K. Sharp c Martin b Atherton ........ 37
P. E. Robinson b Wasim Akram ...... 0
D. Byas not out ................... 35
P. J. Hartley c Watkinson b Atherton . 18
P. Carrick c Hughes b Austin ........ 1
```
```
P. W. Jarvis b Wasim Akram ........
A. Sidebottom b Wasim Akram ......
S. D. Fletcher lbw b Austin ..........
    L-b 9, w 5, n-b 1 ........... 1
1/26 2/59 3/105        (35.3 overs) 18
4/105 5/138 6/161
7/169 8/176 9/182
```

Bowling: Allott 8–1–21–2; Martin 6–0–41–0; Watkinson 8–0–47–0; Wasim Akram 6–0–19–4; Austin 4.3–0–21–2; Atherton 3–0–27–2.

Umpires: B. Leadbeater and N. T. Plews.

YORKSHIRE v ESSEX

At Middlesbrough, August 12. Yorkshire won by 59 runs. Toss: Essex.

Yorkshire

```
*M. D. Moxon c Garnham b Ilott .... 12
A. A. Metcalfe run out ............. 1
†R. J. Blakey c Stephenson b Waugh .. 76
K. Sharp c Hussain b Waugh ........ 30
P. E. Robinson c Waugh b Stephenson . 14
D. Byas c Hussain b Ilott ........... 18
P. Carrick c Hussain b Andrew ....... 30
C. S. Pickles b Andrew ............. 0
```
```
P. J. Hartley not out ...............
P. W. Jarvis b Waugh ...............
A. Sidebottom not out ..............
    L-b 12, w 4 ...............
1/3 2/23 3/124        (9 wkts, 40 overs) 22
4/131 5/149 6/193
7/194 8/194 9/208
```

Bowling: Ilott 8–2–24–2; Andrew 8–2–30–2; Such 4–0–35–0; Topley 7–0–48–0; Waugh 8–0–37–3; Stephenson 5–0–35–1.

Essex

B. R. Hardie c Sidebottom b Jarvis ..	5	M. C. Ilott run out	6
P. Stephenson b Sidebottom	4	S. J. W. Andrew c Metcalfe b Pickles .	5
M. E. Waugh c Pickles b Hartley ...	19	P. M. Such c Metcalfe b Jarvis	5
J. Prichard c Byas b Jarvis	2	B 5, l-b 8, w 1, n-b 1	15
N. Hussain not out	66		—
N. Shahid b Carrick	31	1/11 2/11 3/15 (34.4 overs) 162	
M. A. Garnham c Blakey b Carrick ..	0	4/39 5/105 6/105	
D. Topley c Pickles b Carrick	4	7/124 8/131 9/145	

Bowling: Jarvis 5.4-0-16-3; Sidebottom 8-1-22-1; Hartley 6-0-27-1; Carrick 8-0-46-3; Pickles 7-0-38-1.

Umpires: B. Hassan and A. A. Jones.

YORKSHIRE v MIDDLESEX

At Scarborough, August 26. Yorkshire won by 44 runs. Toss: Yorkshire. Yorkshire's total was their highest in the Sunday League. Haynes took his season's total of runs in the Sunday League to 632, passing C. T. Radley's record for Middlesex of 618 in 1974. Emburey's 30th Sunday League wicket of the season passed by one W. W. Daniel's county record set in 1984.

Yorkshire

M. D. Moxon run out	38	P. Carrick run out	7
A. A. Metcalfe c Carr b Cowans	84		
R. J. Blakey c Ramprakash b Cowans.	63	L-b 6, w 3	9
P. E. Robinson c Weekes b Cowans ...	11		—
D. Byas run out	22	1/60 2/169 3/192 (7 wkts, 40 overs) 271	
C. A. Chapman not out	36	4/204 5/249	
P. J. Hartley b Emburey	1	6/264 7/271	

* W. Jarvis, A. Sidebottom and C. S. Pickles did not bat.

Bowling: Cowans 8-0-43-3; Taylor 8-0-46-0; Hughes 8-1-52-0; Emburey 8-0-57-1; Weekes 4-0-36-0; Haynes 4-0-31-0.

Middlesex

D. L. Haynes lbw b Carrick	60	N. G. Cowans c Blakey b Hartley	0
M. A. Roseberry lbw b Jarvis	9	S. P. Hughes b Jarvis	14
M. R. Ramprakash c Hartley b Carrick	34	N. R. Taylor not out	5
K. R. Brown c Robinson b Hartley	16	L-b 8, w 1	9
D. Carr run out	9		—
J. E. Emburey c Metcalfe b Carrick ..	14	1/19 2/106 3/123 (9 wkts, 40 overs) 227	
P. R. Downton c and b Pickles	28	4/135 5/137 6/152	
P. N. Weekes not out	29	7/190 8/193 9/218	

Bowling: Jarvis 8-0-41-2; Sidebottom 8-0-33-0; Hartley 8-0-51-2; Pickles 8-0-50-1; Carrick 8-0-44-3.

Umpires: J. W. Holder and D. S. Thompsett.

SUNDAY LEAGUE RECORDS

Batting

Highest score: 176 – G. A. Gooch, Essex v Glamorgan (Southend), 1983.

Most hundreds: 11 – C. G. Greenidge; 10 – G. A. Gooch; 9 – W. Larkins, K. S. McEwan and B. A. Richards. 368 hundreds have been scored in the League. The most in one season is 40 in 1990.

Most runs: D. L. Amiss 7,040; C. T. Radley 6,650; D. R. Turner 6,639; P. Willey 6,353; C. G. Greenidge 6,344; G. A. Gooch 6,324; C. E. B. Rice 6,265; G. M. Turner 6,144.

Most runs in a season: 902 – S. J. Cook (Somerset), 1990.

Most sixes in an innings: 13 – I. T. Botham, Somerset v Northamptonshire (Wellingboroug|
School), 1986.

Most sixes by a team in an innings: 18 – Derbyshire v Worcestershire (Knypersley), 1985.

Most sixes in a season: 26 – I. V. A. Richards (Somerset), 1977.

Highest total: 360 for three – Somerset v Glamorgan (Neath), 1990.

Highest total – batting second: 301 for six – Warwickshire v Essex (Colchester), 1982.

Highest match aggregate: 604 – Surrey (304) v Warwickshire (300 for nine) (The Oval), 198|

Lowest total: 23 (19.4 overs) – Middlesex v Yorkshire (Leeds), 1974.

Shortest completed innings: 16 overs – Northamptonshire 59 v Middlesex (Tring), 1974.

Shortest match: 2 hr 13 min (40.3 overs) – Essex v Northamptonshire (Ilford), 1971.

Biggest victories: 220 runs, Somerset beat Glamorgan (Neath), 1990.
   There have been 21 instances of victory by ten wickets – by Derbyshire, Essex (twice|
Glamorgan, Hampshire, Leicestershire (twice), Middlesex (twice), Northamptonshir|
Nottinghamshire, Somerset (twice), Surrey (twice), Warwickshire, Worcestershire (twic|
and Yorkshire (three times). This does not include those matches in which the side battin|
second was set a reduced target.

Ties (30): Nottinghamshire v Kent (Nottingham), 1969, in a match reduced to twenty over|
Gloucestershire v Hampshire (Bristol), 1972; Gloucestershire v Northamptonshire (Bristol|
1972.
Surrey v Worcestershire (Byfleet), 1973.
Middlesex v Lancashire (Lord's), 1974; Sussex v Leicestershire (Hove), 1974.
Lancashire v Worcestershire (Manchester), 1975; Somerset v Glamorgan (Taunton), 197|
Warwickshire v Kent (Birmingham), 1980.
Kent v Lancashire (Maidstone), 1981.
Yorkshire v Nottinghamshire (Hull), 1982; Hampshire v Lancashire (Southampton), 198|
Surrey v Hampshire (The Oval), 1982.
Worcestershire v Nottinghamshire (Hereford), 1983; Lancashire v Worcestershir|
   (Manchester), 1983, in a match reduced to nineteen overs; Warwickshire |
   Worcestershire (Birmingham), 1983, Warwickshire's innings having been reduced to te|
   overs.
Middlesex v Essex (Lord's), 1984.
Essex v Leicestershire (Chelmsford), 1985; Northamptonshire v Lancashire (Northam|
   ton), 1985; Lancashire v Glamorgan (Manchester), 1985.
Kent v Surrey (Canterbury), 1986; Middlesex v Warwickshire (Lord's), 1986; Yorkshire |
   Warwickshire (Leeds), 1986.
Hampshire v Gloucestershire (Southampton), 1987; Hampshire v Derbyshire (Southam|
   ton), 1987.
Essex v Sussex (Ilford), 1988; Surrey v Derbyshire (The Oval), 1988; Sussex v Glamorga|
   (Eastbourne), 1988.
Middlesex v Hampshire (Lord's), 1989; Somerset v Sussex (Taunton), 1989.

Record partnerships for each wicket

239 for 1st	G. A. Gooch and B. R. Hardie, Essex v Nottinghamshire at Nottingham	198|
273 for 2nd	G. A. Gooch and K. S. McEwan, Essex v Nottinghamshire at Nottingham	198|
223 for 3rd	S. J. Cook and G. D. Rose, Somerset v Glamorgan at Neath	199|
219 for 4th	C. G. Greenidge and C. L. Smith, Hampshire v Surrey at Southampton	198|
185* for 5th	B. M. McMillan and Asif Din, Warwickshire v Essex at Chelmsford.	198|
121 for 6th	C. P. Wilkins and A. J. Borrington, Derbyshire v Warwickshire at Chesterfield	197|

32 for 7th	K. R. Brown and N. F. Williams, Middlesex v Somerset at Lord's ...	1988
5* for 8th	D. Breakwell and K. F. Jennings, Somerset v Nottinghamshire at Nottingham	1976
05 for 9th	D. G. Moir and R. W. Taylor, Derbyshire v Kent at Derby	1984
7 for 10th	D. A. Graveney and J. B. Mortimore, Gloucestershire v Lancashire at Tewkesbury	1973

Bowling

Best analyses: eight for 26, K. D. Boyce, Essex v Lancashire (Manchester), 1971; seven for 15, R. A. Hutton, Yorkshire v Worcestershire (Leeds), 1969; seven for 39, A. Hodgson, Northamptonshire v Somerset (Northampton), 1976; seven for 41, A. N. Jones, Sussex v Nottinghamshire (Nottingham), 1986; six for 6, R. W. Hooker, Middlesex v Surrey (Lord's), 1969; six for 7, M. Hendrick, Derbyshire v Nottinghamshire (Nottingham), 1972.

Four wickets in four balls: A. Ward, Derbyshire v Sussex (Derby), 1970.

Hat-tricks (19): A. Ward, Derbyshire v Sussex (Derby), 1970; R. Palmer, Somerset v Gloucestershire (Bristol), 1970; K. D. Boyce, Essex v Somerset (Westcliff), 1971; G. D. McKenzie, Leicestershire v Essex (Leicester), 1972; R. G. D. Willis, Warwickshire v Yorkshire (Birmingham), 1973; W. Blenkiron, Warwickshire v Derbyshire (Buxton), 1974; A. Buss, Sussex v Worcestershire (Hastings), 1974; J. M. Rice, Hampshire v Northamptonshire (Southampton), 1975; M. A. Nash, Glamorgan v Worcestershire (Worcester), 1975; A. Hodgson, Northamptonshire v Somerset (Northampton), 1976; A. E. Cordle, Glamorgan v Hampshire (Portsmouth), 1979; C. J. Tunnicliffe, Derbyshire v Worcestershire (Derby), 1979; M. D. Marshall, Hampshire v Surrey (Southampton), 1981; I. V. A. Richards, Somerset v Essex (Chelmsford), 1982; P. W. Jarvis, Yorkshire v Derbyshire (Derby), 1982; R. M. Ellison, Kent v Hampshire (Canterbury), 1983; G. C. Holmes, Glamorgan v Nottinghamshire (Ebbw Vale), 1987; K. Saxelby, Nottinghamshire v Worcestershire (Nottingham), 1987; K. M. Curran, Gloucestershire v Warwickshire (Birmingham), 1989.

Most economical analysis: 8–8–0–0, B. A. Langford, Somerset v Essex (Yeovil), 1969.

Most expensive analyses: 7.5–0–89–3, G. Miller, Derbyshire v Gloucestershire (Gloucester), 1984; 8–0–88–1, E. E. Hemmings, Nottinghamshire v Somerset (Nottingham), 1983.

Most wickets in a season: 34 – R. J. Clapp (Somerset), 1974, and C. E. B. Rice (Nottinghamshire), 1986.

Most wickets: J. K. Lever 386; D. L. Underwood 346; J. Simmons 307; S. Turner 303; N. Gifford 284; J. E. Emburey 270; J. N. Shepherd 267; E. E. Hemmings 258; T. E. Jesty 249; R. D. Jackman 234.

Wicket-keeping and Fielding

Most dismissals: D. L. Bairstow 255 (231 ct, 24 st); R. W. Taylor 236 (187 ct, 49 st); E. W. Jones 223 (184 ct, 39 st).

Most dismissals in a season: 29 (26 ct, 3 st) – S. J. Rhodes (Worcestershire), 1988.

Most dismissals in an innings: 7 (6 ct, 1 st) – R. W. Taylor, Derbyshire v Lancashire (Manchester), 1975.

Most catches in an innings: 6 – K. Goodwin, Lancashire v Worcestershire (Worcester), 1969, and R. W. Taylor, Derbyshire v Lancashire (Manchester), 1975.

Most stumpings in an innings: 4 – S. J. Rhodes, Worcestershire v Warwickshire (Birmingham), 1986.

Most catches by a fielder (not a wicket-keeper): J. F. Steele 101; G. Cook and D. P. Hughes 94; C. T. Radley 90.

Most catches in a season: 16 – J. M. Rice (Hampshire), 1978.

Most catches in an innings: 5 – J. M. Rice, Hampshire v Warwickshire (Southampton), 1978.

CHAMPIONS 1969-90

John Player League			
1969	Lancashire	1980	Warwickshire
1970	Lancashire	1981	Essex
1971	Worcestershire	1982	Sussex
1972	Kent	1983	Yorkshire
1973	Kent	1984	Essex
1974	Leicestershire	1985	Essex
1975	Hampshire	1986	Hampshire
1976	Kent		*Refuge Assurance League*
1977	Leicestershire	1987	Worcestershire
1978	Hampshire	1988	Worcestershire
1979	Somerset	1989	Lancashire
		1990	Derbyshire

REFUGE ASSURANCE CUP

Middlesex, only one game away from winning the 1990 County Championship, collected their first 40-overs trophy when they beat Derbyshire in the Refuge Assurance Cup final at Edgbaston in September. Previously the closest they had come to success in a 40-overs competition was second to Sussex in the Sunday League in 1982 and the knockout round of the Cup in 1988. In addition to receiving the Refuge Assurance Cup, Middlesex won £6,000, while runners-up Derbyshire received £3,000 to compensate in part for failing to become the first county to achieve the League and Cup double. Lancashire and Nottinghamshire, the losing semi-finalists, each received £1,500. The Man of the Match award was worth £350 in the final and £175 in the semi-finals.

DERBYSHIRE v NOTTINGHAMSHIRE

At Derby, September 5. Derbyshire won by 22 runs. Toss: Nottinghamshire. After two early interruptions because of rain, Barnett and Bowler gave Derbyshire a steady start with an opening partnership of 118. Barnett scored 83 from 89 balls but, as in the final Sunday game, the crucial innings came from Kuiper. He hit 74 from 45 balls, with three sixes and seven fours, helping Derbyshire to add 96 in the last ten overs. At 87 for five in the 23rd over, Nottinghamshire were in trouble, but Robinson and Evans added 112 in thirteen overs to revive their hopes. Robinson's 96 came from 90 balls and contained eight fours. When he was caught at mid-on, Derbyshire regained control in poor light.

Man of the Match: R. T. Robinson.

Derbyshire

*K. J. Barnett c Johnson b Saxelby ...	83
†P. D. Bowler c Evans b Cooper	59
J. E. Morris c Robinson b Evans	0
A. P. Kuiper c Mike b Stephenson	74
T. J. G. O'Gorman not out	20
L-b 12, w 7	19

1/118 2/134 3/168   (4 wkts, 40 overs) 255
4/255

B. Roberts, C. J. Adams, D. E. Malcolm, O. H. Mortensen, A. E. Warner and S. J. Base did not bat.

Bowling: Cooper 8-0-40-1; Stephenson 8-1-49-1; Evans 8-0-58-1; Mike 8-0-48-0; Hemmings 3-0-23-0; Saxelby 5-0-25-1.

Nottinghamshire

B. C. Broad c Barnett b Mortensen	....	28	†B. N. French b Kuiper	0
M. Newell b Warner	....	10	E. E. Hemmings not out	6
P. Johnson b Warner	....	2		
R. T. Robinson c Warner b Malcolm	.	96	L-b 5, w 6, n-b 3	14
M. Saxelby lbw b Base	....	9		
F. D. Stephenson run out	....	7	1/16 2/22 3/48 (8 wkts, 40 overs)	233
K. P. Evans not out	....	55	4/69 5/87 6/199	
G. W. Mike run out	....	6	7/207 8/207	

K. E. Cooper did not bat.

Bowling: Mortensen 8-0-27-1; Warner 8-0-41-2; Malcolm 8-0-45-1; Base 8-0-65-1; Kuiper 8-0-50-1.

Umpires: B. Dudleston and R. Palmer.

LANCASHIRE v MIDDLESEX

At Manchester, September 5. Middlesex won by 45 runs. Toss: Lancashire. Middlesex, beginning with 81 from the first ten overs and finishing with 77 from the last ten, made Lancashire pay for a generally shoddy showing in the field. Haynes and Roseberry (88 balls) both had lives against Watkinson as they put on 153 in 21 overs. In contrast to Allott, whose four overs at the start cost 33 runs, and DeFreitas, 24 from three, Fraser conceded just 6 in his first four overs, and Lancashire had only 28 runs on the board after ten overs. When Fairbrother, after a typically aggressive half-century, was very well caught by Brown at long-off in the 29th over, the possibility of a Lancashire victory faded faster than the light.

Man of the Match: M. A. Roseberry.

Middlesex

D. L. Haynes c Atherton b Hughes	....	72	*J. E. Emburey run out	0
M. A. Roseberry c Allott b Hughes	....	86	N. F. Williams not out	10
M. R. Ramprakash c Lloyd b Austin	..	22	B 5, l-b 6, w 3	14
K. R. Brown not out	....	48		
C. Pooley c Hegg b DeFreitas	......	6	1/153 2/191 3/192 (6 wkts, 40 overs)	272
†P. R. Downton b Watkinson	....	14	4/216 5/245 6/246	

J. P. Hughes, A. R. C. Fraser and P. C. R. Tufnell did not bat.

Bowling: Allott 4-0-33-0; DeFreitas 8-0-71-1; Wasim Akram 5-0-27-0; Watkinson 8-0-50-1; Austin 8-0-40-1; Hughes 8-0-40-2.

Lancashire

G. Fowler b Emburey	....	20	†W. K. Hegg not out	19
M. A. Atherton run out	....	33	I. D. Austin not out	0
G. D. Lloyd c Downton b Fraser	.....	65	B 2, l-b 9, w 1, n-b 3	15
N. H. Fairbrother c Brown b Hughes	..	56		
M. Watkinson c Hughes b Emburey	...	10	1/59 2/66 3/147 (7 wkts, 40 overs)	227
Wasim Akram st Downton b Emburey	.	7	4/167 5/186	
*A. J. DeFreitas c Hughes b Emburey	2	6/190 7/227	

D. P. Hughes and P. J. W. Allott did not bat.

Bowling: Fraser 8-3-28-1; Williams 8-0-32-0; Tufnell 8-0-57-0; Emburey 8-1-39-4; Hughes 8-0-60-1.

Umpires: H. D. Bird and A. G. T. Whitehead.

Refuge Assurance Cup, 1990

FINAL

DERBYSHIRE v MIDDLESEX

At Birmingham, September 16. Middlesex won by five wickets. Toss: Middlesex. Accurate Middlesex bowling, with a noteworthy performance from their 21-year-old off-spinner Weekes, in the team for the injured Williams, contained Derbyshire on a slow pitch. Only Warner's late burst of hitting saw them reach 197 from 151 for six after 35 overs. Haynes and Gatting, whose fitness had been in doubt after he was struck on the elbow three days earlier at The Oval, established the Middlesex reply with 92 in eighteen overs. However, the return of Malcolm and Warner saw three wickets fall in twelve balls, and Middlesex needed 62 from ten overs, 30 from five and finally 7 from the last. Emburey could have been run out as the scores were levelled off the third ball, and Downton hit the next to the mid-wicket boundary for the victory his steady batting had helped secure.

Man of the Match: P. R. Downton.   *Attendance:* 7,212; *receipts* £52,985.

Derbyshire

*K. J. Barnett b Weekes	42	A. E. Warner not out	28
†P. D. Bowler b Hughes	11	S. J. Base not out	1
J. E. Morris c Weekes b Haynes	46	B 1, l-b 9, w 5, n-b 1	16
A. P. Kuiper c Fraser b Weekes	9		
T. J. G. O'Gorman b Fraser	10	1/32 2/81 3/113 (7 wkts, 40 overs) 197	
B. Roberts b Hughes	21	4/116 5/145	
C. J. Adams run out	13	6/151 7/196	

O. H. Mortensen and D. E. Malcolm did not bat.

Bowling: Fraser 8-0-32-1; Cowans 6-0-22-0; Hughes 8-0-45-2; Emburey 7-0-37-0; Weekes 8-1-35-2; Haynes 3-0-16-1.

Middlesex

D. L. Haynes b Malcolm	49	J. E. Emburey not out	3
M. A. Roseberry b Warner	17		
*M. W. Gatting b Malcolm	44	B 1, l-b 5, w 4, n-b 1	11
M. R. Ramprakash c Bowler b Warner	1		
K. R. Brown c Barnett b Malcolm	40	1/23 2/115 3/120 (5 wkts, 39.4 overs) 201	
†P. R. Downton not out	34	4/120 5/191	

P. N. Weekes, S. P. Hughes, A. R. C. Fraser and N. G. Cowans did not bat.

Bowling: Warner 8-0-35-2; Mortensen 8-0-19-0; Malcolm 8-0-41-3; Base 8-0-53-0; Kuiper 7.4-0-47-0.

Umpires: D. J. Constant and M. J. Kitchen.

WINNERS 1988-90

1988 LANCASHIRE beat Worcestershire by 52 runs.
1989 ESSEX beat Nottinghamshire by 5 runs.
1990 MIDDLESEX beat Derbyshire by five wickets.

MINOR COUNTIES CHAMPIONSHIP, 1990

By MICHAEL BERRY and ROBERT BROOKE

The summer of 1990 took on an experimental look for Minor Counties cricket, following the implementation of a reshaped points-scoring system. After years of discussion, bowling bonus points were introduced – one for every two wickets taken in the first innings – and the limitation by which first-innings points were obtained only from the first 55 overs was abolished. It was, inevitably, a curate's egg of a change. The bowling bonus points proved a welcome addition; but from the moment that Berkshire and Oxfordshire extended the first innings of their opening game into the second, and final, afternoon, the absence of the 55-overs yardstick, first used in 1974, fostered much distrust. Agreements between the captains to restrict the length of their first innings served only to reinforce the doubts over the new legislation.

Continued over

MINOR COUNTIES CHAMPIONSHIP, 1990

Eastern Division	P	W	L	Drawn W 1st Inns	Drawn L 1st Inns	Drawn T 1st Inns	NR	Bonus Pts	Total Pts
Hertfordshire NW	9	3	2*	3	1	0	0	34	77
Lincolnshire NW	9	2	2*	2	3	0	0	36	68
Staffordshire NW	8	3	1	2	2	0	1	24	65
Bedfordshire NW	8	3	1	2	2	0	1	22	63
Durham NW	9	1	0	6	2	0	0	33	63
Norfolk NW	9	2	1	1	5	0	0	33	61
Cambridgeshire NW	9	1	2*	3	2	1	0	31	57
Suffolk	9	2	3*	1	3	0	0	24	53
Cumberland	9	0	2	5	1	1	0	30	48
Northumberland	9	0	3*	1	5	0	0	23	34

Western Division	P	W	L	Drawn W 1st Inns	Drawn L 1st Inns	Drawn T 1st Inns	NR	Bonus Pts	Total Pts
Berkshire NW	9	3	1‡	3	2	0	0	26	69
Oxfordshire NW	9	2	1*	4	2	0	0	26	63
Shropshire NW	9	2	0	4	3	0	0	25	60
Buckinghamshire NW	9	2	0	4	3	0	0	25	60
Dorset NW	9	2	3†	0	4	0	0	27	57
Devon NW	9	0	1*	7	1	0	0	32	57
Wiltshire	9	1	3†	3	1	0	1	24	53
Wales	9	1	2	1	5	0	0	28	46
Cheshire	9	1	0	2	5	0	1	16	40
Cornwall	9	1	4	1	3	0	0	17	33

* *Denotes first-innings points (3) in one match lost.*
† *Denotes first-innings points (3) in two matches lost.*
‡ *Denotes tie on first innings (2 pts) in one match lost.*
NW *Denotes qualified for NatWest Bank Trophy in 1991.*
Win = 10 pts, Tie = 5 pts, First-innings win = 3 pts, First-innings tie = 2 pts, First-innings loss = 1 pt, No result = 3 pts.

Note: Where points are equal, priority is given to the county winning the greater number of completed matches. Where this number also is equal, priority is decided according to the nett batting averages.

The modifications, while providing extra interest, did little to alter the formbook. **Hertfordshire** were again at the forefront of the championship, and this time won the title to make up for their double disappointment in 1989. Beaten in both finals then, Hertfordshire took the 1990 championship with a seven-wicket victory over Berkshire in the September final at Luton. Their successful defence of the Eastern Division title revolved largely around the contributions of Andy Needham, John Carr and David Surridge, their shrewd captain. Needham scored 750 runs and took eighteen wickets, Carr scored 365 runs in only four games, and Surridge claimed 29 wickets. Although losing to Staffordshire and Bedfordshire in mid-season, Hertfordshire showed their true worth with a ten-wicket win over Suffolk in their final divisional fixture.

Runners-up in the Eastern Division were **Lincolnshire**, who enjoyed their best season for twenty years. They also reached the final of the Holt Cup at Lord's, but the subsequent dismissal of Neil Priestley, their captain, showed that, despite the success, all was not well behind the scenes. Jim Love, the former Yorkshire stalwart, who made his début in 1990, was chosen to succeed Priestley as captain. Love's 537 championship runs included centuries in both innings against Staffordshire, while Austin Jelfs, a 40-year-old newcomer from the same Harrogate club as Love, took 25 wickets in six games. Ian Pont, having switched from Northumberland, finished with 26 wickets, while Nigel Illingworth performed the season's only hat-trick, in Lincolnshire's Holt Cup semi-final win over Devon.

Staffordshire again just missed out and will rarely have a better chance of reaching the championship play-off. They went into their final fixture, against Lincolnshire, clear at the top of the table. But the batting fell apart in the first innings, and they took only one point from an eight-wicket defeat, while Hertfordshire were closing the gap with eight points from a draw with Durham. David Cartledge and Steve Dean, their swashbuckling openers, both scored in excess of 500 runs, and fast bowler Paul Taylor captured 32 wickets. Had rain not washed out their home games with Bedfordshire – abandoned without a ball being bowled – and Norfolk, Staffordshire could well have been regional winners. However, by beating Shropshire in the qualifying round they did manage to open their account in the Holt Cup, after seven successive unsuccessful years.

Bedfordshire, in beating Cumberland and Hertfordshire in consecutive games, achieved their highest Eastern Division placing of fourth. They gambled with three spinners to beat Cumberland, and successfully chased a target of 302 against Hertfordshire, having begun their campaign in May with victory over Lincolnshire. Mark Briers, an all-rounder who bowled leg-breaks, scored 451 runs and took seventeen wickets in five appearances, while Ray Swann furthered his reputation with 584 runs. Another newcomer in addition to Briers was Gary Palmer, formerly of Somerset.

A last-match triumph over Lincolnshire salvaged **Durham's** season by ensuring them a place in the NatWest Bank Trophy (or Gillette Cup) for the fifteenth successive season. Neil Riddell's final year in charge was especially notable for the return of Peter Kippax, the 49-year-old leg-spinner, after two seasons' absence because of injury. Kippax played in eight of the nine championship games and his 26 wickets included a career-best five for 23 against Cambridgeshire. Paul Burn made 582 runs, Ashok Patel 512, and Gary Brown, a prolific run-scorer for the Minor Counties representative side, would also have passed 500 had he not missed three championship games. Paul Newman of Derbyshire was a Durham newcomer.

The loss of Andy Mack, owing to a heel injury, was a handicap which **Norfolk** could not overcome. The big seam bowler was their major success of 1989, and Norfolk never filled the void. Their captain, Steve Plumb, resigned from the post at the end of the season. Ray Kingshott, the venerable slow left-armer, took 35 wickets, including the season's best analysis of eight for 47, against Northumberland, and Jimmy Lewis established himself with 27. The batting was led by two up-and-coming youngsters in Danny Stamp and Carl Rogers.

Cambridgeshire completed the seven-strong contingent of Eastern Division qualifiers for the NatWest Trophy. Another serious injury to Nigel Gadsby, this time a shattered forearm, blighted their programme, but Stuart Turner again excelled. The 47-year-old former Essex man, bowling off-breaks in the second half of the season, increased his tally of championship wickets in four years to 175, while John Lever, in his first season away from the first-class game, revealed his own versatility by bowling slow left-arm. He managed only twenty wickets, but another newcomer, Ajaz Akhtar, collected 23. Giles Ecclestone, a stylish left-hander destined for greater things, was the leading run-maker with 487 at an average of 60.87.

Suffolk's season started well, but ended disastrously. Chris Gladwin (171 not out) and Mike McEvoy (113 not out) shared a record-breaking unbroken stand of 295 in just 38.5 overs to spearhead a memorable ten-wicket win over Northumberland at Jesmond, and a second win soon followed against Cambridgeshire. But they lost three of their last five games, surrendering miserably to Staffordshire and Hertfordshire. They were not helped by the fact that Gladwin played in only two championship games, or that McEvoy's form deserted him. Andrew Golding, the former Essex and Cambridge University slow left-armer, was their only bowling success, with 28 wickets, but at 34.50 apiece they were not cheap.

Neither Cumberland nor Northumberland managed a single championship victory. It was the second successive season that **Cumberland** had failed to win, and they had to look back to August 1988 for their last taste of championship success. The all-round displays of David Makinson complemented the performances of Chris Stockdale (508 runs) and Malcolm Woods (30 wickets), while there were encouraging late-season débuts by David Pearson and Dipak Patel. Steve O'Shaughnessy's first appearance for **Northumberland** aptly summed up their summer. He registered a pair, did not bowl a ball, and was never seen again. Injury forced Mike Younger to hand over the captaincy to Graeme Morris halfway through the season, and although Northumberland had several consistent run-scorers, their bowling was woefully limited. Jonathon Benn, an opening batsman, had four hundreds in an impressive aggregate of 760 runs.

After finishing as runners-up in the Western Division in the previous three seasons, **Berkshire** finally found the right formula to claim the regional crown. Such was the depth of their bowling that six bowlers collected fourteen or more wickets. David Hartley, a leg-spinner, took the most, but Peter Lewington, their normally productive off-spinner, made only four championship appearances owing to injury. Martin Lickley (838 runs) and Gary Loveday (626) were as dependable as ever as opening batsmen, with Lickley scoring three centuries.

Oxfordshire, the 1989 champions, were runners-up, and had the honour of their captain, 44-year-old Phil Garner, being chosen as the first captain of the newly formed NCA England Amateur XI. A bout of food poisoning afflicted the side in the penultimate game, against Buckinghamshire, as a consequence of which they slumped to an ultimately crucial defeat by 88 runs. Stuart Waterton amassed 883 runs, and Keith Arnold (33 wickets) and Rupert Evans (31) were again greatly influential with the ball. John Abrahams, the former Lancashire captain, had another richly rewarding season for **Shropshire**. His 765 runs and 23 wickets were backed up by Mark Davies, captain John Foster and Tony Parton, all of whom scored in excess of 500 runs, and by Geoff Edmunds, whose slow left-arm bowling resulted in 36 wickets.

Buckinghamshire, who lifted the Holt Cup at Lord's when they beat Lincolnshire, will remember 1990 for their one-day achievements. Paul Atkins was their match-winner, hitting 97 not out and then running out Jim Love with a direct throw from long-on. In the championship Malcolm Roberts, with a Benson and Hedges Cup century at Marlow against Sussex to his name, compiled 921 runs; and Steve Burrow, despite failing to pass three figures in any of his seventeen innings, ran up 743. Burrow, a highly respected all-rounder, also took 27 wickets, while left-arm spinner Tim Scriven was close behind with 24.

Dorset and **Devon** finished on the same number of points, and qualified for the NatWest Bank Trophy, but Devon, without a win, owed their position to their ability to secure both first-innings points and a healthy number of bowling points. For Dorset, Graeme Calway totalled 721 runs, while Julian Shackleton, son of Derek, marked his first full season for the county with 33 wickets. Andy Pugh, Kevin Rice and Nick Folland led the Devon batting with aggregates of more than 500, and Mark Woodman, a tireless and accurate seam bowler, deserved his 29 wickets.

David Turner returned to Minor Counties cricket after 24 years with Hampshire and hit 887 runs, including three hundreds, for his native **Wiltshire**. Paul Bail made 437 in six games, but although Matthew Holland, a teenage slow left-armer, took 21 wickets, their bowling lacked penetration. **Wales** celebrated their first Minor Counties home win when they beat Wiltshire by four wickets at Colwyn Bay in their final match, only their second victory in three seasons in the championship. Andy Puddle captained the side for the first time and led by example with 512 runs, while Tudor Hughes made 454 and Tony Smith, a slow left-armer, collected 23 wickets at a reasonable cost of 25.39 each.

Cheshire, for so long a force in the Western Division, again languished down in the lower reaches. John Hitchmough, a resounding success in 1989, struggled for runs in 1990, with the result that the batting relied heavily on the hard-hitting Steve Crawley and the experienced Ian Cockbain. Andy Greasley, an off-spinner new to Minor Counties cricket, took 22 wickets in just four appearances. Cornwall, though recipients of the wooden spoon for the seventh time in eight seasons, did show signs of improvement with a last-match victory over Dorset. A pre-season fitness course and an early Holt Cup win against Wiltshire had sharpened their resolve, but the unavailability of Steve Williams, a batsman of immense quality, for all but one championship game was a substantial loss. Ed Nicolson and Kevin Thomas gave the batting some backbone but, Chris Lovell apart, the bowling was inadequate.

CHAMPIONSHIP FINAL

BERKSHIRE v HERTFORDSHIRE

At Luton, September 9. Hertfordshire won by seven wickets. Toss: Hertfordshire. MacLaurin's unbeaten 52 saw Hertfordshire to victory with thirteen balls to spare. Berkshire, put in, had lost their way from 88 for one, when Loveday and Mercer succumbed to the first two balls of Smith's flighted slow left-arm spin. Headley grafted his way to an unbeaten 50 in 45 overs, but Hertfordshire in reply always seemed to have plenty in reserve. MacLaurin settled it by twice lifting Lewington, the off-spinner, for six in his final over.

Berkshire

M. G. Lickley c Ligertwood b Merry . .	15	T. P. J. Dodd not out	3
G. E. Loveday c Ligertwood b Smith . .	42		
G. T. Headley not out	50	B 1, l-b 16, w 5, n-b 2	24
D. J. M. Mercer c and b Smith	0		
*M. L. Simmons run out	6	1/25 2/88 3/88 (5 wkts, 55 overs) 171
P. J. Oxley c MacLaurin b Surridge . . .	31	4/97 5/167

M. G. Stear, †M. E. Stevens, J. H. Jones and P. J. Lewington did not bat.

Bowling: Harris 10–1–36–0; Merry 11–2–36–1; Neal 2–0–12–0; Surridge 10–1–31–1; Needham 11–3–24–0; Smith 11–3–15–2.

Hertfordshire

N. P. G. Wright c Stevens b Jones	45	B. G. Evans not out	18
J. D. Carr c Simmons b Jones	16	B 4, l-b 5, w 2, n-b 1	12
A. Needham c Oxley b Lewington	29		
N. R. C. MacLaurin not out	52	1/23 2/81 3/118 (3 wkts, 52.5 overs) 172

†D. G. C. Ligertwood, D. M. Smith, E. P. Neal, W. G. Merry, *D. Surridge and G. A. R. Harris did not bat.

Bowling: Jones 10.5–3–35–2; Headley 5–3–10–0; Stear 10–2–31–0; Dodd 7–1–30–0; Lewington 11–3–30–1; Oxley 9–0–27–0.

Umpires: P. Adams and T. V. Wilkins.

HOLT CUP KNOCKOUT FINAL

BUCKINGHAMSHIRE v LINCOLNSHIRE

At Lord's, August 20. Buckinghamshire won by 16 runs. Toss: Buckinghamshire. Atkins, a 24-year-old batsman on the Surrey staff, proved the key to Buckinghamshire's victory. His 97 not out, which began in a second-wicket stand of 88 with Harwood, was largely responsible for Buckinghamshire's reaching 227 on a slow, unresponsive pitch. Then, when Lincolnshire appeared to be staging a recovery after losing Priestley in the first over, Atkins ran out Love for 47 with a direct throw from long-on. Hibbitt fell to the next ball and Lincolnshire, 116 for four in the 38th over, were suddenly 117 for six. Thereafter they were fighting a lost cause, despite a brave effort from the tail.

Buckinghamshire

A. R. Harwood st Priestley b Fell	52	S. G. Lynch lbw b Love 0
M. J. Roberts c Priestley b Pont	7	T. J. Barry not out 10
P. D. Atkins not out	97	L-b 18, w 2, n-b 2 22
T. J. A. Scriven c Hibbitt b Love	23	
S. Burrow b Love	1	1/23 2/111 3/163 (7 wkts, 55 overs) 227
*N. G. Hames b Love	7	4/165 5/175
B. S. Percy b Illingworth	8	6/197 7/198

†D. J. Goldsmith and C. D. Booden did not bat.

Bowling: Pont 7–3–9–1; Illingworth 10–1–54–1; Jelfs 6–1–30–0; Christmas 11–1–31–0; Fell 11–1–41–1; Love 10–1–44–4.

Lincolnshire

*†N. Priestley c Goldsmith b Barry	2	N. J. B. Illingworth b Barry 31
D. B. Storer b Scriven	23	D. A. Christmas not out 29
N. J. C. Gandon b Barry	3	A. C. Jelfs not out 1
J. D. Love run out	47	B 4, l-b 8, w 4, n-b 3 19
M. A. Fell c Harwood b Scriven	13	
R. C. Hibbitt b Percy	13	1/2 2/19 3/50 (9 wkts, 55 overs) 211
I. L. Pont b Percy	5	4/76 5/117 6/117
J. H. T. Bramhill c Roberts b Burrow	21	7/130 8/154 9/196

Bowling: Barry 11–3–39–3; Booden 11–5–33–1; Burrow 11–5–33–1; Lynch 6–0–32–0; Scriven 7–0–34–2; Percy 9–0–37–2.

Umpires: P. Adams and T. V. Wilkins.

*In the averages that follow, * against a score signifies not out, * against a name signifies the captain and † signifies a wicket-keeper.*

BEDFORDSHIRE

Secretary – A. J. PEARCE, 15 Dene Way, Upper Caldecote, Biggleswade SG18 8DL

Matches 8: Won – Cumberland, Hertfordshire, Lincolnshire. Lost – Norfolk. Won on first innings – Cambridgeshire, Suffolk. Lost on first innings – Durham, Northumberland. Abandoned (No result) – Staffordshire.

Batting Averages

	M	I	NO	R	HI	100s	50s	Avge
R. Swann	7	14	2	584	135*	2	2	48.66
M. P. Briers	5	10	0	451	124	1	2	45.10
S. J. Renshaw	5	7	5	90	34*	0	0	45.00
M. R. Gouldstone	8	16	2	438	60*	0	2	31.28
G. V. Palmer	7	13	2	312	59*	0	2	28.36
P. D. B. Hoare	8	14	2	340	97	0	2	28.33
A. Dean	4	6	2	112	33	0	0	28.00
*J. R. Wake	8	10	2	162	50	0	1	20.25
S. J. Lines	3	6	1	83	47	0	0	16.60
T. C. Thomas	5	6	1	71	42	0	0	14.20
N. G. Folland	3	6	0	61	39	0	0	10.16

Played in seven matches: B. C. Banks 0, 24*, 6, 12*, 0. Played in six matches: †G. D. Sandford 3*, 5, 2, 0*. Played in four matches: P. D. Thomas 22, 15, 0. Played in two matches: K. Gentle 29*, 31, 0. Played in one match: R. G. Blair 6, 2; †G. Conway 0, 0; S. D. L. Davis 7, 17*; R. W. Morris 22, 15; M. R. White 0*; †E. R. Osborn did not bat.

Bowling Averages

	O	M	R	W	BB	5W/i	Avge
M. P. Briers	95	12	405	17	6-45	2	23.82
P. D. Thomas	104.3	17	347	11	3-35	0	31.54
J. R. Wake	194.3	44	620	17	5-51	1	36.47
G. V. Palmer	165	28	595	16	4-32	0	37.18

Also bowled: B. C. Banks 116–23–370–8; A. Dean 37.1–9–131–3; S. J. Renshaw 92–18–300–6; R. Swann 100–25–282–8; M. R. White 15–2–58–2.

BERKSHIRE

Secretary – C. M. S. CROMBIE, Orchard Cottage, Waltham St Lawrence

Matches 9: Won – Cornwall, Devon, Wiltshire. Lost – Dorset. Won on first innings – Cheshire, Oxfordshire, Shropshire. Lost on first innings – Buckinghamshire, Wales.

Batting Averages

	M	I	NO	R	HI	100s	50s	Avge
M. G. Lickley	9	16	3	838	122*	3	4	64.46
G. E. Loveday	9	16	0	626	110	1	6	39.12
P. J. Oxley	9	14	7	258	63*	0	2	36.85
D. J. M. Mercer	9	16	3	470	146*	1	2	36.15
*M. L. Simmons	9	15	4	322	58*	0	1	29.27
G. T. Headley	7	12	1	238	100	1	0	21.63
†M. E. Stevens	9	7	3	43	33	0	0	10.75
M. G. Stear	8	9	4	51	24	0	0	10.20

Played in nine matches: J. H. Jones 2*. Played in five matches: N. B. Fusedale 9*, 17, 2, 9*. Played in four matches: D. J. B. Hartley 2, 0, 1; P. J. Lewington did not bat. Played in three matches: T. P. J. Dodd 37, 94, 0; B. S. Jackson 52, 86, 0*, 9. Played in one match: D. Shaw 61; J. Barrow did not bat.

Bowling Averages

	O	M	R	W	BB	5W/i	Avge
D. J. B. Hartley	84	12	392	18	4-51	0	21.77
P. J. Lewington	139	49	375	15	4-20	0	25.00
G. T. Headley	86.3	15	363	14	3-45	0	25.92
N. B. Fusedale	140	42	389	15	4-36	0	25.93
J. H. Jones ...	165.1	37	536	15	4-41	0	35.73
M. G. Stear ...	144.5	15	544	14	4-59	0	38.85

Also bowled: J. Barrow 12–1–31–0; T. P. J. Dodd 37–5–139–6; B. S. Jackson 50–6–180–3; M. G. Lickley 51.5–13–199–3; D. J. M. Mercer 8.2–2–41–3; P. J. Oxley 73–15–282–6; D. Shaw 9–3–23–2; M. L. Simmons 12–1–76–4.

BUCKINGHAMSHIRE

Secretary – S. J. TOMLIN, Orchardleigh Cottage, Bigfrith Lane, Cookham Dean SL6 9PH

Matches 9: Won – Cornwall, Oxfordshire. Won on first innings – Berkshire, Cheshire, Dorset, Wales. Lost on first innings – Devon, Shropshire, Wiltshire.

Batting Averages

	M	I	NO	R	HI	100s	50s	Avge
M. J. Roberts	9	18	1	921	124	2	5	54.17
S. Burrow	9	17	1	743	86	0	7	46.43
T. J. A. Scriven	8	16	4	445	79*	0	4	37.08
P. D. Atkins	5	10	0	303	63	0	2	30.30
A. R. Harwood	5	10	0	280	83	0	2	28.00
*N. G. Hames	8	15	1	315	53	0	2	22.50
S. G. Lynch	9	13	4	176	38	0	0	19.55
S. M. Shearman	3	6	2	68	35	0	0	17.00
T. J. Barry	9	10	4	94	30	0	0	15.66
G. R. Black	6	10	2	122	45	0	0	15.25

Played in nine matches: C. D. Booden 0*, 2. Played in five matches: †D. J. Goldsmith 0, 3*, 0, 0. Played in three matches: J. N. B. Bovill 3, 4*, 7, 2*; N. Farrow 18, 14, 2, 32*; †C. J. Tungate 4*, 0, 0. Played in two matches: T. Butler 1, 35, 32, 10. Played in one match: P. D. Dolphin 39*, 37; †G. Fryer 3*, 4*; B. S. Percy 1, 15.

Bowling Averages

	O	M	R	W	BB	5W/i	Avge
G. R. Black	73.2	12	248	11	4-43	0	22.54
S. Burrow	194	34	648	27	6-30	1	24.00
T. J. A. Scriven	200	45	706	24	5-23	1	29.41
C. D. Booden	182	39	586	14	4-57	0	41.85
T. J. Barry	221.2	29	862	20	3-42	0	43.10

Also bowled: J. N. B. Bovill 40–3–174–5; S. G. Lynch 102.5–11–425–7; B. S. Percy 14–3–52–3; M. J. Roberts 5–3–9–1.

CAMBRIDGESHIRE

Secretary – P. W. GOODEN, The Redlands, Oakington Road, Cottenham, Cambridge CB4 4TW

Matches 9: Won – Northumberland. Lost – Hertfordshire, Suffolk. Won on first innings – Durham, Norfolk, Staffordshire. Lost on first innings – Bedfordshire, Lincolnshire. Tied on first innings – Cumberland.

Batting Averages

	M	I	NO	R	HI	100s	50s	Avge
G. W. Ecclestone	5	10	2	487	111	1	5	60.87
R. A. Milne	6	11	1	421	134*	1	2	42.10
N. J. Adams	8	15	3	429	102	1	2	35.75
A. M. Cade	7	12	6	206	70*	0	1	34.33
*N. T. Gadsby	4	8	1	239	104*	1	0	34.14
†R. J. Turner	6	11	3	271	52*	0	1	33.87
I. S. Lawrence	8	16	0	393	65	0	3	24.56
Ajaz Akhtar	9	13	2	188	54*	0	1	17.09
S. K. Thomas	5	10	2	123	55	0	1	15.37
S. Turner	8	13	4	130	35*	0	0	14.44
D. P. Norman	5	9	0	126	40	0	0	14.00
S. W. Ecclestone	4	8	1	76	28	0	0	10.85

Played in six matches: J. K. Lever 1, 3, 6, 1, 18*. Played in four matches: M. G. Stephenson 6*. Played in three matches: D. C. Collard 0; A. Howorth 9*, 7, 25. Played in two matches: †M. S. L. Rollinson 0; M. W. Taylor 8*, 4. Played in one match: P. J. Dicks 28, 0; C. R. F. Green 0*, 5; P. A. Redfarn 21; D. M. Cousins did not bat.

Bowling Averages

	O	M	R	W	BB	5W/i	Avge
S. Turner	286.5	79	727	40	7-86	2	18.17
M. G. Stephenson	100.4	34	303	14	5-40	1	21.64
Ajaz Akhtar	208.3	55	579	23	4-16	0	25.17
J. K. Lever	231.1	49	725	20	3-35	0	36.25

Also bowled: N. J. Adams 18–0–71–1; A. M. Cade 3.5–0–25–0; D. C. Collard 68–22–215–4; D. M. Cousins 5.3–1–24–1; N. T. Gadsby 8–3–22–0; C. R. F. Green 1–0–5–0; A. Howorth 63.2–18–182–5; M. W. Taylor 29–8–95–2.

CHESHIRE

Secretary – J. B. PICKUP, 2 Castle Street, Northwich CW8 1AB

Matches 9: Won – Cornwall. Won on first innings – Dorset, Wales. Lost on first innings – Berkshire, Buckinghamshire, Devon, Oxfordshire, Shropshire. No result – Wiltshire.

Batting Averages

	M	I	NO	R	HI	100s	50s	Avge
S. T. Crawley	9	17	4	671	107	2	4	51.61
I. Cockbain	7	12	0	590	106	1	6	49.16
J. Bean	9	15	3	397	58	0	2	33.08
I. J. Tansley	4	8	1	217	78	0	2	31.00
P. A. Davis	4	8	1	188	63	0	1	26.85
J. J. Hitchmough	8	14	1	305	77	0	1	23.46
*N. T. O'Brien	9	15	2	279	63	0	1	21.46
†S. Bramhall	9	11	4	65	21*	0	0	9.28

Played in nine matches: N. D. Peel 0*, 3*. Played in four matches: G. J. Blackburn 0, 14, 8*, 12, 4*; M. G. Boocock 0*, 4*, 11*, 50*; E. McCray 47, 20, 11*, 6, 16; A. D. Greasley did not bat. Played in three matches: J. G. Bacon 8, 1, 27; A. Fox 0*, 0. Played in two matches: J. D. Gray 9*, 1, 18; J. F. M. O'Brien 4, 8, 50*; K. Teasdale 19, 3, 1*; P. Wakefield 4*, 16*, 0, 6. Played in one match: P. H. de Prez 10.

Bowling Averages

	O	M	R	W	BB	5W/i	Avge
A. D. Greasley	138.1	37	471	22	5-96	1	21.40
N. D. Peel	183.1	41	524	15	8-62	1	34.93
S. T. Crawley	111.2	11	375	10	3-46	0	37.50

Also bowled: J. G. Bacon 41–12–140–3; G. J. Blackburn 91.3–27–262–7; M. G. Boocock 79–17–330–7; I. Cockbain 15–5–47–0; P. H. de Prez 34.2–8–129–7; A. Fox 59.3–17–175–6; E. McCray 80.2–20–269–6; J. F. M. O'Brien 48–11–174–5; N. T. O'Brien 27–4–116–1; P. Wakefield 26–5–106–5.

CORNWALL

Secretary – T. D. MENEER, Falbridge, Penvale Cross, Penryn

Matches 9: Won – Dorset. Lost – Berkshire, Buckinghamshire, Cheshire, Shropshire. Won on first innings – Wales. Lost on first innings – Devon, Oxfordshire, Wiltshire.

atting Averages

	M	I	NO	R	HI	100s	50s	Avge
J. C. Thomas ...	6	12	1	414	108*	1	2	37.63
Nicolson	9	18	1	615	77	0	4	36.17
Hooper	6	12	1	348	103*	1	1	31.63
T. Walton	6	12	0	324	69	0	3	27.00
C. Lovell	8	15	2	335	54*	0	1	25.76
G. Furse	8	14	3	276	46	0	0	25.09
Moyle	4	6	2	85	47*	0	0	21.25
A. Coombe	4	7	2	101	34	0	0	20.20
. P. Eva	9	14	7	137	27*	0	0	19.57
Wherry	8	16	0	298	75	0	2	18.62
Turner	5	9	3	97	27*	0	0	16.16
. T. Willetts	9	13	2	122	42	0	0	11.09

Played in four matches: M. Bell 4*, 0*, 0, 8*; A. J. Buzza 1*, 5*, 8*. Played in three atches: D. A. Toseland 0*, 2, 1, 1. Played in two matches: S. Lonsdale 7; S. Pedlar 1, 37, 7. Played in one match: G. G. Watts 1, 19; S. M. Williams 15, 71.

owling Averages

	O	M	R	W	BB	5W/i	Avge
G. Furse	87.4	11	303	12	4-38	0	25.25
C. Lovell	175.3	18	732	25	6-65	1	29.28
. Bell	106	17	378	11	5-72	1	34.36

Also bowled: A. J. Buzza 94–11–380–3; P. A. Coombe 77–15–244–4; S. Lonsdale .4–5–161–3; S. Moyle 67.1–6–283–7; S. Pedlar 7–0–38–2; D. A. Toseland 87.2–16–282–6; Turner 94–8–412–6; R. T. Walton 7–1–34–0; G. G. Watts 18–4–90–2; F. T. Willetts 0–25–1.

CUMBERLAND

Secretary – M. BEATY, 9 Abbey Drive, Natland, Kendal, Cumbria LA9 7QN

atches 9: Lost – Bedfordshire, Staffordshire. Won on first innings – Hertfordshire, Lincolnshire, rfolk, Northumberland, Suffolk. Lost on first innings – Durham. Tied on first innings – mbridgeshire.

atting Averages

	M	I	NO	R	HI	100s	50s	Avge
. R. Moyes	9	13	3	437	137	1	1	43.70
W. Reidy	7	11	1	339	104*	1	1	33.90
J. Stockdale	9	15	0	508	87	0	5	33.86
James	6	8	5	98	36*	0	0	32.66
J. Makinson	8	13	3	291	97	0	2	29.10
A. Burns	7	11	3	180	52*	0	1	22.50
. J. Clarke	4	6	1	98	35	0	0	19.60
. D. Woods	9	6	2	13	7	0	0	3.25

Played in six matches: R. Ellwood 7, 0. Played in five matches: S. Wall 10*, 8, 27, 19; M. Wheatman 3, 2*, 0. Played in four matches: S. Sharp 15, 31, 32, 9, 29. Played in three atches: †S. M. Dutton 3, 30, 26, 6*; D. Patel 48, 11, 62*, 55, 74; S. D. Philbrook 1, 25*, 1, . Played in two matches: D. Halliwell 4, 2; D. Pearson 8, 18, 18, 131*. Played in one match: I. Cooper 0, 17; C. R. Knight 18, 8*; N. Maxwell 19, 1; S. D. Myles 0; N. Pattinson 21, 15; . G. Scothern 19*, 7; G. Bolton did not bat.

Bowling Averages

	O	M	R	W	BB	5W/i	Avg
B. W. Reidy	94	25	289	13	3-28	0	22.
M. D. Woods	242.1	83	704	30	6-47	2	23.
D. J. Makinson	267.2	69	700	29	5-43	1	24.
R. Ellwood	105.3	34	281	10	2-28	0	28.

Also bowled: G. Bolton 36–6–77–5; M. Burns 2–0–7–0; D. Halliwell 39–5–152–2; S. Jam 8–3–32–0; S. D. Myles 14–2–42–2; M. G. Scothern 13–2–52–0; S. Sharp 8–3–27–1; C. Stockdale 1–0–1–0; S. Wall 92.2–20–315–6; D. M. Wheatman 70.5–10–250–5.

DEVON

Secretary – G. R. EVANS, Blueberry Haven, 20 Boucher Road, Budleigh Salterton EX9 6JF

Matches 9: Lost – Berkshire. Won on first innings – Buckinghamshire, Cheshire, Cornwall, Dorse Shropshire, Wales, Wiltshire. Lost on first innings – Oxfordshire.

Batting Averages

	M	I	NO	R	HI	100s	50s	Avg
A. J. Pugh	9	16	3	582	100*	1	3	44.
K. G. Rice	7	14	2	528	93*	0	4	44.0
N. A. Folland	8	16	3	562	109*	1	3	43.2
K. Donohue	4	7	3	111	40*	0	0	27.7
J. K. Tierney	4	7	3	109	46	0	0	27.2
G. P. Randall-Johnson	7	14	4	256	42	0	0	25.6
*J. H. Edwards	9	18	1	395	66	0	3	23.2
R. I. Dawson	9	16	1	343	85	0	2	22.8
†C. S. Pritchard	7	8	5	45	26*	0	0	15.0

Played in nine matches: M. C. Woodman 6*, 4. Played in five matches: J. Rhodes 0 Played in four matches: R. H. J. Jenkins 0*, 23*, 4, 5, 12*. Played in three matches: N. F Gaywood 4, 2, 41*, 1, 26; M. J. Record 5, 6*, 2*. Played in two matches: G. Wallen 9, 3, A. C. Cottam did not bat. Played in one match: S. Cockram 0*; L. R. Hart 13, 4; S. Lott 9* S. A. Moore 2, 28; †R. C. Turpin 17; †P. J. Lucketti and G. W. White did not bat.

Bowling Averages

	O	M	R	W	BB	5W/i	Avg
M. J. Record	62	7	245	16	6-54	1	15.3
M. C. Woodman	286	67	785	29	4-40	0	27.0
J. K. Tierney	91.1	22	338	11	4-57	0	30.7

Also bowled: S. Cockram 12–2–38–0; A. C. Cottam 44.1–7–187–6; R. I. Dawso 41–1–243–5; K. Donohue 112–26–304–9; N. A. Folland 25–3–142–4; N. R. Gaywoo 8.1–2–32–2; L. R. Hart 10–0–47–1; R. H. J. Jenkins 56.2–7–248–9; S. Lott 24–4–89–5; S. A Moore 26.1–7–73–3; J. Rhodes 112–21–443–9; K. G. Rice 44–3–182–5.

DORSET

Secretary – D. J. W. BRIDGE, Long Acre, Tinney's Lane, Sherborne DT9 3DY

Matches 9: Won – Berkshire, Wales. Lost – Cornwall, Shropshire, Wiltshire. Lost on first innings Buckinghamshire, Cheshire, Devon, Oxfordshire.

Batting Averages

	M	I	NO	R	HI	100s	50s	Avge
A. Claughton	5	10	4	283	81	0	3	47.16
S. Calway	9	18	0	721	121	2	4	40.05
M. H. Graham-Brown	6	12	1	368	78	0	3	33.45
D. Reynolds	7	13	3	318	101*	1	1	31.80
A. Pyman	6	8	2	173	71	0	2	28.83
B. Lewis	3	6	1	129	75	0	1	25.80
P. Merriman	9	18	0	443	77	0	3	24.61
Willows	7	13	2	254	59	0	1	23.09
M. Fitzgerald	8	6	4	45	15*	0	0	22.50
H. Shackleton	9	7	3	75	33	0	0	18.75
Stone	9	9	2	131	67	0	2	16.93
R. Taylor	6	9	1	77	24	0	0	9.62
A. R. Wingfield Digby	9	11	2	67	19	0	0	7.44

Played in one match: J. M. Blackburn 4, 6; R. V. J. Coombs 43; S. J. Legg 11, 39; N. Lynn 0*; S. W. D. Rintoul 13, 36*; S. Sawney 6*, 0.

Bowling Averages

	O	M	R	W	BB	5W/i	Avge
R. Taylor	165	39	497	24	5-38	1	20.70
H. Shackleton	290.3	79	759	33	6-67	2	23.00
A. Pyman	93.1	16	365	15	4-29	0	24.33
Stone	221.5	46	666	26	5-59	1	25.61
R. Wingfield Digby	175.2	42	604	12	2-38	0	50.33

Also bowled: J. M. Blackburn 5–0–29–1; G. S. Calway 74.3–17–265–6; R. V. J. Coombs 2–5–103–0; J. M. H. Graham-Brown 2–1–1–0; R. P. Merriman 2–0–9–0; S. Sawney 2–0–62–0; A. Willows 25–4–96–2.

DURHAM

Secretary – J. ILEY, Roselea, Springwell Avenue, Durham DH1 4LY

Matches 9: Won – Lincolnshire. Won on first innings – Bedfordshire, Cumberland, Norfolk, Northumberland, Staffordshire, Suffolk. Lost on first innings – Cambridgeshire, Hertfordshire.

Batting Averages

	M	I	NO	R	HI	100s	50s	Avge
P. Burn	7	13	4	582	105	2	4	64.66
A. S. Patel	8	12	4	512	103*	1	4	64.00
G. K. Brown	6	11	4	417	110*	2	0	59.57
N. A. Riddell	8	9	2	314	92	0	3	44.85
D. Glendenen	9	16	1	413	130	2	1	27.53

Played in eight matches: P. J. Kippax 19, 23, 4*, 7, 58. Played in seven matches: †A. R. Fothergill 12, 10*, 8*, 3, 0. Played in six matches: P. G. Newman 4, 5, 44*, 14, 6; S. Peel 44, 7, 5*, 0. Played in five matches: I. E. Conn 4*, 11, 6*. Played in four matches: G. Clennell 5*; S. Greensword 4, 46*, 26. Played in three matches: P. J. Barnes 50, 34*, 43*, 10, 67; A. Birbeck 15, 9, 1, 1*; J. Tindale 44, 10, 17, 19, 4*; I. Young 2. Played in two matches: †D. Playfor 2, 12; J. F. Sykes 5, 11*; A. C. Day did not bat. Played in one match: S. Ball 2, 0; R. Robson 0; J. Johnston did not bat.

Bowling Averages

	O	M	R	W	BB	5W/i	Avg
A. S. Patel	119.5	35	318	21	5-80	1	15.
P. J. Kippax	220.4	75	531	26	5-23	1	20.
I. E. Conn	144.1	30	452	19	3-19	0	23.
S. Peel	122	25	391	14	4-38	0	27.9
P. G. Newman	175.1	49	519	17	4-65	0	30.

Also bowled: G. K. Brown 39–7–117–1; P. Burn 6–0–34–1; G. Clennell 77–24–224–2; A. (
Day 37–5–147–3; J. D. Glendenen 6–0–33–0; S. Greensword 43–10–133–5; J. Johnst
29–13–45–5; N. A. Riddell 2–0–21–0; J. F. Sykes 15–1–58–1; I. Young 59–7–278–4.

HERTFORDSHIRE

Secretary – D. DREDGE, 38 Santers Lane, Potters Bar EN6 2BX

*Matches 9: Won – Cambridgeshire, Norfolk, Suffolk. Lost – Bedfordshire, Staffordshire. Won
first innings – Durham, Lincolnshire, Northumberland. Lost on first innings – Cumberland.*

Batting Averages

	M	I	NO	R	HI	100s	50s	Avg
A. Needham	8	13	2	750	130*	3	4	68.
J. D. Carr	4	7	1	365	92	0	4	60.8
†D. G. C. Ligertwood	5	7	3	232	81	0	2	58.0
B. G. Evans	5	9	3	292	113*	1	2	48.6
N. P. G. Wright	7	13	2	486	113	1	3	44.1
N. R. C. MacLaurin	4	7	0	173	46	0	0	24.7
M. D. Dale	5	7	2	102	21*	0	0	20.4

Played in eight matches: *D. Surridge 6*, 6*, 9*. Played in six matches: G. A. R. Harris
0, 6. Played in five matches: W. G. Merry 11, 15; D. M. Smith 38*, 8*, 1, 7*. Played in fo
matches: T. S. Smith 7*, 8, 27, 32, 1. Played in three matches: C. N. Cavenor 24, 4*, 7, 19
I. Fletcher 15, 5*, 24, 3, 0; E. P. Neal 20, 12, 11, 2*; †M. W. C. Olley 35, 0, 0; D. G. Price
1*, 1*. Played in two matches: N. J. Ilott 4, 53; D. M. Robinson 12*, 7, 10; C. Thomas
47, 0; †M. C. G. Wright 9, 11, 1*. Played in one match: J. G. Franks 28, 10; G. Hera
21, 20; †S. March 1; R. S. Shakespeare 8, 21.

Bowling Averages

	O	M	R	W	BB	5W/i	Avg
D. M. Smith	93.3	35	215	16	3-31	0	13.4
D. Surridge	224.2	69	488	29	5-24	1	16.8
W. G. Merry	115	27	271	14	4-20	0	19.
A. Needham	192.1	74	417	18	4-26	0	23.
G. A. R. Harris	146	30	502	16	3-59	0	31.3

Also bowled: C. N. Cavenor 38–11–130–3; G. Herath 2–1–5–0; N. R. C. MacLaur
2–1–5–0; E. P. Neal 42–8–151–5; D. G. Price 22.3–1–106–4; R. S. Shakespeare 2–0–10–
T. S. Smith 56.2–20–129–7; P. A. Waterman 87–11–388–8; N. P. G. Wright 1–0–1–0.

LINCOLNSHIRE

Secretary – D. H. WRIGHT, 18 Spencers Road, Ketton, Stamford

*Matches 9: Won – Staffordshire, Suffolk. Lost – Bedfordshire, Durham. Won on first innings
Cambridgeshire, Northumberland. Lost on first innings – Cumberland, Hertfordshire, Norfolk.*

atting Averages

	M	I	NO	R	HI	100s	50s	Avge
. J. C. Gandon	8	14	4	476	103*	1	1	47.60
D. Love	7	14	1	537	103*	2	4	41.30
. B. Storer	8	15	2	497	100	1	4	38.23
'N. Priestley	9	17	1	512	83*	0	2	32.00
. A. Fell	7	13	2	335	130*	1	0	30.45
N. Warman	7	10	1	226	84	0	1	25.11
. C. Hibbitt	7	11	3	189	47*	0	0	23.62
L. Pont	7	9	0	170	81	0	1	18.88
. French	5	7	0	79	23	0	0	11.28
. Marshall	7	8	7	9	6*	0	0	9.00
. A. Christmas	8	6	1	30	10	0	0	6.00

Played in six matches: A. C. Jelfs 17*, 3, 6, 9, 8. Played in four matches: N. J. B. lingworth 0*, 17, 1, 41, 1. Played in two matches: J. R. Airey 28*, 15*; R. T. Bates 16, 1, 6, ; J. H. T. Bramhill 0, 30; P. D. McKeown 6, 3, 9*. Played in one match: P. A. Houghton 4, 14.

owling Averages

	O	M	R	W	BB	5W/i	Avge
. A. Fell	90	20	257	15	4-35	0	17.13
. C. Jelfs	158.5	36	488	25	5-61	1	19.52
. J. B. Illingworth	91	18	298	14	5-38	1	21.28
L. Pont	150.5	26	569	26	6-34	1	21.88
. French	94	20	298	11	3-33	0	27.09
. Marshall	197.2	57	527	17	4-54	0	31.00

Also bowled: J. R. Airey 38-10-77-2; R. T. Bates 11-1-40-0; D. A. Christmas 5.5-15-331-8; N. J. C. Gandon 2-1-1-1; R. C. Hibbitt 1-0-2-0; J. D. Love 75-18-256-7; . D. McKeown 21-0-133-1; D. B. Storer 3-0-27-0.

NORFOLK

Secretary – S. J. SKINNER, 27 Colkett Drive, Old Catton, Norwich NR6 7ND

Matches 9: Won – Bedfordshire, Northumberland. Lost – Hertfordshire. Won on first innings – incolnshire. Lost on first innings – Cambridgeshire, Cumberland, Durham, Staffordshire, Suffolk.

atting Averages

	M	I	NO	R	HI	100s	50s	Avge
. J. Rogers	8	15	2	487	75	0	5	37.46
. M. Stamp	9	17	2	505	81	0	3	33.66
. J. Finney	9	15	3	395	101*	1	2	32.91
. Whitehead	5	8	2	158	33*	0	0	26.33
. B. Dixon	5	7	1	141	49	0	0	23.50
S. G. Plumb	8	13	1	261	58	0	2	21.75
. L. Q. Handley	6	12	0	232	56	0	1	19.33
C. M. Lewis	9	10	1	157	88	0	1	17.44
. R. Thomas	9	11	2	135	42	0	0	15.00
. Kingshott	9	10	3	77	22	0	0	11.00
D. E. Mattocks	5	6	3	29	13	0	0	9.66
. T. Ellis	7	6	3	7	4	0	0	2.33

Played in four matches: †M. M. Jervis 6, 13, 14*, 8. Played in three matches: N. S. Taylor , 17, 4, 46. Played in two matches: B. J. Goodfellow 0*, 0*. Played in one match: D. G. avage 3, 0.

Bowling Averages

	O	M	R	W	BB	5W/i	Avg
S. G. Plumb	125.5	42	358	17	3-39	0	21.0
D. R. Thomas	72.5	12	232	10	4-36	0	23.2
R. Kingshott	279.4	69	878	35	8-47	2	25.0
J. C. M. Lewis ...	189	30	703	27	6-62	1	26.0
M. T. Ellis	101.2	19	348	11	6-60	1	31.6

Also bowled: B. J. Goodfellow 31–5–98–3; D. M. Stamp 5–2–10–0; N. S. Taylc
33–5–144–5.

NORTHUMBERLAND

Secretary – F. J. FARMER, Northumberland County Cricket Ground,
Osborne Avenue, Jesmond, Newcastle upon Tyne NE2 1JS

*Matches 9: Lost – Cambridgeshire, Norfolk, Suffolk. Won on first innings – Bedfordshire. Lost c
first innings – Cumberland, Durham, Hertfordshire, Lincolnshire, Staffordshire.*

Batting Averages

	M	I	NO	R	HI	100s	50s	Avg
J. A. Benn	9	18	1	760	129	4	3	44.7
G. R. Morris	8	16	2	486	118*	1	3	34.7
*M. E. Younger	4	6	0	186	75	0	2	31.0
P. N. S. Dutton	8	16	2	405	111	1	2	28.9
P. G. Cormack	5	10	1	214	110	1	0	23.7
S. C. Dunsford	7	14	2	254	91	0	1	21.1
†N. M. S. Tiffin	6	11	2	170	40	0	0	18.8
T. A. S. Brown	5	9	0	156	48	0	0	17.3
N. B. Campbell	6	9	5	60	27*	0	0	15.0
J. R. Purvis	9	13	4	124	38*	0	0	13.7
R. Perry	5	9	0	108	36	0	0	12.0
P. G. Clark	5	10	1	82	22*	0	0	9.1
P. C. Graham	8	11	4	29	9	0	0	4.1

Played in three matches: †N. H. G. Bates 6*; M. Shepherd 0, 11*; †H. M. Sidney-Wilm<
10, 39, 20, 12*, 37. Played in one match: M. D. Abbott 22; C. S. Gott 4; M. J. Green 0, (
P. Nicholson 3*, 4; S. J. O'Shaughnessy 0, 0.

Bowling Averages

	O	M	R	W	BB	5W/i	Avg
J. R. Purvis	169.4	22	685	20	5-54	1	34.2
P. C. Graham	233.4	51	779	17	3-85	0	45.8
N. B. Campbell	148	22	559	11	2-48	0	50.8

Also bowled: M. D. Abbott 25–4–110–0; J. A. Benn 10–0–74–0; T. A. S. Brown 7–0–37–2
P. G. Cormack 11–1–52–1; S. C. Dunsford 1–0–8–0; P. N. S. Dutton 92–9–454–5; C. S. Go
13.5–3–53–0; G. R. Morris 2–0–17–0; R. Perry 45.1–7–192–8; M. Shepherd 40–1–277–(
H. M. Sidney-Wilmot 5.5–0–50–0; M. E. Younger 64–11–261–3.

OXFORDSHIRE

Secretary – J. E. O. SMITH, 2 The Green, Horton-cum-Studley OX9 1AE

*Matches 9: Won – Wales, Wiltshire. Lost – Buckinghamshire. Won on first innings – Cheshir
Cornwall, Devon, Dorset. Lost on first innings – Berkshire, Shropshire.*

Batting Averages

	M	I	NO	R	HI	100s	50s	Avge
S. N. V. Waterton	9	17	3	883	123*	1	9	63.07
A. Lester	8	16	5	471	98*	0	4	42.81
C. Woods	4	8	0	269	83	0	1	33.62
A. J. Wise	3	6	2	129	58*	0	1	32.25
C. Ford	5	10	0	280	96	0	2	28.00
P. J. Garner	9	17	0	474	69	0	3	27.88
H. C. Hancock	7	13	6	149	51*	0	1	21.28
S. Hartley	9	16	4	235	93*	0	1	19.58
P. Savin	9	11	5	77	16*	0	0	12.83
A. Evans	9	7	1	41	18	0	0	6.83

Played in nine matches: K. A. Arnold 1, 2*, 4, 5*; I. J. Curtis 0*, 0*. Played in three matches: D. A. Hale 5*, 13*; P. M. Jobson 0, 16*, 1, 9. Played in two matches: M. D. Nurton 0, 36, 27. Played in one match: S. V. Laudat did not bat.

Bowling Averages

	O	M	R	W	BB	5W/i	Avge
A. Evans	258.5	71	713	31	5-85	1	23.00
A. Arnold	267.1	57	767	33	5-40	2	23.24
J. Curtis	197.1	48	641	23	5-33	2	27.86
P. Savin	151	30	479	10	4-42	0	47.90

Also bowled: P. J. Garner 8-3-19-0; D. A. Hale 40-7-204-2; J. S. Hartley 61.5-8-243-4; S. V. Laudat 24-5-88-1.

SHROPSHIRE

Secretary – N. H. BIRCH, 8 Port Hill Close, Copthorne, Shrewsbury SY3 8RR

Matches 9: Won – Cornwall, Dorset. Won on first innings – Buckinghamshire, Cheshire, Oxfordshire, Wales. Lost on first innings – Berkshire, Devon, Wiltshire.

Batting Averages

	M	I	NO	R	HI	100s	50s	Avge
Abrahams	7	13	4	765	113*	4	3	85.00
R. Davies	9	15	7	628	114*	2	2	78.50
J. Foster	9	14	2	533	123*	1	2	44.41
Parton	9	16	4	506	119	1	2	42.16
J. R. Weaver ...	7	12	3	256	66	0	2	28.44
B. R. Jones	8	13	1	335	84*	0	3	27.91
B. Wormald	7	6	2	68	21	0	0	17.00
A. B. Byram	8	7	2	76	26	0	0	15.20

Played in nine matches: G. Edmunds 2*, 2. Played in eight matches: A. S. Barnard 3*, 4, 7*. Played in five matches: B. K. Shantry 25, 6, 14*, 9, 0. Played in four matches: J. T. Aspinall 0*. Played in three matches: J. S. Johnson 3, 30, 12, 37, 31. Played in two matches: D. J. Ashley 9*; A. N. Johnson 41, 5, 27*; D. B. K. Page did not bat.

Bowling Averages

	O	M	R	W	BB	5W/i	Avge
G. Edmunds	270.4	68	807	36	8-60	2	22.41
Abrahams	168.5	35	610	23	5-103	1	26.52
B. K. Shantry	110	20	365	13	4-59	0	28.07
B. Wormald	115.5	26	368	10	3-32	0	36.80
A. S. Barnard	176	41	557	11	4-83	0	50.63

Also bowled: J. T. Aspinall 43-4-169-3; A. B. Byram 114-24-422-9; J. B. R. Jones 5-1-104-3; D. B. K. Page 26-3-103-3.

STAFFORDSHIRE

Secretary – W. S. BOURNE, 10 The Pavement, Brewood ST19 9BZ

Matches 8 : Won – Cumberland, Hertfordshire, Suffolk. Lost – Lincolnshire. Won on first innings Norfolk, Northumberland. Lost on first innings – Cambridgeshire, Durham. Abandoned (N result) – Bedfordshire.

Batting Averages

	M	I	NO	R	HI	100s	50s	Avg
D. Cartledge	7	13	2	626	141*	2	4	56.9
S. J. Dean	8	14	2	587	101*	2	2	48.9
D. A. Banks	4	7	3	181	91	0	1	45.2
*N. J. Archer	8	8	3	224	58*	0	2	44.8
J. P. Addison	8	13	2	398	104*	1	0	36.1
P. R. Oliver	8	13	3	358	123*	1	0	35.8
A. J. Dutton	6	6	3	105	28*	0	0	35.0

Played in eight matches: J. P. Taylor 35, 1*, 23*, 0. Played in six matches: †M. Humphries 17, 0*, 14*, 0. Played in five matches: D. W. Headley 1. Played in four matches D. C. Blank 1*; G. D. Williams 14*, 18. Played in two matches: A. D. Hobson 12, 19, 0 †A. N. Mackelworth 15; A. Butler and R. J. Dyer did not bat. Played in one match G. Archer 7; G. Carr 5; N. M. Podmore 1*; J. A. Waterhouse 6.

Bowling Averages

	O	M	R	W	BB	5W/i	Avg
J. P. Taylor	280.3	66	811	32	6-46	1	25.3
D. C. Blank	104.3	22	326	12	3-31	0	27.1
D. W. Headley	135.4	17	465	17	4-38	0	27.3

Also bowled: J. P. Addison 8–0–48–0; G. Archer 2–0–5–0; N. J. Archer 8–2–15–0 A. Butler 7–0–25–0; G. Carr 18–3–73–3; D. Cartledge 62.2–11–228–5; S. J. Dean 1–0–1–0 A. J. Dutton 80–19–198–8; R. J. Dyer 29–11–65–2; N. M. Podmore 25–2–121–1; G. D Williams 64–12–161–5.

SUFFOLK

Secretary – P. HOLLAND, 22 Ashmere Grove, Ipswich IP4 2RE

Matches 9 : Won – Cambridgeshire, Northumberland. Lost – Hertfordshire, Lincolnshire, Stafford shire. Won on first innings – Norfolk. Lost on first innings – Bedfordshire, Cumberland, Durham

Batting Averages

	M	I	NO	R	HI	100s	50s	Avg
S. M. Clements	8	14	2	483	137	1	3	40.2
M. S. A. McEvoy ...	9	17	3	497	113*	1	3	35.5
J. W. Edrich	5	8	2	191	66*	0	2	31.8
A. J. Squire	4	8	0	245	62	0	3	30.6
P. J. Caley	9	15	1	398	101	1	1	28.4
H. J. W. Wright	5	7	2	139	48	0	0	27.8
M. J. Peck	9	15	2	317	80	0	2	24.3
S. J. Halliday	5	10	2	168	39	0	0	21.0
A. K. Golding	8	12	2	186	79	0	1	18.6
*M. D. Bailey	7	8	1	101	24	0	0	14.4
I. D. Graham	6	8	0	107	26	0	0	13.3
†A. D. Brown	9	13	3	112	24	0	0	11.2
R. C. Green	6	6	3	7	5	0	0	2.3

Played in three matches: R. M. Edgeley 1*, 4*. Played in two matches: C. Gladwin 5 171*, 13, 17; P. J. Hayes 1, 20; R. A. Pybus 2*.

Bowling Averages

	O	M	R	W	BB	5W/i	Avge
H. J. W. Wright	111	16	371	13	5-27	1	28.53
A. K. Golding	260.4	45	966	28	6-44	1	34.50
M. D. Bailey	129	25	443	12	4-31	0	36.91
. D. Graham	108.5	20	392	10	3-37	0	39.20

Also bowled: P. J. Caley 43.4–8–137–3; R. M. Edgeley 80–19–256–4; J. W. Edrich
2–1–4–0; C. Gladwin 7–1–15–0; R. C. Green 162–34–551–9; P. J. Hayes 45.5–8–125–3; R. A.
Pybus 47–3–179–8.

WALES MINOR COUNTIES

Secretary – BILL EDWARDS, 59a King Edward Road,
Swansea SA1 4LN

*Matches 9: Won – Wiltshire. Lost – Dorset, Oxfordshire. Won on first innings – Berkshire. Lost on
first innings – Buckinghamshire, Cheshire, Cornwall, Devon, Shropshire.*

Batting Averages

	M	I	NO	R	HI	100s	50s	Avge
A. C. Puddle	9	18	5	512	100*	1	1	39.38
A. W. Harris	4	7	2	181	99	0	1	36.20
C. C. Hughes	7	14	1	454	129*	1	4	34.92
N. G. Roberts	6	12	1	381	95*	0	2	34.63
S. J. Lloyd	4	6	2	121	72*	0	1	30.25
D. W. Evans	5	10	0	269	86	0	2	26.90
S. A. Williams	6	12	0	254	55	0	2	21.16
. D. Hughes	4	8	1	145	50	0	1	20.71
M. A. G. Jones ...	4	7	0	83	30	0	0	11.85
A. C. Smith	6	8	1	76	47	0	0	10.85
C. Williams	8	6	2	13	11	0	0	3.25

Played in five matches: H. G. Rogers 3, 4*, 2. Played in four matches: †M. H. Davies 13, 2,
; †P. Lloyd 7*, 18, 0*, 1; A. Williams 6, 13*, 8*. Played in three matches: G. Edwards 23,
1*, 3, 21. Played in two matches: D. A. Francis 18, 60, 4, 95; M. Kear 48, 2, 4, 3*; R. Morris
, 36, 56, 34; P. D. North 15, 11, 61*, 4; J. Roach 5, 7*; S. G. Watkins 4, 91, 36, 30. Played
n one match: A. R. Davies 1; †A. Shaw 10*, 38; C. Stephens 1*; D. R. Williams 6, 5*.

Bowling Averages

	O	M	R	W	BB	5W/i	Avge
N. G. Roberts	100.5	17	337	15	4-64	0	22.46
A. C. Smith	187.2	46	584	23	5-54	1	25.39
S. J. Lloyd	142.3	45	441	15	4-62	0	29.40
M. G. Rogers	123	30	435	13	3-43	0	33.46
C. Williams	155.1	20	555	11	4-47	0	50.45

Also bowled: A. R. Davies 12–1–49–1; G. Edwards 62–13–210–4; P. D. North
1–16–140–2; J. Roach 75–13–235–4; C. Stephens 18–2–61–1; S. G. Watkins 36.2–6–147–2;
A. Williams 85–19–269–7; D. R. Williams 19.4–1–83–4.

WILTSHIRE

Secretary – C. R. SHEPPARD, 45 Ipswich Street, Swindon SN2 1DB

Matches 9: Won – Dorset. Lost – Berkshire, Oxfordshire, Wales. Won on first innings – Buckinghamshire, Cornwall, Shropshire. Lost on first innings – Devon. No result – Cheshire.

Batting Averages

	M	I	NO	R	HI	100s	50s	Avge
D. R. Turner	9	17	3	887	125*	3	5	63.3
D. R. Parry	3	6	2	244	56*	0	3	61.00
K. N. Foyle	6	11	4	373	87*	0	3	53.28
P. A. C. Bail	6	11	0	437	119	1	4	39.7
C. R. Trembath	4	7	1	204	91	0	1	34.00
D. P. Simpkins	9	14	3	299	100*	1	0	27.1\
S. Williams	9	17	1	428	96	0	2	26.7'
*B. H. White	8	15	0	356	66	0	2	23.7
A. Mildenhall	4	6	3	59	33*	0	0	19.6\
†S. M. Perrin	7	7	1	59	25*	0	0	9.8.
S. J. Malone	8	6	1	41	20	0	0	8.2\

Played in seven matches: M. Holland 3*, 1, 2. Played in five matches: I. G. Osborne 1*, 3*, 0. Played in four matches: D. R. Pike 41, 21, 25*, 33, 32. Played in three matches: N. Prigen 1*, 7*, 18, 8*. Played in two matches: R. R. Savage 4, 16, 21*; †N. Shardlow 1, 7, 0. Played i one match: M. J. Beel 1; J. J. Newman 49, 27; G. Sheppard 0*.

Bowling Averages

	O	M	R	W	BB	5W/i	Avge
C. R. Trembath	129	23	412	17	4-51	0	24.2
M. Holland	145.2	20	632	21	4-106	0	30.00
D. P. Simpkins	189	33	667	17	5-31	1	39.2
S. J. Malone	159.5	12	640	14	4-55	0	45.7

Also bowled: P. A. C. Bail 5-2-10-0; M. J. Beel 7-3-34-1; K. N. Foyle 2-1-5-0; A Mildenhall 96-12-361-9; I. G. Osborne 79-13-260-7; D. R. Pike 51-14-152-6; N. Prigen 37-4-155-5; G. Sheppard 22-2-77-2; B. H. White 2-1-9-0.

TOP TEN MINOR COUNTIES CHAMPIONSHIP AVERAGES, 1990

BATTING

(Qualification: 8 innings)

	M	I	NO	R	HI	100s	Avge
J. Abrahams (*Shropshire*)	7	13	4	765	113*	4	85.00
M. R. Davies (*Shropshire*)	9	15	7	628	114*	2	78.5
A. Needham (*Hertfordshire*)	8	13	2	750	130*	3	68.1
P. Burn (*Durham*)	7	13	4	582	105	2	64.6
M. G. Lickley (*Berkshire*)	9	16	3	838	122*	3	64.4\
A. S. Patel (*Durham*)	8	12	4	512	103*	1	64.00
D. R. Turner (*Wiltshire*)	9	17	3	887	125*	3	63.3
S. N. V. Waterton (*Oxfordshire*)	9	17	3	883	123*	1	63.00
G. W. Ecclestone (*Cambridgeshire*) ...	5	10	2	487	111	1	60.8
G. K. Brown (*Durham*)	6	11	4	417	110*	2	59.5

BOWLING

(Qualification: 20 wickets)

	O	M	R	W	BB	Avge
A. S. Patel (*Durham*)	119.5	35	318	21	5-80	15.14
D. Surridge (*Hertfordshire*)	224.2	69	488	29	5-24	16.82
. Turner (*Cambridgeshire*)	286.5	79	727	40	7-86	18.17
A. C. Jelfs (*Lincolnshire*)	158.5	36	488	25	5-61	19.52
P. J. Kippax (*Durham*)	220.4	75	531	26	5-23	20.42
N. R. Taylor (*Dorset*)	165	39	497	24	5-38	20.70
A. D. Greasley (*Cheshire*)	138.1	37	471	22	5-96	21.40
L. Pont (*Lincolnshire*)	150.5	26	569	26	6-34	21.88
G. Edmunds (*Shropshire*)	270.4	68	807	36	8-60	22.41
H. Shackleton (*Dorset*)	290.3	79	759	33	6-67	23.00
R. A. Evans (*Oxfordshire*)	258.5	71	713	31	5-85	23.00

THE MINOR COUNTIES CHAMPIONS

1895	Norfolk	1925	Buckinghamshire	1961	Somerset II
	Durham	1926	Durham	1962	Warwickshire II
	Worcestershire	1927	Staffordshire	1963	Cambridgeshire
1896	Worcestershire	1928	Berkshire	1964	Lancashire II
1897	Worcestershire	1929	Oxfordshire	1965	Somerset II
1898	Worcestershire	1930	Durham	1966	Lincolnshire
1899	Northamptonshire	1931	Leicestershire II	1967	Cheshire
	Buckinghamshire	1932	Buckinghamshire	1968	Yorkshire II
	Glamorgan	1933	Undecided	1969	Buckinghamshire
1900	Durham	1934	Lancashire II	1970	Bedfordshire
	Northamptonshire	1935	Middlesex II	1971	Yorkshire II
1901	Durham	1936	Hertfordshire	1972	Bedfordshire
1902	Wiltshire	1937	Lancashire II	1973	Shropshire
1903	Northamptonshire	1938	Buckinghamshire	1974	Oxfordshire
1904	Northamptonshire	1939	Surrey II	1975	Hertfordshire
1905	Norfolk	1946	Suffolk	1976	Durham
1906	Staffordshire	1947	Yorkshire	1977	Suffolk
1907	Lancashire II	1948	Lancashire II	1978	Devon
1908	Staffordshire	1949	Lancashire II	1979	Suffolk
1909	Wiltshire	1950	Surrey II	1980	Durham
1910	Norfolk	1951	Kent II	1981	Durham
1911	Staffordshire	1952	Buckinghamshire	1982	Oxfordshire
1912	In abeyance	1953	Berkshire	1983	Hertfordshire
1913	Norfolk	1954	Surrey II	1984	Durham
1914	Staffordshire	1955	Surrey II	1985	Cheshire
1920	Staffordshire	1956	Kent II	1986	Cumberland
1921	Staffordshire	1957	Yorkshire II	1987	Buckinghamshire
1922	Buckinghamshire	1958	Yorkshire II	1988	Cheshire
1923	Buckinghamshire	1959	Warwickshire II	1989	Oxfordshire
1924	Berkshire	1960	Lancashire II	1990	Hertfordshire

RAPID CRICKETLINE SECOND ELEVEN CHAMPIONSHIP, 1990

Sussex were comfortable winners of the Second Eleven Championship, finishing with a 26 point lead over Glamorgan, the runners-up, to take the title for the second time, having won it previously in 1978. They did not feature in the knockout rounds of the 55-overs Bain Clarkson Trophy, though, that competition being won by Lancashire, who beat Somerset by eight wickets in the final.

There was consolation for Somerset in the nomination of their leading batsman, Ricky Bartlett, as the Rapid Cricketline Player of the Year. His 1,393 runs were the second highest aggregate of a season in which a record ten batsmen passed 1,000 runs in the championship nine had done so in 1989, when twelve more matches were played. Sussex's New Zealander Graham Burnett, recorded the highest aggregate (1,432) since S. Jayasinghe's 1,485 for Leicestershire in 1961, achieved in four more innings. In a batsman's season in which only six bowlers took 50 wickets, the Middlesex slow left-armer, Alex Barnett, captured 71, sixteen more than anyone else.

Widespread approval was expressed by players and officials alike for the new format of the championship, whereby all the counties played each other once. It was agreed that this produced a more satisfactory and realistic competition.

As expected, 1990 proved to be a difficult year for **Derbyshire**, who returned to the lower reaches of the table. Often fielding non-contract players, lacking the experience of many opponents, they managed only two wins. Of their eight defeats, three came in the final overs. There were some useful bowling performances from the Young England seamer, Dominic Cork, and from Ewan McCray, a spin bowler whose 50 wickets included six for 122 at Cardiff. McCray also scored 748 runs, with a highest score of 104 at Southampton. He shared the batting honours with Steve Goldsmith, who hit 109 and 163 against Kent at Chesterfield, and Zahid Sadiq, whose aggregate of 892 included 103 at Watford, 106 at Southampton and 112 at Taunton. Of the numerous local players who appeared, Neil Sparham and Paul Shaw played some fine innings.

SECOND ELEVEN CHAMPIONSHIP, 1990

						Bonus points		
Win = 16 points	P	W	L	D	T	Batting	Bowling	Points
1 – Sussex (14)	16	9	1	6	0	45	39	228
2 – Glamorgan (10)	16	7	3	6	0	34	56	202
3 – Surrey (16)	16	5	1	9	1	40	54	182
4 – Nottinghamshire (7) . .	16	6	4	6	0	32	53	181
5 – Kent (3)	16	5	2	9	0	43	46	169
6 – Middlesex (1)	16	4	3	9	0	45	43	152
7 – Warwickshire (2)	16	4	3	9	0	39	46	149
8 – Lancashire (15)	16	3	5	8	0	43	48	139
9 – Essex (12)	16	3	3	10	0	39	49	136
10 – Worcestershire (17) . .	16	2	3	10	1	43	51	134
11 – Hampshire (6)	16	2	5	9	0	45	44	129
12 – Northamptonshire (5) .	16	3	4	9	0	40	35	123
13 – Derbyshire (4)	16	2	8	6	0	33	44	109
14 – Gloucestershire (11) . .	16	2	5	9	0	33	36	101
15 – Somerset (13)	16	1	2	13	0	41	40	97
16 – Leicestershire (8)	16	0	1	15	0	43	47	90
17 – Yorkshire (9)	16	1	6	9	0	33	40	89

1989 positions in brackets.
The totals for Surrey and Worcestershire each include 8 points for a tied match.
The total for Hampshire includes 8 points for levelling the scores in a drawn game.

Essex, once Mark Ilott had been promoted to the first team, generally struggled to bowl sides out twice. His 36 wickets contained match figures of fifteen for 147 from 44.4 overs at Lytham. Still, the slow left-arm bowling of Guy Lovell, an early-season recruit from Cumberland, provided 52 wickets, including returns of eight for 48 against Nottinghamshire and six for 58 against Yorkshire, both at Chelmsford. The batting was again reliable, with Nick Knight and Jon Lewis the leading run-scorers, despite their unavailability early in the season owing to university and college commitments. Lewis followed his 135 against Surrey at Chelmsford in July with 116 not out against them on his first-class début at The Oval at the end of the season. Three centuries each were scored by Keith Butler and the left-handed Knight, the latter's 108 not out at Derby, 141 at Weston-super-Mare and 108 against Yorkshire at Chelmsford coming in successive matches. Adam Seymour overcame the interruption of a broken hand, sustained on his County Championship début, to score 648 runs, and Alastair Fraser also batted well, although his bowling form was inconsistent.

At the end of their best season since they won the championship ten years earlier, runners-up **Glamorgan** could reflect on the crucial defeat in August by the eventual champions, Sussex. While the enterprising captaincy of John Steele was essential to their success, they owed as much to their bowlers, who earned them 56 bonus points – more than any other county. Hamesh Anthony, Steve Bastien, Simon Dennis and Steve Barwick all made significant contributions, particularly in helping win the last three games. In the first and second of these, Dennis returned seven for 46 against Derbyshire at Cardiff and six for 65 at Southampton; in Tune, Bastien, the team's player of the year, took seven for 67 against Lancashire at Cardiff. John Derrick hit two unbeaten hundreds to top the averages, and seven other players contributed three-figure innings, the highest of which was Robert Croft's 149 against Essex at Swansea. Martin Roberts had another good season, effecting 36 dismissals to set beside his 598 runs, including 120 not out at Guildford.

Gloucestershire were another county to find the majority of their opponents were considerably more experienced. This handicap led to three defeats by an innings in August – by Hampshire, Surrey and Warwickshire – although after the first two they in turn inflicted an innings defeat on Derbyshire. Of the 37 players used, Paul Romaines was by far the most successful of the batsmen, his 778 runs in nine matches featuring two centuries, while at the other end of the experience scale promise was shown by sixteen-year-old Darren Blenkiron and Bob Dawson, with maiden centuries respectively at Canterbury and against Middlesex at Bristol. David Graham also hit his maiden hundred at Bristol, against Leicestershire. It was the bowling that gave most cause for concern, with opponents averaging more than 40 runs per wicket and scoring sixteen hundreds. However, seventeen-year-old Jason de la Pena showed potential as an opening bowler, and Ed Milburn took a hat-trick against Lancashire at Bristol, only a dropped catch preventing four wickets in four balls. "Reggie" Williams caught the eye behind the stumps and made the most of his opportunities when deputising with the gloves for Jack Russell. Part way through the season, Andy Stovold took over as captain/coach, and later it was announced that this successful arrangement would continue in 1991.

At **Hampshire**, individual batting performances dominated an otherwise indifferent season, in which a team weakened through injuries managed only two wins and dropped to eleventh place. Tony Middleton was exceptional. He made his maiden first-class hundred, against Kent, on April 27 and then, in his first five innings for the Second Eleven, scored 104 and 144 against Somerset at Southampton, 121 at Bingley, and 100 and 124 against Leicestershire at Bournemouth before returning to the first team on May 19 and scoring 104 not out against Essex five days later. Rupert Cox was hardly less impressive, his aggregate of 1,162 runs also containing five hundreds – 135 against Lancashire at Bournemouth, 134 not out against Derbyshire at Southampton, 128 at Maidstone, 127 at Kidderminster and 102 at Gloucester. Sean Morris, an opening batsman and captain of Durham University, headed the averages with 812 runs at 81.20, including four hundreds: 115 not out against Warwickshire at Southampton, 104 retired hurt at Gloucester, 103 not out at Wellingborough School and 102 against Glamorgan at Southampton. It was not surprising, given such batting strength, that Hampshire gained the most batting bonus points, along with Middlesex and Sussex. Linden Joseph, from Guyana, occasionally bowled with genuine pace and was the leading wicket-taker, just ahead of off-spinner Shaun Udal, whose form improved considerably during the second half of the season.

Kent, the only side to beat the eventual champions, Sussex, doing so by an innings at Eastbourne, finished fifth after an encouraging campaign which saw the emergence of several promising youngsters. Matthew Brimson, David Fulton, Nick Preston and Graham Kersey, all products of the county's youth coaching system, came through with distinction, with Kersey, in particular, developing from a schoolboy wicket-keeper into a capable understudy to Steve Marsh. The Ashford all-rounder, Nigel Llong, progressed as a batsman, with innings of 101 at Marske and 104 not out at Clevedon to accompany a string of fifties. Vince Wells benefited from an extended run in the first team, while Mark Ealham, having had an unsettled start to the season as he moved in and out of the senior side, made a major contribution to the Second Eleven in the last month and finished with 802 runs, including 161 not out against Gloucestershire at Canterbury. Two others to earn first-team calls were the left-arm bowlers, Tim Wren and Min Patel; Wren, at medium-pace, took the most wickets including seven for 34 against Glamorgan at Sittingbourne, and spinner Patel continued his advance on his return from university.

Lancashire, emulating their seniors, challenged the leaders in the championship for two thirds of the season, only to lose four of their last five games and finish eighth, and won the limited-overs Bain Clarkson Trophy. Nick Speak, who took over the captaincy after John Stanworth severed tendons in his hand, again scored the most runs, his 1,274 including 171 against Warwickshire and 119 against Worcestershire, both at Manchester, and 105 at Northampton. Close behind him came Stephen Titchard, whose aggregate of 1,137 contained 139 against Middlesex at Crosby, followed by 117 and 150 without being dismissed at The Oval. John Crawley displayed his rich talent in compiling 870 runs, including 101 at Leicester 100 not out at Northampton and 117 at Shireoaks. Of the bowlers only Ian Folley, with 55 wickets, made much impression, although Peter Martin took seven for 31 at Bristol, Ian Austin six for 54 at Leicester and Wasim Akram five in each innings, for 76, against Derbyshire at Liverpool. The Australian Under-19 captain, Jason Gallian, outstanding for Werneth in the Central Lancashire League, also made a significant all-round contribution.

Beaten by Sussex in their first match, **Leicestershire** drew the rest and were the only side without a win. That they managed to edge into sixteenth ahead of Yorkshire at the bottom of the table was due to their 90 bonus points, the fourth-highest total in the championship. There were maiden centuries for Ben Smith, who headed the batting averages, Andrew Roseberry who scored the most runs, and the Loughborough schoolboy, Chris Hawkes. Smith began the season with 101 not out against Sussex at Leicester, and two weeks later hit 125 not out at Bournemouth; Roseberry made his unbeaten 113 at The Oval, and 110 against Worcestershire at Leicester; and Hawkes hit 122 against Middlesex at Market Harborough. Les Taylor took 36 economical wickets, including seven for 34 at Bournemouth and six for 45 at Canterbury in consecutive matches, and although Lloyd Tennant's tally was three higher, he was 11 runs a wicket more expensive. Paul Nixon had fifteen dismissals in his five matches, and Justin Benson held ten catches in three appearances.

Middlesex, champions and favourites when the season began, were beaten for the first time in four years and dropped to sixth place. This was perhaps inevitable following the promotion of Keith Brown and Mike Roseberry, coupled with first-team demands on the seam bowling resources. Nevertheless they remained a powerful batting side. The left-handed Jason Pooley again passed 1,000 runs, scoring 111 and 201 not out against Somerset at Enfield to follow innings of 158 against Derbyshire at Watford and 100 against Warwickshire at Uxbridge. Matthew Keech found his second season more difficult, but Toby Radford looked sound and Aftab Habib compiled his maiden hundred – 104 at Bristol – in the last match, a promising advance for a player who was too often out for a spectacular thirty. Ian Hutchinson, frequently affected by injuries, had a disappointing season by his standards but scored most runs after Pooley and John Carr, whose three hundreds included 120 and 116 against Derbyshire at Watford. Slow bowling was the side's other strength. Before joining the Young England side, Alex Barnett captured 71 wickets, taking five in an innings five times, including a match return of eleven for 103 against Somerset. Off-spinner Paul Weekes made an ideal partner, and with 641 runs to set alongside his 51 wickets he demonstrated his potential to become a valuable all-rounder. Chas Taylor, an Oxfordshire farmer, was a valuable find whose left-arm fast-medium bowling brought him 21 wickets in seven games, while in Paul Farbrace, who joined the county from Kent, Middlesex had a first-rate wicket-keeper batsman in the tradition of Paul Downton.

Northamptonshire, hampered by injuries throughout the playing staff, called on 41 players in their sixteen championship games. Although they slipped to twelfth, there was consolation in the performances of some young players, notably Richard Montgomerie, Malachy Loye and Russell Warren, each in his first year on the staff. Montgomerie passed 1,000 runs, with scores of 123 against Middlesex at Bedford School and 104 at Canterbury; Loye hit 165 at Southend; and Warren, available for only ten matches owing to school commitments, scored 121 at York, 157 at Shireoaks and 200 not out at Canterbury. Wayne Noon, the Young England captain, kept wicket to a high standard and had an unbeaten 160 at Southend among his batting successes. John Hughes, a lively medium-paced all-rounder, looked promising, and leg-spinner Andy Roberts fully deserved his selection for Young England.

Nottinghamshire began well, playing some fine competitive cricket, but as injuries and first-team calls disrupted the side, they ceased to function as a unit and fell away towards the end. None the less, the progress of some younger players into the senior side was a bonus. Duncan Martindale was the outstanding batsman, his 866 runs at 86.60 including 171 not out at Elland, 140 not out against Warwickshire at Worksop College and 101 not out at Taunton. The fast-scoring Steve Brogan was close behind him with 848 runs, including six fifties and 135 at Heanor. The bowlers, too, did well, with only Glamorgan and Surrey gaining more bowling bonus points. The most wickets were taken by the fast bowlers, Greg Mike and the South African, Dean Laing: Mike's 47 included seven for 41 at Elland and six for 65 against Northamptonshire at Shireoaks, while Laing's best was seven for 64 at Heanor. The younger of the Saxelby brothers, Mark, took four for 1 at Worcester, and several weeks later scored 109 not out at Taunton.

Though involved in a number of close finishes, **Somerset** could manage only one championship win, which left them in fifteenth place. On the other hand, the side went as far as the final in the limited-overs competition. Ricky Bartlett had an outstanding season, scoring 1,393 runs in the three-day games and being named Rapid Cricketline Player of the Year. He hit six hundreds: 134 and 113 not out at Southampton, 153 against Surrey at Yeovil, 109 at Manchester, plus 175 against Derbyshire and 105 against Northamptonshire, both at Taunton. Nick Pringle also passed 1,000 runs, helped by four hundreds, two of them – 130 not out and 111 not out – against Gloucestershire. In that same game, at Bristol, sixteen-year-old Andrew Cottam, a promising slow left-arm bowler, took a hat-trick. The Young England opening bowler, Jeremy Hallett, did well on occasions, but Andrew Caddick, a New Zealander hoping to be qualified for the 1992 season, looked the pick of the seam bowlers. He took six for 42 at Enfield, while another medium-pacer, Daryn Kutner, produced a return of five for 6 at Manchester in Somerset's only victory. Gareth Townsend, who was particularly successful at Taunton, fell just 11 runs short of four figures, and Ian Fletcher, like Harvey Trump and Hallett a product of Millfield School, had a sound first full season.

Surrey climbed from sixteenth in 1989 to third and were able to look back on five wins and some memorable matches. The last fixture, at Worcester, was tied when Surrey were dismissed for 319, having declared at 300 for five in the first innings with Steve Cooper 103 not out in only his second match. Jonathan Robinson's unbeaten 214 not out, in a total of 400 for three declared against Gloucestershire at Guildford, was a personal best, and in the two-wicket defeat of Lancashire at The Oval, five hundreds were scored, three for Surrey. Paul Atkins and Rehan Alikhan made 149 and 103 not out respectively before Surrey declared at 262 for one, and Graham Thorpe made 126 not out in the second innings. Earlier in the season Alikhan had made 151 not out against Leicestershire at The Oval, and Atkins 116 not out at Canterbury. Although spending almost half the season with the first team, Neil Kendrick took 36 wickets, including eleven for 107 in the defeat of Hampshire at The Oval, and Tony Murphy took 28 wickets in his six games. Tony Gray took six for 20 in the rain-affected match at Ilkeston, and all the bowlers benefited from the wicket-keeping of Neil Sargeant, who effected 40 dismissals.

Captained by Keith Greenfield, **Sussex** leapt from fourteenth place to win the title for the first time since 1978. This was particularly encouraging in view of their first team having languished at the foot of the County Championship table for most of the season. Losing only to Kent, they won their first four and last four matches, plus one in July. The key to their success was a settled and varied attack, in which the leg-spin of Andy Clarke complemented the off-breaks of Bradleigh Donelan. Donelan returned match figures of fifteen for 142 as Middlesex were beaten at Hove, and Andy Babington, who, with Clarke, was released at the end of the season, had seven for 52 in the ten-wicket win over challengers Glamorgan at Swansea. The batting was dominated by a New Zealander from Wellington, Graham Burnett, whose aggregate of 1,432 was the highest in the championship in 1990. He struck four hundreds, including 212 against Derbyshire at Hove and 201 at Northampton. Also among the runs was Robin Hanley, whose three hundreds at Hove – 161 against Essex, 139 not out against Derbyshire and 103 against Middlesex – earned him his first-team début in his first season.

A mid-table position accurately reflected the performance of **Warwickshire**, the runners-up in 1989. A young, less experienced side tended to be inconsistent, but there were four hundreds from Jason Ratcliffe – 107 at Worksop, 101 not out at Hinckley, 151 at Southampton and 118 against Derbyshire at Walmley – and two each from Dominic Ostler, Simon Green and the Zimbabwean, Trevor Penney. The leading wicket-takers, with 36 apiece, were off-spinner Adrian Pierson and Gareth Smith, a left-arm seam bowler from Northamptonshire whose match figures of eleven for 97 were instrumental in the innings defeat of Derbyshire. Roger Twose had a good all-round season, highlights of which were his 102 at Swansea and a return of six for 103 against Yorkshire at Moseley. There was recognition for Keith Piper's wicket-keeping with his promotion to the first team, and Warwickshire were fortunate in having as his replacement Piran Holloway, the Young England representative.

Worcestershire moved up from the bottom of the table to tenth place; although they won just twice, with Surrey they accumulated more bonus points (94) than any other side. Both Paul Bent and Gavin Haynes passed 1,000 runs, the first time two Worcestershire players had done so in a championship season, and the first time anyone had reached four figures for the county since J. Robson in 1979. Bent was remarkably consistent, with 174 against Hampshire at Kidderminster, 113 at Manchester, and ten fifties. Martin Weston and Haynes also hit two hundreds each, and there were three from David Leatherdale – 119 not out against Hampshire at Kidderminster, 118 at Colchester and 101 not out at Derby. Stuart Lampitt made a fine all-round contribution to the defeat of Hampshire, hitting an unbeaten century and taking six for 57. In his first season, Steve Herzberg, an English-born all-rounder who grew up in Australia, scored 743 runs as a mid-order batsman, and his 50 wickets, from 505 overs of off-spin, were the most for Worcestershire since J. A. Standen took the same number in 1966. Neal Radford produced the best innings return of the championship with nine for 98 against Northamptonshire at Halesowen, while another fast-medium bowler, Nick Hitchings, took six for 39 against Gloucestershire at Stourbridge.

It was a disappointing season for **Yorkshire**, joint winners in 1987, who finished last. They could manage only one win – over Northamptonshire at York – and were beaten six times; only Derbyshire lost more. Yet there were encouraging individual performances from several of the 30 players used. Craig White, the Yorkshire-born and Australian-bred all-rounder, was soon enlisted in the first team, having made his presence felt with seven for 55 against Leicestershire at Bradford and innings of 209 and 115 without being dismissed at Worcester. In that match wicket-keeper Colin Chapman also reached three figures, and he later followed White into the senior side. Another double-century came from Kevin Sharp, whose 221 not out against Gloucestershire at Todmorden was the season's highest by any batsman in the championship. Bowling was not Yorkshire's strong suit. The left-arm spinner, Matthew Doidge, took the most wickets (24), but with an average of 39.29, and off-spinners Philip Berry and Jeremy Batty, the only others to take twenty, were hardly less expensive.

*In the averages that follow, * against a score signifies not out, * against a name signifies the captain and † signifies a wicket-keeper.*

DERBYSHIRE SECOND ELEVEN

Matches 16: Won – Kent, Yorkshire. Lost – Glamorgan, Gloucestershire, Hampshire, Lancashire, Middlesex, Northamptonshire, Nottinghamshire, Warwickshire. Drawn – Essex, Leicestershire, Somerset, Surrey, Sussex, Worcestershire.

Batting Averages

	M	I	NO	R	HI	100s	Avge
*†B. J. M. Maher	15	23	18	242	61*	0	48.40
S. C. Goldsmith	8	14	1	558	163	2	42.92
G. T. Headley	2	4	0	165	110	1	41.25
A. M. Brown	4	7	0	288	84	0	41.14
G. A. Smith	3	6	0	218	106	1	36.33
C. A. Tweats	3	5	2	109	40*	0	36.33
*. A. Sadiq	14	27	0	892	112	3	33.03
J. Sparham	5	10	0	328	101	1	32.80
F. Shaw	10	20	0	614	86	0	30.70
J. G. O'Gorman	2	4	0	120	51	0	30.00
Peall	4	8	1	189	74	0	27.00
McCray	16	29	1	748	104	1	26.71
G. Cork	9	15	3	244	46	0	20.33
A. Griffith	11	20	0	340	60	0	17.00
R. May	6	11	0	185	33	0	16.81
J. Adams	10	19	4	239	40	0	15.93
W. Sladdin	10	17	4	207	34	0	15.92
M. A. Aduhene	6	12	3	124	33	0	13.77
C. Williams	2	4	0	52	33	0	13.00
N. Weston	3	5	0	64	36	0	12.80
Ahmed	3	6	0	55	28	0	9.16
E. Wall	2	3	0	26	21	0	8.66
J. Slater	9	14	3	87	29	0	7.90
A. Mestecky	2	3	0	11	9	0	3.66
G. Smith	2	3	1	7	4*	0	3.50
R. Spencer	3	5	0	14	9	0	2.80

Played in two matches: S. J. Base 28, 0. Played in one match: G. F. Archer 1, 4; D. R. Eyre *; D. J. Foster 15, 0; †A. D. Gillgrass 31*, 0; L. J. Henshaw 1*; M. Jean-Jacques 2, 12; N. Kingham 0, 15; A. J. McCulloch 20, 17*; R. P. Marsh 11, 6; S. Mohammad 15, 4; P. F. Ridgeway 11, 0*; P. C. P. Simmonite 13, 23; J. F. Trueman 6, 2.

Note: After the first innings of the match v Northamptonshire at Derby, Cork, Goldsmith and Griffith were replaced by Henshaw, McCray and Weston, owing to injuries to first-team players.

Bowling Averages

	O	M	R	W	BB	Avge
*. A. Griffith	101	26	334	12	5-26	27.83
*. W. Sladdin	259.2	65	770	26	4-42	29.61
*. McCray	481.2	108	1,511	50	6-122	30.22
*. J. Base	41	7	158	5	3-70	31.60
*. J. Adams	224.1	57	703	19	5-44	37.00
*. C. Goldsmith	113	33	305	8	2-43	38.12
*. M. A. Aduhene ...	118.5	17	518	12	5-119	43.16
*. G. Cork	181.5	44	672	15	4-95	44.80
*. Peall	60	10	226	5	2-57	45.20
*. J. Slater	125.2	16	483	8	2-43	60.37

Also bowled: I. Ahmed 20–4–55–1; D. R. Eyre 7–0–35–1; D. J. Foster 18–3–64–1; G. T. Headley 19–2–57–2; L. J. Henshaw 11–0–61–0; M. Jean-Jacques 24–2–119–1; A. J. McCulloch 16–3–55–0; B. J. M. Maher 11–0–96–2; M. R. May 2.5–0–20–0; P. A. Mestecky 0–7–140–0; P. F. Ridgeway 16–6–66–0; C. G. Smith 37–3–128–0; G. A. Smith 8–0–69–0; R. R. Spencer 39–6–150–2; R. C. Williams 35–6–127–2.

ESSEX SECOND ELEVEN

Matches 16: Won – Lancashire, Northamptonshire, Yorkshire. Lost – Kent, Surrey, Sussex. Drawn – Derbyshire, Glamorgan, Gloucestershire, Hampshire, Leicestershire, Middlesex, Nottinghamshire, Somerset, Warwickshire, Worcestershire.

Batting Averages

	M	I	NO	R	HI	100s	Avge
N. V. Knight	12	20	5	790	141	3	52.66
J. J. B. Lewis	12	21	3	906	135	1	50.3
K. A. Butler	11	18	3	723	116*	3	48.20
A. C. Seymour	9	18	1	648	70	0	38.1
*K. W. R. Fletcher	10	11	4	255	76	0	36.4
G. W. Ecclestone	2	4	0	137	62	0	34.2
N. Shahid	5	9	0	288	59	0	32.00
M. C. Ilott	8	11	6	154	58	0	30.80
A. W. Lilley	10	17	0	521	191	1	30.6
A. G. J. Fraser	13	23	5	530	85*	0	29.4
B. R. Hardie	3	4	1	83	51	0	27.66
C. A. Miller	7	13	5	212	47	0	26.50
T. D. Topley	5	6	0	134	57	0	22.3
†D. E. East	16	25	3	485	86	0	22.00
A. T. Van-Lint	9	14	0	288	103	1	20.5
D. J. P. Boden	7	11	2	166	81	0	18.4
K. O. Thomas	9	10	2	133	33	0	16.67
P. M. Such	5	6	2	40	32	0	10.00
W. G. Lovell	13	11	4	45	14*	0	6.4
S. J. W. Andrew	4	5	0	24	19	0	4.80

Played in one match: A. Churchill, 28, 47*; N. Hussain 4; I. A. Kidd 2, 15; D. Muneeb 2, 0; P. J. Prichard 12, 51*; A. C. Richards 28, 3.

Bowling Averages

	O	M	R	W	BB	Avge
S. J. W. Andrew	86.1	6	303	16	7-57	18.9
M. C. Ilott	234.1	59	708	36	8-81	19.6
W. G. Lovell	468.2	121	1,438	52	8-48	27.6
T. D. Topley	109	26	315	10	5-32	31.50
C. A. Miller	131	22	475	15	4-53	31.60
K. O. Thomas	202.1	42	623	18	5-50	34.6
A. T. Van-Lint	168.5	33	610	15	3-46	40.60
N. Shahid	91.3	15	306	6	4-60	51.00
A. G. J. Fraser	177.4	24	710	13	3-86	54.6
P. M. Such	184	56	474	8	2-52	59.2.
D. J. P. Boden	119	23	452	4	1-13	113.00

Also bowled: K. A. Butler 0.3–0–11–1; A. Churchill 8–2–28–2; N. V. Knight 3–0–9–0; A. W. Lilley 2–0–16–1; A. C. Richards 15.3–3–70–2; A. C. Seymour 0.2–0–4–0.

GLAMORGAN SECOND ELEVEN

Matches 16: Won – Derbyshire, Gloucestershire, Hampshire, Middlesex, Nottinghamshire, Somerset, Surrey. Lost – Kent, Lancashire, Sussex. Drawn – Essex, Leicestershire, Northampton-shire, Warwickshire, Worcestershire, Yorkshire.

Batting Averages

	M	I	NO	R	HI	100s	Avge
J. Derrick	11	16	3	621	114*	2	47.7
S. P. James	5	10	2	342	105*	1	42.7
P. A. Cottey	7	12	0	512	111	1	42.6
†M. L. Roberts	14	20	4	598	120*	1	37.3
D. L. Hemp	7	11	2	328	67	0	36.4
J. B. Bishop	3	4	1	103	56	0	34.3
S. J. Dennis	5	7	3	136	84	0	34.00
I. Smith	7	11	0	372	118	1	33.8

	M	I	NO	R	HI	100s	Avge
G. C. Holmes	4	7	0	227	125	1	32.42
M. J. Cann	14	24	3	664	84	0	31.61
H. A. G. Anthony	13	17	2	373	73	0	24.86
R. N. Pook	9	16	3	313	100*	1	24.07
K. A. Somaia	12	16	3	296	62	0	22.76
M. Davies	16	16	6	121	31	0	12.10
*J. F. Steele	11	10	6	42	16*	0	10.50
S. Bastien	10	8	2	33	19	0	5.50

Also batted: S. R. Barwick 0*, 9, 1, 4; M. R. J. Brugnoli 1*; M. Burns 5*, 9*; G. M. Charlesworth 15, 0*; R. D. B. Croft 149, 47; A. Dale 0, 71; G. T. Headley 27; S. Kirnon 8, 0; S. D. Lerigo 8, 10; S. Mohammad 65, 6; R. Nancarrow 1*, 0; †A. D. Shaw 2, 15; G. Winterbourne 12. M. J. Newbold and S. Vestegaad did not bat.

Bowling Averages

	O	M	R	W	BB	Avge
S. J. Dennis	175.2	50	513	31	7-46	16.54
S. R. Barwick	251.4	96	522	31	5-35	16.83
. Smith	76.1	23	191	10	3-16	19.10
S. Kirnon	57	17	149	6	3-36	24.83
S. Bastien	313.2	96	862	34	7-67	25.35
H. A. G. Anthony	365.4	84	1,014	38	6-90	26.68
R. D. B. Croft	111	42	330	11	4-100	30.00
M. Davies	250.1	80	629	20	3-33	31.45
K. A. Somaia	139	41	345	10	3-36	34.50
. Derrick	143	30	583	15	3-49	38.86

Also bowled: M. R. J. Brugnoli 11–0–53–1; M. J. Cann 6–1–38–1; P. A. Cottey 5–3–6–0; A. Dale 2–0–2–0; G. T. Headley 19–2–63–1; G. C. Holmes 9–1–28–0; S. D. Lerigo 4–3–57–0; R. Nancarrow 7–1–24–0; R. N. Pook 39–15–89–2; S. Vestegaad 15–0–70–1; G. Winterbourne 10–3–27–0.

GLOUCESTERSHIRE SECOND ELEVEN

Matches 16: Won – Derbyshire, Worcestershire. Lost – Glamorgan, Hampshire, Nottinghamshire, Surrey, Warwickshire. Drawn – Essex, Kent, Lancashire, Leicestershire, Middlesex, Northamptonshire, Somerset, Sussex, Yorkshire.

Batting Averages

	M	I	NO	R	HI	100s	Avge
P. W. Romaines	9	15	4	778	172	2	70.72
D. A. Graham	4	6	1	261	101*	1	52.20
M. W. Alleyne	5	8	2	283	120*	1	47.16
D. A. Blenkiron	4	7	1	260	136	1	43.33
G. D. Hodgson	4	8	1	286	80	0	40.85
A. W. Stovold	13	18	3	497	88	0	33.13
G. A. Tedstone	7	9	1	241	64	0	30.12
B. G. Evans	3	4	1	82	76*	0	27.33
M. W. Pooley	12	14	3	299	74*	0	27.18
E. T. Milburn	12	17	4	345	85	0	26.53
D. C. K. Smith	9	12	0	296	88	0	24.66
N. M. A. Pritchard	12	22	1	489	73	0	23.28
†I. P. Butcher	8	14	0	292	69	0	20.85
M. C. J. Ball	12	11	2	140	45*	0	15.55
. R. Mann	2	4	0	57	19	0	14.25
R. C. J. Williams	6	6	0	85	47	0	14.16
A. D. A. Chidgey	2	4	0	49	19	0	12.25
S. N. Barnes	7	9	2	62	16*	0	8.85

	M	I	NO	R	HI	100s	Avge
J. M. de la Pena	6	7	3	31	14	0	7.75
K. B. S. Jarvis	5	5	2	19	9	0	6.33
N. J. Pitts	6	7	1	37	16*	0	6.16
A. M. Smith	6	9	3	31	17*	0	5.16
P. A. Owen	2	4	1	15	6	0	5.00

Played in five matches: R. M. Bell 0*, 0, 0. Played in two matches: R. I. Dawson 23, 33, 100*; M. J. Rawlings 17. Played in one match: P. Bainbridge 106; D. R. Brown 0*, 11*; G. S. Calway 4; O. S. Chagar 24*, 5; D. A. Graveney 12*, 11; I. A. Kidd 24; J. W. Lloyds 0, 40; P. C. P. Simmonite 8, 6; B. St A. Browne, B. L. Holmes and D. V. Lawrence did not bat.

Bowling Averages

	O	M	R	W	BB	Avge
K. B. S. Jarvis	107.3	37	236	11	4-20	21.45
A. M. Smith	125	24	364	12	3-29	30.33
J. M. de la Pena	100.1	14	373	11	4-47	33.90
E. T. Milburn	212	37	739	20	4-29	36.95
M. C. J. Ball	271.5	49	937	23	5-57	40.73
N. J. Pitts	112	27	372	9	3-83	41.33
S. N. Barnes	188.3	40	614	13	4-70	47.23
M. W. Pooley	209.5	28	807	14	3-46	57.64
R. M. Bell	97	27	220	3	3-48	73.33
M. W. Alleyne	103	20	317	4	2-35	79.25

Also bowled: P. Bainbridge 6.3–0–23–1; D. R. Brown 11–1–51–2; B. St A. Browne 29–7–73–3; G. S. Calway 18–1–64–0; O. S. Chagar 26–9–64–3; D. A. Graveney 57–16–145–4; G. D. Hodgson 1–0–24–0; B. L. Holmes 43–22–73–2; D. V. Lawrence 37.2–5–118–5; J. W. Lloyds 13.5–2–34–0; J. R. Mann 55–13–193–5; P. A. Owen 40–6–138–0; M. J. Rawlings 16–3–64–4; P. W. Romaines 30.5–4–172–4; O. C. K. Smith 64.1–7–246–2.

HAMPSHIRE SECOND ELEVEN

Matches 16: Won – Derbyshire, Gloucestershire. Lost – Glamorgan, Northamptonshire, Surrey, Warwickshire, Worcestershire. Drawn – Essex, Kent, Lancashire, Leicestershire, Middlesex, Nottinghamshire (levelled scores when batting fourth), Somerset, Sussex, Yorkshire.

Batting Averages

	M	I	NO	R	HI	100s	Avge
R. S. M. Morris	8	14	4	812	115*	4	81.20
T. C. Middleton	8	13	0	837	144	5	64.38
*R. M. F. Cox	15	24	3	1,162	135	5	55.33
T. M. Tremlett	11	10	6	217	59*	0	54.25
†A. N. Aymes	15	21	7	689	105*	2	49.21
J. R. Ayling	7	11	2	381	73	0	42.33
I. J. Turner	12	9	5	157	38*	0	39.25
J. R. Wood	10	15	1	513	100*	1	36.64
C. H. Forward	6	8	1	237	63	0	33.85
S. D. Udal	14	17	3	451	100*	1	32.21
R. J. Scott	10	16	1	464	103	1	30.97
W. J. Holdsworth	3	5	1	109	33*	0	27.2
M. J. Russell	3	6	0	144	48	0	24.00
L. A. Joseph	10	12	4	149	43*	0	18.6
D. P. J. Flint	16	12	4	33	15*	0	4.1
K. J. Shine	5	5	0	18	9	0	3.6

Also batted: R. D. Allen 8, 9; P. J. Bakker 8, 7, 0; L. Bryden 0, 8; A. J. Collins 0, 7; D. B. M. Fox 0*; M. Garaway 1, 5; E. S. H. Giddins 17; M. M. King 0, 8, 7*, 3; I. K. Maynard 12; J. P. Osborne 6; †R. J. Parks 4, 2; R. M. Peterson 0, 11; D. J. Skidmore 9, 82*. K. Bird played in one match but did not bat.

Bowling Averages

	O	M	R	W	BB	Avge
P. J. Bakker	91	22	226	13	5-60	17.38
W. J. Holdsworth	101	16	320	16	5-68	20.00
L. A. Joseph	279	54	837	32	5-21	26.15
K. J. Shine	80.1	28	196	7	5-34	28.00
A. J. Turner	274.3	81	745	24	4-113	31.04
T. M. Tremlett	90.5	24	226	7	1-2	32.28
M. M. King	109.3	18	427	13	3-36	32.84
R. J. Scott	118.1	32	313	9	3-24	34.77
S. D. Udal	369.5	97	1,184	30	4-83	39.46
J. R. Ayling	149	37	407	8	2-32	50.87
D. P. J. Flint	318.5	79	1,018	14	3-103	72.71

Also bowled: K. Bird 15–0–67–1; L. Bryden 15–1–58–1; A. J. Collins 22–7–62–2; D. B. M. Fox 23–4–77–1; E. S. H. Giddins 30–5–125–2; T. C. Middleton 3–0–28–0; R. S. M. Morris 1–0–3–0; R. M. Peterson 44–6–156–4; J. R. Wood 4–0–23–0.

KENT SECOND ELEVEN

Matches 16: Won – Essex, Glamorgan, Nottinghamshire, Sussex, Yorkshire. Lost – Derbyshire, Northamptonshire. Drawn – Gloucestershire, Hampshire, Lancashire, Leicestershire, Middlesex, Somerset, Surrey, Warwickshire, Worcestershire.

Batting Averages

	M	I	NO	R	HI	Avge
T. R. Ward	4	8	1	397	201*	56.71
R. M. Ellison	4	7	2	275	105	55.00
N. J. Llong	14	22	5	757	104*	44.52
M. A. Ealham	13	25	4	802	161*	38.19
J. Creed	6	8	4	138	67	34.50
*D. J. M. Kelleher	11	18	1	566	86	33.29
V. J. Wells	12	22	1	698	121	33.23
M. J. Walker	3	4	1	95	47	31.66
D. P. Fulton	5	9	1	249	69	31.12
J. I. Longley	9	17	3	400	77	28.57
M. C. Dobson	15	28	1	683	108	25.29
C. Penn	6	7	1	123	43	20.50
D. R. Penfold	3	5	0	99	43	19.80
†G. J. Kersey	16	24	7	296	51*	17.41
P. S. de Villiers	3	6	0	82	67	13.66
M. M. Patel	4	5	1	42	33	10.50
M. T. Brimson	16	15	2	126	29	9.69
G. D. Myers	3	4	0	38	17	9.50
C. J. Hollins	3	4	0	25	10	6.25
T. N. Wren	10	9	4	23	13*	4.60
N. W. Preston	3	3	1	4	3	2.00

Played in two matches: A. G. E. Ealham 5, 7*, 61*; M. V. Fleming 37*, 50, 136; K. D. Masters 6*, 11*; T. A. Merrick 3, 62, 1. Played in one match: G. R. Cowdrey 69, 6; A. P. Igglesden 0; M. Librizzi 32; S. G. Milroy 0, 7; S. C. Willis 8.

Bowling Averages

	O	M	R	W	BB	Avge
P. S. de Villiers	73	19	168	9	3-60	18.66
T. N. Wren	208.4	43	713	34	7-34	20.97
M. C. Dobson	185.2	57	451	20	3-18	22.55
T. A. Merrick	81	14	235	9	4-90	26.11
M. M. Patel	99.5	38	235	9	4-48	26.11
M. A. Ealham	214.2	37	694	25	3-32	27.76

	O	M	R	W	BB	Avge
C. Penn	159.4	37	494	16	5-89	30.8?
R. M. Ellison	85.5	21	255	8	3-93	31.8?
N. J. Llong	169.5	30	582	18	3-6	32.3?
M. T. Brimson	359.1	89	1,061	32	5-67	33.1?
D. J. M. Kelleher	252	63	748	20	5-36	37.4?
V. J. Wells	113	20	372	9	2-39	41.3?

Also bowled: G. R. Cowdrey 8–3–24–0; M. V. Fleming 24–8–58–3; A. P. Igglesden 26–5–74–2; J. I. Longley 1–0–17–0; K. D. Masters 18–4–64–0; G. D. Myers 3–2–4–0; N. W Preston 34–8–106–3; T. R. Ward 5–2–3–0.

LANCASHIRE SECOND ELEVEN

Matches 16: Won – Derbyshire, Glamorgan, Warwickshire. Lost – Essex, Middlesex, Somerse? Surrey, Sussex. Drawn – Gloucestershire, Hampshire, Kent, Leicestershire, Northamptonshire Nottinghamshire, Worcestershire, Yorkshire.

Batting Averages

	M	I	NO	R	HI	100s	Avge
M. A. Crawley	7	13	4	552	103	2	61.3?
J. P. Crawley	11	20	3	870	117	3	51.1?
D. T. Foy	2	3	2	51	45*	0	51.0?
S. P. Titchard	16	30	6	1,137	150*	3	47.3?
*N. J. Speak	16	31	2	1,274	171	3	43.9?
J. F. Hurst	3	4	2	74	28	0	37.0?
J. E. R. Gallian	9	14	2	411	60	0	34.2?
G. D. Lloyd	9	17	0	556	101	1	32.7?
*†J. Stanworth	8	6	3	97	36	0	32.3?
T. M. Orrell	10	17	1	446	89	0	27.8?
G. Yates	16	23	11	330	58*	0	27.5?
I. Folley	16	15	4	302	78	0	27.4?
R. Irani	12	20	3	322	63	0	18.9?
J. D. Fitton	7	11	0	177	47	0	16.0?
S. J. Speak	2	3	1	18	10	0	9.0?
N. A. Derbyshire	4	4	3	7	5*	0	7.0?
†S. Bramhall	4	3	0	17	8	0	5.6?

Played in seven matches: P. J. Martin 24*, 18. Played in five matches: M. A. Sharp 2, 0 Played in three matches: †T. Wallwork 0, 0. Played in one match: I. D. Austin 20*, 1 S. Clarkson 15, 5; J. Fielding 6; D. Gandy 5; M. E. Parkinson 5*; Wasim Akram 4 G. Chapple, †J. D. Harvey and S. J. Rimmer did not bat.

Bowling Averages

	O	M	R	W	BB	Avge
Wasim Akram	37.2	10	76	10	5-36	7.6?
I. D. Austin	22.3	8	54	6	6-54	9.0?
S. J. Speak	23	4	79	5	4-60	15.8?
D. T. Foy	30	9	67	4	2-21	16.7?
P. J. Martin	216	54	501	25	7-31	20.0?
M. A. Crawley	45	11	132	5	4-58	26.4?
J. E. R. Gallian	198.4	53	591	19	5-62	31.1?
I. Folley	584	130	1,723	55	4-39	31.3?
R. Irani	277.4	54	799	25	5-41	31.9?
M. A. Sharp	92	24	242	7	3-34	34.5?
J. D. Fitton	244	61	663	18	4-100	36.8?
N. A. Derbyshire	54.3	5	228	5	3-7	45.6?
G. Yates	450.5	101	1,439	29	4-88	49.6?

Also bowled: G. Chapple 4–3–4–0; J. Fielding 10–2–27–1; G. D. Lloyd 8–0–46–0; T. M Orrell 10–0–70–0; M. E. Parkinson 11–0–79–0; S. J. Rimmer 12–2–38–0; N. J. Speak 14–1–89–1; S. P. Titchard 10–0–54–2.

LEICESTERSHIRE SECOND ELEVEN

Matches 16: Lost – Sussex. Drawn – Derbyshire, Essex, Glamorgan, Gloucestershire, Hampshire, Kent, Lancashire, Middlesex, Northamptonshire, Nottinghamshire, Somerset, Surrey, Warwickshire, Worcestershire, Yorkshire.

Batting Averages

	M	I	NO	R	HI	100s	Avge
B. F. Smith	14	19	5	701	125*	2	50.07
P. A. Nixon	5	7	3	200	50*	0	50.00
P. N. Hepworth	12	20	5	663	125*	1	44.20
A. I. Gidley	12	15	6	395	92	0	43.88
. Roseberry	16	23	2	829	113*	2	39.47
R. A. Cobb	15	25	3	759	108	1	34.50
D. R. Benson	3	6	0	179	86	0	29.83
J. J. Hawkes	7	8	0	227	122	1	28.37
P. Whitticase	3	4	0	105	43	0	26.25
G. J. F. Ferris	6	6	3	76	32*	0	25.33
A. Gilliver	7	10	1	222	44	0	24.66
F. Plender	14	21	1	492	75	0	24.60
D. J. Millns	9	7	4	73	32*	0	24.33
B. J. Parsons	9	13	2	238	52*	0	21.63
Tennant	14	14	4	145	26	0	14.50
W. K. M. Benjamin	3	3	0	41	22	0	13.66
H. Bell	2	3	0	38	29	0	12.66
. B. Taylor	9	7	3	5	4*	0	1.25

Played in five matches: †C. Bloor 7, 2. Played in two matches: N. Pretorius 0*, 0; R. W. Maddin 14; G. B. Wilson 0. Played in one match: M. P. Briers 7; C. Griffiths 3; W. Matthews ; L. Potter 59, 43; P. Willey 75.

Bowling Averages

	O	M	R	W	BB	Avge
. B. Taylor	270	59	691	36	7-34	19.19
J. J. Hawkes	194.3	65	485	19	5-102	25.52
D. R. Benson	63	20	160	6	2-56	26.66
N. Pretorius	77	18	232	8	4-70	29.00
Tennant	373.4	76	1,181	39	5-72	30.28
B. J. Parsons	271.4	59	793	26	4-39	30.50
W. K. M. Benjamin	76	11	249	8	3-93	31.12
G. J. F. Ferris	121	29	314	10	3-20	31.40
F. Plender	96.4	16	374	10	3-55	37.40
A. I. Gidley	319.5	112	775	20	3-35	38.75
D. J. Millns	212.4	50	579	7	2-50	82.71

Also bowled: M. P. Briers 10–2–34–0; M. A. Gilliver 51.3–7–188–2; C. Griffiths 8–5–78–1; P. N. Hepworth 2–0–8–1; W. Matthews 33–6–101–0; L. Potter 17.4–10–22–1; R. W. Sladdin 44–7–144–1; P. Willey 19.4–7–45–0.

MIDDLESEX SECOND ELEVEN

Matches 16: Won – Derbyshire, Lancashire, Nottinghamshire, Somerset. Lost – Glamorgan, Sussex, Worcestershire. Drawn – Essex, Gloucestershire, Hampshire, Kent, Leicestershire, Northamptonshire, Surrey, Warwickshire, Yorkshire.

Batting Averages

	M	I	NO	R	HI	Avge
J. D. Carr	7	10	0	765	179	76.50
*C. T. Radley	9	10	6	270	67*	67.50
J. C. Pooley	14	23	3	1,021	201*	51.0
R. O. Butcher	10	16	1	602	110	40.13
I. J. F. Hutchinson	13	22	2	644	95	32.20
P. N. Weekes	15	22	2	641	65	32.05
A. Habib	13	21	3	563	104	31.27
†P. Farbrace	10	17	0	529	125	31.11
M. Keech	12	19	4	394	74*	26.26
T. A. Radford	10	15	3	273	74	22.75
R. C. Williams	3	4	0	87	76	21.73
†R. J. Sims	5	8	2	124	44	20.66
C. W. Taylor	7	10	3	129	21*	18.42
M. J. Lowrey	2	4	1	49	28*	16.33
A. A. Barnett	13	15	4	160	54*	14.54
M. J. Thursfield	5	5	1	43	18*	10.75
A. F. Haye	2	3	1	13	13	6.50
J. R. Hemstock	12	11	4	18	6*	2.57

Played in two matches: D. J. Bowett 1, 0*. Played in one match: †P. R. Downton 68; †J. D. Harvey 42; S. Joshi 5, 21; J. W. D. Lishman 0, 7; J. C. Makin 7*; G. R. Mason 0; C. Patel 31*; G. M. Pooley 7; P. C. R. Tufnell 11*; R. S. Yeabsley 1; G. E. Brown and S. P. Hughes did not bat.

Bowling Averages

	O	M	R	W	Avge
J. C. Pooley	17	6	54	4	13.50
S. Joshi	37	10	85	5	17.00
A. A. Barnett	642.4	261	1,404	71	19.77
J. D. Carr	76.2	33	145	7	20.71
P. C. R. Tufnell	63.2	10	166	6	27.66
P. N. Weekes	628.3	204	1,472	51	28.86
C. W. Taylor	197	40	641	21	30.52
R. C. Williams	63.3	14	172	4	43.00
A. F. Haye	43	2	219	4	54.75
M. J. Thursfield	162.3	33	496	9	55.11
J. R. Hemstock	147	33	469	5	93.80

Also bowled: D. J. Bowett 35–13–79–1; R. O. Butcher 4–0–18–0; P. Farbrace 1–0–9–0; A. Habib 4–0–14–0; J. D. Harvey 1–0–2–0; S. P. Hughes 22–6–96–1; I. J. F. Hutchinson 24.5–5–69–1; M. Keech 16–6–48–1; J. W. D. Lishman 22–6–96–1; M. J. Lowrey 21–0–105–0; J. C. Makin 17–4–41–3; G. R. Mason 17–1–80–1; C. Patel 17–0–26–0; T. A. Radford 9–1–58–0; C. T. Radley 1–0–10–0; R. S. Yeabsley 20–4–52–2.

NORTHAMPTONSHIRE SECOND ELEVEN

Matches 16: Won – Derbyshire, Hampshire, Kent. Lost – Essex, Nottinghamshire, Sussex, York-shire. Drawn – Glamorgan, Gloucestershire, Lancashire, Leicestershire, Middlesex, Somerset, Surrey, Warwickshire, Worcestershire.

Batting Averages

	M	I	NO	R	HI	Avge
G. Cook	2	4	1	181	92	60.33
J. N. Snape	2	4	1	175	68*	58.33
R. R. Montgomerie	15	26	3	1,013	123	44.04
M. B. Loye	7	11	3	347	165	43.37
R. J. Warren	10	17	1	668	200*	41.75

	M	I	NO	R	HI	Avge
A. L. Penberthy	5	10	2	318	71	39.75
†W. M. Noon	10	13	2	402	160*	36.54
*D. J. Wild	11	16	1	531	107	35.40
A. R. Roberts	11	19	4	507	102	33.80
P. J. Berry	14	23	2	699	88	33.28
J. W. Govan	12	16	3	423	73*	32.53
J. G. Hughes	12	15	7	259	56	32.37
L. Howell	11	15	2	385	77	29.61
*R. M. Carter	10	8	5	70	23	23.33
R. G. Williams	3	5	0	113	39	22.60
S. J. Brown	7	9	2	90	36	12.85
S. L. Munday	3	3	0	24	21	8.00

Played in three matches: V. Johnson 3, 0*. Played in two matches: W. W. Davis 5, 0; †D. Ripley 26, 49; M. A. Robinson 0; J. Swann 9, 0*; C. Wigham 42, 1*, 14*. Played in one match: I. Ahmed 3, 28; C. Atkins 44; M. P. Briers 7; D. M. Cousins 0; T. de Leede 6, 16; N. A. Felton 59, 125*; H. Hall 3; T. Hancock 35; M. Hunt 5, 0; K. Innes 18, 0; †M. A. Khan 24, 0*; S. Mahboob 2, 0; T. K. Marriott 42*, 1*; C. Rogers 0, 24; M. Sagheer 22, 0*; R. Storr 0*; J. G. Thomas 27; A. Walker did not bat.

Bowling Averages

	O	M	R	W	Avge
R. G. Williams	50	16	84	5	16.80
W. W. Davis	43	11	110	4	27.50
M. A. Robinson	50.5	18	114	4	28.50
J. G. Hughes	250.5	53	770	26	29.61
S. J. Brown	183.2	33	592	19	31.15
A. L. Penberthy	102	29	286	9	31.77
A. R. Roberts	345.4	92	1,077	31	34.74
J. W. Govan	483	118	1,517	36	42.13
V. Johnson	89	21	280	6	46.66

Also bowled: I. Ahmed 8–3–24–1; C. Atkins 23–5–94–2; M. P. Briers 5–1–27–0; G. Cook 1–0–12–0; D. M. Cousins 10–2–41–0; T. de Leede 42–5–131–1; H. Hall 15–4–39–1; T. Hancock 4–0–25–0; L. Howell 16.5–2–71–1; K. Innes 11–1–55–0; S. Mahboob 38–8–93–4; T. K. Marriott 12–4–52–0; R. R. Montgomerie 6–4–8–1; S. L. Munday 60.3–13–195–3; M. Sagheer 14–0–69–1; J. Swann 28–1–166–1; J. G. Thomas 7–2–16–1; A. Walker 34–10–71–0; C. Wigham 41.5–2–184–0; D. J. Wild 160.5–35–593–5.

NOTTINGHAMSHIRE SECOND ELEVEN

Matches 16: Won – Derbyshire, Gloucestershire, Northamptonshire, Warwickshire, Worcestershire, Yorkshire. Lost – Glamorgan, Kent, Middlesex, Sussex. Drawn – Essex, Hampshire, Lancashire, Leicestershire, Somerset, Surrey.

Batting Averages

	M	I	NO	R	HI	100s	Avge
D. J. R. Martindale	8	16	6	866	171*	3	86.60
G. F. Archer	3	5	1	230	99	0	57.50
†C. W. Scott	16	23	7	758	96	0	47.37
M. Saxelby	7	12	1	438	109*	1	39.81
M. Newell	6	11	2	321	64	0	35.66
S. M. Brogan	15	29	3	848	135	1	32.61
R. J. Evans	13	22	3	589	76	0	31.00
M. G. Field-Buss	7	10	2	225	71	0	28.12
P. R. Pollard	9	16	1	393	82*	0	26.20
D. R. Laing	16	26	2	529	72	0	22.04
*J. D. Birch	11	10	3	113	28*	0	16.14
R. T. Bates	5	4	1	48	25*	0	16.00

	M	I	NO	R	HI	100s	Avge
K. P. Evans	6	7	2	76	26*	0	15.20
C. T. McKnight	2	3	1	30	25	0	15.00
G. W. Mike	13	19	0	274	63	0	14.42
W. A. Dessaur	8	12	3	124	39	0	13.77
K. Saxelby	12	14	4	125	36*	0	12.50
R. J. Chapman	4	6	3	32	13	0	10.66
N. A. Hunt	2	4	0	24	12	0	6.00
J. E. Hindson	2	3	0	14	14	0	4.66

Played in one match: J. A. Afford 2, 2; M. A. Fell 33, 15; J. E. Haynes 31, 3; P. Johnson 16*, 11; S. N. Neal 2*, 0; S. Patel 11*; R. A. Pick 35; D. W. Randall 27, 5; D. B. Storer 21, 0; K. Thomas 5; J. F. Trueman 25, 10.

Bowling Averages

	O	M	R	W	BB	Avge
M. Saxelby	70.2	16	237	12	4-1	19.75
K. P. Evans	209.2	53	575	28	5-33	20.53
J. A. Afford	60	21	174	8	5-66	21.75
W. A. Dessaur	69	23	167	7	3-47	23.85
K. Saxelby	344.5	88	1,025	39	5-56	26.28
M. G. Field-Buss	301.5	107	639	24	5-57	26.62
D. R. Laing	394.1	96	1,274	46	7-64	27.69
G. W. Mike	435	96	1,328	47	7-41	28.25
J. D. Birch	31.3	7	151	5	4-54	30.20
R. T. Bates	59.4	14	201	6	2-44	33.50
R. J. Chapman	79	18	261	7	3-73	37.28

Also bowled: R. J. Evans 12-3-40-2; M. A. Fell 42-10-82-2; J. E. Hindson 32-10-73-0; C. T. McKnight 64-17-210-2; M. Newell 5-1-11-0; S. Patel 28-10-82-1; R. A. Pick 32-1-109-1; P. R. Pollard 4-0-49-0; K. Thomas 4-1-20-0.

SOMERSET SECOND ELEVEN

Matches 16: Won – Lancashire. Lost – Glamorgan, Middlesex. Drawn – Derbyshire, Essex, Gloucestershire, Hampshire, Kent, Leicestershire, Northamptonshire, Nottinghamshire, Surrey, Sussex, Warwickshire, Worcestershire, Yorkshire.

Batting Averages

	I	NO	R	HI	Avge
†R. J. Turner	5	3	130	45*	65.00
R. J. Bartlett	24	2	1,393	175	63.31
N. J. Pringle	26	5	1,187	130*	56.52
M. Lathwell	6	1	271	168*	54.20
Keith Parsons	4	2	92	52*	46.00
G. T. J. Townsend	26	4	989	152*	44.95
H. R. J. Trump	8	5	110	63*	36.66
I. Fletcher	27	1	824	137	31.69
J. C. M. Atkinson	13	0	399	97	30.69
M. W. Cleal	12	1	315	57*	28.63
D. M. Kutner	13	3	269	65*	26.90
J. C. Hallett	13	4	225	61	25.00
S. Toogood	3	0	75	53	25.00
S. D. Myles	5	0	111	61	22.20
*†T. Gard	13	6	144	51*	20.57
A. R. Caddick	6	3	60	27	20.00
M. A. Harris	7	0	107	42	15.28
P. J. Rendell	5	0	65	42	13.00
A. C. Cottam	6	2	40	18	10.00

Also batted: P. Bradbury 53*; S. Brodrick 4*, 0; G. Brown 38*, 9; S. Bryan 1; J. J. E. Hardy 104; J. D. Harvey 39, 1; K. Martin 10; K. Moyse 0*, 0*; Kevin Parsons 37, 9; S. M. Priscott 8*, 6; R. A. Pyman 9, 6*; D. Read 4, 0; P. J. Robinson 5, 3*; A. P. van Troost 0; M. Wakefield 12. M. Copping and E. Robinson each played in one match but did not bat.

Bowling Averages

	O	M	R	W	BB	Avge
P. Bradbury	16	0	70	4	2-25	17.50
M. W. Cleal	165	29	477	17	4-49	28.05
A. R. Caddick	241	45	713	24	6-42	29.70
H. R. J. Trump	354.4	91	913	29	5-80	31.48
D. M. Kutner	72.3	12	302	9	5-6	33.55
J. C. Hallett	285.4	46	1,006	28	4-68	35.92
A. C. Cottam	277	62	998	26	5-100	38.38
M. A. Harris	71	9	255	4	1-27	63.75
A. P. van Troost	91	10	392	6	2-80	65.33
P. J. Rendell	99	7	396	4	3-65	99.00

Also bowled: J. C. M. Atkinson 22.1–3–82–3; R. J. Bartlett 6–0–29–0; S. Brodrick 12.5–3–56–2; M. Copping 29–3–96–2; M. Lathwell 25–8–78–1; K. Martin 22–0–90–1; K. Moyse 22.1–3–89–2; S. D. Myles 45.4–4–144–2; Keith Parsons 5–1–14–3; S. M. Priscott 66–7–307–2; R. A. Pyman 29–11–50–1; D. Read 23–3–93–2; E. Robinson 45–14–140–3; P. J. Robinson 18–5–34–3; S. Toogood 64.1–6–305–3; G. T. J. Townsend 1–0–18–0; M. Wakefield 9–3–28–0.

SURREY SECOND ELEVEN

Matches 16: Won – Essex, Gloucestershire, Hampshire, Lancashire, Yorkshire. Lost – Glamorgan. Drawn – Derbyshire, Kent, Leicestershire, Middlesex, Northamptonshire, Nottinghamshire, Somerset, Sussex, Warwickshire. Tied – Worcestershire.

Batting Averages

	M	I	NO	R	HI	100s	Avge
R. I. Alikhan	8	11	4	497	151*	2	71.00
G. P. Thorpe	4	6	1	301	126*	1	60.20
J. D. Robinson	10	16	3	627	214*	1	48.23
*P. D. Atkins	14	21	4	756	149	2	44.47
C. K. Bullen	10	14	4	438	93	0	43.80
A. D. Brown	15	20	1	712	152	1	37.47
A. W. Smith	14	20	3	571	80	0	33.58
M. A. Butcher	15	23	3	627	127	1	31.35
†N. F. Sargeant	14	15	4	308	81	0	28.00
A. Hodgson	4	6	1	136	70	0	27.20
N. M. Kendrick	9	8	2	159	53*	0	26.50
M. A. Feltham	4	5	0	104	61	0	20.80
A. H. Gray	5	3	1	41	24*	0	20.50
D. J. Bicknell	3	4	0	63	35	0	15.75
A. Hollioake	5	6	2	45	16*	0	11.25
N. H. Peters	8	7	1	53	32	0	8.83
A. G. Robson	9	5	1	24	9	0	6.00
J. Boiling	6	5	3	9	4*	0	4.50

Played in six matches: A. J. Murphy 9; C. E. Waller 1*, 2*, 7*. Played in two matches: S. J. Cooper 3*, 103*, 0; D. Foster 6*. Played in one match: M. R. J. Brugnoli 0, 1; M. A. Lynch 56; A. T. Van-Lint 6; A. Giles did not bat.

Bowling Averages

	O	M	R	W	BB	Avge
M. A. Feltham	125.2	33	272	16	6-34	17.00
A. H. Gray	154.4	38	406	22	6-20	18.45
A. J. Murphy	204	52	530	28	5-41	18.92
N. M. Kendrick	345.1	118	694	36	6-56	19.27
C. K. Bullen	312.2	119	577	21	4-63	27.47
J. Boiling	182.3	63	426	14	4-44	30.42
J. D. Robinson	148.3	31	464	15	3-52	30.93
A. G. Robson	272	48	827	22	4-34	37.59
N. H. Peters	153.1	31	543	14	4-36	38.78
S. J. Cooper	89.3	20	273	7	3-96	39.00
A. Hollioake	90	14	357	8	3-46	44.62

Also bowled: P. D. Atkins 17–3–43–0; A. D. Brown 24.3–1–150–1; M. R. J. Brugnoli 12–2–36–1; M. A. Butcher 19–4–62–0; D. Foster 48.4–9–125–4; A. Giles 18–5–42–1; M. A. Lynch 10–3–30–0; N. F. Sargeant 1–0–14–0; A. W. Smith 54–16–170–3; G. P. Thorpe 35–7–148–2; A. T. Van-Lint 39.2–6–135–4; C. E. Waller 29–6–67–1.

SUSSEX SECOND ELEVEN

Matches 16: Won – Essex, Glamorgan, Lancashire, Leicestershire, Middlesex, Northamptonshire, Nottinghamshire, Warwickshire, Yorkshire. Lost – Kent. Drawn – Derbyshire, Gloucestershire, Hampshire, Somerset, Surrey, Worcestershire.

Batting Averages

	M	I	NO	R	HI	100s	Avge
R. Hanley	13	20	3	992	161	3	58.35
G. P. Burnett	16	28	3	1,432	212	4	57.28
*K. Greenfield	14	21	5	840	129	2	52.50
J. W. Hall	6	11	1	433	126*	2	43.30
*D. M. Smith	2	3	0	98	91	0	32.66
†C. H. H. Pegg	4	5	1	125	79*	0	31.25
B. T. P. Donelan ...	13	19	7	341	66	0	28.41
*†I. J. Gould	4	5	0	141	42	0	28.20
J. A. North	10	14	2	324	117	1	27.00
†D. J. Pepperell	4	5	3	54	25*	0	27.00
C. C. Remy	12	19	1	404	48	0	22.44
J. W. Dean	11	13	3	170	36	0	17.00
A. R. Hansford	3	5	2	33	12	0	11.00
A. R. Clarke	13	11	1	105	24	0	10.50
K. Newell	4	5	0	52	23	0	10.40
A. M. Babington ...	10	9	4	50	15	0	10.00
A. R. Cornford	8	11	2	85	23	0	9.44
R. A. Bunting	8	7	0	40	14	0	5.71

Played in five matches: P. W. Threlfall 14, 0. Played in four matches: E. S. H. Giddins 4*. Played in two matches: A. M. A. Aduhene 4*. Played in one match: T. Chadwick 9; T. de Leede 54, 33; †J. Finch 4*; I. A. Kidd 42; †P. Moores 5; H. Nankivell 14, 0*; †J. Smith 2, 1; †M. P. Speight 43; I. C. Waring 0; C. M. Wells 38.

Bowling Averages

	O	M	R	W	BB	Avge
A. R. Clarke	337.3	128	772	42	5-29	18.38
B. T. P. Donelan	363	114	919	46	8-40	19.97
R. A. Bunting	216.3	50	551	27	4-24	20.40
C. C. Remy	163.2	37	388	19	4-44	20.42
E. S. H. Giddins	49	8	198	9	3-20	22.00
A. R. Hansford	36	8	92	4	3-57	23.00
A. M. Babington	208.3	45	590	23	7-52	25.65
J. W. Dean	246	98	607	21	5-63	28.90
P. W. Threlfall	111	25	295	10	3-47	29.50
J. A. North	157.3	36	462	13	5-57	35.53

Also bowled: A. M. A. Aduhene 47–7–157–0; A. R. Cornford 11–4–29–0; T. de Leede 5–4–6–0; K. Greenfield 28–6–64–2; J. W. Hall 2–0–18–0; H. Nankivell 7–2–14–0; D. M. Smith 1–0–3–0; I. C. Waring 4–2–5–0.

WARWICKSHIRE SECOND ELEVEN

Matches 16: Won – Derbyshire, Gloucestershire, Hampshire, Worcestershire. Lost – Lancashire, Nottinghamshire, Sussex. Drawn – Essex, Glamorgan, Kent, Leicestershire, Middlesex, Northamptonshire, Somerset, Surrey, Yorkshire.

Batting Averages

	M	I	NO	R	HI	100s	Avge
Wasim Khan	4	5	1	234	171*	1	58.50
J. D. Ratcliffe	10	18	1	964	151	4	56.70
G. W. Humpage	4	6	0	334	122	2	55.66
D. P. Ostler	9	14	1	707	149	2	54.38
N. M. K. Smith	2	3	1	97	74	0	48.50
S. J. Green	11	15	2	538	122	2	41.38
R. G. Twose	9	14	1	480	102	1	36.92
*T. L. Penney	11	15	3	441	113	2	36.75
†P. C. L. Holloway	8	13	2	383	82	0	34.81
I. G. S. Steer	14	24	5	608	73*	0	32.00
†K. J. Piper	8	13	2	326	64	0	29.63
D. R. Brown	11	13	2	312	60*	0	28.36
A. R. K. Pierson	9	11	5	132	43*	0	22.00
G. J. P. B. Williamson	5	9	1	153	38	0	19.12
O. S. Chagar	10	12	2	156	40	0	15.60
G. Welch	12	15	6	118	22	0	13.11
P. A. Smith	4	7	0	89	34	0	12.71
G. Smith	12	10	3	45	19	0	6.42
P. A. Booth	3	3	0	15	13	0	5.00

Played in three matches: M. P. Clewley 7*, 0*; A. A. Donald 10*, 0. Played in two matches: A. J. Hunt 41, 0; T. A. Lloyd 61, 40; P. Mirza did not bat. Played in one match: Asif Din 54; M. A. V. Bell 3; †M. Burns 22; A. B. Byram 46, 0; D. B. M. Fox 1; A. J. Moles 93, 16; M. J. Pidgeon 5*; G. F. Shephard 38*.

Bowling Averages

	O	M	R	W	BB	Avge
A. A. Donald	88	33	175	13	6-56	13.46
P. A. Booth	101	35	211	11	4-56	19.18
P. A. Smith	92.5	21	228	10	3-29	22.80
N. M. K. Smith	54.1	18	161	7	6-48	23.00
D. B. M. Fox	34	10	97	4	4-54	24.25
A. R. K. Pierson	383.1	123	878	36	4-51	24.38
G. Smith	321	61	931	36	6-53	25.86
R. G. Twose	186.4	41	529	17	6-103	31.11
D. R. Brown	256.2	40	962	24	4-63	40.08
G. Welch	154	35	492	11	5-40	44.72
O. S. Chagar	250	58	713	15	3-60	47.53
M. P. Clewley	63.5	6	264	4	2-38	66.00

Also bowled: Asif Din 11–4–24–2; M. A. V. Bell 21–4–53–2; A. B. Byram 43–7–153–2; S. J. Green 11–1–56–1; P. Mirza 3–0–14–0; D. P. Ostler 7–4–19–1; T. L. Penney 0.4–0–0–0; M. J. Pidgeon 19–6–57–0; K. J. Piper 1–0–8–0; J. D. Ratcliffe 14–3–35–1; I. G. S. Steer 25–5–64–2.

WORCESTERSHIRE SECOND ELEVEN

Matches 16: Won – Hampshire, Middlesex. Lost – Gloucestershire, Nottinghamshire, Warwickshire. Drawn – Derbyshire, Essex, Glamorgan, Kent, Lancashire, Leicestershire, Northamptonshire, Somerset, Sussex, Yorkshire. Tied – Surrey.

Batting Averages

	M	I	NO	R	HI	100s	Avge
M. J. Weston	4	8	1	414	161	2	59.14
N. Davey	2	4	1	172	120	1	57.33
S. R. Lampitt	3	5	1	219	100*	1	54.75
*M. S. Scott	16	10	7	159	70*	0	53.00
D. A. Leatherdale	9	16	2	728	119*	3	52.00
P. Bent	12	24	1	1,116	174	2	48.52
G. R. Haynes	14	25	3	1,043	137	2	47.40
C. M. Tolley	4	7	1	252	62*	0	42.00
J. W. D. Leighton	2	3	1	81	58*	0	40.50
N. V. Radford	4	6	0	236	144	1	39.33
S. Herzberg	15	26	5	743	61*	0	35.38
G. J. Lord	11	20	0	590	94	0	29.50
S. M. McEwan	4	5	2	70	39*	0	23.33
†S. R. Froggatt	4	5	1	81	33	0	20.25
R. P. Gofton	12	18	2	318	141	1	19.87
A. Wylie	6	7	5	38	24	0	19.00
W. P. C. Weston	5	8	0	147	39	0	18.37
I. A. Kidd	3	6	0	100	33	0	16.66
R. D. Stemp	11	12	3	137	39	0	15.22
†S. R. Bevins	14	21	6	218	45*	0	14.53
G. R. Dilley	1	2	0	26	15	0	13.00
M. G. Fowles	3	4	0	18	14	0	4.50
I. T. Wood	4	6	0	26	10	0	4.33

Played in four matches: N. A. Hitchings 10, 0. Played in one match: M. S. Bevins 2; D. M. Cox 16*; S. Grant 29*; P. Mirza 22; S. A. Morgan 0; R. A. Pybus 6; S. G. Reape 9, 8; R. M. Wight 8; R. J. Coyle did not bat.

Bowling Averages

	O	M	R	W	BB	Avge
G. R. Dilley	33.1	6	100	9	6-46	11.11
S. R. Lampitt	52.2	12	162	9	6-57	18.00
D. A. Leatherdale	62	14	188	7	4-63	26.85
P. Bent	77	25	191	7	3-57	27.28
N. A. Hitchings	67.5	11	262	9	6-39	29.11
G. R. Haynes	255.4	65	713	24	4-33	29.70
S. M. McEwan	126	22	432	14	3-21	30.85
S. Herzberg	505	119	1,687	50	5-118	33.74
R. P. Gofton	257.5	50	877	25	3-43	35.08
S. Grant	45	7	178	5	4-78	35.60
N. V. Radford	112.4	21	440	12	9-98	36.66
R. D. Stemp	340.1	110	1,485	35	5-80	42.42
A. Wylie	111.5	14	481	11	2-28	43.72

Also bowled: D. M. Cox 12–1–59–0; M. G. Fowles 21–2–107–2; G. J. Lord 13–4–32–2; P. Mirza 21–6–83–1; R. A. Pybus 19–1–117–0; S. G. Reape 3–0–19–0; C. M. Tolley 44–12–89–1; M. J. Weston 30–8–89–1; W. P. C. Weston 50–9–181–3; R. M. Wight 26–18–28–1.

YORKSHIRE SECOND ELEVEN

Matches 16: Won – Northamptonshire. Lost – Derbyshire, Essex, Kent, Nottinghamshire, Surrey, Sussex. Drawn – Glamorgan, Gloucestershire, Hampshire, Lancashire, Leicestershire, Middlesex, Somerset, Warwickshire, Worcestershire.

Batting Averages

	M	I	NO	R	HI	100s	Avge
C. White	3	6	3	469	209*	2	156.33
K. Sharp	6	11	1	590	221*	2	59.00
*S. N. Hartley	16	24	8	715	105*	2	44.68
C. S. Pickles	5	9	1	309	76	0	38.62
†C. A. Chapman	12	22	0	748	107	1	34.00
B. Parker	5	10	1	270	105	1	30.00
A. P. Grayson	9	17	2	440	90*	0	29.33
S. J. Bartle	6	10	2	230	50	0	28.75
D. Byas	5	9	2	199	79	0	28.42
N. G. Nicholson	14	25	2	583	138	1	25.34
M. J. Doidge	15	27	3	568	81	0	23.66
P. J. Berry	13	17	5	278	119	1	23.16
J. R. Goldthorp	5	8	0	183	59	0	22.87
S. D. Fletcher	6	6	0	132	70	0	22.00
S. Hutton	3	6	0	131	43	0	21.83
M. J. Foster	2	4	0	81	40	0	20.25
S. Bethel	6	10	0	172	96	0	17.20
J. D. Batty	7	7	3	66	29	0	16.50
C. Shaw	13	12	4	85	46*	0	10.62
N. S. Taylor	3	4	0	41	17	0	10.25
I. J. Houseman	8	8	3	23	8*	0	4.60
D. B. Pennett	5	5	1	9	8	0	2.25

Also batted: †D. L. Bairstow 60, 12, 57*; R. J. Blakey 139, 36; D. Gough 0; P. J. Hartley 0, 0; P. W. Jarvis 9; S. A. Kellett 30, 16; D. Mynott 16*, 8*, 17; I. M. Priestley 43.

Note: After the first innings of the match v Hampshire at Bingley, Bairstow was called to Leeds for the Benson and Hedges Cup match v Lancashire and was replaced by Chapman.

Bowling Averages

	O	M	R	W	BB	Avge
C. White	95	37	235	11	7-55	21.36
N. S. Taylor	75.4	15	231	9	4-65	25.66
S. D. Fletcher	151.3	44	433	16	4-48	27.06
A. P. Grayson	106	19	348	10	3-55	34.80
P. J. Berry	310.5	95	732	21	6-77	34.85
J. D. Batty	206.4	31	716	20	5-61	35.80
I. J. Houseman	164	22	714	19	5-52	37.57
S. J. Bartle	46	4	188	5	4-109	37.60
M. J. Doidge	301.5	64	943	24	3-93	39.29
D. B. Pennett	105	13	374	9	2-19	41.55
C. Shaw	184.1	30	680	16	4-58	42.50
C. S. Pickles	126	22	401	9	3-29	44.55

Also bowled: D. Byas 18–2–45–1; M. J. Foster 18–4–55–1; J. R. Goldthorp 5–0–37–0; D. Gough 32–8–77–1; P. J. Hartley 32–4–93–0; P. W. Jarvis 32–9–80–0; N. G. Nicholson 3–0–8–0; I. M. Priestley 26–4–99–1.

SECOND ELEVEN CHAMPIONS

1959	Gloucestershire	1970	Kent	1981	Hampshire
1960	Northamptonshire	1971	Hampshire	1982	Worcestershire
1961	Kent	1972	Nottinghamshire	1983	Leicestershire
1962	Worcestershire	1973	Essex	1984	Yorkshire
1963	Worcestershire	1974	Middlesex	1985	Nottinghamshire
1964	Lancashire	1975	Surrey	1986	Lancashire
1965	Glamorgan	1976	Kent	1987	Kent / Yorkshire
1966	Surrey	1977	Yorkshire	1988	Surrey
1967	Hampshire	1978	Sussex	1989	Middlesex
1968	Surrey	1979	Warwickshire	1990	Sussex
1969	Kent	1980	Glamorgan		

Batting Averages

	M	I	NO	R	HI	100s	Avge
C. White	3	6	3	469	209*	2	156.33
K. Sharp	6	11	1	590	221*	2	59.00
*S. N. Hartley	16	24	8	715	105*	2	44.68
C. S. Pickles	5	9	1	309	76	0	38.62
†C. A. Chapman	12	22	0	748	107	1	34.00
B. Parker	5	10	1	270	105	1	30.00
A. P. Grayson	9	17	2	440	90*	0	29.33
S. J. Bartle	6	10	2	230	50	0	28.75
D. Byas	5	9	2	199	79	0	28.42
N. G. Nicholson	14	25	2	583	138	1	25.34
M. J. Doidge	15	27	3	568	81	0	23.66
P. J. Berry	13	17	5	278	119	1	23.16
J. R. Goldthorp	5	8	0	183	59	0	22.87
S. D. Fletcher	6	6	0	132	70	0	22.00
S. Hutton	3	6	0	131	43	0	21.83
M. J. Foster	2	4	0	81	40	0	20.25
S. Bethel	6	10	0	172	96	0	17.20
J. D. Batty	7	7	3	66	29	0	16.50
C. Shaw	13	12	4	85	46*	0	10.62
N. S. Taylor	3	4	0	41	17	0	10.25
I. J. Houseman	8	8	3	23	8*	0	4.60
D. B. Pennett	5	5	1	9	8	0	2.25

Also batted: †D. L. Bairstow 60, 12, 57*; R. J. Blakey 139, 36; D. Gough 0; P. J. Hartley 0, 0; P. W. Jarvis 9; S. A. Kellett 30, 16; D. Mynott 16*, 8*, 17; I. M. Priestley 43.

Note: After the first innings of the match v Hampshire at Bingley, Bairstow was called to Leeds for the Benson and Hedges Cup match v Lancashire and was replaced by Chapman.

Bowling Averages

	O	M	R	W	BB	Avge
C. White	95	37	235	11	7-55	21.36
N. S. Taylor	75.4	15	231	9	4-65	25.66
S. D. Fletcher	151.3	44	433	16	4-48	27.06
A. P. Grayson	106	19	348	10	3-55	34.80
P. J. Berry	310.5	95	732	21	6-77	34.85
J. D. Batty	206.4	31	716	20	5-61	35.80
I. J. Houseman	164	22	714	19	5-52	37.57
S. J. Bartle	46	4	188	5	4-109	37.60
M. J. Doidge	301.5	64	943	24	3-93	39.29
D. B. Pennett	105	13	374	9	2-19	41.55
C. Shaw	184.1	30	680	16	4-58	42.50
C. S. Pickles	126	22	401	9	3-29	44.55

Also bowled: D. Byas 18-2-45-1; M. J. Foster 18-4-55-1; J. R. Goldthorp 5-0-37-0; D. Gough 32-8-77-1; P. J. Hartley 32-4-93-0; P. W. Jarvis 32-9-80-0; N. G. Nicholson 3-0-8-0; I. M. Priestley 26-4-99-1.

SECOND ELEVEN CHAMPIONS

1959	Gloucestershire	1970	Kent	1981	Hampshire
1960	Northamptonshire	1971	Hampshire	1982	Worcestershire
1961	Kent	1972	Nottinghamshire	1983	Leicestershire
1962	Worcestershire	1973	Essex	1984	Yorkshire
1963	Worcestershire	1974	Middlesex	1985	Nottinghamshire
1964	Lancashire	1975	Surrey	1986	Lancashire
1965	Glamorgan	1976	Kent	1987	{ Kent
1966	Surrey	1977	Yorkshire		Yorkshire
1967	Hampshire	1978	Sussex	1988	Surrey
1968	Surrey	1979	Warwickshire	1989	Middlesex
1969	Kent	1980	Glamorgan	1990	Sussex

FINAL

DURHAM v EXETER

At Liverpool CC, June 20, 21. Durham won by six wickets. Toss: Durham. Wight and Hill gave Exeter a slow but secure start before being parted in the nineteenth over, but the leg-spin of Wasim Raja brought Durham a second wicket before the threatening rain interrupted play until the afternoon. After the resumption Macdonald had Baldwin caught, and there was time for Boiling to capture the vital wicket of Wight before further heavy rain stopped play a second time, with Exeter 99 for four. With the square rapidly disappearing under a sheet of water, and more rain forecast for the following afternoon, the UAU officials decided that play would recommence at ten o'clock next morning, a bold decision that just paid off. Recognising that time was at a premium, Durham's bowlers approached their task with a sense of urgency. Boiling plied his off-breaks skilfully; at the other end, Macdonald combined genuine pace with meticulous line and length. Five wickets fell for the addition of 19 runs, and despite last-wicket defiance from Snelling and Waters, Exeter lasted less than an hour. Yet as the gloom gathered, Durham in turn faltered. Evans was caught in his first over, Morris was run out by Clark's direct throw after a misunderstanding with Longley, who himself soon went, caught behind, playing at a waspish ball from Smith. Much now depended on Wasim Raja, in his last innings as a university cricketer. A motoring accident the previous December had all but ended his life, and the recovery of his cricketing skills had been a triumph of determination and dedication. At first with caution, he turned those skills on the Exeter bowling; but as lunch approached, he widened his range of strokes and accelerated. After the interval Keey lost patience against Wight, the end of an invaluable, intelligent contribution, but there were no further alarms for Durham as Wasim Raja saw them to victory.

Exeter

R. M. Wight c Ellison b Boiling	48	A. M. Smith c Boiling b Macdonald	0
G. F. Hill c Keey b Macdonald	21	R. K. Brook b Macdonald	0
R. Mould b Wasim Raja	0	†J. A. G. Waters not out	10
P. J. A. Baldwin c Longley b Macdonald	13	L-b 4, n-b 2	6
G. R. S. Scovell c and b Boiling	8		—
D. J. Clark lbw b Macdonald	12	1/39 2/45 3/80	(57.1 overs) 134
*M. K. Barker c Longley b Boiling	6	4/90 5/107 6/111	
P. Snelling b Macdonald	10	7/114 8/116 9/118	

Bowling: Macdonald 28.1–5–56–6; Ellison 7–2–10–0; Dakin 2–0–13–0; Wasim Raja 5–0–17–1; Boiling 15–1–34–3.

Durham

*R. S. M. Morris run out	12	†W. M. I. Bailey not out	11
B. G. Evans c Barker b Brook	0	B 2, l-b 1, w 1, n-b 5	9
J. I. Longley c Waters b Smith	16		—
Wasim Raja not out	57	1/6 2/26 3/37	(4 wkts, 44.3 overs) 137
C. L. Keey lbw b Wight	32	4/112	

J. R. C. Dakin, B. C. Ellison, R. H. Macdonald, J. Boiling and S. Patel did not bat.

Bowling: Smith 18–1–59–1; Brook 8–4–13–1; Barker 7–1–30–0; Wight 10.3–4–24–1; Scovell 1–0–8–0.

Umpires: K. Hopley and W. T. Robins.

THE LANCASHIRE LEAGUES, 1990

By CHRIS ASPIN

Batsmen had the best of a season which yielded a rich harvest of runs and records. The leading amateurs were only a little way behind the most successful professionals, though they made far less impact with the ball. As usual, clubs with bowling professionals did best.

East Lancashire won the Lancashire League championship after a gap of six years, thanks largely to Paul Reiffel from Victoria, who took 105 wickets and scored 770 runs. The one other bowler to reach 100 wickets was also an Australian, Colin Miller of South Australia who, playing for Rawtenstall, became only the third man since the league was formed to do the double. The feat had last been accomplished in 1949, by Cec Pepper and Vijay Hazare. Miller was also the match-winner in the Worsley Cup final, taking nine for 25, the season's best return, as Bacup were dismissed for 79 in reply to Rawtenstall's 185 for six.

The decision to replay as many rain-spoiled fixtures as possible helped the record-breakers. These included Miller's fellow-South Australian, Peter Sleep, who scored 1,294 runs for Rishton, and Geoff Parker (Victoria), close behind with 1,250 for Church, both records for their clubs. Craig Smith of Rishton became the fourth amateur in 98 years to score more than 1,000 runs in a season, his total of 1,069 (50.90) including two hundreds and nine fifties. Amateur club records were also set by Paul Simmonite, of Colne, with 970 runs at an average of 44.41, and Chris Bleazard, of Lowerhouse, with 857 (37.26). David Pearson (East Lancashire) scored 968 runs (44.00), and also claimed 53 dismissals to equal the League's 35-year-old wicket-keeping record. Bryan Knowles became the first player to complete 12,000 runs for a single club – he added another 864 for Haslingden at 37.56 – and Peter Wood (Rawtenstall), who made 790 (43.88), passed 10,000. The West Indian, Roger Harper, scored 1,010 runs and took 64 wickets for Bacup. Rishton accumulated a record 4,505 runs, including 323 which Sleep took off the unfortunate Church bowlers. In their first encounter he scored 152 not out and in the second 171 not out.

The leading wicket-takers after Reiffel and Miller were Robert Haynes, the Jamaican leg-spinner, for Accrington and Haslingden's Australian, Mike Whitney. The best amateur returns came from Mark Price (Ramsbottom), with 60 wickets at 19.27, Alan Barnes (Haslingden) with 55 at 20.11, and Jez Hope (Lowerhouse) with 53 at 22.47. Enfield had the dubious distinction of conceding 500 extras during the season.

Rochdale, for whom the South African, David Callaghan, acted as both professional and captain, won the Central Lancashire League championship for the first time since 1956. They ended the season five points ahead of Oldham, who started favourites after signing the West Indian all-rounder, Ezra Moseley. Callaghan was one of four players – three professionals and one amateur – to top 1,000 runs and he was also fifth in the bowling averages. The leading run-maker was an Australian, Geoff Foley, who scored 1,335 for Milnrow, including the season's highest score of 150 against Norden. He was followed by Carl Hooper of Guyana, with 1,118 for Werneth, Nick Hayward, the Stockport amateur, with 1,032 and an average of 39.69, and Callaghan with 1,021. Among fourteen amateurs to score more than 700 runs were Chris Dearden of Littleborough, whose 973 at 32.43 set a new record for the club, and Russell Davies (Norden) with 944 (36.31).

The bowling averages were headed by Cec Wright, the oldest player in the competition, who made light of his 56 years to bowl 357 overs for Crompton and take 67 wickets at 11.78. Two professionals each took 101 wickets – Middleton's South African professional, Brad Osborne, and the Barbadian, Victor Walcott (Littleborough). Moseley took 94 wickets for Oldham, and were similar returns for the Australian Peter Gladigau at Norden and Barrington Browne, the Guyanese fast bowler, at Unsworth. Among the amateurs, Imran Adrees (Radcliffe) took 82 wickets at 16.05, Craig Hopkinson (Royton) 71 at 19.38 and Ian Hayward (Stockport) 65 at 12.25. Werneth won the Lees Wood Cup for the tenth time when they beat Norden by 37 runs in an exciting final, Hooper making 136 not out in a total of 269 for eight. The fastest scoring of the season came from Stockport's Australian professional, Steve Wundke, who hit the Rochdale spinner, Neil Avery, for five consecutive sixes and completed his fifty in twelve balls.

MATTHEW BROWN LANCASHIRE LEAGUE

	P	W	L	D	Pts	Professional	Runs	Avge	Wkts	Avge
East Lancashire	26	21	3	1	102*	P. R. Reiffel	770	45.29	105	11.63
Haslingden	26	19	4	2	90*	M. R. Whitney	151	11.62	81	17.76
Rawtenstall	26	19	7	0	85	C. R. Miller	1,078	51.33	100	15.73
Accrington	26	17	8	0	80*	R. C. Haynes	691	46.07	88	13.89
Bacup	26	16	9	1	72	R. A. Harper	1,010	53.16	64	15.64
Rishton	26	13	12	0	60*	P. R. Sleep	1,294	64.70	71	21.54
Burnley	26	13	13	0	58	Mudassar Nazar	973	40.54	41	27.27
Nelson	26	13	12	1	56	{ B. P. Julian	463	46.30	16	38.38
						{ E. O. Simons	339	48.43	20	20.00
Colne	26	11	14	1	50	H. L. Alleyne	323	29.36	49	16.92
Ramsbottom	26	9	17	0	43	S. Monkhouse	12	3.00	41	25.61
Lowerhouse	26	9	16	0	41*	D. S. Morgan	803	33.46	53	17.55
Todmorden	26	7	16	2	37*	B. Williams	688	31.27	34	29.26
Church	26	4	22	0	19	G. R. Parker	1,250	48.07	48	32.31
Enfield	26	4	22	0	19	C. Killen	663	33.15	50	23.44

* Includes two points awarded in a tied match.

Note: One point awarded for dismissing the opposition.

BROTHER CENTRAL LANCASHIRE LEAGUE

	P	W	L	D	Pts	Professional	Runs	Avge	Wkts	Avge
Rochdale	30	20	4	6	101*	D. J. Callaghan	1,021	40.84	71	14.21
Oldham	30	19	5	6	96	E. A. Moseley	517	28.72	94	13.51
Littleborough	30	19	9	2	86	V. D. Walcott	293	10.85	101	16.17
Werneth	30	18	8	4	84	C. L. Hooper	1,118	43.00	91	16.58
Stockport	30	15	9	6	81*	S. C. Wundke	944	36.31	85	15.64
Middleton	30	16	9	5	80	B. M. Osborne	704	32.00	101	14.76
Heywood	30	16	8	6	77	J. Abrahams	913	39.70	40	27.73
Norden	30	15	10	5	75	P. W. Gladigau	689	23.29	94	14.95
Milnrow	30	13	12	5	66	G. I. Foley	1,335	55.63	48	21.46
Crompton	30	11	13	6	57*	A. Johnston	429	18.65	69	17.94
Clyde	30	10	14	6	52	V. S. Greene	793	36.05	67	17.61
Radcliffe	30	9	15	6	48*	K. W. McLeod	398	18.95	63	24.97
Ashton	30	7	18	5	36	D. Foley	487	21.17	44	24.34
Unsworth	30	6	21	3	30	B. St A. Browne	54	4.05	94	19.37
Royton	30	3	22	5	20	D. Tuckwell	892	31.86	23	29.87
Walsden	30	3	22	6	15	A. G. Daley	803	33.46	77	19.35

* Includes two points awarded in a tied match.

Notes: Five points awarded for an outright win; four for a limited win.
        Averages include cup games.

IRISH CRICKET IN 1990

By DEREK SCOTT

After three years of transition, the Ireland team could glimpse a modicum of light at the end of the tunnel in 1990. They celebrated their first victory since 1987, and by the end of the season appeared to have a settled team. They did not do well in the five one-day games played in May and June against first class opposition, despite fielding their first non-qualified player in the Indian Test batsman, Raman Lamba. But these games pitted Saturday amateur against Test cricketers and county professionals. The three-day matches against mostly amateur opposition, provided real hope for the future; after a run of 21 matches without a win of any sort, Ireland beat MCC, and their games against Wales and Scotland were drawn. In these matches the Irish bowlers took 49 of a possible 50 wickets, and at the reasonable cost of 24.56 runs per wicket. P. McCrum was recalled to share the new ball with A. N. Nelson, whose brother, Noel, was the third seamer. Off-spinner G. D. Harrison had a most successful year, and a leg-spinner, C. Hoey, and slow left-armer, S. Taylor, were waiting in the wings. The batting had become stable, with a new cap, the left-handed S. G. Smyth, adding variety, and the team seemed to flourish on a change of captaincy. After 25 matches leading the side, P. B. Jackson handed the job over to S. J. S. Warke. Jackson's wicket-keeping immediately went from very good to excellent, as did Warke's batting, so the selectors were vindicated.

In early May, the New Zealanders visited Ireland for the first time since 1965 and won the two one-day matches, sponsored by Gilbey's Ulster Games. It was much too soon for the home players to give of their best, but it must be said that these tourists were a pleasure to entertain; and it was a delight for Irish spectators to watch Richard Hadlee take three for 25 in the first game.

Worcestershire were in Dublin in early June for two similar matches, sponsored by JMA, at Castle Avenue. The first was much interrupted by rain and reduced to 34 overs a side, but those lucky enough to be there in mid afternoon saw an unforgettable innings from Graeme Hick. Having reached 50 in 67 minutes, with a six and eight fours off 65 balls, he then took only ten minutes and eleven balls to get to 101 not out, hitting another three fours and six sixes. When the last over began he was 73, but a final six off the last ball of the innings carried him past his century. Furthermore it was not slogging. Next day it was the turn of David Leatherdale, with 76, and Ian Botham, who scored 61 in 44 minutes as Worcestershire totalled 304 all out in 55 overs. Ireland could not match the run-rate, but Smyth scored a splendid 59 not out on his début.

A week later, at Coleraine, came the first three-day match of the season, and Ireland's first victory for three years. MCC were the visitors for a game sponsored by Allied Irish Banks. Another new cap, A. R. Dunlop (69), and the recently appointed captain, Warke (81), were the main contributors to Ireland's first-innings total of 275 for eight declared. When the visitors batted, McCrum and Harrison took three wickets each, with MCC's 243 (A. J. Goldsmith 76) represented a recovery from 160 for eight. On the third morning Ireland reached 64 for two, but then slumped to 99 all out as M. J. Thursfield took five for 15. Ironically this low score probably turned the match in their favour. Had Ireland batted on, there would have been too little time to bowl out their visitors. Chasing 132, MCC were given a flying start by Gehan Mendis of Lancashire; when Harrison bowled him, he had made 49 of his team's 55 runs. Mendis was the fourth man out, and MCC had lost two more wickets, with 46 still required, when the final hour began. However, eight overs were now lost to rain, raising the rate to 4 an over, and when O'Reilly bowled Giles Toogood for 30 MCC, with four overs to go, were 112 for nine and needed 20 to win. They were still 7 runs short when A. T. Crouch was caught on the mid-wicket boundary with five balls remaining. It was Ireland's first win since they defeated MCC at Lord's in 1987.

Ten days later they had to face county opposition again. Sussex overwhelmed them in a nine-wicket win at Downpatrick, in a NatWest Bank Trophy match which could not start until 3.30 p.m. and finished at 7.45 p.m. Six of Ireland's wickets went to Tony Dodemaide, for 9 runs, a performance which earned him the Man of the Match award.

In late July a new venue, Kimmage in Dublin, hosted the annual three-day match against Wales, sponsored by Mycil Products. A good pitch and sunshine brought plenty of runs. Warke declared Ireland's first innings at 299 for four, of which he had made 65 and D. A. Lewis 136 not out in two and a half hours, his maiden international century and the highest score by an Irish batsman against Wales. Bowling for Ireland for the first time, off-spinner Dunlop took five for 26 to give them a 97-run lead, and more consistent batting in the second innings left Wales to score 268 to win in 193 minutes plus twenty overs. They were 124 for four when A. C. Puddle and B. J. Lloyd put on 109 in 85 minutes, but Harrison, who finished with seven for 91, began to spin his way through the lower order. With 4 runs needed from the last ball, the Welsh No. 10 failed to connect and was bowled, leaving the match drawn.

The annual first-class fixture against Scotland was played at Myreside, Edinburgh, in mid-August. The only memorable features for Ireland were Warke's hundred, his second against Scotland, and Harrison's bowling. In 23.2 overs the off-spinner took nine for 113, becoming the only bowler with nine first-class wickets in an innings in the British Isles during 1990, and the first Irishman to achieve the feat since 1957. Warke and Harrison were also Ireland's leading players over the season. In eight matches Warke scored 368 at 36.80, and reached 2,000 career runs to join I. J. Anderson, S. F. Bergin, J. F. Short and A. J. O'Riordan. He was followed by Lewis, who averaged 34.55 from 311 runs, and Dunlop, with 183 runs at 36.60. Newcomer Smyth averaged 47.00 for his 141 runs. Harrison's 26 wickets came at 17.69 each, well ahead of A. N. Nelson, with 13 wickets at 29.38, and McCrum, with 11 at 37.72. Wicket-keeper Jackson claimed his 100th dismissal during the season, and M. F. Cohen earned his 50th cap.

An Irish Under-23 team spent five days in Scotland in August, playing three Scottish Districts Under-23 sides and a two-day game against Scotland Under-23, though the second day was washed out. M. A. Nulty's performances on this tour forced the selectors to recall him for the team to tour Zimbabwe in March 1991, and leg-spinner Hoey was also named for the tour. The Schools eleven was not strong in 1990, and did well to draw with England over two days at Winchester College, after losing to Wales in their three-day match at Ynysygerwn.

The Ulster Bank-sponsored Interprovincial Cup was played according to a new format, whereby the six teams assembled for a festival weekend in the

Northern area and played the nine North/South matches over three days. The remaining six games were played later on various Sundays. Ulster Country were the winners, their first success since 1979. Needing to win their last match against Ulster Town, they did so handsomely – a relief after two years in which they had not lost a match, but had drawn too often to win the tournament they had dominated in the 1970s. The Under-19 interprovincial tournament was won by North-West, while Leinster and Northern Unions shared the Under-15 tournament in Cork. For Leinster, A. Joyce scored 100 not out, 73 and 106 in three matches.

In the Schweppes Cup, a national competition at senior club level, Lurgan recorded their third win in the Cup's nine-year history, recovering from a bad start against Dublin's Clontarf when Ross McCollum struck 91 off 89 balls. Lurgan have become a force in Northern club cricket. In 1989 they won the Northern Union Cup for only the second time, and one year on they claimed their first title in the league, sponsored by Lombard & Ulster Bank, albeit having to share the honour with North of Ireland, joint title-holders three times since 1986 and outright winners in 1987. In the Cup, however, North of Ireland beat holders Lurgan by three wickets in the two-innings final – their nineteenth win since 1889. For only the third time in 26 seasons Waringstown failed to win or share any of the competitions. In the North West, Donemana went back a notch. They did win the Prudential-sponsored league, but only after a play-off with a revitalised Eglinton, who won the Northern Bank Cup to deprive Donemana of their usual league and cup double.

In Dublin the powerful YMCA team won the Belvedere Bond league without losing a game, and the Sportsgear Cup. Their bid for the treble failed when they lost their semi-final of the Wiggins Teape league to Clontarf, the second-best team in the province, who went on to beat Old Belvedere in the final by ten wickets. Clontarf's D. A. Vincent scored thrilling centuries in this and the Sportsgear final, an unprecedented double. During the year it was announced that in 1993 the fourteen senior clubs in the Dublin area would be divided into two leagues of seven, with results over the intervening two seasons determining who should be in which section. All fourteen, however, will compete in the knockout cup and in the Wiggins Teape league in August. In Munster, Waterford won the cup, but surrendered their league title to Limerick. In 1990 County Galway played in this league, which necessitated a 320-mile round trip for fixtures against Waterford.

Exciting prospects for 1991 included the three-week tour of Zimbabwe in March and home matches against the West Indian tourists and against Middlesex in the NatWest Bank Trophy. Ireland also looked forward to the Under-19 tournament in Winnipeg, hoping to repeat the success of their visit to Canada in 1979 when they reached the final of this tournament for the only time.

SCOTTISH CRICKET IN 1990

By J. WATSON BLAIR

While another excellent summer produced a surfeit of runs throughout Scotland, the national side had their best season for many years with four victories, including a memorable one away to Northamptonshire in the Benson and Hedges Cup in May. Following a close encounter with

Nottinghamshire at Titwood in Glasgow, which did not end until after 7.30 p.m. on the second day, the Scotland players left for Northampton by coach. Arriving at their hotel at 3.30 a.m. was not the best preparation for an important match, but the team shrugged off tiredness to win by 2 runs and record their second success in the Benson and Hedges Cup. Ian Philip failed by just 5 runs to become the first Scot to score a century in the competition.

Although they lost their other three Benson and Hedges matches, Scotland's run-rate of 66.66 per 100 balls was the second-best in Group D after Essex, who headed the table with a scoring-rate of 82.35. In addition to Philip's efforts, there were regular contributions from Gordon Greenidge, a new recruit to Scottish colours, the captain, Richard Swan, and Omar Henry, Scotland's player-coach. Scotland met Essex again in the first round of the NatWest Bank Trophy, but Chelmsford has never been a successful ground for them, and Graham Gooch's century set up a nine-wicket victory for the county.

The visit of the Indian tourists in July attracted a large crowd to Titwood for an entertaining 55-overs game. Despite a stand of 122 runs in 81 minutes for the sixth wicket between Henry (74) and Bruce Russell (48), Scotland reached only 196 for seven, a total which the Indians passed with three and a half overs to spare, for the loss of three wickets. However, the following week the recently formed England Amateur XI were beaten by Scotland in what were loosely described as two amateur one-day internationals. Scotland won by 65 runs at Nunholm, Dumfries, and by 2 runs next day at Hamilton Crescent, Glasgow.

August brought the senior internationals to a close with a drawn match against Ireland at Myreside, Edinburgh, followed by the biennial visit to Lord's to play MCC. The former, the only regular first-class match in the calendar of Ireland or Scotland, was disrupted by rain, but Philip registered exactly 100 in Scotland's innings, his second hundred in this fixture. At Lord's, however, Scotland won for the first time since 1874. Gehan Mendis of Lancashire scored 57 out of MCC's first-innings 198 and Scotland declared at 190 for eight before lunch on the second day. A sparkling unbeaten 101 from Steve Wundke, an Australian, enabled MCC to reply with 218 for six declared, setting a target of 227, but Philip with 83, George Salmond (56 not out) and Russell (38 not out) successfully countered the MCC attack, and the clock, to score the winning runs with seven wickets to spare.

In this match the Scots were led to victory by Henry, as Richard Swan was retained by the pressures of business, and at the conclusion of the season the 38-year-old Swan announced that he was giving up the captaincy. A farmer in the Borders, and a stalwart of the Carlton club in the East League, he was educated at Merchiston Castle School and Durham University and first appeared for Scotland in 1974 against MCC. Since then he has represented his country 82 times, a figure surpassed only by Jimmy Brown of Perthshire, and has captained it on 62 occasions – well ahead of Brown, who led Scotland 53 times, and George Goddard (Heriot's FP), 35 times. To the end of 1990, his aggregate of runs in 97 innings for Scotland was 2,105 with a highest score of 100 and an average of 23.38. That total included 49 appearances in limited-overs competitions with the English counties, against whom he scored 1,128 runs with a highest innings of 64 and an average of 23.50. His first-class bowling figures must be rare: against Ireland in 1983 he returned 0.4–0–0–0 (byes from the fourth delivery gave Ireland victory). Swan received special awards from Famous Grouse and the East League for his invaluable contribution to Scottish cricket.

Scotland B began their season with two one-day matches against Durham University at the Racecourse Ground in June, losing the first and winning the second. At the end of July they travelled to Grace Road for a one-day game against Leicestershire Second Eleven, followed by a three-day match with Nottinghamshire Second Eleven at Trent Bridge. With most of the county's contract players on duty, this second game was an uphill struggle for the young Scots. Nottinghamshire declared twice, at 410 for two and 212 for five, and Scotland B replied with 359 for seven declared and 146 for eight to draw. Bruce Patterson scored 125 and 65 for the visitors. A two-day match at Under-23 level between Scotland and Ireland at Cambusdoon in Ayr petered out in a disappointing draw, washed out by rain after an interesting first day. Earlier the Irish side had beaten the North District and drawn with the East and the West in Scotland's Under-23 District Championship.

Scotland's Young Cricketers had a disappointing season. The Under-19 side lost by six wickets to the Welsh Schools in a three-day match at Titwood in mid-May, while the Welsh Under-16s triumphed by the same margin to complete the double. The subsequent visits to Lancashire to challenge the more experienced English Schools produced slightly better results. The Under-19 match was drawn, but in the Under-16 engagement the Scots were beaten in the final over. Sanjay Patel of Clackmannanshire, son of the local professional, scored 112 on his début in representative cricket and looked like developing into a fine batsman.

In the Area Championship, sponsored by Ryden & Partners, the North again won the league section, but they were beaten in the knockout by Edinburgh, who in turn were beaten in the final at Glenpark by Strathclyde West. This match, as well as avenging Strathclyde West's defeat by Edinburgh in the 1989 final, was a personal triumph for Greenock's Peter Duthie, whose performances with both bat and ball undoubtedly turned the game. Grange, champions of Division 1 in the East League, ahead of Royal High and Stenhousemuir, beat Strathmore County to win the Scottish Cup, and also won the Towry Law Cup (formerly the Masterton Trophy) and the Evening Knockout Cup. Division 2 of the Ryden & Partners East League was headed by Watsonians, with Corstorphine as runners-up, Division 3 by Fauldhouse with Marchmont second, and Division 4 by Dalgety Bay followed by Largo. The individual awards went to two Carlton players, Hugh Parker for his batting and Allan McLeod for bowling.

The Western Union competition, sponsored by D. M. Hall, was won by West of Scotland, with Greenock and Ferguslie runners-up and third respectively. The Second Eleven champions were Greenock, and Kelburne won both the Third Eleven and Junior titles. Individual awards went to Duthie of Greenock for batting and, for the second year in succession, to Ronald McGregor (Ferguslie) for bowling. In the final of the West League Cup, Ayrshire beat the holders, West of Scotland, who also lost the Rowan Charity Cup final to Greenock. Throughout the Western Union, professionals played an important role in coaching, not only the senior sides but all players and at various levels, and their value was seen in the success of Western Union clubs in the Bank of Scotland's national age-group leagues. Ayr defeated Strathmore in the final of the Under-18 competition, and Clydesdale Under-15s successfully accounted for Freuchie in their league.

The Scottish Counties Championship was won by Ayrshire on the last Saturday of the season when they defeated their nearest challengers, Strathmore County, beaten finalists in the Scottish Cup at the beginning of the week. Aberdeenshire finished some way back in third place. Lack of sponsorship prevented the staging of the cup competition or awards for best performances. Professionals dominated the averages, but the top amateur bowler, with 23 wickets, was Colin Mitchell of Aberdeenshire, while the Ayrshire and Scotland wicket-keeper, David Haggo, was the leading amateur batsman with 428 runs. Haggo also won the Famous Grouse award for being Scotland's top wicket-keeper. Other Famous Grouse awards went to Duthie as best all-rounder, Philip of Stenhousemuir as best batsman, and McLeod of Carlton as best bowler. The achievements of Grange throughout the season deservedly won the Edinburgh club the title Team of the Year. Of their batsmen, Alec Davies and Chris Warner were consistently outstanding, while David Orr was the star of their three cup successes, scoring 493 runs without being dismissed.

Winners of the other leagues and competitions included – *Strathmore Union*: Aberdeen GSFP. *Three Counties Cup*: Aberdeen GSFP. *Two Counties Cup*: Lawside. *Border League*: Kelso, for the seventh season in succession, with a 100 per cent record. *Border Knockout Cup*: Gala. *Nottinghamshire Sports Small Clubs Cup*: Old Grammarians. *Perthshire Cricket League*: Crieff. *Bon Accord Cup*: Mannofield. *Perthshire League Cup*: Crieff. *Glasgow & District League Division 1*: East Kilbride; *Division 2*: Milngavie & Bearsden; *Division 3*: Old Grammarians. *Glasgow & District Knockout Cup*: Glasgow High/Kelvinside. *North of Scotland League*: Ross County. *North of Scotland Reserve League*: Elgin Second Eleven. *North of Scotland Knockout Cup*: Keith. *North of Scotland Reserve League Cup*: Ross County Second Eleven. *Tony Leicester Cup*: Thornliebank. *Cockspur Cup* (Scottish section): Clydesdale. *Glasgow Evening League Division 1*: Weirs; *Division 2*: Glasgow Academicals. *Glasgow Evening League Knockout Cup*: Vale of Leven. *McLays of Alloa Indoor Sixes*: Ayrshire.

The Scottish Cricket Union experienced an eventful year, with Douglas Lawrence (Royal High FP) faithfully and diligently carrying out his duties as president. His successor in 1991, Andy Little, played cricket and rugby for Glasgow High/Kelvinside for many years, and with more than a share of success. Robin Prentice retired from the office of administrator, and from May 1 a new post, general manager, was created. The first incumbent, Peter Wilkinson, was formerly a lieutenant-colonel in the Royal Marines; after a two-year spell as administrator of the Northern Ireland Cricket Association, he appeared well equipped for the job of maintaining an efficient operation as Scottish cricket looked to increase its commitments. However, the AGM of the Union, in Glasgow on December 19, revealed a considerable financial loss on the year, following a substantial profit in 1989. The post of cricket chairman, vacated by Don Haines (Poloc), was filled by Chris Carruthers, of Fettes College, who has been at the forefront of Scottish youth cricket for many years.

The SCU has been making strenuous efforts to set up a national league to commence in 1992. To date, the response has been mixed: late in 1990 the Western Union clubs rejected the idea, and the more senior clubs in the East League were of a similar mind. Discussions will undoubtedly continue throughout 1991, with sponsorship likely to be the deciding factor. Indeed, sponsorship is now essential if the game is to continue and progress, especially as costs in all departments are escalating. The SCU is indebted to the Scottish Sports Council, the Bank of Scotland, the Clydesdale Bank, the Royal Mail and many others who have provided invaluable financial assistance throughout the years.

PAKISTAN YOUNG CRICKETERS IN ENGLAND, 1990

England's Young Cricketers entertained their Pakistani counterparts for the first time – Pakistan were the only major cricketing country they had not met at Under-19 level – and did well in winning the "Test" series and sharing the honours in the two one-day "internationals". The series was sponsored by Bull as part of their commitment to the new TCCB/NCA Development of Excellence programme at Under-15, Under-17 and Under-19 age-groups.

Well captained by Moin Khan, their wicket-keeper-batsman, and managed and coached by the former Test cricketers, Majid Khan and Haroon Rashid, the young Pakistanis were an attractive touring side, with a number of players who had, or were on the brink of, experience of first-class cricket. Indeed, two of the team, Moin Khan and Zahid Fazal, went on to play for Pakistan in the Test series against West Indies. Touring England in 1990, the team had the good fortune of encountering the kindest of English summers, as well as the benefit of playing their main matches under the watchful, and sometimes stern, eyes of first-class umpires. Certainly, the stridence and frequency of their appealing, at times unwarranted, appeared to lessen as the tour progressed.

England's selectors kept faith, in the main, with the players who had wintered, not altogether successfully, in Australia. In Wayne Noon, the Northamptonshire reserve wicket-keeper, they had an ideal captain, and there were promising batting performances from John Crawley of Lancashire, Piran Holloway of Warwickshire and Matthew Keech of Middlesex. Dominic Cork of Derbyshire bowled quickly and accurately, and scored a match-saving hundred in the Third "Test", while Alex Barnett of Middlesex provided some excellent spells of left-arm spin.

The tour party was: Majid Khan (*manager*), Haroon Rashid (*assistant manager and coach*), Moin Khan (Karachi, *captain*), Ataur Rahman (Lahore), Athar Laeeq (Karachi), Masroor Hussain (Multan), Mujahid Jamshed (Lahore Division), Maqsood Rana (Lahore), Mushahid Afridi (Karachi), Naeem Khan (Sargodha), Naseer Ahmed (Rawalpindi), Rashid Mehmood (Karachi/PNSC), Shahid Hussain (Peshawar), Shakeel Ahmed (Gujranwala), Sohail Ahmed Qureshi (Hyderabad), Tariq Mehmood (Lahore), Zahid Fazal (Gujranwala/PACO).

RESULTS

Matches 14: Won 8, Lost 2, Drawn 4.

Note: None of the matches played was first-class.

v England Under-17: at Southgate CC, July 31. Pakistan Young Cricketers won by 213 runs. Pakistan Young Cricketers 312 for six (55 overs) (Mujahid Jamshed 144, Rashid Mehmood 74); England Under-17 99 for eight (55 overs) (Maqsood Rana four for 20).

v Middlesex Young Cricketers: at Ealing CC, August 1. Pakistan Young Cricketers won by 203 runs. Pakistan Young Cricketers 298 for six (55 overs) (Rashid Mehmood 113, Zahid Fazal 78); Middlesex Young Cricketers 95.

v NCA England Amateur XI: at Esher CC, August 2. Pakistan Young Cricketers won by three wickets. NCA England Amateur XI 188 for seven (55 overs) (M. J. Roberts 60, R. J. Leipe 40); Pakistan Young Cricketers 189 for seven (53.3 overs).

v MCC Young Cricketers: at Charterhouse, August 3, 4, 5. Drawn. Pakistan Young Cricketers 309 for seven dec. (Tariq Mehmood 85, Zahid Fazal 81) and 246 (Zahid Fazal 78); MCC Young Cricketers 397 for nine dec. (T. K. Chadwick 209 not out; Sohail Ahmed Qureshi six for 140) and 76 for six.

v English Schools CA: at NatWest Bank Ground, Beckenham, August 6. Pakistan Young Cricketers won by four wickets. English Schools CA 194 for seven (55 overs) (D. P. Fulton 59; Rashid Mehmood three for 47); Pakistan Young Cricketers 195 for six (Tariq Mehmood 54 not out).

v England Young Cricketers (First one-day "international"): at Lord's, August 8. England Young Cricketers won by 76 runs. Toss: England Young Cricketers. England Young Cricketers 218 for nine (55 overs) (P. C. L. Holloway 32, K. A. Butler 77, W. M. Noon 51; Athar Laeeq four for 40); Pakistan Young Cricketers 142 (42.2 overs) (Masroor Hussain 36, Zahid Fazal 39; J. C. Hallett three for 26, D. G. Cork four for 24).

v England Young Cricketers (Second one-day "international"): at The Oval, August 10. Pakistan Young Cricketers won by 23 runs. Toss: England Young Cricketers. Pakistan Young Cricketers 220 for nine (55 overs) (Rashid Mehmood 38, Shakeel Ahmed 39, Naseer Ahmed 77; D. G. Cork three for 68); England Young Cricketers 197 (52.4 overs) (P. C. L. Holloway 60, M. Keech 32, Extras 32; Athar Laeeq four for 33).

v Combined Services: at RAF Vine Lane, Uxbridge, August 11, 12. Pakistan Young Cricketers won by seven wickets. Combined Services 230 for eight dec. (Capt. J. W. F. Cottrell 45, 2nd Lt R. J. Greatorex 43, Pte J. G. Storey 41, J. Tech. A. Elks 46; Shahid Hussain four for 78) and 164 (Flight Lt A. P. Laws 55; Shahid Hussain six for 49); Pakistan Young Cricketers 220 (Shakeel Ahmed 52, Naseer Ahmed 54; L. Seaman R. Learmouth six for 76) and 178 for three (Shakeel Ahmed 78, Rashid Mehmood 55).

v Northamptonshire Second XI: at Oundle School, August 15, 16, 17. Pakistan Young Cricketers won by 236 runs. Pakistan Young Cricketers 340 (Mujahid Jamshed 163, Tariq Mehmood 54, Moin Khan 50 not out) and 252 for five dec. (Tariq Mehmood 56, Masroor Hussain 52 not out); Northamptonshire Second XI 242 (P. J. Berry 150; Shahid Hussain six for 76) and 114 (R. R. Montgomerie 37; Maqsood Rana four for 30, Shahid Hussain four for 38).

ENGLAND YOUNG CRICKETERS v PAKISTAN YOUNG CRICKETERS

First "Test" Match

At Northampton, August 18, 19, 20, 21. Drawn. Toss: Pakistan Young Cricketers. With the start delayed for two hours by overnight rain, and all of the second day washed out, a draw seemed inevitable. Rashid Mehmood and Mujahid Jamshed gave Pakistan a marvellous start with an opening stand of 156, but Barnett and Roberts, the local leg-spinner, used the conditions well and pegged them to 266 for six at the close. Rashid batted for just over three and a half hours before becoming Roberts's third victim. Some rapid scoring on the third morning prefaced Pakistan's declaration, whereupon England, principally through a stand of 155 in 40 overs between Holloway and Crawley, made their position safe, ending the day at 269 for four. Next day Butler and Roberts tried to accelerate, but Athar Laeeq held things in check and the eventual lead was 54 runs. When Pakistan started their second innings badly, losing three wickets before clearing the deficit, there was the faint possibility of the day going England's way. Instead, Zahid Fazal thwarted them with a remarkable innings of 73, twice clearing the pavilion with tremendous sixes. The ball was not returned the second time.

Pakistan Young Cricketers

Rashid Mehmood st Noon b Roberts	76	– (2) c Roberts b Gough	0
Mujahid Jamshed c Holloway b Barnett	98	– (1) c Roberts b Hallett	7
Shakeel Ahmed c Crawley b Roberts	10	– (6) c Noon b Barnett	5
Zahid Fazal b Barnett	7	– b Grayson	73
Tariq Mehmood lbw b Roberts	3	– (3) c Noon b Gough	24
Naseer Ahmed c Grayson b Gough	57	– (5) c Noon b Barnett	4
*†Moin Khan c Crawley b Barnett	1		
Shahid Hussain b Gough	34	– (7) not out	49
Athar Laeeq not out	3	– (8) c Crawley b Grayson	0
Maqsood Rana (did not bat)		– (9) b Gough	2
Ataur Rahman (did not bat)		– (10) not out	1
L-b 7, n-b 2	9	B 4, l-b 2	6

1/156 2/173 3/184 4/189 5/206   (8 wkts dec.) 298   1/1 2/23 3/45 4/68   (8 wkts) 171
6/213 7/280 8/298   5/100 6/122 7/122 8/162

Bowling: *First Innings*—Gough 13.1–3–45–2; Hallett 13–1–64–0; Cork 14–1–59–0; Barnett 34–14–69–3; Roberts 22–6–54–3. *Second Innings*—Gough 13–1–53–3; Hallett 6–1–25–1; Barnett 16–4–25–2; Cork 1–0–5–0; Roberts 11–1–57–0; Grayson 4–4–0–2.

England Young Cricketers

A. P. Grayson b Athar Laeeq	18	J. C. Hallett c Shakeel Ahmed
P. C. L. Holloway		b Maqsood Rana . 1
lbw b Athar Laeeq .	96	D. Gough lbw b Maqsood Rana 8
J. P. Crawley lbw b Shahid Hussain . . .	93	D. G. Cork c Tariq Mehmood
M. Keech b Shahid Hussain	10	b Shahid Hussain . 13
K. A. Butler c Tariq Mehmood		A. A. Barnett not out 4
b Athar Laeeq .	43	B 3, l-b 7, w 1, n-b 6 17
A. R. Roberts st Shakeel Ahmed		
b Shahid Hussain .	33	1/42 2/197 3/218 4/231 5/300 352
*†W. M. Noon b Ataur Rahman	16	6/304 7/309 8/321 9/344

Bowling: Maqsood Rana 20–2–67–2; Ataur Rahman 19.3–0–72–1; Athar Laeeq 31–8–90–3; Shahid Hussain 49–20–66–4; Rashid Mehmood 18–3–47–0.

Umpires: B. Dudleston and B. J. Meyer.

v **English Schools CA:** at Worksop College, August 24, 25, 26. Drawn. English Schools CA 188 (J. Hodgson 48 not out; Ataur Rahman four for 34) and 342 (G. Archer 98, R. Murray 61, I. Maynard 64, J. Hodgson 48 not out; Ataur Rahman three for 73); Pakistan 263 (Masroor Hussain 105; S. V. Laudat three for 58, A. C. Richards three for 50) and 207 for six (Shakeel Ahmed 61 not out; J. Hodgson three for 60).

ENGLAND YOUNG CRICKETERS v PAKISTAN YOUNG CRICKETERS

Second "Test" Match

At Leeds, August 28, 29, 30. England Young Cricketers won by nine wickets. Toss: Pakistan Young Cricketers. England's victory, with a day to spare, rewarded the players and selectors alike for much hard work, and provided compensation for some earlier disappointments. A stirring, unbeaten 114 by Moin Khan, who hit two sixes and thirteen fours, held England up on the opening day, the Pakistan captain adding 84 for the last wicket with Ataur Rahman, who kept out 57 balls while contributing 6 runs. Otherwise, the only defiance came early on from Zahid Fazal and Shakeel Ahmed in a fourth-wicket partnership of 69. Gough and Cork did sterling work after Hallett had injured a finger, fielding off his own bowling, and they fully deserved the nine wickets they shared. However, Pakistan's 277 took on a better aspect when Moin crowned his day by catching both England openers and sending the home country to supper at 26 for three. That England managed a first-innings lead of 48 was due to Crawley nd the three seam bowlers. The tall, upright Crawley batted for four and a half hours and hit hirteen fours, while Hallett remained unbeaten for four hours, first adding 59 in 30 overs with Gough, following Crawley's dismissal, and then 79 for the last wicket with Cork on a pitch of ncreasingly variable bounce. Having experienced at first hand the problems of batting, Cork hen set about the Pakistanis' second innings, taking the first three wickets in nineteen balls at cost of 2 runs. Hallett's introduction allowed no possibility of a recovery, and in two and a uarter hours the innings was over, leaving England to score just 31 for victory.

Pakistan Young Cricketers

Mujahid Jamshed lbw b Cork	15	– c Noon b Cork	4
Rashid Mehmood c Noon b Gough	7	– b Cork	3
Tariq Mehmood c Noon b Cork	24	– c Holloway b Hallett	11
Zahid Fazal c Keech b Gough	32	– lbw b Cork	1
Shakeel Ahmed lbw b Cork	64	– c Noon b Hallett	9
Naseer Ahmed lbw b Gough	0	– c Crawley b Cork	0
†Moin Khan not out	114	– c Noon b Hallett	6
Shahid Hussain c Butler b Cork	0	– lbw b Hallett	29
Athar Laeeq lbw b Gough	1	– c Grayson b Hallett	4
Naeem Khan c Noon b Roberts	5	– b Gough	1
Ataur Rahman c and b Gough	6	– not out	1
B 1, l-b 6, n-b 2	9	B 5, l-b 4	9
	277		**78**

1/15 2/37 3/48 4/117 5/117   277   1/4 2/13 3/15 4/35 5/36   78
6/157 7/159 8/182 9/193   6/38 7/55 8/67 9/76

Bowling: *First Innings*—Gough 27.2–4–106–5; Hallett 3–0–21–0; Cork 24–8–73–4; Barnett 10–8–47–0; Roberts 12–4–23–1. *Second Innings*—Gough 12–5–18–1; Cork 15–7–18–4; Hallett 13.3–4–33–5.

England Young Cricketers

A. P. Grayson c Moin Khan b Naeem Khan	11	– c Zahid Fazal b Ataur Rahman	9
C. L. Holloway c Moin Khan b Ataur Rahman	8	– not out	20
A. Barnett c Rashid Mehmood b Ataur Rahman	0		
P. Crawley c Moin Khan b Shahid Hussain	84	– (3) not out	5
A. Butler b Naeem Khan	10		
M. Keech lbw b Naeem Khan	22		
R. Roberts c Shakeel Ahmed b Athar Laeeq	17		
†W. M. Noon lbw b Ataur Rahman	25		
C. Hallett not out	55		
D. Gough c Moin Khan b Shahid Hussain	36		
G. Cork lbw b Zahid Fazal	45		
B 1, l-b 7, n-b 4	12		
	325		**(1 wkt) 34**

1/19 2/19 3/25 4/42 5/99   325   1/20   (1 wkt) 34
6/132 7/175 8/187 9/246

Bowling: *First Innings*—Naeem Khan 39–12–81–3; Ataur Rahman 32–10–79–3; Athar Laeeq 35–7–105–1; Shahid Hussain 29–17–36–2; Rashid Mehmood 1–0–4–0; Zahid Fazal 4–0–12–1. *Second Innings*—Ataur Rahman 5–1–19–1; Naeem Khan 4.1–1–15–0.

Umpires: J. W. Holder and D. O. Oslear.

National Association of Young Cricketers: at Millfield School, September 2, 3, 4. Pakistan Young Cricketers won by an innings and 7 runs. Pakistan Young Cricketers 339 (Mujahid Jamshed 127, Zahid Fazal 61; A. Hollioake four for 92); National Association of Young Cricketers 108 (S. V. Laudat 47 not out; Athar Laeeq four for 26, Shahid Hussain four for 28) and 224 (Wasim Khan 82, A. Hollioake 48).

ENGLAND YOUNG CRICKETERS v PAKISTAN YOUNG CRICKETERS

Third "Test" Match

At Taunton, September 7, 8, 9, 10. Drawn. Toss: Pakistan Young Cricketers. The Pakistanis winning the toss for the third time in the series, took full advantage of first use of a benign pitch. They lost Mujahid Jamshed in the first over, but Tariq Mehmood and Shakeel Ahmed set them on their way with a partnership of 227 in 63 overs. Tariq hit eighteen fours in his 106 and Shakeel's 190 contained a six and 27 fours; he had batted for six hours when he succumbed to the new ball. Resuming next day at 384 for three, Pakistan progressed without much difficulty to 561 for five, a declaration which left England to score 412 to avoid following on. At stumps they were 123 for two, and on Sunday, after Ataur Rahman had made an early breakthrough, Keech batted determinedly for four and a half hours while scoring 87. Roberts and Noon helped, but by now Shahid Hussain was flighting his left-arm spin into the bowlers' rough and posing endless problems. By the close, England were batting again and had lost their openers. When Cork, the night-watchman, came to the wicket on Sunday evening, they needed 181 to save an innings defeat; on Monday, the final day, he batted for five hours to deny Pakistan the win which would have levelled the series. Although defence was his main object, he none the less hit seventeen fours in his 110. There was a moment, a three wickets fell to the new ball in ten overs, when it seemed Pakistan might still have a chance, but Roberts and Gough saw off the threat.

Pakistan Young Cricketers

Mujahid Jamshed c Noon b Cork	2	*†Moin Khan not out	5
Tariq Mehmood c Keech b Hallett	106		
Shakeel Ahmed c Hallett b Cork	190	B 2, l-b 10, w 2, n-b 3	1
Zahid Fazal c Noon b Barnett	99		
Masroor Hussain c Keech b Barnett	74	1/2 2/229 3/332 (5 wkts dec.) 56	
Naseer Ahmed not out	21	4/483 5/494	

Shahid Hussain, Ataur Rahman, Athar Laeeq and Naeem Khan did not bat.

Bowling: Cork 37–8–104–2; Gough 23–2–100–0; Butler 2–0–13–0; Hallett 27–10–101–1; Barnett 35–10–111–2; Roberts 39–6–120–0.

England Young Cricketers

A. P. Grayson c Moin Khan b Athar Laeeq	43	– run out	1
P. C. L. Holloway c Moin Khan b Athar Laeeq	38	– c Zahid Fazal b Ataur Rahman	4
J. P. Crawley b Ataur Rahman	41	– b Ataur Rahman	34
K. A. Butler c Moin Khan b Ataur Rahman	19	– (5) b Athar Laeeq	2
M. Keech c Naseer Ahmed b Shahid Hussain	87	– (6) b Shakeel Ahmed b Ataur Rahman	2
A. R. Roberts c and b Naeem Khan	30	– (7) not out	2
*†W. M. Noon c Naseer Ahmed b Shahid Hussain	24	– (8) lbw b Naeem Khan	1
J. C. Hallett lbw b Shahid Hussain	5	– (9) c Shakeel Ahmed b Athar Laeeq	0
D. Gough lbw b Zahid Fazal	3	– (10) not out	1
D. G. Cork b Ataur Rahman	9	– c Naeem Khan b Athar Laeeq	110
A. A. Barnett not out	20		
B 12, l-b 17, w 6, n-b 10	45	B 10, l-b 9, n-b 3	2
	364	(8 wkts) 26	

1/91 2/100 3/148 4/173 5/242   1/5 2/16 3/55 4/127
6/311 7/323 8/326 9/332   5/204 6/240 7/243 8/244

Bowling: *First Innings*—Athar Laeeq 31–10–81–2; Naeem Khan 20–1–46–1; Ataur Rahman 31–8–79–3; Shahid Hussain 54–16–113–3; Zahid Fazal 11–4–16–1. *Second Innings*—Ataur Rahman 26–4–71–3; Naeem Khan 21–5–57–1; Shahid Hussain 31–10–55–0; Athar Laeeq 23–10–50–3; Zahid Fazal 5–2–9–0; Moin Khan 2–0–8–0.

Umpires: B. Dudleston and K. J. Lyons.

ESSO/NAYC UNDER-19 COUNTY FESTIVALS, 1990

By JOHN MINSHULL-FOGG

Essex, not unexpectedly, won the final of the fifth Esso/NAYC County Festivals, beating Hertfordshire by 92 runs at Oxford's Christ Church ground. This was the culmination of a week of cricket which had begun the previous Monday, August 13, with 32 counties taking part and playing mainly on the college grounds at Cambridge and Oxford. Gloucestershire and Buckinghamshire joined the tournament for the first time.

The counties at Oxford, in their groups, were: Somerset, Derbyshire, Hertfordshire and Leinster; Kent, Shropshire, Warwickshire and Durham; Buckinghamshire, Hampshire, Worcestershire and Berkshire; and Staffordshire, Glamorgan, Oxfordshire and Gloucestershire. At Cambridge: Middlesex, Lancashire, Surrey and Suffolk; Essex, Sussex, Norfolk and Cheshire; Yorkshire, Leicestershire, Lincolnshire and Bedfordshire; Nottinghamshire, Northamptonshire, Huntingdon & Peterborough, and Cambridgeshire. Of these, Lancashire, Yorkshire and Warwickshire (twice) had won the tournament previously.

In addition to the two new counties, the 1990 tournament introduced some amendments to the playing conditions. The overs limit was raised from 54 overs to 60 a side, and the start of play was moved forward from 10.30 a.m. to 10.45 a.m. This lengthened the hours of play significantly. Provision was made for a reduction of overs in the event of stoppages for poor weather, but only after one hour's play had been lost. It proved to be not the most ideal of changes and gave rise to a number of difficulties, not the least being the need of young cricketers to find somewhere to eat when matches finished well into the evening. At Oxford, the organisers chose to take an independent line by reverting to the original format for some matches, though the area final was played over the full distance. It produced an upset when Warwickshire, strong and confident favourites for a hat-trick of victories, were beaten by Hertfordshire, a minor county. In the Cambridge area final, Essex beat Surrey to become the first holders of the Norman Yardley Trophy, presented by the family of the late England, Yorkshire and Cambridge University captain for the winners of the Cambridge festival. Essex then travelled to Oxford that Friday evening to take on Hertfordshire the following day.

AREA FINALS

At Cambridge, August 17. Essex won by 38 runs. Toss: Essex. Essex 238 for five (60 overs) (D. J. Robinson 65, A. C. Richards 56 not out); Surrey 200 (55.5 overs) (M. Hodgson 65; T. Kemp five for 55, A. C. Richards four for 90).

At Oxford, August 17. Hertfordshire won by 3 runs. Toss: Warwickshire. Hertfordshire 174 for nine (60 overs) (S. Moffat 44; E. Bourke four for 36); Warwickshire 171 (58.5 overs) (E. Bourke 46; D. Hodges four for 38).

FINAL

ESSEX v HERTFORDSHIRE

At Christ Church, Oxford, August 18. Essex won by 92 runs. Toss: Essex. Batting first on a good pitch, Bate and Robinson gave Essex a sound start with 81 for the first wicket in 27 overs. Bate went on to complete a good half-century, and there was another from Churchill of Hornchurch as Essex piled on the pressure in pursuit of a large total. Hertfordshire in reply were quickly in trouble, losing three wickets for 14, all to Carpenter of Chingford. Benyon, the captain, and Smith, both of the Welwyn club, added 50, but that was the only serious resistance before Kemp and Ranawat, the latter spinning the ball tidily, bowled out the minor county inside their allotted 60 overs.

Essex

M. R. Bate run out	50	R. Slater run out		(
D. J. Robinson b Wilkins	34	A. Ranawat not out		(
*S. C. Ecclestone c Griffin b Skeggs	25	L-b 17, w 3		20
Gul Abbas c Easterbrook b Yeabsley	22			
A. Churchill b Yeabsley	55	1/81 2/118 3/144	(8 wkts, 60 overs)	25?
A. C. Richards c Chippeck b Wilkins	23	4/150 5/189 6/246		
†R. Rollins run out	22	7/251 8/251		

J. Carpenter and T. Kemp did not bat.

Bowling: Easterbrook 8–2–24–0; Skeggs 14–5–43–1; Wilkins 16–1–77–2; Hodges 7–0–34–0; Yeabsley 15–3–56–2.

Hertfordshire

S. Moffat lbw b Carpenter	2	†A. Griffin lbw b Ranawat		(
D. Chippeck b Carpenter	6	D. Hodges not out		3?
S. Crosier c Richards b Carpenter	0	S. Easterbrook st Rollins b Ranawat		?
R. Smith c Robinson b Ranawat	24	B 4, l-b 3, w 8		1?
*D. Benyon c Bate b Ranawat	39	1/5 2/7 3/14	(56.3 overs)	15?
A. Wilkins c Richards b Kemp	5	4/64 5/72 6/101		
M. I. Yeabsley c Ecclestone b Kemp	30	7/101 8/103 9/137		
T. Skeggs run out	0			

Bowling: Slater 5–0–12–0; Carpenter 7–3–18–3; Ecclestone 4–1–9–0; Kemp 21–2–54–2; Ranawat 19.3–3–59–4.

Umpires: D. O. Oslear and R. Palmer.

SCHOOLS CRICKET IN 1990

Of the players capped for English Schools Under-19 in 1989, only M. A. Khan, T. C. Walton and A. C. Richards were available in 1990, C. J. Hawkes, T. A. Radford and R. J. Warren preferring to play for their county Second Elevens. Including the two matches at Lord's, played under the appellation of MCC Schools, fifteen players appeared for the senior Schools side. They were: G. Archer, D. P. Fulton, N. F. Gibbs, J. Hodgson, M. A. Khan, J. Laney, S. V. Laudat, I. Maynard, R. Murray, M. Rawlings, A. C. Richards (captain), J. N. Snape, T. C. Walton, Wasim Khan and W. P. C. Weston. Their schools may be found in the scorecards of matches played at the MCC Festival, Oxford.

As in other cricket arenas in 1990, the bat was dominant, and it soon became apparent from the regional trials that quality bowlers, particularly fast bowlers, were in short supply; a view confirmed at the Oxford Festival, where the majority of wickets fell to the spinners. This imbalance in the attack led to all four international matches being drawn, which was especially disappointing after MCC Schools' fine victory over a strong MCC side at Lord's and their having the best of a draw against NAYC the next day.

The batting was strong right down the order, although there was a tendency for batsmen to get out when seemingly well set. None the less, Archer, Fulton, Wasim Khan, Murray, Snape, Walton and Laney all made significant contributions, and the batting ability of the lower order was in evidence against Welsh Schools and Pakistan Young Cricketers. The main strike bowlers were Weston and Laudat but, with the exception of the Irish match, they were unable to capitalise on an initial breakthrough. The spinners were the leading wicket-takers, both Richards (off-spin) and Hodgson (leg-spin) bowling for long spells with accuracy and good variation. In a side which at times fielded quite brilliantly, Archer and Walton were outstanding, while Marcel Khan kept wicket competently and Richards captained with authority.

The first international was played against Irish Schools at Winchester College on July 26, 27. English Schools batted first, reaching 270 for nine in the allotted 60 overs with Fulton (82), Archer (50), Laney (31) and Snape (36) the main contributors. Weston's fast left-arm bowling then reduced Ireland to 23 for five, but a brave 51 from Taylor led something of a recovery to 121 all out, Weston finishing with five for 38. Following on, the Irish were 95 for five at the close, still in arrears, but the weather cut into the second day, and Ireland occupied the crease long enough in making 170 to leave English Schools only two overs in which to score 22 for victory. Five deliveries brought no run, and when 6 were needed off the last ball, only a single resulted.

At Pontarddulais on July 30, 31, Wasim Khan (105) and Fulton (68) opened with a partnership of 175 after Welsh Schools had put the English in, but some irresponsible batting further down the order led to a final total of only 228 for eight. The Welsh batting was equally disappointing, only J. R. A. Williams (36) putting up much resistance against steady bowling from Laudat (three for 24 off 15 overs) and Richards (four for 37 from 22.2) as the home side were dismissed for 152. With the exception of a positive 40 from Fulton, English Schools batted unconvincingly until an attractive partnership between Marcel Khan (34) and Laudat (39 not out) enabled

Richards to declare at 190 for nine. A target of 267 in two and a half hours plus twenty overs asked a lot of the Welsh, who mustered only 149 for seven from 59 overs.

Against Scottish Young Cricketers at Aigburth, Liverpool, on August 2, 3, English Schools elected to bat on an excellent pitch in superb weather and totalled 263 for six in 60 overs. Fulton (70) was again in good form and Snape fashioned a class innings of 88. The Scots struggled against the in-swing bowling of Walton, who took six for 17 in 9.4 overs, and were all out for 128 in 46.4 overs. When the Scots followed on, however, the English attack was once again unable to repeat its earlier performance, lacking in determination somewhat, and a century from Patel and fifties from Mudie and Garden allowed the visitors the safety of a declaration at 335 for seven and a fairly academic target of 201 in 100 minutes. English Schools were 148 for four (Snape 48, Laney 51 not out) at the close.

English Schools lost their one-day game against Pakistan Young Cricketers at Beckenham on August 6 by four wickets, despite having put up a good performance against strong opponents. Unfortunately, several first-choice players were not available for the three-day fixture at Worksop College on August 24, 25, 26. Given first use of a fresh pitch by Richards's decision to bat, the Pakistani seam attack reduced English Schools to 78 for six at lunch. Another wicket fell soon after, but the depth of batting showed as the last three wickets put on 100, Marcel Khan (25), Laudat (22), Rawlings (22) and especially Hodgson (48 not out) all batting with skill and application. A total of 188 looked useful when the Pakistanis also struggled against the new ball and slumped to 20 for three. However, Tariq Mehmood and Masroor Hussain steadied the innings, and Masroor went on next day to a fine 105. The English bowlers stuck to the task, though, and the visitors' lead was restricted to 75. Batting again, Maynard (64) and Archer added 106 in fine style, and with two overs of the day remaining a score of 247 for three was just reward for sensible strokeplay. However, Archer was dismissed in the penultimate over, missing by 2 runs a well-deserved century, and when in the last over Murray (61) trod on his wicket, the commanding position was gone. Needing 268 in 56 overs, the Pakistanis found themselves 127 for six, but Shakeel Ahmed (61 not out) guided them to 207 for no further loss to frustrate English hopes of victory. This fine, fluctuating game showed English Schools cricket at its best, especially in terms of sportsmanship and attitudes to opponents and umpires.

The Welsh Schools' season was dominated by the batting of the captain, D. L. Hemp, who scored a century in each innings against both Scottish Young Cricketers and Irish Schools. At Titwood, Glasgow, Scottish Young Cricketers declared at 306 for six (S. Millin 76 not out, N. McRae 54), to which Welsh Schools responded with 289 for four declared (Hemp 104 not out, B. Davies 65). Second time around, Scotland were dismissed for 204 (D. Rigby 48; R. Beaumont five for 40, Davies four for 49), whereupon Hemp struck 101 not out and Davies 41 as Wales made 225 for four for victory. At Ynysygerwn, Irish Schools were beaten by 202 runs. Batting first this time, Welsh Schools amassed 367 (Hemp 120, Williams 43, Davies 43; F. Ward three for 86, S. Taylor three for 87) before dismissing Irish Schools for 226 (S. McCready 76 not out; E. P. M. Holland four for 57) and then racing to 237 for one declared (Hemp 102 not out, A. J. Jones 106 not out). A change of batting order was of no avail to the Irish, who were bowled out for 176 (J. Kennedy 50; Davies four for 37).

HMC SOUTHERN SCHOOLS v THE REST

At Wadham College, July 15, 16. HMC Southern Schools won by three wickets. The Rest made a poor start, with two run-outs in the first half-hour contributing to the loss of four wickets for 44 as Yeabsley and Stevens bowled good opening spells. However, Walton and Kendall initiated a recovery and Murphy hit vigorously at the end. Fulton then played the best innings of the match, receiving useful support from the Southern Schools' middle order, and a significant lead looked in prospect until the off-spin of Chetwood and Snape pegged them back. When the Rest batted again, Janes made a solid 60, and with more vigorous knocks from Brand and Snape, Walton was able to set a target of 215 in 53 overs. Walker anchored the early part of Southern Schools' challenge, and a final flourish from Fulton took them to victory with seven balls to spare. The wicket-keeping was competent, Jaggard held three good catches, and the ground fielding of Fulton, Walton and Kendall stood out.

The Rest

Batsman	First innings		Second innings	
C. M. Jaggard (*Merchant Taylors', Northwood*)	run out	9	c Maddock b Stevens	7
A. J. Brooke (*Batley GS*)	lbw b Yeabsley	7	(3) b Yeabsley	4
A. J. Brand (*Merchant Taylors', Northwood*)	run out	9	(5) c Walker b Richards	57
N. Snape (*Denstone*)	b Stevens	4	c Semmence b Richards	39
T. C. Walton (*Leeds GS*)	b Semmence	38	(6) c Maddock b Semmence	22
T. C. Kendall (*Bradfield*)	c Inglis b Stevens	44	(7) b Stevens	0
S. C. Janes (*Hampton*)	lbw b Richards	8	(2) run out	60
J. P. Chetwood (*Eton*)	not out	11	c and b Yeabsley	28
M. Windsor (*Repton*)	b Richards	7	not out	1
G. H. Murphy (*Barnard Castle*)	b Yeabsley	33		
G. Slater (*Ellesmere*)	c Maddock b Yeabsley	0		
Extras		16		23
		186	(8 wkts dec.)	**241**

1/19 2/28 3/29 4/44 5/96 6/129 7/130 8/144 9/186   1/18 2/30 3/112 4/182 5/197 6/197 7/230 8/241

Bowling: *First Innings*—Stevens 16-3-32-2; Yeabsley 12-2-55-3; Semmence 9-5-14-1; Salter 10-2-42-0; Richards 11-2-33-2. *Second Innings*—Yeabsley 7-2-15-2; Stevens 7-1-73-2; Salter 15-5-43-0; Semmence 9-0-42-1; Richards 14-2-49-2.

HMC Southern Schools

Batsman	First innings		Second innings	
C. N. Gates (*Brighton*)	c and b Murphy	16	c Murphy b Slater	20
D. P. Fulton (*Judd*)	c Windsor b Chetwood	67	(8) not out	20
A. C. Richards (*Forest*)	c Jaggard b Chetwood	21	c and b Windsor	0
B. D. Atwell (*Sherborne*)	c Jaggard b Windsor	13	(6) c Janes b Snape	19
M. J. Walker (*King's, Rochester*)	c Snape b Chetwood	21	(2) c Janes b Murphy	63
M. A. Inglis (*Solihull*)	b Snape	26	(5) c Jaggard b Snape	38
A. R. Maddock (*Plymouth*)	c Janes b Snape	23	(4) run out	18
M. J. Semmence (*Hurstpierpoint*)	not out	6	(7) st Janes b Snape	20
R. S. Yeabsley (*Haberdashers' Aske's*)	c and b Snape	1	not out	6
M. Salter (*King Edward VI, Southampton*)	run out	0		
W. Stevens (*Sherborne*)	b Chetwood	0		
Extras		19		14
		213	(7 wkts)	**218**

1/55 2/101 3/117 4/136 5/162 6/206 7/207 8/213 9/213   1/51 2/54 3/111 4/118 5/150 6/185 7/204

Bowling: *First Innings*—Windsor 11-5-17-1; Slater 9-0-47-0; Kendall 3-0-19-0; Murphy 9-1-23-1; Snape 6-1-19-3; Chetwood 15-2-48-4; Walton 7-2-26-0. *Second Innings*—Windsor 7-0-20-1; Slater 10-3-58-1; Chetwood 14-2-48-0; Murphy 8-0-12-1; Snape 5-0-46-3; Walton 3-0-20-0.

ESCA NORTH v ESCA SOUTH

At Keble College, July 15, 16. Drawn. Although ESCA North always had the better of the match, they were unable to break through the solid defence of Gibbs and Hodgson to force the win that had looked likely when ESCA South were 37 for five in pursuit of 241. Strokeplay was not easy on the slow and turning wicket, yet it was still surprising that none of the five batsmen who reached 40 in the first three innings could go on to a half-century. Bourke's off spin and Weston's medium-fast left-arm seam bowling for the North particularly caught the eye, while Hodgson and Jacques both bowled good spells of spin for the South.

ESCA North

*Wasim Khan (*Josiah Mason SFC; Warwicks.*)		
	b Mirza . 2 – c Maynard b Bates	40
G. Archer (*Stafford CFE; Staffs.*) c Morgan		
	b Hodgson . 43	
R. Hughes (*Newbold-on-Avon; Warwicks.*)		
	b Hodgson . 42	
S. V. Laudat (*Oxford CFE; Oxon.*) b Hodgson . 12 – c Gibbs b Jacques		19
†M. A. Khan (*Aylesbury CFE; Oxon.*)		
	c Sims b Bates . 18 – (3) lbw b Mirza	8
R. Murray (*Brigshaw; Yorks.*) b Mirza . 36 – c Jacques b Bates		0
R. A. Kettleborough (*Worksop; Yorks.*)		
	c Bates b Gibbs . 35	
E. Bourke (*Archbishop Grimshaw; Warwicks.*)		
	not out . 2 – (7) not out	31
W. P. C. Weston (*Durham; Durham*) not out . 0 – (5) not out		40
R. Catley (*Ipswich; Suffolk*) (did not bat) . – (2) b Mirza		7
Extras . 43	Extras	14

1/4 2/96 3/96 4/131 5/139   (7 wkts dec.) 233   1/29 2/42 3/77   (5 wkts dec.) 159
6/228 7/233   4/87 5/88

G. Chapple (*West Craven HS; Lancs.*) did not bat.

Bowling: *First Innings*—Rawlings 8–1–19–0; Mirza 12–1–53–2; Jacques 4–0–24–0; Gibbs 12–6–24–1; Bates 10–4–29–1; Hodgson 14–3–48–3. *Second Innings*—Rawlings 11–1–37–0; Mirza 12–1–46–2; Hodgson 7–3–16–0; Bates 12–6–21–2; Gibbs 4–1–9–0; Jacques 10–5–16–1.

ESCA South

H. Morgan (*Westlands; Devon*) c Archer b Bourke 40		
I. Maynard (*QMC Basingstoke; Hants*) b Bourke 23 – c Kettleborough b Bourke		28
J. Laney (*St John's; Wilts.*) lbw b Bourke . 0 – (1) b Weston		1
P. Sims (*Lowestoft CFE; Suffolk*) c and b Bourke . 7 – (3) lbw b Bourke		12
*N. F. Gibbs (*Millfield; Som.*) b Weston . 23 – (6) not out		44
J. Hodgson (*Ranelagh; Berks.*) c Kettleborough		
	b Weston . 23 – (7) not out	18
M. Rawlings (*Filton; Avon*) c Wasim Khan		
	b Weston . 6	
†M. Garaway (*Medina; IOW*) not out . 16 – (4) c Archer b Bourke		0
R. Bates (*Stamford CFE; Lincs.*) not out . 1 – (5) c Archer b Catley		0
Extras . 13	Extras	6

1/60 2/64 3/67 4/84 5/120   (7 wkts dec.) 152   1/6 2/34 3/34   (5 wkts) 109
6/136 7/136   4/35 5/37

P. Mirza (*E. Birmingham; Warwicks.*) and P. T. Jacques (*Millfield; Som.*) did not bat.

Bowling: *First Innings*—Weston 11–5–24–3; Chapple 8–1–20–0; Catley 19–8–41–0; Bourke 18–8–35–4; Kettleborough 4–1–20–0. *Second Innings*—Chapple 10–2–27–0; Weston 8–3–6–1; Bourke 17–10–18–3; Catley 15–4–39–1; Laudat 10–1–16–0.

At Keble College, July 16. Drawn. A. C. Richards's XI 234 for eight dec. (D. P. Fulton 116, R. Hughes 36, Extras 35; P. T. Jacques three for 42, R. A. Kettleborough three for 16); Wasim Khan's XI 227 for seven (Wasim Khan 66, C. M. Jaggard 35, R. Bates 40; P. Mirza three for 48, A. C. Richards three for 63).

At St Edward's School, July 16. N. F. Gibbs's XI won by 54 runs. N. F. Gibbs's XI 259 for five dec. (G. Archer 169, J. Laney 49); T. C. Walton's XI 205 (I. Maynard 38; W. P. C. Weston three for 48).

At Christ Church, July 17. MCC Schools East won by 71 runs in a twelve-a-side match. MCC Schools East 267 for seven dec. (R. Murray 58, T. C. Walton 88, A. C. Richards 35; N. F. Gibbs three for 36, P. T. Jacques three for 95); MCC Schools West 196 (J. Laney 97, M. A. Khan 33; W. P. C. Weston three for 22, A. C. Richards three for 55).

The match at Lord's between MCC and MCC Schools may be found in the MCC section, and that at Lord's between MCC Schools and the National Association of Young Cricketers may be found in Other Matches at Lord's, 1990.

Reports from the Schools:
In a summer memorable for high scoring in county cricket, school records tumbled also. However, it is interesting to note, at a time when there has been concern over the shortening of the summer term because of exams, that a number of schools seem to be playing more matches, with the result that many schoolboy batsmen are getting more innings than in recent years. Eleven from the schools reviewed here passed 1,000 runs: C. N. Gates of Brighton (1,378 at 72.52), C. M. Jaggard (1,364 at 62.00) and A. J. Brand (1,311 at 72.83), both of Merchant Taylors', Northwood, A. R. Maddock of Plymouth College (1,128 at 86.76), J. M. Attfield of Wellingborough (1,116 at 85.84), D. P. Kerkar of Ardingly (1,102 at 61.22), D. Bowen of Enfield GS (1,089 at 64.05), K. A. Graham of King's, Macclesfield (1,075 at 76.78), G. W. White of Millfield (1,061 at 62.41), G. A. H. Awudu of Bedford Modern (1,009 at 56.05) and G. J. Kennis of Tiffin (1,008 at 72.00). Of these only Maddock played fewer than nineteen innings. No batsman recorded a three-figure average, the highest being 97.50 from 780 runs by J. M. A. Inglis of Solihull.

As runs flowed in conditions favouring batsmen, the bowlers often struggled, and a feature of the season was the high proportion of draws. Although they fared better during the poor weather of June, no bowler took 60 wickets, although twelve collected 50 or more. A. R. C. Gilmour of Merchiston Castle had the highest return with 59 at 9.45, while C. J. Eyers of Royal GS Worcester was the outstanding all-rounder with 932 runs and 51 wickets. Notable individual performances included double-centuries by Brand, S. A. I. Dyer of Campbell College, R. C. Weston of The Leys and G. W. White of Millfield. N. C. L. Sinfield of Monkton Combe took all ten wickets v Dauntsey's, who were also the victims of a hat-trick by S. B. Thomas of Wycliffe. Other hat-tricks were performed by S. C. James of King's, Macclesfield, and D. C. Hindle of King's, Ely, who had two in successive matches.

Alleyn's, Ashville College, Bedford, Bradford GS, Canford and Uppingham all participated in the Sir Garfield Sobers International Schools Festival in Barbados, where Canford and Uppingham were perhaps unfortunate not to reach the final. In their semi-final v Harrison's College, Canford were well placed at 40 for three in pursuit of 93 when rain ended play. They lost the replay. The weather similarly rescued Presentation College, who, on a difficult pitch, had been reduced by Uppingham to 6 for five in reply to 66. The English school could not gain the same advantage the next day, and the Trinidad college qualified for the final, which Harrison's College won by ten wickets.

In a relatively successful season, **Abingdon** lost only to RGS High Wycombe in schools matches, and that after a sporting declaration. Their six wins included those v Magdalen College School, Douai and St Edward's, Oxford early in the season and University College School at the end. Frequently batting second in pursuit of a target, the batsmen had limited chances to score consistently, although the opening pair of D. E. Stanley and J. S. Tilley often provided a sound base. Although there was depth in the bowling, the lack of a top-rate spinner was evident. Highlights for **Aldenham** were S. P. Moffat's unbeaten 131 v Liverpool College and a return of six for 23 by M. Okoro v Mill Hill. Unbeaten in their domestic matches, **Alleyn's** enjoyed six wins, their best record for many years, while at the Sir Garfield Sobers festival in Barbados they lost only to the two eventual finalists. The batting of the captain, P. C. Berglund, was the outstanding feature of the summer, especially his 131 not out v Highgate. A. C. Winter, opening the bowling, took 38 wickets in England, plus another twelve in Barbados, and his 116 not out there v Ashville College was the highest score of the tournament. P. Haslam took 24 wickets in his first season as a leg-spinner.

Allhallows managed no wins and were beaten seven times, a disappointing record which they attributed to their batting, bowling and fielding rarely coming good at the same time. The best performance was in the narrow defeat by Exeter School, against whom J. M. Rowe made a splendid unbeaten 122 in a total of 170 for five declared. Rowe, the captain and opening bat, invariably gave the side a good start, and he bowled his off-spin intelligently to take most wickets. R. J. Gilmore was the outstanding bowler at **Ampleforth**, his 51 wickets including a return of seven for 54 v Sedbergh. **Ardingly** won more than half their matches, notably v Lancing, Sevenoaks and St George's, Weybridge, while the only defeats were by Brighton (twice) and Reigate GS. D. P. Kerkar (1,102 runs) and the captain, M. T. E. Peirce (929 runs), both passed the previous record aggregate for the school, as well as taking 38 and 34 wickets respectively. Against Worth, Peirce hit 123 not out in a total of 269 for six, whereupon C. S. Spencer took seven for 12 in eight overs to help dismiss their opponents for 43. **Arnold** were captained by a fifth-former, M. J. Clinning, who was their most successful cricketer, whether as batsman or off-spin bowler. The other top-order batsmen tended to get out in the twenties. I. Best, bowling at medium pace, beat the bat regularly and headed the averages. Victories were recorded v Kirkham GS, Hutton GS, Bangor GS and RGS Clitheroe. A highlight for the unbeaten **Ashville College** XI was an opening partnership of 215 v Bury between the brothers, A. W. and S. R. Alexander.

All fourteen matches played by **Ballymena Academy GS** produced a positive result, ten finishing in their favour. Low-scoring games were the norm on the soft, slow wickets of May and June: Bangor GS were dismissed for 59 (M. McGladdery four for 9) in reply to 80, Antrim GS for 56 in reply to 142, and Larne GS for 85, a total overtaken for the loss of three wickets. In a season of rebuilding, **Bancroft's** results did not reflect accurately the XI's cricket. Fifteen-year-old C. S. Greenhill batted with commendable concentration and determination to total 640 in his first season, just 19 short of the record aggregate, while his opening partner, T. M. Dowling, scored quickly and stylishly, in addition to keeping wicket efficiently. T. C. Dolan, the captain, and T. W. Clark also scored freely, but called on to open the bowling neither was able to produce a match-winning performance. Though somewhat under-bowled, the side's three spinners – J. P. Manning (leg-breaks and googlies), R. Patel (off-breaks) and A. A. Khan (left-arm) – took 67 wickets between them. Under the astute captaincy of M. W. R. McCord, **Bangor GS** enjoyed another profitable season, although inconsistent batting was of continued concern. McCord (slow left-arm) took his wickets for the school to 171 and shared 89 with R. G. Scott, a fast-medium bowler whose aggregate rose to 102. Both players represented Irish Schools.

Barnard Castle failed to live up to expectations; the potentially strong batting performed only moderately, and the bowling tended to lack penetration. Still, they won six matches, notably those v The Edinburgh Academy and St Peter's, York, and enjoyed a successful tour of Denmark. A highlight was the unbeaten hundred v RGS Newcastle by J. G. H. Murphy, who in his final year improved his school figures to 1,684 runs and 137 wickets. **Bedford** beat The Leys, Rugby and Repton and lost to just two schools. R. W. H. Smith scored 578 runs in his second year as captain, with excellent hundreds v MCC and Uppingham, while B. J. A. Miller, as well as keeping wicket tidily, also passed 500 runs. The lower-order also contributed, more than once seeing the side past 200 after a stuttering start. Openers R. J. Stone and M. B. Jenkins toiled manfully, though lacking penetrating pace, but Smith could call on a variety of spin. It was encouraging to see both leg-spinners, A. Focken and D. R. Fossey, operating regularly in tandem. R. M. Pape, an Under-15 fast bowler, marked his début with five for 19 v Repton at the end-of-term festival.

Bedford Modern's excellent season contained victories over Christ's College Cambridge, St Albans, Stamford, The Leys, The Perse, Watford GS, Gentlemen of Bedfordshire and RGS Worcester, who were bowled out for 55 in reply to 224. They lost only to Scots College, from Sydney, in a 40-overs match. The captain, G. A. H. Awudu, scored 1,009 runs with four centuries, his highest being 148 v Nottingham HS, and there were two hundreds from E. R. Osborn. Two promising spinners, A. R. Woodcock (left-arm) and P. D. Brownridge, gave balance and contrast to the three strike bowlers, M. C. Waddingham (left-arm), Awudu and M. J. Rolton, and all five took 25 or more wickets. Among many noteworthy returns, Rolton took eight for 14 v Christ's College, Waddingham six for 13 v Selwyn College, and Awudu seven for 28 v Watford.

Beechen Cliff, who exceeded 200 in seven of their ten innings, finished with five wins, including those v Bristol GS, Kingswood and Lansdown CC's midweek XI. The captain, P. Tisdale, and wicket-keeper S. Bryan hit two hundreds each in four consecutive matches, and among six successive century opening partnerships was a school-record 210 between Tisdale and D. Benton v Wells Cathedral School. Bryan, whose eight innings yielded 604 runs, went on to play for Somerset Second XI. The attack was dominated by A. Piper (fast-medium) and D. Perryman (leg-spin), the only two bowlers to take ten wickets. In schools matches, **Berkhamsted** beat Brentwood, Mill Hill, St Albans, St Lawrence Ramsgate and – having recovered from 18 for six to 124 – Bishop's Stortford. E. P. Shek, the captain, was a consistent left-handed opening bat whose 821 runs included a brilliant 123 v Aldenham, and of the many other batsmen who contributed, D. T. Wotherspoon hit 99 in 80 minutes v Brentwood. A strong attack was spearheaded by R. D. Hilton and M. J. Spooner, with main support coming from medium-pacers J. M. Rennie and R. D. Collett (six for 2 v Kimbolton). B. P. Howard, a young left-arm spinner, gained in confidence during the term and headed the averages. A good season finished with a tour of Holland, where all three matches, played on the mat, were won.

Birkenhead, with a strong side, achieved less than might have been expected, and it was felt that most of the drawn games could have been won. L. C. Parnell, a sensible, positive captain, batted and bowled fast-medium aggressively, and N. D. Cross hit centuries in difficult conditions v King's Macclesfield and Manchester GS; against the latter, Parnell scored 50 not out and then took six for 10 in seventeen overs. The leg-spin of D. A. Allan won two matches, and all the bowlers benefited from the outstanding fielding at short leg of I. G. Berry, who held fourteen catches in eight games. **Bishop's Stortford**, a particularly young side, beat Kimbolton, Dean Close, Wrekin and St Edmund's, Ware, but experienced eight defeats. Unexpectedly brittle batting – an exception being E. M. Peachey's maiden hundred v MCC – and a failure to exploit several commanding positions contributed to their undistinguished record. None the less the bowling was good. R. S. Jayatileke, a Sri Lankan off-spinner, took seven for 6 v Kimbolton, and D. N. Child, the captain, had six-wicket hauls v Berkhamsted and Dean Close. With their Under-17s reaching the South final of the Barclays Bank Cup, and the majority of the First XI expected to return, the college looked to 1991 with optimism.

Bloxham, playing mostly afternoon matches, often found results elusive, particularly on their own excellent pitches, even if batsmen did not always take full advantage of them. Rendcomb, Shiplake, Dean Close and MCC were all beaten. R. D. Beaty performed well both with gloves and bat, proving especially effective in a crisis at No. 7 or No. 8. E. R. H. Wornum (fast-medium in-swing) was the leading bowler, capturing an impressive 41 wickets. With only one win in schools matches and an exciting tie v Taunton, **Blundell's** were left to reflect on their inability either to defend a reasonable total or to score sufficient runs. M. R. N. Hunt, the captain, had a fine season with the bat, but his 524 runs were nearly twice the next aggregate. However, a record of one victory and three defeats in thirteen matches does not do justice to the strong batting side of **Bradfield College**. S. P. Bridgman's 596 runs featured two successive unbeaten hundreds – v Stowe, where he mastered some fiery opening bowling, and v the Old Boys. J. T. C. Kendall, an excellent captain, set a fine example with 25 wickets and 494 runs, his 153 not out v Westminster including a hundred before lunch. His younger brother, W. S. Kendall, also passed 400 runs.

An eventful season for **Bradford GS** culminated in the visit to Barbados for the Sir Garfield Sobers festival in July. The high number of drawn games reflected both a lack of penetration in the bowling and relative inexperience in the batting. Five of the seven victories came in limited-overs games, as did four of the six defeats. The consistent N. J. Gomersall and the captain, D. C. Whitfield, dominated the batting, with the hard-hitting M. J. Savage and the left-handed opener, S. A. W. Davies, also contributing. Slow bowlers D. J. Collinge and M. J. Hannan (left-arm) had encouraging first seasons. **Brentwood**, captained by the Under-19 rugby international, C. J. Wilkins, had a poor summer, with sound batting but a mediocre attack. They were hampered by a crop of injuries to key players, as well as a loss of form by others of whom more had been expected. On the other hand **Brighton College** had an excellent season, winning 14 of their 22 matches and regaining the Langdale Cup when they beat Lancing by 16 runs. C. N. Gates batted superbly, his 1,378 runs being the second-highest in a season by a schoolboy after 1,534 by N. J. Lenham, also of Brighton, in 1984. Fully recovered from a fractured skull, suffered in a road accident at the end of the 1989 season, he hit four hundreds, including 178 not out v Ipswich, and won the *Daily Telegraph* Under-19 batting award. His opening partner and captain, R. D. Oliphant-Callum, made 832 and together they put on 222 unbroken v MCC and 265 v Ipswich. A varied attack was spearheaded by R. I. Lewis, with 45 wickets.

It was a season of rebuilding for **Campbell College**. D. A. Parker, an understanding captain, hit 112 not out v Banbridge Academy, as well as taking 24 economical wickets. Indeed, economy was a feature of the attack, in which four bowlers finished with single-figure averages. S. A. I. Dyer, whose 203 not out v Dungannon Royal School was a record for the college, went on to play for Irish Schools, and there were Ulster Schools honours for R. H. Lucas, the most successful bowler, Parker and C. R. M. Caves. The positive cricket played by **Canford** was apparent from their record of just three draws in sixteen games; Bryanston, Blundell's, the XL Club, Milton Abbey, MCC, RNCC, Wimborne CC and King's, Taunton were all defeated. The captain and opener, J. A. Perry, produced some outstanding performances with the bat, and seam bowler M. W. Forward gave the attack its edge. The real strength of the side, though, lay in the fielding, which was a key factor in their reaching the semi-finals of the Sir Garfield Sobers festival in Barbados.

With eight of **Caterham's** promising 1989 side in the XI again, hopes were high as the season began. However, injury prevented the captain, I. W. Armitage, from bowling, and although S. J. Constantin and S. K. Perera were steady and accurate, they had neither the support nor the penetration to put Caterham in control. K. A. Amaning overshadowed the other batsmen with his strokeplay. Benefiting from a pre-season tour to Southern Spain, a young, rather inexperienced **Cheltenham** XI enjoyed six wins, the most notable being v Haileybury, Pates GS, Free Foresters and St Edward's, Oxford – all achieved when batting second. They were ably led by B. B. Jones, and if his batting was generally disappointing, he did make a fine 102 v Free Foresters. Other hundreds came from two young players, M. C. Cawdron (114 not out v Malvern) and D. R. Hewson (109 v Dean Close). Cawdron, a left-hand opening bat and medium-pace out-swing bowler, collected 578 runs and 23 wickets and with Hewson (412 runs and, with off-breaks, 18 wickets) was selected for West of England Under-15. Hewson later played for England Under-15. D. R. Fulton again took the most wickets with his sharp in-swing, while M. C. Green's seven for 43, bowling left-arm medium, set up the win v St Edward's.

Chigwell's season was built around their Essex Under-19 all-rounders, P. C. Harvey (left-hand bat, right-arm medium) and J. F. Carpenter (right-hand bat, left-arm medium-fast), who provided 1,289 runs and 76 wickets. Harvey hit hundreds v Bancroft's (102 not out off 79 balls), Forest (126) and Wellingborough (119), and had figures of seven for 11 in 6.3 overs v City of London and six for 17 off ten v St Edmund's. Other highlights were a first-ever win v Bishop's Stortford; the defeat of Bancroft's, in which Harvey hit three sixes and fifteen fours in taking his side to 202 from 23 overs in 86 minutes; and the win v Forest, when Chigwell totalled a school-record 292 for seven, to which Harvey and D. R. Evans (96) contributed a record fifth-wicket stand of 182. Other wins were v City of London, Enfield GS, St Edmund's, Latymer and William Hulme's GS, while in schools matches they lost only to Magdalen College School. After a useful start, the **Christ College, Brecon** XI, which had promised so much at Under-17 level, failed to muster the cohesion and determination either to press home an advantage or to save the game. It was felt that the side was too confident and easy-going. Head and shoulders above the rest was the captain, E. P. M. Holland, who again won three more caps for Welsh Schools as a fast bowler who can bat.

Clayesmore's young side performed better than anticipated, losing only three schools matches and achieving some excellent wins, in particular those v Allhallows and King Edward VI, Southampton. They owed much to the leadership and example of their captain, P. Bradbury, who headed both averages and was judged best batsman at the Bearwood festival. There were also noteworthy bowling performances from the young off-spinner, L. Coley, especially his six for 41 v the XL Club. **Clifton's** record eight wins included victories v Colston's, Blundell's, Marlborough, Tonbridge and Winchester in schools games. The captain, J. R. A. Williams's aggregate of 935 runs passed C. M. Trembath's record of 767 in 1979 and included hundreds v Rugby, Marlborough, Tonbridge and MCC. Against Rugby, he and J. P. Parish shared a second-wicket partnership of 250. M. G. N. Windows hit 127 v Millfield on his way to an aggregate of 649 runs, while B. M. O. Gibbs, at fast-medium, was the most successful bowler. Williams played for Welsh Schools Under-19 and captained their Under-16s.

Colfe's, an inexperienced side, worked hard and performed creditably. Even so, they depended heavily on three all-rounders: M. Horder, the captain, M. Quilter and wrist-spinner J. Gledhill-Carr. Of the younger players, T. Shoben and A. Hameed showed run-scoring potential, but as yet lacked consistency, while it was hoped that E. Gratwick (fast-medium) and R. Dennis (off-spin) would develop and strengthen the attack. In a moderately successful season **Colston's** beat King Edward's Bath, Prior Park, Bristol Cathedral School, Truro School and Christ College, Brecon. The captain, J. A. Franklin, I. J. Webb and M. J. Sheedy all scored centuries, with Franklin's 144 v Bristol Cathedral School, 136 v Kingswood and 186 v Hutton GS helping him to a school record aggregate of 906 runs. **Cranleigh's** positive approach brought them wins v the Cryptics, Eastbourne, Cranleigh Village, Epsom and Loretto. Defeats were by MCC, Lancing, King's Canterbury, St John's Leatherhead and Merchant Taylors', Northwood. The high standard of ground fielding was especially noteworthy, as were figures of eight for 44 and six for 44 by H. C. Watkinson and seven for 32 v Epsom by G. B. Atkinson. The batsmen were always looking for runs, but there were few dominating innings.

Dauntsey's, building afresh, began the season tentatively and at half-term were still looking for their first win. The XL Club obliged, after A. N. Field (fast-medium) had taken six for 72, and three more victories followed in the last four matches. The batting was strengthened by newcomer I. D. Hardman, a left-hander, whose 103 v King Edward's, Bath was the only hundred. D. P. Atkins (slow left-arm) took six for 52 on a responsive pitch v Kingswood and Field returned seven for 44 v Wycliffe, who won an exciting game by one wicket in the last over. Under the captaincy of G. M. Gaiger, a good spirit was maintained, even during the frustrating early weeks. **Dean Close,** if somewhat disappointing in terms of results, provided some exciting cricket. Neither of their Gloucestershire Under-19 representatives, C. J. Townsend, the captain, and C. S. Knightley, quite lived up to expectations, although Townsend played some good innings and Knightley, batting left-handed and bowling right-arm medium pace, made a useful all-round contribution. J. M. Bowditch, if not yet accurate enough with the new ball, had his moments.

The young **Denstone** XI, unbeaten and never bowled out, should perhaps have achieved more than four victories – v Wrekin, Old Denstonians, Abbot Beyne and King Edward's, Birmingham. While not quite reproducing his form of 1989, the captain, J. N. Snape, did hit an impressive unbeaten 128 v Worksop and provided seven other fifties. He went on to play for Northamptonshire Second XI and English Schools, and also captained England Under-17 against the touring Pakistanis. **Dover College** began with victory over the Duke of York's Royal Military School, but thereafter won only once more. Weak bowling again put undue pressure on the batsmen, among whom A. S. Burrell showed resolution as an opener and S. J. Schilder played some handsome strokes. The captain, D. M. Rouse, though scoring far fewer runs than in 1989, finished his school days with a total of 1,586. It was the opposite at the **Duke of York's Royal Military School** where, with batsmen losing their wickets in a premature attempt to push the score along, they struggled to compile big totals. On the other hand, the bowlers performed with great credit. G. J. Kennett purveyed his leg-spin with commendable enterprise and looked to give the ball air, while D. J. Reynolds's left-arm swing was always threatening. He returned six for 20 as St Edmund's, Canterbury were bowled out in pursuit of a total of 120. Of the batsmen, N. M. Conway demonstrated a sound technique and showed promise as a wicket-keeper, while the captain, C. N. Conway, generated a good team spirit and led by example in the field.

A record of three wins and five defeats for **Dulwich College** is a little misleading, for three of those losses were sustained while four leading players were on a rugby tour of Australia. Highlights were the defeat of King's, Canterbury and J. H. Potter's 115 v Epsom. The left-handed R. S. Sheldon, captain of the XI, headed the batting. **Durham** began the season by winning their first three games, but defeat by Pocklington on a damp wicket was followed by several drawn games which should have been won. The talented Weston brothers were the mainstay of the side: the captain, W. P. C., opening the batting and bowling, contributed 527 runs and 30 wickets, while his younger brother, R. M. S., opening bat and leg-spinner, scored 643 runs and took 22 wickets. Philip Weston played for English Schools and was chosen to tour New Zealand with England Young Cricketers in 1990-91, and Robin, the England Under-15 captain, received the Sir Jack Hobbs England Under-16 all-round award. Highlights were a nine-wicket win v St Peter's, York and the school's appearance for the third time in five years in the final of the Barclays Bank Under-17 Cup; they were beaten by Richard Huish VI Form College, Taunton.

At **Eastbourne College** the skill and good sense of the captain, A. J. T. Halliday, made for a cheerful, well-motivated side. Potentially gifted young cricketers were encouraged to play some exciting cricket, seen noticeably in the wins v Tonbridge, Christ's Hospital and King's, Canterbury. Halliday's 114 v Christ's Hospital and B. H. Miller's unbeaten 100 v St John's, Leatherhead were major batting moments, while the best performance with the ball was E. G. R. Barrett's return of seven for 13 v Stragglers of Asia. Highlight of an erratic season at the **Edinburgh Academy** was the exciting two-wicket win v Glenalmond, and there were interesting games v Barnard Castle and Scots College, Sydney, the latter winning by just 1 run. J. N. K. Godfrey's captaincy became more enterprising as the season developed, while the innings of 152 v Kelvinside by his fellow-opener, R. W. Cairns, was the highest for the Academy in twenty years. In a season of rebuilding, **Elizabeth College, Guernsey** were content with a record of eight wins, those v Malta and Victoria College, Jersey being particular highlights. Notable individual performances came from the captain, P. J. A. Moody, whose 50 wickets included seven for 30 v Latymer and six for 48 v Victoria, and T. Hollyer-Hill, who scored 103 not out v Reed's in an aggregate of 617 runs.

Ellesmere College beat five sides, including a strong MCC XI, and were one wicket away from a comfortable victory in three of their drawn games. G. N. Phillips (fast-medium) returned seven for 41 v Shrewsbury, and his opening partner, J. G. Slater (fast), took five for 12 v Liverpool College. **Eltham's** strong batting line-up was headed by the consistent left-handed opener, J. M. Ramsey, but their bowling, while capable of containment, struggled to bowl sides out. The college were Kent Cup finalists for the second successive season; in the semi-finals, the captain and leading wicket-taker, F. Kavina (leg-spin), took six for 27 v Judd. **Emanuel** enjoyed an outstanding season, their nine victories including the finals of both the London and Surrey Cup competitions. In the former they recovered from 34 for four in rain-affected conditions to pass Alleyn's 101 with an over to spare; in the latter, a boundary in the last over brought a two-wicket win v KCS Wimbledon. J. C. Cole deputised admirably in the absence, for much of the season, of the captain and all-rounder, M. D. Coe.

After losing two of their first three matches, **Enfield** never looked like losing again until late July. Wins v Hampton, Forest and Scots College, Sydney, and the draws v Haberdashers' Aske's and Merchant Taylors', Northwood, were season's highlights. D. Bowen became the first batsman to score 1,000 runs in a season for the school; of his three centuries, his unbeaten 196 v Reigate GS included a hundred before lunch. Other three-figure innings were played by N. Clydesdale and the captain and wicket-keeper, J. King. N. Lutwyche (off-spin) and M. Stevens (left-arm medium) made a contrasting attack and took 56 and 40 wickets respectively. **Epsom College** won six of their ten matches, including those v St George's Weybridge, Christ's Hospital and – scoring 261 with one ball to spare – KCS Wimbledon. T. R. Newton, a left-handed all-rounder, took 33 wickets, including six for 18 v Lancing, and hit out strongly, while P. E. Roche and N. A. Morris provided the backbone of the batting, the latter playing the side's only three-figure innings.

A record of three wins and three defeats does not do full credit to a good **Eton** side, unbeaten against schools in term and losing only to Eton Ramblers and, in the Silk Trophy festival, to hosts Radley and Shrewsbury. The wins were v St Edward's Oxford, Cranbrook and Harrow at Lord's, where Eton's batsmen played to potential and Harrow were outplayed. J. M. S. Whittington, in his first season, took 49 wickets with his left-arm slow bowling and went on to take 22 more for Berkshire Schools and win the *Daily Telegraph* Under-19 bowling award. In his first schools match for the XI he had figures of 7.3–4–3–8 v St Edward's. The XI was led with rare commitment by all-rounder H. J. P. Chetwood, though in part at the expense of his off-spin bowling. **Exeter School** achieved three of their seven wins on an end-of-term tour to Hereford and Brecon. A consistent batting line-up was headed by D. R. Gannon, whose last two innings produced centuries, while the captain, M. J. Stevenson, bore the brunt of the bowling when injury to M. H. T. Jones (medium-fast) disrupted the attack. However, J. R. Price (slow left-arm) returned good figures on the tour.

It was a disappointing season for **Fettes**, who rarely looked like winning and were beaten eight times. One bright spot was the bowling of the captain, J. R. S. Lloyd, who repeatedly took five wickets in an innings, to finish with 43, and looked a fine prospect. **Forest** won six and lost five of their sixteen fixtures. The distraction of A levels possibly affected the performance of their leading players; the captain, A. C. Richards's aggregate was half that of 1989, for example. Even so, he, P. O'Neill (medium) and wicket-keeper A. Heyes all made major contributions, along with the left-arm spinner, J. Dwyer, who emerged as the leading wicket-taker. Richards went on to captain English Schools and was offered a summer contract for 1991 by Essex, having played for their Second XI in 1990. Under the captaincy of B. Smyth, **Foyle and Londonderry College** won fourteen of their eighteen matches and finished the season as joint holders of the Gordon McCullough Memorial Cup. Their strong attack was spearheaded by J. Brown, who took seven for 19 v Coleraine Academical Institution and, with Smyth and J. McFarland, was selected for Ulster Schools. These three, with T. Dougherty, were the essence of the side's batting strength. Six of **Framlingham's** eight wins came in a run that ended with their only loss – to Kimbolton at the St Lawrence, Ramsgate festival. Success came from their all-round strength: N. I. Barker, S. E. Iliffe, the captain, and W. J. Earl scored consistently, while the opening attack of M. J. Rutterford and J. G. C. Townsend was balanced effectively by the slow left-arm bowling of P. Edwards.

Giggleswick beat Hipperholme GS, Oakwood and the Old Boys, but generally struggled to bowl sides out. **Glenalmond's** young, competitive side were moderately successful in an enjoyable season. Highlights were a fine century v Strathallan by S. C. Scott Elliot and his opening partnership of 158 with J. D. Thomson v Fettes. The captain, R. M. Jebb, bowled leg-spin to good effect for 31 wickets, while the medium pace of J. C. Caldwell provided a further 27. With **Gordonstoun's** senior players in particularly lean form, 1990 was not a vintage year. Poor weather in June led to several matches being cancelled, which, combined with the pressure of exams, meant the season ended on an unsatisfactory note. A highlight for **Grenville College** was their win v rivals West Buckland, against whom R. S. Hann took six for 28. The batting was headed by S. Blakers, an Australian, the consistent J. F. T. Pallister and D. R. Ellacott, who had an outstanding season behind the stumps. Seam bowlers took the most wickets, and a newcomer to the XI, M. J. Graham, though erratic, was fast and hostile. **Gresham's**, though not playing to their true potential for much of the season, finished in fine style with resounding victories v Oakham and Bromsgrove. The individual highlight was an innings of 141 by the captain, I. D. Barnett, v The Leys.

Haberdashers' Aske's were unbeaten. B. Moore (the captain), M. I. Yeabsley and R. Thacker, the top three in the order, made 2,121 between them, with Moore and Yeabsley putting on 225 unbroken for the first wicket v Queen Elizabeth's, Barnet, and three days later, in their next match, opening with 171 v Berkhamsted before being parted. Against Queen Elizabeth's, Yeabsley's younger brother, R. S. Yeabsley, returned eight for 29. The bowling honours were shared between the two brothers, Michael bowling off-spin and Richard medium-fast, supported by Moore (medium). Both Yeabsleys represented Hertfordshire Under-19 and Richard played for Middlesex Second XI and for Devon in the NatWest Bank Trophy; Moore played for Middlesex Young Cricketers and Thacker for Middlesex Under-17. **Hampton** enjoyed four successive wins in May, only for a frustrating string of draws to follow. S. C. Janes and J. E. Sudbury blended sound defence with attacking flair in a successful opening partnership, while seamer S. A. H. Cochrane produced match-winning spells v Latymer and RGS Guildford. The hostility of J. A. Scowen with the new ball and the increasing control of left-arm spinner J. E. Saunders promised well for the future. In schools matches, **Harrow** beat Bedford and St Edward's, Oxford, and lost only to Eton and Zimbabwe Schools; otherwise results were hard to come by on the good, dry wickets of 1990. An unbeaten century by C. E. Williams v Radley was the batting highlight, while among the bowlers R. E. Sexton took 40 wickets in his first season.

The **Harvey GS** recorded fourteen victories and won the Lemon Cup for Kent schools for a record seventh time. They owed much to their opening bowlers, R. J. N. Davis and A. W. Morris (both medium), who took 56 and 50 wickets respectively and were well supported in the field. **Highgate** enjoyed their best season in terms of wins since 1971, thanks particularly to the bowling of T. Gladwin and M. Sylvester, plus some steady batting. Thirteen-year-old E. Gladwin showed much promise with 50 on début, v MCC, and an average of 38.66 from his three innings. The relatively young side of **Hurstpierpoint** beat Seaford, Worth, Whitgift, St John's, Eastbourne and Ellesmere in schools matches, and the Under-17s reached the last four of the Barclays Bank Cup. P. T. Wicker, who hit an unbeaten 100 v St George's, and M. J. Semmence, the captain, were selected for Sussex Young Cricketers. M. J. King, who bowled some brisk spells, took the most wickets, including seven for 35 v Ellesmere; their other three wickets fell for 5 runs to Semmence. **Ipswich** continued their success of 1989, winning five games, losing only once, and finishing the season in style with victory v Dutch Colts at The Hague. The steady batting and leg-spin bowling of R. Catley stood out, while the seam bowling of C. Earley made its mark late on. J. Douglas, in his first season, made hundreds v The Perse and Brighton College, and also headed the bowling averages.

Kelly College, a young side, acquitted themselves well, though occasionally betraying their inexperience. They could bat right down the order – C. P. Insole, the captain, was the most impressive of the batsmen – and only one opposing team exceeded 175 against a steady attack built around J. J. Wood (medium), W. G. Pendrill (left-arm medium) and I. J. Saunders, a promising leg-spinner. Their best victories were v Exeter School and Truro School. **Kimbolton**, disappointing in terms of results, had a successful season in terms of development and attitude, with excellent wins v Berkhamsted and Framlingham providing reward and optimism. The captain, R. J. T. Ramply, a left-hander, headed the batting and forged a useful opening partnership with S. G. Wood, a fine wicket-keeper. The bowling was spearheaded by I. Prideaux (fast-medium), who operated with ideal control and pace. The experienced, well-balanced XI at **King Edward VI College, Stourbridge**, characterised by all-round team effort and fine catching, featured in some exciting finishes. Three of their six wins came in the last over, and close of play in four of the six draws found their opponents' last pair at the crease.

First-ever wins v Canford and St George's, Weybridge were highlights for **King Edward VI, Southampton**, who won eight other matches, retained the Altham Trophy and lost only to Brighton in schools fixtures. B. Quantrill proved to be an able captain, and while his steady batting was well supported by R. T. Markham, it fell to a fourth-form boy, G. R. Treagus, to play the only three-figure innings. The left-arm spinner, R. M. Salter, again exceeded 50 wickets. A difficult season for the young side of **King Edward VII, Lytham** brought no wins, but there were close draws v Arnold and King's, Macclesfield, to suggest the potential for 1991. The captain, P. Macauley, a left-hander, played quality strokes on occasions, and his opening partner, G. Maitland, a promising Under-15 player, headed the averages. P. Young (medium-fast) bowled tirelessly without having much luck or reward. **King Edward's, Birmingham** were pleased to win more matches than they lost at a time when the attack, with the exception of the captain, M. M. Dean, was expected to be only average. The bowling of C. D. Atkin was a bonus. As anticipated, the batting was sound, and an unbroken tenth-wicket stand of 112 v Solihull between N. M. Linehan (81 not out), a colt, and D. A. Bhadri (50 not out) was an unusual highlight.

King's College, Taunton were well captained by W. J. K. Greswell, who had two fine centuries amongst his 625 runs, while the openers, R. E. Berry and C. P. W. Cashell, scored 72 and 93 respectively in a school record opening stand of 178 to beat Blundell's by ten wickets. With most of the XI due to return in 1991, it was an encouraging season. At **King's College School, Wimbledon**, meanwhile, J. Parrish and captain R. Q. Cake formed an opening partnership that few could rival, scoring 833 and 927 runs respectively. H. S. Malik was another to pass 600, while of the bowlers A. M. Denslow (fast-medium) captured 47 wickets in his first season. Cake's sensible but sporting declarations made for some exciting cricket, notably v Epsom (q.v.). **King's, Bruton** beat Taunton School, Canford, Milton Abbey and Queen's, Taunton, losing only to the Old Boys. With seven of the side expected to return in 1991, prospects are good. Five wins were more than might have been expected by **King's Canterbury**. Their inexperienced batting was always likely to be a problem, and indeed several defeats resulted from batting collapses, but their difficulties were compounded by an injury to their opening bowler, M. I. G. Wilkinson. His absence from all but five matches considerably weakened the attack. The well-balanced **King's, Chester** XI recorded ten victories, were unbeaten by schools and lost, in the last over, only to a strong MCC side.

King's, Ely also won ten games, the most memorable of which was the 1-run victory v The Leys in the final of the Cambridgeshire County Cup. They lost to just one school. D. C.

indle, their captain, claimed a hat-trick in successive matches – v Woodbridge (all bowled)
d v King's, Peterborough – and in taking seven wickets in the final match he equalled the
hool record of 49 in a season. C. Q. Taylor, an opening bat, hit hundreds in successive
atches, and A. M. Gallop's 143 not out v King Edward's (King's Lynn) was Ely's best for
me time. Undefeated by schools for the first time in recent memory, **King's, Macclesfield**
st v MCC and beat Bury GS, the Masters' XI, William Hulme's, Arnold, Bolton
hool, Bury GS, Ipswich School and Brighton College. Their Australian opening batsman,
. A. Graham, was outstanding, his 1,075 runs passing by 83 the school record set in 1981 by
Moores, the Sussex wicket-keeper. The attack was led by S. C. James (fast-medium) whose
k for 32 v William Hulme's included a hat-trick, and M. R. Palmer, who opened at fast-
edium but could also ply off-breaks. The batting of **King's, Rochester** was dominated by
. J. Walker, whose 872 runs included 156 not out v Chatham House, 143 not out v the XL
ub, 105 v Maidstone GS and 124 v KCR Common Room. He also took the most wickets
8) and went on to play for Kent Second XI and England Under-17 v Pakistan Young
ricketers. **King's, Worcester** did not play as well as anticipated, injuries and exams affecting
e form of at least two senior players. However, R. Tomlinson, captain and wicket-keeper,
ssed 500 runs for the second successive season, and there was a feeling of satisfaction when
. Thompson, having hitherto struggled for runs, hit an unbeaten century v Reigate on the
d-of-season tour to Victoria College, Jersey.

Kingston GS, a young XI, made good progress; they won five games, and three of their eight
efeats came in the last over. The captain, E. S. Gratton, batted consistently well, his 120 not
t v RGS Guildford lifting the side from 91 for eight. With the ball, M. E. Bendel (fast-
edium) began the season in fine form, only to incur a back injury, and the lack of a good
in bowler was a further handicap. **Kingswood's** batsmen hit a record number of three
undreds, with the captain, G. J. B. Williams's 156 not out in 140 minutes v Colston's a school
est. Unfortunately, moderate bowling resources meant that batting dominance was only
rice converted into victory. The attack of **King William's College, Isle of Man** had similar
mitations, with openers N. C. Capewell and D. R. Norman failing to fulfil earlier promise.
owever, L. R. Clarke, a young medium-pace bowler, responded well to additional
sponsibility. The batting relied heavily on a solid start from the openers, M. L. Craine, the
ptain, and U. A. Nwachuku, an Under-15 colt.

Following a tour to Australia at Easter, **Lancing** had a reasonable season, reaching the final
the Langdale Cup, only to lose to Brighton College. S. Baker dominated with bat and ball,
wling at a lively pace for his 34 wickets and including a fine century v Worth in his 934
ns. For the first time the college were hosts to Malvern, Charterhouse and Rugby in the end-
-term festival. Not surprisingly, the main contributor for unbeaten **Leeds GS** was their
ptain and all-rounder, T. C. Walton, who scored 545 runs, took 49 wickets and went on to
ay for English Schools and England Under-17 v the touring Pakistanis. A fourteen-year-old
ft-hander, I. C. Sutcliffe, developed promisingly as an opening bat, but while R. M.
tkinson bowled his left-arm spin to good effect, Leeds, like many schools, simply could not
wl sides out to exploit winning situations. Pre-eminent at **The Leys** was their left-handed
ening bat, R. C. Weston, who set three new school records. His aggregate of 988 runs
ssed the 977 scored in 1984 by J. D. R. Benson of Leicestershire; his 202 v The Perse (three
xes, 21 fours) overtook Benson's 201 not out in 1983; and he shared in a record opening
rtnership of 219 with M. C. Donnor (82) v the XL Club, going on to 163 not out. Weston
ored 692 runs in June, and missed the opportunity of totalling 1,000 for the season when the
hool's last match was abandoned. Donnor, a Cambridgeshire Under-16 representative,
ored 607 runs and took 23 wickets with his leg-spin. D. J. Woods, the wicket-keeper,
ptained Cambridgeshire Under-17.

Initial promise tailed off into disappointment for **Liverpool College** as technical weaknesses,
some extent countered earlier in the season by spirit and determination, were exposed by
ronger sides. Only J. Q. Harrington, the captain, and the left-handed B. Latto scored
nsistently. With the ball, J. Rushton (medium) bowled steadily, J. Rylance (fast-medium)
owed potential, and Harrington sometimes bowled his leg-breaks to good effect. **Llandovery**
ollege, unbeaten by schools, won half their matches and lost only to Pontyberem CC. Their
rength lay in the batting, headed by S. A. Richards, who batted with style and maturity and
oved to be an excellent captain. He also led the Welsh Independent Schools. On May's
rd wickets, runs flowed, but rain and exams made June a difficult month. B. Rowlands

developed encouragingly as an all-rounder, and his left-arm fast-medium bowling w...
supported by G. D. A. Lyddon-Jones and H. G. Davies (both medium-fast). **Lord Wandswo...
College**, with seven wins to set against a solitary defeat, owed their success to the openi...
attack of N. P. B. Rochford and J. R. Cowles. Both showed genuine pace and hostility an...
sharing 71 wickets, contributed to the dismissal of four sides for less than 100. The captai...
D. A. Robinson, chipped in with 24 wickets from off-breaks. Though the batting was seldo...
tested, fifteen-year-old B. A. Hames opened the innings stylishly and scored the first hundr...
for the school in three years.

Loretto's young side did well on the local circuit, losing only to Merchiston Castle a...
beating Strathallan (all out for 47), Glenalmond (for 54), Fettes, George Watson's a...
Stewart's Melville; but their record was dented during their festival when the batting, capab...
in pursuit of low scores, proved more brittle. Defeats by Bryanston, Cranleigh and Ross...
outweighed the win v St Peter's, York. A. C. F. Mason (left-arm fast) bowled consisten...
well, with figures of six for 31 v Stewart's Melville and four for 9 v Strathallan contributing...
the 81 wickets he shared with the captain, J. A. E. G. Grant (medium). Two left-handers, C....
Hawkes and G. Leeson, were the outstanding cricketers at **Loughborough GS**. Leeso...
opening the batting, hit four hundreds in his 808 runs, while Hawkes contributed 611 runs an...
48 wickets. Hawkes played for Leicestershire Second XI and at the end of the season made h...
County Championship début v Derbyshire. Friars of Derby, Old Loughburians, Leicestershi...
Gentlemen, the XL Club, King Henry VIII Coventry, and Bablake (bowled out for 4...
J. Simpson seven for 13), were all beaten; the one defeat came in the final over v R...
Worcester.

Enterprising cricket earned **Magdalen College School** ten victories. Among the four batsm...
who passed 500 runs, M. B. Bixby and fifteen-year-old N. S. Hawken, scoring 110 and 1...
respectively, put on 212 unbroken for the second wicket v Reading School. S. D. Stinchcom...
(off-spin) again took the most wickets, ably assisted by the wicket-keeping of the captai...
T. H. Boyles, whose 34 dismissals included a school record of seventeen stumpings. **Malve...
College**, in their second-best season since the war, were unbeaten by schools and defeate...
Shrewsbury, Marlborough, Dean Close and Cheltenham, against whom they successfu...
chased 250 in two and a half hours. There were hundreds from P. V. Sykes and J. W. ...
Horton, the captain, while a good seam quartet was spearheaded by C. R. Phillips. S. J. ...
Ferguson, an able wicket-keeper, could put aside the gloves to bowl leg-breaks when requir...

Reservations about the inexperienced batting of **Manchester GS** seemed justified when the...
were bowled out for 119 by Rossall in their first match. However, revealing fine characte...
they improved to beat Bradford GS, Liverpool College, Arnold, William Hulme's, Bury ...
(twice) and King Edward VII, Lytham, losing again only to Bangor GS and Pocklington. T...
batting relied heavily on M. J. P. Ward, who followed scores of 96 not out v Shrewsbury ar...
98 v RGS Lancaster with 106 not out v William Hulme's, 104 v Taunton and 145 not out...
Bury to total 962 runs. L. J. Marland, promoted from the Under-14s to open with War...
possessed a sound technique but as yet lacked the power to dominate. The bowling w...
opened by N. S. Farmer and M. C. Jones, who was often too fast for opposing batsmen, whi...
Ward and Marland, in their differing styles, provided variety with off-spin. The XI were ab...
led by A. M. Dodd. For **Marlborough**, 1990 a disappointing season. Their batting w...
sound enough, but they bowled just one side out and managed only a single win – v ...
Edward's, Oxford. The fielding of J. Simkins and the potential all-round talent of M. E. ...
Harris were noteworthy.

Merchant Taylors', Crosby reported an unspectacular but enjoyable season in which mora...
was good under the captaincy of G. S. Glynne-Jones. However, his inability to bowl, owing ...
injury, weakened the attack. Only three sides were dismissed, and there were heavy defeats ...
the hands of Leeds GS and RGS Lancaster. Glynne-Jones contributed soundly with the ba...
though, to head the averages, and the Doggett brothers looked promising prospects. **Mercha...
Taylors', Northwood** numbered St Albans, Highgate, Watford GS, Aldenham, Universi...
College School, Dulwich, Stowe, Mill Hill, Cranleigh and Bryanston among their reco...
twelve wins. A. J. Brand, the captain, passed 1,000 runs for the second successive season, b...
was beaten to the mark by opener C. M. Jaggard, whose 1,364 runs, including five centurie...
fell 33 short of J. E. Raphael's record aggregate of 1,397 in 1901. Brand's 202 not out ...
Cranleigh in the Loretto festival improved by 1 run the school record he established th...
previous year. They and R. A. Hawkey, who scored 975 runs, made a formidable top thre...

Merchiston Castle, under the captaincy of G. C. Wearmouth, were undefeated by Scottish schools and won v Dollar Academy, George Heriot's, Glenalmond, Dundee HS, Loretto, Strathallan, Fettes and the strong Durham XI (by 97 runs after recovering from 41 for six to declare at 199 for nine). The only schools to beat them were Barnard Castle and RGS Newcastle. In a strong seam attack, A. R. C. Gilmour's excellent line-and-length medium pace brought him 59 wickets, including five for 17 and five for 30 in the two-day game v Fettes. His opening partner, A. A. L. Ramsay, B. R. S. Eriksson, able to swing the ball both ways, and D. W. Hodge (in-swing) lent admirable and accurate support. For **Millfield**, G. W. White became only the third player to score 1,000 runs for the school, his 1,061 including 200 not out v Welsh Schools and 104 v Somerset Second XI. He was followed in the batting by the captain, N. F. Gibbs, who headed the bowling and represented English Schools.

Mill Hill's young side were without a win until the end-of-term festival, where they beat Norwich, Warwick and Plymouth. A colt, D. M. J. Kraft, was the most successful batsman, while the bowling again relied heavily on the slow left-arm skills of the captain, G. E. S. Brock. Although they had no outstanding players, **Milton Abbey's** strength in depth helped them beat St John's Southsea, Clayesmore, Allhallows and Portsmouth GS, the last-mentioned victory coming when Portsmouth, chasing 187, collapsed from 166 for three to 184 all out. In contrast, **Monkton Combe's** season was notable more for individual performances. J. C. L. Sinfield took all ten for 39 in 15.1 overs v Dauntsey's, although he never quite bowled his medium-pace in-swing to such good effect again, and T. Simmons, the captain, compiled a school-record aggregate of 630 runs. His 100 not out v the XL Club was the first hundred for the XI since 1971, and S. Lockyer followed it with another unbeaten century in the eight-wicket win v Fettes at the St Paul's festival. The inexperience of **Monmouth's** bowling told in their record of ten draws in fifteen games. A. J. Jones, by far the most successful batsman, scored 136 v Wellingborough School and, along with J. H. Langworth, played for Welsh Schools. P. A. Clitheroe's leading aggregate of 31 wickets included six for 49 in the six-wicket victory v Colston's.

Newcastle-under-Lyme, unbeaten, experienced little difficulty in bowling sides out. J. Bradbury was their most successful bowler, and wicket-keeper R. M. Davis enjoyed another distinguished season. With the bat M. H. Colclough, an England Under-15 representative, and J. N. Britton both averaged over 70, scoring 100 each v Royal Wolverhampton as they put on a record 219 for the third wicket. The excellent attitude and team spirit of **Nottingham HS** made for an enjoyable and moderately successful season; the high proportion of drawn games was attributed to the good batting wickets and some sides setting safe targets. However, there were a number of exciting finishes, none more so than in the 100th fixture v Trent College (Nottingham 174 for eight dec., Trent 174 for nine).

Oakham's disappointing record stemmed from a lack of application among batsmen, of whom only N. C. Kingham, the captain, and P. M. J. Webb were consistent enough. M. Cullen and Kingham were the pick of the bowlers, invariably bowling a good line and length. Hard work and team spirit brought success to **The Oratory XI**, whose ten wins included those v Magdalen College School, Pangbourne College, St Edmund's, Reading School, Berkshire Gentlemen, the XL Club and Emeriti. J. D. Clarke and D. Olszowski both passed 500 runs, with a century apiece; Clarke hit 125 v Abingdon and Olszowski 101 v Reading in a total of 206 for five from 28 overs. Although the attack lacked the incisive edge of recent years, four bowlers took twenty wickets each. A young **Oundle** side, well led by A. Lee, also played with fine team spirit. They beat The Leys, Oakham, Oundle Rovers, Northamptonshire Amateurs and St Edward's, Oxford, losing only to Felsted (in an overs match) and at the end of the season to Uppingham. A highlight was the fast-medium bowling of A. Richardson v Repton, taking six for 43 in a skilful display.

The Perse again showed themselves capable of scoring prolifically, passing 200 on five occasions, and once going on to 303 for four only to be beaten by The Leys. This illustrates their bowlers' lack of penetration and accuracy; unable to capitalise on their batting strength, the side went without a win. D. Crabb completed three excellent seasons behind the stumps and both E. W. H. Wiseman and R. T. Ragnauth showed promise with the bat. B. J. G. Edgar, an England Under-18 hockey international, scored 158 v Bishop's Stortford – the fourth time in two seasons the school record had been beaten. For their ten victories, set against a single defeat, **Plymouth College** owed much to the magnificent batting of A. R. Maddock, whose 1,128 runs at 86.76 included five centuries. He received sound support from any number of batsmen, all of whom could have scored more runs had the need arisen. Th absence for much of the season of S. W. Nicholson and A. Ginster left a gap in the attack although S. D. Hunt and K. J. Willcock bowled well to share 71 wickets. **Portsmouth GS** di not quite live up to expectations, with only five wins in fifteen games. The captain, J. Osborne, and C. J. Ward both passed 500 runs, while opening bowlers J. R. Compton an H. Rushin took their wickets at a reasonable strike-rate. Inexperience and ill fortune affecte **Prior Park**, who had hoped for more than four wins from potentially their best side for decade. They played to a high standard and were captained with maturity by G. Lee, wh provided the self-belief missing in some of the younger players. J. Power included the side only hundred in his 744 runs, an aggregate not surpassed in recent years, while Lee twice wer close to three figures in compiling 595 runs; he also took 35 wickets with his off-spin J. Smithers's 36 wickets were an excellent return for a seam bowler at the college.

Carried along by a great team spirit, **Queen Elizabeth GS, Wakefield** enjoyed their bes season for many years, winning three games and finishing "moral winners" in six of their nir draws. Much depended on the all-rounder, R. J. Ledger, and opening bat P. M. Dickinson; was significant that the only defeat – v Woodhouse Grove – came when neither performed t potential. Highlight in a successful season for **Queen Elizabeth's Hospital** was the eight-wicke victory v local rivals, Colston's; in other regular schools matches only the powerful Queen' Taunton side beat them. D. C. Taylor, bowling left-arm wrist-spin, captured the most wicket although N. O. McDowell (medium) headed both averages. He was followed in each by th captain, D. N. Bennett (fast-medium), who took six for 42 v Bristol GS. **Queen's, Taunto** with their outstanding depth in batting, were bowled out only once. Schools beaten in seve victories included Bristol GS, Wycliffe, Queen Elizabeth's Hospital, Bishop Vesey's an Taunton. N. J. Burke, who headed the batting, made 103 v King's, Bruton.

An unusual feature of **Radley's** season was their drawing two games with the scores level – Free Foresters and St Edward's, Oxford. In both cases Radley were chasing, and it was fe these should have been added to the wins v Cheltenham, Marlborough, Winchester (scoring off the last ball), Eton and Geelong. They lost only to Stowe and, hosting the festival, won th inaugural Silk Trophy. **Ratcliffe**, with four wins, were unbeaten until the penultimate game, Nottingham HS, and could look back with satisfaction on victory over Mount St Marys an draws with Oakham, Wellingborough and Loughborough. The bowling relied too heavily o the captain, P. G. Meredith, but the batting, while not really strong enough to chase larg totals with confidence, had a more solid look about it. Fifteen-year-old E. J. Meredith heade the averages for the second year. **Reading**, a young and inexperienced XI, enjoyed their cricket, despite winning only once. **Reed's**, capable of making runs, were handicapped by lack of variety in bowling, with too much being done by the specialist batsmen. One of thes M. R. Neal-Smith, took 31 wickets with his off-spin bowling.

Reigate GS were disappointed to lose nine of their 25 fixtures. Consolation came in th batting of A. J. Dewson, whose 680 runs included 102 v Emanuel, M. K. Hynard (110 v Ol Reigatians) and in particular of S. J. Hygate, who had scores of 136 v Victoria College, Jerse and 129 v Portsmouth GS in his 873 runs, the second-highest aggregate for the school afte N. J. Falkner's 1,139 in 1980. Opener C. B. Amos and left-armer R. J. Hathaway provided th bowling support for N. J. Chapman, an outstanding prospect who captured 43 wickets and h 368 runs in his first season. **Rendcomb** began well, winning three of their first four matche and drawing with Cheltenham; but only one more match was won. The left-arm spin of th Gloucestershire Under-19 representative, A. Jones, was the pick of the bowling, whil R. Milner (medium), who took six for 19 v Cheltenham, and R. Hughes (medium away swing), eight for 42 v Bloxham, led the seam attack. Milner, a left-handed opening bat, an J. Carroll both passed 600 runs, but no-one else reached 250.

In schools matches **Repton** registered victories v Pocklington, Oakham, Wellington an King Edward's, Birmingham, and in all games suffered only one defeat. Though eleven game were drawn, there was much exciting cricket, with several going to the last ball and any o four results possible. The side was led by the opening bowler, J. M. Windsor, who took th most wickets; the batting was headed by A. R. Paulett, who scored 105 not out v Pocklingto and M. D. Murray, son of the former West Indian wicket-keeper, D. L. Murray. **Richar Huish College, Taunton** beat the strong Durham side to become the first state school to win th Barclays Bank Under-17 Cup since its inception in 1982; an encouraging result at a time whe cricket in state schools is said to be in decline. With the last pair together, and chasin urham's 140, Huish's opening bowler, N. Hammacott, hit 2 off the last ball to tie the scores, aking them winners by virtue of fewer wickets lost. For thirteen wins in eighteen matches, ey owed much to a batting line-up headed by Kevin Parsons, whose 886 runs in twelve nnings were a school record, his twin brother Keith, the captain, and B. Collins, the last two aking solid all-round contributions. The Parsons, who between them also held 21 catches, layed for Somerset Second XI, as did the seam bowler, K. Moyse.

Rossall's season was one of the most successful for many years. They began by beating anchester GS in their first fixture and followed with seven more wins, including those v rnold, Giggleswick, Stonyhurst and King Edward VII, Lytham. The opening attack was specially hostile and quick, with S. D. Holmes in particular worrying many batsmen when e wickets were hard in May. He took six for 28 v King Edward's. While N. H. Crust was ess successful with the bat than in 1989, he still scored the most runs, and his captaincy was n important factor in the team's success. J. Elliott hit their only century, 100 v Cranleigh in he festival at Loretto. Batting and bowling records were broken at **Royal GS, Guildford**. B. C. ay, the captain, compiled a record aggregate of 673 runs, his 141 v RGS Colchester being oted the outstanding individual performance of the RGS festival. He and N. Kent, whose 00 runs included six fifties, dominated the batting, but the middle order rarely seemed able to onsolidate. A. Thomson's ability to move the ball both ways at medium pace brought him 48 ickets, also a record, including a return of eight for 57 v St Dunstan's. The fact that 28 of his ictims were bowled is a testimony to his accuracy. Newcomers G. Morley and T. Fraser put n good performances at the festival, taking five for 17 v RGS Worcester and six for 34 v RGS igh Wycombe respectively.

Royal GS, Worcester continued their winning ways, beating thirteen sides and losing only Bedford Modern in schools games. The batting was dominated by the first three – D. M. Valker, C. J. Eyers and A. V. Powell – all of whom looked set to make 1,000 runs but faltered t the end. The captain, M. J. N. Taylor, backed them up with 615 runs. Among the bowlers, N. P. Haddock's left-arm spin accounted for 58 wickets, and Eyers, at fast-medium, captured 1 wickets to go with his 932 runs, an impressive all-round performance. Batsmen prospered t **Rugby**, but as a record of twelve draws in fifteen matches suggests, bowlers had to work ard for wickets on the summer's pitches. W. Glazebrook emerged as the leading all-rounder; trong in defence, he also hit hard and straight, and his bowling was tight and tireless. Support ame in both departments from the experienced M. Semmens (fast-medium). **Rydal**, ncouraged by some early-season performances, suffered a setback when they lost control of a ame they should have won, v Liverpool College, and then were completely outplayed by King's, Chester. However, although Rydal finished without a win, with seven of the side xpected to return in 1991, there was cause for optimism.

What was always going to be a difficult season for **St Albans** looked even bleaker when their aptain and leading all-rounder, B. LeFleming, severed both main tendons in his right palm nly months before summer term began. Yet, despite holding the bat with difficulty, he ollected the second-most runs and wickets, as well as taking a record number of catches. . Cornwell's 649 runs included 104 not out v St George's, but of the bowlers, only . Sherman looked capable of bowling sides out. Even so, his 37 wickets were fewer than ad been expected of him. **St Bees** felt they could have improved on their record of four natches won and seven drawn had they possessed a more incisive attack. P. Hoffman headed ne batting averages, and A. Mawson, a colt, showed great potential in scoring the most runs, ncluding the side's only hundred.

St Edmund's, Canterbury anticipated a lacklustre season, yet by the end a young side had een transformed into a confident, cohesive unit, able to overcome the loss of their first four ames and finish with five victories. St Augustine's, Cranbrook, the XL Club and St dmund's Society were teams beaten. A. Hajilou developed the art of astute captaincy, and is unbeaten 117 v St Edmund's Society was the highlight of his significant all-round ontribution. C. R. M. Whittington demonstrated a rare talent with the ball, achieving many ariations of pace, flight and turn, while P. Walker and T. Wong showed all-round promise. t **Edward's, Oxford**, also a young XI, struggled for much of the season, with only wins v towe and the Cryptics to counter nine defeats. The opening batsman, H. Varney, and C. M. itcher, a fast-medium bowler, carried a heavy responsibility, but with most of the side eturning, and some promising colts coming through, the prospects for 1991 are better.

Another school to win just twice was **St George's, Weybridge**. A powerful batting line-up was headed by S. Marsh, whose 871 runs featured his 126 before lunch v Epsom (ten sixes, nine fours), 123 not out v Emeriti (seven sixes, eleven fours) and 182 v KCS Wimbledon (108 minutes, twelve sixes, twenty fours) – the highest for St George's since H. Cannon's 214 in 1901. The bowling, however, lacked the experience needed on good wickets. **St Joseph's, Ipswich** recorded eight wins and five defeats, their mixed fortunes reflecting some sound batting and inconsistent bowling. A highlight in a difficult year for **St Lawrence College, Ramsgate** was the 79-run victory v Kimbolton. The mainstay of the side was O. G. Morris, left-handed batsman and right-arm medium-pace bowler, with good support coming from the left-handed G. Turner, a fast bowler and useful middle-order bat. **St Paul's** could field a highly competent batting XI, but the bowling struggled, especially on the school's pitches at Barnes. B. R. Taberner, captain and wicket-keeper, and T. J. Taberner, his younger brother, played the two three-figure innings, the elder hitting 130 not out v Highgate in the opening match and the younger 101 not out v The Leys on the final day of the season. J. W. Hill, a leg-spinner who took just nine wickets in eight games, set up the win v Mill Hill with the remarkable figures of 18–12–18–6 on a good batting pitch.

St Peter's, York were handicapped by the absence for much of the season of some senior players. Although their results were disappointing, there were good individual performances, notably J. D. Rigby's unbeaten 102 v Yorkshire Gentleman. **Sevenoaks** were another strong batting side whose bowling failed to reach a similar level, even if T. R. Payton's 21 wickets were not due reward for his efforts. Omar Iqbal, the captain, scored 825 runs, the highest aggregate for the school since C. J. Tavaré's 1,036 in 1973, with the most fluent of his four hundreds being 107 v Brentwood in the better of the XI's two wins. **Sherborne's** undefeated XI, in winning more games than any of their predecessors, beat Taunton, King's Taunton, Clifton, Canford, Downside, Blundell's, Geelong College, Marlborough, Cheltenham, Dorset Rangers, Free Foresters and MCC. Their fast bowler, S. W. Stevens, broke the 67-year-old school record with 55 wickets, while the steadiness of A. J. Rutherford (fast-medium) and R. H. F. Pugsley (off-spin) was an ingredient in a successful attack. Wicket-keeper C. R. Lev set an outstanding example for an enthusiastic fielding side which held some splendid catches.

Shiplake reported eight wins; and the game v Lord Wandsworth College ended in a draw with the scores level. A. J. Hall scored most runs and took 56 wickets: in consecutive matches he took nine for 18 v St Bartholomew's and scored 145 not out v Reading School. After an uncertain start, C. P. J. Abbiss emerged as a solid No. 3 batsman and useful stock bowler, while a fourteen-year-old Canadian, P. C. Lefort, showed promise as a left-arm swing bowler. While their batsmen struggled to find early form, **Shrewsbury** endured three consecutive defeats in April; after that they lost only once, and among their four wins was that by 50 runs v Eton in the Silk Trophy festival at Radley. D. J. Bowett, who played for Middlesex Second XI, was again to the fore with 34 wickets and 523 runs, including 139 not out v Zimbabwe Schools. P. W. Trimby's leg-breaks and googlies consistently troubled batsmen, and B. R. Parfitt, son of P. H. Parfitt, showed his batting potential in his seven games, heading the averages.

In a season of rebuilding, **Simon Langton GS** did well to win six matches. N. Jones headed the batting, and the leading wicket-taker was R. Moulton, who captained the side in the absence through injury of R. Stevens. A highlight was the return of seven for 48 v St Edmund's, Canterbury by fourth-former N. Bielby. Excellently captained by J. M. A. Inglis, who was selected for Warwickshire Colts, **Solihull** had six wins to offset their one defeat – in the final of the Birmingham Schools Under-19 competition. Inglis dominated both batting and bowling, but as the season progressed the less-experienced players gained confidence under his guidance. R. A. Kallicharran played some useful innings, as well as moving the ball both ways at medium pace, S. R. Fell brought much-needed steadiness to the middle order, and K. A. Mortimer and P. S. Amiss emerged as a sound opening pair. Mortimer's bowling became more hostile as the season progressed, but S. M. Franklin had a disappointing return by his own standards. Of particular note were successive unbeaten centuries v MCC and King's, Worcester, by Inglis, and his six for 43 v Wolverhampton.

Stowe's bowling earned them five wins, notably that by 100 runs v otherwise unbeaten Radley. The fragility of their middle-order batting, though, led to six defeats. The side was captained with enthusiasm by the wicket-keeper, M. C. G. Atkinson, the third member of his family to lead the school. **Strathallan**, too, looked to their bowling, especially with the ball so ominant in Scottish cricket. Their attack was spearheaded by H. A. D. McKenzie-Wilson ast), with valuable support from the young M. R. Tench (fast-medium). K. L. Salters (right-and bat, slow left-arm bowler) headed both averages. Three all-rounders were prominent in e unbeaten XI of **Sutton Valence**: the captain J. F. Barr (right-hand bat, slow left-arm), Page (medium) and J. Cowell (fast-medium). Highlights were the win v MCC, with a target ' 231 met in the last over; the draw v King's, Rochester, in which Barr made 142 in a total of 35 for three dec.; and Barr's hundred from 73 balls as they achieved 189 for one in 29 overs in ply to Dover College's 208 for five off 81.

Taunton's young side exceeded expectations with seven victories. Memorable were . Tarr's unbeaten 118 v the XL Club and the tie v Blundell's, in which Taunton lost their last icket to the final ball of the match. **Tiffin's** formidable batting line-up was seen to advantage asing runs, the most spectacular wins coming when scoring 249 for six v MCC, 222 for six v Magdalen College School and 283 for seven v Elizabeth College, Guernsey. Opener G. J. ennis became the first since D. G. Ottley in 1962 to score 1,000 runs for the school, his nbeaten 128 v MCC being the most notable of his three hundreds. The captain and No. 4, . D. Nash, had an aggregate of 819, despite missing a month with a broken finger, and hit ur centuries v schools, the highest being 137 v Hampton. He went on to play for Surrey oung Cricketers. Of the bowlers, only B. J. Walters (left-arm spin) performed with match-inning consistency. The leadership skills of the **Tonbridge** captain, J. F. S. Rowland, fostered n excellent spirit and enthusiasm in the XI, which beat Tonbridge CC, Lancing, Free oresters, Haileybury and Felsted, and were just one wicket from victory in four drawn ames. Four of their five defeats came in the last two weeks, only two being v schools. S. J. oel, batting with care and concentration, consistently gave the side a good start, but the iddle order generally failed to build on it. No-one scored a hundred. The bowling honours ere shared by R. P. Ziegler and D. L. Gilbert, who, both medium-fast, troubled batsmen in l matches.

Trent College followed an eleven-match tour of Australia by playing exciting, positive ricket. More than half the eleven draws ended in their favour, three with the opposition nine ickets down. T. A. Ellis's 683 runs included 111 v Bradford GS, and C. M. Winterbottom hit n unbeaten 104 v Pocklington. The bowling was headed by M. T. White and N. D. Johnson, ne latter, under sixteen, making a significant impact in his first year in the XI. Another uccessful season for **Trinity** came as something of a surprise at a time of rebuilding. Capably aptained by the wicket-keeper, S. P. Fairchild, they recorded eleven victories, notably v St Dunstan's, Tiffin, Emanuel and Elizabeth College, Guernsey, and lost just twice, bringing the chool's results against all opposition over three years to 33 won, 5 lost and 29 drawn. S. S. rabhu led the batting with 758 runs, well supported by C. H. Maiden and the left-handed . W. Nowell, while the bowling revolved around two left-arm spinners, P. S. Kember and owell, who shared 84 wickets. Nowell, an Under-14, took seven for 16 v Whitgift. The good ork of the **Truro** bowlers was not backed up by their batsmen, who tended to get out to njudicious strokes when a steadier, more solid approach was called for.

Warwick, with wins v Bablake, Trent, Bishop Vesey's, MCC, Norwich School and King's, Worcester, looked primarily to their batsmen. Most reliable were D. Dalton, S. Ensall and the England Under-15 representative, C. Mulraine, whose 124 not out v MCC was the only entury. Half-centuries from the captain, G. Rawstorne, saw the side to three of these ictories. Fifteen-year-old S. Webb headed the bowling averages with 25 wickets. Un-lefeated, **Wellingborough** beat seven sides, including The Perse, Oakham, Forest, William Iulme's GS and Pocklington. The last two were beaten during the Wellingborough festival, n the final three days of which the captain, J. M. Attfield, hit successive hundreds v Chigwell, Pocklington and Magdalen College School. He dominated the season with a school ecord of 1,116 runs, overshadowing the excellent all-round contribution of N. J. Haste (441 uns and 39 wickets). **Wellington College** had in A. P. D. Wyke a tactically aware captain who, vercoming an injury, took the most wickets, including six for 33 v Charterhouse. The strength of the XI, however, was the depth of their batting, with A. E. Newman and T. N. Sawrey-Cookson particularly effective. Most of the seven wins by **Wellington School** came at he end of term, the best being v BRNC Dartmouth, Queen's Taunton and Christ College, Brecon. R. Fisher batted consistently well, with sound support from G. Wolfendon and S. Palmer, a positive captain, but the bowlers were not helped by the alarming number of dropped catches.

Whitgift enjoyed their best season for some years. In schools matches they beat Dunstan's, Brighton, Reigate and Christ's Hospital, losing only to Hurstpierpoint. The left-handed J. D. G. Ufton, son of D. G. Ufton, established a post-war record of 817 runs 54.46, including 123 not out v St John's, Leatherhead. Hundreds also came from R. Shah 163 not out, and P. M. Horne, 101 not out, in Whitgift's 404 for two off 45 overs v Excelsior Rotterdam. Another 36 wickets by R. J. Targett (fast-medium) took his tally for the school to 108 in three years, and he and all the bowlers were backed by sound fielding: wicket-keeper N. W. J. Edwards effected 31 dismissals (26 ct, 5 st). **Winchester** followed a successful term match tour of Australia at Easter with their best season for some years. Under the captaincy of R. J. Turnill, the experienced side played positive cricket throughout to win six games although a sharper attack might have wrought four more victories. Another experienced XI, that of **Woodbridge**, failed to achieve what had been hoped of them. The captain, B. K. Sindell, led from the front, and scored a fine century v St Joseph's College, but otherwise the batting failed to take advantage of good wickets and never totalled 200. Consequently the bowlers, accurate but not particularly incisive, never had the opportunity to apply pressure.

Woodhouse Grove suffered their only defeat by a school in their first match – v Ashville College. Showing greater application thereafter, they beat Giggleswick, Hipperholme and Queen Elizabeth, Wakefield in schools fixtures. Among a team thought to be the most talented at the school for many years, three all-rounders were prominent, S. N. Lee's leg-spin being well supported by the medium pace of R. D. Webster and C. J. Rika. They also scored the most runs, although the captain and opening bat, D. M. Lawson, would have totalled more had he not missed several matches with a rugby injury. A highlight was Lee's return of six for 31 v Batley. Undefeated by schools, **Worksop College** recorded wins v Ampleforth, Bloxham and Nottinghamshire Club and Ground, as well as participating in an exciting draw v Repton. Their two losses were sustained after declaring. A strong batting side, positive in approach, compiled six totals in excess of 200, with hundreds coming from the captain, J. D. Goode, and two left-handers, R. A. Kettleborough and C. J. Walker. Without much variety, the bowling tended to struggle on the firm home pitches.

Wrekin, with a steady opener in M. R. Savage, their wicket-keeper, lacked a reliable batsman to sustain the middle order. The bowling was the stronger suit, with most opposing sides being bowled out. A. J. Holloway (left-arm spin) took five wickets v schools three times, S R. D. H. Lander was genuinely quick, and S. R. Phillips-Broadhurst, moving the ball about at a lively pace, also registered three five-wicket returns. A highlight was the nine-wicket defeat of Bromsgrove. **Wycliffe** won only twice, but with most of the XI expected to return in 1991, they look forward to an improvement. S. B. Thomas opened the bowling with pace and movement, and took a hat-trick v Dauntsey's, while W. R. Tovey's flighted off-spin troubled many good batsmen and brought him the season's best return of seven for 47 v Bromsgrove. Although some senior batsmen at **Wyggeston & Queen Elizabeth I Sixth Form College** struggled to find form, the depth of batting and the consistent starts provided by S. Kennell ensured that they always scored enough runs. A newcomer to the XI, S. Patel (fast-medium), joined D. Green in constituting a formidable opening attack, but insufficient support meant that advantages gained were not always pressed home.

THE SCHOOLS

(Qualification: Batting 100 runs; Bowling 10 wickets)

* On name indicates captain.   * On figures indicates not out.

Note: The line for batting reads Innings–Not Outs–Runs–Highest Innings–Average; that for bowling reads Overs–Maidens–Runs–Wickets–Average.

ABINGDON SCHOOL

Played 17: Won 6, Lost 3, Drawn 8

Master i/c: A. M. Broadbent

Batting—R. J. Taylor 4-0-169-99-42.25; J. S. Tilley 14-4-355-61*-35.50; D. E. Stanley 7-1-527-83-32.93; *E. J. Tilley 16-1-397-73-26.46; J. S. Taylor 5-1-102-58*-25.50; A. D. Gordon 14-2-234-31*-19.50; J. M. Allen 10-0-173-61-17.30; P. A. B. Page 3-3-144-56-14.40.

Bowling—L. M. Golding 53-10-150-10-15.00; H. E. Wilkinson 70.2-19-246-14-17.57; B. R. Marnane 105.4-24-322-17-18.94; P. A. B. Page 205.2-50-494-25-19.76; J. M. Wallace 147-38-407-18-22.61; J. S. Tilley 46.5-7-229-10-22.90.

ALDENHAM SCHOOL

Played 13: Won 4, Lost 6, Drawn 3

Master i/c: P. K. Smith

Batting—S. P. Moffat 13-3-544-131*-54.40; D. G. Marsh 13-3-389-101*-38.90; C. Robertson 11-3-260-109*-32.50; C. Molyneux 9-2-142-59-20.28; R. Meara 12-0-220-56-18.33; J. Clemow 11-0-196-76-17.81.

Bowling—M. Okoro 134-27-400-27-14.81; R. Robertson 103-21-315-16-19.68; J. Clemow 21-19-384-18-21.33.

ALLEYN'S SCHOOL

Played 15: Won 6, Lost 0, Drawn 9

Master i/c: S. E. Smith

Batting—*P. C. Berglund 15-3-770-131*-64.16; M. Humber 10-6-105-31*-26.25; G. Brook 14-4-119-37-23.80; A. C. Winter 14-2-241-52*-20.08; M. T. Roberts 13-1-219-99*-18.25; C. Ellis 10-1-149-29-16.55; J. Naish 13-2-131-60-11.90.

Bowling—A. C. Winter 166.3-40-395-38-10.39; P. C. Berglund 113-23-278-22-12.63; C. Haslam 118.2-23-333-24-13.87; G. Brook 143-31-360-19-18.94.

ALLHALLOWS SCHOOL

Played 11: Won 0, Lost 7, Drawn 4

Masters i/c: C. G. McNee and M. Hill

Batting—*J. M. Rowe 11-1-279-122*-27.90; J. A. Carstairs 10-0-221-69-22.10; A. C. Coddy 11-0-102-32-9.27.

Bowling—J. M. Rowe 117-20-395-22-17.95; G. D. Moxon 82-17-295-11-26.81.

AMPLEFORTH COLLEGE

Played 17: Won 4, Lost 4, Drawn 9. Abandoned 3

Master i/c: The Revd J. F. Stephens OSB

Batting—A. R. Nesbit 15-2-382-75-29.38; A. J. Finch 14-4-284-39-28.40; R. M. Wilson 17-1-382-84-23.87; T. J. Willcox 16-1-330-57-22.00; T. O. Scrope 17-1-337-71-21.06; R. Finch 12-3-180-95-20.00; R. J. Lamballe 14-1-217-69-16.69; S. B. Pilkington 12-5-102-34*-14.57.

Bowling—D. A. Thompson 77-24-236-15-15.73; R. J. Gilmore 293.4-66-894-51-17.52; R. M. Wilson 69-16-302-10-30.20; S. B. Pilkington 246-55-759-16-47.43.

ARDINGLY COLLEGE

Played 19: Won 10, Lost 3, Drawn 6

Master i/c: T. J. Brooker   Cricket professional: S. S. Sawan

Batting—*M. T. E. Peirce 19–4–929–123*–61.93; D. P. Kerkar 19–1–1,102–150–61.22
A. C. C. Slight 19–5–423–76–30.21; T. D. James 10–2–139–62–17.37; M. J. Newcom
16–0–224–59–14.00; N. Simonin 14–2–145–56–12.08; C. S. Spencer 12–1–129–25–11.72.

Bowling—D. P. Kerkar 156.5–34–491–38–12.92; M. T. E. Peirce 186.1–37–636–34–18.70
C. S. Spencer 141.5–33–508–27–18.81; N. Simonin 112–15–391–19–20.57; M. J. Newcom
63–10–258–10–25.80; T. D. James 68–5–286–11–26.00; S. Skeel 79–13–314–10–31.40.

ARNOLD SCHOOL

Played 13: Won 4, Lost 5, Drawn 4. Abandoned 2

Master i/c: S. Burnage   Cricket professional: J. Simmons MB

Batting—*M. J. Clinning 12–1–451–96*–41.00; P. N. Bentley 12–2–194–47–19.40; R. Che
9–0–135–44–15.00; R. Day 10–1–125–24*–13.88; I. Best 12–0–166–49–13.83; C. Outran
10–0–107–50–10.70.

Bowling—I. Best 157.2–30–534–25–21.36; M. J. Clinning 257.2–73–742–33–22.48; R. Che
124–30–374–13–28.76.

ASHVILLE COLLEGE, HARROGATE

Played 16: Won 6, Lost 0, Drawn 10. Abandoned 2

Master i/c: J. M. Bromley   Cricket professional: P. J. Kippa

Batting—A. W. Alexander 15–2–632–135*–48.61; S. R. Alexander 15–1–382–98–27.28
J. J. C. Moorhouse 13–1–297–101*–24.75; T. P. Loveridge 14–5–187–38–20.77; R. A. Ne
11–2–133–47*–14.77; A. J. B. Casey 13–0–190–33–14.61; K. D. Crack 13–3–131–29*–13.1
Bowling—C. E. Pick 105–20–378–25–15.12; S. R. Alexander 45–11–171–11–15.54; R. A
Neil 81–14–243–13–18.69; A. W. Alexander 116–24–378–19–19.89; K. D. Crac
161–39–452–22–20.54.

BALLYMENA ACADEMY GRAMMAR SCHOOL

Played 14: Won 10, Lost 4, Drawn 0. Abandoned 4

Master i/c: P. G. Davidson

Batting—D. Kennedy 13–0–236–47–18.15; C. Williams 12–0–217–38–18.08; *M. Dunlo
12–1–169–50*–15.36.
Bowling—D. Kennedy 92.4–25–189–29–6.51.

BANCROFT'S SCHOOL

Played 20: Won 4, Lost 9, Drawn 6, Tied 1. Abandoned 1

Master i/c: J. G. Bromfield   Cricket professional: J. K. Lever MB

Batting—C. S. Greenhill 18–5–640–92*–49.23; T. W. Clark 16–1–520–75–34.66; *T.
Dolan 19–2–514–76–30.23; T. M. Dowling 19–1–438–70–24.33; A. A. Kha
11–3–129–37–16.12; R. Patel 17–3–183–29–13.07; J. Pollard 10–1–100–16–11.11; C.
Barlow 15–2–123–39–9.46; J. P. Manning 17–1–127–32–7.93.

Bowling—T. C. Dolan 171–39–594–33–18.00; A. A. Khan 91–15–362–18–20.11; J.
Manning 111.5–13–516–25–20.64; R. Patel 120.3–17–504–24–21.00; T. W. Cla
175.1–56–561–24–23.37.

BANGOR GRAMMAR SCHOOL

Played 21: Won 10, Lost 6, Drawn 5. Abandoned 1

Master i/c: C. C. J. Harte

Batting—P. A. McIlwaine 17–5–316–56*–26.33; M. L. Edwards 9–3–113–68*–18.83; R. G. Scott 19–3–300–103*–18.75; M. N. Wade 17–5–223–51*–18.58; A. J. Irwin 6–2–220–59–15.71; M. S. J. Law 10–2–107–31–13.37; P. J. English 15–2–154–34–11.84; M. W. R. McCord 16–5–118–29*–10.72.

Bowling—R. G. Scott 147.2–36–340–43–7.90; M. W. R. McCord 198.3–63–454–46–9.86; J. A. Skelly 91.5–31–212–20–10.60; C. P. Escott 101–31–241–21–11.47; J. L. Cunningham 72.5–16–200–10–20.00.

BARNARD CASTLE SCHOOL

Played 20: Won 6, Lost 5, Drawn 9. Abandoned 2

Master i/c: C. P. Johnson

Batting—*J. G. H. Murphy 17–5–611–100*–50.91; S. G. Riddell 19–3–316–60–19.75; J. Simon 17–2–296–70*–19.73; R. J. B. Wearmouth 17–3–221–51*–15.78; J. W. Foster 14–2–183–46–15.25; R. Brewis 17–1–227–46–14.18; K. R. Lowe 16–0–175–36–10.93; A. W. Hutchinson 16–3–106–29–8.15.

Bowling—M. R. Rock 37–6–146–11–13.27; J. G. H. Murphy 242–61–646–39–16.56; J. M. Watson 121–21–421–21–20.04; R. Brewis 318–71–916–41–22.34; R. J. B. Wearmouth 54–25–662–26–25.46.

BEDFORD SCHOOL

Played 17: Won 3, Lost 5, Drawn 9. Abandoned 2

Master i/c: D. W. Jarrett   Cricket professional: R. G. Caple

Batting—*R. W. H. Smith 18–3–578–113*–38.53; B. J. A. Miller 19–0–532–88–28.00; D. R. Fossey 10–1–249–61–27.66; A. Focken 19–1–437–54*–24.27; C. S. G. Parke 9–0–119–55–23.80; R. J. Stone 11–3–171–42–21.37; G. I. Green 8–2–112–34*–18.66; P. C. Wynn 17–1–286–99–17.87; N. V. Sinfield 12–1–177–52*–16.09; R. G. Simmonds 14–4–153–36–15.30; M. B. Jenkins 13–0–196–49–15.07.

Bowling—A. Focken 120–35–373–21–17.76; D. G. Stones 131–23–438–21–20.85; M. B. Jenkins 181–36–595–24–24.79; R. J. Stone 146–18–509–17–29.94; R. W. H. Smith 54–26–525–14–37.50.

BEDFORD MODERN SCHOOL

Played 21: Won 8, Lost 1, Drawn 12

Master i/c: N. J. Chinneck

Batting—*G. A. H. Awudu 21–3–1,009–148–56.05; E. R. Osborn 21–3–716–105*–39.77; R. C. Shah 15–4–362–70*–32.90; D. B. Reavill 21–1–446–51–22.30; G. S. Pilgrim 15–5–179–41–17.90; D. E. Jones 11–1–148–52*–14.80; P. A. Wildman 16–2–184–49*–13.14.

Bowling—M. J. Rolton 99.3–24–284–26–10.92; M. C. Waddingham 201.2–50–610–37–16.48; P. D. Brownridge 196.3–58–545–28–19.46; A. R. Woodcock 172.4–38–559–26–21.50; G. A. H. Awudu 203.3–40–646–29–22.27.

BEECHEN CLIFF SCHOOL, BATH

Played 10: Won 5, Lost 1, Drawn 4. Abandoned 2

Master i/c: K. J. L. Mabe   Cricket professional: P. J. Colbourn

Batting—S. Bryan 8-0-604-127-75.50; *P. Tisdale 9-1-570-131-71.25; R. Parke 4-2-140-79-70.00; D. Benton 9-0-226-90-25.11; A. Durrans 6-1-103-64-20.60.

Bowling—D. Perryman 99.1-21-308-19-16.21; A. Piper 83.3-21-260-14-18.57.

BERKHAMSTED SCHOOL

Played 19: Won 10, Lost 4, Drawn 5. Abandoned 1

Master i/c: J. G. Tolchard   Cricket professional: M. Herrin

Batting—*E. P. Shek 19-0-821-123-43.21; D. T. Wotherspoon 18-0-492-99-27.33; T. N Agius 17-6-291-83*-26.45; N. E. Mawdsley 13-4-230-65*-25.55; A. P. Spoone 16-0-353-76-22.06; A. J. Rigden 19-3-255-42-15.93; M. J. Spooner 13-1-181-61-15.08 R. D. Collett 18-1-250-73-14.70.

Bowling—B. P. Howard 81-11-314-21-14.95; J. M. Rennie 156-44-351-21-16.71; R. D Collett 103-22-325-17-19.11; R. D. Hilton 237-60-657-31-21.19; M. J. Spoone 213-42-642-29-22.13.

BIRKENHEAD SCHOOL

Played 14: Won 5, Lost 2, Drawn 7

Master i/c: G. Prescott

Batting—N. D. Cross 10-0-490-116-49.00; S. J. Renshaw 7-4-122-78*-40.66; I. G. Berr 7-1-210-84*-35.00; N. J. Corran 10-4-199-43-33.16; *L. C. Parnell 9-1-233-65-29.12 J. L. Cooper 7-1-105-22-17.50; M. G. Roberts 7-1-101-28*-16.83; D. A. Alla 10-0-162-57-16.20.

Bowling—N. D. Cross 95-26-219-17-12.88; N. J. Corran 135.5-37-287-22-13.04; L. C Parnell 88-31-211-16-13.18; M. G. Roberts 45.3-4-178-12-14.83; D. A. Alla 123.2-30-354-20-17.70; S. J. Renshaw 83.5-25-198-11-18.00.

BISHOP'S STORTFORD COLLEGE

Played 18: Won 4, Lost 8, Drawn 6. Abandoned 1

Master i/c: D. A. Hopper

Batting—E. M. Peachey 13-0-345-100-26.53; L. E. M. Riddell 11-1-243-54-24.30; R. F Hudson 16-4-286-56*-23.83; O. W. R. Haslam 9-2-136-48-19.42; *D. N. Chil 15-0-268-88-17.86; D. F. Gilbert 8-1-116-47-16.57; A. J. P. Brown 14-0-225-71-16.07 R. N. Myers 11-0-120-38-10.90.

Bowling—R. S. Jayatileke 204-71-553-38-14.55; D. N. Child 148.1-27-475-24-19.79 M. J. S. Armitage 81.5-12-261-13-20.07; A. J. P. Brown 88.3-14-341-14-24.35.

BLOXHAM SCHOOL

Played 16: Won 4, Lost 3, Drawn 9. Abandoned 1

Master i/c: J. P. Horton

Batting—R. D. Beaty 15-6-306-62-34.00; S. Hehir 13-1-310-59-25.83; E. R. H Wornum 15-1-289-86*-20.64; A. W. A. Adejumo 12-0-238-56-19.83; S. J Johnson 11-0-201-34-18.27; C. T. G. Carr 11-0-181-40-16.45; R. A. F. Whitto 12-5-101-25*-14.42.

Bowling—E. R. H. Wornum 241.5-60-805-41-19.63; *A. R. Channin 116-14-491-16-30.68; R. A. F. Whitton 194-46-690-22-31.36.